EP 2.1.5 Advance human rights and social and economic justice:
  a. Understand the forms and mechanisms of oppression and discrimination   3, 7, 12, and 13
  b. Advocate for human rights and social and economic justice   3, 7, 12, and 13
  c. Engage in practices that advance social and economic justice   3, 7, 12, and 13

EP 2.1.6 Engage in research-informed practice and practice-informed research:
  a. Use practice experience to inform scientific inquiry   3
  b. Use research evidence to inform practice   3

EP 2.1.7 Apply knowledge of human behavior and the social environment:
  a. Utilize conceptual frameworks to guide the processes of assessment, intervention, and evaluation   3
  b. Critique and apply knowledge to understand person and environment   3

EP 2.1.8 Engage in policy practice to advance social and economic well-being and to deliver effective social work services:

  a. Analyze, formulate, and advocate for policies that advance social well-being   3
  b. Collaborate with colleagues and clients for effective policy action   3

EP 2.1.9 Respond to contexts that shape practice:
  a. Continuously discover, appraise, and attend to changing locales, populations, scientific and technological developments, and emerging societal trends to provide relevant services   3 and 5
  b. Provide leadership in promoting sustainable changes in service delivery and practice to improve the quality of social services   3

EP 2.1.10 Engage, assess, intervene, and evaluate with individuals, families, groups, organizations and communities:
  a. Substantively and affectively prepare for action with individuals, families, groups, organizations, and communities   3, 4, 5, 8, 10, and 13
  b. Use empathy and other interpersonal skills   3, 4, and 5
  c. Develop a mutually agreed-on focus of work and desired outcomes   3, 4, and 5
  d. Collect, organize, and interpret client data   3
  e. Assess client strengths and limitations   3
  f. Develop mutually agreed-on intervention goals and objectives   3, 4, and 5
  g. Select appropriate intervention strategies   3, 4, and 5
  h. Initiate actions to achieve organizational goals   3
  i. Implement prevention interventions that enhance client capacities   3, 4, and 5
  j. Help clients resolve problems   3, 4, and 5
  k. Negotiate, mediate, and advocate for clients   3
  l. Facilitate transitions and endings   3
  m. Critically analyze, monitor, and evaluate interventions   3

For more information about the standards themselves, and for a complete policy statement, visit the Council on Social Work Education website at www.cswe.org.

Adapted with permission from the Council on Social Work Education

EMPOWERING PEOPLE

Empowering people is a theme of this text. Content on empowerment of self and clients is provided in the following chapters:

CHAPTER 1
Social Welfare: Its Business, History, and Future
- The business of social welfare is to empower individuals, groups, families, organizations, and communities to improve their circumstances.

CHAPTER 2
Social Work as a Profession and a Career
- Playing a poor hand well: Empowering at-risk children.
- A goal of social work: Enhance the problem-solving, coping, and developmental capacities of people.
- A goal of social work: Enhance human well-being and eliminate poverty, oppression, and other forms of social injustice.
- The strengths perspective and empowerment.
- Self-awareness and identity formation.

CHAPTER 3
Generalist Social Work Practice
- Role of generalist social worker: Empowerer.
- A therapy group that utilized a strengths perspective.

CHAPTER 4
Poverty and Public Welfare
- Working with discouraged people.

CHAPTER 5
Emotional/Behavioral Problems and Counseling
- Counseling.

CHAPTER 6
Family Problems and Services to Families
- Treatment of incest.

CHAPTER 7
Sexual Orientation and Services to LGBT Individuals
- Social work with LGBT individuals.
- Sex counseling and sex therapy.

CHAPTER 9
Crime, Juvenile Delinquency, and Correctional Services
- The treatment approach.
- Reforming the correctional system.

CHAPTER 10
Problems in Education and School Social Work
- Becoming a creative, critical thinker is the essence of education.
- Expand preschool programs.
- Role of school social worker: Counselor and parent liaison.
- Role of school social worker: Advocate.
- Role of school social worker: Mental health consultant.
- Role of school social worker: Systems change specialist.

CHAPTER 11
Work-Related Problems and Social Work in the Workplace
- Theory Y: Improving productivity and job satisfaction.
- Social work in the workplace.
- Employee assistance programs.

CHAPTER 12
Racism, Ethnocentrism, and Strategies for Advancing Social and Economic Justice
- Cochran Gardens: A grassroots organization that used a strengths perspective.
- Empowerment.
- Strengths perspective: Strategies for advancing social and economic justice.

CHAPTER 13
Sexism and Efforts for Achieving Equality
- Strategies for achieving sexual equality.
- The feminist perspective on therapy.
- Assertiveness training.

CHAPTER 14
Aging and Gerontological Services
- Social work and older adults.
- Development of social roles for older adults.
- Preparation for later adulthood.

CHAPTER 15
Health Problems and Medical Social Services
- Understanding and reducing stress.
- Medical social work.
- Counseling the terminally ill.

CHAPTER 16
Physical and Mental Disabilities and Rehabilitation
- Roles of social workers.
- Empowering consumers of services.

CHAPTER 17
Overpopulation, Misuse of the Environment, and Family Planning
- Confronting environmental problems.
- Social work and family planning.

VALUES AND ETHICS

Content on social work values and ethics is infused throughout the text. Our society is increasingly becoming aware that values and ethics are key determinants of human behavior. Content on social work values and ethics provided in the following chapters:

Introduction to
Social Work and Social Welfare

Empowering People

Eleventh Edition

CHARLES ZASTROW

George Williams College of Aurora University

BROOKS/COLE
CENGAGE Learning·

Australia • Brazil • Japan • Korea • Mexico • Singapore • Spain • United Kingdom • United States

BROOKS/COLE
CENGAGE Learning·

Introduction to Social Work and Social Welfare: Empowering People Brooks/Cole Empowerment Series, Eleventh Edition
Charles Zastrow

Executive Editor: Mark Kerr

Sr Acquisitions Editor: Seth Dobrin

Developmental Editor: Arwen Petty

Assistant Editor: Naomi Dreyer

Editorial Assistant: Coco Bator

Media Editor: Elizabeth Momb

Sr Brand Manager: Elisabeth Rhoden

Market Development Manager: Kara Kindstrom

Sr Content Project Manager: Rita Jaramillo

Art Director: Caryl Gorska

Manufacturing Planner: Judy Inouye

Rights Acquisitions Specialist: Dean Dauphinais

Production Service/Composition: S4Carlisle Publishing Services

Photo Researcher: PreMedia Global

Text Researcher: PreMedia Global

Copy Editor: Kirsten Balayti

Cover Design: Diane Beasley

Cover Images: (clockwise from top left): University students in lecture hall, Clerkenwell; Father with Downs Syndrome son, Monkey Business Images; Elementary school girl, Christopher Futcher; Portrait of mixed race family, Jacqueline Veissid; Senior woman, Lawren; Young male students smiling, Henk Badenhorst

For product information and technology assistance, contact us at
Cengage Learning Customer & Sales Support, 1-800-354-9706.
For permission to use material from this text or product, submit all requests online at **www.cengage.com/permissions**.
Further permissions questions can be e-mailed to
permissionrequest@cengage.com.

Library of Congress Control Number: 2012956197

Student Edition:
ISBN-13: 978-1-285-07717-8
ISBN-10: 1-285-07717-2

Brooks/Cole

20 Davis Drive
Belmont, CA 94002-3098
USA

Cengage Learning is a leading provider of customized learning solutions with office locations around the globe, including Singapore, the United Kingdom, Australia, Mexico, Brazil, and Japan. Locate your local office at **www.cengage.com/global**.

Cengage Learning products are represented in Canada by Nelson Education, Ltd.

To learn more about Brooks/Cole, visit **www.cengage.com/brookscole**

Purchase any of our products at your local college store or at our preferred online store **www.CengageBrain.com**.

Printed in Canada
1 2 3 4 5 6 7 17 16 15 14 13

About the Author

Charles Zastrow, MSW and PhD, is Assistant Director and Professor in the Social Work Program at George Williams College of Aurora University at Williams Bay, Wisconsin. He has worked as a practitioner in a variety of public and private social welfare agencies and has chaired 23 social work accreditation site visit teams for the Council on Social Work Education (CSWE). He has served two terms as a Commissioner on the Commission on Accreditation of CSWE. He has been a Board Member of the Association of Baccalaureate Social Work Program Directors, Inc. (BPD). Dr. Zastrow is a licensed Clinical Social Worker in the State of Wisconsin. In addition to *Introduction to Social Work and Social Welfare*, Dr. Zastrow has written three other social work textbooks: *The Practice of Social Work* (10th ed.), *Social Work with Groups* (8th ed.), *Understanding Human Behavior and the Social Environment* (9th ed.) (with Dr. Karen Kirst-Ashman).

Contributing Authors

DEBRA S. BORQUIST, MSSW, APSW
Child Protection Team Social Worker
University of Wisconsin Health/American Family Childrens Hospital

KATHERINE DRECHSLER, MSW
Adjunct Faculty Member
University of Wisconsin–Whitewater
Doctoral Student in Social Work
Aurora University

RACHEL DUNN, MSW, CAPSW
Field Coordinator
George Williams College of Aurora University

DON NOLAN, MSSW, BCD
Social Worker
Jefferson County Public School System, Wisconsin

MICHAEL WALLACE, MSSW, LCSW
Clinical Social Worker and Lecturer
Social Work Department
University of Wisconsin–Whitewater

MARY R. WEEDEN, MSW, LCSW
Doctoral Candidate, *Loyola University*
Clinical Therapist for Eating Disorders
Assistant Professor, *Concordia University, Wisconsin*

To Kathy,
my wife,
who has invigorated my life!

Brief Contents

Contents

vii

CHAPTER 3

Generalist Social Work Practice   67

© Michael Newman/ PhotoEdit

Steve Hamblin/Alamy

CHAPTER 4
Poverty and Public Welfare   116

© Michael Newman/ PhotoEdit

CHAPTER 5
Emotional/Behavioral Problems and Counseling   141

E Teister/Blickwinkel/Age Fotostock

© Chris Schmidt/iStockphoto.com

© Bettmann/CORBIS

AP Images

Nell Redmond/AP Images for Sprite

© Hulton-Deutsch Collection/Historical/Corbis

CHAPTER 14

Aging and Gerontological Services   453

CHAPTER 15

Health Problems and Medical Social Services   483

AP Photo/Glen Mayne

CHAPTER 16

Physical and Mental Disabilities and Rehabilitation 511

Dibyangshu Sarkar/Afp/Getty Images

CHAPTER 17

Overpopulation, Misuse of the Environment, and Family Planning 533

Preface

In social work, empowering people is the process of helping individuals, families, groups, organizations, and communities increase their personal, interpersonal, socioeconomic, and political strength and influence through improving their circumstances. Social workers seek to develop the capacity of clients to understand their environment, make choices, take responsibility for their choices, and influence their life situations through organization and advocacy. Social workers also seek to gain a more equitable distribution of resources and power among different groups in society. This focus on equity and social justice has been a hallmark of the social work profession. In recent years, social work education has had an increased emphasis on the concept of human rights—which will be discussed in this edition.

This book is designed to stimulate student interest in social work and to provide an experiential "flavor" of what the fields of social welfare and social work are really like. Using a social problems approach, the book describes how people are affected by poverty, child abuse, emotional difficulties, sexism, alcoholism, crime, AIDS, physical and mental disabilities, racism, overpopulation, sexual assault, and other problems. Information on the nature, extent, and causes of such problems is also presented. In teaching introductory courses in social work, a number of my colleagues and I have found that students tend to be more interested when they come face to face with the tragic social conditions that people experience. This book also includes case examples through which the reader is able to identify with people in need of help.

In addition, *Introduction to Social Work and Social Welfare: Empowering People* is designed to:

- Provoke the reader's thinking about some of the controversial contemporary issues in social welfare. I believe developing the student's critical thinking capacities is much more important than teaching unimportant facts to be recited on exams.
- Convey material on social work intervention approaches that the reader can use in working with people to facilitate positive changes.
- Present material on both sides of major social issues confronting our society that the reader can use in arriving at informed positions.
- Provide case examples of the functions, roles, responsibilities, gratifications, and frustrations of social workers that will help the student who is considering a social work major to make an informed career decision.
- Provide a brief historical review of the development of social welfare, social work, and various social services.
- Facilitate the reader in acquiring an international perspective by presenting, in practically every chapter, information on social problems and social services not only in the United States but also in other countries.
- Inform the reader of the Council on Social Work Education's (CSWE) conceptualization of social work education at the baccalaureate and master's levels as delineated in CSWE's *Educational Policy and Accreditation Standards (EPAS)*.
- Help the reader "sort out" his or her value structure in relation to welfare recipients, single parents, ex-convicts, the mentally ill, the divorced,

persons with AIDS, abusive parents, minority groups, those who are prejudiced, and so on. The aim is not to sell any particular set of values but to help the reader arrive at a value system that she or he will be comfortable with and find functional in interacting with others.

Plan of the Book

Part I introduces the student to the fields of social welfare, social work, and human services. These terms are defined, and their relationships to sociology, psychology, and other disciplines are described. A brief history of social welfare and social work is provided, and the future is examined. A discussion of social work as a career and as a profession is included, and this gives the reader a basis for deciding whether to pursue a career in social work.

This part also describes generalist social work practice with systems of all sizes, including individuals, groups, families, organizations, and communities. This conceptualization introduces readers to the knowledge, skills, and values needed for effective social work practice.

Part II focuses on the most common social problems served by the field of social welfare. This part constitutes the main emphasis of the text and describes:

- Contemporary social problems in our society.
- Current social services for meeting these problems.
- Gaps in current services.
- Controversial issues in each service area.
- Proposed new programs to meet current gaps in services.

Numerous case examples provide the reader with a "feeling" awareness of how the problems affect people and convey what it is really like to be a social worker.

This 11th edition updates the information in every chapter. New topics include: Obamacare; safety guidelines for social workers; school bullying; cyberbullying; intersectionality of multiple factors; the Tea Party movement; open adoptions; motivational interviewing; White supremacy; activity theory for older persons; trauma and stress disorders; Dr. Temple Grandin, who is autistic; Arizona's Our Law Enforcement and Safe Neighborhood's Act; evidence-based practice; social work with military personnel, veterans, and their families; the DREAM Act; the Gulf of Mexico oil spill in 2010; and Japan's nuclear plant meltdowns in 2011. The Council on Social Work Education is the national organization that accredits baccalaureate and master's degree programs in social work education in the United States. In 2008 CSWE revised its standards for baccalaureate and master's degree programs in social work educational programs in the United States, known as the *Educational Policy and Accreditation Standards (EPAS)*. A major thrust of *Introduction to Social Work and Social Welfare* is to present material that is consistent with *EPAS*. Three additional themes around which content is organized in this text are vignettes of a "day in the life" of social workers, generalist practice, and ecological perspectives.

The book is intended for use in introductory social work and social welfare courses. It introduces prospective social work majors to the field of social welfare and will help them arrive at career decisions and prepare for future social work courses. For nonmajors, the book provides information about current social problems and social services; the text also gives a framework for analyzing policy issues and for making citizenship decisions on social issues.

A major focus of this edition is to provide text content and skill-building exercises that focus on students acquiring the 10 competencies and 41 practice behaviors of the 2008 EPAS (*Educational Policy and Accreditation Standards*) of the Council on Social Work Education (CSWE). The coverage of these competencies and practice behaviors is facilitated by the following two additional booklets; *The Practice Behaviors Workbook* and *The Instructor Quick-Guide Booklet*.

The Practice Behaviors Workbook is composed of exercises that are explicitly connected to the competencies and practice behaviors of the 2008 EPAS. In addition, there is an assessment process in this workbook that will facilitate students being evaluated on the extent to which they are attaining the competencies and practice behaviors of the 2008 EPAS. The higher a student is assessed in attaining these competencies and practice behaviors, the more likely it is that the student is becoming a competent social worker. The workbook begins with a table that identifies the chapters in the text and the practice exercises in the workbook that relate to the 41 practice behaviors in the 2008 EPAS. (Students will progress in developing the knowledge, skills, and values needed for becoming a competent social worker by conscientiously completing these exercises.)

The *Instructor Quick-Guide Booklet* correlates the core text and accompanying *Practice Behaviors Workbook* to the EPAS 2008 requirements.

The *Quick-Guide Booklet* is designed to assist faculty and their social work departments to monitor the implementation of the EPAS 2008 requirements. The *Booklet* shows: (a) where content is located in the text on the 41 practice behaviors of the EPAS 2008, and (b) a table that identifies where the Dynamic Case Exercises align with the 41 practice behaviors.

An additional advantage of this *Quick-Guide* is that it may be used in preparing self-study documents for accreditation—as documentation that the course in which *Understanding Human Behavior and the Social Environment* is being used is covering the competencies and practice behaviors of the 2008 EPAS. Coverage is provided with text content and with exercises.

Note that **"helping hands" icons** of two hands embracing a sun are located next to content throughout the book. Accredited social work programs must demonstrate that they're teaching students to be proficient in 10 core competencies that are operationalized by the 41 practice behaviors designated by the Council on Social Work Education (CSWE) *Educational Policy and Accreditation Standards* (EPAS). Students require knowledge in order to develop skills and become competent. Our intent here is to specify what chapter content and knowledge coincides with the development of specific competencies and practice behaviors. (This ultimately is intended to assist in a social work program's accreditation process.) Throughout each chapter, icons such as the one located on this page call attention to the location of EPAS-related content. Each icon identifies what competency or practice behavior is relevant by specifying the designated Educational Policy (EP) reference number beneath it. "Competency Notes" are provided at the end of each chapter that describe how EPAS competencies and practice behaviors are related to designated content in the chapter. EPAS competencies and practice behaviors are cited in the inside covers of this book.

Acknowledgments

I wish to express my deep appreciation to the various people who made this book possible. Special thanks to the photo researcher, Vikram Jayabalan. I would like to thank the following colleagues who provided comments on the manuscript for this edition:

I express my gratitude to Mary Weeden, Rachel Dunn, Katherine Drechsler, Debra Borquist, Donald Nolan, and Michael Wallace for being contributing authors.

A sincere thank you to Vicki Vogel for helping in a number of ways with the writing of this text, including preparing the ancillary materials.

A final thank you to the staff at Cengage Learning/ Brooks/Cole for their support and highly professional assistance with the texts I've authored.

—*Charles Zastrow*

CHAPTER **1**

Social Welfare: Its Business, History, and Future

In our industrialized, complex, and rapidly changing society, social welfare activities have become important functions in terms of the money spent, the human misery treated, and the number of people served.[1] This chapter will:

Learning Objectives

EP 2.1.3a

A   Define social welfare and describe its goal.

B   Describe the relationship between social welfare and the following disciplines: sociology, psychology, social work, and human services.

C   Provide a history of social welfare.

D   Describe how the future of social welfare will be affected by technological advances.

E   Illustrate that the future of social welfare will also be partially affected by changes in the American family system. A summary of many of the changes that are occurring in the American family is provided.

Goal of Social Welfare

The goal of social welfare is to fulfill the social, financial, health, and recreational requirements of all individuals in a society. Social welfare seeks to enhance the social functioning of all age groups, both rich and poor. When other institutions in our society, such as the market economy and the family, fail at times to meet the basic needs of individuals or groups of people, then social services are needed and demanded.

In less industrialized societies, people's basic needs have been fulfilled in more direct and informal ways. Even in this country, fewer than 150 years ago most Americans lived on farms or in small towns with extended families and relatives close by. If financial or other needs arose, relatives, the church, and neighbors were there to "lend a helping hand." Problems were visible and personal; everyone knew everyone else in the community. When a need arose, it was taken for granted that those with resources would do whatever they could to alleviate the difficulty. If, for example, the need was financial, personal acquaintance with the storekeeper or banker usually was sufficient to obtain needed goods or money.

Clearly, we are now living in a different era. Our technology, economic base, social patterns, and living styles have changed dramatically. Our commercial, industrial, political, educational, and religious institutions are considerably larger and more impersonal. We tend to live in large urban communities—away from families or relatives—frequently without even knowing our neighbors. We have become much more mobile, often having few roots and limited knowledge of the community in which we live. Vocationally, we have specialized and become more interdependent on others, and as a result we have diminishing control over major aspects of our lives. Our rapidly changing society is a breeding ground for exacerbating former social ills and creating new problems, such as the expanding number of homeless people, higher crime rates, recurring energy crises, terrorism, and the destruction of our environment. Obviously, the old rural-frontier methods of meeting social welfare needs are no longer viable.

It is the business of social welfare:

- To find homes for parentless children.
- To rehabilitate people who are addicted to alcohol or drugs.
- To treat those with emotional difficulties.
- To make life more meaningful for older adults.
- To provide vocational rehabilitation services to persons with a physical or mental disability.
- To meet the financial needs of the poor.
- To rehabilitate juveniles and adults who have committed criminal offenses.
- To end all types of discrimination and oppression.

- To provide services to veterans, including those suffering from traumatic brain injury or posttraumatic stress disorder (PTSD).
- To provide child care services for parents who work outside the home.
- To counteract violence in families, including child abuse and spouse abuse.
- To fulfill the health and legal exigencies of those in financial need.
- To counsel individuals and groups experiencing a wide variety of personal and social difficulties.
- To provide services to people with AIDS and to their families and friends.
- To provide recreational and leisure-time services to all age groups.
- To educate and provide socialization experiences to children who have a cognitive disability* or an emotional disorder.
- To serve families struck by such physical disasters as fires and tornadoes.
- To provide adequate housing for the homeless.
- To provide programs that support and enhance the normal growth and development of all children and adults.
- To provide vocational training and employment opportunities to the unskilled and unemployed.
- To meet the special needs of people of color, migrant workers, and other minority groups.
- To empower individuals, groups, families, organizations, and communities to improve their circumstances.

Social Welfare as an Institution and as a Discipline

The term *social welfare* has different meanings, as it is both an *institution* and an *academic discipline*. The National Association of Social Workers (the primary professional organization for social workers) gives the following definition of social welfare as an institution:

> A nation's system of programs, benefits, and services that helps people meet those social, economic, educational, and health needs that are fundamental to the maintenance of society.[2]

Examples of social welfare programs and services are foster care, adoption, day care, Head Start, probation and parole, financial assistance programs for low-income parents and their children, services to the homeless, public health nursing, sex therapy, suicide counseling, recreational services such as Boy Scouts and YWCA programs, services to minority groups, services to veterans, school social services, medical and legal services to the poor, family planning services, Meals on Wheels, nursing-home services, shelters for battered spouses, protective services for child abuse and neglect, assertiveness-training programs, encounter groups and sensitivity training, public housing projects, family counseling, Alcoholics Anonymous, runaway services, services to people with a developmental disability, and rehabilitation services.

Social welfare programs and social service organizations are sometimes referred to as "social welfare institutions." The purposes of social welfare institutions are to prevent, alleviate, or contribute to the solution of recognized social problems in order to directly improve the well-being of individuals, groups, families, organizations, and communities. Social welfare institutions are established by policies and laws, with the programs and services being provided by voluntary (private) and governmental (public) agencies.

The term *social welfare institution* is applied to various levels of complexity and abstraction. It may be applied to a single program or organization—for example, foster care or Planned Parenthood. Or the term may be applied to a group of services or programs. For example, child welfare services is a social welfare institution that includes such services as adoption, foster care, juvenile probation, protective services, runaway services, day care, school social services, and residential treatment. The highest aggregate level to which the term *social welfare institution* is applied includes *all* of the social programs and organizations in a country that are designed to prevent, alleviate, or contribute to the solution of recognized social problems.

Another meaning of social welfare derives from its role as an academic discipline. In this context, social welfare is "the study of agencies, programs, personnel, and policies which focus on the delivery of social services to individuals, groups, and communities."[3] One of the functions of the social welfare discipline is to educate and train social workers. (Some colleges and universities call their professional preparation programs for social work practice "social work," and others call their programs "social welfare.")

---

*The term *cognitive disability* is used in this text in lieu of *mental retardation*, which has negative connotations.

Social Welfare's Relationship to Sociology and to Other Academic Disciplines

Social welfare has often been confused with "sociology" and "human services." In addition, many people are confused about how social welfare and social work relate to psychology, psychiatry, and other related disciplines. The next few sections seek to clarify these relationships.

Several academic disciplines seek to develop a knowledge base about social problems, their causes, and their alleviation. The most common disciplines are social welfare, sociology, psychology, political science, economics, psychiatry, and cultural anthropology. Figure 1.1 shows the relationship of these disciplines to social welfare.

Each of these disciplines has a distinct focus. The following definitions highlight the similarities and differences among these disciplines:

Sociology: The study of human social behavior, especially the study of the origins, organizations, institutions, and development of human society.

Psychology: The study of mental processes and behavior.

Psychiatry: The study of the diagnosis, treatment, and prevention of mental illness.

Political science: The study of the processes, principles, and structure of government and of political institutions.

Economics: The study of the production, distribution, and consumption of commodities.

Cultural anthropology: The study of human culture based on archeological, ethnographic, linguistic, social, and psychological data and methods of analysis.[4]

Theories and research in these disciplines may or may not, depending on the nature of the content, be considered part of the knowledge base of social welfare. When the theories and research have direct application to the goal of enhancing the social functioning of people, such knowledge can also be considered part of the knowledge base of social welfare. In the past, social welfare has been more of an applied science than a pure science; that is, it has formed its knowledge base primarily from the theories and research of other disciplines and has focused on applying such knowledge through social programs. In recent years, the academic discipline

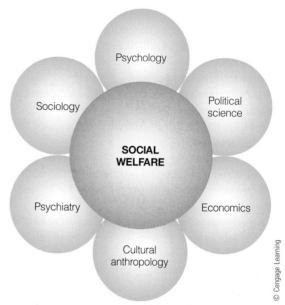

FIGURE 1.1 Overlap of Knowledge Base of Social Welfare with Other Disciplines

of social welfare (called "social work" at many campuses) has been active in research projects and in theory development. This increased research and theory development activity is an indication that social welfare is a discipline that is maturing, as it is now developing much of its own knowledge base.

A few examples may be useful in illustrating how the knowledge base of other disciplines overlaps with social welfare. Sociological research on and conceptualization of the causes of social problems (for example, juvenile delinquency, mental illness, poverty, and racial discrimination) may be considered part of the knowledge base of social welfare. Only through an understanding of such problems can social welfare effectively prevent and control such problems. Sociological studies on the effects of institutions (for example, mental hospitals and prisons) on individuals are currently of considerable interest to and have important application in the field of social welfare. Sociological investigations of other subjects, such as mobility, urbanization, secularization, group formation, race relations, prejudice, and the process of acculturation, have also become part of social welfare's knowledge base because such investigations are directly applicable to enhancing people's social well-being. However, research in other sociological areas, such as studies of social organizations among nonliterate tribes, is usually considered outside the knowledge base of social welfare because such research usually does not have direct applications to the goal of social welfare.

Comparable overlap occurs between social welfare and the other previously mentioned disciplines. Using psychology as an example, studies and theory development in such areas as personality growth and therapeutic techniques can be considered part of the knowledge base of social welfare because they have direct social welfare applications. On the other hand, experimental investigations of, for example, the perceptions and thinking processes of animals do not, at least presently, have such applications and would not therefore be considered part of the social welfare knowledge base.

Social Welfare's Relationship to Social Work

The previously given institutional definition of social welfare is applicable when the relationship between social welfare and social work is examined. *Social welfare* is a more comprehensive term than *social work*; social welfare encompasses social work. Social welfare and social work are primarily related at the level of practice. *Social work* has been defined by the National Association of Social Workers (NASW) as follows:

> *Social work is the professional activity of helping individuals, groups, or communities to enhance or restore their capacity for social functioning and to create societal conditions favorable to their goals.*
>
> *Social work practice consists of the professional application of social work values, principles, and techniques to one or more of the following ends: helping people obtain tangible services; providing counseling and psychotherapy for individuals, families, and groups; helping communities or groups provide or improve social and health services; and participating in relevant legislative processes.*
>
> *The practice of social work requires knowledge of human development and behavior; of social, economic, and cultural institutions; and of the interaction of all these factors.*[5]

The term *social worker* has been defined by the NASW as:

> *Graduates of schools of social work (with either bachelor's or master's degrees), who use their knowledge and skills to provide social services for* clients *(who may be individuals, families, groups, communities, organizations, or society in general).*

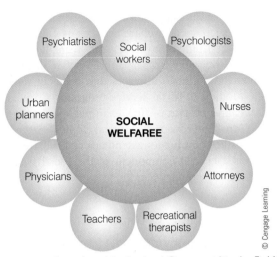

FIGURE 1.2 Examples of Professional Groups within the Field of Social Welfare

> *Social workers help people increase their capacities for problem solving and coping and help them obtain needed resources, facilitate interactions between individuals and between people and their environments, make organizations responsible to people, and influence social policies.*[6]

Almost all social workers are working in the field of social welfare. There are, however, many other professional and occupational groups that may be working in this field, as illustrated in Figure 1.2. Professional people providing social welfare services include attorneys who offer legal services to the poor; urban planners in social planning agencies; physicians in public health agencies; teachers in residential treatment facilities for the emotionally disturbed; psychologists, nurses, and recreational therapists in mental hospitals; and psychiatrists in mental health clinics.

Social Welfare's Relationship to Other Institutions

Social welfare overlaps with such institutions as the family, education, religion, and politics. One of the functions of the family is raising and caring for children. Social welfare assists families by providing services such as counseling, day care, foster care, and adoption. Certain educational courses have both educational and social welfare aspects; for example, social science and physical education courses provide socialization experiences and are important in the social development of youth. Churches have long been interested in people's social well-being and have provided such social welfare services as counseling, financial assistance, day care, and recreation. The overlap between politics and social welfare primarily involves the political processes that occur in regard to the funding of social service programs. Some social welfare programs (for example, public assistance) are controversial political topics. Securing the necessary funding for essential social welfare programs is a crucial component of the social welfare system in any country.

Social Welfare's Relationship to Human Services

Human services may be defined as those systems of services and allied occupations and professions that concentrate on improving or maintaining the physical and mental health and general well-being of individuals, groups, or communities in our society. Alfred Kahn has conceptualized human services as composed of the following four service categories:[7]

1. Personal services (casework, counseling, recreation, rehabilitation, religion, therapy)
2. Protection services (consumer protection, corrections, courts, fire prevention/firefighting, housing-code enforcement, law enforcement, public health services)
3. Information/advising services (consulting, consumer information, education, financial counseling, hotlines, and library services)
4. Maintenance services (child care, unemployment assistance, institutional services, public welfare programs, retirement plans, and Social Security programs)

Kahn indicates that there is a tendency to use the term *human services* for what in the past has been called social welfare.[8] Actually, *human services* is a broader term because it includes services (such as library services, law enforcement, housing-code enforcement, consumer protection, and fire prevention and firefighting) that are usually not considered social welfare services. The term *social welfare* is thus more limited because it focuses on conceptualizing and resolving social problems. *Human services* is a broader term that encompasses social welfare programs. The two terms relate at a *program level*.

A number of universities and colleges now offer a bachelor's degree in human services. Such human services programs consist of courses that have content similar to that which is offered in social work courses. Human services programs do not have a national accreditation review process as rigorous as that provided by the Council on Social Work Education (see Chapter 3). Also, a degree in human services is not as marketable (in demand by social work employers) as a degree in social work; a degree in social work is much more apt to be specified in hiring requirements for social work positions.

Residual View versus Institutional View of Social Welfare

The present social welfare scene is substantially influenced by the past. Currently, there are two conflicting views of the role of social welfare in our society.[9] One of these roles has been termed *residual*—a gap-filling or first-aid role. This view holds that social welfare services should be provided only when an individual's needs are not properly met through other societal institutions, primarily the family and the market economy. According to the residual view, social services and financial aid should not be provided until all other measures or efforts have been exhausted, including the individual's and his or her family's resources. In addition, this view asserts that funds and services should be provided on a short-term basis (primarily during emergencies) and should be withdrawn when the individual or the family again becomes capable of being self-sufficient.

The residual view has been characterized as "charity for unfortunates."[10] Funds and services are seen not as a right (something that one is entitled to) but as a gift, with the receiver having certain obligations; for example, to receive financial aid, recipients may be required to perform certain low-grade work assignments. Associated with the residual view is the belief that the causes of clients' difficulties are rooted in their own malfunctioning—that is, clients are to blame for their predicaments because of personal inadequacies, ill-advised activities, or sins.

Under the residual view, there is usually a stigma attached to receiving services or funds. The prevalence of the residual stigma can be shown by asking, "Have you ever felt a reluctance to seek counseling for a personal or emotional situation you faced because you were wary of what others might think of you?" For almost everyone the answer is yes. An example of this stigma in American society was evidenced in 1968, when Senator Thomas Eagleton was dropped as the vice presidential candidate on the

CASE EXAMPLE 1.1

Blaming the Victim

Jerry Jorgenson and Joyce Mantha decided to get married after dating for 3 years. Both looked forward to a big wedding and a happy future. They had met in college, and now both were working in Mayville, a small town that Jerry had grown up in. Joyce was a kindergarten teacher, and Jerry was manager of a grocery store. Against Jerry's wishes, Joyce drove one weekend to a nearby city to attend a bridal shower with some of her women college friends. The party was still going strong at 2:00 A.M., when Joyce thought it was time to go back to her motel in order to return to Mayville early on Sunday. In the parking lot, Joyce was sexually assaulted. She tried to fight off the assailant and suffered a number of bruises and abrasions. After the assault, a passerby called the police and an ambulance. Joyce called Jerry the next day. At first he was angry at the rapist. But the more he thought about it, the more he assigned blame to Joyce: She went to the party against his wishes, and he erroneously speculated that she dressed and acted in such a way as to interest the rapist (especially because Jerry further assumed that she had been intoxicated).

The weeks that followed became increasingly difficult for Jerry and Joyce. Joyce sensed that Jerry was blaming her for being raped. She tried to talk it out with Jerry, but their "talks" always became shouting matches. Their sexual relationship became practically nil, as Jerry felt his "sexual rights" had been violated, and the few times he made sexual advances he had images of Joyce being attacked by a stranger. They postponed the marriage.

When they first heard about the rape, many townspeople also thought that Joyce had "asked for it" while partying in the big city. Postponement of the marriage was interpreted by the townspeople as evidence for this belief, and they began shunning Joyce. After several months of such treatment, Joyce began to believe that she was at fault and increasingly blamed herself for her predicament. She became despondent and moved back with her parents for refuge.

This story is only one illustration of the tendency in American culture to blame the victim. Others abound. If an adult is unemployed for a long time, often that person is believed to be "lazy" or "unmotivated." Parents who are receiving welfare benefits are erroneously stereotyped as being promiscuous, irresponsible, and lazy. When a marriage breaks up, either the husband or the wife or both are blamed, rather than the relationship being viewed as having deteriorated. When unfortunate circumstances occur (for example, lightning striking someone's home), some people believe it is a punishment for sinful activity. Slapping one's wife is justified by some segments of the population as being a way to "keep her in line" and to "show her who's boss." People living in poverty are often inaccurately viewed as being personally inadequate, incompetent, or lazy or as having a culture that holds them in poverty. The problems of slum housing in inner cities are sometimes traced to the characteristics of "southern rural migrants" not yet "acculturated" to life in the big city. Sadly, blaming the victim sometimes leads to acceptance by the general public of the original victimization, with the result that few efforts are then made to assist current victims or to prevent victimizations in the future.

But perhaps the saddest feature of victim blaming is that the erroneous explanation often becomes a self-fulfilling prophecy. If a teacher is told that a child is a poor learner, that teacher will interact with the child as if he or she were a slow learner. Unfortunately, the child will eventually come to believe the teacher is correct and learn little. Labeling people as lazy, criminal, immoral, or mentally ill strongly influences the expectations others hold for them and simultaneously influences the victims themselves in their expectations and self-definition.

Democratic ticket after it became known that he had once received psychiatric counseling.

The opposing point of view, which has been coined the *institutional view*,* holds that social welfare programs are to be "accepted as a proper, legitimate function of modern industrial society in helping individuals achieve self-fulfillment."[11] Under this view, there is no stigma attached to receiving funds or services; recipients are viewed as being entitled to such help. Associated with this view is the belief that an individual's difficulties are due to causes largely beyond his or her control (for example, a person may be unemployed because of a lack of employment opportunities). When difficulties arise, causes are sought in the environment (society), and efforts are focused on improving the social institutions within which the individual functions.

The residual approach characterized social welfare programs from our early history to the depression of the 1930s. Since the Great Depression, both approaches have been applied to social welfare programs, with some programs largely residual in nature and others more institutional in design and implementation. Social insurance programs, such as Old Age, Survivors, Disability, and Health Insurance (described in Chapter 4), are examples of institutional

---

*The term *institutional view of social welfare* is distinctly different from, and not to be confused with, the term *social welfare institutions.*

programs. Public assistance programs (also described in Chapter 4) are examples of residual programs.

Critical Thinking Question

Which approach to social welfare do you believe is preferable—the residual view or the institutional view? Why?

Liberalism versus Conservatism

The two prominent political philosophies in the United States are liberalism and conservatism. The Republican Party is considered relatively conservative and the Democratic Party is considered relatively liberal. (It should be noted, however, that there are some Democrats who are primarily conservative in ideology and some Republicans who are primarily liberal in ideology.)

Conservatives (derived from the verb "to conserve") tend to resist change. They emphasize tradition and believe that rapid change usually results in more negative than positive consequences. In economic matters, conservatives feel that government should not interfere with the workings of the marketplace. They encourage the government to support (for example, through tax incentives), rather than regulate, business and industry in society. A free-market economy is thought to be the best way to ensure prosperity and fulfillment of individual needs. Conservatives embrace the old adage "that government governs best which governs least." They believe that most government activities constitute grave threats to individual liberty and to the smooth functioning of the free market.

Conservatives generally view individuals as autonomous (that is, as self-governing). Regardless of what a person's situation is, or what his or her problems are, each person is thought to be responsible for his or her own behavior. People are thought to choose whatever they are doing, and they therefore are viewed as responsible for whatever gains or losses result from their choices. People are thought to possess free will, and thus can choose to engage in behaviors such as hard work that help them get ahead or activities such as excessive leisure that contribute to failure (or poverty). Poverty and other personal problems are seen as the result of laziness, irresponsibility, or lack of self-control. Conservatives believe that social welfare programs force hardworking, productive citizens to pay for the consequences of the irresponsible behavior of recipients of social welfare services.

Conservatives generally advocate a residual approach to social welfare programs. They believe that dependency is a result of personal failure and that it is natural for inequality to exist among humans. They assert that the family, the church, and gainful employment should be the primary defenses against dependency. Social welfare should be only a temporary function that is used sparingly; prolonged social welfare assistance will lead recipients to become permanently dependent. Conservatives also believe that charity is a moral virtue and that the "fortunate" are obligated to help the "less fortunate" become productive, contributing citizens in a society. If government funds are provided for health and social welfare services, conservatives advocate that such funding should go to private organizations, which are thought to be more effective and efficient than public agencies in providing services.

Critical Thinking Question

Which political philosophy do you primarily adhere to—conservatism or liberalism? Why?

Conservatives revere the "traditional" nuclear family and try to devise policies to preserve it. They see the family as a source of strength for individuals and as the primary unit of society. They generally oppose abortion, sex education in schools, equal rights for gays and lesbians, public funding of day-care centers, birth control counseling for minors, and other measures that might undermine parental authority or support alternative family forms such as single parenthood.

In contrast, liberals believe that change is generally good, as it usually brings progress. Moderate change is best. They view society as needing regulation to ensure fair competition among various interests. In particular, a free-market economy is viewed as needing regulation to ensure fairness. Government programs, including social welfare programs, are necessary to help meet basic human needs. Liberals advocate government action to remedy social deficiencies and to improve human welfare. They feel that government regulation and intervention are often required to safeguard human rights, to control the excesses of capitalism, and to provide equal chances for success. They emphasize egalitarianism and the rights of minorities.

Liberals generally adhere to an institutional view of social welfare. They assert that because modern society has become so fragmented and complex and because traditional institutions (such as the family) have been unable to meet emerging human needs, few individuals can now function without the help of social services (including work training, job placement services, child care, health care, and counseling). Liberals believe that the personal problems encountered by someone are generally due to causes beyond that person's control. Causes are generally sought in the person's environment. For example, a child with a learning disability is thought to be at risk only if he or she is not receiving appropriate educational services to accommodate the disability. In such a situation, liberals would seek to develop educational services to meet the child's learning needs.

Liberals view the family as an evolving institution and therefore are willing to support programs that assist emerging family forms such as single-parent families and same-sex marriages.

Developmental View of Social Welfare

For years, liberals have criticized the residual approach to social welfare as being incongruent with society's obligation to provide long-term assistance to those who have long-term health, welfare, social, and recreational needs. Conservatives, on the other hand, have been highly critical of the institutional approach. They claim it creates a welfare state with many recipients then deciding to become dependent on the government to meet their health, welfare, social, and recreational needs without seeking to work and without contributing in other ways to the well-being of society. It is clear that conservatives will seek to stop the creation of any major new social program that moves our country in the direction of a welfare society. They currently have the political power (that is, the necessary legislative votes) to stop the enactment of programs that are "marketed" to society as being consistent with the institutional approach.

Is there a view of social welfare that can garner the support of both liberals and conservatives? Midgley contends that the developmental view (or perspective) offers an alternative approach that appears to appeal to liberals, conservatives, and the general public.[12] He defines this approach as a "process of planned social change designed to promote the well-being of the population as a whole in conjunction with a dynamic process of economic development."[13]

This perspective appeals to liberals because it supports the development and expansion of needed social welfare programs. The perspective appeals to conservatives because it asserts that the development of certain social welfare programs will have a positive impact on the economy. (In the past, conservative politicians have opposed the development of many social welfare programs because they claimed such programs would have a negative impact on economic development.) The general public also would be apt to support the developmental perspective. Many voters oppose welfarism because they believe it causes economic problems (for example, recipients choosing to be on the government dole rather than contributing to society by working). Asserting, and documenting, that certain proposed social welfare programs will directly benefit the economy is attractive to voters.

Midgley and Livermore note that the developmental approach is presently not very well defined.[14] It has its roots in the social programs of developing (Third World) countries. Advocates for social welfare programs in developing countries have been successful in getting certain social welfare programs enacted by asserting, and documenting, that such programs have a beneficial impact on the overall economy of the country. Midgley and Livermore note, "the developmental perspective's global relevance began in the Third World in the years of decolonization after World War II."[15] The developmental approach was later used by the United Nations (UN) in its efforts in developing countries to promote the growth of social programs, as the UN asserted such programs had the promise of improving the overall economies of these Third World countries.

What are the characteristics of the developmental approach? It advocates social interventions that contribute positively to economic development. It thus promotes harmony between economic and social institutions. The approach regards economic progress as a vital component of social progress. It promotes the active role of the government in economic and social planning. This is in direct opposition to the residual approach, which advocates that the government should seek to minimize its role in the provision of social welfare programs. Finally, the developmental approach focuses on integrating economic and social development for the benefit of all members of society.

The developmental approach can be used in advocating for the expansion of a wide range of social welfare programs. It can be argued that any social program that assists a person in becoming employable contributes to the economic well-being of a society. It can also be argued that any social program that assists a person in making significant contributions to his or her family, or to his or her community, contributes to the economic well-being of a society. Functional families and functional communities are good for businesses; members of functional families tend to be better employees, and businesses want to be located in prosperous communities that have low rates of crime and other social problems.

A few examples will be cited to illustrate how the developmental approach can be used to advocate for the expansion of social welfare programs. It can be argued that the following programs will be beneficial for the economy because they assist unemployed single parents in obtaining employment: job training; quality child-care programs for children of these parents; and adequate health insurance for these parents and their children so that care is provided to keep them healthy, which will facilitate the parents' ability to work. It can be argued that providing mentoring programs and other social services in school systems will help at-risk children stay in school and eventually contribute to society. When they become adults, these individuals are likely to get jobs and contribute to their families and communities. It can be argued that rehabilitative programs in the criminal justice system will help correctional clients become contributing members of society. It can be argued that the following programs can assist individuals to better handle certain issues and thereby increase their likelihood of becoming contributors to the economy and well-being of society: alcohol and other drug abuse treatment programs, domestic violence services, mental health counseling, nutritional programs, eating disorder intervention programs, stress management programs, and grief management programs.

History of Social Welfare

Early European History

All societies must develop ways to meet the needs of those who are unable to be self-sufficient—the orphaned, the blind, persons with a physical or mental disability, the poor, and the sick. Before the Industrial Revolution, this responsibility was met largely by the family, by the church, and by neighbors. An important value of the Judeo-Christian tradition throughout history—and one that has considerable relevancy for social welfare—is humanitarianism: ascribing a high value to human life and benevolently helping those in need.

With the development of the feudal system in Europe, when a tenant family was unable to meet a relative's basic needs, the feudal lord usually provided whatever was necessary.

The Elizabethan Poor Law

In the Middle Ages, famines, wars, crop failures, pestilence, and the breakdown in the feudal system all contributed to substantial increases in the number of people in need. Former approaches, primarily through the church and the family, were unsuccessful at meeting the needs of many who were unable to be self-sufficient. As a result, many of these individuals were forced to resort to begging. To attempt to solve this social problem, England passed several Poor Laws between the mid-1300s and the mid-1800s. The most significant of these was the Elizabethan Poor Law of 1601, enacted during the reign of Queen Elizabeth I. The fundamental provisions of this Poor Law were incorporated into the laws of the American colonies and have had an important influence on our current approaches to public assistance and other social legislation. (It is interesting to observe that the social problem that these Poor Laws were designed to alleviate was conceptualized not as poverty but, rather, as the ruling class's annoyance with begging.)

The Elizabethan Poor Law established three categories of relief recipients:

1. *The able-bodied poor.* This group was given low-grade employment, and citizens were prohibited from offering them financial help. Anyone who refused to work was placed in stocks or in jail.

2. *The impotent poor.* This group was composed of people unable to work—the elderly, the blind, the deaf, mothers with young children, and those with a physical or mental disability. They were usually placed together in an almshouse (institution). If the impotent poor had a place to live and if it appeared less expensive to maintain them there, they were permitted to live outside the almshouse, where they were granted "outdoor relief," usually "in kind" (food, clothing, and fuel).

3. *Dependent children.* Children whose parents or grandparents were unable to support them were

apprenticed out to other citizens. Boys were taught the trade of their master and had to serve until their 24th birthday. Girls were brought up as domestic servants and were required to remain until they were 21 or married.

This Poor Law did not permit the registration of a person as being in need of charity if his or her parents, spouse, children, or other relatives were able to provide support. Although the law was passed by the English Parliament, the parish (town or local community) was assigned the responsibility of implementing its provisions, with the program expenses to be met by charitable donations and a tax in the parish on lands, houses, and tithes. The Poor Law also stated that the parish's responsibility extended only to those who had legal residence in the parish, which was defined as having been born in the parish or having lived in the parish for 3 years. (Residence requirements are still part of current public assistance programs.) The Poor Law of 1601 set the pattern of public relief under governmental responsibility in both Great Britain and the United States for the next 300 years.

Most of the provisions of the Elizabethan Poor Law were incorporated into the social welfare policies of colonial America. Towns were assigned the responsibility of providing for the needy, almshouses were built to house the unemployable, orphaned children were apprenticed out, and a system of legal residency was established to make it clear that towns were not responsible for meeting the needs of destitute strangers. Conditions in almshouses, it should be noted, were unbelievably deplorable. Into almshouses were packed not only the poor but also the sick, the emotionally disturbed, the blind, the alcoholic, and dependent children. Straw and old cots served for beds, there were no sanitary facilities, and the dilapidated buildings were barely heated in winter.

The Industrial Revolution

In the 17th, 18th, and 19th centuries, the Industrial Revolution flourished in Europe and America. A major reason for its growth was technological advances, such as the development of the steam engine. But the revolution was also made possible by the *Protestant ethic* and the *laissez-faire economic view*. These two themes also had important effects on social welfare. The Protestant ethic emphasized *individualism*, the view that one is the master of one's own

fate. Hard work and self-ambition were highly valued. An overriding goal for human beings set by the Protestant ethic was to acquire material goods. People were largely judged not on the basis of their personalities and other attributes but on how much wealth they had acquired. To be poor was thought to be one's own moral fault.

The laissez-faire economic theory asserted that the economy and society in general would best prosper if businesses and industries were permitted to do whatever they desired to make a profit. Any government regulation of business practices (for example, setting safety standards, passing minimum-wage laws, prohibiting child labor) was discouraged. The Protestant ethic and laissez-faire economics, together, justified such business practices as cutthroat competition, formation of monopolies, deplorable safety and working conditions, and exploitation of the working class through low pay, long hours, and child labor.

The social welfare implications of the Protestant ethic reached their most inhumane level in the theory of *social Darwinism*, which was based on Charles Darwin's theory of evolution. Darwin theorized that higher forms of life evolved from lower forms by the process of survival of the fittest; he had seen in the animal world a fierce struggle for survival that destroyed the weak, rewarded the strong, and produced evolutionary change. Herbert Spencer extended this theory to humanity: Struggle, destruction, and survival of the fit were thought to be essential to progress in human society as well. The theory stated in its most inhumane form that the strong (the wealthy) survived because they were superior, whereas the weak (the needy) deserved to perish; it would be a mistake to help the weak survive. Although leaving the weak to perish was never advocated on a wide scale, the theory did have a substantial influence in curbing the development of innovative and more humane social welfare programs.

Prior to the Industrial Revolution, there were few communities in Europe or America with a population larger than a few thousand. One of the consequences of the Industrial Revolution was the development of large urban areas close to factories. Because employment opportunities were limited in rural areas, many workers moved to cities. With such movement, family and kinship ties were broken, and those who were unable to adapt faced alienation, social breakdown, and a loss of community

CASE EXHIBIT 1.1

Is the Tea Party Movement the Rebirth of Social Darwinism?

The Tea Party movement is a political movement that is generally recognized as conservative and libertarian. (The Libertarian Party is the third largest political party in the United States; it favors minimally regulated, laissez-faire markets; strong civil liberties; reduced government spending; minimally regulated migration across borders; the avoidance of foreign military or economic entanglements with other nations; and respect for freedom of travel to all foreign countries.)

The Tea Party movement endorses reduced government spending, opposition to many current taxation policies, and reduction of the federal budget deficit and the national debt. The name "Tea Party" is a reference to the Boston Tea Party, a protest by colonists who objected to a British tax on tea in 1773 and demonstrated by dumping British tea taken from docked ships into the harbor. Tea Party advocates want to sharply reduce spending on social welfare programs—including Social Security benefits, Medicare, Medicaid, and unemployment insurance (see Chapters 4 and 15 for descriptions of these programs). They also want to curtail the power of trade unions, and are against raising tax rates for millionares.

Robert Reich asserts that the Tea Party is the rebirth of social Darwinism. He writes:

> Social Darwinism offered a moral justification for the wild
> inequities and social cruelties of the late nineteenth century.

It allowed John D. Rockefeller, for example, to claim the fortune he accumulated through his giant Standard Oil Trust was "merely a survival of the fittest." It was, he insisted "the working out of a law of nature and of God."

Social Darwinism also undermined all efforts at the time to build a nation of broadly-based prosperity and rescue our democracy from the tight grip of a very few at the top. It was used by the privileged and powerful to convince everyone else that government shouldn't do much of anything.

Not until the twentieth century did America reject Social Darwinism. We created the large middle class that became the core of our economy and democracy. We built safety nets to catch Americans who fell downward through no fault of their own. We designed regulations to protect against the inevitable excesses of free-market greed. We taxed the rich and invested in public goods–public schools, public universities, public transportation, public parks, public health–that made us all better off.

In short, we rejected the notion that each of us is on his or her own in a competitive contest for survival.[a]

[a]SOURCE: Robert Reich, http://www.readersupportednews.org/opinion2/277-75/7423-focus-the-rebirth-of-social. Reprinted by permission.

---

identity. In an attempt to meet the needs of people living in urban areas, private social welfare services began to spring up in the 1800s—primarily at the initiation of the clergy and religious groups. (A public social welfare agency receives its funds through tax dollars, whereas a private or voluntary agency generally receives a large part of its funds from charitable contributions.*) Because of the lack of development of public social services, private agencies provided most of the funds and services to the needy until the 1930s. In the 1800s, social services and funds were usually provided by upper-middle-class volunteers who combined "charity" with religious admonitions.

Turn of the 20th Century

Around 1880, various segments of the population became aware of the evils of unlimited competition

---

*Some private agencies are now contracting with public agencies to receive public funds to provide services to certain clients. Public agencies are established and administered by governmental units, whereas private agencies are established and administered by nongovernmental groups or private citizens.

and of abuses by those with economic power. It became clear that a few leaders of industry were becoming very wealthy, whereas the standard of living for the bulk of the population was remaining static and only slightly above the subsistence level. One of the theorists who objected to social Darwinism was Lester Ward, who in *Dynamic Sociology* (1883) drew a sharp distinction between purposeless animal evolution and human evolution.[16] Ward asserted that humans, unlike animals, could and should provide social welfare programs to help the needy and that humans have the capacity for regulation through social and economic controls. Ward declared that such programs and controls would benefit everyone. This new thinking was in direct opposition to social Darwinism and laissez-faire economics. It called on the federal government to take on new functions, to establish legislation to regulate business practices, and to provide social welfare programs. As a result, around 1900 there was an awakening to social needs, with the federal government beginning to place some (although limited) funds into such programs as health, housing, and slum clearance.

In the early 1900s, social welfare became more professionalized. Prior to this time, such services were generally provided by well-meaning but untrained volunteers from the middle and upper socioeconomic groups. At this time, people with more formalized training were employed in some positions, and there was an increased interest in developing therapeutic skills and methods in counseling clients. In this era, some of our present patterns of specialization in social welfare programs also developed, such as family services and probation and parole. It was also at this time that the first schools of social work and social welfare were founded in universities.

The Great Depression and the Social Security Act

Before 1930 social services were provided primarily by churches and voluntary organizations, as was financial assistance for people in need. Some cities and some counties had local relief directors who distributed public tax money financed by local governments. In those days, poverty was associated with laziness and immorality. Public relief money was viewed as "pauper aid," and receiving it was a huge social disgrace.

The Roaring Twenties was largely a time of prosperity and festivities. Then, in October 1929, the New York Stock Exchange crashed. Many investors lost their businesses, homes, and life savings. The crash of the stock market was a significant sign that the U.S. economy (along with the whole world's economy) was heading for a severe depression.

The number of people who were unemployed rose from 3 million in the spring of 1929 to 15 million in January 1933.[17] More than 20% of workers were jobless in 1933.[18] Many banks closed. Many farmers and business owners went bankrupt.

In 1931 some states began providing unemployment relief to prevent starvation among the jobless and their families. Herbert Hoover, who was president at the time, believed that only private charity should meet the needs of the unemployed. He thought public relief (state and federal money) would demoralize people and make them permanently dependent on the state and federal governments. His attitude was graphically illustrated in December 1930 when he approved a $45 million bill to feed starving livestock in Arkansas but opposed a $25 million bill to feed starving farmers and their families in the same state.[19]

Nearly 15 million people were unemployed at the height of the Great Depression. These formerly unemployed workers are selling apples as part of a plan devised by the International Apple Association to help meet the demand for jobs.

Chapters of the Community Chest and the Red Cross, as well as other volunteer organizations, were unable to meet the demand for financial assistance in the early 1930s. Because so many people were unemployed, private charities also had trouble raising the funds necessary to help the jobless.

Local and state funds proved inadequate to protect the growing millions of unemployed against hunger, cold, and despair. Many sick people could not pay for, and therefore did not receive, medical care. Children were passed around among neighbors because their parents had no food or were out looking for jobs. The number of suicides increased, as did the incidence of tuberculosis and malnutrition in children. Many middle-class people became penniless, factories lay idle, and stores had few customers.

In 1933, when President Franklin D. Roosevelt took office, 40% of the population in some states was receiving local and state public relief money.[20] Pressure grew for the federal government to bail out the states and counties by helping finance public relief for those living in poverty. Conditions were so desperate that political leaders became concerned

CASE EXHIBIT 1.2

How "Welfare" Became a Dirty Word

Linda Gordon notes:

> In the last half-century, the American definition of "welfare" has been reversed. A term that once meant prosperity, good health, good spirits, and social respect now implies poverty, bad health, despondency, and social disrespect. A word used to describe the health of the body politic now evokes images of its disease-slums, depressed single mothers, neglected children, crime, despair.[a]

How did this reversal of the concept of welfare occur? The term *welfare* could logically apply to hundreds of societal programs that enhance citizens' well-being: pollution control, schools, parks, counseling, recreational programs, regulation of food and drugs, and so on. Yet the general public, from about 1960 to about 2000, viewed "welfare" as the Aid to Families with Dependent Children (AFDC) Program. As a result, the AFDC program and its recipients were stigmatized.

AFDC was one of the programs enacted by the 1935 Social Security Act. The program was not intended by the writers of that act to be inferior to the other Social Security programs that were created. AFDC was intended to be small in terms of number of recipients and temporary, because the framers believed that the model of the family in which the male was the breadwinner and the female the homemaker would be the standard. AFDC was intended to serve the most deserving of all needy groups—namely, helpless mothers left alone with children by heartless men. In 1935 it was believed that mothers should stay home to raise their children; the vast majority of women were married, and it was considered the obligation of the husband to support the family. Unmarried or abandoned mothers, it was thought, should be helped by the government to stay at home for the *welfare* (well-being) of their children.

Linda Gordon notes that the stigmatization of the AFDC program first began on a large scale in the 1950s and 1960s. There were three main reasons.

The role of women began to be redefined in the 1950s and 1960s. More women were entering the workforce, and it began to be expected that women would work outside the home. As a consequence, single mothers on AFDC began to be shamed for being on the welfare rolls. Negative terms such as "lazy," "undeserving," and "charity cases" were hurled at them.

Another development that contributed to the stigmatization was the increasing divorce rate, which left more women alone to raise their children. With AFDC rolls expanding, the general public became more critical of using taxpayers' money to support single mothers and their children.

A third development in the 1950s that contributed to the stigmatization was that African American women began to assert that AFDC was a right they were entitled to as citizens, just like the right to vote. The success of this claim increased not only the number of AFDC recipients but also the proportion of African Americans among the recipients. As a consequence, the stigma attached to welfare intensified, strengthened now by racist animosity.

Responding to the public outrage about the AFDC program, President Clinton (a Democrat) and the Republican-controlled Congress abolished AFDC in 1996 and replaced it with the program titled Temporary Assistance to Needy Families (TANF). TANF was created by the Personal Responsibility and Work Opportunity Reconciliation Act. This program is described later in this chapter and in Chapter 4.

[a]Linda Gordon, "How 'Welfare' Became a Dirty Word," *The Chronicle of Higher Education*, July. 20, 1994, p. B1.

---

that there might be a Socialist or Communist revolution.

President Roosevelt immediately proposed, and Congress passed, temporary emergency programs to provide paid work for some unemployed workers. For those unable to obtain a job, the federal government provided financial assistance.

The depression of the 1930s brought about profound changes in social welfare. Until that time, the belief in individualism was still widely held—that is, the belief that one is the master of one's fate. The depression shattered this myth. It became clear that situations and events beyond individual control can cause deprivation, misery, and poverty. It also became clear that the federal government must play a role in providing financial assistance and social services.

The experience with emergency relief and work programs during the Great Depression demonstrated the need for more permanent federal efforts in dealing with some of the critical problems of unemployment, aging, disability, illness, and dependent children. As a result, in 1935 the Social Security Act was passed, which forms the basis of most of our current public social welfare programs, and federal legislation for the following three major categories of programs was enacted.

Social Insurance

This category was set up with an institutional orientation and provided insurance for unemployment, retirement, or death. It has two main programs: (a) Unemployment Compensation, which provides weekly benefits for a limited time to workers who lose their jobs, and (b) Old Age, Survivors, Disability, and Health Insurance, which provides monthly payments to individuals and their families when a worker retires, becomes disabled, or dies. In everyday conversation, this program is generally referred to as *Social Security*.

Public Assistance

This category has many residual aspects. To receive benefits, an individual must undergo a "means test" in which one's assets and expenses are reviewed to determine if there is a financial need. There were four programs under this category, with the titles indicating eligible groups: (a) Aid to the Blind (people of any age whose vision is 20/200 or less with correction), (b) Aid to the Disabled (people between the ages of 18 and 65 who are permanently disabled), (c) Old Age Assistance (people 65 and older), and (d) Aid to Families with Dependent Children (AFDC) (primarily mothers with children under age 18 and no father in the home). Public assistance programs incorporated several features of the English Poor Laws: There were residence requirements and a means test, some of the aid was "in kind" (such as food), and the benefits were viewed as "charity" rather than aid to which recipients were entitled. In January 1974 three of these programs—Aid to the Blind, Aid to the Disabled, and Old Age Assistance—were combined into one program, Supplemental Security Income (SSI). SSI is described in Chapter 4.

The AFDC program was frequently criticized and stigmatized by politicians and the general public from the 1960s to the 2000s (see Case Exhibit 1.2). The program was abolished in 1996, and replaced by the Temporary Assistance to Needy Families (TANF) program. The TANF program is described in Chapter 4.

Public Health and Welfare Services

Whereas the first two categories provided financial benefits, this category established the role of the federal government in providing social services (for example, adoption, foster care, services to children with a disability, protective services, and services to single parents).

Following the enactment of the Social Security Act, public social welfare services became dominant in terms of expenditures, people served, and personnel. The private role shifted from financial aid to certain specialized service areas. One of the roles of private agencies has been to test the value of new services and approaches. If such new services are found to be cost effective and successful in alleviating human problems, public funds are sometimes requested to provide them on a large-scale basis.

The programs established by the Social Security Act have been controversial. Some authorities credit the act with bringing economic stability to our country and helping to bring us out of the worst depression we have ever seen. Other authorities, including fiscal conservatives, view Social Security expenditures as perpetuating poverty by making people dependent on government for their livelihood. It has been claimed for many years that people would rather live it up on welfare than work. It is also claimed that the expenditures are highly inflationary, as they represent a sizable portion of our federal government's budget.

The basic intent of the Social Security Act was to provide a decent standard of living to every American. President Roosevelt believed that financial security (including public assistance) should not be a matter of charity but a matter of justice. He asserted that every individual has a right to a minimum standard of living in a civilized society. He believed that liberty and security are synonymous; without financial security, people will eventually despair and revolt. Therefore, Roosevelt held the conviction that the very existence of a democratic society depended on the health and welfare of its citizens.[21]

From the 1930s to the 1980s, the federal government gradually expanded its role in providing financial assistance and social programs to Americans suffering from social problems.

The Great Society and War on Poverty

A major push for expansion of social welfare programs came in the 1960s, when President Lyndon Johnson declared a War on Poverty and sought to create what he called a "Great Society." In 1964 Johnson noted in his State of the Union address that one-fifth of the population was living in poverty and that nearly half of all African Americans were poor. Funding for existing social welfare programs was sharply increased, and many new programs were created (such as Head Start, Medicare, and Medicaid*).

The early 1960s was characterized by optimism; there was a feeling that we were on our way to a golden era in which poverty would gradually disappear, racial integration would occur, and other social

---

*Medicare and Medicaid are described in Chapter 15.

problems would be smoothly and painlessly solved. The late 1960s was therefore a shock: Martin Luther King, Jr., and Robert Kennedy were assassinated; many of our inner cities were torched and burned to the ground during protests against racial discrimination; there were substantial increases in crime; there were student protests and riots on campuses over the Vietnam War and other issues; racial minorities and poor people organized to demand their piece of the national financial pie; there was a revolution in sexual values and behaviors; and there was a recognition of other social ills such as the drug problem and the need to preserve the environment.

In the social welfare field, the late 1960s brought a renewed interest in changing the environment, or "the system," to better meet the needs of clients (sociological approach) rather than enabling clients to better adapt and adjust to their life situations (the psychological approach). Social action again became an important part of social work, with some social workers becoming active as advocates of clients, community organizers, and political organizers for social reform.

Conservatism in the 1970s and 1980s

In the 1970s, after the end of the Vietnam War, the turmoil of the late 1960s was replaced for several years with an atmosphere of relative calm on both the foreign and domestic fronts. In contrast to the hope of the 1960s that government programs could cure our social ills, the opposing philosophy emerged that many problems were beyond the capacity of the government to alleviate. Hence, the liberalism of the 1960s, which resulted in the expansion and development of new social programs, was replaced by a more conservative approach in the 1970s and 1980s. Practically no new large-scale social welfare programs were initiated in the 1970s, 1980s, or early 1990s. Unfortunately, other crises (including Vietnam, Watergate, inflation, recession, the Israeli-Arab conflict, energy crises, political turmoil in Iran, the Iran-Contra affair, the 1991 war against Iraq, political turmoil in Haiti, and the large federal budget deficit) received more attention from 1970 to 1995 than our ongoing social problems, which are still problems today. These social problems include dismal living conditions in the inner cities, the AIDS crisis, homelessness, racial discrimination, crime, prison conditions, family violence, the high divorce rate, overpopulation, and the increasing number of people living in poverty.

During President Jimmy Carter's administration (1976–1980), there was increased recognition that the federal government simply did not have the power—no matter how much money it spent—to cure *all* the country's social ills. But instead of a desire for the government to partially allay *many* of these problems, there appears to have been a complete turnaround in philosophy: Many citizens, and many business leaders, began despairing and demanding that government sharply reduce the amount of tax money it was spending on social welfare programs.

In 1980 our domestic economy was in a mess. The rates of both unemployment and inflation were high, and the country had been in a recession for several years. Ronald Reagan was elected president that year and proceeded, as he had promised during his campaign, to make a number of changes to revitalize the economy and to strengthen the military. The following changes were implemented:

- Taxes were sharply cut for both individuals and corporations. These tax cuts resulted in businesses and consumers having more money to spend, which stimulated the economy and led to a reduction in the unemployment rate.
- Military expenditures were sharply increased, which resulted in a strengthening of our armed forces.
- Expenditures for social programs were sharply cut. This massive cutback was the first large-scale federal reduction in social welfare expenditures in our country's history.

In 1988 George Bush was elected president on a conservative platform, and he continued the social welfare policies of the Reagan administration. Bush believed (as did Reagan) that the federal government is not a solution to social problems but in fact is part of the problem (see Case Exhibit 1.3: Everyone Is on Welfare). Reagan and Bush held that federally funded social welfare programs led recipients to become dependent on the government rather than industrious and productive. The Reagan and Bush administrations endorsed an economic program that cut taxes and government spending, eliminated cumbersome federal regulations and red tape that restricted the growth of business and industry, and provided incentives to the private sector for expansion and greater employment. The stated objective was to create a period of prosperity that would "trickle down" to the lowest stratum so that everyone would benefit. The result, however, was that the gap

CASE EXHIBIT 1.3

Everyone Is on Welfare

Although being on welfare is stigmatized in the United States, the reality is that everyone in the country is on welfare! Mimi Abramovitz notes:

> The social welfare system—direct public provision of cash and in-kind benefits to individuals and families, free or at below market cost—is popularly regarded as serving only poor people. However, the record shows that social welfare programs serving the middle and upper classes receive more government funding, pay higher benefits, and face fewer budget cuts than programs serving only poor people.[a]

Social insurance programs (such as Medicare and Old Age, Survivors, Disability, and Health Insurance) primarily serve the middle and upper classes. These social insurance programs pay significantly higher benefits than the public assistance programs for poor people.

Abramovitz notes there are additional welfare benefits for the middle and upper classes:

> ... the tax system has created a "gilded" welfare state that provides the upper and middle classes with a host of benefits

not available to poor people. Tax benefits for the upper-income groups include low-cost government insurance for Oceanside homes, tax-free investments, reduced capital gains taxes, and tax deductions for charitable giving, large medical expenses, investment losses, and many other items.[b]

Corporations also receive welfare—including government grants, tax reductions, support for research and development, tax deferrals, low-interest loans, tax-free enterprise zones, infrastructure subsidies, tax-exempt industrial development bonds, abatements and credits for property and income taxes, and training subsidies channeled through educational institutions. Although few people think of the use of public dollars to increase private profits as welfare, government aid to big business does not differ all that much from government aid to poor families.

[a]Mimi Abramovitz, "Everyone Is Still on Welfare: The Role of Redistribution in Social Policy," *Social Work*, 46, no. 4 (October 2001), p. 299.
[b]Ibid., p. 302.

---

between the rich and the poor widened, with the poor failing to benefit from the improved financial circumstances of the rich.[22] The people who were hurt the most by cutbacks in federally financed social welfare programs were current and former recipients.

What have been the longer-term effects of these cutbacks? Many of our present social problems intensified: The proportion of people living in poverty increased, the income gap between the rich and the poor widened, efforts to reduce racial discrimination slowed, prisons became overcrowded, many of the chronically mentally ill were released from mental hospitals and became homeless without receiving supportive services, the plight of people living in our inner cities worsened, there was an increase in single-parent families, environmental problems (such as acid rain and chemical waste hazards) increased in severity, and the overall number of homeless and hungry skyrocketed.[23]

A Move toward Liberalism— and Back—in the 1990s

Throughout history the predominant philosophy in our society has swung back and forth like a pendulum between the two poles of liberalism and conservatism. Bill Clinton was elected president in 1992. His views on resolving social problems were consistent with a moderate-to-liberal (middle-of-the-road)

orientation. His liberal proposals included a universal health insurance program for all Americans. (This proposal was extensively debated but eventually defeated by a Republican-controlled Congress.)

The move toward liberalism in the early 1990s was short lived. In the congressional elections of 1994, the Republicans (most with a conservative orientation) won majority control of both the Senate and the House of Representatives. (This was the first time in 40 years that Republicans held a majority in the House.) These Republicans had a conservative political agenda and were successful in passing legislation that shifted spending from crime prevention to prison construction, eliminated welfare benefits for unmarried teens with children, abolished the AFDC program, and cut the capital gains tax (a tax cut that primarily benefits the rich).

The Devolution Revolution

In the late 1990s and early 2000s there was a "devolution revolution" with regard to the provision of human services in our society. The term *devolution revolution* refers to the fact that decisions about the provision of key social welfare programs were transferred from the federal government to the state level. One of the major programs affected by the devolution revolution was AFDC.

From 1935 to the mid-1990s, the federal government required all states to provide the AFDC program to eligible families. (The program was created by the 1935 Social Security Act.) This was a public assistance program that provided monthly checks primarily to low-income mothers with children under age 18. The precise parameters of eligibility for AFDC varied from state to state. Payments were made for both the parent (or parents) and the children in eligible families. Financing and administration of the AFDC program were shared by state governments and the federal government. In many states, counties also participated in the financing and administration. In 1996 federal legislation was enacted that dismantled the AFDC program. The concept of poor families being entitled to health and human services as a basic right shifted back to the assumption that helping unemployed people obtain both jobs (thereby reducing the number of people in poverty) and charity can combat local social problems more cheaply than public services can.

Critical Thinking Question

Are you supportive of, or opposed to, the devolution revolution? Why?

The 1996 welfare reform legislation abolished the AFDC program and created Temporary Assistance to Needy Families (TANF). The program guidelines for TANF are: (a) Each state sets its own eligibility rules and amounts for financial assistance. The federal government provides block grants to states to assist in financing the programs that are developed. (b) Recipients of financial benefits receive no more than 2 years of assistance without working, and there is a 5-year lifetime limit of benefits for adults.

In 1935, when the AFDC program was enacted, it was thought best for single mothers to stay at home to raise their children. The 1996 welfare reform legislation asserted that such single mothers (and fathers) have an obligation to work for a living. The safety net for poor families with young children now has some major holes. Clearly, the legislation marks a shift by our society to the residual approach. The profession of social work is being challenged to confront the devolution revolution and to respond to the needs of those who are falling through the holes in the safety net. (The effects

of TANF on families living in poverty are more fully described in Chapter 4.)

Compassionate Conservatism

George W. Bush (the son of George Bush) was elected president, in a very close election, in 2000. His slogan for his social welfare policies was "compassionate conservatism." George W. Bush adhered to a conservative agenda, while at the same time advocating "compassion" for those in need. In 2004, in another close election, he was reelected president. He was a staunch opponent of women's right to choose abortion. He was opposed to passing legislation to legalize gay marriages. He supported increased federal spending for educational programs for low-income school districts and children with disabilities, Pell grants to help poor students attend college, and experimental private-school voucher programs. During his administration, the United States got involved in fighting wars in two countries—Iraq and Afghanistan. Monies that could have been used to support educational and social welfare programs in the United States were instead largely diverted to fighting these wars.

The last few years of the George W. Bush administration were filled with economic problems, including a mortgage crisis. Through the mid-1990s and early years of the 21st century, the number of subprime mortgage loans rose significantly. Partly due to increased competition among mortgage lenders, many lenders began to focus almost exclusively on subprime mortgages. Their mortgage loans to subprime borrowers usually had much higher interest rates. While the loans extended home ownership, many Americans could not really afford the high mortgage payments. In 2007 to the present time, there were huge increases in home foreclosures because people fell behind on their mortgage payments.

Soon, additional and related problems arose. With so many homes on the real estate market, the market value of homes dropped substantially. Lenders experienced sharp losses because many subprime borrowers did not make mortgage payments. A financial crisis ensued, with many large financial institutions experiencing financial instability themselves. This crisis extended to many foreign investors who had put money in U.S. markets, and to foreign markets. Stock markets around the world experienced meltdowns, and a worldwide recession developed. This worldwide financial crisis was exacerbated by additional factors, such as the sharp increase in the price of oil. As a

Barack Obama, the first African American to be elected president in the United States.

result of the turmoil in stock markets, many investors lost substantial portions of their financial portfolios. People spent less. Companies had difficulties. So there were more problems—the number of homeless rose, workers were laid off or terminated, the unemployed were forced to take low-paying jobs that they were overqualified for, and so on.

Barack Obama—A Time for Change

Barack Obama ran on the platform "A time for change!" and was elected president in November 2008. He was the first African American, or biracial American, to be elected president of the United States. Would this be a transcendent moment for improving the respect of White Americans for people of color?

President Obama entered the Oval Office in Washington, D.C., on January 20, 2009. He took office with our country engaged in two wars (Iraq and Afghanistan), having high unemployment (nearly 10%), experiencing a serious recession, and facing a global financial crisis. He was successful in gaining approval of legislation to reform the U.S. health-care industry (called Obamacare); this health-care

legislation has been sharply criticized by conservatives and Tea Party members. The "don't ask, don't tell" policy in the military has been abolished (see Chapter 7). Our country's military involvement in Iraq has ended. Obama has been successful in phasing out detention of prisoners at the Guantanamo Bay detention camp in Cuba. He has an agenda to negotiate substantial reduction in the world's nuclear arsenals, en route to their eventual extinction. In October 2009, he was awarded the Nobel Peace Prize for his efforts to strengthen international diplomacy and cooperation between peoples. In 2011 he successfully oversaw the capture (and killing) of Osama bin Laden, the founder of Al-Qaeda, the organization responsible for the September 11, 2001, attacks on the Twin Towers (New York City) and the Pentagon, and numerous other civilian and military targets.

Conservatives and members of the Tea Party (see Case Exhibit 1.1: Is the Tea Party Movement the Rebirth of Social Darwinism?) sharply criticize Obama for his handling of the economy—as the housing market continues to be depressed and a high rate of unemployment remains. Also, our country continues to be involved in a military conflict in Afghanistan. Troops are scheduled to be withdrawn by the end of 2014.

Barack Obama was reelected President in November, 2012. His agenda for the next four years includes: subsidizing college tuition; increasing U.S. exports; raising taxes on the wealthy; promoting clean energy; reducing the carbon pollution that's causing global warming; creating more manufacturing jobs; reducing the high unemployment rate; cutting the federal deficit; hiring 100,000 more teachers; making sure insurance companies are providing women with contraception; ending the War in Afghanistan; and further implementing Obamacare (see Chapter 15).

Where Do We Stand Today?

Although many people's perception is that the United States spends more on social welfare than any other country in the world, this is far from accurate. Among industrialized nations, we rank very low in the percentage of gross national product spent on social welfare programs.[24] Sweden, for example, proportionately spends over twice as much as the United States.[25]

The status of social welfare today offers more questions than answers. Here are some issues that need to be addressed:

What new services and programs should be developed to combat the worldwide AIDS crisis? How can drug abuse (such as alcohol and cocaine abuse) be more effectively controlled? What new programs should be developed for the homeless? What new services should be provided to the chronically mentally ill, especially those living on the streets of our cities? How can crime be curbed more effectively and the correctional system be made more rehabilitative? What measures should be taken to eliminate racial discrimination? How can we meet the problems of our inner cities?

Should transracial adoptions be encouraged? How should we remedy broken treaties to Native Americans, and what kinds of services need to be developed for Native Americans to alleviate the wide range of social problems they face? Should abortion laws be made more or less restrictive? What additional services need to be developed for veterans suffering from traumatic brain injury or PTSD? How can child pornography be prevented? How can we prevent the Social Security system from going bankrupt? How can we curb fraud in Medicaid, Medicare, and other social welfare programs? How can child

abuse, sexual abuse, and spousal abuse be curbed? How can we prevent suicides, especially the increasing number among teenagers? Should prostitution be legalized? What should be done about the teenage runaway problem?

Should busing to achieve racial integration be expanded or cut back? Do some affirmative action programs involve reverse discrimination against White males? What programs are needed to prevent rape? How can retirement living be made more meaningful? What measures should be taken to protect the civil rights of gays and lesbians? Should legislation be enacted to curb the sale of handguns? Do we really want to provide the funds and services that are necessary to break the cycle of poverty, or do we still believe that many poor people are undeserving in the sense that they would rather be on welfare than working?

The Future

The future direction and nature of social services will be determined largely by technological advances. In the past 80 years, the following advances have resulted in dramatic changes in our lifestyles: auto and air travel, nuclear power, television, birth control methods, automation, new electrical appliances, shopping centers, the discovery of penicillin and other wonder drugs, and computers.

The relationship between technological breakthroughs and changes in social welfare programs generally follows this format: Technological advances foster changes in our lifestyles; lifestyle changes affect changes in our future social, financial, health, and recreational needs; and the latter changes largely determine what changes will be demanded in social service programs.

Predicting what technological breakthroughs will occur and how these advances will affect our lifestyles is highly speculative. Numerous advances are being predicted: space travel to other planets, computers capable of thinking, chip-enhanced brains to increase intelligence, the end of aging, vaccines that will prevent most forms of cancer, artificial hearts and kidneys, vaccines to prevent HIV infection, robots that perform heart (and other) surgeries, tiny jolts of electricity to the brain to treat depression and seizures, and weather and climate control. Because there are more scientists involved in technological research and development now than at any other time in the history of civilization, future technological breakthroughs are likely to occur even more rapidly than in the past. Adjusting psychologically to

CASE EXAMPLE 1.2

Unethical Use of Technology

Dr. Cecil Jacobson was well known for having introduced amniocentesis in the United States for diagnosing defects in unborn
babies. For many years he operated an infertility clinic in Virginia. In March 1992, a federal jury found him guilty of 52 counts
of fraud and perjury. He was charged with defrauding patients
by artificially inseminating them with his own sperm while
claiming to use other donors. He also was charged with tricking
patients into believing they were pregnant when they were not.
(About 3 months after he first told them they were pregnant, he
told them the fetus had died.) The prosecution alleged that
Jacobson may have fathered as many as 75 children through
artificial insemination. He was sentenced to 5 years in prison,
ordered to pay $116,805 in fines and restitution, and required to
serve 3 years' probation after release from prison. This case example illustrates that the new biomedical reproductive technology can be used unscrupulously.

Dr. Cecil Jacobson

rapid lifestyle changes is currently a major problem
and will continue to be one of the most difficult adjustments people will have to make in future years.

At the same time, environmentalists are predicting
that our civilization is in serious danger due to overpopulation, depletion of energy resources, global
warming, excessive use of toxic chemicals, likelihood
of mass famines and starvation, and dramatic declines in the quality of life.

What the future will hold is difficult to predict
accurately. The worst mistake, however, is to take
the "ostrich head in the sand" approach, in which
no effort is made to plan for and control the future.

A key concern for social welfare in the future is
changes in the American family. When there is family breakdown, social services are generally needed.
As the needs of families change, there is a corresponding demand to change social services.

Dramatic Changes Foreseen in the American Family

In viewing the future of the American family, it is
helpful to gain a perspective by taking a quick glance
at some of the changes that have occurred in the
past. Two hundred years ago, marriages were primarily arranged by parents, with economic considerations being the most important determinant of
who married whom. Divorce was practically un-

heard of; now one of two marriages ends in divorce
or annulment.[26] Two hundred years ago, women did
not work outside the home, and children were an
economic asset; now, about 70% of women work
outside the home, and children are a financial
liability.[27] Since colonial days, the family has lost
(or there has been a sharp decline in) a number of
functions: educational, economic production, religious, protective, and recreational.[28] Today the two
main functions that remain are the affectional (or
companionship) and the child-rearing functions.

In our fast-paced society, the family is likely to
change even more dramatically in the future. As in
the past, the family will be affected significantly by
technological changes. Labor-saving devices in the
home (for example, electrical appliances) have been
and still are an important factor in making it possible
for both spouses to work outside the home. Birth
control methods have undoubtedly been an important factor in leading to an increase in premarital
sexual relationships and in extramarital affairs.

The increased use of abortions has been a factor
in sharply reducing the number of children available
for adoption. Many adoption agencies have suspended taking applications from couples desiring
healthy White infants. An ethically questionable
business has developed in which women are paid
to deliver and give up their babies for adoption to
meet the demands of infertile couples who want a
child. Women willing to bypass the normal adoption

CASE EXHIBIT 1.4

Mr. Mom: Men Can Give Birth

Scientists say that the technology now exists to enable men to give birth! Male pregnancy would involve fertilizing a donated egg with sperm outside the body. The embryo would then be implanted into the bowel area, where it could attach itself to a major organ, such as a kidney or the wall of the large intestine. In addition, to achieve pregnancy, men would have to receive hormone treatment to stimulate changes that occur naturally in women during pregnancy. Because the embryo creates the placenta, the embryo theoretically would receive sufficient nourishment. The baby would be delivered by cesarean section.

Any attempt at male pregnancy would carry risks (perhaps some as-yet-unknown risks) for both the man and the embryo. Will some men try it? If people risk their lives climbing Mt. Everest, someone is likely to try this.

SOURCE: http://serendip.brynmawr.edu/exchange/node/1924.

---

channels may sell an unwanted infant for as much as $20,000,[29] even though baby selling in the United States is illegal.

In the future, the American family is likely to be substantially affected by technological breakthroughs in biology and medicine. Let's look at a few developments in these areas—developments that are as alarming as they are intriguing. (See also Case Exhibit 1.4: Mr. Mom: Men Can Give Birth.)

Biomedical Technology

Artificial Insemination

Thousands of babies are born annually in the United States through the process of artificial insemination, with the usage expected to continue to increase in the future.[30] The process of artificial insemination has long been used with livestock because it eliminates all the problems associated with breeding. A breeder can transport a prized animal's frozen sperm across the world and raise a whole new herd of animals almost effortlessly.

Human sperm can be frozen for long periods of time (the length of time has not been determined; it is generally acknowledged that 5 years would be safe with close to 100% assurance). The sperm can then be thawed and used to impregnate a female. This technology has led to the development of a unique new institution, the sperm bank. Sperm banks are usually private enterprises. They collect and maintain sperm, which is withdrawn at some later date to impregnate a woman with a physician's assistance.

The sperm used in artificial insemination may be the husband's (called AIH, for artificial insemination—husband). There may be several reasons for using AIH. It is possible to pool several ejaculations from a man with a low sperm count and to inject them simultaneously into the vaginal canal of his spouse, thus vastly increasing the chance of pregnancy. AIH may also be used for family planning purposes; for example, a man might deposit his sperm in the bank, then undergo a vasectomy, and later withdraw the sperm to have children. High-risk jobs (such as those with a danger of being exposed to radioactive material) might prompt a man to make a deposit in case of sterility or untimely death.

A second type of artificial insemination is called AID (artificial insemination—donor), in which the donor of the sperm is someone other than the husband. AID has been used for several decades to circumvent male infertility. It is also used when it is known that the husband is a carrier of a genetic disease (such as hemophilia). In recent years, increasing numbers of single women who want a child but do not (at least for the near future) want a husband are requesting the services of a sperm bank. The woman specifies the general genetic characteristics she wants from the father, and the bank then tries to match those requests from the information known about donors.

A third type of artificial insemination is of recent origin and has received considerable publicity. Some married couples, in which the wife is infertile, have contracted for another woman to be artificially inseminated with the husband's sperm. Under the terms of the contract, this "surrogate mother" is paid and is expected to give the infant to the married couple shortly after birth. (Surrogate motherhood is the topic of the next section.)

Numerous ethical, social, and legal questions have been raised about artificial insemination. There are objections from religious leaders that this practice is wrong—that God did not mean for people to reproduce in this way. In the case of AID, there are certain psychological stresses placed on husbands and on marriages; the procedure emphasizes the husband's infertility and involves having a baby that he has not fathered. On a broader scale, artificial insemination raises other questions: What are the purposes of marriage and of sex? What will happen to male–female relationships if we do not even have to see each other to reproduce?

Some unusual court cases point to the need for new laws to resolve the questions that are arising. For instance, consider the case of Mr. and Mrs. John M. Prutting. Mr. Prutting was determined by doctors to be sterile as a result of radiation exposure received at work. Without her husband's knowledge, Mrs. Prutting was artificially inseminated. After the birth of the baby, he sued her for divorce on the grounds of adultery.[31]

In another case, a wife was artificially inseminated with the husband's consent by AID. The couple later divorced. When the husband requested child visitation privileges, his wife took him to court on the grounds that he was not the father and thus had no such right. In New York, he won; she later moved to Oklahoma, where the decision was reversed.[32]

Finally, there was a reported case of an engaged couple whose mothers were discovered to have had the same artificial insemination donor. The couple were thus biologically half-brother and half-sister. The marriage would have been incestuous and was therefore canceled.[33]

There are other possible legal implications. What happens if a couple with AIH sperm at a bank cannot pay the bank's bill? Would it become the property of the bank? Could it be auctioned off? If a woman was artificially inseminated by a donor and the child was later found to have genetic defects, could the parents bring suit against the physician, the donor, or the sperm bank? Does the child have a right to know the identity of the donor father?

Sperm banks can also be used in genetic engineering. In the spring of 1980, it was disclosed that Robert Graham had set up an exclusive sperm bank to produce exceptionally bright children. Graham stated that at least five Nobel Prize winners had donated sperm. Over 200 children were born with sperm from this bank. (Dr. Graham died in 1997, and the sperm bank closed 2 years after the death of its creator.) This approach raises questions about whether reproductive technology should be used to produce "superior" children, and what characteristics should be defined as "superior."

Surrogate Motherhood

Thousands of married couples who want children but are unable to reproduce because the wife is infertile have turned to surrogate motherhood. With this type of motherhood, a surrogate gives birth to a baby conceived by artificial insemination using the husband's sperm. (Often the surrogate mother is paid for her services.) At birth the surrogate mother terminates her parental rights, and the child is then legally adopted by the sperm donor and his wife.

Couples using the services of a surrogate mother are generally delighted with this medical technique and believe it is a highly desirable solution to their personal difficulty of being unable to bear children. However, other groups assert that surrogate motherhood raises a number of moral, legal, and personal issues.

Many theologians and religious leaders firmly believe that God intended conception to occur only among married couples through sexual intercourse. These religious leaders view surrogate motherhood as ethically wrong because the surrogate mother is not married to the sperm donor and because artificial insemination is viewed as "unnatural." Some religious leaders also assert that it is morally despicable for a surrogate mother to accept a fee (often between $5,000 and $10,000). They maintain that procreation is a blessing from God and should not be commercialized.

Surrogate motherhood also raises complicated legal questions that have considerable social consequences. For example, surrogate mothers usually sign a nonbinding contract stipulating that the mother will give up the child for adoption at birth. What if the surrogate mother changes her mind shortly before birth and decides to keep the baby? Women who have been surrogate mothers usually report that they become emotionally attached to the child during pregnancy.[34]

Most surrogate mothers to date are married and already have children. A number of issues are likely to arise. How does the husband of a surrogate mother feel about his wife being pregnant by another man's sperm? How does such a married couple explain to their children that their half-brother or half-sister will be given up for adoption to another family? How does such a married couple explain what they are doing to relatives, neighbors, and the surrounding community? If the child is born with a severe mental or physical disability, who will care for the child and pay for the expenses? Will it be the surrogate mother and her husband, the contracting adoptive couple, or society?

In 1983 a surrogate mother gave birth in Michigan to a baby who was born with microcephaly, a condition in which the head is smaller than normal and mental retardation is likely. At first, neither the surrogate mother nor the contracting adoptive couple wanted to care for the child. The adoptive couple refused to pay the $10,000 fee to the surrogate mother. A legal battle ensued. Blood tests were eventually taken that indicated the probable father was not the contracting adoptive father but rather the husband of the surrogate mother. Following the blood tests, the surrogate mother and her husband assumed the care of the child. (This example illustrates another problem with the surrogate motherhood approach: If the surrogate mother engages in sexual intercourse with her partner/husband at about the same time that artificial insemination occurs, the biological father may be the partner/husband.)

In 1986 Mary Beth Whitehead was a surrogate mother who gave birth to a child. She refused to give up the baby for adoption by the genetic father and his wife, even though she had signed a $10,000 contract in which she agreed to give up the child. The genetic father, William Stern, took the case to court, demanding that Whitehead honor the contract she had signed. Whitehead claimed she was the mother of the child and therefore had maternal rights to the child. The case received national attention. In April 1987, in the nation's first judicial ruling on a disputed surrogate contract, the judge ruled that the contract was valid. Just as men have a constitutional right to sell their sperm, women can decide what to do with their wombs.[35] Whitehead appealed this decision to the New Jersey State Supreme Court. In 1988 this court ruled that the contract between Whitehead and the Sterns was invalid because it involved the sale of a mother's right to her child, which violated state laws prohibiting child selling. This decision voided the adoption of the baby by Mrs. Stern; Mr. Stern was given custody, and Whitehead was granted visitation rights.

Test-Tube Babies

In England, on July 24, 1978, Lesley Brown gave birth to the first "test-tube baby." An egg taken from her reproductive system had been externally artificially impregnated using AIH and then implanted in her uterus to complete the normal process of pregnancy. The technique, called embryo transfer, was developed for women whose fallopian tubes are so damaged that the fertilized egg cannot pass through the tubes to the womb as is necessary for it to develop and grow until birth. Following the announcement of this birth, there was a surge of applications from thousands of childless couples asking fertility experts for similar implants.[36]

Another breakthrough in this area occurred in 1984, when an egg donated by one woman was fertilized and then implanted in another woman. Australian researchers in January 1984 reported the first successful birth resulting from a procedure in which an embryo was externally conceived and then implanted in the uterus of a surrogate.[37] This type of surrogate motherhood is a modern-day twist on the wet nurse (a woman who cares for and breast-feeds a child not her own) of earlier times. An unusual application of this new technology occurred in South Africa in 1987, when a grandmother, Pat Anthony, gave birth to her own grandchildren. The daughter was infertile, so her eggs (which had been fertilized in a lab) were implanted into Ms. Anthony. Several months later, Ms. Anthony gave birth to triplets.[38]

This type of surrogate motherhood differs from the earlier version in which the surrogate mother contributes half of the genetic characteristics through the use of her egg. Here the surrogate contributes neither her own egg nor any of the genetic characteristics of the child.

Surrogate pregnancies can, in one respect, be seen as the final step in the biological liberation of women. Like men, women can "sire" children without the responsibility of pregnancy and childbirth.

However, surrogate pregnancies promise to create a legal nightmare. Do the genetic mother and father have any binding legal rights? Can the genetic parents place reasonable restrictions on the surrogate's medical care and diet during the pregnancy? Can the genetic parents require the surrogate mother not to smoke or drink? Could the genetic parents require the surrogate to abort? Could the surrogate abort without the genetic parents' consent? Whose child is it if both the genetic mother and the surrogate mother want to be recognized as the legal mother after the child is born? Will low-income women tend to serve as "holding tanks" for upper-class women's children? Legal experts see far-reaching changes in family law, inheritance, and the concept of legitimacy if laboratory fertilization and childbearing by surrogate mothers become accepted practices.

Human embryo transplants, when combined with principles of genetic selection, allow people who want "superhuman" children to select embryos in which the resultant infant has a high probability of being

CASE EXAMPLE 1.3

Embryo Case Gains International Attention

A South American–born couple, Elsa and Mario Rios, amassed a fortune of several million dollars in real estate in Los Angeles. In 1981 they enrolled in a "test-tube baby" program at Queen Victoria Medical Center in Melbourne, Australia, after their young daughter died. Several eggs were removed from Mrs. Rios and fertilized by her husband's sperm, which had been collected in a laboratory container. One of the fertilized eggs was implanted in Mrs. Rio's womb, but she had a miscarriage 10 days later. The two remaining embryos were frozen so that doctors could try implantation at a later time.

On April 2, 1983, the couple was killed in the crash of a private plane in Chile. Because doctors have successfully thawed and implanted frozen embryos (which have resulted in births), a number of social and legal questions arise:

- Should the embryos be implanted in the womb of a surrogate mother in the hope that they will develop to delivery?
- Are the embryos legal heirs to the multimillion-dollar estate?
- Does life legally begin at conception? If a surrogate mother carries the embryo to birth, is she legally the mother, and is she entitled to some of the inheritance?
- Do embryos conceived outside the womb have rights? If so, what rights? Should these rights be the same as those accorded born humans? (An Australian court ruled in 2008 that the two frozen embryos would be thawed and implanted if a suitable recipient could be found. Doctors rated these aged embryos as having a 5% survival chance. No suitable recipient has been found. This case highlights how the rapid advancement of *in vitro* fertilization (fertilization outside the human body) has outstripped attitudes and laws.

SOURCE: "Quickening Debate over Life on Ice," *Time*, July 1, 2008.

free of genetic defects. The technology also allows parents to choose, with a high probability of success, the genetic characteristics they desire—such as the child's sex, color of eyes and hair, skin color, probable height, probable muscular capabilities, and probable IQ. A superhuman embryo can be formed by combining the sperm and egg of a male and female who are thought to have the desired genetic characteristics.

This breakthrough will raise a number of personal and ethical questions. Couples desiring children may be faced with the decision of having a child through natural conception or of preselecting superhuman genetic characteristics through embryo transplants. Another question that will arise is whether our society will attempt to use this new technology to control human evolutionary development. If the answer is affirmative, decisions will need to be made about which genetic characteristics should be considered "desirable," and questions will arise about who should have the authority to make such decisions. Although our country may not want to control human evolutionary development in this manner, will we not feel it necessary to do so if a rival nation begins a massive evolutionary program? In addition, will parents have the same or somewhat different feelings toward children who result from embryo transplants compared to children who result from natural conception?

Genetic Screening

Practically all states now require mandatory genetic screening programs for various disorders. There are about 2,000 human disorders caused by defective genes, and it is estimated that each of us carries two or three of them.[39] Mass genetic screening could eliminate some of these disorders. One screening approach that is increasingly being used with pregnant women is amniocentesis, which is the surgical insertion of a hollow needle through the abdominal wall and uterus of a pregnant female to obtain amniotic fluid for the determination of chromosomal abnormality. Amniocentesis should be performed between the 13th and 16th weeks of pregnancy.

Another technique for prenatal diagnosis of birth defects is chorionic villus sampling (CVS). It involves taking a sample of cells from the chorionic villus and analyzing them. CVS is preferable to amniocentesis because it can be done in the first trimester of pregnancy, usually around 9 to 11 weeks postconception.

More and more pregnant women are being encouraged to terminate pregnancy if a fetus will be (or is at a high risk of being) genetically inferior. In addition, some genetic disorders can be corrected if diagnosed in time.

Genetic screening programs raise serious questions. Which fetuses should be allowed to continue to grow and which should be aborted? Who shall be

CASE EXAMPLE 1.4

Redefining Motherhood

In August 1990, surrogate mother Anna Johnson filed legal papers seeking parental rights to a child created from the sperm and egg of Mark and Crispina Calvert in California. Ms. Johnson gave birth to the child under a $10,000 surrogacy contract. She was the first surrogate mother to seek custody of a child not genetically related to her. In October 1990, the judge handling the case ruled that Ms. Johnson had no parental rights under California law. The judge assigned permanent custody of the child to the genetic parents. Both the appellate court and the California Supreme Court affirmed the trial court's decision. A precedent appears to have been set, which recognizes that genetics is the primary criterion for determining parentage when a surrogate carries a child genetically unrelated to her.

SOURCE: Susan Peterson and Susan Kelleher, "Surrogate's Loss Could Redefine Motherhood," *Wisconsin State Journal*, Oct. 23, 1990, p. 4A

---

allowed to have children? Who shall make such decisions? Is this a direction our country ought to take?

Genetic screening during pregnancy can be used to detect a wide variety of inherited disorders. For example, Huntington's chorea is an inherited disease in which the principal symptoms are involuntary movements—either rapid, forcible, and jerky or smooth and sinuous. This disorder is often associated with loss of intellectual abilities. Its onset is usually evidenced during middle age. If a fetus is diagnosed as having the gene for this disorder, which usually results in serious mental and physical deterioration in midlife, the pregnant woman and her partner would then be faced with the heart-wrenching decision of whether it would be best to terminate the pregnancy.

The eugenics (scientific breeding) movement was proposed late in the 19th century and embraced by many scientists and government officials. Similar to today, eugenics was designed to improve humanity or individual races by encouraging procreation by those deemed "most desirable" and discouraging it in those judged "deficient." The movement fell into disfavor for a while when Adolf Hitler used it to justify the Holocaust, in which millions of Jews, Gypsies, gays and lesbians, persons with a cognitive disability, and others were exterminated. Are we headed in a similar direction again?

Critical Thinking Question

Would you want to be tested at an early age to obtain information as to which inherited diseases you are likely to have as you go through life? Why or why not?

Cloning

Cloning refers to the process whereby a new organism is reproduced from the nucleus of a single cell. The resultant new organism has the same genetic characteristics of the organism that contributes the nucleus. In effect, it is now possible to make biological copies of humans from a single cell. Biologically, each cell is a blueprint containing all the genetic code information for the design of the organism. Cloning has already been used to reproduce frogs, mice, cattle, sheep, pigs, and other animals.[40]

One type of cloning amounts to a nuclear transplant. The nucleus of an unfertilized egg is destroyed and removed. The egg is then injected with the nucleus of a body cell by one means or another. It should then start to take orders from the new nucleus, begin to reproduce cells, and eventually manufacture a baby with the same genetic features as the donor. The embryo would need a place to develop into a baby—either an artificial womb or a woman willing to supply her own. (The technology for a complete artificial womb is not yet in sight.) The resultant clone would start life with a genetic endowment identical to that of the donor, although learning experiences might alter physical development and personality. The possibilities are as fantastic as they are repulsive. With a quarter-inch piece of skin, one could produce 1,000 genetic copies of any noted scientist or of anyone else! Imagine a professional basketball team composed of two LeBron James and three Kobe Bryants!

In 1993 a university researcher in the state of Washington cloned human embryos using a technique that already was widely used to clone animal embryos. The process involves taking a single human

CASE EXAMPLE 1.5

Clones: Dolly (a Sheep) and Gene (a Calf)

Early in 1997, scientists in Scotland announced they had cloned Dolly, a sheep. In August 1997, scientists in Windsor, Wisconsin, announced they had cloned Gene, a Holstein calf.

Gene was the result of cloning a stem cell from a calf fetus. Stem cells are "blank slates" that have not yet specialized their function. (Examples of specialized cells are liver cells and muscle cells.) Researchers took the nucleus of a cell from the fetus of a calf and inserted the nucleus into a stem cell from a cow in which the genetic material had been removed. The new cell grew into an embryo and was implanted into a cow, where it

grew into Gene. The process used by ABS Global, Inc., in Wisconsin allows for an *infinite* number of copies of a clone to be produced. ABS Global indicated that the technique will allow for fast, reliable duplication of cattle that produce impressive amounts of either beef or milk.

Can the same technique be used to clone a human? Probably.

SOURCE: Rick Barret, "Calf Cloning May Lead to Food, Drug Advances," *Wisconsin State Journal*, Aug. 8, 1997, p. 1A.

embryo and splitting it into identical twins.[41] Because human embryos can be frozen and gestated at a later date, it is now possible for parents to have a child and then, years later, use a frozen cloned embryo to give birth to an identical twin. It is also possible for parents to save identical copies of embryos so that if a child ever needed an organ transplant, the mother could give birth to the child's identical twin, who would be a perfect match for organ donation.

In 2001 biologists at Advanced Cell Technology in Worcester, Massachusetts, announced they had created human embryos through cloning. They removed DNA from a female human egg, and replaced it with the DNA from a body cell. (The embryos died at a very early stage.) The technique used at Advanced Cell Technology was similar to that used to clone the sheep Dolly in 1997 (see Case Example1.5). Their goal is not to create cloned humans but to grow so-called stem cells for medical purposes. Such cells may be used to find cures for diseases like Parkinson's, ALS (Lou Gehrig's disease), diabetes, paralysis, and other thus far incurable conditions.

In 2008 Dr. Samuel Wood and Dr. Andrew French announced that they had successfully created the first five mature human embryos using DNA from adult skin cells. (Their objective was to provide a less-controversial source of viable embryonic stem cells.) The DNA from adult skin cells was transferred to human cells. It is not clear if the embryos produced would have been capable of further development. All the cloned embryos were later destroyed.

Cloning could, among other things, be used to resolve the ancient controversy of heredity versus

environment. But there are grave dangers and perhaps undreamed-of complications. What is to prevent the Adolf Hitlers from making copies of themselves? Will cloning fuel the population explosion? What legal rights will clones be accorded (regarding inheritance, for example)? Will religions recognize clones as having a "soul"? Who will decide which individuals can make clones of themselves? Couples may face the choice of having children naturally or raising children who are copies of themselves.

In the relatively near future, we will progress from cloning human embryonic cells to cloning a human.

Critical Thinking Question

Do you believe it is desirable to clone humans? Why or why not?

Stem Cells

Recent studies suggest that stem cells may hold the secret to treatment, or even cures, for some of our most baffling diseases and injuries, including Alzheimer's, Parkinson's, cancer, diabetes, spinal cord injuries, and other diseases.

Stem cells have the remarkable potential to develop into many different cell types in the body. In addition, in many tissues they serve as a sort of internal repair system, dividing essentially without limit to replenish other cells.

There are currently three types of stem cells: embryonic stem cells, adult stem cells, and induced pluripotent stem cells.

Embryonic stem cells are controversial. They come from the inner cell mass of a blastocyst, the term for a fertilized egg 4 days after conception. (Pro-life advocates argue that using the cells for research or treating diseases is the equivalent of taking a life.)

The primary roles of adult stem cells in a living organism are to maintain and repair the tissue in which they are found. Adult stem cells have been identified in many organs and tissues—including the brain, bone marrow, blood vessels, skeletal muscle, skin, teeth, the heart, and the liver. Unlike embryonic stem cells (which can become all cell types found in the body), adult stem cells are thought to be limited to differentiating into different cell types of their tissue of origin.

Induced pluripotent stem cells are adult cells that have been genetically reprogrammed to a state similar to that of an embryonic stem cells by being forced to express genes and factors characteristic of embryonic stem cells.

Human stem cells can be used to test the effectiveness, and side effects, of new drugs. Human stem cells can be useful in helping scientists better understand the complex events that occur during human development—for example, to identify how undifferentiated stem cells become the differentiated cells that form tissues and organs. Also, the most important potential application of human cells is the generation of cells and tissues that could be used for cell-based therapies to treat a multitude of diseases and medical conditions (including Alzheimer's disease, cancer, spinal cord injuries, burns, heart disease, osteoarthritis, and rheumatoid arthritis).

Much research, however, needs to be done to develop cell-based therapies!

Critical Thinking Question

Are you supportive of, or opposed to, an expansion of stem cell research? Why?

Breaking the Genetic Code

Biochemical genetics is the discipline that studies the mechanisms whereby genes control the development and maintenance of the organism.

Current research focuses on understanding more precisely the roles of DNA (deoxyribonucleic acid) and messenger RNA (ribonucleic acid) in affecting the growth and maintenance of humans. When genes, DNA, and RNA are more fully understood, it may become possible to keep people alive, young, and healthy almost indefinitely. It is predicted that aging will be controlled, and any medical condition (for example, an allergy, obesity, cancer, arthritic pain) will be relatively easy to treat and eradicate. Such possibilities stagger the imagination.

In January 1989, the National Institutes of Health launched a project to map the human genome—that is, to identify and list in order all of the genome's approximately 3 million base pairs. (The genome is the full set of chromosomes that carries all of the inherited traits of an organism—in other words, the "scripts" in our cells that strongly influence health and illness, behavior, special abilities, and life expectancy.)[42] In June 2000, the Human Genome Project announced it had pieced together a "rough draft" of the human genome. It is believed this map will permit scientists to predict an individual's vulnerability to genetic diseases, to treat genetically caused diseases, and possibly to "enhance" a person's genetic potential through the introduction of gene modifications.[43]

Scientists have already discovered the genes that cause a variety of illnesses, such as cystic fibrosis, and demonstrated that gene therapy can be used to correct the underlying defect.[44] The approach uses genetically engineered cold viruses to ferry healthy genes into the body. (Cystic fibrosis results from a mutation in the gene that produces a protein called cystic fibrosis transmembrane conductive regulator. When the protein is missing, thick mucus builds up in the lungs, causing lung damage and eventually death, often by age 30.)

With this potential to break the genetic code to keep people alive and healthy indefinitely, we will be faced with many legal and ethical issues. Perhaps the most crucial issues will be who will live and who will die and who will be permitted to have children. A fountain of youth may occur within our lifetime.

New Family Forms

As we've seen, technology has had profound effects on the family. Now we'll look at some changes in the social structure of our society that are also causing us to redefine our notion of what a family is.

Childless Couples

Traditionally, our society has fostered the perception that there is something wrong with a couple who decides not to have children. Parenthood is regarded legally and religiously as one of the central components of a marriage. In some states, deceiving one's spouse before marriage about the desire to remain childless is grounds for an annulment. Perhaps in the future this myth of procreation will be shattered by the concern about overpopulation and by the high cost of raising children; the average cost of raising a child from birth to age 18 for a two-parent family is estimated to be $226,920. The expenses are for food, shelter, and other necessities.[45]

Postponement of Parenthood until Middle Age or Later

Biological innovations, such as embryo transfers, are now making it possible for women in their 50s and even their 60s to give birth. As a result, couples have more leeway in deciding at what age they wish to raise children. Young couples today are often torn in their time commitments between their children and their careers. In our society, most couples now have children at the busiest time of their lives. Deferring raising children until later in life provides substantial activity and meaning in later adulthood. A major question, of course, is whether such a family pattern will lead to an increase in the number of orphans, as older parents have a higher death rate than younger parents. (An increase in the number of orphans would significantly impact adoption and foster-care services.) Additional questions are whether having older parents would lead to even more gaps in values between the older parents and their young children and whether the older parents would have sufficient energy to keep up with their young children.

Professional Parents

Alvin Toffler predicted that our society will develop a system of professional, trained, and licensed parents to whom a number of natural parents (bioparents) will turn to raise their children.[46] The natural parents would, of course, be permitted frequent visits, telephone contacts, and time to care for the children whenever they desired.

Toffler stated: "Even now millions of parents, given the opportunity, would happily relinquish their parental responsibilities—and not necessarily through irresponsibility or lack of love. Harried, frenzied, up against the wall, they have come to see themselves as inadequate to the tasks."[47] The high rates of child abuse, child neglect, and teenage runaways seem to bear out the assertion that in a large number of families the parent–child relationship is more dissatisfying

than satisfying. Many parents already hire part-time professional parents in the form of nannies and day-care center workers.

In our society, there is currently a belief system that bioparents should care for their children, even if they find the responsibility unrewarding. Only a tiny fraction of bioparents currently terminate their parental rights. Why? Could it be that many parents who have unsatisfying relationships with their children are reluctant to give up their parenting responsibilities because of the stigma that would be attached? Two hundred years ago, divorces were rare mainly because of a similar stigma. Now, with increased acceptance of divorce, one of two marriages is being terminated. Is it not also feasible that a number of parents who cannot choose the characteristics of their children may also find the relationships with some of their children to be more dissatisfying than satisfying? The point is reinforced when it is remembered that a number of pregnancies are unplanned *and* unwanted.

Serial and Contract Marriages

Culturally, religiously, and legally speaking, marriages are still expected to be permanent (that is, for a lifetime). Such a view implies that the two partners made the right decision when they married, that their personalities and abilities complement each other, and that their personalities and interests will develop in tandem for the rest of their lives. All of these suppositions (along with the concept of permanency) are being called into question, however.

With the high rates of divorce and remarriage, some sociologists have pointed out that a small proportion of our population is entering (perhaps unintentionally) into serial marriages—that is, a pattern of successive, temporary marriages.[48] Serial marriages among celebrities have been widely publicized for a number of years. Viewing marriage as temporary in nature may help reduce some of the embarrassment and pain still associated with divorce and perhaps result in an increase in the number of unhappily married people who will seek a divorce. Divorce per se is neither good nor bad; if both partners find that their lives are happier and more satisfying following legal termination, the end result may be viewed as desirable.

The growing divorce rate has resulted in the development of extensive services involving premarital counseling, marriage counseling, divorce counseling, single-parent services and programs, and remarriage counseling for spouses and the children involved. If marriage is increasingly viewed as temporary in nature, divorce may become even more frequent and result in an expansion of related social services.

Several sociologists have proposed that the concept of marriage as temporary be legally institutionalized through a contract marriage. For example, a couple would be legally married for a 2-year period, and (only in marriages where there are no children) the marriage would automatically be terminated unless they filed legal papers for a continuation.[49] A closely related type of contract is the prenuptial agreement, in which a couple prior to marriage specify how their financial assets will be divided if they divorce. (Prenuptial agreements have been criticized as a factor in psychologically setting up an expectation that a divorce is apt to occur.)

Another arrangement embodying the temporary concept is "trial marriage," which is increasingly being tested out by young people. They live together on a day-by-day basis and share expenses. Closely related—and perhaps more common—is the arrangement in which the two maintain separate addresses and domiciles but for several days a month actually live together. (Perhaps this latter form is more accurately described as a "serial honeymoon" than a "trial marriage.") Acceptance of trial marriage is currently being advocated by some religious philosophers, and many states no longer define cohabitation as illegal.

Increasingly, courts are ruling that cohabiting couples who dissolve their living arrangements have certain legal obligations to each other quite similar to the obligations of a married couple.

Open Marriages

O'Neill and O'Neill contrast traditional marriages with "open marriages," of which they are advocates.[50] A traditional or "closed" marriage, the O'Neills assert, embodies concepts such as (a) possession or ownership of mate; (b) denial or stifling of self; (c) playing the "couples game" by doing everything together during leisure time; (d) the husband being dominant and out in the world and the wife being domestic and passive and staying at home with the children; and (e) absolute fidelity. An open marriage, in contrast, offers freedom to pursue individual interests, flexible roles in meeting financial responsibilities, shared domestic tasks, and expansion and growth through openness. In an open marriage, the partners are free to have extramarital relationships or sex without betraying one another. Such a marriage is based on communication, trust, and respect, and it is expected that one partner's growth will facilitate the other partner's development.

Marriage counselors increasingly report that couples have serious interaction difficulties because one spouse has a traditional orientation whereas the other has an open-marriage orientation. The feminist movement and the changing roles of women have brought the conflict between open and closed marriages into public awareness. Marriage counselors now see large numbers of couples in which the wife wants a career, her own identity, and a sharing of domestic responsibilities, but the husband, traditionally oriented, wants his wife to stay home and take care of domestic tasks.

Group Marriages

Group marriage provides insurance against isolation. In the 1960s and 1970s, communes of young people flourished. In the later 1970s and in the 1980s, most communes disbanded. The goals, as well as the structure, of these communes varied widely, involving diverse social, political, religious, sexual, or recreational objectives.

Interestingly, geriatric communes (which have many of the characteristics and obligations of group marriages) are being advocated by a number of sociologists. Such arrangements may be a solution to a number of social problems of older people.

They may provide companionship, new meaning, and interest to the participants' lives, as well as an arrangement in which older adults with reduced functioning capacities can be of mutual assistance to one another. Older adults can thereby band together, pool resources, hire nursing or domestic help if needed, and feel that "life begins at 60." In nursing homes, retirement communities, group homes for older persons, and assisted-living residences, some of the older adults are presently developing relationships that are similar to group marriages.

Same-Sex Marriages

The number of same-sex marriages is on the rise in the United States, particularly in such areas as California and Massachusetts. However, the issue of whether these marriages should be legal according to the laws of given states remains extremely controversial. In 1989 the San Francisco City Council passed an ordinance that legalized such marriages. In opposition, in 1996 Congress passed the Defense of Marriage Act, which allows states to pass laws against same-sex marriages but does not oblige them to do so.

In 2001 the Netherlands was the first country to allow same-sex marriages. Same-sex marriages are also legal in Argentina, Iceland, Canada, Belgium, Norway, Spain, Sweden, and South Africa.

Whether to recognize same-sex marriages has become a major issue in the United States and in many other countries. In the United States, the battle in the courts and at the local, state, and federal levels over same-sex marriage rights is likely to continue for some time. Different courts have ruled inconsistently on whether such marriages should be considered legal. The battle is also going on internationally. For example, the Vatican has a global campaign against the legalization of gay marriages. At the time of writing this edition of the text, same sex-marriages were legal in eight states in the United States: Massachusetts, Maryland, Connecticut, Iowa, Maine, New Hampshire, Washington State, and Vermont. With the passage of Proposition 8, gay marriage is no longer an option in California.

Almost as controversial are the recent decisions by some municipalities and some corporations (such as Disney and Xerox) to extend health and other insurance benefits to the domestic partners of gay and lesbian employees.

Critical Thinking Question

Are you supportive of, or opposed to, the legalization of gay marriage? Why?

Many same-sex couples consider themselves to be married, and an estimated one-third of lesbians and one-fifth of gay males have children from previous heterosexual marriages or relationships.[51] In addition, lesbian couples are increasingly using artificial insemination to have children.

Adoption agencies and the courts are now facing decisions about whether to allow same-sex couples to adopt children. Single people are already being permitted by some agencies and courts to adopt children, so the argument that a child needs both a male and a female figure in the family is diluted.

Questions have been raised as to how children will fare in these families. Hyde and Delamater indicate that three primary questions have been raised:

First, will they show "disturbances" in gender identity or sexual identity? Will they become gay or lesbian? Second, will they be less psychologically healthy than children who grow up with two heterosexual parents? Third, will they have difficulties in relationships with their peers, perhaps being stigmatized or teased because of their unusual family situation?[52]

Research on children growing up in lesbian or gay families, compared with those growing up in heterosexual families, dismisses these fears. Overwhelming numbers of children growing up in lesbian or gay households have a heterosexual orientation. The adjustment and mental health of children in lesbian and gay families are no different from those of children in heterosexual families. Children in lesbian or gay families fare about as well in terms of social skills and popularity as children in heterosexual families.[53]

Transracial Adoptions

Asian and Native American children have been adopted by White parents for more than six decades.[54] About 50 years ago, some White couples began adopting African American children. Questions have arisen about the desirability of placing African American children in White adoptive homes. To answer some of these questions, this author conducted a study comparing the satisfactions derived and problems encountered between transracial adoptive parents and inracial adoptive parents.[55] Transracial adoptions were found to be as satisfying as inracial adoptions. In addition, transracial adoptive children were found to have been accepted by relatives, friends, neighbors, and the general community following placement. The transracial adoptive parents reported that substantially fewer problems had arisen due to the race of the child than even they anticipated before the adoption. They also indicated that they had parental feelings that the child was really their own. They reported becoming "color-blind" following placement—that is, they came to see the child not as African American but as a member of their family.

Unfortunately, none of the children in the study was older than 6. Some observers, a number of whom are African American, have raised questions about whether Black children reared by White parents will experience serious identity problems as they grow older. For example, will they experience difficulty in deciding which race to identify with, in learning how to cope with racial discrimination due to being raised in a White home, and in interacting with both Whites and Blacks due to a (speculated)

In the past few decades transracial adoptions have provided adoptive homes for children of color who might otherwise be raised in a series of foster homes.

confused sense of who they are? On the other hand, advocates of transracial adoption respond by asserting that the parent–child relationship is more crucial to identity formation than the racial composition of the family members. The question, of course, is critical, especially because there is a large number of homeless African American children and a shortage of African American adoptive parents.

One organization that has been strongly opposed to the adoptive placement of African American children in White homes is the National Association of Black Social Workers. This group views such placements as "cultural genocide."[56]

In 1971 Rita J. Simon began studying 204 White families who had adopted children of color. Joined later by Howard Altstein and many generations of graduate students, she went back to talk to the families over a period of 20 years.[57] The researchers interviewed the families in 1971, 1979, 1983, and 1991.

Most of the children they studied now live away from their parents' homes. The majority of adoptees, despite occasional family conflicts, believe that their parents raised them well. If anything, some felt that the parents had overdone it a bit in trying to educate them about their heritage. African American adoptees, for example, complained that too many dinnertime conversations turned into lectures on Black history. The parents, although also acknowledging occasional conflicts, reported satisfaction with their decisions to adopt across racial lines. Fully 90% said they recommended transracial adoption for families planning to adopt. The researchers concluded that children of color who grow up in White families do not become confused about their identities, racial or otherwise.

Comarital Sex

The term *comarital sex* refers to mate swapping and other organized extramarital relations in which both spouses agree to participate. Comarital sex is distinctly different from a traditional extramarital affair, which is usually clandestine, with the straying spouse trying to hide the relationship.

Although some couples appear able to integrate comarital agreements into their lives successfully, others find their marriages breaking up as a consequence.[58] According to marriage counselors, a major reason couples drop out of comarital relationships, and sometimes end their marriage, is because of jealousy, competition, and possessiveness.[59]

The interest in comarital sex and extramarital sex raises the age-old question of whether any *one* individual can satisfy all of the intimate, sexual, and interpersonal needs of another. In the future (and perhaps now), there may be a decrease in comarital and extramarital relationships due to the fear of acquiring AIDS.

Single Parenthood

Although in many people's minds marriage and parenthood "go together," single parenthood is emerging as a prominent form in our society. In many states, it is possible for unmarried people to adopt a children. In addition, an unmarried pregnant woman can refuse to marry and yet keep her child after it is born. Some unmarried fathers have been successful in obtaining custody of their children. Today, although the stigma attached to being single and pregnant is not as strong as it once was, this situation is still seriously frowned on by some.

Similar to single parenthood is the one-parent family, in which a person divorces or legally separates, assumes custody of one or more children, and chooses not to remarry. Although traditionally the mother has been awarded custody of the children, today the courts are occasionally granting custody to fathers. Another arrangement is shared custody, wherein both mother and father have the children part of the time.

Do single parents and one-parent families pose a serious problem? Are children adversely affected by being raised in a one-parent family? Papalia and Olds summarize some of the problems children face in growing up in one-parent families:

> Children growing up in one-parent homes undoubtedly have more problems and more adjustments to make than children growing up in homes where there are two adults to share the responsibilities for child rearing, to provide a higher income, to more closely approximate cultural expectations of the "ideal family," and to offer a counterpoint of sex role models and an interplay of personalities. But the two-parent home is not always ideal, and the one-parent home is not necessarily pathological.[60]

Research indicates that it is better for children to be raised in a non–tension-laden one-parent family than in a tension-laden two-parent family.[61]

Blended Families

Many terms have been used to describe two families joined by the marriage of one parent to another: *stepfamilies, blended families, reconstituted families*, and *nontraditional families*. Here we will use the term *blended families*.

One of two marriages ends in divorce, and many divorcees have children. Most people who divorce remarry someone else within a few years. Moreover, some individuals who are marrying for the first time may have a child born outside of marriage. Thus, various types of blended families are now being formed in our society.

In blended families, one or both spouses have biologically produced one or more children with someone else prior to their current marriage. Often, the newly married couple give birth to additional children. In yet other blended families, the children are biologically a combination of "his, hers, and theirs."

Blended families are increasing in number and proportion in our society, and the family dynamics and relationships are much more complex than in the traditional nuclear family. Blended families, in short, are burdened by much more "baggage" than are two childless adults marrying for the first time. Blended families must deal with stress that arises from the loss (through divorce or death) experienced by both adults and children, which can make them afraid to love and to trust. Previously established bonds between children and their biological parents, or loyalty to a dead or absent parent, may interfere with the formation of ties to the stepparent. If children go back and forth between two households, conflicts between stepchildren and stepparents may be intensified. Sometimes, divorced spouses continue to feud; in these cases, the children are likely to be used as "pawns," thus generating additional strife in the recently formed blended family.

Some difficulties in adjustment for the children are to be expected.[62] Jealousies may arise because the child resents sharing parental attention with the new spouse and with new siblings. Another issue for children is the adjustment to a new parent who may have different ideas, values, rules, and expectations. Sharing space with new people can be a source of stress as well. In addition, if one member of the couple enters the marriage with no child-rearing experience, an adjustment will be necessary by all family members to allow time for the new parent to learn and adapt.

People come into a blended family with ideas and issues based on past experiences. Old relationships and ways of doing things still have their impacts. In discussing blended families, Stuart and Jacobson note that marrying a new partner involves marrying a whole new family.[63] A blended family differs from a traditional family in that more people are involved, including ex-spouses, former in-laws, and an assortment of cousins, uncles, and aunts. The married couple may have both positive and negative interactions with this large supporting cast. If a prior marriage ended bitterly, the unresolved emotions that remain (such as anger and insecurity) will affect the present relationship.

The area of greatest stress for most stepparents is that of child rearing. A stepchild, used to being raised in a certain way, may balk at having to conform to new rules or at accepting the stepparent as a parental figure. Such difficulty is more likely to arise if the stepchild feels remorse over the missing parent. If the husband and wife disagree about how to raise children, the chances of conflict are substantially increased. Stepparents and stepchildren also face the problem of adjusting to each other's habits and personalities. Kompara recommends that stepparents not rush into establishing a relationship with stepchildren; proceeding gradually is more likely to result in a trusting and positive relationship.[64] Kompara also notes that becoming a stepparent is usually more difficult for a woman because children tend to be emotionally closer to their biological mother and to have spent more time with her than with the father.

Three myths about blended families need to be addressed.[65] First, there is the myth of the "wicked stepmother"—the idea that the stepmother is not really concerned about what is best for the children but only about her own well-being. A scene from the children's story *Cinderella* comes to mind. Here, the "wicked stepmother" cruelly keeps Cinderella from going to the ball in hopes that her own biological daughters will have a better chance at nabbing the handsome prince. In reality, stepmothers have been found to establish positive and caring relationships with their stepchildren, provided that the stepmothers have a positive self-concept and the affirmation of their husbands.[66] Stepfathers have also been found to have established healthy relationships with their stepchildren.[67]

A second myth is that "step is less."[68] In other words, stepchildren will never hold the same place in the hearts of parents that biological children do. The fact is that people can learn to love each other and are motivated to bind members of their new family together.

The third myth is that the moment families are joined, they will have instant love for each other.[69] Relationships take time to develop and grow. The idea of instantly strong love bonds is unrealistic. People involved in any relationship need time to get to know each other, test each other out, and grow to feel comfortable with each other.

Stinnet and Walters reviewed the research literature on stepparenthood and came to the following conclusions: (a) integration tends to be easier in families that have been split by divorce rather than by death, perhaps because the children realize the first marriage did not work out; (b) stepparents and stepchildren come to the blended family with unrealistic expectations that love and togetherness will occur rapidly; (c) children tend to see a stepparent of the opposite sex as playing favorites with his or her own children; (d) most children continue to miss and admire the absent biological parent; (e) male children tend more readily to accept a stepparent, particularly if the new parent is a male; and (f) adolescents have greater difficulty accepting a stepparent than do young children or adult children.[70]

Berman and Visher and Visher offer the following suggestions to parents in blended families for increasing the chances of positive relationships between adults and children:[71]

1. *Maintain a courteous relationship with the former spouse or spouses.* Children adjust best after a divorce when there is a harmonious relationship between former spouses. Problems are intensified when former spouses continue to insult each other and when the children are used as weapons ("pawns") by angry former spouses to hurt each other.

2. *Understand the emotions of children.* Although the newlyweds in a recently blended family may be fairly euphoric about their relationship, they need to be perceptive and responsive to the fears, concerns, and resentments of their children.

3. *Allow time for loving relationships to develop between stepparents and stepchildren.* Stepparents need to be aware that their stepchildren will probably have emotional ties to their absent biological parent and that the stepchildren may resent the breakup of the marriage between their biological parents. Some children may even feel responsible for their biological parents' separation. Others may try to make life difficult for the stepparent so that he or she will leave, with the hope that the biological parents will then reunite. Stepparents need to be perceptive and understanding of such feelings and patiently allow the stepchildren to work out their concerns. Stepparents should take time in bonding with their stepchildren.

4. *New rituals, traditions, and ways of doing things need to be developed that seem right and enjoyable for all members of the blended family.* Sometimes it is helpful to move to a new residence that does not hold memories of the past. Leisure time should be structured so that the children spend time alone with the biological parent, with the stepparent, with both, and with the absent parent or parents. In addition, the new spouses need to spend some time alone with each other. New rituals should be developed for holidays, birthdays, and other special days.

5. *Seek social support.* Parents in blended families should seek to share their concerns, feelings, frustrations, experiences, coping strategies, and

triumphs with other stepparents and stepchildren. Such sharing allows them to view their own situations more realistically and to learn from the experiences of others.

6. *Provide organization for the family.* Children need to have their limits defined and consistently upheld. One of the difficulties is that children are faced with a new stepparent attempting to gain control when they have not as yet enjoyed many supportive and positive experiences with their new stepparent. Therefore, it is important for this new stepparent to provide nurturance and positive feedback to stepchildren in addition to making rules and maintaining control.

The Single Life

In our society, women—and, to a lesser extent, men—are brought up to believe that one of their most important goals is to marry. Women who remain unmarried are labeled "old maids." Elaborate rituals have been developed to romanticize engagement and marriage. Unfortunately, many couples discover after the honeymoon that marriage is not always romantic or exciting. Many people deal with unfulfilling marriages with a series of divorces and remarriages.

The person who passes age 25 without getting married gradually enters a new world. The social structures that supported dating—such as college life—are gone, and most people of the same age are married. The attitudes of singles about their status vary widely. Some plan to never get married, as they find their lifestyle exciting and enjoy its freedom. Others desperately search for a spouse, with the desperation increasing as the years wear on. Still others become resigned to being single, and as they grow older, they tend to date less and less—and finally not at all (many of these individuals find other interests to occupy their free time). Statistics show higher rates of depression, loneliness, alcoholism, suicide, drug abuse, and alienation among those who are single.[72]

There are a large number of people over age 18 in the United States who are not married—44% of the adult population.[73]

Concluding Comments

To summarize, it appears that the family of tomorrow will face a future shock. Technological developments (particularly in biology and medicine, for example, cloning and human embryo implants)

may dramatically affect the family, raising a number of ethical, legal, social, and personal questions. In addition, the family is assuming a number of different forms that may dramatically alter the central characteristics of future families. We are now seeing childless couples, postponement of child rearing until middle age or later, professional parents, serial and contract marriages, one-parent families, blended families, comarital sex, open marriages, group marriages for all age groups, same-sex marriages, transracial adoptions, and a growing number of never-married people.

Other forms of marital patterns include interracial marriages and marriages involving partners of very different ages. Because of technological advances and the experimentation with new family forms, the style of living for all families may be substantially changed. Some individuals will probably find these changes exciting, personally satisfying, and functional; others may be less adaptable and find such changes extremely difficult and perhaps even overwhelming, resulting in personal disintegration. In any case, changes that are made in the American family will have important implications for the field of social welfare.

SUMMARY

The following summarizes this chapter's content as it relates to the chapter objectives presented at the beginning of the chapter. Objectives include the following:

A *Define social welfare and describe its goal.*

Social welfare is a nation's system of programs, benefits, and services that helps people meet those social, economic, educational, and health needs that are fundamental to the maintenance of society.

The goal of social welfare is to fulfill the social, financial, health, and recreational needs of everyone in a society. The provision of social services has become one of the most important activities in our society in terms of the money spent, the human misery treated, and the number of people served.

B *Describe the relationship between social welfare and the following disciplines: sociology, psychology, social work, and human services.*

Social welfare overlaps with sociology, psychology, and other disciplines on a knowledge-base level. When theories and research in other academic disciplines have direct applications to the social welfare goal of enhancing the social functioning of people, then this knowledge is also part of the knowledge base of social welfare.

Social welfare overlaps with social work at a practice (service) level. Almost all social workers work in the field of social welfare, but there are also many other professional and occupational groups that work within this field. Social welfare is erroneously conceived at times as synonymous with public assistance, but public assistance is only one of several hundred social welfare programs.

Social welfare institutions are composed of social service programs and social service organizations. The purposes of social welfare institutions are to prevent, alleviate, and contribute to the solution of recognized social problems so as to directly improve the well-being of individuals, groups, families, organizations, and communities.

Human services is a broader term than social welfare.

C Provide a history of social welfare.

Currently there are two conflicting views of the role of social welfare in our society: the residual versus the institutional orientation. The residual approach characterized social welfare programs from early history to the depression of the 1930s, at which time programs with an institutional orientation began to be implemented. Social welfare programs have in the past been influenced (and to some extent still are) by the Protestant ethic, the laissez-faire economic view, social Darwinism, individualism, the Industrial Revolution, and humanitarian ideals. The two prominent political philosophies in the United States are liberalism and conservatism. Liberals generally adhere to an institutional orientation, whereas conservatives tend to adhere to a residual orientation.

D Describe how the future of social welfare will be affected by technological advances.

There are likely to be important changes in the social welfare field in the future, primarily due to anticipated technological advances. In summary form, technological advances largely determine changes in our lifestyles; lifestyle changes largely determine changes in our future social, financial, health, and recreational needs; and the latter changes largely determine changes in needed social service programs.

E Illustrate that the future of social welfare will also be partially affected by changes in the American family system. A summary of many of the changes that are occurring in the American family is provided.

Dramatic changes are also anticipated in the American family of the future due to technological advances in biology and medicine and to the current experimentation with new family forms. Some of these new forms will be found dysfunctional and will be discarded, whereas others will be found satisfying and functional and will probably be incorporated into the "typical" family of the future. The anticipated technological advances and the adoption of new family forms will result in the creation of new social service programs and the expansion of certain existing programs. Unless such changes are carefully examined and planned, our society faces a future shock.

Competency Notes

EP 2.1.3a Distinguish, appraise, and integrate multiple sources of knowledge, including research-based knowledge and practice wisdom. (All of this chapter) This chapter presents introductory content on the business, history, and future of social welfare.

Media Resources

Additional resources for this chapter, including a chapter quiz, can be found on the Social Work CourseMate. Go to CengageBrain.com.

Notes

1. Andrew W. Dobelstein, *Social Welfare: Policy and Analysis*, 2nd ed. (Chicago: Nelson-Hall, 1996).
2. Robert L. Barker, *The Social Work Dictionary*, 5th ed. (Washington, DC: NASW, 2003), p. 408.
3. The *American Heritage Dictionary*, 2nd college ed. (Boston: Houghton Mifflin, 1982).
4. Ibid.
5. National Association of Social Workers, *Standards for Social Service Manpower* (New York: NASW, 1983), pp. 4–5.
6. Barker, *The Social Work Dictionary*, p. 410.

7. Alfred Kahn, *Shaping the New Social Work* (New York: Columbia University Press, 1973), pp. 12–34.

8. Ibid., p. 10.

9. Harold Wilensky and Charles Lebeux, *Industrial Society & Social Welfare* (New York: Free Press, 1965).

10. Ibid., p. 138.

11. Ibid., p. 139.

12. James Midgley, *Social Development: The Developmental Perspective in Social Welfare* (Thousand Oaks, CA: Sage, 1995).

13. Ibid., p. 25.

14. James Midgley and Michelle Livermore, "The Developmental Perspective in Social Work: Educational Implications for a New Century," *Journal of Social Work Education*, 33, no. 3 (Fall 1997), pp. 573–585.

15. Ibid., p. 576.

16. Lester F. Ward, *Dynamic Sociology*; reprint of 1883 ed. (New York: Johnson Reprint, 1968).

17. Walter Trattner, *From Poor Law to Welfare State: A History of Social Welfare in America* (New York: Free Press, 1974).

18. Beulah Compton, *Introduction to Social Welfare & Social Work* (Homewood, IL: Dorsey Press, 1980).

19. Trattner, *From Poor Law to Welfare State*.

20. J. M. Romanyshyn, *Social Welfare: Charity to Justice* (New York: Random House, 1971).

21. Romanyshyn, *Social Welfare: Charity to Justice*.

22. "Poverty Gap Widens, Studies Reveal," *NASW News*, Jan. 1990, p. 19.

23. Linda A. Mooney, David Knox, and Caroline Schacht, *Understanding Social Problems*, 8th ed. (Belmont, CA: Wadsworth/Cengage Learning, 2013).

24. Ibid.

25. Ibid.

26. Ibid.

27. Ibid.

28. Ibid.

29. Diane E. Papalia, Sally Wendkos Olds, and Ruth Duskin Feldman, *Human Development*, 11th ed. (New York: McGraw-Hill, 2009).

30. Janet S. Hyde and John D. DeLamater, *Understanding Human Sexuality*, 11th ed. (New York: McGraw-Hill, 2011).

31. L. Rifken, *Who Should Play God?* (New York: Dell, 1977).

32. Ibid.

33. Ibid.

34. Hyde and DeLamater, *Understanding Human Sexuality*.

35. "Dad Wins Custody of Baby M," *Wisconsin State Journal*, Apr. 1987, p. 1.

36. Hyde and DeLamater, *Understanding Human Sexuality*.

37. "Healthy Baby Is Born from Donated Embryo," *Wisconsin State Journal*, Feb. 4, 1984, sec. 1, p. 2.

38. Stephen Budiansky, "The New Rules of Reproduction," *U.S. News & World Report*, Apr. 18, 1988, pp. 66–69.

39. Mooney, Knox, and Schacht, *Understanding Social Problems*, pp. 455–457.

40. Hyde and DeLamater, *Understanding Human Sexuality*.

41. Ibid.

42. Richard Saltus, "Historic Goal Reached in Human Genome Project," *Wisconsin State Journal*, June 27, 2000, p. 1A.

43. Ibid.

44. "Center for Gene Therapy of Cystic Fibrosis and Other Genetic Diseases," Center for Gene Theory (Iowa City: The University of Iowa, 2007).

45. "The Rising Cost of Raising a Child," http://money.cnn.com/2011/09/21/pf/cost_raising_child/index.htm.

46. Alvin Toffler, *Future Shock* (New York: Bantam Books, 1970).

47. Ibid., pp. 243–244.

48. Mooney, Knox, and Schacht, *Understanding Social Problems*.

49. Ethel Alpenfels, "Progressive Monogamy: An Alternate Pattern?" in *The Family in Search of a Future*, Herbert Otto, ed. (New York: Appleton-Century-Crofts, 1970), pp. 67–74.

50. George O'Neill and Nena O'Neill, *Open Marriage* (New York: M. Evans, 1971).

51. Mooney, Knox, and Schacht, *Understanding Social Problems*.

52. Janet S. Hyde and John D. DeLamater, *Understanding Human Sexuality*, 9th ed. (New York: McGraw-Hill, 2006), pp. 161–162.

53. Ibid., p. 367.

54. David Fanshel, *Far from the Reservation* (Metuchen, NJ: Scarecrow Press, 1972).

55. Charles Zastrow, *Outcome of Black Children–White Parents Transracial Adoptions* (San Francisco: R & E Research Associated, 1977).

56. David L. Wheeler, "Black Children, White Parents: The Difficult Issue of Transracial

Adoption," *Chronicle of Higher Education*, Sept. 15, 1993, p. A16.

57. Ibid., p. A9.

58. Hyde and DeLamater, *Understanding Human Sexuality*, 2011.

59. Ibid.

60. Diane E. Papalia and Sally W. Olds, *Human Development*, 2nd ed. (New York: McGraw-Hill, 1981), p. 326.

61. Papalia, Olds, and Feldman, *Human Development*, pp. 366–369.

62. C. Janzen and O. Harris, *Family Treatment in Social Work Practice*, 2nd ed. (Itasca, IL: F. E. Peacock, 1986), p. 273.

63. R. B. Stuart and B. Jacobson, *Second Marriage: Make It Happy! Make It Last!* (New York: Norton, 1985).

64. D. Kompara, "Difficulties in the Socialization Process of Step-Parenting," *Family Relations*, 29 (1980), pp. 69–73.

65. Janzen and Harris, *Family Treatment*, pp. 275–276.

66. G. L. Shulman, "Myths That Intrude on the Adaptation of the Step-Family," *Social Casework*, 53, no. 3 (1972), pp. 131–139.

67. E. Wald, *The Remarried Family* (New York: Family Service Association of America, 1981).

68. N. Stinnet and J. Walters, *Relationships in Marriage and Family* (New York: Macmillan, 1977).

69. Ibid.

70. Ibid.

71. C. Berman, *Making It as a Stepparent: New Roles/New Rules* (New York: Bantam, 1981); E. Visher and J. Visher, "Stepparenting: Blending Families," in *Stress and the Family: Vol. I. Copying with Normative Transitions*, H. I. McCubbin and C. R. Figley, eds. (New York: Brunner/Mazel, 1983), pp. 87–98; William Kornblum and Joseph Julian, *Social Problems*, 8th ed. (Englewood Cliffs, NJ: Prentice Hall, 1985).

72. Hyde and DeLamater, *Understanding Human Sexuality*, 2011.

73. http://www.unmarried.org/statistics.html.

CHAPTER

Social Work as a Profession and a Career

Social work is one of the primary professions that provide social welfare services. This chapter will:

Learning Objectives

EP 2.1.3a

A   Define the profession of social work.
B   Provide a brief history of social work.
C   Describe the following social work activities: casework, case management, group work, group therapy, family therapy, and community organization.
D   Describe the person-in-environment conceptualization for social work practice.
E   Specify the goals of social work practice.
F   Describe the strengths perspective.
G   Summarize societal stereotypes of social workers.
H   Summarize employment settings and career opportunities in social work.
I   Briefly describe international social work.

A Brief History of Social Work

Social work as a profession is of relatively recent origin. The first social welfare agencies began in the early 1800s in an attempt to meet the needs of people living in urban areas. These agencies, or services, were private agencies developed primarily at the initiation of the clergy and religious groups. Until the early 1900s, these services were provided exclusively by members of the clergy and wealthy "do-gooders" who had no formal training and little understanding of human behavior. The focus was on meeting such basic physical needs as food and shelter and attempting to "cure" emotional and personal difficulties with religious admonitions.

An illustration of an early social welfare organization was the Society for the Prevention of Pauperism, founded by John Griscom in 1820.[1] This society's goals were to investigate the habits and circumstances of the poor, to suggest plans by which the poor could help themselves, and to encourage the poor to save and economize. Toward these ends, its members conducted house-to-house visitation of the poor (a very elementary type of social work).

By the last half of the 1800s, a fairly large number of private relief agencies had been established in large cities to help the unemployed, the poor, the ill, people with a physical or mental disability, and orphans. These agencies' programs were uncoordinated and sometimes overlapped. Therefore, an English innovation—the Charity Organization Society (COS)—caught the interest of a number of American cities.[2] Starting in Buffalo, New York, in 1877, the COS model, was rapidly adopted in many cities. In charity organization societies, private agencies joined together to (a) provide direct services to individuals and families—in this respect, they were forerunners of social casework and of family counseling approaches—and (b) plan and coordinate the efforts of private agencies to combat the pressing social problems of cities—in this respect, they were precursors of community organization and social planning approaches. Charity organizations conducted a detailed investigation of each applicant for services and financial help, maintained a central system of registration of clients to avoid duplication, and used volunteer "friendly visitors" to work with those in difficulty. The friendly visitors were primarily "doers of good works"; they generally gave sympathy rather than money and encouraged the poor to save and to seek employment. Poverty was looked on as the result of a personal shortcoming. Most of the friendly visitors were women.

Concurrent with the COS movement was the establishment of settlement houses in the late 1800s. In 1884 Toynbee Hall became the first settlement house in London; many others were soon formed in larger U.S. cities. Many of the early settlement house workers were daughters of ministers, usually from the middle and upper classes. In contrast to friendly visitors, they lived in the impoverished neighborhoods and used the missionary approach of teaching residents how to live moral lives and improve their circumstances. They sought to improve housing, health, and living conditions; find jobs for neighborhood residents; teach English, hygiene, and occupational skills; and change environmental surroundings through cooperative efforts. Settlement houses used change techniques that are now referred to as social group work, social action, and community organization.

Settlement houses emphasized "environmental reform." At the same time, "they continued to struggle to teach the poor the prevailing middle-class values of work, thrift, and abstinence as the keys to success."[3] In addition to dealing with local problems by local action, settlement houses played important roles in drafting legislation and in organizing to influence social policy and legislation. The most noted leader in the settlement house movement was Jane Addams of Hull House in Chicago (see Case Example 2.1).

It appears that the first paid social workers were executive secretaries of charity organization societies in the late 1800s.[4] At that time, some COSs received contracts from the cities in which they were located to administer relief funds. They then hired people as executive secretaries to organize and train the friendly visitors and to establish bookkeeping procedures to account for the funds received. To improve the services of friendly visitors, executive secretaries established standards and training courses. The first such training course was offered for charity workers in 1898 by the New York Charity Organization Society. By 1904 a 1-year program was offered by the New York School of Philanthropy. Soon many colleges and universities were offering training programs in social work.

Richard Cabot introduced medical social work at Massachusetts General Hospital in 1905.[5] Gradually, social workers were employed in schools, courts, child guidance clinics, and other settings.

Early training programs in social work focused both on environmental reform efforts and on efforts to help individuals adjust better to society. In 1917 Mary Richmond published *Social Diagnosis*, the first text to present a theory and methodology for social work.[6] The book focused on how the worker should intervene with individuals. The process is still used today and involves study (collecting information), diagnosis (stating what is wrong), prognosis (stating the prospect of improvement), and treatment planning (stating what should be done to help clients improve). This text was important because it formulated a common body of knowledge for casework.

In the 1920s, Sigmund Freud's theories of personality development and therapy became popular. The concepts and explanations of psychiatrists appeared particularly appropriate for social workers, who also worked in one-to-one relationships with clients. The psychiatric approach emphasized intrapsychic processes and focused on enabling clients to adapt and adjust to their social situations. Thus, most social workers switched their emphasis from "reform" to "therapy" for the next three decades.

In the 1960s, however, there was a renewed interest in sociological approaches, or reform, by social workers. Several reasons account for this change. Questions arose about the relevance and appropriateness of "talking" approaches with low-income clients who have urgent social and economic pressures. Furthermore, the effectiveness of many psychotherapeutic approaches was questioned.[7] Other reasons for the renewed interest included an increase in the status of sociology and the mood of the 1960s, which raised questions about the relevancy of social institutions in meeting the needs of the population. Social work at present embraces both the reform approach and the therapy approach.

Not until the end of World War I did social work begin to be recognized as a distinct profession. The depression of the 1930s and the enactment of the Social Security Act in 1935 brought about an extensive expansion of public social services and job opportunities for social workers. Throughout the 20th century there was a growing awareness by social agency boards and the public that professionally trained social workers were needed to provide social services competently. In 1955 the National Association of Social Workers (NASW) was formed, which represents the social work profession in this country. The purpose of this association is to improve social

CASE EXAMPLE 2.1

Jane Addams: A Prominent Founder of Social Work

Jane Addams was born in 1860 in Cedarville, Illinois, the daughter of a successful couple who owned a flour mill and a wood mill. Jane graduated from Rockford Seminary (a college in Rockford, Illinois). She briefly attended medical school but was forced to leave because of illness. She then traveled for a few years in Europe, perplexed about what her life work should be. At the age of 25, she joined the Presbyterian Church, which helped her find a focus for her life: religion and humanitarianism—in particular, serving the poor. (Later in her life, she joined the Congregational Church, now known as the United Church of Christ.) Addams heard about the establishment of Toynbee Hall in England and returned to Europe to study this approach. Its staff was composed of college students and graduates, mainly from Oxford, who lived in the slums of London to learn conditions firsthand and to contribute to improving life in the slums with their own financial and personal resources.

Addams returned to the United States and rented a two-story house (later called Hull House) in an impoverished Chicago neighborhood. With a few friends, Addams initiated a variety of group and individual activities for the community. She started a literature reading group for young women and a kindergarten. There were groups focusing on social relationships, sports, music, painting, art, and current affairs. Hull House also provided services to individuals who came asking for immediate help, such as food, shelter, information, and referrals for other services. A Hull House Social Science Club was formed, which studied social problems in a scientific manner and then became involved in social action efforts to improve living conditions. One of its successful efforts was to work for passage of Illinois legislation to prevent the employment of children in area sweatshops. Addams also became interested in the different ethnic groups in the neighborhood. She was fairly successful in bringing the various nationalities together at Hull House, where they could interact and exchange cultural values.

Jane Addams

The success of Hull House served as a model for the establishment of settlement houses in other areas of Chicago and in many large cities in the United States. Settlement house leaders believed that by improving neighborhoods, they would improve communities; by altering communities, they would develop a better society. For her extraordinary contributions, Jane Addams received the Nobel Prize for Peace in 1931.

SOURCE: Adapted from "Jane Addams," by Henry Stroup, in *Social Welfare Pioneers* (Lanham, MD: Rowman & Littlefield Publishers, 1986), pp. 1-29.

---

conditions in society and promote high quality and effectiveness in social work practice. The association publishes (a) several professional journals, most notably *Social Work*; (b) *The Encyclopedia of Social Work*; and (c) a monthly newsletter titled *NASW News*. The newsletter publishes current social work news as well as a list of job vacancies throughout the country.

In recent years, there has been considerable activity in developing a system of certification, or licensing, of social workers. Such a system both helps assure the public that qualified personnel are providing social work services and advances the recognition of social work as a profession. All states have now passed legislation to license or regulate the practice of social work. Although a young profession, social work is growing and gaining respect and recognition.

A Multiskilled Profession

Social work is the professional activity of helping individuals, groups, families, organizations, and communities to enhance or restore their capacity for social functioning and to create societal conditions favorable to their goals.[8] They are graduates of accredited (by the Council on Social Work Education) programs of social work, who have either a bachelor's or master's degree.

Critical Thinking Question

To be really good in a career, you first have to love that career. Do you have a passion to provide social services to clients and to improve the lives of others? Why or why not?

Social work is distinct from other professions (such as psychology and psychiatry) by virtue of its responsibility and mandate to provide social services.

A social worker needs training and expertise in a wide range of areas to handle effectively the problems faced by individuals, groups, families, organizations, and the larger community. Whereas most professions are becoming more specialized (for example, nearly all medical doctors now specialize in one or two areas), social work continues to emphasize a generic, broad-based approach. The practice of social work is analogous to the old, now-fading practice of general medicine. A general practitioner in medicine was trained to handle a wide range of common medical problems; a social worker is trained to handle a wide range of common social and personal problems. Case Example 2.2 highlights some of the skills needed by social workers. These skills include relationship building with clients, interviewing, problem solving, and referral to other organizations (in this case, a support group). Social workers also need to have research and grant-writing skills, program development and fund-raising skills, and knowledge of how to handle ethical/legal issues.

Perhaps the most basic skill that a social worker needs is the ability to counsel clients effectively. Anyone who is unable to do this should probably not be in social work—certainly not in direct service. The second most important skill is the ability to interact effectively with other groups and professionals in the area. A social worker, like a general practitioner, requires a wide range of skills that will enable him or her to intervene effectively in (a) the common personal and emotional problems of clients and (b) the common social problems faced by groups, organizations, and the larger community. Social workers also need an accurate perception of their professional strengths and weaknesses. If a situation arises that a worker knows she or he does not have the training or expertise to handle, then the worker needs to be a "broker" and link those affected with available services.

Critical Thinking Question

Do you believe you have the capacity to become good at counseling and at interacting with others? Why?

A Problem-Solving Approach

In working with individuals, families, groups, organizations, and communities, social workers use a problem-solving approach. Steps in the problem-solving process can be stated in a variety of ways. Here is a simple description of the process:

1. Identify as precisely as possible the problem or problems.
2. Generate possible alternative solutions.
3. Evaluate the alternative solutions.
4. Select a solution or solutions to be used and set goals.
5. Implement the solution(s).
6. Follow up to evaluate how the solution(s) worked.

(Another conceptualization of the problem-solving approach is the change process of social work practice, which is described in Chapter 3.)

Critical Thinking Question

When you have a conflict with someone, do you seek to resolve it by using a problem-solving approach? Why or why not?

Generalist Social Work Practice

The Council on Social Work Education (the national accrediting entity for baccalaureate and master's programs in social work) requires all undergraduate and graduate programs to train their students in generalist social work practice. (Master of Social Work [MSW] programs, in addition, usually require their students to select and study in an area of specialization. MSW programs generally offer several specializations, such as family therapy, administration, corrections, and clinical social work.)

A generalist social worker is trained to use the problem-solving process to assess and intervene with the problems confronting individuals, families, groups, organizations, and communities. Because of the importance of generalist practice, Chapter 3 is devoted to this topic.

CASE EXAMPLE 2.2

A Case Involving Serious Emotional Issues and Domestic Discord

Ken Bientos was referred by his supervisor, Philip Yang, the Employee Assistance Program social worker at the large credit union where he worked. He was a printer at this company. Mr. Bientos had a history of missing many work days, and he also showed symptoms of melancholy.

In meeting with Mr. Yang, Mr. Bientos gradually revealed that he had been married to Francine for the past 14 years. He slowly divulged that their marriage was one that had a long history of marital discord. Mr. Bientos indicated his wife had been diagnosed as bipolar, with a number of cycles of manic behavior and depression. Mr. Bientos stated he also had been diagnosed as bipolar and has been on lithium (antidepressant medication) for the past 11 years.

With both spouses having frequent mood swings, Mr. Bientos stated their marriage was full of severe tension, some episodes of violence, and rarely times of pleasantness. They had a son, Roger, who was now 12 years of age. Roger was described as doing "OK" with the spousal turmoil and also doing "OK" in school.

Mr. Bientos indicated he had tried numerous strategies to persuade his wife to enter into marital counseling with him. He had even twice voluntarily committed himself to a psychiatric hospital for depression—as he was informed that part of his treatment would involve mandated couple's counseling at the hospital. However, both times his wife refused counseling, and both times Mr. Bientos was released after staying for several days.

Mr. Bientos added that occasionally there were physical confrontations with his wife. He stated his wife had a pattern of screaming at him and shoving him when she was irritated with him. A few times he stated he shoved back at her. She usually responded by calling 911. Over his marital years, he indicated he had spent a night in jail on three occasions because of domestic violence.

Mr. Bientos further added that generally after a confrontation with Francine, which usually occurred about once a month, Francine would leave with Roger and stay with her mother, who lived several miles away. Francine then expected Ken to "beg" her and "wine and dine" her to come home.

Mr. Yang indicated this was really severe marital discord and wondered why Mr. Bientos and his wife had not ended their marriage. Mr. Bientos indicated this was his second marriage. He and his first wife also had had a child, and he found it

very difficult to be a "good dad" when he seldom saw that son (Larry), who was now 22 years of age. He stated he did not want to raise another child in a broken relationship. As for why Francine was staying in the marriage, Mr. Bientos stated he did not fully know. He thought partly it was because she was insecure, did not want to be alone, was financially dependent on him, and because she psychologically enjoyed "tormenting" him.

Mr. Yang then asked Mr. Bientos what direction he wanted to head to in the future with his marriage. Mr. Bientos stated he did not know but was leaning toward ending the marriage. Mr. Yang inquired whether Francine would be willing to come in for couples counseling. Mr. Bientos stated he had tried for more than a decade to have this happen, and he had now given up on this. Mr. Yang then stated their meeting time was nearing the end but requested that, prior to the next time they meet (in 5 days), Mr. Bientos complete a homework assignment of writing down a "pro–con" list as to whether it would be desirable to continue the marriage.

Five days later, Mr. Bientos came in with his list. Practically all of his items were on the side of ending the marriage. After considerable discussion, including the possible impact of the divorce on Roger, Mr. Bientos decided to retain a divorce attorney and file for divorce.

It took 14 months for Mr. Bientos to obtain a divorce. He and Francine had major confrontations on custody issues and visitation schedules involving Roger. Joint custody was eventually ordered by the judge. Francine and Ken Bientos also had stormy confrontations over dividing the marital property. During this 14-month time period, Mr. Bientos occasionally met with Mr. Yang to vent his emotions and to problem-solve present and future issues. Mr. Yang also referred Mr. Bientos to a "Rebuilding" support group, which Mr. Bientos found to be quite helpful, as it was a group of men and women who were also going through a divorce and working on rebuilding their lives.

Mr. Bientos stopped by Mr. Yang's office about 4 months after the divorce was finalized. Mr. Bientos expressed gratitude for Mr. Yang's assistance. He indicated he was now emotionally more relaxed and was beginning to date. He also stated that Roger seemed to be doing better because he no longer had to watch the tension and conflict between Francine and himself. Mr. Bientos did indicate, on a negative note, that Francine had increasingly become a "bitter person."

Micro-, Mezzo-, and Macropractice

Social workers practice at three levels: (a) micro—working on a one-to-one basis with an individual; (b) mezzo—working with families and other small groups; and (c) macro—working with organizations and communities or seeking changes in statutes and social policies.

The specific activities performed by workers include, but are not limited to, the following.

Social Casework

Aimed at helping individuals on a one-to-one basis to resolve personal and social problems, casework may be geared to helping clients adjust to their environment or to changing certain social and economic pressures that are adversely affecting them. Social casework services are provided by nearly every social welfare agency that offers direct services to people.

Social casework encompasses a wide variety of activities, such as counseling runaway youths, helping unemployed people secure training or employment, counseling someone who is suicidal, placing a homeless child in an adoptive or foster home, providing protective services to abused children and their families, finding nursing homes for stroke victims who no longer require hospitalization, counseling individuals with sexual dysfunctions, helping alcoholics to acknowledge that they have a drinking problem, counseling those with a terminal illness, serving as a probation or parole officer, providing services to single parents, and working in medical and mental hospitals as a member of a rehabilitation team.

Case Management

Recently, some social service agencies have labeled their social workers *case managers*. The tasks performed by case managers are similar to those of caseworkers. The job descriptions of case managers vary from service area to service area. For example, case managers in a juvenile probation setting are highly involved in supervising clients, providing some counseling, monitoring clients to make certain they are following the rules of probation, linking clients and their families with needed services, preparing court reports, and testifying in court. On the other hand, case managers at a job training center for clients with physical and mental disabilities are likely to be involved in providing job training to clients, counseling clients, arranging transportation, disciplining clients for unacceptable behavior, acting as an advocate for clients, and acting as liaison with the people who supervise clients during their non-work hours (such as at a group home, foster home, residential treatment facility, or the parents' home). Hepworth, Rooney, and Larsen describe the role of a case manager as follows:

A person designated to assume primary responsibility for assessing the needs of a client, arranging and coordinating the delivery of essential goods and services provided by other resources, and working directly with the client to ensure that the goods and services are provided in a timely manner. Case managers must maintain close contact with clients (including sometimes acting to provide

direct casework services) and with other service providers to ensure that plans for service delivery are in place and are subsequently delivered as planned.[9]

Group Work

Group work seeks to facilitate the intellectual, emotional, and social development of individuals through group activities. In contrast to casework or group therapy, it is not primarily therapeutic (except in a broad sense).

Different groups have different objectives, such as improving socialization, exchanging information, curbing delinquency, providing recreation, changing socially unacceptable values, helping to achieve better relations among cultural and racial groups, or explaining adoption procedures and helping applicants prepare for becoming adoptive parents. Activities and focuses of groups vary: arts and crafts, dancing, games, dramatics, music, photography, sports, nature study, woodworking, first aid, home management, information exchange, and discussion of such topics as politics, sex, marriage, religion, and career choice.

Group Therapy

Group therapy is aimed at facilitating the social, behavioral, and emotional adjustment of individuals through the group process. Participants in group therapy usually have emotional, interactional, or behavioral difficulties. Group therapy has several advantages over one-to-one counseling, such as the operation of the *helper therapy* principle, which maintains that it is therapeutic for the helper (who can be any member of a group) to feel he or she has been helpful to others.[10] Group pressure is often more effective than one-to-one counseling in changing maladaptive behavior of individuals, and group therapy is a time-saver in that it enables the therapist to treat several people at the same time. Group therapy has been especially effective for individuals who are severely depressed, have a drinking problem, are victims of rape, are psychologically addicted to drugs, have a relative who is terminally ill, are single and pregnant, are recently divorced, or have an eating disorder.

Family Therapy

Family therapy (a type of group therapy aimed at helping families with interactional, behavioral, and emotional problems) can be used with parent–child interaction problems, marital conflicts, and conflicts with grandparents. Some of the problems dealt with

© Mary Kate Denny/PhotoEdit

Group work is utilized by a wide variety of institutions with equally wide-ranging objectives. This community center offers emergency shelter, counseling, support groups, recreational activities, and educational and career guidance to homeless teenagers in the San Francisco Bay Area.

in family therapy or family counseling include disagreements between parents and youths on choice of friends, drinking and other drug use, domestic tasks, curfew hours, communication problems, sexual values and behavior, study habits and grades received, and choice of dating partners (see Case Exhibit 2.1: Playing a Poor Hand Well).

Community Organization

The aim of community organization is stimulating and assisting the local community to evaluate, plan, and coordinate efforts to provide for the community's health, welfare, and recreation needs. It perhaps is not possible to define precisely the activities of a community organizer, but such activities are likely to include encouraging and fostering citizen participation, coordinating efforts between agencies or between groups, performing public relations, providing public education, conducting research, planning, and being a resource person. A community organizer acts as a catalyst in stimulating and encouraging community action.

Agency settings where such specialists are employed include community welfare councils, social planning agencies, health planning councils, and community action agencies. The term *community organization* is now being replaced in some settings by labels such as *planning, social planning, program development, policy development,* and *macropractice.*

Administration

Administration involves directing the overall program of a social service agency. Administrative functions include setting agency and program objectives, analyzing social conditions in the community, making decisions relating to what services will be provided, hiring and supervising staff members, setting up an organizational structure, administering financial affairs, and securing funds for the agency's operations. Administration also involves coordinating efforts to achieve selected goals, monitoring and revising internal procedures to improve effectiveness and efficiency, and performing whatever functions are required to transform social policy into social

CASE EXHIBIT 2.1

Playing a Poor Hand Well: Empowering At-Risk Children

Many adults who are currently enjoying a happy and productive life grew up under very difficult and stressful conditions. They may have been raised in a high-crime, distressed neighborhood. They may have been abused physically, sexually, or emotionally by a family member. They may have been raised in a series of foster homes. They may have a significant physical or learning disability. Some of these individuals have managed to escape serious emotional damage entirely. Others struggled as children and teenagers with school and had emotional and behavioral difficulties but then turned their lives around in their 20s.

What turned things around for them? Why were they able to play a poor hand well, while many others in similar situations succumbed and lived a life full of despair? In *On Playing a Poor Hand Well*, Mark Katz asserts that by identifying why some people have learned to play a poor hand well, we will then learn to provide avenues through which turning-point experiences and second-chance opportunities can occur for those experiencing severe adversity.

Katz summarizes evidence that a variety of *protective influences* are key to helping a young person find a way to enjoy a happy and productive life. For example, a close-knit family living in a distressed neighborhood can be protective; children may not feel safe on the street, but they feel safe at home. Homeless mothers who place a high priority on ensuring that their children are waiting for the school bus each morning have been protective influences for their children. Parents advocating for a child with special needs and trying to ensure that those needs are met provide protection. The protective influence may be an older brother or sister helping a younger

family member understand a parent's illness. Or it may be an aunt, uncle, or grandparent helping to raise a child because the child's parents may be unable to do so. A school that offers smaller class sizes, which can address each child's unique learning needs and highlight each child's special strengths, talents, and interests, can be protective. Also protective are high-quality recreational programs in distressed neighborhoods that children and teenagers go to after school and stay at for hours.

Mentors and special role models whom children get to know at school, during after-school activities, or through involvement in church or youth groups are protective. Those who overcome childhood adversities often identify a special person in their lives—a teacher, social worker, coach, parent, or counselor—who was always there when needed.

Protection can also come from within. Some children have qualities that draw others toward them in times of need. They may be sparkly. They may excel at developing safety nets for themselves, and when adversity arises, their safety net is there to catch them. Some children are strong academically, or very skilled socially, so that success in the neighborhood and in school comes rather easily. Some children are more resilient, having the capacity to withstand the effects of exposure to known risk factors—for example, having the tendency to reframe adversities as being challenges that they know they have the capacities to overcome.

In working with individuals, groups, and families, social workers can often be a protective influence!

SOURCE: Mark Katz, *On Playing a Poor Hand Well* (New York: Norton, 1997).

services. In social work, the term *administration* is often used synonymously with *management*. In a small agency, administrative functions may be carried out by one person; in a large agency, several people may be involved in administrative affairs.

Other areas of professional activity in social work include research, consulting, supervision, planning, program development, policy development, and teaching (primarily at the college level). Social casework, case management, group work, family work, and community organization constitute the primary professional activities that beginning social workers are likely to provide. All of these activities require counseling skills. (Counseling involves helping individuals or groups resolve social and personal problems through the process of developing a relationship, exploring the problem[s] in depth, and exploring alternative solutions; this

process is described in Chapter 5.) Caseworkers, case managers, group workers, group therapists, and family therapists obviously need a high level of counseling skills in working with individuals and groups. Community organizers need to have relationship skills, to be perceptive, and to be able to assess problems and develop resolution strategies—abilities that parallel or are analogous to counseling skills.

Additionally, social workers must be able to do social histories and link clients with other human services. In some agencies, they are required to do public speaking, prepare and present reports to courts and other agencies, teach parents better parenting techniques, and so forth. Knowledge of evaluative procedures for assessing one's own effectiveness and the effectiveness of social programs is also helpful for the social worker. (Essential skills needed for social work practice are described in more detail in Chapter 3.)

A Medical versus a Systems Model of Human Behavior

From the 1920s to the 1960s, most social work programs used a medical-model approach to assess and change human behavior. This approach was developed by Sigmund Freud. It views clients as "patients." The task of the provider of services is first to diagnose the causes of a patient's problems and then to provide treatment. The patient's problems are viewed as being inside the patient.

People with emotional or behavioral problems are given medical labels, such as schizophrenic, psychotic, borderline personality, or insane. Adherents of the medical approach believe that the disturbed person's mind is affected by some generally unknown internal condition. That unknown internal condition is thought to be due to a variety of possible causative factors: genetic endowment, metabolic disorders, infectious diseases, internal conflicts, chemical imbalances, unconscious use of defense mechanisms, or traumatic early experiences that cause emotional fixations and prevent future psychological growth.

The medical model provided a humane approach to treating people with emotional and behavioral problems. Prior to Freud, the emotionally disturbed were thought to be possessed by demons, viewed as "mad," blamed for their disturbances, and often treated by being beaten or locked up. The medical-model approach emphasized intrapsychic processes and focused on enabling patients to adapt and adjust to their social situations.

In the 1960s, social work began questioning the usefulness of the medical model. Environmental factors were shown to be at least as important in causing a client's problems as internal factors. Research also demonstrated that psychoanalysis was probably ineffective in treating clients' problems.[11] Social work thus shifted some of its emphasis to a reform approach.

A reform approach seeks to change systems to benefit clients. Antipoverty programs (such as Head Start) are examples of efforts to change systems to benefit clients.

Since the 1960s, social work has primarily used a systems approach in assessing human behavior. Social workers are now trained to have a systems perspective in their work with individuals, groups, families, organizations, and communities. The systems perspective emphasizes looking beyond the client's presenting problems to assess the complexities and interrelationships of the client's life situation. A systems perspective is based on systems theory. Key concepts of general systems theory are *wholeness, relationship*, and *homeostasis*.

The concept of wholeness means that the objects or elements within a system produce an entity that is greater than the additive sums of the separate parts. Systems theory is antireductionist; it asserts that no system can be adequately understood or totally explained once it has been broken down into its component parts. (For example, the central nervous system is able to carry out thought processes that would not occur if only the parts were observed.)

The concept of relationship asserts that the patterning and structuring among the elements in a system are as important as the elements themselves. For example, Masters and Johnson found that sexual dysfunctions occur primarily because of the nature of the relationship between husband and wife rather than the psychological makeup of individual partners in a marriage system.[12]

Systems theory opposes simple cause-and-effect explanations. For example, whether a child will be abused in a family is determined by a variety of variables as well as by the patterning of these variables: parents' capacity to control their anger, relationships between child and parents, relationships between parents, degree of psychological stress, characteristics of the child, and opportunities for socially acceptable ways for parents to vent anger.

The concept of homeostasis suggests that most living systems seek a balance to maintain and preserve the system. Jackson, for example, has noted that families tend to establish a behavioral balance or stability and to resist any change from that predetermined level of stability.[13] Emergence of the state of imbalance (generated either within or outside the marriage) ultimately acts to restore the homeostatic balance of the family. If one child is abused in a family, that abuse often serves a function in the family (as indicated by the fact that if that child is removed, a second child is often abused). Or if one family member improves through counseling, that improvement will generally upset the balance within the family; as a result, other family members will have to make changes (adaptive or maladaptive) to adjust to the new behavior of the improved family member.

We turn now to a subcategory of systems theory known as ecological theory, which has become prominent in social work practice.

An Ecological Model of Human Behavior

In recent years, social work has focused increasingly on using an ecological approach. This approach integrates both treatment and reform by conceptualizing and emphasizing the dysfunctional transactions between people and their physical and social environments. Human beings are viewed as developing and adapting through transactions with all elements of their environments. An ecological model explores both internal and external factors. It views people not as passive reactors to their environments but rather as dynamic and reciprocal interactors with those environments.

An ecological model tries to improve coping patterns so that a better match can be attained between an individual's needs and the characteristics of his or her environment. One emphasis of an ecological model is on the person-in-environment. This is depicted in Figure 2.1, which shows that people interact with many systems. With this conceptualization, social work can focus on three separate areas. First, it can focus on the person and seek to develop his or her problem-solving, coping, and developmental capacities. Second, it can focus on the relationship between a person and the systems he or she interacts with and link the person with needed resources, services, and opportunities. Third, it can focus on the systems and seek to reform them to meet the needs of the individual more effectively.

The ecological model views individuals, families, and small groups as having transitional problems and needs as they move from one life stage to another. Individuals face many changes as they grow older. Examples of some of the transitions are learning to walk, entering first grade, adjusting to puberty, graduating from school, finding a job, getting married, having children, seeing one's children leave home, and retiring.

Families also experience transitions. The following are only a few of the events that require adjustment: engagement, marriage, birth of children, parenting, children starting school, children leaving home, and loss of a parent (perhaps through death or divorce).

Small groups also have transitional phases of development. Members of a small group spend time getting acquainted, gradually learn to trust one another, begin to self-disclose more, learn to work together on tasks, develop approaches to handle interpersonal conflict, and face adjustments to the group eventually terminating or to some members leaving.

A central concern of an ecological model is to articulate the transitional problems and needs of individuals, families, and small groups. Once these problems and needs are identified, intervention approaches are selected and applied to help the individuals, families, and small groups resolve the transitional problems and meet their needs.

An ecological model can also focus on maladaptive interpersonal problems and needs. It can seek to articulate the maladaptive communication processes and dysfunctional relationship patterns of families and small groups. These difficulties cover an array

FIGURE 2.1 Person-in-environment conceptualization: people in our society continually interact with many systems, some of which are depicted in this figure.

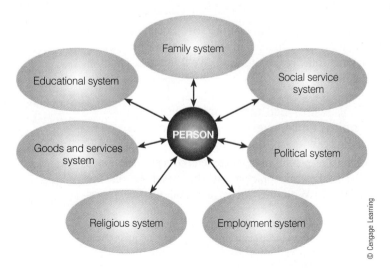

© Cengage Learning

of areas, including interpersonal conflicts, power struggles, double binds,* distortions in communicating, scapegoating, and discrimination. An ecological model seeks to identify such interpersonal obstacles and then apply appropriate intervention strategies.

Critical Thinking Question

When a social worker seeks to assess and change human behavior, which model (medical or person-in-environment) do you believe is more useful? Why?

For example, some parents set too high a price on honesty for their children. In such families, children gradually learn to hide certain behaviors and thoughts and even learn to lie. If the parents discover such dishonesty, an uproar usually occurs. An appropriate intervention in such a family is to open up communication patterns and help the parents to understand that, if they really want honesty from their children, they need to learn to be more accepting of their children's thoughts and actions.

Two centuries ago, people interacted primarily within the family system. Families were nearly self-sufficient. In those days, the "person-in-family" was a way of conceptualizing the main system that individuals interacted with. Our society has become much more complex. Today a person's life and quality of life are interwoven and interdependent on many systems, as shown in Figure 2.1.

Goals of Social Work Practice

The National Association of Social Workers (NASW) has conceptualized social work practice as having four major goals.[14] We'll discuss each of them in turn.

Goal 1: Enhance the Problem-Solving, Coping, and Developmental Capacities of People

Using the person-in-environment concept, the focus of social work practice at this level is on the "person." With this focus, a social worker serves

*A double bind is a psychological dilemma in which the receiver of a message gets conflicting interpersonal communications from the sender or faces disparagement no matter what her or his response to a situation is.

primarily as a *facilitator*. In this role, the worker may take on activities of a counselor, teacher, caregiver (that is, providing supportive services to those who cannot fully solve their problems and meet their own needs), and changer of specific behavior.

Goal 2: Link People with Systems That Provide Them with Resources, Services, and Opportunities

Using the person-in-environment concept, the focus of social work practice at this level is on the relationships between people and the systems they interact with. With this focus, a social worker serves primarily as a *broker*.

Goal 3: Promote the Effectiveness and Humane Operation of Systems That Provide People with Resources and Services

Using the person-in-environment concept, the focus of social work practice at this level is on the systems people interact with. One role a worker may fill at this level is that of an *advocate*. Additional roles at this level are:

- *Program developer:* The worker seeks to promote or design programs or technologies to meet social needs.
- *Supervisor:* The worker seeks to increase the effectiveness and efficiency of the delivery of services through supervising other staff.
- *Coordinator:* The worker seeks to improve a delivery system through increasing communications and coordination among human service resources.
- *Consultant:* The worker seeks to provide guidance to agencies and organizations by suggesting ways to increase the effectiveness and efficiency of services.

Goal 4: Develop and Improve Social Policy

As in Goal 3, the focus of social work practice at this level is on the systems people interact with. The distinction between Goal 3 and Goal 4 is that Goal 3 focuses on the available resources for serving people, whereas Goal 4 focuses on the statutes and broader social policies that underlie such resources. Social workers at this level are *planners* and *policy developers*. In these roles, workers develop and seek adoption of new statutes or policies and propose elimination of those that are ineffective or inappropriate. In these planning and policy development processes, social workers may take an advocate role and, in some instances, an activist role.

The Council on Social Work Education (CSWE) is the national accreditating body for social work education in the United States. It defines the purpose of social work as follows:

The purpose of the social work profession is to promote human and community well-being. Guided by a person and environment construct, a global perspective, respect for human diversity, and knowledge based on scientific inquiry, social work's purpose is actualized through its quest for social and economic justice, the prevention of conditions that limit human rights, the elimination of poverty, and the enhancement of the quality of life for all persons.[15]

This definition of the purpose of social work is consistent with the four goals of social work just mentioned. However, it adds one additional goal of social work, as follows.

Goal 5: Promote Human and Community Well-Being

The social work profession is committed to enhancing the well-being of all human beings and to promoting community well-being. It is particularly committed to alleviating poverty, oppression, and other forms of social injustice. About 15% of the U.S. population has an income below the poverty line.[16] Social work has always advocated for developing programs to alleviate poverty, and many practitioners focus on providing services to the poor.

Poverty is global, as every society has members who are poor. In some societies, as many as 95% of the population lives in poverty. Social workers are committed to alleviating poverty not only in the United States but also worldwide. Alleviating poverty is obviously complex and difficult. Social work professionals work with a variety of systems to make progress in alleviating poverty, including educational systems, health-care systems, political systems, business and employment systems, religious systems, and human services systems.

Oppression is the unjust or cruel exercise of authority or power. In our society, numerous groups have been oppressed—including African Americans, Latinos, Chinese Americans, Native Americans, women, persons with disabilities, gays and lesbians, various religious groups, and people living in poverty. (The listing of these groups is only illustrative, and certainly not exhaustive.) Social injustice occurs when some members of a society have less protection, fewer basic rights and opportunities, or fewer social benefits than other members of that society. Social work is a profession that is committed not only to alleviating poverty but also to combating oppression and other forms of social injustice.

Social justice is an ideal condition in which all members of a society have the same basic rights, protection, opportunities, obligations, and social benefits. Economic justice is also an ideal condition in which all members of a society have the same opportunities to attain material goods, income, and wealth. Social workers have an obligation to help groups at risk increase their personal, interpersonal, socioeconomic, and political strength and influence through improving their circumstances. Empowerment-focused social workers seek a more equitable distribution of resources and power among the various groups in society. Diverse groups that may be at risk include those distinguished by "age, class, color, culture, disability, ethnicity, gender, gender identity and expression, immigration status, political ideology, race, religion, sex, and sexual orientation."[17]

Human rights are commonly understood as inalienable fundamental rights to which a person is inherently entitled simply because he or she is a human being. Human rights are universal (applicable everywhere) and egalitarian (the same for everyone). Examples include: freedom of thought, freedom of religious choice, freedom of peaceful association, and liberty.

Human rights are further discussed in Chapter 3.

Critical Thinking Question

Do you have a desire to improve the living conditions of people who are poor and/or oppressed? Why or why not?

The Strengths Perspective and Empowerment

For most of the past several decades, social work and the other helping professions have had a primary focus on diagnosing the pathology, shortcomings, and dysfunctions of clients. One reason may be that Freudian psychology was the primary theory used in analyzing human behavior. Freudian psychology is based on a medical model and thereby has concepts that are geared to identify illness or pathology.

It has very few concepts to identify strengths. As described earlier in this chapter, social work is now shifting to a systems model in assessing human behavior. This model focuses on identifying both strengths and weaknesses.

It is essential that social workers include clients' strengths in the assessment process. In working with clients, social workers focus on the strengths and resources of clients to help them resolve their difficulties. To utilize clients' strengths effectively, social workers must first identify those strengths.

There is a danger that a primary focus on weaknesses will impair a worker's capacity to identify a client's growth potential. Social workers strongly believe that clients have the right (and should be encouraged) to develop their potentialities fully. Focusing on pathology often undermines this value commitment.

Another reason for attending to clients' strengths is that many clients need help in enhancing their self-esteem. Many have feelings of worthlessness and inadequacy, a sense of being a failure, and a lack of self-confidence and self-respect. Glasser noted that low self-esteem often leads to emotional difficulties, withdrawal, or crime.[18] To help clients view themselves more positively, social workers must first view them as having considerable strengths and competencies.

The *strengths perspective* is closely related to the concept of "empowerment." Empowerment is the process of helping individuals, families, groups, organizations, and communities to increase their interpersonal, personal, political, and socioeconomic strengths so that they can improve their circumstances. The strengths perspective is useful across the life cycle and throughout the assessment, intervention, and evaluation stages of the helping process. It emphasizes people's abilities, values, interests, beliefs, resources, accomplishments, and aspirations.[19]

©JimWest/AgeFotostock

Every community has strengths and resources. Community events are strengths that enrich the lives of those who participate.

According to Saleebey, five principles guide the strengths perspective:[20]

1. *Every individual, group, family, and community has strengths.* The strengths perspective is about discerning these resources. Saleebey notes:

In the end, clients want to know that you actually care about them, that how they fare makes a difference to you, that you will listen to them, that you will respect them no matter what their history, and that you believe that they can build something of value with the resources within and around them. But most of all, clients want to know that you believe they can surmount adversity and begin the climb toward transformation and growth.[21]

2. *Trauma and abuse, illness and struggle may be injurious, but they may also be sources of challenge and opportunity.* Clients who have been victimized are seen as active and developing individuals who, through their traumas, learn skills and develop personal attributes that assist them in coping with future struggles. There is dignity to be drawn in having prevailed over obstacles. We often grow more from crises that we have handled effectively than from contented and comfortable periods in our lives.

3. *Assume that you do not know the upper limits of the capacity to grow and change and take individual, group, and community aspirations seriously.* This principle means workers need to hold high their expectations of clients and form alliances with their visions, hopes, and values. Individuals, families, and communities have the capacity for restoration and rebounding. When workers connect with clients' hopes and dreams, clients are apt to have greater faith in themselves and then put forth the kinds of efforts that can make their hopes and dreams become self-fulfilling prophecies.

4. *We best serve clients by collaborating with them.* A worker is more effective when seen as a collaborator or consultant to a client than when seen as an expert or a professional. A collaborative stance by a worker makes her or him less vulnerable to many of the adverse effects of an expert–inferior relationship, including paternalism, victim blaming, and preemption of client views.

5. *Every environment is full of resources.* In every environment (no matter how harsh), there are individuals, groups, associations, and institutions that have something to give and something that others may desperately need. The strengths perspective seeks to identify these resources and make them available to benefit individuals, families, and groups in a community.

The strengths perspective recognizes that individuals, groups, families, organizations, and communities have challenges, problems, and difficulties. One of the major benefits of the strengths perspective is that it focuses attention on the resources and assets that individuals, groups, families, organizations, and communities have to confront their challenges.

Social Work Stereotypes

The image of the social worker has undergone a more rapid change than that of perhaps any other professional. Sixty-five years ago, there was a stereotype of a social worker as a moralistic upper-middle-class older woman who carried a basket of food and had little understanding of the people she tried to help. The image is much more positive today, reflecting the improved professional nature of the training and services provided. The image is also much more varied.

Dolgoff, Feldstein, and Skolnik summarize some of the current social work stereotypes:

Depending upon who is doing the "name calling," social workers are referred to in many ways: do-gooders, bleeding hearts, radicals intent on changing our society, captives of and apologists for "the establishment," organizers of the poor, and servers of the middle class. All these are ways in which people stereotype social workers and the functions they perform in society.[22]

LeCroy and Stinson in 2004 reported on a study of the public's current perception of the social work profession as examined in a nationally representative, random-digit telephone survey of 386 people.[23] Results of the survey indicated that, for the most part, a majority of the public understands the social work profession and in many ways recognizes its value. One of the questions asked respondents to compare social work's perceived value to the community with that of other professions. Social workers received more "very valuable" ratings than did psychologists, psychiatrists, or counselors;

however, nurses and the clergy received more "very valuable" ratings than social workers. The authors conclude:

> Social workers themselves are best suited to enhance the public's knowledge and opinions about the profession. Although we often seem to gently blend into the background, not attracting too much attention; suffice it to say that if we do not develop a level of comfort with singing our own praises, no one else is likely to step forward to sing them for us.[24]

The U.S. Department of Labor, Bureau of Labor Statistics, has a positive view of social work, as indicated in the following description:

> Social work is a profession for those with a strong desire to help improve people's lives. *Social workers* assist people by helping them cope with and solve issues in their everyday lives, such as family and personal problems and dealing with relationships. Some social workers help clients who face a disability, life-threatening disease, social problem, such as inadequate housing, unemployment, or substance abuse. Social workers also assist families that have serious domestic conflicts, sometimes involving child or spousal abuse. Additionally, they may conduct research, advocate for improved services, or become involved in planning or policy development. Many social workers specialize in serving a particular population or working in a specific setting.[25]

Employment Settings and Opportunities in Social Work

There are currently more employment opportunities in social work than in many other fields. Social services and their delivery are becoming an integral part of our fast-paced existence, and the demand for qualified personnel is expected to expand. If you are looking for the challenge of working with people to improve their social and personal difficulties, then you should seriously consider a career in social work.

From 1960 to 2008, the number of employed social workers grew by over 600%—from 95,000 to 642,000.[26] About 5 out of 10 jobs are in health-care and social assistance industries, and 3 out of 10 are employed by state and local government agencies, primarily in departments of health and human services. Although most social workers are employed in cities or suburbs, some work in rural areas.[27]

The Bureau of Labor Statistics projects the following job outlook for social work positions:

> Employment for social workers is expected to grow faster than the average for all occupations through 2018. Job prospects are expected to be favorable, particularly for social workers who specialize in the aging population or work in rural areas.
>
> *Employment change.* Employment of social workers is expected to increase by 16 percent during the 2008–18 decade, which is faster than the average for all occupations. The growing elderly population and the aging baby boom generation will create greater demand for health and social services, resulting in rapid job growth among gerontological social workers. Employment of social workers in private social service agencies also will increase.
>
> Employment of child, family, and school social workers is expected to grow by about 12 percent, which is as fast as the average for all occupations. Demand for child and family social workers should continue, as these workers are needed to investigate child abuse cases, place children in foster care and with adoptive families. However, growth for these workers may be hampered by the budget constraints of state and local governments, who are amongst the largest employers of these workers. Furthermore, demand for school social workers will continue and lead to more jobs as efforts are expanded to respond to rising student enrollments, as well as the continued emphasis on integrating children with disabilities into the general school population. There could be competition for school social work jobs in some areas because of the limited number of openings. The availability of Federal, State, and local funding will be a major factor in determining the actual job growth in schools.
>
> Mental health and substance abuse social workers will grow by almost 20 percent over the 2008–18 decade, which is much faster than the average. In particular, social workers specializing in substance abuse will experience strong demand. Substance abusers are increasingly being placed into treatment programs instead of being

sentenced to prison. Also, growing numbers of the substance abusers sentenced to prison or probation are increasingly being required by correctional systems to have substance abuse treatment added as a condition to their sentence or probation. As this trend grows, demand will strengthen for treatment programs and social workers to assist abusers on the road to recovery....

Growth of medical and public health social workers is expected to be about 22 percent, which is much faster than the average for all occupations. One of the major contributing factors is the rise in the elderly population. These social workers will be needed to assist in finding the best care and assistance for the aging, as well as to support their families. Employment opportunities for social workers with backgrounds in gerontology should be excellent, particularly in the growing numbers of assisted-living and senior-living communities. The expanding senior population also will spur demand for social workers in nursing homes, long-term care facilities, home care agencies, and hospices.[28]

Widely varying employment settings are available for social workers, including foster care, adoption, probation and parole, public assistance, counseling, services to single parents, day-care services, school social services, services to populations-at-risk, services to veterans, recreational services such as Boy Scouts and YWCA programs, social services in a medical or mental hospital, antipoverty programs, social services in nursing homes and other services to the elderly, marital counseling, drug and alcohol counseling, services to the emotionally disturbed, abortion counseling, family planning services, services to people with a physical disability, sexual counseling, equal rights services, protective services, services in rehabilitation centers, research, social action, and fund-raising. (These settings will be described in detail in the chapters that follow.) In addition to these direct services, there are employment opportunities for those with experience and advanced professional training in social planning, community organization, consultation, supervision, teaching, and administration.

Social work majors who are most likely to secure employment in social work following graduation are those who are outgoing, dynamic, and able to "sell" themselves during an interview as having the competence, confidence, and skills to perform the job

they are applying for. Involvement in groups and extracurricular activities while at college facilitates the development of these capacities, as does volunteer work at one or more social service agencies. Many of our students secure employment through the relationships they develop with staff during their field placement. If they do well at their field placement and a vacancy occurs, they have an inside track in being hired. Also, through acquaintances with staff at an agency, they hear about employment opportunities at other agencies and frequently receive a positive letter of reference from their field placement supervisors.

Students who consider majoring in social work frequently ask: "Is a graduate degree needed to get a job in social work?" It definitely is not. The vast majority of employed social workers hold only a baccalaureate degree. In fact, some agencies prefer to hire a person with a bachelor's degree because it is less expensive. Of course, as in most fields, a master's degree provides higher status, greater promotion opportunities, and perhaps more gratifying work (see Case Exhibit 2.2: Establishing and Maintaining Worker Safety in the Field).

Private Practice of Social Work

Although most social workers are employed by agencies (financed by either public or private funds), growing numbers of social workers in the past two decades have opted to provide counseling (also called psychotherapy) and group therapy on a fee basis. This type of *private practice* is similar to the arrangement in which private physicians provide services to patients.

The social worker may have a private practice on a part-time basis in addition to working full time for an agency. Or the individual may work full time in private practice. Sometimes social workers form a partnership with psychologists and/or psychiatrists to provide psychotherapy and group therapy through a private for-profit clinic. In yet another arrangement, social workers may be employed by a private clinic (which may be owned by a psychologist or psychiatrist) to provide therapy to individuals and groups.

Different states have different laws regulating the structure and operation of private clinics and private practice. Such legislation is intended to protect the public. These laws usually require that the social worker in private practice have a master's degree from an accredited school of social work as well as a few years of supervised practice in counseling individuals and groups.

CASE EXHIBIT 2.2

Establishing and Maintaining Worker Safety in the Field

Social workers are faced with an ever-changing work environment and are often exposed to the possibility of a dangerous situation while working in the field. The executive director of the National Association of Social Workers noted the significance of safety in 2005 when she stated that "As first responders for troubled families, dedicated social workers and caseworkers far too often put their own safety in jeopardy to ensure the safety of others."[a] Situations such as domestic violence, substance abuse, the availability of weapons, and an economy where unemployment and feelings of despair and hopelessness have impacted many individuals and families all increase the risk of danger to a worker. Although few workers are seriously injured during the course of their employment, social work is considered to be one of the most dangerous careers, according to the Occupational Safety and Health Administration, due to these elements of unpredictability.[b] Although there are many reasons for these potentially dangerous situations, according to Trainin-Blank, one of the main reasons that client violence is on the rise is that more workers are seeing clients in their communities and homes, rather than in the office, as service providers move to a focus on community-based delivery of services, rather than the more institutionalized settings and delivery models previously used.[c]

Social worker Teri Zenner may be one of the more well-known social workers killed in the line of duty, as her spouse, in conjunction with Congress, has gone to great lengths after her death to highlight the importance of safety in the workplace. Mrs. Zenner was working as a mental health case manager when she was stabbed to death in 2004 while conducting a home visit with a mentally ill male client. Mrs. Zenner's death brought the potential dangers of the social work field into the spotlight once again, and agencies, as well as Congress, took note of the dangerous work that social workers do. It was after Mrs. Zenner's death that Congress introduced a resolution to raise awareness of these dangers and encouraged agencies to address the issues of safety in the social work field.[d]

Although many workers are out in the community providing services, social workers working in a group home setting, such as Stephanie Moulton also experience violence. Ms. Moulton was killed in January 2011 by a client who had a long history of mental illness and violence. This client had previously served a prison sentence for another vicious beating. According to reports, Ms. Moulton was not aware of her client's violent history or that his family had raised concerns about him not being on his medication days before the killing. When Ms. Moulton was attacked and killed by her client, she was alone with him in the group home.[e]

Fortunately, some workers do escape from these dangerous situations, but may forever bear the wounds of the trauma. In December 2011 a social worker in Kansas City was attacked while making a home visit at a transitional housing complex for homeless youth. The worker was sitting on the couch when the client began choking her and threatened to kill her. The client told the worker that if she performed a sex act, he would allow her to leave, which she was eventually able to do. The client was arrested and charged with one count of attempted forcible sodomy.[f]

For the safety of all workers, as well as those they serve, it is important to establish and maintain safety practices in the field and in the office. It is also important to have these practices encouraged and enforced by agencies. Workers should prepare themselves by learning about the dynamics of addiction and mental illness, as well as other indicators of violence.

When working with individuals and families, there is always the possibility of a capricious situation. However, it is best if workers are able to do their research prior to meeting a client, especially for the first time. This is also important to keep in mind even after working with a person for a duration of time, because elements often change and there is always still the potential for danger. Prior to meeting a client, it is important to gather information, such as who is living in the home; if there is a history of violence with the individual client or in the family; if there is any reported substance abuse or mental health disorders; if firearms are reported to be in the home; or if there are any possible environmental dangers that may pose a risk to the worker. By gathering as much information as possible on the front-end, a worker will be more prepared to respond to any situation once he or she is with the client and less likely to encounter unforeseen danger.

There are a number of different things that social workers can do to prevent becoming a victim of violence. In the age of advanced technology, social workers should be equipped with a cell phone. This may be an agency cell phone or a personal cell phone. Oftentimes a cell phone is the only direct connection to assistance when a worker is out in the community working with clients. It is important that workers keep this cell phone located on their person and charged at all times. If a crisis situation were to arise and the phone is not charged or accessible in that moment, it is a useless tool. An example of this would be keeping a cell phone in a purse where it is hard to find, or leaving it in the car when a worker goes in to a home.

Although it is important to dress as a professional, it is also important for workers to dress for the environment they will be working in. If workers are going to be out in the community completing visits, they should keep in mind the potential for danger and dress accordingly. Comfortable shoes are important, as are clothes that a worker can move quickly in, if necessary. Social workers should also avoid excessive jewelry, handbags, or other clothing items such as scarves that could be grabbed or used to restrain a person. A worker should also consider carrying photo identification, so that if a crisis were to arise, the worker can accurately identify herself and her agency or employer.[g]

(continued)

Social workers frequently carry large caseloads, and schedules are often unpredictable. However, it is always important for a worker to be on time, when possible, and to inform the client if she is going to be late. Tardiness can contribute to a person's frustration and agitation, leading to a potentially hostile environment. It is also good practice for social workers to plan to let someone know where they are going to be and for approximately how long. Many agencies have shared calendars and require workers to use these. By letting other individuals know where a worker intends to be, a worker ensures that if she were not to return or be gone for an unexpected period of time, the agency would know where to find her or where to send assistance. Whether a worker is with a client in a car, home, or office setting it is always important for the worker to be aware of the environment and her location in that environment. Social workers should always place themselves between the client and the exit of their setting. This may mean that a worker has to reposition herself during her interaction with a client, but she should do so as needed. This also may force a worker to decline a seat that the client offers her, which would place her away from the exit. Most importantly when working with clients, workers should always trust their instincts. If a worker is feeling like the situation is escalating and beyond her control, she should leave that situation. She could do this by just exiting the home or office, or she could indicate that she has a call she has to make outside of the home or office and then leave the situation. A worker could also indicate that she forgot some needed paperwork and leave to retrieve it. Most important, if a worker feels that she is in an unsafe situation, she should leave that environment.

Workers often do much of their work in the community and in the privacy of individuals' homes. It is important that a worker always be aware of who is in a home at all times. Oftentimes living situations change, so it is good practice for a worker to always ask who is in the home at the time of each visit. When entering a home, a worker should consider asking for a tour of the residence to assess for any environmental hazards within the home. This is also a good time to identify the layout of the residence and to note the exits of the residence.

When working with clients in the office setting, a worker should always be aware of her building's emergency response plan of action. There are times that workers are in the office during times other than usual business hours. A worker should keep in mind that she should not be in an office building alone with a client. For some workers, they may be providing evening services to better accommodate clients' schedules. The worker should ensure that another colleague is in the building until the conclusion of that session, when possible. If a worker has a client who she knows is agitated or has a history of violence, the worker should consider interacting with that individual in a room designated for this. This room should be centrally located, so that if the worker were to need assistance, other people would be available and aware of the situation.

The worker should also inform the security team, her supervisor, or another coworker of where she will be and about the potential danger, possibly asking someone to check in periodically. This room would also be void of any items that could be potential weapons or pose a threat to the client or worker.

Social workers often find themselves in situations where they are driving to see a client or have a client in the vehicle with them. Before leaving for any appointments, a worker should always ensure that she has enough gas in her vehicle for the trip, which will eliminate a stop either with a client or possibly in a neighborhood the worker is unfamiliar with. When driving in the community, it is important for a worker to know her route and to plan to stay on as many main roads as possible, which can be complicated by working in a rural area. This is important so that if something were to happen, a worker can call for help and be able to describe her exact location. Remaining on main roads also allows for more people to be around and present in the area, which could be beneficial if something were to happen and the worker needed assistance of any sort. If a worker is traveling with a client in her car, she should always insist that the individual wear his or her seatbelt. This is not only a safety precaution and the law, but also a natural restraint if the client were to become agitated and want to lunge at the worker for any reason. As with all working environments, the worker should also ensure to put away any objects, such as pens, paperclips, or other items, that could be used as weapons, because "usually the violence is not premeditated, and the weapon is frequently an object found in the immediate surrounds," according to Trainin-Blank, when incidents of violence do occur.[h] Many workers also suggest keeping an item of distraction in their vehicle.[i] This could be a magazine, a snack, or anything else that could be given to a client if he appears agitated during the ride. The object of distraction could assist the client in refocusing his attention on the object and hopefully divert his attention from the agitating stimuli.

It is important that workers also take precautions when parking their vehicles. When leaving the vehicle, workers should put away any items of value. This could mean disassembling a geographic positioning system (GPS) device or stowing items such as a purse or other electronic devices. Individuals should always park in a well-lit area, close to the entrance of their destination. A driver should also avoid parking behind or near any large vehicles or structures, as these pose as natural ambush points, due to the limited visibility that they create.[j] It is also important that workers keep in mind the dangers of parking in a driveway or alley. If a situation were to arise and the worker needed to leave the location quickly, having to back out of a driveway or an alley can be difficult and slow the worker's exiting time. Parking in a driveway or alley also leaves it possible for someone to block the worker's car in with his own vehicle, creating a safety concern for the worker if she is not able to leave quickly. A parking spot should always be chosen in terms of the ability to drive directly out of it, and quickly. This is true even if it means the worker must walk a little bit further to the destination.

(continued)

Mental rehearsal is another technique used by professionals in all fields and can be beneficial for social workers to practice as well. Mental rehearsal is the skill of picturing oneself in a situation, without actually being there. E. Scott Geller notes that "the more vividly individuals can imagine themselves performing desired behaviors, the greater the beneficial impact of this technique on actual performance."[k] It is wise for workers to utilize mental rehearsal to visualize themselves in undesirable situations. For example, a worker could picture herself being locked in a home with an angry client and how she would escape from that situation. By mentally taking oneself through that circumstance and imagining what one would do in that situation, the body and mind are more likely to respond favorably, rather than to freeze, if that situation were to ever occur. Consequently, the worker would be more prepared to respond to that unsafe scenario by having practiced the response during the mental rehearsal.

Social workers are often faced with individuals who are angry, agitated, hostile, or in a state of crisis. It is important to be familiar and comfortable with basic de-escalation techniques. A worker should always remain calm and self-assured in situations. Although a worker may feel intimidated or tense, it is important not to present in this manner, so as to help alleviate some of the distressing emotions being experienced by the client. Workers should also remain respectful in all interactions. When angry or agitated, clients will often lash out at a worker or become verbally abusive. A worker can empathize with and validate how the client is feeling, but should remain respectful and calm in that dialogue at all times. During the times when clients are escalating or angry, it is important that the worker constantly be assessing the situation for her own safety and that of others and make the decision to leave if necessary.

As workers continue to serve society's most vulnerable individuals, agencies can assist in preparing them to do so by addressing the importance and prevalence of danger in the working environment. As a reactive measure, some agencies are beginning to establish safety committees to address insituations of violence that have already occurred and in hopes of preventing other workers from being placed in these situations. Agencies should also consider creating and implementing policies and procedures related to safety in the workplace. Workers should also be encouraged to trust their judgment and to

ask for assistance when necessary. When workers have experienced violence of any sort, it is important that this is immediately addressed by the agency, and assistance should be provided if legal protection or action needs to be taken on the worker's behalf.

Whether social workers are brand new to the field or have been serving others for years, safety is an important topic to keep at the forefront of their practice and should be revisited often by workers and agencies. Workers should take the time to familiarize themselves with the safety policies and procedures of their agency and to ask about safety precautions and measures. They should also take the time to prepare themselves with self-defense courses and mental rehearsal exercises. Workers can also carry items such as personal panic alarms or pepper spray, if permitted. Most important, workers should always trust their instincts and act accordingly in every situation.

[a]National Association of Social Workers, NASW Communications, "Effort Honoring the Memory of Teri Zenner," Endorsed by the National Association of Social Workers, 2005, http://www.naswdc.org/pressroom.

[b]B. Trainin-Blank, "Safety First: Paying Heed to and Preventing Professional Risks," *The New Social Worker Online*, Summer, 2005, http://www.socialworker.com.

[c]Ibid.

[d]National Association of Social Workers, "Effort Honoring the Memory of Teri Zenner."

[e]M. Valencia, "Giving Voice to Slain Social Worker," *The Boston Globe*, Feb. 8, 2012, http://articles.boston.com.

[f]C. Vendel, "Social Worker Escapes Attacker during Northland Home Visit," *The Kansas City Star*, Dec. 2011, http://www.kansascity.com.

[g]F. Chandler, *Personal Safety Issues for Social Workers* (Madison, WI: National Association of Social Workers Wisconsin Chapter Home Study Program, 2012).

[h]B. Trainin-Blank, "Safety First: Paying Heed to and Preventing Professional Risks."

[i]F. Chandler, *Personal Safety Issues for Social Workers*.

[j]Ibid.

[k]E. S. Geller, "Beyond Safety Accountability: How to Increase Personal Responsibility," 1998, http://www.safetyperformance.com/PreventingInjurywithMentalImagery.pdf.

SOURCE: This exhibit was written by Rachel Dunn, MSW, CAPSW, Field Coordinator for George Williams College of Aurora University.

In most cases, fees for therapy are paid by recipients' health insurance policies. If recipients do not have health insurance coverage, they are expected to pay their own fees for the therapy they receive.

In regards to job prospects in private practice, the Bureau of Labor Statistics predicts:

Opportunities for social workers in private practice will expand, as they are preferred over more costly psychologists. Furthermore, the passage of legislation that requires insurance plans offered

by employers to cover mental health treatment in a manner that is equal to treatment of physical health may increase the demand for mental health treatment.[29]

International Social Work

Social work is now a global profession. It is a recognized profession in Great Britain, Canada, the United States, India, and numerous other countries.

There is a growing recognition that people in all nations are interdependent. In many ways, the world has become, as futurist Marshall McLuhan put it, a "global village."[30] The crises and problems experienced by one country often affect other countries (see Case Exhibit 2.3: Origins of the YMCA).

The nations in our world have become so interdependent that all persons now live in a global community. Significant events in countries far away from us affect all of us, as illustrated by the following examples. Reductions in petroleum production by countries in the Middle East raise petroleum prices, almost immediately, throughout the world (and since petroleum is used in producing practically every product, it leads to global increases in prices). The Great Depression of the United States in the 1930s was felt worldwide. World Wars I and II affected practically every nation. Sharp increases or decreases in the stock markets in Japan and the United States affect stock markets throughout the world and also the overall health of every economy in the world. HIV, which originated in Africa, has affected, in some way, every person in the world. Nearly everyone knows personally someone who has been affected, and the virus has led to changes in sexual behaviors. Drug trafficking is a global phenomenon that affects many families. The collapse of the Berlin Wall in November 1989 signaled the end of the Cold War between the United States and Russia and led to upheavals in many Communist-bloc nations. Those changes have had significant social and economic consequences around the world. The development of e-mail and the Internet has led to rapid sharing of information throughout the world. A major disaster in any part of the world is now shown globally via television and the Internet, and many countries rapidly offer assistance. Terrorists using planes to destroy the Twin Towers in New York City (resulting in the deaths of nearly 3,000 people) on September 11, 2001, spurred an international effort to combat terrorism.

The study of international social work and social welfare is now an imperative that moves us beyond our many self-imposed barriers and allows all of us to be better off in a cooperative global community.

International social work encourages comparative social policy analysis. Two major benefits can be derived from comparative policy analysis in social work. The first is enhanced understanding of one's own system through assessment of its place in the global system. The other is transfer of "technology"—the identification of innovations in other countries that can be adapted to one's home country.

Lynne M. Healy describes the importance of comparative social policy analysis:

It is only possible to fully understand a social welfare system by comparing it with other systems and by assessing a system's place in the worldwide network. Such study may expose widely accepted truisms as mere opinions. Politicians and corporate leaders in the United States, for example, have resisted the idea of paid maternity and paternity leaves, claiming that to grant such leave would destroy American business competitiveness in the world economy. The argument sounds less convincing when compared to the policy and business practices of America's competitors in Western Europe, where almost all countries offer leave with pay not only to new parents but also to employees with ill family members. Thus the comparative view shows that to claim that such a policy is impossible is clearly invalid; more accurately, it can be asserted that parental leave is not a policy priority in the United States.[31]

There is a trend in colleges and universities in many countries to "internationalize" the curriculum. Students need an understanding and appreciation of the diversity that exists internationally (see Case Exhibit 2.4: Manon Luttichau).

Social work educational programs in the United States are increasingly seeking to foster an international perspective for social work majors. This is being done through student exchange programs with other countries, faculty exchange programs with other countries, study-abroad programs (including internships) for social work majors, and new curriculum content on social problems and innovative services in other countries. The Educational Policy and Accreditation Standards (EPAS) of the Council on Social Work Education specifies that: "Social workers recognize the global interconnections of oppression and are knowledgeable about theories of justice and strategies to promote human and civil rights."[32] The Council on Social Work Education also has a Commission on Global Social Work Education. It is composed of educators from around the country who are actively involved in teaching international content and initiating cross-national exchange programs. (This text seeks to facilitate readers acquiring an international perspective by presenting, in practically every chapter, information on social problems

CASE EXHIBIT 2.3

Origins of the YMCA

A number of the social welfare programs in the United States had their origins in other countries. One famous program is the Young Man's Christian Association (YMCA). The first YMCA was founded on June 6, 1844, in London, England, by a young man named George Williams. Williams was a sales assistant in a draper's shop, a forerunner of today's department store. He, and a group of fellow drapers, organized the first YMCA to substitute Bible study and prayer for life on the streets.

At that time, the growth of the railroads and the centralization of commerce and industry brought many rural young men who sought jobs to cities like London. They worked 10 to 12 hours a day, 6 days a week. Far from home, these young men often lived in rooms above their company's shop. (Such a location was often safer than London's tenements and streets.) Outside the shop things were bad—pickpockets, thugs, beggars, drunks, lovers for hire, and abandoned children abounded.

YMCAs proved to be very popular. In the 7 years that followed 1844, 23 more YMCAs were formed in Great Britain, and the approach began to spread to other countries. On November 25, 1851, the first YMCA was organized in Canada—in Montreal. On December 29, 1851, the first YMCA in the United States was founded in Boston.

YMCAs also inspired the formation of the Young Women's Christian Association (YWCA). The first YWCA was organized in London in 1855. The first YWCA in the United States was formed in Boston in 1866. George Williams was knighted by Queen Victoria in 1894 for his YMCA work in Britain and elsewhere. YMCAs are now present in 124 countries.

The programs offered by YMCAs have changed over the years, and there are now considerable variations in services offered at different YMCAs. The worldwide group of YMCAs is now devoted to the physical, intellectual, social, and spiritual well-being of men, but YMCA services are no longer limited to young people, Christians, or even men in some localities.

The YMCA and YWCA movements illustrate that social workers need to have a global perspective—viable social welfare programs are continuing to be developed in other countries.

and social services not only in the United States but also in other countries.)

The International Association of Schools of Social Work (IASSW) is the focal point for social work education around the world. It promotes social work education and the development of high-quality educational programs around the world. It was organized in 1929. Membership, which is open to national associations such as the Council on Social Work Education in the United States, totals over 450 schools from 100 countries.[33]

Critical Thinking Question

Do you have a passion to travel to other countries to understand other cultures, and to work with people of other cultures to improve human well-being?

Social work educational programs vary from country to country; they share certain similarities but also have notable differences.[34] For example, some countries, such as the United States, largely use a person-in-environment model to analyze human behavior, whereas other countries, such as Sweden, still largely use a medical model. (These two models of understanding human behavior are described in Chapter 3.)

The International Federation of Social Workers (IFSW) is an organization comprising more than 50 professional membership associations, including the National Association of Social Workers.[35] Healy describes the goals of the IFSW:

The goals of the federation are to promote social work as a profession with professional standards, training, and ethics; to support the involvement of national associations of social work in policy development; to encourage communications among social workers in various countries; and to present the views of the profession internationally to intergovernment organizations ... A valuable part of the federation's work has been its human rights advocacy for social workers who are held as political prisoners in various parts of the world.[36]

People of all countries are experiencing many of the social problems described in this text, including poverty, mental illness, crime, divorce, family violence, births outside of marriage, AIDS, rape, incest, drug abuse, worker alienation, international terrorism, unemployment, racism, sexism, medical problems, physical and mental disabilities, overpopulation, and misuse of the environment. By studying and analyzing

CASE EXHIBIT 2.4

Manon Luttichau: The Founder of Professional Social Work in Denmark

The global interdependence of social work is demonstrated by the global interchange of ideas that led to professional social work education being established at approximately the same time in a number of countries. As indicated earlier, courses in social work in the United States began to be offered at colleges and universities in the early 1900s.

The first school of social work in Europe was begun in 1899 in Amsterdam and was called the Institute for Social Work Training. Shortly afterward, other European countries also began to offer professional social work programs.

Manon Luttichau was born on April 9, 1900. She is recognized as the most influential person in the founding of professional social work in Denmark. At an early age she became involved in "preprofessional" social work activities that were being established in Denmark; these activities largely involved providing services in settlement houses for young women, including pregnant, single women. "Street work," a form of social work, was also being done in Amsterdam; for example, "street workers" were assisting women near train stations. From 1922 to 1932, Luttichau was an assistant at a private organization, Care for Danish Women, that provided semiprofessional services to young women. During these years, Luttichau traveled to other countries (including the United States) to study how professional social work education was being conceptualized and offered.

On April 1, 1934, she became a "social worker" at the Copenhagen Municipal Hospital. This was a new job title in Denmark, one that she had advocated should be established. In 1936 she formed a planning committee of physicians, lawyers, and others to design professional social work education in Denmark. This committee arranged for classes in social work to be offered, beginning on January 5, 1937. The classes were held in the hospital auditorium, using 29 volunteers as teachers (and using donated space). The classes were collectively called "the Social School in Denmark." Luttichau was the "dean" for the first two groups of students. In 1938 she founded the National Association of Social Workers in Denmark.

Luttichau was a true internationalist. She believed the interchange of ideas and information among countries was essential in developing a profession. She traveled widely, studied the emerging profession of social work in other countries, and highly valued exchanging ideas with social workers in other countries. Luttichau is recognized as the pioneer of professional social work in Denmark. She died in 1995, on her 95th birthday.

SOURCE: Lynne M. Healy, *International Social Work* (New York: Oxford University Press, 2001).

how other countries are combating these problems, social service policy makers and providers in every country can learn to identify more effective programs and service delivery systems. Indeed, some of these problems (such as overpopulation and international terrorism) can be resolved only by coordinated international efforts. Social workers in the future will increasingly need an international perspective in analyzing and combating social problems.

Some international employment opportunities are available for social workers. The United Nations employs some social workers in staff positions for UNESCO (United Nations Educational, Scientific, and Cultural Organization), UNICEF (United Nations Children's Fund), and refugee work. Some units of government in other countries, and some private organizations as well, contract with social workers in the United States to be consultants. Some private national or international organizations (such as Catholic Charities, Worldwide Adoptions, and the Red Cross) have utilized social workers in their international programs.

Self-Awareness and Identity Development

As stated earlier, perhaps the key skill needed to be a competent social worker is the capacity to relate to and counsel individuals. Increasingly, when training social work students, educators are finding that the students who are best able to counsel others are those who know themselves; that is, they have a high level of self-awareness. A counselor has to be perceptive regarding what clients are thinking and feeling. To be perceptive, the counselor must be able to place himself or herself in the client's situation and determine (with the client's values and pressures) what that person is really feeling and thinking. Unless the counselor has a high level of self-awareness, it is very unlikely that she or he will be able to perceive what others are thinking and feeling.

Various approaches have been developed to increase self-awareness, including biofeedback, transcendental meditation, muscle relaxation, Gestalt therapy, identity formation, sensitivity training, and encounter groups.* (Some programs in social work are now offering interpersonal skills courses that are designed to develop self-awareness and interpersonal awareness capacities.)

Identity Formation

One approach to self-awareness—identity formation—will be explored here. Identity formation is the process of determining who you are and what you want out of life. Arriving at an identity you will be comfortable with is one of the most important tasks you will ever have to face. Whether or not you pursue a social work career, the following information on identity could have considerable importance for your future. As noted, it is especially significant for those considering a social work career because knowing oneself substantially enhances one's ability to counsel others.

Identity development is a lifelong process; there are gradual changes in identity throughout the lifetime. During the early years, our sense of who we are is largely determined by the reactions of others (the concept of the "looking-glass self"). For example, if neighbors, for whatever reason, perceive a young male to be a "troublemaker" or a "delinquent," they are then likely to accuse the youth of delinquent acts, treat him with suspicion, and label many of his activities "delinquent." Although frequently accused and criticized, the youth, to some extent, soon begins to realize that enacting the delinquent role also brings certain rewards; it gives him a type of status and prestige, at least from other youths. In the absence of objective ways to determine whether he is a delinquent, he relies on the subjective evaluations of others. Gradually, a vicious cycle develops: The more he is related to as a delinquent, the more likely he is to view himself as a delinquent and the more likely he is to enact the delinquent role.

Glasser indicates that a useful perspective for viewing identity is in terms of a success-versus-failure orientation.[37] Those who develop a success identity view themselves as being generally successful; people who develop a success identity do so through the pathways of *love* and *worth*. People who view themselves as a success must feel that at least one other person loves them and also that they love at least one other person. They must feel that at least one other person believes they are worthwhile, and they must feel they (themselves) are worthwhile.

To develop a success identity, a person must experience both love and worth, particularly during childhood. A person can feel loved but not feel worthwhile. Worth comes through accomplishing tasks and achieving success in the accomplishment of those tasks. A person can feel worthwhile through accomplishing tasks (for example, a successful businessperson) but believe she is unloved because she cannot name someone she loves and who loves her. Experiencing only one of these elements (worth or love) without the other can lead to a failure identity.

A failure identity is likely to develop when a child has received inadequate love or been made to feel worthless. People with a failure identity are likely to be depressed, lonely, anxious, reluctant to face everyday challenges, and indecisive. Escape through drugs or alcohol, withdrawal, criminal behavior, and the development of emotional problems are common.

However, because identity is a lifelong process, significant positive changes can be achieved, even by those with a serious failure identity. An important principle is: *Although we cannot change the past, what we want out of the future, along with our motivation to achieve what we want, is more important (than our past experiences) in determining what our future will be.*

Some of the most important issues you will ever have to face are these:

1. What kind of person do you want to be?
2. What do you want out of life?
3. Who are you?

Without answers to these questions, you will not be prepared to make such major decisions as selecting a career, choosing where to live and what type of lifestyle you want, and deciding whether to marry and whether to have children. Unfortunately, many people muddle through life without ever arriving at answers to these questions. The answers don't come easily. They require considerable thought and much trial and error. During the time you are searching for a sense of who you are, a great deal of anxiety may arise. However, if you are to lead a satisfying, fulfilling

---

*A review of the specific techniques used in these approaches is contained in Richard S. Sharf, *Theories of Psychotherapy and Counseling*, 5th ed. (Belmont, CA: Wadsworth/Cengage Learning, 2011).

life, it is imperative that you know what you want and who you are. Here are some additional questions to aid in identity formation.

Critical Thinking Question

Do you have a fairly well-thought-out sense of who you are and what you want out of life? If not, what do you need to work on?

Questions for Arriving at a Sense of Identity

To determine who you are, answer the following more specific questions:

1. What do you find satisfying/enjoyable? Only after you identify what is meaningful and gratifying will you be able to consciously seek involvement in activities that will make your life fulfilling and avoid activities that are meaningless or stifling.

2. What are your religious or spiritual beliefs?

3. What is your moral code? One possible code is to attempt to fulfill your needs and do what you find enjoyable without depriving others of the ability to fulfill their needs.

4. What are your sexual mores? All of us should develop a consistent code that we are comfortable with and that helps us meet our needs without exploiting others. There is no one right code—what works for me may not work for you because of differences in lifestyle, life goals, and personal values.

5. What kind of a career do you desire? Ideally, you should seek work that is stimulating and satisfying, that you are skilled at, and that earns you enough money to support the lifestyle you desire.

6. What area of the country or world do you want to live in? Variables to be considered are climate, geography, type of dwelling, rural or urban setting, proximity to relatives or friends, and characteristics of the neighborhood.

7. Do you hope to marry? If yes, to what type of person? When? How consistent are your answers here with your other life goals?

8. Do you want to have children? If yes, how many? When? How consistent are your answers here with your other life goals?

9. What kind of image do you want to project to others? Your image consists of your dressing style and grooming habits, emotions, personality, degree of assertiveness, capacity to communicate, material possessions, moral code, physical features, and voice patterns. You need to honestly assess your strengths and shortcomings in this area and try to make improvements in the latter. Seeking counseling in problem areas may be desirable.

10. What do you enjoy doing in your leisure time?

11. Do you desire to improve the quality of your life and that of others? If yes, in what ways? How do you hope to achieve these goals?

12. What type of people do you enjoy being with? Why?

13. What kind of a relationship do you want to have with your relatives, friends, neighbors, and people you meet for the first time?

14. What are your thoughts about death and dying?

15. What do you hope to be doing in 5 years? In 10 years? In 20 years? What are your plans for achieving these goals in these time periods?

To have a fairly well-developed sense of identity, you need to have answers to most, but not all, of these questions. Very few people are able to arrive at rational, fully consistent answers to all the questions.

Be honest about your strengths and shortcomings. Realize that for practically any shortcoming there are specific intervention strategies to bring about improvement.

In addition, expect some changes in your life goals as time goes on. As you grow as a person, changes will occur in your beliefs, attitudes, and values and in the activities that you find enjoyable.

Your life is shaped by different events that result from the decisions you make and the decisions that are made for you. Without a sense of identity, you will not know what decisions are best, and your life will be unfulfilled. With a sense of identity, you will be able to direct your life toward the goals you select and find personally meaningful.

SUMMARY

The following summarizes this chapter's content as it relates to the chapter objectives presented at the beginning of the chapter. Objectives include the following:

A *Define the profession of social work.*

Social work is the professional activity of helping individuals, groups, families, organizations, and communities to enhance or restore their capacity for social functioning and to create societal conditions favorable to their goals. A social worker is a multi-skilled professional. The social worker needs training and expertise in a wide range of areas to be able to deal effectively with problems faced by individuals, groups, families, organizations, and the larger community. Like the general practitioner in medicine, a social worker should acquire a wide range of skills and intervention techniques. Social work is distinct from other careers in that it is the profession that has the responsibility and mandate to provide social services.

The ability to counsel clients effectively is perhaps the most basic skill a social worker needs. Second in importance is probably the ability to interact effectively with other groups and professionals in the community.

B *Provide a brief history of social work.*

Social work as a profession is of relatively recent origin. Individuals were first hired as social workers around 1900, and formalized training in social work was first offered at universities in the early 1900s.

C *Describe the following social work activities: casework, case management, group work, group therapy, family therapy, and community organization.*

Social workers work with individuals, groups, families, organizations, and communities. The social worker helps people increase their capacities for problem solving and coping, helps them obtain needed resources, facilitates interactions between individuals and between people and their environments, helps make organizations responsible to people, and influences social policies. There are several types of professional social work activities: casework, case management, group work, group therapy, family therapy, community organization, administration, research, consulting, planning, supervision, and teaching.

D *Describe the person-in-environment conceptualization for social work practice.*

This perspective views the client as part of an environmental system. This perspective encompasses the reciprocal relationships and other influences between an individual, the *relevant other* or others, and the physical and social environment.

E *Specify the goals of social work practice.*

The five goals of social work practice are to (a) enhance the problem-solving, coping, and developmental capacities of people; (b) link people with systems that provide them with resources, services, and opportunities; (c) promote the effectiveness and humane operation of systems that provide people with resources and services; (d) develop and improve social policy; and (e) promote human and community well-being.

F *Describe the strengths perspective.*

Social work emphasizes empowerment and a strengths perspective (rather than a focus on pathology) in working with individuals, groups, families, organizations, and communities. It is now imperative that social workers have an international perspective, as we live in a global community.

It is essential that social workers include clients' strengths in the assessment process. In working with clients, social workers focus on the strengths and resources of clients to help them resolve their difficulties. To utilize clients' strengths effectively, social workers must first identify those strengths.

There is a danger that a primary focus on weaknesses will impair a worker's capacity to identify a client's growth potential. Social workers strongly believe that clients have the right (and should be encouraged) to develop their potentialities fully. Focusing on pathology often undermines this value commitment.

G *Summarize societal stereotypes of social workers.*

Sixty-five years ago, the stereotype of a social worker was that of a moralistic upper-middle-class older woman carrying a basket of food and having little understanding of the people she tried to help. With the rapid development of social work as a profession, there are now many stereotypes (generally more positive) of what a social worker is.

H *Summarize employment settings and career opportunities in social work.*

Currently there are more employment opportunities available in social work than in many other fields. Widely varying employment settings are available for social workers. Most people employed as social workers do not have a graduate degree. As in most fields, however, individuals with a master's degree in social work generally have higher status and greater promotion opportunities.

It is crucial for social workers to have a high level of self-awareness and a sense of who they are and what they want out of life. Arriving at a sense of identity is one of the most important and difficult quests in life—for everyone. With a sense of identity, you will be able to direct your life toward the goals you select and find personally meaningful.

I Briefly describe international social work.

Social work is now a global profession. It is a recognized profession in Great Britain, Canada, the United States, India, and numerous other countries. There is a growing recognition that people in all nations are interdependent. In many ways, the world has become a "global village." The crises and problems experienced by one country often affect other countries.

Competency Notes

EP 2.1.3a Distinguish, appraise, and integrate multiple sources of knowledge, including research-based knowledge and practice wisdom. (All of this chapter) This chapter describes social work as a profession and a career. It provides a history of social work, and also summarizes the following: micro-, mezzo-, and macropractice; an ecological model of human behavior; the goals of social work practice; the strengths perspective; a medical versus a systems model of human behavior; stereotypes of social workers private practice of social work; and international social work.

Media Resources

Additional resources for this chapter, including a chapter quiz, can be found on the Social Work CourseMate. Go to CengageBrain.com.

Notes

1. Robert M. Bremner, "The Rediscovery of Pauperism," in *Current Issues in Social Work Seen in Historical Perspective* (New York: Council on Social Work Education, 1962), p. 13.
2. Nathan E. Cohen, *Social Work in the American Tradition* (Hinsdale, IL: Dryden Press, 1958), p. 66.
3. Dorothy G. Becker, "Social Welfare Leaders as Spokesmen for the Poor," *Social Casework*, 49, no. 2 (Feb. 1968), p. 85.
4. Ralph Dolgoff and Donald Feldstein, *Understanding Social Welfare* (New York: Harper & Row, 1980), pp. 233–234.
5. Ibid., p. 235.
6. Mary E. Richmond, *Social Diagnosis* (New York: Free Press, 1965).
7. H. J. Eysenck, "The Effects of Psychotherapy," in *Handbook of Abnormal Psychology*, H. J. Eysenck, ed. (New York: Basic Books, 1961), pp. 697–725.
8. Robert L. Barker, *The Social Work Dictionary*, 5th ed. (Washington, DC: NASW, 2003), p. 408.
9. Dean H. Hepworth, Ronald H. Rooney, and Jo Ann Larsen, *Direct Social Work Practice: Theory and Skills*, 5th ed. (Pacific Grove, CA: Brooks/Cole, 1997), pp. 27–28.
10. Frank Riessman, "The 'Helper Therapy' Principle," *Journal of Social Work*, 10, no. 2 (April 1965), pp. 27–34.
11. Richard Stuart, *Trick or Treatment: How and When Psychotherapy Fails* (Champaign, IL: Research Press, 1970).
12. William H. Masters and Virginia E. Johnson, *Human Sexual Inadequacy* (Boston: Little, Brown, 1970).
13. D. D. Jackson, "The Study of the Family," *Family Process*, 4 (1965), pp. 1–20.
14. National Association of Social Workers, *Standards for the Classification of Social Work Practice* (Washington, DC: NASW, 1982), p. 17.
15. Council on Social Work Education, *Educational Policy and Accreditation Standards* (Alexandria, VA: Council on Social Work Education, 2008).
16. http://www.nytimes.com/2011/09/14/us/14census.html?pagewanted=all.
17. Council on Social Work Education, *Educational Policy and Accreditation Standards*.
18. William Glasser, *The Identity Society* (New York: Harper & Row, 1972).
19. A. Weick, C. Rapp, W. P. Sullivan, and W. Kisthardt, "A Strengths Perspective for Social Work Practice," *Social Work*, 34 (1989), pp. 350–354.
20. Dennis Saleebey, The *Strengths Perspective in Social Work Practice*, 2nd ed. (New York: Longman, 1997), pp. 12–15.
21. Ibid., p. 12.
22. Ralph Dolgoff, Donald Feldstein, and Louise Skolnik, *Understanding Social Welfare*, 4th ed. (New York: Longman, 1997), p. 295.
23. Craig W. LeCroy and Erika L, Stinson, "The Public's Perception of Social Work: Is It What We Think It Is?" *Social Work*, 49, no. 2 (April 2004), pp. 164–174.

24. Ibid, p. 174.
25. Bureau of Labor Statistics, U.S. Department of Labor, *Occupational Outlook Handbook, 2010–2011 Edition*, "Social Workers," http://www.bls.gov/ooh/
26. Ibid.
27. Ibid.
28. Ibid.
29. Ibid.
30. See William Kornblum and Joseph Julian, *Social Problems*, 7th ed. (Englewood Cliffs, NJ: Prentice Hall, 1992), p. 468.
31. Lynne M. Healy, *International Social Work* (New York: Oxford University Press, 2001), p. 261.
32. Council on Social Work Education, *Educational Policy and Accreditation Standards*.
33. Lynne M. Healy, *International Social Work*, 2nd ed. (New York: Oxford University Press, 2008).
34. See Idit Weiss, John Gal, and John Dixon, eds., *Professional Ideologies and Preferences in Social Work: A Global Study* (Westport, CT: Praeger Publishers, 2003).
35. Lynne M. Healy, "International Social Welfare: Organizations and Activities," *Encyclopedia of Social Work*, 19th ed. (Washington, DC: NASW, 1995), p. 1505.
36. Ibid.
37. Glasser, *The Identity Society.*

Generalist Social Work Practice

CHAPTER OUTLINE

The focus of this chapter will be on generalist social work practice. This chapter will:

Learning Objectives

EP 2.1.3a

A   Define generalist social work practice.
B   Summarize the change process in social work practice.
C   Describe roles assumed by social workers in social work practice.
D   Discuss social work practice with individuals, families, groups, organizations, and the community.
E   Summarize the knowledge, skills, and values needed for social work practice.
F   Briefly describe educational training for social work practice.

Generalist Social Work Practice Defined

The traditional perception of the social worker has been that of a caseworker, group worker, or community organizer. Practicing social workers know that their roles are more complex than that; every social worker is involved as a change agent (someone who assists in promoting positive changes) in working with individuals, groups, families, organizations, and the larger community. The amount of time spent at these levels varies from worker to worker. But every worker will, at times, be assigned and expected to function effectively at all these levels and therefore needs training in all of them.

The Council on Social Work Education (CSWE)—the national accrediting entity for baccalaureate and master's programs in social work—requires all bachelor's and master's programs to train their students in generalist social work practice. (MSW programs, in addition, usually require their students to select and study in an area of concentration. These programs generally offer several concentrations, such as family therapy, administration, corrections, and clinical social work.)

D. Brieland, L. B. Costin, and C. R. Atherton define and describe generalist practice as follows:

The generalist social worker, the equivalent of the general practitioner in medicine, is characterized by a wide repertoire of skills to deal with basic conditions, backed up by specialists to whom referrals are made. This role is a fitting one for the entry-level social worker.

The generalist model involves identifying and analyzing the interventive behaviors appropriate to social work. The worker must perform a wide range of tasks related to the provision and management of direct service, the development of social policy, and the facilitation of social change. The generalist should be well grounded in systems theory that emphasizes interaction and independence. The major system that will be used is the local network of services....

The public welfare worker in a small county may be a classic example of the generalist. He or she knows the resources of the county, is acquainted with the key people, and may have considerable influence to accomplish service goals, including obtaining jobs, different housing, or emergency food and clothing. The activities of the urban generalist are more complex, and more effort must be expended to use the array of resources.[1]

G. Hull defines generalist practice as follows:

The basic principle of generalist practice is that baccalaureate social workers are able to utilize the problem solving process to intervene with various size systems including individuals, families, groups, organizations, and communities. The generalist operates within a systems and person-in-the-environment framework (sometimes referred to as an ecological model). The generalist expects that many problems will require intervention with more than one system (e.g., individual work with a delinquent adolescent plus work with the family or school) and that single explanations of problem situations are frequently unhelpful. The generalist may play several roles simultaneously or sequentially, depending upon the needs of the client (e.g., facilitator, advocate, educator, broker, enabler, case manager, and/or mediator). They may serve as leaders/facilitators of task groups, socialization groups, information groups, and self-help groups. They are capable of conducting needs assessments and evaluating their own practice and the programs with which they are associated. They make referrals when client problems so dictate and know when to utilize supervision from more experienced staff. Generalists operate within the ethical guidelines prescribed by the NASW Code of Ethics and must be able to work with clients, coworkers, and colleagues from different ethnic, cultural, and professional orientations. The knowledge and skills of the generalist are transferable from one setting to another and from one problem to another.[2]

The Baccalaureate Program Director's organization (BPD) has defined generalist practice as:

Generalist social work practitioners work with individuals, families, groups, communities, and organizations in a variety of social work and host settings. Generalist practitioners view clients and client systems from a strengths perspective in order to recognize, support, and build upon the innate capabilities of all human beings. They use a professional problem-solving process to engage, assess, broker services, advocate, counsel, educate, and organize with and on behalf of the client and client systems. In addition, generalist practitioners engage in community and organizational development. Finally, generalist practitioners evaluate service outcomes in order to continually improve the provision and quality of services most appropriate to client needs.

Generalist social work practice is guided by the NASW Code of Ethics and is committed to improving the wellbeing of individuals, families, groups, communities, and organizations, and furthering the goals of social justice.[3]

The Council on Social Work Education (SWE) in its *Educational Policy and Accreditation Standards* (EPAS) has defined generalist practice as:

Generalist practice is grounded in the liberal arts and the person and environment construct. To promote human and social well-being, generalist practitioners use a range of prevention and intervention methods in their practice with individuals, families, groups, organizations, and communities. The generalist practitioner identifies with the social work profession and applies ethical principles and critical thinking in practice. Generalist practitioners incorporate diversity in their practice and advocate for human rights and social and economic justice. They recognize, support, and build on the strengths and resiliency of all human beings. They engage in research-informed practice and are proactive in responding to the impact of context on professional practice.[4]

The crux of generalist practice involves (a) viewing a problem situation in terms of the person-in-environment conceptualization (described in Chapter 2) and (b) being willing and able to intervene at several different levels, if necessary, while assuming any number of roles. The next section describes the change process in social work practice and illustrates the approach of responding at different levels in a variety of roles.

The Change Process

A social worker uses a *change process* in working with clients. (Clients include individuals, groups, families, organizations, and communities.) The Council on Social Work Education (2008) in its EPAS defines professional social work practice as:

Professional practice involves the dynamic and interactive processes of engagement, assessment, intervention, and evaluation at multiple levels. Social workers have the knowledge and skills to practice with individuals, families, groups, organizations, and communities. Practice knowledge includes identifying, analyzing, and implementing evidence-based interventions designed to achieve client goals; using research and technological advances; evaluating program outcomes and practice effectiveness; developing, analyzing, advocating, and providing leadership for policies and services; and promoting social and economic justice.[5]

Educational Policy 2.1.10(a)—Engagement

Social workers

- substantively and affectively prepare for action with individuals, families, groups, organizations, and communities;
- use empathy and other interpersonal skills; and
- develop a mutually agreed-on focus of work and desired outcomes.

Educational Policy 2.1.10(b)—Assessment

Social workers

- collect, organize, and interpret client data;
- assess client strengths and limitations;
- develop mutually agreed-on intervention goals and objectives; and
- select appropriate intervention strategies.

Educational Policy 2.1.10(c)—Intervention

Social workers

- initiate actions to achieve organizational goals;
- implement prevention interventions that enhance client capacities;
- help clients resolve problems;
- negotiate, mediate, and advocate for clients; and
- facilitate transitions and endings.

Educational Policy 2.1.10(d)—Evaluation

Social workers critically analyze, monitor, and evaluate interventions.[6]

In reviewing this conceptualization of professional social work practice, there are at least eight skills needed by social work practitioners:

1. Engaging clients in an appropriate working relationship.
2. Identifying issues, problems, needs, resources, and assets.
3. Collecting and assessing information.
4. Planning for service delivery.
5. Using communication skills, supervision, and consultation.
6. Identifying, analyzing, and implementing empirically based interventions designed to achieve client goals.
7. Applying empirical knowledge and technological advances.
8. Evaluating program outcomes and practice effectiveness.

The following example illustrates the use of these eight skills in the change process in social work.

Carlos Ramirez is a social worker at a high school in a midwestern state. Four teenagers are suspended for 2 weeks (consistent with school board policy) for drinking alcoholic beverages at school. The case is referred to Mr. Ramirez for intervention.

Phase 1: Engaging Clients in an Appropriate Working Relationship

The first step in the change process is to engage clients in an appropriate relationship. In this case example, there are a number of potential "clients." Clients are the people who sanction or ask for the worker's services, the expected beneficiaries of the service, and those who have a working agreement or contract with the worker. Using this definition, the potential clients in this case are the four teenagers who were suspended (and their parents), as they are the expected beneficiaries of the services; the school system, as it has a working agreement with Mr. Ramirez and it asks him for assistance with this situation; and the other students in the school system (and their parents), as they are also expected beneficiaries.

To be effective, it is essential that a worker seek to form appropriate, professional relationships with all potential clients. A working relationship is facilitated when the worker reflects empathy, warmth, and sincerity. (Chapter 5 contains additional information on forming and maintaining professional relationships with clients.)

Phase 2: Identifying Issues, Problems, Needs, Resources, and Assets

Identifying issues, problems, needs, resources, and assets is the second step in the change process, and it often becomes complex. Mr. Ramirez identifies a variety of issues (questions/concerns/problems), including the following: Do the youths have a drinking problem? Were the youths, disenchanted with the school system, displaying their discontent by breaking school rules? What short-term and long-term adverse effects may the suspensions have on the youths? Will the suspensions have an adverse effect by marking these youths as "troublemakers," thereby leading them into further delinquent behavior? How will the parents of these youths react to the drinking and to the suspensions? What effects will the suspensions have on other students at the school? (A possible positive effect: The suspensions may be a deterrent to other students who consider violating school rules. A possible negative consequence: The suspensions may encourage other students to violate school rules in order to be expelled and relieved of the obligation to attend school.) Will the suspensions create problems for merchants in the community if the expelled youths spend their days on the street? Is the school policy of suspending youths for drinking on school grounds constructive or destructive? Does the school system have a responsibility to add a drug-education component to the curriculum? Do certain aspects of the school system encourage youths to rebel? If so, should these aspects be changed?

Mr. Ramirez is also aware that the school system has a number of resources and assets to confront these issues. The system has a number of professionals (teachers, psychologists, other social workers, nurses, and guidance counselors) who are available to provide services, including in assisting in developing and implementing new programs to address the identified problems, needs, and issues. If need be, the system has funds to hire one or more consultants who are experts in addressing the issues of alcohol and drug use. The school system also has an established bureaucracy (including a school board) that has procedures and policies for establishing new programs. State and federal grant money may also be available for initiating drug prevention programs. The identified issues, problems, and assets will serve as a guide during the next phase (collecting and assessing information).

Phase 3: Collecting and Assessing Information

This phase focuses on an in-depth collection and analysis (assessment) of data to provide the social worker with answers to the issues and problems raised in Phase 1. On some of the issues, useful information can be obtained directly from the clients (including the youths in this example). For example, the question of whether the youths have a drinking problem can perhaps be answered by meeting with them individually, forming a trusting relationship, and then inquiring how often the youth drinks, how much the youth consumes when drinking, and what problems the youth has encountered while drinking. For other issues raised in Phase 1, useful information

must be collected from other sources. For example, the issue of short-and long-term adverse effects of the expulsion on the youths can perhaps be answered by researching the literature on this topic.

Phase 4: Planning for Service Delivery

After information is collected and assessed, Mr. Ramirez and other decision makers in the school system need to decide first whether the school system should provide services in this situation. (Often such a decision involves an assessment as to whether the prospective clients meet the eligibility requirements of the agency.) The decision to provide services in this case is easy to make, as the school system has an obligation to provide services to all enrolled students. The next decision is which services to provide. The next few phases of the change process describe how to decide which services to provide.

Phase 5: Using Communication Skills, Supervision, and Consultation

Effectiveness as a social worker is highly dependent on the worker's communication skills—both oral and writing skills. (Many agency directors assert writing skills are as important as interviewing and counseling skills—workers need to draft a wide variety of reports, such as grant proposals, assessment and treatment plans, court reports, and reports required by the agency.) Also important are the worker's capacities to give presentations; be a witness in court; and communicate effectively with clients, staff, and professionals at other agencies.

Regarding supervision, every agency administrator wants social workers who are "team players" and who respond to supervision in a positive manner—rather than becoming defensive when critical comments and suggestions are given. (In this case example, Mr. Ramirez has frequent meetings with his supervisor, Dr. Maria Garcia, director of pupil services at the high school, about the courses of action that he should take.)

Workers also need to be aware of when consultation may be beneficial and then be willing to utilize such consultation.

In this case example, Mr. Ramirez contacts the state Department of Public Instruction. He discovers this department has a consultant available (at no direct charge to the school system) on alcohol and other drug prevention and treatment programs that have been effective in other parts of the United

States. Mr. Ramirez meets with this individual, Dr. Raul Alvarez, to discuss the issues in his community and to receive information on programs that have been effective.

Phase 6: Identifying, Analyzing, and Implementing Empirically Based Interventions Designed to Achieve Client Goals

There are a variety of potential interventions in this case. Mr. Ramirez can seek to involve the four youths in one-to-one counseling about their drinking patterns and their suspensions. Another intervention would be to offer group counseling at the school for the four youths and for other students having drinking problems. Or, Mr. Ramirez can seek to have the four youths receive individual or group counseling from a counseling center outside the school system. Mr. Ramirez could also seek to have the youths and their parents receive family therapy from a counseling center outside the school system. Yet another intervention strategy is to raise the issue (with parents, the business community, the police department, the school administration, and the school board) as to whether suspension from school for drinking alcoholic beverages is a desirable policy—perhaps "in-school suspension" would be a better policy. An additional intervention strategy is to incorporate educational material on alcohol and other drugs into the curriculum.

Mr. Ramirez discusses these strategies with Dr. Alvarez and obtains his thoughts (based on the results of these interventions being used in other communities) as to which are apt to be most cost effective. (Cost-benefit analysis compares resources used to potential benefits.) Rarely, in real-life situations, can social workers pursue *all* worthy interventions, because of time and resource limitations.

Mr. Ramirez selects as one of his interventions the preventive approach of adding to the curriculum educational material about alcohol and other drugs. Numerous questions related to this intervention now arise for Mr. Ramirez. What specific material should be covered in a drug-education program? Which drugs should be included? (Mr. Ramirez knows that describing certain drugs, such as LSD, may cause some parents to ask whether educational material about seldom-used drugs might encourage some youths to experiment.) *Where* should the drug-education component be added to the curriculum—

in large assemblies with all students required to attend? In health classes? In social science classes? Will the school administration, teachers, school board, students, and parents support a proposal to add this component to the curriculum? What strategy will be most effective in gaining the support of these various groups?

As a first step in this phase, Mr. Ramirez meets with his immediate supervisor, Dr. Maria Garcia, to discuss these issues and to generate a list of alternative strategies. Three strategies are discussed:

1. An anonymous survey could be conducted in the high school to discover the extent of alcohol and other drug use and abuse among students. Such survey results could document the need for drug education.

2. A committee of professional staff in the Pupil Services Department could develop a drug-education program.

3. The Pupil Services Department could ask the school administration and the school board to appoint a committee representing the school board, the school administration, the teachers, the students, the parents, and the Pupil Services Department. This committee would explore the need for and feasibility of a drug-education program.

Mr. Ramirez and Dr. Garcia decide that the best way to obtain broad support for the drug-education program is to pursue the third option. Dr. Garcia meets with the high school principal, who—after some contemplation—agrees to explore the need for such a program. The principal, Ms. Mary Powell, requests the school board to support the formation of a committee. The school board agrees. A committee is eventually formed, and it begins holding meetings. Mr. Ramirez is appointed by Dr. Garcia to be the Pupil Services' representative to this committee.

(In this case example, Mr. Ramirez decides to pursue the following additional interventions: [a] seek to involve the four youths in one-to-one counseling about their drinking patterns and their suspensions—however, only one youth comes to see him on a regular basis; the other three have a pattern of making excuses for not coming: and [b] seek to change the policy of suspending students from school for drinking alcoholic beverages on school grounds to an "in-school suspension" policy. For brevity, this text will focus on the preventive approach of adding to the curriculum educational material about alcohol and other drugs.)

Phase 7: Applying Empirical Knowledge and Technological Advances

One of the first questions raised by some committee members during initial deliberations is, "If a drug-education program is developed, what specific drugs should it include?" Some committee members, as expected, are concerned that providing information about drugs not currently in use among young people in the community may encourage the use of such drugs. As a result, the Pupil Services Department is asked to conduct a student survey to identify the mind-altering drugs currently in use and to discover the extent of such use.

A second (related) issue arising in the committee is the broader question of whether a drug-education program has preventive value, or whether such a program might promote illegal drug use. Mr. Ramirez responds to this issue by suggesting Dr. Raul Alvarez be invited to meet with the committee to discuss this issue. Dr. Alvarez is invited and shares information on the preventive value of a variety of drug-education programs across the nation.

After 14 months of planning and deliberation, the committee presents to the school board its proposal for drug education. The program is designed to be part of the health curriculum in the district's middle schools and high schools.

The drug-education program added to the health curriculum contains the latest research-based knowledge about drugs commonly used by young people in the community. The information about these drugs includes mind-altering effects, characteristics of physical and psychological dependency, and withdrawal and long-term health effects. The curriculum also contains research-based information on the most effective treatment approaches, methods of coping in a family with a drug-abusing member, ways to confront a friend or relative who is abusing, the dangers of driving under the influence of drugs, associations between drug use and sexually transmitted diseases (including AIDS), suggestions for people concerned about their own drug use, and practical ways to say "no" to drugs.

Helpful technological advances applied to this program include computer databases that contain effective drug-education programs used in other school systems, computer software for processing the surveys of student drug use and attitudes in the district, and current films and videotapes that offer age-appropriate drug-education material.

Phase 8: Evaluating Program Outcomes and Practice Effectiveness

To evaluate this preventive approach, the Pupil Services Department decides to conduct an annual survey of a random sample of students to assess the extent of drug use/abuse and to elicit students' thoughts about the merits and shortcomings of the drug-education program. The Pupil Services Department also decides to conduct an annual random survey of the parents of the high school students to obtain information on their thoughts about the merits and shortcomings of this drug-education program and to obtain their suggestions for changes in the program. Such surveys provide a way to monitor and evaluate the program's outcomes.

The final phase of any intervention is termination. The committee that developed the drug-education program has its final meeting after the school board approves the proposal. Most members experience mixed emotions at this meeting. They are delighted that their task is successfully completed, but they feel some sadness because this group, which has become an important and meaningful part of their lives, is now ending. (With any committee, if a close working relationship has formed among members, termination is often a painful process. As issues were addressed, some dependency may have developed, and as a result members may experience a sense of loss when termination occurs.)

A final evaluation is usually a part of terminating. The final evaluation involves more than the assessment of what occurred during monitoring; it emphasizes the usefulness of the entire change process. The final evaluation is also extremely significant to the agency because it indicates whether the agency's services have been beneficial. Each agency needs composite evaluations of all its services to all clients that provide documentation to funding sources to justify continued funding.

A Variety of Roles

In working with individuals, groups, families, organizations, and communities, a social worker is expected to be knowledgeable and skillful in a variety of roles. The particular role that is selected should ideally be determined by what will be most effective, given the circumstances. The following material identifies some, but certainly not all, of the roles assumed by social workers.

Enabler

In this role, a worker *helps* individuals or groups to articulate their needs, to clarify and identify their problems, to explore resolution strategies, to select and apply a strategy, and to develop their capacities to deal with their own problems more effectively. This is perhaps the most frequently used approach in counseling individuals, groups, and families. The model is also used in community practice primarily when the objective is to help people organize to help themselves.

It should be noted that this definition of the term *enabler* is very different from the one used in the area of chemical dependency. There the term refers to a family member or friend who facilitates the substance abuser's continued use and abuse of a drug.

Broker

A broker links individuals and groups who need help (and do not know where it is available) with community services. For example, a wife who is often physically abused by her husband might be referred to a shelter for battered women. Nowadays even moderate-size communities have 200 or 300 social service agencies/organizations providing community services. Even human services professionals may be only partially aware of the total service network in their community.

Advocate

The role of advocate has been borrowed from the legal profession. It is an active, directive role in which the social worker advocates for a client or for a citizens' group. When a client or a citizens' group is in need of help and existing institutions are uninterested (or even openly negative and hostile) in providing services, then the advocate's role may be appropriate. In such a role, the advocate provides leadership for collecting information, for arguing the correctness of the client's need and request, and for challenging the institution's decision not to provide services. The objective is not to ridicule or censure a particular institution but to modify or change one or more of its service policies. In this role, the advocate is a partisan who is exclusively serving the interests of a client or a citizens' group. In being an advocate, a worker is seeking to empower a client or a citizen's group through securing a beneficial change in one or more institutional policies.

Activist

An activist seeks institutional change; often the objective involves a shift in power and resources to a disadvantaged group. Activists are concerned about social injustice, inequity, and deprivation, and their strategies include conflict, confrontation, and negotiation. The goal is to change the social environment to better meet the recognized needs of individuals. Using assertive and action-oriented methods (for example, organizing concerned citizens to work toward improvements in services in a community for people with AIDS), social workers engage in fact-finding, analysis of community needs, research, the dissemination and interpretation of information, mobilization, and other efforts to promote public understanding and support on behalf of existing or proposed social programs. Social action activity can be geared toward a problem that is local, statewide, or national in scope.

Mediator

The mediator role involves intervention in disputes between parties to help them find compromises, reconcile differences, or reach mutually satisfactory agreements. Social workers have used their value orientations and unique skills in many forms of mediation. Examples of target groups in which mediation has been used include disputes that involve divorcing spouses, neighbors in conflict, landlord–tenant disputes, labor–management disputes, and child custody disputes. Mediators remain neutral, not siding with either party, and make sure they understand the positions of both parties. They may help to clarify positions, identify miscommunication about differences, and help those involved present their cases clearly.

Negotiator

A negotiator brings together those who are in conflict over one or more issues and seeks to achieve bargaining and compromise to arrive at mutually acceptable agreements. Somewhat like mediation, negotiation involves finding a middle ground that all sides can live with. However, unlike a mediator, which is a neutral role, a negotiator usually is allied with one of the sides involved.

Educator

The educator role involves giving information to clients and teaching them adaptive skills. To be an effective educator, the worker must first be knowledgeable. Additionally, she or he must be a good communicator so that information is clearly conveyed and readily understood by the receiver. Examples include teaching parenting skills to young parents, providing job-hunting strategies to the unemployed, and teaching anger-control techniques to individuals with bad tempers.

Initiator

An initiator calls attention to a problem—or even to a potential problem. It is important to realize that some problems can be recognized in advance. For example, a proposal to renovate a low-income neighborhood by building middle-income housing units may result in the current residents' becoming homeless. If the proposal is approved, the low-income families won't be able to afford the costs of the middle-income units. Usually the initiator role must be followed by other functions; merely calling attention to problems usually does not resolve them.

Empowerer

A key goal of social work practice is empowerment, which is the process of helping individuals, families, groups, organizations, and communities increase their personal, interpersonal, socioeconomic, and political strength and influence through improving their circumstances. Social workers who engage in empowerment-focused practice seek to develop the capacity of clients to understand their environment, make choices, take responsibility for their choices, and influence their life situations through organization and advocacy. Empowerment-focused social workers also seek to gain a more equitable distribution of resources and power among different groups in society. This focus on equity and social justice has been a hallmark of the social work profession, as evidenced through the early settlement workers such as Jane Addams (see Chapter 2).

Coordinator

Coordinators bring components together in some kind of organized manner. For example, for a multi-problem family it is often necessary for several agencies to work together to meet the complicated financial, emotional, legal, health, social, educational, recreational, and interactional needs of the family members. Someone at an agency needs to assume the role of case manager to coordinate the services from the different agencies to avoid duplication and to prevent the diverse services from having conflicting objectives.

Researcher

Every social worker is at times a researcher. Research in social work practice includes studying the literature on topics of interest, evaluating the outcomes of one's practice, assessing the merits and shortcomings of programs, and studying community needs.

Group Facilitator

A group facilitator is one who serves as a leader for group activity. The group may be a therapy group, an educational group, a self-help group, a sensitivity group, a family therapy group, or a group with some other focus.

Critical Thinking Question

Which of these social work roles would you enjoy fulfilling with clients? Why?

Public Speaker

Social workers occasionally are recruited to talk to various groups (such as high school classes, public service organizations such as Kiwanis, police officers, staff at other agencies) to inform them of available services or to advocate for new services. In recent years, various needed services have been identified (for example, runaway centers, services for battered spouses, rape crisis centers, services for people with AIDS, and group homes for youths). Social workers who have public-speaking skills can explain services to groups of potential clients.

Critical Thinking Questions

Are members of your family currently facing some of these challenges? If so, would some form of family services be useful?

As indicated earlier, a generalist social worker is a change agent (someone who assists in facilitating positive changes) who works with individuals, groups, families, organizations, and the community. To give you a flavor of social work practice in each of these areas, some brief practice-oriented information will be presented.

Social Work with Individuals

A majority of social workers spend most of their time working with individuals in public or private agencies or in private practice. Social work with individuals is aimed at helping people, on a one-to-one basis, to resolve personal and social problems. Social work with individuals encompasses a wide variety of activities, such as counseling runaway youths, helping unemployed people secure training or employment, counseling someone who is suicidal, placing a homeless child in an adoptive or foster home, providing protective services to abused children and their families, finding nursing homes for stroke victims who no longer need to be confined in a hospital, counseling individuals with sexual dysfunctions, helping alcoholics to acknowledge that they have a drinking problem, counseling those with a terminal illness, supervising individuals on probation or parole, providing services to single parents, and coordinating services for individuals who have AIDS.

All of us at times face personal problems that we cannot resolve by ourselves. Sometimes other family members, relatives, friends, or acquaintances can help. At other times we need more skilled intervention to help us handle emotional problems, obtain resources in times of crisis, deal with marital or family conflicts, resolve problems at work or school, or cope with a medical emergency. Furnishing skilled personal help is what social work with individuals is all about.

In their role as change agents in working with individuals, social workers perform many of the functions discussed earlier: enabler, broker, advocate, educator, and so on. An essential skill and role of a social worker is counseling. (Some authorities assert that counseling and relationship skills are the most important abilities needed by social workers.[7] Future chapters will illustrate that social workers counsel people with a wide variety of personal and social problems. See Chapter 5 for guidelines on counseling individuals.)

Social Work with Families

Often the focus of social work services is on the family. A family is an interacting, interdependent system. The problems faced by any individual are usually influenced by the dynamics within a family. Because a family is an interacting system, change in one member affects other members. For example, it has

been noted that the abused child is at times a scapegoat on whom the parents vent their anger and hostility. If the abused child is removed from such a home, another child within the family is likely to be selected as the scapegoat.[8]

Another reason for focusing on the family is that the participation of all members is often needed in the treatment process. For example, other family members can put pressure on an alcoholic to make her or him acknowledge that a problem exists. The family members may all need counseling (or support from a self-help group) to assist them in coping with the alcoholic when she or he is drinking, and these family members may play important roles in providing emotional support for the alcoholic's efforts to stop drinking.

Family Problems

The following is a small listing of some of the infinite number of problems that may occur in families:

- Divorce
- Alcohol or drug abuse
- Unwanted pregnancy
- Bankruptcy
- Poverty
- Terminal illness
- Chronic illness
- Death
- Desertion
- Empty-shell marriage
- Emotional problems of one or more members
- Behavioral problems of one or more members
- Child abuse
- Child neglect
- Sexual abuse
- Spouse abuse
- Elder abuse
- Unemployment of wage earners
- Money management difficulties
- Injury from serious automobile accident involving one or more members
- Cognitive disability in one or more members
- Incarceration or institutionalization of one or more members
- Compulsive gambling by one or more members
- Crime victimization
- Forced retirement of a wage earner
- Alzheimer's disease in an elderly relative
- Involvement of a child in delinquent and criminal activities

- Illness of a member who acquires AIDS
- Runaway teenager
- Sexual dysfunctions of one or more members
- Infidelity
- Infertility

When problems arise in a family, social services are often needed. The types and forms of services that social workers provide to troubled families are extremely varied. We can group them into two major categories: in-home services and out-of-home services.

In-home services are preventive. Although not all are offered literally within the home itself, they are specifically designed to help families stay together. They include financial aid; protective services (services to safeguard children or frail older adults from abuse and neglect); family preservation services (intensive crisis intervention within the home setting where children are so seriously at risk that removal to foster care would otherwise be required); family therapy (intensive counseling to improve family relationships); day care (caretaking services for children or older adults to provide respite for caregivers who might otherwise be overwhelmed, or to permit them to work outside the home); homemaker services (for the same purpose); and family life education (classes, often offered at traditional family service agencies, that cover such topics as child development, parenting skills, communication issues, and so on). Obviously, not all of these services can be provided by social workers, but workers must know where to find them and how to help the family obtain them when needed.

Out-of-home services, on the other hand, are those services that must be operationalized when the family can no longer remain intact. They are a manifestation that something has gone seriously wrong, as the breakup of any family amounts to a tragedy that will have ramifications beyond family boundaries. Although family members usually receive the blame, the larger system (social environment, and the level of support it provides to troubled families) may be called into question. Out-of-home services include foster care, adoption, group homes, institutional care (for example, residential treatment centers), and the judicial system (which provides a different kind of institutional care, prison or jail, for family members who have run into difficulty with the law).

These services require the social worker to perform a variety of roles (broker, educator, advocate, case manager, mediator, and so on).

Satir's Family Therapy Approach

One important social service provided to families is family therapy (also called family counseling). A substantial amount of literature on family therapy has been developed in social work. Numerous theoretical frameworks for family therapy have been advanced. One of the most prominent was developed by Virginia Satir, a psychiatric social worker. Satir's approach to family therapy will be briefly summarized.[9]

Satir stresses clarification of family communication patterns. She notes, in particular, that communication patterns among troubled families tend to be vague and indirect. In other words, rather than speaking clearly for themselves, a marital pair may avoid talking with each other about their needs and desires, or perhaps they talk to each other about what they want through their children. The children are thus maneuvered into the stressful position of speaking for, and therefore allying with, one parent or the other, which precipitates fear of loss of the other parent.

In Satir's view, indirect communication in the troubled family begins with courtship of the marital pair (if not before) and is due to the low self-esteem of the individuals involved. Each spouse-to-be feels worthless but hides these feelings by acting confident and strong. Neither person talks about feeling worthless for fear of driving the potential mate away. So each sees in the other a strong person who will take care of him or her. They marry to gain an extension of the self, but a stronger self who will be able to meet all felt needs; in other words, each marries to "get."[10]

Critical Thinking Question

Are communication patterns in your family vague and indirect, or are they precisely expressed and direct?

Unfortunately, after marriage some of the illusions must fall away. Each spouse is forced to realize at some level that the other spouse is not just an extension of the self. One insists on using a separate toothbrush, for example, while the other wants to share the same one. Such incidents force perceptions of difference, and difference is experienced as bad because it leads to arguments. A desire to fuse and to be cared for conflicts with the other's different felt needs. Facing this difference feels frightening and might lead to arguments that could result in the other's leaving.

Hence each frightened spouse with low self-esteem and high need for the other tries to mask differences as much as possible. On one level, they attempt to please the other to keep him or her; on another level, they fear and resent the other's expressed needs, which they may experience as undesirable.

Because both spouses are in the same uncomfortable position of resenting differences yet needing the other, interpersonal communication gradually becomes more and more indirect. Rather than risk a clear statement such as, "I'd like to get a dog," the spouse desiring a pet might say something like, "Aunt Matilda likes dogs." The hope is that the other spouse will mind-read the intended message and then spontaneously agree to get a dog for the family. However, the receiver of this particular message will more likely communicate a response dealing with Aunt Matilda, bringing disappointment to the speaker. The speaker isn't able to negotiate the desired dog with this type of communication and is left with angry feelings toward the spouse and a sense of unfulfilled needs. However, this state of affairs is experienced as preferable to risking a point-blank denial. Meanwhile, the receiver of the message may become aware of the disappointment or anger of the speaker through nonverbal channels but have no idea what caused it. The spouse, who is also afraid to deal with conflict, will not ask the reason for the apparent upset. So the misunderstanding and tension build.

Satir also notes that communication involves far more than the literal meaning of any words used. First of all, much communication is nonverbal—gestures, facial expressions, voice tone, posture, and the like. Nonverbal communication that matches the meaning of any words used (the words "I am sad" are accompanied by tears and a downturned mouth) is considered *congruent*. The receiver is not likely to misunderstand the meaning of this message because the verbal and nonverbal components agree. However, messages are often *incongruent*. For example, the statement "I am sad" may be accompanied by a grin. Which message should the receiver believe—the words or the facial expression? The receiver is likely to misinterpret unless he or she explicitly asks the sender to explain.

But the person who feels safe only with indirect communication is not likely to ask. Moreover, the sender who becomes skilled at sending incongruent communication for self-protection may even be unaware of the action and will be unable to explain if asked. Satir believes that incongruent communication can lead to misunderstanding in troubled families. Mother, for example, may say to Father in words, "I'm angry with you." However, because she fears rejection if she sends this message too forcefully, she smiles sweetly as she says it. Father may then choose to believe the smile, not take Mother's words seriously, and continue the very behavior that made her use the word *angry*. This is likely to make her angrier, but she may not feel safe enough to express the feeling more congruently. As a result, the communication that is driving the spouses apart goes on.

Another kind of incongruent communication is one that places the receiver in a *double bind*. That is, no matter how one responds, the sender will criticize. Father may say, on the one hand, that all good children should keep their toys picked up, but on the other hand, he tells his son that all "real" boys are messy. The boy who receives both messages will be unable to please Father whether he keeps his toys neat or messy. He may solve the problem by refusing to listen at all. At the extreme, he may pull away from reality to such a degree that he develops a severe emotional disturbance.

Satir's therapeutic goals and techniques are based on her assumption that people have the inherent ability (even drive) to grow and to mature. She feels that we can choose to take responsibility for our own lives and actions and that the mature person will:

1. Manifest himself clearly to others.
2. Be in touch with signals from his internal self, thus letting himself know openly what he thinks and feels.
3. Be able to see and hear what is outside himself as differentiated from himself and as different from anything else.
4. Behave toward another person as someone who is separate and unique.
5. Treat the presence of differentness as an opportunity to learn and explore rather than as a threat or signal of conflict.[11]

To help the members of a troubled family differentiate from one another and learn to own their special unique beings, Satir patiently teaches each person to speak for himself or herself and to send "I-messages." I-messages are nonblaming messages that communicate only how the sender believes the receiver is adversely affecting him or her. For example, suppose a father becomes frightened while riding in a car with his 17-year-old son, who is driving over the speed limit. An I-message that the father might use is, "John, going this fast in a car scares me."

In counseling families, Satir serves as an active, directive, loving role model. She teaches that differentness is normal and should be viewed as a catalyst for growth. She points out incongruent messages and double binds and teaches family members to send clear, congruent messages instead. She uses touch and other nonverbal means, such as family sculpting, to help illustrate to families the unverbalized assumptions they operate by. These techniques take the burden of labeling off the identified client and reveal his or her symptomatic behavior as a product of the family system as a whole.

Family sculpting is used for both assessment and treatment purposes. It involves a physical arrangement of the members of a family, with the placement of each person determined by an individual family member acting as "director." The resulting tableau represents that person's symbolic view of family relationships. Goldenberg and Goldenberg describe family sculpting as follows:

> *The procedure calls for each member to arrange the bodies of all the other family members in a defined space, according to his or her perception of their relationships either at present or at a specific point in the past. Who the sculptor designates as domineering, meek and submissive, loving and touching, belligerent, benevolent, clinging, and so on, and how those people relate to each other becomes apparent to all who witness the tableau. The sculptor is invited to explain the creation, and a lively debate between members may follow. The adolescent boy who places his parents at opposite ends of the family group while he and his brothers and sisters are huddled together in the center conveys a great deal more about his views of the workings of the family system than he would probably be able to state in words. By the same token, his father's sculpture—placing himself apart from all others, including his wife—may reveal his sense of loneliness, isolation, and rejection by his family. The mother may present herself as a confidante of her daughter but ignored by the males in the family, and so forth.*[12]

Satir also analyzes rules in the family. She helps clarify them in the context that some rules may be bad, but the people setting the rules or bound by them are not. She teaches that bad rules can be changed and has the family members negotiate new ones. She insists that each member be heard in her presence, thus teaching respect for each person and each point of view.

Clearly, then, Satir views the family as a system. Working with the family as a whole is the means of relieving the distress of the identified client or of the family itself due to the dysfunctional behavior of the identified client. Her major emphasis in intervention with the family as a system is to clarify their communication patterns and to help them become direct and congruent. Basically, Satir's therapeutic goal of improving methods of communication involves three outcomes. (a) Each member should be able to report congruently, completely, and obviously on what he or she sees, hears, feels, and thinks about himself or herself and others. (b) Each person should relate to his or her uniqueness so that decisions are made in terms of exploration and negotiation rather than in terms of power. (c) Differentness should be openly acknowledged and used for growth.[13]

Social Work with Groups

A group may be defined as:

> *Two or more individuals in face-to-face interaction, each aware of his or her membership in the group, each aware of the others who belong to the group, and each aware of their positive interdependence as they strive to achieve mutual goals.*[14]

Group social work has its historical roots in informal recreational organizations such as the YWCA and YMCA, scouting, Jewish centers, settlement houses, and 4-H clubs.

As was discussed in Chapter 2, George Williams established the Young Men's Christian Association (YMCA) in London in 1844 for the purpose of converting young men to Christian values.[15] Recreational group activities and socialization activities were a large part of the early YMCA's programs.

Settlement houses, which were established in many large cities of this country in the late 1800s, are largely credited for providing the roots of social group work.[16] Settlement houses sought to use the power of group associations to educate, reform, and organize neighborhoods; to preserve religious and cultural identities; and to give emotional support and assistance to newcomers both from the farm and from abroad.

Today almost every social service agency provides one or more of the following types of groups: recreation-skill, education, socialization, and therapy. Most undergraduate and graduate social work programs offer practice courses to train students to lead groups, particularly socialization and therapy groups. There is a national social group work organization, the Association for the Advancement of Social Work with Groups, that holds a yearly symposium and publishes a journal.

The following summary describes a variety of groups in social work: social conversation, recreation, recreation-skill, education, task, problem-solving and decision-making, self-help, socialization, therapy, and sensitivity groups.

Social Conversation Groups

Conversation in these groups is often loose and tends to drift aimlessly. There is no formal agenda. If one topic is dull, the subject is likely to change. Individuals may have some goal (perhaps only to establish an acquaintanceship), but such individual goals may not become the agenda for the entire group. Social conversation is often used for "testing" purposes— for example, to determine how deep a relationship might develop with people we do not know very well. In social work, social conversation with other professionals is frequent, but groups involving clients generally have objectives other than conversation.

Recreation Groups

The objective of these groups is to provide activities for enjoyment and exercise. Often such activities are spontaneous and the groups are practically leaderless. The group service agency (such as YMCA, YWCA, or neighborhood center) may offer little more than physical space and the use of some equipment. Spontaneous playground activities, informal athletic games, and an open game room are examples. Some group agencies that provide such physical space claim that recreation and interaction with others help build "character" and prevent delinquency among youths by offering an alternative to the street.

Recreation-Skill Groups

The objective of these groups is to improve a set of skills while at the same time providing enjoyment. In contrast to recreation groups, an adviser, coach, or instructor is generally present, and there is more of a task orientation. Examples of activities include golf, basketball, needlework, arts and crafts, and swimming. Competitive team sports and leagues may emerge. Frequently such groups are led by professionals with recreational training rather than social work training. Social service agencies that provide such services include the YMCA, YWCA, Boy Scouts, Girl Scouts, neighborhood centers, and school recreational departments.

Education Groups

The focus of such groups is for members to acquire knowledge and learn more complex skills. The leader generally is a professional with considerable training and expertise in the topic area. Examples of topics include assertiveness training, stress management, child-rearing practices, parent training, preparation for adoption, and volunteer training for specialized tasks in a social service agency. These groups may resemble a class, with considerable group interaction and discussion encouraged.

Task Groups

Task groups exist to achieve a specific set of tasks or objectives. The following are just a few examples of task groups that social workers are likely to interact with or become involved in. A *board of directors* is an administrative group charged with responsibility for setting the policy that governs agency programs. A *task force* is a group established for a special purpose; it is usually disbanded after the task is completed. A *committee* of an agency or organization is a group that is formed to deal with specific tasks or matters. An *ad hoc committee,* like a task force, is set up for one purpose and usually ceases functioning after completion of its task. (An ad hoc committee and a task force are essentially the same.)

Problem-Solving and Decision-Making Groups

Both providers and consumers of social services may become involved in problem-solving and decision-making groups. (There is considerable overlap between task groups and this category; in fact, problem-solving and decision-making groups could be viewed as a subcategory of task groups.) Providers of services use group meetings for such objectives as developing a treatment plan for a client or a group of clients, deciding how best to allocate scarce resources, deciding how to improve the delivery of services to clients, arriving at policy decisions for the agency, deciding how to improve coordination efforts with other agencies, and so on.

Potential consumers of services may form a group to meet some current community need. Data on the need may be gathered, and the group may be used as a vehicle either to develop a program or to influence existing agencies to provide services. Social workers may function as stimulators and organizers of such group efforts.

In problem-solving and decision-making groups, each participant often has some interest or stake in the process and stands to gain or lose personally by the outcome. Usually there is a formal leader of some sort, and other leaders sometimes emerge during the process.

Self-Help Groups

Self-help groups are very popular and are often successful in helping individuals with certain social or personal problems. Alfred Katz and Eugene Bender provide a comprehensive definition of self-help groups:

> Self-help groups are voluntary, small group structures for mutual aid, and the accomplishment of a special purpose. They are usually formed by peers who have come together for mutual assistance in satisfying a common need, overcoming a common handicap or life-disrupting problem, and bringing about desired social and/or personal change. The initiators and members of such groups perceive that their needs are not, or cannot be, met by or through existing social institutions. Self-help groups emphasize face-to-face social interactions and the assumption of personal responsibility by members. They often provide material assistance, as well as emotional support. They are frequently "cause"-oriented, and promulgate an ideology or values through which members may attain an enhanced sense of personal identity.[17]

Alcoholics Anonymous, developed by two former alcoholics, was the first self-help group to demonstrate substantial success. A number of other such groups have since been formed. Over 1,100 self-help groups can be located by typing in "American Self-Help Group Clearinghouse" on the Internet. When this website is accessed, type in a keyword of

the support group that you want. Some of these self-help groups are listed in Case Exhibit 3.1.

Many self-help groups stress (a) a confession to the group by every member that she or he has a problem, (b) a testimony to the group recounting past experiences with the problem and plans for handling it in the future, and (c) phone calls to another member whenever one feels a crisis (for example, an abusive parent having an urge to abuse a child); the person who is called stays with the member until the crisis subsides.

There appear to be several reasons why self-help groups are successful. All members have an internal understanding of the problem, which helps them to help others. Having experienced the misery and consequences of the problem, they are highly motivated and dedicated to find ways to help themselves and others who are fellow sufferers. The participants also benefit from the "helper therapy principle"—that is, the helper also gains psychological rewards.[18] Helping others leads the helper to feel "good" and worthwhile and also to put his or her own problems into perspective by seeing that others have problems that may be as serious or even more serious.

Some self-help groups, such as the National Organization for Women, focus on social advocacy and attempt to make legislative and policy changes in public and private institutions. Some groups (such as associations of parents of children with a cognitive disability) raise funds and operate community programs. Many people with a personal problem use self-help groups in the same way that others use social agencies. An additional advantage of self-help groups is that they are generally able to operate with a minimal budget.

Socialization Groups

The objective of such groups generally is to seek to change members' attitudes and behaviors in a more socially acceptable direction. Developing social skills, increasing self-confidence, and planning for the future are other focuses. Leaders of such groups might work with predelinquent youths in group activities to curb delinquency, with youths of diverse ethnic backgrounds to reduce racial tensions, with "at-risk" young children in an elementary school to improve their interpersonal and problem-solving skills and to motivate them to succeed in the school setting, with elderly residents at a nursing home to

CASE EXHIBIT 3.1

Examples of Self-Help Groups

Organization	Service Focus
Abused Parents of America	For parents who are abused by their adult children
Adoptees' Liberty Movement Association	For adoptees searching for their natural parents
Alcoholics Anonymous	For adult alcoholics
American Diabetes Association	Clubs for diabetics, their families, and friends
American Sleep Apnea Association	For people with sleep apnea and their families
Burns United Support Group	For burn victims
Candlelighters Childhood Cancer Foundation	For parents of young children with cancer
Concerned United Birthparents	For parents who have surrendered children for adoption and other adoption-affected people, including those in need of assistance in locating family members
Conjoined Twins International	For families of conjoined twins
Crohn's and Colitis Foundation of America	For people with Crohn's disease and their families
Depressed Anonymous	For depressed people
Divorce Care	For divorced people
Emotions Anonymous	For people with emotional problems
Encephalitis Support Group	For those with encephalitis and their families
Families Anonymous	For relatives and friends of drug abusers
Fortune Society	For ex-offenders, prisoners, and those facing prison and their families
Gam-Anon	For families of gamblers
Gray Panthers	An intergenerational group
Herpes Anonymous	For people with herpes and their families and friends
High Risk Moms, Inc.	For women experiencing a high-risk or problem pregnancy
Impotents World Association	For impotent men and their partners
Make Today Count	For people with cancer and their families
Molesters Anonymous	For men who molest children
National Organization for Women	For women's rights
Overeaters Anonymous	For overweight people
Parents Anonymous	For parents of abused children
Sexaholics Anonymous	For those with sexually self-destructive behavior
WINGS Foundation, Inc.	For men and women traumatized by incest

remotivate them and get them involved in various activities, or with youths at a correctional school to help them make plans for returning to their home community. Leadership of such groups requires considerable skill and knowledge in using the group to foster individual growth and change. Socialization groups are frequently led by social workers (See Case Exhibit 3.3: A Socialization Group at a Shelter for Runaways).

Critical Thinking Question

Do you have a desire to learn to be a group facilitator?

Therapy Groups

Therapy groups are generally composed of members with rather severe emotional or personal problems. Leaders must be highly skilled; they need to be perceptive, to understand human behavior and group dynamics, to have group counseling capacities, to use the group to bring about behavioral changes, to be aware at all times of how each member is affected by what is happening, and to develop and maintain a constructive atmosphere within the group. As with one-to-one counseling, the goal of therapy groups is generally to have members explore their problems in depth and then develop one or more strategies for resolving them. The group therapist often uses one or more of the following psychotherapy approaches as a guide for changing attitudes and behaviors: reality

CASE EXHIBIT 3.2

Contrasting Goals of Therapy versus Sensitivity Groups

Therapy Groups	Sensitivity Groups
Step 1	*Step 1*
Examine problem(s) in depth	Help each person become more aware of himself or herself and how he or she affects others in interpersonal interactions
Step 2	*Step 2*
Explore and then select (from various resolution approaches) a strategy to resolve the problem	Help a person to then develop more effective interaction patterns

therapy, learning theory, rational therapy, transactional analysis, client-centered therapy, psychodrama, and feminist therapy.*

Group therapy is widely used in counseling. It has several advantages over one-to-one therapy. The helper therapy principle generally is operative; members interchange roles and sometimes become the "helper" for someone else's problems. Helping others provides psychological rewards. Groups also help members put their problems into perspective by realizing that others have problems as serious as their own. Groups help members who are having interaction problems to test out new patterns of interacting. Research has shown that it is generally easier to change an individual's attitude in a group than individually.[19] Group pressure can have a substantial effect on changing attitudes and beliefs.[20] Furthermore, group therapy permits the social worker to treat more than one person at a time and thus maximizes the use of professional staff.

In essence, a group therapist uses the principles of one-to-one counseling (discussed in Chapter 5) and of group dynamics to help clients change dysfunctional attitudes and behavior. Often the traditional comprehensive psychotherapy approaches are combined with certain specialized treatment techniques (such as parent effectiveness training and assertiveness training) to help clients resolve personal and emotional problems. The selection of

treatment techniques is based on the nature of the problems.

Sensitivity Groups

Encounter groups, T (training) groups, and sensitivity training (these terms are used somewhat synonymously) refer to group experiences in which people relate to one another in an intimate manner requiring self-disclosure. The goal is to improve interpersonal awareness. An encounter group may meet for a few hours or for a few days.

The goal of sensitivity groups provides an interesting contrast to that of therapy groups (see Case Exhibit 3.2). In therapy the goal is to have each member explore personal or emotional problems in depth and then develop a strategy to resolve them. In comparison, sensitivity groups seek to increase each member's personal and interpersonal awareness and then develop more effective interaction patterns. Sensitivity groups generally do not directly attempt to identify or change specific emotional or personal problems that people have (such as drinking problems, feelings of depression, sexual dysfunctions, and so on). The philosophy behind sensitivity groups is that with increased personal and interpersonal awareness, people will be better able to avoid, cope with, and/or handle specific personal problems that arise.

Sensitivity groups are used in our society for a wide variety of purposes: to train professional counselors to be more perceptive and effective in interpersonal interactions with clients and with other professionals, to train people in management positions to be more effective in their business interactions, to help clients with overt relationship problems become more aware of how they affect others and to develop

*These psychotherapy approaches are described in Richard S. Sharf, *Theories of Psychotherapy and Counseling*, 5th ed. (Belmont, CA: Wadsworth/Cengage Learning, 2011).

© Michael Newman/PhotoEdit

This married couple is receiving counseling from a male–female co-therapy team.

more effective interaction patterns, and to train interested citizens in becoming more aware and effective in their interactions.

Although encounter, marathon, and sensitivity groups are popular and have received considerable publicity, they remain controversial. In some cases, inadequately trained and incompetent individuals have become self-proclaimed leaders and have enticed people to join through sensational advertising. If mishandled, sensitivity groups can intensify personal problems. Many authorities on sensitivity training disclaim the use of encounter groups as a form of psychotherapy and discourage people with serious personal problems from joining such groups.

Social Work with Organizations

Many of my social work students tell me they want to work with individuals, families, and small groups. They also tell me they have little interest in learning about organizations. We have all participated in a number of organizations—schools, clubs at schools, business or social service agencies we have worked for, church organizations, boys and girls organizations

(such as Boy Scouts and Girl Scouts). If you are studying to be a social worker, you will have a field placement at an agency and probably will be seeking a job at a social work agency (organization) after you graduate. Because you may be spending most of your career working for a social work agency, is it not to your benefit to learn about organizations and to learn how to survive and thrive in an organization?

Critical Thinking Question

How high is your interest in learning how to survive and thrive in a social work agency?

An organization is a group of individuals gathered together to serve a particular purpose. The types of purposes (or goals) that people organize themselves to achieve are infinite in number and can range from obtaining basic necessities to attaining world peace. Organizations exist because people working together can accomplish tasks and achieve

CASE EXHIBIT 3.3

A Socialization Group at a Shelter for Runaways

New Horizons is a private temporary shelter facility for runaways in a large midwestern city. It is in a large house that was built 84 years ago. Youths on the run can stay for up to 2 weeks. State law requires that parents be contacted and parental permission received for New Horizons to provide shelter overnight. Services offered include temporary shelter care, individual and family counseling, and a 24-hour hotline for youths in crisis. The facility is licensed to house up to eight youths. Because the average stay is 9 days, the population is continually changing. Intensive counseling is provided for the youths (and often their parents), focusing on reducing family conflicts and on making future living plans. The 14-day limit helps convey to youths and their families, beginning with day 1, that they must work to resolve the reasons for leaving home.

Every evening at 7 P.M. a group meeting is held. All the residents and the two or three staff members on duty are expected to attend. The meetings are convened and led by the staff. This meeting has four main objectives. One is providing a vehicle for residents to express their satisfactions and dissatisfactions with the facilities and program at New Horizons. Sometimes the meeting appears to be primarily a "gripe" session, but the staff members make conscientious efforts to improve those aspects in which the youths' concerns are legitimate. For example, a youth may indicate that the past few days have been "boring," and staff and residents then jointly plan activities for the next few days.

A second objective is to deal with interaction problems that arise between residents or between staff and residents. One resident may be preventing others from sleeping; some youths may refuse to do their "fair share" of domestic tasks; there may be squabbles about which TV program to watch; some residents may be overly aggressive. Because most of the youths face a variety of crises associated with being on the run, many tend to be anxious and under stress. In such an emotional climate, interaction problems are likely to arise. Staff are sometimes intensely questioned about their actions, decisions, and policies. For example, one policy at New Horizons is that each resident must agree not to use alcohol or illegal drugs while staying at the shelter, with the penalty being expulsion. Occasionally a few youths use some drugs and are caught and expelled. Removing a resident from this facility has an immense impact on the others, and at the following group meeting, staff are expected to clarify and explain such decisions.

A third objective is for staff to present material on topics requested by residents. Examples of topics include sex, drugs, gay and lesbian relationships, physical and sexual abuse (a fair number of residents have been abused by family members), ways to avoid being raped, ways to deal with depression and other unwanted emotions, sexually transmitted diseases, legal rights of youths on the run, assertiveness training, ways to make relatives and friends understand why they ran away, and availability of other human services in the community. During such presentations, discussion with residents is encouraged and generally occurs.

The final objective of these group meetings is to convey information about planned daily activities and changes in the overall program at New Horizons.

goals that cannot be achieved as well (or even at all) by an individual.

The importance of organizations in our lives is described by Etzioni:

We are born in organizations, educated by organizations, and most of us spend much of our lives working for organizations. We spend much of our leisure time paying, playing, and praying in organizations. Most of us will die in an organization, and when the time comes for burial, the largest organization of all—the state—must grant official permission.[21]

Netting, Kettner, and McMurtry have summarized the importance of organizations for social work practice:

As social workers, our roles within, interactions with, and attempts to manipulate organizations define much of what we do. Clients often come to us seeking help because they are not able to obtain help from organizations that are critical to their survival or quality of life. In turn, the resources we attempt to gain for these clients usually come from still other organizations.... Social workers with little or no idea of how organizations operate, how they interact, or how they can be influenced and changed from both outside and inside are likely to be severely limited in their effectiveness.[22]

Many disciplines (including business, psychology, political science, and sociology) have generated a prodigious amount of theory and research on organizations. However, in spite of the importance of organizations to social work practice, the amount of social work literature devoted to this topic is somewhat limited. One significant reference in this area is *Social Work Macro Practice*, by Netting, Kettner, McMurtry, and Thomas.[23]

A Therapy Group That Utilized a Strengths Perspective

Several years ago, when I was employed as a social worker at a maximum security hospital for the criminally insane, my supervisor requested that I develop and lead a therapy group. When I asked such questions as "What should the group's objectives be?" and "Who should be selected to join?" my supervisor indicated that those decisions would be mine. No one else was doing any group therapy at this hospital, and the hospital administration thought it would be desirable, for accountability reasons, for group therapy programs to be developed.

Being newly employed at the hospital and wary because I had never led a therapy group before, I asked myself, "Who is in the greatest need of group therapy?" and "If the group members do not improve, or even deteriorate, how will I be able to explain this—that is, cover my tracks?" I concluded that I should select those persons identified as being the "sickest" (those labeled as chronic schizophrenics) for the group. Chronic schizophrenics are generally expected to show little improvement. Thus, if they did not improve, I felt I would not be blamed. However, if they did improve, I thought their progress would be viewed as a substantial accomplishment.

My next step was to invite those persons to join the group. I met with each individually and explained the purpose of the group and the probable topics that would be covered. Eight of the 11 I contacted decided to join. Some of the eight stated frankly that they were joining primarily because it would look good on their record and increase their chances for an early release. The approach I used with the group utilized a strengths perspective. (The strengths perspective is described in Chapter 2, and seeks to identify, use, build, and reinforce the abilities and strengths that people have, in contrast to the pathological perspective, which focuses on their deficiencies.) Many of the principles of reality therapy were also utilized with this group.[a]

At the first meeting, I again presented and described the purpose and focus of the group. The purpose was not to review the members' past but to help them make their present lives more enjoyable and meaningful and to help them make plans for the future. Topics to be covered included how to convince the hospital staff they no longer needed to be hospitalized, how to prepare themselves for returning to their home communities (for example, learning an employable skill while at the institution), what to do when they felt depressed or had some other unwanted emotion, and what actions they should take following their release if they had an urge to do something that would get them into trouble again. I further explained that occasional films covering some of these topics would be shown and discussed. I indicated that the group would meet for about an hour each week for the next 12 weeks (until the fall, when I had to return to school).

This focus on improving their current circumstances stimulated their interest, but soon they found it uncomfortable and anxiety-producing to examine what the future might hold for them. Being informed that they had some responsibility and some control of that future also created anxiety. Their reaction to this discomfort was to state that, because they were labeled mentally ill, they therefore had an internal condition that was causing their strange behavior. Because they were aware that a cure for schizophrenia had not yet been found, they concluded that they could do little to improve their situation.

The members were told their excuses were "garbage" (stronger terms were used), and we spent a few sessions on getting them to understand that the label "chronic schizophrenic" was meaningless. I spent considerable time explaining (as discussed in Chapter 5) that mental illness is a myth; that is, people do not have a "disease of the mind," even though they may have emotional/behavioral problems. I went on to explain that what had gotten them locked up was their deviant behavior, and the only way for them to get out was to stop exhibiting their strange behavior and to convince the other staff that they would not exhibit deviant behavior if released. I added that they held the key for getting released— that key was simply to act "sane."

The next set of excuses they tried held that their broken homes or inferior schools or broken romances or something else in their past had "messed them up," and therefore they could do little about their situation. They were told that such excuses were also "garbage." True, their past experiences were relevant to their being in the hospital. But it was emphasized that what they wanted out of the future, along with their motivation to do something about achieving their goals, was more important than their past experiences in determining what their future would be like.

Finally, after we had worked through a number of excuses, we were able to focus on how they could better handle specific problems: how to handle being depressed, how to stop exhibiting behavior considered "strange," how to present themselves as "sane" to increase their chances of an early release, how they would adjust to returning to their home communities, what kind of work or career they desired on their release, how they could prepare themselves by learning a skill or trade while at this institution, how to examine what they wanted in the future and determine the specific steps they would have to take to achieve their goals, why it was important to continue taking the psychoactive medication that had been prescribed, and so on. In group sessions we also focused on identifying and communicating to each other the unique strengths and assets (including vocational, social, and interactional) that each member had—rather than focusing on their past traumatic experiences.

The results of this approach were very encouraging. Instead of idly spending much of the time brooding about their situation, they became motivated to improve their lives. At the end of the 12 weeks, the eight members of the group spontaneously stated that the meetings were resulting in positive changes in their lives. They requested that another social worker from the hospital be assigned to continue the group after my return to college. This was arranged. Three years later, on a return visit to the hospital, I was informed that five of the eight group members had been released to their home communities. Two of the others were considered to have shown improvement. The final group member's condition was described as "unchanged." These outcomes provide "soft" evidence that this approach to group therapy may have had a positive impact on most of the group members.

[a]William Glasser, *Reality Therapy* (New York: Harper & Row, 1965); and William Glasser, *Reality Therapy in Action* (New York: HarperCollins, 2000).

Earlier in this chapter, in the section titled "The Change Process," we saw an example of the processes a social worker used to achieve organizational change. That section described how a new educational component on alcohol and other drug abuse was added to the curriculum in a school district in a midwestern state. The remainder of this section will present material on how social workers can survive and thrive in bureaucratic systems. A bureaucracy is a type of organization or a subcategory of organization. Distinctive characteristics of a bureaucracy include a vertical hierarchy with power centered at the top; a task-specific division of labor; clearly defined rules; formalized channels of communication; and selection, compensation, promotion, and retention of personnel based on technical competency.

There are basic structural conflicts between helping professionals and the bureaucratic systems in which they work. Helping professionals place a high value on creativity and change. Bureaucracies resist change and are most efficient when no one is "rocking the boat." Helping professionals seek to personalize services by conveying to each client "You count as a person." Bureaucracies are highly depersonalized, emotionally detached systems that view every employee and every client as a tiny component of a large system. In a large bureaucracy, employees *don t* count as "persons"—only as functional parts of a system. Case Exhibit 3.5 lists additional conflicting value orientations between a helping professional and bureaucratic systems.

Any of these differences in value orientations can become an arena for conflict between helping professionals and the bureaucracies in which they work. Knopf has concisely summarized the potential areas of conflict:

The trademarks of a BS (bureaucratic system) are power, hierarchy, and specialization; that is, rules and roles. In essence, the result is depersonalization. The system itself is neither "good" nor "bad"; it is a system. I believe it to be amoral. It is efficient and effective, but in order to be so it must be impersonal in all of its functionings. This then is the location of the stress. The hallmark of the helping professional is a highly individualized, democratic, humanized, relationship-oriented service aimed at self-motivation. The hallmark of a bureaucratic system is a highly impersonalized, valueless (amoral), emotionally detached, hierarchical structure of organization. The dilemma of the HP (helping person) is how to give a

personalized service to a client through a delivery system that is not set up in any way to do that.[24]

Many helping professionals respond to these orientation conflicts by erroneously projecting a "personality" onto the bureaucracy. They describe it using expressions such as *red tape, officialism, uncaring, cruel, the enemy.* Officials of the bureaucracy may be viewed as paper shufflers, rigid, deadwood, inefficient, and unproductive. Knopf states:

The HP (helping person) … may deal with the impersonal nature of the system by projecting values onto it and thereby give the BS (bureaucratic system) a "personality." In this way, we fool ourselves into thinking that we can deal with it in a personal way. Unfortunately, projection is almost always negative and reflects the dark or negative aspects of ourselves. The BS then becomes a screen onto which we vent our anger, sadness, or fright, and while a lot of energy is generated, very little is accomplished. Since the BS is amoral, it is unproductive to place a personality on it.[25]

A bureaucratic system is neither good nor bad. It has neither a personality nor a value system of its own. It is simply a structure developed to carry out various tasks.

A helping person may experience various emotional reactions to conflicts with bureaucratic systems.* Common reactions are anger at the system, self-blame ("It's all my fault"), sadness and depression ("Poor me"; "Nobody appreciates all I've done"), and fright and paranoia ("They're out to get me"; "If I mess up, I'm gone").

Knopf has identified several types of behavior patterns that helping professionals choose in dealing with bureaucracies.[26]

The *warrior* leads open campaigns to destroy and malign the system. A warrior discounts the value of the system and often enters into a win–lose conflict. She or he generally loses and is dismissed.

The *gossip* is a covert warrior who complains to others (including clients, politicians, and the news

---

*This description highlights a number of the negatives about bureaucratic systems, particularly their impersonal nature. In fairness, it should be noted that an advantage of being part of a large bureaucracy is the potential for changing a powerful system to the advantage of clients. In tiny or nonbureaucratic systems, the social worker may have lots of freedom but little opportunity or power to influence large systems or mobilize extensive resources on behalf of clients.

media) about how terrible the system is. A gossip frequently singles out a few officials to focus criticism on. Bureaucratic systems often make life very difficult for the gossip by assigning distasteful tasks, refusing to promote, giving very low salary increases, and perhaps even dismissing.

The *complainer* resembles a gossip but confines complaints to other helping persons, to in-house staff, and to family members. A complainer wants people to agree in order to find comfort in shared misery. Complainers want to stay with the system, and they generally do.

The *dancer* is skillful at ignoring rules and procedures. Dancers frequently are lonely. They are often reprimanded for incorrectly filling out forms, and they have low investment in the system or in helping clients.

The *defender* is timid and dislikes conflict and therefore defends the rules, the system, and bureaucratic officials. Defenders often are supervisors and are viewed by others as being "bureaucrats."

The *machine* is a "bureaucrat" who takes on the orientation of the bureaucracy. Often a machine has not been involved in providing direct services for years. Machines are frequently named to head study committees and policy groups and to chair boards.

The *executioner* attacks persons within an organization with enthusiasm and vigor. An executioner usually has a high energy level and is impulsive. He or she abuses power by indiscriminately attacking and dismissing not only employees but also services and programs. Executioners have power and are angry (although the anger is disguised/denied). They are committed neither to the value orientation of helping professionals nor to the bureaucracy.

Knopf has listed 66 tips on how to survive in a bureaucracy.[27] Some of the most useful suggestions are summarized here:

1. Whenever your needs, or the needs of your clients, are not met by the bureaucracy, use the following problem-solving approach: (a) Precisely identify which of your needs (or the needs of clients) are in conflict with the bureaucracy; this step is defining the problem. (b) Generate a list of possible solutions. Be creative in generating a wide range of ideas. (c) Evaluate the merits and shortcomings of the possible solutions. (d) Select a solution. (e) Implement the solution. (f) Evaluate the solution (see Case Exhibit 3.4. Analyzing a Human Services Organization).

2. Learn how your bureaucracy is structured and how it functions. Such knowledge will reduce fear of the unknown, make the system more predictable, and help in identifying rational ways to best meet your needs and those of your clients.

3. Remember that bureaucrats are people, too, and they have feelings. Communication gaps are often most effectively reduced if you treat them with as much respect and interest as you treat clients.

4. If you are at war with the bureaucracy, declare a truce. The system will find a way to dismiss you if you remain at war. With a truce, you can identify and use the strengths of the bureaucracy as an ally, rather than having the strengths used against you as an enemy.

5. Know your work contract and job expectations. If the expectations are unclear, seek clarity.

6. Continue to develop your knowledge and awareness of specific helping skills. Take advantage of continuing-education opportunities (workshops, conferences, courses). Among other advantages, your continued professional development will assist you in being able to contract from a position of competency and skill.

7. Seek to identify your professional strengths and limitations. Knowing your limitations will increase your ability to avoid undertaking responsibilities that are beyond your competencies.

8. Be aware that you can't change everything, so stop trying. In a bureaucracy, focus your change efforts on those aspects that most need change and that you also have a fair chance of changing. Stop thinking and complaining about those aspects you cannot change. It is irrational to complain about things that you cannot change or to complain about those things that you do not intend to make an effort to change.

9. Learn how to control your emotions in your interactions with the bureaucracy. Emotions that are counterproductive (such as most angry outbursts) particularly need to be controlled. Doing a rational self-analysis on your unwanted emotions (see Chapter 5) is one way of gaining control of them. Learning how to respond to stress in your personal life will also prepare you to handle stress better at work.

10. Develop and use a sense of humor. Humor takes the edge off adverse conditions and reduces negative feelings.

11. Learn to accept your mistakes and perhaps even laugh at some of them. No one is perfect.

CASE EXHIBIT 3.4

Analyzing a Human Services Organization

It is essential that a social worker understand and analyze not only the agency/organization that she or he works for but also the other agencies and organizations that she or he interacts with. Some questions that are useful in analyzing an agency or organization are:

1. What is the mission statement of the organization?
2. What are the major problems of the organization's clients?
3. What services are provided by the organization?
4. How are client needs determined?
5. What percentage of clients are people of color, women, gays or lesbians, elderly, or members of other at-risk populations?
6. What was the total cost of services of this organization in the past year?
7. How much money is spent on each program?
8. What are the organization's funding sources?
9. How much and what percentage of funds are received from each source?
10. What types of clients does the organization refuse?
11. What other organizations provide the same services in the community?
12. What is the organizational structure? For example, does the organization have a formal chain of command?

13. Is there an informal decision-making process and structure at the organization? (That is, are there people who are quite influential and thus exert more influence than would be expected for their formal positions in the bureaucracy of the organization?)
14. How much input do the direct service providers at the organization have on major policy decisions?
15. Does the organization have a board that oversees its operations? If so, what are the backgrounds of the board members?
16. Do employees at every level feel valued?
17. What is the morale among employees?
18. What are the major unmet needs of the organization?
19. Does the organization have a handbook of personnel policies and procedures?
20. What is the public image of the organization in the community?
21. What has been the rate of turnover in recent years among the staff at the organization? What were departing staff members' major reasons for leaving?
22. Does the organization have a process for evaluating the outcomes of its services? If so, what is the process and what are the outcome results?

---

12. Take time to enjoy and develop a support system with your coworkers.

13. Acknowledge your mistakes and give in sometimes on minor matters. You may not be right, and giving in allows other people to do the same.

14. Keep yourself physically fit and mentally alert. Learn to use approaches that will reduce stress and prevent burnout. (See Chapter 15 for a description of approaches to reduce stress.)

15. Leave your work at the office. If you have urgent unfinished bureaucratic business, do it before leaving work.

16. Occasionally take your supervisor and other administrators to lunch. Socializing prevents isolation and facilitates your involvement with and understanding of the system.

17. Do not seek self-actualization or ego satisfaction from the bureaucracy. A depersonalized system is incapable of providing these rewards; you must achieve them on your own.

18. In speeches to community groups, accentuate the positives about your agency. Ask after speeches

that a thank-you letter be sent to your supervisor or agency director.

19. If you have a problem with the bureaucracy, discuss it with other employees, with the focus on problem solving rather than on complaining. Groups are much more powerful and productive than an individual working alone for making changes in a system.

20. No matter how high you rise in a hierarchy, maintain direct service contact. Direct contact keeps you abreast of changing client needs, prevents you from getting stale, and keeps you attuned to the concerns of employees in lower levels of the hierarchy.

21. Do not try to change everything in the system at once. Attacking too much will overextend you and lead to burnout. Start small, and be selective and specific. Double-check your facts to make certain they accurately prove your position before you confront bureaucratic officials.

22. Identify your career goals and determine whether they can be met within this system. If the answer is no, then (a) change your goals, (b) change the bureaucracy, or (c) seek a position elsewhere in which your goals can be met.

CASE EXHIBIT 3.5

Value Conflicts between a Helping Professional and Bureaucracies

Orientations of a Helping Professional	Orientations of Bureaucratic Systems
Desires democratic system for decision making.	Most decisions are made autocratically.
Desires that power be distributed equally among employees (horizontal structure).	Power is distributed vertically.
Desires that clients have considerable power in the system.	Power is held primarily by top executives.
Desires a flexible, changing system.	System is rigid and stable.
Desires that creativity and growth be emphasized.	Emphasis is on structure and the status quo.
Desires that focus be client oriented.	System is organization centered.
Desires that communication be on a personalized level from person to person.	Communication is from level to level.
Desires shared decision making and shared responsibility structure.	A hierarchical decision-making structure and hierarchical responsibility structure are characteristic.
Desires that decisions be made by those having the most knowledge.	Decisions are made in terms of the decision-making authority assigned to each position in the hierarchy.
Desires shared leadership.	System uses autocratic leadership.
Believes feelings of clients and employees should be highly valued by the system.	Procedures and processes are highly valued.

Social Work with the Community

Most social work students do not consider a career in community practice; they feel that they would rather work directly with people. Many believe that community practice involves skills and techniques that are too complex and too abstract to learn. In addition, they perceive community practice as having too few rewards and as involving a lot of boring, unenjoyable work. All of these beliefs are erroneous. The realities are that (a) the most basic skill needed in community practice is the ability to work effectively with people; (b) community practice primarily involves working with individuals and with groups; (c) every practicing social worker occasionally becomes involved in community practice projects; (d) seeing a community project developed, approved, and implemented is immensely gratifying; and (e) community practice efforts are often fun.

Workers in direct practice with individuals or groups are likely to become involved in community development activities when gaps in services or unmet needs are identified for clients they are working with. For example, if there is a rapid increase in teenage pregnancy in a community, a school social worker may become involved in efforts to establish a sex education program in the school system. If there are a number of terminally ill patients and their families are complaining about the way they are treated in a hospital, a medical social worker may become involved in efforts to establish a hospice. If a juvenile probation officer notes a sharp increase in juvenile offenses, the officer may become involved in efforts to have young offenders visit a prison and hear from inmates what prison life is like.

Workers involved in developing needed new services are aware of the human benefits that will result. These payoffs, and the time and effort workers put into community practice projects, often lead them to become highly "ego involved." Success in establishing new services is experienced as a deeply gratifying political victory. On a negative note, a reality is that the development of new services generally involves a number of unanticipated obstacles and requires several times as much time and effort as initially anticipated.

As yet, there is no widely accepted definition of the term *community practice*. The modes of practice performed under this heading have a variety of labels: social planning, community planning, locality development, community action, social action, macro-practice, community organization, and community development.

Community practice will be defined here as the process of stimulating and assisting the local community to evaluate, plan, and coordinate its efforts to provide for the community's health, welfare, and recreation needs. In community practice, a worker's activities include encouraging and stimulating citizen organization around one or more issues, specifying the nature of the problem, coordinating efforts among concerned groups, fact-finding, formulating realizable goals, becoming involved in public relations and public education, conducting research, planning, identifying financial resources, developing strategies to achieve a goal, and being a resource person. Agency settings that employ community practice workers include community welfare councils, the United Way, social planning agencies, health planning councils, neighborhood councils, city planning councils, community action groups, and occasionally some other private or public organization.

Community practice workers become involved in a wide variety of social issues, including civil rights, welfare reform, the needs of poor people, education and health issues, housing, improvement of leisure-time services, race relations, minority-group employment, development of services to counteract alienation of youths, urban redevelopment programs, development of services for teenage runaways and drug users, development of services for the homeless, and development of services for people who are HIV positive or have AIDS.

Disciplines in addition to social work provide training in community practice. These include community psychology, urban and regional planning, health planning, corrections planning, recreation, and public administration.

In recent years, American citizens have organized around a number of issues. Some that have received national attention include labor–management disputes, women's rights issues, problems of farmers, the abortion question, capital punishment, rights for gays and lesbians, tax cuts, school closings in many cities, the national defense budget, nuclear energy, decriminalization of marijuana, massage parlors, nude dancing, affirmative action guidelines on hiring, and environmental concerns.

A Brief History of Community Practice

For centuries people have organized to change social and political conditions. In the 1700s, for example, Americans organized to revolt against the British and fought what has come to be called the Revolutionary War.

Community practice in social work began in the 1800s with the charity organization movement and the settlement house movement.[28]

In the 19th century, private philanthropy bore the major responsibility for the relief of poverty in the United States. During the early 1800s, various private health and welfare agencies were established to provide funds and services (generally combined with religious conversion efforts) to those in need. To avoid duplication of services to the same families, charity organization societies (COSs) were formed to coordinate efforts and to plan for meeting unmet needs.

Reformers associated with the settlement house movement based many of their programs on social action to promote legislation for providing needed services to neighborhoods. These reformers also encouraged neighborhood residents to work together to improve living conditions.

Community welfare councils were first organized in 1908.[29] Continuing the efforts begun by the charity organization movement, these councils served as coordinating organizations for voluntary agencies. The functions of these councils have continued to the present time and include planning, coordinating, avoiding duplication of services, setting standards for services, and improving efficiency and accountability.

Community Chests (now called United Way) were formed around 1920 to serve as centralized campaigns for raising funds for voluntary agencies.[30] In many communities, United Way has been combined with community welfare councils for fund-raising and for the allocation of funds to voluntary agencies.

All social welfare agencies and organizations become involved at times in community practice efforts.

Models of Community Practice

A variety of approaches have been developed to bring about community change. In reviewing these approaches, Jack Rothman and John Tropman categorized them into three models: locality development, social planning, and social action.[31] These models are "ideal types." Actual approaches to community change tend to blend characteristics of all three models. Advocates of the social planning model, for example, may at times use community change techniques (such as extensive discussion and participation by a variety of groups) that are characteristic of the other two models. For analytical purposes, however, we'll view the three models as "pure" forms. (Examples of these three models are found in Case Examples 3.2, 3.3, and 3.4.)

Locality Development Model

The locality development (also called community development) model asserts that community change can best be brought about through broad-based participation by a wide spectrum of people at the local community level. The approach seeks to involve a cross section of individuals (including the disadvantaged and those high up in the power structure) in identifying and solving problems. Some themes emphasized in this model are democratic procedures, a consensus approach, voluntary cooperation, development of indigenous leadership, and self-help.

The roles of the community practitioner in this approach include enabler, catalyst, coordinator, and teacher of problem-solving skills and ethical values. It is assumed that any conflicts among various groups can be creatively and constructively resolved. People are encouraged to express their differences freely and to put aside self-interests to further the interests of their community. The basic theme of this approach is, "Together we can figure out what to do and then do it." The locality development model seeks to use discussion and communication among different factions to reach consensus on which problems to focus on and which strategies or actions to use to resolve these problems. A few examples of such efforts include neighborhood work programs conducted by community-based agencies; Volunteers in Service to America; village-level work in some overseas community development programs, including the Peace Corps; and a variety of activities performed by self-help groups.

Social Planning Model

The social planning approach emphasizes the process of problem solving. It assumes that community change in a complex industrial environment requires highly trained and skilled planners who can guide complex change processes. The role of the expert is crucial to identifying and resolving social problems. The expert or planner is generally employed by a segment of the power structure, such as an area planning agency, city or county planning department, mental health center, United Way board, community welfare council, and so on. Because the social planner is employed by the power structure, there is a tendency for him or her to serve the interests of that structure. Marshaling community resources and facilitating radical social change are generally not emphasized in this approach.

The planner's roles in this approach include gathering facts; analyzing data; and serving as program designer, implementer, and facilitator. Community participation may vary from little to substantial, depending on the community's attitudes toward the problems being addressed. For example, an effort to

design and fund a community center for the elderly may or may not generate a lot of participation by interested community groups, depending on the politics surrounding such a center. Much of the focus of the social planning approach is on identifying needs and on arranging and delivering goods and services to people who need them. In effect, the philosophy is, "Let's get the facts and take the next rational steps."

Critical Thinking Question

How high is your interest in becoming a leader in facilitating positive changes in communities?

Social Action Model

The social action model assumes that there is a disadvantaged (often oppressed) segment of the population that needs to be organized, perhaps in alliance with others, to pressure the power structure for increased resources or for social justice. Social action approaches seek basic changes in major institutions or in basic policies of formal organizations. The objective is redistribution of power and resources. Whereas locality developers envision a unified community, social action advocates see the power structure as the opposition—the target of action. Perhaps the best-known social activist was Saul Alinsky, who advised: "Pick the target, freeze it, personalize it, and polarize it."[32]

The roles of the community practitioner in this approach include advocate, agitator, activist, partisan, broker, and negotiator. Tactics used in social action projects are protests, boycotts, confrontation, and negotiation. The change strategy is one of "Let's organize to overpower our oppressor."[33] The client population is viewed as being "victimized" by the oppressive power structure. Examples of the social action approach include boycotts during the civil rights movement of the 1960s, strikes by unions, protests by antiabortion groups, and protests by African American and Native American groups.

The social action model is not widely used by social workers at present. Involvement in social action activities may lead employing agencies to penalize those social workers with unpleasant work assignments, low merit increases, and withholding of promotions. Many agencies will accept minor and moderate changes in their service delivery systems but are threatened by the prospect of such radical changes as are often advocated by the social action approach.

CASE EXAMPLE 3.2

The Locality Development Model

Robert McKearn, a social worker for a juvenile probation department, noticed in 1999 that increasing numbers of school-age children were being referred to his office by the police department, school system, and parents from a small city of 11,000 people in the county served by his agency. The charges included status offenses (such as truancy) and delinquent offenses (such as shoplifting and burglary). He noted that most of these children were from single-parent families.

Mr. McKearn contacted the community mental health center, the self-help organization Parents Without Partners, the Pupil Services Department of the public school system, the county Social Services Department, and some members of the clergy in the area. Nearly everyone he talked with saw an emerging need to better serve children in single-parent families. The Pupil Services Department mentioned that these children were performing less well academically in school and tended to display more serious disciplinary problems.

Mr. McKearn arranged a meeting of representatives from all the groups and organizations that had been contacted. At the initial meeting, numerous concerns were expressed about the problematic behaviors being displayed by children who had single parents. The school system considered these children to be "at risk" for high rates of truancy, dropping out of school, delinquent activities, suicide, emotional problems, and unwanted pregnancies. Although many problems were identified, no one at this initial meeting was able to suggest a viable strategy to better serve single parents and their children. The community was undergoing an economic recession; therefore, funds were unavailable for an expensive new program.

Three more meetings were held. At the first two, several suggestions for providing services were discussed, but all were viewed as either too expensive or impractical. At the fourth meeting of the group, a single mother representing Parents Without Partners mentioned that Big Brothers and Big Sisters programs in some communities reportedly were of substantial benefit to children raised in single-parent families. This idea seemed to energize the group, and suggestions began to "piggyback." However, members determined that no funds were available to hire staff to run a Big Brothers and Big Sisters program. Then, Rhona Quinn, a social worker in the Public Human Services Department, offered to identify at-risk younger children in single-parent families and to supervise qualified volunteers in a Big Buddy program.

Mr. McKearn mentioned that he was currently supervising a student in an undergraduate field placement from an accredited social work program in a nearby college. Mr. McKearn suggested that perhaps undergraduate social work students could be recruited to be Big Buddies to fulfill their required volunteer experience. Rhona Quinn said she would approve the suggestion if she could have the freedom to screen interested applicants. Arrangements were made over the next 2 months for social work students to be Big Buddies for at-risk younger children from single-parent families. After a 2-year experimental period, the school system found the program to be sufficiently successful that it assigned Ms. Quinn to supervise it half time. Her duties included selecting at-risk children, screening volunteer applicants, matching children with Big Buddies, monitoring the progress of each matched pair, and conducting follow-up to ascertain the outcome of each pairing.

Case Exhibit 3.6 summarizes the three models that have been discussed.

Knowledge, Skills, and Values for Social Work Practice

EP 2.1.1a–
2.1.10m

In its EPAS (2008), the Council on Social Work Education has identified the following knowledge, skills, and values that accredited baccalaureate and master's degree programs are mandated to convey to social work students, which are based on a competency approach.* The Bachelor of Social Work (BSW) curriculum prepares its graduates for generalist practice through mastery of the core competencies. The Master of Social Work (MSW) curriculum prepares its graduates for advanced practice through mastery of the core competencies augmented by knowledge and practice behaviors specific to a concentration.

Core Competencies

EP 2.1

Competency-based education is an outcome performance approach to curriculum design. Competencies are measurable practice behaviors that are comprised of knowledge, values, and skills. The goal of the outcome approach is to demonstrate the integration and application of the competencies in practice with individuals, families, groups, organizations, and communities. The ten core competencies are listed below [EP 2.1.1–EP 2.1.10(d)], followed by a description of characteristic knowledge,

*Reprinted with permission from Council on Social Work Education, *Educational Policy and Accreditation Standards* (Alexandria, VA: Council on Social Work Education, 2008).

CASE EXAMPLE 3.3

The Social Planning Model

In 1999 the board of directors of Lincoln County Social Planning Agency authorized its staff to conduct a feasibility study on establishing a centralized information and referral (I&R) center. Donald Levi (a social planner on the staff) was assigned to direct the study. Mr. Levi collected data showing the following:

- There were more than 350 community service agencies and organizations in this largely metropolitan county of one-half million people. Not only clients but also service providers were confused about what services were available from this array of agencies.
- There was a confusing array of specialized I&R services being developed. (Specialized information and referral services provided I&R services in only one or two areas.) Specialized I&R services were developing in suicide prevention, mental health, cognitive disabilities, day care, adoption services, and alcohol and drug treatment.

Mr. Levi then designed a program model for a centralized information and referral service. The model described a service that would provide I&R services on *all* human and community services in the county. For example, I&R would provide information not only on what day-care services were available but also on where to find public tennis courts and whom to call to remove a stray cat killed in front of your house. The centralized information and referral service number would be widely publicized on television, radio, and billboards and in newspapers and telephone directories. A budget was developed by Mr. Levi for the program costs.

The board of directors of the Lincoln County Social Planning Agency concluded that such a centralized information and referral service would be more efficient and economical than the confusing array that had been developing. The board therefore authorized Mr. Levi to pursue the development of this centralized service.

Mr. Levi conducted a questionnaire survey of all the human service agencies and all the clergy in the county. The results showed that both groups strongly supported the development of a centralized I&R service. In addition, members of the Easter Seal Society felt so strongly that such a service was needed that they contacted Mr. Levi to indicate that they were willing to donate funds for the new program. Mr. Levi was delighted, and an arrangement was worked out for the Easter Seal Society to fund the program for a 3-year demonstration period.

Only one barrier remained. The proposal for this new service needed to be approved by the county board of supervisors, as the proposal required the county to fund the program (beginning 3 years in the future) if the service proved to be effective during the 3-year demonstration phase. Mr. Levi and two members of the board of the Lincoln County Social Planning Agency presented the program proposal to the county board of supervisors. The presentation included graphs showing the savings of a centralized I&R service over specialized I&R services and contained written statements of support from a variety of sources, including city council members, the United Way, human service agencies, and members of the clergy. It was also indicated that there would be no cost to the county for a 3-year demonstration period. At the end of that time, there would be an evaluative study of the merits and shortcomings of the program. Mr. Levi fully expected approval and was speechless when the county board of supervisors said "no." They turned the proposal down because they felt a centralized I&R meant that more people would be referred to county social service agencies, which would raise costs to the county, and because this board was opposed to making a commitment to funding any new social welfare program in the future.

The county continues to be served by less effective specialized I&R services. This case example realistically illustrates that some planning efforts are unsuccessful.

---

values, skills, and the resulting practice behaviors that may be used to operationalize the curriculum and assessment methods. Programs may add competencies consistent with their missions and goals.

Identify as a Professional Social Worker and Conduct Oneself Accordingly

EP 2.1.1 Social workers serve as representatives of the profession, its mission, and its core values. They know the profession's history. Social workers commit themselves to the profession's enhancement and to their own professional conduct and growth. Social workers

- advocate for client access to the services of social work;

- practice personal reflection and self-correction to assure continual professional development;
- attend to professional roles and boundaries;
- demonstrate professional demeanor in behavior, appearance, and communication;
- engage in career-long learning; and
- use supervision and consultation.

Apply Social Work Ethical Principles to Guide Professional Practice

Social workers have an obligation to conduct themselves ethically and to engage in ethical decision making. Social workers are knowledgeable about the

EP 2.1.2

CASE EXAMPLE 3.4

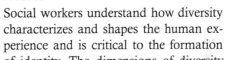

The Social Action Model

Saul Alinsky, a nationally noted social action strategist, provides an example of a creative social action effort. The example also shows that social action efforts are often enjoyable:

> I was lecturing at a college run by a very conservative, almost fundamentalist Protestant denomination. Afterward some of the students came to my motel to talk to me. Their problem was that they couldn't have any fun on campus. They weren't permitted to dance or smoke or have a can of beer. I had been talking about the strategy of effecting change in a society and they wanted to know what tactics they could use to change their situation. I reminded them that a tactic is doing what you can with what you've got. "Now, what have you got?" I asked. "What do they permit you to do?" "Practically nothing," they said, "except—you know—we can chew gum." I said, "Fine, Gum becomes the weapon. You get 200 or 300 students to get two packs of gum each, which is quite a wad. Then you have them drop it on the campus walks. This will cause absolute chaos. Why, with 500 wads of gum I could paralyze Chicago, stop all the traffic in the Loop." They looked at me as though I was some kind of nut. But about two weeks later I got an ecstatic letter saying, "It worked! It worked! Now we can do just about anything so long as we don't chew gum."

SOURCE: Saul Alinsky, *Rules for Radicals* (New York: Random House, 1972), pp. 145–146.

---

value base of the profession, its ethical standards, and relevant law. Social workers

- recognize and manage personal values in a way that allows professional values to guide practice;
- make ethical decisions by applying standards of the National Association of Social Workers Code of Ethics* and, as applicable, of the International Federation of Social Workers/International Association of Schools of Social Work Ethics in Social Work, Statement of Principles;**
- tolerate ambiguity in resolving ethical conflicts; and
- apply strategies of ethical reasoning to arrive at principled decisions.

Apply Critical Thinking to Inform and Communicate Professional Judgments
Social workers are knowledgeable about the principles of logic, scientific inquiry,
EP 2.1.3 and reasoned discernment. They use critical thinking augmented by creativity and curiosity. Critical thinking also requires the synthesis and communication of relevant information. Social workers

- distinguish, appraise, and integrate multiple sources of knowledge, including research-based knowledge, and practice wisdom;

---

*National Association of Social Workers (approved 1996, revised 1999), *Code of Ethics for Social Workers*, (Washington, DC: NASW).

**International Federation of Social Workers and International Association of Schools of Social Work, *Ethics in Social Work, Statement of Principles*. (2004), http://www.ifsw.org.

- analyze models of assessment, prevention, intervention, and evaluation; and
- demonstrate effective oral and written communication in working with individuals, families, groups, organizations, communities, and colleagues.

Engage Diversity and Difference in Practice

Social workers understand how diversity characterizes and shapes the human experience and is critical to the formation **EP 2.1.4** of identity. The dimensions of diversity are understood as the intersectionality of multiple factors including age, class, color, culture, disability, ethnicity, gender, gender identity and expression, immigration status, political ideology, race, religion, sex, and sexual orientation. Social workers appreciate that, as a consequence of difference, a person's life experiences may include oppression, poverty, marginalization, and alienation as well as privilege, power, and acclaim. Social workers

- recognize the extent to which a culture's structures and values may oppress, marginalize, alienate, or create or enhance privilege and power;
- gain sufficient self-awareness to eliminate the influence of personal biases and values in working with diverse groups;
- recognize and communicate their understanding of the importance of difference in shaping life experiences; and
- view themselves as learners and engage those with whom they work as informants.

CASE EXHIBIT 3.6

Three Models of Community Organization Practice According to Selected Practice Variables

Characteristic	Locality Development Model	Social Planning Model	Social Action Model
1. Goals	Self-help; improve community living; emphasis on process goals	Using problem-solving approach to resolve community problems; emphasis on task goals	Shifting of power relationships and resources to an oppressed group; basic institutional change; emphasis on task and process goals
2. Assumptions concerning community	Everyone wants community living to improve and is willing to contribute to the improvement	Social problems in the community can be resolved through the efforts of planning experts	The community has a power structure and one or more oppressed groups; social injustice is a major problem
3. Basic change strategy	Broad cross section of people involved in identifying and solving their problems	Experts using fact gathering and the problem-solving approach	Members of oppressed groups organizing to take action against the power structure, which is the enemy
4. Characteristic change tactics and techniques	Consensus: communication among community groups and interests; group discussion	Consensus or conflict	Conflict or contest: confrontation, direct action, negotiation
5. Practitioner roles	Catalyst; facilitator; coordinator; teacher of problem-solving skills	Expert planner; fact gatherer; analyst; program developer and implementer	Activist; advocate; agitator; broker; negotiator; partisan
6. Views about power structure	Members of power structure as collaborators in a common venture	Power structure as employers and sponsors	Power structure as external target of action, oppressors to be coerced or overturned
7. Views about client population	Citizens	Consumers	Victims
8. Views about client role	Participants in a problem-solving process	Consumers or recipients	Employers, constituents

Advance Human Rights and Social and Economic Justice

EP 2.1.5   Each person, regardless of position in society, has basic human rights, such as freedom, safety, privacy, an adequate standard of living, health care, and education. Social workers recognize the global interconnections of oppression and are knowledgeable about theories of justice and strategies to promote human and civil rights. Social work incorporates social justice practices in organizations, institutions, and society to ensure that these basic human rights are distributed equitably and without prejudice. Social workers

- understand the forms and mechanisms of oppression and discrimination;
- advocate for human rights and social and economic justice; and

- engage in practices that advance social and economic justice.

Engage in Research-Informed Practice and Practice-Informed Research

Social workers use practice experience to inform research, employ evidence-based interventions, evaluate their **EP 2.1.6** own practice, and use research findings to improve practice, policy, and social service delivery. Social workers comprehend quantitative and qualitative research and understand scientific and ethical approaches to building knowledge. Social workers

- use practice experience to inform scientific inquiry and
- use research evidence to inform practice.

Social activists seek basic institutional change. Their tactics range from negotiation and advocacy to confrontation and protests.

Apply Knowledge of Human Behavior and the Social Environment

Social workers are knowledgeable about human behavior across the life course; **EP 2.1.7** the range of social systems in which people live; and the ways social systems promote or deter people in maintaining or achieving health and well-being. Social workers apply theories and knowledge from the liberal arts to understand biological, social, cultural, psychological, and spiritual development. Social workers

- utilize conceptual frameworks to guide the processes of assessment, intervention, and evaluation; and
- critique and apply knowledge to understand person and environment.

Engage in Policy Practice to Advance Social and Economic Well-Being and to Deliver Effective Social Work Services

Social work practitioners understand **EP 2.1.8** that policy affects service delivery, and they actively engage in policy practice. Social workers know the history and current structures of social policies and services; the role of policy in service delivery; and the role of practice in policy development. Social workers

- analyze, formulate, and advocate for policies that advance social well-being; and
- collaborate with colleagues and clients for effective policy action.

Respond to Contexts That Shape Practice

EP 2.1.9

Social workers are informed, resourceful, and proactive in responding to evolving organizational, community, and societal contexts at all levels of practice. Social workers recognize that the context of practice is dynamic, and use knowledge and skill to respond proactively. Social workers

- continuously discover, appraise, and attend to changing locales, populations, scientific and technological developments, and emerging societal trends to provide relevant services; and
- provide leadership in promoting sustainable changes in service delivery and practice to improve the quality of social services.

Engage, Assess, Intervene, and Evaluate with Individuals, Families, Groups, Organizations, and Communities

EP 2.1.10 a–d

Professional practice involves the dynamic and interactive processes of engagement, assessment, intervention, and evaluation at multiple levels. Social workers have the knowledge and skills to practice with individuals, families, groups, organizations, and communities. Practice knowledge includes identifying, analyzing, and implementing evidence-based interventions designed to achieve client goals; using research and technological advances; evaluating program outcomes and practice effectiveness; developing, analyzing, advocating, and providing leadership for policies and services; and promoting social and economic justice.

Engagement

Social workers

EP 2.1.10a

- substantively and affectively prepare for action with individuals, families, groups, organizations, and communities;
- use empathy and other interpersonal skills; and
- develop a mutually agreed-on focus of work and desired outcomes.

Assessment

Social workers

EP 2.1.10b

- collect, organize, and interpret client data;
- assess client strengths and limitations;

- develop mutually agreed-on intervention goals and objectives; and
- select appropriate intervention strategies.

Intervention

Social workers

EP 2.1.10c

- initiate actions to achieve organizational goals;
- implement prevention interventions that enhance client capacities;
- help clients resolve problems;
- negotiate, mediate, and advocate for clients; and
- facilitate transitions and endings.

Evaluation

Social workers critically analyze, monitor, and evaluate interventions.

EP 2.1.10d

Generalist Practice

EP B2.2

Generalist practice is grounded in the liberal arts and the person and environment construct. To promote human and social well-being, generalist practitioners use a range of prevention and intervention methods in their practice with individuals, families, groups, organizations, and communities. The generalist practitioner identifies with the social work profession and applies ethical principles and critical thinking in practice. Generalist practitioners incorporate diversity in their practice and advocate for human rights and social and economic justice. They recognize, support, and build on the strengths and resiliency of all human beings. They engage in research-informed practice and are proactive in responding to the impact of context on professional practice. BSW practice incorporates all of the core competencies.

Advanced Practice

Advanced practitioners refine and advance the quality of social work practice and that of the larger social work profession. They synthesize and apply a broad range of interdisciplinary and multidisciplinary knowledge and skills. In areas of specialization, advanced practitioners assess, intervene, and evaluate to promote human and social well-being. To do so they suit each action to the circumstances at hand, using the

EP M2.2

discrimination learned through experience and self-improvement. Advanced practice incorporates all of the core competencies augmented by knowledge and practice behaviors specific to a concentration.

Signature Pedagogy: Field Education

EP 2.3

Signature pedagogy represents the central form of instruction and learning in which a profession socializes its students to perform the role of practitioner. Professionals have pedagogical norms with which they connect and integrate theory and practice.* In social work, the signature pedagogy is field education. The intent of field education is to connect the theoretical and conceptual contribution of the classroom with the practical world of the practice setting. It is a basic precept of social work education that the two interrelated components of curriculum—classroom and field—are of equal importance within the curriculum, and each contributes to the development of the requisite competencies of professional practice. Field education is systematically designed, supervised, coordinated, and evaluated based on criteria by which students demonstrate the achievement of program competencies.

Critical Thinking Question

Do you have the passion and potential to develop the skills to become a very competent social worker?

Social Work Values

Should the primary objective of imprisonment be rehabilitation or punishment? Should a father who commits incest be prosecuted, with the likelihood that publicity in the community will lead to family breakup, or should an effort first be made, through counseling, to stop the incest and keep the family intact? Should a wife who is occasionally abused by her husband be encouraged to remain living with him? Should abortion be suggested as one alternative for resolving the problems of someone who is single and pregnant? Should youths who are claimed by their parents to be uncontrollable be placed in correctional schools? If a client informs a social worker that he intends to severely injure some third party,

what should the worker do? Suppose a client indicates he is HIV positive but refuses to reveal his condition to his partner, thereby placing the partner in peril through unprotected sexual relations. What action should the social worker take? All of these questions involve making decisions that are based largely on values. Much of social work practice is dependent on making value-based decisions.

Allen Pincus and Anne Minahan concisely define *values* and describe differences between values and knowledge:

> *Values are beliefs, preferences, or assumptions about what is desirable or good for [humans]. An example is the belief that society has an obligation to help each individual realize his fullest potential. They are not assertions about how the world is and what we know about it, but how it should be. As such, value statements cannot be subjected to scientific investigation; they must be accepted on faith. Thus we can speak of a value as being right or wrong only in relation to the particular belief system or ethical code being used as a standard.*
>
> *What we will refer to as knowledge statements, on the other hand, are observations about the world and [humans] which have been verified or are capable of verification. An example is that black people have a shorter life expectancy than white people in the United States. When we speak of a knowledge statement as being right or wrong, we are referring to the extent to which the assertion has been confirmed through objective empirical investigation.*[34]

The National Association of Social Workers (NASW) has formulated a Code of Ethics that summarizes important practice ethics for social workers; this code is presented in Appendix A.

Respect for the Dignity and Uniqueness of the Individual

This value or principle has also been called *individualization,* which means viewing and treating each person as unique and worthwhile. The social work profession firmly believes that everyone has inherent dignity, which is to be respected.

Every human being is unique in a variety of ways—value system, personality, goals in life, financial resources, emotional and physical strengths, personal concerns, past experiences, peer pressures, emotional reactions, self-identity, family relationships, and behavioral patterns. In working with a client, a social worker

---

*L.S. Shulman, "Signature Pedagogies in the Professions," *Daedelus,* (Summer 1994), pp. 52–59.

needs to perceive and respect the uniqueness of the client's situation.

Individualization is relatively easy for a social worker to achieve when clients have values, goals, behavioral patterns, and personal characteristics that are similar to those of the worker. It is harder to achieve when clients have values or behavioral patterns that the worker views as unpleasant. For example, a worker holding traditional middle-class values may have difficulty respecting a client who has killed someone, has raped someone, is filthy, or continually uses vulgar language. A general guideline in such situations is that the worker should seek to accept and respect the client but not the deviant behavior, which needs to be changed. If a worker is not able to convey that she or he accepts the client (but not the deviant behavior), a helping relationship will not be established. In that case, the worker will have practically no opportunity to help the client make constructive changes. A second guideline is that, if a worker views a client as being unpleasant and is unable to establish a working relationship, then the case should be transferred to another worker. The original social worker need not feel disgrace or embarrassment in having to transfer a case for such reasons; it is irrational to expect to like every client or to be liked by every client.[35]

Social workers occasionally encounter "raw" situations. I have worked with clients who have committed a wide range of asocial and bizarre acts, including incest, rape, murder, sodomy, sexual exhibitionism, and grave robbing. Achieving an attitude of respect for people who commit bizarre actions is difficult at times, but rehabilitation will not occur unless the worker develops respect.

Social psychologists have firmly established that our images of ourselves develop largely out of our interactions and communications with others. A long time ago, Charles Cooley labeled this process the concept of the "looking glass."[36] People develop their self-concept in terms of how other people relate to them, as if others were a looking glass or mirror. For example, if you receive respect from others and are praised for your positive qualities, you will feel good about yourself, will gradually develop a positive sense of worth, will be happier, and will seek responsible and socially acceptable ways to continue to maintain the respect of others.

On the other hand, if you are related to by others as if you are irresponsible, you will begin to view yourself as irresponsible and will gradually develop a neg-ative self-concept. With such a view of yourself, you decrease your efforts to act responsibly. In both these examples, the ways that others relate to you (positively or negatively) become a self-fulfilling prophecy.[37]

The principle of individualization also plays a key role in social work treatment. Various problems, needs, goals, and values of clients require different patterns of relationships with workers and different methods of helping. For example, a teenage male who is placed in a group home because his parents find him "uncontrollable" may need an understanding but firm counselor who sets and enforces strict limits. At times the youth may need encouragement and guidance in how to perform better at school. If conflicts develop between the youth and other residents at the group home, the counselor may need to play a mediating role. If the boy is shy, assertiveness training may be needed. If his parents are fairly ineffective in their parenting role, the counselor may seek to have them enroll in a Parent Effectiveness Training (PET) program.[38] If the youth is being treated unfairly at school or by the juvenile court, the counselor may play an advocate role for him and attempt to change the system. If the youth has behavior problems, the social worker will need to explore the underlying reasons and develop an intervention program.

Clients' Right to Self-Determination

This principle asserts that clients have the right to hold and express their own opinions and to act on them, as long as doing so does not infringe on the rights of others. This principle is in sharp contrast to the layperson's perception that social workers seek to "remold" clients into a pattern chosen by the workers. Rather, the efforts of social workers are geared to enhancing the capability of clients to help themselves. Client self-determination derives logically from the belief in the inherent dignity of each person. If people have dignity, then it follows that they should be permitted to determine their own lifestyles as far as possible.

Making clients' decisions and doing everything for them is self-defeating; these actions lead to increased dependency rather than to self-reliance and self-sufficiency. For people to grow, to mature, and to become responsible, they need to make their own decisions and take responsibility for the consequences. Mistakes and emotional pain will at times occur. But that is part of life. We learn by our mistakes and by trial and error. Respect for the client's decision-making ability is associated with the principle that social work is a cooperative endeavor between client and worker (client participation). Social work is done *with* a client, not *to* a client. Plans imposed on people without their active involvement have a way of not turning out well.

Self-determination implies that clients should be made aware that there are alternatives for resolving their personal or social problems. They can choose from several courses of action. (If there is only one course of action, there is no choice and therefore no self-determination.) As we've seen, the role of a social worker in helping clients involves (a) building a helping relationship, (b) exploring problems with clients in depth, and (c) exploring alternative solutions, with the clients then choosing a course of action. This third step is the implementation of the principle of self-determination.

Social workers need to recognize that it is the client who *owns* the problem and therefore has the chief responsibility to resolve it. In this respect, social work differs markedly from most other professions. Most professionals, such as physicians and attorneys, advise clients about what they ought to do. Doctors, lawyers, and dentists are viewed as experts. Clients' decision making in such situations is generally limited to the professional's advice.

In sharp contrast, social workers seek to establish not an expert–inferior relationship but rather a relationship between equals. The expertise of the social worker does *not* lie in knowing or recommending what is best for the client; it lies in assisting clients to define their problems, to identify and examine alternatives for resolving the problems, to maximize their capacities and opportunities to make decisions for themselves, and to implement the decisions they make. Many students, when they first enter social work or some other helping profession, mistakenly see their role as that of "savior" or "rescuer."

When clients reveal to us their concerns (which often lead them to be very miserable and vulnerable), we are erroneously apt to conclude that we *must* find a way to make their lives better. In reality, we have the power to make only our own lives better—not someone else's. With clients who are in dire situations, it is our job to help them problem-solve their dilemmas and to then help them realize there are constructive courses of action they can take to improve their lives. It is up to them to decide whether they will put in the time and effort to implement the courses of action that are likely to result in positive changes for them.

The principle of self-determination is complex and has some limitations. If a client decides to take a course of action that the social worker believes will have adverse effects, the social worker must decide whether to intervene. For example, if an elderly female client chooses to live alone in her home when there is serious concern about her physical capacities to live independently, a social worker has the obligation to point out the dangers and to suggest alternative living arrangements. In this situation, the social worker may decide not to take further action to force her into a safer living environment. On the other hand, if a client tries to commit suicide, the social worker should do everything possible to prevent another attempt.

Furthermore, if a client discusses an intention to harm another person, a social worker must make a judgment about whether to intervene to prevent the client from carrying out his or her intended actions. For example, if a client indicates that he plans to shoot someone and then bolts out of the social worker's office, the worker may choose (and may have a legal obligation) to inform the police and the intended victim.

Critical Thinking Question

Do you believe you have the power to "rescue" people who have serious personal problems?

Confidentiality

Confidentiality is the implicit or explicit agreement between a professional and a client to maintain the privacy of information about the client. An "absolute" implementation of this principle means that disclosures made to the professional are not shared with anyone else, except when authorized by the client in writing or required by law. Because of the principle of confidentiality, professionals can be sued if they disclose unauthorized information that has a damaging effect on the client.

Confidentiality is important because clients are not likely to share their "hidden secrets," personal concerns, and asocial thoughts and actions with a professional who might reveal that information to others. A basic principle of counseling is that clients must feel comfortable in fully revealing themselves to the professional, without fear that their revelations will be used against them.

Confidentiality is absolute when information revealed to a professional is *never* passed on to anyone in any form. Such information would never be shared with other agency staff, fed into a computer, or written in a case record. A student or beginning practitioner tends to think in absolutes and may even naively promise clients "absolute confidentiality."

In reality, absolute confidentiality is seldom achieved. Social workers today generally function as part of a larger agency. In agencies much of the communication is written into case records and shared orally with other staff as part of the service delivery process. Social workers share details with supervisors; many work in teams and are expected to share information with other team members. Thus, it is more precise to describe confidentiality in social work practice as "relative confidentiality."

Confidentiality is a legal matter, and at present there is a fair amount of uncertainty about what legally constitutes a violation and what does not. There have been few test cases in court to define violations of confidentiality.

Today it is generally permissible to discuss a client's circumstances with other professionals within the agency. In some agencies, such as a mental hospital, the input of many professionals (psychiatrists, psychologists, social workers, nurses, physical therapists, and so on) is used in assessing a client and developing a treatment plan.

Many agencies consider it inappropriate to share or discuss the client's case with a secretary. (Yet the secretary does the typing and usually knows as much about each client as the professional staff.)

Most agencies believe it is inappropriate to discuss a client's case with professionals at another agency, unless the client first signs a release form. (However, professionals employed by different agencies do at times informally share information about a client without the client's authorization.)

Currently, nearly all agencies share case information with social work interns. (Whether it is legally permissible to share information with student interns has not yet been determined.)

It is certainly permissible to discuss a case with others for educational purposes if the client is not specifically identified. Yet this is another "gray" area because the person talking about the case will not be able to determine precisely when identifying information is being given. Take the following example.

Some years ago, I was employed at a maximum-security hospital for the criminally insane and had on my caseload a young male who had decapitated his 17-year-old girlfriend. Such a criminal offense is indeed shocking and rare. People in the client's local area will never forget the crime. If I were to discuss this case in a class at a university, I could never be fully certain that no one would be able to identify the offender. There is always the chance that one of the students may be from the client's home community and could recognize the offender.

Another problem area is the thorny question of when a professional should violate confidence and inform others. Again, there are many gray areas surrounding this question.

Most state laws permit or require the professional to inform the appropriate people when a client admits to a past or intended serious criminal act. Yet the question of how *serious* a crime must be before there is an obligation to report it has not been resolved. On the extreme end of the "severity" continuum (for example, when a client threatens to kill someone), it has been established that a professional *must* inform the appropriate people—such as the police and the intended victims.[39]

In regard to the question of how serious a crime must be before it is reported, Suanna J. Wilson notes:

> *How serious must a crime be in order for the professional to take protective measures? Obviously, crimes involving someone's life are sufficiently serious. But what about destruction of personal property, theft, and the hundreds of misdemeanors that are so minor that they are rather easily overlooked? Unfortunately, there seems to be no clear-cut definition of what constitutes a serious crime, and it appears that this will have to be determined by the courts in individual case rulings.[40]*

Without guidelines, a professional must use his or her own best judgment about when a client's actions or communications warrant protective measures and about what those measures should be. Student interns and beginning practitioners are advised to consult their supervisors when questions in this area arise.

A few years ago, I was the faculty supervisor for a student in a field placement at a public assistance agency. The intern had an unmarried mother on his caseload. A trusting working relationship between the intern and the mother was developed. The woman then informed the intern that she was dating a man who was sometimes abusive to her when drunk. She further indicated that there was a warrant for this man's arrest in another state for an armed robbery charge. The student contacted me, inquiring whether it was his obligation to inform the police, thereby violating confidentiality. My response was that he should discuss this with his agency supervisor to find out the agency's policy. The student informed the agency supervisor. The supervisor consulted with the attorney for the agency, who advised that the student should inform the woman that the information she revealed would have to be provided to the authorities. Upon being informed, the woman stomped out of the office, presumably to warn her partner. The police were immediately informed and proceeded to arrest him. The woman was outraged and ended all communication with the professional staff at this agency, as she felt she could no longer trust them. (When professionals are legally obligated to violate confidentiality, the clients involved are apt to react as this mother did.)

Wilson has researched this issue and concludes:

In summary, a professional whose client confesses an intended or past crime can find himself in a very delicate position, both legally and ethically. There are enough conflicting beliefs on how this should be handled, so that clear guidelines are lacking. Social workers who receive a communication about a serious criminal act by a client would be wise to consult an attorney for a detailed research of appropriate state statutes and a review of recent court rulings that might help determine the desired course of action.[41]

There are a number of other circumstances when a professional is permitted, expected, or required to violate confidentiality.* These include:

- When a client formally (usually in writing) authorizes the professional to release information.
- When a professional is called to testify in a criminal case. (State statutes vary regarding guidelines on what information may be kept confidential in criminal proceedings; practitioners must research their own particular statutes in each instance.)
- When a client files a lawsuit against a professional (such as for malpractice).

- When a client threatens suicide. A professional may then be forced to violate confidentiality to save the client's life. Although the treating professional is encouraged to violate confidentiality in such circumstances, there is not necessarily a legal requirement to do so.
- When a client threatens to harm his or her therapist.
- When a professional becomes aware that a minor has committed a crime, when a minor is used by adults as an accessory in a crime, or when a minor is a victim of criminal actions. In such situations, most states require that counselors inform the legal authorities. Again, the question arises of how serious the crime must be before it is reported.
- When there is evidence of child abuse or neglect. Most states require professionals to report the evidence to the designated child protection agency.
- When a client's emotional or physical condition makes his or her employment a clear danger to himself or herself or to others (for example, when a counselor discovers that a client who is an airplane pilot has a serious drinking problem).

All these instances require professional judgment in deciding when the circumstances justify violating confidentiality.

Protecting the confidentiality of files and records in human service organizations is becoming much more difficult as the technology of compiling, storing, and receiving information on clients expands exponentially. With modern computer technology, vast amounts of data can be gathered, recorded, stored, and processed quickly, easily, and inexpensively, Dickson notes:

At one time, a patient's or client's record might have consisted of some basic information on a single file card, or a number of pages of personal data, process notes, and observations. Today, such a record might consist of hundreds of pages of text along with still or moving visual images and recorded sound, all stored on tape, disk, hard drive, or CD-ROM as electronic/magnetic impulses. The record might be copied into a central database of case records, and could be linked with or contain cross-references to other databases containing other records for the same individual, family, or condition. The records could be accessed, sorted, merged, compiled, and transmitted. They could be downloaded and printed, instantly copied, and transmitted by fax or computer modem to

---

*An extended discussion of these circumstances is contained in Suanna J. Wilson, *Confidentiality in Social Work: Issues and Principles* (New York: Free Press, 1978) and in Donald T. Dickson, *Confidentiality and Privacy in Social Work* (New York: Free Press, 1998).

numerous other locations, anywhere in the country or internationally. And with the appropriate linkages, the record could be accessed by other computers or other data systems near and far. Along with all this, the expansion of federal and state government and private third-party insurers in monitoring and reimbursing service delivery has greatly increased the potential for broad access to and dispersion of recorded information.[42]

With computer technology, it is now possible to link or combine a client's health, mental health, social service, juvenile court, adult court, education, and law enforcement records (although there are some legislative acts that prevent certain linkages). At times, individuals have had inaccuracies in their records in computerized databases, which has severely adversely affected them—for example, inaccuracies in credit ratings have prevented a number of people from obtaining a loan.

Preserving privacy and confidentiality in this era of modern electronic technology poses crucial issues in social work. Dickson notes:

Where once a single person might overhear part of a conversation, now a breach of confidentiality might include entire faxed or computer-transmitted records that went awry or were intercepted by a third party. Where once a person overhearing a conversation might tell a few others, now the possibilities for transmitting the intercepted information are enormous. For example, a single item of information or an image now posted on the Internet can be seen, copied, and recopied by literally millions of people around the world.[43]

Even the destruction of records is no longer as simple as it once was. Records can be shredded, torn up, or erased from a computer file, but with modern electronic technology for the reproduction and transmission of information, a record that was assumed to be destroyed or erased may exist in another location, or under another name or identification number. Therefore, it is now important for human service agencies to keep a log of what information about clients has been transmitted when, to where, and in what form.

Because of the dangers of violations of privacy and confidentiality with modern electronic technology, it is crucial that social workers have an in-depth understanding of privacy rights and confidentiality rights of individuals and families. What information

to gather, store, replicate, and transmit, and who has access and for what purposes, have become crucial issues in social work.

Advocacy and Social Action for the Oppressed

Social work recognizes an obligation to advocate for the powerless, oppressed, and the dispossessed. Social work believes that society has a responsibility to all of its members to provide security, acceptance, and satisfaction of basic cultural, social, and biological needs. Only when our basic needs are met can we develop our maximum potentials. Because social work believes in the value of the individual, it has a special responsibility to protect and secure civil rights for all oppressed people and groups. Social workers have a moral responsibility to work toward eradicating discrimination. The civil rights of clients need to be protected to preserve human dignity and self-respect.

Critical Thinking Question
How high is your interest in working for social and economic justice for populations-at-risk?

Accountability

Increasingly, federal and state governmental units and private funding sources are requiring that the effectiveness of service programs be measured. Programs found to be ineffective are being phased out. Although some social workers view accountability with trepidation and claim that the paperwork involved interferes with serving clients, social work has an obligation to funding sources to provide the highest-quality services. Accountability studies have yielded some valuable information. For example, they have demonstrated that orphanages are not the best places to serve homeless children, that long-term hospitalization is not the best way to help the emotionally disturbed, that probation generally has higher rehabilitative value than long-term confinement in prison, that the Job Corps program of the 1960s was too expensive for the outcomes achieved, that most children with a cognitive disability can be better served in their home communities through local programs than by confinement in an institution, and that runaways fare better in runaway centers than in detention or in jail.

Social workers need to become skilled at evaluating their effectiveness in providing services. A wide variety of evaluation techniques are now available to assess effectiveness of current services and to identify unmet needs and service gaps. One of the most useful approaches is management by objectives (MBO). This technique involves identifying the objectives of each program, specifying in measurable terms how and when these objectives are met, and then periodically measuring the extent to which the objectives are met.

Management by objectives is also one of the most useful approaches that a social worker can use to assess his or her own effectiveness. Many agencies are now requiring each of their workers, *with the involvement of their clients*, to (a) identify and specify what the goals will be for each client (generally this is done together with clients during the initial interviews), (b) have the client and the worker then write down in detail what each will do to accomplish the goals (deadlines for accomplishing these tasks are also set), and (c) assess the extent to which the goals have been achieved when the intervention is terminated (and perhaps periodically during the intervention process).

If goals are not being achieved, the worker needs to examine the underlying reasons. Perhaps unrealistic goals are being set. Perhaps the program or the intervention techniques are ineffective. Perhaps certain components of the intervention program are having an adverse effect. Perhaps other factors account for the low success rate. Depending on the cause, appropriate changes need to be made.

On the other hand, if the goals are being met, the worker can use this information to document to funding sources and to supervisors that high-quality services are being provided.

The Institutional Orientation

There are currently two conflicting views of the role of social welfare in our society: the residual orientation versus the institutional orientation. These two views were described at length in Chapter 1. Social work believes in the institutional approach and seeks to develop and provide programs with this orientation. Society must provide opportunities for growth and development that will allow each person to realize his or her fullest potential. Social work believes that society has a responsibility to all its members to provide security, acceptance, and satisfaction of basic cultural and biological needs. Social workers reject the views of rugged individualism and Social Darwinism.

Respect for the Spiritual and Religious Beliefs of Others

A major thrust of social work education is to prepare students for culturally sensitive practice. Because religion and spirituality play important roles in all cultures, it is essential that social workers comprehend the influence of religion and spirituality in human lives. The *Educational Policy and Accreditation Standards* of the Council on Social Work Education now require that accredited baccalaureate and master's programs provide content in these areas so that students develop approaches and skills for working with clients with differing spiritual backgrounds.

Spirituality and religion are separate, though often related, dimensions. Spirituality can be defined as "the general human experience of developing a sense of meaning, purpose, and morality."[44] Key components of spirituality are the personal search for meaning in life, a sense of identity (discussed in Chapter 2), and a value system. In contrast, religion refers to the formal institutional contexts of spiritual beliefs and practices.

Social work's historical roots in religious organizations originated under the inspiration of the Judeo-Christian religious traditions of its philanthropic founders. Jewish scriptures and religious law requiring the emulation of God's creativity and caring have inspired social welfare activities for many centuries. Similarly, the Christian biblical command to love one's neighbor as oneself has been interpreted as a sense of moral responsibility for social service and inspired the development of charity organizations and philanthropy in the United States during the 19th century. Social workers need to be trained for effective practice with religiously oriented clients because many social issues today have religious dimensions, such as abortion, use of contraceptives, acceptance of gays and lesbians, cloning, reproductive technology, roles of women, prayer in public schools, and physician-assisted suicide.

Social workers need an appreciation and respect for religious beliefs that differ from their own. There is a danger that those who believe that their religion is the "one true religion" will tend to view people with divergent beliefs as ill-guided, evil, mistaken, or in need of being "saved." More wars have been fought over religious differences than for any other cause. A major source of intolerance, discrimination,

© Jeff Greenberg/PhotoEdit

It is essential that social workers comprehend the influence of religion and spirituality in their clients' lives.

and oppression is the belief that "my religion is the one true religion; those who believe as I do will go to heaven, while those who believe in some other religion are heathens who will go to eternal damnation" (see Chapter 12).

Furman notes, "The goal of incorporating religious and spiritual beliefs in social work curricula should include a broad array of knowledge of many different religious and spiritual beliefs, primarily to expand students' understanding and sensitivity."[45] Case Exhibit 3.7 summarizes information on four prominent world religions.

Because values play a key role in social work practice, it is essential that social work educational programs (a) help students clarify their values and (b) foster in students the development of values that are consistent with professional social work practice.

Critical Thinking Question

Do you have respect for people whose religious beliefs differ sharply from your own?

Promoting Social and Economic Justice, and Safeguarding Human Rights

Social workers have an obligation to promote social and economic justice for those who are oppressed or victimized by discrimination. The Council on Social Work Education states social work educational programs need to "provide a learning environment in which respect for all persons and understanding of diversity and difference are practiced."[46] In the EPAS (2008), social work educational programs are mandated to have a commitment to diversity, "including age, class, color, culture, disability, ethnicity, gender, gender identity and expression, immigration status, political ideology, race, religion, sex, and sexual orientation."[47] The NASW Code of Ethics states, "Social workers should act to prevent and eliminate domination of, exploitation of, and discrimination against any person, group, or class on the basis of race, ethnicity, national origin, color, sex, sexual orientation, age, marital status, political belief, religion, or mental or physical disability."[48]

The social work profession holds that society has a responsibility to all of its members to provide security, acceptance, and satisfaction of basic cultural, social, and biological needs. Only when individuals' basic needs are met is it possible for them to develop their maximum potentials. Therefore, social workers have a special responsibility to protect and secure civil rights based on democratic principles and a moral responsibility to work toward eradicating discrimination for any reason. Clients' civil rights need to be protected to preserve human dignity and self-respect.

In promoting social and economic justice for oppressed populations, social workers are expected to have an understanding of (1) the consequences and dynamics of social and economic injustice, including the forms of human oppression and discrimination, and (2) the impact of economic deprivation, discrimination, and oppression on populations-at-risk. Social workers have an ethical obligation to understand and appreciate human diversity. They are expected to have and use skills to promote social change that furthers the achievement of individual and collective social and economic justice.

In recent years the Council on Social Work Education has placed increased emphasis on human rights. For example, in the 2008 EPAS statement, Educational Policy 1.1, Values, states, "Service, social justice, the dignity and worth of the person, human rights, importance of human relationships, integrity, competence, and scientific inquiry are the core values of social work."[49]

The 2008 EPAS statement adds, "Each person, regardless of position in society, has basic human rights, such as freedom, safety, privacy, an adequate standard of living, health care, and education. Social workers recognize the global interconnections of oppression and are knowledgeable about theories of justice and strategies to promote human and civil rights."[50]

Reichert, however, has noted that "human rights" has received very limited attention in the social work curriculum and in social work course materials and lectures.[51] Often, a human rights focus is "invisible" in the social work curriculum. Social work literature continually prefers the term "social justice" in analyzing core values relevant to the social work profession.

Social justice is an "ideal" in which all members of a society have the same opportunities, basic rights, obligations, and social benefits. Integral to this value, social workers have an obligation to engage in advocacy to confront institutional inequities, prejudice, discrimination, and oppression.

Human rights are conceived to be fundamental rights to which a person is inherently entitled simply because she or he is a human being. Human rights are thus universal (applicable everywhere) and egalitarian (the same for everyone).

Reichert compares the concept of "human rights" to the concept of "social justice":

Human rights provide the social work profession with a global and contemporary set of guidelines, whereas social justice tends to be defined in vague terminology such as fairness versus unfairness or equality versus inequality.... This distinction gives human rights an authority that social justice lacks. Human rights can elicit discussion of common issues by people from all walks of life and every corner of the world.[52]

What are basic "human rights"? A clear specification of basic human rights has not been agreed upon. A key starting point in articulating such rights is the Universal Declaration of Human Rights (UNDR), developed by the United Nations (UN) Commission on Human Rights in 1948. The human rights that were identified in this document are:

- *All humans are born free and equal in dignity and rights.*
- *Everyone is entitled to all of the rights in the UNDR regardless of any distinction.*
- *The right to life, liberty, and the security of the person*
- *Prohibition of slavery*
- *Prohibition of torture*
- *Right to recognition as a person before the law*
- *All must be treated equally under the law.*
- *Right to a remedy of any violation of these rights*
- *Prohibition of arbitrary arrest, detention, or exile*
- *Right to a fair trial*
- *People shall be presumed innocent until proven guilty.*
- *Right to freedom from arbitrary interference with private life*
- *Right to freedom of movement*
- *Right to seek asylum*
- *Right to a nationality*
- *Right to marry; marriage must be consented to by both parties; the family is entitled to protection from the state*
- *Right to property*
- *Right to freedom of thought, conscience, and religion*
- *Right to freedom of opinion and expression*
- *Right to freedom of assembly and association*
- *Right to participate in the government of one s country*
- *Right to economic, social, and cultural rights necessary for dignity and free development of personality*

CASE EXHIBIT 3.7

Four Prominent Religions: Judaism, Christianity, Islam, and Buddhism

Practicing social workers need a knowledge and appreciation of the religious beliefs and value systems of their clients. The four religions in this exhibit were selected because of their prominence. Readers should know that there are hundreds of other religions in the world.

Judaism

Judaism is the religion of the Jews. Jews believe in one God, the creator of the world who delivered the Israelites out of their bondage in Egypt. The Hebrew Bible is the primary source of Judaism. (The Hebrew Bible was adopted by Christians as part of their sacred writings, and they now call it the Old Testament.) God is believed to have revealed his law (Torah) to the Israelites; part of this law was the Ten Commandments that were given to Moses by God. The Israelites believed God chose them to be a light to all humankind.

Next in importance to the Hebrew Bible is the Talmud, which is an influential compilation of rabbinic traditions and discussions about Jewish life and law. It consists of the Mishnah (the codification of the oral Torah) and a collection of extensive early rabbinical commentary. Various later commentaries and the standard code of Jewish law and ritual (Halakhah) produced in the later Middle Ages have been important in shaping Jewish practice and thought.

Abraham (who lived roughly 2,000 years before Christ) is viewed as an ancestor or father of the Hebrew people. According to Genesis, he came from the Sumerian town of Ur (now part of modern Iraq) and migrated with his family and flocks via Haran (the ancient city of Nari on the Euphrates River) to the "Promised Land" of Canaan, where he settled at Shechem (modern Nablus). After a sojourn in Egypt, he lived to be 175 years old and was buried with his first wife, Sarah. By Sarah he was the father of Isaac (whom he was prepared to sacrifice at the behest of the Lord) and grandfather of Jacob ("Israel"). By his second wife, Hagar (Sarah's Egyptian handmaiden), he was the father of Ismael, the ancestor of 12 clans. By his third wife, Keturah, he had six sons who became the ancestors of the Arab tribes. He was also the uncle of Lot. (Interestingly, Abraham is regarded by Judaism, Christianity, and Islam as an important ancestor or father in their religions.)

All Jews see themselves as members of a community that originated around the time in which Abraham lived. This past lives on in its rituals. The family is the basic unit of Jewish ritual, although the synagogue has come to play an increasingly important role. The Sabbath, which begins at sunset on Friday and ends at sunset on Saturday, is the central religious worship. The synagogue is the center for community worship and study. Its main feature is the "ark" (a cupboard) containing the handwritten scrolls of the Pentateuch (the five books of Moses in the Hebrew Bible, comprising Genesis, Exodus,

Leviticus, Numbers, and Deuteronomy). A rabbi is primarily a teacher and spiritual guide.

There is an annual cycle of religious festivals and days of fasting. The first of these is Rosh Hashanah, the Jewish New Year, which falls in September or October. During this New Year's Day service, a ram's horn is blown as a call to repentance and spiritual renewal. The holiest day in the Jewish year is Yom Kippur, the Day of Atonement, which comes at the end of 10 days of penitence following Rosh Hashanah; Yom Kippur is a day devoted to fasting, prayer, and repentance for past sins. Another important festival is Hanukkah, held in December, commemorating the rededication of the Temple in Jerusalem after the victory of Judas Maccabees over the Syrians. Pesach is the Passover festival, occurring in March or April, commemorating the exodus of the Israelites from Egypt; the festival is named after God's passing over the houses of Israelites when he killed the firstborn children of the Egyptian families.

Christianity

Christianity is a religion practiced in numerous countries that is centered on the life and work of Jesus of Nazareth in Israel. It developed out of Judaism. The earliest followers were Jews who, after the death and resurrection of Jesus, believed him to be the Messiah, or Christ, promised by the prophets in the Old Testament. He was declared to be the Son of God. During his life, he chose 12 men as disciples, who formed the nucleus of the church. This communion of followers believed that Jesus would come again to inaugurate the "kingdom of God." God is believed to be one in essence but threefold in person, comprising the Father, Son, and Holy Spirit or Holy Ghost (together known as the Trinity). Jesus Christ is also wholly human because of his birth to Mary. The Holy Spirit is the touch or "breath" of God that inspires people to follow the Christian faith. The Bible is thought to have been written under the Holy Spirit's influence.

Jesus Christ was the son of Mary and Joseph, yet also the Son of God created by a miraculous conception by the Spirit of God. He was born in Bethlehem (near Jerusalem) but began his ministry in Nazareth. The main records of his ministry are the New Testament gospels, which show him proclaiming the coming of the kingdom of God and in particular the acceptance of the oppressed and the poor into the kingdom. The duration of his public ministry is uncertain, but it is from John's Gospel that one gets the impression of a 3-year period of teaching. He was executed by crucifixion under the order of Pontius Pilate, a Roman ruler. The date of death is uncertain but is considered to be when Jesus was in his early 30s.

At the heart of the Christian faith is the conviction that through Jesus's death and resurrection, God has allowed humans to find salvation. Belief in Jesus as the Son of God,

(continued)

along with praying for forgiveness of sin, brings absolution of all sin. Many Christians believe that those who ask for forgiveness of their sins will join God in heaven, while unbelievers who do not ask for forgiveness of their sins will be consigned to hell. The gospel of Jesus was proclaimed at first by word of mouth, but by the end of the first century A.D., it was written and became accepted as the authoritative scripture of the New Testament. Through the witness of the 12 earliest leaders (apostles) and their successors, the Christian faith, despite sporadic persecution, spread through the Greek and Roman world. In A.D. 315, it was declared by Emperor Constantine to be the official religion of the Roman Empire. It survived the breakup of the Empire and the "Dark Ages," largely through the life and witness of groups of monks in monasteries. The religion helped form the basis of civilization in the Middle Ages in Europe. Since the Middle Ages, major denominations of Christianity have formed as a result of differences in doctrine and practice.

Islam

Islam is the Arabic word for "submission" to the will of God (Allah). It is also the name of the religion originating in Arabia during the 7th century through the prophet Muhammad. Followers of Islam are known as Muslims, or Moslems.

Muhammad was born in Mecca. He was the son of Abdallah, a poor merchant of the powerful tribe of Quaraysh, hereditary guardians of the shrine in Mecca. Muhammad was orphaned at 6 and raised by his grandfather and uncle. His uncle Abu Talib trained him to be a merchant. At the age of 24, he entered the service of a rich widow, Khadijah, whom he eventually married. They had six children. While continuing as a trader, Muhammad became increasingly drawn to religious contemplation. Soon afterward, he began to receive revelations of the word of Allah, the one and only God. These revelations given to Muhammad by the angel Gabriel over a period of 20 years were eventually codified into the Quran (Koran). The Quran commanded that the numerous idols of the shrine should be destroyed and that the rich should give to the poor. This simple message attracted some support but provoked a great deal of hostility from those who felt their interests threatened. When his wife and uncle died, Muhammad was reduced to poverty, but he began making a few converts among the pilgrims to Mecca. He eventually migrated to Yathrib. The name of this town was changed to Medina, "the City of the Prophet." This migration known in Arabic as the *hijra*, marks the beginning of the Muslim lunar calendar. After a series of battles with warring enemies of Islam, Muhammad was able to take control of Mecca, which recognized him as chief and prophet. By A.D. 360, he had control over all Arabia. Two years later, he fell ill and died in the home of one of his nine wives. His tomb in the mosque at Medina is venerated throughout Islam.

Islam embraces every aspect of life. Muslims believe that individuals, societies, and governments should all be obedient to the will of God as set forth in the Quran. The Quran teaches there is one God, who has no partners. He is the creator of all things and has absolute power over them. All persons should commit themselves to lives of giving praise and grateful obedience to God, as everyone will be judged on the day of resurrection. Those who have obeyed God's commandments will dwell forever in paradise, whereas those who have sinned against God and have not repented will be condemned eternally to the fires of hell. Since the beginning of time, God has sent prophets (including Abraham, Moses, and Jesus) to provide the guidance necessary for the attainment of eternal reward.

There are five essential religious duties known as "the pillars of Islam." (a) The *shahadah* (profession of faith) is the sincere recitation of the twofold creed: "There is no god but God and Muhammad is the Messenger of God." (b) The *salat* (formal prayer) must be performed at fixed hours five times a day while facing toward the holy city of Mecca. (c) Almsgiving through the payment of *zakat* ("purification") is regarded primarily as an act of worship and is the duty of sharing one's wealth out of gratitude for God's favor, according to the uses stated in the Quran. (d) There is a duty to fast (*saum;* abstain from food and drink between sunrise and sunset) during Ramadan, the ninth month of the Muslim year. (e) The pilgrimage to Mecca is to be performed, if at all possible, at least once during one's lifetime.

Shariah is the sacred law of Islam and applies to all aspects of life, not just religious practices. This sacred law is found in the Quran and the sunnah (the sayings and acts of Muhammad).

Buddhism

Buddhism originated in India about 2,500 years ago. The religion derived from the teaching of Buddha (Siddharta Gautama). Buddha is regarded as one of a continuing series of enlightened beings.

Buddha was born the son of the rajah of the Sakya tribe in Kapilavastu, north of Benares. His personal name was Siddharta, but he was also known by his family name of Gautama. At about age 30, he left the luxuries of the court, his beautiful wife, and all earthly ambitions. He became an ascetic, as he practiced strict self-denial as a measure of personal and spiritual discipline. After several years of severe austerities, he saw in meditation and contemplation the way to enlightenment. For the next four decades, he taught, gaining many followers and disciples. He died at Kusinagara in Oudh.

The teaching of Buddha is summarized in the four noble truths, the last of which asserts the existence of a path leading to deliverance from the universal human experience of suffering. A central tenet of Buddhism is the law of karma, by which good and evil deeds result in appropriate rewards or punishments in this life or in a succession of rebirths. It is believed that the sum of a person's actions is carried forward from one life to the next, leading to an improvement or deterioration in that person's fate. Through a proper understanding of the law

(continued)

CASE EXHIBIT 3.7 *(continued)*

of karma, and by obedience to the right path, humans can break the chain of karma.

The Buddha's path to deliverance is through morality (*sila*), meditation (*samadhi*), and wisdom (*panna*). The goal is nirvana, which is the "blowing out" of the fires of all desires and the absorption of the self into the infinite. All Buddhas ("enlightened ones") are greatly revered, with a place of special accordance being given to Gautama.

There are two main branches of Buddhism dating from its earliest history. Theravada Buddhism adheres to the strict and narrow teachings of the early Buddhist writings; in this branch, salvation is possible for only the few who accept the severe

discipline and effort to achieve it. Mahayana Buddhism is more liberal and makes concessions to popular piety; it teaches that salvation is possible for everyone. It introduced the doctrine of the bodhisattva (or personal savior). A bodhisattva is one who has attained the enlightenment of a Buddha but chooses not to pass into nirvana and voluntarily remains in the world to help lesser beings attain enlightenment; this view emphasizes charity toward others. Mahayana Buddhism asserts that all living beings have the inner potential of Buddha nature. Buddha nature is a kind of spiritual embryo that holds out the promise to all people that they can eventually become Buddhas because they all have the potential for Buddhahood.

- *Right to work and equitable compensation*
- *Right to rest and leisure from work*
- *Right to an adequate standard of living, including food, clothing, housing, and medical*
- *Right to education*
- *Right to participate in cultural activities and to share in scientific achievements*
- *Right to a world order in which these rights can be realized*
- *Each has duties to their community; rights shall be limited only in regards to respecting the rights of others.*
- *None of the rights may be interpreted as allowing any action to destroy these rights.*[53]

Every member nation of the UN has approved this Declaration. Yet it is not legally binding on any nation. Because this Declaration articulates human rights in somewhat vague terms, it is sometimes difficult to determine when (or if) a country/government is violating basic human rights.

Most countries now recognize that safeguarding human rights has evolved into a major, worldwide goal. Yet identifying violations is currently an imprecise science. It is common for a government to accuse other governments of violating human rights, while at the same time "overlooking" its own violations, Reichert states:

The United States, compared to many other countries, fails to fulfill its obligation to promote human rights for all. . . . For instance, our failure to provide adequate health care for children and all expectant mothers violates the same Universal Declaration of Human Rights that U.S. political leaders continually call upon to denigrate China, Cuba, and Iraq, among other countries. The infant

mortality rate is higher in the United States than in any other industrialized nation . . . and, within the U.S. itself, infant mortality rates are disparate among racial groups, with African-American infants suffering a mortality rate more than twice that of non-Hispanic whites.[54]

It is hoped that greater attention to articulating basic human rights will lead countries to initiate programs that safeguard such rights for all citizens. Increased attention to articulating and protecting basic human rights has promise of being a key countervailing force to facilitate curbing discrimination against people of color, women, people with disabilities, gays and lesbians, and other groups currently victimized by discrimination.

Social Work Education

Two-Year Associate Programs

During the past three decades, many community colleges and technical schools have begun offering 2-year associate programs related to social work education. These programs provide training for a wide range of associate degrees with such titles as:

- Social Work Aide/Social Service Associate/Social Service Technician
- Probation and Parole Aide
- Mental Health Associate/Mental Health Aide
- Human Services Technician/Human Services Aide
- Child Care Technician/Residential Child Care Aide
- Community Service Assistant/Community Services Technician/Community Social Service Worker

Many of these programs are accredited by the Council for Standards in Human Service Education. The programs must demonstrate the rigor of their courses in order to be accepted. Associate degree credits are transferring to 4-year institutions with increasing frequency.

As yet, associate degrees are not accredited by the Council on Social Work Education (CSWE). (The CSWE reviews social work baccalaureate and master's programs throughout the United States to determine whether individual programs meet the standards to warrant accreditation.) Standardization of associate programs in social work probably will not be achieved unless the CSWE decides to review associate programs for accreditation.

Undergraduate and Graduate Education

The Council on Social Work Education reviews for accreditation those undergraduate and graduate programs in social work that apply for accreditation. The CSWE sets standards for social work education and promotes and improves the quality of education in social work programs. Students who attend schools with accredited programs are assured that the quality of education meets national standards and generally have an advantage in securing employment following graduation because social welfare agencies prefer hiring graduates from accredited programs.

Until the early 1970s, undergraduate study in social work was generally recognized as an academic or preprofessional education; only the master's degree was recognized as a professional degree in social work. However, because a majority of people employed as social workers did not (and still do not) have a graduate degree, the need for professional training at the baccalaureate level was recognized. Effective July 1, 1974, accreditation requirements for undergraduate programs were substantially changed to emphasize professional preparation. In fact, the CSWE required that an accredited baccalaureate program "shall have as its primary stated educational objective preparation for beginning professional social work practice."[55] Secondary objectives for baccalaureate programs include (a) preparation of students for graduate professional education in social work and (b) preparation for intelligent, informed citizenship that brings an understanding of a wide range of social problems, intervention techniques to resolve such problems, and an understanding of social welfare concepts.

Master of Social Work (MSW) programs as a rule require 2 years of academic study. However, numerous graduate programs are granting advanced standing to students holding an undergraduate major in social work. Advanced standing (up to 1 academic year of credit) is given on the basis of the number of "core" courses taken as an undergraduate. Core courses are those that are required in both undergraduate and graduate programs and include classes in social welfare policy and services, social work practice, human behavior and the social environment, social research, and field placement.*

The Council on Social Work Education has an accreditation standard that states:

> *Advanced standing is awarded only to graduates holding degrees from baccalaureate social work programs accredited by CSWE, those recognized through its International Social Work Degree Recognition and Evaluation Service, or covered under a memorandum of understanding with international social work accreditors.*[56]

Because of the professional preparation focus of graduate programs, fieldwork is an important component of all MSW programs. Students spend an average of 2 to 3 days per week at an agency while receiving intensive supervision.

Although there is some variation in the format and structure of master's programs, almost all of them have the following two components: (a) Part of the program has a generic social work practice focus. Courses taken to meet this generic practice focus are similar (and at some schools identical) to the core courses of an undergraduate program. Some schools offer this generic focus during the first year, a few offer it during the first semester, and others have course content in this area for both years. (b) For the second part of the program, the student selects a concentration area from several available options and then takes courses in this study area. There is considerable variation among graduate schools in the concentration options that are offered.

Some of the concentration options are policy analysis, planning, research and administration, community organization, direct practice with individuals and small groups, direct practice with large groups, program development, community mental health, family

---

*Guidelines for granting advanced standing in MSW programs differ among schools; interested students should therefore consult with the graduate schools they want to attend.

functioning, health care, clinical practice, inner-city neighborhood services, social work in school systems, child welfare, consultation, aging, and crime and delinquency.

Individuals with MSW degrees often, within a year or two following graduation, assume supervisory or administrative responsibilities.

At the advanced graduate level, two additional programs are offered by some schools: (a) a "third year" program aimed at strengthening the professional skills of the student and (b) a Doctor of Social Work (DSW) or Doctor of Philosophy (PhD) degree. The doctoral program requires 2 or more years of postgraduate studies.

SUMMARY

The following summarizes this chapter's content as it relates to the chapter objectives presented at the beginning of the chapter. Objectives include the following:

A *Define generalist social work practice.*

The Council on Social Work Education in its *Educational Policy and Accreditation Standards* (EPAS) has defined generalist practice as:

> *Generalist practice is grounded in the liberal arts and the person and environment construct. To promote human and social well-being, generalist practitioners use a range of prevention and intervention methods in their practice with individuals, families, groups, organizations, and communities. The generalist practitioner identifies with the social work profession and applies ethical principles and critical thinking in practice. Generalist practitioners incorporate diversity in their practice and advocate for human rights and social and economic justice. They recognize, support, and build on the strengths and resiliency of all human beings. They engage in research-informed practice and are proactive in responding to the impact of context on professional practice.*[57]

B *Summarize the change process in social work practice.*

The change process in social work practice involves social workers using the following eight skills:

1. Engaging clients in an appropriate working relationship.
2. Identifying issues, problems, needs, resources, and assets.
3. Collecting and assessing information.
4. Planning for service delivery.
5. Using communication skills, supervision, and consultation.
6. Identifying, analyzing, and implementing empirically based interventions designed to achieve client goals.
7. Applying empirical knowledge and technological advances.
8. Evaluating program outcomes and practice effectiveness.

C *Describe roles assumed by social workers in social work practice.*

Social workers are expected to be knowledgeable and skillful in filling a variety of roles, including enabler, broker, advocate, activist, empowerer, mediator, negotiator, educator, initiator, coordinator, researcher, group facilitator, and public speaker.

D *Discuss social work practice with individuals, families, groups, organizations, and the community.*

Social work with individuals is aimed at helping people on a one-to-one basis to resolve personal and social problems.

When there are problems in a family, social services are often needed. There is extensive variation in the types and forms of services that are provided by social workers to troubled families. One of the many social services provided to families is family therapy.

Almost every social service agency now provides some group services. The focus of social work groups has considerable variation, including social conversation, recreation, recreation-skill development, education, task, problem solving and decision making, self-help, socialization, therapy, and sensitivity training. The goal in therapy groups is generally to have each member explore, in depth, his or her personal or emotional problems and to develop a strategy to resolve those problems. In contrast, sensitivity groups seek to foster increased personal and interpersonal awareness and to develop more effective interaction patterns.

An organization is a collectivity of individuals gathered together to serve a purpose. The roles of social workers within organizations, and their interactions with organizations (including their attempts to manipulate organizations), define much of what social workers do. There are basic structural conflicts between helping professionals and the bureaucratic systems in which they work. Numerous suggestions are presented on how social workers can survive and thrive in a bureaucracy.

Community practice is the process of stimulating and assisting the local community to evaluate, plan, and coordinate efforts to meet its needs. Social work is one of several disciplines that provide training in community practice. Practically all social workers, in one capacity or another, become involved in community practice efforts. Three models of community practice are locality development, social planning, and social action. The locality development model asserts that community change can best be brought about through broad participation of a wide spectrum of people at the local community level. The basic theme is, "Together we can figure out what to do and then do it." The social planning model emphasizes the process of problem solving. The role of the expert is stressed in identifying and resolving social problems. The theme of this approach is, "Let's get the facts and take the next rational steps." The social action model seeks to organize an oppressed group to pressure the power structure for increased resources or for social justice. The basic theme of this approach is, "Let's organize to overpower our oppressor."

E *Summarize the knowledge, skills, and values needed for social work practice.*

The 10 competencies identified in the *Educational Policy and Accreditation Standards* (EPAS) of the CSWE identify the knowledge, skills, and values needed for social work practice. This chapter presents these competencies.

The value base of social work includes: respect for the dignity and uniqueness of each individual; clients' right to self-determination; confidentiality; advocacy and social action to ensure the rights of those who are oppressed; accountability; an institutional orientation; respect for the spiritual and religious beliefs of others; and promoting social and economic justice and safeguarding human rights.

F *Briefly describe educational training for social work practice.*

The primary educational objective for undergraduate social work programs accredited by the CSWE is preparation for beginning professional social work practice. All accredited undergraduate and graduate social work programs are required to train their students for generalist practice. (MSW programs, in addition, usually require their students to select and study in an area of concentration.)

Whether or not you decide to pursue social work as a career, you can get involved in combating human problems.

Competency Notes

EP 2.1.3a Distinguish, appraise, and integrate multiple sources of knowledge, including research-based knowledge and practice wisdom. (All of this chapter) This chapter describes generalist social work practice. It summarizes the following: roles of social workers; social work with individuals, families, groups, organizations, and the community; knowledge, skills, and values for social work practice; and social work education.

EP 2.1.1a through EP 2.1.10m All the competencies and practice behaviors of the 2008 EPAS (pp. 93–99). This section reprints the knowledge, skills, and values needed for social work practice, as stated in the 2008 EPAS.

Media Resources

Additional resources for this chapter, including a chapter quiz, can be found on the Social Work CourseMate. Go to CengageBrain.com.

Notes

1. Donald Brieland, Lela B. Costin, and Charles R. Atherton, eds., *Contemporary Social Work: An Introduction to Social Work and Social Welfare,* 3rd ed. (New York: McGraw-Hill, 1985), pp. 120–121.
2. G. H. Hull, *Social Work Internship Manual* (Eau Claire: University of Wisconsin-Eau Claire, Department of Social Work, 1990), p. 17.
3. BPD, "Definition of Generalist Practice," discussed and advanced by the BPD Social Work Continuum Committee and approved by the BPD Board of Directors, 2006.
4. Council on Social Work Education, *Educational Policy and Accreditation Standards* (Alexandria, VA: Council on Social Work Education, 2008).
5. Ibid., reprinted with permission from the Council on Social Work Education.
6. Ibid.
7. Felix P. Biestek, *The Casework Relationship* (Chicago: Loyola University Press, 1957).

8. Alfred Kadushin, *Child Welfare Services*, 3rd ed. (New York: Macmillan, 1980).

9. Virginia Satir, *Conjoint Family Therapy*, rev. ed. (Palo Alto, CA: Science & Behavior Books, 1967); Virginia Satir, *Peoplemaking* (Palo Alto, CA: Science & Behavior Books, 1972).

10. Satir, *Conjoint Family Therapy*, pp. 8–10.

11. Ibid., p. 92.

12. Irene Goldenberg and Herbert Goldenberg, *Family Therapy*, 3rd ed. (Pacific Grove, CA: Brooks/Cole, 1991), p. 242.

13. B. Okun and L. Rappaport, *Working with Families: An Introduction to Family Therapy* (North Scituate, MA: Duxbury Press, 1980), p. 93.

14. David W. Johnson and Frank P. Johnson, *Joining Together: Group Theory and Group Skills*, 5th ed. (Boston: Allyn & Bacon, 1994), p. 13.

15. Gerald L. Euster, "Services to Groups," in *Contemporary Social Work*, Donald Brieland, Lela B. Costin, and Charles R. Atherton, eds. (New York: McGraw-Hill, 1975), p. 227.

16. Ralph Dolgoff and Donald Feldstein, *Understanding Social Welfare* (New York: Harper & Row, 1980), pp. 27–42.

17. Alfred H. Katz and Eugene I. Bender, *The Strength in Us: Self-Help Groups in the Modern World* (New York: Franklin-Watts, 1976), p. 9.

18. Frank Riessman, "The 'Helper Therapy' Principle," *Journal of Social Work* (April 1965), pp. 27–34.

19. Johnson and Johnson, *Joining Together*.

20. Ibid.

21. A Etzioni, *Modern Organizations* (Englewood Cliffs, NJ: Prentice Hall, 1964), p. 1.

22. F. E. Netting, P. M. Kettner, and S. L. McMurtry, *Social Work Macro Practice*, 2nd ed. (New York: Longman, 1998), pp. 193–194.

23. F. E. Netting, P. M. Kettner, S. L. McMurtry, and M. L. Thomas, *Social Work Macro Practice*, 5th ed. (New York: Pearson, 2012).

24. R. Knopf, *Surviving the BS (Bureaucratic System)* (Wilmington, NC: Mandala Press, 1979), pp. 21–22.

25. Ibid., p. 25.

26. Ibid.

27. Ibid.

28. A. Panitch, "Community Organization," in *Contemporary Social Work*, 2nd ed., Donald Brieland, Lela B. Costin, and Charles R. Atherton, eds. (New York: McGraw-Hill, 1980), pp. 124–125.

29. Neil Gilbert and Harry Specht, "Social Planning and Community Organization: Approaches," *Encyclopedia of Social Work*, 17th ed. (Washington, DC: NASW, 1977), pp. 1412–1425.

30. Ibid.

31. Jack Rothman and John E. Tropman, "Models of Community Organization and Macro Practice Perspectives: Their Mixing and Phasing," in *Strategies of Community Organization*, 4th ed., Fred Cox, John Erlich, Jack Rothman, and John E. Tropman, eds. (Itasca, IL: F. E. Peacock, 1987), pp. 3–26.

32. Saul Alinsky, *Rules for Radicals* (New York: Random House, 1972), p. 130.

33. Saul Alinsky, *Reveille for Radicals* (New York: Basic Books, 1969), p. 72.

34. Allen Pincus and Anne Minahan, *Social Work Practice: Model and Method* (Itasca, IL: F. E. Peacock, 1973), p. 38.

35. Albert Ellis and R. Harper, *A New Guide to Rational Living* (North Hollywood, CA: Wilshire Books, 1975).

36. C. H. Cooley, *Human Nature and the Social Order* (New York: Scribner's, 1902).

37. William Glasser, *The Identity Society* (New York: Harper & Row, 1972).

38. Thomas Gordon, *Parent Effectiveness Training* (New York: Wyden, 1973).

39. "*Tarasoff* v. *Regents of University of California:* The Psychotherapist's Peril," *University of Pittsburgh Law Review*, 37 (1975), pp. 159–164.

40. Suanna J. Wilson, *Confidentiality in Social Work: Issues and Principles* (New York: Free Press, 1978), pp. 116–117.

41. Ibid., p. 121.

42. Donald T. Dickson, *Confidentiality and Privacy in Social Work* (New York: Free Press, 1998), pp. 124–125.

43. Ibid., p. 125.

44. K. Miley, "Religion and Spirituality as Central Social Work Concerns," paper presented at Midwest Biennial Conference on Social Work Education, LaCrosse, WI, April 9–10, 1992, p. 2.

45. L. E. Furman, "Religion and Spirituality in Social Work Education," paper presented at Midwest Biennial Conference on Social Work Education, St. Paul, MN, April 28–29, 1994, p. 10.

46. Council on Social Work Education, *Educational Policy and Accreditation Standards*.

47. Ibid.

48. National Association of Social Workers, *Code of Ethics,* Revised and adopted by the 1996 Delegate Assembly of NASW (Washington, DC: NASW Press, 1996), p. 27.

49. Council on Social Work Education, *Educational Policy and Accreditation Standards.*

50. Ibid.

51. E. Reichert, *Challenges in Human Rights: A Social Work Perspective* (New York: Columbia University Press).

52. Ibid., p. 41.

53. United Nations, *Universal Declaration of Human Rights.* Adopted December 10, 1948. GA, Res. 2200 AXXI (New York: United Nations). Reprinted by permission.

54. Reichert, *Challenges in Human Rights*, p. 8.

55. Council on Social Work Education, *Standards for the Accreditation of Baccalaureate Degree Programs in Social Work* (New York: CSWE, 1974), p. 13.

56. Council on Social Work Education, *Educational Policy and Accreditation Standards.*

57. Ibid.

Poverty and Public Welfare

Poverty has always been one of the most serious social problems in the United States. (In most other countries, it is even more severe.) In our modern, civilized society, one of six Americans is poor.[1] This chapter will:

Learning Objectives

EP 2.1.3a

A   Describe the extent of poverty and the effects of living in poverty.

B   Discuss the income and wealth gaps between the rich and the poor in the United States.

C   Summarize the causes of poverty and identify the population groups with the lowest income levels.

D   Outline current programs to combat poverty and discuss their merits and shortcomings.

E   Present strategies to reduce poverty in the future.

F   Describe a social worker's role in motivating people who are discouraged.

The Problem

In 2012 over 46 million people, about 15% of our population, were living below the poverty line.[2] (The poverty line is the level of income that the federal government considers sufficient to meet basic requirements of food, shelter, and clothing.) A cause for alarm is that the rate of poverty is higher now than it was in 1980, and the poverty rate in 2012 was nearly as high as it was in 1966.[3]

Poverty does not mean simply that poor people in the United States are living less well than those of average income. It means that the poor are often hungry. Many are malnourished, with some turning to dog food or cat food for nourishment. Poverty may mean not having running water, living in substandard housing, and being exposed to rats, cockroaches, and other vermin. It means not having sufficient heat in the winter and being unable to sleep because the walls are too thin to deaden the sounds from the people living next door. It means being embarrassed about the few ragged clothes that one has to wear. It means great susceptibility to emotional disturbances, alcoholism, and victimization by criminals, as well as a shortened life expectancy. It means lack of opportunity to advance oneself socially, economically, or educationally. It often means slum housing, unstable marriages, and few chances to enjoy the finer things in life—traveling, dining out, movies, plays, concerts, and sports events.

The infant mortality rate of the poor is more than double that of the affluent.[4] The poor have less access to medical services and receive lower-quality health care from professionals. The poor are exposed to higher levels of air pollution, water pollution, and unsanitary conditions. They have higher rates of malnutrition and disease. Schools in poor areas are of lower quality and have fewer resources. As a result, the poor achieve less academically and are more likely to drop out of school. They are also more likely to be arrested, indicted, and imprisoned, and they are given longer sentences for the same offenses committed by the nonpoor. They are less likely to receive probation, parole, or suspended sentences.[5]

Poverty also often leads to despair, low self-esteem, and stunted growth—including physical, social, emotional, and intellectual growth. Poverty hurts most when it leads to a view of the self as inferior or second class.

We like to think that the United States is a land of equal opportunity and that there is considerable upward class mobility for those who put forth effort. The reality is the opposite of this myth. Extensive research has shown that poverty is almost "escape proof." Children raised in poor families are likely

Steve Hamblin/Alamy

We like to think that we live in a land of equal opportunity and that upward mobility today is possible for all those who put forth the effort. But the reality is otherwise: poverty is virtually "escape proof."

to live in poverty in their adult years. Most people have much the same social status their parents had. Movement to a higher social status is an unusual happening in practically all societies, including the United States.[6]

A Brief History of Our Response to the Poor

The way a society cares for its needy reflects its values. In nonliterate societies, the needs of those who were not self-sufficient were met by family or other tribal members. During the medieval period in Europe, poor relief was a church responsibility.

The famous Elizabethan Poor Law of 1601 in England combined humanitarianism with the Protestant ethic. This law was enacted because the general public viewed begging (not poverty) as a social

problem. The law established three separate programs: (a) The able-bodied poor were offered work. If they refused, they were whipped, imprisoned, or sent back to their birthplace. (b) The impotent poor (the elderly and disabled) were either given public relief or placed in almshouses. (c) Children whose parents could not provide for them were bound out as apprentices to other adults. This Poor Law established the principles of categorical relief by distinguishing between the able-bodied (undeserving) poor and the impotent (deserving) poor. Nearly all the principles contained within this Poor Law became incorporated into the "relief" programs of colonial America.

In the 19th century, a controversy raged in both England and the United States between advocates of workhouses and supporters of "outdoor relief" (assistance to people in their own homes). Outdoor relief raised concerns about fraud, and citizens feared that cash handouts might destroy moral fiber. On the other hand, workhouses (also called almshouses) were generally overcrowded and unsanitary; contrary to their stated goal, they offered no activity for the able-bodied. Also in the 19th century, the first social service organizations sprang up in urban areas to serve the needy. These organizations were private and church sponsored and primarily offered food and shelter. They attempted to solve personal problems with religious admonitions.

As you will recall from the discussions in Chapters 1 and 2, Americans, until the Great Depression, believed in the myth of individualism—that is, each person is master of his or her own fate. Those in need were viewed as lazy, as unintelligent, or as justly punished for their sinful ways (see Case Exhibit 4.1).

The Great Depression of the 1930s called into question the individualism myth. Nearly one-third of the workforce was unemployed.[7] With large numbers of people out of work, including those from the middle class, a new view of relief applicants developed: These people were not essentially different from others who were caught up in circumstances beyond their control. Private relief agencies (including private agencies receiving funding support from local governing entities) were unable to meet the financial needs of the unemployed. There was a rapid breakdown in traditional local methods of aiding the poor.

Harry Hopkins, a social worker from Iowa, was appointed by President Franklin Roosevelt to oversee national employment programs and emergency

The Ideology of Individualism

Wealth is generally inherited in this country; few individuals actually move up the social-status ladder on their own. Having wealth opens up many doors (through education and contacts) for children to make large sums of money when they become adults. For children living in poverty, there is little chance to escape when they become older. Yet the individualism myth is held by many. It states that the rich are personally responsible for their success and that the poor are to blame for their failure. The main points of this individualism myth are:

1. Each individual should work hard and strive to succeed in competition with others.
2. Those who work hard should be rewarded with success (such as wealth, property, prestige, and power).

3. Because of extensive employment opportunities and because of equal opportunity legislation, those who work hard will in fact be rewarded with success.
4. Economic failure is an individual's own fault and reveals lack of effort and other character defects.

In our society, the poor are blamed for their circumstances. As a result, a stigma has been attached to poverty, particularly to those who receive public assistance (welfare). Although the belief in individualism is less strongly held now than it was prior to the Great Depression of the 1930s, remnants still remain today.

assistance. Hopkins became one of Roosevelt's closest advisers and exerted considerable influence in designing and enacting the 1935 Social Security program. As indicated in Chapter 1, this program was of major significance because it initiated the federal government's role in three areas: (a) social insurance programs, (b) public assistance, and (c) social services.

After 1935 the economy of our country slowly began to recover. Some of those who had been living in poverty began to enjoy a more affluent lifestyle—even though many other Americans remained in poverty. The poor were left behind and forgotten. Public concern shifted to World War II in the early 1940s and then to other issues, such as the feared spread of communism and the Korean War. From the 1940s through the 1950s, poverty was no longer recognized or addressed as a major problem—even though large segments of the population continued to live in abject poverty.

In 1960 John Kennedy saw large numbers of people in many states living in degrading circumstances due to poverty. He made this a central issue in his national presidential campaign. Hence, poverty was once again defined as a major social problem.

In 1962 Michael Harrington published *The Other America*, which graphically described the plight of the fifth of our population who were living in poverty.[8] The media publicized the poverty issue, and public concern about this problem increased dramatically.

In 1965 President Lyndon Johnson launched his War on Poverty and his plan for creating the "Great Society." Eliminating poverty became one of our nation's highest priorities. Various programs were established: Head Start, Volunteers in Service to America (VISTA), Job Corps, Title I Educational Funding, Community Action Program, Youth Corps, and Neighborhood Legal Services.

Although these programs reduced poverty somewhat, the optimistic hope of the early 1960s that poverty could be eradicated was short lived. In the late 1960s, the Vietnam War drained resources that would otherwise have been spent on domestic programs. It also turned attention away from poverty and finally drove Johnson from office. During periods of economic growth, it is easier for a society to allocate resources to the poor in an effort to share the national wealth.

In the mid-1970s, after the end of the Vietnam War, the turmoil of the late 1960s was replaced for several years by an atmosphere of relative calm on both the foreign and domestic levels. In contrast to the hope of the 1960s that government programs could cure our social ills, the opposing philosophy emerged that many problems were beyond the capacity of the government to alleviate. Hence the liberalism of the 1960s, which resulted in the expansion and development of new social programs, was replaced by a more conservative approach in the 1970s and 1980s. Practically no new large-scale social welfare programs were initiated in those two decades.

Government interest in helping the poor waned considerably. Ronald Reagan was elected in 1980, partly on a program designed to give tax cuts to the rich and to provide decreased funds and services to the poor. Allegations of welfare fraud, high tax rates, and increasing relief roles replaced poverty as a national concern. Welfare again became a political "whipping boy." Since the 1970s, there has been a shift away from a liberalized extension of public responsibility to help the poor.

Past history suggests that as government expenditures to help the poor (and the marginally poor) decrease, the proportion of the population living in poverty increases. Since 1980 there have been significant cutbacks in federal funding of programs for the poor, and the proportion of people living in poverty has risen.[9]

In 1988 George Bush was elected president on a conservative platform, and he continued the social welfare policies of his predecessor. The Reagan and Bush administrations endorsed an economic program that cut taxes (which primarily benefited the rich) and cut government spending on social welfare programs (which primarily hurt the poor). The result was that the income gap between the rich and the poor widened.[10] The people who were hurt the most were recipients of federally financed social welfare programs who received reduced services and sharp reductions in financial assistance.

Bill Clinton was elected president in 1992. During his campaign, Clinton promised "to end welfare as we know it." He was referring specifically to federal entitlement programs, particularly Aid to Families of Dependent Children (AFDC). AFDC was a major component of the so-called social safety net of measures designed to prevent poverty from turning into starvation and abject destitution. The conservative sweep of both houses of Congress in 1994 and President Clinton's endorsement of welfare reform legislation prior to the 1996 presidential election were important political steps toward the most far-reaching changes in support for poor families and individuals since the 1930s. The 1996 welfare reform legislation (also known as the Personal Responsibility and Work Opportunity Reconciliation Act) ended the 60-year-old AFDC program. This legislation replaced the AFDC program with Temporary Assistance to Needy Families (TANF).

Under 1996 welfare reform legislation, parents whose household incomes fall below a given level (depending on the size of the household) are no longer entitled to federal funds administered through state and county welfare agencies. Instead, states now receive block grants (that is, large sums of money earmarked for assistance to the poor) from the federal government. Federal requirements of these block grants specify that recipients of financial benefits cannot receive more than 2 years of financial assistance without working, and there is a 5-year limit on benefits for adults. (States have the option of exempting up to 20% of their recipients from these requirements and time limits.) In 1935, when the AFDC program was enacted as a component of the Social Security Act, it was thought that single mothers should stay at home to raise their children. The 1996 welfare reform legislation asserts that single mothers (and fathers) now have an obligation to work for a living.

The assumption underlying the TANF program was that, in order to avoid a long-term welfare class, all jobless people should work, whether or not they have children. In line with this view, public assistance was changed from a form of support for family welfare to a temporary means of helping people until they become part of the labor force.

What will be the long-term effects of this welfare-to-work legislation? Will the legislation harm poor people, particularly poor children? (Later in this chapter we will review results of the studies conducted on the merits and shortcomings of TANF.) The long-term effects of TANF are, as yet, not fully known.

George W. Bush was elected president in 2000 and reelected in 2004. During his administration there were no major changes in federal social welfare programs; much of his administration's focus was on the war in Iraq.

Barack Obama was elected president in November 2008. He ran on a platform that had the component of reducing the inequality of wealth and income between the rich and the lower/middle classes in our society. From about 2007 to the present, there was a global recession. Many large corporations responded by trimming their workforce and cutting their expenditures. The rate of those unemployed increased (to nearly 10% in the United States), and the percent in poverty increased—while corporations prospered.[10] The result has been that the rich became richer, the poor became poorer, and the size of the middle class decreased—with some middle-class individuals moving to a lower income status.[11] The gap between the rich and poor in the United States has in fact widened. Case Exhibit 4.2 highlights income disparities in the United States.

CASE EXHIBIT 4.2

Personal Income Disparities Are Astounding

In some countries in the world, the average per capita income is less than $500 per year. In the United States, over 46 million people (about 15% of the population) are living in poverty. (In 2012 the poverty threshold for a family of four was $22,350.)

In the fall of 1997, Kevin Garnett signed a 6-year deal for $123 million with the Minnesota Timberwolves, a professional team in the National Basketball Association (NBA). The deal, which amounted to an average of $20.5 million per year, was (at the time) the richest long-term sports contract. Kevin Garnett was only 20 years old when he signed. He joined the NBA after high school, without ever attending (or playing basketball in) college.

In the fall of 2007, Alex Rodriguez signed a 10-year deal for $275 million with the New York Yankees (a professional baseball team). The deal of $27.5 million per year then became the richest long-term sports contract.

In a single year (June 1998 to June 1999), the personal worth of Bill Gates (the richest person in the world) rose $39 billion, from $51 billion to $90 billion!

During this 1-year period, he made an astounding average of $750 million per week, which is over $100 million per day! Bill Gates is the chairman of Microsoft Corporation.

Globally, Kornblum and Julian note:

A growing gap between the haves and the have-nots exists throughout the world. One-fifth of the world's people live in the richest nations (including the United States), and their average incomes are 15 times higher than those of the one-fifth who live in the poorest nations. In the world today there are about 160 billionaires and about 2 million millionaires, but there are approximately 100 million homeless people. Americans spend about $5 billion per year on diets to lower their caloric intake, while 400 million people around the world are undernourished to the point of physical deterioration.[a]

[a]William Kornblum and Joseph Julian, *Social Problems*, 14th ed. (Boston: Pearson, 2012), p. 188.

The Rich and the Poor

Throughout most countries in the world, wealth is concentrated in the hands of a few individuals and families. Poverty and wealth are closely related in that abundance for a few is often created through deprivation of others.

There are two ways of measuring the extent of economic inequality. *Income* refers to the amount of money a person makes in a given year. *Wealth* refers to a person's total assets—real estate holdings, cash, stocks, bonds, and so forth.

The distribution of wealth and income is highly unequal in our society. Like most countries, the United States is characterized by *social stratification;* that is, it has social classes, with the upper classes having by far the greatest access to the pleasures that money can buy.

Critical Thinking Question

What changes would you have to make if you were forced to live on $2 a day?

Although this chapter focuses on poverty in the United States, it is important to note that there is a

growing gap between the rich and the poor in most countries. Kornblum and Julian note:

These growing disparities between rich and poor throughout the world have a direct bearing on the situation of the poor in the United States because American jobs are being "exported" to areas where extremely poor people are willing to accept work at almost any wage. World poverty also contributes to environmental degradation, political instability, and violence, which drain resources that could be used to meet the nation's domestic needs.[12]

In the United States, the top 1% of all households have over one-third of all personal wealth.[13] The distribution of income is even more unequal: the wealthiest 20% of households in the United States receive over 50% of all income, whereas the poorest 20% receive less than 5% of all income.[14]

In the words of a pastoral letter issued by a committee of Roman Catholic bishops, "The level of inequality in income and wealth in our society...must be judged morally unacceptable."[15] Paul Samuelson, an economist, provides a dramatic metaphor of the disparity between the very rich and most people in the United States:

If we made an income pyramid out of a child's blocks, with each layer portraying $1,000 of

CASE EXAMPLE 4.1

Wealth Perpetuates Wealth and Poverty Perpetuates Poverty

The following summaries of the life experiences of two people illustrate that in the United States, wealth perpetuates wealth and poverty perpetuates poverty.

Tim Mills is the son of wealthy parents (both of whom also had parents in the upper social class). Tim Mills's mother, Suzanne, is a successful stockbroker, and his father, David, is a successful attorney. (Their household income is in excess of $300,000 per year.) After Tim was born, he was always dressed in the finest clothes money could buy, and his parents focused on providing extensive early stimulation and the highest-quality educational experiences. He attended expensive private schools in kindergarten, elementary school, middle school, and high school. The schools had low student-to-teacher ratios, so Tim Mills received extensive attention from his teachers. Tim's parents were always highly involved in the parent–teacher associations in the school systems, which encouraged the teachers to give Tim extra attention, and also to praise him frequently, which contributed to Tim developing a positive self-concept and a high level of self-confidence.

Tim's parents liked to travel to other countries two or three times a year, and they always took Tim along, which contributed to his learning to understand and appreciate diversity and other cultures. It also led Tim to understand that he needed to attain a college education to secure a high-paying position and have the privileges that money can buy.

Tim's mother and father had friends who were also in their community's power elite. Tim was introduced to this higher circle and made friends with the children of the parents in this power elite. In this sphere of the power elite, he acquired skills and confidence in his ability to socialize and to increasingly participate in the decisions made by this power elite. After graduating from high school, he attended a prestigious private college on the East Coast, which many of his high school friends also attended. Upon graduation from the 4-year college, he attended a prestigious law school and graduated with honors. His father's connections helped him join a distinguished law firm as a corporate attorney upon receiving his law degree. A year after graduating from law school, he married Virginia DeMarco, a lawyer he met in law school

who had a similar upper-class background. Five years later, their annual household income was in excess of $500,000.

In contrast, the following summary of Marcee Calvello's life describes how poverty and dismal living conditions lead to despair, hopelessness, and failure.

Marcee Calvello was born and raised in New York City. Her father had trouble holding a job because he was addicted to cocaine, and her mother was an alcoholic who divorced her husband when Marcee was 3 years old. Marcee's mother at first sought to provide a better home for Marcee and her three brothers. She worked at a minimum-wage job. However, her addiction to alcohol consumed most of her time and money. Neighbors reported the children were living in abject neglect, and protective services workers removed Marcee and her brothers to foster care. Marcee was placed in a series of 17 different foster homes. In one of these homes, her foster father sexually assaulted her, and in another a foster brother assaulted her. Being moved from foster home to foster home resulted in frequent school changes. Marcee grew distrustful of the welfare system, schoolteachers and administrators, men, and anyone else who sought to get close to her.

When she turned 18, the state no longer paid for her foster care. She got a small efficiency apartment that cost her several hundred dollars a month. Because she dropped out of school at age 16, she had few marketable job skills. She worked for a while at some fast-food restaurants. The minimum wage she received was insufficient to pay her bills. Eight months after she moved into her apartment, she was evicted. Unable to afford another place, she started living in the subway system of New York City. She soon lost her job at McDonald's because of poor hygiene and an unkempt appearance.

Unable to shower and improve her appearance, she has not been able to secure another job. For the past 2 years she has been homeless, living on the street and in the subway. She has given up hope of improving her situation. She now occasionally shares IV needles and has been sexually assaulted periodically at night in the subway by men. She realizes she is at high risk for acquiring the AIDS virus but no longer cares very much. Death appears to be, to her, the final escape from a life filled with victimization and misery.

income, the peak would be far higher than the Eiffel Tower, but almost all of us would be within a yard of the ground.[16]

More than 1.2 billion people—one in five people on this planet—survive on less than $1 a day.[17] Nearly half of the world's population lives on less than $2 a day.[18]

Given the enormous wealth of the richest 20%, it is clear that a simple redistribution of some of the

wealth from the top one-fifth to the lowest one-fifth could easily wipe out poverty. Of course, that is not politically acceptable to members of the top fifth, who have the greatest control of the government. It should also be noted that many of these rich families avoid paying income taxes by taking advantage of tax loopholes and tax shelters.

An estimated 50 million Americans are hungry, due to lack of financial resources, for at least some period of time each month.[19] Millions of those who go hungry in the United States are children.

Critical Thinking Question

Do you believe there should be a redistribution of some of the wealth from the top one-fifth to the lowest one-fifth in this country?

Hunger can have devastating effects on young children, including causing mental retardation. The brain of an infant grows to 80% of its adult size within the first 3 years of life. If supplies of protein are inadequate during this period, the brain stops growing. The damage is irreversible, and the child will have a permanent cognitive disability.[20]

Coleman and Cressey describe the respective effects of wealth and poverty:

The economic differences between the rich, the poor, and the middle class have profound effects on lifestyles, attitudes toward others, and even attitudes toward oneself. The poor lack the freedom and autonomy so prized in our society. They are trapped by their surroundings, living in run-down, crime-ridden neighborhoods that they cannot afford to leave. They are constantly confronted with things they desire but have little chance to own. On the other hand, wealth provides power, freedom, and the ability to direct one's own fate. The wealthy live where they choose and do as they please, with few economic constraints. Because the poor lack education and money for travel, their horizons seldom extend beyond the confines of their neighborhood. In contrast, the world of the wealthy offers the best education, together with the opportunity to visit places that the poor haven't even heard of.

The children of the wealthy receive the best that society has to offer, as well as the assurance that they are valuable and important individuals. Because the children of the poor lack so many of the things everyone is "supposed" to have, it is much harder for them to develop the cool confidence of the rich. In our materialistic society people are judged as much by what they have as by who they are. The poor cannot help but feel inferior and inadequate in such a context.[21]

Defining Poverty Is a Policy Problem

Despite all the research on poverty, we have yet to agree on how to define the condition. A family of four living on a farm that earns $20,000 per year may not view themselves as being "poverty stricken," especially if they have no rent to pay, are able to grow much of their own food, and are frugal and creative in securing essential needs. On the other hand, a family of four earning $20,000 per year in a city with a high cost of living may be deeply in debt, especially if they pay high rent and are confronted with unexpected medical bills.

The usual definitions of poverty are based on lack of money, and annual income is the measure most commonly applied. There are two general approaches to defining poverty: the absolute approach and the relative approach.

The *absolute approach* holds that a certain amount of goods and services is essential to an individual's or family's welfare. Those who do not have this minimum amount are viewed as poor. The fundamental problem with this approach is that there is no agreement as to what constitutes "minimum" needs. Depending on the income level selected, the number and percentage of the population who are poor change substantially, along with the characteristics of those defined as poor.

A serious problem with the absolute definition of poverty is that it does not take into account the fact that people are poor not only in terms of their own needs but also in relation to others who are not poor. That is, poverty is relative to time and place. Those Americans labeled poor today would certainly not be poor by the standards of 1850; nor would they be viewed as poor by standards existing in India or in other less developed countries. In the 1890s, no one felt particularly poor because of not having electric lights; yet today a family without electricity is usually considered poor.

It is important to realize that the experience of poverty is based on conditions in one's own society. People feel poor or rich with reference to others around them, not with reference to very poor or very rich people elsewhere in the world. To the poor in the United States, it is of little comfort to be informed that they would be regarded as well off (according to their income and wealth) if they lived in Ethiopia (or some other impoverished country).

In some geographic areas, poverty and affluence exist side by side.

The *relative approach* states, in essence, that a person is poor when his or her income is substantially less than the average income of the population. For example, anyone in the lowest one-fifth (or tenth or fourth) of the population is regarded as poor. By defining poverty in these terms, we avoid having to define absolute needs, and we also put more emphasis on the inequality of incomes. With a relative approach, poverty will persist as long as income inequality exists. The major weakness with a relative approach is that it tells us nothing about how badly, or how well, the people at the bottom of the income distribution actually live. With poverty measures, ideally, we want to know not only how many people are poor but also how desperate their living conditions are.

The federal government has generally chosen the absolute approach in defining poverty. The poverty line is raised each year to adjust for inflation. In 2012 the government set the poverty line at $22,350 for a family of four.[22]

Who Are the Poor?

An encouraging trend is that the proportion of the population below the poverty line has gradually decreased in the past 100 years. Prior to the 20th century, a majority of Americans lived in poverty. In 1937 Franklin D. Roosevelt stated: "I see one-third of a nation ill-housed, ill-clad, ill-nourished."[23] In 1962 the President's Council of Economic Advisors estimated that one-fifth of the population was living in poverty.[24] In 2012 about 15% of the population was estimated to be below the poverty line. An alarming concern is that, since 1978, there has been an increase in the proportion of the population that is poor.[25]

Poverty is concentrated in certain population categories, including one-parent families, children, the elderly, large families, and people of color. Educational level, unemployment, and place of residence are also related to poverty.

One-Parent Families

Most one-parent families are headed by a female, and 31% of female-headed families are in poverty, compared to 11% for two-parent families.[26] Single mothers who are members of a racial minority (for example, African Americans, Latinos, Native Americans) are particularly vulnerable to poverty, as they are subjected to double discrimination (race and sex) in the labor market.

Women who work full time are paid on the average only about 77% of what men who work full time are paid.[27] Many single mothers are unable to work due to lack of transportation, the high cost of day-care facilities, and inadequate training. Of the families living in poverty, approximately half are headed by a single mother.[28] About 3 of 10 children in this country are now living apart from one parent, and because of increasing divorce rates, separations, and births outside marriage, it is estimated that nearly one of two children born today will spend part of the first 18 years in a family headed by a single mother.[29] Single-parent families now constitute more than 20% of all families in the United States.[30] The increase in one-parent families has led to an increase in the feminization of poverty. Female-householder, no-husband-present families have become the archetypal poverty-stricken family.

Critical Thinking Question

Which would you rather have—two children, or over one-half million more to spend?

Children

Twenty-six percent of children under the age of 18 are living in poverty.[31] More than one-half of these children live in families with an absentee father.[32]

Older Adults

Many older adults depend on Social Security pensions or public assistance (in the form of Supplemental Security Income) for their basic needs. Since the initiation of the 1964 War on Poverty programs, the population group that has benefited most has been older adults. Programs such as Medicare and Supplemental Security Income, as well as increases in monthly payments under the Old Age, Survivors, Disability, and Health Insurance Program, have reduced the poverty rate among the older adults from over 25% in 1964 to around 10% at the present time.[33]

Large Families

Large families are more likely than smaller ones to be poor, partly because more income is needed as family size increases. The average cost of raising a child from birth to age 18 for a married couple is estimated to be $226,920. The expenses are for food, shelter, and other necessities.[34]

People of Color

Roughly half (48%) of those below the poverty line are White.[35] Although more Whites than any other race live in poverty, the *proportion* of various ethnic populations living in poverty is another matter. African Americans are nearly three times more likely to live in poverty than Whites.[36] Twenty-six percent of Native Americans, 25% of African Americans, and 23% of Latinos have incomes below the official poverty level, as compared to about 10% of the non-Latino White population.[37] Racial discrimination is a major reason most racial minorities are disproportionately poor.

Education

Attainment of less than a ninth-grade education is a good predictor of poverty. A high school diploma, however, is not a guarantee that one will earn wages adequate to avoid poverty, as many of the poor have graduated from high school. A college degree is an excellent predictor of avoiding poverty; only a small proportion of those with a college degree are impoverished.[38]

Employment

Being unemployed is, of course, associated with being poor. However, being employed is not a guarantee of avoiding poverty; about 1.5 million heads of families work full time, but their income is below the poverty level.[39] The general public (and many government officials) wrongly assumes that employment is the key to ending poverty. However, jobs alone cannot end poverty.

Place of Residence

People who live in rural areas have a higher incidence of poverty than those in urban areas. In rural areas, wages are low, unemployment is high, and work tends to be seasonal. The Ozarks, Appalachia, and the South have pockets of rural poverty with high rates of unemployment.[40]

People who live in deteriorated areas of cities constitute the largest geographical group in terms of numbers of poor people. The cities of the Northeast and Midwest have particularly large deteriorated areas. Poverty is also extensive on Native American reservations and among seasonal migrant workers.

All these factors indicate that some people are more vulnerable to poverty than others. Michael Harrington, who coined the term *other America* for the poor in the United States, notes that the poor made the simple mistake of:

> *Being born to the wrong parents, in the wrong section of the country, in the wrong industry, or in the wrong racial or ethnic group. Once that mistake has been made, they could have been paragons of will and morality, but most of them would never even have had a chance to get out of the other America.*[41]

Causes of Poverty

There are a number of possible causes of poverty:

- High unemployment
- Poor physical health
- Physical disabilities
- Emotional problems
- Extensive medical bills
- Alcoholism
- Drug addiction
- Large families
- Job displacements due to automation
- Lack of an employable skill
- Low educational level
- Households with young children headed by females only
- Lack of cost-of-living increases for people on fixed incomes

- Racial discrimination
- Being labeled an "ex-convict" or "crazy"
- Residence in a geographic area where jobs are scarce
- Divorce, desertion, or death of a spouse
- Gambling
- Budgeting problems and mismanagement of resources
- Sex discrimination
- Consequences of being a crime victim
- Anti-work-ethic values
- Underemployment
- Low-paying jobs
- Having a cognitive disability
- Retirement

This list is not exhaustive. However, it shows that there are many causes of poverty. Eliminating the causes of poverty would require a wide range of social programs. Poverty interacts with almost all other social problems—emotional problems, alcoholism, unemployment, racial and sex discrimination, medical problems, crime, gambling, and so on. The interaction between poverty and these other social problems is complex. As indicated, these other social problems are contributing causes of poverty. Yet, for some social problems, poverty is also a contributing *cause* of those problems (such as emotional problems, alcoholism, and unemployment). Being poor intensifies the effects (the hurt) of all social problems.

The Culture of Poverty

To some extent, poverty is passed on from generation to generation in a cycle (Figure 4.1). Why? Some authorities argue that the explanation can be found in a "culture of poverty." Oscar Lewis, an anthropologist, is one of the chief proponents of this cultural explanation.[42]

Lewis examined poor neighborhoods in various parts of the world and concluded that people are poor because they have a distinct culture or lifestyle. The culture of poverty arises after extended periods of economic deprivation in highly stratified capitalistic societies. Such economic deprivation is brought about by high rates of unemployment for unskilled labor and by low wages for those who are employed. Such economic deprivation leads to the development of attitudes and values of despair and hopelessness. Lewis describes these attitudes and values as follows:

The individual who grows up in this culture has a strong feeling of fatalism, helplessness, dependence,

and inferiority, a strong present-time orientation with relatively little disposition to defer gratification and plan for the future, a high tolerance for psychological pathology of all kinds.[43]

Once developed, this culture continues to exist, even when the economic factors that created it (for example, lack of employment opportunities) no longer exist. The culture's attitudes, norms, and expectations serve to limit opportunities and prevent escape. A major reason the poor remain locked into their culture is that they are socially isolated. They have few contacts with groups outside their own culture and are hostile toward the social services and educational institutions that might help them escape poverty. They reject such institutions because they perceive them as belonging to the dominant class. Furthermore, because they view their financial circumstances as private and hopeless and because they lack political and organizational skills, they do not take collective action to resolve their problems.

The culture-of-poverty theory has been controversial and widely criticized. Eleanor Leacock argues that the distinctive culture of the poor is not the *cause* but the *result* of their continuing poverty.[44] She agrees that the poor tend to emphasize "instant gratification," which involves spending and enjoying one's money while it lasts. But she argues that instant gratification is a result of being poor, because it makes no sense to defer gratification when one is pessimistic about the future. Deferred gratification is a rational response only when one is optimistic that postponing pleasures today by saving money will reap greater benefits in the future. (Interestingly, studies have found that when residents of deteriorated neighborhoods obtain a stable, well-paying job, they then display the middle-class value of deferred gratification.)[45] Because of poverty, Leacock argues, the poor are forced to abandon middle-class attitudes and values, which are irrelevant to their circumstances.

In an even stronger indictment, William Ryan criticizes the culture-of-poverty theory as being simply a classic example of "blaming the victim."[46] Blaming the poor for their circumstances is a convenient excuse, according to Ryan, for refusing to endorse the programs and policies thought necessary to eradicate poverty. The real culprit is the social system that allows poverty to exist. Ryan says bluntly that the poor are not poor because of their culture but because they do not have enough money.

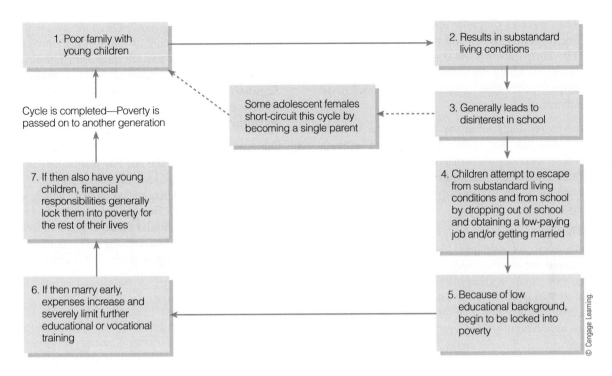

FIGURE 4.1 Cycle of Poverty

Critical Thinking Question

Do you believe the culture-of-poverty theory is valid?

Pro and con arguments for the culture-of-poverty theory persist. There are many reasons, both external and internal, why a person may be poor. External reasons include high rates of unemployment and underemployment; racial discrimination; automation, which throws people out of work; lack of job training programs; sex discrimination; a shortage of antipoverty programs; and inflation. Internal reasons include physical or mental impairment, alcoholism, obsolete job skills, early parenthood, lack of education, and lack of interest in taking available jobs.

Functions of Poverty

Obviously, poverty is dysfunctional—mainly to the poor themselves, but also to the affluent. However, the realization that poverty also has some functions in society can help us understand why some decision makers are not actively seeking to eradicate it.

Eleven functions are provided by the poor to affluent groups:

1. They are available to do the unpleasant jobs no one else wants to do.
2. Their activities subsidize the more affluent (for example, domestic service for low pay).
3. They help create jobs (for example, jobs for social workers who provide services to the poor).
4. They purchase poor-quality goods that otherwise could not be sold.
5. They serve as examples of deviance to be frowned on by the majority, thereby supporting dominant norms.
6. They provide an opportunity for others to practice their "Christian duty" of helping the less fortunate.
7. They make mobility more likely for others because they are removed from the competition for good education and good jobs.
8. They contribute to cultural activities (for example, by providing cheap labor for the construction of monuments and works of art).
9. They create cultural forms (such as jazz and the blues) that are often adopted by the affluent.

10. They serve as symbolic opponents for some political groups and as constituents for others.
11. They often absorb the costs of change (for example, by being the victims of high levels of unemployment that result from technological advances).[47]

Furthermore, denigrating the poor has the psychological function for some Americans of making them feel better about themselves.

Ehrenreich further elaborates on how the working poor are, in reality, the major philanthropists in our society:

> When someone works for less pay than she can live on—when, for example, she goes hungry so that you can eat more cheaply and conveniently—then she has made a great sacrifice for you, she has made you a gift of some part of her abilities, her health, and her life. The "working poor," as they are approvingly termed, are in fact the major philanthropists of our society. They neglect their own children so that the children of others will be cared for; they live in substandard housing so that other homes will be shiny and perfect; they endure privation so that inflation will be low and stock prices high. To be a member of the working poor is to be an anonymous donor, a nameless benefactor, to everyone else.[48]

Partly because poverty is functional, our society makes only a halfhearted effort to eliminate—or even reduce—it. To do so would result in a redistribution of income from the rich to the poor, a policy generally seen as undemocratic (sometimes communistic), even by the not-so-affluent. Because the rich control the political power, proposals that would eliminate poverty (such as guaranteed annual income programs) have generally met with opposition. Gans emphasizes this point:

> Legislation in America tends to favor the interests of the businessman, not the consumers, even though the latter are a vast majority; of landlords, not tenants; of doctors, not patients. Only organized interest groups have the specific concerns and the time, staff, and money to bring their demands before government officials....The poor are powerless because they are a minority of the population, are not organized politically, are often difficult to organize, and are not even a homogeneous group with similar interests that could be organized

> into a single pressure group....Given the antagonism toward them on the part of many Americans, any programs that would provide them with significant gains are likely to be voted down by a majority. Legislative proposals for a massive antipoverty effort...have always run into concerted and united opposition in Washington.[49]

Our government has the resources to eliminate poverty—but not the will. In the last 100 years our country has been able to find billions of dollars in resources within a few months when we go to war (which has happened several times). But our government has not been willing to allocate similar funds to improve living conditions for the homeless and for millions of other people who are living in poverty in this country.

Social Insurance Programs

Because poverty relates to nearly every other social problem, almost every existing social service—to some extent—works to combat poverty (including Alcoholics Anonymous, health care programs, vocational rehabilitation, Parents Without Partners, foster care, adoption, day care, Head Start, housing programs, urban renewal, and community action programs). Such programs indirectly reduce poverty by alleviating related social problems. These programs are too numerous to describe fully in this text. This section will instead describe social insurance programs, and the next section will describe public assistance programs. (Social insurance programs are financed by taxes on employees, on employers, or on both. Public assistance program benefits are paid from general government revenues.)

Old Age, Survivors, Disability, and Health Insurance (OASDHI)

This social insurance program was created by the 1935 Social Security Act. Generally, OASDHI is referred to as "Social Security" by the public. It is the largest income insurance program and is designed to partially replace income that is lost when a worker retires or becomes disabled. Cash benefits are also paid to survivors of "insured" workers.

Payments to beneficiaries are based on previous earnings. The rich as well as the poor are eligible if insured. Benefits are provided to fully insured workers at age 65 or older (somewhat smaller benefits can be taken at age 62).

The full retirement age is gradually increasing for those who are born after 1937, as shown on the following chart:

YEAR OF BIRTH	FULL RETIREMENT AGE
1937 (or earlier)	65
1938	65 and 2 months
1939	65 and 4 months
1940	65 and 6 months
1941	65 and 8 months
1942	65 and 10 months
1943–54	66
1955	66 and 2 months
1956	66 and 4 months
1957	66 and 6 months
1958	66 and 8 months
1959	66 and 10 months
1960 (and later)	67

Dependent husbands or wives over age 62 and dependent children under age 18 (there is no age limit on disabled children who become disabled before 18) are also covered under the retirement benefits.

Participation in this insurance program is compulsory for most employees. The program is financed by a payroll tax assessed equally to employer and employee. The rate has gone up gradually. Eligibility for benefits is based on the number of years in which Social Security taxes have been paid.

A major concern has been the financial soundness of OASDHI. Since 1935 the Social Security (FICA) tax has led to a buildup in the trust fund for OASDHI. But the liberalization of benefits and the increased number of recipients in recent years have raised concern about the system paying out more than it takes in. In times of high unemployment and recession, the number of workers paying into OASDHI is decreased. The decline in the birthrate, along with a steady increase in the retired population, may jeopardize the financial soundness of the program; the number of recipients is increasing at a faster rate than the number of workers paying into the system. If OASDHI is to remain financially sound, benefits may have to be scaled back, FICA taxes increased, or both.

Medicare

In 1965 Congress enacted Title XVIII (Medicare) to the Social Security Act. Medicare has two parts: hospital insurance and medical insurance. Hospital insurance helps pay for inpatient hospital care, inpatient care in a skilled nursing facility, home health care, and hospice care. Medical insurance helps pay for medically necessary doctors' services, outpatient hospital services, and a number of other medical services and supplies that are not covered by the hospital insurance part of Medicare. The hospital insurance part is financed by a surcharge on the Social Security taxes paid by employers and employees. The medical insurance part is a voluntary insurance plan for which enrollees are charged a monthly premium. (More than two-thirds of the costs of the medical insurance premium is paid from general revenues of the federal government.) Medicare, a public health insurance program, is described more fully in Chapter 15.

Unemployment Insurance

This program was also created by the 1935 Social Security Act and provides benefits to workers who have been laid off or, in certain cases, fired. Unemployment insurance is financed by a tax on employers. The amount and duration of weekly benefits vary from state to state. In many states, the unemployed are eligible for benefits for about a year. To be eligible in most states, a person must (a) have worked a certain number of weeks in covered employment; (b) be ready, willing, and able to work; (c) file a claim for benefits and be registered in a public employment office; and (d) demonstrate that unemployment is due to a lack of work for which she or he is qualified.

Unemployment insurance benefits help individuals and families who become unemployed due to a lack of work. In our society, in which employment is valued highly, being without work can be a demeaning experience. In the past three decades, the unemployment rate has ranged from 3% to 11% of able-bodied workers. High rates clearly indicate a lack of available jobs. Yet the unemployment insurance program has been sharply criticized by claims that some of the unemployed would rather collect insurance benefits than make a concerted effort to obtain employment.

Workers' Compensation Insurance

This program provides both income and assistance in meeting medical expenses for injuries sustained on a job. The program was enacted after a series of lawsuits by injured employees against employers—the only recourse employees had. The first workers' compensation program was the Federal Employees

Compensation Act of 1908. Individual states gradually passed workers' compensation laws modeled after the program for federal employees. By 1920 all but six states had such laws, but it was not until 1948 that all states had adequate coverage.[50] Cash benefits are paid for total or temporary disability or death. Medical benefits cover hospital and doctors' fees. Rehabilitation benefits are also available for those needing after-care and retraining to again become employable. Workers' compensation is financed by a tax on employers.

Public Assistance Programs

Public assistance is sometimes viewed as synonymous with "welfare" by the general public, yet there are hundreds of other social welfare programs. Public assistance has primarily residual aspects, and applicants must undergo a "means test" that reviews their assets and liabilities to determine their eligibility for benefits.

Adherents of the residual view of public assistance generally hold the following opinions:

1. Assistance should be made as unpleasant as possible to discourage its use. This is to be accomplished by giving relief in kind (for example, food or clothes) rather than money, by continually reevaluating need, by making it only temporary, by stopping it and/or threatening prosecution if illegitimacy is involved, and by removing children from their own homes when these homes do not meet minimal standards.

2. Relief should also be made unpleasant by requiring recipients to work for it regardless of the nature of the work, how depressed the wage, or whether the requirement would be used as a means for securing cheap labor; notwithstanding, income from this work is still labeled relief.

3. Assistance should be discouraged by making payments too low for anyone to really want it. It is argued by advocates of this approach that assistance in amounts greater than would be received by the lowest paid, most menial worker would encourage individuals to seek assistance in lieu of employment.

4. Outsiders should be prevented from seeking help (they may receive only emergency aid and only for short periods).

5. People should be forced to remain at their jobs or to return to employment; this is accomplished by denying assistance to anyone who is guilty of a "voluntary quit."[51]

In contrast, the institutional view of public assistance (generally held by social workers) assumes or advocates the following:

1. Adequate income and the elimination of hunger and destitution should be provided for all citizens as an instrument of social policy.

2. Relief should be extended to applicants who can qualify under eligibility requirements; that is, subjective, biased, and capricious considerations should be removed. Relief should be based on need as it is determined to exist by objective, rather than subjective, criteria and as a legally determined right.

3. It is assumed that workers generally prefer income from employment over public welfare and that motivations to work are built into the economy in the form of social, cultural, and economic advantages to the employed man or woman.

4. Psychological and social barriers sometimes stand in the way of rehabilitation and employment. Counseling and other services may be needed to restore certain individuals to economic and social self-sufficiency.

5. Preservation of the independence and self-respect of the applicant for assistance is a prime consideration in the administration of programs of relief.

6. A punitive approach defeats the purpose for which assistance is used—namely, the restoration of the individual to normal functioning; it deepens feelings of inadequacy and dependency, causes embarrassment and humiliation, and brings destructive psychological defenses into play.

7. There are many pulls in society that make work more appealing than public welfare, such as a higher standard of living and the prestige and sense of importance one receives from gainful employment.[52]

Public assistance programs have several distinguishing features:

- *Programs have a means test.* Individuals applying for assistance have their income and assets examined to determine whether their financial needs meet the eligibility requirements. The means test is designed to ensure that individuals receiving assistance do not already have sufficient resources for a minimum level of subsistence. Resources that are examined include both earned and unearned income. Earned income is money in the form of salary or wages. Unearned income includes benefits from other public and private financial programs, gifts, life insurance annuities, stock dividends, rental income, inheritances, support payments from relatives, and so on.

- *Eligibility and benefit levels are determined on a case-by-case basis.* All applications for assistance are closely reviewed on an individual basis. Although there are federal, state, and local guidelines on eligibility and on allowable benefits, the staff who administer public assistance have substantial discretion in deciding whether a client will receive special allowances in addition to basic benefits. Staff also have discretion in deciding which social services and other resources might be mobilized on behalf of the client. Eligibility determination, along with benefit-level determination, is a cumbersome, lengthy process involving extensive review of documents.
- *Benefits are viewed as charity.* In contrast to social insurance benefits, to which recipients are viewed as legally entitled, public assistance benefits are perceived as charity. In this country, poor people are not considered to have a constitutionally established right to a minimum income. (In comparison, some foreign countries, such as Great Britain, recognize the right of those in poverty to be maintained and protected by government.)
- *Program benefits are paid from general government revenues.* Public assistance benefits at the federal, state, and local levels are financed through taxes on personal income and on property.

The main public assistance programs include Supplemental Security Income, General Assistance, Medicaid, food stamps, housing assistance, and Temporary Assistance to Needy Families (which was enacted in 1996 to replace Aid to Families with Dependent Children).

Supplemental Security Income

Under the Supplemental Security Income (SSI) program, the federal government pays monthly checks to people in financial need who are 65 years of age and older or who are blind or disabled at any age. To qualify for payments, applicants must have no (or very little) regular cash income, own little property, and have little cash or few assets that could be turned into cash (such as stocks, bonds, jewelry, or other valuables).

The SSI program became effective January 1, 1974, and replaced the following programs that were created by the 1935 Social Security Act: Old-Age Assistance, Aid to the Blind, and Aid to the Permanently and Totally Disabled. SSI is the first federally administered assistance program. All other public assistance programs are administered through state and local governments. The word *supplemental* refers to the fact that, in most cases, payments *supplement* whatever income may be available to the claimant. Even OASDHI benefits are supplemented by this program.

SSI provides a guaranteed minimum income (an income floor) for the aged, the blind, and the disabled. Aged, blind, and disabled are defined as follows:

Aged: 65 or over.
Blind: Vision no better than 20/200 (even with glasses) or tunnel vision (limited visual field of 20° or less).
Disabled: A physical or mental disability that prevents a person from doing any substantial gainful work and is expected to last at least 12 months or result in death.

Administration of SSI has been assigned to the Social Security Administration. Financing of the program is through federal tax dollars, primarily income taxes.

General Assistance

The General Assistance (GA) program is supposed to serve those needing temporary, rather than long-term, financial support. It is designed to provide financial help to those in need who are ineligible for any other income-maintenance program. No clearly stated eligibility requirements exist for general assistance. GA is the only public assistance program that receives no federal funds. It is usually funded by property taxes. In some large cities, the state contributes substantially toward meeting the costs of GA. In most localities, however, the program is financed and administered at the local level through the county or township or by a village or city. In many local governmental units, a political official has arbitrary jurisdiction over whether an applicant receives help. Most expenditures for GA are for medical care. In-kind payments (food, medical care, clothes, and items other than money) are frequent. Whenever feasible, communities usually attempt to move GA recipients into federally funded public aid programs to reduce local expenses.

Payments for GA tend to be minimal and grudgingly made to discourage people from applying and from becoming dependent on welfare. With in-kind and voucher payments, GA conveys to recipients the suspicion that they are incapable of managing their

AP Photos/Tony Dejak

Under the 1996 Welfare Reform Act, states are responsible for job training programs that lead to employment within 2 years of receiving benefits.

own affairs. Because able-bodied unemployed men and women sometimes find it necessary to seek GA benefits, GA has been viewed as a public assistance program for the "undeserving poor." In some parts of the country, GA has demoralizing effects because many local program directors hold—and convey to recipients—a negative attitude about providing assistance.

In recent years, some states and counties have terminated their GA programs.

Medicaid

This program provides hospital and medical care to certain poverty-stricken people. Those eligible are individuals who have very low income and assets. Because Medicaid is a joint federal/state program, the laws governing eligibility and benefits vary in different geographic areas. Generally, recipients of SSI and other public assistance programs are eligible. In addition, states have the option to include people who are able to provide for their own daily living but

whose income and resources are not sufficient to meet all their medical costs.

Medicaid is administered by the states, with financial participation by the federal government. Direct payments are made to providers of services. As is required for every public assistance program, Medicaid applicants must undergo a means test.

Food Stamps

Tragically, an estimated 50 million people in the United States (the most powerful and one of the richest countries in the world) do not have enough food to eat.[53] Many of those with inadequate diets are poor. Not only does an insufficient diet affect the individual, but research suggests that severe nutritional deficits in expectant mothers also may lead to irreversible brain defects in their children.

The food stamp program is designed to combat hunger and to improve the diets of low-income households by supplementing their food-purchasing ability.

Housing Assistance

Similar to food stamps and Medicaid, housing assistance is an "in-kind" program rather than a cash program. Generally, such assistance is provided in the form of public housing, usually large housing projects that are owned and operated by the government. In a public housing project, the tenants have lower, subsidized rents. Because they pay less than the market value of their apartments, they are effectively receiving an income transfer.

There are also housing assistance programs for low-income people who are renting and even buying their homes and apartments in the private market. In these programs, the rent or mortgage payment is reduced, with the Department of Housing and Urban Development (HUD) making up the difference.

Temporary Assistance to Needy Families

In 1986 Charles Murray proposed in his controversial book *Losing Ground* that the government should eliminate welfare benefits for all working-age adults.[54] He contended that court decisions, bureaucratic reforms, and antipoverty programs in our society have actually made the poor worse off by creating a dependency. In essence he asserted people on welfare decide that being on the government dole is better than working.

Murray was especially critical of the Aid to Families of Dependent Children (AFDC) program. He asserted that it provided an incentive for single women to want to have children in order to receive welfare payments. He also asserted that increases in crime and drug abuse, poor educational performance in schools, and deteriorating conditions in inner cities stem largely from the increase in single-parent families, which he attributed to government programs that support such families. His solution to overhauling the AFDC program was simple: "If you want to cut illegitimate births among poor people,...I know how to do that. You just rip away every kind of government support there is."[55]

Critics of this approach were horrified. They argued that Murray's plan would make innocent children suffer for their parents' inadequacies, which seems doubly unfair given that two of three AFDC beneficiaries were children. If the AFDC program were eliminated without any program to replace it, many more children undoubtedly would end up homeless and hungry. Murray's response was that single mothers who are unable to care for their children should place them for adoption. He further asserted that terminating the AFDC program would force single women to think twice about getting pregnant and would force more low-income males to refrain from fathering children outside of marriage.

Although there was little support for eliminating the AFDC program without replacing it, political decision makers in the early 1990s became more interested in replacing AFDC with a program that forced unemployed single mothers (and single fathers) to take a job.

In the 1994 elections, Republicans (mostly conservatives) won a majority of seats in the House of Representatives for the first time in 40 years and had control of both houses of Congress. The new House speaker, Newt Gingrich, proposed there be no AFDC benefits for unmarried teens and their children. In addition, he proposed that AFDC recipients be prohibited from receiving benefits for more than 5 years, with states having the option of reducing the time limit for welfare benefits to 2 years.

When Bill Clinton was campaigning for the presidency in 1992, he promised to "end welfare as we know it."[56] In 1994 he proposed attacking the costly national problem of welfare dependency with a plan that would force growing numbers of young welfare mothers into public or private jobs. The objective of the plan was to make young single mothers self-sufficient by giving them money and child care while they received job training—but then to cut off their cash benefits after no more than 24 months. Those who were unable to find jobs would be given temporary tax-subsidized work, usually at the minimum wage, either in the private sector or in community service.

In 1996 President Clinton and the Democrats and Republicans in Congress compromised on welfare reform and passed the Personal Responsibility and Work Opportunity Reconciliation Act. Key provisions of this act are:

- The federal guarantee of cash assistance for poor families with children (under the AFDC program) is ended. Each state now receives a capped block grant (lump sum) to run its own welfare and work programs.
- The head of every family has to work within 2 years, or the family loses its benefits. After receiving welfare for 2 months, adults have to perform community service unless they have found regular jobs. (States can choose not to have a community service requirement.)

- Lifetime public welfare assistance is limited to 5 years. (States can establish stricter limits.) Hardship exemptions from this requirement are available for up to 20% of recipients in a state.
- Communities must provide child care to TANF participants.
- States can provide payments to unmarried teenage parents only if a mother under 18 is living at home or in another adult-supervised setting and attends high school or an alternative educational or training program as soon as the child is 12 weeks old.
- States are required to maintain their own spending on public welfare at 75% of their 1994 level or 80% if they failed to put enough public welfare recipients to work.
- States cannot penalize a woman on public welfare who does not work because she cannot find day care for a child under 6 years old.
- States may deny Medicaid to adults who lose welfare benefits because of a failure to meet work requirements.
- A woman on public welfare who refuses to cooperate in identifying the father of her child must lose at least 25% of her benefits.
- Future legal immigrants who have not yet become citizens are ineligible for most federal welfare benefits and social services during their first 5 years in the United States. SSI benefits and food stamp eligibility ended for noncitizens, including legal immigrants, receiving benefits in 1996.[57]

The Personal Responsibility and Work Opportunity Reconciliation Act abolished the AFDC program and replaced it with the TANF program. No longer is cash assistance to the poor an entitlement. It is now short term and varies from state to state.

Because each state has considerable leeway in designing its version of TANF, it is accurate to indicate there are 50 versions of TANF. Taking advantage of the flexibility allowed by the federal legislation, some states modified TANF services by setting stricter time limits on how long someone in poverty could receive cash assistance. For example, Georgia and Florida set their limits at 48 months, Montana and Indiana at 24 months, and Utah at 36 months.[58] Cash amounts given to TANF participants vary widely from one state to another, with Alabama and Mississippi on the low end, and California and New York on the high end.[59] As indicated in Case Exhibit 4.3, TANF is a controversial program.

Critical Thinking Questions

Do you believe it is better for a single mom with young children to be working outside the home (with her children in day care) than for her to be at home with her children? Do you believe it is better for a married woman to be working outside the home than for her to be at home with her children?

Proposed Welfare Alternative Program: Family Allowance Program

The United States is the only Western industrialized country without a family allowance program. Under a family allowance program, the government pays each family a set amount based on the number of children in the household. If payments were large enough, a program like this could aid in eliminating poverty, particularly in large families.

There are some strong criticisms of family allowance plans. If payments were made to all children, the program would be very expensive and much of the money would go to nonpoor families. This problem could be solved (as Denmark has done) by varying the family allowance payments with income and terminating payments after a certain income is reached. (However, such an approach would then involve a means test and continue to stigmatize recipients.) A second criticism is that such a program would provide an incentive to increase the birthrate at a time when overpopulation is a major concern. A final criticism is that it would not provide payments to single individuals and childless couples who are poor.

At the time of revising this text, the Republican Party (particularly the Tea Party contingent) is advocating that our country needs to make sharp cutbacks in a variety of social programs, including Social Security payments, Medicare, and Medicaid. With the current political climate, there is practically no chance that an expensive new social program, such as a family allowance program, will be enacted.

Social Work and Public Welfare

The preamble to the Code of Ethics of the National Association of Social Workers states:

The primary mission of the social work profession is to enhance human well-being and help meet

CASE EXHIBIT 4.3

Temporary Assistance to Needy Families

This is a controversial program.

Numerous studies have been conducted, and are continuing to be conducted, on the effects of Temporary Assistance to Needy Families. Supporters of the program tout several benefits. Critics cite a number of shortcomings.

Supporters of the program cite the following benefits:

- Employment of young single mothers (ages 18–24) has increased.
- Employment of never-married mothers has increased.
- The number of Americans on cash assistance (the AFDC program compared to TANF) has plummeted.
- Teenage birthrates have fallen since 1996. One motivation for the passage of the 1996 Welfare Reform Act was the desire to change policies that conservatives claim reward early childbearing by single mothers. The Welfare Reform Act denies public assistance payments to teenage mothers, except under the following conditions: States can provide payments to unmarried teenage parents only if a mother under 18 is living at home or in another adult-supervised setting and attends high school or an alternative educational or training program as soon as the child is 12 weeks old. The underlying reason behind denying welfare payments to most teenage mothers is to send a message to teenagers that having babies will not be financially rewarded.
- Almost all mothers (and fathers) who are working state they prefer work to welfare. Having a job may be more psychologically beneficial to the parents and to their children than being on a stigmatized welfare program. Some of these working parents may rise in socioeconomic status and have an increased sense of self-worth and a higher living status. Eventually these families will have more total income than when they received cash assistance. In such families, the children are apt to be proud of their working mothers (or parents), and such children are apt to follow their mothers' (or parents') example.

Critics of TANF site the following shortcomings:

- Most mothers who leave the welfare rolls find jobs, but a large minority do not. Moreover, some of those who find jobs soon lose them and do not reappear on the welfare rolls.
- Some former welfare recipients are making successful transitions to work, often after many years of welfare dependency. Yet even the more successful job holders experience economic hardship and often must ask for help from family and friends. Incomes are rising at the top, but not at the bottom.
- The long-term impact of welfare reform on both single mothers and their children could well turn out to be like the long-term impact of deinstitutionalization on the mentally ill; good for some but terrible for others.
- There have been significant increases in the proportion of poor people, especially single mothers and their children,

who are not covered by health insurance. Once people leave welfare to begin working, they may not be eligible for Medicaid, and their employers may not offer health insurance.
- Many working mothers report problems finding satisfactory child care. There is some evidence that young children are being left alone, sometimes for long periods. Will welfare reform end up helping parents but hurting their children?
- The people who have been kicked off the welfare rolls are pushing down wages for low-skilled workers in the United States. People desperate for food and shelter are being hired for lower wages than those currently employed, who may lose their jobs to former welfare recipients. Flooding the labor market with thousands of desperate workers has helped to lower labor costs for businesses. The welfare overhaul has depressed the median wage of all women workers. Increased competition for jobs makes it easier for employers to pay less, and harder for unions to negotiate good contracts.
- The group that has benefited most by welfare reform is employers—as this group now has a much larger pool of applicants for low-income jobs. Welfare reform has led to increased economic hardship for many low-income parents and their children.
- States now have much more choice in determining whom they will assist, what requirements they will impose upon those who receive aid, and what noncash supports those families will receive. As a result, there is much more disparity between states than existed under AFDC. With this disparity between states, two children in identical situations in different states now live with very different realities. One may have household resources above the poverty level; stable, high-quality child care; and health insurance, while the other may have none of these.
- A majority of those who receive TANF do not make it above the poverty line, as TANF benefits are often below the poverty line. In addition, many of those who obtain a job often remain in poverty because the jobs are often minimum-wage (or slighly above) jobs that are below the poverty line.
- There is a serious danger that many TANF recipients will be trapped into long-term poverty. TANF programs provide almost no opportunities, via paid benefits, for TANF recipients to continue their education beyond high school. As a result, TANF recipients are likely to obtain minimum-wage jobs and other "dead-end work" (work involving poor pay, scant fringe benefits, and little opportunity for advancement). The education offered to TANF recipients does not prepare or qualify them for higher-end work.

SOURCE: William Kornblum and Joseph Julian, *Social Problems*, 14th ed. (Boston: Pearson, 2012), p. 217.

basic human needs of all people, with particular attention to the needs and empowerment of people who are vulnerable, oppressed and living in poverty.[60]

The Educational Policy and Accreditation Standards (EPAS) of the Council on Social Work Education states that one of the purposes of the social work profession is: "the elimination of poverty."[61]

These two statements clearly assert that the profession of social work and social work professionals have an obligation to work toward alleviating poverty.

Since the enactment of the 1935 Social Security Act, numerous social services have been provided to public assistance recipients. The particular services provided vary widely from area to area (depending on state and county decisions) but include counseling, day care, protective services, foster care, services to people with a physical or mental disability, information and referral, homemaker services, financial counseling, assistance in child rearing, family planning, health services, vocational training, and employment counseling. Large numbers of social workers are employed to provide such services.

Until 1972 social services and financial assistance were combined, and social workers were involved in financial eligibility determination. The 1972 Amendments to the Social Security Act separated services and assistance. Now public assistance recipients are informed of available social services and of their right to request such services. Financial eligibility is determined by staff who generally are not social workers.

Social workers find many gratifications in helping people with personal or social problems. Yet social work is frequently frustrating. The sources of these frustrations include:

- Having extensive paperwork.
- Trying to meet the needs of clients when those needs are not served by existing programs.
- Trying to change the huge public welfare bureaucratic structure to better meet the needs of clients. (The public welfare system is slow to change to meet emerging needs and is filled with extensive "red tape.")
- Having a larger caseload than one can optimally and effectively serve.

- Trying to keep informed about the numerous changes (program, organizational, and eligibility determination) that occur on an ongoing basis.
- Dealing with discouraged clients who lack the necessary motivation to work toward improving their circumstances. Social work "interns" in field placement and new social workers frequently report this as their greatest frustration and a severe "reality shock." They anticipate that, after carefully working out an "intervention plan" with a client to resolve some problem, the client will follow through. Unfortunately, in many cases this does not happen. Future appointments may be broken by the client, and even if the client responsibly keeps appointments, she or he is likely to have excuses for not following through on commitments. These excuses can usually be interpreted to represent a lack of motivation.

Working with Discouraged People

The key variable in determining if clients will make positive changes in their lives is whether they have the motivation to make the efforts necessary to improve their circumstances. Failure in counseling or social work generally occurs when clients do not become motivated.

EP 2.1.10a, b, c, f, g, i, j

Many public assistance recipients are discouraged. Continued economic pressures and generally a long series of past "failure" experiences when they have tried to improve their circumstances frequently have sapped their motivation. Discouraged people tend to travel through life in an unhappy "rut" that is dull, stagnating, and generally unfulfilling but that is seen by them as normal and predictable. For them, extensive efforts to improve their circumstances are viewed as risky and frightening. Many feel it is safer to remain in their rut than to try something new that might further expose their weaknesses and result in psychological "hurt."

Seeking a job, finding transportation, and making day-care arrangements could be seen as overwhelmingly difficult for an unskilled single mother (on public assistance) who has never been employed previously. For a wife with five children who periodically is physically beaten by her husband, seeking counseling or making separation arrangements may be seen as highly risky because the future would be uncertain; she may also fear that such actions would only make her husband more abusive. For a person with a drinking problem who has recently lost his last two jobs, giving up drinking may be seen as giving up his main "crutch."

To motivate a discouraged person, the social worker has to be an "encouraging person." According to Lewis Losoncy, an encouraging person does the following:

Has complete acceptance for the discouraged person and conveys "I accept you exactly as you are, with no conditions attached." (She or he should not, however, convey acceptance of the deviant behavior that needs to be changed.)

Has a nonblaming attitude so that the discouraged person no longer feels a need to lie, pretend, or wear a mask.

Conveys empathy that she or he is aware and can to some extent feel what the discouraged person is feeling.

Conveys to the discouraged person that she or he is genuinely interested in the counselee's progress and conveys that the counselee is an important, worthwhile person. For discouraged people to believe in themselves, they generally need an encouraging person who conveys the idea that they are important and worthwhile.

Notices (rewards) every small instance of progress—for example, if the person is wearing something new, the counselor says "That's new, isn't it? It really looks good on you." This is particularly valuable during the beginning of the relationship.

Conveys to the discouraged person that she or he has confidence in that person's capacity to improve.

Conveys sincere enthusiasm about the discouraged person's interests, ideas, and risk-taking actions.

Has the capacity to be a nonjudgmental listener so that the discouraged person's real thoughts and feelings can be expressed freely, without fear of censure.

Has the time to spend listening and understanding the discouraged person as fully as possible. Motivating a discouraged person takes a long, long time. Discouraged people generally have a long history of failures.

Has a sincere belief in the discouraged person's ability to find a purpose in life.

Allows the person to take risks without judging him or her.

Reinforces efforts made by the discouraged person. The important thing is that one tries and not necessarily whether one succeeds. By making efforts to improve, there is hope.[62]

SUMMARY

The following summarizes this chapter's content as it relates to the chapter objectives presented at the beginning of the chapter. Objectives include the following:

A *Describe the extent of poverty and the effects of living in poverty.*

About 15% of our population lives below the poverty line. Poverty is relative to time and place. An agreed-on definition of poverty does not exist. The usual definitions are based on a lack of money, with annual income most commonly used to gauge who is poor. Income is defined using either an absolute approach or a relative approach. The pain of poverty involves not only financial hardships but also the psychological implications that being "poverty stricken" have for a person.

B *Discuss the income and wealth gaps between the rich and the poor in the United States.*

Huge income and wealth gaps exist between the highest fifth and lowest fifth in our society, and social mobility (movement up the social-status ladder) occurs rarely. Wealth perpetuates wealth and poverty perpetuates poverty. The ideology of individualism and the Protestant ethic still stigmatize the poor in our society.

C *Summarize the causes of poverty and identify the population groups with the lowest income levels.*

Those most likely to be poor include female heads of households, children, people of color, the elderly, large families, those with limited education, the unemployed, and those living in pockets of poverty and high unemployment.

The causes of poverty are numerous. Poverty is interrelated with most other social problems. Therefore, almost every social service combats poverty to some extent. Some researchers have noted that the poor have a set of values and attitudes that constitutes a culture of poverty. There is now considerable controversy about whether this culture *perpetuates* poverty or is simply an *adaptation* to being poor.

In some ways, poverty is functional for society. For this and other reasons, some decision makers are not actively seeking to eradicate it.

D *Outline current programs to combat poverty and discuss their merits and shortcomings.*

The major income maintenance programs to combat poverty were created by the 1935 Social Security Act. The federal government's role in providing social insurance programs and public assistance programs was initiated by this act.

Social insurance programs (which are consistent with the institutional view of income transfers) receive less criticism than public assistance programs (which are consistent with the residual view of income transfers). A danger of punitive, stigmatized public assistance programs is that poverty and dependency may be passed on to succeeding generations.

In 1996 welfare reform legislation was enacted that focuses on putting adult public assistance recipients with children to work. In 1935, when the AFDC program was enacted, it was thought best for single mothers to stay at home to raise their children. The 1996 Welfare Reform Act, which created TANF, maintains that single mothers (and fathers) must work.

E *Present strategies to reduce poverty in the future.*

The United States is the only Western industrialized country without a family allowance program. Under a family allowance program, the government pays each family a set amount based on the number of children in the household. If payments were large enough, a program like this could aid in eliminating poverty, particularly in large families.

F *Describe a social worker's role in motivating people who are discouraged.*

Although the profession of social work has gratifications, it also has frustrations, including dealing with mounds of paperwork and red tape, working in a bureaucratic structure that is slow to respond to emerging needs, and working with discouraged people who do not follow through on "intervention plans" to improve their circumstances. To motivate discouraged clients, the social worker has to be an "encouraging person."

Competency Notes

EP 2.1.3a Distinguish, appraise, and integrate multiple sources of knowledge, including research-based knowledge and practice wisdom. (All of this chapter) This chapter focuses on poverty and public welfare. It provides a history of our response to the poor; describes the rich and the poor; identifies the population groups who are poor; summarizes the causes of poverty; and describes the culture and functions of poverty. It also outlines social insurance programs and public assistance programs, and describes a social worker's role in motivating people who are discouraged.

EP 2.1.10a Substantively and affectively prepare for action with individuals, families, groups, organizations, and communities

EP 2.1.10b Use empathy and other interpersonal skills

EP 2.1.10c Develop a mutually agreed-on focus of work and desired outcomes

EP 2.1.10f Collect, organize, and interpret client data

EP 2.1.10g Assess client strengths and limitations

EP 2.1.10i Implement prevention interventions that enhance client capacities

EP 2.1.10j Help clients resolve problems (pp. 136–137) Information is presented on the social worker's role in motivating people who are discouraged.

Media Resources

Additional resources for this chapter, including a chapter quiz, can be found on the Social Work CourseMate. Go to CengageBrain.com.

Notes

1. "U.S. Poverty Rate Climbed to 15.1 Percent Last Year, Total Number Hit All-Time Record," *Huffington Post* (Jan. 5, 2012), p. 9.

2. Ibid.

3. Ibid.

4. Ibid.

5. Ibid.

6. William Kornblum and Joseph Julian, *Social Problems*, 14th ed. (Boston: Pearson, 2012), pp. 188–194.

7. Marilyn Flynn, "Public Assistance," in *Contemporary Social Work*, 2nd ed., Donald Brieland, Lela Costin, and Charles Atherton, eds. (New York: McGraw-Hill, 1980), p. 165.

8. Michael Harrington, *The Other America* (New York: Macmillan, 1962).

9. Kornblum and Julian, *Social Problems*, pp. 187–191.

10. "U.S. Poverty Rate Climbed to 15.1 Percent Last Year, Total Number Hit All-Time Record," *Huffington Post*, p. 9.

11. Ibid.

12. Kornblum and Julian, *Social Problems*, p. 188.

13. Ibid., p. 189.

14. Ibid., p. 189.

15. Quoted in Kornblum and Julian, *Social Problems*, p. 190.

16. Ibid., p. 189.

17. Kornblum and Julian, *Social Problems*, pp. 191–192.

18. Ibid., p. 191.

19. http://www.feedingamerica.org.

20. Ian Robertson, *Social Problems*, 2nd ed. (New York: Random House, 1980), p. 31.

21. James W. Coleman and Donald R. Cressey, *Social Problems*, 4th ed. (New York: Harper & Row, 1990), p. 161.

22. "U.S. Poverty Rate Climbed to 15.1 Percent Last Year, Total Number Hit All-Time Record," *Huffington Post*.

23. Second inaugural address of President Franklin D. Roosevelt (Jan. 20, 1937).

24. President's Council of Economic Advisors, *Economic Report of the President* (Washington, DC: U.S. Government Printing Office, 1964), pp. 56–57.

25. Kornblum and Julian, *Social Problems*, pp. 187–191.

26. Ibid., p. 198.

27. Ibid., p. 259.

28. Ibid., p. 198.

29. Ibid., pp. 198–199.

30. Ibid., pp. 198–199.

31. Ibid., pp. 198–199.

32. Ibid., pp. 198–199.

33. Ibid., p. 197.

34. "The Rising Cost of Raising a Child," http://money.cnn.com/2011/09/21/pf/cost_raising_child/index.htm.

35. Kornblum and Julian, *Social Problems*, p. 200.

36. Ibid., p. 200.

37. Ibid., p. 200.

38. Ibid., pp. 194–195.

39. Ibid., p. 193.

40. Ibid., pp. 200–201.

41. Harrington, *The Other America*, p. 21.

42. Oscar Lewis, "The Culture of Poverty," *Scientific American*, 215 (Oct. 1966), pp. 19–25.

43. Ibid., p. 23.

44. Eleanor Leacock, ed., *The Culture of Poverty: A Critique* (New York: Simon & Schuster, 1971).

45. Elliott Liebow, *Tally's Corner: A Study of Negro Street-Corner Men* (Boston: Little, Brown, 1967); Ulf Hannertz, *Soulside: An Inquiry into Ghetto Culture and Community* (New York: Columbia University Press, 1969); Leacock, *The Culture of Poverty*.

46. William Ryan, *Blaming the Victim*, rev. ed. (New York: Vintage Books, 1976).

47. Thomas Sullivan, Kendrick Thompson, Richard Wright, George Gross, and Dale Spady, *Social Problems: Divergent Perspectives* (New York: Wiley, 1980), p. 390.

48. Barbara Ehrenreich, *Nickel and Dimed* (New York: Henry Holt and Co., 2001), p. 221.

49. Herbert J. Gans, *More Equality* (New York: Pantheon, 1968), pp. 133–135.

50. Helen M. Crampton and Kenneth K. Keiser, *Social Welfare: Institution and Process* (New York: Random House, 1970), p. 73.

51. These conservative views are summarized by Samuel Mencher, "Newburgh: The Recurrent Crisis in Public Assistance," *Social Work*, 7 (Jan. 1962), pp. 3–4.

52. Rex A. Skidmore and Milton G. Thackeray, *Introduction to Social Work*, 2nd ed. (Englewood Cliffs, NJ: Prentice Hall, 1976), pp. 111–112.

53. "U.S. Poverty Rate Climbed to 15.1 Percent Last Year, Total Number Hit All-Time Record," *Huffington Post*.

54. Charles Murray, *Losing Ground: American Social Policy, 1950–1980* (New York: Basic Books, 1986).

55. Quoted in David Whitman, "The Next War on Poverty," *U.S. News & World Report*, Oct. 5, 1992, p. 38.

56. Quoted in Kornblum and Julian, *Social Problems*, p. 213.
57. Ralph Dolgoff, Donald Feldstein, and Louise Skolnik, *Understanding Social Welfare*, 4th ed. (White Plains, NY: Longman, 1997), pp. 217–218.
58. Ira Colby and Sophia Dziegielewski, *Social Work: The People's Profession* (Chicago: Lyceum Books, 2001), p. 155.
59. Kornblum and Julian, *Social Problems*, pp. 213–217.
60. Preamble to the Code of Ethics of the National Association of Social Workers, as adopted by the Delegate Assembly of Aug. 1996.
61. Council on Social Work Education, *Educational Policy and Accreditation Standards (EPAS)* (Washington, DC: Council on Social Work Education, 2008).
62. Lewis Losoncy, *Turning People On* (Englewood Cliffs, NJ: Prentice Hall, 1977).

Emotional/Behavioral Problems and Counseling

Everyone, at times, has emotional problems and/or behavioral difficulties. This chapter will:

Learning Objectives

EP 2.1.3a

A Describe the nature and extent of emotional and behavioral difficulties.

B Discuss the concept of mental illness.

C Present a theory about the causes of chronic mental illness.

D Present information about the homeless.

E Discuss controversial issues in the mental health field.

F Present research on the relationship between social structure and the rate of mental illness.

G Describe treatment approaches for emotional and behavioral problems.

H Describe the role of social work in the mental health field.

I Present information about counseling and counseling techniques.

A Perspective on Emotional and Behavioral Problems

Several years ago, I worked as a counselor at a maximum-security hospital for the "criminally insane." A number of the residents at this hospital had committed bizarre crimes due to emotional and behavioral problems. I'll describe a few of these situations to give you an idea of what I encountered.

In one case, a 22-year-old male had decapitated his 17-year-old friend. In another, a married male with four children had been arrested for the fourth time for exposing himself. In still another, a male had dug up several graves and used corpses to "re-decorate" his home. Another married man had been committed after it was discovered that he was in-volved in incestuous relationships with his 11- and 12-year-old daughters. Another man had been com-mitted after trying to deliver sermons in local taverns and after repeatedly maintaining that clouds fol-lowed him around in whatever direction he was

Critical Thinking Questions

Do any members of your extended family have an emotional or behavioral issue? If so, do you have any thoughts on how the issue or issues might be resolved?

going. Another inmate had brutally killed his father with an ax. Bizarre? Yes, definitely!

Is there a way to explain why these men did what they did? A variety of interpretations have been offered by different authorities, most of whom assert that they acted strangely because they were mentally ill.

Albert Ellis, a prominent psychologist, has ad-vanced a different explanation that offers consider-able promise for understanding and treating people who commit bizarre offenses. Ellis asserts that if we look at what the offenders were thinking when they committed unusual offenses, we will be able to gain an understanding of (a) why the bizarre actions oc-curred, (b) what would have prevented them from happening, and (c) what services are now needed to prevent the offenders from again getting into trou-ble after their release.[1] In a nutshell, Ellis asserts that the primary determinant of all of our actions is our thoughts (that is, thoughts → actions).

At the maximum-security hospital, Ellis's inter-pretation was applied to the gravedigger's case. Jim Schmidt (the name has been changed) was 46 years old when he began digging up graves and redecorat-ing his home. His mother had died 3½ years earlier. Unfortunately, his mother was the only person who had provided meaning to his life. He was shy and had no other friends, and the two had lived together in a small rural community for the past 22 years.

After his mother's death, he became even more isolated. Being very lonely, he wished his mother were still alive. As happens with many people who lose someone close, he began dreaming that she was still alive. His dreams appeared so real that, on awakening, he found it difficult to believe his mother was definitely dead. He then began thinking that his mother could in fact be brought back to life and that bringing corpses of females to his home would help bring his mother back. (Now, to us this idea certainly appears irrational. But being isolated, Jim had no way of checking what was real and what was not.) He decided to give the idea a try.

Jim, of course, needed counseling (then and now). Such services would help him adjust to his mother's death, find new interests in life, become more involved with other people, and exchange thoughts with others to check out what is real and what is not.

Nature and Extent of Emotional and Behavioral Problems

Emotional and behavioral problems are two comprehensive labels covering an array of disturbances: depression, excessive anxiety, feelings of inferiority or isolation, alienation, sadistic or masochistic tendencies, marital difficulties, broken romances, parent–child relationship difficulties, hyperactivity, unusual or bizarre behavior, aggressiveness, phobias, child or spousal abuse, compulsive or obsessive behavior, guilt, shyness, violent displays of temper, vindictiveness, nightmares or insomnia, sexual deviations, eating disorders, and so on.

Each problem has unique and sometimes numerous potential causes. Depression, for example, may stem from biochemical imbalances, from the loss of a loved one or of something highly valuable, from feelings of guilt or shame, from knowledge of an undesirable impending event (for example, discovery of a terminal illness), from aggression turned inward, from certain physical factors such as menopause, from feelings of inadequacy or inferiority, from self-denigrating thoughts, or from feelings of loneliness or isolation. Literally hundreds of thousands of books have been published on the causes and treatments of the wide array of emotional and behavioral problems.

One of every four Americans (age 18 and older) experiences some form of emotional or behavioral disorder at some point during any given year.[2] These disorders range from mild depression and anxiety to suicide ideation or a severe eating disorder such as anorexia (see Case Exhibit 5.1). Every year more than 6 million people receive mental health care in the United States.[3]

What Is Mental Illness?

Much of the language relating to emotional and behavioral disturbances has become a part of everyday conversation. We use a number of terms to express a judgment (often unfavorable) about someone's unusual behavior or emotions; for example, we say that he or she is *crazy, weird, psychotic, neurotic, insane, sick, uptight,* or *mad,* or is having a *nervous breakdown* or acting like a *space cadet.* Amazingly, we act as if the label accurately describes the person, and we then relate to that person as if the label were correct and all-encompassing. However, it is impossible to precisely define any of these terms. What, for example, are the specific characteristics that distinguish a "psychotic" or a "space cadet" from other people?

There are two general approaches to viewing and diagnosing people who display emotional disturbances and abnormal behaviors: the medical model and the interactional model (which asserts that mental illness is a myth).

Medical Model

This model views emotional and behavioral problems as mental illness, comparable to physical illness. Medical labels (for example, schizophrenia, paranoia, psychosis, insanity) are thus applied to emotional problems. Adherents of the medical approach believe that the disturbed person's mind is affected by some generally unknown internal condition. That condition, they assert, might be due to genetic endowment, metabolic disorders, infectious diseases, internal conflicts, unconscious use of defense mechanisms, or traumatic early experiences that cause emotional fixations and prevent future psychological growth.

The medical-model approach arose in reaction to the historical notion that emotionally disturbed individuals were possessed by demons, were mad, were to be blamed for their disturbances, and were to be "treated" by being beaten, locked up, or killed. The medical model led to a perception of the disturbed as in need of help. It also stimulated research into the nature of emotional and behavioral problems and promoted the development of therapeutic approaches.

CASE EXHIBIT 5.1

Eating Disorders: A Continuing Problem

Eating disorders continue to present as a serious issue within the United States and other industrialized nations. Problems with this illness have also now emerged in developing countries such as Asia, Latin America, and India, possibly as a result of the impact of global economic development and the changing status of women in these cultures.[a] Although eating disorders primarily affect women, there has been an increase in males affected with this illness.

Lasègue in 1873 and Gull in 1874 designated the term *anorexia nervosa* (AN) in separate cases in which they reported young females who were starving themselves. Descriptions of this illness became more frequent in the late 19th century.[b] Anorexics exhibit a drive for perfection and the pursuit of thinness. These individuals refuse to maintain a normal body weight for their height. Their weight places them below 85% of their ideal weight range. Anorexics display an intense fear of gaining weight or becoming fat, even though they may be extremely underweight. Body distortion is associated with the affected individual's denial of being underweight. Postmenarcheal females suffering from anorexia will lose their menses for at least three consecutive cycles, and in premenstrual girls puberty can be delayed. Anorexia nervosa is subcategorized as being the restrictive type, in which individuals will severely limit their intake to only a few hundred calories per day and do not engage in bingeing or purging behaviors, or the binge-eating/purging type, which is characterized by frequently engaging in binge-eating or purging behaviors. The primary age of onset is during early to mid-adolescence.[c]

Bulimia nervosa (BN), as noted in the current diagnostic criteria, was relatively obscure until the latter part of the 20th century.[d] It is now considered more common than anorexia nervosa. Bulimic individuals strive to prevent weight gain or lose weight through binge/purge behaviors. Self-loathing, feeling ineffective, and low self-esteem may lead to bulimia nervosa. Triggers to binge/purge incidents can vary, but stress and an inability to feel a sense of control may precede an event. Most often in secrecy, a bulimic will consume huge amounts of high-calorie foods in a relatively short time period, such as 2 hours. Afterward, the person feels extremely, and frequently painfully, full. Episodes of bingeing are followed with purging, primarily through the vomiting of food, but methods can include the use of laxatives, diuretics, other medication, or enemas, as well as excessive exercising. The frequency of bingeing and purging can wax and wane, with incidents occurring one or two times a week up to several times a day over a period of 3 months. Adolescents are most commonly affected by bulimia nervosa.[e]

Serious medical complications can arise with both disorders, and the incidence of death with AN appears to be higher than with BN.[f] A recent review of mortality rates for this population suggested the risk factors of AN patients may need to be staged, similar to cancer, in an effort to more effectively measure the incidence and death risks of this disease.[g] Cardiac abnormalities, changes in brain function, osteoporosis, anemia, gastrointestinal problems, and altered blood chemistry may be seen in both anorexics and bulimics. Individuals with either disorder may exhibit symptoms of fatigue, sleep difficulties, and depression. In addition, individuals who binge and purge by vomiting often suffer from dental problems related to the loss of tooth enamel and gum disease due to the hydrochloric acid in the vomitus.[h]

Although not listed as a specific diagnosis in the *Diagnostic and Statistical Manual* (DSM-IV-TR)[i], binge-eating disorder (BED) has become increasingly prevalent, affecting up to 8% of the obese population. Multiple subcategories are evident, but this population is characterized by rapid consumption of food until uncomfortably full, distressed feelings over this behavior, obesity, failed efforts at dieting, and altered self-esteem. Individuals who are categorized as having BED appear to have eating behavior that differs from those of persons diagnosed with bulimia nervosa, being more disorganized. Presentation typically occurs between ages 30 and 50, with women having a higher incidence than men.[j] Research on BED is relatively recent, with the literature revealing varied results for treatment efficacy and outcomes.[k]

In all age categories, obesity has dramatically increased and can lead to an eating disorder. The risk factors for developing an eating disorder include biological, social, familial, and cultural aspects. There is no single theoretical perspective, and eating disorders represents a myriad of complex, intertwining factors in their development. Other psychiatric disorders may present along with an eating disorder, and need to be assessed and treated along with the eating disorder.[l] A recent study of 292 female twins demonstrated there is a relationship between disordered eating and depressive symptoms, 70% of which is explained by genetic factors.[m]

Treatment options include inpatient, outpatient, group, individual, and residential therapies. Key factors for successful treatment often include a multidimensional team approach, incorporating physicians, nurses, social workers, and dieticians. Education about nutrition and health is integrated with psychotherapy, body-image and self-esteem exercises, and ongoing support. The goals of treatment include a resolution or reduction in maladaptive behaviors, addressing the psychological and physiological issues, and weight restoration for anorexia. Treatment is expensive, usually several thousand dollars, and can take up to 8 years or even longer, depending on the severity of the situation and the length of chronicity.[n] Current prevention programs have been found to be more effective when focused on high-risk adolescent girls who were provided forms of interactive interventions, offered multiple sessions, and provided with content related to addressing maladaptive attitudes and behaviors.[o]

SOURCE: This exhibit was written by Mary R. Weeden, MSW, LCSW, doctoral candidate at Loyola University and clinical therapist for eating disorders; Assistant Professor, Concordia University, Wisconsin.

[a]Richard A. Gordon, "Eating Disorders East and West: A Culture-Bound Syndrome Unbound," in *Eating Disorders and Cultures in*

(continued)

Transition, Mervat Nasser, Melanie A. Katzman, Richard A. Gordon, eds. (New York: Taylor & Francis Inc. 2001), pp. 3–4.

[b]Joseph A. Silverman, "Anorexia Nervosa: Historical Perspective on Treatment," in *Handbook of Treatment for Eating Disorders*, David M. Garner and Paul E. Garfinkel, eds. (New York: Guilford Press, 1997), pp. 4–5.

[c]American Psychiatric Association, *Diagnostic and Statistical Manual of Mental Disorders* (DSM-IV-TR), 4th ed., text revision (Washington, DC: Author, 2000).

[d]Gerald F. M. Russell, "The History of Bulimia Nervosa," in *Handbook of Treatment for Eating Disorders*, David M. Garner and Paul E. Garfinkel, eds. (New York: Guilford Press, 1997), p. 20.

[e]American Psychiatric Association, *Diagnostic and Statistical Manual of Mental Disorders*.

[f]Nancy D. Berkman, Kathleen N. Lohr, and Cynthia M Bulik, " Outcomes of Eating Disorders: A Systematic Review of the Literature," *International Journal of Eating Disorders*, 40, no. 4 (2007), pp. 293–309.

[g]Agneta M. Rosling, Pär Sparen, Claes Norring, and Anne-Liis von Knorring, "Mortality of Eating Disorders: A Follow-up Study of Treatment in a Specialist Unit 1974–2000," *International Journal of Eating Disorders*, 44, no. 4 (2011), pp. 304–310.

[h]Claire Pomeroy and James Mitchell, "Medical Complications of Anorexia Nervosa and Bulimia Nervosa," in *Eating Disorders and Obesity*, Christopher Fairburn and Kelly D. Brownell, eds. (New York: Guilford Press, 2002), pp. 278–284.

[i]American Psychiatric Association, *Diagnostic and Statistical Manual*.

[j]Carlos M. Gilo, "Binge Eating Disorder," in *Eating Disorders and Obesity*, Christopher Fairburn and Kelly D. Brownell, eds. (New York: Guilford Press, 2002), pp. 178–180.

[k]Kimberly A. Brownley, Nancy J. Berkman, Jan A. Sedway, Kathleen N. Lohr, and Cynthia M. Bulik, "Binge Eating Disorder Treatment: A Systematic Review of Randomized Controlled Trials," *International Journal of Eating Disorder*, 40, no. 4 (2007), pp. 337–348.

[l]Ulrike Schmidt, "Risk Factors for Eating Disorders," in *Eating Disorders and Obesity*, Christopher Fairburn and Kelly D. Brownell, eds. (New York: Guilford Press, 2002), p. 247.

[m]Jennifer D. Slane, S. Alexandra Burt, and Kelly L. Klump, "Genetic and Environmental Influences on Disordered Eating and Depressive Symptoms," *International Journal of Eating Disorders*, 44, no. 7 (2011), pp. 605–611.

[n]David M. Garner and Lawrence D. Needleman, "Sequencing and Integration of Treatment," in *Eating Disorders and Obesity*, Christopher Fairburn and Kelly D. Brownell, eds. (New York: Guilford Press, 2002), p. 53.

[o]Eric Stice and Heather Shaw, "Eating Disorder Prevention Programs: A Meta-Analytic Review," *Psychological Bulletin*, 130, no. 2 (2004), pp. 206–227.

The major evidence for the validity of the medical-model approach comes from studies suggesting that some mental disorders, such as schizophrenia, may be influenced by genetics (heredity). The bulk of the evidence for the significance of heredity comes from studies of twins. For example, identical twins have been found to have a concordance rate (that is, if one has it, both have it) for schizophrenia of about 50%.[4] The rate of schizophrenia in the general population is about 1%.[5] So when one identical twin is schizophrenic, the other is 50 times more likely than the average to be schizophrenic. This suggests a causal influence of genes, but not genetic determination, as concordance for identical twins is only 50%, not 100%.

The medical model has a lengthy classification of mental disorders defined by the American Psychiatric Association (see Case Exhibit 5.2).[6] The DSM-IV-TR categories are used in the systems of reimbursement from health insurance policies to mental health providers for the provision of psychotherapy to individuals and groups.

Interactional Model

Critics of the mental-illness approach assert that medical labels have no diagnostic or treatment value and frequently have an adverse effect.

Thomas Szasz, in the 1950s, was one of the first authorities to state that mental illness is a myth—that it does not exist.[7] Szasz's theory is interactional; it focuses on the processes of everyday social interaction and the effects of labeling on people. Beginning with the assumption that the term *mental illness* implies a "disease in the mind," Szasz discusses the inappropriateness of calling such human difficulties "mental illnesses" and categorizes all of the so-called mental illnesses into three types of emotional/behavioral disorders:

1. *Personal disabilities*, such as excessive anxiety, depression, fears, and feelings of inadequacy. Another term for personal disabilities is *unwanted emotions*. Szasz says these so-called mental illnesses may appropriately be considered "mental" (in the sense that thinking and feeling are considered "mental" activities), but they are not diseases.

2. *Antisocial acts*, such as bizarre homicides and other social deviations. Homosexuality used to be in this category but was removed from the American Psychiatric Association's list of mental illnesses in 1974. Szasz says such antisocial acts are only social deviations; they are neither "mental" nor "diseases."

3. *Deterioration of the brain with associated personality changes*. This category includes the "mental illnesses" in which personality changes result following brain deterioration from such causes as Alzheimer's disease, arteriosclerosis, chronic alcoholism, general paresis, AIDS, or serious brain damage caused by an accident. Common symptoms are loss of memory, listlessness, apathy, and deterioration of personal grooming habits. Szasz says these disorders can appropriately be considered "diseases," but they are diseases of the brain rather than diseases of the mind.

CASE EXHIBIT 5.2

Major Mental Disorders as Defined by the American Psychiatric Association

Disorders Usually Diagnosed in Infancy, Childhood, or Adolescence

These include, but are not limited to, mental retardation, learning disorders, communication disorders (such as stuttering), autism, attention-deficit/hyperactivity disorders, and separation-anxiety disorder.

Delirium, Dementia, and Amnestic and Other Cognitive Disorders

These include delirium due to alcohol and other drug intoxication, dementia due to Alzheimer's disease or Parkinson's disease, dementia due to head trauma, and amnestic disorder.

Substance-Related Disorders

This category includes mental disorders related to abuse of alcohol, caffeine, amphetamines, cocaine, hallucinogens, nicotine, and other mind-altering substances.

Schizophrenia and Other Psychotic Disorders

This category includes delusional disorders and all forms of schizophrenia (such as paranoid, disorganized, and catatonic).

The essential feature of a delusional disorder is the presence of one or more delusions that persist for at least 1 month. A *delusion* is something that is falsely believed or propagated. An example is the persecutory type in which an individual erroneously believes he or she is being conspired against, cheated, spied on, followed, poisoned or drugged, harassed, or obstructed in the pursuit of long-term goals.

Schizophrenia encompasses a large group of disorders, usually of psychotic proportion, manifested by disturbances of language and communication, thought, perception, affect, and behavior that last longer than 6 months.

Mood Disorders

These include emotional disorders such as depression and bipolar disorders. A bipolar disorder is a major affective disorder with episodes of both mania and depression, which was formerly called *manic-depressive psychosis*. Bipolar disorder may be subdivided into manic, depressed, or mixed types, on the basis of current symptoms.

Somatoform Disorders

These are psychological problems that manifest themselves as symptoms of physical disease (for example, hypochondria). Hypochondria is a chronic preoccupation with shifting health concerns and symptoms, a fear or conviction that one has a serious physical illness, the search for medical treatment, inability to accept reassurance, and either hostile or dependent relationships with caregivers and family.

Anxiety Disorders

This category includes phobias, posttraumatic stress disorder (PTSD), generalized anxiety disorder, acute stress disorder, and substance-induced anxiety disorder. A phobia is characterized by an obsessive, persistent, unrealistic, intense fear of an object or situation. A few common phobias are *acrophobia* (fear of heights), *algophobia* (fear of pain), and *claustrophobia* (fear of closed spaces).

Dissociative Disorders

This category includes problems in which part of the personality is dissociated from the rest, such as dissociative identity disorder (formerly called multiple personality disorder).

Sexual and Gender Identity Disorders

This category includes sexual dysfunctions (such as hypoactive sexual desire, premature ejaculation, male erectile disorder, male and female orgasmic disorders, and vaginismus), exhibitionism, fetishism, pedophilia (child molestation), sexual masochism, sexual sadism, voyeurism, and gender identity disorders (such as cross-gender identification).

Eating Disorders

This category includes anorexia nervosa, bulimia nervosa, and compulsive overeating.

Sleep Disorders

This classification includes insomnia and other problems with sleep (such as nightmares and sleepwalking).

Impulse-Control Disorders

These disorders relate to the inability to control certain undesirable impulses (for example, kleptomania, pyromania, and pathological gambling).

Adjustment Disorders

These involve difficulty in adjusting to the stress created by such common events as unemployment or divorce.

Personality Disorders

This category refers to an enduring pattern of inner experience and behavior that deviates markedly from the expectations of the individual's culture, is pervasive and inflexible, has an onset in adolescence or early adulthood, is stable over time, and leads to distress or impairment. Examples include the following:

- *Paranoid.* A pattern of distrust and suspiciousness such that others' motives are interpreted as malevolent.
- *Schizoid.* A pattern of detachment from social relationships and a restricted range of emotional expression.

(continued)

- *Schizotypal.* A pattern of acute discomfort in close relationships, cognitive or perceptual distortions, and eccentricities of behavior.
- *Antisocial.* A pattern of disregard for, and violation of, the rights of others.
- *Borderline.* A pattern of instability in interpersonal relationships, self-image, and affects, and impulsivity.
- *Histrionic.* A pattern of excessive emotionality and attention seeking.
- *Narcissistic.* A pattern of grandiosity, need for admiration, and lack of empathy.
- *Avoidant.* A pattern of social inhibition, feelings of inadequacy, and hypersensitivity to negative evaluation.
- *Dependent.* A pattern of submissive and clinging behavior related to an excessive need to be taken care of.
- *Obsessive-Compulsive.* A pattern of preoccupation with orderliness, perfectionism, and control.

Other Conditions

This category covers a variety of other disorders that may be a focus of clinical attention. The category includes parent–child relational problems; partner relational problems; sibling relational problems; child victimization of physical abuse, sexual abuse, and neglect; adult victimization of physical and sexual abuse; malingering; bereavement; academic problems; occupational problems; identity problems; and religious or spiritual problems.

SOURCE: American Psychiatric Association, *Diagnostic and Statistical Manual of Mental Disorders (DSM-IV-TR)*, 4th ed., text revision (Washington, DC: Author, 2000).

According to Szasz, the notion that people with emotional problems are mentally ill is as absurd as the belief that the emotionally disturbed are possessed by demons: "The belief in mental illness as something other than man's trouble in getting along with his fellow man is the proper heir to the belief in demonology and witchcraft. Mental illness exists or is real in exactly the same sense in which witches existed or were real."[8]

In actuality, there are three steps to becoming labeled mentally ill: (a) The person displays unwanted emotions (such as depression) or some strange, deviant behaviors; (b) the emotions or behaviors are not tolerated by family or local community, and as a result, the person is referred for an evaluation to a mental health professional; and (c) the mental health professional, usually a psychiatrist, happens to believe in the medical model and assigns a mental-illness label. Thomas Scheff and David Mechanic provide independent evidence that whether the family or community will tolerate the deviant behavior and whether the mental health professional believes in the medical model are more crucial in determining whether someone will be assigned a label of mentally ill than are the emotions or behaviors exhibited by the person.[9]

The point that Szasz and many other writers are striving to make is that people *do* have emotional problems, but they *do not* have a mystical mental illness. Terms that describe behavior are very useful—for example, depression, anxiety, obsession, compulsion, excessive fear, hallucinations, feelings of failure. Such terms describe personal problems that people have. But the medical terms are not useful because there is no distinguishing symptom that would indicate whether a person does or does not have the "illness." In addition, Caplan points out there is considerable variation among cultures regarding what is defined as a mental illness.[10] (Russia, for example, used to define protests against the government as a symptom of mental illness.) The usefulness of the medical model is also questioned because psychiatrists frequently disagree on the medical diagnosis to be assigned to those who are disturbed.[11]

In a dramatic study, psychologist David Rosenhan demonstrated that professional staff in mental hospitals could not distinguish "insane" patients from "sane" patients.[12] Rosenhan and seven "normal" associates went to 12 mental hospitals in five different states claiming they were hearing voices; all eight were admitted. After admission, these pseudopatients stated that the voices had stopped, and they behaved normally. The hospitals, unable to distinguish their "sane" status from the "insane" status of other patients, kept them hospitalized for an average of

CASE EXAMPLE 5.1

A Mental-Illness Model Interpretation

Dan Vanda was arrested for stabbing his parents to death. He was 22 years old and had always been described as a "loner" by neighbors. In elementary school, junior high, and high school, he was frequently absent, had no close friends, and received mostly failing grades. School records showed that teachers had informed protective services on three occasions that they believed his parents were abusing and neglecting him. Protective services' records indicated that his parents were uncooperative but that sufficient evidence could not be found to justify placement in a foster home.

At the time of his arrest, Dan appeared confused. He said he was in communication with King David (the David in the Bible who slew Goliath), who told him to slay his parents because they were out to get him. He tended to ramble on with incoherent statements from the Bible, and he also stated that people were often controlled by cosmic rays. At his arrest, he

appeared to be expecting congratulations for what he had done rather than incarceration.

The court ordered a 90-day observation period in a maximum security hospital for the mentally ill to determine his sanity.

Neighbors and school officials could add little to explain his actions. He had dropped out of school at age 16. Neighbors felt that he was "weird" and had ordered their children not to associate with him. They reported that they sometimes saw him butchering birds. When they asked him why, he said he was being advised by Alfred Hitchcock (director of the film *The Birds*) to do this to prevent an attack.

Psychiatrists concluded that Dan was paranoid schizophrenic. It was felt his insanity was such that he would not be able to understand the nature of court proceedings connected with his offense. With this recommendation, the court committed him indefinitely to a maximum security psychiatric hospital.

19 days. All were then discharged with a diagnosis of "schizophrenia in remission."

The use of medical labels, it has been asserted, has several adverse effects.[13] People labeled mentally ill believe that they have a disease for which there may be no known "cure." The label gives people an excuse for not taking responsibility for their actions (for example, pleading innocent by reason of insanity). Because there is no known "cure," the disturbed frequently idle away their time waiting for someone to discover a cure rather than assuming responsibility for their behavior, examining the reasons for their problems, and making efforts to improve. Other undesirable consequences of being labeled mentally ill are that the individuals may lose some of their legal rights; may be stigmatized in social interactions as being dangerous, unpredictable, untrustworthy, or of "weak" character; and may find it difficult to secure employment or receive a promotion.[14]

The question of whether mental illness exists is indeed important. The assignment of mental-illness labels to disturbed people has substantial implications for how the disturbed will be treated, for how others will view them, and for how they will view themselves. Cooley's "looking-glass-self" approach crystalizes what is being said here.[15] The "looking glass" means we develop our self-concept in terms

of how other people react to us. People are likely to respond to those labeled mentally ill as if they were mentally ill. As a result, those labeled mentally ill may well define themselves as being different or "crazy" and begin playing that role. Authorities who adhere to the interactional model raise a key question: "If we relate to people with emotional/behavioral problems as if they are mentally ill, how can we expect them to act in emotionally healthy and responsible ways?"

Compared to a physical illness, a diagnosis of a mental illness carries a greater stigma. In 1972 Senator Thomas Eagleton was forced to withdraw his candidacy for vice president on the Democratic ticket after it was revealed that he had received electroshock treatments for depression. The leaders of the Democratic party feared that the public would perceive someone who had once received psychiatric help as too "unstable" and "dangerous" to be in line for the presidency. On the other hand, Franklin Roosevelt had a physical disability resulting from polio, but he was elected president four times.

Szasz also argues that the mental-illness approach is used (perhaps unintentionally) as a means of control over people who do not conform to social expectations.[16] The former Soviet Union had a long history of labeling dissenters (including literary figures and intellectuals who would be respected in this country) as mentally ill and then sending them to concentration camps or to insane asylums. In the past, psychiatrists in Russia often concluded that people who did not accept the Marxist–Leninist philosophy were psychologically impaired.

Are some psychiatrists using mental-illness labels to control the behavior of nonconformists in our country? Szasz asserts that they are and uses the example of homosexuality—listed as a mental disorder by the American Psychiatric Association until 1974. As another example, Szasz cites Dana L. Farnsworth, a Harvard psychiatrist and an authority on college psychiatric services:

> *Library vandalism, cheating and plagiarism, stealing in the college or community stores or in the dormitories, unacceptable or antisocial sexual practices (overt homosexuality, exhibitionism, promiscuity), and the unwise and unregulated use of harmful drugs are examples of behavior that suggest the presence of emotionally unstable persons....*[17]

Mental-illness labels do have a "boundary" effect; they define what behaviors a society defines as "sick," with pressures then being put on citizens to avoid such behaviors. Szasz's point is that a number of nonconformists are adversely affected by the use of the medical model to control their behavior.

Adherents to the interactional approach assert that mental illness is a myth. They maintain that people are labeled mentally ill for two main reasons: They may have an intense unwanted emotion, or they may be engaged in dysfunctional (or deviant) behavior. Assigning a mental-illness label to unwanted emotions or dysfunctional behaviors does not tell us how the emotions or behaviors originated, nor does it tell us how to treat such emotions and behaviors. The material presented later in this chapter on rational therapy does both: It gives us an approach for identifying the sources of unwanted emotions and dysfunctional behaviors and provides strategies for changing them.

Critical Thinking Questions

Which approach (the medical approach or the interactional approach) do you believe is more accurate in identifying why someone has an emotional or behavioral problem? Why?

Labeling as the Cause of Chronic "Mental Illness"

A question is frequently raised about Szasz's assertion that mental illness is a myth: "If you assert that mental illness doesn't exist, why do some people go through life as if they are mentally ill?" Thomas Scheff has developed a sociological theory that provides an answer.[18] Scheff's main hypothesis is that labeling is the most important determinant of people's displaying a chronic (long-term) mental illness.

Scheff begins by defining how he determines, for research purposes, who is mentally ill. Before giving his definition, he notes:

> *One source of immediate embarrassment to any social theory of "mental illness" is that the terms used in referring to these phenomena in our society prejudge the issue. The medical metaphor "mental illness" suggests a determinate process which occurs within the individual: the unfolding and development of disease. In order to avoid this assumption, we will utilize sociological, rather than medical, concepts to formulate the problem.*[19]

He goes on to state that the symptoms of mental illness can be viewed as violations of social norms and that he uses the term *mental illness* only to refer to those assigned such a label by professionals (usually psychiatrists).

Scheff indicates that thousands of studies have been conducted that seek to identify the origins of long-term mental disorders. Practically all of this research has focused on internal causes (for example, metabolic disorders, unconscious conflicts, chemical imbalances, heredity factors). These research efforts have been based on medical and psychological models of human behavior. Yet, amazingly, in spite of this extensive investigation, the determinants of chronic mental disorders (for example, schizophrenia) are largely unknown.

Scheff suggests that researchers may be looking in the wrong direction. He asserts that the major determinants are not inside a person but in social processes—that is, in interactions with others. Here's a brief summary of his theory.

Everyone, at times, violates social norms and commits acts that could be labeled as symptoms of mental illness. For example, a person may occasionally get in fights with others, experience intense depression or grief, be highly anxious, use drugs or alcohol to excess, display a fetish, or commit a highly unusual or bizarre act.

CASE EXAMPLE 5.2

Questioning the Usefulness of the Mental-Illness Concept

While working at a mental hospital, I was assigned the case of Kevin Tanko (name has been changed), a 19-year-old male who had shot and killed two people in the City-County Courthouse in a medium-size city in a midwestern state. Two psychiatrists diagnosed him as schizophrenic, and a court found him "innocent by reason of insanity." He was then committed to the mental hospital where I was employed as a social worker.

Why did Mr. Tanko kill these two people—one was the county coroner and the other was a secretary for a business (she came to the courthouse simply to deliver some papers)? Mr. Tanko had never met either of these people. Labeling Mr. Tanko as insane provides an explanation to the general public that he committed these tragic murders because he was "crazy." But does such a label explain why he killed these two people whom he had never met before, rather than killing someone else or committing some other bizarre act? Does the label explain what would have prevented him from committing these murders? Does the label suggest the kind of treatment that will cure him? The answer to all these question is, of course, "no."

What Is Schizophrenia?

As noted earlier, schizophrenia is commonly defined as a psychotic condition characterized by disturbances of language and communication, thought, perception, affect, and behavior and lasting longer than 6 months. People who have Alzheimer's disease exhibit all these symptoms. Are they schizophrenic? No. What about those with a severe or profound cognitive disability who have a mental age of less than 2? They have these symptoms but are not considered schizophrenic. What about people who go into a coma following a serious accident? They also fit the definition but are not considered schizophrenic. The 19-year-old male who committed these murders knew these acts were wrong, was aware of what he was doing, was in contact with reality, and told me his reasons for doing what he did. Then why was he labeled schizophrenic?

Many authorities are now asserting that there is no definition of symptoms that separates people who have this "disease" from those who do not. I generally agree with Albert Ellis's assertion that the reasons for the occurrence of any deviant act can be determined by examining what the offender was thinking prior to and during the commission of the act.[a]

The Reasons Underlying the Two Murders

After Mr. Tanko described what had happened, it was understandable (even though bizarre) why he had done what he did. His account also identified the specific problems he needs help with. He described himself as the "black sheep" of the family, who, at the time of the murders, was experiencing several personal crises.

His father was a well-known surgeon, and his mother was an established accountant. He had an older brother who was attending medical school. He also had an older sister who had graduated from law school and was now a corporate attorney. Kevin Tanko never had a close relationship with either his brother or sister. His parents viewed Kevin as being "lazy," and they were upset because Kevin as yet did not have much of a focus in his life. When Kevin was younger, his parents disliked Kevin's friends. His parents viewed the friends as being unmotivated youths who dressed slovenly and who repeatedly became involved in petty delinquent acts for which they were arrested, including shoplifting, curfew violations, underage drinking, and possession of marijuana. Kevin also had a history of being arrested for such offenses.

Kevin Tanko's grades were insufficient to get him admitted to the public university located in the city in which the Tanko family lived. Mr. and Mrs. Tanko, however, made a substantial financial donation to this university, and subsequently Kevin Tanko was admitted. Mr. and Mrs. Tanko told Kevin they would pick up the financial costs of attending college if he agreed to discontinue seeing his friends. Kevin reluctantly agreed.

In his first year at the university, Kevin found an apartment to live in with two other male college freshmen. All three of these freshmen partied a lot and occasionally smoked marijuana. All three frequently skipped classes, and all three were placed on "final probation" by the university because of their very low grades. Mr. and Mrs. Tanko were very upset with Kevin's grades. They informed him that they were going to substantially reduce his allowance and that his grades had to improve next semester; if not, they would stop giving him any money.

For the first 2 weeks of the spring semester Kevin tried his best to go to his classes and also to study. To have spending money, he took two part-time jobs as a waiter at two different restaurants. To make additional money, Kevin and his two roommates began holding beer parties at their apartment. They would purchase two half-barrels of beer, as one of the roommates had a fake I.D. They would then charge $6 per person for others (mostly under the legal drinking age) to drink all that they wanted. About the 3rd week of the semester, things started really going bad for Kevin. His girlfriend, Jocelyn, broke up with him. Kevin felt sorry for himself. He started drinking more and smoking more pot. Two weeks later he showed up for work stoned for one of his waiter jobs and was fired immediately. Kevin became more and more stressed out. He was upset because Jocelyn told him she never would date him again. He started missing classes and realized he was flunking out of college. His parents unexpectedly stopped by when he was inebriated and made it clear they were furious with the way he was living.

(continued)

CASE EXAMPLE 5.2 *(continued)*

Three days later Kevin and his two roommates were giving a party, and police officers raided the party, arrested 57 people for underage drinking, and arrested Kevin and his two roommates for selling beer to minors. Kevin spent the night in jail, and the next day was bailed out by his furious parents. The police chief decided to set an example of trying to end college beer parties by writing tickets to Kevin and his roommates that amounted to a total of $13,500.

Upon returning home, Kevin was angry and frustrated. His thought processes were the following: "To h_____ with it. Everything is going bad for me. I'm flunking out of school. My girlfriend dumped me. I've been fired from one of my jobs. My parents are furious with me. I've got this huge fine to pay, and have no money. Life sucks. I wish I were dead, but I don't have the courage to kill myself. I hate that police chief for deciding to make an example of me. He's largely to blame for all my troubles. I'm going to saw off the barrel of the shotgun I own. Then I'll put it under my trench coat and march into his office and blow him away. I probably will be shot to death trying to escape—but then my miseries will be over with."

That's what Kevin tried to do. He sawed off his shotgun, loaded it, and walked into the City-County Courthouse. (At that time the courthouse did not have a metal detector.)

Upon arriving at the door of the police department, an officer stopped him because Kevin was perspiring and acting suspiciously. The officer asked him to unbutton his trench coat. Kevin turned around and started running away. The officer was momentarily stunned by Kevin's actions and did not immediately pursue him.

Kevin's thought processes then became "To h_____ with it. I'm such a loser. I can't even shoot the guy I wanted to shoot. I'll just kill as many people as I can before I get shot." He took out his shotgun and shot the first two people he encountered—the county coroner and a secretary who was delivering papers at the courthouse. Both died almost immediately.

A few seconds later, Kevin was shot in the leg and the back by the police officer who initially stopped him. Kevin survived. He eventually went to court, was found innocent by reason of insanity, and was sent to a mental hospital for the so-called "criminally insane."

From talking with Kevin and identifying his thinking before and during these homicides, I was able to pinpoint certain factors that led to these murders: his thoughts that everything was going wrong in his life; his wanting to strike out at others for the miseries he was feeling; his thoughts about his financial problems and his failures in college; his thoughts about his

parents being furious with him and viewing him as the black sheep in the family; and his thoughts about his girlfriend, whom he deeply loved, ending the relationship.

Such thoughts help to explain why he decided to kill some people, whereas the label *schizophrenia* does not. If the foregoing problems had been identified and treated prior to the murders, the slayings might have been prevented. What Kevin needed was to find more of a career focus in his life. He needed to improve his relationships with his parents and siblings. He needed to get help for his excessive drinking and heavy use of marijuana. He needed to receive help for managing his anger. He needed to learn and practice stress management techniques. These specific problems are the ones that will have to be addressed during his hospitalization. In no way do I feel that Kevin should be excused for his actions, as implied by the term *innocent by reason of insanity*. But he does need help for these problems. (In 10 or 12 years, he will probably be released; if these problems are not rectified, he will be a danger to society upon his release.)

If you are wondering how anyone could reach a point at which he does something as bizarre as killing two people, remember that it is necessary to attempt to view the situation from the deviant person's perspective. You must try to consider all the circumstances, pressures, values, and belief systems of the deviant person.

Another example highlights the fact that practically anyone will do something bizarre when circumstances become desperate. A number of years ago a passenger plane crashed in the Andes Mountains in the wintertime. A number of people were killed, but there were nearly 30 survivors. Rescue efforts initially failed to locate the survivors, who took shelter from the cold in the wreckage of the plane. The survivors were without food for more than 40 days before they were finally rescued. During this time, they were faced with the choice of dying of starvation or cannibalizing those who had died. It was a desperate, difficult decision. (Psychologically, many people who commit a bizarre act feel they are facing a comparably desperate decision.) In this situation, all but one of the initial crash survivors chose cannibalism. The one who refused died of starvation.

[a]Albert Ellis, *A Guide to Rational Living*, 3rd ed. (New York: Wilshire, 1998).

SOURCE: From The Personal Problem Solver, Charles Zastrow and Dae Chang, eds. Copyright © 1977 by Prentice Hall. Reprinted by permission of Charles Zastrow.

Usually the person who has unwanted emotions or who commits deviant acts is not identified (labeled) as mentally ill. His or her emotions and actions are ignored, unrecognized, or rationalized some other manner.

Occasionally, however, such norm violations are perceived by others as "abnormal." The offenders are

then labeled mentally ill and consequently are related to as if they were mentally ill. Being highly suggestible to cues from others, they then begin to define and perceive themselves as mentally ill.

Traditional stereotypes define the mentally ill role, both for those who are labeled mentally ill and for the people they interact with. Those labeled mentally ill are often rewarded for enacting that social role. They are given sympathy and attention and are excused from holding a job, fulfilling other role requirements, and being held responsible for their wrongdoings.

In addition, those labeled mentally ill are punished for attempting to return to conventional roles. They are viewed with suspicion and implicitly considered to still be insane. They may have considerable difficulty obtaining employment or receiving a job promotion.

Such pressures and interactions with others gradually lead to changes in their self-concept; they begin to view themselves as different, as insane. Often a vicious circle is created. The more they enact the mentally ill role, the more they are defined and treated as mentally ill; the more explicitly they are defined as mentally ill, the more they are related to as if they are mentally ill, and so on. Unless this vicious circle is interrupted, it will lead to a career of long-term mental illness. Scheff's conclusion is that the labeling is the single most important determinant of chronic mental illness.

Accordingly, significant changes are needed in diagnostic and treatment practices. Mental health personnel are frequently faced with uncertainty in deciding whether a person has a mental disorder. An informal norm has been developed to handle this uncertainty: When in doubt, it is better to judge a well person ill than to judge an ill person well. This norm is based on two assumptions: (a) A diagnosis of illness results in only minimal damage to one's status and reputation. (b) Unless the illness is treated, it will become progressively worse. However, both these assumptions are questionable. Unlike medical treatment, psychiatric treatment can drastically change a person's status in the community; for example, it can remove rights that are difficult to regain. Furthermore, if Scheff is right about the adverse effects of mental-illness labeling, then the exact opposite norm should be established to handle uncertainty (when in doubt, do not label a person mentally ill). This would be in accord with the legal approach, "When in doubt, acquit" or "A person is innocent until proved guilty."

Critical Thinking Question

How has your self-concept and your life been impacted by negative or positive labeling from others?

If labeling is indeed a major determinant of mental illness, then certain changes are called for in treating violators of social norms. One is to attempt to maintain and treat people with problems in their local community without labeling them mentally ill or sending them to a mental hospital where their playing the role of the mentally ill is likely to be reinforced. The field of mental health has, in the past several years, been moving in this direction. Another outgrowth of Scheff's theory would be increasing public education efforts to inform the general population of the nature of emotional/behavioral problems and the adverse effects that result from inappropriate labeling.

Other Issues

There are other issues at stake in the field of mental health. These include care for the homeless, the civil rights of those labeled mentally ill, the improper use of the insanity plea to excuse criminals from their actions, the use (or misuse) of drugs in "treating" supposedly mentally ill people, and the merits and shortcomings of managed mental health-care systems.

The Homeless

One of the population groups that has received considerable media attention is the homeless. Having hundreds of thousands of people homeless in the richest nation in the world is a national disgrace. The number of homeless Americans is large and growing larger. The exact number is unknown, but estimates range from 1 million to over 3 million people.[20] Many of the homeless are living on the street, in parks, in subways, or in abandoned buildings, seeking food from garbage cans.

It has been estimated that between 20% and 25% of the homeless suffer from serious and chronic forms of mental illness.[21] Discharged from institutions without the support they need, tens of thousands of former patients live on the street in abominable conditions. Instead of providing support services for discharged patients, many states have a deinstitutionalization program of simply drugging people and dumping them into the street.

Such an approach is a far cry from what was envisioned 60 years ago when federal authorities embarked on an ambitious program to phase out large state hospitals and move the disturbed to more

© AP Photo/Ron Edmonds

Although the number of homeless in America is unknown, estimates range from 1 million to more than 3 million people. Many sleep in streets, subways, parks, abandoned buildings, and cars. Our nation's capital is no exception.

humane and convenient treatment in communities. This commendable goal has not been fulfilled. Federal, state, and local governments have failed to provide enough housing, transitional care, and job training to integrate patients into society. In many areas of the country, a revolving-door policy prevails: Patients are discharged from state hospitals, only to return to the hospitals again because of a lack of community support.

It is true that institutional care not only is expensive ($10,000–60,000 per month for full-service programs)[22] but frequently also stifles the intellectual, social, and physical growth of patients. But tragically, the necessary support services have not been developed in most communities to serve discharged patients.

There are a variety of reasons for the large increase in the number of homeless. Deinstitutionalization of state mental hospitals is one cause. Cutbacks in social services by the federal government is

another. Urban renewal projects have demolished low-cost housing in many areas. The shift from blue-collar jobs to service and high-tech jobs in our society has sharply reduced the demand for unskilled labor. Another factor has been a recent trend to ignore members of our society who are unable to fend for themselves. Most of the homeless are such because they cannot afford the housing that is available; our country does not have a commitment to a social policy of providing affordable housing to the poor. The majority of the homeless are not mentally ill, but simply too poor to afford available housing.

Solutions to the dismal conditions in which the homeless are living include low-cost housing, job training and placement programs, and community services for those with emotional problems. Is our society willing to provide the necessary resources to meet the needs of the homeless? Deplorably, the answer is, "No. Not at present."

Civil Rights

State laws have permitted the involuntary confinement of people in mental hospitals, which can be seen as an infringement of their civil right to liberty. Although state laws vary, in some jurisdictions, people can be hospitalized without their consent and without due process.[23] Often all that is required for confinement is the statement of a physician.[24]

When I worked at a hospital for the "criminally insane," there was a patient who was originally arrested on a disorderly conduct charge for urinating on a fire hydrant. Some neighbors thought he might be mentally ill, so the judge ordered that he be sent to a mental hospital for a 60-day observation period to determine his sanity. The hospital judged him "insane" and "incompetent to stand trial" on the charge. He was not considered a threat to himself or to others. But because of the hospital's finding, the judge confined him to a maximum-security hospital for the criminally insane. When I met him there, he had already been hospitalized for 9 years—for committing an offense for which, if found guilty, he probably would only have been required to pay a small fine. Involuntary confinement has been a controversial practice for years.

Today, in most jurisdictions, people cannot be involuntarily confined unless they commit illegal acts (such as aggravated assaults or suicide attempts) that demonstrate they are a threat either to themselves or to others. Such a policy provides some assurance that emotionally disturbed individuals' right to liberty will be safeguarded. But the policy also has been sharply criticized. Emotionally disturbed people who provide warning signs of doing bodily harm to others cannot be involuntarily confined unless they actually commit an illegal act. As a result, the civil right of others to safety in our society is sometimes infringed upon.

Striking an acceptable balance between the disturbed person's right to liberty and society's right to safety and protection is complex. Throughout our nation's history, policies on this issue have swung back and forth on the continuum between these two sets of rights.

Another problem in some mental hospitals is that patients do not receive adequate treatment, even after several years of confinement. Lack of treatment became a civil rights violation when, in 1964, Congress established a statutory right to treatment in the Hospitalization of the Mentally Ill Act.[25]

Decisions about providing treatments such as electroconvulsive therapy (which has questionable value and may cause brain damage) also raise civil rights questions. The severely disturbed are often unable to make rational choices about their own welfare. Permission of relatives is sometimes obtained, but this still denies patients their fundamental rights.

A closely related issue is the extent to which patients in mental hospitals have the right to refuse treatment. Nolen-Hoeksema notes:

One of the greatest fears of people committed against their will is that they will be given drugs or other treatments that rob them of their consciousness, their personality, and their free will. Many states now do not allow mental institutions or prisons to administer treatments without the informed consent of patients. Informed consent means that a patient accepts treatment after receiving a full and understandable explanation of the treatment being offered and making a decision based on his or her own judgment of the risks and benefits of the treatment.[26]

Some states recognize that patients in mental hospitals have the right to refuse treatment, whereas other states do not. In some of the states that recognize the right to refuse treatment, there are provisions that this right can be overruled in certain circumstances. For example, if a patient is psychotic or manic, it may be judged that she or he cannot make a reasonable decision; thereby, the decision must be made by others.

Patients' psychiatrists and perhaps families sometimes seek court rulings allowing the mental hospital to administer treatment even if patients refuse treatment. Judges usually agree with the requests of psychiatrists or families to force treatment on patients.[27]

Plea of Innocent by Reason of Insanity

In 1979 a San Francisco jury found Dan White innocent by reason of insanity on charges of the premeditated murder of Mayor George Moscone and Supervisor Harvey Milk. This verdict was rendered even though testimony clearly showed that the murders had been carefully planned and carried out by White.[28] The general public was as shocked by the jury's decision as it had been by the crime. White was confined in a mental hospital for a few years and then released in 1984. (He subsequently committed suicide.)

In 1982 John Hinckley, Jr., was found innocent by reason of insanity for the attempted assassination of President Reagan a year earlier. Three other people were also injured by Hinckley in the assassination attempt. He is currently receiving treatment in a mental hospital.

In another case, Kenneth Bianchi (called the Hollywood "Hillside Strangler") was accused of murdering 13 women in the Los Angeles area and 2 more in Washington state in the 1970s. Six different psychiatrists examined him and came to three different conclusions about his mental state: Two judged him sane, two judged him insane, and two were undecided.[29]

Cases such as those of White, Hinckley, and Bianchi have forced the courts and psychiatrists to examine more carefully the plea of innocent by reason of insanity. As indicated earlier, the terms *mental illness* and *mental health* are poorly defined. Mental illness (insanity) may not even exist. In a number of trials involving the insanity plea, it has become routine for the prosecuting attorney to use as witnesses those psychiatrists who are likely to judge the defendant "sane," whereas the defendant's attorney uses as witnesses those psychiatrists who are likely to arrive at an "insane" recommendation. An authority notes:

Among psychiatrists, there is nothing remotely approaching a consensus on what constitutes insanity. Moreover, psychiatrists themselves concede that they lack reliable means for determining whether a person was insane in any sense at the time of a crime. All too often, they must rely heavily on the accused's behavior and on what he tells them—two types of data that a shrewd defendant can carefully orchestrate.[30]

Defendants are increasingly becoming aware that they can probably get a psychiatrist to label them insane by "acting crazy," such as by openly performing indecent acts or by claiming to hear voices.

The argument for eliminating the insanity plea is that people are literally using it to get away with murder and other serious felonies. Instead of forcing people to take responsibility for their felonies, the insanity plea excuses them for their crimes. The plea enables a clever defendant or attorney to seek refuge from criminal punishment.

When a person is acquitted by reason of insanity, she or he is generally sent to a mental institution. Under the law, a person is kept there until doctors determine he or she is no longer dangerous and a judge concurs. Sadly, the measures for determining "no longer dangerous" are as untrustworthy as those used to assign a mental-illness label.

Critical Thinking Questions

Do you believe the insanity defense should be abolished? Why or why not?

For example, E. E. Kemper, III, spent 5 years in a hospital for the criminally insane after murdering his grandparents. Kemper convinced psychiatrists and the judge that he was cured by giving rational answers to a battery of psychological tests. (He had memorized the answers prior to the tests.) Three years after his release, he was again arrested for brutally killing eight women—including his mother.[31]

Psychiatrist Lee Coleman urges that the insanity defense be eliminated altogether to resolve this dilemma. Doing so would allow courts to deal with the guilt or innocence of an individual without interference from psychiatrists. Coleman states: "Victims are no less injured by one who is mentally sound and violent."[32] Coleman further urges that if the convicted individual later wishes help for emotional or behavioral problems, he or she can then request it.

Because of the controversy over the insanity plea, a number of states have revised their laws surrounding it. One approach adopted by a number of states is to have a two-step process in which the jury first determines whether the defendant is innocent or guilty. If the verdict is guilty, the jury then decides if that person is sane or insane. (If found insane, the

defendant is usually sent to a maximum-security mental hospital.) At least three states—Montana, Idaho, and Utah—have abolished the insanity defense entirely, but there's evidence that those who would have used the plea are now just found incompetent to stand trial and end up in the same hospitals.

Use of Psychotropic Drugs

Psychotropic drugs include tranquilizers, antipsychotic drugs (such as Thorazine), and antidepressants. Since their discovery in 1954, these drugs have been credited with markedly decreasing the number of patients in state and county hospitals from 550,000 in 1955 to less than 100,000 at the present time.[33] Psychotropic drugs do not "cure" emotional problems but are useful in reducing high levels of anxiety, depression, and tension.

Americans make extensive use of psychotropic drugs, particularly tranquilizers, such as Valium, Librium, and Miltown. Most general practitioners prescribe tranquilizers for the large number of patients who complain of tension and emotional upset. Lithium and Prozac have been found to be fairly effective in reducing depression in a number of clients and are now widely prescribed by physicians.

"Popping pills" (both legal and illegal) has become fashionable, but the dangers of excessive drug use include physical and psychological dependency and unwanted side effects. There is also the danger that, because drugs provide temporary symptom relief, users may avoid making the necessary changes in their lives to resolve the problems causing the anxiety, depression, or tension. Physicians face a dilemma in balancing the benefits of psychotropic drugs against the dangers of abuse, particularly when such drugs are sought by patients for extended periods of time. Because psychotropic drugs provide only temporary relief for a patient's *symptoms* (such as anxiety and depression), many authorities urge that patients also receive counseling or psychotherapy to help resolve the underlying emotional difficulties.

Managed Mental Health Care*

Social workers are the largest group of mental health providers in the country.[34] There are clinical social workers across the United States treating adults,

---

*Michael Wallace, MSSW, LCSW, was a contributing author for this section.

Many complex issues are raised as health-care delivery is shifting from practice based on fee-for-service to managed-care systems.

adolescents, and children for a variety of mental health concerns ranging from emotional/behavioral disturbances to serious debilitating mental illnesses. Social workers practice in a variety of settings, including private practice, inpatient psychiatric hospitals, outpatient mental health clinics, veterans hospitals, prisons, and nursing homes. Increasingly in our society, mental health care is being provided by managed health care systems. In fact according to the trade association America's Health Insurance Plans, 90% of insured Americans are now enrolled in plans with some form of managed care.[35]

Managed health care is a generic term used to describe a variety of methods of delivering and financing health-care services designed to contain the costs of service delivery while maintaining a defined level of quality of care. At its best, it is perceived as a system in which appropriate control, structure, and accountability enable the most efficient use of health resources to achieve maximal health outcome. (To date, there is a lack of agreement as to what is the

"best" system.) At its worst, it is perceived as a system in which no real dollars are saved, and money is diverted to administrative operations and profits at the expense of needed patient services. Because managed health care tends to have more to do with managing cost than managing care, health-care delivery has shifted from practice based on fee-for-service (in which the social worker is directly reimbursed by the insurance company) to managed-care systems.

An example of a managed-care system is the health maintenance organization (HMO). As noted, the majority of Americans with private insurance are now enrolled in managed-care plans. HMOs have become a major component of managed mental health care offered by employers to their employees and family members. HMOs tend to have two major functions: One entails establishing policies and procedures that regulate benefits, payments, and providers. The second involves employing gatekeepers to review and authorize services.[36] Both functions serve the purpose of containing costs in the plans of managed mental health care, which is mainly done by restricting client benefits. Examples of restrictions include:

- limiting the number of visits for outpatient psychotherapy
- increasing the use of psychotropic medication as the primary treatment approach
- restricting the number of days covered for inpatient care
- limiting the number of dollars per year for mental health care per person
- limiting the number of dollars per lifetime for mental health care per person
- increasing deductibles
- increasing copayments
- requiring that services be preapproved by a gatekeeper HMO "case manager" for the types and costs of services provided

Managed Care and Evidence-Based Practice

Basing one's practice on the best available evidence is often referred to as *evidence-based practice* (EBP). The concept of EBP evolved in the field of medicine in response to the realization that many patients did not receive the most effective treatments available, sometimes with unfortunate outcomes. The assumption was that practitioners were not informed about the best treatments or perhaps were influenced more by authority and tradition than by empirical evidence.[37] The evolving paradigm of EBP not only emphasized the importance of empirical evidence in one's practice but also included skills for finding the best evidence and applying it to one's work. EBP is now well established in medical schools and is rapidly being adopted in social work programs as well.[38]

EBP is actually a broader concept than just using evidence-informed interventions. It incorporates using one's clinical expertise and the client's values and preferences when deciding what intervention to use. Evidence-based intervention should be used only when the worker is competent to do the intervention and it is compatible with the client's wishes and situation.

Although the term *evidence-based interventions* implies that some interventions are "evidence-based" and others are not, it is an oversimplification to think of EBP that way. There are many types of empirical evidence, ranging from the findings of randomized clinical trials (highly controlled control group studies), to simple follow-up studies, to descriptive studies and evolving best practices. EBP considers all of the evidence that is available and uses it to inform one's choice of intervention, consistent with one's professional competence and the client's preferences. For this reason it seems more accurate to describe this approach as "evidence-informed practice" than simply EBP.

Some EBP advocates argue that to treat anyone using treatments without known effectiveness is unethical. Also, some advocates assert that if one treatment program works better than other available treatment approaches, professionals have an ethical obligation to use it in order to best serve clients/patients. Advocates also have asserted that only interventions with demonstrated effectiveness should be supported financially. This assertion links demonstrations of effectiveness with funding through managed care systems.[39]

Social workers should be committed to giving clients the most current and effective treatments possible. However, there is considerable debate about EBP and how it should be applied to social work practice.[40]

This is partly because EBP is based on evidence-based medicine (EBM); the primary focus of EBM is the diagnosis of symptoms to determine which procedures and/or medications to prescribe. This approach may work well in medicine, but its applicability to social work in mental health needs to be questioned.

There is concern over the tendency of EBP to focus on the symptoms and to ignore other issues/concerns effecting the client's well-being. This approach goes against the traditional bio/psycho/social/cultural/spiritual/environmental approach used by social workers in both the assessment and treatment of mental health illness. In addition, some have criticized EBP on philosophical grounds, arguing that an evidence-based, rational model of decision making does not fit the realities of individualized, contextualized practice, especially nonmedical practice, wherein problems are less well defined.[41]

For example, conditions that have known biological causes, such as bipolar disorder and schizophrenia, are seen as primarily requiring psychopharmacological interventions only. This approach only looks at symptom reduction (e.g., decrease of mania), ignoring all other factors that may be contributing to the person's condition (such as stress, lack of employment, etc.).

With EBP, managed-care companies are also putting pressure on social workers and other mental health professionals to produce empirical treatments with proven outcomes.[42]

They are the driving force in promoting empirically supported treatments (ESTs).[43] This approach may well effect how social workers in mental health work with their clients, as EBP is increasingly dictating the types of treatments therapists can provide.[44]

EBP tends to ignore one of the hallmarks of good social work practice—individualizing clients. Social workers do not simply treat the problem, they build a therapeutic relationship; identify needs, goals, and resources; and emphasize mutuality in the relational context.[45]

The relationship between worker and client, the therapeutic alliance, has been demonstrated to have significant influences across numerous studies.[46] Thus, nearly half of the outcome relies on fundamental skills and abilities that must be fostered in social workers, apart from the type of treatment offered. The therapeutic alliance has long been identified as the key to successful outcomes for clients. In fact, research on treatment outcomes suggest that four factors can account for much of the improvement in clients: client or extra-therapeutic factors (40%); relationship factors (30%); placebo, hope, and expectancy factors (15%); and model/technique factors (15%).[47] We need to ensure that social workers are learning to build these therapeutic relationships as a proven intervention.

Because managed mental health care focuses on managing costs, a number of ethical dilemmas arise for social workers. The following are a few examples:

- The social worker's primary responsibility is to promote the well-being of clients (National Association of Social Workers [NASW] Code of Ethics). This may conflict with an HMO's focus on saving money or corporate profitability. Treatment is often dictated by what an HMO prescribes as "best" cost-saving practice, rather than what may be in the best interest of the client.
- The increased use of EBP can reduce clients to a set of symptoms instead of "respecting the uniqueness and worth of the individual." This also ignores the person-in-environment approach. In addition, if insurance companies insist that practitioners only use their approved list of treatments, it takes the decision-making power away from the client and the social worker, denying the client's right to self-determination.
- Social workers should respect a client's right to privacy. Social workers should protect the confidentiality of all information obtained in the course of professional service and should not disclose confidential information to third-party payers unless a client has authorized such disclosure. Because of contractual obligations a social worker may have with an HMO, providers are typically required to share a client's diagnosis, treatment plan, medication, social history, and so on. Often, this type of information is viewed and shared by HMO staffs that have no direct connection with the case at hand.
- Social workers should take reasonable steps to avoid abandoning a client who is still in need of services (NASW Code of Ethics). By their very nature, HMOs are designed to limit the number of treatment sessions, and any additional services must go through, at times, a cumbersome approval process. If the HMO refuses to authorize needed treatment, some social workers may be put into the position of providing pro bono (without cost) services to clients with serious ongoing needs.

The introduction of managed health care has raised additional complex issues, including:

- To what degree does the use of EBP work for or against the best interests of the client?
- How is quality of care defined and who defines it?
- What are the provisions for access to care for people considered at high health risk? For example, there have been instances in which a mental health-care provider has recommended inpatient care for a highly suicidal client, but the utilization review mechanism has denied reimbursement, with the client then subsequently taking his or her life![48]
- Who has legitimate access to clients' mental health records? Expanded review of care decisions and computerization means more sneaky eyes seeing personal mental health care information. Complex issues surrounding confidentiality arises with managed care.
- Do managed care efforts to streamline care and keep costs down lead to treating symptoms, not underlying causes? For example, prescribing drugs that provide symptom relief is cheaper than long-term psychotherapy.
- Does managed care lead to a system in which those therapists who see more people in less time are rewarded, while those therapists who provide longer-term care to fewer people are punished? (The answer is "Yes!")
- Because managed-care systems have policies that limit expenses, coverage limits can be a heavy

burden for people who need expensive medication and psychotherapy to treat such chronic mental disorders as bipolar disorder.

- A client's right to self-determination is a core value of social work practice. Self-determination implies that clients should be made aware of alternatives regarding their treatment and that they have a right to choose which of these courses of action they wish to take. In certain managed-care situations, a client can be denied psychotherapy for refusing to take medication as part of his or her treatment. Such a managed-care mandate conflicts with a client's right to choose his or her treatment. If the client chooses not to receive medication, the social worker is in the awkward position of having to choose between not providing needed psychotherapy or providing psychotherapy free of charge.

Increasing numbers of social workers in the mental health field find themselves at odds with the restrictions and dictates of HMOs. The result is that some social workers have begun to set up self-pay systems in which a client pays out of pocket for services at a reduced rate, thereby avoiding any contact with HMOs.

Social Structure and Mental Illness

EP 2.1.9a

Sociologists have conducted a number of studies on the relationships between social factors and the rate of mental illness. Questions they have tried to answer include: Is social-class status related to the rate of mental illness? Does illness occur more in urban areas, in suburbs, or in rural areas? Which age groups are more prone to be affected? Are men or women more likely to be affected? (As indicated earlier, there is a question as to whether mental illness exists. In this section, the term *mental illness* is used to refer to those labeled mentally ill.)

Social Class

The poor are more likely to be labeled mentally ill. People living below the poverty line in the United States are much more likely than those with incomes twice the poverty line to have serious psychological disorders.[49] A variety of explanations may help to understand these results. Perhaps the poor are less likely to seek treatment when emotional problems first begin to develop; they therefore become

mentally ill before receiving help. Perhaps they are under greater psychological stress. Perhaps their attitudes, values, educational histories, and living conditions make them more susceptible to becoming mentally ill. Perhaps mental illness leads to lower status.

Or there may be *no* actual difference in severity and rate of emotional problems among social classes. It is possible that psychiatrists are less likely to assign a mental-illness label to a person of higher status because of the stigma associated with the label. In addition, psychiatrists may have less understanding of the value systems of the poor and therefore be more likely to label behavior of lower-class patients as deviant or mentally ill.

As for why higher rates of mental illness are found in the lowest socioeconomic class, evidence is increasingly being found to support the "drift hypothesis."[50] The drift hypothesis holds that social class is not a cause but a consequence of mental disorder. Studies are indicating that a wide variety of mental illnesses impair individuals' ability to develop their skills and advance in the world of work, and thus prevent them from attaining social mobility.[51] Studies have also found that mentally ill people who have a higher class level tend to "drift" downward to the lowest socioeconomic class because their illness results in a lowered social status and a decrease in earning power.[52]

Critical Thinking Questions

Do you believe the drift hypothesis is valid in explaining why higher rates of mental illness are found in the lowest socioeconomic class? Why or why not?

A number of studies have also found social-class differences in quality of treatment of those labeled mentally ill.[53] Lower-class patients often receive lower-quality care (often just custodial care when hospitalized) and have lower rates of release when hospitalized in a mental institution.

Urbanization

There is some evidence that cities, particularly inner-city areas, have a higher rate of mental illness than rural areas.[54] This finding may be due to overcrowding and to the deteriorated quality of life—dirt, noise, crime, transportation problems, inadequate housing, unemployment, drugs—which create a higher level of emotional problems. Also, mental health facilities tend to be located in and around urban areas, which increases the probability that urban dwellers with emotional problems will be identified and treated.

Recent research on child development and crowding offers evidence that children growing up in crowded apartments, child care facilities, and neighborhoods are at a higher risk of developing severe mental disorders in later life. Overcrowding for children has also been found to be associated with difficulties in behavioral adjustment at school, lowered academic achievement, and impaired parent–child relationships.[55]

Age

Most severe and disabling physical illnesses (such as heart disease and cancer) tend to strike adults in the later years of their working lives. In contrast, mental illness tends to begin early in life. With mental illness, 50% of all lifetime cases begin by age 14.[56] Three-quarters begin by age 24.[57] These statistics indicate that mental disorders can be viewed as the chronic diseases of the young. Anxiety disorders (including panic attacks) often begin in the teenage years. Eating disorders and mood disorders typically begin in late adolescence. Substance abuse disorders typically begin in the early 20s.

The risk of mental disorders declines as people mature out of the high-risk younger years. It should be noted, however, that older adults are more apt than middle-aged adults to suffer from depression (which is partially due to the low status that older adults have in our society; low status leads to a crushing sense of uselessness and isolation). Additionally, older adults may experience disturbances associated with degeneration of brain cells from such causes as arteriosclerosis and chronic alcoholism.[58]

Marital Status

People who are single, divorced, or widowed have higher rates of mental disorder than married people. Married adults have lower levels of depression and anxiety compared to those who are single.[59]

Sex

Men and women are equally likely to be treated, but the nature of the diagnosis varies. Women are more likely to be diagnosed as suffering from anxiety, depression, and phobias and to be hospitalized in a mental institution. Men are more likely to be diagnosed as having a personality disorder.[60]

The vast majority of psychiatrists are men, and there is evidence that psychiatrists are more apt to consider sexual promiscuity or aggressive behavior in women a mental disorder as compared to in men.[61]

Race

Compared with Whites, African Americans are more likely to be diagnosed as mentally ill, and their rate of hospitalization is substantially higher.[62] There are several sociological explanations for these trends. African Americans may be under greater psychological pressure due to discrimination. Or the higher rates may stem from their lower social status, as a greater proportion of people in the lower social classes are diagnosed as mentally ill. Or because most psychiatrists are White, a lack of awareness of the lifestyles of African Americans may lead psychiatrists to more readily assign the label "mentally ill" to African Americans who may differ in class, status, cultural values, and cultural background.

Combatants in Wars

Combatants in wars are apt to experience higher rates of mental illness than the general population, often, the mental health services provided to them are inadequate. Kornblum and Julian state the following about soldiers returning from combat duty in Iraq and Afghanistan:

Once called shell shock or combat fatigue, what is now known as post-traumatic stress disorder, or PTSD, was frequently confused with cowardice or weakness and was a severe problem in past wars. Now mental-health researchers understand that an individual may develop PTSD after witnessing or experiencing any traumatic event. The treatment of soldiers with PTSD may improve as a result of a recent, highly publicized study of the mental-health needs of soldiers returning from Iraq and Afghanistan, conducted a few months after their return. It found that one in eight American GIs serving in those countries reported symptoms of PTSD. The symptoms of this disorder may be quite severe and can include flashbacks, nightmares, feelings of detachment, irritability, trouble concentrating, and sleeplessness…The research also showed that fewer than half of returned soldiers with symptoms of PTSD seek help, mostly out of fear of being stigmatized or hurting their careers.[63]

Treatment

Brief History

Although the history of treatment for the emotionally disturbed is fascinating, it is also filled with injustices and tragedies. George Rosen explains that most societies have developed unique ways of viewing mental illness and treating those so labeled.[64] In some societies, deviants have been highly valued and even treated as prophets with supernatural powers. In others the emotionally disturbed have been viewed as evil and even feared as possessing demonic powers. In medieval times, for example, the emotionally disturbed were viewed as possessed by demons; they were "treated" by flogging, starving, and dunking in hot water to drive the devils out. During a brief period in our colonial history, certain disturbed individuals were viewed as "witches" and were burned at the stake. Prior to the 19th century, the severely disturbed in the United States were confined in "almshouses," received only harsh custodial care, and often were chained to the walls.[65]

In the 19th century, a few mental institutions in France, England, and the United States began to take a more humanitarian approach to treating the disturbed. Although the severely disturbed were still confined in institutions, they began to be viewed either as having an illness or as having an emotional problem. The physical surroundings were improved, and efforts were made to replace the harsh custodial treatment with a caring approach that recognized each resident as a person deserving respect and dignity. Unfortunately, these humanitarian efforts were not widely accepted, in part because they were considered too expensive. Most of the severely disturbed continued to be confined in overcrowded, unsanitary dwellings with inadequate care and diet.

In 1908 Clifford Beers's book *A Mind That Found Itself* was published.[66] Beers had been confined as a patient, and the book recounted the atrocities occurring in this "madhouse." The book reached a wide audience and sensitized the public to the emotional trauma experienced by those confined. Under Beers's leadership, mental health associations were formed that advocated the need for improved inpatient care and initiated the concept of outpatient treatment.

Between 1900 and 1920, Sigmund Freud developed his psychoanalytic theories about the causes and treatment of emotional problems. According to Freud, emotional problems were mental illnesses that resulted from early traumatic experiences, internal psychological conflicts, fixations at various stages of development, and unconscious psychological processes. Most members of the counseling professions (psychiatry, clinical psychology, social work) accepted, from the 1920s to the 1950s, Freud's and other psychoanalytic theorists' views with regard to diagnosing and treating the disturbed. Due to Freud's influence, the public adopted a more humanitarian approach to treating the disturbed.

However, in the 1950s, questions began to arise about the effectiveness of the psychoanalytic method. It was expensive and lengthy (an analysis took 4 or 5 years), and research studies began to show that the rate of improvement for those undergoing analysis was no higher than that for people receiving no treatment.[67] Since the 1950s, a variety of counseling approaches have been developed that reject most or all of the concepts underlying psychoanalysis; these newer approaches include behavior modification, rational therapy, reality therapy, transactional analysis, family therapy, feminist intervention, and client-centered therapy.[68]

Certain segments of the medical profession have continued to maintain, since the 19th century, that mental illness is akin to other physical illnesses. They assert that infectious diseases, genetic endowment, and metabolic imbalances are the causes of mental disorders.[69] However, only a few specific organic causes have been identified. General paresis, for instance, which is a progressive emotional disorder, has been linked to syphilis; pellagra, another disorder, has been found to result from a dietary deficiency.

The notion that mental disorders are physiological led to certain medical treatments that now appear to be tragedies. In the 18th century, bloodletting was widely practiced. In the early 20th century, prefrontal lobotomies (surgical slashing of the frontal section of the brain) were performed to "remove" the mental illness. Lobotomies have little therapeutic value, cause lasting brain damage, and result in patients becoming docile and having a cognitive disability.

Critical Thinking Question

What services do you believe need to be provided to discharged mental patients?

CASE EXHIBIT 5.3

Asylums and Total Institutions

In 1961 Erving Goffman wrote *Asylums*, which described life inside state mental hospitals. Goffman indicates that such mental hospitals are "total institutions." (Other total institutions are prisons, boot camps, monasteries, and convents.) In a total institution, a resident is cut off from society for appreciable periods of time and required to lead a regimented life. Inside an asylum, residents are stripped of their clothing and deprived of contact with the outside world. Total institutions seek to control residents fully and to resocialize and remake their lives. The fear of expulsion is often a major control mechanism. Long-term confinement in asylums usually causes people to lose their capacities to respond in an independent, rational fashion and undermines their ability to cope with the outside world.

Total institutions teach residents to accept the staff's view of right and wrong, eroding residents' capacities to think independently. Such actions as questioning the therapeutic value of treatment programs are taken not as signs of mental stability but as a symptom of sickness. The "good" patient, from the staff's point of view, is one who is undemanding, docile, and obedient. In general, mental hospitals downgrade patients' feelings of self-esteem and emphasize their failures and inadequacies. Uniform furniture and clothing, a regimented routine, and a custodial atmosphere encourage patients to be docile and unassertive. The use of the medical-model approach to emotional problems encourages patients to view themselves as sick and in need of help. Such "resocialization" actually hinders residents from making a successful return to society. There is a high probability that long-term hospitalization will do more harm than good. The film *One Flew over the Cuckoo's Nest* vividly illustrates the resocialization process described by Goffman.

SOURCE: Erving Goffman, *Asylums: Essays on the Social Situation of Mental Patients and Other Inmates* (New York: Doubleday, 1961).

Current Trends

In the past 50 years, there have been two major developments in the treatment of the severely disturbed. The first was the discovery and use of psychoactive drugs, both tranquilizers and antidepressants. The initial hope was that such drugs would cure severe disturbances, but it was soon realized that they provide primarily symptom relief and thereby enable the disturbed person to be more accessible to other therapy programs and approaches.[70] The second development was deinstitutionalization. Mental health practitioners realized that mental hospitals, instead of "curing" the disturbed, were frequently perpetuating disturbed behavior via long-term hospitalization. That is, the disturbed were labeled mentally ill and came to define themselves as "different" and enact the insane role.[71] They also became adapted to the relaxed, safe life of a hospital; the longer they stayed, the more they perceived the outside world as threatening.

Mental health professionals now use hospitalization only for those whose emotional problems pose a serious threat to their own well-being or to that of others. Psychotherapy and drug therapy are the main treatment approaches used in mental hospitals. In most cases now, hospitalization for an emotional problem is brief.

The concept of deinstitutionalization has brought about a significant expansion of services designed to meet the needs of the disturbed in their home community, including community-based mental health centers, halfway houses, rehabilitation workshops, social therapeutic clubs, and foster-care services for the disturbed.

A criticism of the deinstitutionalization approach has been that some communities have returned long-term patients to society *without* developing adequate community-based support services. The result is that many of the patients who have been discharged are living with families, friends, or on the street and are receiving little or no counseling and/or medical services.

Recent investigations have revealed incidents of discharged mental patients living in squalor in unlicensed group homes, in low-quality hotels, and on the street.[72] Many are victims of crime, fire, and medical neglect. Some are fed rancid food and exposed to rats and cockroaches. Sometimes such former patients set fires and abuse others; a few commit homicide or suicide.

Treatment Facilities: Community Mental Health Centers

Treatment services for emotional/behavioral problems are provided by nearly every direct-service social welfare agency, including public welfare agencies, probation and parole agencies, penal institutions, school social services, family service agencies, adoption agencies, private psychotherapy clinics, sheltered workshops, social service units in hospitals, and nursing homes. However, in many communities, mental health centers are a primary resource for serving those with emotional problems.

Community mental health centers were given their impetus with the passage by the federal government of the Community Mental Health Centers Act of 1963. This act provided for transferring the care and treatment of the majority of "mentally ill" people from state hospitals to their home communities. The emphasis is on local care, with the provision of comprehensive services (particularly to underprivileged areas and people).

Other emphases are (a) early diagnosis, treatment, and return to the community; (b) location of centers "near and accessible to" the populations they serve; and (c) the provision of comprehensive care consisting of five basic components: inpatient care, outpatient care, partial hospitalization (that is, day, night, and weekend care), emergency care, and consultation/education. Services provided are expected to relate to a wide range of problem areas and population groups, such as the disturbed, older persons, minorities, and people with alcohol and other drug-related problems.[73]

Professionals in a community mental health center may include psychiatrists, social workers, psychologists, psychiatric nurses, specialized consultants, occupational and recreational therapists, paraprofessionals, and volunteers. Typical services include outpatient care, inpatient care, alcohol and chemical abuse treatment, work evaluation, occupational therapy, family and group therapy, transportation services, counseling of children and adults, crisis intervention (including 24-hour emergency care), community education, and field training of students in the helping professions.

Community mental health services have in recent years received increasing criticism. Studies have found that some community mental health services are ineffective and inadequate.[74] Patients still have high readmission rates and inadequate levels of adjustment to the community.[75] Many centers have been ineffective in dealing with the personal and societal problems of large numbers of poor people because many of these so-called comprehensive centers provide little more than traditional inpatient and outpatient care for middle-class patients.[76]

On the other hand, proponents of community mental health centers argue that the centers have shown impressive results. For example, their programs have reduced the number of people in state and county mental hospitals from 550,000 in 1955 to less than 100,000 at the present time.[77]

Social Work and Mental Health

Social workers were first employed in the mental health field in 1906 to take social histories of newly admitted patients to Manhattan State Hospital in New York City.[78] Since then they have been involved in providing a variety of preventive, diagnostic, and treatment services.

Over the years, there has been a shift in emphasis from treating the individual to treating the family. Social workers, psychologists, and psychiatrists now function interchangeably as individual, family, and

© Mary Kate Denny/PhotoEdit

Many social agencies offer counseling and therapy to people with emotional problems. Art therapy is one activity these professionals use in working with children at a private medical center.

group therapists. All three professional groups are also involved in designing and administering mental health programs. Other professionals involved in working as a team in mental health facilities include psychiatric nurses, occupational therapists, and recreational therapists.

The number of social workers providing mental health services in the United States is larger than the number of psychiatrists or clinical psychologists providing such services.[79] Many social agencies, in addition to community mental health centers, provide counseling and psychotherapy to people with emotional problems. Such agencies include schools, family counseling agencies, social service departments, hospitals, adoption agencies, and probation and parole departments. An increasing number of clinical social workers are opening private practices to provide individual, family, and group therapy for a variety of emotional problems. Increasingly, payments from public and private insurance programs reimburse social workers for providing therapy on a private basis.

The NASW has been promoting state licensing (or registration) requirements to assure the public that social work practitioners, especially those in private practice, meet high standards of competency. All states have now enacted legislation to license social workers.

The NASW has also established a national Register of Clinical Social Workers. Requirements for membership are:

- A master's or doctoral degree in social work from a graduate school accredited by the Council on Social Work Education (CSWE).
- Two years or 3,000 hours of postgraduate clinical social work experience, supervised by a clinical social worker with at least 2 years of experience.
- Active membership in the Academy of Certified Social Workers (ACSW) or a state license that requires an examination.[80]

At one time, the social work role in the mental health field was generally considered subordinate to psychiatry. But with a growing recognition that emotional problems are primarily problems in living rather than organic in nature, social workers are increasingly employed in agencies to provide counseling and psychotherapy without supervision by a psychiatrist.

LeCroy and Stinson asked 386 people in a random digit telephone survey the "perceived value to the community" of social work compared with that of other professions. Social workers received more "very valuable" ratings (60.8%) than did counselors (58.3%) psychologists (44.5%), and psychiatrists (41.9%).[81]

The primary therapy approach used to treat people with emotional or behavioral problems is psychotherapy or counseling. (I use these two terms interchangeably, as there do not appear to be clearcut distinctions between the two.) Counseling is a broad term covering individual, family, and group therapy. A skilled counselor has knowledge of (a) interviewing principles and (b) comprehensive and specific treatment approaches. The next section discusses these two areas and is designed to give you a "flavor" of what counseling is composed of. Additional theoretical material covering these two areas is presented in social work practice and field placement courses. Through role-playing of contrived counseling situations and, later, through working with clients, social work students gain skill and confidence in putting this material into practice. Sharpening and further developing one's counseling skills do not end with acquiring a degree in a counseling field; they are ongoing, lifelong processes.

Counseling

Counseling services are provided by practically every direct service social welfare agency. Some agencies, such as social service departments and mental health centers, provide counseling services covering almost all emotional or interpersonal problems. Other more specialized agencies provide counseling designed for specific problems that require considerable background knowledge and training in using highly developed treatment techniques. (Such areas include drug abuse counseling, therapy for eating disorders, genetic counseling, and sex therapy.)

EP 2.1.10a, b, c, f, g, i, j

The capacity to counsel effectively is one of the key skills needed by social workers; in fact, it may be *the* most important skill. Acquiring in-depth skill at counseling in one area (for example, marriage or adoption counseling) prepares that person for counseling in other areas. Because this skill is transferable, undergraduate and graduate social work programs can take a generic, broad-based approach to social work training. The emphasis is placed on

CASE EXHIBIT 5.4

Summary of Key Guidelines in Counseling Clients

1. Establish a working relationship
   a. Introduce yourself and begin with a little small talk.
   b. Have the client talk about his or her concerns by saying something like "Do you have some concerns you'd like to talk about today?"
   c. After the client discusses his or her concerns for 3 or 4 minutes, "connect" with the feelings by saying something like, "How are you feeling about this?" "This must really be difficult for you," or "I sense you're feeling (such and such) about this." Such "connections" with a client generally facilitate the client comprehending that

the counselor understands and cares about his or her feelings and concerns. Such "connections" validate the client's feelings and concerns.
2. Explore the client's concerns in depth.
3. Explore alternative solutions to the concerns with the client.
   a. In doing this, please *first* ask the client what he or she has tried, and what he or she is thinking about trying.
   b. Don't give advice, but instead phrase your resolution options as suggestions, such as "Have you thought about trying _____?"

---

in-depth training in counseling rather than on training in specialized counseling areas.

How to Counsel*

Counseling someone with personal problems is neither magical nor mystical. Although training and experience in counseling are beneficial, everyone has the potential of helping another by listening and talking through difficulties. Counseling with a successful outcome can be done by a friend, neighbor, relative, hairdresser, banker, or bartender, as well as by social workers, psychiatrists, psychologists, guidance counselors, and the clergy. This is not to say that everyone will be successful at counseling. Professional people, because of their training and experience, have a higher probability of being effective. But competence and empathy, rather than degrees or certificates, are the keys to desirable outcomes.

There are three phases to counseling: (a) building a relationship, (b) exploring problems in depth, and (c) exploring alternative solutions. Successful counseling gradually proceeds from one phase to the next, with some overlapping of the stages. For example, in many cases, while exploring problems, the relationship between the counselor and the counselee continues to develop; while exploring alternative solutions,

the problems are generally being examined in greater depth. A format that is useful for social workers to use in counseling others is presented in Case Exhibit 5.4.

Building a Relationship

The following are guidelines for building a relationship with a client:

1. Seek to establish a nonthreatening atmosphere in which the counselee feels safe to communicate fully his or her troubles while feeling accepted as a person.

2. In initial contacts with the counselee, you need to "sell" yourself—not arrogantly, but as a knowledgeable, understanding person who may be able to help and who wants to try.

3. Be calm. Do not laugh or express shock when the counselee begins to open up about problems. Emotional outbursts, even if subtle, will lead the counselee to believe that you are not going to understand his or her difficulties, and he or she will usually stop discussing them.

4. Generally be nonjudgmental and nonmoralistic. Show respect for the counselee's values, and do not try to sell your values. The values that work for you may not be best for someone else in a different situation. For example, if the counselee is premaritally pregnant, do not attempt to force your values toward adoption or abortion. Let the counselee decide on a course of action after a full examination of the problem and an exploration of the possible solutions.

---

*This section on "How to Counsel" is reprinted from an article of the same title written by me in *The Personal Problem Solver*, Charles Zastrow and Dae Chang, eds. Copyright © 1977 by Prentice Hall. Reprinted by permission of Charles Zastrow.

5. View the counselee as an equal. Rookie counselors sometimes make the mistake of thinking that, because someone is sharing intimate secrets, the counselor must be very important; they then end up creating a superior/inferior relationship. If counselees feel that they are being treated as inferior, they will be less motivated to reveal and discuss personal difficulties.

6. Use "shared vocabulary." This does not mean using the same slang words or the same accent as the counselee. If the counselee sees your speech as artificial, it may seriously offend him or her. You should use words that the counselee understands and that are not offensive.

7. The tone of your voice should convey the message that you empathetically understand and care about the counselee's feelings.

8. Keep confidential what the counselee has said. All of us by nature have urges to share "juicy secrets" with someone else. But, if the counselee discovers that confidentiality has been violated, a working relationship may be quickly destroyed.

9. If you are counseling a relative or a friend, there is a danger that, because you are emotionally involved, you may get upset or into an argument with the other person. If that happens, it is almost always best to drop the subject immediately, as tactfully as possible. Perhaps, after tempers cool, the subject can be brought up again. Or it may be best to refer the counselee to someone else. Many professionals refuse to counsel friends or relatives because emotional involvement interferes with the calm, detached perspective that is needed to help clients explore problems and alternative solutions.

Exploring Problems in Depth

Following are suggestions to guide counselors in helping clients explore problems in depth:

1. Many rookie counselors make the mistake of suggesting solutions as soon as a problem is identified, without exploring the problem in depth. For example, an advocate of abortions may advise this solution as soon as a single female reveals that she is pregnant. A counselor should take the time to discover whether this person is strongly opposed to abortions, really wants a baby, or intends to marry soon.

2. In exploring problems in depth, the counselor and counselee need to examine such areas as the extent of the problem, its duration, its causes, the counselee's feelings about the problem, and the physical and mental capacities and strengths the counselee has to cope with the problem, before exploring alternative solutions. For example, if a single female is pregnant, the counselor and counselee need to explore the following questions: How does the person feel about being pregnant? Has she seen a doctor? About how long has she been pregnant? Do her parents know? If so, what are their feelings and concerns? Has the female informed her partner? What are his feelings and concerns? What does she feel is the most urgent situation to deal with first? Answers to such questions will determine the direction of counseling. The most pressing, immediate problem might be to inform her parents, who may react critically, or it might be to secure medical services.

3. When a problem area is identified, a number of smaller problems may occur (for example, planning how to tell her partner, obtaining medical care, obtaining funds for medical expenses, deciding where to live, deciding whether to leave school or work during the pregnancy, deciding whether to keep the child, and making plans for what to do after the child is delivered or the pregnancy is terminated). Explore all these subproblems.

4. In a multiproblem situation, the best way to decide which problem to handle first is to ask the counselee which one she or he perceives as most pressing. If the problem can be solved, start with exploring that subproblem in depth and developing together a strategy for the solution. Success in solving a subproblem will increase the counselee's confidence in the counselor and thereby will further solidify the relationship.

5. Convey empathy, not sympathy. Empathy is the capacity to show that you are aware of and can to some extent feel what the counselee is feeling. Sympathy is also sharing of feelings, but it has the connotation of pity. The difference is subtle, but empathy is oriented toward problem solving, whereas sympathy usually prolongs problems. For example, if you give me sympathy when I'm depressed, I'll keep telling you my sad story over and over, each time having an emotional outpouring supported by your sympathy, without taking any action to improve the situation. This process only reopens old wounds and prolongs my depression.

6. "Trust your guts." The most important tool you have as a counselor is yourself (your feelings

and perceptions). You should continually strive to place yourself in the client's situation (with the client's values and pressures). To use the earlier example, if the client is 17 years old, single, and pregnant, and has parents who are very critical of the situation and want her to have an abortion, a competent counselor would continually strive to feel what she is feeling and to perceive the world from her perspective, with her goals, difficulties, pressures, and values. It probably never happens that a counselor is 100% accurate in placing himself or herself in the counselee's situation, but 70% to 80% is usually sufficient to gain an awareness of the counselee's pressures, problems, and perspectives. This information helps the counselor to determine what additional areas need to be explored, to decide what to say, and to figure out possible solutions. In other words, a counselor should ask "What is this person trying to tell me, and how can I make it clear that I understand not only intellectually but empathetically?"

7. When you believe that the client has touched on an important area of concern, you can encourage further communication by:

a. Nonverbally showing interest.
b. Pausing. Inexperienced counselors usually become anxious when there is a pause, and they hasten to say something—anything—to have conversation continue. This is usually a mistake, especially when it leads to a change in the topic. Pausing will also make the counselee anxious, give him or her time to think about the important area of concern, and then usually motivate him or her to continue conversation in that area.
c. Using neutral probes. Examples are: "Could you tell me more about it?" "Why do you feel that way?" "I'm not sure I understand what you have in mind."
d. Summarizing what the client is saying. You might offer: "During this past hour you made a number of critical comments about your spouse; it sounds like some things about your marriage are making you unhappy."
e. Reflecting feelings. Examples are: "You seem angry" or "You appear to be depressed about that."

8. Approach socially unacceptable issues tactfully. Tact is an essential quality of a competent counselor. Try not to ask a question in such a way that the answer will put the respondent in an embarrassing position. Suppose, for instance, you are counseling a male with poor personal hygiene who has been discharged from a variety of jobs and does not know why. The man explains that employers initially compliment him on his work productivity and then tend, a few weeks later, to discharge him without informing him why. After several possible explanations have been explored and eliminated, you as the counselor may tactfully say "I'm wondering if your personal appearance and hygiene may be a reason for the dismissals. I notice you haven't shaved for a few days, and I sense you may not have bathed for a few days either. Do you think this may be an explanation?" It's very important to confront clients with ineffective actions that are having substantial negative effects on their lives.

9. When pointing out a limitation that a counselee has, also mention and compliment him or her on any assets. Discussion of a limitation will literally make the counselee feel that something is being laid bare or taken away. Complimenting him or her in another area will give something back.

10. Watch for nonverbal cues. A competent counselor will generally use such cues to identify when a sensitive subject is being touched on, as the client will show anxiety by changing tone of voice, fidgeting, yawning, assuming a stiff posture, or appearing flushed.

11. Be honest. An untruth always runs the risk of being discovered. If that happens, the counselee's confidence in you will be seriously damaged and perhaps the relationship seriously jeopardized. But being honest goes beyond not telling lies. The counselor should always point out those shortcomings that are in the counselee's best interest to give attention to. For example, if someone is being fired from jobs because of poor grooming habits, this needs to be brought to his or her attention. Or, if a trainee's relationship skills and personality are not suited for the helping professions, that person needs to be "counseled out" in the interests of clients and in the trainee's own best interests.

12. Listen attentively to what the counselee is saying. Try to hear his or her words not from your perspective but from the counselee's. Unfortunately, some counselors are caught up in their own interests and concerns, and they do not "tune out" their own thoughts while the counselee is speaking. This guideline seems very simple, but it is indeed difficult for many to follow.

Exploring Alternative Solutions

The following are guidelines for exploring alternative solutions with a client:

1. After (or sometimes while) a subproblem is explored in depth, the next step is for the counselor and the counselee to consider alternative solutions. In exploring alternative solutions, it is almost always best for the counselor to begin by asking something like "Have you thought about ways to resolve this?" The merits, shortcomings, and consequences of the alternatives thought of by the counselee should then be tactfully and thoroughly examined. If the counselee has not thought of certain viable alternatives, the counselor should mention these, and the merits and shortcomings of these alternatives should also be examined. For example, in the case of the unwed pregnant teenager, if she decides to continue the pregnancy to full term, possible alternatives for the subproblem of making plans for living arrangements include keeping the child, getting married, seeking public assistance, finding foster care after delivery, filing a paternity suit, placing the child for adoption, and obtaining the assistance of a close relative to help or care for the child.

2. The counselee usually has the right to self-determination—that is, to choose the course of action among possible alternatives. The counselor's role is to help the counselee clarify and understand the likely consequences of each available alternative but generally not to give advice or choose the alternative for the counselee. If the counselor were to select the alternative, there would be two possible outcomes: (a) The alternative may prove to be undesirable for the counselee, in which case the counselee will probably blame the counselor for the advice, and the future relationship will be seriously hampered. (b) The alternative may prove to be desirable for the counselee. This immediate outcome is advantageous; but the danger is that the counselee will then become overly dependent on the counselor, seeking his or her advice for nearly every decision in the future and generally being reluctant to make decisions independently. In actual practice, most courses of action have desirable and undesirable consequences. For example, if the unmarried mother is advised to keep her child, she may receive considerable gratification from being with and raising the child, but at the same time she may blame the counselor for such possible negative consequences as long-term financial hardships and a restricted social life.

The guideline of not giving advice does *not* mean that a counselor should not suggest alternatives that the client has not considered. On the contrary, it is the counselor's responsibility to suggest and explore all viable alternatives with a client. A good rule to follow is that, when a counselor believes a client should take a certain course of action, this idea should be phrased as a suggestion ("Have you thought about …?") rather than as advice ("I think you should…").

3. Counseling is done *with* the counselee, not to or *for* the counselee. In general, the counselee should take responsibility for those tasks that she or he has the capacity to carry out, and the counselor should attempt to do only those that are beyond the capacities of the counselee. As with giving advice, doing things *for* counselees may create a dependency relationship. Furthermore, successful accomplishment of tasks by counselees leads to personal growth and better prepares them for taking on future responsibilities.

4. The counselee's right to self-determination should be taken away only if the selected course of action has a high probability of seriously hurting others or the counselee. For example, if it seems likely that a parent will continue to abuse a child or that a counselee will attempt to take his or her own life, intervention by the counselor is called for. For most situations, however, the counselee should have the right to select his or her alternative, even when the counselor believes that another alternative is a better course of action. Frequently, the counselee is in a better position to know what is best for him or her; if the alternative is not the best, the counselee will probably learn from the mistake.

5. Attempt to form explicit, realistic "contracts" with counselees. When the counselee does select an alternative, he or she should clearly understand what the goals will be, what tasks need to be carried out, how to do the tasks, and who will carry out each of them. It is often desirable to build into the "contract" a time limit for the accomplishment of each task. For example, if the unmarried mother decides to keep her child and now needs to make long-range financial plans, this goal should be understood and specific courses of action decided on—seeking public assistance, seeking support from the alleged father, securing an apartment within her budget, and so on. Furthermore, who will do what task within a set time limit should be specified.

6. If the counselee fails to meet the terms of the "contract," do not punish, but do not accept excuses. Excuses let people off the hook; they provide

temporary relief, but they eventually lead to more failure and to a failure identity. Simply ask "Do you still wish to try to fulfill your commitment?" If the counselee answers affirmatively, another deadline acceptable to the counselee should be set.

7. Perhaps the biggest single factor in determining whether the counselee's situation will improve is the motivation to carry out essential tasks. A counselor should seek to motivate apathetic counselees. One of the biggest reality shocks of inexperienced helping professionals is that many clients, even after making commitments to improve their situation, do not have the motivation to carry out the steps outlined.

8. One way to increase motivation is to clarify what will be gained by meeting the commitment. When counselees fulfill commitments, reward them verbally or in other ways. Avoid punishment if commitments are not met. Punishment usually increases hostility without positive lasting changes. It also serves as only a temporary means of obtaining different behavior; a person who is no longer under surveillance will usually return to the "deviant" behavior.

9. Sometimes the counselee lacks the confidence or experience to carry out certain tasks. In this case it is helpful to "role-play" the tasks. For example, if a pregnant unwed teenager wants help in deciding how to tell her partner about the pregnancy, role-playing the situation will assist her in selecting words and developing a strategy for informing him. The counselor can first play her role and model an approach, while she plays her partner's role. Then the roles should be reversed so that the teenager practices telling her partner.

Other helpful hints for counseling could be given here, but the basic format is to develop a relationship, explore problems in depth, and then explore alternative solutions. These guidelines are not to be followed dogmatically; they will probably work 70% to 80% of the time. Learn to trust your own feelings, perceptions, relationship capacities, and interviewing skills.

One final important guideline is that the counselor should refer the counselee to someone else, or at least seek a professional counselor to discuss the case with, for any of the following situations: if the counselor feels that she or he is unable to empathize with the counselee; if the counselor feels that the counselee is choosing alternatives (such as seeking an abortion) that conflict with the counselor's basic value system; if the counselor feels that the problem is of such a nature that she or he will not be able to help; and if a working relationship is not established.

A competent counselor knows that she or he can work with and help some people but not all. If you encounter a client you feel you cannot help, it is in that person's best interests, as well as your own, to refer the client to someone else who can.

Comprehensive and Specialized Counseling Approaches

In addition to a good grasp of interviewing principles, an effective counselor needs a knowledge of comprehensive counseling theories and of specialized treatment techniques to diagnose precisely what problems exist and decide how to intervene effectively. There are a number of contemporary comprehensive counseling approaches: psychoanalysis, rational therapy, client-centered therapy, Adlerian psychotherapy, behavior modification, Gestalt therapy, reality therapy, transactional analysis, neurolinguistic programming, and encounter approaches.* These therapy approaches generally present theoretical material on (a) personality theory, or how normal psychosocial development occurs; (b) behavior pathology, or how emotional/behavioral problems arise; and (c) therapy, or how to change unwanted emotions and dysfunctional behaviors.

An effective counselor generally has a knowledge of several treatment approaches. Depending on the unique set of problems presented by the client, the counselor picks and chooses from his or her "bag of tricks" the intervention strategy that is likely to have the highest probability of success. In addition to comprehensive counseling approaches, there are a number of specialized treatment techniques for specific problems, such as assertiveness training for people who are shy or overly aggressive, relaxation techniques for people experiencing high levels of stress, specific sex therapy techniques for such difficulties as premature ejaculation or orgasmic dysfunction, and parent effectiveness training for parent–child relationship difficulties. An effective counselor strives to gain a working knowledge of a wide variety of treatment techniques to increase the likelihood of being able to help clients.

For illustrative purposes, one comprehensive therapy approach, rational therapy, will be summarized.

---

*A good summary of contemporary global counseling approaches and of specialized treatment techniques is in Richard S. Sharf, *Theories of Psychotherapy and Counseling*, 5th ed. (Belmont, CA: Wadsworth/Cengage Learning, 2011).

Rational Therapy

The two main developers of rational therapy are Albert Ellis and Maxie Maultsby.[82] The approach potentially enables those who become skillful in rationally analyzing their self-talk to control or get rid of any undesirable emotion or any dysfunctional behavior.

It is erroneously believed by most people that our emotions and our actions are determined primarily by our experiences (that is, by events that happen to us). On the contrary, rational therapy has demonstrated that the primary cause of all our emotions and actions is what we tell ourselves about what happens to us.

All feelings and actions occur according to the following format:

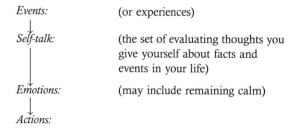

Events:	(or experiences)
Self-talk:	(the set of evaluating thoughts you give yourself about facts and events in your life)
Emotions:	(may include remaining calm)
Actions:	

An example will illustrate this process.

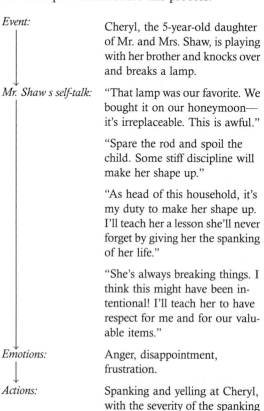

Event:	Cheryl, the 5-year-old daughter of Mr. and Mrs. Shaw, is playing with her brother and knocks over and breaks a lamp.
Mr. Shaw s self-talk:	"That lamp was our favorite. We bought it on our honeymoon— it's irreplaceable. This is awful."
	"Spare the rod and spoil the child. Some stiff discipline will make her shape up."
	"As head of this household, it's my duty to make her shape up. I'll teach her a lesson she'll never forget by giving her the spanking of her life."
	"She's always breaking things. I think this might have been intentional! I'll teach her to have respect for me and for our valuable items."
Emotions:	Anger, disappointment, frustration.
Actions:	Spanking and yelling at Cheryl, with the severity of the spanking bordering on abuse.

If, on the other hand, Mr. Shaw gives himself a different set of self-talk, his emotions and actions will be quite different:

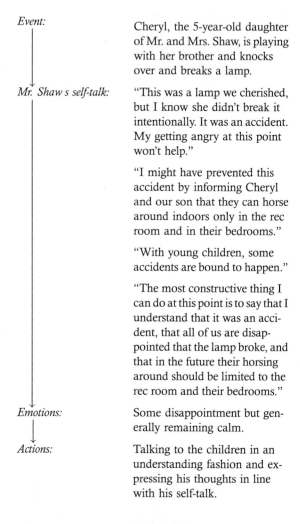

Event:	Cheryl, the 5-year-old daughter of Mr. and Mrs. Shaw, is playing with her brother and knocks over and breaks a lamp.
Mr. Shaw s self-talk:	"This was a lamp we cherished, but I know she didn't break it intentionally. It was an accident. My getting angry at this point won't help."
	"I might have prevented this accident by informing Cheryl and our son that they can horse around indoors only in the rec room and in their bedrooms."
	"With young children, some accidents are bound to happen."
	"The most constructive thing I can do at this point is to say that I understand that it was an accident, that all of us are disappointed that the lamp broke, and that in the future their horsing around should be limited to the rec room and their bedrooms."
Emotions:	Some disappointment but generally remaining calm.
Actions:	Talking to the children in an understanding fashion and expressing his thoughts in line with his self-talk.

The most important point about the preceding processes is that our self-talk determines how we feel and act; by changing our self-talk, we can change how we feel and act. Generally we cannot control events that happen to us, but we have the power to think rationally and thereby change *all* of our unwanted emotions and ineffective actions. This is the rehabilitative aspect of the conceptualization.[83]

The self-talk we give ourselves about specific events that happen to us is often based on a variety of factors, including our beliefs, attitudes, values, wants, motives, goals, and desires.[84] For example, the self-talk a married woman might give herself on being informed by her husband that he wants a divorce would be influenced by her desire (or lack of desire) to remain married, by her values and beliefs about being a divorcée, by her attitudes toward her husband, by her present goals (and whether getting a divorce would be consistent or inconsistent with them), and by her beliefs about the reasons her husband says he wants a divorce.

Another important point about self-talk is that, with repeated occurrences of an event, a person's emotional reaction becomes nearly automatic. That is, the person rapidly gives himself or herself a large set of self-talk gradually acquired through past experiences. For example, a few years ago, I counseled a woman who became intensely upset and depressed every time her husband came home intoxicated. In examining her emotional reactions, it became clear that, because of the repeated occurrences, she would rapidly tell herself the following on seeing him inebriated:

- "He's making a fool of himself and of me."
- "He's foolishly spending money we desperately need."
- "For the next few hours, I'm going to have to put up with his drunken talk and behavior. This is awful."
- "He loves drinking more than he loves me because he knows I don't want him to get drunk."
- "Woe is me."

Critical Thinking Questions

First identify any unwanted emotions or dysfunctional actions that you currently have—or have had in the past. Do you believe that your thoughts are (or were) the primary determinant of these emotions or actions? Do you believe that changing your thoughts in a more positive and rational direction will be therapeutic for you?

Changing Unwanted Emotions

There are five ways to change an unwanted emotion. Three are constructive: getting involved in a meaningful activity, changing the negative and irrational thinking underlying the unwanted emotion, and changing the distressing event. Two are destructive: abuse of alcohol, drugs, and food; and suicide. We will discuss each of the five in turn.

Meaningful Activity

Practically everyone encounters day-to-day frustrations and irritations—having a class or two that aren't going well, working at a job that's unpleasant,

or coping with a dull social life. Dwelling on such irritations will spawn such unwanted emotions as depression, anger, frustration, despair, or feelings of failure. Which of these emotions a person has will directly depend on the person's self-talk.

Meaningful enjoyable activity, however, produces satisfaction and a healthful distraction from unwanted emotion. Individuals can learn the value of meaningful activity by writing an "escape" list of activities they find motivating, energizing, and enjoyable—taking a walk, playing golf or tennis, going to a movie, shopping, doing needlework, visiting friends, and so on. By having an "escape" list of things they enjoy doing, individuals can nip unwanted emotions in the bud. By getting involved in things they enjoy, they can use enjoyable activities to take their minds off their day-to-day concerns and irritations. The positive emotions they experience will stem directly from the things they tell themselves about the enjoyable things they are doing.

In urging individuals to compile and use an escape list, rational therapy is not suggesting that people should avoid doing something about unpleasant events. If something can be done to change a distressing event, all constructive efforts should be tried. However, we often do not have control over unpleasant events and cannot change them. Although we cannot change unpleasant events, we always have the capacity to control and change what we tell ourselves about the unpleasant events. This latter focus is often helpful in learning to change our unwanted emotions.

Changing Self-Talk

A second approach to changing unwanted emotions is to identify and then alter the negative and irrational thinking that leads to them. Maultsby (1977) developed *rational self-analysis* (RSA), which is very useful in alleviating undesirable emotions. An RSA has six parts, as shown in Case Exhibit 5.5.

The goal in RSA is to change unwanted emotions (such as anger, guilt, depression, or shyness). An RSA is done by recording the event and self-talk on paper.

Part A (facts and events): Simply state the facts or events that occurred.

Part B (self-talk): Write all of your thoughts about A. Number each statement (1, 2, 3, 4, and so on). Write either "good," "bad," or "neutral" after each self-talk statement to show how you believe each B-section statement reflects on you as a person. (The RSA in Case Example 5.3 illustrates the mechanics of an RSA.)

CASE EXHIBIT 5.5

Format for RSA

A	D(a)
Facts and Events	Camera Check of A
B	D(b)
Self-Talk	Rational Debate of B

1. _____
2. _____
   and so on

1. _____
2. _____
   and so on

C	E
Emotional Consequences of B	Emotional Goals and Behavioral Goals for Similar Future Events

Part C (emotional consequences): Write simple statements describing your gut reactions and emotions stemming from your self-talk in B.

Part D(a) is written *only* after you have written sections A–C. Part D(a) is a "camera check" of part A. Reread part A and ask yourself, "If I had had a video of what happened, would it verify what I wrote as 'fact'?" Videos record facts, not personal beliefs or opinions.

An example in part B of a personal opinion mistaken as a fact is, "Karen made me look like a fool when she laughed while I was trying to make a point." Under D(a) (video check of A), the opinion part of this statement is corrected by writing only the factual part: "I was attempting to make a serious point when Karen laughed." Then add the personal opinion part of the statement to B ("Karen made me look like a fool").

Part D(b) challenges and thus may change negative and irrational thinking. Take each B-section statement separately. Read B-1 first and ask yourself whether it is inconsistent with any of the five questions for rational thinking. It will be irrational if it does one or more of the following:

1. Is not based on objective reality.
2. Hampers you in protecting your life.
3. Hampers you in achieving your short- and long-term goals.
4. Causes significant trouble with other people.
5. Leads you to feel emotions that you do not want to feel.

If the self-talk statement is consistent with the five questions for rational thinking, merely write "that's rational." If, however, the self-talk statement meets one or more of the guidelines for irrational thinking, then think of an alternative "self-talk" to that B statement. This new self-talk statement is crucially important in changing your undesirable emotion and needs to (a) be rational and (b) be a self-talk statement you are willing to accept as a new opinion for yourself. After writing down this D(b-1) self-talk in the D(b) section, then consider B-2, B-3, and so on, in the same way.

Under Part E, write down the new emotions you want to have in similar future A situations. In writing these new emotions that you desire, keep in mind that they will follow from your self-talk statements in your D(b) section. This section may also contain a description of certain actions you intend to take to help you achieve your emotional goals when you encounter future As.

Rational self-challenges will work only if clients actively practice using the rational self-challenges they develop. Self-challenges work best when used by clients every time they start the original negative, irrational self-talk.

Changing the Distressing Event

A third way to change unwanted emotions is to change the distressing event. There are an infinite number of distressing events: losing a job, the

CASE EXAMPLE 5.3

Using Rational Therapy: Coping with a Sexual Affair

A 21-year-old woman, Cindy, sought counseling after she was informed by her boyfriend, Jim, that a few months earlier he had become sexually involved with another woman, Linda. Jim and Cindy had dated fairly steadily for the past 2 years. Both were attending the same college. Prior to their summer break, they were having frequent arguments and decided not to see each during the summer. When they returned to college in the fall, they resumed their relationship. A few weeks later, Jim (after Cindy questioned him) informed her that he once had sex with Linda.

Cindy told the counselor that she wanted to better handle her unwanted emotions about this affair. After discussing her feelings in some depth, the counselor informed her that she could counter her undesirable emotions by doing a rational self-analysis (based on rational therapy). This involves writing down:

A. The facts and events that occurred.
B. The self-talk a person gives himself or herself.
C. The emotions a person experiences.
D. An examination of the statements in section A to determine whether they are factual or whether they belong to section B (a person's self-talk). This section is written *only* after sections A, B, and C are written.
E. Positive and rational self-talk challenges to the negative and irrational self-talk in section B (this segment is the main therapeutic part of the process).
F. The emotional and behavioral goals a person has.

For this process to be therapeutic, the person must practice replacing the irrational self-talk with rational self-talk. In writing an RSA, the person first writes in the left column the components A, B, and C; then he or she comes back to the beginning to write in the right column the components D, E, and F. The following RSA should be read with this A-B-C/D-E-F format in mind.

A	D
Facts and Events	*Factual Check of A*
My boyfriend, Jim, informed me that he had sexual relations with Linda after a party at which they had both been drinking.	This is all factual. I know this because Jim told me himself. Jim and I are very close, and I know he would not lie to me.

B	E
My Self-Talk	*My Rational Debates of B*
B-1.	E-1.
It's not fair! How could Jim do such a thing to me?	Jim had sex with Linda. I'll just have to accept that. Because people are human and fallible, it's a mistake to expect that I will always be treated with fairness by others. Besides, Jim and I had broken up, so I'm sure they didn't have me in mind when they did it. At the time they were sexually involved, neither Jim nor I had any commitment to each other. In truth, I also considered getting sexually involved this summer and perhaps would have if I had met the right guy.

B-2.	E-2.
That creep just had sex with Linda because he was horny.	Jim probably had sex with Linda for other reasons. I know he's not the type to "use" a woman merely for relief of his sexual tensions. It's also a mistake to label him a creep. No one is a creep. People are humans. If I mislabel him as a creep, it may lead me to view him in terms of an inaccurate label.

B-3.	E-3.
Jim and Linda had no good reasons for doing what they did. They only did it because they were both drunk. What a couple of jerks!	I do believe that alcohol had something to do with the fact that Jim and Linda had sex. I know for a fact that Jim becomes much less inhibited when he's had a few drinks. I don't know about Linda, though. The drinking can't be the only reason they had sex. Maybe they felt attracted to each other and wanted to have sex. I've got to remember that this summer Jim and I had no commitments to each other, and therefore I don't have the right to expect that he would be celibate to please me. Also, it's a mistake for me to refer to Jim or Linda as a "jerk." People are people.

B-4.	E-4.
Linda must be some kind of cheap tramp. Only a tramp would have sex with a guy she didn't love.	I don't even know Linda, so I shouldn't judge her like this. Furthermore, I have no way of knowing how Linda felt about Jim. Maybe she felt she loved him at the time. A woman isn't necessarily loose if she has sex with a guy.

(continued)

CASE EXAMPLE 5.3 *(continued)*

B-5.

Jim must think he's some kind of stud now.

E-5.

Jim has told me that he has had sex with only two women. My idea of a "stud" is a guy who thinks he can have sex with any woman who comes along. I know Jim better than that. He doesn't think he could conquer any woman—nor would he try to.

B-6.

Jim and I will never again be able to have a good sexual relationship of our own now that he has someone else to compare me to. I just know that he'll be thinking of Linda from now on.

E-6.

Jim and I love each other. Jim told me that he does not love Linda. Just because Jim had sex with Linda does not mean our relationship will always be adversely affected. We can communicate easily during sex, and it has always been satisfying so far. It would be silly for Jim to compare our entire relationship to the one night he spent with Linda.

B-7.

This is the worst thing that Jim could have done.

E-7.

This is not the worst thing that Jim could have done. What he did was not a crime, like murder or rape, which would have been worse. The situation would be worse if Jim had slept with Linda while he was still seeing me. I'm glad to know that he would never do that.

B-8.

Now that I know Jim had sex with Linda, our whole relationship will be ruined.

E-8.

The fact that Jim had sex with Linda does not have to ruin our relationship. The event occurred in the past. It's over. Past sexual experiences should have no bearing on the future of our relationship. I want the relationship to continue, and I don't want to see it ruined.

B-9.

I should never have broken up with Jim. Then he would never have slept with Linda. It's all my fault.

E-9.

It's not my fault at all. I broke up with Jim because I felt it was the best thing to do at the time. I know Jim would not have been unfaithful to me had we still been dating, but we weren't dating at the time this happened. I had no way of knowing he would go to bed with Linda, and knowing would not have changed my decision to break up with him. It's not my fault because I wasn't even involved.

B-10.

From now on, whenever I hear Linda's name mentioned, I'm going to have a fit! I won't be able to handle it!

E-10.

When I hear Linda's name mentioned, I don't have to respond by having a fit. I can handle my feelings by being calm and not letting the mention of her name bother me.

C

My Emotions

I feel guilty, hurt, angry, upset, and jealous.

F

My Emotional and Behavioral Goals

I want to get over my unwanted emotions that I have had about this affair. I want to put this affair in our past. At the time it happened, Jim and I had no commitments to each other. What is important to Jim and me is our present and future relationship, not what happened one evening after Jim and I had broken up.

---

breakup of a romantic relationship, receiving failing grades, being in an automobile accident, and so on. In some cases, constructive action can be taken to change the distressing event. For example, if a man is terminated from a job, he can seek another, when he finds one, he will feel better. If a student is getting failing grades, a conference with the instructor may give the student some ideas about how to improve the grades. If the suggestions appear practical and have merit, the student will feel better.

Not all distressing events can be changed. For example, a woman may have a job that she needs and be forced to interact with other employees who display behaviors she dislikes. If that individual cannot change the behaviors of the others, the only other constructive option is to "bite the bullet" and adapt to the circumstances. However, when it is practical to change distressing events, they should be changed. When constructive changes in events are made, a person is then apt to feel better because he or she will then (in all likelihood) be having more positive self-talk related to the constructive changes that have been made.

Destructive Ways of Dealing with Unwanted Emotions

There are two destructive ways to deal with unwanted emotions which, unfortunately, some people use. (I want to make it clear that I strongly discourage using either of the following two ways. I present them only to complete the list of ways to deal with unwanted emotions.) One method is to temporarily relieve intense unwanted emotions through the use of alcohol, other drugs, or food. When the effects of the drug wear off, the person's problems and unwanted emotions remain, and there is a danger that through repeated use the person will become dependent on the drug. Some people overeat for the same reasons—loneliness, insecurity, boredom, and frustration. The process of eating and the feeling of having a full stomach provide temporary relief from intense unwanted emotions. Such people are apt to become overweight or bulimic—or both.

SUMMARY

The following summarizes this chapter's content as it relates to the chapter objectives presented at the beginning of the chapter. Objectives include the following:

A *Describe the nature and extent of emotional and behavioral difficulties.*

Emotional and behavioral problems are two comprehensive labels covering an array of problems. All of us, at times, experience emotional and behavioral problems. Serious or severe emotional problems are sometimes labeled "mental illnesses."

B *Discuss the concept of mental illness.*

The history of treatment for the emotionally disturbed is fascinating but also is filled with injustices and tragedies. In the past, the disturbed have been viewed in a variety of ways, ranging from prophets to evil people possessed by demonic powers. Recent major developments in treatment are the discovery and use of psychoactive drugs and the trend toward deinstitutionalization.

A major controversy is whether mental illness exists. Adherents of the medical approach believe that the disturbed person's mind is affected by some generally unknown internal condition. Critics of the medical model assert that disturbed people display

a social deviation or have an emotional problem but do not have a disease of the mind. Further, the critics assert that mental-illness labels have no diagnostic or treatment value and frequently have an adverse effect.

C *Present a theory about the causes of chronic mental illness.*

Thomas Scheff asserts that labeling people as mentally ill is the most important determinant of people displaying a chronic mental illness.

D *Present information about the homeless.*

The large number of homeless people in our nation is a national disgrace. Many of the homeless are thought to suffer from serious and chronic forms of mental illness. Discharged from mental institutions without the support they need, tens of thousands of former mental patients live on the street in abominable conditions.

E *Discuss controversial issues in the mental health field.*

A major issue in the mental health field is civil rights concerns over involuntary confinement, inadequate treatment, and enforced use of treatments that have adverse side effects. Other issues include the usefulness of the innocent by reason of insanity plea, the extent to which psychotropic drugs should be used, and the adequacy of the services provided by local communities to emotionally disturbed individuals who are no longer (because of deinstitutionalization) being sent to state mental hospitals. The emergence of managed mental health-care systems raises a number of issues, including the extent to which such systems are restricting the provision of needed services to persons with emotional or behavioral difficulties.

F *Present research on the relationship between social structure and the rate of mental illness.*

Sociologists have found a number of associations between social factors and mental illness. Higher rates of diagnosed mental illness have been found in the lower socioeconomic classes; in inner cities as compared to rural areas; among teenagers, young adults, and older persons; among unmarried people; and among African Americans as compared to Whites. Men and women are about equally likely to receive treatment; women are more likely to be diagnosed as suffering from anxiety, depression, and phobias and to be hospitalized. Men are more likely to be labeled as having a personality disorder. Lower-class patients often receive lower-quality care.

G *Describe treatment approaches for emotional and behavioral problems.*

The main therapy approach used to treat people with emotional and behavioral problems is psychotherapy or counseling. Counseling services are provided by practically every direct service social welfare agency. Drug therapy is also used at times.

H *Describe the role of social work in the mental health field.*

The ability to counsel others effectively is perhaps the most important skill needed by social workers. To be a competent counselor, it is essential to have a working knowledge of interviewing principles and of a wide range of treatment approaches.

I *Present information about counseling and counseling techniques.*

There are three distinct phases to counseling: building a relationship, exploring problems in depth, and exploring alternative solutions. One approach to counseling, rational therapy, is presented in this chapter.

Competency Notes

EP 2.1.3a Distinguish, appraise, and integrate multiple sources of knowledge, including research-based knowledge and practice wisdom. (All of this chapter) This chapter describes the nature and extent of emotional and behavioral difficulties. It analyzes the concept of mental illness; theorizes about the causes of mental illness; presents information on mental illness among the homeless population; summarizes the relationship between social structure and the rate of mental illness; and describes the role of social work in the mental health field. It also presents information about counseling and counseling techniques.

EP 2.1.9a Continuously discover, appraise, and attend to changing locales, populations, scientific and technological developments, and emerging societal trends to provide relevant services. (pp. 159-160) This section presents information on the relationship between the rate of mental illness and the following social factors: social class,

urbanization, age, marital status, sex, race, and combatants in wars.

EP 2.1.10a Substantively and affectively prepare for action with individuals, families, groups, organizations, and communities.

EP 2.1.10b Use empathy and other interpersonal skills.

EP 2.1.10c Develop a mutually agreed-on focus of work and desired outcomes.

EP 2.1.10f Collect, organize, and interpret client data.

EP 2.1.10g Assess client strengths and limitations.

EP 2.1.10i Implement prevention interventions that enhance client capacities.

EP 2.1.10j Help clients resolve problems. (pp. 164-175) Introductory material is presented about counseling and counseling techniques in working with individuals, families, and groups.

Media Resources

Additional resources for this chapter, including a chapter quiz, can be found on the Social Work CourseMate. Go to CengageBrain.com.

Notes

1. Albert Ellis, *A Guide to Rational Living*, 3rd ed. (New York: Wilshire, 1998).
2. William Kornblum and Joseph Julian, *Social Problems*, 14th ed. (Boston: Pearson, 2012), p. 67.
3. Ibid., p. 67.
4. Ronald J. Comer, *Fundamentals of Abnormal Psychology*, 6th ed. (New York: Worth, 2010).
5. Ibid.
6. American Psychiatric Association, *Diagnostic and Statistical Manual (DSM-IV-TR) of Mental Disorders*, 4th ed., text revision (Washington, DC: Author, 2000).
7. Thomas S. Szasz, *The Myth of Mental Illness*, rev. ed. (New York: HarperCollins, 1984); Thomas S. Szasz, *Insanity: The Idea and Its Consequences*, rev. ed. (Portland, OR: Book News Inc., 1999).
8. Thomas S. Szasz, "The Myth of Mental Illness," in *Clinical Psychology in Transition*, John R.

Braun, comp. (Cleveland: Howard Allen, 1961), p. 27.

9. Thomas Scheff, *Being Mentally Ill*, rev. ed. (New York: Aldine de Gruyter, 1999); David Mechanic, "Some Factors in Identifying and Defining Mental Illness," *Mental Hygiene*, 46 (Jan. 1962), pp. 66–74.

10. P. J. Caplan, *They Say You're Crazy* (Reading, MA: Addison-Wesley, 1995).

11. Ibid.

12. David L. Rosenhan, "On Being Sane in Insane Places," *Science*, 179 (Jan. 1973), pp. 250–257.

13. Comer, *Fundamentals of Abnormal Psychology*.

14. Ibid.

15. Charles H. Cooley, *Human Nature and the Social Order* (New York: Seribneris, 1902).

16. Szasz, *Insanity: The Idea and Its Consequences*.

17. Ibid., p. 17.

18. Scheff, *Being Mentally Ill*.

19. Ibid., p. 31.

20. http://www.nationalhomeless.org.

21. Ibid.

22. http://www.residentialtreatmentcenter.net.

23. Comer, *Fundamentals of Abnormal Psychology*.

24. Ibid.

25. The President's Commission on Mental Health, *Report to the President from the President's Commission on Mental Health*, vol. 1 (Washington, DC: U.S. Government Printing Office, 1978).

26. Susan Nolen-Hoeksema, *Abnormal Psychology*, 3rd ed. (McGraw-Hill, 2004), p. 691.

27. Ibid., p. 691.

28. "Psychiatric Testimony Clouds Justice in the Courtroom," *Freedom*, Feb. 1980, p. 1.

29. Ibid., p. 4.

30. "Behind Growing Outrage over Insanity Pleas," *U.S. News & World Report*, May 1999, p. 41.

31. Ibid., p. 42.

32. "Psychiatric Testimony Clouds Justice in the Courtroom," p. 4.

33. Kornblum and Julian, *Social Problems*, p. 90.

34. Darlene Grant, "Clinical Social Work" in Terry Mizrahi and Larry E. Davis, Editors in Chief, *Encyclopedia of Social Work*, 20th ed., vol. 1 (Washington, DC: NASW Press, 2008), pp. 317–326.

35. "Fast Facts." America's Health Insurance Plans. HealthDecisions.org.

36. E. R. Wagner, "Types of Managed Care Organizations," in P. R. Kongstvedt, ed. *The Managed Care Handbook* (Gaithersburg, MD: Aspen Press, 2001). pp. 33–45.

37. E. Gambrill, "Evidence-Based Practice and Policy: Choices Ahead," *Research on Social Work Practice,* 16 (2006), pp. 338–357.

38. A. Rubin, "Proceedings of the Conference on Improving the Teaching of Evidence-Based Practice in Social Work" [Special Issue], *Research on Social work Practice*, 17, no. 5, (2007).

39. E. Gambrill, "Evidence-Based Practice: An Alternative to Authority-Based Practice," *Families in Society: Journal of Contemporary Human Services*, 80, no. 4 (1999), pp. 341–350.

40. K. B. Adams, H. C. Matto, and C. W. LeCroy, "Limitations of Evidence-Based Practice for Social Work Education: Unpacking the Complexity," *Journal of Social Work Education* 45, no. 2 (2009); and E. Gambrill, "Evidence-Based Practice and Policy: Choices Ahead."

41. E. J. Millen and D. L. Streiner, "The Evidence for and against Evidence-Based Practice," *Brief Treatment and Crisis Intervention,* 4 (2004), pp. 111–121.

42. K. J. Long, L. Homesley, and J. S. Wodarski, "The Role for Social Workers in the Managed Health Care System: A Model for Evidence-Based Practice," in *Social Work in Mental Health: An Evidence-Based Approach*, B. A. Thyer and J. S. Wodarski, eds. (Hoboken, NJ: Wiley, 2007).

43. J. Deegar and D. M. Lawson, "The Utility of Empirically Supported Treatments," *Professional Psychology: Research and Practice*, 34, no. 3 (2003), pp. 271–277.

44. B. E. Wampold and K. S. Bhati, "Attending to Omissions: A Historical Examination of Evidence-Based Practice Movements," *Professional Psychology: Research and Practice*, 35, no. 6 (2004), pp. 563–570.

45. Adams, Motto, and LeCroy, "Limitations of Evidence-Based Practice for Social Work Education."

46. J. C. Norcross and M. J. Lambert, "The Therapy Relationship," *Evidence-Based Practices in Mental Health: Debate and Dialogue on the Fundamental Questions*, J. C. Norcross, L. E. Beutler, and R. F. Levant, eds. (Washington, DC: American Psychological Association, 2006), pp. 208–217; and B. Wampold, *The Great Psychotherapy Debate:*

Models, Methods and Findings (Mahwah, NJ: Erlbaum, 2001).

47. B. L. Duncan and S. P. Miller, *The Heroic Client* (San Francisco: Jossey Bass, 2000).

48. Rich Furman and Carol L. Langer, "Managed Care and the Care of the Soul," *Journal of Social Work Values and Ethics*, 3, no. 6 (2006), pp. 42–53.

49. Kornblum and Julian, *Social Problems*, pp. 78–80.

50. Ibid., p. 79.

51. Ibid., p. 79.

52. Ibid., p. 79.

53. Ibid., pp. 78–79.

54. Ibid., p. 80.

55. Ibid., p. 80.

56. Ibid., p. 82.

57. Ibid., p. 82.

58. Ibid., pp. 82–83.

59. Ibid., pp. 79–83.

60. Ibid., pp. 79–83.

61. Ibid., pp. 79–83.

62. Ibid., p. 81.

63. Ibid., pp. 76–77.

64. George Rosen, *Madness in Society: Chapter in the Historical Sociology of Mental Illness* (New York: Harper & Row, 1969).

65. Ibid., pp. 172–195.

66. Clifford W. Beers, *A Mind That Found Itself* (New York: Longman, Green, 1908).

67. H. J. Eysenck, "The Effects of Psychotherapy: An Evaluation," *Journal of Consulting Psychology,* 11 (1955), pp. 319–324.

68. A good summary of these theories is in Richard S. Sharf, *Theories of Psychotherapy and Counseling,* 5th ed. (Belmont, CA: Wadsworth/Thomson Learning, 2011).

69. Miriam Siegler and Mumphrey Osmond, *Models of Madness, Models of Medicine* (New York: Harper & Row, 1974).

70. Joseph Mehr, *Human Services* (Boston: Allyn & Bacon, 1980), p. 88.

71. Erving Goffman, *Asylums: Essays on the Social Situation of Mental Patients and Other Inmates* (New York: Doubleday, 1961).

72. Kornblum and Julian, *Social Problems*, pp. 89–91.

73. Ibid., pp. 88–89.

74. Ibid., pp. 88–89.

75. Ibid., pp. 88–89.

76. Ibid., pp. 88–89.

77. Ibid., p. 90.

78. Anthony J. Vattano, "Mental Health," in *Contemporary Social Work,* 2nd ed., Donald Brieland, Lela B. Costin, and Charles R. Antherton, eds. (New York: McGraw-Hill, 1980), p. 293.

79. Ira Colby and Sophia Dziegielewski, *Introduction to Social Work: The People s Profession,* 3rd ed. (Chicago: Lyceum Books, 2010).

80. National Association of Social Workers, 1993 *Register of Clinical Social Workers,* 7th ed. (Washington, DC: Author, 1993), pp. v–vi.

81. Craig W. LeCroy and Erika L. Stinson, "The Public's Perception of Social Work: Is It What We Think It Is?" *Social Work,* 49, no. 2 (April 2004), p. 170.

82. Ellis, *A Guide to Rational Living;* Maxie Maultsby, *Help Yourself to Happiness* (Boston: Marborough/Herman, 1975).

83. Ibid.

84. Charles Zastrow, *You Are What You Think* (Chicago: Nelson-Hall, 1993).

CHAPTER

Family Problems and
Services to Families

CHAPTER OUTLINE

Diverse Family Forms

The American Family: Past and Present

Problems in the Family

Following a short introduction to various family forms throughout the world, this chapter will:

Learning Objectives

EP 2.1.3a

A   Present a brief history of changes in the American family since colonial days.

B   Describe current problem areas in the American family, including divorce, empty-shell marriages, family violence, sexual abuse of children, births outside of marriage, and rape. Also describe current social services for family problems.

Diverse Family Forms

The family is a social institution that is found in every culture. The U.S. census defines *family* as a group of two or more persons related by blood, marriage, or adoption. It should be noted that such a definition does not cover a number of living arrangements in which the members consider themselves to be a family, such as:

- A husband and wife raising two foster children who have been in the household for several years.
- Two lesbians in a loving relationship who are raising children born to one of the partners in a previous heterosexual marriage.
- A man and woman who have been living together for years in a loving relationship but have never legally married.

A broader definition of family that encompasses all of the above is: a family is a kinship system of all relatives living together or recognized as a social unit.[1] Such a definition recognizes unmarried same-sex and opposite-sex couples and families, foster families, and any relationships that function or feel like a family.

Families take a variety of forms in different cultures. In some societies, husband and wife live in separate buildings. In others, they are expected to live apart for several years after the birth of a child. In many societies, husbands are permitted to have more than one wife. In a few countries, wives are allowed to have more than one husband. Some cultures permit (and even encourage) premarital and extramarital intercourse.

Some societies have large communes where adults and children live together. There are also communes in which the children are raised separately from adults. In some cultures without communes, surrogate parents rather than the genetic parents raise the children. Some societies encourage certain types of gay and lesbian relationships, and a few recognize gay marriages as well as heterosexual marriages.

In many cultures, marriages are still arranged by the parents. Some societies do not recognize the existence of romantic love. Some cultures expect older men to marry young girls. Others expect older women to marry young boys. Some expect a man to marry his father's brother's daughter; others insist that he marry his mother's sister's daughter. Most societies prohibit the marriage of close relatives, yet a few subcultures encourage marriage between brothers and sisters or between first cousins. In a few societies, infants are married before they are born (if the baby is of the wrong sex, the marriage is dissolved). In some societies, a man, on marrying, makes a substantial gift to the bride's father; in others, the bride's father gives a substantial gift to the new husband.

People in each society generally feel strongly that their particular pattern is normal and proper; many feel the pattern is divinely ordained. Suggested changes in their particular form are usually viewed with suspicion and defensiveness; changes are often sharply criticized as being unnatural, immoral, and a threat to the survival of the family.

In spite of these variations, practically all family systems can be classified into two basic forms: the extended family and the nuclear family.

Extended families like this one are still the predominant pattern in many developing countries.

An *extended family* consists of a number of relatives living together, such as parents, children, grandparents, great-grandparents, aunts, uncles, in-laws, and cousins. The extended family is the predominant pattern in preindustrial societies. The members share various agricultural, domestic, and other duties.

A *nuclear family* consists of a married couple and their children living together. The nuclear family emerged from the extended family. Extended families tend to be more functional in agricultural societies in which many "hands" are needed. The nuclear family is more suited to the demands of complex industrialized societies because its smaller size and potential geographic mobility make it more adaptable to changing conditions—such as the need to relocate to obtain a better job.

In the United States and a number of other countries, a third family form is emerging: the single-parent family. Single-parent families are created in a variety of ways, such as by an unmarried person adopting a child, an unmarried woman giving birth to a child, and a married couple divorcing with one parent (usually the woman) assuming custody of the children. Single-parent families now constitute about 29% of all families in the United States.[2]

Some family forms have been discriminated against, such as a single-parent household, or a gay or lesbian couple with children.

The American Family: Past and Present

The Family in Preindustrial Society

We often view the family as a stable institution in which few changes occur. Surprisingly, a number of changes have taken place since colonial and frontier days.

Prior to the 1800s, the economy in our country was predominantly agricultural. The majority of people lived on small farms in rural areas. In preindustrial society, transportation was arduous and travel was constricted. The family was nearly self-sufficient;

most of what it consumed was produced on the farm. The house and the farm were the center of production. The most common family type was the extended family, with each member having specific roles and responsibilities. Because there were many tasks on small farms, the extended family was functional; it contained a number of family members to carry out those tasks.

Economic considerations influenced family patterns. Marriage was highly valued, as was having many children. A large family was needed to do all the tasks involved in planting and harvesting crops and in raising cattle and other animals. With more children, a married couple could cultivate more acreage and thereby become more profitable. Children were thus important economic assets. Parents wanted their sons to marry robust, industrious women who could substantially contribute to the work that needed to be done.[3]

Cuber, John, and Thompson have noted that preindustrial American society developed a *monolithic code* of cultural beliefs that was accepted by most people during this era.[4] A monolithic code permits only one acceptable pattern of behavior. Components of this code were:

1. Adults were expected to be married. Women were expected to marry in their teens or early twenties. Those who delayed marriage or did not ever marry were referred to as "old maids" and "spinsters."

2. Marriage was considered permanent—for life. Divorce was rare and highly disapproved of.

3. An individual was expected to place the welfare of the family unit ahead of his or her individual preferences. For example, an individual's choice about who she or he wanted to marry was considered less important than the parents' notions about what was best for the family as a unit.

4. Sexual relations were restricted to marriage. There was a double standard: Women who had premarital or extramarital affairs were more harshly criticized and stigmatized than men who did so.

5. Married couples were expected to have children. Children were not only considered an economic asset but were also viewed as a religious obligation, based on the biblical ethic of "be fruitful and multiply."

6. Parents were expected to take care of their children, whatever the cost. Children were expected to obey and honor their parents. When parents became partially disabled (for example, from old age), children were expected to care for them.

7. The father was the head of the family and made the important decisions. Women and children were expected to be subordinate to him. There were numerous advantages to being male. Women left their parents' home upon marriage and moved into the husband's home (usually near or in his parents' home). Male children were more highly valued than female children, partly because males would remain home after marrying. The woman's place was in the home, and she was expected to do the cooking, washing, cleaning, and a variety of other domestic tasks. Thus, American preindustrial society was clearly patriarchal.

These beliefs were so strongly held by most people that they were considered the morally decent way to live. To violate them was viewed as going against nature and against God's will. (As we'll see, remnants of this code still remain in American society.)

The Family in Industrial Society

The Industrial Revolution, which began roughly 200 years ago, greatly changed family life. Factories and large-scale business organizations replaced small family farms as centers of economic production. Urbanization accompanied industrialization, and most people now live in urban or semiurban areas. Products that were mass produced on assembly lines or produced using complex equipment and technology became much cheaper than those produced on small family farms or in small family shops.

As the family gradually began losing its economic-productive function, other changes followed. Fewer people were needed in families to fill essential economic roles. Smaller families became more functional for industrialized societies because they could more readily relocate to fill employment openings that arose.

Gradually there was a shift toward individualism. A key component of individualism is the belief that the desires of the individual should take precedence over those of the family. As a result, it became increasingly recognized that the choice of a mate should be based on personal preference, not family need.

In addition, with the loss of the economic-productive function, children became economic liabilities; that is, they did nothing to increase family income but still had to be clothed, fed, and sheltered. As a response, parents began having fewer children.

There have been numerous other changes. No longer is the wisdom of the elderly as highly valued, partly because children are now trained and educated in institutionalized settings. In a rapidly changing industrial society, the job skills of older workers often become obsolete. As a result, the elderly are less esteemed than they once were.

Gradually women won the right to vote, and in the past six decades, the feminist movement has been calling into question the "double standards" of sexual morality. Women are also seeking egalitarian relationships with men. An increasing number of women are entering the labor force and seeking employment in settings (such as police departments) that were once considered appropriate only for men. Sexuality is more openly discussed today, and there has been an increase in the rate of sexual relations outside of marriage.[5] However, recent concern about AIDS has led many adults to reduce their sexual contacts. (The chances of acquiring AIDS increase with the number of sexual partners one has.)

Still, remnants of the monolithic code remain. Some people continue to find it objectionable if a married couple divorce or choose not to have children, or if a single person becomes pregnant or decides never to marry.

In 1938 sociologist William Ogburn summarized changes in function the American family has undergone as a result of industrialization and technological advances:[6]

1. The economic-productive function has been lost. In most families, financial resources are now acquired outside the home.

2. The protective function has been lost. The protective function is now being met by such agencies as police departments, hospitals, insurance companies, and nursing homes.

3. The educational function has been sharply reduced. Schools, day-care centers, and Head Start programs have taken on much of this function.

4. The family is less likely to be the center for religious activity.

5. The recreational function has largely been reduced. Each family member is now more likely to join recreational groups outside the home.

6. The status recognition function has been sharply reduced. Individuals now receive recognition through their own achievements in organizations outside the family, such as at school, at work, and in social and religious groups.

7. The family has retained its affectional function. Members receive social and emotional gratification from the family and also have many of their companionship needs met by the family.

Most authorities agree with Ogburn's assessment that many of the functions of the American family have been lost or sharply reduced. It has been noted, however, that the modern family retains certain functions that Ogburn overlooked. Following are five essential functions that families perform to help maintain continuity and stability in modern industrial society.[7]

Replacement of the Population

Every society must have some system for replacing its members. Because practically all societies consider the family as the unit in which children are produced, societies have defined the rights and responsibilities of the reproductive partners within the family unit. These rights and responsibilities help maintain the stability of society, although they are defined differently from one society to another.

Care of the Young

Children require care and protection until at least the age of puberty. The family is a primary institution for rearing children. Modern societies have generally developed supportive institutions to help in caring for the young—for example, medical services, day-care centers, parent training programs, and residential treatment centers.

Socialization of New Members

To become productive members of society, children must be socialized into the culture. Children are expected to acquire a language, to learn social values and mores, and to dress and behave within the norms of society. The family plays a major role in this socialization process. In modern societies, a number of other groups and resources are involved in this process. Schools, the mass media, peer groups, the police, movies, books, and other written materials are important influences in the socialization process. (Sometimes these different influences clash by advocating opposing values and attitudes.)

Regulation of Sexual Behavior

Failure to regulate sexual behavior would result in clashes between individuals due to jealousy and exploitation. Unregulated sexual behavior would probably also result in large numbers of births outside of marriage—children for whom no fathers could be held responsible. Every society has rules that regulate sexual behavior within family units. Most cultures, for example, have incest taboos, and most disapprove of extramarital sex.

Source of Affection

Spitz has demonstrated that humans need affection, emotional support, and positive recognition from others (including approval, smiles, encouragement, and reinforcement for accomplishments).[8] Without such affection and recognition, a person's emotional, intellectual, physical, and social growth is stunted. The family is an important source for obtaining affection and recognition because members generally regard one another as among the most important people in their lives and gain emotional and social satisfaction from these relationships. (As noted earlier, Ogburn identified this function as the primary one remaining in modern families.)

This brief sketch of American family history shows that, although a number of changes have occurred, the family retains several important functions. We will now turn to an examination of problem areas for today's American family: divorce, empty-shell marriages, family violence, sexual abuse, births outside of marriage, and rape.

Problems in the Family

Divorce

Our society places a higher value on romantic love than do most other societies. Cultures in which marriages are arranged by parents, love generally has no role in mate selection. In the United States, however, romantic love is a key factor in forming a marriage.

American children are socialized from an early age to believe in the glories of romantic love. "Love conquers all," it is asserted. Magazines, films, TV programs, and books continually portray "happy ending" romantic adventures. All of these breathtaking romantic stories suggest that every normal individual falls in love with that one special person, gets married, and lives happily ever after. This ideal rarely happens.

About one of every two marriages ends in divorce.[9] This high rate has been gradually increasing; before World War I, divorce seldom occurred.

Divorce usually leads to a number of difficulties for those involved. First, those who are divorcing face many emotional concerns, such as a feeling that they have failed, doubt over whether they are able to give and receive love, a sense of loneliness, concern over the stigma attached to getting a divorce, worry about the reactions of friends and relatives, concern over whether they are doing the right thing by parting, and fear about whether they will be able to make it on their own. Many people who are considering separation feel trapped because they believe they can neither live with nor without their spouse. Dividing up the personal property is another matter that frequently leads to bitter differences of opinions. If there are children, there are concerns about how the divorce will affect them.

There are also other issues that need to be decided. Who will get custody of the children? (Joint custody is now an alternative; with joint custody, each parent has the children for part of the time.) If one parent is awarded custody, controversies are likely to arise over visiting rights and child support payments. Each spouse often faces the difficulties of finding a new place to live, making new friends, doing things alone in a couple-oriented society, trying to make it on one's own financially, and thinking about the hassles connected with dating.

Going through a divorce is very difficult. People are less likely to perform their jobs well and are more likely to be fired during this time period.[10] Divorced people have a shorter life expectancy.[11] Suicide rates are higher for divorced men than for married men.[12]

Divorce per se is no longer automatically assumed to be a social problem, although some of its consequences still are. On the other hand, there is increasing recognition that in some marriages (in which there is considerable tension, bitterness, and dissatisfaction) divorce is sometimes a solution. It may be a concrete step that some people take to end the unhappiness and to begin a more productive and gratifying life. Further, there is increasing awareness that a divorce may be better for the children because they may no longer be subjected to the tension and unhappiness of a marriage that has gone sour.

The rising divorce rate does not necessarily mean that more marriages are failing. It may simply mean that more people in unhappy marriages are dissolving them rather than continuing to live unhappily.

Reasons for Marital Happiness

There are many sources of marital breakdown: alcoholism, economic strife caused by unemployment or

CASE EXHIBIT 6.1

Romantic Love versus Rational Love

Achieving a gratifying, long-lasting love relationship is one of our paramount goals. The experience of feeling "in love" is exciting, adds meaning to life, and gives us a good feeling about ourselves.

Unfortunately, few people are able to maintain a long-term love relationship. Most individuals encounter problems, like falling in love with someone who does not love them, falling out of love with someone after an initial stage of infatuation, being highly possessive of someone they love, or having substantial conflicts with the loved one because of differing sets of expectations about the relationship. Failures in love relationships are more often the rule than the exception.

The emotion of love is often viewed (erroneously) as a feeling over which we have no control. A number of common expressions (erroneously) connote or imply that love is a feeling beyond our control: "I *fell* in love." "It was love at first sight." "I just couldn't help it." "He swept me off my feet." It is more useful to think of the emotion of love as based primarily on our self-talk (that is, what we tell ourselves) about a person we meet. Romantic love can be diagrammed as follows:

Event
Meeting or becoming acquainted with a person who has *some* of the overt characteristics you seek in a lover.
↓

Self-talk
"This person is attractive and personable and has *all* of the qualities I admire in a lover/mate."
↓

Emotion
Intense infatuation; a feeling of being romantically in love; a feeling of ecstasy.

Romantic love is often based on self-talk that stems from intense, unsatisfied desires and frustrations rather than on reason or rational thinking. Unsatisfied desires and frustrations include extreme sexual frustration, intense loneliness, parental and personal problems, and extensive desires for security and protection.

A primary characteristic of romantic love is to idealize the person with whom we are infatuated as "perfect"; that is, we notice that this person has some overt characteristics we desire in a lover and then conclude that this person has *all* the desired characteristics.

A second characteristic is that romantic love thrives on a certain amount of distance. The more forbidden the love, the stronger it becomes. The more social mores are threatened, the stronger the feeling. (For example, couples who live together and later marry often report that living together was more exciting and romantic.) The greater the effort required to be with each other (for example, traveling long distances), the more

intense the romance. The greater the frustration (for example, loneliness or sexual needs), the greater the ecstasy.

The irony of romantic love is that, if an ongoing relationship is achieved, the romance usually withers. Through sustained contact, the person in love gradually comes to realize what the idealized loved one is really like—simply another human being with certain strengths and limitations. When this occurs, the romantic love relationship either turns into a rational love relationship or is found to have significant conflicts and dissatisfactions and then is terminated. For people with intense unmet needs, the latter occurs more frequently.

Romantic love thus tends to be temporary and based on make-believe. A person experiencing romantic love never loves the real person—only an idealized imaginary person.

Rational love, in contrast, can be diagrammed in the following way:

Event
While being aware of and comfortable with your own needs, goals, identity, and desires, you become well acquainted with someone who reflects, to a fair extent, the characteristics you desire in a lover or spouse.
↓

Self-talk
"This person has many of the qualities and attributes I seek in a lover or spouse. I admire this person's strengths, and I am aware and accepting of his (her) shortcomings."
↓

Emotion
Rational love.

The following are ingredients of a rational love relationship: (a) You are clear and comfortable about your desires, identity, and goals in life; (b) you know the other person well; (c) you have accurately and objectively assessed the loved one's strengths and shortcomings and are generally accepting of the shortcomings; (d) your self-talk about this person is consistent with your short- and long-term goals; (e) your self-talk is realistic and rational so that your feelings are not based on fantasy, excessive need, or pity; (f) you and this person are able to communicate openly and honestly so that problems can be dealt with when they arise and so that the relationship can continue to grow and develop; (g) you and the other are able to give and receive, show kindness and affection, and know and do what pleases the other person.

Because love is based on self-talk that causes feelings, it is we who create love. Theoretically, it is possible to love anyone by making changes in our self-talk. On the other hand, if we are in love with someone, we can gauge the quality of the relationship by analyzing our self-talk to determine the nature of our attraction and the extent to which our self-talk is rational and in our best interests.

other financial problems, incompatibility of interests, infidelity, jealousy, verbal or physical abuse of spouse, and interference in the marriage by relatives and friends.

As noted earlier, many people marry because they believe they are romantically in love. If this romantic love does not grow into rational love, the marriage is likely to fail. See Case Exhibit 6.1 for a description of romantic love versus rational love. Unfortunately, young people in our society are socialized to believe that marriage will bring them continual romance, resolve all their problems, and be sexually exciting, thrilling, and full of adventure. (Most young people need only look at their parents' marriage to realize such romantic ideals are seldom attained.) In actuality, living with someone in a marriage involves carrying out the garbage, washing dishes and clothes, being weary from work, putting up with one's partner's distasteful habits (for example, poor hygiene or belching), changing diapers, and dealing with conflicts over such things as finances and differences in sexual interests. *To make a marriage work, each spouse must put considerable effort into that relationship.*

Critical Thinking Questions

Have you been romantically involved with someone and you thought that person had all of the qualities you could ever want in a mate? What happened to that relationship?

Another factor that is contributing to an increasing divorce rate is the unwillingness of some men to accept the changing status of women. Many men still prefer a traditional marriage in which the husband is dominant and the wife plays a supportive (subordinate) role as child rearer, housekeeper, and the husband's and family's emotional support. Many women are no longer accepting such a status and are demanding egalitarian marriages in which making major decisions, doing the domestic tasks, raising the children, and bringing home paychecks are shared responsibilities.

Today more than 70% of American women with children under 18 work outside the home.[13] These women are no longer as heavily reliant financially on their husbands. Women who are able to support themselves financially are more likely to seek a divorce if their marriages go sour.[14]

Another factor contributing to the increasing divorce rate is the growth of individualism. Individualism involves the belief that people should seek to actualize themselves, to be happy, to develop their interests and capacities to the fullest, and to fulfill their own needs and desires. The interests of the individual take precedence over those of the family. People in our society have increasingly come to accept individualism as a way to go through life. In contrast, people in more traditional societies and in extended families are socialized to put the interests of the group first, with their own individual interests viewed as less important. With America's growing belief in individualism, people who are unhappily married are much more likely to dissolve the marriage and seek a new life.

Yet another reason for the rise in the divorce rate is the growing acceptance of divorce in our society. With less stigma attached to divorce, more unhappily married people are now ending those marriages.

An additional factor in the increasing divorce rate is that modern families no longer have as many functions as did traditional families. Education, food production, entertainment, and other functions once centered in the family are now largely provided by outside agencies. Kenneth Keniston notes:

> *In earlier times, the collapse of a marriage was far more likely to deprive both spouses of a great deal more than the pleasure of each other's company. Since family members performed so many functions for one another, divorce in the past meant a farmer without a wife to churn the cream into butter or care for him when he was sick, and a mother without a husband to plow the fields and bring her the food to feed their children. Today, when emotional satisfaction is the bond that holds marriages together, the waning of love or the emergence of real incompatibilities and conflicts between husband and wife leave fewer reasons for a marriage to continue. Schools and doctors and counselors and social workers provide their supports whether the family is intact or not. One loses less by divorce today than in earlier times, because marriage provides fewer kinds of sustenance and satisfaction.[15]*

Case Exhibit 6.2 identifies variables that predict whether a marriage will or will not last.

Divorce Laws

In the past, society attempted to make the breakup of marriages almost impossible. One way it did this was through laws that made a divorce difficult to

CASE EXHIBIT 6.2

Facts about Divorce

Age of spouses: Divorce is most likely to occur when the partners are in their 20s.

Length of engagement: Divorce rates are higher for those who had a brief engagement.

Age at marriage: People who marry at a very young age (particularly teenagers) are more likely to divorce.

Length of marriage: Most divorces occur within 3 years after marriage. There is also an increase in divorce shortly after the children are grown. This may occur partly because some couples wait until their children leave the nest before dissolving an unhappy marriage.

Social class: Divorce occurs more frequently at the lower socioeconomic levels.

Education: Divorce rates are higher for those with fewer years of schooling. Interestingly, divorce occurs more fre-

quently when the wife's educational level is higher than the husband's.

Residence: Divorce rates are higher in urban areas than in rural areas.

Second marriages: The more often individuals marry, the more likely they are to get divorced again.

Religion: The more religious individuals are, the less likely they are to divorce. Divorce rates are higher for Protestants than for Catholics or Jews. Divorce rates are also higher for interfaith marriages than for same faith marriages.

SOURCE: William Kornblum and Joseph Julian, *Social Problems*, 14th ed., (Boston: Pearson, 2012), pp. 332–334.

---

obtain. After one spouse petitioned the court for a divorce, there were long waiting periods before that divorce could be obtained. Divorce courts also followed the "adversary" judicial procedures in which the spouse seeking the divorce had to document that the other spouse was guilty of some offense, such as adultery, desertion, or cruel and inhuman treatment. In many cases, the actual reasons for the divorce (such as no longer finding the relationship satisfying) bore little relationship to the grounds on which the court allowed that divorce. Often the marital partners contrived a story that fit the legal requirements.

In most divorces, both partners contribute to the marital breakdown. Yet traditional divorce laws erroneously assumed that one partner was guilty and the other party innocent. Traditional divorce laws often intensified the trauma that both partners were undergoing and pitted the partners against each other. Moreover, the process was very expensive.

Because of these difficulties, most states have now passed "no fault" divorce laws, which allow the couple to obtain a divorce fairly rapidly by stating to the court that they both agree their marriage has irreparably broken down. (The adversary process is still available for any spouse who chooses to use it.)

Issues that are still often contested between the two partners in divorce proceedings involve the division of property, alimony or maintenance (a financial allowance paid to one spouse by the other for support after the divorce), child support payments, and

custody of the children. In the past, courts invariably awarded the woman custody of the children, child support payments, and alimony (particularly if she was not employed). However, a large percentage of the men failed to make some, or all, of their child support and alimony payments, which left their former wives in dire financial straits.

Changes in sex roles and the increased employment of women have led to changes in divorce settlements. Most states have enacted legislation allowing courts to require that the woman make alimony payments to her former husband (although few courts have as yet issued such orders). Custody of the children is still generally given to the mother, although this assignment is no longer automatic. An increasing number of fathers are requesting custody of their children and are making it known that they resent the sexist bias of many courts, which assumes that a mother is better qualified to raise children.

A critical point about divorce is that when it occurs, many of the costs are paid by society. In families of average income or less, the burden of divorce-related poverty falls on society as a whole. Examples of such costs include subsidized housing, public sector make-work jobs, and payments to lawyers who are involved in collecting support for women and children.

The recent willingness of courts to award custody to the father has a hidden cost to society. Fathers often threaten a protracted custody battle. As a result, mothers who want custody of their children without a fight are routinely forced to "barter" custody in exchange for reduced child support payments. Because such payments are so low, these women and their children then qualify for financial assistance with Temporary Assistance to Needy Families (TANF). See Chapter 4 for a description of TANF.

Custody battles between fathers and mothers are becoming common in divorce cases. Typical custody battles may take as long as 2 years and cost thousands of dollars for attorneys, expert witnesses, and court costs. During this process, the parents are likely to use the children as "pawns" against each other. They bribe the children with large allowances, relax discipline, and indulge outrageous whims of their children. They may also try to turn their children against the other parent by "bad-mouthing" him or her. Custody battles are not only costly but also emotionally damaging to all family members.

In many states now, children over age 14 are allowed to select the parent with whom they wish to live if that parent is "fit." As a way of avoiding custody battles and the situation in which women barter reduced child support payments for custody, Richard Neely recommends that, for children under 14, custody be awarded to the primary caretaker parent, who is defined as:

> …the parent who: (1) prepares the food; (2) changes the diapers, dresses, and bathes the child; (3) takes the child to school, church, and other activities; (4) makes appointments with a doctor and generally watches over the child's health; and (5) interacts with the child's friends, the school authorities, and other adults engaged in activities that involve the child. It is not surprising that the "primary caretaker" is usually the mother, but that need not be the case.[16]

Critical Thinking Questions

Do you think fathers should have as much right to be awarded custody of the children as the mothers when divorce occurs? Why or why not?

Empty-Shell Marriages

In empty-shell marriages, the spouses feel no strong attachments to each other. Outside pressures keep the marriage together rather than feelings of warmth and attraction between the partners. Such outside pressures may include business reasons (for example, an elected official wanting to convey a stable family image), investment reasons (for example, husband and wife may have a luxurious home and other property that they do not want to lose by parting), and outward appearances (for example, a couple living in a small community may remain together to avoid the reactions of relatives and friends to a divorce). In addition, a couple may believe that ending the marriage would harm the children or be morally wrong.

John F. Cuber and Peggy B. Harroff have identified three types of empty-shell marriages.[17] In a *devitalized relationship*, husband and wife lack excitement or any real interest in each other or their marriage. Boredom and apathy characterize this relationship. Serious arguments are rare.

In a *conflict habituated relationship*, husband and wife frequently quarrel in private, or they may also quarrel in public, or they may put up a façade of being compatible. The relationship is characterized by considerable conflict, tension, and bitterness.

In a *passive-congenial relationship*, both partners are not happy but are content with their lives and generally feel adequate. The partners may have some interests in common, but those interests are generally insignificant. The spouses contribute little to each other's real satisfactions. This type of relationship generally has little overt conflict.

The number of empty-shell marriages is unknown: It may be as high as (or even higher than) the number of happy marriages. The atmosphere in empty-shell marriages is usually joyless. Members do not share and discuss their problems or experiences with each other. Communication is kept to a minimum. There is seldom any spontaneous expression of affection. Children in such families are usually starved for love and reluctant to have friends over to visit because they are embarrassed about how their parents interact.

The couples in these marriages engage in few activities together and display no pleasure in each other's company. Sexual relations between the partners, as might be expected, are rare and generally unsatisfying. Outsiders may perceive that the partners (and often the children) appear insensitive, cold, and callous to each other. Yet closer observation will reveal that the spouses are highly aware of each other's weaknesses and sensitive areas, and they manage to mention them frequently to hurt each other.

William J. Goode compares empty-shell marriages to marriages that end in divorce:

Most families that divorce pass through a state—sometimes after the divorce—in which husband and wife no longer feel bound to each other, cease to cooperate or share with each other, and look on one another as almost a stranger. The "empty shell" family is in such a state. Its members no longer feel any strong commitment to many of the mutual role obligations, but for various reasons the husband and wife do not separate or divorce.[18]

It is not known how many empty-shell marriages end in divorce. It is likely that a fair number eventually do. Both spouses must put considerable effort into making a marriage work to prevent an empty-shell marriage from gradually developing.

Marriage Counseling

The primary social service for people who are considering a divorce or who have an empty-shell marriage is marriage counseling. (Those who do obtain a divorce may also need counseling to work out adjustment problems, such as adjusting to single life. Generally such counseling is one-on-one, but at times it may include the ex-spouse and the children, depending on the nature of the problem.)

Marriage counseling is provided by a variety of professionals, including social workers, psychologists, guidance counselors, psychiatrists, and members of the clergy. It is also provided (to a greater or lesser extent) by most direct social service agencies.

Marriage counselors generally use a problem-solving approach in which (a) problems are first identified, (b) alternative solutions are generated, (c) the merits and shortcomings of the alternatives are examined, (d) the clients select one or more alternatives to implement, and (e) the extent to which the problems are resolved by the alternatives is later assessed. Because the spouses "own" their problems, they are the primary problem solvers.

A wide range of problems may be encountered by married couples. For example, the couple may experience sexual problems, financial problems, communication problems, problems with relatives, conflicts of interest, infidelity, conflicts on how to discipline and raise children, or drug or alcohol problems. Marriage counselors attempt to have spouses precisely identify their problems and then use the problem-solving format to seek to resolve the issues.

In some cases, couples may rationally decide that a divorce is in their best interest.

In marriage counseling, there is considerable effort by the counselor to see both spouses together during sessions. Practically all marital conflicts involve both partners and therefore are best resolved when both partners work together on resolving them. (If the spouses are seen separately, each spouse is likely to become suspicious of what the other is telling the counselor.) By seeing both together, the counselor can facilitate communication between the partners. (When spouses are seen individually, they are also more likely to exaggerate the extent to which their mate is contributing to the disharmony.) Joint sessions allow each partner the opportunity to refute what the other is saying. Only in rare cases is it desirable to hold an individual session with a spouse. For example, if one of the partners wants to work on unwanted emotions concerning a past incestuous relationship, it may be desirable to meet individually with that spouse. (When an individual session is held, the other spouse should be informed of why it is being held and what will be discussed.)

Critical Thinking Questions

Can you identify a couple that is in an empty-shell marriage? If so, why do you believe this couple has reached this stage?

If some of the areas of conflict involve other family members (such as the children), it may be desirable to include these other members in some of the sessions. For example, if a father is irritated that his 14-year-old daughter is often disrespectful to him, the daughter may be invited to the next session to work on this subproblem.

Additional Marriage-Related Services

Although marriage counseling and divorce counseling are the primary social services for resolving marital conflicts, other related services are available.

Premarital counseling services are designed for couples who are considering marriage. Such services help clients assess whether marriage is in their best interest and also help them to prepare for the realities of marriage. Conflicts that people are having while dating are also worked on, and other topics, such as birth control, are explored.

The self-help organization *Parents Without Partners (PWP)* serves divorced people, unwed mothers or fathers, and stepparents. It is partially a social group, but it is also an organization that helps members with the adjustment problems of raising a family alone.

A recent development in social services is *divorce mediation*, which helps divorcing spouses to resolve (as amicably as possible) such issues as dividing the personal property, deciding custody and child support issues, and working out possible alimony arrangements.

Some agencies are now offering *relationship workshops* and *encounter couple groups*, which are designed to help those who are dating or who are married to improve their relationships through sharing concerns and improving communication patterns.

Violence in Families

We tend to view the family as a social institution in which love and gentleness abound. Sadly, the opposite is often true, with violence pervasive in American families.

Beatings, stabbings, and assaults are common in many families. The extent of violence in families is largely unknown, as much of it is unreported. Violence in families is not limited to child abuse and spouse abuse. The number of children who assault their parents is greater than the number of children abused by their parents.[19] *Elder abuse* is increasingly receiving attention. This term refers to the physical or psychological mistreatment of older adults. The perpetrator may be the son or daughter of the older adult, a caregiver, or some other person.

One of the more notable victims of elder abuse was Mickey Rooney. He began as a child movie star and acted in more than 200 movies. In March 2011, he gave an emotional testimony on elder abuse before a U.S. senate panel. Rooney said he had been victimized for years by two of his stepchildren. He stated they bullied and threatened him, making him "effectively a prisoner in his home." He added they took his money, denied him his medication, and withheld food from him. Rooney told the senators if it can happen to him, it can happen to anyone.[20]

The varied forms of mistreatment of older persons are typically grouped into the following eight categories:

- *Physical abuse.* The infliction of physical pain or injury, including bruising, punching, restraining, or sexually molesting.

- *Psychological abuse.* The infliction of mental anguish, such as intimidating, humiliating, and threatening harm.
- *Financial abuse.* The illegal or improper exploitation of the victim's assets or property.
- *Neglect.* The deliberate failure or refusal to fulfill a caregiving obligation, such as denial of food or health care or abandoning the victim.
- *Sexual abuse.* Nonconsensual sexual contact with an older person.
- *Self-neglect.* Behaviors of a frail, depressed, or mentally incompetent older person that threaten her or his own safety or health, such as failure to eat or drink adequately, or to take prescribed medications.
- *Abandonment.* Desertion of vulnerable elder by anyone who has assumed the responsibility for care or custody of that person.
- *Violating personal rights.* Rights that may be violated include the older person's right to privacy and to make her or his personal and health decisions.

Violence between children is also common. Some children even use a weapon (such as a knife or a gun) when having conflicts with their siblings.

Patterns of family violence appear to be learned in families. Abused children (when they become adults and parents) are more likely to abuse their children. Also, adults abused as children by their parents who then become the primary caregivers for those parents are more likely to abuse their elderly parents.

The victims of family violence—battered children, battered parents, and battered wives—have common disadvantages. They are generally smaller in size, have less physical strength, and usually feel helpless in relation to the aggressors (primarily because they depend on their aggressors for physical, financial, and emotional support).

Before the 1960s, little attention was given to violence in families, partly because the family was viewed as a sacred institution and a private domain: What went on within families was viewed as a personal concern and the responsibility of family members alone—not outsiders. Over the past five decades, there has been an increasing awareness that violence in families is a major social problem.

Family fights constitute the single largest category of calls to police. The highest rate of police fatalities arises from responses to disturbance calls, and domestic violence cases make up a large proportion of such calls.[21] Suzanne Steinmetz and Murray Straus have noted: "It would be hard to find a group or an institution in American society in which violence is more of an everyday occurrence than it is within the family."[22] Violence not only causes physical harm in families; each incident also weakens the loyalty, affection, and trust among members that are basic to positive family functioning.

One explanation of why family violence occurs is based on the theory that frustration often provokes an aggressive response. A husband or wife who is frustrated at work may come home and take out that frustration on the spouse or the children. A young child frustrated by the action of a sibling may take a poke at him or her. Steinmetz and Straus observe: "In a society such as ours, in which aggression is defined as a normal response to frustration, we can expect that the more frustrating the familial and occupational roles, the greater the amount of violence."[23]

In another explanation, John O'Brien has noted that family members often use physical force to gain an advantage.[24] A parent spanks a child for disciplinary reasons. A sister may shove her brother out of the way in an attempt to obtain something they both want. O'Brien suggests that family members are likely to resort to physical force when other resources are nonexistent, diminished, or exhausted. Thus, an alcoholic husband who feels he has lost the respect of his family may resort to physical abuse as a last-ditch effort to assert his authority.

Spouse Abuse

Spouse abuse, particularly wife beating, was unfortunately tolerated for many years but has now become an issue of national concern. The problem leaped into the spotlight in 1994 following the death of Nicole Brown Simpson, who was savagely stabbed to death, and the arrest of her former husband (O. J. Simpson) for the murder. At least eight times prior to her death, police had been called to the Simpson home after Nicole claimed she was battered by O. J.[25] (Two years later in a civil trial, O. J. was found guilty of murdering his wife and Ronald Goldman.)

It is not just wives who are abused. Husbands are slapped or shoved with about the same frequency as are wives.[26] The greatest physical damage, however, is usually suffered by women. Studies show that men cause more serious injuries largely because they are physically stronger.[27]

E Teister/Blickwinkel/Age Fotostock

Spouse abuse has become an issue of national concern, and new services have been developed to treat domestic violence.

More than 10% of all murder victims are killed by spouses.[28] Women tend to endure cruelty and abuse much longer than men, at times because they feel trapped due to unemployment and financial insecurity. Spouse abuse is sometimes precipitated by the victim; that is, the recipient of the abuse may be the first to use verbal or physical violence in the incident.[29] However, the dominant theme in American spouse abuse is the systematic use of violence and the threat of violence by some men to "keep their wives in line." That is to say, there is a traditional belief held by some segments of our society that husbands have a right to control what their wives do and to force them to be submissive.

Domestic violence from husbands, male partners, or other family members happens so often that violence is the major cause of injury to women.[30] Injuries from woman battering are more common than those from rape, mugging, or even auto accidents.[31]

Incidents of physical abuse between spouses are not isolated, but tend to recur frequently in a marriage. Spouse abuse occurs as often among the well educated as among the less educated.[32]

Most wives who are severely beaten by their husbands do not seek to end the marriage. Wives are more likely to remain in the home if (a) the violence is infrequent, (b) they were abused by their parents when they were children, or (c) they believe they are financially dependent on their husbands.[33]

Many authorities believe spouse abuse is related to a norm of tolerating violence in American families. Straus notes:

There seems to be an implicit, taken-for-granted cultural norm which makes it legitimate for family members to hit each other. In respect to husbands and wives, in effect, this means that the marriage license is also a hitting license.[34]

Critical Thinking Questions

Have you had a relationship in which you were being physically or emotionally abused? If so, why did you stay in the relationship as long as you did?

Several studies have found that a sizable number of both men and women believe it is appropriate for a husband to hit his wife "every now and then."[35]

Men batter women for a variety of reasons. Many men have a poor self-image; they are insecure about their worth as breadwinners, fathers, and sexual partners. They tend to have a stereotyped view of their wives as playing a submissive role and as needing to be controlled. Many men use alcohol and other drugs to excess and are much more likely to be violent when intoxicated or high.

In battered-spouse families, a cycle of violence tends to be continually repeated as follows: A battering incident occurs, and the wife sustains injuries. The husband feels remorse, but he also fears his wife may leave or may report the abuse to the police, so he tries to "honeymoon" her into thinking he is a good husband who won't abuse her again. (He may even send flowers, buy expensive gifts, or be overly attentive.) Gradually the "honeymoon" efforts on his part cease, and tensions about work or family matters again begin to build inside him. As the tension builds, a minor incident sets him off, often while he's intoxicated, and he again batters his wife. The battering/honeymoon/tension-building/battering cycle tends to be repeated again and again.

Abusive husbands often isolate their spouses and make them dependent. They try to make their wives sever ties with relatives and friends. They ridicule their wives' friends and relatives, and they usually create an embarrassing scene when the wife is with those friends or relatives. The wife then ends contact with friends and relatives to "keep peace." Abusive husbands make their wives dependent on them by continually ridiculing them, which lowers the women's self-esteem and leads them to play a submissive role. Husbands also create financial dependency, such as by creating barriers that prevent their wives from seeking highpaying employment.

A surprising number of battered women do not permanently leave their husbands for a variety of reasons. Many are socialized to play a subordinate role to their husbands, and the husbands use violence and psychological abuse to make them feel too inadequate to live on their own. Some women believe it is their moral duty to stick it out to the end—that marriage is forever, for better or for worse. Many hope (in spite of the continuing violence) that their husbands will change. Some fear that, if they try to leave, their husbands will retaliate with even more severe beatings. A fair number do not view leaving as a viable alternative because they feel financially dependent. Many have young children and do not believe they have the resources to raise children on their own. Some believe the occasional beatings are better than the loneliness and insecurity connected with leaving. Some dread the stigma associated with separation or divorce. These women are captives in their own homes.

Fortunately, new services in recent years have been developed for battered women. Shelter homes for battered women and their children have been established in many communities. These shelters give abused women an opportunity to flee from their abusive situation. The women also generally receive counseling, assistance in finding a job, and legal help. Services to battered women now include "safety planning," which is an empowerment approach to help women develop a repertoire of resources to maintain their safety. In some areas, programs are also being established for the husbands. These programs include group therapy for batterers, anger management programs for batterers, marriage counseling for both spouses, and 24-hour hotlines that encourage potential spouse abusers to call when they are angry. (Unfortunately, many batterers refuse to participate in such programs.) Many communities also have public information programs (for example, short television announcements) to inform battered women that they have a legal right not to be abused and that there are resources to stop the abuse.

In an effort to treat domestic abuse as seriously as crimes between strangers, many states have enacted a domestic abuse law that requires police to make an arrest (of either spouse, but usually the husband) if physical abuse has occurred and injury or threat of further harm exists. Police face criminal or civil penalties under the law if they do not make a mandated arrest.[36]

As services for battered wives become more widely available, we may expect an increasing number of these women to flee from their homes and refuse to return until they have some guarantee of their safety.

Child Abuse and Neglect

Although definitions of child abuse and neglect vary somewhat from state to state, Alfred Kadushin and Judith Martin summarize these kinds of situations as including:

- Physical abuse.
- Malnourishment; poor clothing; lack of proper shelter, sleeping arrangements, attendance, or supervision. (Includes "failure to thrive" syndrome, which describes infants who fail to grow and develop at a normal rate.)
- Denial of essential medical care.
- Failure to attend school regularly.
- Exploitation, overwork.
- Exposure to unwholesome or demoralizing circumstances.
- Sexual abuse.
- Somewhat less frequently, the definitions include emotional abuse and neglect involving denial of the normal experiences that permit a child to feel loved, wanted, secure, and worthy.[37]

The consequences of child abuse and neglect can be devastating. Gelles notes:

Researchers and clinicians have documented physical, psychological, cognitive, and behavioral consequences of physical abuse, psychological abuse, sexual abuse, and neglect. Physical damage can range from death, brain damage, and permanent disabilities to minor bruises and scrapes. The

psychological consequences can range from lowered sense of self-worth to severe psychiatric disorders, including dissociative states. Cognitive problems range from severe organic brain disorders to reduced attention and minor learning disorders. Maltreated children's behavioral problems can include severe violent and criminal behavior and suicide as well as inability to relate to peers.[38]

Physical Abuse   In the past 60 years, there has been considerable national concern about the "battered child syndrome." Abused children have been beaten using a variety of objects, including bare fists, electric cords, ropes, rubber hoses, baseball bats, belts, sticks, pool cues, wooden shoes, broom handles, chair legs, and books. Some are kicked, or burned with open flames (such as cigarette lighters). Some are scalded by hot liquids. Others are strangled or suffocated by pillows. Some are drowned in bathtubs. Others are stabbed, bitten, thrown violently to the floor or against a wall, or stomped on.

Broken bones are common, so are black eyes, severe bruises, fractured ribs, and lost teeth. Sometimes concussions and skull fractures occur. Case Example 6.1 describes just one example of physical abuse.

Physical abuse involves beating a child to the point at which some physical damage is done. The line between physical abuse and harsh parental discipline is difficult to define. Silver et al. note:

If a parent punishes a child with a belt, is it after the fourth slash with the belt that parental rights end and child abuse begins; is it after the belt raises a welt over two millimeters that it becomes abuse versus parental rights?[39]

Definitions of abuse vary. Some are narrow in scope, restricting abuse to actual serious injury sustained by the child; broader definitions include intent to harm the child and verbal abuse.

In the late 1960s, in response to a growing national concern about child abuse, all states adopted child-abuse and neglect-reporting laws. Such laws are essentially a case-finding device. They require professionals (such as physicians, social workers, counselors, hospital administrators, school administrators, nurses, and dentists) to report suspected cases of child abuse to certain specified agencies, such as the local police department and the county welfare department.

The true extent of child abuse is unknown. Accurate data are difficult to get for two reasons: the failure of citizens and professionals to report suspected cases and the reluctance of abused children to talk. Many battered children, believing their punishment is deserved, keep mute when interviewed by those who might help, and they develop negative self-images.

A significant result of child abuse is that violence breeds violence. George C. Curtis reports evidence showing that abused children may "become tomorrow's murderers and perpetrators of other crimes of violence."[40] When they become parents, there is also a high probability they will become abusive parents.[41] Theoretically, abuse generates an unusually high degree of hostility, which, in future years, may be channeled into violence. A disproportionate number of rapists, murderers, robbers, and spouse abusers were child-abuse victims when they were younger. Abused children are high risks to become runaways, which exposes them to other kinds of victimization and sometimes results in their being involved in criminal activity, such as shoplifting, theft, or prostitution.

Although in rare cases abuse is nonrecurrent, generally it is repeated. Nonrecurrent abuse is usually difficult to document, as the abuser can contrive a plausible explanation for the one-time injuries received by the child.

Gelles reviewed studies on the characteristics of parents and caregivers who are most at risk of abusing their children and found:

- Abuse was more likely to occur among parents with limited education and few employment skills, among non-White families, and among mother-headed, single-parent families.
- In many of the families, there was evidence of "family discord" and stress due to limited financial resources. (It is possible that the higher incidence of abuse in the lower classes may partly result from the fact that middle- and upper-class parents are in a better position to conceal the abuse.)
- Mothers are more likely to abuse their children than fathers. The reasons for this gender difference are probably related to the fact that mothers tend to spend more time with children, and mothers in our society are considered more responsible for the children's behavior than are fathers.
- More than two-thirds of abused children are permitted to remain in their homes by protective services even after abuse is determined. (Protective services are described later in this chapter.)[42]

Physical Neglect   In contrast to child abuse, child neglect is more a problem of omission than of commission. Specific types of physical neglect include (a) child abandonment; (b) environmental neglect—letting a child live in filth, without proper clothing, unattended, unsupervised, or without proper nourishment; (c) educational neglect, in which a child is allowed to be excessively absent from school; and (d) medical neglect, in which no effort is made to secure needed medical care for the child. Although child neglect has received less national attention than child abuse, it is the most common situation in which protective services agencies must intervene.

In rare cases, such as child abandonment, the parent rejects the parental role. In most child-neglect cases, however, the parent inadequately performs the role. Kadushin and Martin define a typical neglectful mother as physically exhausted, mentally impoverished, emotionally deprived, and socially isolated.[43] Parental neglect is more likely to be found among those who are poverty stricken or who live on marginal incomes.

Vincent De Francis provides the following description of what a social worker encountered in investigating a neglect complaint:

What I saw as I entered the room was utter, stark disorganization. The room was a combined kitchen-dining room. At the other end of the room, two scrawny, owl-eyed, frightened children—a girl of about four and a boy of three—stared silently at me. Except for thin cotton undershirts, they were stark naked. They had sore crusts on their legs and arms. They were indescribably dirty, hair matted, body and hands stained and covered with spilled food particles. Sitting on a urine-soaked and soiled mattress in a baby carriage behind them was a younger child—a boy about two.

The floor was ankle-deep in torn newspapers. There were feces in about a half-dozen spots on the floor, and the air was fetid and saturated with urine odor.

There were flies everywhere. What seemed like giant roaches were crawling over the paper-strewn floor. The kitchen sink and gas stove were piled high with greasy and unwashed dishes, pots, and pans.[44]

CASE EXAMPLE 6.1

Physical Abuse and Murder

Chicago—Jody Marie Olcott lived only 102 days. She died on November 16, 2007. The coroner's report showed that she had suffered more injuries than most people who live into late adulthood. Charged with second-degree murder in her death was her father, Malcom Olcott, age 34.

Jody Marie was born on August 5, 2007. Her unmarried parents lived together. Her mother, Judy Forbes, worked as a waitress. Her father was unemployed and felt considerable "pressure" over being unemployed and now having parental responsibilities.

Jody's first 2 months were quite normal. Her pediatrician saw her early in October and reported that she had gained nearly 2 pounds and appeared in good health. Shortly after that, Jody's nightmare began. The pathologist who examined Jody after her death noted that she suffered from at least five broken ribs caused about a month earlier by kicking or by punching with a fist.

The pathologist noted that about 10 days before her death she had received bruises to her head, chest, and left elbow. Also, at about the same time, she had received burn marks on her buttocks and her head. The district attorney acknowledged that Mr. Olcott had admitted (at the time of his arrest) to setting Jody on top of a space heater.

The pathologist's report also noted one of Jody's knees was broken, and the other was badly sprained, "possibly resulting from the child being picked up by her legs and then her legs being snapped." At the time of her death, Jody's weight had dropped to 6 pounds—1 pound less than when she was born.

The blow that caused Jody's death occurred during the night of November 15. Ms. Forbes was at her waitressing job at a fast-food restaurant. The district attorney stated that Mr. Olcott was feeling on edge with his financial and family responsibilities. He began drinking. Jody was crying, as she had done for the past several days (probably from the pain of all her injuries). Mr. Olcott stated he just couldn't take the incessant crying. He grabbed Jody and tossed her about 10 feet—hoping she'd land on the sofa. Jody missed the sofa and landed on her head on a hardwood floor. Mr. Olcott told the police that during the next few hours Jody stopped crying but appeared to have trouble breathing and sometimes vomited. When Ms. Forbes came home that evening, she found that Jody did not appear to be breathing. She called for an ambulance. Jody was pronounced dead on arrival, with the cause of death being a blood clot caused by a skull fracture. Ms. Forbes was asked by the police why she did not report the violence occurring to Jody over the past several weeks. Ms. Forbes stated, "Malcom told me if I went to the police, he would leave me and have nothing more to do with me."

Emotional Neglect   Meeting a child's affectional needs is as important to normal growth and development as meeting his or her physical needs. Yet emotional neglect is difficult to define and document in the precise terms required by law.

The National Clearinghouse on Child Neglect and Abuse defines emotional neglect as:

> ... *failure to provide the child the emotional nurturing or emotional support necessary for the development of a sound personality, as for example, subjecting the child to rejection or to a home climate charged with tension, hostility, and anxiety-producing occurrences which result in perceivable problems in children.*[45]

Interpreted broadly, the problem with this definition is that practically every parent at times is guilty of such neglect. Other definitions of emotional neglect encounter the same problem. Nevertheless, there is solid agreement that some children do suffer from emotional neglect, even when they are adequately cared for physically.

Emotional neglect is very difficult to document in court. When emotional neglect is accompanied by physical neglect, protective services agencies make a case based on the physical neglect. (See Case Example 6.2: Is This Emotional Neglect?)

Sexual Abuse   Sexual abuse (or incest) within families has in recent years become an issue of national concern. It is discussed at length later in this chapter.

Unwholesome or Demoralizing Conditions   Children who are exposed to their parents' continued prostitution, criminal activity, drug addiction, and severe alcoholism are also considered in need of protective services. Such exposure is deemed injurious to the moral development of children.

Exploitation   This category involves forcing a child to work for unreasonably long hours or encouraging a child to beg, steal, or engage in prostitution.

Abusive and Neglectful Parents   No single cause can fully explain why parents abuse or neglect their children. Available research indicates that abusive

CASE EXAMPLE 6.2

Is This Emotional Neglect?

The following case example raises a number of as-yet-unanswered questions surrounding emotional neglect.

Gary, age 9, was the only child of Mr. and Mrs. Jim N. The N. family lived in a suburb of a metropolitan area, and Gary's physical needs were adequately met. Yet Gary was not doing well in school. He repeated the first grade and now is repeating the third grade.

Gary was referred for psychological testing and was found to have a very low self-concept. His self-concept was so negative that he refused to study math for fear of failing and would not participate in any competitive games with peers. He instead preferred to play by himself, with toys appropriate to children of an age level of 5.

A home study found that Mr. N. was a stoic, unaffectional person who was seldom at home, as he spent long hours operating a service station he owned. Mrs. N. had such a distasteful personality and disposition that she was unable to hold a job and had no close friends. Below average in intellectual function-ing, she completed only the ninth grade. In her interactions with Gary, she was observed to have a short tolerance level, to frequently berate and criticize him, and to call him "stupid" and "an idiot." Gary appeared somewhat fearful of her and tried to avoid interacting with her. Both parents refused to take parent effectiveness training or to receive counseling.

- Are Gary's personal problems (negative self-image) a result of interactions with his parents or of some other factors (for example, school environment, a past traumatic experience, or an inherited disposition)?

- Even if it is assumed that his problems are due to his parental interactions, how can this be proved in court?

- Would his personal problems be reduced or intensified if he were removed from his home and placed in foster care? For example, would moving him to a foster home lead him to feel rejected by his parents or to blame himself for the move because he erroneously assumed he was "bad"?

and neglectful parents may have little in common. The following factors[46] have been found to be associated with parents who abuse their children:

- Some abusive parents were themselves abused as children. If not abused, they generally had a lack of stable love relationships in their childhood and an inadequate gratification of early emotional needs.

- Although abuse, like neglect, is more heavily concentrated among the lower classes, it is more randomly distributed through the population than is neglect.

- Frequently, one child in a family is singled out to be the target of the abuse. Many reasons appear to account for this. The child may be viewed as mentally slow or as a potential delinquent. Where there is marital conflict, one child may be chosen as the victim because of a resemblance to the disliked spouse. One child may cry more, be more hyperactive, or be more demanding of parental care. The child may be punished because he or she was conceived prior to marriage, is illegitimate, or is the result of an unwanted pregnancy.

- In some cases, the abused child contributes to the process by placing greater than normal burdens on parental patience by having severe temper tantrums; by having feeding, speech, or toilet-training problems; and/or by being restless, negative, unresponsive, listless, whiny, or fussy.

- The child who is the victim may, in disturbed families, be essential for the psychic stability of the family. It appears that some disturbed families need a "whipping boy" or "scapegoat" to maintain an equilibrium within the family. Sometimes when an abused child is removed, another is selected to be the victim and thereby fulfills the "stability" role.

- Abusive parents often show an absence of guilt, have a tendency toward social isolation, have a high level of overall aggressiveness, are prone to impulsivity, and tend to have emotional problems, feelings of inadequacy, and a low tolerance of criticism.

- Environmental stress factors (for example, marital problems), economic pressures, and social isolation sometimes help trigger abuse.

- Abusive parents tend to believe in strict discipline and to view misbehavior by their children as willful, deliberate disobedience. Also characteristic is a high demand for the child to perform to gratify the parent.

- Alcohol/drug abuse plays an important contributing role in some cases.

The following factors[47] have been identified as associated with child neglect:

- The preponderance of families comes from the lower socioeconomic classes. Financial deprivation is a major contributing factor. Many also have inadequate housing.
- A high percentage (60% in some studies) are one-parent families, generally headed by a female.
- Neglectful parents frequently have an atypically large number of children.
- A fair number of neglectful mothers are below normal in intellectual capacity.
- Neglectful parents (particularly the mothers who have the most contact with children) are physically and emotionally exhausted, have health problems, are socially withdrawn or isolated, are frustrated, are apathetic, and lack hope. Such factors lead them to be "indifferent" toward their children.
- Neglectful parents tend to have been emotionally deprived during their early childhood years. Similar to abusive parents, they lacked stable affectional relationships when they were young. Such early childhood experiences appear to lead to later emotional inadequacies and then, when combined with severe financial and environmental stress, result in physical and emotional exhaustion.
- Neglectful parents are not without intrapsychic distress but are generally less emotionally disturbed than abusive parents. Similar to abusive parents, they tend to be socially isolated.

Protective Services

Under the concept of *parens patriae*, the state is ultimately a parent to all children. When the natural parents neglect, abuse, or exploit a child, the state has the legal right and responsibility to intervene. Protective services has been defined as "a specialized casework service to neglected, abused, exploited, or rejected children. The focus of the service is preventive and nonpunitive and is geared toward rehabilitation through identification and treatment of the motivating factors which underlie" the problem.[48]

Brief History   In colonial days, a child was regarded as chattel (an item of personal property). This gave parents the right to sell the child, exploit his or her labor, offer the child as a sacrifice, or even kill the child at birth. Although most communities regulated and restricted such behaviors, it was not until the era of industrialization that children were

considered to have any rights. These rights have gradually been expanded. In the early 20th century, child labor laws were finally enacted, prohibiting parents from exploiting the labor of their children.

Agencies providing protective services in America trace their origin to the case of Mary Ellen in 1875.[49] Mary Ellen was severely beaten and neglected by the couple who had raised her since infancy. Concerned community citizens were unaware of any legal approach to protect her. In desperation, they appealed to the Society for the Prevention of Cruelty to Animals. (It's interesting to note that at this time organizations existed to protect animals, but not children.) Mary Ellen was brought to the court's attention by this society. She was given protection by the court and was placed with another family. The abusive couple were sentenced to prison. Following this dramatic case, the Society for the Prevention of Cruelty to Children was formed in New York. Gradually other such societies throughout the United States were formed, laws protecting children from abuse and neglect were enacted, and agencies providing protective services were established.

Almost from the start, protective services had two focuses: a law enforcement approach and a rehabilitative approach. The law enforcement focus emphasized punishment for the abusive or neglectful parents, whereas the rehabilitative approach emphasized the importance of helping the parents and keeping the family together rather than disrupting it. Since the early 1900s, protective services have generally taken the rehabilitative approach.

Since the late 1960s, there has been a dramatic growth of interest in services to prevent and treat child abuse. With this interest came, in 1975, passage of Title XX to the Social Security Act, making protective services mandatory for each state and providing federal reimbursement for most costs. A federal Child Abuse Prevention and Treatment Act, passed in January 1974, provides direct assistance to states to help them develop child abuse and child neglect programs.

Processes in Protective Services   Extensive efforts have been made to encourage parents who have mistreated their children (or feel they may mistreat them) to request agency services voluntarily. Radio and TV announcements, along with posters, announce the availability of stress hotline services that parents may call in many communities.

Parents who mistreat their children, however, do not generally seek help. Currently, initiation of services most often results from the legal requirement of mandatory reporting by professionals of suspected abuse, physical neglect, sexual abuse, and emotional injury. The list of professionals required to report includes, among others, social workers, school personnel, doctors, day-care workers, counselors, legal personnel, nurses, and dentists. The agencies to which reports are made include the local police department, the county welfare department, and the county sheriff. The law grants civil and criminal immunity to the professionals required to make such reports and also specifies penalties for failure to report.

Each state has the legal right and responsibility to intervene when a child is abused, neglected, or exploited. This right and responsibility are delegated to protective services (in many states protective services is located within human services departments).

Case finding is almost always through a complaint referral. Complaints generally are filed by neighbors, relatives, or family friends—in addition to those professionals already mentioned who are required by law to report abuse. A complaint is a report of a possible neglect or abuse situation that needs exploration. The complainant may remain anonymous. Occasionally, unfounded complaints are made to harass a parent.

Some complainants feel guilty about making a report, and they are given reassurance that they are performing a very useful function that is necessary to protect and safeguard children. They are also informed that their identity (name) will not be revealed to the family against which the report has been made.

All complaints are then investigated by the protective services agency. Some agencies arrange for the initial visit by telephone. Others prefer an unannounced visit, which has the advantage of allowing the social worker to view the home environment in its day-to-day appearance. The initial approach is direct and frank. The social worker conveys that a concern about potential danger to a child has been expressed and needs to be explored; if a potential danger does exist, the worker's responsibility and interest are to be helpful to both the parents and their children.

The social worker attempts to obtain an objective and accurate description of the situation. Specific information relevant to the complaint is sought.

For example, if the complaint is that a child appears malnourished and is frequently absent from school, specific questions are asked about the daily diet of the child, any illnesses he or she has had, and the specific dates and reasons why the child has been absent from school. Such details are necessary to determine whether the child is in fact in danger and what help (if any) is needed. The information is also essential as evidence if a petition is made to the court to remove the child from the home. Obtaining this information must be done tactfully because it is also important that the social worker try to develop a working relationship with the parents.

During this evaluation process, the social worker almost always attempts to see the child who allegedly has been endangered. If abuse or neglect exists, the objective is to convey to the parents that the focus of protective services is to prevent further neglect or abuse and to alleviate the factors that are now a danger to the child. Because many families charged with abuse or neglect have multiple problems, services may be far ranging (involving, for example, services related to health, education, finances, housing, counseling, employment, parent effectiveness training, day care, and so on).

When there is no evidence of neglect or abuse, the case may be closed after the initial interview. For families with serious problems, continued services may be provided for years.

If the child is clearly in danger (for example, is a victim of repeated severe abuse) or if the parents are unable or unwilling to make changes essential for the long-term well-being of the child, the youngster may have to be removed from the home. Protective services agencies view court action as "a means of protecting the child rather than prosecuting the parents."[50]

If the social worker decides it is necessary to remove the child from the home, the parents' voluntary consent is first sought. If it is not received, a petition is made to the court requesting that the child receive protection. (Court action is atypical in protective services; studies suggest that most cases are closed without it.)[51]

After a petition is filed, a preliminary hearing is held within a few weeks. Parents are permitted to be represented by an attorney, and the normal adversarial court procedures are followed. The social worker must support the petition with documented facts. The judge has the responsibility of protecting the rights not only of the child but also of the parents. At the preliminary hearing, the parents are asked if they will consent to or contest the petition. If they decide to contest and if evidence of abuse and neglect is substantiated, a trial is held.

In making a disposition, a number of avenues are open to the judge. She or he may decide that there is not sufficient evidence of neglect or abuse to warrant any action. Or the judge can place the child under supervision of the court while permitting him or her to remain at home. Such supervision puts pressure on the family to make needed changes, with the threat of the child being removed if the changes are not made. The judge also has the option of placing the child under protective legal custody. Under this arrangement, legal custody is assigned to a social agency, which then has the authority to remove the child if essential changes are not made. The judge can also terminate the parents' legal rights and place the child under guardianship of the agency. Under this disposition, the child is automatically removed from the home.

For children who are in imminent danger, many jurisdictions have provisions that allow either the protective services agency or the family court to remove the child immediately. Such children are then usually placed in a temporary foster home. When a child is removed for emergency reasons, a court hearing must be held within 24 hours to determine the appropriateness of the action. Unless the court is satisfied that protection of the child requires removal from the home, the child must be returned to his or her parents.

Involuntary Services Protective services cannot withdraw from the situation if it finds that the parents are uncooperative or resistant. For most social services, clients are voluntary recipients. Protective services is one of the few services in which participation is involuntary (probation and parole are other examples).

Because protective services is involuntary, and because provision of services is based on an "outside" complaint, the recipients are likely to view the services as an invasion of privacy. The initial contact by the social worker may arouse hostility, be viewed as a threat to family autonomy, and perhaps raise some guilt about incidents in which the parents have mistreated their children in the past. Having one's functioning as a parent questioned and explored arouses substantial emotional feelings. Although the focus of protective services theoreti-

cally is rehabilitative and nonpunitive, protective services clients generally view the services as punitive and investigatory.

Some recipients of protective services remain hostile and resistant throughout the time services are provided. Others, in time, form a productive working relationship with the agency, in which case positive changes are much more likely to occur. A few individuals are cooperative from the beginning, perhaps because they recognize that their family needs help.

In working with parents who neglect or abuse their children, the social worker must show respect for the parents as people while in no way conveying acceptance of their mistreatment. The worker needs to convey empathy with their situation, be warm, and yet be firm about the need for positive changes. This approach is illustrated in the following interview:

The C. family was referred to the child welfare agency by a hospital which treated the 6-year-old boy, Wade, for a broken arm suffered in a beating by his mother.

Both parents said they whipped the children because they believed in firm discipline, and they challenged the worker's right to question this. Mr. C. again attempted to avoid the subject of Wade's beating by describing at length how strict his parents had been with him.

Again the worker brought the conversation back to the C.'s own disciplinary practices by saying that children had to be dealt with firmly, but the injury of a child was a serious matter. He added, "I can understand that one may be so upset he has trouble controlling himself." Mrs. C. hesitatingly said, "I was so upset and too angry," and broke into tears. The worker replied that, if together they could try to understand why Mrs. C. gets so upset, perhaps the behavior would not continue. Mr. C., who had been silent for a while, said he realized it was serious and that he did not approve of Mrs. C. beating the children but did not know what to do. He had told her that this was bad for the youngsters, but she continued. Mrs. C. remarked that looking back on Wade's beating was a terrible experience. She did not realize she had injured him until his arm became swollen. She supposed it was her anger and her temper that did it. She would like to talk to someone and she does need help.[52]

The protective services worker must be ready to perform a variety of roles: teacher, enabler, adviser, coordinator of treatment, intervener, supporter, confidante, and expediter. The focus must be on constantly identifying concrete needs, selecting intervention approaches, and providing specific services. Workers must also be ready to collaborate with other professional groups: the doctors treating the child, schoolteachers, lawyers, and judges.

A wide variety of treatment resources are used in attempting to make the needed changes. Crisis nurseries, extended day-care centers, and emergency foster homes provide short-term shelter to relieve a potentially damaging crisis situation. Parent effectiveness training programs, group therapy, and family life education programs sometimes are useful in curbing the abuse or neglect. Homemakers relieve the frustrated, overburdened mother of some of the daily load of child care. Emergency relief funds are sometimes provided to meet immediate rent, heat, food, and electricity expenses. Behavior modification programs, such as modeling and role-playing, have been used to change the behaviors of parents toward their children. "Emergency parents" have been used in some communities to go into a home and stay with a child who has been left unsupervised and unprotected. Psychotherapy and counseling have also been provided by protective services workers and other professionals. A self-help group, Parents Anonymous, is described in Case Exhibit 6.3. (Very few communities have the resources to provide all of these services. In many cities, the primary intervention resources available to protective services workers are their own counseling capacities and their ability to remove from the home children who are in danger.)

Kadushin and Martin have reviewed studies on the effectiveness of protective services and conclude:

In summary, the evaluation studies suggest that the agencies have achieved some modest measure of success. The amount of change one might reasonably expect the agencies to effect must be assessed against the great social and personal deprivation characteristic of the client families. Even the modest success achieved may have been more than could have been expected initially.

The resources available to treat these families are limited. The technology available to the worker in trying to effect change in such families is blunt and imprecise....

Scarce resources backed by a weak technology applied to a group of involuntary, disturbed clients resistive to change and living in seriously deprived circumstances would seem to guarantee the likelihood of limited success.[53]

Social workers have found protective services to be demanding. Burnout occurs at a higher rate among protective services workers than in many other social welfare areas.

Multidisciplinary Teams and Child Advocacy Centers*

Child protection is a complex and challenging area involving numerous professionals, agencies, and systems. In many communities today, child protective services agencies are teaming with multiple other agencies in order to jointly investigate and provide the best possible outcome for children and families. Multidisciplinary teams (MDTs) are formed with a variety of agencies to collaborate on child abuse and neglect cases. Each individual agency representative brings his or her specific roles and obligations to the team, but all with one common goal of addressing the protection of the children in the community. The multidisciplinary team often includes social service agencies, medical professionals, criminal justice personnel such as law enforcement and prosecutors, mental health providers, community members, educators, and victim services coordinators. As communities create MDTs, they develop written protocols to address interagency agreements, territorial concerns, definition of roles, conflict resolution, and tackle complex issues such as confidentiality. They may also create mission statements and memorandums of understanding (MOUs) to facilitate the most effective teaming and review of cases.[54]

In addition, many communities have also created child advocacy centers (CACs), which serve to be a "one-stop-shop" for children and families, child protective services, and other involved agencies such as law enforcement. CACs offer a child an appropriate and friendly environment with expert interviewers and access to video and audio technology. Additionally, they provide a neutral facility where involved professionals can conduct joint investigative interviews regarding reports of child abuse and neglect. This interagency collaboration allows for multidisci-

*This section was written by Debra S. Borquist, MSSW, APSW, Child Protection Team Social Worker, University of Wisconsin Health/American Family Children's Hospital.

plinary case reviews, case tracking, referrals for medical examinations, mental health evaluation and treatment, advocacy, a criminal justice system liaison, and coordination with other needed services. Compared to independent child protective services investigations, joint investigations with law enforcement were shown to have many positive outcomes for children. Additional advantages of CACs include higher-quality services to children and families, cost savings, community collaboration, and improved accountability.[55]

Family Preservation Programs With the implementation of mandatory child abuse and child neglect reporting in the 1960s, the number of reports of suspected abuse and neglect skyrocketed. In many cases in which abuse or neglect was determined to be occurring, the maltreated children were placed in temporary placements—typically foster homes. By the end of the 1960s, there was increasing concern about the number of children in foster care and the cost. There was widespread questioning of both the need to remove so many children from their biological homes and the effectiveness of foster care as a means of dealing with abused or neglected children. As a result, intensive family preservation programs were developed as a mechanism for protecting children and preserving families.

Family preservation is a model of intervention developed specifically for work with families in which the placement of one or more of the children is imminent. Gelles describes family preservation services as follows:

The essential feature is that family preservation services are intensive, short-term, crisis interventions. Services are provided in the client's home, although social workers do not actually move in. The length of home visit is variable—it is not confined to the "50-minute" clinical hour. Services are available 7 days a week, 24 hours a day, not just during business hours Monday through Friday. Caseloads are small—two or three families per worker. Soft services, such as therapy and education, and hard services, such as food stamps, housing, a homemaker, and supplemental Social Security, are available.[56]

Family preservation services are typically limited to 4 to 6 weeks.

Initial evaluations of intensive family preservation programs were uniformly enthusiastic. They were claimed to be successful in protecting the children involved and in saving costs by reducing placement of children outside the home. In recent years, however, there has been an increasing level of criticism of family preservation programs. Gelles concludes: "To date, no evaluation study that uses a randomly assigned control group has found that intensive family preservation programs reduce placement, costs or the risk of maltreatment."[57] There is a danger that failing to remove children who are being abused in a home actually places those children at risk of reabuse or even fatal abuse.

Patrick Murphy describes one family preservation case that ended in tragedy:

In December 1991, the aunt of a 3-year-old girl told the family services department that her sister and her sister's lover had physically abused the child. State investigators confirmed the abuse: the child had bruises and rope burns on her body. Instead of bringing the case to court, the department provided a housekeeper and a social worker who between them went to the home a total of 37 times over the next 90 days. The housekeeper helped the mother clean up and make dinner. The social worker took her out for meals and shopping.

On March 7, 1992, the aunt telephoned the family services agency again, pleading that the child was still being abused. The agency ignored her. On March 17, the agency closed the case with a glowing report on how well the family was doing. Several hours later, the girl was dead. An autopsy revealed that boiling water had been poured on her genitals and that she had been struck on the head with a blunt instrument. Her body was covered with 43 scars, bruises and rope burns, most of which had been made in the previous few weeks. She weighed 17 pounds.[58]

Family Group Conferencing The family group conferencing approach with abused or neglected children originated in New Zealand. The approach has now been adopted in many other countries, including in the United States.

When evidence of child abuse by child protective services or the police has been documented, some child protective services agencies are now offering the parents of the affected children the option of using the family group conferencing approach to attempt to improve the parenting and end future abuse. The process is first explained to the parents. If the parents agree to involve their extended kinship network in planning, the process is then implemented.

CASE EXHIBIT 6.3

Parents Anonymous (PA)

Self-help organizations (such as Alcoholics Anonymous, Parents and Friends of Lesbians and Gays, Over-eaters Anonymous, and Weight Watchers) have had considerable rehabilitative success. One such group, Parents Anonymous (PA), has been particularly effective at helping individuals who have abused or neglected their children.

PA was established in 1970 in California by Jolly K., who was desperate to find help to meet her needs. For 4 years, she had struggled with an uncontrollable urge to punish her daughter severely. One afternoon she attempted to strangle the child. She sought help from the local child-guidance clinic and was placed in therapy. When asked by her therapist what she could do about this situation, she formed an idea: "If alcoholics can stop drinking by getting together, and gamblers can stop gambling, maybe the same principle would work for abusers, too."[a] With her therapist's encouragement, she formed Mothers Anonymous in 1970 and started a few local chapters in California. Now the organization has chapters in most areas of the United States and Canada, and the name has been changed to Parents Anonymous because fathers who abuse their children are also eligible to join.

PA uses some of the basic therapeutic concepts of Alcoholics Anonymous. It is a crisis intervention program that offers two main forms of help:

1. Regular group meetings in which members share experiences and feelings and learn to control their emotions better.
2. Personal and telephone contact among members during periods of crisis, particularly when a member feels a nearly uncontrollable desire to take his or her anger or frustration out on a child.

Parents may be referred to PA by a social agency (including protective services) or may be self-referrals who are aware they need help.

Cassie Starkweather and S. Michael Turner describe why some parents who abuse their children would rather participate in a self-help group than receive professional counseling:

It has been our experience that most [abusive] parents judge themselves more harshly than other more objective people tend to judge them. The fear of losing their children frequently diminishes with reassurance from other members that they are not the monsters they think they are.

Generally speaking, PA members are so afraid they are going to be judged by others as harshly as they judge themselves that they are afraid to go out [to] seek help. Frequently, our members express fears of dealing with a professional person, seeing differences in education, sex, or social status as basic differences that would prevent easy communication or mutual understanding.

Members express feelings of gratification at finding that other parents are "in the same boat." They contrast this

with their feelings about professionals who, they often assume, have not taken out the time from their training and current job responsibilities to raise families of their own.[b]

PA emphasizes honesty and directness. In the outside world, parents who are prone to abuse their children learn to hide this problem because society finds it so detestable. In contrast, the goal in PA is to help parents admit and accept the fact that they are abusive. The term abuse is used liberally at meetings. PA has found that this insistence on frankness has a healthy effect. Parents are relieved because finally they have found a group of people who are able to accept abusive parents for what they really are. Furthermore, it is only after they are able to admit they are abusive that they can begin to find ways to cope with this problem.

During PA meetings, parents are expected to say why they believe they are abusive to their children, and the members challenge one another to find ways to curb the abuse. Members also share constructive approaches that have been successful for them, and efforts are made to help one another develop specific plans for dealing with potentially abusive episodes. Members learn to recognize danger signs and then to take the necessary action to avoid committing abuse.

PA stresses protecting people's anonymity and confidentiality. This protection permits group members to discuss their experiences and asocial thoughts without risk of public disclosure. The fact that they are sharing their experiences with other parents who have abused children assures their being able to "confess" without danger of humiliation, recrimination, or rejection.

Group members develop a sense of "oneness," and often the group becomes a surrogate family. Each member is given the phone numbers of all others in the group and is urged to reach for the phone instead of the child when feeling distressed. Members are gradually transformed into "lay professionals" who are able to help other abusers and who perceive themselves as skillful at this because they have, at one time, been child abusers.

The group leader or chapter chairperson is always a parent who at one time abused a child. Members can identify more readily with an abuser than they can with a professional therapist. Among the reasons PA is successful is that it diminishes the social isolation of abusive parents and provides them with social supports.[c]

[a]Phyllis Zauner, "Mothers Anonymous: The Last Resort," in *The Battered Child*, Jerome E. Leavitt, ed. (Morristown, NJ: General Learning Press, 1974), p. 247.
[b] Cassie L. Starkweather and S. Michael Turner, "Parents Anonymous: Reflections on the Development of a Self-Help Group," in *Child Abuse: Intervention and Treatment*, Nancy C. Ebeling and Deborah A. Hill, eds. (Acton, MA: Publishing Sciences Group, 1975), p. 151.
[c]Check the parents Anonymous website at http://parentsanonymous.org.

The family decision-making conference is facilitated by a professional person (often associated with child protective services). The professional person is usually called "the family group coordinator." Three characteristics are central to family group conferencing:

1. Family is widely defined to include extended family members, as well as other people who are significant to the family.
2. The family is given the opportunity to prepare the plan.
3. The professionals involved with the family must agree to the plan, unless it is thought to place the child at risk.

The coordinator prepares and plans for the first meeting of the extended family. Such planning may take weeks.

Downs, Moore, McFadden, and Costin describe the initial planning process:

This involves working with the family; identifying concerned parties and members of the extended kinship network; clarifying their roles and inviting them to a family group meeting; establishing the location, time, and other logistics; and managing other unresolved issues. At the meeting the coordinator welcomes and introduces participants in a culturally appropriate manner, establishes the purpose of the meeting, and helps participants reach agreement about roles, goals, and ground rules. Next, information is shared with the family, which may involve the child protection workers and other relevant professionals such as a doctor or teacher involved with the child.[59]

In the New Zealand model, the coordinator and other professional withdraw from the meeting in the next stage to allow the family privacy for their deliberations. (Some programs in the United States and other countries allow the coordinator to remain in the meeting.) The kinship network makes plans to respond to the issues that are raised, including developing a plan for the safety and the care of the child. The coordinator and/or protective services retain the right to veto a family plan if they believe the child will not be protected. (In reality, a veto is rarely used.) Several meetings (over several days) may be necessary to develop the family plan.

Downs, Moore, McFadden, and Costin summarize the challenges faced by social workers with this approach:

Working with family group decision making requires a new approach to family-centered practice.

The social worker must expand his or her ideas about the family to recognize the strength and centrality of the extended kinship network, particularly in communities of color. Use of the strengths perspective is critical. The worker must understand the greater investment of kin in the well-being of the child and should also understand that, even when parts of the kinship system may seem to be compromised or dysfunctional, the healthier kinfolk can assess and deal with the problem. One of the greatest challenges for the social worker is incorporating the sharing of power or returning of power to the kinship network. Many social workers trained as family therapists or child welfare workers have assumed a power role and may find it difficult to relinquish a sense of control.[60]

There are several advantages of family group conferencing. It facilitates getting the extended family involved in meeting the needs of the abused/neglected child or children and in meeting the needs of their parents. It reduces government intervention in people's lives. It recognizes the strengths of kinship networks to provide assistance to at-risk families. It reduces the number of children placed in foster homes. (Frequently, with this approach one or more extended family members temporarily take in the abused/neglected child, which then gives the parents an opportunity to receive whatever they need to become more stable and to learn better parenting skills.)

Family group conferencing has also been adapted to respond to other family issues, such as families with an adjudicated delinquent.

Critical Thinking Question

What do you see as the strengths and shortcomings of family group conferencing?

Rights of Children versus Rights of Parents   Earlier in American history, the law guarded the rights of parents but gave little attention to the rights of children. In recent years, defining and protecting the rights of children have received national attention, as indicated by a variety of child advocacy efforts and the specification of various "bill of rights for children" proclamations. Protective services, particularly in contested court cases, encounters the problem of defining the respective rights of parents and children. The balance of rights between parents and children varies from community to community.[61]

Some of the situations in which this balance becomes an issue are the following. If parents, for religious reasons, are opposed to their child's receiving medication for a serious health problem, should the state intervene? Should the state intervene when an unmarried parent is sexually promiscuous yet is meeting his or her children's basic physical and emotional needs? Should the state intervene when a child is being raised in a gay or lesbian family or in a commune where lifestyles and mores are substantially different? Should the state intervene in families in which a child has serious emotional problems and the parents refuse to seek professional help? Should the state intervene in certain ethnic settings when educational needs are not being met? Should intervention occur when a father uses harsh discipline by whipping a child two or three times a week? Should the state intervene in families in which there is long-term alcoholism and serious marital discord? Should the state intervene when a child is living in filth, has ragged clothing, and seldom bathes, even though his or her emotional and social needs are being met?

Different workers, different judges, and different communities would probably disagree on what should be done. The reluctance to intervene may have tragic consequences, as indicated in the following case:

> In 1953, a boy of 13 was referred to a children's court because of chronic truancy. A psychiatric examination established the fact that the boy was "drawn to violence" and represented "a serious danger to himself and to others." Psychiatric treatment was recommended by the psychiatrist and social workers concerned with the boy's situation. The mother refused to accept the recommendation and refused to bring the boy back for treatment. Should the mother have been forced to accept treatment for the boy? This is a question of limits of protection intervention. Nothing was done. Ten years later the boy, Lee Harvey Oswald, assassinated President Kennedy.[62]

Part of the difficulty in deciding when to intervene is that no one is accurately able to predict what effects intervention will have on the children, particularly if the children are removed and placed in foster homes. Sometimes a placement in a foster home works out well, and other times it doesn't—with such children often eventually being placed in a series of different foster homes. Such serial placements may have severe adverse consequences for these children.

Sexual Abuse of Children

This section will describe child molestation and incest. The category of "incest victims" is, in actuality, a subcategory of sexually abused children.

Child Molestation

Child molestation is the sexual abuse of a child by an adult. Sexual abuse includes not only sexual intercourse (genital or anal) but also oral–genital contact, fondling, and behaviors such as exposing oneself to a child and photographing or viewing a child for the molester's erotic pleasure. Although legal definitions of various forms of sexual contact between older and younger people are clearly delineated in statute books, the central feature that makes the behavior abusive is that the sexual act is designed for the erotic gratification of the older, more powerful person. In child sexual abuse, the child is used as an object for the immediate gratification of another person, generally with no regard for the short- or long-term consequences for the child.

Child molestation is generally regarded as one of the most despicable sexual offenses in our society. The public fears—rightly—that this type of sexual abuse will destroy the innocence of the child and may lead to severe psychological trauma, interrupting the child's (and subsequent adult's) normal sexual development.

How extensive is child molestation? Many studies have been conducted to determine the incidence of child sexual abuse, and they indicate that approximately one in three girls and one in six boys have experienced sexual abuse.[63]

More than 90% of child molesters are males.[64] A number of factors partially explain this gender imbalance: (a) Men in our culture are socialized toward seeing sexuality as focused on sexual acts rather than as part of an emotional relationship. (b) Men are also socialized to be more aggressive and to believe that appropriate sexual partners are smaller and younger than themselves. In contrast, women are socialized to think that appropriate partners are larger and older than they are. (c) Finally, women in our culture are much more often caregivers of children and therefore are more attuned than men to children's emotional needs. A person who is closely involved since birth with taking care of a child is far less likely to view children in sexual ways than is someone who has had more incidental contact.

In the past few decades, there have been several well-publicized cases of child molestation. In 1979 John Wayne Gacy was arrested and convicted in Chicago for enticing 33 male adolescents into his home, sexually assaulting them, and then killing and burying them under his home. He was executed for these crimes in 1994. On March 11, 1977, Roman Polanski (a noted film director) was arrested in Los Angeles and charged with unlawful sexual intercourse, child molestation, supplying a minor with the drug Quaalude, oral copulation, sodomy, and rape via the use of drugs. A teenage girl was the alleged victim of these charges. After a plea bargain, he confessed to and was found guilty of only the first charge. While awaiting sentencing, he fled the United States and has never returned. In 1991 Jeffrey Dahmer in Milwaukee (who was on probation for molesting a 13-year-old boy in 1988) confessed to sexually assaulting, murdering, and dismembering 17 males, some of whom were teenagers. In 1993 Michael Jackson, the immensely popular singer, was accused of prolonged sexual contact with a 13-year-old boy; in 1994 the boy's parents withdrew a civil lawsuit for damages against Jackson after he paid them several million dollars. Beginning in 2001, and continuing to the present time, a national and international scandal has arisen in the Roman Catholic church as it has been revealed that some priests over a number of years had molested children and teenagers. The church hierarchy compounded the abuse by not referring the cases to the police or to protective services, but instead transferred the priests to other parishes—where the transferred priests then molested other children and teenagers. In 2011 there were allegations that former Pennsylvania State University football assistant coach Jerry Sandusky sexually assaulted or had inappropriate contact with at least eight underage boys on or near university property. In June 2012 he was found guilty of 45 charges of sexual abuse (both anal and oral sex) with 10 victims. It is likely that he will spend the rest of his life in prison.

Who are child molesters? The stereotype is that a molester is a stranger who lurks in the dark, waiting to pounce on a child who is walking or playing alone. The fact is that in most cases the offender is an acquaintance, friend, or relative.[65] (If the offender is a relative, the abuse is called incest.) Scores of parents, stepparents, scout leaders, child care workers, and people from all walks of life have been found to be child molesters. Force is rarely used. The abuser generally gains sexual access to the child by manipulation and enticement rather than by use of a threat of force or harm. The nature of the abuse ranges on a continuum from inappropriate touching to actual intercourse.

In a small proportion of cases, the child may even initiate the contact. However, such initiation does not justify the adult's becoming an active participant and almost always indicates that the child has been sexually abused previously. (It is *always* the adult's responsibility for any abuse that occurs, and never the child's.)

A. Nicholas Groth has identified two categories of child molesters: fixated and regressed.[66] A *fixated* child molester's primary sexual object choice is children; he would always prefer a child as a sexual partner over an adult. These men are also known as pedophiles. Pedophilia is a sexual disorder characterized by recurrent sexual fantasies and urges or behaviors involving sexual activity with children.[67] A *regressed* child molester is a person whose usual sexual interest is in adult partners, but when faced with massive stress (marital difficulty, loss of job, a death in the family, and so on), he "regresses" emotionally (becomes a psychologically younger person) and acts out sexually toward children to meet his needs. Regressed child molesters generally seek female children as partners; fixated molesters are generally interested in male children. Most incest perpetrators are of the regressed type; they generally function well in society, are in a stable heterosexual relationship, but manage stress inappropriately by acting out sexually toward children. Some molesters have been found to engage in a variety of other inappropriate sexual behaviors, including voyeurism (peeping Toms), exhibitionism, and even rape of adult women.[68] They apparently exercise little control over their sexual impulses; when a child becomes available, he or she becomes a victim.[69]

Critical Thinking Question

What are the best ways to reduce the amount of sexual abuse by Roman Catholic priests?

Even though the most attention in the media and among protective services workers is given to the sexual assault of girls in families (primarily incestuous relationships), recent research indicates that child molesters who abuse boys outside the home victimize children in far larger numbers. In an innovative study, Abel and his colleagues discovered that child molesters of boys reported an average (mean) of 150 victims, whereas child molesters of girls reported an average of 20 victims.[70] So why is less attention given to sexual abuse of boys as compared to abuse of girls? The most significant reason is that girls are far more likely to report sexual victimization; boys tend to think it would be "unmasculine" for them to report they were sexually victimized. It is thought by many authorities that child molestation of boys is the most underreported major crime in America.

How traumatic is molestation for the child? The factors that have the most emotional impact on child (and later adult) development seem to include (a) the relationship between the child and the adult (it is more damaging to the further development of trust to be abused by someone you are close to than by a stranger); (b) the frequency and duration of the abuse; (c) the actual sexual behaviors engaged in; (d) the number of perpetrators; (e) the reactions of other people if the abuse becomes revealed; (f) the child's general mental and emotional health and coping strategies; and (g) the availability and use of professional intervention by the victim, the abuser, and others (such as the parents). The most helpful interventions following child sexual abuse occur when all significant parties (professionals, parents, siblings, and so forth) believe the child's report, when the perpetrator takes full responsibility for his or her actions, and when the child has forums that promote understanding and healing at various stages in his or her later development.

Incest

Incest is defined as sexual relations between blood relatives. Typically, the definition is extended to include sex between certain nonblood relatives, such as between a stepparent and a child. In the past, families generally attempted to hide this type of abuse, and it usually was not reported. Now, with an increased openness about human sexuality, there is a greater willingness for family members to seek professional help.

In the largest proportion of incest cases reported to the police, the sexual abuse is between father or stepfather and daughter.[71] However, most incest cases are never reported to the police. Brother/sister incest is actually the most common form.[72] This may or may not constitute sexual abuse. If the children are approximately the same age and the sexual activity is mutual and not coerced, this type of incest may be considered normal sexual experimentation. However, if the children are more than a few years apart in age, the potential exists for the younger child to be coerced into activity she or he is not comfortable with. At that point, consent no longer exists, and nonconsenting sex is sexual abuse.

Most often incest occurs in the child's home. The child is usually enticed or pressured, rather than physically forced, to participate. The age range of the abused child is from several months to adulthood, although most reports involve teenagers.[73] Children are unlikely to report the sexual abuse because they often have loyalties toward the abuser and realistically fear the consequences for themselves, for the abuser, and for the family.

Causes of Incest Why does incest occur? Students of sexology have long known that people frequently use sexual behavior to achieve nonsexual rewards. For example, a teenage boy might wish to have intercourse with his girlfriend (sexual behavior) not primarily because he loves her or because he seeks sexual gratification but rather to enhance his status with his friends and therefore gratify his ego (nonsexual reward).

Adults who are threatened by and fearful of the rejection of other adults often turn for reassurance to children, who are nonthreatening and generally unconditionally loving. This need for acceptance can lead to the adult's initiating sexual behavior (especially if the adult had been sexually abused as a child, as is often the case) because many people view sexual behavior as the ultimate acceptance and ego validation. Most child molesters intend no harm to their victims; they are psychologically needy people who use children in their own battle for emotional survival.

Effects of Incest Blair and Rita Justice have studied the consequences of incest at three different points in time: while the incest is going on, when the incest is discovered, and years after its occurrence.[74] It is important to bear in mind that incest is a symptom of a disturbed family system.

First we will look at the effects while the incest is occurring. A daughter who has sex with her father often gains special power over him; she controls a very important secret. The daughter can receive special privileges from the father, which makes the other siblings (and even the mother) jealous. Role confusion often occurs. The daughter is still a child, but at times she is a lover and an equal to her father. Victims are deprived of the opportunity to explore and discover their sexuality by themselves or with a peer partner of their choice. Instead, this normal sexual development is violated by an adult imposing his exploitative behavior. The daughter often does not know if her father is going to act as a parent or as a lover, so she is confused about whether she should respond to him as a child or as a sexual partner. The mother may become both a parent and a rival to her daughter. Siblings may also become confused about who is in charge and how to relate to their sister who is receiving special privileges. Fathers in an incestuous family may become jealous and overpossessive of their daughters.

As the daughter grows older, she wants to be more independent and to spend more time with other teenagers. Often she grows more resentful of her father's possessiveness. To make a break from the father, she may run away or tell someone about the incest. Or she may passively resist the father's rules, for example, by ignoring curfews.

In a small number of cases, the incest is discovered when the daughter becomes pregnant. (Genetically, incest may have adverse consequences, as it leads to inbreeding. The offspring are more apt to have lower intelligence, physical performance difficulties, and genetic defects.[75]) At times the incest is discovered by the mother, who then may try to stop it by reporting it to the police. (Sometimes the mother discovers the incest but remains quiet.)

If the incest is reported to the police and criminal charges are filed against the father, the entire family is usually caught up in a traumatic, time-consuming, confusing, and costly legal process. When there is legal involvement, the daughter is often subjected to embarrassing and humiliating interrogation. She may feel, at times, that her account of the incest is not believed. Or she may feel that blame is being placed on her rather than on her father. Once she is recognized as a victim of incest, she may be approached sexually by other men who now view her as "fair game."[76] Often she is removed from the home to prevent further abuse. In addition, the mother and father suffer considerable embarrassment and humiliation. Their marriage may become so conflictful that it ends in divorce.

The long-term effects of incest vary from child to child. Younger children usually do not fully realize the significance of the sexual behavior and tend to suffer less guilt than adolescent victims. However, with young children there is always the danger that, as they grow older and learn about society's taboos against incest, they may start blaming themselves for having participated. Possible long-term effects on the daughter include low self-esteem, guilt, depression, and fear.[77]

The daughter may also become angry at both parents for not protecting her and at the father for exploiting her. Moreover, she may believe that she is somehow to blame for what happened; she may feel tainted by the experience and see herself as worthless or as "damaged goods." Because of her guilt and anger, she may in future years develop difficulties in expressing her sexuality and relating to men. She may feel unable to trust men because she was betrayed and severely hurt by her father, whom she deeply trusted. Some victims seek to blot out their pain and loneliness through self-destructive behavior such as prostitution, drug abuse, or suicide.

If the incest is ongoing and unreported and the victim is an older child, she may attempt to avoid the abuser by running away from home. If she flees, there is a strong possibility that she will become a prostitute to support herself, in part because she has been taught, dysfunctionally, that her sexuality is valued by men and is her most valuable asset. She is also likely to abuse drugs as a method of escaping the life situation she is trapped in.

Some victims during their childhood years seek to deny or suppress the traumas associated with incest. When they become adults, they may experience difficulties in developing relationships with others. Because relationships are founded on trust, and because the victims' fundamental trust in others (and therefore their ability to trust their own judgment of others) has been violated, they often fear making commitments to others in an attempt to protect themselves from further hurt. Many of these victims finally acknowledge as adults the traumas they experienced as children. Therapy is highly recommended for these adult victims to help them come to terms with the pain and suffering of having been violated by someone they trusted.

Treatment of Incest   Documented cases (cases in which evidence verifies that incest has occurred) are handled by protective services, which was described earlier. Because incest is only one symptom of a disturbed family, treating these families is difficult and complex. In the past when incest was reported, the victim (usually a teenage girl) was generally placed in a foster home, further victimizing her. Such action was likely to reveal the sexual abuse to the local community. Often neighbors, relatives, and friends expressed shock and began shunning all members of the family. The disruption usually intensified the marital conflict between husband and wife and generally led to permanent dissolution of the family. In some instances, the husband was also prosecuted, which even further intensified the family conflicts.

In recent years, a number of social service agencies have been seeking to keep the family intact, particularly when all three of the members involved (husband, wife, and victim) express a desire to maintain the family. A typical intervention requires the father's removal from the home for a period of 6 months to 1 year, during which time all family members are involved in individual and group treatment. The incest perpetrator must acknowledge to his or her family that he or she was entirely responsible for the sexual abuse, is sorry it happened, and will make the necessary lifestyle and value changes to ensure that the abuse will not recur. The nonabusing parent (typically the mother) is taught assertiveness. Intervention with the nonabusing parent and victim is geared toward improving their relationship, which is usually very damaged. The victim (typically the daughter) is helped to process his or her anger, guilt, and confusion. Eventually all family members are seen in therapy together to help them build, perhaps for the first time, a healthy, functional family system.

Births Outside of Marriage

Women between the ages of 15 and 24 constitute about 40% of the total population of women of childbearing age—yet they account for roughly 70% of births outside of marriage.[78] More than a million teenage women become pregnant each year. Most of these pregnancies are unplanned and unwanted and result from misinformation or lack of access to birth control. Roughly 60% of these teenagers have babies, with the remainder ending the pregnancy through abortion or miscarriage.[79] Two of every five American women giving birth to their first child were not married when they became pregnant.[80] Four of five teenage marriages end in divorce; many of these marriages were preceded by a pregnancy.[81] For those who are unmarried when the child is born, over 90% decide to keep the baby rather than give it up for adoption.[82]

About 70% of African American babies are born to single women.[83] African American women have a substantially higher rate of birth outside of marriage than White women.[84] Coleman and Cressey give the following reasons for the high birthrate among single African American women:

Although the causes are not entirely clear, several factors stand out. First and foremost, blacks are much more likely to be poor than whites, and the illegitimacy rate is much higher among poor people from all ethnic groups. Second, the prejudice and discrimination that have been aimed at blacks for so many years have hit particularly hard at black males from poor homes. The extremely high rate of unemployment among this group makes it much harder to live up to the expectations of fatherhood, and fathers who feel inadequate to meet the needs of their families are far more likely to withdraw and leave their support to the welfare department. Third, the pattern of early pregnancy and single-parent homes has been passed down from one generation to the next in the black underclass.[85]

The higher birthrates among single non-White women do not necessarily mean that unmarried non-Whites are more likely to be promiscuous. Perhaps non-Whites have less access to contraceptives. Perhaps they may be less likely to seek an abortion, or they may be less likely to marry the father before the birth of the child.

Although teenage women represent roughly 25% of the population of childbearing age, they account for over 45% of all births outside of marriage.[86] These statistics emphasize that birth outside of marriage is a problem that is disproportionately faced by adolescents. Teenagers who marry when pregnant are nearly as likely to be single parents sometime in the future (due to divorce) as are those who are unmarried at the time of the child's birth.

Many adolescents are not adequately informed about the reproductive process and tend not to use contraceptives. Some teenage women think that, if they take a birth control pill once a week, they're okay; some believe it's safe to have sex standing up; some are afraid birth control will harm them or their future babies.[87]

The good news in recent years is that teenage birthrates have fallen.[88] The lingering bad news is that American teenagers are still having babies at higher rates than are teenagers in other industrial nations.[89]

Many unmarried mothers are simply not prepared—by education, work experience, or maturity—to undertake the dual responsibility of parenthood and economic support. As a result, society inevitably must contribute to the support of these children through public assistance payments and social welfare services.

Fifty years ago, both premarital intercourse and births outside of marriage were considered immoral in our society. (In fact, children born outside of marriage were labeled "illegitimate" and were usually stigmatized as much as the mother. The terms *illegitimate* and *illegitimacy* persist today, even though they stigmatize innocent people.) In the 1940s, Alfred Kinsey found, however, that high percentages of the population had experienced premarital intercourse.[90] Since the Kinsey studies, attitudes toward premarital intercourse have become more tolerant; today, few people are virgins when they marry.

Attitudes toward birth outside of marriage have also become somewhat more tolerant. Few parents now send their pregnant daughter off to a maternity home to avoid "disgracing" the family. However, we sometimes see the unusual situation in which parents tolerate premarital intercourse yet strongly disapprove if their daughter becomes pregnant.

Why are births outside of marriage seen as a social problem by most Americans? There are many answers to this question. Some parents still feel "disgraced" if their daughter becomes pregnant. Some single pregnant women (and their parents) view it as a problem because difficult decisions need to be made about whether to end the pregnancy. If it is decided not to have an abortion, decisions need to be made about adoption, continued education or employment, a possible marriage, living arrangements, and perhaps welfare assistance. The father of the child must make decisions about his role and the extent to which he will seek to provide emotional and financial support.

Some people see birth outside of marriage as a social problem—a sign of a breakdown in the traditional family and a symptom of moral decay. Others assert that it is a problem mainly because the great majority of these children are born to women who are simply not yet prepared—by experience, education, or maturity—to be a parent or to provide for a family financially. Authorities who view birth outside

of marriage as a problem for this reason are concerned about the effects on the child of being raised by a mother who is in many ways merely an older child herself. They are also concerned about the effects on the mother of trying to maintain a one-parent family with limited financial and personal resources. Finally, some authorities view birth outside of marriage as a problem because of the high cost to society of having to make welfare payments to large numbers of single-parent families (see Chapter 4).

Is the social stigma attached to birth outside of marriage functional? Certainly it is not to either the child or the mother. On the other hand, some authorities have argued that the stigma is functional to society because it discourages births outside of marriage and thereby helps perpetuate the nuclear family, which provides a structure for the financial support and socialization of children. In response to this view, it can be argued that this punitive approach may not be the optimal way to reduce the incidence of births outside of marriage. The Sex Information and Education Council of the United States (SIECUS) asserts that a more effective approach would involve quality educational programs about responsible sexuality. SIECUS asserts that the goals of sex education should be:

1. *Information* To provide accurate information about human sexuality, including: growth and development, human reproduction, anatomy, physiology, masturbation, family life, pregnancy, childbirth, parenthood, sexual response, sexual orientation, contraception, abortion, sexual abuse, and HIV/AIDS and other sexually transmitted diseases.

2. *Attitudes, values, and insights* To provide an opportunity for young people to question, explore, and assess their sexual attitudes in order to develop their own values, increase self-esteem, develop insights concerning relationships with members of both genders, and understand their obligations and responsibilities to others.

3. *Relationships and interpersonal skills* To help young people develop interpersonal skills, including communication, decision-making, assertiveness, and peer refusal skills, as well as the ability to create satisfying relationships. Sexuality education programs should prepare students to understand their sexuality effectively and creatively in adult roles. This would include helping young people develop the capacity for caring, supportive, noncoercive, and mutually pleasurable intimate and sexual relationships.

Martin Bernetti/AFP/Getty Images

Programs now exist in many cities to freely distribute condoms to teenagers and young adults. Such programs have two objectives: to reduce teen pregnancy and to curb the spread of HIV.

Critical Thinking Questions

If you are sexually active, do you use safe sex practices? If not, why?

4. *Responsibility* To help young people exercise responsibility regarding sexual relationships, including addressing abstinence, how to resist pressures to become prematurely involved in sexual intercourse, and encouraging the use of contraception and other sexual health measures. Sexuality education should be a central component of programs designed to reduce the prevalence of sexually related medical problems, including teenage pregnancies, sexually transmitted diseases including HIV infection, and sexual abuse.[91]

Even with over 1 million teenagers becoming pregnant each year, the question of whether to provide sex education is still a controversial issue in many school systems. Apparently, many people believe sex education will lead to promiscuity and to teenage pregnancies. Advocates of sex education argue that such programs reduce the number of teenage pregnancies.

Health clinics located in or near high schools appear particularly effective in reducing the number of teenage pregnancies. Such clinics provide birth control information and also prescribe contraceptives for sexually active people.[92] Critics of this approach assert that making birth control information and contraceptives more readily available will simply increase sexual activity. The response of the health clinics to this criticism is that learning accurate information about human reproduction in an educational setting is more desirable than the alternative of receiving largely inaccurate information from peers on the street.

The peril of AIDS has given sex education in schools a major boost. The best way of stopping the transmission of AIDS is through quality sex education programs that provide accurate information on safe sex practices.[93]

One motivation for the passage of the 1996 welfare reform act was the desire to change policies that conservatives claim reward early childbearing by single mothers. The welfare reform act denies public assistance payments to teenage mothers, except under the following conditions: States can provide payments to unmarried teenage parents only if a mother under 18 is living at home or in another adult-supervised setting and attends high school or an alternative educational or training program as soon as the child is 12 weeks old. The underlying reason behind denying welfare payments to some teenage mothers is to send a message to teenagers that having babies will not be financially rewarded; that is, conservatives hope this will discourage teenage women from becoming pregnant.[94] Interestingly, teenage birthrates have fallen in recent years—perhaps the conservatives are right on this issue.[95]

A program that has had success in teen pregnancy prevention is computerized infant simulators.[96] Mooney, Knox, and Schacht describe this approach:

> *Some teen pregnancy prevention programs use computerized infant simulators to give adolescents a realistic view of parenting. Computerized infant simulators are realistic, life-sized computerized "dolls" that are programmed to cry at random intervals (typically between 8 and 12 times in 24 hours) with crying periods lasting typically between 10 and 15 minutes. The "baby" stops crying only when the caregiver "attends" to the doll by inserting a key into a slot in the infant simulator's back until it stops crying. The infant simulator records data, including the amount of time the caregiver took to attend to the infant (insert the key) and any instances of "rough handling," such as dropping, hitting, or shaking the doll. Participants who are found to neglect or handle the doll roughly may receive a private counseling session and may be required to take a parenting class.*[97]

Single-Parent Services

Services to single women who become pregnant have become known as single-parent services. A high proportion of pregnant single women decide to carry the baby to full term and then keep the child. The scope of single-parent services extends from predelivery to postdelivery. Single-parent services are provided by certain public agencies (such as human services departments or the public welfare department) and by private agencies (such as Catholic Social Services and Lutheran Social Services).

Typical single-parent services include:

- *Alternatives counseling:* The pregnant single woman is helped to make decisions about carrying the baby to full term, having an abortion, keeping the child, terminating parental rights, deciding on foster placement, and undergoing adoption counseling. (Workers in single-parent services generally refrain from revealing their own values about abortion and the other alternatives to the clients because clients have the legal right to make their own decisions in these matters.)

- *Physical and mental childbirth preparation:* Clients are informed about the effects of drug and alcohol abuse on the embryo. They are prepared for childbirth, given pre- and postnatal counseling, and provided with information on the effects of venereal diseases. Clients also receive mental and physical health counseling.

- *Counseling on legal issues:* Areas covered include paternity action, procedures for termination of parental rights, legitimation and/or adoption procedures, rights to attend school, and procedures involved in receiving public assistance.

- *Counseling on interpersonal relationships:* Such counseling focuses on the client's relationships with the alleged father, parents and other relatives, and significant others.

- *Alternative living arrangements:* Alternatives include a maternity home, the home of parents or other relatives, and foster homes.

- *Alleged-father counseling:* This involves informing him about his rights and responsibilities, counseling him on his concerns, and providing birth control counseling and perhaps premarital counseling.

- *Family planning counseling:* Birth control information is provided for both parents, and perhaps referral to a family planning clinic is made.

- *Educational and employment counseling:* Here, information is provided about remaining in educational programs (including home study programs) or about employment opportunities and work-training programs.

- *Self-development counseling:* This may include a variety of areas such as identity formation, assertiveness training, sexual counseling, rape counseling, and so on.

- *Financial and money management counseling:* This includes eligibility for public assistance, food stamps, and Medicare.
- *Child care:* After a baby is born, single-parent services assists the mother in making child-care arrangements (such as day care) when needed. Such assistance may include financial assistance for child care.
- *Child development counseling:* New parents receive counseling on caring for young children and meeting their physical, social, and emotional needs.

In providing social services to single parents, social workers seek first to establish a helping relationship (see Chapter 4). If the client is single and pregnant, the worker tries to convey that she (not her parents) has the right and responsibility to decide among the alternatives of carrying the child to delivery, having an abortion, keeping the baby after delivery, placing the baby in foster care, or putting the baby up for adoption. To help a client make such decisions, the worker uses a problem-solving approach. That is, he or she helps the client:

1. Define her problems.
2. Identify the alternatives.
3. Make a pro/con list for each alternative.
4. Evaluate the alternatives.
5. Select one or more alternatives.
6. Implement, and later evaluate, the alternatives that are chosen.

Most single parents decide to keep their babies, and the proportion making this decision has been increasing. The social stigma of single parenthood has weakened. In addition, unmarried single parents are not as conspicuous as they have been in the past because we now have single foster parents, single adoptive parents, and a large number of one-parent families following a divorce.*

---

*I do not want to take a position on whether, in general, unmarried mothers should keep their babies. Being a parent at a young age has some rewards. But it is certainly an immense responsibility. An unmarried mother often has little time to enjoy young adulthood. Dating, pursuing a career, and having the necessary funds to meet wants and desires are more or less restricted. Most workers in single-parent services feel that it is usually in the long-range best interest of the child and the mother to consider placing the child for adoption. In working with unmarried mothers, however, workers in single-parent services seek to refrain from expressing their views. They instead seek to have the single mother carefully analyze the pros and cons of the available alternatives. Deciding whether to keep the baby is a very difficult, emotionally taxing responsibility.

Ursula Myers (a former supervisor of a single-parent unit at a social services agency) describes the small minority of single parents who decide to terminate parental rights:

> *In our experience, the woman who terminates her parental rights is generally long-range goal, reality oriented. The stigma of single parenthood is for her perceptually more marked. She sees the coming child as an encumbrance or as totally out of place in her present and future world, her immediate culture, and her internal mental health system. She is usually aware that her pregnancy is untimely and that she cannot cope with the vital needs of an infant at this point in her life. The separation process can result in a broad spectrum of responses, all perfectly normal and human. Both or either parent may feel a sense of loss, grief, emptiness, and unreality. There may be a sense of relief and even pleasure at terminating for some, while others may become depressed and withdrawn. Some work through the grief process to a point of rational and emotional acceptance, while others may completely sever themselves from the pregnancy by "cutting out" that part of their lives and/or totally denying its reality.*[98]

Foster Care and Adoption

If a single mother relinquishes her parental rights, the child is usually placed temporarily in foster care. Some single parents who are unsure about whether to give up parental rights may also place their child in foster care until they make a decision. (Foster care, as was discussed earlier, is also used for children who are removed from their parents for neglect or abuse.)

The goals of foster care are to protect the children, to rehabilitate the parents, and generally to return the children to their genetic parents as soon as it is feasible. Foster care is the temporary provision of substitute care for children whose parents are unable or unwilling to meet the child's needs in their own home. Except for emergency placement, legal custody of the child is usually transferred, by court action, from the child's parents to the agency responsible for foster placement. (Removal of a child from the parents' legal custody is carefully weighed by the court in an effort to protect the parents' rights while at the same time providing protection to the child.)

Foster parents face the difficult task of being expected to provide love and affection to foster children without becoming too emotionally attached. The placement is temporary, and separating is easier when strong emotional bonds have not been established between foster parents and foster children. One of the tragic aspects of some foster placements is that the genetic parents never attain the capacity to care for their children. If they do not relinquish parental rights, the children may end up being raised in a series of foster homes. When this happens, a serious question arises about whether a child's right to be raised in a stable, healthy environment is being preserved. Children who are shuffled among foster homes are likely to experience considerable emotional trauma over relating to and later separating from a variety of parental figures.

Agencies seek to attain quality care in foster placements by studying and selecting applicants for foster parenthood, licensing foster parents, and monitoring each home after a child is placed. While the children are in foster care, the genetic parents have visitation rights. In neglect and abuse cases, the hours of visitation are usually arranged through the court and supervised by the foster placement agency. Single parents who decide to relinquish their parental rights often choose not to visit the foster home because they are in the process of separating emotionally from their child.

If the genetic mother relinquishes her rights, the alleged father does not automatically receive custody of the child. He must first be adjudged the father of the child by a court of law. Then, to obtain custody, he must also convince the court of his fitness and ability to care for the child. (If the mother decides to keep her child, she need not legally demonstrate her fitness.) For a child to be eligible for adoptive placement, both the genetic mother and the alleged father must relinquish their parental rights. In recent years, many more people have applied for adoptive parenthood than there are children available for adoption. In particular, there are many more applicants for White, healthy infants than there are available babies.

Adoptive placement agencies carefully study, select, and prepare for parenthood applicants who want a child. After a child is placed, the agency monitors the placement until it is finalized by court action. Courts generally wait several months after a child is placed before finalizing a placement. Only in very rare circumstances is a child removed from an adoptive home. The purpose of this waiting period is to ascertain, as thoroughly as possible, that the placement is working out well.

As fully as possible, the medical histories of both biological parents are compiled to provide physical health and genetic information to the adoptive parents. Efforts are also made by placement agencies to meet the wishes of the biological parents concerning the physical characteristics, religious affiliation, racial characteristics, and geographical location of the adoptive parents.

A recent trend in adoptions is "open adoption," whereby the genetic and adoptive parents become officially known to each other (see Case Exhibit 6.4: Open Adoptions). (In the past, adoptive placement agencies usually did not tell the adoptive parents who the genetic parents were, nor did they tell the genetic parents who the adoptive parents were.) Some adoptive and genetic parents even maintain contact with each other. Another trend is for some adoptive children (when they become young adults) to seek out and make contact with their genetic parents.

Not all adoptions are arranged by state-licensed agencies. Although professionally frowned on, some attorneys (for a substantial fee) arrange adoptions for couples seeking a child. These attorneys sometimes pay a fee (which they charge to the adoptive couple) to the birth mother to offset some of her expenses for carrying the pregnancy to term and then relinquishing parental rights. (See Case Exhibit 6.5: The Adoption and Safe Families Act (ASFA) of 1997, and Its Application.)

Rape

Forced intercourse is a commonly committed violent crime in the United States. More than 90,000 cases are reported annually, and many more instances go unreported.[99] Victims of rape are hesitant to report the crime for a variety of reasons. They may feel that reporting the case will do them no good because they have already been victimized. They sometimes fear that they may be humiliated by the questions the police will ask. They are reluctant to press charges because they fear the reactions of the general public and of people close to them, including their boyfriends or husbands. Many fear that, if they report the offense, the rapist will try to attack them again. Some victims just want to try to forget about it. Others fail to report it because they do not want to testify in court. But perhaps the most common reason women fail to report sexual assault is that they feel—usually wrongly—that they somehow contributed to the rape's occurrence. This is especially true in the most frequent type of rape—that by an acquaintance.

CASE EXHIBIT 6.4

Open Adoptions

An open adoption is an adoptive family and birth family keeping in contact for the benefit of a child. Contact in an open adoption can mean different things to different families. Contact may include one or more of the following between the birth mother, adoptive parents, and adoptive child: regularly scheduled visitation (monthly, bi-monthly, weekly); holiday and birthday visits in the home or at neutral locations; phone calls; text messages; e-mails; cards; letters; and update packages (such as homework samples or pictures).

Open adoptions have pros and cons. On a positive note, the adoptee will have some contact with the birth family, so he or she will not have the feeling of a "missing piece" in his or her life, as some adoptees in closed adoptions feel. The adoptee is also apt to receive answers to the question "why was I placed for adoption?" The adoptee will also have access to background information on her or his heritage and ancestry; this background information would include medical and genetic information on physical health and mental health issues.

The birth parents would benefit by having information on how their child is developing, and being able to participate (with limited contact) in their child's development. The adoptive family may be grateful for the extra support provided by the birth parent/family's love for the child.

There are also "cons" to an open adoption. Unmet expectations can be an issue for both the adoptive family and the birth family. For example, an adoptive couple may want the birth parent to play a lesser role in the child's life, while a birth parent may expect the adoptive couple to use somewhat different strategies in raising the child. Severe conflicts can arise if birth parents and adoptive parents do not "mesh" well. With open adoptions, it is essential that the birth family and the adoptive couple communicate and resolve up front what the boundaries are in regard to phone calls, visitation, and birth parent input in the raising of the child.

In many states, rape is defined as a crime that only males can commit. Although the great majority of male rape victims are raped by men (frequently in prison settings), a few men are raped by women.[100] Research shows that men may respond with an erection in emotional states such as anger and terror.[101] Research indicates that men who have been raped by women experience a rape trauma syndrome that is very similar to the rape trauma syndrome (soon to be described) of female victims.

An unusual case of a woman raping a male (in this case it was statutory rape) occurred in Seattle. Mrs. Mary Kay Letourneau was a highly respected elementary school teacher. She was married, age 34, and the mother of four children. In 1997 she pleaded guilty to second-degree child rape of a 13-year-old boy who was a former student of hers. She acknowledged that she had a 6-month affair with this young teenager. She became pregnant by him and delivered a baby girl. In November 1997, a judge sentenced her to 6 months in jail and to 3 years' participation in an outpatient sex offender treatment program for committing second-degree rape of a child. A few months later, she violated the rules of probation by having contact with the teenager and was sentenced by a judge to prison for over 7 years. This sexual contact resulted in Mary Kay Letourneau again becoming pregnant, and she later delivered another baby girl. On August 4, 2004, Letourneau was released from prison. On April 16, 2005, she married this male lover (Vili Fualaau)—he was 22 at that time, and she was 43.[102]

A similar case occurred in 2008 when Kelsey Peterson, at age 26, pleaded guilty to fleeing to Mexico with a 13-year-old male student so she could have sex with him. Ms. Peterson admitted to having sex with the boy, beginning when he was 12 years old and a student at Lexington Middle School in Omaha, Nebraska, where she taught math. In October 2007 they fled to Mexico, and a week later she was arrested in Mexico. Both Ms. Peterson and the boy were returned to the United States. She struck a plea bargain with the court and in September 2008 was sentenced to 6 years in prison.

There is no profile that fits all rapists. They vary considerably in terms of motivation for committing the rape, prior criminal record, education, occupation, marital status, and so on. In a majority of cases, the rapist and his (or her) victim know each other on a first-name basis. A significant proportion of rapes are date rapes.

Rape is primarily an aggressive act and secondarily a sexual act. That is, it is a sexual expression of aggression, not an aggressive expression of sexuality. Many people wrongly believe that rape occurs

CASE EXHIBIT 6.5

The Adoption and Safe Families Act (ASFA) of 1997, and Its Application

"On November 19, 1997, President Clinton signed into law the Adoption and Safe Families Act of 1997. This legislation, passed by the Congress with overwhelming bipartisan support, represents an important landmark in Federal child welfare law. It established unequivocally that our national goals for children in the child welfare system are safety, permanency, and well-being. The passage of this new law gave an unprecedented opportunity to build on the reforms of the child welfare system that had begun in recent years in order to make the system more responsive to the multiple, and often complex, needs of children and families. The law reaffirmed the need to forge linkages between the child welfare system and other systems of support for families, as well as between the child welfare system and the courts, to ensure the safety and well-being of children and their families. The law also gave renewed impetus to dismantle the myriad barriers that may exist between children waiting in foster care and permanency."[a]

The ASFA embodied a number of key principles that needed to be considered in order to implement the law:

- The safety of children is the paramount concern that must guide all child welfare services.
- Foster care is a temporary setting and not a place for children to grow up.
- Permanency planning efforts for children should begin as soon as a child enters foster care and should be expedited by the provision of services to families.
- The child welfare system must focus on results and accountability.
- Innovative approaches are needed to achieve the goals of safety, permanency, and well-being.

Example

Terri and Donald met through mutual friends when they were juniors in high school. They began dating almost immediately and felt they had a lot in common. Terri and Donald used both alcohol and drugs on a regular basis and eventually dropped out of school. Terri had a history of sexual abuse (perpetrated by an uncle) and struggled with mental health issues, mainly anxiety and severe anger outbursts. Donald's parents had significant histories of drug and alcohol abuse, and were both in and out of jail for most of his childhood. As a result, Donald experienced long periods of depression where he was unable to function in daily life.

Terri and Donald never legally married but moved in together into Terri's mother's apartment when they were 18 years old. Within 3 years, the couple had three children. The stress of the three young children, financial challenges, untreated mental health issues, drug and alcohol abuse, and so on took a toll on the young family and negatively affected the care of the children. Terri and Donald struggled to meet the multiple needs

of their young children and often left them in the care of Terri's aging mother, until she was moved to an assisted living facility.

Neighbors and family reported that the children generally appeared dirty, thin, emotionally withdrawn, and lagging in their physical development. The oldest child also had unexplained bruises on his legs and arms (some in the shape of an adult size handprint). There were many occasions when the children were left alone while the parents were out "partying" and heavily involved with drugs and alcohol. Neighbors tried to help out but grew tired of the couple's irresponsible behavior. Shortly after the third child was born, a neighbor heard the young children crying one evening. He had made a number of attempts to knock on the door and to try to find the parents. Given the young ages of the children, he quickly grew concerned for their safety and contacted the police and child protective services. The children were immediately taken into custody by child protection and placed in foster care.

Under the previous child welfare laws and philosophy, in particular, the 1984 Family Preservation and Support Services Act (P.L. 96–272), "the law states that the state must make reasonable efforts to prevent or eliminate the need for removing a child from his home, or if the child has been removed, then the state must make reasonable efforts to reunify the child with his family in a timely manner."[b]

Under ASFA, there has been a significant shift in addressing these types of cases. Although family reunification and preservation are still possibilities, they are no longer child protective social workers' initial response. The law now stresses that the "child's health and safety shall be the paramount concern in determining what is reasonable, and consistent with the plan for timely, permanent placement of a child."[c]

In this example, the parents would still be offered services to address their mental health issues, drug and alcohol concerns, parenting challenges, education and job skill issues, housing, and so on. But unlike in the past, the parents would not have a lot of time to make their changes. Under the ASFA, if children are in foster care for 15 out of the previous 22 months, the child protection agency must file a termination of parental rights and move the children toward adoption (unless special circumstances apply and a judge determines otherwise).

The case study also brings to the light the issue of alcohol and drug treatment for parents in the child welfare system. "In 1997, a study of state child welfare agencies estimated that 67 percent of parents in the child welfare system required substance abuse treatment services."[d] Given the limited access to treatment for these issues and the challenges of sobriety, the new time frame for filing a termination of parental rights (children placed in foster care for 15 of the previous 22 months) is a huge challenge for clients seeking and working in a treatment program. It also brings up ethical and resources issues for the child protection agencies and juvenile court system.

(continued)

The Adoption and Safe Families Act—Is It Working?

The ASFA was enacted primarily to address the problem of too many children in the foster care system for long periods of time. The goals included increasing permanent placements for children by facilitating more adoptions for children in foster care. According to the U.S. General Accounting Office's 2003 report, "although the number of adoptions has increased 57% from the time ASFA was an active through fiscal year 2000 and the lack of comparable pre- and post-ASFA for data makes it difficult to determine the role of ASFA in this increase or changes in foster care outcome."[e] Despite the limited data that states were able to provide the federal government, they were able to identify some of the issues related to the continued lag of children in foster care and issues related to permanent placements for children.

There were a number of barriers identified by the states in their response to the federal survey regarding the implementation of ASFA.[f] One area of ongoing concern is related to the juvenile court process. Reported issues included insufficient number of judges or court staff, insufficient training for court personnel, and issues related to the possibility of judges not being supportive of ASFA's permanency goals. Other identified barriers included difficulty adhering to the timeline of filing for termination of parental rights within the 15-of-22-months requirement. Some states reported concern that this timeframe "push children through the child welfare system too quickly." States also identified situations where they did not want to file for termination of parental rights—for example, when children were teenagers and had strong ties to biological families. There were also situations where a child's special needs were so significant that an agency was not able to find an appropriate adoptive home for the child. Additionally, if a child was placed in foster care and the ASFA timing indicated that a termination of parental rights should be filed in court, but the child welfare agency was "reasonably confident" that the parents would be able to reunify within a couple of months, the agency did not file termination of rights as required. Last, issues concerning limited access to services for parents were identified as a barrier, particularly regarding substance abuse treatment.

A positive outcome was that many states reported that they were using the ASFA's additional federal adoption incentive payments to implement a number of strategies to enhance adoption resources and facilitate permanent placements for children. Some states have created new recruitment videos, done more to promote National Adoption Month in November, and hired additional recruiters for foster and adoptive families.

The federal government continues to work with states in terms of collecting reliable data related to foster care outcomes, permanency, effective child welfare practices, and efforts to improve the child welfare system.

Questions for classroom discussion:

Review the section in this chapter on the specifics regarding child abuse and neglect. What are your major child welfare concerns for Donald and Terri's children?
Review the section in this chapter "Rights of Children versus Rights of Parents." In the example of Donald and Terri, do you agree or disagree with the decision to intervene and remove the children from the parental home?
Do you believe these issues could have been addressed with the children remaining in the home or being returned as soon as the parents were found? Review the sections "Family Preservation Programs" and "Family Group Conferencing." Do you believe either or both of these programs could have benefited this family? Why or why not?
Review the section in this chapter "Rights of Children versus Rights of Parents." Apply this idea to the case example. In addition, how do issues of culture and diversity impact families in the child protective system? Do parents have the right to raise their children as "they see fit," based on their cultural values and beliefs?
Do you believe parents should get a number of chances to get their children returned to them? Should these children ever be returned to these parents? How does the ASFA impact this young family?
What would need to happen for you to feel comfortable returning these children to their parental home? What if they can't meet the CPS expectations before their time is up (meaning the children are in foster care for 15 out of the last 22 months)? Do you agree with the basic components of the ASFA? Why or why not?

This exhibit was written by Debra S. Borquist, MSSW, APSW, Child Protection Team Social Worker, University of Wisconsin Health/American Family Children's Hospital.
[a]U.S. Department of Health and Human Services, Administration for Children, Youth and Families, http://www.acf.hhs.gov/programs/cb/laws_policies/policy/pi/pi9802.htm.
[b]The National Casa Association, 1997, http://www.casanet.org/reference/asfa-summary.htm.
[c]Ibid.
[d]Child Welfare League of America, 2001, http://www.cwla.org.
[e]http://www.gao.gov/assets/110/109829.pdf.
[f]http://www.childwelfare.gov/adoption/nam/.

because the rapist cannot control his sexual arousal or because he is "oversexed." Rape is, instead, the mismanagement of aggression; the rapist's gratification (if any) comes not from the sexual act but rather from the expression of anger or control through the extreme violation of another's body.

There are a number of typologies for classifying rapists, depending on numerous variables. One straightforward model was developed by A. Nicholas Groth,[103] who describes rapists as falling into one of three categories: the anger rapist, the power rapist, and the sadistic rapist.

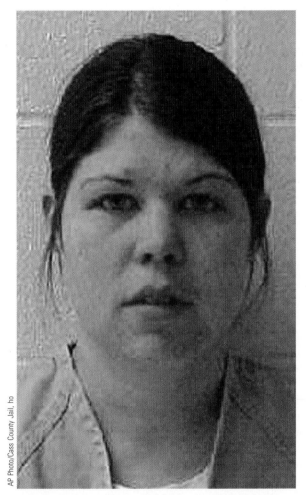

Kelsey Peterson, a schoolteacher, pleaded guilty in 2008 to fleeing to Mexico with a 13-year-old male student so she could have sex with him.

and suffering. His offenses often are ritualistic and involve bondage and torture, particularly to the sexual organs.

We live in a society that promotes aggression and represses sexuality. In the United States, males are socialized to be aggressive, even in seeking sexual gratification. For example, men are often expected to play the "aggressive" role in sex. In our culture, sex and aggression are frequently confused and combined. In Swedish culture, where sexual information is readily available in the media but depictions of aggression are not, the incidence of rape is low. According to Janet Hyde, the confusion of sex and aggression in socialization practices may lead males to commit rape:

> *It may be, then, that rape is a means of proving masculinity for the male who is insecure in his role. For this reason, the statistics on the youthfulness of rapists make sense; youthful rapists may simply be young men who are trying to adopt the adult male role, who feel insecure about doing this, and who commit a rape as proof of their manhood. Further, heterosexuality is an important part of manliness. Raping a woman is a flagrant way to prove that one is a heterosexual.*[104]

(See Case Exhibit 6.6 for more about aggression and sexuality.)

Date Rape

In a study by Struckman-Johnson of female college students, 22% stated that they had been victimized by at least one incident of forced sexual intercourse on a date.[105] The study demonstrates that date rape is not a rare occurrence.

In some cases, date rape seems to result from the mistaken belief on the part of the man that, if he spends money on the woman, he is entitled to (or she is implicitly giving consent to) sexual rewards. The traditional view in dating relationships has been that, when the woman says "no," she really means "yes." Unfortunately, media depictions of this misinformation abound, from John Wayne movies to such classics as *Last Tango in Paris* and *Gone with the Wind*. For example, in the movie The *Quiet Man*, John Wayne plays a macho, quiet Irishman. He courts a feisty woman played by Maureen O'Hara, but to no avail. Only after beating up a mean rival, spanking the woman in front of the townspeople, and literally dragging her home does he win her compliance and cooperation. The underlying message seems to be that

The *anger rapist* performs his act to discharge feelings of pent-up anger and rage. He is brutal in the commission of his assault, using far more force than is necessary to gain sexual access to his victim. His aim is to hurt and debase his victim; forced sex is his ultimate weapon.

The *power rapist* is interested in possessing his victim sexually, not harming her. He acts out of underlying feelings of inadequacy and is interested in controlling his victim. He uses only the amount of force necessary to gain her compliance. Sometimes he will kidnap his victim and hold her under his control for a long period of time, perhaps engaging in sexual intercourse with her numerous times.

The *sadistic rapist* eroticizes aggression; that is, aggressive force creates sexual arousal in him. He is enormously gratified by his victim's torment, pain,

AP Photo/Cass County Jail, ho

"real men" obtain power, status, and sexual gratification by violating women sexually—a very dangerous message indeed!

Leon, a college student, described his thinking processes prior to a date rape:

It's time for me to make my move. Tonight her every dream will come true when I show her what it's like to be with a real man. It'll be the perfect ending to an evening she'll never forget. I knew that she was after more than dinner and dancing from the moment that I picked her up. I mean, check out that dress she's wearing, those fancy jewels, that sexy perfume, and those looks she has been giving me—they're unmistakable. Now that she has agreed to a nightcap at my place, we can end the evening in style. I'll just slide a little closer to her on the couch, slip my arm around her shoulder, and kiss her neck….Does she really think that moving away and saying "No!" will stop me? I guess all women play that game. I dropped a bundle on this date and now it's time for her to pay up. Boy, the guys will be impressed to know that I scored with such a classy number. Even if she wanted to, she couldn't stop someone as powerful as me. Besides, everyone knows that when a woman says "No!" she really means "Yes!"

The vast majority of date rapes go unreported. In fact, many of the female victims of sexual assault do not interpret the assault as such.[106] When the victims view themselves as being "in love" with the perpetrator, there is a tendency to see the rape as being within the realm of acceptable behavior.

Kanin studied 71 unmarried college men who were self-disclosed date rapists and compared them to a control group of unmarried college men.[107] The date rapists tended to be sexually predatory. When asked how frequently they attempt to seduce a new date, 62% of the date rapists said "most of the time," compared with 19% of the controls. The date rapists also were much more likely to report using a variety of manipulative techniques on their dates, including falsely professing love, getting the dates high on alcohol or other drugs, and falsely promising to go steady or get engaged.

Men need to learn that "no" means "no." Date-rape educational programs are needed in elementary, secondary, and college settings. Laws against date rape should be more vigorously enforced. And society (including the mass media) must stop glamorizing rape and instead report it as a serious crime that takes a devastating toll on its victims.

Effects on Victims

Ann Burgess and Lynda Holmstrom have found that rape generally constitutes a severe crisis for the victims and that aftereffects often persist for 6 months or longer.[108] They analyzed the reactions of 92 victims of forcible rape and labeled the series of emotional changes experienced by the victims the "rape trauma syndrome."[109]

Critical Thinking Questions

If you are a female, what is your set of strategies for seeking to prevent being sexually assaulted? If you are a male, are you aware of the long-term negative effects that a woman may experience if she is sexually assaulted?

This syndrome occurs in two phases: an acute phase and a long-term reorganization phase. The acute phase begins immediately after the rape (or attempted rape) and may last for several weeks. Victims have an expressive reaction in which they are likely to cry and have feelings of anger, fear, humiliation, tension, anxiety, and a desire for revenge. During this phase, victims also usually have periods of controlled reaction in which they mask or deny their feelings and appear calm, composed, or subdued. Victims undergo many physical reactions during this phase, such as stomach pains, nausea, headaches, insomnia, and jumpiness. In addition, some women who had been forced to have oral sex reported irritation or damage to the throat. Some who had been forced to have anal intercourse reported rectal pain and bleeding. Two feelings were especially common: fear and self-blame. Many women feared future physical violence or continued to suffer from the fear of being murdered during the attack. The self-blame is related to the tendency on the part of the victim and others to "blame the victim." The women often spent hours agonizing over what they thought they had done to bring on the attack or over what they could have done to fight off the attacker. Common self-criticisms are, "If only I hadn't walked alone," "If only I had bolt-locked the door," "If only I hadn't worn that tight sweater," and "If only I hadn't been dumb enough to trust that guy."

The *long-term reorganization phase* follows the acute phase. At this point, victims may experience a variety of major disruptions. Some women who have been

CASE EXHIBIT 6.6

Initiating Kissing and Sexual Intimacy

This author occasionally asks students in some of his classes the following question: "Assume you are out on your first or second date with someone you find very attractive. You really desire to kiss and hug this person. What would you do to seek to initiate this activity?"

Many students respond that they would use body language to convey their interest. To this response I usually ask "Tell me, specifically, what types of body language would you use?" Students usually are unable to give a specific answer to this question.

Think about your past romantic experiences. How did you, or the person you were with, convey an interest in kissing and hugging?

Body language sends ambiguous messages. We may misread the body language of someone. Sadly, romantic movies and soap operas usually model that participants in romantic encounters use body language to determine the other person's interests in a romantic relationship.

If someone does not want to be kissed by you, and you kiss them, you may see physical reactions of that person rejecting you—and in rare cases even slapping you in the face. (Some sexual harassment complaints are now being filed over unwanted kissing.)

Why is it that our society socializes us to convey romantic interests through body language?

Why is it that traditionally males (in male–female relationships) are expected to initiate an interest in hugging and kissing? In our contemporary society that advocates equality between the sexes, should not females have the same right to initiate hugging and kissing (in male–female relationships)?

Michael J. Domitrz in *May I Kiss You?* makes a strong case that we would be better off by using verbal communication to seek to convey our interest in hugging and kissing a person we are highly attracted to.[a] Would not saying something like the following be more constructive and respectful than seeking to use body language? "I am very attracted to you. I'd really like to give you a kiss. Would that be OK with you?"

A second question I sometimes ask my students is: "Assume you have been dating someone you are highly attracted to for quite a length of time. You have kissed and hugged this person a number of times, but yet have not become sexually intimate. Also assume you desire to become sexually intimate. What would you do to seek to initiate this activity?"

Again, many students respond that they would convey this message through body language. (Again, movies and soap operas often convey that this is the best way of sending such a message.) Sadly, the high number of date rapes clearly document that body language (along with physical force) is not the most constructive or respectful way of conveying such a message.

Often, female students respond to this question by saying it is "up to the male" to initiate such moves. Should not females in our society have the same rights as men in this area?

Domitrz in *May I Kiss You?*[b] again makes a strong case that your interest in initiating sexual intimacy with someone is best conveyed, and most respectfully conveyed, by a verbal communication, such as the following: "I find you highly attractive. I really desire to become intimate with you. Could you tell me your thoughts about this?" Such a question shows your respect for the other person, and it conveys your feelings with much greater clarity than body language. (If you use body language and start groping someone, aren't you sending confusing, and perhaps alarming messages—which even makes you vulnerable to a sexual assault charge?)

Another advantage of using verbal communication is that it enhances the chances that you (and the person you are with) will have an honest discussion about the limits and types of sexual intimacy (such as oral sex being the type and limit) that are desired. Verbal communication also can facilitate a discussion of using contraceptives if sexual intercourse is agreed upon.

[a]Michael J. Domitrz, *May I Kiss You?* (Greenfield, WI: Awareness Publications, 2003).
[b]Ibid.

raped outdoors may develop a fear of going outdoors; others who have been raped indoors may develop a fear of being indoors. Some are unable to return to work, particularly if the rape occurred there. Some quit their job and remain unemployed for a long time. Many fear the rapist will find them and assault them again. To attempt to avoid this recurrence, they may move (sometimes several times), change their telephone number, or get an unlisted number. Some develop sexual phobias and have severe difficulties in returning to their regular sexual behaviors. In some cases, it takes several years before the victim returns to her previous lifestyle.

In addition, if the victim reports the rape, the police investigation and the trial (if it occurs) are further crises that are experienced. Police and the courts have a history of abusive and callous treatment of rape victims. The police have, at times, conveyed the idea that the victim was fabricating the assault or had willingly agreed to have sex but then changed her mind. The police often ask embarrassing questions about the details of the rape without showing much understanding or sympathy. In court it is common for the defense attorney to imply that the victim provoked the defendant. Victims are sometimes made to feel as if they are the ones who are on trial.

CASE EXHIBIT 6.7

How to Attempt to Prevent Rape

There have been a number of suggestions to help women prevent rape and fight off an attacker. These suggestions include having and using secure locks on doors, not walking alone at night, and learning self-defense measures such as judo, aikido, tae kwon do (Korean karate), or jujitsu. Being assertive when saying "no" to unwanted sexual advances is particularly useful in preventing acquaintance rape.[a] Exercising regularly and keeping in shape are also recommended to give the potential victim the strength to fight back and the speed to run fast. Some experts recommend poking an attacker in the eyes or kneeing him in the groin. Other experts recommend that every woman have a psychological strategy to use if attacked, such as telling the rapist that she has cancer of the cervix or a sexually transmittable condition (such as being HIV positive). If other preventive measures fail, some experts urge dissuading the attacker by regurgitating on him, which can be accomplished by sticking one's finger down one's throat. Another last-ditch strategy is to urinate on him.

Women have many tools to harm their attacker. They include smashing the nose or Adam's apple, kicking his knee, smashing the instep, gouging the eyes, and grabbing and squeezing his groin. Pencils, pens, a book, an umbrella, a briefcase, and a purse are all items that can be used to fend off an attacker.

It is important that each woman have a strategy, or set of defensive measures, she would seek to use if an attack occurred. No one type of advice can apply to all situations because the rapist may respond quite differently to the victim's fighting back, depending on whether he is primarily a power, anger, or sadistic rapist. Therefore, any woman who physically survives a rape should be viewed as having utilized a successful strategy.

On a broader sociological level, feminists urge a revision in our sex-role socialization practices. Margaret Mead has noted that rape does not occur in societies in which males are socialized to be nurturant rather than aggressive.[b] To reduce rape sharply, Janet S. Hyde recommends the following changes in socialization practices:

> If little boys were not so pressed to be aggressive and tough, perhaps rapists would never develop. If adolescent boys did not have to demonstrate that they are hypersexual, perhaps there would be no rapists....
>
> Changes would also need to be made in the way females are socialized, particularly if women are to become good at self-defense. Weakness is not considered a desirable human characteristic, and so it should not be considered a desirable feminine characteristic, especially because it makes women vulnerable to rape.... While some people think that it is silly for the federal government to rule that girls must have athletic teams equal to boys' teams, it seems quite possible that the absence of athletic training for girls has contributed to making them rape victims....
>
> Finally, for both males and females, we need a radical restructuring of ideas about sexuality. As long as females are expected to pretend to be uninterested in sex and as long as males and females play games on dates, rape will persist.[c]

[a]Janet S. Hyde, *Understanding Human Sexuality,* 5th ed. (New York: McGraw-Hill, 1994), p. 496.
[b]Margaret Mead, *Sex and Temperament in Three Primitive Societies* (New York: Morrow, 1935).
[c] Hyde, *Understanding Human Sexuality,* p. 498.

Of late, fortunately, many police departments have developed sensitive crime units with specially trained officers to intervene in cases of rape and child sexual assault. With such units, victims are less likely to be further victimized by authorities. Furthermore, a number of states have enacted "shield" evidence laws, which prohibit defense attorneys from asking questions about the victim's previous sexual experiences (except with the alleged rapist) during a rape trial. (In the past, defense attorneys sought to imply that the victim was promiscuous and therefore probably seduced the defendant.)

Because rape and its aftereffects are extremely traumatic, Burgess and Holmstrom urge counseling for victims to (a) provide support and allow the victims to vent their feelings, (b) lend support and guidance during the medical tests and police interrogation,

(c) provide similar support during the trial, and (d) provide follow-up counseling for emotional reactions to the rape.[110]

Burgess and Holmstrom also note that, because a majority of rapes are not reported, many of the victims have a silent rape reaction.[111] Many nonreporters not only fail to report the rape to the police but also choose to tell no one about it. They are likely to experience the same adjustment problems as victims who report the rape experience. However, the trauma for nonreporters is often intensified because they have no way of expressing or venting their feelings. Some nonreporters eventually seek professional counseling for other problems, such as depression, anxiety, or inability to have orgasms. Often such problems are then found to stem from the rape. Women who have had unreported rape experiences should be helped to talk about them so they can gradually learn to deal with the trauma. A number of communities now have rape crisis centers that provide counseling, medical services, and legal services to victims.

SUMMARY

The following summarizes this chapter's content as it relates to the chapter objectives presented at the beginning of the chapter. Objectives include the following:

A *Present a brief history of changes in the American family since colonial days.*

The family is a social institution that is found in every culture. Yet there are substantial variations in family patterns and forms. Most families throughout the world can be classified as either extended or nuclear. Our culture has moved from an extended family system (before the Industrial Revolution) to a nuclear family system. In a number of countries, a third family form, the single-parent family, is now emerging.

No society has ever existed without the institution of the family. Five essential functions performed by the modern family are replacing the population, caring for the young, socializing new members, regulating sexual behavior, and providing affection.

B *Describe current problem areas in the American family, including divorce, empty-shell marriages, family violence, sexual abuse of children, births outside of marriage, and rape. Also describe current social services for family problems.*

One of two marriages ends in divorce. Divorce per se is not a social problem, but the consequences sometimes are. Reasons for the high divorce rate in our society include the extensive emphasis on romantic love, the changing status of women (who are now increasingly more financially independent), the growth of individualism, the growing acceptance of divorce, and the loss of certain functions in the modern family.

In empty-shell marriages, the spouses feel no strong attachments to each other. Three types were described: devitalized relationships, conflict habituated relationships, and passive-congenial relationships. Some empty-shell marriages eventually end in divorce. Marriage counseling is the primary service available to spouses contemplating a divorce or to spouses with an empty-shell marriage.

Spouse abuse, child abuse, and elder abuse occur in more than half of all U.S. households. In the past five decades, family violence has become recognized as one of our major social problems.

With spouse abuse, the greatest physical damage is usually sustained by women. Although husbands are slapped or shoved with about the same frequency as wives, they are not controlled through violence to the extent that battered wives are. Spouse abuse appears to be related to a norm of tolerating violence in American families. A sizable number of men and women believe it is acceptable for a husband to occasionally hit his wife. Services (for example, shelter homes) are increasingly being developed in many communities for battered wives.

Large numbers of children are victims of child abuse or neglect. Physical abuse is dramatic and has received considerable national attention. Child neglect has received less national attention, even though it occurs more frequently than physical abuse. *Physical abuse, physical neglect*, and particularly *emotional neglect* are terms that are somewhat ambiguous and difficult to define precisely. The primary service designed to curb child abuse and neglect is protective services.

Sexual abuse of children was discussed. Child molestation is the sexual abuse of a child by an adult. Most child molesters are males. Approximately one in three girls and one in six boys have experienced sexual abuse. The extent to which abused children are traumatized varies considerably between victims and is dependent on a number of factors. A subcategory of sexual abuse of children is incest. In the largest proportion of incest cases reported to the police, the sexual abuse is between father (or stepfather) and daughter. The long-term effects of incest vary from child to child. Documented cases of incest are handled by protective services. Children who are traumatized after being sexually abused can often benefit from receiving counseling.

Premarital intercourse is fairly common and is now often tolerated in our society. If a single woman becomes pregnant, however, there may be considerable turmoil within families. Birth outside of marriage has become somewhat more accepted in our society, yet it is still viewed as a social problem. There is considerable variation in the reasons why it is viewed as a problem ranging from assertion that it is a sign of the moral decay and collapse of the family to a concern about the difficulties that the single parent and her child will encounter. A disproportionately high number of births outside of marriage occur among teenagers, suggesting a need for quality educational programs about responsible sexuality. Single-parent services is the primary social service for women who are single and pregnant and for unmarried mothers and fathers.

Forced intercourse is a commonly committed violent crime in the United States. Many cases of rape are not reported to the police. Rape is primarily an aggressive act and secondarily a sexual act. Date rape happens quite frequently, and many cases go unreported. Rape generally constitutes a severe crisis for the victims, and the aftereffects often persist for 6 months or longer. Many of the victims have a series of emotional reactions that has been termed "rape trauma syndrome." Those suffering are in need of counseling.

Competency Notes

EP 2.1.3a Distinguish, appraise, and integrate multiple sources of knowledge, including research-based knowledge and practice wisdom. (All of this chapter) This chapter briefly describes diverse family forms. A brief history of changes in the American family since colonial days is then presented. Most of the chapter focuses on describing current problem areas in the American Family, and the social services that are available for these problems. Problem areas described include divorce, empty-shell marriages, family violence, sexual abuse of children, births outside of marriage, and rape.

Media Resources

Additional resources for this chapter, including a chapter quiz, can be found on the Social Work CourseMate. Go to CengageBrain.com.

Notes

1. Linda A. Mooney, David Knox, and Caroline Schacht, *Understanding Social Problems*, 8th ed. (Belmont, CA: Wadsworth/Cengage Learning, 2013), p. 136.
2. William Kornblum and Joseph Julian, *Social Problems*, 14th ed. (Boston: Pearson), p. 330.
3. Philippe Aries, "From the Medieval to the Modern Family," in *Family in Transition*, Arlene S. Skolnick and Jerome H. Skolnick, eds. (Boston: Little, Brown, 1971), pp. 90–104.
4. John F. Cuber, Martha Tyler John, and Kenrick S. Thompson, "Should Traditional Sex Modes and Values Be Changed?" in *Controversial Issues in the Social Studies: A Contemporary Perspective*, Raymond H. Muessig, ed. (Washington, DC: National Council for the Social Studies, 1975), pp. 87–121.
5. Janet S. Hyde and John D. DeLamater, *Understanding Human Sexuality*, 11th ed. (McGraw-Hill, 2011).
6. William F. Ogburn, "The Changing Family," *The Family*, 19 (July 1938), pp. 139–143.
7. George P. Murdock, *Social Structure* (New York: Free Press, 1949); Ogburn, "The Changing Family, " pp. 139–143; William J. Goode, "The Sociology of the Family," in *Sociology Today*, Robert K. Merton, Leonard Broom, and Leonard J. Cottrell, eds. (New York: Basic Books, 1959); Talcott Parsons and Robert F. Bales, *Family, Socialization and Interaction Process* (Glencoe, IL: Free Press, 1995); Coleman and Kerbo, *Social Problems*, pp. 36–38.
8. René Spitz, "Hospitalism: Genesis of Psychiatric Conditions in Early Childhood," *Psychoanalytic Study of the Child*, 1 (1945), pp. 53–74.
9. Kornblum and Julian, *Social Problems*, p. 332.
10. Ibid., pp. 332–336.
11. Ibid., pp. 332–336.
12. Ibid., pp. 332–336.
13. Ibid., p. 393.
14. Ibid., pp. 332–336.
15. Kenneth Keniston, *All Our Children: The American Family under Pressure* (New York: Harcourt Brace Jovanovich, 1977), p. 21.
16. Richard Neely, "Barter in the Court," *The New Republic*, Feb. 10, 1986, p. 17.
17. John F. Cuber and Peggy B. Harroff, "Five Types of Marriage," in Skolnick and Skolnick, *Family in Transition*, pp. 287–299.
18. William J. Goode, "Family Disorganization," in *Contemporary Social Problems*, 4th ed., Robert K. Merton and Robert Nisbet, eds. (New York: Harcourt Brace Jovanovich, 1976), p. 543.
19. Richard J. Gelles, *Intimate Violence in Families*, 3rd ed. (Thousand Oaks, CA: Sage Publications, 1997).
20. http://www.cbsnews.com/stories/2011/03/02/national/main20038443.shtml.
21. Kornblum and Julian, *Social Problems*, pp. 344–346.
22. Suzanne K. Steinmetz and Murray A. Straus, *Violence in the Family* (New York: Dodd, Mead, 1974), p. 3.
23. Ibid., p. 9.

24. John O'Brien, "Violence in Divorce Prone Families," *Journal of Marriage and the Family*, 33 (Nov. 1971), pp. 692–698.
25. Steven V. Roberts, "Simpson and Sudden Death," *U.S. News & World Report*, June 27, 1994, pp. 26–32.
26. Gelles, *Intimate Violence in Families*.
27. Ibid.
28. Ibid.
29. Ibid.
30. Ibid.
31. Ibid.
32. Ibid.
33. Murray A. Straus, Richard Gelles, and Suzanne Steinmetz, *Behind Closed Doors: A Survey of Family Violence in America* (Garden City, NY: Doubleday, 1979).
34. Ibid.
35. Gelles, *Intimate Violence in Families*.
36. Andrea Saltzman and Kathleen Proch, *Law in Social Work Practice* (Chicago: Nelson-Hall, 1990), pp. 296–307.
37. Alfred Kadushin and Judith A. Martin, *Child Welfare Services*, 4th ed. (New York: Macmillan, 1988), pp. 218–327.
38. Gelles, *Intimate Violence in Families*, p. 66.
39. Larry Silver, C. C. Dublin, and R. S. Lourie, "Does Violence Breed Violence? Contribution from a Study of the Child-Abuse Syndrome," *American Journal of Psychiatry*, Sept. 1969, pp. 404–407.
40. George C. Curtis, "Violence Breeds Violence—Perhaps?" in *The Battered Child*, Jerome E. Leavitt, ed. (Morristown, NJ: General Learning Press, 1974), p. 3.
41. Gelles, *Intimate Violence in Families*.
42. Ibid.
43. Kadushin and Martin, *Child Welfare Services*, pp. 243–244.
44. Vincent De Francis, *Special Skills in Child Protective Services* (Denver: American Humane Association, 1958), p. 11.
45. American Humane Association, *National Analysis of Official Child Neglect and Abuse Reporting* (Denver: American Humane Association, 1978), p. 27.
46. C. Henry Kempe and Ray E. Helfer, *Helping the Battered Child and His Family* (Philadelphia: Lippincott, 1972); Kadushin and Martin, *Child Welfare Services;* Leavitt, *The Battered Child;* Gelles, *Intimate Violence in Families*.
47. Ibid.
48. Kadushin and Martin, *Child Welfare Services*, p. 218.
49. Sallie A. Watkins, "The Mary Ellen Myth: Correcting Child Welfare History," *Social Work*, 35, no. 6 (Nov. 1990), pp. 500–503.
50. Ellen Thomson, *Child Abuse—A Community Challenge* (Buffalo, NY: Henry Stewart, 1971), p. 44.
51. Gelles, *Intimate Violence in Families*.
52. Anna Mae Sandusky, "Services to Neglected Children," *Children*, Jan.–Feb. 1960, p. 24.
53. Kadushin and Martin, *Child Welfare Services*, p. 291.
54. Mark Ellis, "Forming a Multidisciplinary Team to Investigate Child Abuse," http://idcartf.org/Forming_MDTs.pdf.
55. Bernie Sue Newman and Paul C. Pendleton, "Child Abuse Investigations: Reasons for Using Child Advocacy Centers and Suggestions for Improvement," *Child and Adolescent Social Work Journal*, vol. 22 (April 2005), pp. 165–181; Lisa Snell, "Child Advocacy Centers: One Stop on the Road to Performance-Based Child Protection," http://www.policyarchive.org/handle/10207/bitstreams/5820.pdf.
56. Gelles, *Intimate Violence in Families*. p. 152.
57. Ibid., p. 153.
58. Patrick Murphy, "Family Preservation and Its Victims," *The New York Times*, Jun. 19, 1993, p. 21.
59. Susan W. Downs, Ernestine Moore, Emily J. McFadden, and Lela B. Costin, *Child Welfare and Family Services*, 6th ed. (Boston: Allyn & Bacon, 2000), p. 295.
60. Ibid., 295.
61. Gelles, *Intimate Violence in Families*.
62. Kadushin and Martin, *Child Welfare Services*, p. 315.
63. Hyde and DeLamater, *Understanding Human Sexuality*.
64. Ibid.
65. Ibid.
66. A. Nicholas Groth, "The Incest Offender," in *Intervention in Child Sexual Abuse*, Suzanne M. Sgroi, ed. (Lexington, MA: Lexington Books, 1982), pp. 215–239.
67. Hyde and DeLamater, *Understanding Human Sexuality*.
68. G. G. Abel, J. V. Becker, J. Cunningham-Rathner, M. S. Mittelman, and J. L. Rouleau, "Multiple Paraphilic Diagnoses among Sex Offenders,"

Bulletin of the American Academy of Psychiatry and the Law, 16, no. 2 (1988), pp. 153–168.

69. R. Karl Hanson, Rocco Gizzarelli, and Heather Scott, "The Attitudes of Incest Offenders," *Criminal Justice and Behavior*, 21, no. 2 (June 1994), pp. 187–202.

70. G. G. Abel, J. V. Becker, M. S. Mittelman, J. Cunningham-Rathner, J. L. Rouleau, and W. D. Murphy, "Self-Reported Sex Crimes of Nonincarcerated Paraphiliacs," *Journal of Interpersonal Violence*, 2, no. 1 (1987), pp. 3–25.

71. Hyde and DeLamater, *Understanding Human Sexuality.*

72. Ibid.

73. Ibid.

74. Blair Justice and Rita Justice, *The Broken Taboo: Sex in the Family* (New York: Human Sciences Press, 1979).

75. Hyde and DeLamater, *Understanding Human Sexuality.*

76. Justice and Justice, *The Broken Taboo*, p. 177.

77. Judith Siegel, Jacqueline M. Golding, Judith A. Stein, M. Audrey Burnam, and Susan B. Sorenson, "Reactions to Sexual Assault," *Journal of Interpersonal Violence*, 5 (1990), pp. 229–246.

78. Kornblum and Julian, *Social Problems*, pp. 337–339.

79. Ibid.

80. Ibid.

81. Ibid.

82. Ibid.

83. Ibid.

84. Ibid.

85. James W. Coleman and Donald R. Cressey, *Social Problems*, 4th ed. (New York: Harper & Row, 1990), p. 136.

86. Kornblum and Julian, *Social Problems*, pp. 337–339.

87. Ibid., pp. 337–339.

88. Ibid., pp. 337–339.

89. Ibid., pp. 337–339.

90. Alfred C. Kinsey, W. B. Pomeroy, and C. E. Martin, *Sexual Behavior in the Human Male* (Philadelphia: Saunders, 1948): Alfred C. Kinsey, W. B. Pomeroy, C. E. Martin, and P. H. Gebhard, *Sexual Behavior in the Human Female* (Philadelphia: Saunders, 1953).

91. Sex Information and Educational Council of the United States, *Guidelines for Comprehensive Sexuality Education* (New York: Author, 1991).

92. Hyde and DeLamater, *Understanding Human Sexuality.*

93. Ibid.

94. Kornblum and Julian, *Social Problems*, pp. 337–339.

95. Ibid.

96. Diane de Anda, "'Baby, Think It Over' Evaluation of an Infant Simulation Intervention for Adolescent Pregnancy Prevention," *Health and Social Work*, 31, no. 1 (2006), pp. 26–35.

97. Linda A. Mooney, David Knox, and Caroline Schacht, *Understanding Social Problems*, 6th ed. (Belmont, CA: Wadsworth/Cengage Learning, 2009), p. 203.

98. Ursula S. Myers, "Illegitimacy and Services to Single Parents," in *Introduction to Social Welfare Institutions*, 2nd ed., Charles Zastrow, ed. (Homewood, IL: Dorsey Press, 1982), p. 176.

99. Hyde and DeLamater, *Understanding Human Sexuality.*

100. Ibid.

101. Philip Sarrel and William Masters, "Sexual Molestation of Men by Women," *Archives of Sexual Behavior*, 11 (1982), pp. 117–132.

102. "Mary Kay Letourneau Released," *Wisconsin State Journal*, Aug. 5, 2004, p. 2A.

103. A. Nicholas Groth, *Men Who Rape* (New York: Plenum Press, 1979).

104. Janet S. Hyde, *Understanding Human Sexuality*, 5th ed. (New York: McGraw-Hill, 1994), p. 492.

105. Cindy Struckman-Johnson, "Forced Sex on Dates: It Happens to Men, Too," *Journal of Sex Research*, 24 (1988), pp. 234–241.

106. M. P. Koss, T. E. Dinero, C. A. Siebel, and S. L. Cox, "Non-stranger Sexual Aggression: A Discriminant Analysis of the Psychological Characteristics of Undetected Offenders," *Sex Roles*, 12 (1985), pp. 981–992.

107. Eugene J. Kanin, "Date Rapists: Differential Sexual Socialization and Relative Deprivation," *Archives of Sexual Behavior*, 14 (1985), pp. 219–232.

108. Ann W. Burgess and Lynda Holmstrom, *Rape: Victims of Crisis* (Bowie, MD: Robert J. Brady, 1974).

109. Ann W. Burgess and Lynda Holmstrom, "Rape Trauma Syndrome," *American Journal of Psychiatry*, 131 (1974), pp. 981–986.

110. Ibid.

111. Ibid.

CHAPTER **7**

Sexual Orientation and Services to LGBT Individuals

I regard sex as the central problem of life.... Sex lies at the root of life, and we can never learn to reverence life until we know how to understand sex.
—Havelock Ellis[1]

Amazingly, we were able to put a man in space before we learned to understand the physiology of sexual orgasms.[2] This chapter will:

Learning Objectives

EP 2.1.4a–d; 2.1.5a–c

A   Present a brief look at sexual expression in history and in other cultures.

B   Present a historical review of scientific studies of sexuality.

C   Present material on sexual orientation, including definitions of terms, hate crimes against gays and lesbians, myths and facts about gays and lesbians, incidence of same-sex sexual orientation, causes of same-sex sexual orientation, life experiences of gays and lesbians, the process of coming out, current issues for gays and lesbians, conversion therapy, information about transgenderism, and social work with LGBT (lesbian, gay, bisexual, or transgender) individuals.

Sex in History and in Other Cultures

Practically every conceivable sexual activity and conjugal arrangement, to some degree, has been socially acceptable to at least some people. Intercourse for procreation only, oral–genital relations, premarital sex, adultery, anal intercourse, monogamy, polyandry (more than one husband), polygyny (more than one wife), gay and lesbian relationships, lifelong celibacy—each has been a method of responding to sexual desire that has been socially approved by some human community. Not even incest, which is among the most widely prohibited of sexual relationships, has been universally tabooed.[3] Some ancient cultures encouraged incest in royal families as a way to maintain the wealth and power among a small number of people and as a way to ensure the purity of the royal line.

Gay and lesbian relationships in ancient Greece were not only acceptable but encouraged. There is a wide range of attitudes toward same-sex relationships in various cultures. At one extreme are societies that strongly disapprove of same-sex relationships for people of any age. In contrast, some societies tolerate gay and lesbian behavior for children but disapprove of it in adults. Yet other societies actively force all their male members to engage in some gay relationships, usually in conjunction with puberty rites.[4] No matter how a particular society views same-sex relationships, the behavior always occurs in some individuals; thus, same-sex relationships are found in all societies.[5]

Societies differ considerably in their rules regarding premarital sex. Inhabitants of the Trobriand Islands encourage premarital sex because it is thought to be an important preparation for marriage. Some societies permit young boys and girls to play husband and wife even before puberty. In Asia the Lepcha society believes that girls need sexual intercourse to mature.[6] In contrast, in many Muslim and South American cultures, premarital chastity for women is highly revered: a female who has premarital sex is likely to be shamed and ostracized. However, in some other developing countries, some low-income parents sell their adolescent daughters as prostitutes, particularly to tourists.

There are some cultures in which rape is practically nonexistent, as among the Arapesh of New Guinea. In that society, males are socialized to be peaceful and nonaggressive. In contrast, in the Gussi tribe in Kenya, the rate of rape is several times higher

CASE EXHIBIT 7.1

Sexuality in Mangaia

Mangaia is an island in the South Pacific. The Mangaians have elaborate rituals that use sex for pleasure and for procreation.

Mangaian boys around the age of 7 or 8 are instructed how to masturbate. At about age 13, they have a superincision ritual (in which a slit is made on the full length of the skin on the top part of the penis). This ritual initiates them into manhood. As part of this ritual, they are also given instruction in how to kiss, how to bring a female partner to orgasm several times before they have an orgasm themselves, and how to perform cunnilingus (a form of oral sex). Approximately 2 weeks later, each boy is introduced to sexual intercourse with an experienced woman. She demonstrates intercourse in various positions and further instructs him on how to delay ejaculation to have simultaneous orgasms with his partner.

Mangaian girls also receive sexual instruction from adult women. Thereafter, Mangaian boys and girls actively seek each other out, and many have coitus nearly every night. Teen-age girls are raised to believe virility in a male is proof of his desire for her. In particular, a male is expected to be able to vigorously continue the in-and-out action of intercourse for 15 to 30 minutes or longer while the female moves her hips back and forth in a rhythmic motion. Any male who is unable to perform this act is looked down on.

By age 20, the average male is likely to have had 10 or more female partners, and the average "nice" female will have had 3 or 4 successive male partners. Mangaian parents encourage such sexual experiences because they want their daughters and sons to find a marriage partner with whom they are sexually compatible. At around age 18, Mangaians typically have sex every night. Men are brought up to believe that bringing their partner to orgasm is one of the chief sources of sexual pleasures for a man.

SOURCE: Janet S. Hyde and John D. DeLamater, *Understanding Human Sexuality*, 9th ed. (Boston: McGraw-Hill, 2006), pp. 10–11.

than in the United States. In this tribe, both men and women are socialized to be aggressive and competitive—and women often resist sexual relations, even with their husbands.[7]

It has been fairly common throughout history for soldiers to rape the women of the societies they conquered. In the past, Eskimo husbands offered male guests the privilege of spending the night with their wives, and it was considered a serious insult for guests to refuse. White slaveowners in U.S. history often prohibited their slaves from marrying, and some attempted to improve the characteristics of African American children by mating female slaves with an African American male who was considered to have desirable characteristics. Some persons with a cognitive disability in various societies have been sterilized in an effort to prevent them from having children. Hitler, in Nazi Germany in the 1930s and 1940s, mated women with certain soldiers in an effort to "breed" offspring with the characteristics he considered desirable.

Some parents in Europe believe that fathers should have intercourse with their daughters to teach them about sex, although this practice is most often viewed as an excuse for incest or sexual abuse. Although there is a myth in our society that older adults do not and should not engage in sexual activity, many older adults are sexually active and may have more than one partner. In many cultures, males greet each other with a kiss and a hug.

Sex-change operations have been occurring since the early 1930s. They became well publicized in 1952, when Christine Jorgensen announced to the world that she had undergone surgery to change her from being biologically male to biologically female. As is often the case with sexual matters that are little understood by the larger society, Jorgensen's surgery met with widespread disapproval. Nonetheless, several thousand people have since undergone such operations.[8]

Clearly, what is defined as acceptable and unacceptable sexual behavior varies from culture to culture and from one time period to another (see Case Exhibit 7.1: Sexuality in Mangaia). Let's look briefly at the history of our changing sexual attitudes and mores.

Perhaps the major influence on the current attitudes toward sex in Western culture has been the Judeo-Christian tradition. The Old Testament approved of sexual intercourse only within marriage. The purpose of intercourse, it was asserted, should be to conceive children. Masturbation, gay and lesbian relationships, and all other sexual expressions outside of marriage were viewed as sinful.

Early Christianity prohibited premarital and extramarital sexual relations. It viewed the purposes

CASE EXHIBIT 7.2

Learning Sexual Behavior via Scripts

Sociologists have made a major contribution to our understanding of human sexuality by asserting that sexual behavior (as well as most other human behavior) is developed through learning "scripts." *Scripts* (as in a play) are plans that we learn and then carry around in our heads. These scripts enable us to conceptualize where we are in our activities and provide us with direction for completing those activities and accomplishing our goals. Scripts are also devices for helping us to remember what we have done in the past.

Sexual scripts result from elaborate prior learning in which we acquire an etiquette of sexual behavior. According to this script approach, little in sexual activity is spontaneous. Scripts tell us who appropriate sexual partners are, what sexual activity is expected, where and when the activity should occur, and what the sequence of the different sexual behaviors should be.

Rose and Frieze asked male and female college students to make a list of the things that a woman or man typically do on a first date.[a] Hyde and DeLamater summarize the findings:

The hypothetical script written by many of the participants included a core sequence of acts: dress, pick up, get to know, evaluate, eat, make out, and go home. This is the first-date script. This script is also influenced by contemporary views of gender roles. Males were portrayed as proactive, taking the initiative: pick up the female, pay for the date, attempt to make out, and ask for another date. Females were portrayed as reactive: be picked up, be treated, accept or reject the male's attempt to make out, and accept or reject an invitation to another date. The widely shared nature of this script enables relative strangers to interact smoothly on their first date.[b]

[a]S. Rose and I. H. Frieze, "Young Singles' Contemporary Dating Scripts," *Sex Roles*, 28 (2006), pp. 499–509.
[b]Janet S. Hyde and John D. DeLamater, *Understanding Human Sexuality*, 11th ed. (Boston: McGraw-Hill, 2011), p. 37.

of sexual intercourse as being procreation, and strengthening the bond between husband and wife. This remains the official position of the Roman Catholic Church.

The Protestant Reformation, which began in the 16th century, advocated a strict and repressive sexual code. The Protestant ethic that emerged at the time emphasized the importance of hard work and asserted that it was morally wrong to engage in pleasurable activities of any kind. Denying sexual urges and refraining from sexual activities except to procreate were seen as virtues. A major immigrant group that began colonizing America in the 17th century, the Puritans, rigidly adhered to this ascetic (self-denial of pleasurable activities) life.

The views promulgated by the Protestant ethic became incorporated into what has become known as "Victorian morality." The name is derived from the reign of Queen Victoria of England. Victorian morality was prominent in the 19th and early 20th centuries. John Gagnon and Bruce Henderson note:

The Puritan-dominated sex ethic became that of penny-pinching Adam Smith.… The moral values of the new middle classes, with their belief in hard work, delayed gratification, and avoidance of pleasure, including the sexual, were to triumph during *the Victorian age, not only in England but in most of Western Europe.*[9]

Victorian morality all but banished sexuality from discussion in respectable relationships. Modesty was stressed to the point of extreme prudishness. In polite conversations, simple anatomical terms such as *legs* or *breasts* were taboo; these body parts instead were referred to as limbs and bosoms. The limbs (legs) of tables were often covered by long tablecloths so that sexual feelings would not be aroused. Women did not get "pregnant"; they were "in a family way" and were expected to remain at home during their "condition." In Philadelphia men and women were not allowed to visit art galleries together for fear their modesty might be offended by the classical statues (on which fig leaves were added to the genital areas to minimize their offensiveness).[10]

Middle- and upper-class women, before marriage, were expected to be virgins. There were considered to be two types of females: The good women were virgins—undamaged property—who were fit to marry. The bad were "fallen women" who were sexually active premaritally. They were pitied but not consoled because their "fall" was attributed to their own weakness. They were no longer deemed fit to marry but were nevertheless considered available for nonmarital relations with men. A popular myth throughout this period held that men were inherently more sexual than women. This led to the development—still very prevalent today—of two standards of acceptable behavior (the so-called double standard). Although it was hoped that men would remain chaste, because of their "animal natures" they were seldom criticized for having premarital and extramarital relations. Prostitutes and lower-class women were proper outlets for men's excessive sexual urges, which were too beastly to impose on their wives. J. John Palen notes:

> From this division of women—good and bad, mothers and whores—came the double standard that implicitly allowed men to be sexually active but that forbade "nice girls" even to think about such things. Overt sexuality was condemned, while covert premarital or extramarital sex among men was tolerated as a necessary evil, given the male's more pressing sexual urges.[11]

Researchers have since found that the female sex drive is as strong as that of the male. Interestingly, even during the repressive years of the Puritan and Victorian eras, there were always certain segments advocating more liberal expressions of sexuality. For example, in the Victorian era, there was a profitable trade in erotic drawings and novels.

Since the early 1900s, there have been dramatic changes in sexual attitudes and behaviors. For example, recent surveys indicate most males and females in the United States have engaged in premarital intercourse by the age of 19, and most young women (ages 18 to 24) are not virgins at marriage.[12] One of the most striking features of the sexual revolution of the past few decades is the increased popularity of mouth–genital (oral–genital) sex.[13]

The 1970s in the United States were viewed as a time of sexual permissiveness and experimentation during which many people engaged in sexual behaviors that were previously uncommon. Since then there has been a partial reversal of this permissive trend, with a general movement toward fewer partners, more emphasis on long-term relationships, and a more gradual development of the sexual aspects of a relationship. This reversal has been attributed to a general dissatisfaction with sexual behavior divorced from intimacy, as well as to the very real threat of increased susceptibility to sexually transmitted diseases for people who have sexual contact with multiple partners.[14]

Critical Thinking Questions

One sign of emotional and sexual maturity is having a set of sexual values that you are comfortable with and that works for you while also not hurting others. Have you formulated this kind of value system? If not, what do you need to do to progress in formulating such a value system?

In the 1980s, 1990s, and early 2000s, there has been substantial publicity about seemingly new epidemics of sexually transmitted diseases, including genital herpes and AIDS. The AIDS epidemic has been likened to a modern-day plague. Cures have not yet been found for either genital herpes or AIDS. Publicity about AIDS and the realization that prevention cannot be guaranteed short of sexual abstinence or sexual monogamy with an uninfected partner have led millions of people to shift their patterns of sexual behavior by adding precautions (for example, using condoms). Several of the tenets of the sexual revolution, such as the belief that sexual intercourse between relative strangers could be enjoyed purely for recreational pleasure and without consequences, are being rejected in the face of new challenges.

At present, ambiguity and confusion abound over what ought to be the sexual code and behavior of Americans. On the conservative end of the spectrum are groups such as the Catholic Church and some fundamentalist religious organizations. They advocate that sex be for procreation only and restricted to heterosexual married people. Such groups express alarm that increased sexual permissiveness will destroy the moral fiber of the family and ultimately result in the destruction of our society.

At the liberal end of the spectrum are groups and individuals holding that sex can legitimately be enjoyed for recreation as well as for procreation. They assert that the ways in which sexuality is expressed should be of no concern except to those consenting adults who participate.

Expressions of this liberal attitude are visible throughout society. Sexual topics are presented frankly and openly by the mass media, including television, magazines, and newspapers. Nudity is displayed in movies, in magazines, and on television. No longer are women who have premarital sex considered unfit for marriage. One factor that appears to have led to the increases in premarital and extramarital relations is the increased availability of birth control devices, particularly the pill.[15]

Because of the widely conflicting codes advocated by parents, peers, and other pressure groups in our society, many individuals go through considerable turmoil in arriving at a personal code of sexual behavior that they can be comfortable with and seek to live by.

Shockingly, worldwide there are several countries that have laws in which gay and lesbian behaviors are subject to the death penalty. These countries include Afghanistan, Iran, Pakistan, Saudi Arabia, Sudan, United Arab Emirates, and Yemen.[16] A global perspective on laws and social attitudes regarding gay and lesbian relationships reveals that countries vary tremendously in their treatment of same-sex sexual behavior—from acceptance and legal protection to intolerance and criminalization. More countries have laws prohibiting gay relationships than laws prohibiting lesbian relationships.[17]

Formal Study of Sex

Prior to the 20th century, there were practically no scientific studies of sexuality. Since about 1900, the work of four social scientists has had profound effects on our understanding of human sexuality: Sigmund Freud, Alfred Kinsey, and the team of William Masters and Virginia Johnson.

Sigmund Freud

Sigmund Freud was a psychoanalyst who theorized in his writings (from 1895 to 1925) that the sex drive was a fundamental part of human life. Freud realized that many people had sexual conflicts. He made sexuality a central focus of his theories and defined most emotions and behaviors as being primarily sexual in nature. He interpreted "sexuality" broadly; he thought of it as including physical love, affectional impulses, self-love, love for parents and children, and friendship associations.

Freud advanced a number of controversial theories. He asserted that everyone, from birth on, has sexual interests. He stated that boys at an early age (around age 3) fall sexually in love with their mother and fear their father will discover this interest and then castrate them (a fear referred to as castration anxiety). Girls, on the other hand, at about the same age (age 3) fall sexually in love with their father. They discover that they do not have a penis, and

their desire to have one leads to penis envy. Girls conclude that they lost their penis at an earlier age when their mother discovered their sexual interest in their father. That is, they believe their mother castrated them because of their love for their father. Girls also experience castration anxiety, but it stems from their belief that having been castrated makes them inferior to males.

Freud's notion that sexuality was a critical part of human development initially provoked shock and outrage. Before his time, it was thought that sexual interests played only a minor role in human development. Gradually his theories came to have a liberating effect, as sexuality slowly became recognized as playing a key role in personality development. Freud's theories also led to increased communication about sexuality and stimulated scientific investigations of this topic.

Perhaps Freud's greatest contribution was this change he effected on our attitudes toward sexuality. Unfortunately, he developed a number of hypotheses that he advanced as "truths" without scientifically testing their validity. Consequently, some of Freud's specific hypotheses about sexuality have been hotly disputed and widely challenged—for example, his hypotheses involving castration anxiety in boys and castration anxiety and penis envy in girls. In recent years, a storm of criticism of Freudian theory has arisen from feminists. Feminists are particularly offended by Freud's assumption that the female is biologically inferior to the male because she lacks a penis. They ask what is so intrinsically valuable about a penis that makes it better than a clitoris, a vagina, or a pair of ovaries? Feminists argue that psychoanalytic theory is essentially a male-centered theory that has adverse effects on women as it asserts females are biologically inferior to males.

Alfred Kinsey

In 1948 Alfred C. Kinsey, an American zoologist, published *Sexual Behavior in the Human Male*, which was based on interviews with 5,300 White American men. This study investigated sexual practices and found that the actual sexual behavior of males differed substantially from the stated moral values of the time. One-third of the respondents had had at least one same-sex experience since puberty; 83% had had premarital relations; half of those who were married had had extramarital affairs; and 92% had masturbated to orgasm.[18]

The studies of pioneer sexologist Alfred Kinsey revealed the discrepancy between Americans' sexual mores and their sexual practices.

Five years later, in 1953, Kinsey published *Sexual Behavior in the Human Female*, which was based on interviews with 5,940 White American women.[19] This study showed, to some extent, that the double standard was still operating. But it also found that women were not as asexual as was commonly thought. More than half of these respondents had had premarital relations, and one-fourth of those who were married had had extramarital relations. (It should be noted that Kinsey's studies lacked racial diversity in that he studied no people of color. Therefore, any conclusions he drew can be applied to White Americans only.)

Kinsey's findings were widely publicized by the mass media. For the first time, society was con-fronted with the wide gaps that existed between sexual mores and sexual practices. Kinsey's studies may have led people to become freer in their sexual behavior or at least to feel less guilt about sexual behavior that was inconsistent with traditional sexual mores. The studies certainly challenged the belief that women were basically uninterested in sex.

William Masters and Virginia Johnson

In 1957 William Masters and Virginia Johnson began their study of the physiology of human sexual response, which culminated in the publication of their classic text *Human Sexual Response*.[20] Their contribution to the scientific understanding of human sexual response has been enormous, and their findings have generally withstood the test of others' replications.

Masters and Johnson were the first to provide accurate information about the physiology of human sexual response based on laboratory observations of people's responses rather than their personal reports. Their findings destroyed a number of myths. Freud, for example, had asserted that vaginal orgasm in women was superior to clitoral orgasm. Masters and Johnson found that the clitoris was the organ having the most nerve endings (and therefore the area of greatest pleasure) in a female's genitals. The clitoris was essentially the main structure being stimulated in both clitoral orgasm and vaginal orgasm, and therefore there were no physiological differences between these orgasms. This finding enhanced the sex lives of many women who were fruitlessly searching for the vaginal orgasm—many of whom felt that they were inadequate or that they were missing out on something. Other important findings were that men and women are able to enjoy sexual activity into advanced age and that some women have numerous orgasms in succession.

On completion of this research, Masters and Johnson began to treat people with sexual dysfunctions, such as premature ejaculation in males and failure to achieve orgasm in females. They departed radically from the prevailing thinking of the day, which viewed sexual dysfunction as a by-product of other individual or relationship problems. They identified the relationship of the two partners as the client, rather than one person or the other, and indeed required both partners to participate in the process of therapy. They did what many others had thought untenable—they dealt primarily with the sexual problem and treated people in short-term (2 weeks) therapy. Extremely successful results were achieved, and their methods and outcomes were subsequently published in *Human Sexual Inadequacy*.[21] They also demonstrated there is no evidence that relief of a sexual problem led (as Freud asserted) to the formation of a replacement problem. Most contemporary forms of sex therapy are based on Masters and Johnson's original work.

Variances Rather Than Sexual Problems

Human beings are capable of expressing their sexuality in an amazing variety of ways due to both biological determinants and learning. Everyone has some form of a sex drive, but how it is expressed is shaped by biological predispositions, rituals, acceptable role models, trial and error as to what is pleasurable and what is not, and the attitudes of others (parents, peers, teachers, and so forth). Gagnon and Henderson note that the learning of ways to express our sexuality is closely related to the process of forming our gender identity (our self-concept of maleness or femaleness):

> We assemble our sexuality beginning with gender identity, and we build upon that the activities we come to think of as fitting to ourselves. Our belief in what is correct and proper results more from our social class, religion, style of family life, and concepts of masculinity and femininity than from the specifically sexual things that we learn.[22]

One approach to studying the wide variety of sexual behaviors is the social problems approach. This approach seeks to classify as social problems any sexual behavior that differs from a norm to such a great extent that a significant number of people (or a number of significant people) feel that something should be done about it. This approach requires delineation of the code or norm of acceptability. However, there is no consensus about which sexual expressions are acceptable and which are not. In addition, as the Kinsey study showed, there is a vast difference between the purported sexual norms of society and people's actual sexual behavior.

Another shortcoming in using the social problems approach is that those acts that would be identified as social problems would then be stigmatized as "sick," "degenerate," or "perverted." During the Victorian era, our society suffered too much from the efforts of some to make value judgments about what is inap-

propriate sexual behavior. This text will not attempt to force any specific sexual code onto readers—too many other groups are still trying to do this. Instead of the term *social problems*, the term *sex variances* will be used to refer to sexual expressions that are of concern to certain segments of our society.

Definitions of acceptable and nonacceptable sexual behavior tend to change over time. Some behaviors that were once widely condemned are now generally accepted. Masturbation, for example, used to be viewed as sinful, immoral, and unhealthy but now is widely practiced and is recommended by sex therapists as a way to learn about one's sexuality. Not long ago, oral sex was considered immoral or wrong, but today many people engage in oral sex.[23]

It may be argued that laws in a society can be used to determine acceptable and unacceptable sexual expressions. Any sexual acts that are legally prohibited could therefore be identified as unacceptable. However, many of our present laws relating to sexual behaviors were enacted during the Victorian era and remain highly conservative. There is a considerable time lag between changes in laws relating to sexuality and changes in attitudes and norms about sexuality. Acts that are currently still illegal in at least some states include premarital sex, oral sex, masturbation, extramarital sex, cohabitation, and intercourse in any position other than the missionary position. Historically, severe penalties were imposed for those found guilty of "sex crimes." For example, the 17th-century Puritans made extramarital sex a crime punishable by death. Until 2003 Georgia had a state statute that specified that oral sex between consenting adults was a felony punishable by not less than 1 year or more than 20 years in jail.[24]

Laws, to some extent, are an indicator of how societies feel about certain sexual behaviors. For example, the stiff penalties for rape and child molestation suggest strong disapproval. Yet for the reasons just cited, laws cannot be used as the only measure of prevailing views about acceptable sexual behavior in a society.

Sexual Orientation

The purpose of this section is to try to provide a better understanding of people's sexual orientations, whether heterosexual, gay or lesbian, transgender, or bisexual. Also, this section will seek to provide an understanding of homophobia (the fear and hatred of gays and lesbians).

Some Definitions

When we look at sexual orientation, there are a variety of terms we need to understand. Some of these terms will be briefly defined.

Sexual Orientation

Sexual orientation is the direction of one's sexual interest toward members of the same, opposite, or both sexes. Three aspects of sexual orientation are attraction, behavior, and identity. Sexual attraction may be to partners of the same or opposite sex or to both sexes. Behavior refers to sexual activities with partners of the same or opposite sex, or with both sexes. Identity refers to one's view of oneself as heterosexual, gay or lesbian, or bisexual.

Homosexual

The sexual or erotic orientation of a person for members of the same sex is referred to as homosexuality. It should be noted that using the term homosexual to describe a gay or lesbian individual is offensive and is similar to using the "n-word" to describe African Americans. The negative connotation of the word homosexual came from two sources: some religions who are against homosexuality, and from early psychoanalysis—which stigmatized gay and lesbian relationships.[25]

Gay

The term *gay* is preferred by many people with a same-sex orientation, primarily males, in describing themselves and their sexual orientation. Gay men prefer the term *gay* instead of *homosexual* because it does not have the negative connotations frequently associated with the word *homosexual*.

The term *gay* is sometimes used to refer to both males and females who have a same-sex sexual orientation. This chapter will primarily use the term *gay* to refer to males with a same-sex sexual orientation.

Lesbian

A woman whose sexual or erotic orientation is for other women is a lesbian. Many people who are heterosexual use the term *gay* to refer to both lesbians and gay men. Many lesbians, however, have expressed concern that men are given precedence over women when the term *gay* is used by itself to refer to both genders.

Heterosexual

The sexual or erotic orientation of a person for members of the opposite sex is referred to as heterosexuality.

Bisexual

A person who is sexually attracted to members of either gender is bisexual. Many people who view themselves as being heterosexual have had same-sex experiences at some time during their lives.[26]

The policy statement of the National Association of Social Workers (NASW) on gays, lesbians, and bisexuals is as follows:

> *It is the position of NASW that same-gender sexual orientation should be afforded the same respect and rights as other-gender orientation. Discrimination and prejudice directed against any group are damaging to the social, emotional, and economic well-being of the affected group and of society as a whole. NASW is committed to advancing policies and practices that will improve the status and well-being of all lesbian, gay, and bisexual people.*[27]

Transgender Person

A person whose gender identity is the opposite of his or her biological gender. To some extent, such people tend to feel trapped in the body of the opposite gender. Another term that is sometimes used for a transgender person is transsexual. Most transgender people prefer the term transgender because the term transsexual emphasizes "sex," and gender identity involves so many more facets of an individual's personality and life circumstances.

The term *transgender* is sometimes also used to refer to a broader spectrum of people, namely those whose appearance and behaviors do not conform to the gender roles ascribed by society for people of a particular sex.[28] These include people who prefer to wear the clothing generally worn by the opposite gender and who adopt behaviors commonly exhibited by that gender. The term *transgender* can refer to a range of people, including transsexual people, transvestites, and cross-dressers.[29]

Transgender persons generally face a number of life challenges that are not experienced by heterosexual individuals. A few will be mentioned. When they fill out an application (for example, for a job) and they are asked to check "male" or "female," do they check their biological gender or their psychological gender? They encounter substantial discrimination in seeking a job. If arrested, they often encounter negative reactions from both fellow prisoners and police officers. When receiving medical exams or medical help, they may encounter discriminatory reactions from prejudiced or uninformed medical staff. When seeking to use a public bathroom, do they choose the one that is consistent with their biological sex, or their psychological gender?

Transgender people have sexual orientations ranging from heterosexual to bisexual to gay or lesbian. In the past, a person's gender role was considered to either be male or female. A more accurate perspective is that one's gender identity is on a continuum, with most people at either end of a female-to-male scale, but a significant minority exist somewhere in between.

Crossport, a non-profit social support organization serving transgender individuals, notes:

> Transgender behavior has been around since the dawn of civilization. There are records of males and females crossing over throughout history and in virtually every culture. It is simply a naturally occurring part of all societies. In many cultures such as native American and eastern countries, a transgendered person was thought to be a blessing to the family, tribe or society as they were considered to have a higher spiritual nature.[30]

Transsexual Individual

A transsexual is a person who has a persistent desire to transition to living as, and being perceived as, the sex that is consistent with his or her gender identity. Typically, this desire is driven by an extreme discomfort with his or her current sex. Transsexuals transitioning from male to female are often referred to as "MTFs." Similarly, female-to-male transsexuals are frequently referred to as "FTMs."

Transsexual transitions are complex processes. Such a transition involves the following four processes, as described by Karen Kirst-Ashman:

> First, they enter counseling to make certain that they are aware of their true feelings and that they understand the potential ramifications of changing genders. Second, they undergo a "real-life test" where they actually live and undertake their daily activities as a person of the opposite gender. Third, they receive extensive hormone treatments to align their bodies with the opposite gender as much as possible—a process that they must continue for the rest of their lives. For example, female-to-male transgender people would take male hormones to encourage facial and body hair growth, while male-to-female transgender people would take female hormones to encourage the softening of body tissue and the redistribution of body fat. The fourth step involves undergoing surgery where genitals

and other areas of the body are surgically altered to more closely resemble the opposite gender. Of course, changes are primarily cosmetic because construction of internal organs is impossible. Genital tissue is used to create a penislike organ and scrotum for female-to-male transgender people, and a vaginal canal and labia for male-to-female transgender people. Other physical alterations might include breast implants or breast removal, or decreasing the size of a biological male's Adam's apple.

In the past, male-to-female operations were more common, but today female-to-male operations are catching up in frequency. Female-to-male surgery is generally more complex. In view of the physical pain and discomfort, in addition to the high cost, many transgender people choose not to pursue surgery.[31]

LGBT

This term is often used to refer collectively to lesbians, gays, bisexuals, and transgender individuals.

Homophobia

Homophobia is the hatred or fear of gays, lesbians, and bisexuals. Homophobia sometimes leads to acts of violence, discrimination, and hostility toward LGBT individuals. Discrimination toward LGBT individuals comes in many forms. Homophobic individuals may engage in discriminatory actions at work, at school, at clubs, and in many other areas. Such discriminatory actions often stem from the erroneous perception that same-sex sexual activity is immoral. Homophobic people frequently think they are superior to LGBT individuals. Such beliefs are often reinforced by some churches and religions that maintain same-sex sexual behavior is a sin and runs counter to the will of God, as expressed in certain biblical passages.

Critical Thinking Questions

Have you made derogatory comments about gays or lesbians, or participated in telling or listening to jokes about gays and lesbians? If so, should you make changes in these areas in the future (as such jokes are a factor in perpetuating negative stereotypes)?

Surveys have found that a majority of Americans regard same-sex sexual activity as "very obscene and vulgar" and as a "curable disease."[32] Gays and lesbians are also often viewed as harmful to American life. The negative view of gay and lesbian behavior in this country is indicated by the array of derogatory slang terms for gays and lesbians. (Similar attitudes and different derogatory terms have been applied in the past to various ethnic minorities, including the Irish, Italians, African Americans, and Latinos.) Gays and lesbians have frequently been the victims of antigay hate crimes.[33] (See Case Exhibit 7.3: Causes of Homophobia.)

Such negative attitudes can have considerable psychological impact on gay and lesbian people. It can be devastating to learn that a majority of Americans consider your natural interests and behaviors to be vulgar and obscene. Some gays and lesbians therefore seek to hide their sexual orientation, and they live in constant fear of being "outed." Some believe (often correctly) that discovery will result in being fired from their job or being ostracized by friends and relatives. Tragically, some gay and lesbian youths become so despondent that they commit suicide. The suicide rate of gay and lesbian adolescents is significantly higher than that of heterosexual teenagers. This is a sad and extreme example of the ultimate costs of bigotry.

Intersex Individuals

Intersex persons are people who are born with atypical reproductive anatomies. They are sometimes called "hermaphrodites," but that term is considered pejorative. It is estimated that approximately 2% of births have some degree of intersexuality.[34] Conditions can range from not visible at birth to very visible, sometimes doctors have a difficult time assigning a sex to an intersex baby.

The birth of an intersex child has historically been considered a medical emergency that has to be fixed by surgery. Surgery has then been performed, sometimes without the full knowledge or consent of the parents, in order to make the child appear to be more male or female, dependent on the sex assignment chosen by the physician. Intersex persons may experience feelings of being transgender and may wish to transition away from the sex that was assigned to them at birth.

Androgynous Person

An androgynous individual is a person who expresses both feminine and masculine characteristics or features. Other people are apt to find it difficult to decide whether to refer to that person as female or male. An androgynous person may or may not identify as transgender, and may or may not have a desire to transition to the opposite gender.

Cross-Dresser

This term generally refers to men who wear clothing and accessories designed for women (in their private lives). Cross-dressers are sometimes called "transvestites," but that term is considered pejorative. Many cross-dressers cite stress relief, comfort, or being able to express their feminine side as reasons for their cross-dressing. Persons who cross-dress are not likely to cross-dress at work for fear of discrimination or harassment. Many cross-dressers are heterosexual, married men who are comfortable with being male. Unlike transsexuals, cross-dressers generally do not seek to change their physical characteristics, nor do they desire to live full-time as females.

Women who are more comfortable wearing men's clothing are more accepted in American society, and therefore they generally are not referred to as cross-dressers.

Drag Queen/King

A drag queen is a male who impersonates a female for entertainment purposes (typically singing and dancing to music). A drag king is a female who impersonates a male. Persons who "do drag" may or may not consider themselves transgender. For some, it is simply a performance; for others, it is a way to express their transgender inclinations.

Hate Crime

A hate crime is an unlawful act of violence motivated by prejudice or bias (see Case Example 7.1: The Murder of Matthew Shepard). Hate-crime laws call for tougher sentencing when prosecutors can prove that the crime committed was motivated by prejudice or bias. Although state laws vary, current statutes permit federal prosecution of hate crimes committed on the basis of a person's protected characteristics of race, religion, ethnicity, gender, sexual orientation, nationality, gender identity, class, social status, political affiliation, age, and disability. On October 28, 2009, President Obama signed the Matthew Shepard (see Case Example 7.1) and James Byrd, Jr. Hate Crimes Prevention Act, which expanded existing U.S. federal hate-crime laws to apply to crimes motivated by a victim's actual or perceived gender, gender identity, sexual orientation, or disability.

James Byrd, Jr. was an African American who was murdered by three White men, alleged to be White supremacists, during a racially motivated crime in Jasper, Texas, on June 7, 1998. Byrd was dragged for about 3 miles behind a pickup truck that swerved from side to side, after his killers wrapped a logging chain around his ankles. Byrd was killed when his body hit the edge of a culvert, severing his head and right arm. The three perpetrators were found guilty of murder; one was executed, a second is on death row, and a third was given a life sentence.

Myths and Facts about Gays and Lesbians

There are several erroneous myths about gays and lesbians:

Myth 1: People are either homosexual or heterosexual.

Fact: Alfred Kinsey found that being gay or lesbian and heterosexuality are not mutually exclusive categories. Most people have had sexual thoughts, feelings, and fantasies about members of the same sex as well as about members of the opposite sex. Kinsey proposed a seven-point rating scale to categorize sexuality, with exclusive heterosexuality at one end and exclusive same-sex sexual orientation at the other (Case Exhibit 7.4). Kinsey noted:

The world is not divided into sheep and goats.... Only the human mind invents categories and tries to force facts into pigeonholes. The living world is a continuum in each and every one of its aspects. The sooner we learn this concerning human sexual behavior, the sooner we will reach a sound understanding of the realities of sex.[35]

Myth 2: Same-sex sexual behavior is universally disapproved of in all cultures.

Fact: Some cultures accept, and even encourage, same-sex sexual behavior. A young male in ancient Greece was sometimes given a boy slave who served as a sexual partner until the boy was old enough to marry a woman. It was also common for older married men to form a same-sex relationship with a young boy. Today all males among the Siwans of North Africa are expected to engage in same-sex sexual relationships throughout their lives.[36] Among the Aranda of central Australia, there are relationships between young boys and unmarried men, with these liaisons generally ending at marriage.[37]

Myth 3: Gay men are generally "effeminate," and lesbians are generally "masculine." The stereotype is that gay men are limp-wristed, talk with a lisp, and have a "swishy" walk; lesbians are believed to have short hair and to wear clothes that are normally worn by males.

Critical Thinking Question

Have you had fantasies about members of the same sex or had sexual contact with someone of the same sex?

Fact: Most gays and lesbians are indistinguishable in appearance and mannerisms from heterosexuals.[38] This myth probably comes from confusing same-sex sexual behavior with transvestism —wearing the clothing of the opposite gender for sexual arousal. Transvestism and same-sex attraction are different: Most transvestites are heterosexual.[39] Interestingly, whereas our culture erroneously associates gay men with effeminacy, the ancient Greeks and Romans associated same-sex attraction with aggressive masculinity (as among the Spartan warriors). Hyde notes:

The belief that gay men are feminine and that lesbians are masculine represents a confusion of two important concepts: gender identity (sense of maleness or femaleness) and sexual orientation (heterosexual or homosexual). The gay person differs from the majority in who the erotic and emotional partner is, but the gay person does not typically differ from the majority in gender identity. That is the gay man chooses a partner of the same gender, but his identity is quite definitely masculine. He thinks of himself as male and has no desire to be a female. The same holds true for the lesbian; although her erotic and emotional orientation is toward other women, she is quite definitely a woman and typically has no desire to be a man.[40]

Myth 4: Gays and lesbians are "sick" and different in personality characteristics from heterosexuals.

Fact: Clinical projective tests do not reliably distinguish between gays or lesbians and heterosexuals. Studies of gays or lesbians and heterosexuals have found no differences between the two groups in personality traits or in general

CASE EXHIBIT 7.3

Causes of Homophobia

Bigotry has been in existence in the United States ever since Christopher Columbus first landed in 1492. There have been many victims—Native Americans, women, members of some religious groups, African Americans, Latinos, and many others. It is no longer acceptable (for the most part) for people to be overtly anti-Semitic, racist, or sexist, or to express negative feelings about persons with a disability. The one bigotry that remains acceptable in large portions of the American society is bigotry against gays and lesbians.

Homophobia is an irrational fear of gays and lesbians; most homophobic people are "homophobic" because of fixed negative attitudes and prejudiced behaviors toward gays and lesbians. Interestingly, same-sex sexual behavior was admired in some past cultures and is fully accepted in some cultures today. Why are there so many homophobic people in our society? Homophobic attitudes are learned; they are certainly not inherited. How are such attitudes learned?

There are several roots of homophobia in our society. Some religions are fundamentally a part of the problem; the religions that instill homophobic attitudes are those that view same-sex sexual behavior as "evil" or a "sin" and that assert that people who engage in same-sex activities are likely (unless they repent) to be sent by God to eternal damnation. Some homophobic people have erroneously assumed that the high rate of AIDS/HIV infection among gay men provides "evidence" that same-sex sexual behavior is against God's wishes and is a way for God to punish gay people.

Some studies confirm the theory that some homophobic people use hostility and violence against gays and lesbians to reassure themselves about their own sexuality.[a] If one feels insecure about one's own sexuality (as many adolescents do), one way of reassuring oneself is by verbally or physically attacking gays and lesbians.

The greatest portion of anti-homosexual bias, psychologists say, arises from a combination of fear and self-righteousness.[b]

Homophobic persons frequently perceive gays and lesbians "as a proxy for all that is evil," according to Gregory Herek, a psychologist who has researched homophobia. "Such people see hating gay men and lesbians as a litmus test for being a moral person."[c] Another researcher, Bob Altemeyer, found that those with the strongest feelings of hostility toward gays and lesbians often fear that the world and society are in jeopardy. "They see homosexuality as a sign that society is disintegrating and as a threat to their sense of morality," said Altemeyer in an interview with the New York Times. "Their self-righteousness makes them feel they are acting morally when they attack homosexuals."[d]

Once a person has an antigay bias, that bias is difficult to change. Despite the fact that gays and lesbians are not prone to child molesting, many homophobic people continue to believe that gay men are child molesters. Furthermore, according to Herek, "once parents perceive a threat to their children, their emotionality makes them prone to simplistic thinking. It is such emotionality that makes anti-gay stereotypes so hard to change."[e]

Furthermore, a study in stereotyping showed that when homophobic people encounter gays and lesbians, they have a tendency to remember primarily the negative details that support their prejudice.[f] As one becomes more convinced that gays and lesbians are "evil" and a "threat," one is apt to take that next step by engaging in discrimination or violence against gays and lesbians.[g]

[a]Daniel Goleman, "Studies Discover Clues to the Roots of Homophobia," New York Times, July 10, 1990.
[b]Ibid.
[c]Quoted in Goleman, "Studies Discover Clues to the Roots of Homophobia," p. C11.
[d]Ibid.
[e]Ibid.
[f]Daniel Goleman, "Studies Discover Clues to the Roots of Homophobia."
[g]Ibid.

adjustment.[41] The only difference is their sexual orientation.

Homosexuality was listed as a mental disorder by the American Psychiatric Association until 1973. For a number of years preceding 1973, gays and lesbians demonstrated at psychiatric conventions, demanding that same-sex sexual orientation no longer be considered a mental disorder. In 1973, after several years of heated controversy, the board of trustees of the American Psychiatric Association voted to strike homosexuality from its official list of mental diseases. Thomas Szasz (a psychiatrist) asserted around this time that psychiatrists and others

who labeled same-sex sexual orientation an illness were merely taking the place of the church in identifying gays and lesbians and punishing them for their sexual behavior.[42]

Myth 5: One partner in a homosexual liaison generally plays the "active" or masculine role in sexual activity and the other plays the "passive" or feminine role.

Fact: Most gays and lesbians play both roles and (similar to heterosexuals) experiment with a variety of arousal techniques. There is no single form of same-sex sexual expression or identity. In reality there is as wide a divergence among gays and lesbians as among heterosexuals.

CASE EXHIBIT 7.4

The Continuum of Sexuality According to Kinsey

1	2	3	4	5	6	7
Exclusively heterosexual	Heterosexual with incidental same-sex experience	Heterosexual with substantial same-sex experience	Equal heterosexual and same-sex experience	Same-sex with substantial heterosexual experience	Same-sex with incidental heterosexual experience	Exclusively same-sex

SOURCE: Adapted from Alfred C. Kinsey et al., *Sexual Behavior in the Human Male* (Philadelphia: Saunders, 1948), p. 638.

Some gays and lesbians are married to someone of the opposite sex and are genuinely bisexual, enjoying the sex act with either male or female partners. Most gays and lesbians who are married to someone of the opposite sex are more comfortable in same-sex relationships but are married for the sake of domestic stability, companionship, and respectability. Some gays and lesbians candidly acknowledge their sexual orientation and live their same-sex sexual activity openly. Others are not willing to "come out" (publicly acknowledge their sexual orientation) because they fear they may then be discriminated against. Some gays and lesbians refuse to view themselves as being same-sex oriented primarily from abhorrence at being identified with a socially outcast minority.

The question is sometimes asked: "What do gays and lesbians do in bed?" Most of their activities are similar to those in which heterosexuals engage. Foreplay generally includes kissing, hugging, and petting. Gay men may engage in mutual masturbation, oral–genital sex, interfemoral intercourse (in which one man's penis moves between the thighs of the other), and anal intercourse. Lesbians may engage in mutual masturbation, oral–genital sex, and more infrequently, tribadism (one partner lying on top of the other and making thrusting movements so that both receive genital stimulation); a rarer practice among lesbians is the use of a dildo by one female to stimulate the other.

Myth 6: Gay men primarily seek out young boys.

Fact: Gay men are no more attracted to children than are heterosexuals, and same-sex child molesting is less common than its heterosexual counterpart. Most child molesting is done by heterosexual men and involves young girls.

Strangely, people who worry that gay male teachers will try to seduce young boys in a school do not seem to worry that heterosexual male teachers will try to seduce young girls—and the latter occurs much more frequently.[43]

Myth 7: Gays and lesbians are to blame for AIDS, which is a punishment from God for their behavior.

Fact: Although gay males are a high-risk group for contracting the AIDS virus in our society, very few cases have been reported among lesbians.[44] (Gay men are at high risk for acquiring AIDS because of the transfer of body fluids that occurs during anal intercourse.) AIDS is a life-threatening disease not only for gay men but also for heterosexuals. The growth in the spread of AIDS is currently fastest among heterosexuals.[45] Gays and lesbians are not the cause of AIDS. Blaming this deadly disease on the group that, in the United States, has suffered and died most disproportionately from it is a classic and regrettable case of blaming the victims. Although it is true that the largest single risk group of people with AIDS in the United States is gay men, it is ludicrous to assume they caused this health crisis. AIDS is caused by a virus. It is even more ludicrous to assert that gay men would want to deliver the disease on the world after first spreading it among themselves. Quite to the contrary, the gay male community in the United States has been in the forefront of educating people about behavior that minimizes the transmission of the disease. Gay men have radically altered their sexual behavior patterns, as evidenced by a substantial drop in the rate of transmission of this disease among this group in the past two decades. (Expanded material on AIDS is presented in Chapter 15.)

CASE EXAMPLE 7.1

Hate Crime: The Murder of Matthew Shepard

Matthew Shepard was a gay University of Wyoming freshman. He died in the early morning of October 12, 1998, from severe injuries due to a brutal beating and torture in Laramie, Wyoming. Six days earlier, on October 6, Matthew Shepard had been found tied to a fence, savagely beaten, and comatose. Two men, Aaron McKinney and Russell Henderson, both 21 years old and high school dropouts, were convicted of the murder. The two men had met Mr. Shepard in a bar and led him to believe that they, too, were gay. They lured him from the bar to ride in their pickup truck. In the truck they began beating him with a revolver. They then got out and tied him to a fence, beat him more, and left him for dead. The motive was generally believed to be an effort to torture and rob someone who was gay.

Studies show that gays, lesbians, and bisexuals have substantially higher rates than heterosexuals of the following: being assaulted with a weapon, being physically assaulted, experiencing vandalism or other property crimes, being threatened with violence, and being verbally harassed because of their sexual orientation.

SOURCE: http://www.mathewshepard.org.

Critical Thinking Question

Do you have judgmental tapes in your head about LGBT people?

Incidence of Gay and Lesbian Orientation

Determining the extent of same-sex sexual activity is difficult. First, there are definitional problems because most people are not exclusively heterosexual or same-sex oriented. Second, because of the stigma attached to same-sex sexual behavior, some people are reluctant to acknowledge homosexual thoughts, feelings, or acts.

Kinsey found that 4% of White males and 2% of White females were exclusively same-sex oriented— that is, never had sex with someone of the opposite sex. He further estimated that 37% of American males have had one or more same-sex experiences to orgasm and that 10% of American males have long periods of more or less exclusive same-sex oriented.[46] Other research has resulted in somewhat lower estimates.[47] After reviewing several studies, Janet S. Hyde and John D. DeLamater conclude:

How many people are homosexual and how many are heterosexual?—is complex. Probably about 90 percent of men and 90 percent of women are exclusively heterosexual. About 10 percent of men and women have had at least one same-gender sexual experience in adulthood. About 2 percent of men and 1 percent of women are exclusively homosexual.[48]

Causes of Sexual Orientation

People are often curious about the causes of same-sex sexual orientation. Why are some people erotically attracted to members of the same gender and others to members of the other gender? Social, behavioral, and biological scientists have examined and argued this question for decades. Let's see what they have learned.

First, you cannot study the question of why one becomes gay or lesbian without studying the larger question of what determines sexual object choice for anyone, heterosexual or gay/lesbian. Why do we get aroused by a woman, or a woman with particular attributes, or a man of a certain body type? Is this something we've learned? Are we born with a "script" that determines our sexual object choice?

Many researchers and theoreticians have advanced hypotheses in an effort to explain this complex and important question. Some believe that the biology of an individual determines heterosexuality or same-sex orientation. Some studies have shown chemical differences between the two groups, but it is impossible to determine causation from the results of these studies. In other words, are the chemical differences between people responsible for this behavior, or does their behavior somehow alter their body chemistry?

Other theorists posit that childhood experiences determine heterosexuality or same-sex orientation. Here we have the causation question again. If we determined that a certain child had more sex play with a child of the same gender and grew to be gay or lesbian in adult life, can we say that this sex play led to same-sex sexual orientation? Perhaps the increased sex play grew out of an inborn desire and erotic potential toward gratification from such play. That is, the behavior grew out of a predisposition toward same-sex sexual orientation; the predisposition did not grow out of the behavior.

The most comprehensive study of this question to date was undertaken by researchers at the Alfred C. Kinsey Institute for Sex Research.[49] The researchers, Alan P. Bell, Martin S. Weinberg, and Sue Kiefer Hammersmith, studied 979 gays and lesbians and 477 heterosexual men and women, gathering a large amount of information about their lives in an effort to determine critical and statistically significant differences between these two groups. They analyzed their data using a method called "path analysis," which enabled them to examine a large number of independent variables (such as parental traits, parent and sibling relationships, and gender conformity) to determine *causation* of sexual orientation and not merely association between variables. Their significant findings were as follows: (a) By the time boys and girls reach adolescence, their sexual orientation is likely to be determined, even though they may not yet have become sexually very active. (b) The gays and lesbians in the study were not particularly lacking in heterosexual experiences during their childhood and adolescent years. They were distinguished from their heterosexual counterparts, however, in finding such experiences ungratifying. (c) Among both the men and women in the study, there was a powerful link between gender nonconformity and the development of same-sex sexual orientation. (Gender nonconformity refers to children who prefer engaging in activities generally associated in this culture with the other gender—for example, boys playing with dolls.)

What do these findings suggest? First, they show that sexual orientation is established early in life, perhaps long before adolescence. Although every person has the potential to behave sexually in the manner he or she chooses, one's true sexual orientation may be set before birth or at a very early age and then no longer be influenced by the environment. Many same-sex oriented people behave as if they are heterosexual in this society because there are so many sanctions against being gay or lesbian. However, their preferred sexual partner, in the absence of these negative sanctions, would be someone of the same gender. Human beings certainly have the ability to respond sexually to people who are not their most preferred sexual partner, but to do so requires going against the current of their innermost inclinations. We can freely choose various behaviors; we cannot freely choose who or what "turns us on." The question of what causes a person's sexual orientation to be set (either as gay/lesbian, bisexual, or heterosexual) before birth or at a very early age has not yet been answered. (It appears that some people are naturally heterosexual in orientation and others are naturally gay/lesbian, just as some people are naturally left-handed and others are naturally right-handed.)

The possibility that sexual orientation is more a matter of nature than of nurture got a boost in a 1991 study that reported differences in the brains of gay men and heterosexual men. The research focused on the hypothalamus, the region of the brain thought to control sexual behavior. The results were striking. Certain groups of nerve cells in the hypothalamus were more than two times larger in heterosexual men than in gay men. The hypothalamus of a gay man appears to be closer in structure to that of a heterosexual woman than to that of a heterosexual man.[50]

Studies of separated twins were conducted in 1991 and 1993 at the Boston University School of Medicine. It was found that there was greater likelihood of both twins in a pair being gay/lesbian if they were identical (shared the same genes) than if they were fraternal (did not share the same genes).[51] Another study in 1993 found additional evidence that same-sex sexual orientation is genetically determined. Evidence of a "gay gene" was found when researchers studied the X chromosome in 40 pairs of gay brothers. In this group, 33 shared identical genetic markers in the tip of the X chromosome, suggesting with more than 99% certainty that the sexual orientation of the men was genetically influenced.[52]

After reviewing the studies conducted on the origins of sexual orientation, Hyde and DeLamater conclude the causes of sexual orientation are as yet unknown:

> *We have examined a number of theories of sexual orientation and the evidence supporting or refuting them. What is the bottom line? Which theory is correct? The answer is, We don't know yet, we do not know what causes sexual orientation.*[53]

Life Experiences of Gays and Lesbians

In the past, a number of states enacted laws banning consensual sex between adults of the same sex. A 2003 U.S. Supreme Court decision struck down such laws. The ruling enshrines for the first time a broad constitutional right to sexual privacy. As recently as 1960, every state had a sodomy law. Sodomy laws specified that certain intimate sexual acts between two adults of the same sex are illegal and can be prosecuted. Sodomy was defined as copulation with a member of the same sex or with an animal and included anal and oral copulation. Gradually, since 1960, these laws were slowly being repealed by court decisions, or blocked by state courts. Gay rights groups hailed the 2003 Supreme Court decision as "historic." The decision, involving *Lawrence et al. v. Texas*, resulted in sodomy laws in Texas and other states being declared unconstitutional because they violated people's right to privacy.

The Gay Liberation Movement has been seeking to change negative attitudes and end discriminatory acts toward gays and lesbians, yet many people still view gays and lesbians as psychologically "sick"—as having a form of mental illness. (Until 1973 the American Psychiatric Association defined homosexuality as a mental illness.)

The Gay Liberation Movement is composed of groups such as the Gay Liberation Front, the National Gay Task Force, and the International Union of Gay Athletes. This social movement contends (along with many social scientists) that same-sex sexual orientation is not a perversion or sickness but is simply a different lifestyle. Their arguments have met with mixed reactions. Some states have repealed anti-gay/lesbian legislation, and several cities have passed gay civil rights ordinances that prevent discrimination against police officers, teachers, and other city employees who are gay or lesbian. Other cities and states have rejected bills that sought to ban discrimination against gays and lesbians.

When Bill Clinton was running for president in 1992, he promised to reverse the 50-year-old policy aimed at keeping gays and lesbians out of the military. After his election, he tried in 1993 to lift the ban by executive order but encountered strong resistance in the Pentagon and Congress. After months of hearings and negotiations, Congress passed and Clinton signed a bill that has been referred to as "Don't ask, don't tell." New recruits to the military no longer could be asked by military personnel about their sexual orientation; however, anyone who openly engaged in same-gender sexual conduct could be discharged. As part of the policy, the Pentagon promised to end purges of military personnel who keep their same-sex sexual behavior private. (Many gay activists considered this policy as onerous as the original prohibition.)

From 1993 to 2011, gay rights organizations campaigned for banning the "Don't ask" legislation. In 2011, President Obama signed into law the repeal of the ban on open service for gays and lesbians in the military known as "Don't ask, don't tell." This repeal means the military can no longer prevent gays and lesbians from serving openly in its ranks.

In 1996 Congress passed, and President Clinton signed, the Defense of Marriage Act, which allows states to refuse to recognize gay marriages performed in other states. The Defense of Marriage Act prevents one partner in a same-sex sexual relationship from claiming Social Security, veteran's, or other federal benefits in the event of the other's death or disability. It also bars gay and lesbian couples from filing joint income-tax returns, even if they live under the same roof and share everything else.

Courts are increasingly hearing cases involving gay rights issues. Some judges are supportive of gay rights issues, whereas others are not, as illustrated by the following two conflicting decisions (both of which were made in 1993). A federal judge in Virginia denied a lesbian mother custody of her son solely because of her sexuality; he awarded custody to the boy's grandmother. However, in Boston a state supreme court ruling made two lesbians the first gay couple to win approval to adopt a child in Massachusetts.[54]

In most places, gay and lesbian people may be denied private employment because of their sexual orientation. Federal civil service regulations forbid such discrimination in public employment.

The NASW in *Social Work Speaks* summarizes additional forms of discrimination for lesbian, gay, and bisexual people:

Despite the successes of the gay rights movement, there continues to be discrimination against LGB people. Thirty-five states do not protect LGB people from discrimination in employment, education, credit, housing, and other public accommodation. Six states do not allow lesbians or gay men to adopt (Florida and Mississippi) or foster children (North Dakota, Utah, Arkansas, and Oklahoma).... Thirteen states passed state constitutional amendments that prohibit same-sex marriage (although the courts in Louisiana struck down its amendment). Alabama, Arizona, Mississippi, South Carolina, and Texas prohibit any discussion of homosexuality in school or "mandate that any references to homosexuality be exclusively negative."[55]

America's schools are not safe places for LGBT youth. More than two-thirds (69%) of known gay and lesbian students have been physically, verbally, or sexually harassed at school.[56] Homophobic language (for example, being called "faggot" or "dyke") is pervasive in U.S. schools. Homophobic language is used not only by students but also by some faculty and school staff.[57] Known gay and lesbian students are sometimes punched, kicked, injured with a weapon, or pushed because of their sexual orientation.

Given the harsh treatment of LGBT youth in school settings, it is not surprising that 40% of LGBT youth report their schoolwork being negatively affected by conflicts over sexual orientation.[58] Some skip some school days because they feel it is unsafe for them to attend. More than one-fourth of gay and lesbian youth drop out of school—usually to escape the violence, harassment, and alienation they endure there.[59] LGBT youth reporting high levels of victimization at school also have higher levels of suicidal thoughts, suicide attempts, and sexual risk behaviors than heterosexual peers reporting high levels of at-school victimization.[60]

Antigay hate is also common among college students. Many young adults believe that antigay harassment and violence is socially acceptable.[61]

Because of negative attitudes and discriminatory acts, some gays and lesbians go to extensive lengths to hide their sexual behavior. They fear discrimination and even loss of employment. They also fear the stigma and embarrassment that they and their families would receive if they "came out." Some gays and lesbians marry someone of the opposite sex and may even hide their same-sex encounters from their spouses. Leading a double life, with fear of criminal penalties if one's sexual orientation were discovered, is stress producing.

Many larger cities now have gay/lesbian communities that provide an escape from the pressures of leading such a double life. These communities may offer recreational and leisure-time activities and may serve to socialize new entrants into the gay/lesbian subculture. They are often located in a certain geographical area of a city and generally have shops, restaurants, and hotels that are owned and patronized primarily by gay and lesbian customers. The "gay bars" are perhaps the most visible establishments in such communities. Gay bars provide opportunities for their clientele to drink, socialize, and find a sexual partner or a lover. Some gay bars look just like any other bar from the outside, while others have names (such as The Gay Closet) that indicate the clientele.

Critical Thinking Question
If a LGBT person in a school was being victimized, would you seek to intervene in that person's defense?

Unlike other minority-group members, gay/lesbian youths grow up as minorities within their own families. People of color, for example, are socialized—trained—by their parents, older siblings, and relatives about functioning in a society that is likely to discriminate against them. Gay and lesbian youths have no such training ground, as most are raised in heterosexual families. This makes gay/lesbian-identified institutions (the most visible and approachable of which is the gay bar) very important in the life of a gay or lesbian young adult. Most gays and lesbians patronize these gay bars for only a brief period (primarily while they are formulating their gay/lesbian identity). After this phase, they generally prefer social contact with other gays and lesbians in environments where the focus is not on alcohol and superficial interactions.

There is a wide variation in the lifestyles of gays and lesbians, as is true for heterosexuals. In addition, gays and lesbians tend to differ somewhat in their sexual attitudes and practices. Lesbians are more likely to equate sex with love. They tend to engage in sex with fewer partners than do gay men. Their relationships tend to last longer and to be based more on love and affection. Lesbians may be less likely to acknowledge their sexual orientation publicly or to participate in a gay/lesbian community.[62]

Lesbians are better able to conceal their sexual orientation because the public is less suspicious of two women living together or otherwise being close to each other. Most lesbians have had sexual relationships with men.[63]

A bisexual person's sexual orientation is toward both women and men. The proponents of bisexuality argue that it has the advantage of allowing more variety in one's sexual and human relationships than either exclusive same-sex relationships or exclusive heterosexuality. On the other hand, some heterosexuals may devalue those who are known to be bisexual. In addition, people who are bisexual may be

The specter of AIDS has had a tremendous impact on gay/lesbian communities, particularly on gay men. Gay/lesbian communities have been active in encouraging federal and state governments to (a) recognize the dangers of AIDS, (b) provide research funds to develop treatments for those who are infected with the AIDS virus, and (c) provide research funds to develop approaches to preventing the spread of AIDS.[66] Gay/lesbian communities have also been advocates of safer sex practices, and many gay men have made responsible and dramatic changes in their sexual practices. Gay/lesbian communities have also developed support systems for people with AIDS.

Coming Out

There are significant variations in the gay experience, depending on whether or not one is "out of the closet." Covert ("in the closet") gays and lesbians may spend only a few hours a month engaging in secret same-sex behavior. They seek to keep their sexual orientation secret. They may even be heterosexually married, have children, and be a respected career person in a heterosexual community. The overt ("out of the closet") gay or lesbian may live almost entirely in a gay/lesbian community (particularly if he or she lives in a large city such as San Francisco or New York that has a large gay/lesbian subculture). In such an area, the gay or lesbian person may have relatively few contacts with heterosexuals.

There are varying degrees of being out of the closet. Some gays and lesbians are out with trusted friends, but not with casual acquaintances. Some gays and lesbians are out with trusted friends and relatives but not at work. Some are out with everyone. Many factors enter into who gays and lesbians choose to be out to, including community values, social class, occupation, geographic area, personality, family values, marital status, and so on.

The process of coming out is a major psychological event. It involves acknowledging to oneself, and then to others, that one is gay or lesbian. The person is psychologically vulnerable during this time period. Hyde and DeLamater describe the usual experiences of someone who comes out:

Following the period of coming out, there is a stage of exploration, in which the person experiments with the new sexual identity; the person makes contact with the lesbian and gay community and practices new interpersonal skills. Typically, next comes a stage of forming first relationships. These relationships are often short-lived and characterized by

Despite the negative and even hostile view many Americans still have of same-sex sexual orientation, more gay men and women now openly acknowledge their sexual orientation.

viewed with suspicion or downright hostility by the gay/lesbian community.[64] Some gays and lesbians view bisexuals as "fence-sitters" who betray the gay/lesbian movement as they can pretend to be "straight" when it is convenient and gay (or lesbian) when it is convenient.[65]

There is a diversity of bisexuals. Some bisexuals (referred to as 50:50 bisexuals) have equal preferences for men and for women. Some bisexuals have a preference for one gender but are accepting of sex with the other. Some are sequentially bisexual; they have only one lover at a time, sometimes a man and sometimes a woman. Some are simultaneously bisexual; they have both a male and a female lover at the same time. Some are transitory bisexuals who are passing through a bisexual phase on the way to becoming exclusively heterosexual or same-sex oriented. Others are enduring bisexuals who maintain their bisexual preferences throughout their life span.

CASE EXHIBIT 7.5

Same-Sex Marriages

In 1989, the city of San Francisco became the first government in the United States to grant marriage licenses to same-sex couples. At the time of this writing, same-sex marriages are legal in eight states in the United States: Massachusetts, Maryland, Connecticut, Iowa, Maine, New Hampshire, Washington state, and Vermont. With the passage of Proposition 8, gay marriage is no longer an option in California.

Some states have passed a law allowing gay and lesbian people to form "civil unions" that provide essentially the same rights and responsibilities as those inherent in a heterosexual marriage. Such rights include child custody, probate court, workers' compensation, and family leave benefits. However, these rights are not transferable to other states if the couple moves. Other states (such as Connecticut, New Jersey, and New Hampshire) have also approved civil unions.

On the state level, several states approved constitutional amendments codifying marriage as an exclusively heterosexual institution. Gay rights activists in some of these states have filed challenges to these new amendments. The battle over whether to recognize same-sex marriages is likely to continue for years.

Internationally, legal recognition of same-sex relationships has become more widespread. In 2001 the Netherlands became the first country in the world to offer full, legal marriage to same-sex couples. In recent years, Belgium, Spain, Sweden, Norway, South Africa, and Canada have legalized gay marriages. Other countries recognize same-sex registered partnerships, which are federally recognized relationships that convey most but not all of the rights of marriage. Some of the countries that provide this recognition are Australia, Brazil, Denmark, Finland, France, Germany, Greenland, Great Britain, Hungary, Israel, Italy, New Zealand, and Portugal.

Mooney, Knox, and Schacht summarize the arguments for recognizing same-sex marriages.

Advocates of same-sex marriage argue that banning same-sex marriages or refusing to recognize same-sex marriages granted in other states is a violation of civil rights that denies same-sex couples the many legal and financial benefits that are granted to heterosexual married couples. For example, married couples have the right to inherit from a spouse who dies without a will; to avoid inheritance taxes between spouses; to make crucial medical decisions for a partner and take family leave to care for a partner in the

AP Photo/Bas Czerwinski

(continued)

event of the partner's critical injury or illness; to receive Social Security survivor benefits; and to include a partner in his or her health insurance coverage. Other rights bestowed on married (or once-married) partners include assumption of spouse's pension, bereavement leave, burial determination, domestic violence protection, reduced-rate memberships, divorce protections (such as equitable division of assets and visitation of partner's children), automatic housing lease transfer, and immunity from testifying against a spouse.[a]

Opponents of same-sex marriages do not want to legitimize same-sex sexual relationships as a socially acceptable lifestyle. Those who view same-sex sexual relationships as sick, unnatural, or immoral do not want their children to learn that a same-gender sexual relationship is an accepted and "normal" lifestyle. The most common argument against same-sex marriage is the assertion that it undermines the stability and integrity of the heterosexual family.

[a]Linda A. Mooney, David Knox, and Caroline Schacht, *Understanding Social Problems*, 6th ed. (Belmont, CA: Wadsworth/Cengage Learning, 2009), pp. 455–456.

---

jealousy and turbulence, much like many heterosexual dating relationships. Finally, there is the integration stage, in which the person becomes a fully functioning member of society and is capable of maintaining a long-term, committed relationship.[67]

Prior to coming out, the person needs to first conclude that she or he is lesbian or gay in sexual orientation. According to Cass, this identity development process occurs in six phases:

1. *Identity confusion:* The person has had a history of assuming a heterosexual identity, as heterosexuality is the expectation in our society. As same-sex attractions or behaviors occur, the person becomes confused as to "who am I?"

2. *Identity comparison:* The person now ponders whether "I *may* be gay/lesbian." There are apt to be questions of personal worth as the comfortable heterosexual identity is fading away.

3. *Identity tolerance:* The person comes to believe that "I probably am gay/lesbian in sexual orientation." The person now seeks out same-sex persons to have intimate relationships with and also forms contact with the gay subculture, hoping for affirmation. The nature and quality of these initial contacts are critical to the extent of psychological trauma that is experienced in coming out.

4. *Identity acceptance:* The person now concludes, "I am gay/lesbian," and accepts (rather than tolerates) this identity.

5. *Identity pride:* The person dichotomizes people into gays and lesbians (who are good and important people) and heterosexuals (who are apt to be intolerant and discriminating). A strong identification with the gay/lesbian community occurs, and the person increasingly comes out of the closet to others.

6. *Identity synthesis:* The person no longer believes gays and lesbians are "us," and heterosexuals are "them." The person recognizes that there are some good and supportive heterosexuals. In this final stage, the person is also able to synthesize public and private sexual identities.[68]

The Boston Women's Health Book Collective has characterized the process of coming out as involving four stages:

1. *Coming out to oneself:* This stage involves thinking about oneself as a person who is lesbian or gay, instead of as one who is heterosexual. During this stage, individuals experiment with the label of being gay or lesbian. They contemplate what such a label will mean concerning their life. The individual ponders advantages and disadvantages of being openly gay/lesbian. An advantage is the decreased fear and anxiety; he or she could stop pretending to be someone (a heterosexual person) that he or she is not. Another advantage is the opportunity for social activities and support systems with other lesbian and gay people. Disadvantages might include the negative reactions of some friends and family members and future discrimination in employment and social settings.

2. *Meeting and getting to know other lesbian and gay people:* This stage involves searching for a support system, a community, to identify with and belong to. At this stage the person begins forming new friendships and seeks to associate with other gays and lesbians who understand what it is like to come out and who are easy to talk to about it.

3. *Telling friends and relatives:* The advantages and disadvantages of coming out (and who to come out to) need to be assessed. It is not necessary to tell all close friends, relatives, and colleagues if the person

concludes the reactions of some homophobic people may be highly negative. For example, a senior in college may have a parent who is highly homophobic and is apt to react by no longer providing financial support for attending college. In such a situation, the senior may decide to wait to graduate before informing his or her parents.

4. *Publicly acknowledging that one is lesbian or gay:* Again, the person needs, at this phase, to assess the positive and negative consequences of coming out. Many gays and lesbians choose not to come out of the closet fully, due to the criticism, rejection, or discrimination that they may face. Some authorities on this issue recommend that each person consider what is best for him or her.[69] In opposition to this view, other authorities assert that one cannot be free to be oneself without honesty and openness to everyone.[70]

Critical Thinking Question

Do you believe same-sex marriages should be legally recognized?

Current Issues for Gays and Lesbians

As mentioned earlier, a major issue is whether civil rights laws should be enacted to protect gays and lesbians from discrimination in housing, employment, military service, and other areas. Gays and lesbians argue that they are refused jobs in teaching, in the military, and in many private corporations. They also are commonly the targets of blackmailers who threaten to reveal their sexual orientation. They assert that legal protection for gay rights will not turn heterosexuals into gays and lesbians. Having long been the victims of abuse and exploitation, they now want the same protection that other minorities receive.[71]

Those who oppose civil rights laws for gays and lesbians assert that gays are not like other minority groups who are discriminated against based on physical characteristics (African Americans, women, people with a disability). They believe that gays and lesbians choose their sexual orientation, which can be changed if they so desire. A number of other objections are also given by opponents: Legislation to protect gay rights would indicate approval of same-sex sexual behavior, which in fact they consider unnatural. Permitting gays and lesbians to teach in school would unwisely expose children to gay atti-

tudes and activities and would probably lead to increased same-sex experimentation. In addition, if sanctions were relaxed, same-sex sexual behavior would flourish, the stability of the family would be threatened, birthrates would drop drastically, and society would be severely damaged. (This is, of course, highly unlikely; with or without social sanctions, gays and lesbians constitute only a small minority of any society. And social support is unlikely to significantly increase behavior so basic to one's being as sexual orientation.)

As can be seen, arguments on both sides of this issue are intense. And there are other concerns as well. As stated in Case Exhibit 7.5, some states are now legally recognizing same-sex marriages. Proponents of gay/lesbian marriages assert that gays and lesbians ought to be permitted to receive the same personal gratifications and financial advantages through marriage that are available to heterosexuals. Opponents view these marriages as sacrilegious, as a violation of the purpose of marriage, and as a threat to the stability of the traditional family.

A growing number of corporations (including Disney, IBM, and Xerox) now extend health insurance and other benefits to members of same-sex unions, despite vociferous criticism from conservative organizations. The state of Vermont and some municipalities (such as Madison, Wisconsin) have granted same-sex couples all benefits given to heterosexual couples. Laws and policies concerning these issues are generally referred to as "domestic partnership" policies. If benefits are extended to members of same-sex unions, the question arises as to whether benefits should also be extended to unmarried partners in heterosexual relationships who are living together.

Related issues involve rights of gays and lesbians to adopt children and to retain custody of their own children after divorce. As we've seen, in some court cases, lesbian mothers have won custody of their children; in other cases, courts have decreed that lesbian behavior is sufficient evidence that a person is unfit to be a parent. At issue in gay/lesbian adoptions and custody battles is whether gays and lesbians would pass on their sexual orientation to the child. Initial research findings suggest that this is unlikely.[72] We as a society continue to be confused about how sexual orientation might influence—if at all—other important aspects of life, such as child rearing or work performance.

If a gay or lesbian person becomes critically ill and needs hospitalization, his or her partner may

CASE EXHIBIT 7.6

Does Conversion Therapy for Gays and Lesbians Work?

Conversion therapies for gays and lesbians have been around for more than 100 years. The goal is to convert their sexual orientation to heterosexuality. Many earlier techniques were downright inhumane. They included giving gay men electrical shocks while they viewed slides of nude men (this was a crude behavioral therapy approach). The conversion techniques also included brain surgery and castration. All these approaches assumed that same-sex sexual behavior was an illness that could be cured. None were successful.

In recent years, more humane treatments have been tried, including approaches based on rational therapy (see Chapter 5 for a description).

Because gays, lesbians, and bisexuals are not mentally ill and are as well adjusted as heterosexuals, Hyde and DeLamater conclude "such therapies make no sense."[a] Such therapies have a chance of working only with the few gays and lesbians who are highly motivated to want to convert to a heterosexual lifestyle. It makes no sense to change a gay into a straight against his or her will.[b] Hyde and DeLamater conclude, "In sum, it is probably about as easy to change a homosexual person into a happy heterosexual as it is to change a heterosexual person into a happy homosexual—that is, not very."[c]

It is not gay men and lesbians who need to change; it is negative attitudes and discrimination against gay people that need to be abolished.

[a]Janet S. Hyde and John D. DeLamater, *Understanding Human Sexuality*, 9th ed. (Boston: McGraw-Hill, 2006), p. 373.
[b]Ibid.
[c]Ibid.

---

be denied visiting privileges. A lesbian or gay partner has no legal rights because she or he does not fall under the legal definition of family. Lesbian and gay people are therefore encouraged to draw up a legal document to address the medical power of attorney; such a document may also address visitation rights, the right to be consulted about giving or withholding consent about medical decisions, and in case of death, the right to personal effects and the right to make funeral arrangements.

In case of death of one's partner, inheritance issues are also problematic. Gay and lesbian partners have no rights unless there is a will. Without a will, all inheritance is given to legal family members. Therefore, gay and lesbian people are strongly encouraged to have a will made. Such wills need to be carefully drafted to cover all contingencies. For example, a funeral director informed me of a lesbian couple in which the older partner willed all of her assets to the younger partner. The younger partner unexpectedly died first; she had not made a will. As a result, the older partner did not receive any inheritance, was forbidden by the deceased's family members from receiving any personal effects, and (as a final insult) was prohibited by the deceased's family members from even attending the funeral!

Over time, our society has become more tolerant; years ago, efforts to suppress same-sex sexual behavior were so strong that no newspaper even dared to print the word *homosexual*. Today this orientation is no longer an unmentionable deviancy. It is discussed on the airwaves, in newspapers and magazines, and in political debates. It is depicted in movies and on TV. Openly gay candidates for political office in the United States are increasingly being elected. Officially sanctioned support groups for gays are being established in high schools. Domestic partnerships between gay couples have been officially recognized in dozens of cities, and numerous corporations are granting partners of their gay/lesbian employees the same benefits heterosexual spouses receive. Discrimination on the basis of sexual orientation is now illegal in a number of states and in nearly 200 cities and counties.[73]

A Brief Introduction to Transgenderism

Cross-dressing and other transgender behaviors are merely a form of personality expression. No individual is 100% masculine or femine. We all have characteristics, traits, and even body chemistry pertinent to the opposite sex. Some of us have these to a higher degree than others. A transgender person is simply expressing that opposite sex part of his or her personality, which is stronger and more ingrained than in most people.

Typical cross-dressers do not need to cross-dress all the time because the feminine aspect of males (and the masculine aspect of females) does not require 100% expression. What causes transgender behavior in the first place? No one knows. There has been considerable research on this phenomenon but with no conclusive findings. Theories of both psychological and biological causality have been forwarded, and it is quite likely there are different causes for different individuals.

Transgender people do not choose to be transgender. It is innate to their total person. (Hardly anyone would choose a transgender lifestyle, which has been so strongly stigmatized by society.)

Can transgenderism be "cured"? No, many psychological and medical therapies have been tried, but none have been found to have a lasting effect on curbing the desire to cross-dress or to curb the desire to engage in other ways to express transgenderism. The best "cure" is for a transgender individual to become self-accepting and for our society to understand and be respectful of this behavior and appreciate the value of diverse individuals in our culture. Frankly, most well-adjusted transgender individuals are not interested in a "cure." They enjoy their lifestyle. For many cross-dressers, spending time in their other sex persona is comfortable and stress relieving—it is like a minivacation.

Chances are you know one or more transgender people and simply do not realize it. A transgender person usually keeps her or his behavior very secret because of the negative societal stigma. Every one of us has been programmed since birth regarding proper gender roles and behavior. Consequently, many transgender people experience severe, needless guilt and shame regarding their transgender behavior.

Social Work with LGBT Individuals

The two most prominent social work organizations in the United States (the Council on Social Work Education and the National Association of Social Workers) have identified LGBT individuals as populations-at-risk. These organizations also consider it the obligation of all social workers to work toward ending the discrimination and oppression experienced by LGBT individuals in our society.

Many social workers have negative views of people who are gay or lesbian. As a first step in working with gays and lesbians, it is crucial for social workers to confront their own homophobia. Zastrow and Kirst-Ashman note:

One of the worst things a practitioner can do is negatively label a lesbian or gay client and criticize that client for her or his sexual orientation. This contradicts the basic social work value of the client's right to self-determination. A negatively biased practitioner can unknowingly work against a client's development and maintenance of a positive self-image.[74]

Another recommendation in working with gays and lesbians is for a social worker to become familiar with gay/lesbian lifestyles and with the gay/lesbian resources in that worker's geographic area. This knowledge is necessary in order to help connect gay and lesbian clients with the resources available to them. (It is also helpful for the social worker to know people within the gay/lesbian community who can update the practitioner on new resources and events.)

It is critical that social workers become aware of services available to LGBT individuals in a community. Gays and lesbians need various services that address specific aspects of gay/lesbian life. These services include support groups for gays and lesbians who are in the process of coming out, support groups for people who are questioning their sexual orientation, legal advice for gay or lesbian parents seeking child custody, and couple counseling for lesbian or gay partners.

In addition to making appropriate referrals, social workers need to be involved in educating others about the special issues confronting LGBT individuals. They also need to act as advocates for the rights of gays and lesbians. Sexual orientation needs to be addressed as simply another aspect of human diversity. Political candidates in favor of gay/lesbian rights need to be supported. Agencies that discriminate against LGBT individuals need to be confronted, informed, and pressured to provide needed services in a fair and unbiased manner. Finally, social workers need to be active in generating community support to strongly oppose hate crimes in which LGBT individuals are the victims.

As for transgender individuals, our society needs to find ways to assist those who do not fit into assigned, rigid, bipolar gender roles in exploring other alternatives. The NASW's policy statement on providing services to transgender individual is that people of diverse gender (including transgender individuals) should be afforded the same rights and respect as any other people.[75]

Critical Thinking Question

Odds are that you have cross-dressed in the past. If this is true, was it a "pleasant" experience?

Because transgender people often experience guilt and shame about expressing their other sex persona, connecting them to a support group is highly beneficial. One value of a support group for transgender individuals is that it allows them to "compare notes" with others and helps them come to terms with their true gender foundation. Societal reaction to transgender behavior is the most significant problem experienced by a transgender person. Transgender behavior is not a particular individual's "mental" problem—it is a societal one because of how society views the behavior.[76]

SUMMARY

The following summarizes this chapter's content as it relates to the chapter objectives presented at the beginning of the chapter. Objectives include the following:

A *Present a brief look at sexual expression in history and in other cultures.*

Practically every conceivable sexual activity is socially acceptable to some groups of people. What is defined as acceptable and unacceptable sexual behavior varies from culture to culture and from one time period to another. Judeo-Christian values, the Puritan influence, and Victorian morality contributed in our history to repression of sexual expression. At present, ambiguity and confusion abound over what ought to be the sexual code and behavior of Americans. For the past several decades, our society has been undergoing a revolution in sexual values and mores.

B *Present a historical review of scientific studies of sexuality.*

The work of four social scientists has had profound effects on our understanding of human sexuality: Sigmund Freud, Alfred Kinsey, and the team of William Masters and Virginia Johnson. This text uses a social variance approach to examining sexual concerns rather than a social problems approach because there is as yet no general consensus about which sexual acts are acceptable and which are not.

C *Present material on sexual orientation, including definitions of terms, hate crimes against gays and lesbians, myths and facts about gays and lesbians, incidence of same-sex sexual orientation, causes of same-sex sexual oreintation, life experiences of gays and lesbians, the process of coming out, current issues for gays and lesbians, conversion therapy, information about transgenderism, and social work with LGBT individuals.*

Sexual orientation was discussed at some length. Gay activists prefer the term *gay* to *homosexual*, as the latter is sometimes used as a derogatory label, and because there are so many negative connotations to the term *homosexuality*.

Gays, lesbians, and bisexuals are frequently the target of hate crimes. Numerous myths and facts were presented about gays and lesbians. Gays and lesbians, for example, have been found to be as well adjusted as heterosexuals.

About 10% of men and women have had at least one same-gender sexual experience in adulthood. About 2% of men and 1% of women are exclusively gay/lesbian.

There are a variety of theories about the causes of same-sex sexual orientation (and heterosexuality). Sexual orientation is established early in life, perhaps long before adolescence. As yet, we do not know what causes sexual orientation.

In most places, gays and lesbians may be denied private employment because of their sexual orientation. Many large cities now have gay and lesbian communities. The specter of AIDS has had a tremendous impact on gay/lesbian communities, particularly on gay men.

There are significant variations in the gay/lesbian experience, depending on whether or not one is "out of the closet." The process and psychological turmoil of coming out were described.

Numerous current issues affect gays and lesbians. There are movements in many states to pass legislation to legally recognize marriages of couples of the same gender. (There are also efforts in many states to pass amendments codifying marriage as an exclusively heterosexual institution.) There is a movement to urge employers to extend benefits to partners of employees in same-sex couples. There are inheritance issues in gay and lesbian relationships. Courts struggle with whether to allow gay and lesbian couples to adopt. Courts also struggle with child custody cases in which one of the spouses in a divorce is acknowledged to be gay or lesbian.

Progress is slowly being made in recognizing the civil rights of gays and lesbians. Discrimination on the basis of sexual orientation is now illegal in a number of states.

Social workers need to confront their homophobic beliefs. Prominent social work organizations have identified gays and lesbians as populations-at-risk. These organizations assert it is the obligation of all social workers to work toward ending the discrimination and oppression experienced by gays, lesbians, and bisexuals in our society. Using therapy approaches to seek to convert a gay or lesbian to being heterosexual is ineffective and is probably unethical—unless requested by the gay or lesbian client.

A transgender person is someone whose gender identity is the opposite of his or her biological gender. The term *transgender* can refer to a range of people, including transsexual people, transvestites, crossdressers, and female impersonators. Transgender people have varying sexual orientations ranging from heterosexual to bisexual to same-sex orientation. People of diverse gender orientations—including transgender individuals—should be afforded the same respect and rights as any other person. The chapter ended with a section on social work with LGBT individuals.

Competency Notes

EP 2.1.3.a Distinguish, appraise, and integrate multiple sources of knowledge, including research-based knowledge and practice wisdom.

EP 2.1.4.a, b, c, d The competency "Engage diversity and difference in practice," and the four practice behaviors associated with this competency

EP 2.1.5.a, b, c The competency "Advance human rights and social and economic justice," and the three practice behaviors associated with this competency (All of this chapter)

This chapter provides a summary of sex in history and in other cultures, and it presents a historical review of scientific studies of sexuality. Material is presented on sexual orientation, including definitions of terms, hate crimes, myths and facts about gays and lesbians, incidence of gay and lesbian rela-

tionships, causes of gay and lesbian orientations, life experiences of gays and lesbians, the process of coming out, current issues for gays and lesbians, conversion therapy, transgenderism, and social work with LGBT individuals.

Media Resources

Additional resources for this chapter, including a chapter quiz, can be found on the Social Work CourseMate. Go to CengageBrain.com.

Notes

1. Havelock Ellis, *Sex and Marriage: Eros in Contemporary Life* (Westport, CT: Greenwood Press, 1977), p. 42.
2. David A. Schulz, *Human Sexuality* (Englewood Cliffs, NJ: Prentice Hall, 1979), p. 4.
3. Don Grubin, "Sexual Offending: A Cross Cultural Comparison," in *Annual Review of Sex Research*, vol. 3, John Bancroft, Clive M. Davis, and Howard J. Ruppel, Jr., eds. (Lake Mills, IA: Society for the Scientific Study of Sex, 1993), pp. 201–217.
4. Janet S. Hyde and John D. DeLamater, *Understanding Human Sexuality*, 11th ed. (Boston: McGraw-Hill, 2011).
5. Ibid.
6. John Gagnon and Bruce Henderson, *Human Sexuality: The Age of Ambiguity* (Boston: Little, Brown, 1975), p. 14.
7. Hyde and DeLamater, *Understanding Human Sexuality*.
8. Ibid., pp. 306–308.
9. Gagnon and Henderson, *Human Sexuality: The Age of Ambiguity*, p. 16.
10. J. John Palen, *Social Problems* (New York: McGraw-Hill, 1979), p. 544.
11. Ibid.
12. Hyde and DeLamater, *Understanding Human Sexuality*.
13. Ibid., pp. 204–206.
14. Ibid.
15. Ibid., pp. 145–150.
16. Linda A. Mooney, David Knox, and Caroline Schacht, *Understanding Social Problems*, 8th ed. (Belmont, CA: Wadsworth/Cengage Learning, 2013), p. 345.
17. Ibid., pp. 345–347.

18. Alfred C. Kinsey, W. B. Pomeroy, and C. E. Martin, *Sexual Behavior in the Human Male* (Philadelphia: Saunders, 1948).

19. Alfred C. Kinsey, W. B. Pomeroy, C. E. Martin, and P. H. Gebhard, *Sexual Behavior in the Human Female* (Philadelphia: Saunders, 1953).

20. William H. Masters and Virginia E. Johnson, *Human Sexual Response* (Boston: Little, Brown, 1966). For a layperson, an excellent summary is Ruth Brecher and Edward Brecher, *An Analysis of Human Sexual Response* (New York: Signet Books, 1966).

21. William H. Masters and Virginia E. Johnson, *Human Sexual Inadequacy* (Boston: Little, Brown, 1970). For a layperson, an excellent summary is Fred Belliveau and Lin Richter, *Understanding Human Sexual Inadequacy* (New York: Bantam Books, 1970).

22. Gagnon and Henderson, *Human Sexuality: The Age of Ambiguity*, p. 14.

23. Hyde and DeLamater, *Understanding Human Sexuality*, pp. 204–206.

24. Ibid.

25. http://www.joekost.com/homosexual/_n_word .html.

26. Hyde and DeLamater, *Understanding Human Sexuality*.

27. NASW, *Social Work Speaks: 2009–2012*, 8th ed. (Washington, DC: NASW Press), p. 220.

28. R. Crooks and K. Baur, *Our Sexuality*, 8th ed. (Belmont, CA: Wadsworth, 2002), p. 62.

29. NASW, *Social Work Speaks: 2009–2012*, pp. 342–348.

30. Crossport, "Frequently Asked Questions," http://www.crossport.org/faq.html.

31. Karen K. Kirst-Ashman, "Transsexual and Transgender People," in *Understanding Human Behavior and the Social Environment*, 8th ed. Charles H. Zastrow and Karen K. Kirst-Ashman, eds. (Belmont, CA: Brooks/Cole, 2010), p. 558.

32. Hyde and DeLamater, *Understanding Human Sexuality*, pp. 314–317.

33. Ibid.

34. Ibid., p. 93.

35. Kinsey et al., *Sexual Behavior in the Human Male*, p. 639.

36. Hyde and DeLamater, *Understanding Human Sexuality*, pp. 332–335.

37. Thomas Sullivan, Kenrick Thompson, Richard Wright, George Gross, and Dale Spady, *Social Problems* (New York: Wiley, 1980), p. 537.

38. Hyde and DeLamater, *Understanding Human Sexuality*, pp. 343–345.

39. Ibid., pp. 343–345.

40. Janet S. Hyde, *Understanding Human Sexuality*, 5th ed. (New York: McGraw-Hill, 1994), p. 424.

41. Hyde and DeLamater, *Understanding Human Sexuality*, pp. 325–326.

42. Hyde and DeLamater, *Understanding Human Sexuality*, pp. 377–379.

43. Ibid., pp. 436–445.

44. Ibid., pp. 436–445.

45. Kinsey et al., *Sexual Behavior in the Human Male;* Kinsey et al., *Sexual Behavior in the Human Female.*

46. Hyde and DeLamater, *Understanding Human Sexuality*, pp. 324–325.

47. Ibid., pp. 324–325.

48. Ibid., p. 325.

49. Alan P. Bell, Martin S. Weinberg, and Sue Kiefer Hammersmith, *Sexual Preference* (Bloomington: Indiana University Press, 1981).

50. Charlene Crabb, "Are Some Men Born to Be Homosexual?" *U.S. News & World Report*, Sept. 9, 1991, p. 58.

51. William F. Allman, "The Biology-Behavior Conundrum," *U.S. News & World Report*, July 26, 1993, pp. 6–7.

52. Ibid., pp. 6–9.

53. Hyde and DeLamater, *Understanding Human Sexuality*, p. 332.

54. Kim I. Mills, "Was 1993 'The Year of the Queer'?" *Wisconsin State Journal*, Jan. 1, 1994, p. 4A.

55. NASW, *Social Work Speaks*, p. 219.

56. Mooney, Knox, and Schacht, *Understanding Social Problems*, pp. 362–364.

57. Ibid.

58. Ibid.

59. Ibid.

60. Ibid.

61. Ibid.

62. Karlein M. G. Schrewrs, "Sexuality in Lesbian Couples: The Importance of Gender," in *Annual Review of Sex Research*, vol. 4, John Bancroft, Clive M. Davis, and Howard Ruppel, Jr., eds. (Lake Mills, IA: Society for the Scientific Study of Sex, 1994), pp. 49–66.

63. Hyde and DeLamater, *Understanding Human Sexuality*, p. 332.

64. Ibid., pp. 502–503.

65. Ibid.

66. Mooney, Knox, and Schacht, *Understanding Social Problems*, p. 443.

67. Hyde and DeLamater, *Understanding Human Sexuality*, p. 318.

68. Vivienne Cass, "Homosexual Identity Formation: A Theoretical Model," *Journal of Homosexuality*, 4 (1979), pp. 219–235.

69. Boston Women's Health Book Collective, *The New Our Bodies, Ourselves*, 12th ed. (New York: Simon and Schuster, 2005).

70. Charles Zastrow and Karen Kirst-Ashman, *Understanding Human Behavior and the Social Environment*, 8th ed. (Pacific Grove, CA: Brooks/Cole, 2010), pp. 574–577.

71. Mooney, Knox, and Schacht, *Understanding Social Problems*, pp. 364–374.

72. Ibid., pp 364–374.

73. Hyde and DeLamater, *Understanding Human Sexuality*, pp. 502–503.

74. Zastrow and Kirst-Ashman, *Understanding Human Behavior and the Social Environment*, p. 581.

75. NASW, *Social Work Speaks*, p. 345.

76. North Alabama Gender Center, "Transgender 101," p. 5.

CHAPTER

Drug Abuse and Drug Treatment Programs

Practically everyone has taken one or more drugs and, on a few occasions, used a drug to excess. A large proportion of our population, as we will see, currently abuses drugs. This chapter will:

Learning Objectives

EP 2.1.3.a

A   Define drugs and drug abuse.

B   Provide a brief history of our drug-taking society.

C   Present sociological theories of drug abuse.

D   Describe drug subcultures.

E   Summarize facts about and effects of commonly used drugs.

F   Describe rehabilitation programs for drug abuse.

G   Present suggestions for curbing drug abuse in the future.

Drugs and Drug Abuse

Pharmacologically, a drug is any substance that chemically alters the function or structure of a living organism.[1] This definition would include food, insecticides, air pollutants, water pollutants, acids, vitamins, toxic chemicals, soaps, and soft drinks. Obviously this interpretation is too broad to be useful. For our purposes, a definition based on context is more appropriate. In medicine, for example, a drug is any substance that is manufactured specifically to relieve pain or to treat or prevent diseases and other medical conditions.

In a social problems approach, a *drug* is any habit-forming substance that directly affects the brain and the nervous system. It is a chemical that affects moods, perceptions, body functions, or consciousness, and that has the potential for misuse because it may be harmful to the user.

Drug abuse is the regular or excessive use of a drug when, as defined by a group, the consequences endanger relationships with other people, are detrimental to the user's health, or jeopardize society itself. This definition identifies two key factors that determine what is considered drug abuse in a society: The first is the actual drug effects, and the second is a group's perception of the effects.

Society's perceptions of the ill effects of a drug are often inconsistent with the actual effects. In our society, moderate use of alcohol and tobacco is accepted by many Americans, even though moderate use of

both can cause serious health problems. Excessive drinking of coffee (containing caffeine) is accepted in our society but can also lead to health problems. In the 1930s, our society was convinced that marijuana was a dangerous drug; it was said to cause insanity, crime, and a host of other ills. Now available evidence suggests that it may be no more dangerous than alcohol.[2] The occasional use of heroin has been thought for years to be highly dangerous, but evidence now indicates that occasional users suffer few health consequences and can lead productive lives.[3]

The dominant social reaction to a drug is influenced not only by the actual dangers of the drug but also by the social characteristics and motives of the groups that use it. Heroin is considered dangerous because its use has been popularly associated with inner-city residents and high crime rates. Society is generally accepting of the use of pills by middle-aged people to reduce stress and anxiety but less accepting of college students using the same pills "to feel good" and "to get high." Surprisingly, legal drugs (such as alcohol and tobacco) are more often abused and cause more harm in our society than illegal drugs.

One of the most widely used drugs today is aspirin. Millions of Americans use it to relieve pain and other discomforts. Taken in excessive amounts, however, aspirin can be harmful, causing gastrointestinal bleeding, ulcers, and other ailments.

Other over-the-counter drugs (those available without a physician's prescription) can be and are abused. Laxatives, for example, which are taken for constipation, can damage the digestive system. Large doses of vitamins A and D are toxic.

Prescription drugs are also frequently abused. Among the most abused prescription drugs are tranquilizers, painkillers, sedatives, and stimulants. Many Americans are obsessed with taking pills, and many prescription drugs have the potential to be psychologically and physiologically addicting. Drug companies spend millions in advertisements in an effort to convince consumers that there is something wrong with them—that they are too tense, that they are taking too long to fall asleep, that they should lose weight, that they are not "regular" enough—and that their medications will solve these problems. Unfortunately, many Americans accept this easy symptom-relief approach and end up depending on pills rather than making life changes to improve their health (such as learning stress reduction techniques, changing their diets, and deciding to exercise regularly).

Because a drug is legal and readily available does not mean it is harmless. Alcohol and tobacco are legal, but both may seriously damage our health. The rationale determining the acceptability of a drug is often illogical. Drugs favored by the dominant culture (such as alcohol in our society) are generally acceptable, whereas those favored by a small subculture are usually outlawed. It is interesting to note that in many parts of North Africa and the Middle East, marijuana is a legal drug and alcohol is outlawed.[4] Our country imposes severe penalties on the use of cocaine, but in certain areas of the Andes Mountains that substance is legal and widely used.[5]

A characteristic of habit-forming drugs is that they lead to a *dependency*, with the user developing a recurring craving for them. This dependency may be physical, psychological, or both. When physical dependency occurs, the user will generally experience bodily withdrawal symptoms, which may take many forms and range in severity from slight tremblings to fatal convulsions. When psychological dependency occurs, the user feels psychological discomfort if use is terminated. Users also generally develop a *tolerance* for the drug, which means that they have to take increasing amounts over time to achieve a given effect. Some drugs (such as aspirin) do not create tolerance.

Drug addiction is somewhat difficult to define. In its broadest usage, the term refers to an intense craving for a particular substance. All of us have intense cravings—such as for ice cream, strawberry shortcake, potato chips, or chocolate. To distinguish drug addiction from other intense cravings, some authorities have erroneously defined drug addiction as the physiological dependency that a person develops after heavy use of a particular drug. Most addicts, however, experience periods when they "kick" their physical dependency, yet their psychological craving continues undiminished; as a result, they soon return to using their drug of choice. It is therefore more useful to define drug addiction as the intense craving for a drug that develops after a period of physical dependency from heavy use.[6]

Why are Americans so involved in using and abusing drugs? There are numerous reasons: to feel good, to get high, to escape from reality, to obtain relief from pain or anxiety, and to relax or sleep. Drugs definitely meet a functional need (such as providing temporary relief from unwanted emotions) but can have serious side effects. On a broader level, many segments of our society encourage and romanticize the use of drugs. Former senator Frank Moss, for example, comments on the role played by advertisements and commercials:

> It is advertising which mounts the message that pills turn rain to sunshine, gloom to joy, depression to euphoria, solve problems, and dispel doubt. Not just pills: cigarette and cigar ads; soft drinks, coffee, tea, and beer ads—all portray the key to happiness as things to swallow, inhale, chew, drink, and eat.[7]

A Brief History of Our Drug-Taking Society

When the Pilgrims set sail for America in 1620, they loaded on their ships 14 tons of water—plus 10,000 gallons of wine and 42 tons of beer.[8] Ever since, Americans have been widely using and abusing drugs.

During and after the Civil War, thousands of injured soldiers were treated with narcotics to relieve their pain; many became addicted. Narcotics addiction was a serious problem from the 1860s to the first decade of the 20th century. At the turn of the century, about 1% of the population was addicted to a narcotic drug—the highest rate in our history.[9] At that time, opiates (including heroin and morphine) were readily available for a variety of purposes. They were used to treat such minor ailments as stomach pains and to ease the discomfort of infants during teething. Pharmacies, grocery stores, and mail-order houses did a prosperous business in selling opiates. Such sales were legally stopped in 1914 by the Harrison Narcotics Act, which required that narcotic drugs be dispensed only through prescriptions by licensed physicians.

In colonial times, tobacco was a popular substance for chewing, and after 1870 its use for smoking increased greatly. For a brief time shortly after 1900, its sale was prohibited in 14 states because it was thought to be a "stepping-stone" to alcohol use and to lead to sexual deviance, insanity, and impotence. The laws banning the sale proved ineffective and were repealed after World War I. Today tobacco is one of our most widely used—and abused—drugs, despite what we know about the health hazards of smoking.

Marijuana use has occurred throughout our history. In the mid-19th century, it was often smoked by writers and artists in the larger cities. Shortly after the beginning of the 20th century, Latinos and African Americans began smoking it. The drug was then thought to lead to "unruly" behavior, and the first laws prohibiting its use and distribution were passed in the South. The rest of the states soon enacted similar legislation. In 1937 the director of the Federal Bureau of Narcotics labeled marijuana the "assassin of youth." The mass media jumped on this campaign and began publishing stories stereotyping marijuana users as "crazed drug fiends." Later, to continue receiving funds for his bureau, the director asserted that marijuana was dangerous, as it was a "stepping-stone" to narcotic drugs.[10] Marijuana, in the 1960s and 1970s, became increasingly popular among youths, college students, drug subcultures, and the general population. Its use and effects remain a controversial issue.

Alcohol use has continued unabated ever since the Pilgrims landed. The first governor of Massachusetts complained of excessive drunkenness in his colony, and since that time, there have always been some segments of American society that have viewed alcohol use as a social problem. The American Temperance Union was formed in the early 1800s. It was later followed by the Women's Christian Temperance Union, the Anti-Saloon League, and several other temperance organizations. Alcohol was viewed as responsible for many social ills: crime, the collapse of the family, and unemployment. Immigrants, the poor, and certain minority groups were the major consumers of alcohol at that time. Under pressure, several states passed legislation prohibiting the sale and distribution of alcoholic beverages in the latter half of the 19th century. By the start of World War I, nearly half the population resided in "dry" areas.

The 18th Amendment to the Constitution, which prohibited the sale of alcohol, was ratified in 1919. Prohibition had begun. But people continued to drink, and the law was virtually unenforceable. It gave impetus to organized crime. Moonshiners (people who distilled or sold liquor illegally) and speakeasies (places where illegal alcoholic beverages were sold) flourished. Prohibition became a political embarrassment, and the United States was a laughingstock around the world. In 1933 the 18th Amendment was repealed. Following Prohibition the use of alcohol became more widespread.[11] People in the middle and upper-middle classes also began drinking on a rather large scale. As a result, alcohol was no longer viewed as the scourge of society.

It is interesting to note that whereas narcotics made a transition from respectability to disrepute in the past 100 years, alcohol made exactly the opposite transition.

Sociological Theories of Drug Abuse

A number of biological, psychological, and sociological theories have been advanced to explain drug abuse. Summarizing all of these theories is beyond the scope of this text, but three sociological theories will be presented for illustrative purposes: anomie theory, labeling theory, and differential association.

Anomie Theory

This theory stems largely from the work of Emile Durkheim[12] and Robert Merton.[13] Merton used anomie to explain deviant behavior. Anomie is a condition in which the acceptance of approved standards of conduct is weakened. Every society has both approved goals (such as making a lot of money) and approved means for attaining these goals (such as high-paying

© Bettmann/CORBIS

In 1919 the 18th Amendment, which prohibited the sale of alcohol, was ratified and thus an era of speakeasies, bootleg liquor, and "bathtub" gin began. Here authorities are destroying barrels of bootleg liquor.

jobs). When certain members of society want these goals but have insufficient means for attaining them, a state of anomie results, and these individuals then seek to achieve the desired goals through deviant means. Applied to drug abuse, this theory asserts that if people are prevented from achieving their goals, they may be "driven to drink" or to use other drugs. The drugs may be used as an escape—to avoid the suffering caused by failure to achieve goals—or they may be used as a substitute for the "highs" that users had originally hoped to experience from successfully accomplishing their goals.

Merton asserts that drug abuse can be reduced if society (a) sets realistic goals that people can attain and then (b) establishes legitimate means, available to everyone, for attaining these goals. However, anomie theory fails to explain drug abuse by people who appear to be achieving their goals.

Labeling Theory

This theory was developed by a number of researchers.[14] Labeling theorists view drug abuse as largely stemming from occasional users' being labeled "abusers." Initially, occasional users indulge in drug use that is disapproved of by others—such as getting drunk or smoking marijuana. These users do not at this point view themselves as abusers. However, if their use is discovered and made an issue by significant other people (such as parents, police, or teachers), and if they are then publicly labeled a "drunkard," "pothead," or "dope user," they are more closely watched. Under this closer surveillance, if they continue to occasionally be found using drugs, the label is gradually confirmed. Their significant others may begin to relate to them in terms of the label, causing these occasional users to view themselves as people who truly are whatever label is applied. When this happens, the occasional user is likely to embark on a "career" as a habitual drug abuser.

Labeling theory asserts that drug abuse can be reduced by avoiding labeling—that is, by refusing to treat occasional drug users as if they were "abusers." However, it fails to explain drug abuse among "closet alcoholics" and others who are already drug abusers before being labeled as such.

Differential Association

This theory, developed by Edwin Sutherland,[15] asserts that behavior is determined primarily by the values and actions that are considered important by the small, intimate groups one interacts with. Applied to drug abuse, differential association theory asserts that people will learn and take on the drug use norms of the small groups they associate with. These groups include family, neighborhood peer groups, and religious and social groups. Differential association has been used to explain differences in alcoholism rates among ethnic and religious groups.

There are, for example, marked differences in alcohol use patterns between the Irish, Italians, and Jews in the United States. The Italian subculture (both in Italy and in this country) widely accepts the moderate use of alcohol, particularly at mealtimes. Serving wine with meals is part of the dietary customs; even the young partake of it. Excessive drinking, however, is frowned on. As a result, although alcohol is widely used in the Italian community, drunkenness and alcoholism are relatively rare.[16]

Similarly, the Jewish community uses alcohol widely, including as a component in religious rituals. As with Italian families, the use of alcohol in controlled social settings minimizes its potential negative effects. And because there are strong norms against drunkenness and abuse, alcoholism among American Jews is rare.[17]

In contrast, the Irish subculture tolerates periodic episodes of excessive drinking, particularly by single males. Such drinking is seen as a way to relieve tension and frustration. With such norms, there is a relatively high rate of alcoholism among Irish American males.[18]

It is, of course, possible for people to be resocialized into the drug use norms of another subculture. For example, a teenager raised in a family opposed to marijuana use may become attracted to a high school group that places a high value on smoking marijuana. This teenager may then, through the principles of differential association, become resocialized by this new group into using marijuana.

Critical Thinking Question

Identify three people you are aware of who are abusing drugs. Why do you believe each of these people is abusing drugs?

As noted, there are many other theories (including psychological and biological ones) concerning the causes of drug abuse.[19] No single theory is sufficient for identifying all causes, and each theory may or may not apply in any given case.

Drug Subcultures

A person's decision about whether to use a drug depends not only on his or her personality characteristics and family background but also on the attitudes of peers. These views determine which drugs are used, how often they are used, how much is used at any one time, and what other activities will be engaged in when drugs are used.

A group of peers who advocates the use of one or more drugs can be called a *drug subculture*. Most drug taking occurs in a social group that approves the use of the drug. In a classic study, "Becoming a Marijuana User," Howard Becker found that the peer group plays a crucial role in the individual's learning to smoke marijuana.[20] The group introduces the novice to smoking and teaches the new smoker to recognize the pleasant experiences associated with a "high." Membership in this drug subculture also encourages further drug use and instructs the newcomer to reject established norms and instead to accept the norms of this group.

Drug subcultures appear to function similarly in relation to different drugs. They are more likely to develop around the use of illegal rather than legal drugs. Use of alcohol (among teenagers), marijuana, heroin, LSD, PCP, and cocaine generally occurs in drug subcultures.

In many cities in the United States, numerous gangs (composed of juveniles and young adults) have formed and become involved in widespread use and distribution of illegal drugs. Frequently, gang members also engage in other crimes (such as thefts and burglaries) to financially support their drug habits.

Although drug subcultures are often dysfunctional for society, they do serve important functions for the user. They provide instruction on how to use the drug, including guidelines on the safety limits of dosages. They help handle adverse effects, assist in obtaining the drug, and provide protection from arrest when the drug is being used. They also provide a party-type atmosphere to enhance enjoyment of the effects of the drug.

Facts about and Effects of Commonly Used Drugs

Depressants

In this section, we will examine the following drugs, which are classified as depressants: alcohol, barbiturates, tranquilizers, Quaalude, and PCP. For a complete listing of the drugs discussed in this chapter and their effects, see Table 8.1.

Alcohol

Alcohol is the most abused drug in American society. Still, its use is so accepted that few Americans view alcohol as a serious social problem. Social drinking is highly integrated into the customs of our society. In many areas of the country, the local pub is a center (particularly for men) for meeting and socializing with friends and neighbors. Going out and getting "high" or even "smashed" is a favorite pastime of college students. Taverns and nightclubs are primary sites for meeting and entertaining dates. Businesses frequently use cocktail lounges to wine and dine customers. In some communities, it is the custom to have "a second church service" at a local watering hole after the weekly church service is over. Because of the pervasiveness of alcohol in our society, this chapter will devote considerable attention to its use, abuse, and treatment.

Alcohol is a colorless liquid that is a component of beer, wine, brandy, whiskey, vodka, rum, and other intoxicating beverages. The average American over the age of 21 consumes an average of 21.8 gallons of beer, 2.5 gallons of wine, and 1.4 gallons of hard liquor a year.[21] The vast majority of American teenagers and adults drink alcohol.

Drinking has become so entrenched into our customs that, unfortunately, people who do not drink are sometimes viewed as "weird," "stuck up," or "killjoys" and are often assumed to have something wrong with them. The serving of alcoholic beverages is expected at many rituals and ceremonies for adults: weddings, birthday parties, Christmas parties, graduations, and the like. Some formal religious rites also include alcohol (for example, wine as the blood of Christ during Communion). Many popular songs highlight drinking. But it is not the use of alcohol at rituals and ceremonies that causes most problems. Because most American alcohol use is informal and relatively uncontrolled, it can easily become excessive without the safeguards that are built into the drinking patterns of many ethnic groups.

The type of alcohol found in beverages is ethyl alcohol. (It is also called grain alcohol because most of it is made from fermenting grain.) Many drinkers believe that alcohol is a stimulant because it relaxes tensions, lowers sexual and aggressive inhibitions, seems to facilitate interpersonal relationships, and usually leads those who have a few drinks to talk more. It is, however, very definitely a depressant to the central nervous system. Its chemical composition and effects are very similar to those of ether (an anesthetic used in medicine to induce unconsciousness).

Alcohol slows mental activity, reasoning ability, speech ability, and muscle reactions. It distorts perceptions, slurs speech, lessens coordination, and slows memory functioning and respiration. In increasing quantities, it leads to stupor, sleep, coma, and finally, death. A hangover (the aftereffects of too much alcohol) may cause headache, thirst, muscle aches, stomach discomfort, and nausea.

The effects of alcohol vary with the percentage of alcohol in the bloodstream as it passes through the brain. Generally, effects are observable when the concentration of alcohol in the blood reaches one-tenth of 1%. Five drinks (each containing 1 ounce of 86-proof alcohol, 12 ounces of beer, or 3 ounces of wine) in 2 hours will result in a blood alcohol concentration of one-tenth of 1% for a 120-pound person. (The heavier the person, the more drinks it takes to increase the level of alcohol in the blood.) Table 8.2 shows the effects of increasing percentages of alcohol in the blood.

In 1990, scientists discovered that women's stomachs are less effective than men's at breaking down alcohol; as a result, women generally become intoxicated more quickly. Men have in their stomachs substantially more dehydrogenase (an enzyme) than do women. This enzyme breaks down much of the alcohol in the stomach before it reaches the bloodstream. This finding may also help explain why medical complications, including cirrhosis of the liver, anemia, and gastrointestinal bleeding, develop more rapidly in alcoholic women than in alcoholic men.[22]

Who Drinks? The primary factors related to whether an individual will drink and how much alcohol a drinker will use include biological factors, socioeconomic factors, gender, age, religion, and urban–rural residence.[23]

- *Biological Factors:* Close relatives of an alcoholic are four times more likely to become alcoholics themselves, and this tendency holds true even for children who were adopted away from their biological families at birth and raised in a nonalcoholic family. Such findings clearly suggest that drinking and alcoholism are due in part to biological factors. Some Asian populations have highly negative reactions to alcohol, which tend to diminish their risk of becoming alcoholics.
- *Socioeconomic Factors:* Drinking is more frequent among younger men at higher socioeconomic levels, and less frequent among older women at lower levels.
- *Gender:* Men are more likely to use and abuse alcohol than are women. Still, recent decades have seen a dramatic increase in alcoholism among adult women. Why? One explanation is that cultural taboos against heavy drinking among women have weakened. Another explanation is that increased drinking is related to the changing roles of women in our society.
- *Age:* Older people are less likely to drink than younger people, even if they were drinkers in their youth. Heavy drinking is most common at ages 21 to 30 for men and ages 31 to 50 for women.
- *Religion:* Nonchurchgoers drink more than regular churchgoers. Heavy drinking is more common among Episcopalians and Catholics, whereas conservative and fundamentalist Protestants are more often nondrinkers or light drinkers. Few Jews are heavy drinkers.

Table 8.1 Drugs of Abuse: Facts and Effects

Drug	Dependence Potential		Tolerance	Duration of Effects (hours)	Usual Methods of Administration
	Physical	Psychological			
Narcotics					
Opium	High	High	Yes	3 to 6	Oral, smoked
Morphine	High	High	Yes	3 to 6	Injected, smoked
Heroin	High	High	Yes	3 to 6	Injected, sniffed
Depressants					
Alcohol	High	High	Yes	1 to 12	Oral
Barbiturates	High	High	Yes	1 to 16	Oral, injected
Tranquilizers	Moderate	Moderate	Yes	4 to 8	Oral
Quaalude	High	High	Yes	4 to 8	Oral
Stimulants					
Caffeine	High	High	Yes	2 to 4	Oral
Cocaine	Possible	High	Yes	2	Injected, sniffed
Crack	Possible	High	Yes	2	Smoked
Amphetamines	Possible	High	Yes	2 to 4	Oral, injected
Butyl nitrate	Possible	Unknown	Probable	Up to 5	Inhaled
Amyl nitrate	Possible	Unknown	Probable	Up to 5	Inhaled
Hallucinogens					
LSD	None	Degree	Yes	variable	Oral
Mescaline and Peyote		Unknown			Oral, injected
Psilocybin psilocin					Oral
PCP					Oral, injected
MDMA (Ecstasy)					Oral, injected, smoked
Cannabis					
Marijuana	Degree	Moderate	Yes	2 to 4	Oral, smoked
Hashish	unknown				
Nicotine (Tobacco)	High	High	Yes	2 to 4	Smoked, chewed
Anabolic steroids	None	High	Unknown	Unknown	Oral

© Cengage Learning.

- *Urban–Rural Residence:* Urban residents are more likely to drink than rural residents.

In the past two decades, there has been a decline in drinking, especially of hard liquor, in many segments of the American public.[24] For example, some business executives have switched from having martini luncheons to jogging and working out. In the 1980s and 1990s, the federal government put considerable financial pressure on states to raise the legal drinking age to 21 or else have federal highway funds withheld. All states have now raised the drinking age to 21. Secondary schools, colleges, and universities have initiated alcohol awareness programs. Many businesses and employers offer Employee Assistance Programs, which are designed to provide treatment services to alcoholics and problem drinkers. Drunk-driving laws have become stricter, and police

Possible Effects	Effects of Overdose	Withdrawal Symptoms
Euphoria, drowsiness, respiratory depression, constricted pupils, nausea	Slow and shallow breathing, clammy skin, convulsions, coma, possible death	Watery eyes, runny nose, yawning, loss of appetite, irritability, tremors, panic, chills and sweating, cramps, nausea
Slurred speech, disorientation, drunken behavior, loss of coordination, impaired reactions	Shallow respiration, cold and clammy skin, dilated pupils, weak and rapid pulse, coma, possible death	Anxiety, insomnia, tremors, delirium, convulsions, possible death
Increased alertness, excitation, euphoria, dilated pupils, increased pulse rate and blood pressure, insomnia, loss of appetite	Agitation, increase in pulse rate and blood pressure, loss of appetite, insomnia Agitation, increase in body temperature, hallucinations, convulsions, tremors, possible death	Apathy, long periods of sleep, irritability, depression, disorientation
Excitement, euphoria, giddiness, loss of inhibitions, aggressiveness, delusions, depression, drowsiness, headache, nausea	Loss of memory, confusion, unsteady gait, erratic heartbeat and pulse, possible death	Insomnia, decreased appetite, depression, irritability, headache
Illusions and hallucinations, poor perception of time and distance	Longer and more intense "trip" episodes, psychosis, possible death	Unknown
Euphoria, relaxed inhibitions, increased appetite, disoriented behavior, increased heart and pulse rate	Fatigue, paranoia, possible psychosis, time disorientation, slowed movements	Insomnia, hyperactivity, decreased appetite
Increased alertness, excitation, euphoria, dilated pupils, increased pulse rate and blood pressure, insomnia, loss of appetite	Agitation, increase in pulse rate and blood pressure, loss of appetite, insomnia	Apathy, long periods of sleep, irritability, depression
Moodiness, depression, irritability	Virilization, edema, testicular atrophy, gynecomastia, acne, aggressive behavior	Possible depression

departments and the courts are more vigorously enforcing these laws. Organizations such as Mothers Against Drunk Driving (MADD) and Students Against Drunk Driving (SADD) have been fairly successful in creating greater public awareness of the hazards of drinking and driving. A cultural norm seems to be emerging that it is no longer stylish to have too much to drink. Despite these promising trends, however, rates of alcohol use and abuse in the United States remain extremely high.

Reasons for Drinking As discussed earlier, social patterns influence people to drink in a wide variety of situations, such as at happy hours, before and after dinner, and at parties.

There are also individual reasons for drinking. Some people drink because alcohol acts as a "social lubricant," relaxing them so that they feel more at ease interacting with others. Some drink simply to relax. Others use alcohol as a kind of anesthetic, to

Table 8.2 Percentages of Alcohol in the Blood and Its Effects

Alcohol	Effects
.05%	Lowered alertness and a "high" feeling
.10	Decreased reactions; reduced coordination (legally drunk in most states)
.20	Massive interference with senses and motor skills
.30	Perceptions nearly gone; understanding nearly gone
.40	Unconsciousness
.50	Potential death

SOURCES: Adapted from Oakley S. Ray, *Drugs, Society, and Human Behavior* (St. Louis, MO: Mosby, 1972), p. 86; Erich Goode, *Drugs in American Society* (New York: Knopf, 1972), pp. 142–143.

dull the pain of living and to take their minds off their problems. Some excessive drinkers seek a continual "buzz" to avoid facing life. Others drink occasionally to get "high." Some insomniacs drink so that they will sleep (often they pass out). Drinking before a flight is common for persons with a fear of flying because alcohol has a tranquilizing effect. Also, people often drink to temporarily get rid of unwanted emotions such as loneliness, anxiety, depression, feelings of inadequacy, insecurity, guilt, and resentment.

Alcoholism is a rather imprecise term because there is no clear-cut distinction between a problem drinker and an alcoholic. Nevertheless, a useful definition of alcoholism is *the repeated and excessive use of alcohol to the extent that it is harmful to interpersonal relations, to job performance, or to the drinker's health.*

Whether a person will be labeled an alcoholic depends to a large extent on the reactions of his or her employers, family, friends, associates, and community. For example, the "drier" the community in which one lives, the less alcohol and the fewer the problem incidents involving alcohol it takes for someone to be defined as an alcoholic.

People's reactions to drinking vary considerably. Some individuals can drink large amounts quite regularly while appearing sober—although their driving is affected, and they may have a high likelihood of becoming alcoholic in the future. Some people drink heavily without experiencing hangovers, although hangovers are functional because they let people know they have ingested too much alcohol and discourage further binges. Generally, as we've seen, the greater the weight of the drinker, the more she or he can consume before becoming intoxicated.

Many alcoholics who stop drinking must abstain *totally;* if they start again, they will have a

compulsive, uncontrollable urge to go on a series of binges. Because of this, Alcoholics Anonymous asserts that "Once an alcoholic, always an alcoholic." There is some evidence (highly controversial) that certain alcoholics can, after treatment, return to social drinking.[25] However, this finding has been highly criticized by a number of treatment organizations because it has led some alcoholics who had quit drinking to try to drink lightly, with the result that they immediately returned to excessive drinking.

Each alcoholic in the United States affects at least four other people close to him or her—including spouse, family, or employer. A majority of alcoholics are male, but the proportion of female alcoholics has risen in the past 40 years.[26] Contrary to popular stereotypes, only an estimated 5% are homeless.[27] Most are ordinary people.

Some people become alcoholic quite soon after they start drinking. Others may drink for 10, 20, or 30 years before becoming addicted. An alcoholic may be only psychologically dependent on alcohol, but most are also physically dependent.

Health Problems Caused by Alcohol The life expectancy of alcoholics is 10 to 12 years lower than that of nonalcoholics.[28] There are several reasons for this. Alcohol, over an extended period of time, gradually destroys liver cells, leaving scar tissue in their place. When the scar tissue is extensive, a medical condition called cirrhosis of the liver occurs. This condition causes more than 27,000 deaths per year in the United States.[29]

Alcohol has no healthy food value, although it contains a high number of calories. Heavy drinkers, as a result, have a reduced appetite for nutritious food, frequently suffer from vitamin deficiencies, and are highly susceptible to infectious diseases.

Heavy drinking also causes kidney problems, contributes to a variety of heart ailments, is a factor that leads to diabetes, and also appears to contribute to cancer. It is a contributing cause of ulcers and impotency in males. In addition, heavy drinking is associated with thousands of suicides each year.[30] Death can occur from drinking an excessive amount of alcohol—for example, from depression of the respiratory system or from the drinker choking on vomit while unconscious.

Interestingly, for some as-yet-unknown reason, the life expectancy for light to moderate drinkers

CASE EXHIBIT 8.1

Drug-Related Deaths of Famous People

There are hundreds of famous people whose deaths were drug related. The following are a few examples. Their ages at death are in parentheses ( ).

John Belushi (33), actor and comedian; heroin and cocaine overdose

Len Bias (22), basketball star; died of cocaine overdose before ever playing in the NBA

Lenny Bruce (40), comedian; morphine overdose

Richard Burton (59), actor; alcohol-related causes

Truman Capote (59), writer; liver disease complicated by phebitis and multiple drug intoxication

Kurt Cobain (27), musician; heroin overdose and a shotgun wound in head

Tommy Dorsey (51), jazz musician and band leader; choked to death while sleeping with the aid of drugs

Chris Farley (33), comedian; cocaine and morphine overdose

W. C. Fields (67), performer and actor; complications of alcoholism

Sigmund Freud (83), psychoanalyst; long-term cocaine use; physician-assisted morphine overdose

Judy Garland (47), singer and actress; disputed drug overdose as cause of death

Andy Gibb (30), singer; cardiac damage strongly exacerbated by cocaine and alcohol abuse

Bobby Hatfield (63), singer and musician; heart attack triggered by cocaine overdose

Billie Holiday (44), jazz singer; cirrhosis of the liver attributed to longtime alcohol and heroin abuse

Whitney Houston (48), pop singer; overdose of cocaine, alcohol, and other drugs

Howard Hughes (70), aviator, engineer, industrialist, movie producer; liver failure—autopsy showed lethal amount of codeine and Valium in body

Michael Jackson (41), pop singer; personal physician gave lethal dose of propofol

Janis Joplin (27), singer and musician; heroin overdose

Alan Ladd (50), actor; acute overdose of alcohol and barbiturates (probable suicide)

Heath Ledger (28), actor; combined drug intoxication of various prescription drugs, including oxycodone

Billy Martin (61), baseball player and manager; alcohol-related auto accident

Marilyn Monroe (36), actress; overdose of barbiturate-based sleeping pills

River Phoenix (23), actor; overdose of heroin and cocaine

Elvis Presley (42), singer; heart attack brought on by overdose of barbiturates

Freddie Prinze (22), comedian, actor; self-inflicted gunshot wound while under the influence of Quaaludes

Anna Nicole Smith (39), actress, reality show star; lethal combination of chloral hydrate and various benzodiazepines

Sid Vicious (21), musician; heroin overdose, disputed suicide

Keith Whitley (33), country singer; alcohol poisoning

Hank Williams (29), country singer; drugs and probably alcohol

Amy Winehouse (28), singer; alcohol poisoning

Natalie Wood (43), actress; drowned while intoxicated

---

exceeds that for nondrinkers.[31] Perhaps an occasional drink helps people relax and thereby reduces the likelihood of life-threatening stress-related illnesses.

Combining alcohol with other drugs can have disastrous and sometimes fatal effects. Sometimes two drugs taken together have a *synergistic* interaction, meaning that they create an effect much greater than either would produce alone. For example, sedatives like barbiturates (often found in sleeping pills) or Quaalude, when taken with alcohol, can so depress the central nervous system that a coma or even death may result.

Other drugs tend to have an *antagonistic* response to alcohol, meaning that one drug negates the effects of the other. Many doctors now caution patients not to drink while taking certain prescribed drugs because the alcohol will reduce, or even totally negate, the beneficial effects of these drugs.

Whether drugs will interact synergistically or antagonistically depends on a wide range of factors:

the properties of the drugs, the amounts taken, the user's tolerance to them, the amount of sleep the user has had, the kind and amount of food that has been eaten, and the user's overall health. The interactive effects may be minimal one day and extensive the next.

Withdrawal from alcohol once the body is physically addicted may lead to delirium tremens (DTs) and other unpleasant reactions. The DTs are characterized by rapid heartbeat, uncontrollable trembling, severe nausea, and profuse sweating.

Drinking and Driving Alcohol is a significant contributing factor in approximately 40% of all automobile fatalities and in many serious automobile injuries.[32] Each year nearly a million people in the United States are arrested for driving under the influence of alcohol.[33] One of the most noted persons to die in an alcohol-related accident was Princess Diana of Britain, age 36, who died in August

1997. The driver of the car, Henri Paul, was legally drunk when the crash occurred in a tunnel in Paris, France. Mothers Against Drunk Driving is having considerable success in getting states to enact and enforce stricter drunk-driving laws. In addition, the news media (particularly television and radio) have been airing public service programs and announcements to educate the public about the consequences of drunk driving (see Table 8.2).

Alcohol and Crime   About one-ninth of all arrests for minor crimes are alcohol related: public drunkenness, violations of liquor laws, disorderly conduct, and vagrancy.[34]

Alcohol is also a contributing factor in many major crimes. In a majority of homicides, aggravated assaults, sexual crimes against children, and sexually aggressive acts against women, the offender had been drinking.[35] This is not to say that alcohol is the main cause of these crimes. However, it appears to be a contributing factor that increases the likelihood of such crimes.

Critical Thinking Questions

Have you ever driven while intoxicated? If so, what are your strategies for avoiding doing this in the future?

Effects of Alcohol Abuse on the Family   In the past, if there was a problem drinker in the family, it was almost always the husband. Now the likelihood is increasing that it could be the wife or one (or more) of the teenagers.

Heavy drinking is a contributing factor to many family problems: child abuse, child neglect, spouse abuse, parent abuse, financial problems, unemployment of wage earners, violent arguments, and unhappy marriages. Marriage to an alcoholic often ends in divorce, separation, or desertion. Children of an alcoholic parent have higher rates of severe emotional and physical illnesses.[36] (See Case Exhibit 8.2: Fetal Alcohol Syndrome.)

Sharon Wegscheider indicates that members of alcoholic families tend to assume roles that both protect the chemically dependent person from taking responsibility for his or her behavior and actually serve to maintain the drinking problem. She

identifies several roles that are typically played by family members in addition to the chemically dependent person: the chief enabler, the family hero, the scapegoat, the lost child, and the mascot.[37]

The chief enabler's main purpose is to assume the primary responsibility for the family functioning. The abuser typically continues to lose control and relinquishes responsibility. The chief enabler, on the other hand, takes on more and more responsibility and begins making more and more family decisions. A chief enabler is often the parent or spouse of the chemically dependent person.

Conditions in families of chemically dependent people often continue to deteriorate as the dependent person loses control. A positive influence is needed to offset the negative. The family hero fulfills this role. The family hero often is the "perfect" person who does well at everything he or she tries. The hero works very hard at making the family appear to be functioning better than it is. In this way, the family hero provides the family with self-worth.

Another typical role played by someone in the chemically dependent family is the scapegoat. Although the alcohol abuse is the real problem, a family rule may mandate that this fact be denied and the blame be placed elsewhere. Frequently, another family member is targeted with the blame. The scapegoat often behaves in negative ways (for example, gets caught for stealing, runs away, becomes extremely withdrawn), which draws the spotlight to him or her. The scapegoat's role is to distract attention away from the dependent person and onto something else. This role helps the family avoid addressing the problem of chemical dependency.

Often there is also a lost child in the family. This is the person who seems rather uninvolved with the rest of the members yet never causes any trouble. The lost child's purpose is to provide relief to the family from some of the pain it is suffering. At least there is someone in the home who neither requires much attention nor causes any stress. The lost child is simply there.

Finally, chemically dependent families often have someone playing the role of mascot. The mascot is the person who probably has a good sense of humor and appears not to take anything seriously. Despite how much the mascot might be suffering inside, he or she provides a little fun for the family.

In summary, alcoholism is a problem affecting the entire family. Each member is suffering over

CASE EXHIBIT 8.2

Fetal Alcohol Syndrome

Prior to the 1940s, it was thought that the uterus was a glass bubble that totally separated the fetus from the outside world and fully protected the fetus from whatever drugs the mother happened to be using. Since then, medical science has learned that chemical substances are readily transferred from the mother's uterine arteries, across the placental membrane, into the baby's umbilical vein, and then to the baby's entire body.

When a pregnant woman drinks any alcoholic beverage (including beer and wine), the alcohol easily crosses the placenta, and the fetus attains blood alcohol levels that are similar to those in the mother. Heavy alcohol consumption by pregnant mothers can cause a variety of conditions in the new baby that, taken together, have been labeled fetal alcohol syndrome. These conditions include cognitive disabilities and developmental delays, overall growth retardation before and after birth, and various congenital malformations of the face, head, skeleton, and heart. These babies are more likely to be born prematurely, to have a low birth weight, to be hyperirritable, and to have neurological defects and poor muscle tone. They also have a higher infant mortality rate. The chances of

microcephaly (a condition in which the baby has a small brain and skull and is mentally retarded) are increased.

The more alcohol a pregnant woman ingests, the greater the probability that her baby will have fetal alcohol syndrome. Studies suggest that, if a pregnant woman has five or more drinks at any one time, her baby will have a 10% chance of developing fetal alcohol syndrome. If she drinks lightly over a prolonged period, the syndrome may also occur. An average of 1 ounce per day results in a 10% risk; an average of 2 ounces per day results in a 20% risk.

The U.S. Public Health Service recommends that pregnant women not drink alcohol. Just as a mother would not give a glass of wine to her newborn, she should not give it to her unborn baby. Other drugs (such as tobacco, marijuana, cocaine, and heroin) during pregnancy also endanger the unborn child.

SOURCES: Mike Samuels and Mary Samuels, "Pregnancy: How Smoking and Drugs Endanger Baby," *Wisconsin State Journal*, Jul. 2, 1986, sec. 2, p. 1; Diane E. Papalia, Sally W. Olds, and Ruth D. Fiedman, *Human Development*, 10th ed. (Boston: McGraw-Hill, 2007), pp. 93–94.

the dependency, yet each assumes a role in order to maintain the family's status quo and to help the family survive. Family members are driven to maintain these roles, no matter what.

Alcohol and Industry   Alcoholism costs business and industry billions of dollars annually. This figure reflects losses in terms of sick leave, absenteeism, missed or late work assignments, and on-the-job accidents.

Alcoholism Gene Theory   Alcoholism has long been assumed to be caused by both environmental and genetic factors. There has been considerable controversy in recent years, however, concerning the alcoholism gene theory.

Alcoholism has been found to run in families. In addition, children of alcoholic (biological) parents who are adopted at an early age have a significantly higher chance of becoming alcoholic than do children in the general population.[38]

Biological research has primarily focused on the role of genetics in predisposing an individual to drug use. Research suggests that persons who experience severe early-onset alcoholism may be genetically predisposed.[39]

Mooney, Knox, and Schacht note:

Biological theories of drug use hypothesize that some individuals are physiologically predisposed to experience more pleasure from drugs than others and, consequently, are more likely to be drug users. According to these theories, the central nervous system, which is composed primarily of the brain and spinal cord, processes drugs through neurotransmitters in a way that produces an unusually euphoric experience. Individuals not so physiologically inclined report less pleasant experiences and are less likely to continue use.[40]

Critical Thinking Question

To what extent do you believe that biological factors predispose a person to be alcoholic?

Avoiding Treatment for Alcoholism   Many alcoholics (perhaps the majority) do not seek help because they *deny* they have a drinking problem. In an attempt to prove they can drink like any other person, they wind up sneaking drinks, excusing their drinking behavior, or blaming others ("If you had a job like mine, you'd drink too!"). There are many reasons why

Date-Rape Drugs

In the mid-1990s, Rohypnol became known as the date-rape drug. Since that time a number of women have been sexually assaulted after the drug was slipped into one of their drinks (both alcoholic and nonalcoholic). Rohypnol often causes blackouts, with complete loss of memory. Female victims who are slipped the drug and then raped often cannot remember any details of the crimes.

Rohypnol is a sedative related to Valium but 10 times stronger. It is legally available in more than 60 countries for severe insomnia but is illegal in the United States (many drugs—such as cocaine and heroin—are, too, but are widely used and abused). Much of the illegal Rohypnol in the United States is smuggled in from Mexico and Colombia.

Rohypnol is also popular with teens and young adults (both males and females) who like to combine it with alcohol for a quick punch-drunk hit. Another reason for its popularity is that it's relatively inexpensive, often being purchased on the street for $1 to $5 per pill. In some jurisdictions, drivers are now tested for Rohypnol when they appear drunk but register a low alcohol level. (Rohypnol is also addictive, and there is a potential for lethal overdosing.)

Because of the ease with which Rohypnol can be slipped into a drink, rape crisis centers are urging women never to take their eyes off their drinks. In 1997 the marketer of Rohypnol, Hoffmann-LaRoche, announced it will only sell a new version that would cause any liquid that it is slipped into to have a blue color. In response to the reformulated blue tablets, people who intend to commit a sexual offense facilitated by Rohypnol are now serving blue tropical drinks and punches in which the blue dye can be disguised.

Other sedatives have similar effects. Gamma hydroxy butyrate (GHB) is another drug that is increasingly being used as a date-rape drug. GHB is a central nervous system depressant that is approved as an anesthetic in some countries. It can be readily made at home from a mixture of chemicals purchased in stores normally used in cleaning, such as lye. Just 1 gram of this liquid home brew provides an intoxicating experience equivalent to 26 ounces of whiskey. Similar to Rohypnol, GHB is slipped into the drinks of intended victims.

---

alcoholics refuse to admit the severity of their condition. Alcoholism is highly stigmatized. It is viewed as a disease, and alcoholics may not want to perceive themselves as "sick." Some see alcohol as essential to their lives. They socialize through drinking and are able to relax, fall asleep, or escape from their problems. Thus, they may choose to keep drinking even though they know it is ruining their health, destroying their reputation in the community, getting them fired at a variety of jobs, and breaking up their family. In many ways, alcohol becomes their "best friend," which they refuse to abandon—even if it kills them.

If an alcoholic is to be helped, this denial of their problem must be confronted. (We will discuss denial further in the section on rehabilitation programs.)

Barbiturates

Barbiturates, which are derived from barbituric acid, depress the central nervous system. Barbiturates were first synthesized in the early 1900s, and there are now more than 2,500 different varieties. They are commonly used to relieve insomnia and anxiety, to treat epilepsy and high blood pressure, and to relax patients before or after surgery. Barbiturates are illegal unless obtained by a physician's prescription.

Taken in sufficient doses, barbiturates have effects similar to strong alcohol. Users experience relief from inhibitions, have a feeling of euphoria, feel "high" or in good humor, and are passively content. However, these moods can change rapidly to gloom, agitation, and aggressiveness. Physiological effects include slurred speech, disorientation, staggering, confusion, drowsiness, and impaired coordination.

Prolonged heavy use of barbiturates can cause physical dependency, with withdrawal symptoms similar to those of heroin addiction. Withdrawal is accompanied by body tremors, cramps, anxiety, fever, nausea, profuse sweating, and hallucinations. Many authorities believe barbiturate addiction is more dangerous than heroin addiction, and it is considered more resistant to treatment than heroin addiction. Abrupt withdrawal can cause fatal convulsions. One forensic pathologist noted: "Show me someone who goes cold turkey (the sudden and complete halting of drug use) on a bad barbiturate habit, and I'll show you a corpse."[41]

Barbiturate overdose can cause convulsions, coma, poisoning, and sometimes death. Barbiturates are particularly dangerous when taken with alcohol because the alcohol acts synergistically to magnify the potency of the barbiturates. Accidental deaths due to excessive doses are frequent. Often the user becomes groggy, forgets how much has been taken, and continues to take more until an overdose level has been reached. Barbiturates are also the most popular suicide drug. A number of famous people (for example, Marilyn Monroe) have fatally overdosed on barbiturates.

Generally, barbiturates are taken orally, although some users inject them intravenously. Use of barbiturates, like alcohol, may lead to traffic fatalities.

Tranquilizers

Other depressants are the drugs classified as tranquilizers. Common brand names are Librium, Miltown, Serax, Tranxene, and Valium. They reduce anxiety, relax muscles, and act as sedatives. Users have a moderate potential of becoming physically and psychologically dependent. Tranquilizers are usually taken orally, and the effects last 4 to 8 hours. Side effects include slurred speech, disorientation, and behavior resembling intoxication. Overdoses are possible and result in cold and clammy skin, shallow respiration, dilated pupils, weak and rapid pulse, coma, and possibly death. Withdrawal symptoms are similar to those from alcohol and barbiturates: anxiety, tremors, convulsions, delirium, and sometimes death.

Quaalude and PCP

Both Quaalude and PCP are depressants. (PCP also produces effects similar to those of hallucinogens.)

Methaqualone (better known by its patent name, Quaalude) resembles barbiturates and alcohol in its effects, although it is chemically different. It has the reputation of being a "love drug" because users believe it makes them more eager for sex and enhances sexual pleasure. These effects probably stem from the fact that it lowers inhibitions (similar to alcohol and barbiturates). Quaalude also reduces anxiety and gives a feeling of euphoria. Users can become both physically and psychologically dependent. Overdose can result in convulsions, coma, delirium, and even death. Most deaths occur when the drug is taken together with alcohol, which vastly magnifies its effects. Withdrawal symptoms are severe and unpleasant. Abuse of the drug may also cause hangovers, fatigue, liver damage, and temporary paralysis of the limbs.

The technical name for PCP is phencyclidine, and its street name is "angel dust." PCP was developed in the 1950s as an anesthetic, but this medical use soon ended because patients displayed symptoms of severe emotional disturbance after receiving it. PCP is legal today only for tranquilizing elephants and monkeys, which apparently do not experience the adverse side effects.

PCP is used primarily by young people who are unaware of its hazards. It is usually smoked, often after being sprinkled on a marijuana "joint." It may also be sniffed, swallowed, or injected. PCP is a very dangerous drug. It distorts the senses, disrupts balance, and leads to an inability to think clearly. Larger amounts of PCP can cause a person to become paranoid, can lead to aggressive behavior (even violent murder), and can create temporary symptoms of a severe emotional disturbance. Continued use can lead to the development of a prolonged emotional disturbance. Overdose may result in coma or even death.

Research has not as yet concluded whether PCP induces physical or psychological dependency. The drug has a potential to be used (and abused) extensively because it is relatively easy to prepare in a home laboratory and because the ingredients and recipes are widely available. An additional danger of PCP is that even one-time users sometimes have flashbacks in which hallucinations are reexperienced, even long after use has ceased. It may be that many accidents and unexplained disasters are caused by someone's previous use of PCP or some other undetectable hallucinogenic substance.

Stimulants

In this section, we will examine the following drugs classified as stimulants: caffeine, amphetamines, cocaine and crack, amyl nitrate, and butyl nitrate.

Caffeine

Caffeine is a stimulant to the central nervous system. It is present in coffee, tea, cocoa, Coca-Cola, and many other soft drinks. It is also available in tablet form (for example, No-Doz).

Practically all Americans use caffeine on a daily basis. It reduces hunger, fatigue, and boredom and improves alertness and motor activity. The drug appears to be addictive because many users develop a tolerance for it. A further sign that it is addictive is that heavy users (for example, habitual coffee drinkers) will experience withdrawal symptoms of mild irritability and depression. Excessive amounts of caffeine cause insomnia, restlessness, and gastrointestinal irritation and can even, surprisingly, cause death.

Because caffeine has the status of a "nondrug" in our society, users are not labeled criminals, there is no black market for it, and no subculture is formed to give support in obtaining and using the drug. Because caffeine is legal, its price is low compared to that of other drugs. Users are not tempted to resort to crime to support their habit. Some authorities assert that our approach to caffeine should serve as a model for the way we react to other illegal drugs (such as marijuana) that, they feel, are no more harmful than caffeine.[42]

Amphetamines

Amphetamines are called "uppers" because of their stimulating effects. When prescribed by a physician, they are legal. Some truck drivers have obtained prescriptions to stay awake and alert during a long haul, with a few becoming addicted. Dieters have received prescriptions to help them lose weight and have also found that the pills tend to give them more self-confidence and buoyance. College students have used them to stay awake and alert while studying. Others who have used amphetamines to increase alertness and performance for relatively short periods of time include athletes, astronauts, and executives. Additional nicknames for these drugs are *speed, ups, pep pills, black beauties,* and *bennies.*

Amphetamines are synthetic drugs. They are similar to adrenalin, a hormone from the adrenal gland that stimulates the central nervous system. The better known amphetamines include Dexedrine, Benzedrine, and Methedrine. Physical reactions to amphetamines are extensive: Consumption of fat stored in body tissues is accelerated, heartbeat is increased, respiratory processes are stimulated, appetite is reduced, and insomnia is common. Users feel euphoric and stronger and have an increased capacity to concentrate and to express themselves verbally. Prolonged use can lead to irritability, deep anxiety, and an irrational persecution complex that can provoke sudden acts of violence.

Amphetamines are usually taken orally in tablet, powder, or capsule form. They also can be sniffed or injected. "Speeding" (injecting the drug into a vein) produces the most powerful effects but also the greatest harm. An overdose can cause a coma, with possible brain damage, and in rare cases death may occur. Speeders may develop hepatitis, abscesses, convulsions, hallucinations, delusions, and severe emotional disturbances. Another danger is that, when sold on the street, the substance may contain impurities that are additional health hazards.

An amphetamine high is often followed by mental depression and fatigue. Continued amphetamine use leads to psychological dependency. It is unclear whether amphetamines are physically addicting because the withdrawal symptoms are uncharacteristic of withdrawal from other drugs. Amphetamine withdrawal symptoms include sleep disturbances, apathy, decreased activity, disorientation, irritability, exhaustion, and depression. Some authorities see these withdrawal symptoms as indicative of physical addiction.[43]

One of the legal uses of certain amphetamines is in the treatment of hyperactivity in children. Hyperactivity (also called hyperkinesis) is characterized by a short attention span, excessive motor activity, restlessness, and shifts in moods. Little is known about the causes of this condition. As children become older, the symptoms tend to disappear, even without treatment. Interestingly, some amphetamines (Ritalin is a popular one) have a calming and soothing effect on children; the exact opposite effect occurs when Ritalin is taken by adults. It should be noted that treatment of "uncontrollable" children with amphetamines has frequently been abused. Some of the children for whom Ritalin is prescribed are not really hyperactive. They are normal children who simply refuse to submit to what their teachers and parents consider appropriate childhood behavior. As a result, these children are labeled "problem children" and are introduced into the world of taking a mood-altering drug on a daily basis.

An amphetamine that has had increasing illegal use in recent years is methamphetamine hydrochloride, known on the street as "meth" or "ice." In liquid form, it is often referred to as "speed." Under experimental conditions, cocaine users often have difficulty distinguishing cocaine from methamphetamine hydrochloride. There is a danger this drug may be increasingly abused, as its "high" lasts longer than that from cocaine and the drug can be synthesized relatively easily in laboratories from products that are sold legally in the United States. Methamphetamine hydrochloride (Desoxyn) is legally used to treat obesity as one component of a "last-resort" weight-reduction regimen. There is, however, a serious side effect of this drug when used for weight reduction: The user's appetite returns with greater intensity after the drug is discontinued.

Cocaine and Crack

Cocaine is obtained from the leaves of the South American coca plant. It has a chic status in this country and is rapidly replacing other illegal drugs in popularity. Although legally classified as a narcotic, it is in fact not related to the opiates from which narcotic drugs are derived. It is a powerful stimulant and anti-fatigue agent.

In the United States, cocaine is generally taken by sniffing and absorbed through the nasal membranes. The most common method is sniffing through a straw or a rolled-up bank note; this is known as "snorting." It may also be injected intravenously, and in South America the natives chew the coca leaf. It may be added in small quantities to a cigarette and smoked. Cocaine has been used medically in the past as a local anesthetic, but other drugs have now largely replaced it for this purpose.

Cocaine constricts the blood vessels and thereby leads to increased strength and endurance. It also is thought by users to increase creative and intellectual powers. Other effects include a feeling of euphoria, excitement, restlessness, and a lessened sense of fatigue. Some users of cocaine claim that it heightens or restores their virility and enables them to prolong intercourse for long periods.[44]

Larger doses or extended use may result in hallucinations and delusions. A peculiar effect of cocaine abuse is *formication*—the illusion that ants, snakes, or bugs are crawling on or into the skin. Some abusers have such intense illusions that they literally scratch, slap, and wound themselves trying to kill these imaginary creatures.

Physical effects of cocaine include increased blood pressure and pulse rate, insomnia, and loss of appetite. Frequent users may experience weight loss or malnutrition due to appetite suppression. Physical dependency on cocaine is considered a low to medium risk. However, the drug appears to be psychologically habituating; withdrawal usually results in intense depression and despair, which drive the person back to taking the drug.[45] Additional effects of withdrawal include apathy, long periods of sleep, extreme fatigue, irritability, and disorientation. Serious tissue damage to the nose can occur when large quantities of cocaine are "sniffed" over a prolonged time period. Regular use may result in habitual sniffling and sometimes leads to an anorexic condition. High doses can cause

agitation, increased body temperature, and convulsions. A few people who overdose may die if their breathing and heart functions become too depressed.

Crack (also called "rock") is obtained from cocaine. The inert ingredients are separated from the cocaine by mixing it with water and ammonium hydroxide. The water is then removed from the cocaine base by means of a fast-drying solvent, usually ether. The resultant mixture resembles large sugar crystals, similar to rock sugar. Crack is highly addictive. Some authorities claim that one use is enough to lead to addiction. Users generally claim that, after they have finished one dose, they immediately crave another.

Crack is usually smoked, either in a specially made glass pipe or mixed with tobacco or marijuana in a cigarette. The effects are similar to those of cocaine, but the "rush" is more immediate, and the drug gives an intensified high and has an even greater orgasmic effect.

An overdose is more common when crack is injected than when it is smoked. Withdrawal effects include an irresistible compulsion to have the drug, as well as apathy, long periods of sleep, irritability, extreme fatigue, depression, and disorientation.

Communal use of needles spreads AIDS. Cocaine and crack can have serious effects on the heart, straining it with high blood pressure, with interrupted heart rhythm, and with raised pulse rates. Cocaine and crack may also damage the liver. Severe convulsions can cause brain damage, emotional problems, and sometimes death. Smoking crack may also damage the lungs.

Amyl Nitrate and Butyl Nitrate

Amyl nitrate ("poppers") is prescribed for patients at risk of certain forms of heart failure. It is a volatile liquid that is sold in small bottles. When the container is opened, the chemical begins to evaporate (similar to gasoline). If the vapor is sniffed, the user's blood vessels are immediately dilated, and there is an increase in heart rate. These physical changes create feelings of mental excitation ("head rush") and physical excitation ("body rush"). The drug is legal only by prescription, but (as with many other drugs) illicit dealers readily obtain and distribute it.

Butyl nitrate is legally available in some states without a prescription and has an effect similar to that of amyl nitrate. Trade names under which it is sold are Rush and Locker Room. Similar to amyl nitrate, the vapor is sniffed. It is available at some sexual aid and novelty stores.

Both these drugs have been used as aphrodisiacs and as stimulants while dancing. The drugs have some short-term, unpleasant side effects that may include fainting, headaches, and dizziness. A few deaths have been reported due to overdoses. Both these drugs are classified as stimulants.

Narcotics

The most commonly used narcotic drugs in the United States are the opiates (such as opium, heroin, and morphine). The term *narcotic* means "sleep inducing." In actuality, drugs classified as narcotics are more accurately called analgesics, or painkillers. The principal effect produced by narcotic drugs is a feeling of euphoria.

The opiates are all derived from the opium poppy, which grows in many countries. Turkey, Southeast Asia, and Colombia have in our recent past been major sources of the opiates. The drug opium is the dried form of a milky substance that oozes from the seed pods after the petals fall from the purple or white flower. Opium has been used for centuries.

Morphine is the main active ingredient of opium. It was first identified in the early 1800s and has been used extensively as a painkiller. Heroin was first synthesized from morphine in 1874. It was once thought to be a cure for morphine addiction but later was also found to be addicting. Heroin is a more potent drug than morphine.

Opium is usually smoked, although it can be taken orally. Morphine and heroin are either sniffed (snorted) or injected into a muscle or a vein (called "mainlining"), which maximizes the drugs' effects.

Opiates affect the central nervous system and produce feelings of tranquility, drowsiness, or euphoria. They also generate a sense of well-being, which makes pain, anxiety, or depression seem unimportant. Tony Blaze-Gosden notes:

> It has been described as giving an orgasmlike rush or flash that lasts briefly but memorably. At the peak of the euphoria, the user has a feeling of exaggerated physical and mental comfort and well-being; a heightened feeling of buoyancy and bodily health, and a heightened feeling of being competent, in control, capable of any achievement, and being able to cope.[46]

Overdoses can cause convulsions, coma, and in rare cases, death by respiratory failure. All opiates are now recognized as highly addictive.

Heroin is the most widely abused opiate. In addition to the aforementioned effects, heroin slows the functioning parts of the brain. The user's appetite and sex drive tend to be dulled. After an initial feeling of euphoria, the user generally becomes lethargic and stuporous. Contrary to popular belief, most heroin users take the drug infrequently and do not as a rule become addicted.[47]

Opiate addiction occurs when the user takes the drug regularly for a period of time. Whether addiction will occur depends on the opiate taken, the strength of the dosages, the regularity of use, the characteristics of the user, and the length of time taken. Addiction can occur within a few weeks. Users rapidly develop a tolerance and may eventually need a dose that is up to 100 times stronger than a dose that would have been fatal during the initiation to the drug.[48]

The withdrawal process is very unpleasant. Symptoms include chills, cramps, sweating, nervousness, anxiety, runny eyes and nose, dilated pupils, muscle aches, increased blood pressure, severe cramps, nausea, and fever. Most addicts are obsessed with securing a fix to avoid these severe withdrawal symptoms.

Addiction to opiates is extremely difficult to break, partly because intense craving for the drug may recur periodically for several months afterward.

Most opiate addicts are under age 30, of low socioeconomic status, and poorly educated. A disproportionate number are African Americans. Distribution and addiction to narcotic drugs occur primarily in large urban centers.

When heroin was first discovered in the late 1800s, it was initially used as a painkiller, as a substitute for people addicted to morphine, and as a drug taken by many to experience euphoria. A fair number of people became addicted, and in the early 1900s, laws were passed to prohibit its sale, possession, and distribution.

Heroin abuse continues to be regarded by some Americans as our most serious drug problem. This stereotype does not appear warranted because only a tiny fraction of the U.S. population has ever tried heroin. The number of people addicted to heroin is minuscule compared to the number addicted to alcohol or tobacco. In addition, drugs such as alcohol and barbiturates contribute to many more deaths.

One reason why heroin retains its reputation is that users are thought to be "dope fiends" who commit violent crimes and reject the values of contemporary society. Addicts, however, are unlikely to commit such

CASE EXHIBIT 8.4

Babies Who Are Crack Exposed

In the 1980s, a flurry of media reports suggested a link between women's cocaine use during pregnancy and a range of damaging effects on babies. Some media articles stated these babies would have permanent brain damage, suggesting they would have severe cognitive disabilities for the remainder of their lives. A *Washington Post* column by Charles Krauthammer (7/30/89), for example, stated "The inner-city crack epidemic is now giving birth to the newest horror: a bio-underclass, a generation of physically damaged cocaine babies whose biological inferiority is stamped at birth."

Now, however, researchers who have followed these children who were exposed to cocaine before birth have concluded that the long-term effects of such exposure on children's brain development and behavior appear to be relatively small. Cocaine is undoubtedly bad for the fetus. But experts say its effects are less severe than those of alcohol and are comparable to those of tobacco. (Sometimes the media seizes on supposed medical phenomenon and hypes it beyond recognition, distorting facts irresponsibly or simply getting the "facts" wrong.) It appears the lack of good prenatal care, use of tobacco and alcohol, and poverty are more serious factors in poor fetal development among pregnant cocaine users than cocaine itself.

Source: http://www.fair.org/index.php?page=3702.

violent crimes as rape or aggravated assault. They are more likely to commit crimes against property (shoplifting, burglary, pickpocketing, larceny, and robbery) to support their habit.[49] Prostitution for female addicts is also common. Because the severe withdrawal symptoms begin about 18 hours after the last fix, addicts who have experienced these symptoms will do almost anything to avoid them.

Unsanitary injections of heroin may cause hepatitis and other infections. Communal use of needles can spread AIDS. Also, the high cost of maintaining a heroin habit—often more than $100 daily—may create huge financial problems for the user.

Because the price of illicit narcotic drugs is so high, organized crime has made huge profits in the smuggling and distribution of these drugs. Often narcotics are diluted with dangerous impurities, which pose serious health hazards for the users.

Hallucinogens

Hallucinogens were popular as psychedelic drugs in the late 1960s. These drugs distort the user's perceptions, creating hallucinatory impressions of "sights and sounds" that do not exist. The five hallucinogens most commonly used in this country are mescaline (peyote), psilocybin, psilocin, LSD, and ecstasy. All are taken orally—swallowed in capsule form, eaten on a sugar cube, or licked from the back of a stamp.

Peyote is derived from a cactus plant. Mescaline is the synthetic form of peyote. Psilocybin and psilocin are found in approximately 90 different species of mushrooms (called "magic mushrooms"). Both peyote and psilocybin have had a long history of use among certain Native American tribes. Members of the Native American Church, a religious organization, have won the legal right to use peyote on ceremonial occasions.[50]

A very popular hallucinogen is LSD (lysergic acid diethylamide). LSD is a synthetic material derived from a fungus (ergot) that grows on rye and other plants. It is one of the most potent drugs known; a single ounce will make up to 300,000 doses.

The effects of LSD vary greatly depending on the expectations and psychological state of the user and on the context in which it is taken. The same person may experience differing reactions on different occasions. Users report "seeing" sounds and "hearing" colors. Colors may seem unusually bright and shift kaleidoscopically, and objects may appear to expand and contract. LSD users become highly suggestible and easily manipulated, including sexually.

Bizarre hallucinations are also common. The experience may be peaceful or may result in panic. Some users have developed severe emotional disturbances that resulted in long-term hospitalization. Usually a "trip" will last 8 to 16 hours. Physical reactions include increased heartbeat, goose bumps, dilated pupils, hyperactivity, tremors, and sweating. Aftereffects include acute anxiety or depression. Flashbacks sometimes occur after the actual drug experience. They may happen at any time and place, with no advance warning. If the user is driving a car when a flashback occurs, the condition could be life threatening for everyone in the vicinity. Users develop tolerance to the drug very rapidly, with larger doses being needed in the future to achieve the desired effects. Cessation of use, even for a few days, will restore sensitivity to the drug, enabling the user to again take smaller quantities to experience the effects.

The effects and dangers of mescaline, psilocybin, and psilocin are similar to those of LSD. LSD is, however, the most potent of the hallucinogens.

Ecstasy was developed and patented in the early 1900s as a chemical forerunner in the synthesis of pharmaceuticals. Chemically, ecstasy is similar to the stimulant amphetamine and the hallucinogen mescaline, and can produce both stimulant and psychedelic effects. Effects last approximately 3 to 6 hours, although confusion, depression, sleep problems, anxiety, and paranoia have been reported to occur even weeks after the drug is taken. Ecstasy is used sometimes by young adults at all-night dance parties, such as "raves." The stimulant effects of ecstasy enable users to dance for extended periods.

Ecstasy use in high doses can be extremely dangerous. It can lead to dehydration, hypertension, and heart or kidney failure. It can cause a marked increase in body temperature. Chronic use of ecstasy can produce long-lasting, perhaps permanent, damage to the neurons that release serotonin and thus result in memory impairment.

Tobacco

The use of tobacco has now become recognized as one of the most damaging drug habits in the United States. Smoking can cause emphysema, cancer of the mouth, ulcers, and lung cancer. Users have a reduced life expectancy. Smoking significantly increases the risk of strokes and heart disease, particularly in women who use birth control pills.[51] Smoking by a pregnant woman sometimes leads to miscarriages, premature births, and underweight infants. Yet in spite of these widely publicized hazards, many Americans continue to smoke.[52]

Critical Thinking Question

Make a list of all of the drugs, including prescribed drugs, that you are currently using. Are there any that you know you should cut back on, or stop using? Circle these.

Tobacco is the number-one killer drug, contributing to far more deaths than all other drugs combined.[53] It is estimated to lead to 430,000 deaths per year in the United States.[54] This is more than double the number of deaths caused by alcohol abuse and hundreds of times the number of deaths caused by cocaine.[55] Most of these deaths result from heart disease and lung cancer due to cigarette smoking. However, more than 2,000 deaths per year result from fires caused by smoking.[56] There is also substantial evidence that "passive smoking" (breathing the smoke from others' cigarettes, cigars, or pipes) is hazardous to health. One source of such evidence is the finding that young children whose parents smoke have a higher incidence of pneumonia and other respiratory disorders than young children whose parents do not smoke.[57]

The attitudes of Americans toward tobacco use are gradually becoming more negative. Increasingly, we are viewing tobacco as a dangerous drug, and nonsmokers are perceiving smokers as pariahs. Some authorities are now predicting that cigarettes will eventually be outlawed in many countries.

In 1988 the surgeon general of the United States, C. Everett Koop, declared that tobacco is as addictive as heroin or cocaine.[58] Koop defined people who are addicted to tobacco as drug addicts.

Nicotine, the primary drug in tobacco, has remarkable capacities; it can act as a depressant, a stimulant, or a tranquilizer. Smokers quickly develop a tolerance for nicotine and gradually increase consumption to one or two packs or more a day.

There are special clinics and a variety of other educational and therapeutic programs to help people quit smoking. Tobacco is a very habit-forming drug. Withdrawal from use leads people to become restless, irritable, and depressed and to have an intense craving to smoke. Studies show that only a minority of smokers who make determined efforts to quit actually succeed.[59]

In the biggest civil settlement in U.S. history, tobacco companies agreed in 1998 to pay more than $240 billion to the 50 states to settle claims against the industry for health-care costs blamed on tobacco-related illnesses. The payments to the states are distributed over 25 years (payments began in 2000). Some of the funds will go to a foundation to study how to reduce teen smoking. A major objective of the deal is to discourage children from smoking by restricting advertising and by imposing sharp limits on the ways that cigarettes are marketed.

Marijuana

Marijuana ("grass" or "pot") comes from the hemp plant *Cannabis sativa*. This plant grows throughout the world, and its fibers are legally used to produce rope, twine, paper, and clothing.

The main use of the plant now, however, centers on its dried leaves and flowers—marijuana—and on its dried resin—hashish. Both marijuana and hashish may be taken orally but are usually smoked. Hashish is several times more potent than marijuana.

The effects of marijuana (and hashish) vary, as with any other drug, according to the mood and personality of the user, the circumstances, and the quality of the drug. Marijuana has sedative properties and creates in the user a sense of relaxed well-being and freedom from inhibition. There may also be mild hallucinations that create a dreamy state in which the user experiences fantasies. Smokers become highly suggestible and may engage in actions (such as sexual activities) they might otherwise avoid. The drug may induce feelings of joyousness, hilarity, and sociability. It may lead to talkativeness, disconnected ideas, a feeling of floating, and laughter. Sometimes marijuana intensifies sensory stimulation, creates feelings of enhanced awareness and creativity, and increases self-confidence.

The threat of physical dependency is rated low; the threat of psychological dependency is rated moderate. Withdrawal, however, may be very unpleasant, with the user suffering from insomnia, hyperactivity, and loss of appetite.

The short-term physical effects of marijuana are minor: a reddening of the eyes, dryness of the throat and mouth, and a slight increase in heart rate. There is some evidence that continued use by young teenagers will result in their becoming apathetic, noncompetitive, and uninterested in school and other activities.[60]

Frequent users may have impairments of short-term memory, concentration, judgment, and coordination. They may find it difficult to read, to understand what they read, or to follow moving objects with their eyes. Users may feel confident that their coordination, reactions, and perceptions are quite normal while they are still experiencing the effects of the drug; under these conditions, such activities as driving a vehicle may have tragic consequences to them and to others. Marijuana use by pregnant women may also contribute to malformations in fetuses, much like the effects of alcohol use.

An overdose of the active ingredients of cannabis can lead to panic, fear, confusion, suspiciousness, fatigue, and sometimes, aggressive acts. One of the most frequently voiced concerns about marijuana is that it will be a "stepping-stone" to other drugs. About 60% of marijuana users "progress" to other drugs.[61] However, other factors, such as peer pressure, are probably more crucial determinants of which mind-altering drugs people will "advance" to using.

The attempt to restrict marijuana use through legislation has been described as a "second prohibition,"[62] with similar results: Large numbers of people are using the drug in disregard of the law. The unfortunate effect of laws that attempt to regulate victimless acts (crimes, as defined by law) is that they criminalize the private acts of many people who are otherwise law abiding. They also foster the development of organized crime and the illicit drug market.

For years heated debates have raged about the hazards of long-term marijuana use. Some studies claim that it causes brain damage, chromosome damage, irritation of the bronchial tract and lungs, and a reduction in male hormone levels. These findings have not been confirmed by other studies, and the controversy rages on.[63]

Marijuana may be useful in treating glaucoma, asthma, certain seizure disorders, and spastic conditions, and in controlling severe nausea caused by cancer chemotherapy.[64]

One of the reversible short-term health effects of marijuana use is impairment of motor coordination, which adversely affects driving or machine-operating skills. The drug also impairs short-term memory, slows learning abilities, and may cause periods of confusion and anxiety. There is evidence that smoking marijuana may affect the lungs and respiratory system in much the same way that tobacco smoke does and may be a factor in causing bronchitis and precancerous changes.

In 1996 voters in California and Arizona approved the medical use of marijuana (for example,

CASE EXHIBIT 8.5

Steroid Use in Baseball

On March 30, 2006, baseball commissioner Bud Selig asked former Senator George Mitchell to investigate steroid use in baseball. On December 13, 2007, Mitchell released his report. The report found steroid use among former and current players to be rampant.

Eighty-six former and current players were named in the report. (It is thought that there are many other users among baseball players who have not as yet been identified.) Steroids have been part of baseball's banned substance list since 1991; however, testing of major league players did not begin until 2005.

Seven Most Valuable Player Award Winners were named in the report, along with 31 All Stars—at least one for every position. Some of the biggest names in baseball are alleged to have been users. Those named included Barry Bonds, Roger Clemens, Mark McGwire, David Justice, Jason Giambi, Gary Sheffield, Miguel Tejada, Lenny Dykstra, Rafael Palmeiro, Andy Pettitte, and Chuck Knoblauch. (Some of these players have denied, under oath, that they used steroids.)

To avoid testing positive for steroids, many athletes looking for an edge have turned to human growth hormone, HGH, to build muscle. It is difficult to detect, and the best test available has a window of detection of only 48 to 72 hours.

---

for treating symptoms of AIDS, cancer, and other diseases). However, the Clinton administration threatened sanctions against doctors who prescribed it. In 1997 a panel of experts convened at the National Institutes of Health stated that marijuana shows promise in treating painful symptoms of some diseases and urged its medical use to be studied further.[65] Seven other states soon passed legislation that allowed marijuana to be used for medical purposes.

In 2001 the U.S. Supreme Court ruled that federal law definitely classifies the use of marijuana as illegal and that marijuana has no medical benefits worthy of an exception.[66] The High Court did not strike down state laws allowing medical use of marijuana, but left those distributing the drug for that purpose open to prosecution.

In 2005 the U.S. Supreme Court upheld the power of Congress to legislate to prohibit the possession and use of marijuana for medical purposes, even in the states that permit it. This ruling does not invalidate laws in the states that have approved medical marijuana, but it does deflate these states' power to protect users and doctors who prescribe the drug. The controversy over the medical use of marijuana will probably continue to be an issue.

At the time of the revision of this text, 16 states and the District of Columbia have enacted laws to legalize medical marijuana.

Anabolic Steroids

Anabolic steroids are synthetic derivatives of the male hormone testosterone. Although steroids have been banned for use by athletes in sporting competition, they are still used by some athletes, bodybuilders, and teenagers who want to look more muscular and brawny. From early childhood, many boys have been socialized to believe that the ideal man looks something like Mr. Universe. Some well-known athletes are known to have taken the steroid shortcut to muscularity and increased running speed. A number of prominent baseball players have admitted using steroids, and many more are suspected of using steroids. In 2005 Major League Baseball began testing players for steroid use (see Case Exhibit 8.5)

Some young male bodybuilders use steroids to promote tissue growth and to endure arduous workouts, routinely flooding their bodies with 100 times the testosterone they produce naturally.[67] Most steroid users are middle class and White.

Steroid-enhanced physiques are a hazardous prize. Steroids can cause temporary acne and balding, upset hormonal production, and can damage the heart and kidneys. Doctors suspect that they may also contribute to liver cancer and atherosclerosis.[68] For teens the drugs can stunt growth by accelerating bone maturation. Male steroid users have also experienced shrinking of the testicles, impotency, yellowing of the skin and eyes, and development of female-type breasts. In young boys, steroids can have the effect of painfully enlarging the sex organs. In female users, the voice deepens permanently, breasts shrink, periods become irregular, the clitoris swells in size, and hair is lost from the head but grows on the face and body.

Steroid drug users are prone to moodiness, depression, and irritability and are likely to experience difficulty in tolerating stress. Some formerly easygoing males display raging hostility after prolonged use, ranging from being obnoxious to continually provoking physical fights. Some users become so depressed that they commit suicide.

Steroid users generally experience considerable difficulty in terminating use of the drugs. One reason is that bulging biceps and ham-hock thighs soon fade when steroid use is discontinued. Concurrent with the decline in muscle mass is the psychological feeling of being less powerful and less "manly." Most users who try to quit wind up back on the drugs. A self-image that relies on a steroid-enhanced physique is difficult to change.

Rehabilitation Programs

Rehabilitation programs for alcohol abuse are very similar to those for most other drugs. We'll begin by looking closely at the treatment of alcoholism.

2.1.10.a

Alcohol Treatment Programs

Alcohol often becomes the "best friend" of alcoholics. Alcohol is something they can count on to relieve their anxieties and the stresses they encounter in everyday living. Alcoholics are reluctant to give up their "best friend," so they deny they have a problem with drinking.

It used to be standard practice for drug counselors to recommend intense confrontation by family members, friends, employers, and counselors to declare that the alcoholic has a problem with drinking. For example, Tim Bliss stated:

In confronting the alcoholic, documentation of incidents that occurred while drinking becomes extremely important. This is particularly important because the alcoholic may have blackouts. These are periods of amnesia as opposed to passing out or unconsciousness. Both are due to excessive drinking. Many times during confrontation it is important that the entire family be present to reinforce the incident. In documenting the incident, one should be instructed to write down the date and time, and to be as specific as possible in describing the situation.[69]

Such confrontation usually led the alcoholic to become defensive and distrusting of the confronters. In recent years, many substance abuse counselors believe *motivational interviewing* is a more effective approach to lead an alcoholic to acknowledge that she or he has a problem and needs help. (See Case Exhibit 8.6: Motivational Interviewing.)

If the alcoholic continues to deny that a problem exists, there are some guidelines for what family members should and should not do. "Nagging" the alcoholic will only increase family arguments and may provoke the alcoholic into verbally or physically abusing someone, particularly when he or she is inebriated. Family members often make the mistake of assuming they are responsible for getting the alcoholic to stop drinking, and they feel guilty or frustrated if the person continues to drink. They, however, do not *own* the drinking problem; the alcoholic is the one responsible for the drinking and is the one who determines whether he or she will stop drinking. When a person is drunk, yelling and screaming at him or her will accomplish nothing (except perhaps to make other family members more upset). What is more productive for the other family members is to isolate themselves from the alcoholic when she or he is drunk—perhaps by going shopping, taking a walk, or if need be, locking themselves in a room.

Critical Thinking Question

If a member of your extended family is currently abusing (severely) a drug, do you believe motivational interviewing would be beneficial?

There are three self-help groups that family members can attend. Al-Anon is for spouses and other family members of alcoholics. The program reaches out to people affected by another person's drinking regardless of whether the alcoholic recognizes his or her problem. It helps members learn the facts about alcoholism and ways to cope with an

Motivational Interviewing

Change may be the one true constant in our lives. Yet the goal of achieving long-term behavioral change, which motivates many individuals to seek treatment, is often elusive and difficult to achieve. It is not enough to only discuss and understand behaviors and feelings around a certain issue. The goal must be to help individuals seek and examine their core issues; to help them experience physiological changes and emotional responses congruent with a new understanding of their choices and reactions. The challenge then becomes how social workers encourage and support individuals with this change process.

Motivational interviewing is not a technique but rather a style, a facilitative way of being with people. Motivational interviewing is a direct, client-centered, counseling style for eliciting behavior change by helping clients explore and resolve ambivalence.[a] This facilitative style encourages self-motivation for positive change within individuals. The development of motivational interviewing in the early 1980s by William R. Miller and Stephen Rollnick was out of response to substance abusers in treatment who had high dropout rates, high relapse rates, and poor outcomes overall in treatment. This lack of progress in treatment caused social workers to view the individuals as resistant and unmotivated to change. The question of why *do* people change became the foundation of developing motivational interviewing. Instead of dismissing challenging clients as unmotivated and unable to change, motivational interviewing skills allow social workers to become equipped with the skills to enhance motivation and to help clients become active in the change process.

The spirit that embraces the motivational interviewing style is the ability of the social worker to form a therapeutic partnership with the client. This collaborative manner is nonjudgmental. The social worker's tone is not one of imparting wisdom, insight, or reality, but rather of eliciting the client's internal view of the situation. The social worker draws out ideas, feelings, and wants of the client. Drawing out motivation, finding intrinsic motivation for change, and bringing it to the surface for discussion is the essence of motivational interviewing. The responsibility for change is left totally with the client.

Fundamentals of Motivational Interviewing

The fundamentals of motivational interviewing are a combination of strategies and techniques based on existing models of psychotherapy and behavior change techniques. These strategies and techniques serve as catalysts for increasing motivation to change and for maintaining the change. The following are fundamental principles of motivational interviewing.

Express Empathy

Empathy involves seeing the world through the client's eyes, thinking about things as the client thinks about things, feeling things as the client feels them, and sharing in the client's experiences. Expression of empathy is critical to the motivational interviewing process. When clients feel that they are understood, they are more apt to open up and share their own experiences. Having clients share experiences in depth allows the social worker to assess when and where they need support and what barriers there may be to the change planning process. When clients perceive the social worker as empathetic, they become more open to gentle challenges by the social worker about lifestyle changes. Clients become more comfortable openly examining their ambivalence about change and less likely to defend their ideas of possible denial. The social worker's accurate understanding of the client's experience facilitates change.

The following are some examples of the social worker's possible empathic responses to a client who states, "I've been trying to quit smoking for years, but I just haven't been able to quit."

"You must be feeling pretty frustrated."

"Quilting smoking is very difficult. I sense your pain in struggling with this. I will do my best to help you to find a way to quit for good."

"I applaud you for wanting to quit. Being able to quit is very difficult because of the craving to smoke. Are you wiling to try some strategies for quitting that have worked for others?"

Support Self-Efficacy

Self-efficacy is the belief that one is capable of performing in a certain manner to attain certain goals.

A client's belief that change is possible is an important motivator to succeeding in making a change. As clients are held responsible for choosing and carrying out actions to change in the motivational interviewing approach, the social worker focuses his or her efforts on helping the client stay motivated. Supporting clients' sense of self-efficacy is a great way of helping individuals stay motivated. The belief that there is no right way to change can help develop a belief within an individual that he or she can make a change. The social worker wants the client to develop the argument for change. Change should be derived from within the individual, not from outside the individual. One technique for helping a client assess his or her willingness to change is the following Readiness to Change Rule.

On the following scale (show client) from 1 to 5, what number best reflects how ready you are *at the present time* to change your (the behavior)?

Circle One

Not Ready to Change	Thinking of Changing	Undecided/ Uncertain	Somewhat Ready	Very Ready to Change
1	2	3	4	5

The social worker needs to operate at the same level of change where the client is in order to minimize resistance and gain cooperation.

For example, if a client states he is "Somewhat Ready" to give up drinking alcoholic beverages, the social worker may

(continued)

gently inquire, "What will it take for you to be very ready to give up drinking?"

In a group setting, the power of having other people in group who have changed a variety of behaviors during their lifetime gives the other members in group proof that people can change. Another effective strategy for enhancing self-efficacy is to explore a client's past successes (around the specific behavior or other behaviors).

Roll with Resistance

In motivational interviewing, the social worker does not fight resistance but "rolls with it." Statements made by the client demonstrating resistance are not challenged. Instead, the social worker uses the client's momentum to further explore the client's views. Using this approach, resistance tends to be decreased rather than increased, as clients are not being reinforced for being argumentative to the social worker's statement. Motivational interviewing encourages clients to develop their own solutions to problems that they themselves have defined. Thus, there is no real power in the client–social worker relationship for the client to challenge. In exploring client concerns, social workers invite new ways of thinking about things but do not impose their ways of thinking on the client.

A useful technique when a client is resisting change is using a reflection, where the social worker is responding to resistance with nonresistance by repeating the client's statement in a neutral form. An example of this would be if a social worker asks a client, "I would like to talk to you about the night you were arrested for smoking marijuana." The client responds, "What's to talk about? The police and you have already made your mind up that it was my fault." The social worker would respond with the reflection, "So you feel like your opinion doesn't matter?" instead of responding with a statement reflecting the facts documented in the police report. Rolling with resistance avoids confrontations with clients on issues they have.

Develop Discrepancy

"Motivation for change occurs when people perceive a discrepancy between where they are and where they want to be."[b]

Social workers help clients examine the discrepancies between their current behavior and what they have identified as their future goals. When clients perceive that their current behaviors are not leading toward some important future goal, they become more motivated to make life changes. Social workers respectfully and gently help clients gain insight that some of their current ways of living may lead them away from instead of toward their goals.

If a client states he has a problem with drinking alcoholic beverages but is uncertain if he is ready to commit to no longer drinking, the social worker can create a gap between where he is currently and where he wants to be with the following types of statements/questions:

"What will your life be like 10 years from now if you continue to use?"

"How do you believe your life will improve if you stop drinking?"

"Tell me some of the good things, and less good things, about your drinking."

"What was your life like before you started having problems with drinking?"

Stages of Change

Researchers have found that people go through a process when they make positive changes, and this process can be conceptualized in a series of steps or stages. The Stages of Change Model, part of the Transtheoretical Model of Change, outlines the process of change that individuals go through when they successfully make changes in their lives.[c]

Brief Definition of Each Stage of Change

Stage	Basic Definition
1. PRECONTEMPLATION	A person is not seeing a need for a lifestyle change.
2. CONTEMPLATION	A person is considering making a change but has not decided yet.
3. PREPARATION	A person has decided to make changes and is considering how to make them.
4. ACTION	A person is actively doing something to change.
5. MAINTENANCE	A person is working to maintain the change or new lifestyle. There may be some temptations to return to the former behavior or even small relapses.

Motivational interviewing is designed to help clients in stages 1, 2, or 3 to move toward stages 4 and 5. The stages of change are dynamic—a person may move through them once or recycle through them several times before reaching success and maintaining a behavior change over time. Individuals may move back and forth between stages on any single issue or may simultaneously be in different stages of change for two or more behaviors. Embedded in the spirit of motivational interviewing is the need to meet the client where he or she is. The stages of change help to identify where a person is in the change process.

The essence of motivational interviewing embodies the following social work concepts:

- Developing hope
- Empowerment
- Self-determination
- Starting where consumers/clients are at.
- Respect for clients/consumers
- The strengths perspective
- Developing coping skills
- Recovery takes place as a series of small steps
- Recovery should focus on consumer/client choice
- Crisis is seen as involving opportunity
- Recovery can occur even if symptoms reoccur

(continued)

CASE EXHIBIT 8.6 *(continued)*

- Supportive relationships from helping professionals who convey they believe in the consumer's/client's potential to recover
- The consumer/client developing a sense of meaning and overall purpose to sustain the recovery process

Source: This exhibit was written by Katherine Drechsler, MSW, adjunct faculty member at the University of Wisconsin–Whitewater. She is also a doctoral student in social work at Aurora University.

[a]William R. Miller and Stephen Rollnick, *Motivational Interviewing: Preparing People to Change Addictive Behavior* (New York: Guilford Press, 1981).
[b]W R. Miller, A. Zweben, C. C. Diclente, and R. G. Rychtarik, *Motivational Enhancement Therapy Manual: A Clinical Research Guide for Therapists Treating Individuals with Alcohol Abuse and Dependence* (Rockville, MD: National Institute on Alcohol Abuse and Alcoholism, 1992), p. 8.
[c]J. O. Prochaska and C. C. DiClemente, "Trans-Theoretical Therapy: Toward a More Integrative Model of Change," *Psychotherapy: Theory, Research and Practice*, 19, no. 3 (1982), 276–288.

---

alcoholic. Alateen is for teenage children of alcoholics and helps adolescents to understand alcoholism and to learn effective ways to cope with problems. Adult Children of Alcoholics helps adults cope with issues they are still struggling with that largely stem from being raised in an alcoholic family.

If the alcoholic does acknowledge a drinking problem, many treatment programs are available. The best-known and most successful program is Alcoholics Anonymous, which is further described in Case Exhibit 8.7.

There appear to be several reasons why such self-help groups are successful. The members have an intrinsic understanding of the problem that helps them to help others. Having experienced the misery and consequences of the problem, they are highly motivated and dedicated to find ways to help themselves and others who are fellow sufferers. The participants also benefit from the "helper therapy principle"; that is, the helper gains psychological rewards by helping others.[70] Helping others leads the helper to feel "good" and worthwhile and also enables the helper to put his or her own problems into perspective by seeing that others have problems that are as serious, or even more serious. From the viewpoint of new members who are still drinking, having people around who have successfully stopped provides role models of abstinence and gives them reason to believe that they too can break the grip of alcohol abuse.

At one time, intoxicated people were just thrown into jail to sober up. (Unfortunately, this is still happening in some places.) Many communities, however, have now switched to a treatment approach.

Most alcohol treatment facilities offer both inpatient and outpatient programs. Outpatient treatment usually serves clients who have the potential to stop using alcohol while living at home. If the client is unable to live at home or is still drinking excessively, inpatient treatment will usually be recommended. Those who go through an inpatient program receive subsequent follow-up treatment on an outpatient basis. Inpatient treatment can last anywhere from a few days to 3 months, depending on the patient's problems and the treatment program. Inpatient treatment is usually intense, including one-on-one therapy, group therapy, an orientation to Alcoholics Anonymous, and occupational and recreational therapy. Outpatient treatment is not as intense, usually lasts from 3 to 6 months, and offers the same forms of treatment.

Critical Thinking Question

If some members of your extended family are addicted to a drug, would any of these programs be useful for them?

Outpatient and inpatient services are provided in some medical hospitals, in drug rehabilitation centers, and in community mental health centers. Many communities also have halfway houses that serve the alcoholic who is unable to live with family members but is not yet ready to live alone.

Most larger companies now sponsor alcohol treatment programs (as a component of employee assistance programs, described in Chapter 11) for their employees. These programs seek to identify problem drinkers in their early stages and then intervene before severe problems arise. The problem

Alcoholics Anonymous

In 1929 Bill Wilson was a stock analyst. When the stock market crashed that year, he lost most of his money and turned to alcohol. A few years later, his doctor warned him that his continued drinking was jeopardizing his health and his life. Bill W. underwent what he perceived as a spiritual experience, and he made a commitment to stop drinking. He also discovered that, through discussing his drinking problem with other alcoholics, he was helped to remain sober. One of the people he talked with was Robert Smith, an Ohio doctor and also an alcoholic. Together they formed Alcoholics Anonymous (AA), a self-help group composed of recovering alcoholics.

AA stresses the following precepts: (a) confessing to the group that one has a drinking problem, (b) recounting to the group past experiences with the drinking problem and plans for handling the problem in the future, and (c) phoning another member of the group whenever one feels an intense urge to drink. The person called will do whatever can be done to keep the caller "dry," including coming over to stay with the person until the urge subsides.

Today AA has chapters in over 100 countries. Local chapters (around 25 people per chapter) meet once or twice a week for discussions. These sessions resemble traditional group therapy but without the presence of a trained professional leader.

Bill W. and Dr. Bob, as they were known within AA, remained anonymous until their deaths. Local chapters still follow procedures similar to the original ones—the sharing of similar experiences in order to abstain from taking the first drink (which is "one too many") and the thousandth (which is "not enough").

AA is widely recognized as the treatment approach that has the best chance of helping an alcoholic. Testimony to its value is that hundreds of other self-help groups with treatment principles based on the AA model have now been formed to deal with other personal problems—for example, Overeaters Anonymous, Narcotics Anonymous, Prison Families Anonymous, Debtors Anonymous, Gamblers Anonymous, Emotions Anonymous, Emphysema Anonymous, Adult Children of Alcoholics, and many more.

An AA Meeting

AA has helped more people overcome their drinking problems than all other therapies and methods combined.

AA is supported entirely by voluntary donations from the members at meetings. There are no dues or fees. Each chapter is autonomous, and free of any outside control by the AA headquarters in New York City or by any other body. There is no hierarchy in the chapters. The only office is that of the group secretary. This person chooses a chairperson for each meeting, makes the arrangements for meetings, and sees that the building is open, the chairs are set up, and the tea and coffee put on. The group secretary holds office for only a limited time period; after a month or two the secretary's responsibilities are transferred to another member.

The only requirement for membership in AA is a desire to stop drinking. All other variables (such as economic status, social status, race, religion) do not count. Members can even attend meetings while drunk, as long as they do not disturb the meeting.

AA meetings are held in a variety of physical locations—churches, temples, private homes, business offices, schools, libraries, or banquet rooms of restaurants. The physical location is thus unimportant.

When a newcomer first arrives, he or she will usually find people setting up chairs, placing ashtrays, putting free literature on a table, and making coffee. Other members will be socializing in small groups. Someone is apt to introduce himself or herself and other members to the newcomer. If someone is shy about attending the first meeting alone, he or she can call AA and someone will take the person to the meeting and introduce him or her to the other members.

When the meeting starts, everyone sits down around tables or in rows of chairs. The secretary and/or chairperson, and one or more speakers, sit at the head of the table or on a platform if the meeting is in a hall.

The chairperson opens with a moment of silence, which is followed by a group recitation of a nondenominational prayer. The chairperson then reads or gives a brief description of Alcoholics Anonymous and may read or refer to a section of the book *Alcoholics Anonymous* (a book that describes the principles of AA and gives a number of case examples).

Then, the chairperson usually asks if anyone is attending for the first, second, or third time. The new people are asked to introduce themselves according to the following: "Hello, my name is [first name], and this is my first [second, third] meeting." Those who do not want to introduce themselves are not pressured to do so. New members are the lifeblood of AA, and are the most important people at the meeting in the members' eyes. (All the longer-term members remember their first meeting and how frightened and inhibited they felt.)

If the group is small, the chairperson usually then asks the longer term members to introduce themselves and say a few words. If the group is large; the chairperson asks volunteers among the longer term members to introduce themselves by saying a few words. Each member usually begins by saying, "My name is [first name]; I am an alcoholic" and then discloses a few thoughts or feelings. (The members do not have to say they are alcoholic, unless they choose to do so. Each member sooner or later generally chooses to say this, to remind himself or herself that he or she is an addictive drinker who is recovering and that alcoholism is a lifelong disease, which must be battled daily.) Those who introduce themselves usually say whatever they feel will be most helpful to the newcomers. They may talk about their first meeting, or their first week without drinking, or something designed to make the newcomers more comfortable. Common advice for the newcomers is to get the phone numbers of other members after

(continued)

CASE EXHIBIT 8.7 *(continued)*

the meeting so that they can call a member when they feel a strong urge to drink. AA considers such help as vital in recovering. The organization believes members can remain sober only through receiving the help of people who care about them and who understand what they are struggling with.

AA members want newcomers to call when they have the urge to drink, at any time day or night. The members sincerely believe that by helping others they are helping themselves to stay sober and grow. Members indicate that such calling is the newcomer's ace in the hole against the first drink, if everything else fails. They also inform newcomers that it is good to call others when lonely, just to chat.

In his own words, a newcomer explains how AA began to help him:

> Here's what happened to me. When I finally hit bottom and called AA for help, a U.S. Air Force officer came to tell me about AA. For the first time in my life, I was talking to someone who obviously really understood my problem, as four psychiatrists had not, and he took me to my first meeting, sober but none too steady. It was amazing. I went home afterward and didn't have a drink. I went again the next night, still dry, and the miracle happened a second time. The third morning my wife went off to work, my boys to school, and I was alone. Suddenly I wanted a drink more than I had ever wanted one in my life. I tried walking for a while. No good. The feeling was getting worse. I tried reading. Couldn't concentrate. Then I became really desperate, and although I wasn't used to calling strangers for help, I called Fred, an AAer who had said that he was retired and would welcome a call at any time. We talked a bit; he could see that talking on the phone wasn't going to be enough. He said, "Look, I've got an idea. Let me make a phone call, and I'll call you back in ten minutes. Can you hold on that long?" I said I could. He called back in eight, asking me to come over to his house. We talked endlessly, went out for a sandwich together, and finally my craving for a drink went away. We went to a meeting. Next morning I was fine again and now I had gone four days without a drink.[a]

After such discussion, speakers may describe their life of drinking, how drinking almost destroyed their life, how they were introduced to AA, their struggles to remain sober one day at a time, how AA has helped them, and what their life is now like.

At the end of a meeting the chairperson may ask the newcomers if they wish to say anything. If they do not wish to say much, that is okay. No one is pressured to self-disclose what they do not want to reveal.

Meetings usually end after the chairperson makes announcements. (The collection basket for donations is also passed around. New members are not expected, and frequently not allowed, to donate any money until after the third meeting. If someone cannot afford to make a donation, none is expected.) The group then stands, usually holding hands, and repeats in Unison the Lord's Prayer. Those who do not want to join in this prayer are not pressured to do so. After a meeting the members socialize. This is a time for newcomers to meet new friends and to get phone numbers.

AA is a cross-section of people from all walks of life. Anonymity is emphasized. It is the duty of every member to respect the anonymity of every person who attends. Concern for anonymity is a major reason for two kinds of meetings in AA, open and closed. Anyone is welcome at open meetings. Only people with drinking problems are allowed at closed meetings. Therefore, if a person feels uncomfortable going to an open meeting and has a drinking problem, then closed meetings are an alternative.

Members do not have to believe in God to get help from AA. Many members have lost, or never had, a faith in God. AA does, however, assert that faith in some higher power is a tremendous help in recovery because such a belief offers a source of limitless power, hope, and support whenever one feels one has come to the end of one's resources.

How does AA help? New members, after years of feelings of rejection, loneliness, misunderstanding, guilt, and embarrassment, find they are not alone. They feel understood by others who are in similar predicaments. Instead of being rejected, they are welcomed. They see that others who had serious drinking problems are now sober, apparently happy that way, and are in the process of recovering. It gives them hope that they do not need alcohol to get through the day and that they can learn to enjoy life without alcohol. They find that others sincerely care about them, want to help them, and have the knowledge to do so.

At meetings they see every sort of personal problem brought up and discussed openly, with suggestions for solutions being offered from others who have encountered similar problems. They can observe that group members bring up "unspeakable" problems without apparent embarrassment, and that others listen and treat them with respect and consideration. Such acceptance gradually leads newcomers to share their personal problems and to receive constructive suggestions for solutions. Such a disclosure leads individuals to look more deeply into themselves and to ventilate deep personal feelings. With the support of other members, newcomers gradually learn how to counter strong desires to drink, through such processes as calling other members.

Newcomers learn that AA is the means of staying away from that first drink. AA also serves to reduce the stress that compels people to drink by providing a comfortable and relaxed environment and by having members helping each other to find ways to reduce the stresses encountered in daily living. AA meetings and members become a safe port that is always there when storms start raging. AA helps members to be programmed from negative thinking to positive thinking. The more positive a member's thinking becomes, the more stress is relieved, the better he or she begins to feel about himself or herself, the more the compulsion to drink decreases, and the more often and more effectively the person begins to take positive actions to solve his or her problems.

[a]Clark Vaughan, *Addictive Drinking* (New York: Penguin, 1984), pp. 75–76.

CASE EXAMPLE 8.1

Therapy with a Heroin Addict

Tim Bliss, a drug counselor, describes the following efforts to treat an addict:

> Many times the drug counselor feels he or she isn't making any progress in the recovery process of the heroin addict. Counseling the heroin addict takes a special type of counselor—one who can walk the walk and talk the talk so to speak. To counsel, first off, it takes an extreme amount of dedication, concentration, and effort.
>
> The client I worked with was a 30-year-old black, married male with three children. The history was as follows. The client will be referred to as Bob. Bob was raised in an urban area; he was the middle child and seemingly led a normal childhood. As he reached his early teens, he got more and more involved with drinking and drugs. He graduated from high school and went into the army soon after graduation. This is where many problems arose. Bob had several bouts with the army ranging from insubordination to disorderly conduct. He started chipping [occasionally using] heroin and became quite involved in the drug culture overseas in Germany. He then married a white German woman and brought her back to the United States, where they have lived for the past 10 years. Bob then became involved in an armed robbery and claimed he was innocent; yet he spent three years in prison. After his prison time ended, Bob secured a job at a local factory; this lasted approximately one and one-half years at which time he was fired for excessive absenteeism. The excessive absenteeism was a result of episodic drinking and drug abuse.
>
> Prior to Bob's going to prison, he was involved in the Black Panthers [a militant black separatist organization]. What was interesting was that he was married to a white, which had to be a conflict with Bob.
>
> In general Bob seemingly had quite a conflict being black. He wanted at times to be white, and yet at other times wanted to be married to a black instead of a white.
>
> Bob became increasingly involved with drugs, and in time developed a habit with heroin. This led to his involvement in both the criminal justice system and treatment.
>
> Fortunately, there was a federal grant at this time that could divert criminal justice clients to alcohol or drug treatment centers. Bob became involved in a local alcohol treatment center while on probation. However, due to the fact that he was a heroin addict, treatment was ineffective. Within a very short period of time after discharge, Bob was back to "junk." He was then involved in another armed robbery and this time was facing 7 to 10 years for several counts of armed robbery and burglary. At this point I became involved with the client. Bob was out on bond and was awaiting his court date. Throughout this time period Bob was seen on an outpatient treatment basis. Urine drug screens were taken, and all turned up negative for opiates for about four weeks. Then Bob started chipping...heroin [again]. A therapeutic community which treated heroin addicts had been contacted to arrange an intake interview with Bob. The therapeutic community was a six- to nine-month intensive inpatient treatment program. Their philosophy was that the drug of choice was only a symptom and what needed to be changed was the lifestyle.
>
> The court date was finally reached, and it was time for Bob to "face the music." The therapeutic community had interviewed Bob, and he was accepted into their program. I had arranged for a psychologist to run a series of tests on Bob to determine statistically his chances for succeeding in treatment. The results of this testing were that Bob would have one-third of a chance of succeeding in treatment, one-third not succeeding, and one-third of no change at all. Obviously statistics were against Bob, but in outpatient treatment he had demonstrated that he was sincere and did want to change. So with that, this counselor and Bob's probation officer felt treatment was the best alternative rather than incarceration. The presiding judge was approached with this alternative, and he accepted it. However, Bob was found guilty, so the judge imposed a stayed sentence of seven years to be served if Bob did not successfully complete treatment.
>
> The following week Bob was transferred to the therapeutic community. He stayed there approximately six months, at which time the community voted that he be terminated, unsuccessfully completing treatment. Bob was voted out for a number of reasons: (1) he wasn't following instructions when reprimanded by staff, (2) overall he was an extremely bad influence on the rest of the community as he was always gaming people, not being able to be honest with himself or others, (3) he was breaking cardinal rules, which meant that when he would get angry other members of the community were actually afraid to be around him as they were afraid he might get physically violent. The incident that resulted in Bob's termination was that he was reprimanded for an incident that involved a female client. Supposedly Bob had intercourse with the female, and the female admitted this to staff in one of the community's "cop to" groups. (A "cop to" simply means people in the community who have done something wrong, or are feeling guilty, talk about it in one of these groups.)
>
> The staff told Bob he was on a communication ban (no talking) the following day; they also requested he wear a five-foot sign with some writing on it. This kind of reprimand might seem ineffective or silly to some of us; however, it is quite effective in an atmosphere like a therapeutic community, especially on a long-term basis. Bob didn't follow through the next day, and a vote was taken; he was transferred to the county jail where he would await a decision by the probation officer, the judge, and the original referring agent.
>
> We had decided Bob was still amenable to treatment. However, this would entail a more highly structured treatment environment, a facility that dealt more with the hard-core heroin addict.
>
> Meanwhile Bob was becoming increasingly bitter sitting in jail thinking about what had occurred, and also becoming anxious due to the fact he was facing seven years in prison.
>
> The probation officer and original treatment staff involved with Bob found a treatment facility that would be most favorable to any kind of successful treatment for Bob. The judge also went along with this.
>
> Bob, after about two weeks of sitting in jail, was transferred on a Friday afternoon to this treatment facility. Friday evening he called his wife and absconded from treatment. He has not been heard of since, and consequently his probation has been revoked. When caught, he will be sent to prison.

(continued)

CASE EXAMPLE 8.1 *(continued)*

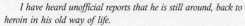

I have heard unofficial reports that he is still around, back to heroin in his old way of life.

This is not a success story, obviously, but all too often that's all we ever hear. The field is challenging; however, this case history is also a real part of treatment, that oftentimes a therapist has to realize his or her own limitations and accept reality as it is. Not everyone is a success, and no matter what you do, you can't change that. All we can do is seek as much knowledge about

the field as possible and utilize every tool available to motivate clients in changing their behavior. Only after this can we say "I gave it my best shot, and that's all there is."

SOURCE: From "Drugs—Use, Abuse, and Treatment," by Tim Bliss from Zastrow, Introduction to Social Welfare Institutions, 3E. © 1986 Cengage Learning.

drinkers are referred to appropriate community resources. If the employee uses such help, there are no adverse work consequences. Considerable pressure may be placed on the employee to participate, with the threat of eventual discharge if she or he refuses help and continues to display lowered work productivity due to drinking.

Most therapists now believe that alcohol is used to meet some need—the need for socialization, relaxation, escape, and so on. If treatment is to be successful, it must provide alternatives for satisfying these needs: by helping the alcoholic to find a new circle of friends, to learn other ways to relax, to learn to handle life's problems better—whatever may be the unique needs of the drinker. This theory of *functional need equivalents* has been applied to addictions in addition to alcohol abuse.

Other Drug Treatment Programs

There is a stereotype that "once an addict, always an addict." This attitude has hampered efforts to rehabilitate those who are chemically dependent. Statistical evidence in the past tended to confirm this myth. More recent evidence, however, suggests that drug addicts *can* successfully kick their habits.[71]

Physical dependency on practically any drug can be ended with a detoxification program. Generally, the user will undergo some intense and highly painful withdrawal symptoms for the first few days or even for a few weeks. Psychological dependency is more difficult to end. Because drugs meet psychological needs, they are functional. Users receive certain psychic rewards (feelings of relaxation, euphoria, more alertness, less pain, escape from reality and problems). The psychological needs met by taking a drug are often unique to each user. To end the dependency, it is necessary for treatment programs to discover what psychological needs are being met for each user and then teach the user new (drug-free) ways to meet those needs.

Inpatient Programs

Community mental health centers, specialized chemical abuse rehabilitation centers, and some medical hospitals provide inpatient treatment programs. Detoxification lasts from 24 hours to 3 weeks, depending on the severity of withdrawal. Additional inpatient care lasts 2 to 3 more weeks in a chemically free environment. Inpatient care is designed for those chemically dependent individuals who are unable to end the dependency while remaining in the community. Inpatient treatment is highly expensive; it may cost $20,000 or more for a 30-day stay.

Outpatient Programs

Outpatient care, which is usually less intense than inpatient care, generally lasts 3 to 6 months. It is designed for people who no longer need inpatient care, as well as for those who have a good chance of terminating their habit without having to be hospitalized. Outpatient care consists of counseling, medical services, and vocational services. Such services are provided by community mental health centers, specialized rehabilitation centers for treating chemical abuse, medical hospitals, and outpatient clinics for chemical abuse.

Self-Help Programs

Modeled after Alcoholics Anonymous, there are many self-help programs for abusers. They include Narcotics Anonymous, Pill Addicts Anonymous, Cocaine Anonymous, Pills Anonymous, and Marijuana Anonymous.[72]

Halfway Houses

Halfway houses assist those who have been hospitalized (and detoxified) to reenter the community at their own pace. They also serve those who are psychologically dependent and want to kick a habit but do not need to be hospitalized. Halfway houses provide counseling services (both one-to-one and group) to help residents remain drug free and work on resolving other personal problems they face. Residents also receive vocational training, assistance in finding a job, and room and board. Many halfway houses employ staff who were former addicts. Recovered drug abusers are often more effective than professional staff in relating to the residents and in breaking down the barriers of denial, anger, isolation, and hostility that addicts feel. Former addicts also provide a model, as they are evidence that addiction is a curable disease. Halfway houses emphasize the importance of residents' assuming responsibility for their actions and behaviors.

Treatment Using Drugs

Analogous to the use of Antabuse with alcoholics (see Case Exhibit 8.8), some chemicals are used in therapeutic programs to treat certain drug addictions.

Methadone, which has received considerable publicity, is used to treat heroin addiction. Methadone is a synthetic narcotic and is sufficiently similar to heroin to satisfy the addict's physical craving. It prevents the anguish of heroin withdrawal symptoms but does not induce a high. Methadone thus allows a heroin addict to function fairly normally in a community. (It is usually not effective for heroin users who are unwilling to give up their "high.")

Methadone itself is addictive. Moreover, it does not cure addicts of their addiction to heroin. It simply *maintains* addicts in their communities without their having to use heroin. Methadone is controversial, and many authorities object to treating heroin addicts by making them dependent on another drug.

Methadone is available (legally) only through approved programs. In the first few weeks of treatment, addicts are usually required to report daily to the treatment center to receive their dose. As with any other drug that is in demand, an illicit market has developed in methadone. Some heroin addicts use methadone to tide them over when they cannot obtain heroin; others sometimes seek to treat themselves by taking methadone instead of heroin. As

with heroin, an overdose of methadone can result in death.

Scientists have also developed narcotic antagonists that prevent opiate (morphine and heroin) users from experiencing euphoria. Two of the best-known opiate antagonists are naloxone and cyclazocine. These drugs prevent addicts from feeling the euphoria they crave and thereby help motivated addicts to kick the habit.

Understanding and Treating Codependency

Codependent people are so trapped by a loved one's addiction that they lose their own identity in the process of obsessively managing the day-to-day trauma created by the addict. Codependency is unhealthy behavior learned amid chaos. Some codependents are as dysfunctional as the addict, if not more so. Living with addiction triggers excessive caregiving, suppression of one's own needs, feelings of low self-worth, and strained relationships.

Critical Thinking Questions

Do you know someone who is codependent? If so, what kind of treatment program may be beneficial for that person?

Many codependents grow up in a dysfunctional family. (Some are adult children of alcoholics.) They marry or become romantically involved with someone who abuses alcohol or some other drug. To some extent, the addict fills the need of the codependent—to be a caregiver, to feel inferior, and so on. Codependency can thus be viewed as a normal reaction to abnormal stress.

The addict may terminate the use of his or her drug of choice, but the codependent's dysfunctional behaviors generally continue, unless he or she receives treatment. There are a variety of treatment approaches for codependents: individual psychotherapy, group therapy, and self-help groups (such as Al-Anon, Adult Children of Alcoholics, and Codependents Anonymous). For many codependents, treatment involves recognition that they have a life and an identity separate from the addict, that the addict alone is responsible for his or her substance abuse, and that their life and the addict's will improve by terminating their caregiving and enabling behaviors. Through treatment, many codependents regain (or gain for the first

CASE EXHIBIT 8.8

Antabuse Treatment

Antabuse, developed in Copenhagen in 1947, is a drug that is useful for helping an alcoholic stay sober. When taken, it makes a patient's system react adversely to even small quantities of alcohol. Shortly after a person drinks an alcoholic beverage, Antabuse causes intense flushing, increased pulse rate, and nausea, often to the point of vomiting.

Before beginning treatment, the patient is detoxified. Then the drug is administered for several consecutive days, along with small doses of alcohol. The small amounts of alcohol are used to help the patient recognize the strong and uncomfortable effects that will occur while drinking.

Antabuse is not a cure-all for drinking because the reasons for drinking still remain. An alcoholic, if she or he chooses, can simply stop taking the drug and resume drinking. However, Antabuse is useful as part of a comprehensive treatment program involving counseling, vocational and social rehabilitation, and AA. By taking Antabuse, a person is forced to remain sober and is thereby more likely to respond to other therapies.

time) their own identity and banish the self-destructive habits that sabotage their happiness.

Suggestions for Curbing Drug Abuse in the Future

It is, of course, important to treat current drug abusers. But perhaps it is even more important to prevent nonabusers from becoming abusers. This section discusses six preventive approaches: educational programs, prevention of illegal drug trafficking across borders, employee drug-testing programs, stricter laws and enforcement, decriminalization of drug use, and the treatment approach in the Netherlands.

Educational Programs

More programs are appearing that give students as well as the general public a realistic understanding of drug use and abuse. Quality programs teach (a) what effects commonly used drugs produce, (b) how to recognize signs of abuse, (c) how to responsibly decide when and when not to use drugs, (d) how to help someone who overdoses, (e) how to help friends and relatives who are abusing drugs, (f) what treatment resources and programs are available in the community, (g) what to do if you think you may have a drug problem, (h) what to do if a relative or friend refuses to acknowledge his or her drug problem, and (i) how to help abusers learn drug-free ways of meeting their psychological needs.

Educational programs in the past often used scare tactics such as showing pictures of fatal automobile crashes after drug use, suggesting that drug users end up on "skid row," and indicating that experimenting with small quantities of drugs would forever ruin the users' lives. Such tactics are now viewed as ineffective. The young see their parents, other adults, and peers using drugs (particularly alcohol) without dire consequences (generally). These alarmist approaches wound up destroying the credibility of the educators.

Fortunately, books, curriculum guides for teachers, and audiovisual materials now available paint a more realistic picture of drug use and abuse.

In the past five decades, the mass media and the schools have launched major campaigns to prevent drunk driving, alcohol abuse, smoking, and illegal drug use. Extensive drug abuse prevention programs are now under way in elementary schools, middle schools, high schools, and colleges. These programs, which are tailored to the age level of the students at which they are targeted, include McGruff, the Crime Dog, at the kindergarten level; D.A.R.E. (Drug Abuse Resistance Education), a police-sponsored program, at the elementary school level; and various clubs, retreats, and lock-ins at middle and high school levels. They use a variety of approaches, including pointing out the risks of drug use, providing accurate information on drugs and their effects, offering instructions on how to assertively say "no" to peer pressure to use drugs, providing enjoyable drug-free activities, and enhancing students' self-esteem.

With drug and alcohol abuse increasingly portrayed in the media and in the schools as risky and dangerous rather than glamorous and fashionable, overall drug and alcohol use appears to be declining for adults.[73] It is highly unlikely that the United States will ever become drug-free. Certain drugs do have valid medical use. But the abuse of drugs can and should be curbed.

One reason why the United States has one of the highest rates of drug abuse in the world is the erroneous view that "there's a pill for everything."

John Boykin/PhotoEdit

An AA meeting.

Americans tend to believe that medical technology can solve every ill the body encounters, and we use this belief to absolve ourselves of the responsibility of maintaining a healthy lifestyle. At the same time, the tendency to self-medicate is a common response when we feel worthless, "stressed out," or mistreated by society. In a culture where medication is so much the norm (a view that is boosted by advertising from the massive alcohol, pharmaceutical, and tobacco industries), it is easy to turn to drugs, alcohol, or tobacco as a way of relieving stress or forgetting about one's all-too-real problems. Public education is definitely needed to convey that drug use does not *solve* life's problems—it *intensifies* them.

Prevention of Illegal Drug Trafficking across Borders

Small-time drug dealers often make enormous profits, middle-level dealers frequently become millionaires, and the top drug barons are billionaires. Clearly, illegal drug trade across borders of countries is a big, highly profitable endeavor. One way of combating the illegal drug trade is to take the kind of action that will put drug barons out of business.

The United States and other countries have spent millions of dollars trying to prevent illegal drugs from being smuggled across borders. A few drug shipments are confiscated, and a few transporters of drugs are arrested. But drug barons are generally successful in finding increasingly creative ways to smuggle drugs across borders. If drug trafficking across borders is to be stopped, more effective steps need to be taken.

One way to combat drug trafficking across borders would be for all the countries of the world to agree among themselves to treat this activity as an international crime, indictable by international law.

An international court to administer this law could be established as a division of the United Nations. This court could have an investigative force with the authority to enter drug-producing countries to gather evidence against the drug barons who are masterminding the production, manufacture, and distribution of illegal drugs across borders. Countries would be expected to arrest and extradite for trial to this international court any individuals indicted for masterminding drug trafficking across borders. Those found guilty could be penalized with a life sentence, with no chance of parole. The United Nations could be empowered to impose trade sanctions against any country that refused to arrest and extradite indicted drug barons. (No country can survive today without international trade and finance.) In addition, armed forces of the United Nations could be made available to those governments that are too weak to combat the private armies employed by some of the notorious drug barons.

The U.S. government is continuing its efforts to put drug barons in foreign countries out of business. The U.S. government has given financial and other assistance to other governments (such as in Mexico and in Colombia) to help in arresting and extraditing drug barons to this country to face drug trafficking charges.

Employee Drug-Testing Programs

In 1986 the President's Commission on Organized Crime recommended that both government and private industry launch drug-testing programs for employees. The commission asserted that such examinations would help curb a drug abuse epidemic that drains billions of dollars annually from American society and erodes the nation's quality of life.[74]

Many major U.S. companies require applicants or employees to provide urine for an analysis that can detect the use of such drugs as cocaine, marijuana, heroin, and morphine. The tests are also given in the military, in a few sensitive federal agencies, and in many drug-treatment facilities. Local governments in many communities are now requiring random drug testing of employees in certain job categories, such as bus drivers.

Professional baseball, basketball, and football organizations also have drug-testing programs. For example, the National Football League requires all players to take a mandatory urine test prior to the start of the regular season and two unscheduled tests during the regular season. If a player tests positive, he is first required to receive treatment. If he relapses twice (as identified by two positive tests over a period of time), he is permanently banned from the league. The National Basketball Association and the National Football League have already banned several players for repeated drug violations.

Drug-testing programs are recommended in the interest of safety, health, and increased productivity. The programs are a clear signal that companies are serious about addressing the hazards caused by drugs. Employees who test positive are generally given an opportunity to enter treatment programs.

If further drug tests reveal continued use of illegal drugs, the employee is usually discharged.

Opponents of drug testing assert that such programs violate civil liberties, including the Constitution's ban on unreasonable searches.[75]

Stricter Laws and Enforcement

It is clear from public opinion polls that the most popular approach to curbing drug abuse is enactment of stricter laws and more rigid enforcement of laws involving drug abuse. In the past four decades, a variety of such laws have been passed.

In 1984 federal legislation was enacted that placed considerable pressure on states to raise the minimum drinking age to 21 years; states that do not comply risk losing federal matching funds for highways. All states have now raised the minimum drinking age to 21. Most states have reduced the legal alcohol levels required for conviction of drunken driving and toughened penalties for driving while intoxicated. With regard to tobacco, most states have passed "clean indoor air" laws, requiring nonsmoking areas in restaurants and, in many cases, banning smoking entirely in public places. To combat illegal drugs, various state and local governments established a policy of confiscating property (such as cars or boats) used to carry or store drugs, even small amounts of marijuana for personal use. As we've seen, drug testing in the workplace is becoming more widespread.

Have these efforts worked? Drug, alcohol, and tobacco use appears to be declining in our society. But it's hard to tell how much of the current decline is due to stricter laws and enforcement and how much is due to increased awareness of the risks of drug and alcohol abuse and smoking.

Decriminalization of Drug Use

Over the past century, a number of laws have prohibited the use of a variety of drugs. Penalties for violators have become harsher. Yet the proportion of the population using drugs remains high, and jails and prisons are filled with people who have been arrested for drug law violations. Drug legislation makes possession of illegal drugs a crime with penalties in some cases equivalent to or in excess of those for such criminal acts as grand larceny and second-degree murder. In the past, states have sentenced people for up to 25 years—and even life—for selling or giving small quantities of marijuana to another

CASE EXHIBIT 8.9

Drug Abuse as a Disease: The Netherlands

The United States primarily uses a punitive approach with anyone found guilty of possessing or using prohibited drugs. Some advocates of a treatment approach to the drug problem point to the Netherlands as a model.

Coleman and Kerbo describe the Dutch approach:

Dutch drug policy is an interesting combination of four elements. The first is the official tolerance of "soft drugs" (marijuana and hashish—a condensed form of marijuana). Although sale is technically illegal, many cafes openly sell marijuana without fear of arrests or fines. The second is a tough enforcement effort aimed at the dealers of hard drugs, such as heroin and cocaine, that are often smuggled into Rotterdam, the world's largest port. The third element of Dutch policy is the decriminalization of all users. No one is jailed for merely using or possessing small amounts of any drug. Finally, the Dutch have made treatment and maintenance programs easily available to all addicts.[a]

What have been the effects of this approach? The Netherlands, since the program's inception a number of years ago, has seen a sharp decline in the number of heroin addicts and an increase in their average age (indicating that fewer younger people are becoming addicted). In addition, the Netherlands did not experience the cocaine epidemic that happened in the United States.

Numerous studies show it is much less expensive to treat abusers than to toss them into jail.[b]

Critics of this treatment approach are skeptical that it would work in the United States. They claim the Netherlands is less susceptible to drug abuse because it has less of a poverty problem (the country has a much more generous welfare system), and it does not have large and deteriorating urban areas. Critics also note that the Netherlands has the additional problem of "drug tourism"—an increasing number of travelers are going to the Netherlands specifically to buy marijuana.

[a]J. W. Coleman and H. R. Kerbo, *Social Problems*, 8th ed. (Upper Saddle River, NJ: Prentice Hall, 2002), p. 412.
[b]Thomas K. Grose, "Abuse as a Disease, Not a Crime," *U.S. News & World Report*, March 26, 2007, pp. 43–44.

---

person. Such harshness discredits the criminal justice system and contributes to disrespect for the law.

Until recently, drug legislation in this country has been designed to punish users rather than to treat abusers or to prevent use of drugs. Does it really do any good to arrest and jail (sometimes weekly) habitual drunks?

The public's general lack of accurate information about drugs has led to irrational fears about drug use and abuse. For example, there is the fear that use of marijuana will always be a stepping-stone to use of narcotic drugs. There are unwarranted fears about the negative effects of such drugs as heroin and opium. These irrational fears have led citizens to demand that harsh legislation be enacted to attempt to curb the use of drugs.

However, it is increasingly recognized that punitive legislation often does not work. Prohibition demonstrated that outlawing alcohol would not end its use. In an analogous vein, laws prohibiting the use of other drugs have been largely responsible for the enormous growth of organized crime and the illicit drug trade. Prison wardens cannot even keep drugs out of their own prisons.

Some authorities are now urging that drug laws be revised to emphasize treatment rather than punishment of addicts and to make penalties for the possession of drugs more consistent with the actual dangers. It seems irrational to send to prison (at a huge expense to taxpayers) a person who possesses one joint of marijuana (a drug that may be less dangerous than alcohol).

Changes in certain drug laws in the past five decades are emphasizing rehabilitation and reducing harsh penalties for the sale and possession of certain drugs. Many of these revisions have centered on marijuana.

In 1972 the National Commission on Marijuana and Drug Abuse recommended changes in state and federal laws regarding marijuana. The commission urged that the private possession of marijuana for personal use and the distribution of small amounts without profit to the distributor no longer be considered offenses.[76] Since this 1972 report, a number of states have passed laws decriminalizing the use of marijuana.[77]

Laws have also been passed mandating that those arrested for public drunkenness receive treatment rather than simply being thrown into jail. In some areas of the country, individuals who acknowledge that they are addicted to a hard drug (such as heroin) are now given treatment without risking arrest or incarceration. Such programs are experimental and often controversial. (See Case Exhibit 8.9.)

Critical Thinking Question

What are the best ways to curb drug abuse in the United States?

SUMMARY

The following summarizes this chapter's content as it relates to the chapter objectives presented at the beginning of the chapter. Objectives include the following:

A *Define drugs and drug abuse.*

A drug is any habit-forming substance that directly affects the central nervous system; it affects moods, perceptions, bodily functions, or consciousness. Drug abuse is the regular or excessive use of a drug when, as defined by a group, the consequences endanger relationships with others, are detrimental to a person's health, or jeopardize society itself. The dominant social reaction to a drug is influenced not only by the actual dangers of the drug but also by the social characteristics and motives of the groups that use it. Legal drugs are abused more often and cause more harm in our society than illegal drugs. Many drugs produce psychological or physical dependency (addiction), or both. Often users develop a tolerance for a drug, which means that they need steadily increasing dosages. Drug addiction is the intense craving for a drug that develops after a period of physical dependency from heavy use.

B *Provide a brief history of our drug-taking society.*

Drugs have been used, and abused, for centuries in our society. As time moves along, there are changes in the extent to which various drugs are used and abused.

C *Present sociological theories of drug abuse.*

Sociological theories of drug abuse include anomie theory, labeling theory, and differential association.

D *Describe drug subcultures.*

A group of peers that advocates the use of one or more drugs is a drug subculture.

E *Summarize facts about and effects of commonly used drugs.*

Social costs of drugs include property crime (generally committed to support a habit), automobile accidents, economic losses, health problems, disrespect for the law, family disruption, spouse and child abuse, financial crises for users, and adverse psychological effects on individuals.

Our society romanticizes and encourages the use of several drugs through commercials, films, books, and TV programs. Widely advertised drugs include alcohol, tobacco, caffeine, and over-the-counter drugs.

The most commonly used drugs include depressants (alcohol, barbiturates, tranquilizers, Quaalude, PCP), stimulants (caffeine, amphetamines, cocaine, crack, amyl nitrate, butyl nitrate), narcotics (opium, heroin, morphine), hallucinogens (peyote, psilocybin, psilocin, LSD, and ecstasy), tobacco, marijuana, and anabolic steroids. Alcohol is by far the most widely abused drug in our society.

F *Describe rehabilitation programs for drug abuse.*

Treatment programs for drug abuse include inpatient and outpatient services provided by community mental health centers, some medical hospitals, and specialized chemical abuse rehabilitation centers. Additional programs include self-helps groups and halfway houses.

G *Present suggestions for curbing drug abuse in the future.*

Drug abuse will probably never cease in this country, but the extent of the abuse can certainly be reduced. Punitive laws, as Prohibition demonstrated, do not deter drug use for many people and often encourage the development of organized crime and an illicit drug market. Suggestions for curbing abuse include expanding quality educational programs that give accurate information about drugs, indicting drug barons who mastermind the production and distribution of illegal drugs, using employee drug-testing programs, enacting stricter laws and increasing enforcement activity against violations involving drug abuse, and decriminalizing drug use to encourage a treatment approach rather than a punitive approach.

Competency Notes

EP 2.1.3.a Distinguish, appraise, and integrate multiple sources of knowledge, including research-based knowledge and practice wisdom. (All of this chapter) This chapter defines drugs and drug abuse, and provides a brief history of drug

use and abuse in our society. It presents three sociological theories of drug abuse, and describes drug
subcultures. It summarizes facts about and effects of
commonly used drugs. It describes rehabilitation programs for drug abuse and presents suggestions for
curbing drug abuse in the future.

**EP 2.1.10.a Substantively and affectively prepare
for action with individuals, families, groups,
organizations, and communities.** (pp. 275-284)
This section provides introductory material on how
to intervene with substance abusers, and it summarizes
services for substance abusers and their families.

Media Resources

Additional resources for this chapter, including a chapter quiz, can be found on the Social Work CourseMate.
Go to CengageBrain.com.

Notes

1. *Webster s New Collegiate Dictionary* (Springfield,
   MA: Merriam-Webster, 1990).
2. William Kornblum and Joseph Julian, *Social
   Problems*, 14th ed. (Boston: Pearson, 2012), pp.
   100–101.
3. Howard Abadinsky, *Drug Use and Abuse: A Comprehensive Introduction*, 7th ed. (Belmont, CA:
   Wadsworth, 2010).
4. Ibid.
5. Ibid.
6. James W. Coleman and Harold R. Kerbo, *Social
   Problems*, 8th ed. (Upper Saddle River, NJ: Prentice Hall, 2002), p. 389.
7. Quoted in Earle F. Barcus and Susan M.
   Jankowski, "Drugs and the Mass Media," *The
   Annals of the American Academy of Political and
   Social Science*, 417 (1975), p. 89.
8. Ian Robertson, *Social Problems*, 2nd ed. (New
   York: Random House, 1980), p. 438.
9. Leon G. Hunt and Carl D. Chambers, *The Heroin
   Epidemics* (New York: Spectrum Books, 1976).
10. Alfred R. Lindesmith, *The Addict and the Law*
    (Bloomington: Indiana University Press, 1965),
    p. 228.
11. Joseph Gusfield, *Symbolic Crusade: Status Politics
    and the American Temperance Movement* (Urbana:
    University of Illinois Press, 1963).
12. Emile Durkheim, *Suicide: A Study in Sociology*,
    trans. John Spaulding and George Simpson
    (New York: Free Press, 1951).
13. Robert Merton, *Social Theory and Social Structure*,
    2nd ed. (New York: Free Press, 1968).
14. See Charles H. Cooley, *Human Nature and the
    Social Order* (New York: Scribner's, 1902);
    Howard S. Becker, *Outsiders: Studies in the Sociol-
    ogy of Deviance* (New York: Free Press, 1963).
15. Edwin H. Sutherland and Donald R. Cressey,
    Principles of Criminology, 7th ed. (Philadelphia:
    Lippincott, 1966).
16. Kornblum and Julian, *Social Problems*, p. 107.
17. Ibid.
18. Ibid.
19. For a review of these theories, see Abadinsky,
    Drug Use and Abuse.
20. Howard S. Becker, "Becoming a Marijuana
    User," *American Journal of Sociology*, 59 (Nov.
    1953), pp. 235–242.
21. Kornblum and Julian, *Social Problems*, p. 104.
22. "Why Liquor Is Quicker for Women," *U.S. News
    & World Report*, Jan. 22, 1990, p. 13.
23. The material in this section is summarized from
    studies that were reviewed in Kornblum and
    Julian, *Social Problems*, pp. 105–107.
24. Ibid., pp. 104–105.
25. See David J. Armor, J. Michael Polich, and
    Harriet G. Stambul, *Alcoholism and Treatment*
    (New York: Wiley Interscience, 1978).
26. Kornblum and Julian, *Social Problems*, p. 106.
27. Ibid., p. 111.
28. Ibid., p. 109.
29. Ibid., p. 110.
30. Ibid.
31. John E. Farley, *American Social Problems*, 2nd ed.
    (Englewood Cliffs, NJ: Prentice Hall, 1992),
    p. 237.
32. Kornblum and Julian, *Social Problems*, p. 110.
33. Ibid.
34. Ibid.
35. Ibid., p. 110.
36. Ibid., p. 111.
37. Sharon Wegscheider, *Another Chance: Hope and
    Health for the Alcoholic Family* (Palo Alto, CA:
    Science & Behavior Books, 1981).
38. Brenda C. Coleman, "Study Adds to Alcohol-
    ism Gene Theory," *Wisconsin State Journal*, Apr.
    18, 1990, p. 1A.
39. Linda A. Mooney, David Knox, and Caroline
    Schacht, *Understanding Social Problems*, 8th ed.

(Belmont, CA: Wadsworth/Cengage Learning, 2013) p. 71.

40. Ibid.

41. Wayne W. Dunning and Dae H. Chang, "Drug Facts and Effects," in *The Personal Problem Solver*, Charles Zastrow and Dae H. Chang, eds. (Englewood Cliffs, NJ: Spectrum Books, 1977), p. 177.

42. John Timson, "Is Coffee Safe to Drink?" *Human Nature*, Dec. 1978, pp. 57–59.

43. Abadinsky, *Drug Use and Abuse*.

44. Tony Blaze-Gosden, *Drug Abuse* (Birmingham, Great Britain: David & Charles Publishers, 1987), p. 99.

45. Abadinsky, *Drug Use and Abuse*.

46. Blaze-Gosden, *Drug Abuse*, p. 95.

47. Abadinsky, *Drug Use and Abuse*.

48. Ibid.

49. Ibid.

50. Robertson, *Social Problems*, p. 450.

51. Abadinsky, *Drug Use and Abuse*.

52. J. John Palen, *Social Problems for the Twenty-first Century* (Boston: McGraw-Hill, 2001), p. 380.

53. Timothy Noah, "A Hit or a Miss for Mr. Butts?" *U.S. News & World Report*, Jun. 30, 1997, pp. 22–24.

54. Kornblum and Julian, *Social Problems*, p. 42.

55. Ibid.

56. Ibid.

57. Ibid.

58. Lynn Rosellini, "Rebel with a Cause: Koop," *U.S. News & World Report*, May 30, 1988, pp. 55–63.

59. Noah, "A Hit or a Miss for Mr. Butts?"

60. Kornblum and Julian, *Social Problems*, p. 113–116.

61. "About Marijuana," *Hope Health Letter*, 14, no. 4 (Apr. 1991), p. 7.

62. John Kaplan, *Marijuana: A New Prohibition* (New York: World, 1970).

63. National Academy of Sciences, *Marijuana and Health* (Washington, DC: U.S. Government Printing Office, 1982).

64. Ibid.

65. Warren E. Leary, "Panel Recommends Marijuana Studies," *Wisconsin State Journal*, Feb. 21, 1997, p. 2A.

66. Brenda Ingersoll, "High Court Nixes Marijuana," *Wisconsin State Journal*, May 15, 2001, p. 1A.

67. A. Toufexis, "Shortcut to the Rambo Look," *Time,* Jan. 30, 1989, p. 78.

68. Ibid.

69. Tim Bliss, "Drugs—Use, Abuse, and Treatment," in *Introduction to Social Welfare Institutions*, Charles Zastrow, ed. (Homewood, IL: Dorsey Press, 1978), p. 301.

70. Frank Riessman, "The 'Helper Therapy' Principle," *Journal of Social Work*, Apr. 1965, pp. 27–34.

71. Abadinsky, *Drug Use and Abuse*.

72. Over 1,100 self-help groups can be located by typing in "American Self-Help Group Clearinghouse" on the Internet. When this website is accessed, type in a keyword of the support group that you want.

73. Palen, *Social Problems for the Twenty-first Century*, p. 382.

74. "A Test-Tube War on Drugs?" *U.S. News & World Report*, Mar. 17, 1986, p. 8.

75. Alvin P. Sanoff, "Baseball's Drug Menace," *U.S. News & World Report*, Mar. 17, 1986, p. 57.

76. National Commission on Marijuana and Drug Abuse, *Drug Use in America: Problem in Perspective*, Second Report (Washington, DC: U.S. Government Printing Office, Mar. 1973).

77. Kornblum and Julian, *Social Problems*, pp. 113–116.

CHAPTER

Crime, Juvenile Delinquency, and Correctional Services

Being victimized by crime is the social problem that many Americans are most concerned about. Types of crimes include murder, battery, aggravated assault, burglary, theft, arson, forcible rape, drug trafficking, and white-collar crime. What can be done to prevent these and other offenses? This chapter will:

Learning Objectives

EP 2.1.3a

A   Discuss the nature and extent of crime.
B   Present crime causation theories.
C   Describe types of crime.
D   Describe the criminal justice system (the police, the courts, and the correctional system).
E   Suggest ways to reduce crime and delinquency.
F   Discuss the role of social work in providing correctional services.

Nature and Extent of Crime

What Is Crime?

A *crime* is simply an act committed or omitted in violation of a law. A *law* is a formal social rule that is enforced by a political authority. Usually the state (or the power elite that controls the state) specifies as crimes those acts that violate certain strongly held values and norms. Not all behaviors that violate norms are prohibited by law; in some cases, informal processes (such as social disapproval) regulate norm violations. For example, a swimmer's failure to aid a drowning person is not a criminal act, although it is usually considered morally wrong.

Norms and values change over time, and therefore so do laws. When norms change, there is often a time lag before laws based on the outdated norms are changed. Some areas still have obsolete laws that prohibit card playing on Sundays and sexual intercourse (even between married couples) in any position other than the missionary position. Certain norms and values differ among cultures and societies; therefore, so do laws. In many Arab countries, the use of alcohol is illegal but the use of marijuana is acceptable; in the United States the reverse is generally the law.

Everyone, at one time or another, has violated some law. Whether a violator becomes a convicted offender depends on a number of factors, including whether he or she is arrested, how forcefully the prosecuting attorney wants to present the case, how effective the defense attorney is, whether there are witnesses, and how the offender presents himself or herself in court.[1]

With thousands of laws on the books, police, prosecuting attorneys, and judges have considerable discretion over which laws to ignore, which to enforce, and how strongly to enforce them. This discretionary power offers many opportunities for criminal justice officials to choose whom to arrest and whom to release. The act of applying the law often involves issues of political power and favorable treatment for certain groups and classes. Because this power usually resides with the White middle- and upper classes, the poor and minority groups are often (intentionally or unintentionally) treated more harshly. For example, authorities are substantially less vigorous in enforcing white-collar crime than they are in enforcing vagrancy laws in middle- and upper-class neighborhoods. (The middle- and upper-class power structure generally seeks to enforce vagrancy laws "to keep bums and other undesirables off the streets, or at least out of respectable neighborhoods."[2])

How Extensive Is Crime?

Crime is one of the most serious problems facing our nation. Former President Richard Nixon on several occasions called crime our "number-one enemy" and remarked that "we must declare war against it."

CASE EXHIBIT 9.1

Number of Offenses Reported for Some of the Major Crimes in the United States—2010

Violent Crime	1,246,248
Murder and nonnegligent manslaughter	14,748
Forcible rape	84,767
Robbery	367,832
Aggravated assault	778,901
Property crime	9,082,887
Burglary	2,159,878
Larceny-theft	6,185,867
Motor vehicle theft	737,142

SOURCE: U.S. Department of Justice, Federal Bureau of Investigation, *Crime in the United States—2010*, http://www.fbi.gov/ucr/cius2010/offenses/index.html.

(Ironically, Nixon and many of his top administrative officials later faced criminal charges—with some imprisoned—in connection with the Watergate affair.*)

The most comprehensive statistical summary of crime in the United States is the annual publication of *Crime in the United States* by the Federal Bureau of Investigation (FBI).[3] (This report used to be called *Uniform Crime Reports*.) *Crime in the United States* lists the crimes and arrests in this country as reported by law enforcement agencies. Case Exhibit 9.1 provides summary information on the number of offenses reported for some of the most serious crimes in the United States.

Critical Thinking Question

What crimes have you committed? All of us have violated one or more laws—such as jaywalking, speeding while driving, getting into a physical fight, parking in a no-parking zone, and so on.

---

* The Watergate affair involved a break-in in the early 1970s at the Democratic National Committee headquarters (housed in the Watergate building in Washington, DC) by persons who were clandestinely employed to help reelect Nixon. Nixon and some of his top aides then committed a variety of offenses in an effort to cover up this break-in. Nixon was eventually forced to resign from the presidency after the cover-up was revealed. He received a pardon by his successor as president, Gerald Ford, for his alleged crimes.

Many Americans feel unsafe in their own neighborhoods at night, and a high proportion own guns, largely for self-protection. Case Exhibit 9.1 demonstrates graphically why people are so fearful today, as a large number of crimes are committed daily in the United States.

How does the crime rate in the United States compare to the rates in other countries? This question is difficult to answer for a couple of reasons. Different countries define their crimes in somewhat different ways—for example, prostitution is a crime in some countries but not in others. In addition, many other countries do not collect accurate statistics on the extent of crime in their homelands. There is, however, one crime that every country defines in the same way and for which they collect accurate data. That crime is murder.

The United States has by far the highest rate of murder of any industrialized nation.[4] Coleman and Kerbo give the following explanation for the high level of violence in the United States:

The high level of violence in America is often seen as a holdover from the rowdy days of frontier expansion. According to this view, violence became a way of life as an unending stream of settlers fought among themselves and with native peoples for land and profit.... Furthermore, America is an extremely wealthy nation, but, compared with other Western countries, it has a bigger gap between the rich and the poor and inferior welfare and social programs. Thus, those at the bottom of the social hierarchy tend to be more frustrated and desperate, and more resentful of those who possess the wealth they are denied.[5]

Who Is Arrested?

Those who are arrested for crimes are disproportionately likely to be males, young, members of a racial minority, and city residents.

Males are arrested about three times as often as females.[6] (Only in juvenile runaway, embezzlement, and prostitution cases are females arrested more often.) There are two major reasons why males are more often arrested. One is sex-role socialization, which encourages males to be more aggressive and daring, whereas females are encouraged to be more passive and conforming to rules and norms. The second reason is the tendency of police officers and the courts to deal more leniently with female offenders.[7] However, in the past three decades, crime among females has been increasing faster than that among males,[8] which may be a negative side effect of women's challenging their traditional sex roles.

Young people appear to commit far more than their share of crime, including the crimes that are classified by the FBI as most serious—rape, murder, robbery, arson, burglary, aggravated assaults, auto theft, and larceny.[9] A partial explanation of the high arrest rate among juveniles and young adults is that they may be less skillful than older adults in avoiding arrest. In addition, they tend to commit crimes (such as auto theft) that are highly visible to the police. Even when all these factors are taken into account, it is still the case that the young commit more crimes than the old.

There are differences in arrest rates among various racial and ethnic groups. Chinese Americans and Japanese Americans have the lowest arrest rates in the country.[10] The arrest rate for African Americans is three times higher than for Whites.[11] One reason for this higher rate is that a higher proportion of the African American population is poor or unemployed, and there are high correlations between poverty (and unemployment) and the types of crime classified by the FBI as most serious. An additional reason for the higher arrest rate among certain minority groups may be racial prejudice. Numerous studies have shown that the probability of arrest, prosecution, conviction, and incarceration for an offense decreases as the social status of the offender increases. In one study, judges were given fact sheets on a hypothetical case and asked to recommend an appropriate sentence. The fact sheets contained the following information:

"Joe Cut," 27, pleaded guilty to battery. He slashed his common-law wife on the arms with a switchblade. His record showed convictions for disturbing the peace, drunkenness, and hit-run driving. He told a probation officer that he acted in self-defense after his wife attacked him with a broom handle. The prosecutor recommended not more than five days in jail or a $100 fine.[12]

Half of the fact sheets identified "Joe Cut" as White, and the other half identified him as African American. The judges who thought he was White recommended a sentence of 3 to 10 days, whereas those who thought he was African American recommended a sentence of 5 to 30 days.

Another major reason for higher arrest rates among African Americans is the use of racial profiling by police forces.[13]

Simply put, the high number of these groups who are arrested is partially the result of police targeting them in the first place. Racial profiling refers to the tendency of police departments to view members of certain minority groups as more likely to commit crimes than the general population, and to then use that assumption in making decisions about who to arrest for traffic violations, whose suitcases to search in customs investigations, and so on. One source of evidence of racial profiling is a report from the New Jersey attorney general that showed that 77% of the motorists stopped and searched by New Jersey state troopers are African American or Hispanic, even though only 13.5% of the drivers on New Jersey highways are African American or Hispanic.[14]

In addition, lack of access to high-quality legal services, along with patterns of bias in jury selection, also help account for much higher conviction rates among people of color. These patterns of racial injustice are examples of what is known as *institutional racism*. A major reason African Americans make up a disproportionate share of prison populations (as compared to Whites) is institutional racism. African Americans and Hispanic Americans are more than twice as likely as Whites to be searched, arrested, or subdued with force when stopped by police.[15]

Cole and Smith state:

The evidence of racial profiling in the criminal justice system is not limited to traffic enforcement....

African American women returning from abroad were nine times as likely as white women to be subjected to x-ray searches at airports, even though white women were found to be carrying illegal contraband twice as often as were African American women.[16]

Since September 11, 2001, many Arab Americans have also been victimized by ethnic profiling.

A majority of reported crimes and reported arrests are in large cities, as compared to suburbs and rural areas. Within large cities, crime tends to occur in sections that are changing rapidly and that have a high concentration of low-income and transient inhabitants. Arrest rates are substantially lower in more stable, higher-income, residential areas. Crime is lower in the suburbs than in the cities and lower still in the rural areas.[17]

How Accurate Are Official Crime Statistics?

As described earlier, the FBI annually compiles *Crime in the United States* based on data from law enforcement agencies throughout the country on crimes committed and arrests made. This report focuses primarily on violent crimes and on property crimes.

Critical Thinking Questions

Have you been a victim of a crime—such as having something stolen? Practically all of us have been a victim. What could you have done differently to avoid being victimized? Reflecting on this last question may help you to avoid being victimized in the future.

There are a number of problems connected with this report. Actual crime rates are substantially higher than the official rates. Kornblum and Julian estimate that crimes reported to the police account for about 33% of actual offenses and about 50% of violent crimes.[18] Victims often do not report crimes to the police because (among other reasons) they feel that nothing can be done.[19] Most crimes go unsolved.

Crime in the United States focuses on crimes that are more likely to be committed by people of lower social and economic status. It does not reflect the types of crimes typically committed by higher-income groups: fraud, false advertising, bribery, embezzlement, industrial pollution, tax evasion, and so on. If white-collar crimes were included in the re-

port, and if law enforcement authorities were more vigorous in enforcing such laws, the profile of a typical criminal would very likely be older, wealthier, whiter, and more suburban than suggested by the *Crime in the United States.*

Self-report studies, in which respondents are asked anonymously the details of any crimes they may have committed, reveal that "close to 100 percent of all persons have committed some kind of offense, although few have been arrested."[20] In what way, then, do those who are arrested differ from those who are not? For one thing, those who are not caught tend to commit a crime only rarely, whereas those who are arrested tend to break the law more frequently.[21] Perhaps a better explanation, however, lies in the types of crimes committed. Those arrested may be committing the kinds of crimes that are more strictly enforced by law enforcement agencies. The poor, for example, may be more likely to commit high-risk, low-yield crimes such as larceny, burglary, or robbery. In contrast, the wealthier are more likely to commit low-risk, high-yield crimes such as income tax evasion and false advertising.

Even with a large proportion of unreported crimes, statistics show a rapid increase in crime in the early 1970s. The crime rate continued to increase in the late 1970s, but in the early 1980s it leveled off. In the early 1990s, the rate of violent crimes and property crimes began to decrease, and there has been a slow decrease through the early 21st century.[22] Sociologists believe the recent decline is due to the waning of the crack epidemic in the largest metropolitan centers, the rapid increase in the number of prison inmates, and increases in the size of police forces throughout the nation (such increases are designed to deter people from committing crimes).

Strictly speaking, *Crime in the United States* is not fully comparable among jurisdictions. At times it is even inconsistent from one year to the next within the same reporting unit. A major reason for this difficulty is that each of the 50 states has its own unique criminal code. For example, an offense that is classified as burglary in one state may be classified as larceny or robbery in another; what is classified as sexual assault in one state may be considered a less serious offense in another. Because states occasionally make changes in their criminal codes, inconsistencies may arise from one year to the next within the same reporting unit because of changes in definitions of offenses. Furthermore, individual officers interpret the law differently as they carry out their duties.

Finally, crime statistics are at times manipulated by the police and public officials. Data may be skewed to show higher rates of crime, perhaps to help document the need for a federal or state grant or to politick for a budget increase in personnel or facilities. More often than not, however, police and public officials are under considerable pressure to keep the crime rate low. By manipulating statistics, they can reclassify certain serious crimes into different, less serious categories.

In summary, *Crime in the United States* of the FBI provides an indication of the rates and trends of certain crimes in the United States. Yet these statistics overlook white-collar crime, are affected by police-reporting practices, and must be viewed against the fact that many crimes are unreported. It further appears that the poor, the undereducated, and minorities have been the victims not only of selective law enforcement but also of misleading statistics on crime. Some sociologists have contended that, because higher-income classes are far more involved in white-collar crime (which is often ignored by law enforcement agencies), they may actually have a higher rate of crime than the lower classes.[23]

Crime Causation Theories

A variety of theories about the causes of crime have been advanced by several disciplines. Space limitations permit only a summary of the more prominent theories. Case Exhibit 9.2 identifies these prominent theories along with their approximate dates of origin. As you read about each of these theories, ask yourself the following questions: Is this theory helpful in explaining why a person committed a rape (or burglary, murder, drug-trafficking offense, aggravated assault, kidnapping, embezzlement, and so on)? Is the theory useful in suggesting a correctional plan to prevent a recurrence of the offense?

Early Theories

Three of the earliest theories on the causes of crime were *demonology*, the *classical/neoclassical theory*, and the *Marxist–Leninist theory*.

Demonology

For centuries many nonliterate societies conceived of crime as caused by evil spirits. This belief is commonly referred to as *demonology*. It was thought that those who engaged in deviant behavior were possessed by the devil. The only way to cure the criminal act was to remove the evil spirit through prayer, through a ritual, or by torture (sometimes to the point of death). This theory is no longer prominent, partly because scientific study has found no evidence that lawbreakers are possessed by evil spirits. Remnants of the theory remain, however, as seen in satanic cults, rock lyrics with satanic themes, and movies (such as *Friday the 13th* and *The Exorcist*) depicting people possessed by demons.

Classical and Neoclassical Theory

The classical and neoclassical schools were based on hedonistic psychology. Classical theory asserted that a person makes a decision about whether to engage in criminal activity based on the anticipated balance of pleasure and pain. Each individual was assumed to have a free will and to act solely on the basis of the anticipated hedonistic calculations. Advocates of this school considered this to be a full and exhaustive explanation of causality. Applied to corrections, this approach urged that clear-cut punishments be assigned to each offense so the prospective offender could calculate anticipated pleasures and pains. The penalties assigned were to be slightly more severe than anticipated pleasures to discourage criminal activity. The neoclassical school accepted the basic notion of hedonistic calculations but urged that children and "lunatics" be exempt from punishment because of their inability to calculate pleasures and pains responsibly. Judicial discretion was also urged for certain mitigating circumstances (for example, an offense now referred to as involuntary manslaughter).

Although correctional systems in the 19th century were based primarily on the neoclassical approach, classical/neoclassical theory has waned in popularity. Some elements of it can still be found in our legal/judicial system—particularly the emphasis on using punishment to deter crime. The theory has been severely criticized because it does not allow for other causes of crime and because the punitive approach it advocates has not been very

CASE EXHIBIT 9.2

Prominent Theories of Crime

Theory	Approximate Date of Origin
Early theories	
Demonology	Nonliterate societies
Classical/Neoclassical	1775
Marxist–Leninist	1850
Physical and mental trait theories	
Phrenology	1825
Lombrosian	1900
Mental deficiency	1900
Morphological	1920
Psychological theories	
Psychoanalytic	1900
Psychodynamic problem solving	1920
Frustration–aggression	1950
Self-talk	1975
Sociological theories	
Labeling	1900
Differential association	1939
Societal control	1950
Deviant subcultures	1955
Anomie	1957
Critical	1995

successful in curbing further criminal activity. In addition, hedonistic psychology ignores the fact that much human behavior is determined by values and morals rather than by the pleasure-versus-pain calculation.

Marxist–Leninist Theory

Marxist–Leninist theory assumes that all crime results from the exploitation of workers and from intense competition among people. Crime disappears, according to neo-Marxists, when society achieves a "classless" status. The basic tenet of communism is, "From each according to his ability, to each according to his need." Socialist countries (such as Cuba and North Korea) have in the past sought to formulate their societies on the principles advocated by Karl Marx. Class differentials are much less prominent in socialist countries as compared to capitalist nations.

Although Marx asserted that crime would be sharply reduced in socialist countries because there would be less class conflict, substantial criminal activity does occur in these countries. (The extensiveness of criminal activity is difficult to determine because these countries publish almost no crime-rate reports.) The continued existence of crime in socialist countries is not taken by socialists as evidence that the theory is defective; rather, it is explained as being the result of old capitalistic traditions and ideologies and the imperfect application of Marxist theory. (Many socialist countries in recent years have been discarding Marxist principles and are moving toward incorporating capitalistic incentives into their economies.)

Physical and Mental Trait Theories

You may have noticed in Case Exhibit 9.2 that the first "physical and mental trait theory," *phrenology*, actually originated before Marxist–Leninist theory. Although it falls chronologically into the category of "early theories," it is more closely related to "trait theories" and will be discussed in this section along with three other trait theories: the

Lombrosian, the *mental deficiency*, and the *morphological* theories.

Phrenology

Phrenology was popular until the turn of the 20th century. Phrenologists maintained that criminal behavior was related to the size and shape of the human skull. They closely scrutinized the grooves, ridges, and number of bumps on a skull. The shape of the brain, which was influenced by the shape of the skull, was thought to be sufficient to predict criminal activity. Although there were isolated incidents in which offenders with "criminal-prone" skulls were treated more harshly than other offenders, this approach was not widely incorporated into correctional systems. Scientific studies have found no evidence of correlations between criminal behavior and the shape of the skull.

Lombrosian Theory

Around the beginning of the 20th century, biological/constitutional theories were popular. The prototype of such theories was Cesare Lombroso's theory of the "born criminal." This school maintained that a criminal inherits certain physical abnormalities or stigmata, such as a scanty beard, low sensitivity to pain, distorted nose, large lips, or long arms. The more such stigmata a person had, the more he or she was thought to be predisposed to a criminal career. People with several stigmata were thought to be unable to refrain from criminal activity unless their social environment was unusually favorable. The theory that criminals have distinct physical characteristics was refuted by Charles Goring, who found no significant physical differences in a study comparing several thousand criminals with several thousand noncriminals.[24]

Mental Deficiency Theory

The mental deficiency theory replaced the Lombrosian school when the latter fell into disrepute. Mental deficiency theory asserted that criminal behavior resulted from "feeblemindedness," which was alleged to impair the capacity to acquire morality and self-control or to appreciate the meaning of laws. As mental tests became standardized and widely used, it was discovered that many criminals achieved average or above-average intelligence scores. The theory waned in popularity in the 1930s. Neither the Lombrosian nor the mental deficiency approach had a lasting, significant effect on corrections.

Morphological Theory

Closely related to the mental deficiency and Lombrosian theories is morphological theory, which asserted that there is a fundamental relationship between psychological makeup and physical structure. The most popular variant of this theory was William Sheldon's, developed in the 1940s. Sheldon described three body categories: endomorph (obese), mesomorph (muscular), and ectomorph (lean). To the mesomorph he ascribed an unusual propensity to criminal activity. Sheldon did not assert that mesomorphs were inherently criminally prone. Rather, he asserted that this physique was associated with a distinctive type of temperament, characterized by such traits as love of physical adventure, abundance of restless energy, and enjoyment of exercise. Mesomorphy thus produced energetic, aggressive, and daring types of individuals, such as generals, athletes, and politicians, as well as criminals. Morphological approaches like Sheldon's are still popular in southern European and South American countries. Scientific studies, however, have found little evidence that muscular people are more likely to commit crimes than people who are lean or overweight.

Psychological Theories

Psychological theories about crime attribute its causes to the criminal's thought processes, which are seen as relatively unrelated to overall societal conditions. These theories include the *psychoanalytic, psychodynamic problem-solving, frustration–aggression,* and *self-talk* approaches to understanding criminal behavior.

Psychoanalytic Theory

Psychoanalytic theory is not a single coherent theory but a variety of hypotheses developed by psychoanalysts since the turn of the 20th century from the pioneering work of Sigmund Freud. Generally, these theories postulated that delinquent behavior results when the restraining forces in the superego (one's conscience and self-ideal) and the ego (mediator among the superego, the id, and reality) are too weak to curb the instinctual, antisocial pressures from the id (source of psychic energy). Human nature was seen as largely determined by id instincts, which were basically antisocial and immoral in character. This theory postulated that current behavior was largely controlled by early childhood experiences. Deviant behavior was viewed as stemming from unconscious conflicts, fixations, and repressed traumatic experiences.

The psychiatric school, of which psychoanalysis is a large component, has had a significant influence on corrections because it asserts that some offenders commit illegal acts because they are insane. Criminal justice systems frequently call on psychiatrists to determine the "sanity" of accused offenders. If someone is judged by the court to be "innocent by reason of insanity," he or she is sent to a mental hospital, instead of to a jail, to recuperate.

Psychiatry has also classified individuals into numerous categories in terms of their "mental" functioning. One category, *sociopath*, has had considerable relevancy for corrections. A sociopath is a person who is thought to have no moral constraints against engaging in criminal activity, doing so whenever it is personally advantageous, even though others may be hurt.

Since 1950 Thomas Szasz and others have seriously questioned the medical-model approach to emotional problems and have asserted that mental illness is a myth.[25] Szasz believes that people have emotional problems, but not a "disease of the mind," as implied by the medical model (see Chapter 5). Courts, however, continue to use the mental-illness model.

Psychoanalytic theory is increasingly falling into disfavor. One reason is the finding that people with emotional problems who undergo psychoanalysis are no more likely to improve than a comparable group who receives no therapy.[26]

Psychodynamic Problem-Solving Theory

Psychodynamic problem-solving theory views deviant behavior as contrived by the personality as a way of dealing with some adjustment problem. The problem is generally perceived as a conflict among various ingredients of the personality: wishes, drives, fears, strivings, loyalties, codes of ethics, and so on. Situational factors are generally deemphasized.

A serious shortcoming of the theory is that it is often extremely difficult (if not impossible) to determine precisely which wishes, drives, fears, or ethics motivated someone to commit a crime. For example, the following internal desires have all been advanced as motivations for committing rape: unfulfilled sexual desires, a desire for violence, and feelings of inferiority. All are theorized to be temporarily alleviated during rape as the offender feels a sense of power and superiority. When a sexual assault occurs, it is nearly impossible to determine the extent to which each of these internal desires contributed to the assault. Frequently, when using this theory, only speculations can be made about why a crime occurred, as few "tools" exist to check the accuracy of the speculations.

Frustration–Aggression Theory

Frustration–aggression theory asserts that frustration often provokes an aggressive response. Thus, violence is seen as a way to release the tension produced by a frustrating situation. An unemployed husband, unable to pay the bills or find a job, for example, may beat his wife. Some authorities viewed the burning and rioting in our inner cities in the 1960s as a reaction by African Americans to the frustration of living in a society that promises equality but does not provide it.

Critical Thinking Question

Identify a crime that you committed. What were the thought processes that led you to commit this crime?

Frustration–aggression theory provides an explanation for only violent crimes. It does not attempt to explain other kinds of criminal behavior, such as prostitution, fraud, and forgery.

Self-Talk Theory

Self-talk theory is a psychological approach for identifying the underlying motives for committing a crime.[27] According to this theory, the reasons for any criminal act can be determined by examining what the offender was thinking prior to and during the time the crime was committed (see Case Example 9.1). A shortcoming of the theory is that, when offenders discuss what they were thinking during a crime, they often seek to slant what they reveal in a socially acceptable way.

Sociological Theories

Sociological theories focus on societal factors that influence people to commit crimes. For ease in understanding these theories, we will examine them out of chronological order (see Case Exhibit 9.2) as follows: *differential association theory, anomie theory, deviant subcultures theory, societal control theory, labeling theory,* and *critical theory.*

CASE EXAMPLE 9.1

Self-Talk Theory: A Presidential Assassination Attempt

On March 30, 1981, President Ronald Reagan was shot in Washington, D.C., by a .22-caliber bullet, which pierced the left side of his chest and collapsed his left lung. Also injured were a secret service agent, a Washington policeman, and White House press secretary James Brady. Fortunately, all four men survived. Arrested for this assassination attempt was John W. Hinckley, Jr., 25, the son of a multimillionaire Colorado oil executive.

Born into wealth, John Hinckley has been described as a loner and a drifter, a misfit who craved fame. In high school, Hinckley was an average student but had few friends. He went to college for 7 years off and on but never graduated. His father was a self-made millionaire, and his brother was vice president of his father's firm. His family members were known as strong Reagan supporters.

John Hinckley became infatuated with actress Jodie Foster, although they had never met. In the film *Taxi Driver*, Jodie Foster played a teenage prostitute. The film was about a disturbed loser (played by Robert DeNiro) who stalks a political figure. This film appears to have influenced Hinckley's assassination attempt, as he wrote in an unmailed letter to Ms. Foster:

> I would abandon this idea of getting Reagan in a second if I could only win your heart and live out the rest of my life with you, whether it be in total obscurity or whatever. I will admit to you that the reason I'm going ahead with this attempt now is because I just cannot wait any longer to impress you....
>
> Jodie, I'm asking you to please look into your heart and at least give me the chance with this historical deed to gain your respect and love.[a]

Apparently, John Hinckley shot the president because he believed that such an action would impress Jodie Foster and lead to a relationship with her.

When attorneys, judges, police officers, and other criminal justice officials search for the motive for an offender committing a crime, they are really searching to identify the cognitions (that is, the self-talk) that led the offender to commit a crime.

[a]John S. Lang, "John Hinckley—A Misfit Who Craved Fame," *U.S. News & World Report*, Apr. 13, 1981, p. 26.

Differential Association Theory

Edwin Sutherland, perhaps the best-known criminologist in contemporary sociology, advanced his famous theory of differential association in 1939. The theory asserts that criminal behavior is the result of a learning process that primarily occurs in small, intimate groups—family, neighborhood peer groups, friends, and so on. In essence, "A person becomes delinquent because of the excess of definitions favorable to violation of law over definitions unfavorable to violation of law."[28] Whether a person decides to commit a crime is based on the nature of present and past associations with significant others. People internalize the values of the surrounding culture. When the environment includes frequent contact with criminal elements and infrequent contact with noncriminal elements, a person is likely to engage in delinquent or criminal activity.

Past and present learning experiences in intimate personal groups thus define whether a person should violate laws; for those deciding to commit crimes, the learning experiences also include the choice of which crimes to commit, the techniques of committing these crimes, and the attitudes and rationalizations for committing these crimes. Thus, a youth whose most admired person is a member of a gang involved in burglaries or drug trafficking will seek to emulate this model, will receive instruction in committing these crimes from the gang members, and will also receive approval from the gang for successfully committing these crimes.

The theory does little to explain such crimes as arson and embezzlement, in which the offender often has no exposure to others who have committed such crimes.

Anomie Theory

Robert Merton applied anomie theory to crime.[29] This approach views criminal behavior as resulting when an individual is prevented from achieving high-status goals in a society. Merton begins by noting that every society has both approved goals (for example, wealth and material possessions) and approved means for attaining these goals. When certain members of society share these goals but have insufficient access to approved means for attaining them, a state of anomie results. (Anomie is a condition in which acceptance of the approved standards of conduct is weakened.) Unable to achieve the goals through society's legitimately defined channels, they then seek to achieve them through illegal means.

AP Photo/Sasa Kralj

Confrontation among gang members. According to one theory, gangs develop delinquent subcultures that solve the status problems of working-class adolescents, especially those rejected by middle-class society.

Merton asserts that higher crime rates are likely to occur among groups that are discriminated against (that is, groups that face additional barriers to achieving the high-status goals). These groups include the poor and racial minorities. Societies with high crime rates (such as the United States) differ from those with low crime rates because, according to Merton, they tell all their citizens they can achieve, but in fact they block achievement for some people.

Anomie theory has difficulty explaining why white-collar crime (which is committed primarily by individuals who are seldom discriminated against) is perhaps the most common type of crime committed in this country.[30]

Deviant Subcultures Theory

Deviant subcultures theory is another explanation for crime. This theory asserts that some groups develop their own attitudes, values, and perspectives, which support criminal activity. Walter Miller, for example, argues that American lower-class culture is more conducive to crime than middle-class culture.[31] He asserts that lower-class culture is organized around six values—trouble, toughness, excitement, fate, smartness (ability to con others), and autonomy—and allegiance to these values produces delinquency. Miller concludes that the entire lower-class subculture is deviant in the sense that any male growing up in it will accept these values and almost certainly violate the law.

Albert Cohen advanced another subculture theory.[32] He contended that gangs develop a delinquent subculture that offers solutions to the problems of young male gang members. A gang gives them the chance to belong, to amount to something, to develop their masculinity, and to fight middle-class

CASE EXAMPLE 9.2

The Saints and the Roughnecks: A Study Showing the Effects of Labeling and of Expectations of Significant Others

William Chambliss, in a dramatic study, examined factors affecting delinquency within two groups of adolescents at the same high school. One group was composed of middle- and upper-class boys (the Saints), and the other was composed of lower-class boys (the Roughnecks). The Saints were often truant from school, harassed citizens and the police, openly cheated on exams, vandalized homes, drank excessively, and drove recklessly. Teachers, school officials, and the police largely ignored their acts because they were viewed as basically good boys. They were almost never arrested by the police, and hardly anything negative appeared in their school records. These youths were regarded as harmless pranksters, were allowed to "sow their wild oats," and were expected to succeed in life. Interestingly, the success expectations appeared to be a major factor in determining their futures; practically all of the Saints went on to college and white-collar careers.

On the other hand, the Roughnecks, who committed fewer, although similar, offenses, were labeled "deviants." Because they didn't have cars as the Saints did, the Roughnecks were confined to an area where they were more easily recognized and substantially more often arrested. The police and school officials expected that they would fail—and they did. These "delinquents" did poorly in school and went on to low-status jobs or criminal careers.

One additional factor that led to fewer arrests for the Saints was their apologetic nature whenever they were stopped by a police officer. They were polite and penitent and pled for mercy when stopped. In contrast, there was a high level of dislike and distrust between the police and the Roughnecks. When stopped by police, they came across as "tough" kids who displayed disdain and hostility—and as a consequence were more frequently arrested.

This study of the Saints and Roughnecks demonstrates that both labeling and the expectations of significant others can have a substantial effect on behavior.

SOURCE: William Chambliss, "The Saints and the Roughnecks," *Society*, 2, no. 11 (Nov.–Dec. 1973), pp. 24–31.

---

society. In particular, the delinquent subculture, according to Cohen, can effectively solve the status problems of working-class boys, especially those who are rejected by middle-class society. Cohen contends that the main problems of working-class boys revolve around status.

As with the previous theories, deviant subculture theories are unable to explain white-collar crime and other crimes committed by the middle and upper classes.

Societal Control Theory

Control theories ask the question, "Why do people *not* commit crimes?" Theories in this category assume that all of us would "naturally" commit crimes and therefore must be constrained and controlled by society from breaking the law. Control theorists have identified three factors for preventing crime. One is the internal controls that build up through the process of socialization; a strong conscience and a sense of personal morality prevent most people from breaking the law. A second factor is a strong attachment to small social groups (for example, the family), which is thought to prevent individuals from breaking the

law because they fear rejection and disapproval from the people who are important to them. A third factor (taken from the classical school) is that people do not break the law because they fear arrest and incarceration.

Control theories assume that basic human nature is asocial or evil. Such an assumption has never been proved. Theories that perceive humans as having an evil nature are unable to explain altruistic and other "good" deeds performed by people.

Labeling Theory

Labeling theorists, similar to differential association theorists, assert that criminals *learn* to break the law. Labeling theory focuses on the process of branding people as criminals and on the effects of such labeling. Contrary to control theory, this theory holds that labeling a person as a delinquent or a criminal encourages rather than discourages criminal behavior.

Charles Cooley developed a labeling theory with his concept of the "looking-glass self."[33] This theory argues that people develop their self-concept (sense of who and what they are) in terms of how others relate to them, as if others were a looking glass or mirror. For example, if a neighborhood identifies a young boy as a "troublemaker" or "delinquent," neighbors are likely to relate to the youth as if he were not to be trusted. They may accuse him of delinquent acts, and they will label his semidelinquent and aggressive behavior "delinquent." This labeling process also results in a type of prestige and status for the boy, at least from his peers. In the absence of objective ways to gauge whether he is, in fact, a "delinquent," the youth will rely on the subjective evaluations of others. Thus, gradually, as he is related to as a "delinquent," he begins to perceive himself in that way and enacts the delinquent role.

Labeling theory is unable to explain why some offenders stop committing crimes after being arrested and convicted.

Critical Theory

This theory argues that the capitalist economic system is the root cause of our crime problem. Supporters of this theory assert that capitalism fosters crime by encouraging, and even requiring, the exploitation of one group by another and by promoting the selfish quest for personal gain as if it were the inevitable goal of all human behavior.[34] (Readers will note the similarities of this theory to Marxist–Leninist theory, which was described earlier.) Critical theory fails to explain why crime occurs in Communist societies, which do not have a capitalist economic system.

Usefulness of Theories

These theories identify some of the reasons why crime occurs, especially why crime rates are higher within some groups than within others. One of the most important questions in criminology is, "Do these theories identify the reasons why an offender committed a specific crime (for example, an aggravated rape)?" The answer, unfortunately, is that most theories are not very useful in identifying the causes for specific crimes. Also, they are not very useful in explaining why one individual commits forgery, another commits rape, and yet another burglarizes someone. Without knowing why a crime occurs, it is extremely difficult to develop an effective rehabilitation approach to curb repeat offenders.

Theories that attempt to explain all types of crime have a built-in limitation. Crime is a comprehensive label covering a wide range of offenses, including purse snatching, auto theft, rape, check forgery, prostitution, drunkenness, possession of narcotics, and sexual exhibition. Obviously, because the natures of these crimes vary widely, the motives or causes underlying each must vary widely. Therefore, it is unlikely that any theory can adequately explain the causes of all crimes. It may be more productive to focus on developing more limited theories that attempt to identify the causes of specific offenses (for example, drunkenness, incest, auto theft, rape, or fraud) rather than to develop additional comprehensive theories.

Now let's take a detailed look at specific types of criminal offenses.

Critical Thinking Questions

What is your favorite theory as to why people commit crimes? Why do you prefer this theory?

Types of Crime

We tend to think that crime is a well-defined phenomenon and to have stereotyped views about who criminals are. Actually, criminal offenses and the characteristics of lawbreakers are almost as varied as noncriminal offenses and law abiders. Many diverse forms of behaviors are classified as crimes, with the only major common thread being a violation of a criminal statute. Because it is impossible to look at all crimes, we will examine the more important ones. Keep in mind that the following categories are not mutually exclusive.

Organized Crime

Organized crime is a large-scale operation. Illegal activities are carried out as part of a well-designed plan developed by a large organization seeking to maximize its overall profit. Activities that lend themselves to organized crime include illegal gambling, drug dealing, fencing (receiving and selling stolen goods), prostitution, bootlegging, and extortion (in the form of selling protection). Large-scale operations are more cost efficient than small-scale operations in certain illegal activities. For example, in drug trafficking, drugs are smuggled into a country and distributed on a large scale, with corrupt officials paid off to reduce the risks of arrest and prosecution.

It appears that most organized crime efforts start on a small scale, generally with one small organization that carries on a particular crime, such as extortion or gambling. The group then expands to control this activity within a given neighborhood or city by absorbing or destroying the competition. Eventually the organization expands its activities into other crimes and begins to operate in larger regions or even nationwide.

A major characteristic of organized crime is that many of its activities are not predatory (such as robbery, which takes from its victims). Instead, organized crime generally seeks to provide to the public desired goods and services that cannot be obtained legally (drugs, gambling, prostitution, loan money). For its success, organized crime relies on public demand for illegal services.

Because of the obvious emphasis on secrecy in organized crime, only limited information is available about the extent of offenses, the leaders and members of organized crime, or the nature of the internal organization.

Organized crime in the United States is thought to revolve primarily around the Mafia (also called the Cosa Nostra). Its leadership is Italian American, with the lower ranks drawn from a variety of other ethnic groups. The Mafia developed largely during the 1920s and 1930s, when criminal groups organized to supply illegal alcohol during Prohibition. It has grown into a loose network of American regional syndicates or groups. These syndicates coordinate their efforts through a "commission" composed of the heads of the most powerful "families."[35] At the head of each family is a "don," who has absolute authority over the family unless overruled by the commission. Each don is assisted by an underboss and a counselor. Next in the hierarchy are "lieutenants," each of whom supervises a group of "soldiers" who are involved in illegal enterprises. Contrary to public opinion, the Mafia is not an international syndicate of Sicilian lawbreakers; rather, it is a network of syndicates that were developed and organized in this country. The *Godfather* books and films paint a fairly realistic picture of the structure and operations of organized crime.

The costs to society and to our economy from organized crime are enormous. Through gambling and drug traffic, the lives of many individuals and their families are traumatized. Labor racketeering and infiltration of legitimate businesses lead to higher prices for goods, lower-quality products, the forced closing of some businesses, the establishment of monopolies, the unemployment of workers, misuse of pension and welfare benefits, and higher taxes. Through corruption of public officials (a necessary component of many illegal ventures), organized crime leads to public cynicism about the honesty of politicians and the democratic process. It also leads to higher taxes and mismanagement of public funds.

In the past five decades the FBI made immense progress in its battle against organized crime. The heads of many of the nation's Mafia families were indicted, convicted, and incarcerated. In addition, thousands of organized crime members were arrested and convicted of a variety of offenses. Experts credit this breakthrough to a number of factors. The FBI now devotes a significant proportion of its workforce to combating organized crime[36] and has been making increased use of electronic eavesdropping. The FBI also is working more closely with state law enforcement authorities and with Italy to curb organized crime. Recently law enforcement agencies have been successful in getting large numbers of gang members to violate the traditional code of *omertà*—conspiracy of silence. Fearing lengthy stays in prison, where they could be vulnerable to mob-ordered murders, many underworld figures are joining a witness-protection effort that provides informants with new identities (including fake biographies) and homes in a different area of the country.

Despite these efforts, no one sees an end to the mob's influence any time soon. Many of the old leaders have been replaced by a "new breed" of leadership, who have a greater familiarity with the world of high finance and legitimate business. Organized crime is developing new marketplace scams, including counterfeiting consumer credit cards and airline tickets, bootlegging gasoline (thereby avoiding payment of federal and state gasoline taxes), and selling fraudulent tax shelters.[37] In addition, new organizations unassociated with the Mafia have emerged to import and distribute illegal drugs.[38] These include organizations that are smuggling drugs in from Mexico and Colombia.

Let's examine the major crime efforts: gambling, drug trafficking, loan sharking, infiltrating legitimate businesses, labor racketeering, and prostitution.

Gambling

Illegal gambling takes place on a wide scale and generates enormous profits. Illegal operations include lotteries, off-track betting, illegal casinos, "numbers," and dice games. Such operations can be located practically anywhere—in a restaurant, garage, tavern, apartment complex, or even on business premises.

Drug Trafficking

Drug trafficking is an industry that makes billions of dollars annually in the United States. With such profits, it is little wonder that organized crime is involved in the importation and distribution of drugs such as cocaine, heroin, marijuana, crack, amphetamines, and hallucinogens. A recent trend in the illicit drug trade in the United States is the growth of new organizations unassociated with older crime "families." Some of these new organizations have ethnic group identities, such as Colombian, Chinese, Vietnamese, Puerto Rican, Nigerian, African American, or Russian.[39]

Loan Sharking

This crime involves lending money at interest rates above the legal limit. Interest rates have been reported to go as high as 150% a week.[40] Syndicated crime can ensure repayment by the threat of violence. Major borrowers from loan sharks include gamblers who need to cover losses, drug users, and small-business owners who are unable to obtain credit from legitimate sources.

Infiltrating Legitimate Businesses

The huge profits from illegal activities provide organized crime with the capital to enter into legitimate operations, including the entertainment industry, banking, insurance, restaurants, advertising firms, bars, the automotive industry, and real estate agencies—to name but a few.

Infiltrating legitimate business provides organized crime with tax covers for its members, gives them a certain respectable status in the community, and offers additional profit-making opportunities. With its cash reserves, a syndicate can temporarily lower prices and bankrupt competitors. It can also use strong-arm tactics to force customers to buy its goods and services.

Labor Racketeering

This activity involves the systematic extortion of money from labor unions and businesses. Racketeers can extort money from union members by forcing them to pay high union dues and fees in order to obtain and secure employment. Racketeers can shortchange employees by paying less than union wages and by misusing the union's pension and welfare funds. Finally, racketeers can extort money from employers by forcing them to make payoffs for union cooperation (for example, to avoid a strike).

Prostitution

Because prostitutes offer a service for which some people are willing to pay high prices, prostitution can be a highly profitable endeavor, which makes it appealing to organized crime. Mobsters serve as brokers for prostitutes and customers and also protect them from arrest and prosecution by bribing law enforcement officials. Organized crime has also gotten involved in other sex-related forms of crime, such as the illegal distribution of pornographic films and magazines.

White-Collar Crime

John Johnson and Jack Douglas have noted that the most costly—and perhaps the most frequent—crimes are committed by "respectable" middle-class and upper-class citizens.[41] White-collar crimes are work-related offenses committed by people of high status.[42]

Offenses against customers include false advertising, stock manipulation, violations of food and drug laws, release of industrial waste products into public waterways, illegal emissions from industrial smokestacks, and price-fixing agreements. In the 1980s and early 1990s, there was extensive fraud in the savings and loan industry that led to the industry's collapse. The federal government had to cover many of the losses. It cost taxpayers an estimated $500 billion, with large amounts of unprotected savings also lost by individual investors.[43] This savings and loan scandal helps to illustrate that white-collar crimes cost more money than all other types of crimes put together.[44]

The case of stock speculator Ivan Boesky provides a classic example of white-collar crime. Boesky personally made over $100 million on illegal insider trading (acting on information not available to the public). Brokers who possess inside information (such as knowledge of an impending corporate merger or a change in the financial condition of a company that will affect the price of its stock) are prohibited from profiting from that information themselves or from selling it to others who may be able to profit from it. In 1986 Boesky admitted his illegal activities, paid the Securities and Exchange Commission $100 million in fines and illicit profits, and was later convicted of conspiracy to file false documents with the federal government. Boesky's crimes precipitated a wave of additional allegations of insider trading, which have rocked the financial

Bernard Madoff was convicted in a giant Ponzi scheme in which investors lost 50 billion dollars.

community in recent years. For these multimillion-dollar offenses, Boesky was imprisoned only 2 years.

In December 2008, Bernard Madoff was arrested by the FBI and charged with securities fraud. His investment firm was one of the five most active firms in the development of the NASDAQ. He served as its chairman of the Board of Directors. In March 2009, Madoff pleaded guilty to 11 federal felonies and admitted to turning his wealth management business into a massive Ponzi scheme that defrauded thousands of investors of billions of dollars. He was sentenced to 150 years in prison, the maximum allowed. The amount of money missing from client accounts, including fabricated gains, was almost $50 billion.[45]

A Ponzi scheme is a fraudulent investment operation that involves paying abnormally high returns to investors out of the money paid in by subsequent investors, rather than from the profits from any real business. The scheme is named after Charles Ponzi who became notorious for using the strategy after emigrating to the United States from Italy in 1903.

The $50 billion allegedly lost by Madoff makes this fraud one of the biggest in history. Investors who lost millions of dollars (some their life savings) include individuals, banks, charities, and Wall Street investors. Several charities were severely affected by Madoff's Ponzi scheme, including charities formed by Steven Spielberg and Nobel laureate Elie Wiesel.

Embezzlement is an offense in which an employee fraudulently converts some of the employer's funds for personal use through altering company records. Embezzlers who take large sums of money are usually thought to be respectable citizens and trusted employees. They are often motivated by financial problems that their regular income cannot handle, such as gambling debts, financial demands of a lover or spouse, or extensive medical bills for a relative.[46] Sullivan et al. note: "Embezzlers rationalize their theft by convincing themselves that they are merely 'borrowing' the money, that their employers are really crooks who deserve to lose the money, or that the employers will not miss the funds."[47]

Embezzlement occurs at all levels of business, from a clerk stealing from petty cash to the president of a company stealing large investment sums. Many cases go undetected or unprosecuted. Often an informal arrangement is worked out whereby the embezzler agrees to pay back the amount stolen and seeks employment elsewhere—a solution that is often more effective than prosecution for recovering the stolen funds. Because a scandal involving employee dishonesty threatens the employer's public image and hurts future business, companies often prefer to handle the offense informally and privately.

Other examples of white-collar crime include income tax evasion, expense-account fraud, and misuse of government funds by business organizations.

American society, unfortunately, is generally tolerant of white-collar crime. A pickpocket who repeatedly steals small sums of money will likely go to prison, whereas someone who repeatedly fails to report large earnings on income tax returns is unlikely to face prosecution. This acceptance of white-collar crime appears to be due largely to the attitude that the victim is a large, impersonal organization (for example, the government or a large corporation) that will be unaffected. People who would never think of taking an item from a private home might feel no qualms about stealing "souvenirs" (towels, sheets, ashtrays) from hotels.

White-collar crime raises serious questions about our conceptions of crime and criminals. It suggests that crime is not necessarily concentrated among the young, the poor, and racial minorities and in our inner cities. Why, in our society, are burglars and pickpockets severely punished and stigmatized, whereas white-collar criminals who commit far more costly offenses are seldom prosecuted or viewed as criminals? Could it be due to the power structure of our society, in which the middle and upper classes define their own offenses as "excusable," but those committed by powerless groups as "intolerable"?

Corporate Crime

One type of white-collar crime involves corporate crimes. (Corporate crime is listed as a separate category here because of the recent attention it has received.) Some examples of corporate crimes include illegal labor practices, insider trading in finan-

cial institutions, environmental crimes, illegal credit card manipulations, defrauding of pension plans, bribery of public officials, falsification of company records, intimidation of competitors and employees, and fraud.

One example of corporate crime is the WorldCom scandal of the early 2000s. WorldCom was an American Telecommunications company. WorldCom engaged in what has been called the largest accounting fraud in history. It exaggerated its worth by $ 9 billion. Shareholders and investors lost billions of dollars, while top executives made millions by selling their stock in the company prior to revealing the accounting fraud.[48]

Computer Crime

Computer crimes involve the use of computers and the Internet to commit acts against people, public order, property, or morality. Cybercriminals have learned new ways to do old tricks. There are a variety of ways to commit computer crimes. The following are a few examples.

Hacking, or unauthorized computer intrusion, is one common example. After breaking into a computer, a hacker can do nearly an infinite number of illegal activities. Hackers can post insulting messages and steal valuable data, including credit card information, Social Security numbers, and company secrets.[49]

Cole and Smith describe other crimes committed by hackers:

Some use computers to steal information, resources, or funds. These thefts can be aimed at simply stealing money or they can involve the theft of companies' trade secrets, chemical formulas, and other information that could be quite valuable to competing businesses. Others use computers for malicious, destructive acts, such as releasing Internet viruses and "worms" to harm computer systems. In addition, there are widespread problems with people illegally downloading software, music, videos, and other copyrighted materials.[50]

Nude photos, with the aid of a digital camera, can be taken of a person and then displayed worldwide on the Internet. Some use the Internet to illegally gamble, disseminate child pornography, and advertise sexual services.

Cole and Smith describe additional computer crimes:

The global nature of the Internet presents new challenges to the criminal justice system. For example, in 2008, a Colombian man was sentenced to nine years in prison by a U.S. district court for installing keystroke logging software on computers in hotel business centers and other public-access computer locations. He collected personal information, such as bank account numbers and passwords, from 600 people who used those computers. Subsequently, the personal and financial information enabled him to steal $1.4 million. The FBI arrested him during one of his trips to the United States...

In another example, stolen credit card numbers are sold on the Internet, primarily by dealers based in countries that were formerly part of the Soviet Union. Computer hackers steal large numbers of credit card numbers from the computer systems of legitimate businesses and sell the numbers in bulk to dealers who sell them throughout the world via members-only websites. Credit card fraud costs online merchants more than $1 billion each year.[51]

The increase in hacking has also led to an increase in identity theft, which is the use of someone else's identification (e.g., birth date or Social Security number) to obtain credit. No one knows exactly how widespread this form of theft is, but recent estimates indicate that one in four Americans has been affected by identity theft and that the overall value of losses due to identity theft is over $4 billion.[52] The average victim (it is estimated) spends about 600 hours and $1,400 clearing her or his name and credit records after the crime has been committed.[53]

Hate Crime

Hate crimes have been added to the penal codes in nearly every state in the United States. Hate crimes are violent acts aimed at individuals or groups of a particular race, ethnicity, religion, sexual orientation, disability, class, nationality, age, gender, gender identity, social status, or political affiliation. The laws also make it a crime to vandalize religious buildings and cemeteries or to intimidate another person out of bias.

Examples of hate crimes include setting African American churches on fire, defacing a Jewish family's home by swastikas and anti-Semitic graffiti, assaulting a gay or lesbian college student, inserting and igniting a cross in the lawn of an African American family, and vandalism against Arab Americans. With hate crimes, judges can impose a higher sentence when they find a crime was committed with a bias motive.[54]

Public-Order Crimes

Public-order offenders constitute the largest category of criminals; their activities far exceed reported crimes of any other type. Public-order crimes include traffic violations, prostitution, vagrancy, pornography, gambling, drunkenness, curfew violations, loitering, use of illegal substances, fornication, and homosexuality between consenting adults. (Some of these actions are illegal in certain jurisdictions and legal in others.) Laws that make such behaviors criminal are primarily designed to regulate people's private lives. The laws exist because powerful groups within society regard these acts as "undesirable." Public-order offenders rarely consider themselves criminals or view their actions as crimes.

Because public-order crimes are considered less serious (by at least some segments of the population) and because these crimes consume excessive money and time that police and the courts could devote to reducing more serious crime, there have been efforts to decriminalize or repeal some of these laws. Alexander Smith and Harriet Pollack state:

For every murderer arrested and prosecuted, literally dozens of gamblers, prostitutes, ... and derelicts crowd our courts' dockets. If we took the numbers runners, the kids smoking pot, and winos out of the criminal justice system, we would substantially reduce the burden on the courts and the police.... Moral laws that do not reflect contemporary mores or that cannot be enforced should be removed from the penal code through legislative action because, at best, they undermine respect for the law.[55]

Critical Thinking Question

Have you been victimized by a crime that meets the legal definition of a hate crime?

Criminal penalties for such crimes may also do more harm than good. For example, treating someone arrested for homosexual activity as a hardened criminal may well damage the person's self-concept and status in the community. Criminal penalties may also force the offenders to form a subculture to continue their illegal activity with greater safety. Such subcultures (for instance, of gays/lesbians and drug users) serve to separate them even further from the rest of society.

Sex Offenses

Sex offenses include forcible rape, prostitution, soliciting, statutory rape, fornication, sodomy, homosexuality, adultery, and incest.

In most states, only males are legally liable for rape by force. Forcible rape is a highly underreported crime. Why? In about half of the cases, the attacker is a friend or acquaintance of the victim; therefore, some victims think police action will only create more interpersonal problems. Many victims are reluctant to report the offense because they believe (perhaps realistically) they have nothing to gain and more to lose by making a report, including social embarrassment, interrogation by sometimes unsympathetic law enforcement officials, and humiliating public testimony in court about the offense. A danger to society of underreporting rape is that the rapist is less likely to fear apprehension and thus more likely to seek out other victims.

Statutory rape involves sexual contact between a male who is of a legally responsible age (usually 18) and a female who is a willing participant but is below the legal age of consent (16 in some states and 18 in others). In most states, females are not defined as being liable for committing statutory rape. In some states, a charge of statutory rape can be made on the basis of sexual contact other than sexual intercourse (such as oral–genital contact).

Increased attention is now being given to sexual abuse of children. Such abuse includes sexual intercourse (genital or anal), masturbation, oral–genital contact, fondling, and exposure. There is no unambiguous definition of sexual abuse. Sexual intercourse with children is definitely abuse, but other forms of contact are more difficult to judge as abusive. At some point, hugging, kissing, and fondling become inappropriate. Abusers may be parents, older siblings, extended relatives, friends, acquaintances, or strangers. (Sexual abuse is discussed in greater length in Chapter 6.)

Certain sex offenses (such as incest, rape, and same-sex sexual contact with a minor) incite considerable repugnance among the general public, which results in harsh punishments for offenders. Unfortunately, less attention is given to helping the victims cope with their exploitation or to rehabilitating the offenders.

Human Trafficking

Internationally, human trafficking is increasingly recognized as a major social problem. Human trafficking is the recruitment, transportation, or receipt of people for the purposes of slavery, forced labor, or servitude. It is a multibillion-dollar-a-year industry. Trafficking victims typically are recruited using deception, fraud, coercion, the abuse of power, or outright abduction.

Adult victims may be forced into prostitution or other forms of sexual exploitation, forced labor, or slavery. Child victims may be forced into prostitution, illicit international adoption, or trafficking for early marriage. They may also be recruited as child soldiers, beggars, or for membership in a religious cult.

Human trafficking differs from people smuggling. With smuggling, people voluntarily request the smuggler's service for a fee. On arrival at their destination, the smuggled people are usually free. On the other hand, trafficking victims are enslaved. The trafficker takes away the basic human rights of the victim. Victims are sometimes tricked and lured by false promises or physically forced. Traffickers use both coercive and manipulative tactics such as deception, intimidation, feigned love, isolation, physical force, and even force-feeding with drugs.

In some areas such as Russia, Hong Kong, Japan, and Colombia, human trafficking is controlled by large criminal organizations.[56] Trafficked victims are usually the most vulnerable and powerless minorities in a region.

Women are particularly at risk for sex trafficking, that is, forced into prostitution. For example, traffickers in a foreign country may promise young women the prospect of job training and a better life in the United States, and then they are forced into prostitution when they arrive. Thousands of children are sold into the global sex trade every year—often they are kidnapped or even sold by their own families.

Thousands of male (and sometimes female) children have also been forced to be child soldiers. Men are at risk of being trafficked for unskilled work—predominantly involving forced labor.

The following two case stories are illustrative of the forms of human trafficking that take place around the world. The stories come from a U.S. State Department report. (The United States federal government has taken a firm stance against human trafficking both within its borders and beyond. Human trafficking is a federal crime under Title 18 of the United States Code.) The material remains in its original state.

Central Africa

Mary, a 16-year-old demobilized child soldier forced to join an armed rebel group in Central Africa, remembers: "I feel so bad about the things that I did. It disturbs me so much that I inflicted death on other people. When I go home I must do some traditional rites because I have killed. I must perform these rites and cleanse myself. I still dream about the boy from my village whom I killed. I see him in my dreams, and he is talking to me, saying I killed him for nothing, and I am crying."

Cambodia

Neary grew up in rural Cambodia. Her parents died when she was a child, and, in an effort to give her a better life, her sister married her off when she was 17. Three months later she and her husband went to visit a fishing village. Her husband rented a room in what Neary thought was a guesthouse. But when she woke the next morning, her husband was gone. The owner of the house told her she had been sold by her husband for $300 and that she was actually in a brothel. For five years, Neary was raped by five to seven men every day. In addition to brutal physical abuse, Neary was infected with HIV and contracted AIDS. The brothel threw her out when she became sick, and she eventually found her way to a local shelter. She died of HIV/AIDS at the age of 23.[57]

According to the U.S. State Department, between 600,000 and 800,000 men, women, and children are trafficked across international borders annually, and millions more are trafficked within their own countries.[58]

Homicide and Assault

Criminal homicide involves the unlawful killing of one person by another. Criminal assault is the unlawful application of physical force on another person. Most homicides are unintended outcomes of physical assaults. People get into physical fights because one (or both) is incensed about the other's actions and decides to retaliate. Provoking actions may include ridicule, flirting with the other's spouse or lover, or failure to repay a debt. Fighting is often an attempt by one or both to save face when challenged or degraded. Homicides frequently are "crimes of passion," occurring during a violent argument or other highly charged emotional situation.

Yet some homicides are carefully planned and premeditated, including most gangland killings, killings to obtain an inheritance, and mercy killings. Homicides are also associated with robberies, during which the victim, the robber, or a law enforcement official may be shot.

Contrary to public stereotypes, the majority of murders occur between relatives, friends, and acquaintances.[59] Because of the overt physical damage from assault and homicide, these crimes generate the most fear. The police have a higher arrest rate (around 70%) in homicide cases than with any other crime—partly because they devote extensive attention to murders and partly because the questioning of the victim's friends, neighbors, and relatives usually identifies the killer.[60] Alcohol is frequently an important contributing factor in murders and assaults, as slightly over half of all those in prison for violent crimes report they were under the influence of alcohol or other drugs at the time of their offense.[61]

Theft

This category of crime refers to illegally taking someone's property without the person's consent. Offenses range from pickpocketing and burglary to sophisticated multimillion-dollar swindles. Thieves range from grocery store clerks who take small amounts of food to people who concoct highly professional confidence schemes to swindle others out of thousands of dollars.

The most successful thieves (labeled professional thieves by the noted criminologist Edwin H. Sutherland[62]) engage in confidence games, forgery, expert safecracking, counterfeiting, extortion (for example, blackmailing others who are involved in illegal acts), and organized shoplifting. Most such crimes require that professional thieves appear personable and trustworthy and that they be good actors to convince others that they are somebody who they are not. Professional thieves use sophisticated, nonviolent techniques. Their crimes are carefully planned, and they tend to steal as a regular business. They define themselves as thieves, have a value system supportive of their career, and often are respected by their colleagues and by law enforcement officials. Because of their cunning and skill, they seldom are arrested. They often justify their activities by claiming that they are simply capitalizing on the fact that all people are dishonest and would probably also be full-time thieves if they had sufficient skills.

CASE EXAMPLE 9.3

Murder and the Fall of an American Hero

Orenthal James (O. J.) Simpson was born and raised on Connecticut Street in Potrero Hill, a poor neighborhood in San Francisco, which O. J. once described as "your average Black ghetto." His father, Jimmy, a custodian and cook, left home when O. J. was 5. Jimmy, who was gay, died of AIDS in 1985. O. J.'s mother, Eunice, worked long hours as a hospital orderly to support her four children.

As a youth, O. J. joined gangs, picked fights, stole hubcaps, shot craps, and played hooky from school. After a gang fight at age 15 landed him briefly in jail, Lefty Gordon, the supervisor of the local recreational center, arranged for baseball great Willie Mays to meet with O. J. The meeting left a lasting impression on O. J., who stated, "He made me realize that we all have it in ourselves to be heroes."

O. J. applied himself to football. He didn't have the grades for a 4-year school, so he attended City College of San Francisco, where he set records as a running back. In his junior year, he transferred to the University of Southern California. O. J. led USC to two Rose Bowls, and in his senior year, he won the Heisman Trophy, given annually to the best player in college football.

© AP Photo/Vince Bucci, Pool

O. J. Simpson

After his triumphs at USC, O. J. was drafted by the National Football League. In 1973, while playing halfback for the Buffalo Bills, he broke the single-season rushing record held by Jim Brown.

The world of advertising in the 1970s was searching for a "breakthrough Black man" who had the right look, the right smile, and the right nickname. O. J. was it. His magnetic image won him several lucrative advertising contracts.

Even before his retirement from pro football after 11 seasons, he started acting in movies and on TV. He became a sports broadcaster for NBC and ABC. He was also inducted in the football Hall of Fame.

But apparently there was another side to O. J. Simpson. A married man with two children, he met Nicole Brown, a very attractive teenager. Shortly after she turned 19, they began living together. Eventually they married, had two children of their own, and lived a glamorous life in their West Los Angeles mansion. However, on at least eight occasions, police were called to their home to settle domestic fights. In 1989, after one particularly brutal fight, witnesses said O. J. had repeatedly screamed "I'll kill you!" The Los Angeles city attorney filed charges against Simpson for wife beating, and he pleaded no contest.

In 1992 Nicole and O. J. finally divorced. Afterward they continued to see each other, and O. J. hoped for a reconciliation. But in the spring of 1994, friends say Nicole shattered O. J.'s dreams by telling him she had decided not to reconcile.

During the evening of June 12, 1994, Nicole Brown Simpson was brutally stabbed to death outside her condominium. Also brutally stabbed to death was Ronald Goldman, a friend of hers who reportedly was returning a pair of sunglasses she had left earlier in the evening at the restaurant in which he worked.

A few days later, O. J. was arrested and charged with these murders. In 1995 a jury in a criminal trial proceeding found O. J. innocent of these two murders. In 1996 a jury in a civil court proceeding found O. J. responsible for the wrongful deaths of Nicole Brown Simpson and Ronald Goldman, and he was ordered to pay more than $30 million in damages to the families of these two victims. (O. J. Simpson, at the time of this revision, had paid only a small amount of this court-ordered judgment.)

In September 2007, Simpson faced more legal troubles when he was arrested in Las Vegas and subsequently charged with numerous felonies, including burglary with a firearm, assault with a deadly weapon, robbery with a deadly weapon, first degree kidnapping with use of a deadly weapon, coercion with use of a deadly weapon, conspiracy to commit robbery, conspiracy to commit kidnapping, and conspiracy to commit a crime. The charges stemmed from an incident in which a group of men led by Simpson entered a room at the Palace Station hotel/casino and took sports memorabilia at gunpoint. He was found guilty of all charges on October 3, 2008. On December 5, 2008, he was sentenced to at least 15 years in prison. He will be eligible for parole in 2017.

Semiprofessional thieves engage in armed robberies, burglaries, holdups, and larcenies that do not involve much detailed planning. Some semiprofessional thieves work alone, holding up service stations, convenience stores, liquor stores, and the like. Semiprofessionals often wind up spending substantial portions of their lives in prison because they commit the types of crimes that are harshly punished by courts. They also tend to be repeat offenders for similar crimes. Often they define themselves as products and victims of a corrupt and unjust system, having started their careers in low-income and ghetto neighborhoods. They adjust fairly well in prison because other inmates often have similar backgrounds, lifestyles, and views on life. However, as a group they are poor parole risks.[63]

Amateur thieves are individuals who steal infrequently. In contrast to professional and semiprofessional thieves, these individuals generally define themselves as respectable law-abiding citizens. Their criminal acts tend to be crude, unsophisticated, and unplanned, with some offenders being juveniles. Examples of offenses by this group include stealing from employers, shoplifting, stealing an unguarded bicycle, taking an auto for a joyride, taking soda from a truck, and breaking into a home to take CDs or beer. Businesses and industries suffer substantial losses from amateur thieves who are either employees or customers.

Juvenile Delinquency
Crime Among Youths

According to official crime statistics, about 20% of all people arrested are under age 18.[64] Many of these arrests are for crimes that have already been discussed—thefts, robberies, assaults, and rapes. Yet one reason why juveniles have such a high arrest rate is that a majority of the arrests are for status offenses —that is, acts that are defined as illegal if committed by juveniles but not if committed by adults. Status offenses include being truant, having sexual relations, running away from home, being ungovernable, violating curfew, and being beyond the control of parents.

Police arrests of lower-class juveniles are far higher than for middle and upper-class juveniles.[65] This is partly due to the fact that police are more inclined to arrest lower-class juveniles than middle and upper-class juveniles.[66] After reviewing a number of studies on the relationships between delinquency and poverty, Kornblum and Julian conclude that these two variables are interrelated in a complex manner. Middle- and upper-class juveniles tend to commit nuisance crimes at about the same rates as lower-class youths, but lower-class youths commit higher rates of serious crimes, such as homicide.[67]

Gangs

Juvenile gangs have existed for many decades in the United States and in other countries. In recent years in the United States, there have been increases in the number of gangs, the number of youths belonging to gangs, gang youth drug involvement, and gang violence. Violent, delinquent urban gang activity has become a major social problem in the United States. The scientific knowledge base about delinquent gangs is very limited. Longres notes:

> No consensus exists for a definition of a youth gang. In addition, no agreed upon recording system exists, and no data on gang offenses are collected in systematic ways by disinterested agencies. Furthermore, attempts to eradicate gangs through social service and criminal justice programs have met with little success.[68]

The inadequacy of the knowledge base about delinquent gangs is a major obstacle to developing effective intervention strategies with this population. There have been numerous definitions of gangs, but no consensus exists on their distinguishing characteristics.[69] The lack of consensus is indicated by the numerous and diverse categories that have been used by different investigators to classify gangs: corner group, social club, conflict group, pathological group, athletic club, industrial association, predatory organization, drug addict group, racket organization, fighting-focused group, defensive group, unconventional group, criminal organization, turf group, heavy metal group, punk rock group, satanic organization, skinhead group, ethnic or racial group, motorcycle club, and scavenger group.[70]

An illustration of a categorization is provided by Morales, who classified youth gangs into four types: criminal, conflict, retreatist, and cult/occult.[71]

Criminal gangs have as a primary goal material gain through criminal activities, including theft of property from people or premises, extortion, fencing, and drug trafficking (especially of rock cocaine).

Conflict gangs are turf oriented. They engage in violent conflict with individuals of rival groups that invade their neighborhood or commit acts that they consider degrading or insulting. Respect is highly valued and defended. Latino gangs often fall into this category. Sweeney notes that the Code of the Barrio mandates that gang members watch out for their neighborhood and be willing to die for it.[72]

Retreatist gangs focus on getting "high" or "loaded" on alcohol, cocaine, marijuana, heroin, or other drugs. Individuals tend to join this type of gang to secure continued access to drugs. In contrast to criminal gangs that become involved with drugs for financial profit, retreatist gangs become involved with drugs for consumption.

Cult/occult gangs engage in devil or evil worship. *Cult* refers to systematic worshiping of evil or the devil; *occult* implies keeping something secret or hidden or a belief in supernatural or mysterious powers. Some occult groups place extensive emphasis on sexuality and violence, believing that by sexually violating an innocent child or virgin, they have defiled Christianity. Not all cult/occult gangs are involved in criminal activity. Unlike the other three gang types, which are composed primarily of juveniles, the majority of occult groups are composed of adults.

Contradictions abound in conceptualizing delinquent gangs. Gangs are believed to be composed largely of ethnically homogeneous adolescents (African American, Latino, and Asian youths); yet some gangs composed of White youths exist. Most gang members are believed to be between ages 12 and 18, yet recent evidence indicates some gangs include and may be controlled by adults.[73] Gangs are believed to be composed of males; yet some gangs have female members, and a few gangs consist exclusively of females.[74] Gangs are believed to be primarily involved in drug trafficking; yet some delinquent gangs have other illegal foci, such as burglary, robbery, larceny, or illegal drug consumption. Gang activity is thought to be primarily located in large inner-city areas; yet gang activity is flourishing in many smaller cities and in some suburbs.[75]

Currently, there are inadequate statistical data on the number of gangs, the number and characteristics of members, and their criminal activities. Longres notes:

> *Statistics on gangs and their criminal behavior are not obtained easily. Many cities have gang control units that collect data but do not report them in any systematic way. Even when such data are obtained, they are difficult to interpret because no uniform definition of gang offenses exists, no recording system has been in place long enough to*

discern trends, and arrest data from police departments may reflect bias. Additionally, no uniform definition of a gang-related offense exists across police jurisdictions even within the same state, city, or county.[76]

Spergel presents documentation that gangs primarily develop in those local communities that are often socially disorganized and/or impoverished.[77] Gang members typically come from families in which the parents lack effective parenting skills and communities in which the school systems give little attention to students who are falling behind in their studies, youths are exposed to adult crime groups, and youths feel there is practically no opportunity to succeed through the legitimate avenues of education and a good-paying job. Spergel asserts that youths join gangs for many reasons—security, power, money, status, excitement, and new experiences—particularly under conditions of social deprivation or community instability. In essence, he presents a community disorganization approach to understanding the attraction of joining a gang.

In a very real sense, a delinquent gang is created because the needs of youths are not being met by the family, neighborhood, or traditional community institutions (such as the schools, police, and recreational and religious institutions). Some useful changes suggested by Spergel are reduced access to handguns; improved educational resources; access to recreation, job training, jobs, family counseling, and drug rehabilitation; and mobilization of community groups and organizations to restrain gang violence (such as neighborhood watch groups). Social policy changes are also needed at state and national levels to funnel more resources to urban centers. Funds are needed to improve the quality of life for city residents, including youths, so that the needs of youths are met in ways other than through gang involvement.[78]

The Criminal Justice System

The criminal justice system consists of the police, the courts, and the correctional system. It is perceived by many Americans as cumbersome, ineffective, irrational, and unjust, fostering a perception that "crime does pay." Some segments of the population are suspicious of the police and believe that they abuse their powers. Other segments, particularly the middle and upper classes, see the police as unduly hampered in their work by cumbersome arrest and interrogation procedures designed to protect the civil rights of suspected offenders.

Courts are sharply criticized for their long delays in bringing cases to conclusion and for their sentencing procedures. Many Americans believe that courts are not harsh enough on offenders. Courts are also criticized for (a) varying widely in the harshness of sentences meted out for apparently similar offenses and (b) giving harsh sentences to "ordinary offenders" but light fines to white-collar offenders.

Prisons, too, have been sharply criticized, as they are viewed as failing to rehabilitate their populations. The rate of recidivism (that is, return to crime) is alarmingly high. Over half of those released from prison later return after being convicted of another crime.[79] Indeed, far from rehabilitating inmates, prisons are accused of being schools for crime.

In all societies, criminal justice systems face a conflict between two goals: crime control and due process. The crime-control goal involves the need to curb crime and protect society from lawbreakers. It emphasizes speedy arrest and punishment for those who commit crimes. The due-process goal involves the need to protect and preserve the rights and liberties of individuals. Some societies are police states that use strong-arm tactics to control their citizens, displaying little concern for individual rights. At the other extreme are societies in which individuals flagrantly break the law, with the government having neither the power nor the respect of its citizens to uphold the law. American society seeks to strike a balance between the conflicting goals of crime control and due process, but the struggle is constant. At times the same individual may seek to have one goal emphasized in one situation but the conflicting goal emphasized in a different setting. For example, a homeowner may want speedy justice when her house is burglarized but may seek to use all the due-process protections when accused of income tax evasion.

We will now take a closer look at each of these three components of the criminal justice system.

The Police

Police officers are the gatekeepers for the criminal justice system. Whom they arrest determines whom the courts and corrections will have to deal with. As we have seen, nearly everyone commits an occasional crime. Police cannot arrest everyone, or the jails, courts, and prisons would be overloaded and our society would collapse. Therefore, police exercise considerable discretion in which laws they vigorously enforce and which types of offenders they arrest. For example, police are more likely to arrest lower-income than middle-income youths.

Only a small part of a police department's effort is directly focused on making arrests. Police officers classify as "criminal" only about 10% to 20% of the calls and incidents they handle on a given day.[80]

David Peterson has noted that the role of a police officer is usually best conceptualized as that of a "peace officer" or even "social worker" rather than as a "law enforcement officer":

> A prominent theme in the literature dealing with the work behavior of the police stresses that the role of the uniformed patrol officer is not a strict legalistic one. The patrol officer is routinely involved in tasks that have little relation to police work in terms of controlling crime. His activities on the beat are often centered as much on assisting citizens as upon offenses; he is frequently called upon to perform a "supportive" function as well as an enforcement function. Existing research on the uniformed police officer in field situations indicates that more than half his time is spent as an amateur social worker assisting people in various ways. Moreover, several officers have suggested that the role of the uniformed patrol officer is not sharply defined and that the mixture of enforcement and service functions creates conflict and uncertainties for individual officers.[81]

Service functions of police may include giving first aid to injured people, rescuing trapped animals, and directing traffic. When police do perform law enforcement functions, they squarely face trying to achieve the proper balance between the crime-control model and the due-process model. There is considerable pressure to swiftly apprehend certain lawbreakers—murderers, rapists, and arsonists. Yet they are expected to perform according to the due-process model so that the legal rights of those arrested are not violated. James Coleman and Harold Kerbo note: "Police officers operate more like diplomats than like soldiers engaged in a war on crime."[82]

In many areas of the nation, police do not have sufficient resources to do their job effectively. Often there is also considerable hostility toward police officers. Part of this hostility may result from the fact that everyone commits an occasional crime; people may be suspicious of police officers because they fear possible apprehension. In addition, some people (particularly the poor and minority group members) have been harassed by being picked up for crimes they clearly did not commit and by being subjected to long "third-degree" interrogations. Also, some hostility toward the police stems from well-publicized incidents of police corruption (for example, taking bribes), particularly in larger cities.

The Courts
How the Courts Work

Criminal justice in the United States is an adversary system. That is, a prosecuting attorney first presents the state's evidence against a defendant, and that defendant, presumed innocent until proved guilty, then has an opportunity to refute the charges with the assistance of a defense attorney.

Contrary to public opinion, more than 90% of convictions in the United States are obtained not in court but through plea bargaining between the prosecuting attorney and the defendant, who is often represented by a defense attorney in the plea-bargaining process.[83] For a plea of guilty, a suspect may receive a more lenient sentence, have certain charges dropped, or have the charge reduced to a less serious offense. Plea bargaining is not legally binding in court, but the judge usually goes along with the arrangement. Plea bargaining is highly controversial. It does save taxpayers considerable expense because court trials are costly. But it may in some cases circumvent due-process protections if an innocent person charged with some serious offense is pressured into pleading guilty to a reduced charge.

There are four key positions in a court: the prosecuting attorney, the defense attorney, the judge, and the jury.

Prosecuting attorneys have considerable discretionary authority in choosing whether to seek a conviction for those arrested and how vigorously to prosecute a defendant. Prosecuting attorneys are either elected or appointed to office and are therefore political figures who must periodically seek reelection or reappointment. Therefore, they seek to prosecute most vigorously the cases they perceive the community is most concerned about. Prosecuting attorneys usually focus police departments' attention on which violations will be further processed by the criminal justice system.

Defense attorneys are supposed to represent their clients' interest before the criminal justice system. Impoverished individuals are provided, at the state's expense, a court-appointed attorney. The skills and competency of the defense attorney are major factors in determining whether a defendant will be found innocent or guilty if there is a trial. The wealthy not only can retain the best attorneys but also can afford additional resources (such as private investigators) to help prepare a better defense.

Sometimes the poor are shortchanged by court-appointed defense attorneys, who tend to be young, inexperienced practitioners, or less competent older lawyers, who resort to this type of practice in order to survive professionally. Because these defense attorneys depend on the good opinion of their legal colleagues (including judges and prosecuting attorneys) to stay in practice, the client's best interest sometimes receives secondary priority.[84]

If a defendant is prosecuted for a minor offense, the case is generally presented before a lower-court judge without a jury. For a serious offense, the defendant first receives a preliminary hearing, which is solely for the benefit of the suspect. At the hearing, the prosecutor presents evidence against the suspect, and the judge decides whether that evidence is sufficient to warrant further legal proceedings. If the evidence is insufficient, the suspect is discharged. If the evidence is sufficient, the accused is held over to await a court trial. (Often the held-over cases are then decided by plea bargaining before they go to trial.)

A jury is supposed to be a cross section of the community. However, there is a tendency for retired persons, housewives with grown children, and the unemployed—those who are not inconvenienced by the duty—to be overrepresented on juries. Juries use the standard of reasonable doubt to decide if the prosecution has provided enough evidence for conviction. To obtain the conviction of a defendant charged with a crime, all 12 members of the jury must vote "guilty." A hung jury occurs when a jury is unable to reach a decision. Because of group pressure, only rarely does a lone juror produce a hung jury.

Under the bail system, accused people are allowed to deposit money or credit with the court to obtain a release from jail while awaiting trial. Bail is designed to ensure that the suspect will appear for trial. The amount of bail is set by the court and varies according to the offense and the judge's attitudes toward the suspect. The bail system severely discriminates against the poor. Anyone unable to raise enough money must stay in jail while awaiting trial, which may take several months. Those who cannot post bail have less opportunity to prepare a good defense because they are locked up. Also, their cases are further prejudiced when they do appear in court because they are brought into the courtroom in handcuffs and often without proper grooming. Being locked up before trial is a form of punishment that runs counter to the notion that the suspect is innocent (and should be treated as such) until proved guilty. In some cases, a suspect spends more time in jail awaiting trial than she or he spends in jail if found guilty.

After defendants have been found guilty or have pleaded guilty, they return to the courtroom for sentencing. Judges usually have fairly wide discretion in assigning sentences; for example, they can place one murderer on probation, commit another to prison, and in those states where capital punishment is legal, order the execution of a third. Judges base their sentences on such factors as the seriousness of the crime, the motives for the crime, the background of the offender, and their attitudes toward the offender.

Judges vary greatly in the extent to which they send convicted offenders to prison, use probation, or assign fines. Concern about disparities in sentences has grown in recent years. Coleman and Cressey note:

> Judges and other sentencing authorities are on the spot. They are supposed to give equal punishments, no matter what the social status of the defendants involved. Yet they are supposed to give individual punishments because the circumstances of each crime and the motivations of each criminal are always different and a just punishment for one burglar or car thief may be completely inappropriate for another.... As judges try to satisfy these conflicting demands, they are bound to be denounced as unfair. The judge's task, like the police officer's task, is to walk a thin line between the crime control model and the due process model, balancing demands for repressing crime against demands for human rights and freedom.[85]

Juvenile Courts

The first juvenile court was established in Cook County, Illinois, in 1899. The philosophy of the juvenile court is that it should act in the best interests of the child, as parents should act. In essence, juvenile courts have a treatment orientation. Adult criminal proceedings focus on charging the defendant with a specific crime, on holding a public trial to determine whether the defendant is guilty as charged, and on sentencing the defendant if he or she is found guilty. In contrast, the focus in juvenile courts is on the current psychological, physical, emotional, and educational needs of children, as opposed to punishment for misdeeds. Reform or treatment of the child is the goal, even though the child or his or her family may not necessarily agree that the court's decision is in the child's best interests.

Of course, not all juvenile court judges live up to these principles. In practice, some juvenile judges focus more on punishing than on treating juvenile offenders. There is also a danger that court appearances by children can have adverse labeling effects. A Supreme Court decision in the famous *Gault* case of May 15, 1967, restored to juveniles procedural safeguards that had been ignored—including notification of charges, protection against self-incrimination, confrontation, and cross-examination.[86] There is currently considerable effort to have juvenile probation officers provide informal supervision for youths who commit "minor" violations. With informal supervision, youthful offenders receive counseling and guidance and do not appear in court.

Correctional Systems

Current correctional systems in the United States and throughout the world contain conflicting objectives. Some components are punishment oriented, whereas others are treatment oriented. A manifestation of this confusion is the existence, side by side, of correctional programs intended primarily for deterrence and retribution and other programs designed to reform offenders. Only rarely do punitive and treatment components complement each other. Generally, the two components, when combined, result in a system that is ineffective and inefficient in curbing criminal activity. In the past three decades, correctional systems have moved toward a more punitive approach.

The Punitive Approach

Throughout history various approaches have been used to punish offenders. These methods include physical torture, social humiliation, financial penalties, exile, the death penalty, and imprisonment.

Physical Torture Most societies have at one time or another used this method. Specific examples of corporal (bodily) punishment have included stocks, whipping, flogging, branding, hard labor, confinement in irons and cages, arm twisting, and mutilation of body parts. Corporal punishment was particularly popular during the medieval period. Virtually no types of corporal punishment are assigned today by European or U.S. courts.

Social Humiliation   Reducing the social status of an offender is another method of punishment. This approach flourished in the 16th and 17th centuries, and remnants exist today. Specific techniques included some that also had corporal-punishment facets: the stocks, the pillory, the ducking stool, branding, and the brank. (The brank was a small cage that was placed over the offender's head. It had a bar that was inserted into the mouth of the offender to prevent him or her from talking; occasionally this bar had spikes in it.) Some of these punishments were temporary—for example, the stocks—whereas others had a permanent effect on the offender—for example, branding. One of the objectives of the permanent method was to deter future crime by publicly humiliating offenders. However, the techniques frequently had the opposite effect, as they overtly labeled the offender, thereby making it difficult for him or her to secure employment and earn a living in a law-abiding manner.

Deprivation of civil rights is another approach that has been used for centuries to humiliate the convicted offender socially. The principal rights that are taken away from convicted felons by most states in this country are (a) the right to vote while in prison or while on probation or parole; (b) the right to hold public office; (c) the right to practice certain professions, such as the law; and (d) the right to own or possess firearms.[87]

Financial Penalties   The use of fines in criminal law became widespread in this country about a century ago and is now by far the most frequent court approach to punishing offenders. More than 75% of all penalties imposed at present are fines.[88] The advantages of a fine are (a) it provides revenue to the state; (b) it costs the state almost nothing to administer, especially in comparison to the cost of imprisonment; (c) the amount of the fine can easily be adjusted to the enormity of the offense, the reaction of the public, and the wealth and character of the offender; (d) it inflicts a material type of suffering; and (e) it can easily be paid back if the alleged offender is later found innocent. A serious disadvantage is that it is highly discriminatory toward the poor, who have less ability to pay. Sweden has found a way to curb this discrimination by the creation of day fines, in which the offender pays the equivalent of the amount earned in a specified number of days of work rather than a flat amount as a fine.

Courts are also increasingly requiring, in their sentencing decisions, that the offender make restitution payments to the victim that are in line with the amount of injury. This kind of reaction to crime is more treatment oriented, as it attempts to give the offender an opportunity to "make good." Restitution is, of course, also advantageous to the victim. Restitution and reparation are used most frequently for minor offenses. Generally, the offender is placed on probation, with restitution being a condition of probation. Some of the work of probation departments now involves acting as a collection agency to obtain restitution payments from probationers.

Exile   Almost all societies have exiled certain offenders, particularly political criminals. Deportation on a large scale, however, has been used only since about the 16th century. The United States has been deporting alien criminals for decades. In addition, many counties and municipalities in the United States give people accused or convicted of a crime a set number of hours to "get out and stay out" of their jurisdiction.

Death Penalty   The extent to which the death penalty has been used and the methods for executing offenders have varied considerably in different societies. Criminals have been hanged, electrocuted, shot, burned, gassed, drowned, boiled in oil, broken at the wheel, guillotined, stoned, put in an iron coffin, pierced with a sharp stake, stabbed with a sword, and poisoned. In essence, almost every lethal method has at one time or another been used by some society.

The death penalty has been used in the United States throughout most of our history. In colonial America, "witches" in some communities were burned at the stake. While the West was being developed, individuals who stole a horse or committed certain other crimes were sometimes shot or hanged (sometimes by a lynch mob or a "kangaroo court"). From the time of the Civil War until the recent past, African Americans in the South who were thought to have committed a serious crime against Whites (for example, rape) were sometimes lynched. Gas chambers, firing squads, lethal injections, hangings, and electric chairs are the current methods of execution used in the United States.

From 1967 to 1977, the death penalty was not used in this country, partly due to U.S. Supreme Court decisions that ruled the penalty unconstitutional. In October 1976, the Supreme Court changed its position on this issue and ruled that states may execute murderers under certain guidelines. On January 17, 1977, Gary Gilmore was the first person in a decade to be executed, and the sensational case attracted national attention. Gilmore was convicted of ruthlessly killing several people. The continued use of the death penalty remains a controversial national issue.

The primary argument for using the death penalty for certain crimes is that it is assumed to have a deterrent effect. This assumption is questionable, as statistics generally do *not* show a corresponding decrease in serious crime rates when a country adopts the death penalty.[89] Also, there is no clear-cut evidence that when a country discontinues use of the death penalty, there will be an increase in serious crimes.[90] Additional arguments for use of the death penalty are that (a) some crimes (such as brutal, premeditated murder) are so abominable that the offender deserves the ultimate punishment and (b) it is less expensive to society to put hardened criminals to death than to incarcerate them for life. (In reality, executing someone is more expensive than lifetime incarceration, as huge amounts of legal expenses are incurred on the appeals that precede an execution.)

Critical Thinking Questions

Are you in favor of, or opposed to, the death penalty being used in the United States? Why?

Arguments against use of the death penalty are as follows: (a) it constitutes cruel and unusual punishment, being the ultimate punishment; (b) if the convicted person is later found innocent, the penalty is irreparable; (c) the "eye for an eye" approach is inconsistent with civilized, humanitarian ideals; (d) the "right to life" is a basic right that should not be infringed on; and (e) the death penalty appears to be assigned in a discriminatory manner (African Americans and Latinos are proportionately much more likely than Whites to be sentenced to death).

Imprisonment   The penal system currently plays an enormous role in our society. Thousands of people are incarcerated each year. As noted, the recidivism rate (return to prison after release) is estimated to be over 50%, which raises questions about the effectiveness of prisons in curbing future criminal activity.[91] Since 1970 several large-scale prison revolts (for example, Attica Prison, in New York, in 1971 and New Mexico State Penitentiary in 1980) have raised the concern of the general public.

Conditions within prisons prior to the 20th century were deplorable. Frequently the young were placed with hardened criminals, and women were not separated from men. Only custodial care was provided, often with "hard-labor" work projects. There were a number of prison reform studies from 1700 to 1850 that criticized within prisons the use of intoxicating liquors, sexual orgies, gambling, and the personal lewdness of security officers. Some prisons kept inmates in solitary confinement for months at a time, and corporal punishment was frequently used.

Since 1800 prisons have become more specialized. Jails are used for shorter sentences and for those awaiting trial. Separate institutions have been built for the young, for women, and for those labeled as criminally insane. Prisons also have various degrees of security: maximum, moderate, and minimum. Special programs have been developed to meet individual needs of inmates (for example, alcohol and drug abuse programs, educational and vocational training, medical and dental programs, and recreational programs).

Prisons are still distasteful and sometimes physically dangerous institutions. There is now the danger of AIDS being transmitted by sexual assaults in prison. However, in the past 100 years, the horrors of prison life have been somewhat reduced. In addition to rehabilitative programs, strides have been made in safeguarding civil rights of inmates, abandoning long-term solitary confinement, improving methods of discipline, promoting contact between inmates and the outside world, providing libraries, reducing the monotony of prison life, and improving diet, ventilation, and cleanliness within the facilities. Gone are such humiliating approaches as shaving the head, chaining inmates, issuing striped clothing, and using the ball and chain. Also, corporal-punishment methods, such as whipping, are no longer officially approved. The most severe punishment that remains for many prisoners is their constant fear of being victimized by their fellow inmates.

Since 1975 there has been a dramatic increase in the number of people sentenced to prison by the courts.[92] Part of this increase is due to the mushrooming of drug-related convictions, including drug trafficking convictions. Another reason is that our society has become more conservative and therefore is demanding a more punitive approach (imprisonment) to handling convicted offenders. As a result of the increased use of imprisonment, many prisons are currently overcrowded. An alternative to imprisonment that is used for less serious criminal offenders is home confinement with the use of electronic surveillance monitors to ensure that the convicted offenders remain at home.

The first American institution built specifically to house juvenile offenders was opened in New York City in 1825. There are now more than 300 state and local training schools for juveniles. It has always been contended that such institutions are not prisons, but schools to educate and reform the young. However, until the recent past, most were best described as prisons in terms of functions, methods of discipline, and daily routine. Even today a few are still prison oriented. One of the most significant developments in juvenile institutions was cottage-type architecture, which provides a more homelike setting. The first such juvenile homes were established in Massachusetts and Ohio in 1858. These settings facilitate, but do not necessarily ensure, a treatment orientation.

Objectives of Incarceration   The conflict between the punitive approach and the treatment approach to corrections is strikingly clear in our penal system. Until a few centuries ago, the purpose of incarceration was strictly to punish an offender. From 1900 to 1970, there was an increased emphasis on treatment and a shift away from punishment. There were several reasons for this shift. Practically all prisoners return to society, and it was concluded that punitive approaches alone do not produce the desired reformation. Locking a person in an artificial environment, without providing rehabilitative programs, does not sufficiently prepare that person to be a productive citizen on his or her return. Moreover, in this era of accountability, the 50% recidivism rate is unacceptable, especially because the annual cost of incarceration per inmate is more than $35,000.[93]

In the past three decades, however, the pendulum has swung back to using a more punitive approach in our prison system. Increased concerns about community protection and the effects of crime on victims and a greater emphasis on wanting criminals to pay for their crimes have been factors that have led to a shift away from the treatment approach.

The specific objectives for imprisonment are (a) to reform offenders so they will no longer commit crimes; (b) to incapacitate criminals so they cannot commit crimes for a period of time, thereby protecting society; (c) to achieve retribution for the victim and, to some extent, for the state; and (d) to serve as a warning to the general public, thereby having a deterrent effect. A major problem with these objectives is that some components conflict with others. The infliction of pain and suffering is aimed at meeting the retribution and deterrence objectives, but most punitive approaches are counterproductive in terms of having reformative value.

There are also some dangers with using imprisonment. Association with other offenders may result in inmates learning additional lawbreaking techniques. Moreover, incarceration may label the offender as a "lawbreaker." According to labeling theory, if convicted offenders are related to as "dangerous, second-class citizens who are law violators," they may begin to perceive themselves as being "law violating."[94] Once they perceive themselves as law violators, labeling theory asserts they will then play that role upon their release.

In addition, as Sutherland and Cressey note, "Hatred of the criminal by society results in hatred of society by the criminal."[95] Relating to criminals as being dangerous, segregating them, and making them keep their distance (both while they are incarcerated and following their release) may force them into a career of criminal activity.

A third danger of long-term imprisonment is "institutionalization." Some prisoners, especially those who have had problems in adjusting to outside society, may eventually prefer prison life to outside society. After several years, they may actually feel more comfortable being confined (with their basic needs met) than having to return to the world outside, which will have undergone substantial change since their entry into prison. They will also have established a circle of friends within the prison from whom they receive respect. If they encounter problems on their return to society (for example, being unemployed and broke), they may yearn at some level to return to prison.

The Treatment Approach

There are literally hundreds of treatment programs in the corrections system. Space limitations prevent an exhaustive discussion of these programs, but a brief summary of major approaches will be covered in this section. It is necessary, however, to remember that the punitive approach has the continuous effect of decreasing the efficiency and effectiveness of treatment programs.

Individualized treatment for offenders has been increasingly popular since the 19th century. It developed as a reaction to the classical school, which advocated uniform penalties for criminals. Throughout history, however, there has been a dual standard of justice, with the rich and politically influential being (a) much less likely to be charged with a crime; (b) much less likely to be found guilty when accused because of their "character," position in society, and better legal representation; and (c) much less likely to receive a severe sentence if found guilty.

Counseling   Both one-to-one counseling and group counseling are used in prisons and by probation and parole officers. The aim is to identify the specific problems of each offender (including the reasons that motivated him or her to become involved in criminal activity) and then to develop programs for solving these problems. The inmate's needs may be extensive and numerous, including medical, psychological, and financial issues; drug use and abuse patterns; family and peer relationships; housing; education; vocational training; and employment. Attention is also given to the criminal's attitudes, motives, group and peer relationships, and rationalizations regarding criminality.

The effectiveness of counselors (social workers, probation and parole officers, psychologists, vocational rehabilitation counselors) is somewhat mitigated by their "dual" role perception by offenders. Some inmates view them as true helpers, whereas others view them as authority figures in control of rewards and punishments. Offenders with the second perception are reluctant to discuss socially unacceptable needs and motives or to establish a close relationship for fear that information divulged will be used against them.

Prison Education   Education in prison has two objectives: (a) to give inmates formal academic training comparable to schools and (b) to resocialize inmates' attitudes and behaviors. To accomplish these objectives, prisons use TV programs, movies, libraries, lectures, classroom instruction in academic subjects (covering elementary, secondary, and sometimes even college material), religious programs, group discussions, and recreational programs. However, the bitter attitude that most inmates have toward prison and the prison administration often interferes with their accomplishing educational objectives.

Vocational Training   The objective of these programs is to give inmates a job skill suitable to their capacities that will prepare them for employment on release. The quality of such programs in institutions throughout the country varies greatly. In many prisons, vocational training is defined as the maintenance work of the institution: laundry, cooking, custodial work, minor repairs, dishwashing. For a period of time, vocational training was considered the main component of rehabilitation, but now rehabilitation is seen as covering many other areas.

Prison Labor   The idea that prisoners should perform work has always existed. Originally, labor in prisons was seen as a method of punishment. England, for example, for a long time had inmates carry a cannonball on treadmills that had a meter measuring the number of units of work produced. For each meal, inmates had to produce a certain number of units. Additional units were assigned for misconduct.

Currently there are two conflicting conceptions of work: (a) it should be productive and train inmates for employment upon their release and (b) it should be hard, unpleasant, or monotonous for retributive purposes. The second view is still rationalized by some authorities as also having a reformative function; it is thought to teach discipline, obedience, and conformity and to develop an appreciation for avoiding criminal activity.

Convict labor has been used for building roads, running agricultural farms, fighting fires, conducting insect control programs, doing lumber-camp work, doing laundry, making state license plates, and performing a wide variety of other tasks. Work and educational release programs in jails and in some prisons allow release of inmates during the day so they may work or attend school but be locked up in the evening.

Good Time   Good-time legislation permits a prison review board to release a prisoner early if she or he has maintained good conduct. Most good-time laws specify that, for every month of acceptable behavior, a certain number of days will be deducted from the sentence. Good-time laws are designed to make inmates responsible for their conduct, to provide an incentive for good conduct and rehabilitation efforts, and to reduce discipline problems within prisons.

Indeterminate sentences, which were first established in the 1800s, have similar objectives. Many sentences are indeterminate, with a minimum and a maximum limit on the amount of time an inmate can be incarcerated. In recent years, however, a movement to return to determinate sentencing has gained considerable support.

Parole and Probation   Parole is the conditional release of a prisoner serving an indeterminate or unexpired sentence. It is granted by an administrative board (parole board) or by an executive. Parolees are considered "in custody" and are required to maintain acceptable conduct and avoid criminal activity. Parole is designed both to punish (certain behavior is restricted, and there is a threat of return to prison) and to treat the offender (a parole officer generally counsels and helps the parolee meet his or her needs).

Probation is granted by the courts. It involves suspending the sentence of a convicted offender and giving him or her freedom during good behavior under the supervision of a probation officer. Probationers are viewed as undergoing treatment. There is, however, the threat of punishment; if the conditions of probation are violated, the offender will be sent to prison. Similar to parole, probation contains reformation and retribution components.

Probation and parole officers have a dual role responsibility: a police role and a rehabilitative role. The probation and parole officer functions in the "police" or authority role by closely monitoring the activities of probationers and parolees to observe whether they are violating laws or violating the conditions of their parole/probation. Those being supervised are continually aware that the probation/parole officer has the authority to initiate procedures to revoke the probation/parole, which will send them to prison. Many probationers and parolees are distrustful of the criminal justice system and are therefore wary of anyone (including probation and parole officers) associated with this system.

This police role conflicts at times with the second primary function of probation and parole officers: the rehabilitative role. For rehabilitation to be most effective, the counselee must trust the counselor, must feel free to reveal socially unacceptable attitudes and activities to the counselor, and must form a close working relationship with the counselor. Obviously, those probationers and parolees who view their supervising officer primarily in the police role are likely to avoid forming a counseling relationship with that person.

How to Reduce Crime and Delinquency

The heading of this section may be inappropriate. Societies have been trying for centuries to reduce crime through a number of different approaches, yet the rate of crime seems to fluctuate independently of direct crime-suppression efforts. About 40 years ago, former President Nixon declared war on crime, and the federal government has since spent billions trying to curb crime. Yet the rate of crimes being committed continues to fluctuate—sometimes increasing, and sometimes decreasing. The prospects for reducing crime in the future remain uncertain because we do not as yet know enough about how to prevent people from committing crimes or how to reform them after they do. Nevertheless, this section will summarize major approaches that have been advanced to improve the situation. (You will note that some of the proposals are contradictory.) We will consider three general areas:

1. Increasing or decreasing sentences.
2. Reforming the correctional system.
3. Preventing crime in the first place.

Increasing or Decreasing Sentences

There are conflicting opinions concerning the appropriateness of various sentences as related to the crime committed. Suggestions to improve the effects of various sentences include shortening the times between arrest, conviction, and punishment; imposing harsher sentences; permanently imprisoning repeat offenders; increasing prosecution of white-collar criminals; creating uniform sentences; decriminalizing victimless offenses; and imposing stricter gun control.

Instituting Swift and Certain Punishment

It is generally agreed that the deterrent value of punishment decreases as the time lag between the crime and the eventual punishment increases. Only a fraction of those who commit crimes are arrested, and only a fraction of those arrested are ever found guilty.

All too often, crime does pay—particularly white-collar crime and organized crime. Criminal court proceedings commonly drag on for months and even years. During this time, offenders use due-process maneuvers in the hope that public anger over their crimes will dissipate and they will either be found innocent or have the charges reduced. Swifter action in catching, convicting, and punishing a greater percentage of lawbreakers will, it is argued, lead to greater respect for the law and curb crime. The argument against swifter action is that it would conflict with due-process protections and might result in a higher number of innocent people being arrested, convicted, and incarcerated.

Imposing Harsher Sentences

This approach is also based on the assumption that punishment has a deterrent effect. Advocates demand longer prison sentences and increased use of capital punishment. The reasoning is that lengthier sentences will reduce crime because criminals obviously cannot victimize citizens when they are locked up.

Opponents of this approach claim that longer sentences may increase crime rates rather than reduce them. Because practically all people sent to prison return to society, lengthier sentences may simply increase the bitterness of those serving time, reduce their respect for our laws and criminal justice system, and give them extended training in breaking the law through association with other hardened criminals. Opponents also note that imprisonment is expensive for society; it costs more per year to send someone to prison than to college.

Separating Repeat Offenders from Society

Crimes of violence (arson, rape, armed robbery, murder) are of particular concern to society, as are certain other offenses, such as repeated hard-drug trafficking. According to some authorities, repeated arrests and convictions for these offenses demonstrate that the offenders are so dangerous that protection of society must become the primary concern. It is further asserted that, because past efforts at reformation have not been effective, future efforts are not likely to be either. For repeat offenders of serious crimes, we should just "throw away the key." Our courts are in fact heading in this direction by locking up "repeaters" for longer periods of time.

A particular problem with this proposal is that serious crimes of violence are often committed by juveniles. As we've seen, juvenile courts use a "child-saving" approach: Their main focus is not on the nature of the crime but on treatment or rehabilitation. A number of states now allow juveniles arrested for homicide and other violent crimes to be charged and tried as adults. In adult court, convicted juveniles can then be given sentences commensurate with the seriousness of their offenses.

Advocating that repeat lawbreakers who commit serious crimes be locked up for long periods is an admission of rehabilitation failure. On the other hand, it is a proclamation that potential victims have rights too and that their rights take priority over the rights of repeaters.

Getting Tougher on White-Collar Crime

In the early 1970s, many high-ranking officials in the Nixon administration (which was pledged to "law and order") were accused of committing such offenses as illegal wiretapping, tax fraud, destruction of evidence, misappropriation of campaign funds, extortion, bribery, conspiracy to pervert the course of justice, and conspiracy to violate civil rights. Many of these officials were convicted but received very light sentences (often in special federal prisons referred to as "resorts") in comparison to the harsher sentences given to ordinary burglars and thieves. Former President Nixon was pardoned by President Gerald Ford prior to facing criminal charges. The Watergate scandal aroused a major discussion about the mild way in which white-collar crime is handled in our society. Yet today, white-collar crime is still largely ignored or glossed over by the police, the courts, and the correctional system. (It should be noted that organized crime is also increasingly involved in white-collar type offenses.)

It has been argued that more vigorous arrests, prosecution, and sentencing of white-collar crime and organized crime would lead to increased respect for the law by all citizens and would reduce crime. But that would require the White power structure in our society to encourage the police and the courts to arrest and prosecute its own members. In actuality, that power structure is more interested in prosecuting the crimes that are committed by members of the powerless groups in our society.

Creating Uniform Sentences

As noted earlier, there are wide variations in sentences imposed on different convicted offenders for the same crime. If justice is to be equal for all, then variables such as the economic status, race, and gender of the offender should not influence his or her sentence. Sentencing one murderer to death while putting another on probation undermines respect for the law and the criminal justice system. One way to reduce the disparity in sentences is to make them subject to appeal; currently the harshness of a sentence cannot be appealed. A second way is to take legislative action to reduce the latitude that is given to judges in imposing sentences for each type of conviction.

The move toward greater uniformity in sentencing in recent years does address somewhat the need for equality of treatment, but it also reduces the opportunity for individualized justice, which is a hallmark of our system. In addition, more uniform sentences (especially the imposition of mandatory minimums) has increased the average length of stay in prisons and contributed to prison overcrowding.

Decriminalizing Public-Order Offenses

Prohibition is the classic example of creating problems by outlawing a public-order activity. Prohibition made it a crime to manufacture, distribute, or drink alcohol. Police spent substantial time and resources trying to enforce this law but were largely unsuccessful. Instead, Prohibition led to bootlegging and fostered the rise of organized crime.

Today, public-order crimes are still with us—gambling, marijuana use, fornication, and prostitution, to name just a few. If such actions were decriminalized, immense resources in money and time could be diverted to confronting the more serious crimes. There is some movement to decriminalize certain offenses; for example, Nevada now allows prostitution in a few counties. In the past three decades, police departments have been less vigorous in making arrests for smoking marijuana, and there are efforts to decriminalize this activity in several states. Gambling laws are beginning to undergo change, as some states have now set up legal gambling activities, such as lotteries, casinos, and pari-mutuel betting on horse races and dog races.

Imposing Stricter Gun Control

In the past 50 years, John F. Kennedy, Robert Kennedy, Martin Luther King, Jr., Anwar Sadat, and John Lennon were killed by shootings. In 1981 there were assassination attempts on President Reagan and on the pope. More than 14,000 homicides and more than 360,000 robberies are committed annually in the United States.[96] Many homicides and armed robberies involve the use of a handgun. The number of Americans killed by handguns exceeds the number of Americans killed in wars declared by the United States in the past 100 years![97] States that have a higher proportion of guns have higher rates of homicides, suicides, and deaths during domestic disputes.[98] A number of special-interest groups have advocated an end to the sale of handguns except for approved and limited purposes.

In the past decade, Congress and the federal government have moved somewhat in the direction of imposing stricter gun controls. In 1993 the Brady Bill was enacted, which requires that gun buyers wait 5 business days and undergo a background check by police. (The Brady Bill was named in honor of James Brady, former presidential press secretary who was shot and severely wounded in the 1981 assassination attempt on President Reagan.) Supporters and opponents of the Brady Bill agree that the enactment of this bill will not stop the majority of criminals from obtaining firearms. In 1994 Congress passed, and President Clinton signed, a crime bill banning 19 types of assault-style firearms, which are used primarily to rapidly kill a number of people.

The major opposition to passing stricter gun control laws comes from the gun lobby (a coalition of several powerful organizations, including the National Rifle Association), which is funded by sports enthusiasts and firearms manufacturers.

Reforming the Correctional System

Perhaps the first step in improving the correctional system is to clarify its presently conflicting objectives, some of which are punitive in nature and others of which are treatment oriented. When the general public and public officials are confused about what the primary objective for incarceration should be, prison administrators and inmates will also be confused, making rehabilitation difficult.

If our society decides that retribution, deterrence, and vengeance should be the primary goals, then we can expect a continued high rate of recidivism and continued high crime rates because those being punished will become increasingly bitter and hostile toward society. However, from a social benefits viewpoint, the primary objective of a correctional system should be to curb future criminal activity of incarcerated offenders in the least expensive way. The current prison system is not only ineffectual in preventing recidivism, but it is also expensive. The national average per capita cost for institutionalization of adult felons is many times greater than the cost of probation services to adults.

If the correctional system had rehabilitation as its primary objective, a number of changes would occur. For example, sentencing of wrongdoers is now based primarily on the nature of their past deeds. If a convicted person has previously committed serious felonies, a long incarceration is likely. A reformative approach would, instead, focus on identifying ways to curb the supervisee's (or offender's) tendency to break the law. Involved in this identification process would be an assessment of the reasons why the person is committing crimes and a determination of how the offender can legally obtain what he or she wants. Needed services would then be specified, and the responsibilities of the supervisee would be identified—such as maintaining or securing employment, enrolling in an educational or vocational program, receiving counseling or family therapy, undergoing medical or drug treatment, paying debts, and/or making restitution. Removal from society would generally be used only after the supervisee failed to meet the requirements of the supervision plan (for example, restitution) or when the supervisee was a definite threat to society.

Let's consider two examples that illustrate this approach:

1. A 17-year-old female runs away from home, has very limited employment and educational skills, and therefore turns to prostitution for financial reasons. Instead of assigning fines after each arrest, would it not make more sense to identify her needs (such as financial needs, educational needs, need for legal employment that pays her more than prostitution, and need to resolve the conflicts with her parents) and then provide her with services to meet these needs?

2. A 32-year-old male is arrested for burglarizing 43 homes in wealthy neighborhoods over a span of 4 months. The man is unemployed, and he states that he committed the burglaries to support his cocaine habit. Instead of sending him directly to prison at taxpayers' expense, authorities could identify his needs (such as job training, employment, and drug treatment) and then provide him with services to meet those needs. As part of such a rehabilitative approach, he would be required (over a realistic period of time) to make restitution to the victims. He would be informed that additional convictions or any other failure on his part to fulfill the terms of the rehabilitative plan would result in a lengthy prison sentence.

With this approach, supervisees would become acutely aware that they have the choice and the responsibility to decide which of two avenues to pursue: continuation of criminal activity (resulting in a lengthy prison sentence) or a more law-abiding, productive, and respectable future. If they chose the latter, they would be given access to services (for example, counseling and vocational training) available to assist them, but they would also be made aware of the responsibility and effort required on their part.

With more than 1 million people behind bars, the United States imprisons a higher proportion of its population than any other nation.[99] Marc Mauer notes:

> *The same policies that have helped make us a world leader in incarceration have clearly failed to make us a safer nation. We need a fundamental change of direction, towards proven programs and policies that work to reduce both imprisonment and crime. We've got to stop jailing and start rehabilitating.*[100]

Diversion Programs

Labeling theory suggests that the criminal justice system perpetuates crime by branding offenders and interacting with them as if they were delinquents and criminals. Diversion programs have therefore been developed in a number of communities to divert first-time or minor offenders from entering the criminal justice system; as an alternative, they receive services from community agencies.

One such program is "deferred prosecution," which some communities now provide. Adults who are arrested for the first time for a minor offense (such as shoplifting) are referred by either a judge or a prosecuting attorney to deferred prosecution prior to standing trial. Deferred prosecution programs provide, over a period of several weeks, small-group sessions that are geared to helping the members refrain from committing additional crimes. The case is dismissed if the defendant (a) pays for any damages, (b) is not re-arrested while participating in the program, and (c) attends all the group meetings.

Many diversion programs focus on keeping juveniles out of juvenile courts and criminal courts by instead referring them to treatment programs handled by community agencies. Juveniles, for example, may be referred for counseling (from social workers, probation officers, or psychologists); they may receive help for emotional or family problems; or they may receive help with schoolwork.

Many communities have Scared Straight programs, which were initially developed at a prison in Rahway, New Jersey. Juveniles who have committed offenses are taken to visit a prison, where inmates harshly describe prison life. Prison conditions are also observed firsthand. The objective is to expose juveniles to the realities of life in prison so that the threat of imprisonment will motivate them to stop breaking the law. It is not yet certain, however, that this exposure has a deterrent effect on juveniles.

Transitional Programs

A variety of transitional programs are now offered to offenders. While in jail or prison, a person may be allowed to work in the community during the daytime. School-release programs allow inmates to attend college or a technical school during the day. Halfway houses have been used as an alternative to sending a person to prison; they allow residents to work or go to school in their home community. Halfway houses have also been used to help inmates just released from prison to readjust to society. If offenders misbehave while in halfway houses, there is the threat of being sent back to jail or prison.

Critical Thinking Questions

What do you believe are the best approaches for reducing the crime rate? Why do you prefer these approaches?

A goal of transitional programs is for inmates to maintain and develop strong ties to the noncriminal elements in their home community. The programs seek to reduce or alleviate the negative effects of incarceration and provide opportunities and resources for rehabilitation.

Preventing Crime

Theoretically, there are four ways to prevent crime:

1. Make the punishment for violating a law so severe that lawbreakers will be deterred from committing crimes. Studies on the use of capital punishment, however, suggest that even this severest penalty does not deter crime.

2. Keep the convicted lawbreakers in prison. Such an approach would be very expensive—especially, because practically everyone occasionally commits a crime.

3. Change the economic, social, and political conditions that breed crime. Among the numerous proposals that have been advanced are improve family life; improve the educational system to make education an exciting, growth-producing experience for students; end racial discrimination; end racial profiling by police departments; provide equal opportunities for achieving success for all citizens, including the poor and minority groups; provide full employment and a decent living wage for all able-bodied people; improve housing conditions and living conditions in our inner cities; and curb alcohol and drug abuse.

4. Educate the general public on how to avoid becoming a victim of crime. This fourth approach will be discussed in some detail and involves reducing opportunities for crime to occur. This approach is highlighted because it is one everyone should be aware of and participate in.

Dae Chang describes this approach, which developed from victimology, an area of study in criminology:

> *Research shows that much crime—and by far the greatest portion of street crime and burglary—is the result of opportunity and luck rather than of careful and professional planning.*
>
> *Someone sees an "opportunity"—in an open window, an empty house, a person alone in a dark alley—and acts on it. Muggers look for likely victims, not specific individuals, burglars, for a house they can enter, not a particular address. Preselected targets frequently are chosen precisely because they are seen as "easy marks."*
>
> *Who is the victim of a crime? What causes crime? Who causes crime? There are some startling answers to these questions. In the majority of cases, the victim contributes, and in some cases is a major cause of a criminal act. All of us are potential victims. We frequently present the criminal or an individual with an invitation to commit a crime. We entice him, advertise to him, coax him, give him the opportunity, and even implant the idea into his head. Through our carelessness, open disregard for our personal possessions, forgetfulness, attitudes, vanity, etc., we frequently invite someone to commit a criminal act either directly at ourselves or to our possessions. We also invite bodily harm upon ourselves by our actions in public and private. Our habits, attitudes, dress, etc. all are signals to the people who would be enticed into crime.*[101]

In effect, one must ask oneself, "Is what I'm currently doing, or failing to do, making me vulnerable to becoming a victim of a crime?" Case Exhibit 9.3

CASE EXHIBIT 9.3

Precautions to Prevent Becoming a Crime Victim

At Home

- Bolt doors and windows, and use exterior lighting to frustrate burglary techniques.
- Engrave identification numbers on possessions to curb fencing of stolen property.
- If you leave home for part of the evening, make it look as though someone is home. Leave some lights and music on. Or leave the television on, keeping it low so that it sounds as if people are inside talking or the family is home watching TV.
- Double-secure sliding-glass doors by placing lengths of metal rod or wooden dowels in the lower tracks to prevent the doors from being opened.
- Put in exterior lighting over front and back doors. Also, cut back shrubbery that might be used to hide intruders.
- If you hear someone breaking in at night, let the intruder know you have heard the noise, but avoid a confrontation. Chances are the person will leave as fast as possible. If you confront the intruder unexpectedly, you could get hurt. Instead, yell, "Get the shotgun!"—even if you are alone. Or yell to the neighbors or call the police.
- One of the best places to have a strong deadbolt lock is on the inside of your bedroom door.
- A dog that barks a lot may deter an intruder. The yapping of the dog will make the intruder wary that someone else will hear the barking, so the intruder will probably exit in a hurry.
- Do not leave the key to your home under the doormat, in the mailbox, or on top of the door ledge.
- Be cautious about inviting door-to-door salespeople into your home. Many communities now require salespeople to carry an identification card.
- Do not leave possessions on lawns or in your driveway at night. If left, bicycles, barbecue grills, power tools, and lawn mowers are easily removed.
- Do not leave important papers, expensive jewelry, or large sums of money at home. Rent a bank security deposit box, which protects valuables not only from burglars but also from fires and natural disasters.
- When going on an extended vacation, arrange for a friend to check your home every few days. Do not let newspapers or mail pile up. The post office will hold your mail at no cost while you are away. Inexpensive timers can be purchased to activate lights, radios, or TVs to give the impression you are home.
- When you expect a visitor and are unable to be home, do not leave a telltale note outside: "Welcome—will be back at 8 P.M. Walk in and make yourself at home. Door is unlocked." Burglars readily accept such invitations.
- Women are advised to list only their last name and initials on mailboxes and in phone directories.

In an Automobile

- Flashy equipment on autos will invite theft or break-ins. If you have mag wheels, a radar detector, a portable GPS, fancy wheel covers, and other expensive gadgets, your car will draw attention. The place you park your car can be an invitation for it to be stolen or broken into. Always lock your car, put valuables in the trunk, and never leave the key in the ignition.
- If you leave your car someplace for a few days (for example, at an airport), it will be nearly theft-proof if you pull the center wire out of the distributor in addition to locking the car and taking the keys. (Before pulling the wire, make sure you know how to put it back!)
- Remove identification from key chains so that, if your keys are lost or stolen, no one knows what the keys will open.
- Do not hitchhike or pick up hitchhikers. Hitchhiking has led to a significant number of robberies and assaults. If you cannot avoid hitchhiking, be very selective as to whom you ride with.

In Public

- Avoid carrying large sums of money. If forced to do so, take along a second wallet containing three or four bills and some expired credit cards, which you can give a thief if confronted.
- When in a crowd, place your wallet in a safe place (for example, front pocket, a waist pocket, or a buttoned back pocket) to frustrate pickpocketing efforts.
- Never leave a purse unattended.
- Avoid going into a dark parking lot. It may be cheaper to call a taxi than risk being mugged.
- There are a variety of approaches to avoid becoming a victim of rape, including physical techniques of self-defense (for example, the martial arts) and distasteful approaches (for example, vomiting or urinating on the rapist, informing the potential rapist you have tested positive for HIV, sharply squeezing the genitals of the rapist, and poking your fingers into the rapist's eyes). Women should become familiar with these approaches and select a few that they would be comfortable with and prepared to use should an attack occur.

presents a number of specific precautions to prevent becoming a crime victim.

Social Work and the Criminal Justice System

Role of Social Work

The primary focus of social work in the criminal justice system has been on the correctional component. Social workers have frequently been employed as probation and parole officers, as social workers in a prison, and as social workers at a correctional halfway house. There are only a few police departments that employ social workers to provide social services to individuals and families with whom police come in contact.

To a lesser extent, social workers have been employed in programs that are primarily preventive (as compared to correctional) in nature. For example, in the juvenile gang arena, a wide variety of programs have attempted to reduce delinquent gang activities. These have included detached worker programs, in which workers join gangs and seek to transform antisocial into prosocial attitudes and behaviors; drug treatment programs for gang members who have a chemical addiction; programs to support and strengthen families, particularly single-parent families in urban areas; programs to prevent dropping out of school and to provide academic support (such as mentoring programs); and family preservation programs (see Chapter 6 for a description).

Many probation and parole officers are trained in social work. One of the important responsibilities of a probation and parole officer is to prepare a presentence report. This is a social history of the offender that is prepared to help guide the judge in sentencing. A sample presentence report appears in Case Exhibit 9.4.

In the field of corrections, there are two important factors influencing treatment: custody–treatment conflict and offenders' "con games." Social workers need to understand how these factors operate.

Factors Influencing Treatment

Custody–Treatment Conflict

In prison settings, administrators emphasize custody. More than 90% of the money spent in such institutions goes for custody.[102] When custody policies clash with treatment programs, treatment almost always comes in second. Prison administrators are primarily concerned with preventing escapes, curbing riots, and calming internal disruptions. New social workers in prison settings soon realize rehabilitation is not the primary focus.

Social workers in prisons, and those who work as probation and parole officers, are often viewed by offenders as part of the larger authoritarian bureaucracy that caught and convicted them. Many offenders are distrustful of social workers because they feel the social workers are "monitoring" or "policing" them.

Offenders' "Con Games"

Since the 1930s, the criminal justice system has promoted both individual and group therapy. Prison administrators and directors of probation and parole programs have required offenders to participate in treatment programs. Obviously, compelling clients to submit to treatment interventions can inhibit establishment of rapport with offenders. Yet enforced treatment is commonplace in corrections.

Offenders are highly skilled at "conning" professional staff through persuasion, deceit, and manipulation. Most convicted offenders disdain correctional staff. This disdain is strengthened when they see therapy forced on them. Inmates realize that they must participate in such activities as individual and group counseling in order to have a good record. If imprisoned on an indeterminate sentence (as is common in most states), a good record will get them released on parole sooner. If they are on probation or parole, offenders may see their participation in "treatment" programs as a way to get the probation/parole officer to do things for them or to overlook minor violations of the rules for probation and parole.

The social worker should be aware that many offenders who request professional assistance have no genuine interest in self-improvement but are seeking to manipulate the worker.

CASE EXHIBIT 9.4

Presentence Report

Walworth County Court
June 23, 2010
   Name: James LaMartina
   Address: 408 Walnut St. Delavan, WI 54987
   Legal Residence: Same
   Age: 34
   Date of Birth: 5-8-76
   Sex: Male
   Race: Caucasian
   Citizenship: U.S.A.
   Education: 11th grade
   Marital Status: Married
   Dependents: Two (wife and a 4-year-old son)
   Soc. Sec. No.: 393-42-9067
   FBI No.: 287 1237
   Detainers or Charges Pending: None
   Offense: Second-degree sexual assault
   Penalty: Imprisoned not more than 10 years and/or fined
     not more than $10,000
   Plea: Guilty
   Verdict:
   Custody: Posted bail of $5,000
   Prosecuting Attorney: Richard Jorgenson, Assistant District
     Attorney
   Defense Counsel: Donald Hauser

Offense: Official Version

Officers Karen Davenport and David Erdmier stated they arrested Mr. LaMartina in Lakeland County Park at 12:30 A.M. on June 5, 2010, for having sexual intercourse with a 17-year-old minor. Mr. LaMartina and the minor were in the backseat of the offender's car and were reported to be unclothed.

Mr. LaMartina stated he had met the woman in Don's Hillside Tavern earlier in the day. He stated that this was the first time he had met her and did not know her age—he assumed she was an adult. A check with Donald Leesburg, owner of the tavern, indicated that Mr. LaMartina was a frequent patron of the tavern but that the woman was not a regular patron. The owner further stated that the night of June 4, 2010, was busy. He noted that Mr. LaMartina was there earlier that evening, but the owner was unaware whether Mr. LaMartina had met this woman at the tavern.

The minor appeared intoxicated at the time of the arrest. Her driver's license the night of the arrest revealed her age to be 17 years and 2 months. She was returned home by the police to her parents, who were very angry; Officers Davenport and Erdmier had to restrain the father from physically hitting her.

Defendant's Version of Offense

Mr. LaMartina stated that he frequently stopped at Don's Hillside Tavern after work with fellow workers from the con-

struction company he has worked with for the past 6 years. Mr. LaMartina stated that this evening was the first time he had met this woman. He mentioned he began buying drinks for her and for the two other women friends she was with. He stated that she had drunk considerably more than he had. He emphasized that he assumed she was at least 21 years of age (the legal drinking age in this state).

Around midnight he asked her if she wanted a ride home, which she accepted. He drove instead to Lakeland County Park, where he emphasized she willingly agreed to go to the backseat with him and willingly became sexually involved. When asked whether he had become sexually involved with other women, Mr. LaMartina became defensive and refused to answer.

Prior Record

Date	Offense	Disposition
9-2-2003	Disorderly conduct	$80 fine
10-11-2006	Driving motor vehicle while under the influence	$510 fine and group dynamics course

Personal History

The defendant was born in Fort Atkinson, Wisconsin, on May 8, 1968, the older of two children. His parents were dairy farmers. He attended public schools and completed the 11th grade. He received mainly Cs and Ds in school and left school to help on the farm. He had a number of friends in school and was active in several sports, including the high school varsity basketball and baseball teams.

The defendant's father, Leonard, died following a stroke when the defendant was 22 years of age. His mother, Loretta, is still living on the family farm in rural Jefferson County. The defendant ran the farm for 6 years after his father's death and then sold the cattle in order to work for Johnstone's Road Construction Company. The farm appeared to be only marginally successful when the defendant had dairy cattle. The defendant still plants and harvests crops on the farm.

The defendant's sister, Janine, is 28 years of age and has been married for the past 6 years to Dennis Richter, a dairy farmer in Dane County.

Mr. LaMartina has been married for the past 8 years to Sue Heinz (maiden name). Sue is 32 years of age and graduated from Carthage College 10 years ago. She taught elementary school for the first 4 years of their marriage but has not taught school for the past 4 years—since their son, Tim, was born. She and James LaMartina have lived in the LaMartinas' farmhouse since their marriage.

Sue LaMartina separated from her husband shortly after she heard he was arrested. She and her son are now staying with her parents. She has ambivalent feelings about her husband. She stated that he can be a good father and husband,

(continued)

but she is intensely irritated about his drinking and about his staying out late at night with his "cronies." She stated that she suspected he may occasionally have been having affairs with other women, but this incident is "the last straw." She stated that she is seeing a counselor at the mental health center, has contacted an attorney, and is contemplating a divorce.

Mr. LaMartina stated that he does not want a divorce and appears sincerely remorseful about the family problems he has created. He stated that if he and his wife can reconcile, he will change his ways. He will not stay out late or become involved with other women. Mr. LaMartina has asked his wife to attend marriage counseling with him, but she indicated she is still too emotionally hurt and embarrassed to be able to discuss the incident.

There is some evidence that Mr. LaMartina has been drinking to excess for several years. Mr. LaMartina denies this, but his frequent stops after work at a tavern and his past arrest record suggest otherwise. The future of his marriage, however, appears to be a more immediate problem needing attention.

Evaluative Summary

The defendant is a 34-year-old male who entered a plea of guilty to second-degree sexual assault. The defendant was arrested for having sexual intercourse with a 17-year-old woman

he met, apparently for the first time, earlier that evening at a tavern. The defendant apparently did not know the woman was a minor. The defendant's wife has separated from him following this arrest and is contemplating a divorce. The defendant expressed considerable remorse about the embarrassment and domestic strife he has caused.

Mr. LaMartina has a 4-year-old son and has no prior felony arrest record. He may at times drink to excess. He completed 11 years of schooling and has run a dairy farm. For the past 6 years, he has been a road construction worker. His employer reports that he is dependable and has been a good worker.

Recommendation

It is recommended that the defendant be fined and placed on probation. If placed on probation, the defendant expresses willingness to seek counseling for his domestic problems. This counseling should also at some future time explore whether he has a drinking problem. The future of his marriage, however, needs first attention.

Respectfully submitted,

Ralph Franzene
Probation and Parole Officer
State of Wisconsin

SUMMARY

The following summarizes this chapter's content as it relates to the chapter objectives presented at the beginning of the chapter. Objectives include the following:

A *Discuss the nature and extent of crime.*

Crime is one of the most serious problems facing our nation. Serious, violent crime has reached alarming proportions. In addition, the criminal justice system (the police, the courts, and prisons) is perceived as relatively ineffective in curbing crime.

Everyone, at one time or another, has violated some laws. Those arrested for crimes are disproportionately likely to be male, young, a member of a racial minority, and a city resident. If white-collar crime and organized crime were more vigorously prosecuted, the "typical" criminal would more likely be older, White, and a suburban resident.

Official crime statistics are inaccurate for a variety of reasons. Many crimes go unreported. Police and courts vigorously enforce only certain crimes. Police-reporting practices are affected at times by political

considerations, such as reclassifying serious offenses as less serious to attempt to make police departments appear more effective in curbing serious crimes. In terms of number of people victimized and financial costs to society, it appears that white-collar crime is our most serious type. Yet it is less vigorously enforced by the police and the courts.

B *Present crime causation theories.*

Various theories about the causes of crime have been advanced. These theories identify some of the reasons crime occurs. But we do not have a complete understanding of all the reasons for crime. With the crime rate continuing to increase, it is also clear that we do not as yet know how to reduce crime effectively.

C *Describe types of crime.*

Types of crime include organized crime, gambling, drug trafficking, loan sharking, labor racketeering, prostitution, white-collar crime, computer crime, hate crime, public-order crime, sex offenses, human trafficking, homicide and assault, theft, and juvenile delinquency.

D *Describe the criminal justice system (the police, the courts, and the correctional system).*

Current correctional systems throughout the world reflect conflicting objectives; some components are punishment oriented, whereas others are treatment oriented. Generally, the two components, when combined, result in a system that is confusing and ineffective in curbing criminal activity. There is a danger that prisons may serve as schools for crime and may have a labeling effect that leads to future criminal activity.

E *Suggest ways to reduce crime and delinquency.*

Numerous proposals have been advanced for reducing crime, including administering swift and certain punishment, imposing harsher sentences, separating repeat offenders from society, getting tougher on white-collar crime, creating uniform sentencing, decriminalizing public-order offenses, ending racial profiling by police forces, imposing stricter gun control, reforming the correctional system to emphasize the treatment approach, increasing use of diversion and transitional programs, and educating citizens on how to avoid becoming crime victims. Some of these proposals contradict others. Although each proposal has some research support, no proposal has conclusively been proved valid in reducing crime.

The ways in which societies have punished convicted offenders are as atrocious as the atrocities offenders have inflicted on victims. The "eye-for-an-eye" retributive approach generally is ineffective in curbing future crime.

F *Discuss the role of social work in providing correctional services.*

The primary focus of social work in the criminal justice system has been on the correctional component. Social workers have frequently been employed as probation and parole officers, as social workers in a prison, and as social workers at a correctional halfway house. There are only a few police departments that employ social workers to provide social services to individuals and families with whom police come in contact.

To a lesser extent, social workers have been employed in programs that are primarily preventive (as opposed to correctional) in nature.

Competency Notes

EP 2.1.3a Distinguish, appraise, and integrate multiple sources of knowledge, including research-based knowledge and practice wisdom.

(All of this chapter) This chapter describes the nature and extent of crime, and presents crime causation theories. It describes types of crime, and also describes the criminal justice system. It suggests ways to reduce crime and delinquency, and summarizes the role of social work in providing correctional services.

Media Resources

Additional resources for this chapter, including a chapter quiz, can be found on the Social Work CourseMate. Go to CengageBrain.com.

Notes

1. Vincent N. Parrillo, John Stimson, and Ardyth Stimson, *Contemporary Social Problems*, 2nd ed. (New York: Macmillan, 1989), pp. 127–158.
2. William Kornblum and Joseph Julian, *Social Problems*, 14th ed. (Boston: Pearson), p. 137.
3. U.S. Department of Justice, Federal Bureau of Investigation, *Crime in the United States—2010*, http://www.fbi.gov/ucr/cius2010/offenses/index.htm.
4. Kornblum and Julian, *Social Problems*, pp. 142–144.
5. James W. Coleman and Harold R. Kerbo, *Social Problems*, 8th ed. Upper–Saddle River, NJ: Prentice Hall, 2002), p. 433.
6. Kornblum and Julian, *Social Problems*, p. 161.
7. Ibid., p. 161.
8. Ibid., p. 161.
9. Ibid., pp. 162–163.
10. Ibid., p. 165.
11. Ibid., p. 165.
12. Donald Jackson, "Justice for None," *New Times*, Jan. 11, 1974, p. 51.
13. Kornblum and Julian, *Social Problems*, pp. 165–166.
14. Ibid., p. 166.
15. Ibid., pp. 165–166.
16. George Cole and Christopher Smith, *The American System of Criminal Justice*, 12th ed. (Belmont, CA: Thomson Wadsworth, 2010), p. 108.
17. *Crime in the United States—2010.*
18. Kornblum and Julian, *Social Problems*, pp. 139–140.
19. Ibid.
20. Coleman and Kerbo, *Social Problems*, pp. 431–432.
21. Ibid.
22. Kornblum and Julian, *Social Problems*, pp. 134–136.

23. H. E. Pepinsky and R. Quinney, *Criminology as Peacemaking* (Bloomington: Indiana University Press, 1991).

24. Charles Goring, *The English Convict* (London: His Majesty's Stationery Office, 1913).

25. Thomas Szasz, *The Myth of Mental Illness* (New York: Hoeber-Harper, 1961).

26. H. J. Eysenck, "The Effects of Psychotherapy," *International Journal of Psychiatry*, 1 (1965), pp. 97–144.

27. Charles Zastrow and Ralph Navarre, "Self-Talk: A New Criminological Theory," *International Journal of Comparative and Applied Criminal Justice*, Fall 1979, pp. 167–176.

28. Edwin H. Sutherland and Donald R. Cressey, *Criminology*, 8th ed. (Philadelphia: Lippincott, 1970), p. 10.

29. Robert K. Merton, *Social Theory and Social Structure* (New York: Free Press, 1968), p. 232.

30. John M. Johnson and Jack Douglas, eds., *Crime at the Top: Deviance in Business and the Professions* (Philadelphia: Lippincott, 1978).

31. Walter B. Miller, "Lower Class Culture as a Generating Milieu of Gang Delinquency," *Journal of Social Issues*, 14 (1958), pp. 5–19.

32. Albert Cohen, *Delinquent Boys: The Culture of the Gang* (New York: Free Press, 1955).

33. Charles Cooley, *Human Nature and the Social Order* (New York: Scribner's, 1902).

34. Gary Cavendar, "Alternative Approaches: Labeling and Critical Perspectives," in *Criminology: A Contemporary Handbook*, Joseph F. Sheley, ed. (Belmont, CA: Wadsworth, 1995), pp. 186–199.

35. Stewart Powell, Steven Emerson, and Orr Kelly, "Busting the Mob," *U.S. News & World Report*, Feb. 3, 1986, pp. 24–31.

36. Kornblum and Julian, *Social Problems*, pp. 150–151.

37. Ibid.

38. Ibid.

39. Coleman and Kerbo, *Social Problems*, pp. 425–426.

40. Kornblum and Julian, *Social Problems*, pp. 150–151.

41. Johnson and Douglas, *Crime at the Top*.

42. Kornblum and Julian, *Social Problems*, p. 145.

43. Ibid., p. 147.

44. Coleman and Kerbo, *Social Problems*, pp. 426–427.

45. Kornblum and Julian, *Social Problems*, p. 146.

46. Ibid., p. 145.

47. Ibid., p. 145.

48. Linda A. Mooney, David Knox, and Caroline Schacht, *Understanding Social Problems*, 8th ed. (Belmont, CA: Wadsworth/Cengage Learning, 2013), pp. 112–113.

49. Ibid., p. 114.

50. Cole and Smith, *The American System of Criminal Justice*, p. 24

51. Ibid., p. 25.

52. Kornblum and Julian, *Social Problems*, p. 153.

53. Ibid., p. 153.

54. Kornblum and Julian, *Social Problems*, pp. 154–155.

55. Alexander B. Smith and Harriet Pollack, "Crimes without Victims," *Saturday Review*, Dec. 4, 1971, pp. 27–29.

56. Mooney, Knox, and Schacht, *Understanding Social Problems*, p. 101.

57. U.S. State Department, *Victim Stories*, 2006, available at http://2001-2009.state.gov/g/tip/c16482.htm.

58. Ibid.

59. Kornblum and Julian, *Social Problems*, pp. 142–143.

60. Ibid., p. 142.

61. Ibid., p. 110.

62. Edwin H. Sutherland, *The Professional Thief* (Chicago: University of Chicago Press, 1937).

63. Charles H. McCaghy and Stephen A. Cernkovich, *Crime in American Society*, 2nd ed. (New York: Macmillan, 1987), pp. 245–247.

64. *Crime in the United States—2010*.

65. Kornblum and Julian, *Social Problems*, p. 153.

66. Ibid.

67. Ibid.

68. J. F. Longres, "Youth Gangs," in National Association of Social Workers, *Encyclopedia of Social Work: 1990 Supplement* (Silver Spring, MD: NASW, 1990), p. 320.

69. A. P. Goldstein, *Delinquent Gangs: A Psychological Perspective* (Champaign, IL: Research Press, 1991).

70. Ibid.

71. Armando T. Morales, "Urban and Suburban Gangs: The Psychosocial Crisis Spreads," in *Social Work: A Profession of Many Faces*, 9th ed., Armando T. Morales and Bradford W. Sheafor, eds. (Needham Heights, MA: Allyn & Bacon, 2001), pp. 404–407.

72. T. A. Sweeney, *Streets of Anger, Streets of Hope* (Glendale, CA: Great Western, 1980), p. 86.

73. Morales, "Urban and Suburban Gangs: The Psychosocial Crisis Spreads," pp. 397–431.

74. Ibid.

75. Ibid.

76. Longres, "Youth Gangs," p. 325.

77. I. A. Spergel, *The Youth Gang Problem: A Community Approach* (New York: Oxford University Press, 1995).

78. Ibid.

79. Kornblum and Julian, *Social Problems*, pp. 172–173.

80. Coleman and Kerbo, *Social Problems*, p. 442.

81. David M. Peterson, "The Police Officer's Conception of Proper Police Work," *The Police Journal*, 47 (1974), pp. 102–108.

82. Coleman and Kerbo, *Social Problems*, p. 442.

83. http://www.enotes.com/criminal-law-reference/plea-bargaining.

84. Don C. Gibbons, *Society: Crime and Criminal Behavior*, 5th ed. (Englewood Cliffs, NJ: Prentice Hall, 1987), p. 439.

85. James W. Coleman and Donald R. Cressey, *Social Problems*, 6th ed. (New York: HarperCollins, 1996), p. 407.

86. Alan Neigher, "The *Gault* Decision: Due Process and the Juvenile Court," *Federal Probation*, 31, no. 4 (Dec. 1967), pp. 8–18.

87. Cole and Smith, *The American System of Criminal Justice*, pp. 595–596.

88. Ibid., p. 518.

89. Kornblum and Julian, *Social Problems*, p. 171.

90. Ibid., pp. 170–171.

91. Cole and Smith, *The American System of Criminal Justice*, p. 576.

92. Ibid.

93. Ibid.

94. Ibid.

95. Sutherland and Cressey, *Criminology*, p. 354.

96. *Crime in the United States—2010*.

97. Cole and Smith, *The American System of Criminal Justice*, p. 130.

98. Ibid.

99. Ibid.

100. Marc Mauer, quoted in "Prison Ratio Highest in U.S.," *Wisconsin State Journal*, Jan. 5, 1991, p. 3A.

101. Dae H. Chang, "How to Avoid Becoming a Victim of Crime," in *The Personal Problem Solver*, Charles Zastrow and Dae H. Chang, eds. (Englewood Cliffs, NJ: Prentice Hall, 1977), pp. 348–349.

102. Cole and Smith, *The American System of Criminal Justice*, p. 563.

CHAPTER

Problems in Education and School Social Work

CHAPTER OUTLINE

In 1957 the United States and the Soviet Union were involved in an unofficial race to be first to place a satellite in orbit. The race became a symbol of international honor and prestige. The Soviets won when they successfully launched *Sputnik* I into orbit. Why did the United States lose? There were numerous reasons. However, the general public blamed the American educational system for neglecting subjects that were vital to national survival. For example, one outspoken critic, Max Rafferty, stated, "Instead of offering a four-year program of studies in mathematics, history, foreign languages, and other disciplines [high schools] encourage students to divert themselves with ceramics, stagecraft, table decorating, upholstering, and second-year golf."[1] Following these events, the American educational system was called on to emphasize mathematics, natural science, and other courses that would enable our country to successfully compete with the Soviets. This historical incident is just one of many that could be cited to illustrate that when events in our society do not go as the public wants, the educational system in the United States is often, rightly or wrongly, a target of blame. Today, one of the countries that American children are competing with is China, as China is an economic power that is rivaling the United States. Can our children outperform children from less democratic countries? This chapter will:

Learning Objectives

EP 2.1.3a

A Summarize problems that school systems currently face.

B Present proposals for improving education.

C Discuss ideas for improving educational opportunities for children of low-income and minority families.

D Summarize the functions of school social workers and describe several roles for school social work practice.

Problematic Areas in Education

The educational system has frequently been asked to resolve and alleviate social problems. For example, it is currently being called on to help reduce racism and sexism by developing new curricula designed to change the attitudes of school-age children. (The school setting is one of the places where real integration of the races is likely to occur.) The educational system is expected to provide students of low-income families with the education and job-training skills that will enable them to escape from a life of poverty, even though children living in poverty often come with fewer enriching life experiences and less motivation for academic achievement than more affluent children. It must identify and refer for treatment those children who have emotional or learning problems and those who abuse alcohol and other drugs.

The school system is a mechanism for conveying a sense of citizenship responsibility and for countering antisocial and delinquent attitudes. In addition, it is required to refer to protective services any children who are suspected of being physically abused, neglected, or sexually abused.

The educational system in a democratic society is the "great equalizer" that should create a common bond and give equal opportunity to all. Sometimes the educational system is perceived as a social problem itself because it is not meeting the expectations of society. Education is in a crisis of controversy, indecision, and decreasing public vocal and financial support. The self-confidence, morale, and motivation of teachers are often low. Some schools have been accused of perpetuating, rather than alleviating, social inequality for the poor and for minorities.

Although recent improvements have occurred, student scores on achievement tests are lower than they were 50 years ago.[2] Some schools are so victimized by vandalism and violence that students and teachers are as concerned with survival as with education. In some schools alienated students have shot their classmates and teachers; fear of victimization is now the culture of some of our schools.

The educational system in our country faces a number of crises. This section will examine the following problems: the question of the quality of education, the issue of equal access to a quality education, confusion about the goals of education, and intolerable working conditions in some school settings.

The Question of Quality

In 2007 the National Center for Education Statistics released the National Assessment of Adult Literacy, a report that studied the literacy abilities of a representative sample of U.S. adults 16 years or older. Three types of literacy were measured: quantitative (e.g., balancing a checkbook), prose (e.g., reading a newspaper), and document (e.g., reading a transportation schedule). The report indicated 30 million people in the United States are estimated to have below basic literacy skills. Seven million of these individuals were estimated to be non-English speakers.[3]

The percentage of eighth graders who are "proficient" in mathematics in the United States was found in one study to be less than one-third. Only 31% of these eighth graders were proficient in reading. The study also found only 18% of 12th graders were proficient in science.[4]

U.S. students continue to be outperformed by students in other developed countries. Of the 30 countries of the Organization for Economic Co-operation and Development (OECD), only four countries have lower high school graduation rates than the United States—Mexico, New Zealand, Spain, and Turkey. In addition, U.S. 15-year-olds placed 27th out of these 30 OECD countries on mathematical achievement.[5]

Based on the results of ACT tests (a college admissions test, 70% of would-be-college students are unprepared for college expectations in reading, writing, or mathematics.[6]

Equal Access to Quality Education

An egalitarian society has a responsibility to provide equal opportunity for a high-quality education to all its citizens. Our society has generally failed to meet this responsibility, especially with respect to minority groups and the poor.

Numerous studies have found social class to be the single most effective predictor of achievement in school.[7] Students from the middle and upper classes tend to achieve higher grades, stay in school longer, and get higher scores on standardized achievement tests. There are two primary explanations for this relationship; one focuses on family background and the other on school systems.

The family background explanation ascribes the inequality to the fact that lower-class children live in a very different environment from middle- and upper-class children. The theory asserts that lower-income homes tend to have fewer magazines, newspapers, and books, and less access to computers and the Internet. Lower-income parents usually have less education and are less likely to act as role models to encourage high academic expectations. In fact, they may give the message, "I didn't do well in math either." Because lower-class families tend to be larger and to be headed by a single parent, it is said, their children receive less guidance and educational encouragement.[8] Because of such factors, poor children may be less likely to view education as a means of achieving in society and less likely to develop educational goals. Further, poor children are more likely to be hungry and undernourished, which also inhibits their motivation to learn. In contrast, middle- and upper-class families tend to place a higher value on education and therefore put more time and effort into helping their children do homework in order to do well in school. Middle- and upper-class children may also have heard from the time they first started kindergarten that they would be going to college. While a high school diploma may be seen as an achievement for a child from a lower-class background, a college degree is often a minimal expectation for an upper-middle-class child.

School systems are primarily geared for educating middle- and upper-class students. Youngsters who live in wealthy tax districts benefit from having more money spent on their schools than students who live in poorer districts. About 40% of the funds for public schools in this country come from local school district taxes.[9] Because most of this money is derived from property taxes, school districts with numerous expensive homes have much more revenue for their schools. For example, in the state of New York, schools teaching the poorest students receive $2,319 per student less than schools teaching the wealthiest students.[10]

CASE EXAMPLE 10.1

The Pygmalion Effect

The Pygmalion effect means "self-fulfilling prophecy." The principles of a self-fulfilling prophecy are:

- We form certain expectations of people or events.
- We communicate those expectations with various verbal and nonverbal cues.
- People tend to respond to these cues by adjusting their behavior to match them.
- The result is that the original expectation becomes true.

This creates a circle of self-fulfilling prophecies.

Robert Rosenthal and Lenore Jacobson performed an intriguing experiment to demonstrate that teachers' expectations of students can increase students' IQ scores. They called this self-fulfilling prophecy the Pygmalion Effect. (The word "Pygmalion" is taken from George Bernard Shaw's play "Pygmalion," in which a professor makes a bet that he can teach a poor flower girl to speak and act like an upper-class lady, and is successful.)

These experimenters began by giving a standard IQ test to students in 18 classrooms of an elementary school. (The teachers were told that the test was the Harvard Test of Inflected Acquisition—no such test exists.) The researchers then randomly selected 20% of the students and informed their teachers that the test results predicted remarkable progress for these students in the coming school year. When the students were re-tested 8 months later, those who had been expected to be remarkable achievers showed a significantly greater increase in IQ scores than the others. The researchers concluded that this increase was due to the higher expectations of the teachers, who then worked more intensively with these students. If the expectations of teachers do indeed affect student achievement and IQ test scores, lower-class and minority students may be at a disadvantage; most teachers are White, middle class, and have a tendency to expect less from lower-class and minority students.

SOURCE: Robert Rosenthal and Lenore Jacobson, *Pygmalion in the Classroom* (New York: Harper & Row, 1969).

Mooney, Knox, and Schacht note that making schools heavily dependent on local financing has several consequences:

- Low-socioeconomic-status school districts are poorer because less valuable housing means lower property values; in the inner city houses are older and more dilapidated; and less desirable neighborhoods are hurt by "White flight," with the result that the tax base for local schools is lower in deprived areas.
- Low-socioeconomic-status school districts are less likely to have businesses or retail outlets where revenues are generated; such businesses have closed or moved away.
- Because of their proximity to the downtown area, low-socioeconomic-status school districts are more likely to include hospitals, museums, and art galleries, all of which are tax-free facilities. These properties do not generate revenues.
- Low-socioeconomic-status neighborhoods are often in need of the greatest share of city services; fire and police protection, sanitation, and public housing consume the bulk of the available revenues. Precious little is left over for education in these districts.

- In low-socioeconomic-status school districts a disproportionate amount of the money has to be spent on maintaining the school facilities, which are old and in need of repair, so less is available for the children themselves.[11]

The educational reformer Jonathon Kozol says in *Savage Inequalities* that the United States maintains two separate and unequal school systems, one for poor minority inner-city children and another for the more affluent.[12] Poor children sometimes attend Third-World-condition schools with poorly qualified teachers, while a bus ride away there are well-equipped schools with highly qualified teachers. The average reading level of Black 17-year-olds is about that of White 13-year-olds.[13]

Most teachers have middle-class backgrounds, which may mean they are better able to establish relationships with middle- and upper-income children, with whom they have more in common. There is also evidence that teachers expect less of poor children academically and behaviorally than they expect of middle- and upper-class children. In turn, low-income students tend to respond to such expectations by underachieving and misbehaving.[14] Thus, the expectation becomes a self-fulfilling prophecy (see Case Example 10.1).

Critical Thinking Questions

Should state and federal governments contribute more tax money to fund local school districts in order to move toward greater access to quality education in poorer school districts? Why or why not?

Many school systems place students in one of several different tracks or ability groups. In high school, the so-called most promising are placed in college preparatory courses, whereas others go into "basic" or vocational classes. Lower-class and minority students are much more likely to be placed in the basic or vocational track[15] and are not exposed to college-oriented math, science, and literature.

In addition, because such students have little contact with college-bound students, they are less likely to aspire to a college education. Without a vocational or 4-year college education, they have very limited opportunities to obtain high-paying jobs.

When federal or state governments have large budget deficits, public school systems are often victimized by funding cuts.

The small proportion of low-income and minority students who do pursue a college education generally do not have the financial resources to attend prestigious colleges and universities. Also, they have greater difficulty competing academically with wealthier students, partly because they have to work (at least part time) to offset some of their expenses.

Minority students are particularly likely to have inferior educational opportunities. Until 1954, Blacks attended segregated schools in the South that were markedly inferior to those attended by Whites. In 1954 the U.S. Supreme Court, in *Brown* v. *Board of Education*, ruled that racial segregation in public schools was unconstitutional. Although *de jure* (legal) segregation ended, *de facto* (actual) segregation remained in many communities with significant proportions of non-Whites.

Schools in such communities tend to remain segregated because housing is segregated. To deal with this problem, the Supreme Court ruled that school districts must seek racial balance in schools. In some school districts, busing was used to attain a racial balance. Studies indicate that segregation has been reduced *within* school districts but has increased *between* districts.[16] This increase is largely due to "White flight"—that is, Whites leaving the inner cities and moving to suburbs. In some communities, courts have ordered busing between school districts, and some Whites have responded by sending their children to private schools. In many large cities (such as Baltimore, Chicago, Cleveland, and Detroit), public schools are approaching 90% minority enrollment.[17]

In 1991 the Supreme Court declared that busing to achieve integration, when ordered, need not continue indefinitely, although the Court did not say precisely how long is enough. The ruling allows communities to end court-ordered busing if they can convince a judge they have done everything "practicable" to eliminate "vestiges of past discrimination" against minorities. In many inner cities, minority students continue to be segregated in dangerous, crowded, and inferior schools.

Urban Latinos and African Americans are not the only ones who have inferior educational opportunities: Native Americans, Alaskan Eskimo, and migrant workers also lack access to high-quality schools. Many Native Americans attend reservation schools, which are inferior in quality.

For Latinos, bilingual/bicultural education is an issue of intense debate. With bilingual/bicultural

CASE EXHIBIT 10.1

Will the Computer Age Further Divide the Rich and the Poor?

In a 1999 speech to educators in Washington, D.C., William Daley, former secretary of commerce, called attention to the gap in technology skills between young people from more affluent homes (who have computers and Internet access) and those from low-income (often African American or Hispanic) families, who have none. Daley noted, "All this is creating what can be called a digital divide. And it is a divide that is growing. But we can't let this happen. Computer skills are just too important for getting a good job in today's economy."[a]

Not only are poor families less likely to have computers in their homes than affluent families, the school districts in which poor families primarily live are also less likely to have up-to-date computer equipment as compared to more affluent school districts.

Even if poor school districts have computer equipment, the teachers may not be able to upgrade computers on a regularly scheduled basis and may not be able to use newer, expensive equipment such as Smart Boards. Also, the teachers in those districts are less likely to utilize such computer technology, as poor school districts tend to have less qualified teachers.[b]

In our society, practically all those holding higher-paying positions must be computer literate. Those who are not computer literate are increasingly being employed in the lower-paying (often minimum-wage) positions. The advent of the computer age may be a new factor that widens the gap between the rich and the poor.

[a]William Daley, "Bridging the Digital Divide," *Presidents & Prime Ministers*, 8 (Jul. 1999), p. 25.
[b]William Kornblum and Joseph Julian, *Social Problems*, 12th ed. (Upper Saddle River, NJ: Pearson, 2007), pp. 372–373.

education, students are taught wholly or partly in their native language until they can speak English fairly fluently, and in some cases longer. One side argues that preserving the culture and language of minorities is a worthwhile (or essential) goal of public education. The opposing side believes that minority students will be best prepared to compete effectively in American society if they are "immersed" in English-language instruction; moreover, bilingual education is expensive and reinforces separateness because it is a factor in keeping people of color living in ethnic communities.

Critical Thinking Questions

Do you support or oppose using school busing to achieve racial integration? Why?

A few years ago, California banned bilingual education in any publicly funded school. Latino students must now be taught exclusively in English even if they do not understand it.

Given all these factors, it is not surprising that there are significant differences in educational achievement between Whites and African Americans and between Whites and Latinos. Latino and African American students are substantially more likely to drop out of high school as compared to Whites.[18] Latinos and African Americans (as compared to Whites) have substantially higher rates of functional illiteracy. Those who are functionally illiterate are unable to read or write a simple sentence in any language.[19] (There are very few jobs in our society for the functionally illiterate.)

Critical Thinking Question

Do you support or oppose bilingual education in publicly funded schools?

Confusion about the Goals of Education

There is agreement that school systems should teach the basic skills of reading, writing, and arithmetic. However, considerable controversy exists over what other values, knowledge, and skills schools should teach.

- Feminists criticize school systems for teaching and perpetuating sexism—for example, by discouraging females from pursuing careers in science and math (technologically oriented college majors often receive the highest-paying jobs in our society).
- There is controversy over the extent to which school systems should offer educational programs to prevent sexual assaults and date rapes.
- Controversy exists over what roles the schools should play in educating students about sexual harassment and intervening to prevent harassment and bullying.

- There is controversy in some districts about whether to promote, or discourage, bilingual education for students whose primary language is not English.
- With the increasing trend to "mainstream" special education students into regular classes, there is increasing discussion of the rights of the non–special education students to be in a classroom that is not disrupted by the behavior of others.
- Schools have been criticized for helping to perpetuate the class system.
- There is considerable disagreement about the extent to which sex education should be taught in the school system.
- There is disagreement on whether prayers should be allowed in public schools (or before high school athletic events), even though the Supreme Court has ruled that prayers in public schools violate the principle of separation of church and state.
- There is disagreement about the emphasis that should be placed on teaching such subjects as music, sports, and family and consumer education.
- There is disagreement on the extent to which school systems should be used to combat racism, stop drug abuse, prevent unwed pregnancies, help people with a disability, reduce delinquency, and curtail bullying.
- There is controversy over whether schools should focus more on developing the creative thinking capacities of students or on teaching academic content.
- Now that the threat of AIDS has arisen, there is controversy over whether school systems should offer information on contraceptive methods that help to prevent AIDS.
- There is controversy regarding what school systems should teach about same-sex relationships.

In recent years, there has been a conservative trend in our society that has been expressed as a "back-to-basics" movement in school systems. Educational conservatives are opposed to schools being experimental, custodial (for the emotionally disturbed), or recreational facilities and to their offering "frill" and elective courses or "social services" by school social workers. This movement is calling for the establishment of clear standards of achievement for students, "criteria mastery" as the basis for grade promotion, participation by students in varsity sports only when certain grade levels are achieved, increased attention to academic subjects and to the teaching of "core values," more testing and homework, longer school hours, and sterner discipline. The movement also urges that teachers receive salary increases based on merit rather than seniority (the underlying assumption is that such a system would motivate teachers to do a better job in the classroom). The trend toward more standardized testing and/or passing of a general test as a high school graduation requirement is also a part of this movement.

There are controversies, however, within the back-to-basics movement. Are goals such as "learning to get along with others" and "communicating effectively" components of a "basic" education? Are "the basics" the same for all students?

A variety of other questions have been raised about education. Should private schooling be financially supported by refunding to those families who send their children to private schools the amounts they spend on public education through taxes? Should public colleges and universities collect more of their funds through higher student tuitions (which makes it more difficult for students of low-income families to attend)? What changes in school curricula need to be made to train students for the high-technology jobs that are opening up in our society? Clearly there is a need for increased consensus on the priorities and goals in education. This will be difficult to achieve. Similar to a bunch of people standing around trying to figure out how to fix the front porch, everyone has an idea. There appears to be no definitive right or wrong answer. Teachers are not necessarily the experts, and some politicians make careers of criticizing the quality of education in public schools.

Intolerable Working Conditions for Some Teachers

On April 20, 1999, two students who were attending Columbine High School near Denver opened fire on their fellow students and teachers (see Case Exhibit 10.2). Twelve students and one teacher were shot to death, and 21 additional students were injured. The two shooters then shot and killed themselves. The tragedy was the most deadly at that time of numerous shootings that have taken place in school settings. Bomb threats occur yearly in almost all school districts, causing considerable stress to students, parents, and teachers.[20]

CASE EXHIBIT 10.2

What Caused the Columbine Massacre?

The massacre at Columbine High School, near Denver, Colorado, was the most devastating school shooting in U.S. history. On April 20, 1999, two students attacked the school of 1,945 students. During lunch hour, in less than 15 minutes, student gunmen Eric Harris (age 18) and Dylan Klebold (age 17) shot and killed 12 students and one teacher and wounded 21 people. The gunmen apparently wanted to kill as many people as possible. The massacre could have been worse. Harris and Klebold had also placed more than 30 bombs in the school but were not able to detonate them because the police responded quickly. When police arrived, Eric Harris killed himself by firing a shotgun shell into his mouth. Dylan Klebold apparently killed himself by shooting himself in the right temple.

Why did Harris and Klebold commit these horrendous crimes? We will never fully know because both killed themselves before they could be questioned. However, Eric Harris left a diary as well as notes on his computer that provide us with substantial clues to the thought processes of the two gunmen. (The two gunmen had linked their personal computers on a network.)

The diary indicated the two teenagers planned to kill upward of 500 students in their school using guns and homemade bombs. They also planned to attack other schools and then run into the surrounding neighborhood and the downtown area and kill neighbors on the street and in apartment buildings. Finally, they intended to either escape the United States and go live on an island or hijack an airplane and crash it into the heart of New York City. They had been planning the attack on Columbine High for about a year.

Some of the thought processes of Eric Harris that were in his diary are as follows:

I hate the f _ _ _ _ world.... If you recall your history, the Nazis came up with a "Final Solution" to the Jewish problem: Kill them all. Well in case you haven't figured it out yet, I say "Kill mankind." No one should survive....I live in Denver, and dammit, I would love to kill almost all of its residents.

Harris railed against every conceivable person of color, expressing his hate in very negative terms. Harris had a nondiscriminating hate against practically everyone, according to a source who has read the diary, including rich people, poor people, martial arts experts, Star Wars fans, people who mispronounce words, people who drive slowly in the fast lane, and so on.

The diary indicated the two gunmen planned to take their lives if cornered by the police, which they did. The diary also indicated they just wanted to achieve notoriety, which they did, by hurting and killing as many people as they could. According to the diary, they also thought they were being teased, abused, and mistreated by other students at Columbine High. Harris and Klebold admired Hitler, Nazism, and Nazism's "Final Solution." Harris and Klebold viewed themselves as being superior to others, to the extent that they thought they constituted a *two-man master race*.

SOURCE: Dave Cullen, "'Kill Mankind. No One Should Survive,'" Sept. 23, 1999, available at http://www.salon.com/news/feature/1999/09/23/journal.

In surveys, half of all teachers say that, if they had the opportunity to choose careers again, they would not select teaching.[21] Many factors contribute to disenchantment with teaching: low pay, low prestige, inadequate preparation, increased alternative job opportunities for women, and intolerable working conditions. College graduates can earn substantially more money in many other areas: accounting, engineering, computer science, or sales, for example.

Intolerable working conditions in school systems include some teachers in secondary schools being threatened by students and even being physically attacked. Cyberbullying of teachers and principals is occurring more frequently. In some schools, teachers spend as much time trying to keep peace and order (babysitting) as they do teaching. There are high rates of drug and alcohol abuse among students, and teachers are forced to confront this issue, often without much preparation. Many school districts have insufficient instructional supplies. High student-to-teacher ratios are another concern—the more students, the more difficult it is for teachers to give individualized instruction.

Many teachers do not feel adequately prepared to teach protective behavior (such as how to protect oneself against sexual assaults), alcohol and drug abuse education, and similar topics.

An amazing statistic is that fewer than one in five new teachers is still in the profession after 10 years;[22] many leave because of the distressing working conditions. The United States ranks last of all the major industrialized nations in how generously it compensates its teachers.[23]

On April 20, 1999, two students at Columbine High School (near Denver) opened fire on fellow students and their teachers. Twelve students and one teacher were shot to death. This memorial commemorates the tragic event.

School Bullying and Cyberbullying

Each day, an estimated 160,000 students in the United States refuse to go to school because they dread the verbal and physical aggression of their peers.[24] Many more students attend school in a chronic state of depression and anxiety. Bullying can be physical, verbal, or emotional; and is usually repeated over a period of time.

Physical bullying includes shoving, kicking, punching, pushing, tickling, headlocks, school pranks, teasing, fighting, inappropriate touching, and use of available objects as weapons. Verbal bullying includes directing profanity at the victim; name calling; commenting negatively on someone's appearance, clothes, body, and so on; tormenting; and harassment. Emotional bullying includes spreading malicious rumors, harassment, whispering to another in front of the victim, face-making, eye rolling, keeping the victim out of a group, and the silent treatment.

Cyberbullying is any bullying done through the use of technology. Cyberbullying can be as simple as continuing to send e-mails to someone who has said she or he wants no further contact with the sender. It may also include threats, sexual remarks, hate speech, and posting false statements as facts aimed at humiliation. It may include disclosing the victim's personal data (e.g., name and address) on websites and then publishing material in the victim's name that defames or ridicules the victim. It includes sending embarrassing (including nude) pictures of the victim to others.

The American Society for the Prevention of Cruelty to Children describes the effects of bullying and cyberbullying on victims:

Bullying can result in reluctance to go to school and truancy, headaches and stomach pains, reduced appetite, shame, anxiety, irritability, aggression and depression. Bullying is a direct attack on a student's status, sense of belonging and core identity, and often results in low self-esteem. The effects of bullying often continue many years into adulthood. In the most extreme cases, targets have taken out their anger and despair through school shootings or by committing suicide.[25]

The American Society for the Prevention of Cruelty to Children also describes the effects of bullying on school systems:

For the school, the costs of bullying are countless hours consumed in tackling a problem that is resistant to change, truancies, reduced student retention, low teacher morale, negative perceptions of the school by the wider community and parent hostility. The school campus becomes a place where diverse youth are marginalized and where no–one feels safe. As students become alienated from school, academic performance declines. Schools are increasingly sued for failing to provide a safe learning environment and are being held liable for the harassment, violence and suicides caused by bullying.[26]

Strategies to Improve Education

Michael Rutter and his associates evaluated a number of high schools and concluded what most parents already know: "Schools do indeed have important impact on children's development, and it does matter what school a child attends."[27] Rutter found that the best schools required more homework, maintained high academic standards, had well-understood and well-enforced discipline standards, and yet created a comfortable and supportive atmosphere for students.[28] This section will examine four proposals for improving the school system: increased incentives for teachers, improvement of the curriculum, parental choice of schools, and expanded preschool programs.

Increase Incentives for Teachers

Perhaps the only way to encourage more high-quality college students to enter the teaching profession, and to raise the morale of existing teachers, is to increase incentives for teaching. Incentives might include increased pay, expanded in-service training, provision of sufficient school supplies, increased availability for classroom use of high-tech equipment (computers, film, and videotape equipment), and improved working conditions.

A controversial recommendation is the creation of a "master teacher" rank that would recognize and reward ability and dedication to teaching. There is growing evidence that superior teaching can have immense positive effects on students. Pedersen and Faucher found a high correlation between outstanding first-grade teaching and later adult success of students, all of whom came from an inner-city neighborhood.[29] Master teachers would be paid substantially more and have added responsibilities, such as curriculum design and supervision of new teachers. Teachers' unions have generally opposed the concept, fearing that criteria other than ability and dedication (such as favoritism) will be used in making such selections. Unions also tend to be opposed to basing higher pay and promotion on merit because the merit concept conflicts with the preferred union concept of basing pay on seniority.

To assist new teachers so they have a better experience and thereby an increased desire to stay in education, some school districts now use mentoring systems. The new teacher has someone (who is experienced in teaching at that school and who is not a supervisor) to rely on for advice and support. This mentor is a guide, a support system, and a knowledge resource in teaching styles and curriculum.

Improve the Curriculum

If few new resources are required, practically everyone is in favor of this proposal. However, a major question is: In what directions should the curriculum be improved? As noted earlier, considerable confusion exists as to the goals of a quality education. In the 1960s and early 1970s, there was criticism of the rigidity and authoritarianism in schools, which led to increases in the number of electives in high schools and colleges and a reduction in the number of basic "academic" classes. Alternative schools were created for students who found traditional schools to be "stifling." History and social studies classes were revised to include content on significant contributions made by Native Americans, African Americans, Latinos, and other minority groups. New courses were developed that attempted to make schoolwork more relevant to the lives of minority students.

In the past five decades, concern has shifted. There is a focus on the decline in academic achievement, and school systems are returning to "stiffer" academic programs. In fact, many of the requirements for basic academic courses that were dropped in the 1960s and early 1970s have been reinstated. There has been a move toward teaching basic skills (reading, writing, and arithmetic) and away from teaching electives (sociology, psychology, or specialized areas of literature and history). As part of this movement, children are also taught to respect authority, be patriotic, and lead moral lives. Some schools have reestablished strict dress codes and sought to curb unconventional behavior.

Consistent with the back-to-basics movement, Congress passed, and President George W. Bush signed, a bill in 2002 that requires all states to test students in the third through the eighth grades annually in math and reading. (See Case Exhibit 10.3: No Child Left Behind.)

At the same time, a critical thinking movement is taking place, which focuses on developing the thinking capacities of students. This approach encourages students to make observations and to critically analyze issues. It stresses class discussions and downplays lectures, emphasizes critical analysis over rote learning, and advocates assessing student understanding through use of essay tests rather than objective tests. In some ways, the critical thinking movement conflicts with the back-to-basics movement. The latter places greater emphasis on learning and remembering facts; the former asserts that memorizing is much less important than developing thinking capacities. The critical thinking movement has fueled the expansion of advanced placement classes where students can receive some college credit while still in high school.

Another debate centers around computer-based or aided instruction. Computers are and will be a part of the educational experience—but will the benefits outweigh the shortcomings? Will basic spelling and math computation become ignored so that the student will not be able to write a coherent letter or figure out the comparative costs of two items without a palm-size computer?

Americans agree that our educational system needs to be improved, but there is vast disagreement on what the curriculum goals should be.

Critical Thinking Questions

Which approach do you believe will better improve education—the back-to-basics movement or the critical thinking movement? Why?

Allow Parental Choice of Schools

Under a parental choice system, not only are parents entitled to enroll their children in public schools outside their geographic district, but state tax dollars go to the school that wins the enrollment. By creating market incentives, the thinking goes, academically superior schools should thrive, while inferior schools would either have to improve their performance or face bankruptcy. A voucher system is usually used for implementing a parental choice system; the voucher system is a program in which the government gives vouchers to students that may be used to pay for education at any school that they or their parents choose.

CASE EXHIBIT 10.3

No Child Left Behind—Will It Be Discontinued?

President George W. Bush's education plan, No Child Left Behind (NCLB), was signed into law in January 2002. It has the following concepts, principles, and provisions:

The Challenge: For too long, America's education system has not been accountable for results and too many children have been locked in underachieving schools and left behind.

The Solution: Information is power; testing and gathering independent data are the ways to get information into the hands of parents, educators, and taxpayers.

Testing: Until teachers and parents recognize what their students know and can do, they can't help them improve. Testing will raise expectations for *all* students and ensure that no child slips through the cracks.

- Every state must set clear and high standards for what students in each grade should know and be able to do in the core academic subjects of reading, math, and science.

- States will measure each student's progress toward those standards with tests aligned with those higher standards.

- Test scores will be broken out by economic background, race and ethnicity, English proficiency, and disability. That way parents and teachers will know the academic achievement of each group of students and can work to ensure that no child will be left behind.

- Testing tells parents, communities, educators, and school boards which schools are doing well. If a school takes a challenging population and achieves great results, testing will show that. If a school is allowing certain groups to fall behind year after year, testing will expose that too.

- Every child in grades three through eight, and in one grade in high school, will be tested annually as to their math and reading abilities.

(continued)

CASE EXHIBIT 10.3 *(continued)*

Accountability: States must describe how they will close the achievement gap and make sure all students, including those who are disadvantaged, achieve academic proficiency. They must produce annual state and school district report cards that inform parents and communities about state and school progress. Schools that do not make progress must provide supplemental services, such as free tutoring or after-school assistance; take corrective actions; and, if still not making adequate yearly progress after 5 years, make dramatic changes to the way the school is run. Scores in lower-scoring school systems must show annual improvement; the goal is for all students to reach proficiency in math and reading in 12 years. Lagging schools will receive up to $1,000 per child from the federal government; however, if these schools don't improve after 3 years, pupils may transfer to another public or charter school. Under the legislation, schools with low scores that do not improve after 5 years will have to replace poorly performing staff or develop new curriculum.

The program has been functioning now for over a decade. It has now become clear that NCLB is problematic, for a variety of reasons. For example, accountability efforts required that, to make adequate progress, all student groups (e.g., African American, White, Hispanic, Native American, students with a disability, those of limited English proficiency) must obtain a set level of achievement in both mathematics and reading. If one student group does not reach the set levels, then the entire school receives a failing grade, and is subject to severe sanctions. (A few years after 2002 the original NCLB regulations were changed to allow for alternative testing of students with a disability and for those with limited English proficiency. In addition, because many schools were "Failing," the deadlines for making adequate yearly progress in mathematics and reading were extended to 2014 for all states.)

There have been additional concerns, including the following:

- NCLB provides an incentive for school systems to encourage students who are low scoring on the standardized tests to drop out, so that those students' scores will not adversely impact the school's average scores in the future.
- The focus on standardized testing (all students in a state taking the same test under the same conditions) encourages teachers to teach a narrow subset of skills that increase test performance rather than teaching students to be creative, critical thinkers.

- Some schools are only focusing their instruction on core subjects (reading, writing, mathematics, and science). As a result, programs such as art appreciation and health education are receiving very little attention. Instruction in the following areas appears to have decreased as a result of NCLB—the arts, elementary social studies, physical education, foreign languages, history, civics, and literature.
- Standardized tests in English are "culturally biased" against students who are learning English as a second language. The schools that provide English as a second language are also adversely impacted by the standardized test.
- Schools have little incentive to teach gifted students to meet their potential.
- When teachers feel they must "teach to the test," they risk losing the "teachable moments" when children are inspired to explore new areas of learning and develop their creative thinking capacities.
- Critics of NCLB argue that it unfairly burdens the states, which must pay for most of the financial costs of NCLB.
- Test scores on adequate yearly progress have not significantly improved in recent years.
- The Black–White achievement gap (with Whites attaining higher test scores) remains considerably large.
- Other developed nations continue to surpass U.S. performance on international assessments.

In February, 2012, President Barack Obama "freed" 10 states from the strict and sweeping requirements of NCLB. The move is probably a tacit acknowledgement that the law's main goal, getting all students to a set level in mathematics and reading by 2014, is not within reach. A total of 28 other states have signaled that they too are going to ask for this "freed" waiver.

Under the waiver, the states must show they will prepare children for college and careers, set new targets for improving achievements among all students, develop meaningful teacher and principal systems, reward the best-performing schools, and focus help on the ones doing the worst.

SOURCES: Department of Education, *No Child Left Behind Is Working* (Washington, DC: U.S. Department of Education, 2006); Linda A. Mooney, David Knox, and Caroline Schacht, *Understanding Social Problems*, 8th ed. (Belmont, CA: Wadsworth/Cengage Learning, 2013), pp. 253–255.

Parental choice of schools is currently being tried in a number of states. Initial findings indicate that the reasons parents and students opt out of one school for another are often unrelated to academics.[30] In some cases, the parents select schools with lower educational standards to increase the chances that their son or daughter will graduate—or will graduate with higher grades. Other parents pick schools near their work for convenience reasons. Some parents select

schools that will increase the chances of their son or daughter playing on a varsity sports team. In many cases, transportation problems force parents to select the school closest to their home.

A major problem with parental choice of schools is that it has the potential to undermine the neighborhood school concept. This concept holds that the neighborhood school should be a center of community living, with its facilities used by both youngsters

CASE EXHIBIT 10.4

Becoming a Creative, Critical Thinker Is the Essence of Education

New trends and ideas seem to be forever occurring in education. While some educational theorists rediscover the "3Rs," others imagine computer workstations on every desk. Among teachers, there is a growing distrust of the "idea of the month" and a renewed interest in doing what they do best—teaching. In this atmosphere Alfie Kohn is a contemporary writer who is interested more in what teachers do than in the latest curricular movement of the newest program to change American educators. At the same time, he has published provocative critiques of the educational establishment. In *The Schools Our Children Deserve*, Kohn asserts that turning students into enthusiastic learners is more important than what is learned.[a] Kohn asks,

> What's wrong with this picture—Abigail is given plenty of worksheets to complete in class as well as a substantial amount of homework. She studies to get good grades, and her school is proud of its high standardized test scores. Outstanding students are publicly recognized by the use of honor rolls, awards assemblies, and bumper stickers. Abigail's teacher, a charismatic lecturer, is clearly in control of the class: students raise their hands and wait patiently to be recognized. The teacher prepares detailed lesson plans well ahead of time, uses the latest textbooks, and gives regular quizzes to make sure kids stay on track.[b]

His answer is: "Just about everything."[c] He argues that memorization of facts, endless drills of multiplication problems, blind obedience to the teacher, long periods of time sitting behind desks, and the latest fad of standardized tests and graduation requirements harm the educational process more than they help it. Kohn is an outspoken critic of using standardized tests as a means of measuring educational achievement. He asserts standardized testing needlessly pits students against one another and ultimately leads to mediocrity. When students become obsessed with how well they're doing in school, they often lose interest in what they're doing, and ultimately they think less deeply. Worse, he asserts that when standardized tests are used to measure how well students are doing, intellectual life is squeezed out of classrooms, and the

classrooms then become test-prep centers. The "back-to-basics" philosophy of teaching treats children as passive receptacles into which forgettable facts are poured. Standardized tests force teachers to spend time preparing to take them instead of helping the students to become critical, creative thinkers.

Kohn then argues in "Punished by Rewards? A Conversation with Alfie Kohn" that teachers need to bribe students to learn and excessively praise those who do because the process of learning is fundamentally boring and inefficient.[d]

He asserts that a better teaching and learning equation is one in which learning is regarded as an active process in which students need to be given a creative and active role, and he argues that the product of learning is not facts and skills. Although the learning of facts and skills will occur, he asserts the key product of learning is the development of an ability to critically, creatively, and individually think and problem solve. The essence of teaching is involving students in a community—their classroom. Students are involved in processes such as cooperative learning (group problem solving), mentoring relationships (with older and/or younger students), and hypothesis-testing experiments that build an ability and a desire to learn. To Kohn, standardized testing cannot measure what is ultimately most important—the ability to think for oneself.

As might be expected, Kohn's ideas have been met with considerable skepticism and criticism. Yet he is an example of a theorist who can think "outside of the box," and in this way is a model for social workers who know some of the old methods just do not work. We all need to be open to new ways of solving complex problems.

[a]Alfie Kohn, *The Schools Our Children Deserve: Moving beyond Traditional Classrooms and "Tougher Standards"* (New York: Houghton Mifflin, 1999).
[b]Ibid., p. 1.
[c]Ibid.
[d]Ron Brandt, "Punished by Rewards? A Conversation with Alfie Kohn," *Educational Leadership*, 53, no. 1 (Sept. 1995).

and adults for a variety of purposes: education, recreation, leisure activities, social gatherings, sporting events, and community meetings. If parents in a neighborhood send their children to different schools, the neighborhood school will not become a center of community life.

Another drawback of parental choice is that many children are not in a position to travel to faraway schools. These children (some of whom are already educationally disadvantaged) may then be "left behind" in the worst districts, which become further

impoverished as money follows students to better-financed schools. Another issue would be special education students and students who have behavior problems. These children might not be accepted in private schools, leaving them isolated in public schools whose funds may be sharply reduced due to the transfer of the brightest students to private schools.

In addition, providing federal or state funds to parochial schools raises constitutional questions as to whether such an approach violates the principle of separation of church and state.

Critical Thinking Questions

Do you support or oppose the parental choice system? Why?

Some authorities in the United States advocate an increase in the number of *charter schools*, as a way of improving school systems. Charter schools are publicly funded elementary or secondary schools that have been freed from the regulations, rules, and statutes that apply to other public schools in exchange for some type of accountability for producing certain results. The results are specified in each schools charter. An example of a specified charter result is "improved educational outcomes."

The founders of charter schools are often parents, teachers, or activists who feel restricted by traditional public schools. State-run charter schools (schools not affiliated with local school districts) are often established by universities, nonprofit groups, or some government entities. The rules and structures of charter schools depend on state authorizing legislation and differ from state to state charter schools, like school vouchers, are designed to expand schooling options and to increase the quality of education through competition. Studies of the educational achievement of students who attend charter schools indicate the students achieve at about the same levels as students who attend traditional public schools.[31]

Expand Preschool Programs

There is increasing evidence that the most cost-effective approach to improving the results of education is to expand the number of preschool programs so that many more preschool children can be enrolled. There is considerable research indicating that attending a quality preschool program will have a number of long-term positive effects.

Recent results from a 25-year Chicago longitudinal study found that low-income children who had a high-quality early education program were more likely to graduate from high school and less likely to be arrested.[32]

Noreen S. Ahmed–Ullah states:

The report shows children who attended an established preschool program in Chicago Public Schools completed high school at higher rates, improved living standards, stayed out of jail and had less likelihood of substance abuse into adulthood.[33]

The 1,400 children in the study attended high-quality preschools that (a) had a focus on language arts and numerical skills, (b) emphasized intense parental involvement, and (c) had well-paid and highly educated teachers.

In 1999 the University of North Carolina reported that high-quality child care starting in infancy had a positive long-term educational effect.[34] UNC's Abecedarian Project followed up with approximately 100 infants who enrolled in the study two decades previously. The study found that low-income children who received early educational intervention had higher reading and math skills, as well as moderately higher cognitive test scores.

The Perry Preschool Project studied 123 African American children from low-income families in Ypsilanti, Michigan.[35] The children were randomly divided into an experimental group that received a high-quality preschool program and a control group that was not enrolled in a preschool program. The preschool program was staffed by a team of four highly trained teachers. Most of the 58 children in the experimental group participated in the program for 2 years, at the ages of 3 and 4. The children in the two groups were followed then until age 27. The results were dramatic. The children in the experimental group had higher scholastic performance during the school years, had lower arrest rates, had higher-paying jobs, had lower rates of receiving welfare assistance, had higher graduation rates from high school, were less likely to have births outside of marriage, and had higher rates of attending college.

These studies suggest that high-quality preschool programs have long-term benefits for those children who attend and for the broader society. Quality preschool programs have proved to improve the following for those enrolled:

- Social and emotional skills
- Language, reading, and math skills
- Cognitive development
- Positive attachments and relationships to the mother, caregivers, and peers
- Their future: higher incomes, higher educational achievement, improved marital status, and higher-status employment

In addition, attending quality preschool programs reduces the chances of the following:

- Failure to pass a grade level and enrollment in a special education program
- Criminal behavior and delinquency
- Aggressive and problem behavior

A student in a special education program receives individualized, one-to-one instruction.

Sadly, in too many child-care programs in our society, wages are low, there is overcrowding, staff morale is low, and many of the staff are not educated as teachers.

Critical Thinking Question

Do you believe programs such as Head Start (for low-income children) should be expanded and the quality of preschools improved? Such an approach may be the most cost-effective way of improving the quality of education in this country.

Toward Equal Educational Opportunity

As we've seen, educational opportunities are often lacking for minorities and the poor in this country. Nearly everyone agrees that there should be equal educational opportunity for all. But there is considerable disagreement on how this can be achieved.

Three proposals for progressing toward equal educational opportunity are:

1. Reforming school financing so that an equal amount of money is spent on each student's education
2. Establishing special compensatory educational programs for disadvantaged students
3. Integrating students from different ethnic backgrounds into the same school

Reform of School Financing

Schools in wealthy districts tend to receive considerably more money per student than schools in poor districts. Currently, a majority of the revenue for school districts in practically all states comes from local property taxes. Decaying inner cities are especially hard-pressed to finance school systems, and many schools in these areas are inferior.

There is growing opposition in the United States to using property tax dollars as the primary source of revenue for funding school systems. Taxpayers on fixed incomes (such as the retired elderly) are increasingly unable to pay large annual increases in their property tax bills. In 1993 taxpayers in Michigan voted to abolish using property tax revenues to fund the public school system in that state. In 1994 voters in Michigan approved a constitutional amendment to raise the state sales tax and cigarette tax as the primary sources of supporting the state's schools. One result of this action in Michigan is movement toward equalizing among school districts the amount of money spent on each student's education.[36] Some other states are moving in a similar direction.

Another suggestion for equalizing the amount of money spent on each student's education is for the federal government to pay for all primary and secondary education, giving the same amount of money per student to each school. Critics of this approach assert that schools in this country have excelled because of local control and involvement. If the funding shifted to the federal government, critics say, the result would be greater federal control and increased red tape, meaning that a huge federal bureaucracy would undoubtedly evolve.

Compensatory Education

Many authorities believe that special programs and extra assistance would improve achievement levels of the poor and minorities. A variety of programs already exist.

Most school districts have pupil services departments that seek to assess the academic, social, and emotional needs of children who are not progressing well in school. Once an assessment of a child is completed, programs are developed to meet the unique learning needs of the child. A wide variety of services may be provided depending on the identified needs. There are special classes for the emotionally disturbed and for those with learning disabilities. Counseling is sometimes provided. Some students are referred for drug abuse, and some are referred for visual or hearing difficulties. Pupil services departments are staffed by a variety of professionals— school psychologists, social workers, and guidance counselors. In 1975 Congress passed the Education for All Handicapped Children Act, now known as PL 94-142. This law addresses the numerous physical, developmental, learning, and social–emotional problems that hamper the education of children. In sweeping legislation, the law mandated that all school districts identify students with these problems

and then develop specialized programs to meet their needs. Unfortunately, many low-income school districts, because of financial constraints, have not been able to meet the objectives of this bill. (The 2004 Individuals with Disabilities Act has replaced PL 94-142—see Case Exhibit 10.5.)

In many states, programs are being developed to prevent children from dropping out of school. Dropping out represents an enormous loss to those individuals and to society because of lost potential productivity. The estimated lifetime earnings of high school graduates are more than $200,000 higher than those of dropouts.[37] Programs for "at-risk" students are a response to the need to help high school students stay in school and learn practical job skills.

Some elementary and secondary school systems now have reading, writing, and arithmetic programs during the summer for students who need assistance in these areas. A variety of compensatory educational programs have been established at the college level as well. These include noncredit courses in English and mathematics, tutoring, and various testing programs. Many colleges have special provisions for the admission of minority students who do not meet standard admission requirements, and these students are encouraged to utilize the educational opportunity programs that are available. (Students who attended inferior elementary and secondary school systems in inner cities are often two to four grade levels behind in reading, writing, and arithmetic and therefore need educational opportunity programs to have a chance to succeed in college.) Some states, such as Florida, now have scholarship programs to provide higher-education funds to low-income high school students who academically are doing well in high school.

Educational opportunity programs have become an accepted part of most colleges and universities. A stickier question involves special admissions of minority students to graduate and professional schools. Supporters believe that these affirmative action admissions are attempts to compensate for the inferior school systems and other discriminations that minorities have been subjected to in the past. On the other hand, because competition is intense for the limited admissions into these schools, White students complain that they are the victims of reverse discrimination—that they are being rejected even though their entrance exam scores are higher than those of some minority students who are accepted. The legal status of this affirmative action policy has not as yet been fully resolved.

Effective Integration

As discussed earlier, school busing has been used to attempt to integrate students within school districts. Many Whites in large cities have responded by moving to suburbs or sending their children to private schools. Some big cities, through court orders, are experimenting with merging suburban school districts with inner-city school districts and then busing children within each district. The extent to which such merging will occur is questionable. There is a major problem with distance, as some suburban communities are so far from inner cities that students would have to spend a large part of their day on a bus. Most White parents in suburbs would not raise serious objections to a small number of inner-city children being bused to their schools in the suburbs. However, most suburbanites (fearing potential violence and a lower-quality education) would object to their children being bused to inferior school systems in inner cities. Many White parents, if faced with such a court order, would probably respond by placing their children in private schools.

The ideal way to integrate neighborhood schools is through integration of residential areas so that neighborhood schools are then automatically integrated. Such integration would provide ongoing opportunities for interracial cooperation and friendships for children and for adults. The chances of this proposal working, however, are minute. People of different ethnic and racial groups generally are reluctant to live together in the same neighborhood. In addition, many members of minority groups cannot afford to live in affluent neighborhoods, and White residents of such neighborhoods object to having low-cost housing built in their communities.

Another possible avenue toward integration is through the use of "magnet" schools in cities. Magnet schools are ones that offer special courses, programs, or equipment. Examples would be a fine arts middle school or high school and a school emphasizing curriculum in the area of computer science. Proponents of magnet schools hope that placing such schools in inner-city areas would draw students from suburbs because of the excellent educational opportunities they could offer.

The prospects of significant federal help for inner-city schools in the near future are not bright. In this era of trying to reduce the federal deficit through budget cutbacks, the chances of the enactment of a bold new federal program to channel resources to financially distressed school districts are remote.

John E. Farley summarizes the significance to all Americans of providing equal educational opportunities for minorities and the poor:

If the overall effectiveness of the educational system is poor, American productivity will suffer, and our standard of living will likely fall in our increasingly competitive world. Likewise, if we fail the large and growing proportion of our young people who are African American, Hispanic, or from low-income homes of any race, the result will be the same. Failing to educate those who account for such a large and growing share of the future labor force will have a similar destructive impact on America's productivity and its standard of living.[38]

Curbing Bullying and Cyberbullying

Kidpower is a nonprofit leader in bullying and cyberbullying prevention. It recommends the following safety actions that parents, schools, and school children should take:[39]

1. *Address bullying.* Bullying is a destructive force in the lives of many children.
2. *Make bullying against the rules.* Schools need to have a clear written Violence and Harassment Prevention Policy. If a school does not have such a policy, parents need to advocate that such a policy be developed. Parents also need to be role models for their children by not allowing people to bully them.
3. *Teach children to be alert, calm, and confident.* Bullies tend to pick on children who act scared. An alert, assertive presentation of self often stops most bullying before it starts.
4. *Teach children target denial skills.* Target denial is an official martial arts technique that means, "Don't be there." Physically, it means to seek to avoid being around a bully. Emotionally, it means to respond to attempts at emotional harassment by seeking to leave by smiling and cheerfully saying "No thanks," instead of acting scared or angry.
5. *Teach children the protective power of words.* Kidpower states:

Teach kids to protect themselves from hurtful words by imagining throwing them into a trashcan instead of taking them inside their hearts or their heads.

Teach kids not to let insults, rude behavior, or guilt trips trigger them into feeling intimidated or emotionally coerced by a bully. Kids need to learn how not to let what others say or do control their choices. They also need to learn how not to behave in emotionally damaging ways towards others. Teach kids how to set clear strong verbal boundaries in a respectful assertive way with people they know.[40]

6. *Teach children to defend themselves physically.*
   As a last resort, when children cannot physically leave a bully, they need to have learned how they can hurt the bully so that the bully will no longer seek to hurt them.
7. *Teach children to get help.*
   Kidpower states:

   Most of the time kids just need someone to listen so they won't feel alone. Being able to talk about problems can help a child figure out what to do and put things into perspective—getting our kids into the habit of talking to us can also alert us to more serious issues.[41]

8. *Give children the chance to practice.*
   Parents and teachers can teach children how to use the above techniques by role-playing possible bullying scenarios with them. Children learn more by doing than by being told what to do.

In addition, Suppes and Wells assert that school systems should model zero tolerance for bullying. Teachers should not bully students. Nonteaching staff should not be allowed to bully students. Administrators should not be allowed to bully teachers and staff. Coaches should not be allowed to bully athletes. There should be zero tolerance of parents who seek to bully teachers. There should be zero tolerance of cyberbullying.[42]

Parents and teachers can use the following suggestions to curb cyberbullying:

1. Instruct students to never pass along harmful or cruel messages or images.
2. Train students to delete suspicious e-mail messages without opening them.
3. At home, parents need to supervise their children's time online. Placing the computer in a common area is a step in this direction.
4. Schools need to develop a formal policy for curbing cyberbullying.
5. Instruct students on how to block communication from cyberbullies.

6. Encourage students to assertively ask friends who are cyberbullying to stop.
7. Encourage parents and teachers to talk to students about the importance of telling a teacher or parent about any cyberbullying that they become aware of.
8. Parents and teachers need to investigate the reasons why a student is withdrawn, depressed, or reluctant to attend school or social events.

School Social Workers: A Response to Crisis*

Given the problems within the educational system and the societal difficulties that schools have been asked to erase, it is not surprising that specialists, such as school social workers, have become part of the school system. School social work is a relatively new role. Before 1960 there were few school social workers, and they were employed primarily by large urban school systems (for example, New York City and Chicago). In fact, one of the earliest papers on school social workers was first published in 1955.[43] School social work, then, must be discussed within the context of its evolving role.

Before doing this, however, it is necessary to have a method of analyzing behavior so that we have an initial base for understanding the nature of children's problems in schools. It is a practical necessity for any school social

EP 2.1.10a

worker to understand the dynamics of behavior because social workers have been and will continue to be closely involved with problematic behavior in children. In 1975 Congress enacted the Education for all Handicapped Children Act (now known as Individuals with Disabilities Education Act). This statute mandates that each local school district must provide full and appropriate educational opportunities to all children with a disability. Much of the definition of social work services offered in Individuals with Disabilities Education Act specifies (a) defining the nature of social or behavioral problems, (b) using individual or family counseling skills, and (c) using other resources to make an impact on behavioral, emotional, and social problems.

---

*This section was written especially for this text by Don Nolan, MSSW, school social worker.

In 2005 President George W. Bush signed the most recent reauthorization of what is now known as the Individuals with Disabilities Education Act. The reauthorization is closely linked with what has been termed No Child Left Behind (NCLB) legislation, described earlier in this chapter. NCLB mandates that public school students, regardless of disability, economic status, ethnicity, or native language, need to meet state academic standards in reading, language arts (primarily writing skills), math, science, and social studies. In essence, by the year 2014, students will be expected to have grade-level academic skills in these areas. Yearly testing in specified grades (third, fourth, fifth, sixth, seventh, eighth, and one year in high school) will monitor every child in every public school district in the country.

Thus, the identification of students with behavioral, emotional, and/or motivational difficulties is now only the first step in providing educational services to students with disabilities. To "pass" the mandated state academic tests, there now will need to be programs that treat these difficulties so that the difficulties interfere minimally with academic achievement. Such legislation provides a new opportunity for school social workers—both as treatment (counseling) specialists and as professionals who can provide research expertise on "what works" in areas such as mental health treatment and substance abuse prevention and in areas that relate to resiliency (the ability to overcome adversity) and youth development programs.

Additionally, the federal government's NCLB achievement mandates are now being applied to special education students. Specialized and individualized education, not remedial education, must be offered to these students in order to increase their chances of achieving a year's academic progress (as measured by test scores) in a school year. Many special education students have "achievement gaps" because their test scores are apt to be lower than those students in regular classes. When placed in a special education program, nearly all these students have a need for special education programming because of their academic delays. There is a need for school social work services for these students because many have difficulties in motivation, high anxiety levels, and emotional self-control issues. Such problems need to be dealt with in order to increase the likelihood that these students will progress academically.

The Nature of Behavior

We will begin with the premise that behavior is purposeful—that we do things for a reason. We may not always know exactly why we are doing something because we don't analyze each of our behaviors. But we always respond to a given situation with a set of beliefs, with a history of past attempts to solve a problem, and within the context of our present environment.[44]

In using his rational–emotive behavior therapy, Albert Ellis looks at behavior within the context of what he calls its ABCs. In essence, he says when a highly charged emotional consequence (C) follows a significant activating event (A), Event A may seem to, but actually does not, cause C. Instead, emotional consequences are largely created by the individual's belief system (B). An example follows.[45]

A. Activating event: Someone calls you a jerk.
B. Your belief system: "He's right, I am a useless, unworthy, selfish person. I didn't know my shortcomings were that obvious to others. I need to apologize and then quietly leave."
C. Your emotional consequence: Depression and feelings of inferiority and guilt.

This belief system not only determines the emotional consequence (C), it also primarily determines how the person will react to A. In the above example, the person is apt to apologize for the actions that led to being called a jerk and then slowly walk away.

This belief system is based, no matter what our age, on opinions we have about ourselves and others in relation to our perceptions about our place in the larger world. The person, then, can decide on a course of action given certain circumstances. Children, like adults, do not act in a random fashion. They act in relation to decisions they have made about the consistency and stability of their relationships with adults and other children. There are antecedents of behavior that often depend on *decisions* they have made about their abilities, not on their *actual* abilities. Thus, although it may seem that a girl is misbehaving when she approaches new situations, in reality she may have decided from past experience that she will have little success in the task and is thus misbehaving because she does not want to face the fear of another failure. The child has made a decision, although it may be based on what can be termed a *mistaken belief system*.[46] She wrongly assumes that failure means she is worthless and that trying is not important. To understand how to alter that self-perception, one must look more closely at some primary goals of behavior.

Similar to Ellis, Rudolf Dreikurs postulated that the force behind every human action is a goal. We all know some of what we want, although often we do not consciously act on those goals but rather on unanalyzed means of achieving them. It is possible to understand the psychological motivation of the child if one develops diagnostic skills to analyze four goals of misbehavior: attention getting, power seeking, revenge seeking, and assuming a disability.[47] Some children try to get attention, to always be the focal point for others, because they believe that otherwise they are worthless. Other children attempt to prove their power in the belief that only if they can do what they want and defy adult pressure can they be important. Still others may seek revenge: The only means by which they feel significant is to hurt others, just as they feel hurt by them. Others may display actual or imaginary disabilities in order to receive sympathy or be left alone so that nothing is demanded of them. The crucial point is that, whatever behaviors children display, there are always reasons for them.

Anyone who has worked extensively with children in any situation can readily remember youngsters who were acting out these goals. For example, Ted, who is constantly in front of the teacher interrupting and is always calling attention to himself by "forcing" the teacher to repeatedly reprimand him, is clearly seeking attention. Juan, who is usually confrontational, who is noncompliant to reasonable requests from the teacher, and who rejects praise and social reinforcers from the teacher, is in a power struggle. Noriko, who physically injures others and who usually puts others and herself down, is probably seeking revenge for some perceived wrong. Odell, who is withdrawn, who sinks down in his desk, who is shy with classmates, and who fears new situations, is probably displaying a disability.

We must, of course, be careful not to overgeneralize or analyze too quickly, and we must remember that the child could be displaying these behaviors because of dysfunctional family patterns or because of medical or psychiatric problems. Behavior is complicated and can be deceptive at times. However, if we use the goals-of-behavior construct, with its philosophy of purposeful behavior and actions, we have a starting point for responding to these behaviors. Thus, given a general philosophy of behavior as it applies to the educational system, we can talk about specific ways of intervening to solve problems.

Traditional School Social Work Roles

Because many school systems have never had social workers on their staff, the responsibility for elucidating the many roles of social work and the potential value of these functions often remains with the new school social worker. This will be a long and at times frustrating process, for any fundamental change in basic system services will affect the balance and direction of all services. Consequently, the social worker must be in a position to prove that the change she or he brings will ultimately benefit the system and thus be worth the uneasiness that the other staff will feel in adjusting to a new person in a different and challenging role. Persistence and what Albert Ellis terms self-awareness (being perceptive and accepting of one's strengths and limitations) will be needed initially.[48]

Let's look at some traditional roles for school social work practice: caseworker, group worker, truant officer, counselor, and parent liaison.

Caseworker

Intervention has always been the essence of social work. Social workers have responded with a variety of methods to the problems caused by the complexities of modern society. Casework, traditionally, has been one of the first methods used in any given area; it encompasses the more clinical and best-known aspects of social work. Basically, social workers have had to prove their worth; that is, they have had to prove that they do something different from what was already being done. Because social workers have substantial training in family dynamics, they can analyze and diagnose common problems in the dysfunctional family. This is a skill that others in the typical school system do not have, and thus it is viewed as an area of particular expertise for the school social worker.

Consider the case of Mike, age 10, who had a number of problems. He was physically aggressive toward other children and was prone to act with outbursts of emotion and anger when put in new or different situations. He had poorly developed coping skills and came to school after weekends or vacations in an angry, irritable mood. The family consisted of five children and his mother. His father was no longer living at home but visited on occasion. Mike's emotional problems, and particularly his violent attitudes, were accentuated after these visits. In addition, Mike wore dirty, unkempt clothing, which always seemed either too small or much too big. Mike's behavior in class was, of course, a problem. His goals of misbehavior were a combination of attention seeking and power seeking. In an attempt to change this behavior pattern, the social workers, using a casework strategy, (a) made a referral to the county department of social services to make sure that the family was getting all services that were available—for example, medical services, and counseling; (b) modified Mike's behavior at school by devising a system of reinforcers that were important to him; (c) made sure that Mike had an opportunity for success in academic areas in school by helping the teacher understand the difficulties in Mike's life so she could individualize for his needs; (d) tried to help the mother understand that Mike should not be put in situations in which he had to adopt a negative attitude to get attention from adults; and (e) contacted the father about developing more of a relationship with his son. All of this takes considerable time and energy. In casework a consistent, organized, step-by-step approach is used. Casework thus becomes a one-to-one involvement with a family in an attempt to solve a problem.

Now let's look at Phyllis, age 6, who had a hearing disability. She was in a special education program 4 hours a day. There were a number of problems: noncompliant behaviors when Phyllis knew what was wanted of her, a difficulty in communicating in any way, and a number of medical problems. In consultation with others, the caseworker decided that a home intervention program was necessary. Consistency was needed in the sign language program between home and school. Behavior management was lacking in the home, for Phyllis was not expected to do any work there; the only demands were bathroom skills. The parents needed help in developing reasonable goals and expectations for Phyllis and then following through on a program. Medically, Phyllis needed extensive diagnostic work at a nearby hospital. The caseworker made contact with the hospital, arranged for a meeting, and then made sure that follow-up came from the hospital. Again, the social worker set specific goals and followed them in an attempt to solve a multitude of problems. Much of the emphasis in the caseworker model is on doing things that teachers are not prepared for and do not have the time to do. The goals are not strictly educational but have the purpose of enabling children to achieve in school.

Group Worker

As casework came to be considered too costly and perhaps outmoded in some areas of social work practice,[49] school social workers found another method of intervening in school problems: group work. Essentially, the rationale was that the social worker could influence the lives and educational success of too few people when using the casework approach. A group approach also assumes that, by sharing experiences, students can put their own problems in perspective and can learn new strategies for resolving school-related and personal problems. A few examples of a group approach follow.

Ms. Tanner's fifth-grade class was a problem for her. Specifically, four boys regularly would not listen, clowned around, and did little work in class. In fact, they were doing less well academically than in the past year and were starting to "hang out" together, often getting into trouble on the playground. An intervention strategy was designed: the creation of groups as a means of solving these problems. Two groups of five boys were created, with two of the "problem" boys in each group. The groups worked in specific high-interest areas; for example, one group worked on a science project that involved creating a metric unit for the third grade, while the other studied the principles of flight and aerodynamics, making kites, paper airplanes, and wooden models. There were a number of planned goals for each group. First, the social worker wanted to create new friendships and show the disruptive children models of more appropriate behavior that could be as rewarding as attention-getting behavior. Second, cooperation was fostered in conjunction with the principles of peer pressure. All children worked toward step-by-step, cooperative goals; unless all helped, none could reach their goal. Finally, the social worker wanted everyone—the target boys, their peers in the class, and their teacher—to realize that the boys could be productive and successful so that both the teacher's and students' perceptions would be altered. The social worker also discussed with Ms. Tanner how classroom cooperative groups could be used to provide additional successful educational experiences for these four boys as well as others in the class.

In another case, group experience involved high school freshmen who were failing in their initial coursework. Study habits, poor motivation, and a negative attitude toward school success were the main concerns. In this case, the social worker organized a group of students who took a special course focused on ways of studying. The course was named "Ten Ways to Beat the System" and was structured in a way that allowed the student to learn enjoyable ways to become successful in school. At the same time, a number of older students were organized to meet informally with the freshmen to discuss some positive aspects of high school. In addition, these upperclassmen offered guidance about classes and which teachers to select for future.

Many school districts are now offering a variety of groups that are often led by social workers. Examples include *assertiveness training* for students who are shy or nonassertive, *anger control* for students who frequently lose their temper or are aggressive, *relationship building* for students who have difficulty making friends, *coping with loss* for students whose parents divorce or who have experienced the death of a loved one, *student assistance programs* for students who are using or abusing alcohol or other drugs, and *school-age mothers* for students who are pregnant or are raising a child.

Truant Officer

Social workers in the school have performed a number of other roles, including that of truant officer. Often the truant officer functions as an advocate for the child. There are times when acting as an agent of social control (the law, the system) need not be looked at negatively. A case in point is a multiproblem family with three boys in high school. Although none of the boys had reached the legal age after which school was no longer compulsory, the parents decided to keep the boys at home so they could help the father in his job as a farmhand. The boys had mentioned to different teachers that they feared this was about to happen, but they were afraid to tell their father that they wanted to stay in school. The social worker was able to intervene in this case by using the truancy laws to inform the parents that they had no choice but to send their sons to school. In this case, the undesirable role of truant officer was transformed into one that was advantageous for the children involved. It was also a means of helping to promote the concept of equal access. Given the high truancy and dropout rates in larger cities, the approach of combining the services of truant officers with creative or alternative approaches to education can benefit children.

Another example shows how a school social worker used the truancy laws as an "access point" to intervene with a family. In this case, Jose appeared to have emotional (perhaps psychiatric) difficulties. Jose's parents were reluctant to see a counselor, Jose often did not attend school. By using a truancy

referral to the county department of social services, counselors from that agency were able to build a relationship with the family, which eventually resulted in Jose being referred to the agency's child psychiatrist where he received psychotropic medication. With the medication and the counseling that Jose received from the county department of social services, his behavior gradually improved.

The truant officer role may also be a way of helping parents. Sometimes teens become too powerful in their families and may refuse to go to school. In this instance, a truancy referral may help parents reassert their authority and/or assist them diagnostically if other problems are causing their child to be excessively rebellious.

Counselor and Parent Liaison

The social worker as a counselor and/or parent liaison or parent trainer is also a fairly common role in school social work. Often teachers will expect the school social worker to be the liaison between themselves and parents. And it is frequently assumed that the social worker will defend and justify the actions or educational planning of the teacher. This can cause somewhat strained relations between the social worker and the rest of the teaching staff, especially when a worker agrees with a parent that the school system ought to make changes in its educational programs to better serve the children. This role requires a lot of tact and prior planning, as well as a relatively assertive view toward expanding social work services.

In the role of counselor, the social worker brings a number of skills to the situation. As school social work services have developed, there has been a trend toward perceiving the social worker as a therapist rather than as an academic counselor. This distinction has been more than semantic because advanced professional (master's degree) training has greatly increased the diagnostic and psychological skills of school social workers relative to other school professionals (such as guidance counselors). Thus, a school social worker can be seen as both a specialist in the diagnosis of emotional difficulties in children and as the support staff person with the most extensive psychiatric and medically based training.

Newer School Social Work Roles

In essence, role development and expansion are of critical concern to school social workers. When they join a school system, a number of expectations and specific job-related demands will be placed on them. There are bound to be conflicts because the older roles encompassing casework, group work, counselor, or parent liaison may not provide enough flexibility to meet the demands of the change effort. As a result, school social workers have adapted by developing newer approaches to their role. We'll now look at eight of these newer approaches: advocate, behavioral specialist, mental health consultant, alcohol and other drug abuse specialist, individual education plan (IEP) team member, violence prevention specialist, systems change specialist, and program research specialist.

Advocate

One of the most provocative roles for the social worker has become that of advocate.[50] In the school setting, an advocate is someone who understands and is not intimidated by large complicated systems and can help a family or child face the educational bureaucracy or deal with other social systems.

This can be a particularly useful role when working with families who are not well acquainted with the educational system. For instance, in an early education program that is geared to helping prekindergarten children who show evidence of developmental delay, the social worker can use the advocate role to help the parents understand their rights under the law, including their rights to appeal program decisions if they feel the programs do not fit the needs of their child. The social worker can explain who is teaching what materials and why this should help the child progress. She or he can be the person who follows the child in the program so that the parents can have contact with someone they have rapport with and with whom they feel comfortable asking questions. The social worker can also be the person who makes them aware of applicable medical or social service agencies that are available to give them a better knowledge of their child or offer supportive services when these are needed. The social worker can be a person to talk to about the complexities, difficulties, fears, or guilt associated with raising a child who in some way is different from other children.

Another more general function is to advocate for parents as a group in meetings with teachers, administrators, or school boards. An example might be in the area of homework. Academic expectations have dramatically increased in the past decade, such that much of what was high school algebra and biology are now commonly taught in seventh and eighth grades. Teaching staffs need to understand that there are many parents who cannot tutor their children in their homework once the children are beyond sixth or seventh grade. Instead of complaining about lack of parental help, teachers and administrators need assistance in developing more creative ways of helping students, such as peer helpers, study skill groups, and/or extra time for students to meet with the teacher before or after class.

Another example would be in the area of parent/teacher conferences. Parents often dread these meetings because they feel belittled or embarrassed by the teacher. However, the teacher could get more support from parents if he or she started conferences by first making some positive comments about the child and his or her abilities and values. The teacher should also ask parents to do only what is practical and realistic. School social workers can assist teachers in developing this new approach to conferences—which is apt to benefit the child as well as the teacher.

Thus, a combination of all of these functions expands the role of home liaison and enables the advocate to meet needs that have not previously been met in the school context.

Behavioral Specialist

There has been a trend at some major universities toward training school social workers in one discrete, highly recognizable skill. Within this context, emphasis is often put on the social worker's becoming a behavioral specialist, a person who understands and can systematically apply behavior modification principles. Within the schools, a knowledge of how to alter behavior has immediate and long-term applicability. Using behavioral skills, the social worker can provide guidance in general learning principles as applied to overall teaching and can develop specific programs for children who are having difficulty adjusting to the normal classroom routine. The following is a case example.

Phillip, age 9, was having difficulty paying attention and was usually noncompliant to directions. His teacher was having trouble understanding his behavior and motivating him to be involved in usual classroom activities—for example, doing independent work in math and reading, participating in small-group activities, and cooperating in play arrangements. A social worker with behavioral training was asked to intervene. After observing the antecedents of the noncompliant behavior and recording baseline data of on-task or attending behaviors in non-academic situations,[51] the social worker was able to put together a program. The program included (a) the planned use of social reinforcers (praise from the teacher); (b) a reward system built around interest in science (other work had to be done before the work in science could begin); and (c) a system that involved ignoring Phillip's verbal noncompliance while reinforcing compliance with praise and tangible rewards, such as permitting him to help with a special project. In this way, Phillip's behaviors were changed in a relatively short time.

Within current special education legislation, there is a requirement to establish a behavior intervention plan for any student with an emotional disturbance who has behavior problems. Behavior modification skills are crucial in the development of this plan.

Mental Health Consultant

A school social worker can also function as a mental health consultant to other staff members. Curriculum today is no longer as simple as reading, writing, and arithmetic (if this ever was the case). Although there is currently substantial concern about teaching the "basics" in education, teachers must still seek to improve old curriculum and develop new materials and new teaching styles. Because social workers have training in the social psychology of individual behavior, they can serve as consultants on the mental health and human relations aspects of curriculum and on teaching style. With this focus, the social worker plays a preventive role, seeking to help teachers motivate students via stimulating materials. She or he can help create a teaching approach that is not threatening but intriguing, questioning, and supportive of the process of learning. Naturally, the social worker would also be involved in helping teachers to individualize education—to devise materials and teaching styles that meet the needs of all children, no matter what their current academic level.

The school social worker can also lead efforts in Positive Behavior Interventions and Supports (PBIS), which relates to creating positive school climates and recognition systems for students who are performing well socially and academically. PBIS also helps in preventing students from bullying one another.

The social worker can help create a systematized approach to monitoring progress and then create new techniques to facilitate remediation when necessary. To accomplish these goals, it may be necessary to organize brainstorming sessions with all the teachers or to begin an investigation of the materials available on a number of topics.

In this way, social workers can help provide guidance in curriculum development, with an overall emphasis on human relations. The inclusion of specific human relations goals in teaching has often been overlooked, even though many problems in the schools (such as trouble on the playground and problems with special and regular education classes) can be seen as directly attributable to a lack of human relations materials. Children need to learn that "different is okay," that cultural or racial differences can be enjoyed rather than feared, that all people deserve respect as human beings, and that values are learned concepts that can be changed.[52] School social workers, because of their training and unique place in the school, can provide the perspective needed to devise such a curriculum and help create systems for implementation.

Another more complex role in this area, and one that requires advanced training, is to help evaluate whether children might have significant emotional or psychiatric difficulties. There has been a significant increase in the number of children who have been diagnosed by the medical and/or child psychological disciplines as having attention-deficit-hyperactivity disorder (ADHD) or other emotional/behavioral disorders (such as a major depression or bipolar disorder). Because of the unique skills and roles of the school social worker, he or she can be a liaison to the mental health and/or medical community by making appropriate referrals and by assisting in follow-up care. Often parents will be confused about their child's behavioral or emotional development. Parents will then need assistance in understanding what may be "naughty behavior" or "going through a stage" as opposed to behaviors that indicate the possibility of a more serious problem. It is imperative in these latter situations that the child and the parents be referred to qualified specialists or clinics and that communication then take place between mental health providers and schools. As the first mental health specialist that parents are apt to see, it is also important that parents feel the school social worker is supportive and nonjudgmental. This will raise the likelihood that they will actually go to a clinic for professional treatment. It is equally important that teachers receive assistance in understanding the nature of child psychiatric problems and how to help affected children.

Given that school social workers, along with guidance counselors and school psychologists, are most likely to provide mental health referrals in school systems, it is important that these professionals have a solid foundation in mental health diagnosis and treatment. Adolescents with mental health disorders are at increased risk of poor school performance and involvement in the juvenile justice system.

Alcohol and Other Drug Abuse Specialist

Drug use and abuse continue to be a major problem in our society. From the days of Prohibition, various segments of society have addressed the "evils" of alcohol and other drug use. Today, with the tragic loss of lives associated with drunk driving and with the much-publicized drug-overdose deaths of sports and entertainment figures, there is a growing realization of the need for drug prevention programs. Programs having a punitive interventive focus have not been successful. Thus, there has been a recent emphasis on prevention, and schools have become the mechanism for drug prevention programs.

Because schools generally do not have trained specialists in this area, many school districts have hired school social workers to consult with parents and to refer students who are abusing drugs to appropriate inpatient or outpatient treatment centers. Social workers, because of their knowledge of chemical dependency, their training in interviewing, their skills in interacting with parents, and their knowledge of community resources, have become the logical choice to spearhead the development of prevention programs. They have also been asked to become curriculum specialists in this area. Thus, as part of their overall responsibilities, many school social workers help develop teaching curriculum on drug use and abuse for elementary, middle, and high schools. In this respect, social workers are responding to changes in society and in the family, as education seeks to accomplish more and more societal goals.

Many school districts have developed intervention programs for students who either have become chemically dependent or are concerned about the possibility of this occurring. Student Assistance Programs (SAPs), often led by school social workers, offer a group approach in this area. Groups for students who have returned from alcohol or other drug treatment centers, groups for students who want to know more about the mood-altering effects of alcohol and other drugs, and groups for students who are concerned about others' use of chemicals have become commonplace in many schools. There may also be groups for students affected by others' (such as parents') use of alcohol or other drugs. In this latter area, students learn that they have not caused their parents' problems and that they cannot control their parents' drinking behavior. They also learn how to cope so as to be successful at school.

Individual Education Plan Team Member

Another role of the social worker that is gaining increasing popularity involves using his or her skills in conjunction with other members on a team. The school social worker may join with other professionals (psychologist, speech therapist, special education teacher, physical therapist, and regular education teacher) to determine the special educational needs and particular programming appropriate for certain children. This is an area of implementation of the 2004 Individuals with Disabilities Education Act (see Case Exhibit 10.5). On an individual education plan (IEP) team, the social worker might be involved (a) with an initial assessment of the child and the family, with special emphasis on family functioning and the child's social and adaptive skills; (b) with the parents clinically, either through family counseling and role analysis or through training in special techniques, such as behavior modification or crisis intervention; or (c) in teacher observation, training, and support.

The point here is that the social worker acts as part of a team—as a member with certain discrete skills and knowledge—and in conjunction with the team, seeks to alleviate problems. Although this may appear to be a somewhat constricting role, in that other methods may seem to offer more independence, it can be a useful way to find gaps in services and to decrease overlap among individual skills. It has its advantages, especially if one is responsible for a school (or a school system) with a large population. One particular advantage is the learning that takes place for the social worker as she or he interacts with other professionals on the team.

A somewhat different type of team is "team consultation" provided by a pupil service team. Similar to the IEP team, this team has members from many disciplines—in fact, often the same members as the previously described IEP team. However, this team's consultation approach differs in that it is a consultation/prevention resource to teachers. Instead of a child being formally referred as a client with a potential

The 2004 Individuals with Disabilities Act

The Individuals with Disabilities Education Act (IDEA) is the primary federal program that authorizes state and local aid for special education and related services for children with disabilities. The IDEA was formerly known as the Education for All Handicapped Children Act. The 2004 IDEA requires that public schools create an Individualized Education Program (IEP) for each student who is found to be eligible for special education services. The IEP is the cornerstone of a student's educational program and must be designed to meet the unique educational needs of each child in the "least restrictive environment" appropriate to the needs of that child. ("Least restrictive environment" means that a student with a disability should have the opportunity to be educated with nondisabled peers to the greatest extent possible.) When a child qualifies for services, an IEP team is convened to design an education plan. The IEP team must include the child's parents, at least one of the child's regular education teachers, a special education teacher, and someone who can interpret the educational implications of the child's evaluation (such as a social worker, school psychologist, or school administrator). Parents are considered to be equal members of the IEP team along with the school staff. Because school social workers have educational training in assessment, research, and evidence-based practice, they often are key members on IEP teams in developing and implementing IEP plans.

emotional/behavioral disability, the pupil service team seeks to find ways to help the child, the teacher, or the parents immediately. An illustration of a prevention effort by this type of team is the team consulting with teachers on how to work more effectively with children who have been diagnosed as having attention deficit hyperactivity disorder.

Violence Prevention Specialist

Schools are often said to be a microcosm of the larger society. In many of our cities, violence toward others has become a major problem, and it is not limited to adults. Offenses committed by juveniles have become more serious in nature. In many inner cities, gangs have become such a destructive force that some school districts now have instituted dress codes in an attempt to counter the influence of gang symbols (the wearing of certain apparel or colors is thought to be a factor in developing and maintaining a "gang identity"). Student violence against teachers has also increased, creating a climate in some schools of fear and intimidation. Police liaison officers are now common in many schools.

The tragedy of Columbine High School brought more fear into school systems. Threat assessment is now part of a school social worker's new role. As schools and the larger society try to balance personal rights with group safety, it is necessary to have skillful individuals who do not over- or under-react to threats.

Violence prevention is yet another area where schools have traditionally not employed specialists. Some 30 to 40 years ago, in a slower-paced and more stable society, the school principal would usually enforce whatever discipline was necessary. (The principal often solicited parent cooperation in administering strict, often punitive, consequences to students who violated school rules.) Today gangs have become the "family" of far too many teens. The use of such drugs as crack and cocaine has caused an increase in addictive behaviors and aggression toward others. The methods of maintaining behavioral control in schools have changed, and school social workers are in a unique position to again demonstrate leadership and knowledge of human behavior.

Teachers need to develop more effective ways of working with students who are prone to become violent or aggressive. School social workers can help train teaching staff to become effective in nonviolent intervention techniques. For example, teachers can be instructed in helping students to learn anger-control techniques. Students can be taught how to reframe their angry thought processes so that they express their anger in assertive and nonviolent ways rather than in aggressive ways. They can also be instructed in how to walk away from a potential fight, and they can learn indirect ways of expressing their anger (such as by hitting a punching bag or by jogging). Teachers who have learned to guide students in anger-control techniques also regain a sense of "being in charge."

Another example of an effective technique for reducing student violence is peer mediation, whereby students mediate their interpersonal conflicts. School social workers develop a training plan to teach a core

An Example of the Systems Change Role

Andy recently moved into the elementary school's attendance area. He is in the fourth grade and has been in five previous school districts. He has a speech and language disability and a learning disability. He seems socially immature for his age and his misarticulation of words makes him difficult to understand. He has been at his new school for 2 months, and although he is getting special education help for learning and speech difficulties, another problem has arisen. The main special education teacher comes to see the school social worker because this student is making her "gag," and she states she is "not going to put up with it any longer." This student has a problem with bowel control; the soiling of his undergarments creates a disconcerting smell. The teacher forcefully states "something must be done." She suggests the student be sent home every time he has a problem—until he or his parents "fix" the problem. The parents do not have a telephone, and therefore she wants the school social worker to go speak to them.

How else can we problem-solve this case? Using a systems model, more information is needed; then an action plan can be developed. The school social worker goes to see the parents to obtain information—but not to complain to them or to intimidate them. It turns out that Andy has had this difficulty for 3 to 4 years. They state he saw a doctor within the past year, and the doctor said that he did not have a medical problem causing this condition. The school social worker obtains a release of information from the parents to speak to the doctor and says he will be back. In a telephone conversation, the doctor says he believes Andy gets impacted because of constipation problems, in part because he has never established a good routine for bowel movements. The doctor had suggested that Andy's parents establish a routine for Andy and also add more fiber to his diet.

Other information from the home visit: Andy's parents do not have a lot of money and his father is currently unemployed. His mother is employed at a low-income job as a maid at a motel.

The social worker then put together an action plan with the following goals: (a) help Andy's father get connected with the local county job service office—at the very least there are part-time jobs available in the community; (b) establish a bathroom routine or schedule at school with Andy using the private bathroom in the main office instead of the student bathrooms; (c) encourage the parents to set a bathroom schedule for Andy at home in the morning and evening; (d) have Andy bring some extra clothing to school to be kept there in case a change of clothes is needed; (e) purchase high-fiber (and good-tasting) bars for Andy to "earn" as reinforcers for assignment completion (special education money can be used for this purpose); and (f) get Andy involved in one of the school counselor's friendship groups.

Using this model, the social worker is designing a planned change approach and recognizing motivations for change and problems resulting from change. Andy is the focus for a problem and is not *the* problem. He is the *access point* for the interconnection among a number of systems: social service agencies, special education teachers, children with friendship problems, and children with learning disabilities. As far as the school social worker is concerned, Andy is a catalyst for the creation of a system that can better serve other children like Andy in the future.

group of students the skills of active listening, compromising, and problem solving. Through training and supervision, this core group can then mediate conflicts that occur in the school, potentially preventing smaller disagreements from becoming violent conflicts. The influence of the social worker is then greatly enhanced, as many more students are ultimately "seen" through the core group of trained students.

Another approach to minimize school violence is the formation of violence prevention teams formed from the police department, schools, and youth-serving agencies. Too often, agencies and schools are involved only in intervention efforts. Because of their unique position and skills and because of the system coordination expectations in their job, school social workers can take a leadership role in developing a team effort for the prevention of violence that

uses the resources and energies of professionals from many systems.

An example of such a project is the development of a "teen court." Through school, police departments, social service agencies, and judges working together, some teens may have to explain their actions to a group of their peers and then have consequences developed by people their own age. (Often, teens are most influenced by their peers.)

Systems Change Specialist

Allen Pincus and Anne Minahan postulate that the focus of social work practice should be the interaction between people and systems in the social environment.[53] If we look at schools as a natural access point for families (most families must deal with schools at some point in their existence), social workers should be able to perform a unique role in the schools. Given the complex nature of society today, most people need to enhance their problem-solving abilities. Social workers can help in this regard by linking people to systems and improving existing service and delivery mechanisms. This role model can involve situations of equal access or integration, the development of programs to deal with changing family patterns, or issues relating to the quality of education. Schools are a critical link in the total societal resource system. Indeed, the neighborhood school is often the system with which the average citizen feels most comfortable. Thus, we must examine our schools and look for the inadequacies in their educational structure. The questions we need to answer are: What do we really need to determine success for the student? How can we use the materials and personnel in the most efficient way? Through a system of assessing present data, determining goals, and forming active systems for the purpose of exercising influence, one can answer these questions and ultimately build a better, more accessible, more demand-based school program.

The social worker has a large role to play in this process, for he or she can become an organizer, a leader, a catalyst toward change, a liaison for the needs and wishes of the families, and a specialist in devising systems to meet change-oriented goals. Typical focuses are on discovering (a) the particular deficiencies in the school and the community, (b) under- or unserved populations, and (c) the programs that are needed to get children back in school and to curb juvenile delinquency. Another focus might be to analyze the interaction among the components in the systems in schools, or between the schools and the county departments of social services, to see, for example, whether these components are really working together or whether they have underlying assumptions that work at cross-purposes.

As a systems change specialist, a social worker is an institutional change agent, a person analyzing ongoing programs and proposed new programs. The systems change approach seeks to change the goals of the traditional school social worker. The traditional goals were to help the child adapt to the school, to use the learning opportunities available, and to modify student behavior or parent–child relationships to alleviate problems in the school. With the systems approach, the goals are to analyze which parts of the system are activating stress in a given situation and then to alter that system so that equilibrium is again maintained. One must find and prioritize targets

for change, acknowledging that different approaches must be used to solve different problems.

This approach should become clearer if we analyze a typical problem (see Case Example 10.2) that might be referred to a school social worker. By reevaluating and refocusing the problem, the systems change specialist makes the goals clearer and more meaningful.

Another example of the systems change role relates to the previously discussed issues of alcohol use and abuse by students. Using a systems modality, a school social worker might focus on seeking to change a community's acceptance of teen use of alcohol. A change effort could involve the social worker forming a group of concerned community leaders, such as representatives from the clergy, the police, business, social services, service clubs such as the Rotary, parents, teens, and others to develop a plan to increase community knowledge of the dangers of alcohol use. The ultimate goal is to decrease teen use of alcohol by strategies such as improved parental supervision of teens, increased police enforcement of current laws, parent networks to decrease home parties, and community development of alternative activities to teen drinking. An advantage of this approach is that substantially more teens and their families will potentially benefit than if the school social worker meets on a one-to-one basis with teens who are using or abusing alcohol. It also recognizes that in 7 hours a day, school cannot do everything. Parents and the community must help in facilitating the development of children.

Program Research Specialist

Facilitating positive youth development, resiliency, and character development are additional approaches that can be used to alleviate potential problem behavior in school-age children and improve school systems. Research on positive youth development has shown that the development of emotional attachment to at least one caring adult, the development of a positive identity with goals and an orientation to the future, the development of decision-making skills and self-determination skills, and the development of competence through success in learning and social accomplishments are all important factors in helping teens reduce risky behaviors and enhancing their likelihood of becoming successful adults.[54] Research on resiliency has shown that resilient children and adults have thought processes that foster a positive identity, the formation of constructive goals, an orientation to the future, sound decision-making and problem-solving skills, and time management skills.[55]

An important focus for school social workers is on evidence-based practice. Social workers need to research and identify which programs best facilitate positive youth development, resiliency, and character development. They then should serve as consultants to school decision makers in these areas. There are many programs that claim they will facilitate growth in these areas. Some programs are much more effective than others. Another area in which school social workers can serve as consultants to school decision makers is in identifying effective drug and alcohol prevention programs. Research shows that some programs in this area have a positive impact on youth, whereas others are ineffective.[56] There is a need for school social workers to look at the research and identify what programs actually produce what results.

There is increasing emphasis in school systems on data decision making. A thorough understanding of research methodology and statistical probability will help in becoming competent in data decision making. Developing standards for evaluating the effectiveness of programs or curriculums will help school districts spend money wisely.

Superman/Superwoman

This is, of course, a bit facetious, but as you enter the field of school social work, you may feel you need to be "super" in order to accomplish all the things you need to do for children at risk and their families. In this context, a school social worker can do numerous "little things" that add up to a better school climate and a better life, at least at school, for others. A school social worker can offer a sincere feeling of "being welcome" to parents. She or he can bring a smile and some reassurance to children that they really are "good enough." She or he can bring a sense of hope that life will be all right. She or he can bring a voice for the disadvantaged and those with a disability to the "table" when fiscal decisions are made. She or he can bring a feeling of energy by developing other ways of looking at issues and by framing issues within an optimistic perspective, often giving his or her clients the sense that their problems are rather small ones that can be constructively combated. She or he can bring a clinical set of skills in certain mental health areas—skills that do not exist elsewhere in the school setting. She or he can bring access to community resources. Finally, she or he

can bring the awareness that less-than-perfect behavior and events in a sometimes chaotic world are understandable (often predictable) and are changeable when one uses social work principles and methods.

Critical Thinking Question

Are you interested in pursuing a career as a school social worker?

SUMMARY

The following summarizes this chapter's content as it relates to the chapter objectives presented at the beginning of the chapter. Objectives include the following:

A *Summarize problems that school systems currently face.*

Education, which in the past has been called on to resolve a variety of social problems, is now recognized as a social problem itself. Education is currently facing a variety of crises and issues.

Numerous indicators raise questions about the quality of education in this country. For example, scores on the Scholastic Aptitude Test, which is taken annually by high school seniors, are significantly lower than they were 50 years ago.

A second problematic area is that school systems are providing inferior educational opportunities for the poor and for members of minority groups. Less money is spent per student on education in low-income school districts and in school districts in which high proportions of minority students live. In our society, academic achievement is highly correlated with socioeconomic status.

A third problematic area is that there is considerable confusion about the desirable goals of education. There is agreement that schools should teach the basic skills of reading, writing, and arithmetic. However, there is controversy among different interest groups concerning the other learning goals that education should strive to attain.

A fourth problematic area is intolerable working conditions for teachers in some school settings. Intolerable conditions include low pay and low prestige, drug and alcohol abuse among students, physical threats and assaults from some students, insufficient instructional supplies, and high student-to-teacher ratios.

A fifth problematic area is school bullying and cyberbullying. Victims of such bullying are frequently severely traumatized.

B *Present proposals for improving education.*

Four proposals for improving education in this country are to increase incentives for teachers, to improve the curricula, to allow parents to choose the school to which they will send their children, and to expand preschool programs. One of the controversial proposed incentives for teaching is the creation of master-teacher positions that would reward excellence in teaching. A major problem with seeking to improve the curriculum is a lack of agreement about what the curriculum should teach students. Under the parental choice of schools approach, it is theorized that market incentives would be created whereby academically superior schools would thrive and inferior schools would have to improve or face bankruptcy.

Suggestions are given for parents, teachers, and students to curb bullying and cyberbullying.

C *Discuss ideas for improving educational opportunities for children of low-income and minority families.*

Three proposals were presented for seeking to work toward equal education opportunities for low-income and minority students: (a) reform school financing to spend an equal amount of money on each student's education, (b) establish special compensatory educational programs for disadvantaged students, and (c) integrate students from different ethnic and racial backgrounds into the same schools.

D *Summarize the functions of school social workers and describe several roles for school social work practice.*

There are several roles for school social work practice. Traditional roles include those of caseworker, group worker, truant officer, counselor, and parent liaison. Newer roles include advocate, behavioral specialist, mental health consultant, alcohol and other drug abuse specialist, individual education plan team member, violence prevention specialist, systems change specialist, and problem research specialist.

School social workers cannot solve all of the problems in education. Difficulties with integration, differences over goals, problems with the quality of the teaching staff, and changing roles and expectations in the family are all very complex and demanding problems. However, new ideas and creative approaches can be developed within the role of a systems change specialist, who can help the educational system address the problems of education and ultimately seek solutions.

Competency Notes

EP 2.1.3a Distinguish, appraise, and integrate multiple sources of knowledge, including research-based knowledge and practice wisdom. (All of this chapter) This chapter summarizes problems that school systems currently encounter, and presents proposals for improving education. It discusses ideas for improving educational opportunities for children of low-income and minority families. It summarizes the functions of school social workers and describes several role models for school social work practice.

EP 2.1.10a Substantively and affectively prepare for action with individuals, families, groups, organizations, and communities. (pp. 350-361) Introductory material is presented on school social work practice.

Media Resources

Additional resources for this chapter, including a chapter quiz, can be found on the Social Work CourseMate. Go to CengageBrain.com.

Notes

1. Quoted in William Kornblum and Joseph Julian, *Social Problems*, 6th ed. (Englewood Cliffs, NJ: Prentice Hall, 1988), p. 394.
2. William Kornblum and Joseph Julian, *Social Problems*, 14th ed. (Boston: Pearson, 2012), pp. 360–361.
3. National Center for Education Statistics, *Literacy in Everyday Life: Results from the 2003 National Assessment of Adult Literacy*, April 4, 2007. Available at http://nces.ed.gov/naal.
4. Linda A. Mooney, David Knox, and Caroline Schacht, *Understanding Social Problems*, 8th ed. (Belmont, CA: Wadsworth/Cengage Learning, 2013), pp. 244–245.
5. Ibid.
6. Ibid.
7. Kornblum and Julian, *Social Problems*, 14th ed., pp. 363–365.
8. Ibid.

9. Mooney, Knox, and Schacht, *Understanding Social Problems*, pp. 247–249.

10. Ibid., p. 248.

11. Ibid., pp. 238–239.

12. Jonathon Kozol, *Savage Inequalities* (New York: Crown, 1991).

13. Kornblum and Julian, *Social Problems*, 14th ed., pp. 364–367.

14. Ibid., pp. 364–367.

15. Ibid., pp. 364–367.

16. Ibid., pp. 364–367.

17. Mooney, Knox, and Schacht, *Understanding Social Problems*, pp. 240–241.

18. Kornblum and Julian, *Social Problems*, 14th ed., pp. 364–367.

19. Ibid., pp. 364–367.

20. Ibid., pp. 374–375.

21. Ibid.

22. Ibid.

23. Ibid.

24. "Bullying," http://www.americanspcc.com/education/bullying/.

25. Ibid.

26. Ibid.

27. Michael Rutter, *15,000 Hours: Secondary Schools and Their Effects on Children* (Cambridge, MA: Harvard University Press, 1979).

28. Ibid.

29. Eigil Pedersen and Therese Annette Faucher, with William W. Eaton, "A New Perspective on the Effects of First-Grade Teachers on Children's Subsequent Adult Status," *Harvard Educational Review*, 48 (1978), pp. 1–31.

30. Kornblum and Julian, *Social Problems*, 14th ed., p. 371.

31. Mooney, Knox, and Schacht, *Understanding Social Problems*, p. 328.

32. Noreen S. Ahmed-Ullah, "Study: Preschool Boosts Low-Income Students," *Chicago Tribune*, June 9, 2011.

33. Ibid.

34. Patricia Simms, "Life-Altering Outcomes," *Wisconsin State Journal*, Apr. 3, 2002, pp. A1, A7.

35. High/Scope Educational Research Foundation, *Perry Preschool Project* (Ypsilanti, MI: High/Scope Press, 2011).

36. "Michigan's Model," *U.S. News & World Report*, p. 16.

37. Kornblum and Julian, *Social Problems*, 14th ed., p. 355.

38. John E. Farley, *American Social Problems*, 2nd ed. (Englewood Cliffs, NJ: Prentice Hall, 1992), p. 480.

39. "Bullying Prevention," http://www.kidpower.org/resources/articles/dealing-with-bullying.html.

40. Ibid.

41. Ibid.

42. Mary A. Suppes and Carolyn C. Wells, *The Social Work Experience*, 6th ed. (Boston: Pearson, 2013), p. 259.

43. See Mildred Sikkema, "The School Social Worker Serves as a Consultant," *Casework Papers* (New York: Family Service Association of America, 1955), pp. 75–82.

44. Alan Guskin and Samuel Guslan, *A Social Psychology of Education* (Reading, MA: Addison-Wesley, 1970), pp. 1–3.

45. Albert Ellis, *Humanistic Psychotherapy* (New York: McGraw-Hill, 1973), pp. 55–69.

46. Ibid.

47. Rudolf Dreikurs, Bernice Grunwald, and Floy Pepper, *Maintaining Sanity in the Classroom* (New York: Harper & Row, 1971), pp. 17–21.

48. Ellis, *Humanistic Psychotherapy*, pp. 129–133.

49. Joel Fisher, "Is Casework Effective?" *Social Work*, 18 (Jan. 1973), pp. 5–21.

50. See Mary J. McCormick, "Social Advocacy: A New Dimension in Social Work," *Social Casework*, 51 (Jan. 1970), pp. 3–11.

51. For a more detailed discussion of behavior modification, see Beth Sulzer and G. Roy Mayer, *Behavior Modification Procedures for School Personnel* (New York: Holt, Rinehart & Winston, 1972).

52. Sidney Simon, *Values Clarification* (New York: Hart, 1972), pp. 20–21.

53. Allen Pincus and Anne Minahan, *Social Work Practice: Model and Method* (Itasca, IL: F. E. Peacock, 1973), pp. 3–9.

54. William Glasser, *Choice Theory: A New Psychology of Personal Freedom* (New York: Harper Perennial, 1999).

55. Ibid.

56. Ibid.

CHAPTER 11

Work-Related Problems and Social Work in the Workplace

A question that is commonly asked when two strangers meet is, "What do you do for a living?" Work is a central focus in our lives. Work not only enables us to earn money to pay bills, but it can also provide a sense of self-respect, a circle of colleagues and friends, and a source of self-fulfillment. A challenging job can help us grow intellectually, psychologically, and socially. Work also largely determines our place in the social structure. We are, to a great extent, defined by our work.

In our society, we value the "work ethic"; that is, we consider work to be honorable, productive, and useful. Unemployed, able-bodied people are often looked down on. This chapter will:

Learning Objectives

EP 2.1.3a

A   Present a brief history of work.

B   Describe three major problems involving work: alienation, unemployment, and occupational health hazards. Also, summarize current efforts and proposed new approaches to combat these problems.

C   Describe social work in the workplace, which is an emerging field of social work practice.

A Brief History of Work

Work has not always been so esteemed. The ancient Greeks, for example, viewed work as a curse imposed on humanity by the gods. Work was thought to be an unpleasant and burdensome activity that was incompatible with being a citizen and developing one's mind. The Greeks therefore used slaves and justified slavery on the grounds that it freed citizens to spend their time in philosophic contemplation and cultural enrichment. Aristotle remarked: "No man can practice virtue who is living the life of a mechanic or laborer."[1]

Although the Romans viewed commercial banking as acceptable employment, practically all other occupations were considered vulgar and demeaning.

The ancient Hebrews viewed work ambivalently. On the one hand, they regarded it as a drudgery or a grim necessity. On the other hand, they saw it as an expression of love for God.

The early Christians also were ambivalent toward work. They viewed working as doing penance for Original Sin. (The Christian interpretation of the Bible asserts that Original Sin began with Adam and Eve disobeying God in the Garden of Eden.)

But they also believed that people needed to work to make their own living and to help those in need.

The Protestant Reformation, which began in the 17th century, brought about profound changes in social values concerning work. Work became highly valued for the first time. One of the Protestant reformers, Martin Luther, asserted that labor was a service to God. Since that time, work has continued to be viewed as honorable and as having religious significance.

Another Protestant reformer, John Calvin, had an even more dramatic effect on changing social views toward work. Calvin preached that work is the will of God. Hard work, good deeds, and success at one's vocation were taken to be signs that one was destined for salvation. God's will was that people should live frugally (that is, spend very little money) and should use profits from work to invest in new ventures, which in turn would bring in more profits for additional investments, and so on. Idleness or laziness came to be viewed as sinful. One religious group that was heavily influenced by Calvin's teachings was the Puritans. The Puritans also developed a strong ascetic lifestyle—that is, the practice of denying worldly pleasures as a demonstration of religious

CASE EXHIBIT 11.1

Max Weber and the Protestant Ethic

In 1904 the German sociologist Max Weber published what has become one of the most provocative theories in sociology. In *The Protestant Ethic and the Spirit of Capitalism*, Weber asserted that the Protestant ethic encouraged and made possible the emergence of capitalism. Weber theorized that the ideas of Puritanism (advocated by Martin Luther and John Calvin) provided the value system that led to the transformation from traditional society to the Industrial Revolution.

Weber noted that Puritan Protestantism embraced the doctrine that people were divinely selected for either salvation or damnation. There was nothing people could do to alter their fate. No one knew for sure whether she or he was destined for eternal salvation or eternal damnation. However, people looked for signs from God to suggest their fate. Because they

also believed that work was a form of service to God, they concluded that success at work (making profits) was a sign of God's favor. They therefore worked very hard to accumulate as much wealth as possible.

Because the Protestant ethic viewed luxury and self-gratification as sinful, the profits acquired were not spent on luxuries. Instead, profits were reinvested into new ventures to increase incomes.

Such new ventures included building factories and developing new machines. Thus, according to Weber, the Industrial Revolution began, and capitalism was born.

Source: Max Weber, *The Protestant Ethic and the Spirit of Capitalism*, rereleased (New York: Scribner's, 1958).

---

discipline. Calvin's teachings were widely accepted and formed a new cultural value system that became known as the Protestant ethic. This ethic has three core values: hard work, frugality, and asceticism.

The values advanced by the Protestant ethic have continued throughout our history. For example, Benjamin Franklin cleverly praised these values in several axioms:

> *A penny saved is a penny earned.*
> *Time is money.*
> *After industry and frugality, nothing contributes more to the raising of a young man than punctuality.*
> *He who sits idle … throws away money.*
> *Waste neither time nor money; an hour lost is money lost.*[2]

Former President Nixon, in a speech on welfare reform, declared that labor had intrinsic value, that it had a strong American tradition, and that it was consistent with religious teachings. Nixon added: "Scrubbing floors and emptying bedpans have just as much dignity as there is in any work done in this country—including my own.... Most of us consider it immoral to be lazy or slothful."[3]

Although we no longer value the frugal, ascetic lifestyle of Puritanism, we still believe strongly in the ethic of hard work. An able-bodied person, to gain approval from others, is expected to be employed (or at least to be receiving job training). People on welfare are often looked down on. There

remains a strong link between amount of income and sense of personal worth. The more people are paid, the more highly they are regarded by others and the more highly they regard themselves.

People in low-status jobs are generally unable to form a satisfying identity from their jobs. Having an assembly-line job, for example, often leads workers to view themselves as personally insignificant. They routinely perform the same task day in and day out— such as attaching nuts to bolts. Many such workers feel embarrassed about not having a better job.

Because our work has immense effects on our self-concept, having a degrading, boring, and dehumanizing job can damage our psychological well-being. We judge ourselves not only by how much we earn but also by whether our job is challenging and satisfying and helps us to grow and develop.

Trends in the American Workforce

In the past 100 years, unions have generally been growing in power in this country, which has led to significant pay increases and fringe benefits for employees. Since 1980, however, the power balance between unions and management has shifted more toward management. In a number of businesses, management has been asking that employees take zero wage increases (or even pay cuts), with the threat of moving the business elsewhere or closing the doors permanently. Employees have generally chosen, with considerable reluctance, to accept management's offers rather than to strike and risk losing their jobs.

In the past 100 years, the nature of work and the composition of the workforce have changed radically in our society. Eight changes seem especially prominent: the increase in white-collar workers, the emergence of an employee society, specialization, the increase in women in the workforce, the emphasis on intrinsic rewards, the emphasis on high technology, the growth of low-paying jobs, and outsourcing in a global factory.

Increase in White-Collar Workers

In colonial times, most people made a living working on small farms, either their own or someone else's. We have since moved from an agricultural economy to a modern industrial economy.

In 1900, 27% of the labor force were farm workers, and 18% were white-collar workers. In the early 2000s, only about 2% of the labor forces consisted of farming, forestry, and fishing workers, whereas about 60% were white-collar workers.[4] The immense productivity of our industrial system has made it possible for 2% of the workforce to feed all of us! Farm workers (farmers, farmhands, and farm managers), once the largest occupational group, are now one of the smallest.

White-collar workers (professionals, clerical personnel, sales personnel, managers), once the smallest occupational group, are now the largest. This group surpassed blue-collar workers in terms of numbers in 1956.[5]

Work in industrial societies can be grouped into three categories: primary, secondary, and tertiary.

Primary industry is the gathering or extracting of undeveloped natural resources, such as farming, mining, or fishing. In the early stages of industrialization, most workers are employed in this category.

Secondary industry involves turning raw materials into manufactured goods, such as processed food, steel, and automobiles. In the middle stages of industrialization, most workers are employed in this category. Most of these workers are blue-collar workers.

Critical Thinking Questions
What are your views of work? What kind of work career do you desire?

Tertiary industry involves service activities of one kind or another, such as dental care, medical services, automobile maintenance, sales, and pest control. In advanced societies such as ours, most workers are employed in service activities, primarily in white-collar jobs. Now, more than 60% of our workforce is employed in tertiary industry.[6] Work in this category is generally cleaner and more pleasant than work in primary and secondary industries.

Emergence of an Employee Society

No longer are Americans likely to be self-employed, as they generally were in colonial times. Less than 10% of the workforce now classifies themselves as self-employed.[7] A few small-business owners, small family-owned farms, independent shopkeepers, and independent carpenters and artists still remain. But small owner-operated businesses increasingly are finding it difficult to compete against well-organized corporations and businesses. The vast majority of workers are employed by someone else: large corporations, the government, and so forth. Even physicians, who once were largely self-employed as general practitioners, now generally work for a medical clinic or some other organization.

Specialization

The 1850 census listed a total of only 323 distinct job titles in the United States.[8] There are now more than 22,000 job titles—68 times as many different occupations.[9] Some of the unusual jobs one can choose for a career are clock winder, tea taster, and water smeller. With this extensive specialization, production of goods is now fragmented into repetitive and monotonous tasks, with each worker contributing only a small portion of the final product. A worker on an assembly line commented:

The assembly line is no place to work, I can tell you. There is nothing more discouraging than having a barrel beside you with 10,000 bolts in it and using them all up. Then you get a barrel with another 10,000 bolts, and you know every one of those 10,000 bolts has to be picked up and put in exactly the same place as the last 10,000 bolts.[10]

Specialization has contributed substantially to the development and provision of highly sophisticated products and services. But it has also created problems. Workers find it difficult to take pride in their work when they realize they are merely a replaceable adjunct to a machine or a process and when they contribute only a small part to the final product. Such specialization often results in job dissatisfaction. Those who are trained for a single narrowly defined job that later becomes obsolete are often without marketable skills for other openings. Specialization has also created problems of worker cooperation and coordination for managers of organizations. Our society has become highly interdependent because of specialization. With interdependency, disruption in one work area may gravely affect the whole economy. For example, our country is now heavily dependent on the utilization of computers. At times, computer viruses have shut down the daily operations of some major corporations/businesses, which has disrupted, nationally, the workflow for a few days.

Increase in Women in the Workforce

The labor force consists of people 16 years of age and over who are employed or who are actively seeking work (the unemployed).

Women are increasingly entering the labor force. In 1900 only 20% of all adult women were in paid employment, compared to more than 70% at present.[11] Women, however, still tend to be employed in the less prestigious, lower-paying positions (as will be discussed further in Chapter 13). Women who work full time are paid, on the average, only about three-fourths of what men who work full time are paid.[12] Non-White women, subjected to double discrimination, earn even less.

Emphasis on Intrinsic Rewards

Intrinsic rewards come from the nature of the work itself. Work that offers intrinsic rewards is fulfilling and challenging, helps one grow socially and emotionally, contributes to physical fitness, promotes a sense of accomplishment through the use of one's talents, generates a feeling of self-respect, provides interest and enjoyment, offers an opportunity to meet new friends, and so on. In the past, people took a job primarily for its extrinsic rewards—a paycheck that would enable them to pay their bills. In the past 40 years, workers have become increasingly concerned about the intrinsic rewards prospective jobs will provide.[13]

Emphasis on High Technology

Our society's economy is becoming increasingly based on high technology, such as computers and

GRANTPIX/Jupiterimages

It is difficult to be excited to go to work when the job involves assembling the same equipment 8 hours a day, 40 hours a week, as the days go by.

advanced communication systems. Automation and robots are now doing more of the work that was previously done by blue-collar workers.

Technology is a double-edged sword. Every major technological innovation has both freed humans from previous hardships and created new, unanticipated problems. For example, the development of nuclear power is an important source of energy, but a nuclear mishap has the potential to kill thousands (and even millions) of people. Technology can be defined as the totality of means used to provide objects necessary for human comfort and sustenance.

Technological innovations are causing major changes in the type of work available to Americans. Blue-collar and agricultural jobs are declining, and jobs in high-technology fields (such as computers and communications) are increasing. People who are laid off or discharged in industries (such as the

A female African American astronaut has broken through gender and racial barriers.

The Growth of Low-Paying Jobs

Despite the increase in the total number of jobs in the American economy in the past two decades, average wage and salary income (adjusted for inflation) declined in most industries.[14] A major reason for this trend has been the extensive growth in low-wage jobs. For example, there has been extensive expansion of minimum-wage jobs in the fast-food industry. There has also been significant expansion of part-time employment (that is, jobs offering fewer than 35 hours of work per week). More part-time jobs are now created each month than full-time jobs.[15] Employers are also more likely now, as compared to two decades ago, to hire temporary employees (for example, limited-term positions).[16] By hiring part-time and temporary employees, employers avoid paying many fringe benefits (such as health-care insurance and retirement plans). Another reason for the growth in low-paying jobs is a continued shift of the labor force out of manufacturing and into service jobs. As plants have closed and manufacturing jobs have been exported to less developed countries, displaced workers have been forced to accept jobs in services and trade, which have twice the proportion of low-wage jobs as the manufacturing sector.[17] Many manufacturing corporations in the 1990s and early 21st century emphasized *downsizing* their number of full-time employees.

Critical Thinking Question

It has been said that to excel in any work position, you first must have a passion for doing that line of work. What kind of work do you have a passion for doing?

Outsourcing in a Global Factory

Multinational corporations (corporations headquartered in one country that pursue business activities in one or more foreign countries) are transforming the world's economy with "global factories." Such corporations are no longer confined to producing their products in just one country. High-speed transportation enables these corporations to get raw materials and finished products from one location to another anywhere in the world. Such transportation systems enable multinational companies to take advantage of the supply of cheap labor in developing

steel industry) in which jobs are declining face immense obstacles in obtaining employment that pays comparable wages. On the other hand, people who are trained for high-tech positions have excellent career opportunities. In the employment market, technological advances are a boon for some and a disaster for others. Automobile executives welcome the coming of robots to the assembly line because robots are cutting production costs. Unemployed assembly-line workers with home mortgages are cursing the use of robots.

There is a growing concern among many educational, political, and civil rights leaders that as we come to depend increasingly on computers and other technological innovations, only a select portion of the population will have the skills needed to function well in our society. Those who lack such skills may find themselves trapped in lower-class positions.

CASE EXAMPLE 11.1

Job Dissatisfaction

Mary and Robert Buyze met in college and were married shortly after Mary graduated in 2005. Bob had graduated a year earlier. Bob majored in history and Mary in psychology. Both shared the American dream of having a home in the suburbs, a motorboat, and two cars. Because both had graduated from college, they were optimistic that they were well on their way. They fantasized about taking a yearly trip to such places as Acapulco, Europe, Jamaica, and Hawaii.

It is now 6 years later. Bob is 29 and Mary is 28. They have yet to take a trip and now have two young children. They are deeply in debt, having tried to buy much of their dream with credit. They purchased a run-down "starter" home with two bedrooms that was advertised as a "fixer's delight." Unexpected repairs to the furnace, the roof, and the plumbing have plunged them even deeper into debt, as have medical expenses, food, and clothing for the family.

What is even sadder is that they both have jobs they dislike. Bob has been a life insurance salesman for a small company for the past three and a half years. Bob states:

I took the job because I couldn't find anything else. There were no job openings for historians when I graduated, so I took a variety of odd jobs, none of which I enjoyed. I was a truck driver, manager of a pizza place, taxicab driver, car salesman—and much of the time I was unemployed.

I hoped when I took this job that I would finally be able to make good money. It just hasn't worked out. I hate selling insurance. Most of the time, I randomly call people from the telephone directory and urge them to buy a policy. It's like begging for money for a charity. I absolutely despise having to put myself in a position of peddling policies—and being nice and charming to people who at times end up slamming the phone down and hurting my eardrum. But I have no choice. I've got so many bills to pay that I can't afford not to work. I also hate to see Mary having to work with the kids so young. But again, we have no choice. What really hurts is that both of us

are slaving away at jobs we don't like. Yet, with all the bills we have to pay, we hardly are able to buy Christmas presents.

Mary is a clothing store clerk. She also was unable to get a job in her field (psychology). After graduating, she worked for 2 years as a secretary, which paid about the same as her present job—slightly above the minimum wage. She quit being a secretary shortly before their first child (Rob) was born; she disliked secretarial work even more than her present job. A few months after Rob's birth, she began working part time in the job she now holds full time. Mary states:

When I was in college, I guess I was too idealistic. I expected to get a challenging job that would help me grow as a person and also pay well. That just hasn't happened. What I earn now is very little, especially after having to pay the babysitter. This job at times is boring, especially during the months when business is slow. November and December are just the opposite—we're running all the time, and I'm exhausted by the end of the day. It's feast or famine. But my day doesn't end when I leave the store. I've got cooking, washing, and cleaning to do—plus trying to find time to spend with the children. The last 4 years since the kids were born have been a nightmare—changing diapers, getting up in the middle of the night, taking care of sick kids. Don't get me wrong—I wouldn't trade them in, but some days I really wonder where I went wrong. What really hurts is that we have almost nothing financially to show for our efforts.

I tell you, some mornings I'm so worn out when I get up and so unhappy with work that tears roll out of my eyes when I drive to work. What's just as bad is that I know that Bob hates his job as much as I do. Increasingly, when he has a bad day, he drinks too much—and that is worrying me more and more. I'm in a dead-end job with no chance for advancement, and I can't afford to give it up. Is this all there is to life?

---

countries. For example, U.S. baseball manufacturers send the materials for their product—yarn, leather covers, cement, and thread—to Haiti, where baseballs are assembled for wages far below those paid for similar work anywhere in the United States.

Outsourcing is the practice of locating plants that produce products for American markets in Third World nations where the corporation can take advantage of lower wage rates. Outsourcing in effect "exports" manufacturing jobs from the United States to the Third World. (Some authorities have referred to this phenomenon as deindustrialization in the United States.)

Problems in the Work Setting
Alienation

Alienation has a specific sociological meaning: *the sense of meaninglessness and powerlessness that people experience when interacting with social institutions they consider oppressive and beyond their control.* The term *worker alienation* was originally used by Karl Marx. (Perhaps because Marx has been associated with communism, the subject of worker alienation has tended to be neglected in our country.) Marx suggested that worker alienation occurs largely because workers are separated from ownership of the means of production and from any control over the final product of their labor. They thus feel powerless and view their work as meaningless. Marx described alienation as follows:

> In what does this alienation consist? First, that work is external to the worker, that it is not part of his nature, that consequently he does not fulfill himself in his work but denies himself, has a feeling of misery, not well-being, does not develop freely a physical and mental energy, but is physically exhausted and mentally debased.... His work is not voluntary but imposed, forced labor.... Finally, the alienated character of work for the worker appears in the fact that it is not his work but work for someone else, that in work he does not belong to himself but to another person.[18]

According to Marx, specialization is a major cause of alienation. With specialization workers are forced to perform an unfulfilling task repeatedly. Because people use only a fraction of their talents, work becomes an enforced, impersonalized activity rather than a creative venture.

Marx believed that worker alienation would eventually lead to such discontent that the workers would band together and revolt against owners. Another reason workers would revolt is that they would realize they were exploited by the dominant class, who prosper from their toil.

Marx's prediction of a class revolution has not come true in the United States. Marx did not foresee the effectiveness of collective bargaining and new technology in improving the conditions of workers during the 20th and 21st centuries. Interestingly, even workers in socialist countries such as Cuba experience considerable alienation. (Marx had predicted that there would be less alienation in socialist countries.)

It may be that much of the alienation that Marx attributed to capitalistic societies was really caused by industrialism. Workers in this country, contrary to what Marx predicted, continue to have basic trust and faith in the American capitalistic system. Many workers have made financial investments in stocks, bonds, real estate, savings, and so forth. To a significant extent, they are also part of the dominant class. Marx saw a struggle between only two classes— owners and workers. He did not foresee considerable overlap between these classes, nor did he foresee the development of a large middle class that tends to include both investors and workers. Because of Americans' faith in our system and their disdain of communism, it is highly unlikely that there will be a class revolution in our country in the foreseeable future.

In fact, the working class has not successfully staged a socialist revolution in any industrialized country. The socialist revolutions that have occurred—in the former Soviet Union, China, Cuba, and so forth—have all taken place in developing or preindustrial countries. It is important to note that even China and, especially, Russia are increasingly using the profit motive (a key component of capitalism) as an incentive to work and as a method to stimulate their economies.

In addition, it appears that Marx's theories about the evils of a capitalistic economy are being rejected by many of the societies (such as the former Soviet Union and Poland) that tried to establish economic systems based on Marxist principles. These countries have concluded that, unless they use capitalistic incentives, they cannot motivate their citizens to produce at desired rates. Some authorities are now asserting that Marx's theories about economic production have been tried and tested and have been found to have failed miserably. In terms of productivity, the economies of Eastern Europe that have been based on Marx's theories have fallen far behind those of Western Europe (which have been using capitalistic incentives). In 1990 posters of Karl Marx bearing the caption, "Workers of the World! Forgive me" were selling widely in eastern Germany.[19] (Marx had coined the slogan, "Workers of the World! Unite.")

Sources of Alienation

Alienation has many sources. Specialization has led workers to feel that they have meaningless jobs and are contributing insignificantly to the business. It is difficult, for example, for assembly-line workers to take pride in producing an automobile when they attach only an ignition wire.

Working for a large business or corporation and knowing that you can readily be replaced leads to feelings of powerlessness and lowered self-esteem. Not being involved in the decision-making process and being aware that supervisors do not want workers to "make waves" also lead to feelings of powerlessness and meaninglessness.

In some businesses, machines have been developed to do most of the work. This automation (for example, assembly lines in the auto industry) has led

CASE EXAMPLE 11.2

The Hawthorne Effect

In 1927 in Chicago, the Hawthorne Works of the Western Electric Company began a series of experiments designed to discover ways to increase worker satisfaction and productivity. Hawthorne Works primarily manufactured telephones, with the plant operating on an assembly-line basis. Workers needed no special skills in this production process and performed simple repetitive tasks. The employees were not unionized. Management speculated that, if they found ways to increase job satisfaction, the employees would work more efficiently and productivity would increase.

The company tested a number of factors potentially related to productivity. These factors included rest breaks, better lighting, changes in the number of work hours during the day, changes in the wages paid, improved food facilities, and so on.

The results were surprising. Productivity increased, as expected, with improved working conditions. But it also increased when working conditions worsened. (One way that working conditions were worsened was by substantially dimming the lighting.) The finding that productivity increased when working conditions worsened was unexpected and led to additional study to find an explanation.

The investigators discovered that participation in the experiments was extremely attractive to the workers. They felt they had been selected by management for their individual abilities, and so they worked harder, even when working conditions became less favorable. There were additional explanations. The workers' morale and general attitude toward work improved, as they felt they were receiving special attention from management. By participating in this study, they were able to work in smaller groups, and they also became involved in making decisions. Working in smaller groups allowed them to develop a stronger sense of solidarity with their fellow workers. Being involved in decision making decreased feelings of meaninglessness and powerlessness about their work.

The results of this study have become known as the "Hawthorne effect" in sociological and psychological research. The Hawthorne effect holds that when subjects know they are participants in a study, this awareness may lead them to behave differently and thereby substantially influence the results of the study.

SOURCE: Fritz J. Roethlisberger and William J. Dickson, *Management and the Worker* (Cambridge, MA: Harvard University Press, 1939).

---

workers to feel they are insignificant cogs in the production process. Even the pace at which they work is controlled by the assembly-line machinery. Jobs that offer little opportunity to be creative also contribute to alienation. Such jobs include typist, receptionist, janitor, garbage collector, assembly-line worker, or telephone operator. Most American workers do not hold jobs they had planned for; they are doing what they do for such reasons as "simple chance" or "lack of choice." As a result, many people feel trapped in their jobs.[20]

Alienation also derives from jobs that do not provide opportunities to learn, a sense of accomplishment, or the chance to work with compatible people. Many authorities believe that alienation leads to acts of disruption in the production process—work of poor quality, high rates of absenteeism, and vandalism or theft of company property.

Dissatisfaction with one's job is a useful indicator of alienation at work. Studies on job satisfaction show wide differences, according to vocation, in worker satisfaction with their jobs. Many jobs are simply dull. For workers who already earn enough to live adequately, additional income cannot always offset the meaninglessness of such jobs.

Confronting Alienation and Job Dissatisfaction

One of the best-known efforts to increase worker satisfaction and productivity was that of Hawthorne Works, a division of Western Electric Company in Chicago. The results were surprising, as described in Case Example 11.2.

Many employers have become aware that job dissatisfaction reduces efficiency and productivity. There are a number of ways to increase job satisfaction. The first step is to find out precisely what the workers are dissatisfied about. Then changes can be made. In one job setting, workers may be most concerned about safety conditions (as in coal mining); in another they may be most concerned about boring, repetitive work (as on an assembly line); in another it may be wages (as for jobs that pay only the minimum wage); in yet another it may be lack of recognition (as for clerical workers who make their supervisors look good).

A wide variety of changes can be made to improve job satisfaction. The following list is far from exhaustive:

- Find ways to make the work challenging and interesting.
- Provide opportunities for career advancement.

- Provide in-service training on relevant aspects of the work—for example, stress management programs for stressful jobs.
- Increase wages, salaries, and fringe benefits.
- Involve workers in the decision-making process.
- Have social get-togethers to help improve group morale.
- Give workers more of the profits through a profit-sharing program.
- Have a reward system to recognize significant contributions made by workers.
- Institute employee policies that generate a sense of job security.
- Allow workers some control over their schedules—for example, through flextime. Workers are more satisfied in jobs in which they feel they have some decision-making responsibilities and some control over their work schedules. They don't like punching a time clock, whereas flextime is appealing. The idea behind flextime is to have most workers present during the busiest time of the day but to leave the remaining hours up to the discretion of the workers. Those who want to start earlier, so they can leave earlier, can do so. Those who want to come in later and stay later also have this option. In some places, it is possible with flextime to work 4 days a week (10 hours per day) and thereby have an extra day off.

  Many government agencies and private companies are now on flexitime. Although supervisors have found it is more difficult to coordinate work schedules when using flextime, absenteeism declines and productivity increases under such a program.
- Make the work setting as free of hazards as possible.
- Have promotion-from-within policies, training programs, personnel policies that ensure equal opportunity for advancement and education, and good physical facilities and conveniences (lounges, cafeterias, gyms, and the like).

Critical Thinking Questions

Of the jobs you've held, which did you like the least? Why did you dislike it? How could it have been made more satisfying to you?

Various programs involve employees in *participative management*. For example, in *consultive management*, managers consult with their employees (either individually or in small groups) and encourage them to think about job-related issues and contribute their own ideas before decisions are made. *Democratic management* goes even further; it systematically allows employee groups to make a number of major decisions. An example of democratic management is the practice of allowing work teams to hire, orient, and train new employees. *Self-managing teams* are a subcategory of democratic management; they are autonomous work groups that are given a high degree of decision-making authority and are expected to control their own behavior and work schedules, with compensation usually based on the team's overall productivity.

Quality circles are work-improvement task forces in which managers and employees meet regularly to allow employees to air grievances (which in itself has a ventilating effect in reducing job dissatisfaction), to identify problems that hinder productivity, and to offer suggestions for alleviating these concerns. *Suggestion programs* are formal procedures to encourage employees to recommend work improvements, often in writing; in many companies, employees whose suggestions result in cost savings receive monetary awards. *Stock trusts* allow employees to buy or receive stock in the company, thereby becoming partial owners; a benefit of stock trusts is that they act as an incentive for higher productivity among employees. *Employee ownership* occurs when employees provide the capital to purchase control of an existing company; employee ownership generally increases employee interest in the company's financial success and acts as an incentive for workers to remain with the company.[21]

A number of American companies have increased productivity by conducting "climate surveys," in which workers are asked to vent their concerns and to criticize their jobs. Sometimes such surveys identify problematic situations that can be improved through relatively minor changes. Even when the problems cannot be resolved, work tensions are often temporarily reduced just by allowing workers to let off steam.

Theory Y managers have been found to substantially improve productivity and job satisfaction, as compared to Theory X managers (see Case Exhibit 11.2).

Unemployment

The Costs of Unemployment

As illustrated in Case Example 11.3, unemployment can have devastating effects. Most obviously, it

CASE EXHIBIT 11.2

Theory Y: Improving Productivity and Job Satisfaction

Douglas McGregor categorized management thinking and behavior into two types—Theory X and Theory Y.

Theory X managers view employees as incapable of much growth. Employees are perceived as having an inherent dislike for work, and it is presumed that they will attempt to evade work whenever possible. Therefore, X-type managers believe they must control, direct, force, or threaten employees to make them work. Employees are also viewed as having relatively little ambition. Theory X managers believe employees seek to avoid taking on new responsibilities and prefer to be directed. X-type managers therefore spell out job responsibilities carefully, set work goals without employee input, use external rewards (such as money) to force employees to work, and punish employees who deviate from established rules. Because Theory X managers reduce responsibilities to a level at which few mistakes can be made, work usually becomes so structured that it is monotonous and distasteful. The assumptions of Theory X are, of course, inconsistent with what behavioral scientists assert are effective principles for directing, influencing, and motivating people.

In contrast, *Theory Y managers* view employees as wanting to grow and develop by exerting physical and mental effort to accomplish work objectives to which they are committed. Y-type managers believe that internal rewards, such as self-respect and personal improvement, are stronger motivations than external rewards (money) and punishment. A Y-type manager also believes that, under proper conditions, employees will not only accept responsibility but seek it. Most employees are assumed to have considerable ingenuity, creativity, and imagination for solving the organization's problems. Therefore, employees are given considerable responsibility in order to test the limits of their capabilities. Mistakes and errors are viewed as necessary phases of the learning process, and work is structured so that employees can have a sense of accomplishment and growth.

Employees who work for Y-type managers are generally more creative and productive, experience greater work satisfaction, and are more highly motivated than employees who work for X-type managers. Under both management styles, expectations often become self-fulfilling prophecies.

SOURCE: Douglas McGregor, *The Human Side of Enterprise* (New York: McGraw-Hill, 1960).

---

reduces (sometimes to below poverty levels) the amount of income that a family or single person receives. Short-term unemployment, especially when one receives unemployment compensation (described in Chapter 4), may have only minor consequences. But long-term unemployment inflicts numerous problems. Long-term unemployment often leads to extreme personal isolation. Work is a central part of many people's lives. When unemployment occurs, work ties are severed. As a result, many of the unemployed see friends less, cease participating in community life, and become increasingly isolated.[22]

Long-term unemployment causes attitude changes that persist even after reemployment.[23] Being laid off (or fired) is often interpreted by the unemployed as a sign of being incompetent and worthless. Self-esteem is lowered, they are likely to experience depression, and they feel alienated from society. Many suffer deep shame and avoid their friends. They feel dehumanized and insignificant and see themselves as an easily replaced statistic. They also tend to lose faith in our political and economic system, with some blaming the political system for their problems. Even when they find new jobs, they do not fully recover their self-esteem.

There is a strong association between unemployment and emotional problems. During an economic recession, mental hospital admissions increase. The suicide rate increases, indicating an increase in depression. Also higher during times of high unemployment are the divorce rate, the incidence of child abuse, and the number of peptic ulcers (a stress-related disease).[24] Just the threat of unemployment can lead to emotional problems.

In many cases, the long-term unemployed are forced to exhaust their savings, sell their homes, and become public assistance recipients. A few turn to crime, particularly the young. The unemployed no longer enjoy the companionship of their fellow workers. They often experience feelings of embarrassment, anger, despair, depression, anxiety, boredom, hopelessness, and apathy. These feelings may lead to alcoholism, drug abuse, insomnia, stress-related illnesses, marital unhappiness, and even violence within the family. The work ethic is still prominent in our society: When people lose their jobs, they devalue themselves and also miss the sense of self-worth that comes from doing a job well.

As more and more women have entered the labor force, the consequences of unemployment for single

CASE EXAMPLE 11.3

American Dream Becomes Economic Nightmare through Unemployment

Lorraine and Jim Dedrick thought they had it made. They had a five-bedroom, stone-foundation home on a lake, a landscaped yard, two well-behaved children, a car, a van, a motorboat, and a sailboat. The home, the vehicles, and the boats were bought on timed payments. Because both were working, they were confident that they could easily make the monthly payments. Mrs. Dedrick describes what happened.

My husband worked at Pana Corporation (a car- and truck-axle manufacturing plant). He was a crew supervisor and was making over $40,000 a year. I was, and still am, a legal secretary.

When the layoffs started in spring 2007, we didn't think it would touch Jim. He had 6 years of seniority. But by March of 2008, we knew a layoff was inevitable. Pana Corporation was not doing well financially. When the layoff came in June of 2008, we weren't surprised.

At first we weren't worried. Jim thought it would be nice to have a summer off and looked forward to doing some fishing and some fixing up around the house. Because he was 39 years old and had worked steadily since he was 18, I also thought a few months' break would do him good. He was of course able to draw unemployment benefits, and with my salary I was certain we could get by. Surely Pana Corporation would recover, and he would be called back in the fall.

In late summer, however, a rumor started and quickly spread throughout the plant that Pana was going to close its plant. In September they announced the plant was going to close.

Both of us immediately became alarmed. Jim started looking for other work in earnest. Unfortunately, there were no comparable jobs in the area.

Jim applied at many different jobs but had no luck. I know of nothing worse than to see a once-proud, secure person come home each evening with the look on his face that he has once again been rejected. Jim began developing stomach problems from the rejections, and I started having, and still have, tension headaches. We used to go out a lot, laugh, and have a good time. Now we not only cannot afford it, but we no longer have an interest.

Jim grabbed at every straw. He even went to apply for jobs in Milwaukee and Chicago. In the last year, he appears to have aged 10 years.

In February of 2009, his unemployment benefits ended. Bill collectors began hounding us. We soon depleted all our savings. We got so many calls from bill collectors that we took out an unlisted telephone number. Never before were we unable to pay our bills.

The months since February have been hell. Increasingly we have gotten into arguments. Whenever I bring my check home, Jim has a pained look on his face, as he feels he's not doing his share. I try to tell him that it's not his fault, but whenever we talk about it, he appears hurt and becomes angry.

At the end of February, he began to advertise by word of mouth that he was an independent carpenter. He's good with his hands. Unfortunately, the few jobs he got have as yet not even paid for the extra tools he's had to buy. It has only gotten us deeper into debt.

When I drive to work, the tears often fall. It's my only time alone. Driving home I often cry as I think about our situation and know I'll have to face Jim's sad look.

We don't associate much with friends now. They either pity us or have that arrogant "I told you so" look in response to our optimism when Jim was first laid off.

It just doesn't look like Jim is going to be able to get a job in this area. Next week he's going to Atlanta—we've heard there are a lot of job openings there.

Dennis, our 12-year-old son, is alternately sad and angry about the possibility of leaving this area. He's got a lot of friends and loves to go boating, fishing, and sailing. Having to take your son away from something he really loves is one of the most difficult things I'll probably ever have to do.

Karen, our daughter, who's 15, really had a bad year at school. Her grades fell, and when we asked her why, she said, "What's the use in studying—won't help in getting a job." That remark hurt deeply, probably because it may have a ring of truth in it.

It looks like we're going to have to give up our dream house on this lake. (Tears came to Mrs. Dedrick as she spoke.) We've lived here for the past 5 years and really loved it. This is our first real home. We've added on a patio, a bedroom, and enlarged the living room. We also spent a lot of time in painting and fixing it up. It's really become a part of us. If Jim gets a job in Atlanta, we'll be forced to sell. We checked what market prices are, and there's no way we're going to get what we put into this house.

A few years ago, we thought we were starting to live the American dream. This past year and a half has been hell. Here we are broke, unhappy, and about to lose our home. At our age, starting life over is almost more than we can take.

women with children have assumed ever-greater importance. Newman found that middle-class women who experience divorce "typically have to make do with 29 to 39 percent of the family income they had before divorce."[25] When these women are in the labor force and experience unemployment, it is often difficult for them to support their families while looking for new jobs. Typically they had interrupted their careers for marriage and child rearing, and they now find themselves less competitive in the labor market than men who have been working more or less continuously.

Widespread unemployment also sharply cuts government tax revenues. When tax revenues are reduced, federal departments are forced to cut services at a time when the services are most needed. Such cuts further add to alienation and despair.

High unemployment also leads to high rates of underemployment. Underemployment occurs when people are working at jobs below their level of skill. College graduates, for example, may be forced to take unskilled road construction work or become clerical workers.

Who Are the Unemployed?

In the past few years, there has been a serious economic downturn (worldwide!). In the United States the unemployment rate has been near 9%.

In the past four decades, the national unemployment rate has ranged from 4% to 11%. Official statistics are compiled by the Bureau of Labor Statistics. The bureau, usually monthly, makes a survey of households randomly selected from the total population.

Virtually all of us will be unemployed at some point during our working years. There is some variation from time to time in the groups that are most vulnerable to unemployment. In the late 1970s and early 1980s, unemployment was particularly high among steel workers and automobile workers. In the mid-1970s, PhDs in the liberal arts and social sciences had high unemployment rates. In the early 1980s, the housing industry was in a slump, and there were high unemployment rates among carpenters and construction workers. In the middle and late 1980s, there were high rates of unemployment among workers in the petroleum production industry. In the 1990s and early 2000s, businesses and corporations were downsizing their workforces, including administrative positions; as a result, there were high unemployment rates among middle-level managers. In 2007 to 2012, there was a major downturn in new home building. The downturn was partially triggered by subprime mortgages, which eventually led to a large increase in home foreclosures. Due to the downturn in new home building, many workers in the home-building industry became unemployed.

Some groups have chronically high unemployment rates. These groups include African Americans and Latinos, teenagers, women, older workers, the unskilled, the semiskilled, and people with a disability.

High unemployment among African Americans and Latinos is partly due to racial discrimination. Unfortunately, there is truth in the cliché that minorities are "last to be hired, first to be fired." Another reason for high unemployment is their lower average level of educational achievement, which leaves them unqualified for many of the available jobs. (Lower educational levels and lack of marketable job skills are largely due to *past* discrimination.)

High unemployment among women also stems partly from discrimination. Many employers (most of them men) are still inclined to hire a man before a woman, and many jobs are still erroneously thought to be "a man's job." Women have also been socialized to seek lower-paying jobs, to not be competitive with men, and to believe their place is in the home and not in the workforce (see Chapter 13 for a fuller discussion).

Myths about older workers—age 50 and over—make it more difficult for them to obtain a new job if they become unemployed. They are *erroneously* thought to be less productive, more difficult to get along with, more difficult to train, clumsier, more accident prone, less healthy, and more prone to absenteeism than younger workers (see Chapter 14 for a further discussion of these myths, along with a review of research studies that refute these stereotypes). An additional problem for unemployed older workers is that younger people are often available at salaries far below what the older applicants were paid at their last job.

Unemployment is high for teenagers and young people. This is partly because many of them have not received the training that would provide them with marketable skills.

Employers are willing to hire unskilled workers when they have simple repetitive tasks to be performed. But unskilled workers are the first to be laid off when there is a business slump. These workers can readily be replaced if business picks up. Highly skilled workers are more difficult to replace. Also, employers have much more invested in skilled workers, as they have spent more time training them.

Blue-collar workers are more affected by economic slumps than white-collar workers. Industries that employ large numbers of blue-collar workers—housing, road construction, manufacturers of heavy equipment such as tractors, the auto industry—are quickly and deeply hit by recessions and often forced to lay off workers. As noted earlier, the number of blue-collar jobs is decreasing, whereas white-collar jobs are increasing. A major reason for this decline is *automation*, whereby the system of production is increasingly controlled by means of self-operating machinery. Examples of automation include the automobile assembly line and direct-dial telephone (which displaced thousands of telephone operators). Robots are now replacing workers in a number of industries, particularly for doing simple repetitive tasks.

People with a disability have very high unemployment rates. There are many stereotypes that contribute to these high rates, as described at some length in Chapter 16. There is a tendency in our society to conclude that because a person has a disability in one area he or she also has other disabilities. For example, those with a physical disability are sometimes thought to be less intelligent and less effective in social interactions. Numerous studies have found that when people with a disability are hired, they usually dispel all of the negative myths that surround them.[26] Kornblum and Julian conclude:

> An overwhelming majority prove to be dedicated, capable workers; they have only a slightly higher than average absentee rate, and their turnover rate is well below average. They are neither slower nor less productive than other workers and have excellent safety records.[27]

Reasons for the High Unemployment Rate

The reasons for the high unemployment rate in this country are numerous and complex. First, it should be noted that, even when a society has "full employment," there will always be some people capable of working who are temporarily unemployed. Some people will be changing jobs. Some recent graduates or dropouts have not as yet found a job. Some people who have had prolonged illness could be starting to look for a job. For these reasons, most countries generally consider full employment to exist when the unemployment rate does not exceed 2% to 3% of the workforce.

In many areas of the country, there are more people in the workforce than there are available jobs. Automation in many industries has reduced the number of workers needed and made certain job skills (such as blacksmithing) obsolete. Planting and harvesting machines in agriculture, for example, have drastically reduced the number of people needed in producing food. Picking beans, digging potatoes, and picking cotton and corn once required large numbers of workers, but such work is now done by machines.

From the end of World War II until around 1965, there was a "baby boom," when large numbers of children were born. For the past 45 years, these baby-boom children have been growing up and entering the labor force in large numbers. The past few decades have also seen women being liberated from the cultural expectation that they should remain at home. Millions of females are now employed or seeking full- or part-time work. This increase in the number of workers seeking employment has added to the unemployment rate.

As discussed earlier, outsourcing in a global factory is exporting manufacturing jobs from the United States to the Third World. For example, global sportswear companies headquartered in the United States are paying young girls and women in Indonesia less than $2 *per day* to assemble shoes that will be exported and sold in the United States.[28]

Another factor involves foreign trade. A decrease in orders of American products for foreign customers forces U.S. companies to cut back their production and, often, to lay off workers.

Excessively dry summers in our country sharply reduce the amount of food produced. The law of supply and demand therefore drives up the price of available food. Consumers are less able to buy other products, and companies are then forced to cut back production and lay off workers.

High interest rates make it too costly for consumers to buy homes, automobiles, and other expensive items that are normally purchased with a loan. The demand for such items goes down, and again businesses have to cut back production and lay off workers.

Still another major reason for the high unemployment rate in this country is that we have a structural unemployment problem; that is, large numbers of unemployed people are not trained for the positions that are open. In recent years, many blue-collar jobs have disappeared (as in the steel industry), while high-skill jobs have opened in other areas (such as in the high-tech field of computers). As people become trained for current positions, the employment needs of our economy will again shift; thus, there will continue to be disharmony between skills needed for vacant positions and skills held by unemployed people.

Factors That Reduce Unemployment

Many factors increase the number of jobs and thereby reduce the unemployment rate. Lower interest rates encourage consumers to purchase more items through loans and with credit. Consumers buy more, stimulating companies to produce more to meet the demand and thus to hire more people. Lower interest rates have a direct effect on businesses. Companies often borrow money to purchase capital items (for example, additional machinery to produce their goods or buildings to expand the business) to increase production. When interest rates are lower, businesses borrow more money to increase production, which usually creates additional jobs.

Wars almost always reduce the unemployment rate. Some workers are drafted, and their former jobs become available for people who are unemployed. Furthermore, it takes many additional jobs to provide the military with the products needed to fight a war—bullets, bombs, tanks, fighter planes, food, medicine, and so on.

Businesses and governments in many other countries take a much more paternalistic approach to employees and to ensuring that there will be jobs for those who are unemployed. In the United States, when an economic slump occurs, businesses usually lay off workers. By contrast, in Japan businesses are much less likely to lay off workers; indeed, they seek to have their employees spend their entire working lives with the same company. Governments in many other countries attempt, when there is an economic slump, to create jobs for those who are unemployed. Germany, for example, pays the unemployed to receive work training.

The development of new products opens up many new jobs. The invention of the automobile, airplane, television, computer, hair dryer, and refrigerator created jobs not only for factory workers but also for managers, repair personnel, sales personnel, insurance personnel, and so on.

Confronting Unemployment

Economists agree that the ideal way to overcome unemployment is through increased economic growth. They disagree, however, about the causes of a sluggish economy and about the best way to stimulate an economy.

Rapid economic growth, however, is a mixed blessing. It historically has had adverse effects on the natural environment because it leads to more rapid consumption of scarce resources (see Chapter 17). Once again we see that a solution to one problem often creates or aggravates another problem; in sociological terms, the solution has both functional and dysfunctional aspects.

In the early 1980s, the economy was in a slump, with high unemployment and high inflation rates. President Reagan stimulated the economy through a tax cut to individuals and to businesses. The tax cut gave individuals more buying power and businesses additional money to reinvest to increase production. Reagan's plan worked: The economy was stimulated, production increased, more jobs were created, and the unemployment rate went down. Reagan's plan also included immense cuts in federal spending for social welfare programs and for educational programs. The cuts were designed to reduce the inflation rate. (Big spending by the federal government has often been blamed as a major contributor to inflation.) For the most part, Reagan's plan worked. The economy was again stimulated, and the rates of unemployment and inflation were cut nearly in half. Unfortunately, massive tax cuts (along with sharp increases in military spending) led to other problems, including cuts in social programs that have increased the rates of poverty, homelessness, hunger, and a variety of other social problems.

Economics is a complicated and complex area. Certainly it is a mistake to assume that tax cuts will always stimulate the economy and lead to reductions in unemployment and inflation. For example, a case can be made that high rates of inflation and unemployment in the 1970s were due to rising oil prices, and drops in these rates in the 1980s were due not to tax cuts but to declining oil prices. Petroleum is the major source of energy in producing practically all goods. When the price of petroleum goes up, the cost of production increases, which raises the price of all commodities and results in inflation. With inflation, the public cannot buy as much, which results in an oversupply of goods. Industries then lay off workers, which increases the unemployment rate. When the price of petroleum goes down, the cost of producing goods goes down, which reduces prices and thereby reduces the rate of inflation. Also, the public can purchase more goods at lower prices, which reduces the supply of available goods. Industries are then stimulated to produce more goods, which they do by hiring more employees—thus reducing the unemployment rate.

In 2008 the association between increases in oil prices and increases in the rate of inflation and the rate of unemployment appears to have occurred again. There were sharp increases in the price of oil, which were followed by increases in the unemployment rate and the rate of inflation.

At the time of the revision of this text (2012), there is (and has been for the past 4 years) a very high unemployment rate—near 9%. Most Democrats have proposed a large multibillion-dollar job-creation initiative. As part of the proposal, Democrats suggest an "infrastructure bank" that would make loans to support highway and rail construction projects. Most Republicans are opposed to such a job-creation initiative. They assert that tax cuts for businesses and corporations are the best way—as businesses and corporations would then use their tax savings to create more jobs to expand the profitability of their businesses and corporations.

One proposal for reducing unemployment rates is for the government to subsidize private companies to maintain their payrolls (instead of laying off people) during economic recessions. Many foreign governments do this.

Geographically, there have always been areas of high unemployment, and areas that are booming and needing more workers. It has been suggested that the government could take a more active role in identifying geographic areas where employers are seeking employees, publicizing what jobs are available in these regions, and providing assistance in paying relocation expenses for unemployed workers who are willing to move from areas of high unemployment.

Another proposal is for the government to expand its role in providing job training to the unskilled and semiskilled and to those workers whose skills have become obsolete. Germany, as an example, not only provides such work training but also usually pays workers during the weeks or months they are learning new job skills.

Critics of the above proposals argue that extensive government efforts in any of these areas would sharply increase government spending and thereby increase the rate of inflation. They also maintain that government-supplied jobs would merely be a stopgap measure that would not solve the overall problem of joblessness. According to these critics, government should not be in the business of creating "make-work" jobs.

Occupational Health Hazards

A number of occupational health hazards affect workers. These include on-the-job accidents, work-related illnesses, and job stress.

On-the-Job and Work-Related Health Hazards

Every year over 4 million workers in the United States suffer nonfatal occupational injuries and illnesses. This is a rate of 5 cases per 100 full-time workers.[29]

There are a variety of on-the-job injuries: noise–induced hearing loss, fractures, sprains, strains, and cuts. The most common injuries are disorders associated with repeated motion, such as carpal tunnel (a wrist disorder that can cause severe pain, numbness, and tingling) and tendinitis (inflammation of the tendons).[30]

At least 100,000 Americans die of job-related injuries and diseases each year.[31] Occupations that have the highest fatality rates are agriculture, fishing, and forestry; mining; transportation; and construction.[32]

Currently, one of the most controversial occupational hazards is the use of nuclear power for energy purposes. Many nuclear power plants have already been built. In 1979 an accident at the nuclear plant at Three Mile Island in Pennsylvania released small amounts of radioactive particles into the air. Although thousands of people in the surrounding area were evacuated, authorities feared a serious threat from the released radioactivity. In 1986 an accident at the nuclear power plant in Chernobyl, Russia, released massive amounts of radioactivity into the atmosphere. More than 20 people died within a few days; exposure to smaller amounts of radiation has resulted in early deaths for tens of thousands of other people in Chernobyl from cancers of the bone marrow, breast, and thyroid. These accidents have raised a worldwide concern about the dangers of using nuclear energy to produce electricity.

A serious problem involving occupational hazards is that some substances take years before their deadly effects appear. Asbestos is a prime example. Asbestos is a mineral that has multiple uses, from construction to beer brewing. It has been handled by workers in a wide range of industries. Three decades ago, it was discovered that employees who had worked extensively with asbestos later became high risks to develop cancer. It was not only the workers who were in danger but also their spouses and children who were exposed to clinging asbestos particles on the workers' clothes. The government is now advising people who have been exposed to asbestos to undergo periodic medical examinations for early detection and treatment of cancer.

Mesothelioma was once a rare form of cancer; it attacks the abdominal organs and the lining of the lungs and is usually fatal. This type of cancer has now become relatively common among asbestos workers. Manufacturers and insurers had known for half a century that asbestos workers were dying prematurely from mesothelioma, but it was not until the mid-1970s that this became public knowledge.

Asbestos may be only the tip of the iceberg. There are more than 2,400 suspected carcinogens (cancer-causing substances). Only a few of them have been so designated and regulated by the government.

Rubber workers are exposed to a variety of carcinogens and are dying of cancer of the prostate, cancer of the stomach, leukemia, and other cancers of the blood and the lymph-forming tissues.

Steelworkers, especially those handling coal, are becoming victims of lung cancer at excessive rates. Workers exposed to benzidine and other aromatic amines (often used in producing dyestuffs) have excessively high rates of bladder cancer. Dry cleaners, painters, printers, and petroleum workers are exposed to benzene, which is a known leukemia-producing agent. Miners of iron ore, uranium, chromium, nickel, and other industrial metals fall victim to a variety of occupationally related cancers. Insecticide workers, farmworkers, and copper and lead smelter workers are exposed to inorganic arsenic, a carcinogen that results in high rates of lymphatic cancer and lung cancer.

One of the gravest health dangers involves the chemical industry. This industry was born amid the technological innovations of World War II and has been rapidly growing ever since. Chemicals are now involved in the manufacture of practically every product we use—our clothing, the processed food we eat, the soaps we wash with, our televisions, and our automobiles. These chemicals have been found to cause certain diseases, such as cancer, birth defects, heart problems, nervous disorders, weight loss, and sterility. (DDT will be described in Chapter 17; it is a chemical that has been found to be a carcinogen.) There is some evidence that saccharin (used in the past in diet soft drinks) may be a carcinogen.

It is extremely difficult to prove that a substance causes cancer. Scientists disagree about how much evidence is needed to document a causal relationship. In addition, cancer and certain other diseases (such as respiratory disorders) can take several years to appear after exposure. When a segment of the population has a high incidence of cancer, it is often difficult to identify the cancer-causing substances they were exposed to years earlier.

Simply documenting that certain chemicals are hazardous does not automatically mean they will be taken off the market. For example, there is solid evidence that tobacco is a health hazard, yet many Americans continue to smoke.

When given the choice of being unemployed or working in an industry that is a recognized health hazard (such as coal mining), people often elect to work. Because of the high cost of meeting safety standards, businesses commonly drag their feet in complying with government regulations and sometimes threaten to relocate to other countries when the government pressures them. In many occupational areas, such as textile mills, there is considerable controversy regarding what should be considered "safe" levels of exposure to substances.

In the past five decades, the federal government has become increasingly involved in seeking to reduce occupational illnesses. In 1970 it passed the Occupational Safety and Health Act, which established two new organizations to combat occupational hazards. The Occupational Safety and Health Administration (OSHA) was created in the Department of Labor to establish health standards for industry. The National Institute for Occupational Safety and Health (NIOSH) was created in the Department of Health and Human Services to research occupational hazards.

In 1976 the federal government enacted the Toxic Substances Control Act, which established systems and guidelines for screening and controlling dangerous substances. With the rapid development of chemicals and other substances, OSHA and NIOSH face formidable tasks in testing the effects of all of these substances and in setting and enforcing safety limits for substances found to be health hazards.

Job Stress

Diseases and medical conditions are caused by a variety of factors: what we eat; exposure to germs, viruses and bacteria; genetics; too much or too little sun; lack of exercise; lack of sleep; and stress. Most standard textbooks in medicine assert that stress is a contributing factor in 50% to 80% of all diseases.[33] That is, there are a number of diseases that are stress-related or psychosomatic in origin. One of the main sources of stress is job pressures. Practically any job has stresses. Some of the more stressful jobs are inner-city school teacher, police officer, air traffic controller, medical intern, and firefighter. (Stress is further described in Chapter 15.) The list of stress-related illnesses includes bronchial asthma, peptic ulcer, ulcerative colitis, mucous colitis, hay fever, arthritis, hyperthyroidism, enuresis, hypertension, alcoholism, insomnia, cancer, migraine headache, impotency, atopic dermatitis, amenorrhea, and chronic constipation. Stress is also one of the causes of emotional disorders.

Employers are becoming increasingly aware of the cost of stress to employees and to their businesses: absenteeism, low productivity, short- and long-term stress-related illnesses, job alienation and job dissatisfaction, marital difficulties, and emotional disorders. Therefore, many companies are sponsoring stress management programs to help their employees learn to reduce stress through techniques such as meditation, relaxation, hypnosis, exercise programs (such as jogging), time management, biofeedback, and hobbies.[34]

Social Work in the Workplace

Social work in the workplace has had a variety of other titles in recent years, including industrial social work, occupational social work, and employee assistance. No term has yet emerged as "preferred." In this section, we will primarily use the terms *social work in the workplace* and *occupational social work*.

Occupational social work is generally viewed as an emerging specialization. Social workers in the past three decades have been employed in industry in increasing numbers and in a variety of settings and roles. However, the roots of occupational social work go back in time much further than most people realize.

A Brief History

In the late 1800s, there was a welfare movement in American business. Programs and services were developed to help employees in work-related areas as well as with personal or domestic problems (such as marital conflicts). This movement grew steadily into the 1920s. By 1926, 80% of the 1,500 largest companies in the United States had at least one type of welfare program for employees.[35]

The welfare movement emerged at this time for several reasons. Businesses were growing so large that personal contact between personnel and labor was practically nonexistent. In addition, an increasing percentage of the labor force was made up of women and non-English-speaking immigrants whom management did not understand. Employee turnover, employee sabotage, and the development of labor organizations also stimulated management's interest in the welfare movement. The threat of government regulation in the area of employee welfare also influenced businesses to take action.

The programs that were developed during this welfare movement required staff to provide the services. The positions that emerged became known as social secretaries, welfare secretaries, or social welfare secretaries. With little previous knowledge on which to draw, these secretaries developed methods and techniques through experimentation. One popular approach was that of group work. It was soon discovered that the formation of groups benefited employees in both work- and non-work-related areas. For example, groups that formed for socialization or recreation fostered employee morale, which was reflected in work production and attitude. In addition to working directly with the employees, these secretaries performed many administrative duties such as handling pension and insurance programs.

The number of positions of welfare secretaries declined sharply in the 1930s for several reasons. Labor leaders tended to oppose such positions because they felt the secretaries were antiunion. (All too often, management urged welfare secretaries to mold employees into loyal workers and to fight unionization.) Laborers came to react negatively to the paternalistic character of the position. With the Great Depression in the 1930s, many businesses were forced to cut back on welfare programs.

Aspects of the welfare secretary's role still exist. Many of these functions are now included in what is called personnel or human relations services, such as handling grievances, linking employees who need help with available resources, and processing health insurance and pensions.

In the 1960s and early 1970s, large corporations developed training programs for inexperienced, long-term unemployed people, including members of minority groups. Directors of these training programs learned that many of the trainees needed help in a variety of areas, such as child care, interpersonal skills, family problems, personal problems, and adequate housing and transportation. In the past four decades, industries have increasingly been employing social workers to provide services in these areas.

The development of employee assistance programs (EAPs) has also been a major factor in the emergence of occupational social work. The EAP movement had its roots in the development of alcoholism programs in the 1930s and 1940s. Originally these programs were operated by industrial physicians or were informal programs staffed by recovering alcoholics. Employee assistance programs now focus primarily on the restoration of employees' job performance when alcohol or other drug abuse, emotional or personal problems, or changes in the nature of a job have interfered. Occupational social work is now sometimes erroneously considered synonymous with EAP. However, EAP is essentially a specific performance-focused program, whereas (as we will see) occupational social work is much broader in scope.

There are now thousands of EAPs across the United States. They are staffed by people with a variety of backgrounds: social work, psychology, counseling, medicine, nursing, alcohol and drug abuse counseling, business administration, economics, and management.[36] The professional staff members of EAPs have generally completed some specialized training in alcohol and drug abuse counseling, mental health, and/or employee assistance programming.

The Status of Social Work in the Workplace

Businesses and industries perceive occupational social work as an emerging area for social work practice. Many social work programs have added content on occupational social work in their curricula for social work students who want a career in industry. Occupational social work has the potential to become one of the higher-paying areas for social work practice because most businesses and industries have considerable financial resources.

Common job titles used to describe the functional positions of occupational social workers in business and industrial settings are employee assistance program coordinator, employee counselor, substance abuse service coordinator, affirmative action officer, employee resources manager, occupational safety and health officer, community relations consultant, corporate relocation officer, training consultant, charitable allocations analyst, human resources policy adviser, career planning and development counselor, urban affairs adviser, outplacement specialist, and coordinator of corporate health and wellness programs. In an emerging field, there is always considerable confusion over what the specific tasks and functions of the professionals should be. This is particularly true in occupational social work.

Social workers might help employees deal with problems in the following areas: child care, financial problems, family problems, retirement planning, affirmative action, alienation, legal problems, health problems, mental health problems, alcohol and substance abuse, and recreation problems. Social workers might become involved in providing training and staff development programs. They might serve as advocates in developing programs to combat hazardous working conditions. They might design and implement stress management programs. They might provide consultation regarding the physical or social environment within the company. They might help strikers meet basic needs. They might become involved in community relations—for example, acting as a representative of the business in fund-raising and/or planning for community services. They might propose new job designs to replace boring, tedious, assembly-line work. Thus, occupational social workers have many more functions than simply being involved in operating direct service programs. Paul Kurzman and Sheila Akabas note:

> Social workers may…be called on to consult with management on its human resource policy, donations to tax-exempt activities, collective bargaining demands, or other dimensions of emerging corporate efforts at social responsibility. Professionals may be expected to analyze legislation, administer health and welfare benefit systems, or assist in developing programs designed to attract unorganized workers to trade union membership.[37]

Leo Perlis, longtime community relations director of the American Federation of Labor–Congress of Industrial Organizations (AFL–CIO) cautions that an occupational social worker needs knowledge of labor-management relations to avoid direct involvement in the adversarial relationship between labor and management.[38] (Occupational social workers should not make the mistake of many welfare secretaries who became identified with the side of management.)

Other professionals in industry are already providing services similar to those of occupational social work, so questions of turf are arising. Such other professionals include psychiatrists, psychologists, drug and alcohol counselors, nurses, and experts in personnel management. It would seem that the profession of social work needs to develop models of occupational social work that will clarify to management, labor, and other helping professionals what it can realistically provide.

Businesses and industries do not provide social services for humanitarian reasons. Social workers in the workplace are expected to be accountable by demonstrating that their services promote improved productivity and reduce tardiness and absenteeism and make it easier to retain members of the company's workforce, many of whom have received expensive training.

There are at least five ways in which social services may be sponsored in business and industry:

1. Sponsorship by management in companies with or without a union
2. Sponsorship by the union
3. Sponsorship by both management and labor, with social workers employed by management and dually monitored by both management and labor
4. Private consultantships by social workers under contract to union or management to provide services to workers and/or the organization
5. Sponsorship by a community mental health center or family service agency that has a specific contractual arrangement with the company.[39]

Research is needed to identify the merits and shortcomings of each of these approaches to sponsorship.

Employee Assistance Programs

Most social services in the workplace are currently provided by EAPs. Social work practitioners are the primary professional group that provides staff for EAPs.[40] As noted earlier, other professionals (such as psychologists and guidance counselors) may also be employed by EAPs. In addition to being located in businesses and industries, EAPs are mandated in federal government agencies and many city and county governments, as well as in the military.

It is essential that EAPs operate outside the disciplinary system of an organization. Donald Brieland, Lela Costin, and Charles Atherton describe the importance of employees' feeling free to use EAP services without adverse reactions from management:

Employees ideally should come for help in the early stages of difficulties but are understandably reluctant to share information that management could use against them. Therefore, we have seen that employees tend to conceal problems from both management and fellow workers. After they are referred by management or by a supervisor or union steward for help, the employee may feel labeled as a problem. If they are confronted by management, they fear loss of their job or discrimination in promotion. Managers have similar fears about revealing their own personal problems. Sometimes getting help is specified as a condition for retaining a job. Workers have to be convinced of the ultimate value of getting help.[41]

It is also essential for employees to be aware that what they say to EAP staff will remain confidential; otherwise, they will be reluctant to discuss their personal concerns and circumstances openly. Sometimes management finds confidentiality a difficult concession to make because it is paying the bill, but there is no other way to establish trust with employees. Brieland, Costin, and Atherton note:

Social workers in industry need a written agreement to guarantee that the services they provide will be confidential and also to spell out the guidelines for referral to other community resources....

Management or supervisors who refer the employee should be concerned with job performance but not with diagnosis. If they detect problems they expect some response. One way to handle the issue is to submit a statement indicating that the employee was in contact with the EAP and to provide a brief statement of general progress later.[42]

The primary services provided by EAPs are alcohol and drug abuse counseling, counseling for emotional difficulties, family counseling, career counseling and education, credit counseling, and retirement planning. Each of these areas will be briefly described.

Alcohol and Drug Abuse Counseling

The major focus of EAPs has been on alcohol and drug abuse. It is well recognized that alcohol and drug abuse costs businesses and industries millions of dollars in productivity each year through lower-quality work, absenteeism, tardiness, and deterioration of well-trained employees. EAPs tend to view alcoholism and other drug use as a disease and to emphasize total sobriety or total abstinence rather than a reduction in use. Alcoholics Anonymous and Narcotics Anonymous are also promoted in the treatment process. Inpatient hospital treatment is sometimes used, but outpatient efforts are preferred because they cost less and because they do not involve loss of work time. Some EAPs provide treatment to those who are chemically dependent, whereas other EAPs serve as brokers by arranging for treatment with other resources.

Students seeking a career in social work in the workplace are advised to become knowledgeable about drug and alcohol abuse through coursework and probably a field internship in the treatment of chemical dependency. Employees who have a chemical dependency that is affecting their work are generally offered treatment by EAP staff; such treatment is paid for by the employer (generally through health insurance programs). Employees who refuse treatment encounter the risk of being fired.

Counseling for Emotional Difficulties

EAPs also provide services to employees who have emotional problems, such as depression. As with alcohol and drug abuse treatment, EAP staff either provide treatment services for emotional difficulties or serve as brokers by arranging for treatment with other resources.

Family Counseling

Brieland, Costin, and Atherton summarize the primary family problems that EAPs become involved in:

> Stresses involving the spouse and other family members are an important concern. Not only does the employee take family problems to the workplace but he or she brings workplace problems home and displaces them on family members. Marriage counseling and child care are the most common needs. Separation and divorce take their toll in stress on the job. Child abuse and family violence increasingly come to the attention of the assistance program. These behaviors may lead to criminal prosecution. If publicity results, assault may lead to rejection in the workplace, even though no sentence results.[43]

EAPs either provide counseling in these areas or refer employees and their families to other therapists. If the family dispute involves court action, as in the case of spouse abuse, the court may ask the employer to provide an evaluation, which is then often conducted by staff of the EAP.

Financial problems for families are usually created when employees are laid off. EAP staff may help employees to obtain unemployment benefits. Because layoffs may contribute to increased drinking and to child and spouse abuse, EAPs can provide counseling and referral services for such difficulties during layoffs. For employees who need child care, EAPs may play a broker role in helping to link them with child-care services.

Career Counseling and Education

EAPs have become involved in two areas of career counseling: helping employees to set and achieve specific career goals and helping them to learn and use stress management techniques. In the first area, EAPs may administer, or arrange for, aptitude tests. They may also help employees to understand the promotion and advancement opportunities within the company. EAPs help employees to enroll in educational programs that enhance their physical and mental health and increase their skills on the job. Many companies provide or pay for training that will facilitate promotion. Some companies will also pay for courses that increase employees' assertiveness, personal adjustment, self-understanding, and problem-solving capacities. (Many EAPs are reluctant to provide assistance to employees who are seeking a job outside the company.)

EAPs also provide, or arrange for, workshops and seminars on stress management techniques. Such techniques include using relaxation exercises, hypnosis, time management, or positive thinking; developing hobbies and exercise programs; improving interpersonal relationships; learning to solve problems; and establishing a positive sense of self. Employees who are experiencing burnout or severe job stress may receive counseling by EAP staff or be referred elsewhere for therapy.

Credit Counseling

Many EAPs have become involved in providing assistance to employees who are having financial difficulties and need credit counseling. One aspect of this involves debt counseling, in which the workers receive assistance in renegotiating their payments to creditors over a longer period of time. They are also encouraged to make a commitment to defer further credit purchases until the financial burden is reduced. Often they also receive financial counseling on developing a budget to meet their financial needs.

Critical Thinking Question

Are you interested in pursuing a career in social work in the workplace?

In some states, creditors can claim part of the debtor's wages through legal garnishment. In such cases, the employer must deduct a portion of the employee's wages, which is then paid to the creditor to pay off the debt. This process reveals the credit problems to the employer. (Some employers may view a worker with bad credit as a problematic employee and may then discharge her or him.) EAP staff members may get involved in cases of legal garnishment to help employees straighten out their financial circumstances.

Some EAPs also provide financial planning assistance to employees who are burdened with alimony and child support payments.

Retirement Planning

In recent years, employees have shown increased interest in retirement planning. EAPs can arrange retirement-planning workshops and seminars for employees. A wide variety of programs can be explained, including Social Security benefits, individual retirement account (IRA) plans, pension plans, profit-sharing plans, stock option plans, and tax-sheltered annuity plans.

EAP staff should be knowledgeable about the retirement plans available from the firm in order to help individuals make intelligent decisions. EAP staff may also provide assistance to employees nearing retirement. Such employees need to plan not only for their financial needs but also for what they will do to maintain a high level of positive mental and physical activity.

Occupational social work appears to be a challenging new growth area for social work. But careful planning is needed to avoid the mistakes that led to the demise of welfare secretaries. Because there are more than 100 million workers in the United States, employees and their families constitute a massive target population. Business and industry could hire every graduating social worker and hardly dent their payrolls.[44]

SUMMARY

The following summarizes this chapter's content as it relates to the chapter objectives presented at the beginning of the chapter. Objectives include the following:

A *Present a brief history of work.*

Work is highly esteemed in our society. Under the influence of the Protestant ethic, work has become a moral obligation. It is also a source of self-respect and an opportunity to form friendships, and it may be a source of self-fulfillment and an opportunity to use one's talents. To a large extent, our work determines our social status and defines who we are. Before the Protestant Reformation, work was denigrated and even considered a curse by some societies.

There have been significant changes or trends in the nature of work and the composition of the workforce in the past few decades. The number of white-collar workers has increased, and the number of farmers and blue-collar workers has decreased. Most workers are now employees rather than self-employed. Work is increasingly becoming specialized, and considerable automation is occurring. More women are entering the labor force. Workers are now seeking intrinsic rewards (rewards that come from the nature of the work itself). Our economy emphasizes high technology. Those who are well educated in high-tech areas have a promising future, whereas the unskilled face increased prospects of being trapped in the lower socioeconomic class. In the past three decades, there has been extensive growth in low-paying jobs. There has also been a trend to outsource manufacturing jobs to Third World countries. (Some authorities have referred to this phenomenon as deindustrialization in the United States.)

B *Describe three major problems involving work: alienation, unemployment, and occupational health hazards. Also, summarize current efforts and proposed new approaches to combat these problems.*

Alienation appears to be a serious problem for many workers. Sources of alienation include specialization, automation, lack of involvement in the decision-making process, performance of routine and repetitive tasks, and lack of opportunity to be creative or to use one's talents fully. Alienation may lead to poor-quality work, absenteeism, job turnover, and low productivity. Job dissatisfaction is one measure of alienation. Available studies indicate conflicting results about how satisfied American workers are with their jobs. Numerous techniques have been proposed for reducing worker alienation and job dissatisfaction.

In the past four decades, the unemployment rate has ranged between 4% and 11%, which is considered high. Long-term unemployment has serious adverse effects: depletion of savings, loss of self-respect, loss of friends, isolation, and feelings of embarrassment, anger, despair, depression, anxiety, boredom, hopelessness, and apathy. It may be a factor leading to emotional problems, suicide, alcoholism, and stress-related illnesses.

Groups that have chronically high rates of unemployment are African Americans and Latinos, teenagers, women, older workers, the unskilled, the semiskilled, and people with a disability. The reasons for high unemployment among these groups, as well as among the total workforce, are numerous and complex.

Economists agree that the ideal way to cure unemployment is through rapid economic growth. They disagree, however, about the causes of a sluggish economy and about the best ways to stimulate it.

There are three main occupational health hazards: on-the-job accidents, conditions that lead to work-related physical diseases (for example, high rates of lung cancer among asbestos workers), and job stress. The numerous untested chemicals that are increasingly being used may pose the greatest health danger in the future. Many chemical substances have a delayed reaction in which an illness (such as cancer) appears several years after exposure.

C *Describe social work in the workplace, which is an emerging field of social work practice.*

Social work in the workplace is an emerging field for social work practice. Most social services in the workplace are currently provided by employee assistance programs (EAPs). EAP services include alcohol and drug abuse counseling, counseling for emotional difficulties, family counseling, career counseling and education, credit counseling, and retirement planning.

Competency Notes

EP 2.1.3a Distinguish, appraise, and integrate multiple sources of knowledge, including research-based knowledge and practice wisdom. (All of this chapter) This chapter presents a brief history of work. It describes three major problems involving

work—alienation, unemployment, and occupational health hazards—and it summarizes current efforts and proposed new approaches to combat these problems. It ends with describing social work in the workplace, which is an emerging field of social work practice.

Media Resources

Additional resources for this chapter, including a chapter quiz, can be found on the Social Work CourseMate. Go to CengageBrain.com.

Notes

1. Aristotle, *Politics*, Book 3, sec. V, Benjamin Jowett, trans. (Oxford: Clarendon Press, 1945).
2. Quoted in Thomas Sullivan, Kenrick Thompson, Richard Wright, George Gross, and Dale Spady, *Social Problems: Divergent Perspectives* (New York: Wiley, 1980), p. 300.
3. Quoted in Ian Robertson, *Social Problems*, 2nd ed. (New York: Random House, 1980), p. 87.
4. William Kornblum and Joseph Julian, *Social Problems*, 14th ed. (Boston: Pearson, 2012), pp. 390–392.
5. Ibid.
6. Ibid., pp. 390–392.
7. Ibid.
8. Seymour Wolfbein, *Work in American Society* (Glenview, IL: Scott, Foresman, 1971), p. 45.
9. Kornblum and Julian, *Social Problems*, p. 395.
10. Charles R. Walker and Robert Guest, *Man on the Assembly Line* (Cambridge, MA: Harvard University Press, 1952), pp. 54–55.
11. Kornblum and Julian, *Social Problems*, pp. 392–394.
12. Ibid., p. 393.
13. Ibid., pp. 401–402.
14. James W. Coleman and Harold R. Kerbo, *Social Problems*, 10th ed. (New York: Vango Books, 2009), pp. 88–94.
15. Ibid.
16. Ibid.
17. Ibid.
18. Karl Marx, *Selected Writings in Sociology and Social Philosophy*, T. B. Bottomore, trans. (New York: McGraw-Hill, 1964), p. 47.
19. Charles Fenyvesi, "Trade Marx," *U.S. News & World Report*, Mar. 12, 1990, p. 23.

20. Kornblum and Julian, *Social Problems*, pp. 401–402.

21. Keith Davis and John W. Newstrom, *Human Behavior at Work*, 8th ed. (New York: McGraw-Hill, 1989), pp. 232–249.

22. Kornblum and Julian, *Social Problems*, pp. 400–401.

23. Ibid.

24. Ibid.

25. K. Newman, *Falling from Grace* (New York: Free Press, 1988), p. 202.

26. Kornblum and Julian, *Social Problems*, p. 48.

27. Ibid., p. 48.

28. Thomas J. Sullivan, *Social Problems*, 4th ed. (Needham Heights, MA: Allyn & Bacon, 1997), p. 61.

29. Linda A. Mooney, David Knox, and Caroline Schacht, *Understanding Social Problems*, 8th ed. (Belmont, CA: Wadsworth/Cengage Learning, 2013), p. 214.

30. Ibid., pp. 214–215.

31. Kornblum and Julian, *Social Problems*, p. 403.

32. Ibid., p. 403.

33. Mastha Davis, Elizabeth R. Eshelman, and Matthew McKay, *The Relaxation and Stress Reduction Workbook*, 5th ed. (Enumclaw, WA: Idyll Arbor, 2002).

34. Ibid.

35. Philip R. Popple, "Social Work Practice in Business and Industry, 1875–1930," *Social Service Review*, 55 (June 1981), pp. 257–269.

36. Sheila H. Akabas, "Employee Assistance Programs," in *Encyclopedia of Social Work*, 20th ed., ed. by Terry Mizrahi and Larry E. Davis, (Washington DC: NASW Press, 2008), 2, pp. 115–118.

37. Paul A. Kurzman and Sheila H. Akabas, "Industrial Social Work as an Arena for Practice," *Social Work*, 26 (Jan. 1981), p. 53.

38. Leo Perlis, "The Human Contract in the Organized Workplace," *Social Thought*, 3 (Winter 1977), p. 49.

39. "Industrial Social Work Movement Expanding," *NASW News*, 23 (Feb. 1978), p. 7.

40. Nan Van Den Bergh, "Employee Assistance Programs," *Encyclopedia of Social Work*, 19th ed. (Washington, DC: NASW, 1995), p. 842.

41. Donald Brieland, Lela B. Costin, and Charles R. Atherton, *Contemporary Social Work*, 3rd ed. (New York: McGraw-Hill, 1985), p. 334.

42. Ibid., pp. 342–343.

43. Ibid., p. 343.

44. Van Den Bergh, "Employee Assistance Programs."

Racism, Ethnocentrism, and Strategies for Advancing Social and Economic Justice

We see ethnic and racial conflict—riots, beatings, murders, and civil wars—nearly every time we turn on the evening news. In recent years, there have been clashes resulting in bloodshed in such countries as Egypt, Libya, Iraq, Iran, Syria, Afghanistan, and Somalia. Practically every nation with more than one ethnic group has had to deal with ethnic conflict. The oppression and exploitation of one group by another are particularly ironic in democratic nations because these societies claim to cherish freedom, equality, and justice. In reality, in all societies, the dominant group that controls the political and economic institutions rarely agrees to share (equally) its power and wealth with other groups. This chapter will:

Learning Objectives

EP 2.1.3a; 2.1.4a, b, c, d; 2.1.5a, b, c

A   Define and describe ethnic groups, ethnocentrism, racial groups, racism, prejudice, discrimination, oppression, and institutional discrimination.

B   Outline the sources of prejudice and discrimination.

C   Summarize the effects and costs of discrimination and oppression.

D   Present background material on racial groups: African Americans, Latinos, Native Americans, and Asian Americans.

E   Outline strategies for advancing social and economic justice.

F   Describe social work's commitment to ending racial discrimination and oppression.

G   Forecast the pattern of race and ethnic relations in the United States in the future.

Ethnic Groups and Ethnocentrism

An ethnic group has a sense of togetherness, a conviction that its members form a special group, and a sense of common identity or "peoplehood." An *ethnic group* is a distinct group of people who share cultural characteristics, such as religion, language, dietary practices, national origin, and a common history, and who regard themselves as a distinct group.

Practically every ethnic group has a strong feeling of *ethnocentrism*, which is characterized or based on the belief that one's own group is superior. Ethnocentrism leads members of ethnic groups to view their culture as the best, as superior, as the one that other cultures should adopt. Ethnocentrism also leads to prejudice against foreigners, who may be viewed as barbarians, uncultured people, or savages.

Feelings of ethnic superiority within a nation are usually accompanied by the belief that political and

economic domination by one's own group is natural, morally right, in the best interest of the nation, and perhaps also God's will. Ethnocentrism has contributed to some of the worst atrocities in history, such as the American colonists' nearly successful attempt to exterminate Native Americans and Adolf Hitler's mass executions of more than 6 million European Jews and millions more gypsies, people with disabilities, and other minority group members.

Critical Thinking Question

Do you believe that the ethnic group you belong to is superior?

In interactions between nations, ethnocentric beliefs sometimes lead to wars and serve as justifications for foreign conquests. At practically any point in the past several centuries, at least a few wars have occurred between nations in which one society has been seeking to force its culture on another or to eradicate another culture. For example, Israel has been involved in bitter struggles with Arab countries in the Middle East for more than six decades over territory ownership. Currently, Shiites, Kurds, and Sunnis are struggling with each other in Iraq.

Race and Racism

Although a racial group is often also an ethnic group, the two groups are not necessarily the same. A *race* is believed to have a common set of physical characteristics. But the members of a racial group may or may not share the sense of togetherness or identity that holds an ethnic group together. A group that is both a racial group and an ethnic group is Japanese Americans; they are thought to have some common physical characteristics and also have a sense of "peoplehood." On the other hand, White Americans and White Russians are of the same race, but they hardly have a sense of togetherness. In addition, there are ethnic groups that are composed of a variety of races. For example, a religious group (such as Roman Catholics) is sometimes considered an ethnic group and is composed of members from diverse racial groups.

In contrast to ethnocentrism, racism is more likely to be based on physical differences than on cultural differences. *Racism* is the belief that race is the primary determinant of human capacities and traits and that racial differences produce an inherent superiority of a particular race. Racism is frequently a basis of discrimination against members of other "racial" groups.

Similar to ethnocentric ideologies, most racist ideologists assert that members of other racial groups are inferior. Some White Americans in this country have gone to extreme and morally reprehensible limits in search of greater control and power over other racial groups.

Prejudice, Discrimination, and Oppression

Prejudice is a preconceived adverse opinion or judgment formed without just grounds or before

sufficient knowledge. Prejudice, in regard to race and ethnic relations, is making negative prejudgments. Prejudiced people apply racial stereotypes to all or nearly all members of a group according to preconceived notions of what they believe the group to be like and how they think the group will behave. Racial prejudice results from the belief that people who have different skin color and other physical characteristics also have innate differences in behaviors, values, intellectual functioning, and attitudes.

The word *discrimination* has two very different meanings. It may have the positive meaning of the power of making fine distinctions between two or more ideas, objects, situations, or stimuli. However, in minority-group relations it is the unfair treatment of a person, racial group, or minority; it is an action based on prejudice.

Racial or ethnic discrimination involves denying to members of minority groups equal access to opportunities, residential housing areas, membership in religious and social organizations, involvement in political activities, access to community services, and so on.

Prejudice is a combination of stereotyped beliefs and negative attitudes, so that prejudiced individuals think about people in a predetermined, usually negative, categorical way. Discrimination involves physical actions—unequal treatment of people because they belong to a category. Discriminatory behavior often derives from prejudiced attitudes. Robert Merton, however, notes that prejudice and discrimination can occur independently. In discussing discrimination in the United States, he describes four different "types" of people:

1. *The unprejudiced nondiscriminator*, in both belief and practice, upholds American ideals of freedom and equality. This person is not prejudiced against other groups and, on principle, will not discriminate against them.

2. *The unprejudiced discriminator* is not personally prejudiced but may sometimes, reluctantly, discriminate against other groups because it seems socially or financially convenient to do so.

3. *The prejudiced nondiscriminator* feels hostile to other groups but recognizes that law and social pressures are opposed to overt discrimination. Reluctantly, this person does not translate prejudice into action.

4. *The prejudiced discriminator* does not believe in the values of freedom and equality and consistently

discriminates against other groups in both word and deed.[1]

An example of an unprejudiced discriminator is the owner of a condominium complex in an all-White middle-class suburb who refuses to sell a condominium to an African American family because of fear (founded or unfounded) that the sale would reduce the value of the remaining units. An example of a prejudiced nondiscriminator is a personnel director of a fire department who believes Latinos are unreliable and poor firefighters but complies with affirmative action efforts to hire and train Latinos.

It is very difficult to keep personal prejudices from eventually leading to some form of discrimination. Strong laws and firm informal social norms are necessary to break the causal relationship between prejudice and discrimination.

Discrimination is of two types: de jure and de facto. *De jure* discrimination is legal discrimination. The so-called Jim Crow laws in the South gave force of law to many discriminatory practices against African Americans, including denial of the right to trial, prohibition against voting, and prohibition against interracial marriage. Today, in the United States, there is practically no de jure discrimination because such laws have been declared unconstitutional.

De facto discrimination refers to discrimination that actually exists, whether legal or not. Acts of de facto discrimination often result from powerful informal norms that are discriminatory. Marlene Cummings gives an example of this type of discrimination and urges victims to confront it assertively:

> *Scene: department store. Incident: Several people are waiting their turn at a counter. The person next to be served is a black woman; however, the clerk waits on several white customers who arrived later. The black woman finally demands service, after several polite gestures to call the clerk's attention to her. The clerk proceeds to wait on her after stating, "I did not see you." The clerk is very discourteous to the black customer; and the lack of courtesy is apparent, because the black customer had the opportunity to observe treatment of the other customers. De facto discrimination is most frustrating...; the customer was served. Most people would rather just forget the whole incident, but it is important to challenge the practice even*

> *though it will possibly put you through more agony. One of the best ways to deal with this type of discrimination is to report it to the manager of the business. If it is at all possible, it is important to involve the clerk in the discussion.[2]*

Oppression is the unjust or cruel exercise of authority or power. Members of minority groups in our society are frequently victimized by oppression from segments of the White power structure. Oppression and discrimination are closely related, as all acts of oppression are also acts of discrimination.

Racial and Ethnic Stereotypes

Stereotypes are generalizations, or assumptions, that people make about the characteristics of all members of a group, based on an image (often wrong) about what people in a group are like.

Racial and ethnic stereotypes involve attributing a fixed and usually inaccurate or unfavorable conception to a racial or ethnic group. Stereotypes are closely related to the way we think, as we seek to perceive and understand things in categories. We need categories to group things that are similar in order to study them and to communicate about them. We have stereotypes about many categories, including mothers, fathers, teenagers, communists, Republicans, schoolteachers, farmers, construction workers, miners, politicians, Mormons, and Italians. These stereotypes may contain some useful and accurate information about a member in any category. Yet each member of any category will have many characteristics that are not suggested by the stereotypes and is apt to have some characteristics that run counter to some of the stereotypes.

Racial stereotypes involve differentiating people in terms of color or other physical characteristics. For example, historically there was the erroneous stereotype that Native Americans become easily intoxicated and irrational when using alcohol. This belief was then translated into laws that prohibited Native Americans from buying and consuming alcohol. A more recent stereotype is that African Americans have a natural ability to play basketball and certain other sports. Although at first glance, such a stereotype appears complimentary to African Americans, it has broader, negative implications. The danger is that if people believe the stereotype, they may also feel that other abilities and capacities (such as intelligence, morals, and work productivity) are also determined by race. In other words, believing this positive stereotype increases the probability that people will also believe negative stereotypes.

Racial and Ethnic Discrimination

Gunnar Myrdal pointed out that minority problems are actually majority problems.[3] The White majority determines the place of non-Whites and other ethnic groups in our society. The status of different minority groups varies in our society because Whites apply different stereotypes to various groups; for example, African Americans are viewed and treated differently from Japanese Americans. Elmer Johnson notes, "Minority relationships become recognized by the majority as a social problem when the members of the majority disagree as to whether the subjugation of the minority is socially desirable or in the ultimate interest of the majority."[4] Concern about discrimination and segregation has also received increasing national attention because of a rising level of aspiration among minority groups who demand (sometimes militantly) equal opportunities and equal rights.

Our country was supposedly founded on the principle of human equality. The Declaration of Independence and the Constitution assert equality, justice, and liberty for all. Yet in practice, our society has always discriminated against minorities.

From its earliest days, our society has singled out certain minorities to treat unequally. A *minority* is a group, or a member of a group, of people of a distinct religious, ethnic, racial or other group that is smaller or less powerful than society's controlling group. The categories of people who have been singled out for unequal treatment in our society have changed somewhat over the years. In the late 1800s and early 1900s, people of Irish, Italian, and Polish descent were discriminated against, but that discrimination has been substantially reduced. In the 19th century, Americans of Chinese descent were severely discriminated against. However, this also has been declining for many decades.

As time passes, new minorities are recognized as the victims of discrimination. For example, women, people with a disability, and gays and lesbians have always been discriminated against, but only in the past 60 years has there been extensive national recognition of this discrimination.

Race as a Social Concept

Ashley Montague considers "race" to be one of the most dangerous and tragic myths in our society.[5] Race is erroneously believed by many to be a biological classification of people. Yet there are no clearly delineating characteristics of any "race," and no "racial" group has unique or distinctive genes. Throughout history the genes of different societies and racial groups have been intermingled. In addition, biological differentiations of racial groups have gradually been diluted through such sociocultural factors as changes in preferences of desirable characteristics in mates, effects of different diets on those who reproduce, and such variables as wars and diseases in selecting those who will live and reproduce.[6]

Despite definitional problems, it is necessary to use racial categories in the social sciences because race has important (though not necessarily consistent) social meanings for people. To have a basis for racial classifications, a number of social scientists have used a social, rather than a biological, definition. A social definition is based on the way members of a society classify one another by physical characteristics. For example, a frequently used social definition of an African American is anyone who either displays overt Black physical characteristics or is known to have a Black ancestor.[7] The sociological classification of races is indicated by different definitions of a race among various societies. In the United States, anyone who is not "pure White" and is known to have a Black ancestor is considered to be Black, whereas in Brazil, anyone who is not "pure Black" is classified as White.[8]

Race, according to Ashley Montague, becomes a dangerous myth when it is assumed that physical traits are linked with mental traits and cultural achievements.[9] Every few years, it seems, some noted scientist stirs the country by making this erroneous assumption. For example, Herrnstein and Murray asserted that Whites, on the average, are more intelligent, as IQ tests show that Whites average scores of 10 to 15 points higher than African Americans.[10] Herrnstein and Murray's findings have been sharply criticized by other authorities as falsely assuming that IQ is largely genetically determined.[11] These authorities contend that IQ is substantially influenced by environmental factors, and

Discrimination Against Arab Americans and American Muslims

Following the September 11, 2001, attacks on the World Trade Center and the Pentagon, Arab Americans and American Muslims have been the victims of numerous hate crimes. Emert gives some examples:

> In Texas, a Pakistani Muslim storeowner was murdered. In California, an Egyptian Christian was killed. In a Chicago suburb, hundreds of men and women chanting, "USA, USA" marched on a local **mosque** and were stopped by police. In Brooklyn, an Islamic school was pelted with rocks and bloody pork chops (Muslims are forbidden to eat pork). Fire-bombings of mosques and Islamic centers occurred in Chicago, Seattle, Texas and New York.[a]

Mosques, Arab community centers, and Arab-owned businesses have been vandalized, women and girls wearing the traditional Muslim head covering, the hijab, have been harassed and assaulted.

Stereotypes abound of Arab Americans, and they are mostly negative. The Western image of the Arab is as Ali Baba, Sinbad, the thief of Baghdad, White slave owners, harem dwellers, and sheiks. The facts are that harems and polygamy have been abolished, for the most part, in the Arab world, and only a small number of Arab nations have "sheiks." Arabs are almost always portrayed on TV or in movies as evil or foolish. One *Sesame Street* character, always dressed like an Arab, is always the one that teaches negative words like "danger." In movies, they're always portrayed as villains or financial backers of espionage plots.

It is important for all of us to remember what happened to Japanese Americans after Pearl Harbor was attacked in 1941. Emert notes:

> After the unexpected attack on Pearl Harbor on December 7, 1941, distrust, fear and anger against the 130,000 Japanese-Americans living in the United States at that time intensified, especially in California where an enemy invasion was anticipated. About 115,000 Japanese lived on the West Coast, and their presence was considered a security threat. Americans questioned the loyalty of these Japanese people even though 80,000 of them were second-generation, natural-born U.S. citizens. There was fear that these Japanese-Americans would resort to sabotage or treason to aid America's enemies.
>
> Public leaders like the California Governor, Attorney General, and U.S. military commanders supported the idea of a mass evacuation of all Japanese from the West Coast. Beginning on March 22, 1942, approximately 110,000 Japanese were transported to 15 temporary assembly centers in California, Oregon, Washington and Arizona. Several months later, they were moved to 10 permanent relocation centers scattered throughout the country. These Japanese-Americans lost nearly everything they owned. They were forced to sell their homes and businesses at rock bottom prices.[b]

In September 2001, after 9-11, the U.S. Senate passed a resolution calling for the protection of the "civil rights and civil liberties of all Americans, including Arab-Americans and American Muslims."[c] Virtually all major Arab American organizations and American Muslim organizations have condemned the actions of Osama bin Laden's militant fringe.

Some factual information about Arab Americans and American Muslims may be useful. There are about 4 million Arab Americans in the United States, which is about 2% of the population. There are 21 separate Arab nations, but the United States and United Nations only recognize 19 of them.[d]

There's no simple definition of who an "Arab" is. That word refers to those who speak the Arabic language, but almost every country's version of Arabic is different from another's (e.g., Jordanian Arabic is quite different from Algerian Arabic), and to make matters worse, several Arab countries have internal ethnic groups who speak a totally different form of Arabic or some non-Arabic language.

American Muslims and Arab Americans are different groups in the United States. There is some overlap between these two groups, with some American Muslims being of Arab ancestry. Most Arab Americans are not Muslim, and most Muslim Americans are not of Arab background. Many Arab Americans are Christians, some are Hindu, a few are agnostics, and a few are atheists. Arab Americans are an ethnic group, and Muslims are a religious group.

Islam, with approximately 1.3 billion followers worldwide, is second to Christianity among the world's religions.[e] Schaefer notes that Christianity and Islam are faiths that are very similar:

> Both are monotheistic (i.e., based on a single deity) and indeed worship the same God. Allah is the Arabic word for God and refers to the God of Moses, Jesus, and Muhammad. Both Christianity and Islam include a belief in prophets, an afterlife, and a judgment day. In fact, Islam recognizes Jesus as a prophet, though not the son of God. Islam reveres both the Old and New Testaments as integral parts of its tradition. Both faiths impose a moral code on believers, which varies from fairly rigid proscriptions for fundamentalists to relatively relaxed guidelines for liberals.[f]

(Christianity and Islam are more fully described in Chapter 3.)

In regard to the ethnic background of American Muslims in the United States, Schaefer gives the following estimates:

> Based on the most recent studies, there are at least 2.6 million and perhaps as many as 3 million Muslims in the United States. About two-thirds are U.S.-born citizens. In terms of ethnic and racial background, the more acceptable estimates still vary widely. Estimates range as follows:

- 20–42 percent African American
- 24–33 percent South Asian (Afghan, Bangladeshi, Indian, and Pakistani)
- 12–32 percent Arab
- 15–22 percent "others" (Bosnian, Iranian, Turk, and White and Hispanic converts)[g]

[a]P. B. Emert "Discrimination against Arab-Americans: Learning from the Past," 2007, http://www.njsbf.org/njsbf/student/respect/winter02-1.cfm.
[b]Ibid.
[c]Ibid.
[d]R. T. Schaefer, *Racial and Ethnic Groups*, 13th ed. (Boston: Pearson, 2012) p. 263.
[e]Ibid.
[f]Ibid., p. 263. Reprinted by permission.
[g]Ibid., p. 264. Reprinted by permission.

it is likely that the average achievement of African Americans, if given similar opportunities to realize their potentialities, would be the same as Whites. Also, it has been charged that IQ tests are racially slanted. The tests ask the kinds of questions that Whites are more familiar with and thereby more apt to answer correctly.

Elmer Johnson summarizes the need for an impartial, objective view of the capacity of different racial groups to achieve:

> Race bigots contend that, the cultural achievements of different races being so obviously unlike, it follows that their genetic capacities for achievement must be just as different. Nobody can discover the cultural capacities of any population or race... until there is equality of opportunities to demonstrate the capacities.[12]

Most scientists, both physical and social, now believe that, in biological inheritance, all races are alike in every significant way. With the exception of several very small, inbred, isolated nonliterate tribes, all racial groups appear to show a wide distribution of every kind of ability. All important race differences that have been noted in personality, behavior, and achievement appear to be due to environmental factors.

Many Americans classify themselves as "mixed-race" or "multiracial," as they have parents of different races. Tiger Woods (a noted golfer), for example, has a multiracial background, with a Caucasian, African American, Native American, and Asian heritage.

Institutional Racism and Institutional Discrimination

In the past four decades, institutional racism has become recognized as a major problem. Institutional racism refers to discriminatory acts and policies against a racial group that pervade the major macro-systems of society, including the legal, political, economic, and educational systems. Some of these discriminatory acts and policies are illegal, whereas other are not.

In contrast to institutional racism is the term *individual racism*, which Barker defines as:

> The negative attitudes one person has about all members of a racial or ethnic group, often

resulting in overt acts such as name-calling, social exclusion, or violence.[13]

Carmichael and Hamilton make the following distinction between individual racism and institutional racism:

> When white terrorists bomb a black church and kill five black children, that is an act of individual racism, widely deplored by most segments of society. But when in the same city... five hundred black babies die each year because of the lack of proper food, shelter, and medical facilities, and thousands more are destroyed and maimed physically, emotionally, and intellectually because of conditions of poverty and discrimination in the black community, that is a function of institutional racism.[14]

Institutional discrimination is the unfair treatment of an individual that is due to the established operating procedures, policies, laws, or objectives of large organizations (such as governments, corporations, schools, police departments, and banks).

Discrimination is built, often unwittingly, into the structure and form of large organizations. The following examples reflect institutional racism:

- A family counseling agency with branch offices assigns its less skilled counselors and thereby provides lower-quality services to an office located in a minority neighborhood.
- A human services agency encourages White applicants to request funds for special needs (for example, clothing) or to use certain services (for example, day-care and homemaker services), whereas non-White clients are not informed (or are less enthusiastically informed) of such services.
- A human services agency takes longer to process the requests of non-Whites for funds and services.
- A police department discriminates against non-White staff in terms of work assignments, hiring practices, promotion practices, and pay increases.
- A real estate agency has a pattern of showing White homebuyers houses in White neighborhoods and African American homebuyers houses in mixed or predominantly African American areas.
- A bank and an insurance company engage in redlining, which involves refusing to make loans or

issue insurance in areas with large minority populations.

- A probation and parole agency tends to ignore minor rule violations by White clients but seeks to return non-White parolees to prison for similar infractions.
- A mental health agency tends to label non-White clients "psychotic" while ascribing a less serious disorder to White clients.
- White staff at a family counseling center are encouraged by the executive board to provide intensive services to clients with whom they have a good relationship and are told to give less attention to clients "they aren't hitting it off well with," resulting in fewer services provided to non-White clients.

And what are the results of institutionalized racism? The unemployment rate for non-Whites has consistently been over twice that for Whites. The infant mortality rate for non-Whites is nearly twice as high as for Whites. The life expectancy for non-Whites is several years less than for Whites. The average number of years of educational achievement for Native Americans, Hispanics, and African Americans is considerably less than for Whites.[15]

There are many examples of institutional racism in school systems. Schools in White suburbs generally have better facilities and more highly trained teachers than schools in minority neighborhoods. Minority families are, on the average, less able to provide the hidden costs of "free" education (higher property taxes in the neighborhoods where the best schools are located, transportation, class trips, clothing, and supplies), and therefore, their children become less involved in the educational process. Textbooks generally glorify the White race and give scant attention to minorities. Jeannette Henry writes about the effects of history textbooks on Native American children:

What is the effect upon the student, when he learns from his textbooks that one race, and one alone, is the most, the best, the greatest; when he learns that Indians* were mere parts of the landscape and wilderness which had to be cleared out, to make way for the great "movement" of white population across the land; and when he learns that Indians were killed and forcibly removed from their ancient homelands to make way for adventurers (usually called "pioneering goldminers"), for land grabbers (usually called "settlers"), and for illegal squatters on Indian-owned land (usually called "frontiersmen")? What is the effect upon the young Indian child himself, who is also a student in the school system, when he is told that Columbus discovered America, that Coronado "brought civilization" to the Indian people, and that the Spanish missionaries provided havens of refuge for the Indians? Is it reasonable to assume that the student, of whatever race, will not discover at some time in his life that Indians discovered America thousands of years before Columbus set out upon his voyage; that Coronado brought death and destruction to the native peoples; and that the Spanish missionaries, in all too many cases, forcibly dragged Indians to the missions?[16]

Even in school districts that use busing to attempt to achieve integration, institutional discrimination may occur. One method of discriminating is to use a track system. Most White children are placed in an "advanced" track, receiving increased educational attention from teachers, whereas most non-White children are placed in a "slower learner" track, receiving less educational attention.

Our criminal justice system also has elements of institutional racism. The justice system is supposed to be fair and nondiscriminatory. The very name of the system, *justice*, implies fairness and equality. Yet in practice, there is evidence of racism. Although African Americans constitute only about 12% of the population, they make up about 44% of the prison population. (There is considerable debate about the extent to which this is due to racism as opposed to differential crime rates by race.) The average prison sentence for murder and kidnapping is longer for African Americans than for Whites. Nearly half of those sentenced to death are African Americans.[17] Police departments and district attorneys' offices are more likely to vigorously enforce laws against the kinds of crimes committed by lower-income groups and minority groups than those committed by middle- and upper-class White

---

*The term *Indian* was originally used by early European settlers to describe the native populations of North America. Because of its non-native derivation and the context of cultural domination surrounding its use, many people, particularly Native Americans, object to the use of the word. The term *Native American* is now generally preferred. Some authorities now prefer the term "First Nations People" instead of "Native Americans." This text will use the term "Native Americans."

groups. Poor people (a disproportionate number of non-Whites are poor) are substantially less likely to be able to post bail. As a result, they are forced to remain in jail until their trial, which may take months or sometimes more than a year to come up. Unable to afford the expenses of a well-financed defense (including the prices charged by the most successful criminal defense teams), they are more likely to be found guilty.

White Privilege

An underexposed part of racism in America is that White people (and White men in particular) have privileges that other Americans do not have. Following is a list of some of these privileges:

- White people can go shopping alone and be pretty well assured that they will not be followed or harassed.
- White people have no problem finding housing to rent or purchase in an area they can afford and want to live in.
- White people can feel assured that their children will be given curricular materials in school that testify to the existence of their race.
- White people can go into any supermarket and find the staple foods that fit with their cultural traditions.
- When White people use checks, credit cards, or cash, they can be sure that their skin color is not being taken into account when their financial reliability is questioned.
- White people are never asked to speak for all White people.
- White people can go into a hairdresser's shop and find someone who can cut their hair.
- White people can be sure that their neighbors in nice and affordable neighborhoods will be neutral or pleasant to them.
- White people can assume that police officers will provide protection and assistance.
- White people can be sure that their race will not count against them if they need legal or medical help.[18]

Causes of Racial Discrimination and Oppression

No single theory provides a complete picture of why racial discrimination and oppression occur. The sources of discrimination are both internal and external to those who are prejudiced. We'll now look at several explanations for this behavior.

Projection

Projection is a psychological defense mechanism by which we attribute to others characteristics that we are unwilling to recognize in ourselves. Many people have personal traits they dislike. They have an understandable desire to get rid of such traits, but this is not always possible. These people may then "project" some of these traits onto others (often to some other group in society), thus displacing the negative feelings they would otherwise direct at themselves. In the process, they reject and condemn those onto whom they have projected the traits.

For example, a minority group may serve as a projection of a prejudiced person's fears and lusts. People who view African Americans as lazy and preoccupied with sex may be projecting their own internal concerns about their industriousness and their sexual fantasies onto another group. It is interesting to note that although some Whites view Blacks as promiscuous, sexually indiscreet, and immoral, historically it has generally been White men who pressured Black women (particularly slaves) into sexual encounters. Perhaps these White males felt guilty about their sexual desires and adventures and dealt with their guilt by projecting their own lusts and sexual conduct onto African American males.

Frustration–Aggression

Another psychic need satisfied by discrimination is the release of tension and frustration. All of us at times become frustrated when we are unable to achieve or obtain something we desire. Sometimes we strike back at the source of our frustration, but many times direct retaliation is not possible. For example, we may be reluctant to tell our employers what we think of them when we feel we are being treated unfairly because we fear repercussions.

Some frustrated people displace their anger and aggression onto a scapegoat. The scapegoat may not be limited to a particular person but may include a group of people, such as a minority group. Like people who take out their job frustrations on their spouses or family pets, some prejudiced people vent their frustrations on minority groups. (The term *scapegoat* derives from an ancient Hebrew ritual in which a goat was symbolically laden with the sins of the entire community and then chased into the wilderness. It "escaped"—hence the term *scapegoat*. The definition was gradually broadened to apply to anyone who bears the blame for others.)

Insecurity and Inferiority

Still another psychic need that may be satisfied by discrimination is the desire to counter feelings of insecurity or inferiority. Some insecure people feel better about themselves by putting down another group; they then can tell themselves that they are "better than" those people.

Authoritarianism

One of the classic works on the causes of prejudice is *The Authoritarian Personality*, by T. W. Adorno et al.[19] Shortly after World War II, these researchers studied the psychological causes of the development of European fascism and concluded that there was a distinct type of personality associated with prejudice and intolerance. The *authoritarian personality* is inflexible and rigid and has a low tolerance for uncertainty, has a great respect for authority figures and quickly submits to their will, and highly values conventional behavior while feeling threatened by unconventional behavior in others. To reduce this threat, this personality type labels unconventional people as "immature," "inferior," or "degenerate" and thereby avoids any need to question his or her own beliefs and values. The authoritarian personality views members of minority groups as unconventional, degrades them, and expresses authoritarianism through prejudice and discrimination.

History

There are also historical explanations for prejudice. Charles F. Marden and Gladys Meyer note that the racial groups now viewed by prejudiced White people as being second class are ones that have been conquered, enslaved, or admitted into our society on a subordinate basis.[20] For example, Africans were imported as slaves during our colonial period and stripped of human dignity. Native Americans were conquered, and their culture was viewed as inferior.

Competition and Exploitation

Our society is highly competitive and materialistic. Individuals and groups compete daily to acquire more of the available goods. These attempts to secure economic goods usually result in a struggle for power. In our society, Whites have historically sought to exploit non-Whites. As just mentioned, they have conquered, enslaved, or admitted non-Whites into our society on a subordinate basis. They then use their powers to exploit non-Whites through cheap labor—for example, as sweatshop factory laborers, migrant farmhands, maids, janitors, and bellhops.

Members of the dominant group know they are treating the subordinate group as inferior and unequal. To justify such discrimination, they develop an ideology (set of beliefs) that their group is superior and that it is right and proper for them to have more rights, goods, and so on. Often they assert that God divinely selected their group to be dominant. Furthermore, they assign inferior traits (lazy, immoral, dirty, stupid) to the subordinate group and conclude that the minority need and deserve less because they are biologically inferior.

Socialization Patterns

Prejudice is also a learned phenomenon, transmitted from generation to generation through socialization processes. Our culture has stereotypes of what different racial group members "ought to be" and how they "ought to behave" in relationships with members of certain outgroups. These stereotypes provide norms against which a child learns to judge people, things, and ideas. Prejudice, to some extent, is developed through the same processes by which we learn to be religious and patriotic, to appreciate and enjoy art, or to develop our value system. Racial prejudice, at least in certain segments in our society, is thus a facet of the normative system of our culture.

Critical Thinking Question

If a social worker believes his or her religion is the one true religion, can that social worker fully accept clients who are members of some other religious faith?

Belief in "The One True Religion"

Some people are raised to believe that their religion is the one true religion and that they will go to heaven, whereas everyone who believes in a different religion is a heathen who will go to eternal damnation. A person with such a belief system comes to the conclusion that he or she is one of "God's chosen few," which leads that person to value himself or herself over "heathens." Feeling superior to others often leads such a person to devalue "heathens" and then treat them in an inferior way. The influence of the "one true religion" has led to an extensive number of wars between societies that each thought its religion was superior. These societies thought they were justified in spreading their chosen religion through any possible means, including physical force, which has resulted in wars.

The belief in the one true religion may be one of the most crucial determinants in developing an attitudinal system of racial prejudice. (It should be noted, as elaborated upon later in this chapter and in Chapter 3, religion does have a number of beneficial components for many people.)

White Supremacy

White supremacy is the belief, and promotion of that belief, that White people are superior to people of other racial backgrounds. The term is sometimes used to describe a political ideology that advocates social and political dominance by Whites. The belief in White supremacy has frequently been a factor that has led Whites to discriminate against people of color.

White supremacy was a dominant belief in the United States before the American Civil War and for decades after Reconstruction. In some parts of the United States, many people who were considered non-White were disenfranchised, and barred from holding most government jobs well into the second half of the 20th century. Many U.S. states banned interracial marriage through anti-miscegenation laws until 1967, when these laws were declared unconstitutional. White lenders often viewed Native Americans, Chinese Americans, and other people of color as inferior. Bradley notes that most U.S. presidents who were in office prior to the 20th century (and in the early 20th century) believed in White supremacy—one of those presidents was Abraham Lincoln.[21] Lincoln believed that Whites and Blacks could not coexist in the same nation. He promoted his idea of colonization—that is, resettling blacks in foreign countries. He urged blacks be resettled in Central America, because of the similarity of climate condition to Africa.[22]

White supremacy was also a dominant belief in many other countries, as in South Africa under apartheid. The Ku Klux Klan still advocates and asserts White supremacy.

The Eye of the Beholder

No one of these theories explains all the causes of prejudice, which has many origins. Taken together, however, they identify a number of causative factors. All these theories assert that the causative factors of prejudice are in the personality and experiences of the person holding the prejudice, not in the character of the group against whom the prejudice is directed.

A novel experiment documenting that prejudice does not stem from contact with the people toward whom it is directed was conducted by Eugene Hartley. He gave his participants a list of prejudiced responses to Jews and African Americans and to three groups that did not even exist: Wallonians, Pireneans, and Danireans. Prejudiced responses included statements such as, "All Wallonians living here should be expelled." The respondents were asked to state their agreement or disagreement with these prejudiced assertions. The experiment showed that most of those who were prejudiced against Jews and African Americans were also prejudiced against people whom they had never met or heard anything about.[23]

The Effects and Costs of Discrimination and Oppression

Racial discrimination is a barrier in our competitive society to obtaining the necessary resources to lead a contented and comfortable life. Being a victim of discrimination is another obstacle that has to be overcome. Being discriminated against because of race makes it more difficult to obtain adequate housing, financial resources, a quality education, employment, adequate health care and other services, equal justice in civil and criminal cases, and so on.

Discrimination also has heavy psychological costs. All of us have to develop a sense of identity about who we are and how we fit into a complex, swiftly changing world. Ideally, it is important that we form a positive self-concept and strive to obtain worthy goals. Yet as we have noted before, according to Cooley's "looking-glass self," our idea of who we are and what we are is largely determined by the way others relate to us.[24] When members of a minority group are treated by the majority group as if they are inferior, second-class citizens, it is substantially more difficult for them to develop a positive identity. Thus, people who are the objects of discrimination encounter barriers to developing their full potential as human beings.

Young children of groups who are the victims of discrimination are likely to develop low self-esteem at an early age. African American children who have been subjected to discrimination tend to prefer White dolls and White playmates over Black.[25]

Pinderhughes has noted that the history of slavery and oppression of African Americans, combined with racism and exclusion, has produced a "victim system":

A victim system is a circular feedback process that exhibits properties such as stability, predictability, and identity that are common to all systems. This particular system threatens self-esteem and reinforces problematic responses in communities, families and individuals. The feedback works as follows: Barriers to opportunity and education limit the chance for achievement, employment, and attainment of skills. This limitation can, in turn, lead to poverty or stress in relationships, which interferes with adequate performance of family roles. Strains in family roles cause problems in individual growth and development and limit the opportunities of families to meet their own needs or to organize to improve their communities. Communities limited in resources (jobs, education, housing, etc.) are unable to support families properly and the community all too often becomes an active disorganizing influence, a breeder of crime and other pathology, and a cause of even more powerlessness.[26]

Discrimination also has high costs for the majority group. It impairs intergroup cooperation and communication. Discrimination also is a factor in contributing to social problems among minorities (for example, high crime rates, emotional problems, alcoholism, and drug abuse), all of which have cost billions of dollars in social programs. Albert Szymanski argues that discrimination is a barrier to collective action (such as unionization) among Whites and non-Whites (particularly people in the lower income classes) and therefore is a factor in perpetuating low-paying jobs and poverty.[27] Less affluent Whites who could benefit from collective action are hurt.

The effects of discrimination are even reflected in life expectancy. The life expectancy of non-Whites is several years less than that of Whites in the United States.[28] The fact is that non-Whites tend to die earlier than Whites because they receive inferior health care, food, and shelter.

Finally, discrimination in the United States undermines some of our nation's political goals. Many other nations view us as hypocritical when we advocate human rights and equality. To make an effective argument for human rights on a worldwide scale, we must first put our own house in order by eliminating racial and ethnic discrimination. Few Americans realize the extent to which racial discrimination damages our international reputation. Non-White foreign diplomats to America often complain about being victims of discrimination, as they are mistaken for being members of American minority groups. With most of the nations of the world being non-White, our racist practices severely damage our influence and prestige.

Intersectionality of Multiple Factors

The Council on Social Work Education's *Education Policy and Accreditation Standards* (EPAS) (2008) states: "The dimensions of diversity are understood as the intersectionality of multiple factors including age, class, color, culture, disability, ethnicity, gender, gender identity and expression, immigration status, political ideology, race, religion, sex, and sexual orientation."[29]

Intersectionality holds that the classical models of oppression within society (such as those based on race, ethnicity, religion, gender, class, age, or disability) do not act independently of one another; instead, these forms of oppression interrelate, creating a system of oppression that reflects the "intersection" of multiple forms of discrimination. Intersectionality is a theory to analyze how social and cultural categories intertwine. For example, intersectionality asserts there are vast differences in the life experiences of an African American male, 57 years old, upper class, and healthy as compared to an African American female, 75 years old, indigent, and legally blind.

In working with clients, social workers need to view individuals in terms of "intersectionality."

Stereotyping and Multiculturalism: A Perspective

The Code of Ethics of the National Association of Social workers states:

Social workers should not practice, condone, facilitate, or collaborate with any form of discrimination on the basis of race, ethnicity, national origin, color, sex, sexual orientation, age, marital status, political belief, religion, or mental or physical disability.[30]

Similar to most other social work texts, this text presents descriptive information on these groups. By presenting descriptive information, it has traditionally been thought such information will increase social workers' capacities to be culturally competent with these groups.

It is important to note that some social work authorities are now raising questions as to whether presenting descriptive information about these groups leads to stereotypes and prejudices against these groups.[31] For example, if we describe women as being more emotional than men, and men as being more rational than women, such a perception and categorization often steers expectations for an individual or a group. Such perceptions and categorizations are often inaccurate when applied to an individual member of a group, as well as to the group as a whole.

Another example may help to further clarify this perspective. There is a perception that Asian Americans are a "model minority" as they are viewed as an "overachieving, supersuccessful ethnic group without significant problems."[32] If we perceive Asian Americans as overachieving, and supersuccessful, it raises a number of questions that may negatively impact those labeled as Asian Americans. A few of these questions are the following: Will it lead Asian American children to feel undue pressure to be supersuccessful? Will it lead those Asian Americans who are not supersuccessful to view themselves as failures? Will social service agencies and policy makers tend to ignore developing human service programs for Asian Americans because they are already perceived to be supersuccessful? Will providers of services (such as dentists, car dealers, plumbers, electricians) tend to charge Asian Americans more because they are apt to be perceived to be "wealthy"?

It should be noted that the stereotyping of Asian Americans as being overachieving and supersuccessful misrepresents the diverse experiences of Asian Americans by glossing over huge differences within a group of people who come from more than two dozen countries, most of which have their own distinct language and culture. In this regard, Ziauddin Sardar notes:

White people ... look at me and exclaim: "Surely, you're Asian." However, there is no such thing as an Asian. Asia is not a race or identity: it is a continent. Even in Asia, where more than half of the world's population lives, no one calls him or herself "Asian." ... In the U.S., the Asian label is attached to Koreans, Filipinos, and Chinese. In Britain, we do not use the term Asian to describe our substantial communities of Turks, Iranians, or Indonesians, even though these countries are in Asia.[33]

There is a danger that presenting descriptive information about a group may lead to negative stereotyping and then overt discrimination. For example, there is descriptive information that indicates African Americans tend to have higher rates (compared to Whites) of poverty, being homeless, births outside of marriage, dropping out of school, criminal arrests, and criminal convictions.[34] Does such information lead to the expectation by non–African Americans that African American individuals they meet are apt to "fit" such descriptive information? For example, the poverty rate for African Americans is about 25%, while for Whites it is 10%.[35] Will this lead a non–African American to expect that African American individuals they encounter are apt to be "poor"? What may be ignored by the non–African American is that most African Americans (75%) are not living in poverty.

This text will continue to use the traditional approach of presenting descriptive information about the diverse categories identified in the EPAS for two reasons.[36] One, most social work educators deduce that the EPAS was written with the expectation that descriptive information will be presented in the social work curriculum on these categories. Two, the social work authorities who are concerned about descriptive information being presented have *not* arrived at a new definition of diversity that enables us to develop a knowledge base of information about the diverse groups identified in the EPAS who have been victimized in the past (and currently) by discrimination. This author urges readers to be aware of the dangers of stereotypes being generated by descriptive information about the diverse groups identified in this text.

An additional caveat about diversity will be mentioned. Everyone has multicultural diversity. We differ from one another in terms of variables such as age, economic status, education, family type, gender, personality type, ethnicity, religion, geographic origin, sexual orientation, communication types, attire, language, political views, physical abilities, lifestyle, and so on. Therefore, when we meet someone who, for example, is Japanese American, it is essential to recognize that there are so many other facets of that individual than his or her ethnicity.

Background of Racial Groups

The largest racial group in the United States is the White race, which is the majority group, both in numbers (about 70% of the population[37]) and in power. The 2000 census showed that Latinos surpassed African Americans as a share of the total U.S. population. Latinos now compose 13% of the population.[38] African Americans compose 12% of the population.[39] The other non-White groups constitute about 2% of our population and primarily include Native Americans and people of Japanese, Chinese, and Filipino descent. There are also small numbers of the following non-White groups: Aleuts, Asian Indians, Eskimo, Hawaiians, Indonesians, Koreans, and Polynesians. In educational attainment, occupational status, and average income, most of these non-White groups are clearly at a disadvantage as compared with the White groups. (The two major non-White groups that now approach Whites in socioeconomic status are Japanese Americans and Chinese Americans.)

African Americans

The United States has always been a racist nation. Although our country's founders talked about freedom, dignity, equality, and human rights, the economy of the United States prior to the Civil War depended heavily on slavery.

Many slaves came from cultures that had well-developed art forms, political systems, family patterns, religious beliefs, and economic systems. However, because their culture was not European, slave owners viewed it as being of "no consequence" and prohibited slaves from practicing and developing their art, language, religion, and family life. For want of practice, their former culture soon died in the United States.

The life of a slave was harsh. Slaves were viewed not as human beings but as chattel to be bought and sold. Long, hard days were spent working in the field, with the profits of their labor going to their White owners. Whippings, mutilations, and hangings were commonly accepted White control practices. The impetus to enslave Blacks was not simply racism; many Whites believed that it was to their economic advantage to have a cheap supply of labor.

Cotton growing, in particular, was thought to require a large labor force that was cheap and docile. Marriages between slaves were not recognized by the law, and slaves were often sold with little regard to marital and family ties. Throughout the slavery period and even afterward, African Americans were discouraged from demonstrating intelligence, initiative, or ambition. For a period of time, it was even illegal to teach them to read and write.

Some authorities have noted that the opposition to the spread of slavery preceding the Civil War was due less to moral concern for human rights and equality than to the North's fears of competition from slave labor and the rapidly increasing migration of free Blacks to the North and West.[40] Few Whites at that time understood or believed in the principle of racial equality—not even Abraham Lincoln, who thought Blacks were inferior to Whites. In 1858 in a speech in Charleston, Illinois, Lincoln asserted:

> I will say, then, that I am not, nor ever have been in favor of bringing about in any way the social and political equality of the white and black races; that I am not, nor ever have been, in favor of making voters or jurors of Negroes, nor of qualifying them to hold office, nor to inter-marry with White people ... and inasmuch as they cannot so live, while they do remain together there must be the position of superior and inferior, and I as much as any other man am in favor of having the superior position assigned to the White race.[41]

Following the Civil War, the federal government failed to develop a comprehensive program of economic and educational aid to African Americans. As a result, most of them returned to economic dependency on the same planters in the South who had held them in bondage. Within a few years, laws were passed in the southern states prohibiting interracial marriages and requiring racial segregation in schools and public places.

A rigid caste system in the South hardened into a system of oppression known as "Jim Crow." The system prescribed how African Americans were supposed to act in the presence of Whites, asserted White supremacy, embraced racial segregation, and denied political and legal rights to African Americans. Those who opposed Jim Crow were subjected to burnings, beatings, and lynchings. Jim Crow was used to "teach" African Americans to view themselves as inferior and to be servile and passive in interactions with Whites.

World War II opened up new employment opportunities for African Americans, who migrated to the North in large numbers. Greater mobility afforded by wartime conditions led to upheavals in the traditional caste system. Awareness of disparity between the ideal and the real led many people to try to improve race relations, not only for domestic peace and justice but also to answer criticism from abroad. With each gain in race relations, more African Americans were encouraged to press for their rights.

A major turning point in civil rights history was the 1954 U.S. Supreme Court decision in *Brown* v. *Board of Education*, which ruled that racial segregation in public schools was unconstitutional. Since then there have been a number of organized efforts by both African Americans and certain segments of the White population to secure equal rights and opportunities for minorities. Attempts to change deeply entrenched racist attitudes and practices have produced much turmoil: the burning of our inner cities in the late 1960s,* the assassination of Martin Luther King, Jr., and clashes between militant Black groups and the police. There have also been significant advances. Wide-ranging legislation has been passed, protecting civil rights in areas such as housing, voting, employment, and the use of public transportation and facilities. During the riots in 1968, the National Advisory Commission on Civil Disorders warned that our society was careening "toward two societies, one Black, one White—separate and unequal."[42]

America today is not the bitterly segregated society that the riot commission envisioned. African Americans and Whites now more often work together and lunch together—yet few really count each other as friends.

Schaefer provides a brief summary of the current status of African Americans in the United States:

African Americans have made significant progress in many areas, but they have not kept pace with White Americans in many sectors. African Americans have advanced in formal schooling to a remarkable degree, although in most areas residential patterns have left many public schools predominantly Black or White. Higher education also reflects the legacy of a nation that has operated two schooling systems: one for Blacks and another

for Whites. Gains in earning power have barely kept pace with inflation, and the gap between Whites and Blacks has remained largely unchanged. African American families are susceptible to the problems associated with a low-income group that also faces discrimination and prejudice. Housing in many areas remains segregated, despite growing numbers of Blacks in suburban areas. African Americans are more likely to be victims of crimes and to be arrested for violent crimes. The subordination of Blacks is also apparent in health care delivery. African Americans have made substantial gains in elective office but still are underrepresented compared with their numbers in the general population.[43]

We, as a nation, have come a long way since the U.S. Supreme Court's decision in 1954. But we still have a long way to go before we eliminate African American poverty and oppression. Living conditions in some African American communities remain as bleak as they were when our inner cities erupted in the late 1960s.

Two developments have characterized the socioeconomic circumstances of African Americans in recent years. A middle class has emerged that is better educated, better paid, and better housed than any group of African Americans that has gone before it. However, as middle-class African Americans move to better neighborhoods, they leave behind those who are living in poverty. The group that has been left behind generates a disproportionate share of the social pathology that is associated with a deteriorating urban neighborhood, including high rates of crime, unemployment, drug abuse, school dropouts, births outside of marriage, and families receiving public assistance.

More than half of all African American children are being raised in single-parent families.[44] However, many of the children living in single-parent families are living in family structures composed of some variation of the extended family. Many single-parent families move in with relatives during adversity, including economic adversity. In addition, African American families of all levels rely on relatives to care for their children while they work.

Schaefer summarizes five strengths identified by the National Urban League that allow African American families to function effectively in a racist society:

1. *Strong kinship bonds:* Blacks are more likely than Whites to care for children and the elderly in an extended family network.

---

*On April 4, 1968, Martin Luther King, Jr., was killed by a White assassin's bullet. His death helped trigger extensive rioting in 40 cities; in many places, whole blocks were burned down.

CASE EXHIBIT 12.2

The Africentric Perspective and Worldview

African American culture has numerous components. It has elements from traditional African culture; elements from slavery, Reconstruction, and subsequent exposure to racism and discrimination; and elements from "mainstream" White culture. An emerging perspective is the *Africentric perspective*,[a] which acknowledges African culture and expressions of African beliefs, values, institutions, and behaviors. It recognizes that African Americans have retained, to some degree, a number of elements of African life and values.

The Africentric perspective holds that the application of Eurocentric theories to explain the behavior and ethos of African Americans is often inappropriate. Eurocentric theories of human behavior reflect concepts that were developed in European and Anglo-American cultures. Eurocentric theorists have historically vilified people of African descent and other people of color. Such theorists have explicitly or implicitly claimed that people of African descent are pathological or inferior in their social, personality, or moral development.[b] The origins of this denigration can be found in the slave trade, as slave traders and owners were pressed to justify the enslavement of Africans. The fallout of Eurocentric theories is the portrayal of African cultures as "uncivilized" and as having contributed practically nothing of value to world development and human history.

The Africentric perspective seeks to dispel the negative distortions about people of African ancestry by legitimizing and disseminating a *worldview* that goes back thousands of years and that exists in the hearts and minds of many people of African descent today. The concept of worldview involves one's perceptions of oneself in relation to other people, objects, institutions, and nature. It focuses on one's view of the world and one's role and place in it. The worldviews of African Americans are shaped by unique and important experiences, such as racism and discrimination, an African heritage, traditional attributes of the African American family and community life, and a strong religious orientation.

The Africentric perspective also seeks to promote a worldview that will facilitate human and societal transformation toward moral, spiritual, and humanistic ends and that seeks to persuade people of different cultural and ethnic groups that they share a mutual interest in this regard. The Africentric perspective rejects the idea that the individual can be understood apart from others in his or her social group. It emphasizes a collective identity that encourages sharing, cooperation, and social responsibility.

The Africentric perspective also emphasizes the importance of spirituality, which includes one's moral development and attaining meaning and identity in life. The Africentric perspective views oppression and alienation as the major sources of human problems in the United States. Oppression and alienation are generated not only by prejudice and discrimination but also by the European worldview that teaches people to see themselves primarily as material, physical beings seeking immediate pleasure for their physical, material, or sexual desires. It is further asserted that this European worldview discourages spiritual and moral development.

The Africentric perspective has been used to provide explanations of the origins of specific social problems. For example, violent crimes by youths are thought to be a result of the limited options and choices they have to advance themselves economically. Youths seek a life of street crime as a logical means to cope with, and protect against, a society that practices pervasive employment discrimination (associated with minimum wages, layoffs, lack of opportunities for education or training, and a wide gap between the rich and the poor). These youths believe that they can make more money from a life of street crime than from attending college or starting a legitimate business with little start-up capital. Turning to a life of crime is also thought more likely to occur in a society that uses the European worldview, which de-emphasizes spiritual and moral development, as individuals then have little or no awareness of collective and social responsibility.

The Africentric perspective values a more holistic, spiritual, and optimistic view of human beings. It supports the "strengths perspective" and "empowerment" concepts of social work practice, which are described later in this chapter.

[a]W. Devore and E. G. Schlesinger, *Ethnic-Sensitive Social Work Practice*, 4th ed. (Needham Heights, MA: Allyn & Bacon, 1996).
[b]J. H. Schiele, "Afrocentricity: An Emerging Paradigm in Social Work Practice," *Social Work*, 41 (May 1966), pp. 284–294.

2. *A strong work orientation*: poor Blacks are more likely to be working, and poor Black families often include more than one wage earner.
3. *Adaptability of family roles*: in two-parent families, the egalitarian pattern of decision making is the most common. The self-reliance of Black women who are the primary wage earners best illustrates this adaptability.
4. *Strong achievement orientation*: working-class Blacks indicate a greater desire for their children to attend college than working-class Whites. Even a majority of low-income African Americans want to attend college.
5. *A strong religious orientation*: since the time of slavery, Black churches have been the impetus behind many significant grassroots organizations.[45]

Although it is a reality that many African American families are headed by single mothers, it would be a serious error to view such family structures as inherently pathological. A single parent with good parenting skills, along with a supportive extended family, can lead to healthy family functions.

Religious organizations that are predominantly African American have tended not only to have a spiritual mission but also to have been highly active in social action efforts to combat racial discrimination. Many prominent African American leaders, such as Martin Luther King, Jr., and Jesse Jackson, have been members of the clergy. African American churches have served to develop leadership skills and as social welfare organizations to meet basic needs, such as clothing, food, and shelter. African American churches are support systems for troubled individuals and families.

Many African Americans have had the historical experience of being subjected to negative evaluations by school systems, social welfare agencies, health care institutions, and the justice system. Because of their past experiences, African Americans are likely to view such institutions with apprehension. Schools, for example, have erroneously perceived African Americans as being less capable of developing cognitive skills. Such perceptions about school failure are often a self-fulfilling prophecy. If African American children are expected to fail in school systems, teachers are likely to put forth less effort in challenging them to learn, and African American children may then put forth less effort to learn, resulting in a lower level of achievement.

Some of the attitudes and behaviors exhibited by African Americans who seek services from White social agencies are often labeled resistant. However, the attitudes and behaviors can better be viewed as attempts at coping with powerlessness and racism. For example, if there are delays in provision of services, African Americans may convey apathy or disparage the agency because they interpret the delay as being due to racism; they then respond in ways they have learned in the past to handle discrimination.

Latinos

Latinos are Americans of Spanish origin. They constitute diverse groups bound somewhat together by their language, culture, and ties to Roman Catholicism. This broad categorization includes Mexican Americans (Chicanos), Puerto Ricans, Cubans, people from Central and South America and the West Indies, and others of Spanish origin (Figure 12.1). The Latino population is growing at a much faster rate than the rest of the population.[46] There are three main reasons for this rapid growth: a tendency to have large families, a continual inflow of immigrants (particularly from Mexico), and the high proportion of Latinos in this country who are of childbearing age.

Mexican Americans

The largest Latino group in the United States is Mexican Americans. Although many Americans are unaware of the fact, Mexican Americans have had a long history of settlement and land ownership in what is now the United States. In the 1700s and 1800s, there were a number of small Latino communities in what later became the American Southwest—in areas that have since gained statehood (including Texas, Arizona, New Mexico, and California). These early Latinos were generally small landholders. In the 1800s, Whites moved into these regions, and competition for good land became fierce. Many Mexican Americans had their land taken away by large White-owned cattle and agricultural interests. Texas was once part of Mexico. In 1836 the settlers (including many of Spanish descent) staged a successful insurrection against the Mexican government and formed an independent republic. In 1845 Texas was annexed to the United States. As a consequence, many of the Mexican settlers became U.S. citizens.

Since the 1850s, there has been a steady migration of Mexicans to the United States, with a number of immigrants entering this country illegally. The average income in Mexico is much lower than in the United States, so the quest for higher wages and a better life has lured many Mexicans to this country.

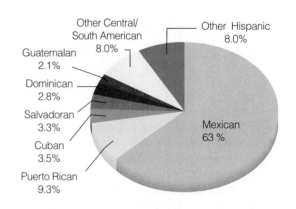

FIGURE 12.1 Hispanic Population

Source: *The Hispanic Population: 2010.* C2010BR-404. Accessible at http://www.census.gov/prod/cen2010/briefs/c2010br-04.pdf.

César Chávez formed the first successful labor union to represent migrant workers about 40 years ago. His nationwide boycotts of table grapes picked by underpaid workers and contaminated with pesticides have inspired other collective action by Chicanos.

Relations between Whites and Mexican Americans have on occasion become vicious and ugly. Similar to Black–White confrontations, there have been many riots between Whites and Mexican Americans.

Many Mexican Americans live in barrios (Spanish-speaking sections of U.S. cities that have deteriorated) in cities such as Los Angeles, Denver, and Chicago. Although some are moving up in socioeconomic status, most have low-paying jobs.

A smaller number of Mexican Americans are employed in temporary seasonal work, largely on farms. Some migrate north in the summer to be farm laborers and return to the Southwest in the fall. In terms of acculturation and assimilation, these migrant workers are among the least "Americanized" of all ethnic groups.[47] They are reluctant to seek help from social agencies, partly because of their pride and partly because of language and cultural barriers.

An increasingly large segment of this ethnic group is becoming involved in the "Chicano" movement. Chicanos are Americans of Mexican origin who

resent the stereotypes that demean Mexican Americans—particularly the image of laziness, because many are performing some of the hardest physical labor in our society. The origin of the word *Chicano* is not clear, but until the last generation it was a derogatory term Whites used for Mexican Americans. Now the word and the people have come full circle, and *Chicano* has taken on a new, positive meaning. The Chicano movement asserts that social institutions must become more responsive to the needs of Chicanos. Chicano-studies programs have been developed at a number of universities.

The civil rights activities of African Americans have provided encouragement for the Chicanos' militant stance. In addition, second- and third-generation Mexican Americans have fewer ties to Mexico than did their elders, and they are oriented more toward the majority American culture in terms of aspirations and goals. Yet similar to African Americans, Mexican Americans generally have low-paying jobs, high rates of unemployment, and high levels of poverty. They also have high rates of infant mortality, low levels of educational attainment, and high levels of substandard housing. Their standard of living is no better than that of African Americans.

Chicano men, as contrasted to Anglo men, have been described as exhibiting greater pride in their maleness.[48] *Machismo*—a strong sense of masculine pride—is highly valued among Chicano men and is displayed by males to express dominance and superiority. Machismo is demonstrated differently by different people. Some may seek to be irresistible to women and to have a number of sexual partners. Some resort to displaying weapons or fighting. Some interpret machismo to mean pride in one's manhood, honor, and ability to provide for one's family. Others boast of their achievements, even those that never occurred. Recent writers have noted that the feminist movement, urbanization, upward mobility, and acculturation are contributing to the decline of machismo.[49] Chicanos also tend to be more "familistic" than Anglos. Familism is the belief that the family takes precedence over the individual.[50]

In the 1970s and 1980s, César Chávez unionized migrant workers in California, organized several strikes, and led successful nationwide boycotts of fruit and vegetables picked by underpaid workers. Powerful White economic interests made several violent attempts to break these strikes. Chávez's campaigns provided an example and incentive for other collective action by Chicanos. The future is likely to see Chicanos becoming an increasingly powerful political force with which to be reckoned.

Puerto Ricans

After World War II, many Puerto Ricans migrated to the mainland United States, largely because of population pressure and insufficient job opportunities on the island. Although they are found in all the states, they have settled mainly in New York City, New Jersey, Illinois, Florida, California, Pennsylvania, and Connecticut. Those migrating from Puerto Rico were from the higher socioeconomic classes in their home society. Although their earnings on the mainland are higher than in Puerto Rico, they have experienced lower job status than Anglos and many live in substandard housing.

For Puerto Ricans, the Spanish culture has been dominant, but they have also been influenced by the Taino, American, African, and European cultures. In Puerto Rico, status is based on culture or class, not skin color, and interracial marriages are common.

On entering the mainland United States, many Puerto Ricans understandably become puzzled by the greater emphasis given to skin color here.

The island of Puerto Rico is in a commonwealth arrangement with the United States, and citizenship was extended to Puerto Ricans living on the island by the Jones Act of 1917.[51] As a commonwealth, its people have privileges and rights different from those on the mainland. They are subject to military service, selective service registration, and all federal laws. Yet they cannot vote in presidential elections and have no voting representation in Congress. Puerto Ricans pay a local income tax but no federal income tax. There is currently considerable controversy in Puerto Rico as to whether the island should seek independence from the United States, seek statehood, or remain a commonwealth.

The role of the United States in Puerto Rico has produced an economy that is strong by Caribbean standards, but remains well below that of the poorest areas of the United States. It has a high rate of unemployment, poor housing, a high rate of poverty, and inadequate health care.

Cubans

Most Cuban Americans are recent migrants to the United States. Many are political refugees, having fled Cuba following the takeover of the government by Fidel Castro in 1959. Many of these Cuban Americans are well educated and have managerial or professional backgrounds. Large numbers have settled in southern Florida, particularly in the Miami area.

In 1980 Castro opened the doors of his socialist island, and more than 100,000 more Cubans fled to this country. Many of these latest arrivals, some of whom had been imprisoned in Cuba for a variety of crimes, were from the lower class. (Castro apparently sent them to the United States to reduce the costs of the correctional system in Cuba.) Many of these most recent arrivals have also settled in southern Florida, where they have experienced confrontations with Euro-Americans, a high rate of crime, and other adjustment problems.

Compared with other recent immigrant groups and with Latinos as a whole, Cuban Americans are doing well. Cuban Americans have college completion rates twice those of other Latinos.[52] Many Cuban Americans have settled in southern Florida, particularly in Dade County (Metsopolitan Miami), with its warm climate and proximity to other Cubans and Cuba itself. Cuban Americans and other Latin American immigrants have helped transform Miami from a quiet resort to a boomtown.

Critical Thinking Questions

Assume you are single. Are there ethnic or racial groups from which you would be hesitant to date someone? If so, what ethnic or racial groups are these, and does such hesitancy suggest some racial or ethnic biases on your part?

Native Americans

When Columbus first came to America in 1492, there were about 1 million Native Americans grouped into more than 600 distinct societies.[53] Tribal wars between groups were common, and there were wide variations among tribes in customs, culture, lifestyle, languages, and religious ceremonies. The Whites gradually expanded their settlement, moving westward and slowly usurping native land. Colonists and pioneers adopted a policy that amounted to deliberate extermination of Native Americans. The saying "The only good Indian is a dead Indian" became popular. Whites took their lands away, depleted the buffalo herds on which many tribes depended for survival, slaughtered tribes, and indirectly killed many others by leading forced marches in freezing weather and bringing diseases and famine.[54] Unable to mobilize a common defense, all native tribes were defeated by 1892.

In 1887 Congress passed the General Allotment Act, which empowered Congress unilaterally to revise treaties made with Native Americans. This action opened the way for land-hungry Whites to take productive native land. From 1887 to 1928, the land held by Native Americans decreased from 137 million acres to 50 million acres, with most of the remaining property being some of the least productive real estate in the country.[55]

Contact with the White culture has undermined Native Americans' traditional living patterns. It has been said that "the buffalo are gone"—meaning that Native Americans can no longer sustain themselves through hunting and fishing. Segregation to reservations has further damaged their pride and sense of self-worth. Government programs now attempt to meet subsistence needs, but they also serve to pauperize Native Americans. Native Americans on reservations have high rates of suicide, alcoholism, illiteracy, poverty, homicide, child neglect, and infant mortality.

Earlier in the 20th century, the plight of Native Americans was largely ignored because of their isolation on remote reservations. Through the Bureau of Indian Affairs (BIA), they received the most paternalistic treatment by the government of all minorities. For many years, the BIA had programs designed to destroy Native American culture, religion, and language. Today the bureau has become a symbol of frustration and despair.[56]

In the 1960s and 1970s, the plight of the Native Americans received national attention, and many Whites became actively involved in their problems. In the past, films depicted the "glorious" victories of the Whites over "savages." Now we know that early White settlers exploited the Native Americans by taking away their land and destroying their way of life.

During most of the 20th century, Native Americans were not very active in civil rights activities. However, in the 1960s and 1970s, there were some organized efforts to make changes. Like African Americans and Chicanos, Native Americans staged some widely publicized demonstrations, such as one at Wounded Knee, South Dakota, in the 1970s.

In 1978 the U.S. Congress enacted the Indian Child Welfare Act (PL 95-608), which seeks to protect Native American families and tribes. Recognizing that Native American children are the most important resource of the tribes, the act establishes federal standards for involuntary removal of Native American children from their families and provides a legal mechanism for tribes to assume jurisdiction over Native American children who have been involuntarily removed by state and local authorities.

Casinos have become a major source of revenue for many Native American tribes in numerous states.

Miguel Gandert/Corbis

The act is therefore designed to promote the security and stability of Native American families and tribes. When a child is removed from a Native American family, the tribe must be notified, and preference must be given to placing the child with relatives, tribal members, or other Native American families. Despite this critical piece of federal legislation, many Native American children continue to be placed in foster care or for adoption with non–Native American families.[57] A significant hindrance to the implementation of PL 95-608 is the lack of awareness of social workers concerning the act's mandates.

High rates of poverty and other social problems continue among Native Americans. Schaefer notes:

Native Americans have to choose between assimilating to the dominant White culture and maintaining their identity....

The reservations are economically depressed, but they are also the home of the Native American people spiritually and ideologically, if not always physically....

For Native Americans, the federal government and White people are virtually synonymous.[58]

Some tribes are taking legal action to recover land that was illegally usurped from them. The Nonintercourse Act of 1870 stated that any land transaction between Indians and others not approved by Congress is null and void. Many such transactions were not ratified by Congress. Some tribes have brought legal claims for land and for rights to minerals and rivers, and some of these claims have already been upheld. Two tribes in Maine have won their claim to half the land in the state. In Alaska, Native Americans have been awarded $1 billion and 40 million acres of land in compensation for illegal seizures of their territory in the past.[59]

In recent years, Native American tribes have opened gambling casinos in many states. These casinos have become very popular and highly profitable. (Recent court decisions about federal treaties with Native Americans permit substantial tax breaks on these profits.) Many Native American tribes that are operating casinos are using some of the profits to fund social and educational programs for their tribal members. (See Case Exhibit 12.3.)

Asian Americans

Asian Americans in the United States include the Japanese, Chinese, Filipinos, Koreans, Burmese, Hmongs, Indonesians, Guamanians, Samoans, South Vietnamese, and Thais. A large number of South Vietnamese immigrated to this country in the mid-1970s following the Vietnam War. Contrary to a popular stereotype, Asians are not homogeneous. Each ethnic group has its own history, religion, language, and culture. These Asian American groups also differ in terms of group cohesion, levels of education, and socioeconomic status. Just as it is wrong to view all Europeans as the same, it is an error to view all Asians as a single entity.

Like other disenfranchised groups, Asian Americans are victimized by discrimination. Immediate problems include housing, education, income maintenance, unemployment and underemployment, health care, and vocational training and retraining. Because of language and cultural barriers, many needy Asians (particularly new immigrants and the elderly) do not seek services to which they are entitled. The two most prominent Asian groups in this country are Japanese Americans and Chinese Americans.

Japanese Americans

Until 1900 few Japanese migrants came to the United States, partly because of legal restrictions against their migration and partly because of the unfriendly reception they received in this country.

After the turn of the century, Japanese migration increased. Immigrants settled primarily on the West Coast. By 1941 (when Pearl Harbor was attacked), there were few distinctive Japanese American settlements outside the West Coast other than in New York City and Chicago. During World War II, Japanese Americans' loyalty was viewed with intense suspicion, and they severely felt the impact of prejudice, war hysteria, and the denial of certain civil rights. On March 2, 1942, the commander of the Western Theater of Operations established "relocation centers" (concentration camps) to which Japanese Americans living on the West Coast were sent. The confused policies of our nation during this war are indicated by the fact that 33,000 Japanese Americans served in the armed forces for the United States, while 110,000 Japanese Americans were confined in concentration camps.[60] Not only were their civil rights violated, but they also were forced to sell their property. (In comparison, Americans of German or Italian descent were not similarly persecuted, even though the war was fought against Germany and Italy as well as Japan.) Following the war, the return of Japanese Americans to the

Ethical Dilemma: Are Native American Casinos a Benefit or a Detriment?

In 1988 Congress passed the Indian Gaming Regulatory Act, which recognized the right of Native American tribes in the United States to establish gambling and gaming facilities on their reservations as long as the states in which they are located have some form of legalized gambling. A majority of states have now made arrangements with Native American tribes to have casinos. Gambling operations vary among casinos but may include off-track betting, casino tables such as blackjack and roulette, sports betting, video games of chance, telephone betting, slot machines, and high-stakes bingo. The vast majority of gamblers are non–Native Americans. The actual casinos are a form of tribal government enterprise rather than private business operations.

The economic impact on some reservations has been enormous. Many casinos take in millions of dollars in profits annually. Schaefer does note that only about one-third of the recognized Native American tribes have casinos.[a] Tribes that have opened casinos have greatly reduced their rate of unemployment because the casinos tend to hire a number of members of the tribe (they also employ non–Native Americans). The revenue generated has helped spur economic development on land owned by the tribe. On reservations with casinos, the percentage of people on welfare has dropped. Tribes are using their profits for the betterment of the reservation and its people. They are building schools, colleges, and community centers; setting up education trust funds and scholarships; investing in alcohol and drug treatment programs; financing new business enterprises (entrepreneurships); and putting in water and sewer systems on the reservations. The national prominence of tribal casinos has also given Native American leaders potential political clout with federal, state, and local governments.

There are also some drawbacks. One negative effect is gambling addiction. In many communities where casinos have been built, there are dramatic increases in the number of people who become addicted to gambling. Such an addiction may lead to higher rates of domestic violence and alcoholism. Another negative aspect of gambling is that those who can least afford to gamble usually are the most affected. The poor spend a greater percentage of their income on gambling than the wealthy, giving gambling the same effect on incomes as regressive taxes, with the poor being hit the hardest.

Opposition to gambling on reservations has arisen from both Native Americans and non–Native Americans. Some Native Americans fear losing their traditional values to corruption and organized crime. Some Native Americans fear that as more and more casinos are built, the gambling market will become saturated with casinos competing with one another "for the same dollar," with the tribes eventually being left with empty casinos and high unemployment rates (again). Some tribal members feel that casinos trivialize and cheapen their heritage. The issue of who shares in gambling profits has led to heated conflicts in some tribal communities as to who is a member of the tribe.

Non–Native American critics sharply question the special economic status being afforded to Native Americans in being able to operate casinos, and they assert that there should be an even playing field.

[a]Richard T. Schaefer, *Racial and Ethnic Groups*, 13th ed. (Boston: Pearson, 2012), pp. 163–165.

West Coast met with some initial opposition, but among Whites a counter-reaction soon developed that emphasized fair play and acceptance.

Since 1946 Japanese Americans have settled in other parts of the country, and their socioeconomic status is now approaching that of Whites. Japanese Americans now have a higher level of educational achievement than White Americans.[61]

An act of Congress in 1988 granted $20,000 to each of the Japanese Americans who were interned during World War II. This act is a hopeful signal of greater intergroup cooperation in the future.

Chinese Americans

In the 1800s, the Chinese were encouraged to immigrate to the United States to do mining, railroad construction, and farmwork. These immigrants soon encountered hostility from some Whites, particularly in western states, because of their willingness to work for low wages. Their racial and cultural distinctiveness also made them targets for scapegoating, especially during periods of high unemployment. Charles Henderson, Bok-Lim Kim, and Ione D. Vargus describe the extent to which Chinese Americans were subjected to racism during this time period:

Racism against Asians is shown in the 1854 decision of the California Supreme Court in The People vs. Hall. *The appellant, a white Anglo-American, had been convicted of murder upon the testimony of Chinese witnesses. Was such evidence admissible? The judge ruled that Asians should be ineligible to testify for or against a white man. This ruling opened the floodgate for anti-Chinese abuse, violence, and exploitation. Group murders, lynchings, property damage, and robbery of the Chinese were reported up and down the West Coast. Because of the harsh treatment of the Chinese, any luckless person was described as not having a "Chinaman's chance."*[62]

In the early 1900s, Chinese Americans were concentrated largely on the West Coast, but since the 1920s, they have tended to disperse throughout the nation. They have settled in large cities, and many live in Chinatowns in cities such as Los Angeles, San Francisco, New York, Boston, and Chicago.

The struggles of China against Japan before and during World War II brought about a more favorable image of Chinese Americans. Nevertheless, some discrimination continues. They have been subjected to less discrimination in Hawaii than on the mainland, as Hawaii is much closer to being a pluralist society than the rest of the country. Chinese Americans now have a higher level of educational achievement than White Americans.[63] Although Chinese Americans still tend to intramarry, they are now more likely to marry a member of another racial group than was true in the past. An increasing number are also moving out of Chinatowns to live in suburbs and in other areas.

Strategies for Advancing Social and Economic Justice

Social justice is an ideal condition in which all members of a society have the same basic rights, protection, opportunities, obligations, and social benefits. Economic justice is also an ideal condition in which all members of a society have the same opportunities for attaining material goods, income, and wealth. A wide range of strategies have been developed to reduce racial and ethnic discrimination and oppression, thereby advancing social and economic justice. These strategies include the following: mass media appeals, strategies to increase interaction among the races, civil rights laws, activism, school busing, affirmative action programs, confrontation of racist remarks and actions, minority-owned businesses, and grassroots organizations.

Mass Media Appeals

Newspapers, magazines, radio, and television at times present information designed to explain the nature and harmful effects of prejudice and to promote harmony among humanity. The mass media are able to reach large numbers of people simultaneously. By expanding public awareness of discrimination and its consequences, the media can counteract the influence of racial extremists. But the mass media have limitations in changing prejudiced attitudes and behaviors; they are primarily providers of information and seldom have a lasting effect in changing deep-seated prejudices through propaganda. Broadcasting such platitudes as "all people are brothers and sisters" and "prejudice is un-American" is not very effective. Highly bigoted people are often unaware of their own prejudices. Even if they are aware of them, they generally dismiss mass media appeals as irrelevant or as propaganda. However, the mass media probably have had a significant impact in reducing discrimination by showing non-Whites and Whites harmoniously interacting in commercials, on news teams, and on other TV fare.

Greater Interaction among the Races

Increased contact among races is not in itself sufficient to alleviate racial prejudice. In fact, increased contact may, in some instances, highlight intergroup differences and increase suspicions and fear. George Simpson and J. Milton Yinger reviewed a number of studies and concluded that prejudice is likely to be increased when contacts are tension laden or involuntary.[64] Prejudice is likely to subside when individuals are placed in situations in which they share characteristics in nonracial matters (for example, as coworkers, fellow soldiers, or classmates). Equal-status contacts, rather than inferior–superior contacts, also reduce prejudices.[65]

Civil Rights Laws

In the past 50 years, equal rights have been legislated in employment, voting, housing, public accommodation, and education. A key question is, "How effective are laws in curbing racial discrimination and reducing racial prejudice?"

Proponents of civil rights legislation make certain assumptions. The first is that new laws will reduce discriminatory behavioral patterns. The laws define what was once "normal" behavior (discrimination) as now being "deviant" behavior. With time, attitudes are expected to change and become more consistent with the forced nondiscriminatory behavior patterns.

A second assumption is that the laws will be enforced. Civil rights laws enacted after the Civil War

CASE EXAMPLE 12.1

Rosa Park's Act of Courage as a Spark for the Civil Rights Movement

On December 1, 1955, Rosa Parks was waiting for a bus in Montgomery, Alabama. She was in a hurry because she had a lot of things to do. When the bus arrived, she got on without paying attention to the driver. She rode the bus often and was aware of Montgomery's segregated seating law that required African Americans to sit at the back of the bus.

In those days in the South, Black people were expected to board the front of the bus, pay their fare, and then get off and walk outside the bus to reboard at the side door near the back. But she noted that the rear was already crowded, with standing room only. Black passengers were even huddled on the back steps of the bus. It was apparent to Rosa that it would be all but impossible to reboard at the back. Besides, bus drivers sometimes drove off and left Black passengers behind, even after accepting their fares. Rosa Parks spontaneously decided to take her chances. She paid her fare in the front of the bus, walked down the aisle, and took a seat in the area reserved for Whites. At the second stop, a White man got on and had to stand.

The bus driver saw the White man standing and ordered Rosa Parks to move to the back. She refused, thinking, "I want to be treated like a human being." Two police officers were called, and they arrested her. She was taken to city hall, booked, fingerprinted, jailed, and fined. Her arrest—and subsequent appeal all the way to the U.S. Supreme Court—served as a catalyst for a yearlong boycott of the city's buses by Blacks, who composed 70% of all bus riders. The boycott inspired Martin Luther King, Jr., to become involved. It ended when the Supreme Court declared Montgomery's segregated seating laws unconstitutional. Rosa Parks's unplanned defiance of that law sparked the civil rights movement. This movement not only promoted social and economic justice for

Paul J. Richards/AFP/Getty Images

Rosa Parks

African Americans but also inspired other groups to organize to advocate for their civil rights. These groups include other racial and ethnic groups, women, the elderly, people with a disability, and gays and lesbians.

SOURCE: Marie Ragghianti, "I Wanted to Be Treated Like a Human Being," *Parade*, Jan. 19, 1992, pp. 8–9.

were seldom enforced and gradually eroded. It is also unfortunately true that some officials will find ways of evading the intent of the law by eliminating only the extreme, overt symbols of discrimination without changing other practices. Thus, the enactment of a law is only the first step in the process of changing prejudiced attitudes and practices. However, as Martin Luther King, Jr., noted, "The law may not make a man love me, but it can restrain him from lynching me, and I think that's pretty important."

Activism

The strategy of activism attempts to change the structure of race relations through direct confrontation of discrimination and segregation policies. Activism employs three types of politics: the politics of creative disorder, the politics of disorder, and the politics of escape.[66]

The *politics of creative disorder* operates on the edge of the dominant social system and includes school boycotts, rent strikes, job blockades, sit-ins (for example, at businesses that are alleged to discriminate), public marches, and product boycotts. This type of activism is based on the concept of nonviolent resistance. A dramatic illustration of nonviolent resistance involved Rosa Parks (see Case Example 12.1). The famous Montgomery bus boycott that her behavior provoked had an even more important psychological impact: It suggested that people of color had rights equal to those of Whites and that united nonviolent resistance could overturn discriminatory laws.[67]

The *politics of disorder* reflects alienation from the dominant culture and disillusionment with the political system. Those discriminated against resort to mob uprising, riots, and other forms of violence.

In 1969 the National Commission on Causes and Prevention of Violence reported that 200 riots had occurred in our inner cities in the previous 5 years.[68] In the early 1980s, there were riots in Miami and in some other inner cities. In 1992 there were devastating riots in Los Angeles following the acquittal of four White police officers who had been charged with using excessive force in arresting Rodney King, an African American; the brutal arrest had been videotaped. In 2001 there was rioting in Cincinnati after an African American was shot and killed by a White police officer. Most of these riots have involved minority group aggression against White-owned property.

The *politics of escape* is characterized by passionate rhetoric about how minorities are being victimized. But because the focus is not on arriving at solutions, the rhetoric is not productive, except perhaps for providing an emotional release.

The principal value of activism or social protest seems to be the stimulation of public awareness of certain problems. The civil rights protests in the 1960s made practically all Americans aware of the discrimination to which non-White groups were being subjected. As a result, at least some of the discrimination has ceased, and race relations have improved. Continued protest beyond a certain (admittedly indeterminate) point, however, appears to have little additional value.[69]

Affirmative Action Programs

Affirmative action programs provide preferential hiring and admission requirements (for example, admission to medical schools) for minority applicants. The programs apply to all minority groups, including women. They require employers to (a) make active efforts to locate and recruit qualified minority applicants and (b) in certain circumstances, have hard quotas under which specific numbers of minority members must be accepted to fill vacant positions (for example, a university with a high proportion of White male faculty members may be required to fill half of its faculty vacancies with women and members of other minority groups). Affirmative action programs require that employers demonstrate, according to a checklist of positive measures, that they are not guilty of discrimination.

A major dilemma with affirmative action programs is that preferential hiring and quota programs create reverse discrimination, in which qualified majority group members are sometimes arbitrarily excluded. There have been several successful lawsuits involving reverse discrimination. The best-known case to date has been that of Alan Bakke, who was initially denied admission to the medical school at the University of California, Davis, in 1973. He alleged reverse discrimination because he had higher grades and higher scores on the Medical College Admissions Test than several minority applicants who were admitted under the university's minorities quota policy. In 1978 his claim was upheld by the U.S. Supreme Court in a precedent-setting decision.[70] The Court ruled that strict racial quotas are unconstitutional, but it did not rule against the use of race as one among many criteria in making admissions decisions.

Henderson, Kim, and Vargus summarize some of the views of Whites and minority groups about affirmative action:

> The minority worker in white agencies often asks himself: "Why have I been hired?" ... The worker may meet resistance from white colleagues if he or she is a product of "affirmative action," seen by some white people as simply "reverse discrimination." Whites may be quick to say that competence is what counts. Blacks perceive this as saying that they are not competent. Considering the many ways in which whites have acquired jobs, blacks wonder why competence is now suggested as the only criterion for employment. For every white professional who may dislike affirmative action to compensate for past exclusions and injustices, there is a black professional who feels that it is tragic that organizations have had to be forced to hire minorities.[71]

Supporters of affirmative action programs note that the White majority expressed little concern about discrimination when its members were the beneficiaries instead of the victims. They also assert that there is no other way to make up rapidly for past discrimination against minorities, many of whom may presently score slightly lower on qualification tests simply because they did not have the opportunities and the quality of training that the majority group members have had.

Affirmative action programs raise delicate and complex questions about achieving equality through preferential hiring and admissions policies for minorities. Yet no other means has been found to end obvious discrimination in hiring and admissions.

Gaining admission to educational programs and securing well-paying jobs are crucial elements in the quest for integration. The history of immigrant groups that have "made it" (such as the Irish, the Japanese, and the Italians) suggests that equality will be achieved only when minority group members gain middle- and upper-class status and thus become an economic and political force to be reckoned with. The dominant groups then become pressured into modifying their norms, values, and stereotypes. For this reason, a number of authorities have noted that the elimination of economic discrimination is a prerequisite for achieving equality and harmonious race relations.[72] Achieving educational equality among races is also crucial because lower educational attainments lead to less prestigious jobs, lower incomes, lower living standards, and the perpetuation of racial inequalities from one generation to the next.

In the mid-1990s, the future of affirmative action became a hotly debated national issue. In the 1996 presidential campaign, several Republican presidential hopefuls urged that affirmative action programs be ended. A *Wall Street Journal/NBC News* survey found that two of three Americans were opposed to affirmative action.[73]

The assault on affirmative action gathered strength from a slow-growth economy, stagnant middle-class incomes, and corporate downsizing, all of which make the question of who gets hired— or fired—more volatile. Minority candidates who receive positions that are perceived by other workers as the result of affirmative action are often viewed by the other workers with suspicion, which sometimes results in toxic tension in the workplace. Critics note that such tension has not brought us a color-blind society (which was the hope), but instead has brought us an extremely color-conscious society. As a result, critics assert that affirmative action is now a highly politicized and painful remedy that has stigmatized many of those it was meant to help. Affirmative action is now perceived by many in our society as a system of preferences for the unqualified. Critics further assert that affirmative action may have been necessary 50 years ago to ensure that minority candidates received fair treatment to counter the social barriers to hiring and admission that stemmed from centuries of unequal treatment. But today such programs are no longer needed. They maintain it is wrong to discriminate against White males for the sole reason of making up for the injustices that somebody's great-grandfather may have done to somebody else's great-grandfather. They believe it is wrong for the daughter of a wealthy African American couple to

be given preference in employment over the son of a homeless alcoholic who happens to be White.

Supporters of affirmative action assert, "If we abandon affirmative action, we return to the old-boys' network." They believe affirmative action has helped a number of women and people of color to attain a good education and higher-paying positions, and thereby to remove themselves from the ranks of the poor. They maintain that, in a society where racist and sexist attitudes remain, it is necessary to have affirmative action to give women and people of color a fair opportunity at attaining a quality education and well-paying jobs.

In 1996 voters in the state of California passed Proposition 209, which explicitly rejects the idea that women and other minority group members should receive special consideration when applying for jobs, government contracts, or university admission. This affirmative action ban became law in California in August 1997. In addition, numerous lawsuits have been filed objecting to reverse discrimination. If the courts rule in favor of those filing the lawsuits, the power of affirmative action programs will be sharply reduced. In November 1997, the U.S. Supreme Court rejected a challenge to the California law that ended racial and gender preferences in that state. This Supreme Court action clears the way for other states and cities to ban affirmative action.

Is there a middle ground for the future of affirmative action? Zuckerman recommends:

> The vast majority of Americans would probably accept a return to the original notion of affirmative action—an aggressive outreach to minorities to make sure they have a fair shot. They would probably see a social benefit in accepting that racial justice might be relevant in a tiebreaker case, or might even confer a slight advantage. The goal must be a return to policies based on evenhandedness for individuals rather than for groups. Then employers can concentrate on whether a minority applicant is the right person for the job rather than being moved by whether the applicant looks litigious. All employees could take it for granted that they had a fair shot.[74]

Critical Thinking Questions

Do you support or oppose present-day affirmative action programs? Why?

A number of authorities are now proposing race-blind policies that will not create reverse discrimination but will address past patterns of racism and the inequalities engendered by racism. Such policies would deal with the needs of people on a class basis rather than in terms of race of ethnic status. An example of a race-blind social policy in the interests of increasing equality of opportunity is the practice recently established by Harvard University and other private universities of awarding full scholarships to accepted students whose families earn less than $50,000 per year.[75]

Confrontation of Racist and Ethnic Remarks and Actions

Jokes and sarcastic remarks related to race help shape and perpetuate racist stereotypes and prejudices. It is important that both Whites and non-Whites tactfully but assertively indicate that they do not view such remarks as humorous or appropriate. It is also important that people tactfully and assertively point out the inappropriateness of racist actions by others. Such confrontations have a consciousness-raising effect, making explicit the belief that subtle racist remarks and actions are discriminatory and harmful. Gradually these confrontations will reduce racial prejudices and actions.

Noted author, lecturer, and abolitionist Frederick Douglass stated:

> Power concedes nothing without a demand—it never did, and it never will. Find out just what people will submit to, and you've found out the exact amount of injustice and wrong which will be imposed upon them. This will continue until they resist, either with words, blows, or both. The limits of tyrants are prescribed by the endurance of those whom they oppress.[76]

Critical Thinking Questions

Why do people make racist jokes and comments? Who finds them amusing, and why?

Minority-Owned Businesses

Many people aspire to run their own business. Running one's own business is particularly attractive to many members of minority groups. It means an opportunity to increase one's income and wealth. It is also a way to avoid some of the racial and ethnic discrimination that occurs in the work world, such as the "glass ceiling" that blocks the promotion of qualified minority workers.

Since the 1970s, federal, state, and local governments have attempted to assist minority-owned businesses in a variety of ways. Programs have provided low-interest loans to minority-owned businesses. Set-aside programs stipulate that government contracts must be awarded to a minimum proportion, usually 10% to 30%, of minority-owned businesses. Some large urban areas have created enterprise zones that encourage employment and investment in blighted neighborhoods through the use of tax breaks. The number of minority-owned businesses has slowly been increasing; yet only a small fraction of the total number of people classified as a member of a minority group has benefited from government support of minority-owned businesses.[77]

Grassroots Approaches to Improving Deteriorating Neighborhoods

Deteriorating neighborhoods in cities are a national disgrace. The United States is the richest and most powerful country in the world, yet we have been unable to improve living conditions in deteriorating neighborhoods.

Our country has tried a variety of approaches to improve living conditions in deteriorating neighborhoods. Programs and services provided include work training, job placement, financial assistance through public welfare, low-interest mortgages to start businesses, Head Start, drug and alcohol treatment, crime prevention, housing, rehabilitation, day-care services, health care services, and public health services.

One of the most comprehensive undertakings to assist inner cities was the Model Cities Program, which was part of the War on Poverty in the 1960s. Several inner cities were targeted for this massive intervention. The program tore down dilapidated housing and constructed comfortable living quarters. Salvageable buildings were renovated. In addition, these Model City projects had a variety of programs that provided job training and placement, health care services, social services, and educational opportunities. The results are more than depressing. The communities have again become slums, and living conditions are as bleak, or bleaker, than at the start of the Model City interventions.[78]

To date, practically all programs that have endeavored to improve deteriorating neighborhoods have had, at best, only short-term success. No other conclusion can be made. Deteriorating neighborhoods continue to have abysmal living conditions. In the 1980s, 1990s, and early 2000s, the federal government appears to have given up trying to improve living conditions; federal programs for deteriorating neighborhoods have either been eliminated or sharply cut back.

Our society, for better or worse, is materialistic. The two main legitimate avenues for acquiring material goods are by getting a good education and obtaining a high-paying job. It appears that many residents of deteriorating neighborhoods realize the prospects are bleak for them getting a good education (when only inferior schools exist in their areas) or obtaining a high-paying job (when they have few marketable job skills). As a result, many turn to illegitimate ways to get material goods (shoplifting, drug trafficking, robbery, and con games). Many also turn to immediate gratification (including sex and drug highs). A value system is developing that includes being resigned to being dependent on the government through welfare for a substandard lifestyle.

One promising approach to improving inner cities is grassroots organizations. These organizations can sometimes effect positive, long-lasting changes in a variety of settings, including inner cities. Grassroots organizations are community groups, composed of community residents who work together to improve their surroundings. (It may be that lasting changes can be made only in neighborhoods whose residents are inspired to improve their community.) The following is a description of a successful grassroots effort in Cochran Gardens in St. Louis, Missouri.[79]

Cochran Gardens was once a low-income housing project typical of many deteriorating housing projects in large urban areas. It was strewn with rubbish, graffiti, and broken windows, and its residents were plagued by frequent shootings, crime, and drug trafficking.

Bertha Gilkey grew up in this housing project. Had it not been for her, this neighborhood might have continued to deteriorate. As a youngster, Gilkey believed the neighborhood could improve if residents worked together. As a teenager she attended tenant meetings in a neighborhood church. When she was 20 years old, she was elected to chair this tenants' association. The neighborhood has since undergone gradual, yet dramatic, positive changes.

Gilkey and her group started with small projects. They asked tenants what realistically achievable things they really wanted. There was a consensus that the housing project needed a usable laundromat. The project's previous laundromats had all been vandalized, and the only working laundromat in the projects had no locks. In fact, the entry door had been stolen. Bertha and her group requested and received a door from the city housing authority. The organization then held a successful fund-raiser for a lock. The organization next held a fund-raiser for paint, and that too was a success. The organization then painted the laundromat. The residents were pleased to have an attractive, working laundromat, and its presence increased their interest in joining and supporting the tenants' association. The association then organized to paint the hallways, floor by floor, of the housing project. Everyone who lived on a floor was responsible for being involved in painting their hallway's floor. Gilkey stated:

Kids who live on the floor that hadn't been painted would come and look at the painted hallways and then go back and hassle their parents. The elderly who couldn't paint prepared lunch so they could feel like they were a part of it too.[80]

The organization continued to initiate and successfully complete new projects to spruce up the neighborhood. Each success inspired more and more residents to take pride in their neighborhood and to work toward making improvements. While improving the physical appearance of this housing project, Gilkey and the tenants' organization also reintroduced a conduct code for the project. A committee formulated rules of behavior and elected monitors on each floor. The rules included no loud disruptions, no throwing garbage out of the windows, and no fights. Slowly, residents got the message, and living conditions improved, one small step at a time.

The building was renamed Dr. Martin Luther King, Jr., Building. (Symbols are important in community-development efforts.) The organization also held a party and a celebration for each successfully completed project.

Another focus of Gilkey's efforts was to reach out to children and adolescents. The positives were highlighted. The young people wrote papers in school on "What I like about living here." In art class they built a cardboard model of the housing project that included the buildings, streets, and playground. Such efforts were designed to build the self-esteem of the young people and to instill a sense of pride in their community.

In the 1980s, Cochran Gardens was a public housing project with flower-lined paths, trees, and grass—a beautiful and clean neighborhood filled with trusting people who had a sense of pride in their community. The high-rise buildings were completely renovated. There was a community center, and there were tennis courts, playgrounds, and townhouse apartments to reduce density in the complex. Cochran Gardens was managed by the tenants. The association (named Tenant Management Council) ventured into owning and operating certain businesses: a catering service, day-care centers, health clinics, and a vocational training program.

The Cochran success was based on principles of self-help, empowerment, responsibility, and dignity. Gilkey stated,

> This goes against the grain, doesn't it? Poor people are to be managed. What we've done is cut through all the bullshit and said it doesn't take all that. People with degrees and credentials got us in this mess. All it takes is some basic skills. ... If we can do it in public housing, it can happen anywhere. (qtd. in Boyte, 1989, p. 5)[81]

In the 1990s Bertha Gilkey focused her attention nationally, serving as co-chair of the New York–based National Congress of Neighborhood Women, where she negotiated for government grants that supported the establishment of tenant management associations in New York and other cities.

Gilkey hired a professional manager, an accountant, and other staff to run Cochran Gardens in the early 1990s. In 1998, city authorities took over the management of Cochran Gardens, citing mismanagement by the tenant association. The buildings rapidly deteriorated under city management. Rental vacancies rapidly increased. By the end of 2008, all but one of the Cochran Gardens buildings had been demolished.

Although Cochran Gardens had a sad ending, the community prospered for over 30 years. It remains a symbol of the viability of grassroots efforts.

The accomplishments of Cochran Gardens suggest that federal, state, and city governments can improve inner-city conditions by encouraging and supporting (including financially) grassroots efforts. Social workers can use their macro practice skills as catalysts in the formation of grassroots organizations. Once such organizations are formed, social workers can provide invaluable assistance by helping them identify community needs and then plan and implement interventions to meet those needs.

Ethnic-Sensitive Social Work Practice

Traditionally, professional social work practice has used the medical model for the delivery of services. This is a deficit model that focuses on identifying problems within a person. The medical model largely ignores environmental factors that impact the person-in-situation. A major shortcoming of a deficit model is that it ignores strengths and resources. (When one emphasizes only the shortcomings of a person, that person's self-esteem is apt to be severely affected negatively, as that person is likely to define him- or herself in terms of the shortcomings and, in the process, overlook strengths and resources.)

Ethnic-sensitive practice seeks to incorporate understanding of diverse ethnic, cultural, and minority groups into the theories and principles that guide social work practice.[82] It is based on the view that practice must be attuned to the values and dispositions related to clients' ethnic group membership and social class position. Ethnic-sensitive practice requires that social workers have an in-depth understanding of the effects of oppression on racial and ethnic groups.

Another important conceptual framework is the "dual perspective."[83] This concept is derived from the view that all people are a part of two systems: (a) the dominant system (the society that one lives in), which is the source of power and economic resources, and (b) the nurturing system, composed of the physical and social environment of family and community. The dual perspective concept asserts that the adverse consequences of an oppressive society on the self-concept of a person of color can be partially offset by the nurturing system.

Ethnic-sensitive practice requires that social workers be aware of and seek to redress the oppression experienced by ethnic groups. It assumes that each ethnic group and its members have a history with roots in the past that have a bearing on the members' perceptions of current problems. For example, the individual and collective history of many African Americans leads to the expectation that family resources will be available in times of trouble.[84]

Ethnic-sensitive practice, however, assumes the present is most important. For example, many Mexican American and Puerto Rican women currently feel tension as they attempt to move beyond traditionally defined gender roles into the mainstream as students and paid employees.[85]

Ethnic-sensitive practice introduces no new practice principles or approaches. Instead, it urges the adaptation of prevailing therapies, social work principles, and skills to take account of ethnic reality. Regardless of which practice approach is used, three concepts and perspectives that are emphasized are empowerment, the strengths perspective, and culturally competent practice.

Empowerment

This concept has been defined as the process of helping individuals, families, groups, organizations, and communities to increase their interpersonal, personal, political, and socioeconomic strengths so that they can improve their circumstances. In working with an ethnic or racial group, empowerment counters the negative image or stereotypes of a group, which have been rendered through a long history of discrimination, with a positive value or image and an emphasis on the ability of each ethnic group member to influence the conditions of his or her life. Empowerment counters hopelessness and powerlessness with an emphasis on the ability of each person to address problems competently, beginning with a positive view of oneself. Empowerment counters oppression and poverty by helping ethnic groups and their members to increase their ability to make and implement basic life decisions.

Strengths Perspective

The strengths perspective is closely related to empowerment. The strengths perspective seeks to identify, use, build, and reinforce the abilities and strengths that people have in contrast to the medical perspective, which focuses on their deficiencies. It emphasizes people's abilities, interests, aspirations, resources, beliefs, and accomplishments.

For example, some strengths of African Americans in the United States include the more than 100 predominantly African American colleges and universities; fraternal and women's organizations; and social, political, and professional organizations. Many of the schools, businesses, churches, and organizations that are predominantly African American have

developed social service programs such as family support services, mentoring programs, food and shelter services, transportation services, and educational and scholarship programs. Through individual and organized efforts, self-help approaches and mutual aid traditions continue among African Americans. African Americans tend to have strong ties to immediate extended family. They tend to have a strong religious orientation, a strong work and achievement orientation, and egalitarian role sharing.[86]

Culturally Competent Practice

Projections indicate that by the middle of the 21st century nearly half the population of the United States will be people of color.[87] Social workers will be dealing with people who are increasingly diverse, politically more active, and more aware of their rights. It is therefore incumbent upon social workers to become increasingly culturally competent. To become culturally competent, social workers need to (a) become aware of culture and its pervasive influence, (b) learn about their own cultures, (c) recognize their own ethnocentricity, (d) learn about other cultures, (e) acquire cultural knowledge about their clients, and (f) adapt social work skills and intervention approaches accordingly.[88]

In 2001 the National Association of Social Workers approved the following 10 standards for cultural competence in social work practice:

1. **Ethics and Values**—*Social workers shall function in accordance with the values, ethics, and standards of the profession, recognizing how personal and professional values may conflict with or accommodate the needs of diverse clients.*

2. **Self-Awareness**—*Social workers shall seek to develop an understanding of their own personal, cultural values and beliefs as one way of appreciating the importance of multicultural identities in the lives of people.*

3. **Cross-Cultural Knowledge**—*Social workers shall have and continue to develop specialized knowledge and understanding about the history, traditions, values, family systems, and artistic expressions of major client groups that they serve.*

4. **Cross-Cultural Skills**—*Social workers shall use appropriate methodological approaches, skills, and techniques that reflect the workers' understanding of the role of culture in the helping process.*

5. **Service Delivery**—*Social workers shall be knowledgeable about and skillful in the use of services available in the community and broader society and be able to make appropriate referrals for their diverse clients.*

6. **Empowerment and Advocacy**—*Social workers shall be aware of the effect of social policies and programs*

Neil Redmond/AP Images for Sprite

Ethnic-sensitive practice includes the concept of empowerment and the strengths perspective, which focus on the positive resources and abilities of individuals and groups. For example, organized efforts, such as student unions, fraternities, and sororities, can help consolidate a group's focus on academic success and achievement.

on diverse client populations, advocating for and with clients whenever appropriate.

7. **Diverse Workforce**—*Social workers shall support and advocate for recruitment, admissions and hiring, and retention efforts in social work programs and agencies that ensure diversity within the profession.*

8. **Professional Education**—*Social workers shall advocate for and participate in educational and training programs that help advance cultural competence within the profession.*

9. **Language Diversity**—*Social workers shall seek to provide or advocate for the provision of information, referrals, and services in the language appropriate to the client, which may include use of interpreters.*

10. **Cross-Cultural Leadership**—*Social workers shall be able to communicate information about diverse client groups to other professionals.**

*Reprinted from *NASW Standards for Cultural Competence in Social Work Practice* (Washington, DC: NASW, 2001). Copyrighted material reprinted with permission from the National Association of Social Workers, Inc.

It is a mistake for a social worker to conclude that working effectively with a different cultural group presents insurmountable barriers and obstacles. In actuality, the similarities between worker and clients almost always outweigh the dissimilarities.

The major professional social work organizations have in the past few decades taken strong positions to work toward ending racial discrimination and oppression. The National Association of Social Workers, for example, has lobbied for the passage of civil rights legislation.

Critical Thinking Question

Are you currently committed to working toward ending racial and ethnic discrimination and advancing social and economic justice?

The Council on Social Work Education's EPAS requires that baccalaureate and master's programs in social work include content on racism, diversity, human rights, and the promotion of social and economic justice.[89] Professional social work education is committed to preparing social work students to understand and appreciate cultural and social diversity. Students are taught to understand the dynamics and consequences of oppression, and they learn to use intervention strategies to combat social injustice, oppression, and their effects. The Association of Black Social Workers also has been very active in combating racial prejudice and discrimination.

Social workers have an obligation to work vigorously toward ending racial and ethnic discrimination and advancing social justice. The social work professional needs to recognize the reality of practice in a culturally diverse environment. Social workers do have many of the prejudices and misperceptions of the general society, and the tendency to use one's own prejudices and stereotypes poses dangers for the well-meaning practitioner. For example, a social worker assigned to a Native American client might perceive the client's quietness as a sign that the client is being uncooperative or that the client is fully agreeing with the worker. It is possible that neither assumption is accurate. As a general rule, a Native American will not challenge or correct a worker who is off track because to do so would violate "noninterference." Noninterference is a basic value of Native American culture; it asserts that one should handle unwanted attempts at intervention with withdrawal—emotional, physical, or both.[90]

Another response pattern of White social workers that is counterproductive with Native Americans is the attempt to maintain direct eye contact. Such face-to-face eye contact is considered rude and intimidating by many Native Americans.[91]

A bilingual practitioner working in a Chicano community may not understand all aspects of the language. For example, the special language of the barrio often contains words with a variety of connotations that differ from formal Spanish.[92] As a consequence, the worker who does speak Spanish must be acutely alert to the possibility that words may have very different meanings for clients living in a barrio.

The Future of American Race and Ethnic Relations

The past few decades have been a struggle for minorities as they have tried to hold onto past gains in the face of reactions against minority rights. Vowing to take "big government" off the back of the American people and to strengthen the economy by giving businesses the incentive to grow and produce, the Reagan administration (1980–1988) largely removed the federal government from its traditional role as initiator and enforcer of programs to guarantee minority rights. The George Bush administration (1988–1992) continued to follow a similar strategy. The federal government under the Reagan and George Bush administrations asserted that private businesses were in the best position to correct the problems of poverty and discrimination. (Because businesses generally profit from paying low wages, most companies in the 1980s and early 1990s did not aggressively seek to improve the financial circumstances and living conditions of minorities.) Perhaps because of the federal government's shift in policies, minorities were less active in the 1980s and 1990s (as compared to the 1960s and 1970s) in using the strategy of activism. In the 1980s and 1990s, minority groups were experiencing difficulties in maintaining the gains they had achieved 2 decades earlier in the job market through affirmative action and Equal Employment Opportunity programs. Bill Clinton, elected president in 1992, ran on a platform that promised a more active role by the federal government in promoting social and economic justice for all racial and ethnic groups in this country.

Bill Clinton's views on resolving social problems were consistent with a moderate (middle-of-the-road) to liberal orientation. His liberal proposals that would have benefited populations-at-risk included a health insurance program for all Americans and significantly expanded educational and training programs for individuals on welfare to help them become self-supporting.

The move toward liberalism in the early 1990s was, however, short-lived. In the congressional elections of 1994, the Republicans won majority control of both the Senate and the House of Representatives. (This was the first time in 40 years that Republicans held a majority in the House.) Most of these Republicans had a conservative political agenda that included shifting spending from crime prevention to prison construction, eliminating affirmative action programs, reducing spending for many social welfare programs, and reducing the amount of taxes paid by high-income individuals. Such proposals were not, in the Clinton administration, enacted into law.

George W. Bush was elected president in 2000 in a very close election. He ran on a largely conservative agenda. His top priority was cutting taxes, and both houses of Congress passed tax cuts in 2001. (These tax cuts widened further the income gap between the rich and the poor.) George W. Bush had few proposals that were specifically directed at benefiting people of color. He advocated for increased funding for historically black colleges. In addition, he appointed African Americans and Latinos to some high-level positions in his administration.

Barack Obama was elected president in 2008. The election of an African American as president demonstrates our country has made significant progress in White Americans having respect for African Americans and for other people of color.

What will be the pattern of race relations in the future? Milton Gordon has outlined three possible patterns of intergroup relations: Anglo-conformity, the melting pot, and cultural pluralism:

> Anglo-conformity *assumes the desirability of maintaining modified English institutions, language, and culture as the dominant standard in American life. In practice, "assimilation" in America has always meant Anglo-conformity, and the groups that have been most readily assimilated have been those that are ethnically and culturally most similar to the Anglo-Saxon group.*
>
> The melting pot *is, strictly speaking, a rather different concept, which views the future American society not as a modified England but rather as a totally new blend, both culturally and biologically, of all the various groups that inhabit the United States. In practice, the melting pot has been of only limited significance in the American experience.*
>
> Cultural pluralism *implies a series of coexisting groups, each preserving its own tradition and culture, but each loyal to an overarching American nation. Although the cultural enclaves of some immigrant groups, such as the Germans, have declined in importance in the past, many other groups, such as the Italians, have retained a strong sense of ethnic identity and have resisted both Anglo-conformity and inclusion in the melting pot.*[93]

Members of some European ethnic groups (such as the British, French, and Germans) have assimilated the dominant culture of the United States and are now integrated. Other European ethnic groups (such as the Irish, Italians, Polish, and Hungarians) are now nearly fully assimilated and integrated.

Cultural pluralism appears to be the form that race and ethnic relations are presently taking. There has been a renewed interest on the part of a number of ethnic European Americans in expressing their pride in their own customs, religions, and linguistic and cultural traditions. We see slogans like, "Kiss Me. I'm Italian," "Irish Power," and "Polish and Proud." African Americans, Native Americans, Latinos, and Asian Americans are demanding entry into mainstream America—but not assimilation. They want to coexist in a plural society while preserving their own traditions and cultures. This pride is indicated by slogans such as "Black Is Beautiful" and "Red Power." These groups are finding a source of identity and pride in their own cultural backgrounds and histories.

Some progress has been made toward ending discrimination since the *Brown* v. *Board of Education* Supreme Court decision in 1954. Yet equal opportunity for all people in the United States is still only a dream.

SUMMARY

The following summarizes this chapter's content as it relates to the chapter objectives presented at the beginning of the chapter. Objectives include the following:

A *Define and describe ethnic groups, ethnocentrism, racial groups, racism, prejudice, discrimination, oppression, and institutional discrimination.*

- An ethnic group is a distinct group of people who share a common language, set of customs, history, culture, race, religion, or origin.
- Ethnocentrism is an orientation or set of beliefs that holds one's own culture, ethnic or racial group, or nation as superior to others.
- Race is a social concept, and is the way in which members of a society classify each other by physical characteristics.
- Racism is stereotyping and generalizing about people, usually negatively, because of their race; commonly a basis of discrimination against members of racial minority groups.
- Prejudice is an opinion about an individual, group, or phenomenon that is developed without proof or systematic evidence.
- Discrimination is the prejudgment and negative treatment of people based on identifiable characteristics such as race, gender, religion, or ethnicity.

- Oppression is the social act of placing severe restrictions on a group or institution.
- Institutional discrimination is prejudicial treatment in organizations based on official policies, overt behaviors, or behaviors that may be covert but approved by those with power.

B *Outline the sources of prejudice and discrimination.*

Theories about the sources of discrimination and oppression involve projection, frustration–aggression, insecurity and inferiority, authoritarianism, historical explanations, competition and exploitation, socialization processes, and the belief that there is only one true religion. Institutionalized racism is pervasive in our society and involves discrimination that is built into our social institutions, such as the legal system, politics, employment practices, health care, and education.

C *Summarize the effects and costs of discrimination and oppression.*

Our country has always been racist and ethnocentric, but there has been progress in the past five decades in alleviating prejudice and discrimination. Yet we cannot relax. Discrimination continues to have tragic consequences for those who are its victims. Individuals who are targets of discrimination are excluded from certain types of employment, educational and recreational opportunities, certain residential housing areas, membership in certain religious and social organizations, certain political activities, access to some community services, and so on. Discrimination is also a serious obstacle to developing a positive self-concept and has heavy psychological and financial costs. Internationally, racism and ethnocentrism severely damage our credibility in promoting human rights.

D *Present background material on racial groups: African Americans, Latinos, Native Americans, and Asian Americans.*

There are numerous White and non-White groups in our nation, each with a unique culture, language, and history and with special needs. This uniqueness needs to be understood and appreciated if we are to progress toward racial and ethnic equality. Summary information is presented in this chapter on a number of non-White groups.

E *Outline strategies for advancing social and economic justice.*

Strategies for advancing social and economic justice include mass media appeals, increased interaction among races, civil rights legislation, protests and activism, affirmative action programs, minority-owned businesses, confrontation of racist and ethnic remarks and actions, confrontation of the problems in inner cities, and grassroots organizations.

F *Describe social work's commitment to ending racial discrimination and oppression.*

As a profession, social work has an obligation to work vigorously toward ending racial and ethnic discrimination and oppression, thereby advancing social and economic justice. Social workers have an obligation to implement the principles of ethnic-sensitive practice. In working with diverse clients, three additional principles are critical: empowerment, the strengths perspective, and culturally competent practice.

G *Forecast the pattern of race and ethnic relations in the United States in the future.*

Three possible patterns of intergroup race and ethnic relations in the future are Anglo-conformity, the melting pot, and cultural pluralism. Cultural pluralism is the form that race and ethnic relations are presently taking and may well take in the future.

Competency Notes

EP 2.1.3a Distinguish, appraise, and integrate multiple sources of knowledge, including research-based knowledge and practice wisdom.

EP 2.1.4a, b, c, d The competency "Engage diversity and differences in practice," and the four practice behaviors associated with this competency.

EP 2.1.5a The competency "Advance human rights and social and economic justice," and the three practice behaviors associated with this competency. (All of this chapter) This chapter describes a number of terms involving discrimination against racial and ethnic groups. It outlines the sources of prejudice and discrimination, and summarizes the effects and costs of discrimination and oppression. It presents background information on a variety of racial groups. It outlines strategies for advancing social and economic justice, and describes social work's commitment to ending racial discrimination and oppression. It ends by forecasting the pattern of race and ethnic relations in the United States in the future.

Media Resources

Additional resources for this chapter, including a chapter quiz, can be found on the Social Work CourseMate. Go to CengageBrain.com.

Notes

1. Robert Merton, "Discrimination and the American Creed," in *Discrimination and National Welfare*, Robert M. MacIver, ed. (New York: Harper, 1949).
2. Marlene Cummings, "How to Handle Incidents of Racial Discrimination," in *The Personal Problem Solver*, Charles Zastrow and Dae H. Chang, eds. (Englewood Cliffs, NJ: Prentice Hall, 1977), p. 200.
3. Gunnar Myrdal, *An American Dilemma* (New York: Harper, 1962), p. 144.
4. Elmer H. Johnson, *Social Problems of Urban Man* (Homewood, IL: Dorsey Press, 1973), p. 344.
5. Ashley Montague, *Man s Most Dangerous Myth: The Fallacy of Race,* 4th ed. (Cleveland, OH: World, 1964).
6. Johnson, *Social Problems of Urban Man*, p. 350.
7. Richard T. Schaefer, *Racial and Ethnic Groups*, 13th ed. (Boston: Pearson, 2012), pp. 175–184.
8. Paul Ehrlich and Richard Holm, "A Biological View of Race," in *The Concept of Race*, Ashley Montague, ed. (New York: Free Press, 1964), p. 82.
9. Montague, *Man s Most Dangerous Myth*.
10. R. J. Herrnstein and C. Murray, *The Bell Curve: The Reshaping of American Life by Differences in Intelligence* (New York: Free Press, 1994).
11. G. R. LeFrancois, *The Lifespan*, 5th ed. (Belmont, CA: Wadsworth, 1996).
12. Johnson, *Social Problems of Urban Man*, p. 50.
13. Robert Barker, ed., *The Social Work Dictionary*, 5th ed. (Washington, DC: NASW, 2003), p. 215.
14. S. Carmichael and C. V. Hamilton, *Black Power: The Politics of Liberation in America* (New York: Vintage Books, 1967).
15. Schaefer, *Racial and Ethnic Groups*.
16. Jeanette Henry, *The Indian Historian*, 1 (Dec. 1967), p. 22.
17. Schaefer, *Racial and Ethnic Groups*, pp. 210–211.
18. Peggy McIntosh, *White Privilege: Unpacking the Invisible Knapsack* (Wellesley, MA: Wellesley College Center for Research on Women, 1998).
19. T. W. Adorno, E. Frenkel-Brunswik, D. J. Devinson, and R. N. Sanford, *The Authoritarian Personality* (New York: Harper & Row, 1950).
20. Charles F. Marden and Gladys Meyer, *Minorities in American Society* (New York: American Book, 1962).
21. J. Bradley, *The Imperial Cruise: A Secret History of Empire and War* (Boston: Little, Brown & Company, 2009).
22. P. W. Magness and S. P. Page, *Colonization after Emancipation* (Columbia, MO: University of Missouri Press, 2011).
23. Eugene Hartley, *Problems in Prejudice* (New York: King's Crown Press, 1946).
24. C. H. Cooley, *Human Nature and the Social Order* (New York: Scribner's, 1902).
25. J. W. Coleman and D. R. Cressey, *Social Problems*, 5th ed. (New York: HarperCollins, 1993).
26. E. Pinderhughes, "Afro-American Families and the Victim System," in *Ethnicity and Family Therapy*, M. McGoldrick, J. K. Pearce, and J. Giordana, eds. (New York: Guilford Press, 1982).
27. Albert Szymanski, "Racial Discrimination and White Gain," *American Sociological Review*, 41 (June 1976), pp. 403–414.
28. Schaefer, *Racial and Ethnic Groups*, p. 212.
29. Council on Social Work Education, *Educational Policy and Accreditation Standards: 2008* (Washington, DC: Author, 2008).
30. NASW, *The National Association of Social Workers Code of Ethics* (amended) (Washington, DC: NASW, 1999).
31. M. E. Mor Barak, *Managing Diversity: Toward a Globally Inclusive Workplace* (Thousand Oaks, CA: Sage Publications, 2005).
32. *Chicago Tribune*, "Model Minority Doesn't Tell?" Jan. 3, 1998, p. 18.

33. Ziauddin Sarder, "More Hackney Than Bollywood," *New Statesman*, July 30, 2001, pp. 14–16.
34. Schaefer, *Racial and Ethnic Groups*, pp. 197–210.
35. Ibid., p. 202.
36. Council on Social Work Education, *Educational Policy and Accreditation Standards*.
37. Schaefer, *Racial and Ethnic Groups*.
38. Ibid.
39. Ibid.
40. Charles H. Henderson and Bok-Lim Kim, "Racism," in *Contemporary Social Work*, Donald Brieland, Lela Costin, and Charles Atherton, eds. (New York: McGraw-Hill, 1975), p. 180.
41. Excerpted from a speech by Abraham Lincoln in Charleston, IL, in 1858, as reported in Richard Hofstader, *The American Political Tradition* (New York: Knopf, 1948), p. 116.
42. Quoted in David Gelman, "Black and White in America," *Newsweek*, Mar. 7, 1988, p. 19.
43. Schaefer, *Racial and Ethnic Groups*, p. 197. Reprinted by permission.
44. Ibid.
45. Ibid., p. 207. Reprinted by permission.
46. Michael Barone, "The Many Faces of America," *U.S. News & World Report*, Mar. 19, 2001, pp. 18–20.
47. Schaefer, *Racial and Ethnic Groups*, p. 242.
48. Ibid.
49. Ibid.
50. Ibid., p. 253.
51. Ibid., pp. 245–248.
52. Ibid., p. 228.
53. Johnson, *Social Problems of Urban Man*, p. 349.
54. Dee Brown, *Bury My Heart at Wounded Knee* (New York: Holt, Rinehart & Winston, 1971).
55. Helen M. Crampton and Kenneth K. Keiser, *Social Welfare: Institution and Process* (New York: Random House, 1970), p. 104.
56. Schaefer, *Racial and Ethnic Groups*, pp. 155–166.
57. Communication with Mace J. Delosme, Arcata, CA.
58. Schaefer, *Racial and Ethnic Groups*, pp. 170–171. Reprinted by permission.
59. Ian Robertson, *Social Problems*, 2nd ed. (New York: Random House, 1980), p. 218.
60. Johnson, *Social Problems of Urban Man*, p. 349.
61. Schaefer, *Racial and Ethnic Groups*, p. 316.
62. Charles Henderson, Bok-Lim Kim, and Ione D. Vargus, "Racism," in *Contemporary Social Work*, 2nd ed., Donald Brieland, Lela Costin, and Charles Atherton, eds. (New York: McGraw-Hill, 1980), p. 403.
63. Schaefer, *Racial and Ethnic Groups*, pp. 306–310.
64. George E. Simpson and J. Milton Yinger, *Racial and Cultural Minorities*, 3rd ed. (New York: Harper & Row, 1965), p. 510.
65. Thomas Sullivan, Kenrick Thompson, Richard Wright, George Gross, and Dale Spady, *Social Problems* (New York: Wiley, 1980), p. 437.
66. Johnson, *Social Problems of Urban Man*, pp. 374–379.
67. Cummings, "How to Handle Incidents," p. 197.
68. Sullivan et al., *Social Problems*, p. 438.
69. Ibid., p. 439.
70. Allan P. Sindler, *Bakke, DeFunis, and Minority Admissions: The Quest for Equal Opportunity* (New York: Longman, Green, 1978).
71. Henderson, Kim, and Vargus, "Racism," p. 403.
72. Schaefer, *Racial and Ethnic Groups*, pp. 76–77.
73. S. V. Roberts, "Affirmative Action on the Edge," *U.S. News & World Report*, Feb. 13, 1995, pp. 32–39.
74. M. B. Zuckerman, "Fixing Affirmative Action," *U.S. News & World Report*, Mar. 20, 1995, p. 112.
75. William Kornblum and Joseph Julian, *Social Problems*, 14th ed. (Boston: Pearson, 2012), p. 255.
76. Quoted in Cummings, "How to Handle Incidents," p. 201.
77. Schaefer, *Racial and Ethnic Groups*.
78. Ibid.
79. Harry C. Boyte, "People Power Transforms a St. Louis Housing Project," *Occasional Papers* (Chicago: Community Renewable Society, Jan. 1989), pp. 1–5; J. Deparle, "Cultivating Their Own Gardens," *New York Times*, Sept. 30, 2007.
80. Quoted in Harry C. Boyte, "People Power Transforms a St. Louis Housing Project," *Occasional Papers* (Chicago: Community Renewable Society, Jan. 1989), p. 5.
81. Ibid.
82. W. Devore and E. G. Schlesinger, *Ethnic-Sensitive Social Work Practice*, 4th ed. (Needham Heights, MA: Allyn & Bacon, 1996).
83. D. G. Norton, "Diversity, Early Socialization, and Temporal Development: The Dual Perspective Revisited," *Social Work*, 38, no. 1 (Jan. 1993), pp. 82–90.

84. Devore and Schlesinger, *Ethnic-Sensitive Social Work Practice*.

85. Ibid.

86. A. Billingsley, *Climbing Jacob's Ladder: The Enduring Legacy of African-American Families* (New York: Simon & Schuster, 1993).

87. Surjit S. Dhopper and Sharon E. Moore, *Social Work Practice with Culturally Diverse People* (Thousand Oaks, CA: Sage, 2001).

88. Ibid.

89. Council on Social Work Education, *Educational Policy and Accreditation Standards* (EPAS) (Washington, DC: CSWE, 2008).

90. Jimm G. Good Tracks, "Native American Noninterference," *Social Work*, 18 (Nov. 1973), pp. 30–34.

91. Ronald G. Lewis and Man Keung Ho, "Social Work with Native Americans," *Social Work*, 20 (Sept. 1975), pp. 378–382.

92. Dolores G. Norton, "Incorporating Content on Minority Groups into Social Work Practice Courses," in *The Dual Perspective* (New York: Council on Social Work Education, 1978).

93. Milton Gordon, "Assimilation in America: Theory and Reality," *Daedalus*, 90 (Spring 1961), pp. 363–365.

CHAPTER **13**

Sexism and Efforts for Achieving Equality

Women who work full time are paid only about three-fourths as much as men who work full time.[1] Jobs held mainly by women (such as nurse or elementary school teacher) are paid at rates that average 20% less than those for equivalent jobs held mainly by men.[2] About one-fourth of single families headed by a female have incomes below the poverty line.[3] This chapter will:

Learning Objectives

EP 2.1.3a;
2.1.4a, b, c, d;
2.1.5a, b, c

A   Present a history of sex roles, sexism, and sexual harassment.
B   Describe traditional sex-role expectations.
C   Examine whether there is a biological basis for sexism.
D   Describe traditional sex-role socialization practices.
E   Examine the consequences of sexism for males and females.
F   Describe the sex-role revolution in our society.
G   Present strategies for achieving sexual equality.
H   Summarize social work's commitment to combating sexism.

History of Sex Roles and Sexism

In almost every known society, women have had lower status than men.[4] Women have been bound by more social restrictions and have consistently received less recognition for their work than have men. Women have been regarded differently than men, not only biologically but also emotionally, intellectually, and psychologically. Double standards have often existed for dating, for marriage, and for social and sexual conduct.

Most religions (including Judaism, Christianity, Hinduism, and Islam) in their traditional doctrines ascribe inferior status to women. This tradition continues in most countries, even though women attend religious services more often, hold firmer religious beliefs, pray more often, and are more active in church programs.[5] Many societies have concluded that it is divinely ordained that women should play a secondary and supportive role to men. In many Christian religions, such as the Roman Catholic Church, women cannot become ministers or priests. Some orthodox Jewish men offer a daily prayer of thanks to God for not having made them a woman. In almost all houses of worship, God is referred to as "He."

Hunter–gatherer societies provide insight into the processes that have resulted in women's lower status. Such societies usually lived in small bands consisting of several mating couples and their dependents. Men generally were the hunters, and women were the gatherers of nuts, plants, and other foods. There are several explanations for this role differentiation. Males were supposedly better suited to hunting because they were physically stronger and could run faster. The infant mortality rate was very high in these bands, so it was necessary for the women to be pregnant or nursing throughout most of their childbearing years to maintain the size of the band. The need to tend to children largely prevented women from leaving the camp for days at a time to hunt large game. Even though women often gathered more food than men obtained through hunting, the male's hunting activities were viewed as more prestigious.

Women spent much of their adult lives pregnant, nursing infants, and raising children. Because they were forced to remain around the home, they were also assigned the "domestic tasks" of cooking, serving, and washing. Once these sex roles became part of tradition, the distinctions were perceived not only as practical but also as "natural."

Gradually more behavior patterns were added to these sex-role distinctions. Because men were trained at hunting, these skills led them to be recognized as the defenders of their band in case of attack from other groups. Child-rearing patterns were developed to teach boys to value aggression and to be leaders.

CASE EXHIBIT 13.1

The Ideal Wife, According to Buddhism

Most traditional religions hold that women should have a submissive and supportive role to men. For example, Buddhism asserts that the ideal wife should be:

> ... like a maid-servant. She serves her husband well and with fidelity. She respects him, obeys his commands, has no wishes of her own, no ill-feeling, no resentment, and always tries to make him happy.[a]

[a] *The Teaching of Buddha* (Tokyo: Kosaido. 1966), p. 448.

Girls, on the other hand, were taught to be passive and dependent and to provide emotional support to the males.

Before the Industrial Revolution, practically all societies had come to assign distinct roles to men and women. Females generally performed domestic and child-rearing activities, whereas males were involved in what were then considered the productive* (such as hunting and economic support) and protective functions for the family. Women in preindustrial societies also engaged in food production and economic support, such as making clothes, growing and harvesting garden crops, and helping on the farm. But their specific responsibilities were often viewed as inferior and requiring fewer skills.

The 19th-century Industrial Revolution brought about dramatic changes in sex roles. Men, instead of working on a small farm, left the home to work in a factory or other setting to provide economic support. The economic role of women declined because they were no longer performing economically productive tasks. Women's roles became increasingly defined as child rearing and housework. But the amount of time required to perform these functions declined for several reasons. Families had fewer children. With compulsory education, older children went to school. Gradually, labor-saving devices reduced the need for women to perform time-consuming domestic tasks (baking bread, canning vegetables, and washing). As the traditional roles of women began to change, some females started to pursue activities (for example, outside employment) that had traditionally been reserved for men. With these changes, sex roles began to blur.

The struggle for women's rights in the United States has been going on for nearly two centuries. In the early 19th century, women who were working for the abolition of slavery complained that they, too, were denied such rights as voting. (An 1840 antislavery conference even refused to seat women, as the male delegates gave impassioned speeches about the moral imperative to end slavery.)

In 1848 two feminists, Susan B. Anthony and Elizabeth Stanton, organized the first women's rights caucus, which was held in the state of New York.[6] These early leaders demanded suffrage (the vote for women) and the reform of many laws that were openly discriminatory toward women. It took more than 70 years, until 1920, to pass the 19th Amendment to the Constitution, which gave the vote to women. The suffrage movement was marked by jailings of feminist militants and fierce controversy. Many feminists equated winning the right to vote with achieving sexual equality. As a result, after 1920 the "women's movement" was nearly dormant for the next 40 years.

In the early 1900s, some modern birth control techniques became available. This advance gave women greater freedom from the traditional roles of child rearing and housework.

During World War II, large numbers of women were employed outside the home for the first time, to fill the jobs of men who had been drafted into the military. At that time, more than 38% of all women 16 years of age and over were employed outside the home, causing a further blurring of traditional sex roles.[7]

The 1960s saw a resurgence of interest in sex-role inequality for a variety of reasons. The civil rights movement had a consciousness-raising effect that made people more aware of and concerned about inequalities. This movement to curb racial discrimination through social action also served as a model, suggesting to a number of concerned women that

---

*The use of the term *productive* indicates the higher status that was assigned to the role of men. In actuality, the roles of women were as, or even more, "productive" in completing essential tasks.

CASE EXHIBIT 13.2

Female Genital Mutilation: An Extreme Example of Sexism

Female circumcision, or more accurately, female genital mutilation (FGM), is commonplace in more than half of the African countries and in parts of the Middle East. The details of FGM vary somewhat from culture to culture and from region to region, but the basics are the same.

Shannon Brownlee and Jennifer Seter describe FGM as follows:

> Sometime between infancy and adulthood, all or part of a girl's external genitalia is cut away with a knife or razor blade, usually with no anesthetic. In most cases, the clitoris and the labia minora are removed. In the most extreme form, known as infibulation, the external labia are also scraped and stitched together with thread or long thorns, leaving only a tiny opening for urine and menstrual blood. The opening must be widened on the woman's wedding night.
>
> The pain lasts far longer than the operation. Many of the 85 million to 110 million women who have endured FGM suffer ill effects ranging from reduced or lost sexual sensation to infections, persistent pain, painful intercourse,

infertility, and dangerous childbirth. The purpose is to diminish sexual appetite, in order to maintain a girl's virginity—and thus her marriageability.[a]

Anthropologists believe that the first clitoridectomies, like chastity belts, were a means for husbands to ensure that their children were truly their own; FGM reduces a woman's interest in sex and thus in extramarital affairs. Today young women in many African countries who have not undergone the procedure are shunned as oversexed, unmarriageable, and unclean. Currently FGMs are usually performed by select older women, who are held in high esteem in their societies.

Feminist organizations in the United States tend to view FGM as the gender oppression to end all oppressions. Yet most international human rights organizations have been slow to condemn the practice, arguing that it is inappropriate to interfere with other people's cultural practices.

[a]Shannon Brownlee and Jennifer Seter, "In the Name of Ritual," *U.S. News & World Report*, Feb. 7, 1994, pp. 56–58.

---

sexual discrimination also could be alleviated through social action. More women attended college and thereby became more informed about inequalities. As females moved into new occupational positions, they became increasingly aware of discriminatory practices. Moreover, there was an explosion of research suggesting that sex-role differences were not innately determined but were in fact the result of socialization patterns that were discriminatory toward women.

Studies have found dramatic differences in socialization patterns between males and females. Boys are given more sports equipment and task-oriented toys (such as construction sets) to play with, whereas girls are given dolls and toys relating to marriage and parenthood.[8] During the first few months of life, girls receive more distal stimulation (such as looking and talking) from their parents, whereas boys receive more proximal stimulation (such as rocking and handling).[9] Fathers tend to play more aggressively with sons than with daughters.[10]

Betty Friedan, in her 1963 book *The Feminine Mystique*, provided the ideological base for the resurgence of the women's movement.[11] The term *feminine mystique* referred to the negative self-concept, lack of direction, and low sense of self-worth among women. The book served as a rallying point for women and

led Friedan and others to form the National Organization for Women (NOW) in 1966. Today NOW is the largest women's rights group in the country and an influential political force. NOW and other women's groups have been working to end sexual discrimination, to achieve sexual equality, to end sexual double standards, and to improve the self-identity of women.

The Civil Rights Act of 1964, intended primarily to end racial discrimination, also prohibited discrimination on the basis of gender.

In 1972 the Equal Rights Amendment (ERA) received congressional approval but required ratification by three-fourths (38) of the states to become the 27th Amendment to the Constitution. The ERA stated: "Equality of rights under the law shall not be denied or abridged by the United States or any state on account of sex." Time ran out on the ERA in 1982 when, after 10 years of extensive political action, it narrowly failed to gain the support of enough states to be ratified.

Emotions ran high on both sides of the question of ERA ratification. Proponents asserted that it would be an important legal step toward true gender equality for women.[12] Opponents argued that passage of the ERA would mean that women could be drafted into the armed forces, would lose preferential

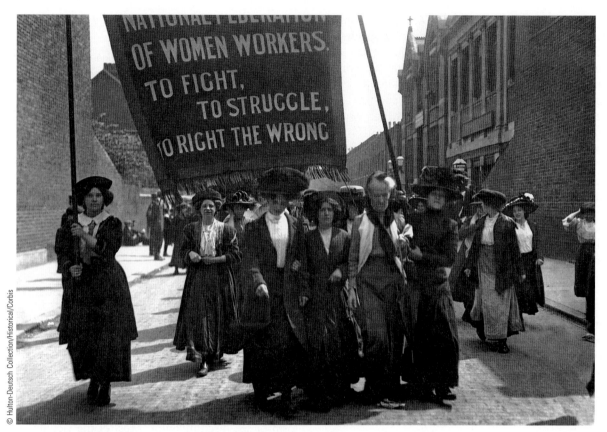

The primary goal of these suffragettes—equal voting rights in national and state elections—has been a reality for more than 80 years. But in spite of affirmative action programs and other important gains of the 1970s and 1980s, full political and economic parity between men and women is yet to come.

treatment in divorce actions, and would become equally liable for alimony, child support, and spouse support. They asserted that labor laws giving preferential treatment to women would need to be revised, such as limits on the amount of weight women may lift on the job. Opponents also argued that "maternity leaves" would have to be made available to husbands who want to stay home with a newborn child.[13] A number of women concluded that the ERA would be more detrimental than beneficial to females, and they actively opposed its passage.

Various statutes have been passed to prevent sex discrimination. The federal Equal Pay Act of 1963 and a number of similar state laws require equal pay for equal work. As mentioned earlier, the Civil Rights Act of 1964 outlaws discrimination on the basis of race, color, sex, or religion. Executive Order 11246, as amended by Executive Order 11375 on October 13, 1967, forbids sex discrimination by federal suppliers and contractors and provides procedures for enforcement. In addition, numerous court decisions have set precedents establishing the illegal-

ity of sex discrimination in hiring, promotions, and rates of pay.[14] Several landmark decisions have required employers to pay female employees millions of dollars in compensation for past wage discriminations. In 1988, for example, the State Farm Insurance Company in California agreed (in a multimillion-dollar settlement) to pay damages and back wages to thousands of women who had been refused jobs as insurance agents over a 13-year period. The women had been told that a college degree was required for agents, even though men were hired without degrees.

Critical Thinking Questions

In your extended family, are men or women the primary decision makers—or is there equality between the sexes in decision making? Do men in your extended family tend to hold higher-status (and higher-paying) jobs?

The Equal Credit Act of 1974 bars discrimination on the basis of marital status or gender in credit transactions. Many states have passed laws prohibiting discrimination against pregnant women in hiring, training, and promotion. Despite these laws, acts, and precedents, however, substantial illegal sex discrimination still occurs, which women often have to fight on a case-by-case basis. For example, some high schools prohibit pregnant or married girls from attending classes, although unmarried fathers and married boys are allowed to attend.

Affirmative action programs apply to women as well as to certain racial minorities. Women are considered a minority group because for generations they have been subjected to discrimination and have been denied equal opportunities.

The following employers are required to have affirmative action programs: government contractors and suppliers, recipients of government funds, and businesses engaged in interstate commerce. Affirmative action applies primarily to job vacancies. Employers must demonstrate active efforts to locate and recruit minority applicants (defined to include women), must demonstrate positive efforts to increase the pool of qualified applicants (for example, special training programs for minorities), must give hiring preference to minority applicants, and in some cases must set hard quotas that specify numbers of minority members that must be accepted to fill vacant positions. The clout of affirmative action programs is in the threat of loss of government funds if employers do not have such programs effectively in place.

As noted in Chapter 12, there is an active backlash against affirmative action programs that could curtail their effectiveness. The following are examples. In 1996 a California ballot initiative abolished gender and racial preferences in government programs that included state colleges and universities, and voters in Washington state passed a similar initiative in 1998. In 1999 the governor of Florida signed an executive order ending that state's affirmative action program. However, affirmative action is still viable. For example, in 2003 the U.S. Supreme Court held that universities have a "compelling interest" in having a diverse population and therefore may take minority status into consideration when making admissions decisions.[15]

Critical Thinking Questions

Do you support or oppose the continuance of affirmative action programs? For example, do you believe that colleges and universities should have lower admission standards for members of underrepresented racial and ethnic groups? Why or why not?

Sexual Harassment

The Equal Employment Opportunity Commission defines sexual harassment as follows:

Unwelcome sexual advances, requests for sexual favors, and other verbal and physical conduct of a sexual nature constitute sexual harassment when this conduct explicitly or implicitly affects an individual's employment, unreasonably interferes with an individual's work performance, or creates an intimidating, hostile, or offensive work environment.[16]

Sexual harassment has become recognized as a form of sex discrimination. Most of the victims are women; men rarely are the objects of unwanted sexual advances.

Horton, Leslie, and Larson identify some of the victims of sexual harassment:

Sexual harassment is an ancient practice. Attractive female slaves were routinely bought as sex playthings, and domestic servants were often exploited. If the Victorian housemaid denied her bed to a lecherous master, he dismissed her; if she admitted him, she soon became pregnant and disgraced, and his wife dismissed her. Either way, she lost!

Sexual harassment can be found anywhere, but is likely to be a problem only where men have supervisory or gatekeeper power over women. The "casting couch" is a well-known feature of show business, and women in many occupations can escape unwelcome attentions only by quitting their jobs, often at a sacrifice. Sexual harassment on the campus has also surfaced, with many female graduate students claiming that senior professors claimed sexual privileges as the price for grades, degrees, and recommendations.[17]

Types of Sexual Harassment

Sexual harassment falls into three categories: verbal, nonverbal, and physical. The following examples may represent sexual harassment if the behavior is clearly unwelcome and not reciprocated.

Verbal

- Sexual innuendo ("So you're majoring in packaging? I love your packaging.")
- Suggestive comments ("Those jeans really fit you well.")
- Sexual remarks about a person's clothing, body, or sexual activities ("I noticed you lost weight. I'm glad you didn't lose your gorgeous chest, too.")
- Sexist insults or jokes or remarks that are stereotypical or derogatory to members of the opposite sex ("Women should be kept barefoot, pregnant, and at the edge of town.")
- Implied or verbal threats concerning one's grades or job ("It's simple. If you want to pass this course, you have to be nice to me, and sex is the nicest thing I can think of.")
- Sexual propositions, invitations, or other pressures for sex ("My office hours are too limited. Why don't you drop by my house tonight? We'll have more privacy and time to get to know each other.")

- Use of employment position to request dates or sexual favors

Nonverbal

- Visual sexual displays; unwanted display of pornographic pictures, posters, cartoons, or other materials
- Body language (such as leering at one's body or standing too close)
- Whistling suggestively
- Mooning or flashing
- Obscene gestures
- Actions that involve gender-directed favoritism or disparate treatment

Physical

- Patting, pinching, and any other inappropriate touching or feeling
- Bra snapping
- Brushing against the body
- Grabbing or groping
- Attempted or actual kissing or fondling
- Coerced sexual intercourse
- Attempted or actual sexual assault

The definition of what is and what is not sexual harassment is somewhat vague. Repeated, unwanted touching is certainly harassment. A 1986 U.S. Supreme Court decision broadened the definition. Today a hostile work environment in which a woman feels hassled or degraded because of constant unwelcome flirtation, lewd comments, or obscene joking may be sufficient grounds for a lawsuit.[18] A number of colleges and universities in recent years have defined sexual harassment to include consenting sexual relationships between faculty and adult students. The rationale is that students are in a lower power position and may suffer adverse consequences if they refuse.

Sexual harassment (see Case Exhibit 13.3) is distinct from flirtation, flattery, a request for a date, and other acceptable behavior occurring in the workplace or the classroom. It is also distinct from other forms of harassment that do not involve conduct of a sexual nature. Sexual harassment is a type of sexual coercion that relies on the power of the perpetrator to affect the victim's economic or academic status and does not necessarily involve physical force. According to U.S. law, sexual harassment is a form of sexual discrimination in employment and education that is prohibited by Title VII of the Civil Rights Act of 1964. Sexual harassment is defined as:

> *Unwelcome sexual advances, requests for sexual favors, and other verbal or physical conduct of a sexual nature constitute sexual harassment when 1.) submission to such conduct is made either explicitly or implicitly a term or condition of an individual's employment; 2.) submission to or rejection of such conduct by an individual is used as a basis for employment decisions affecting such an individual; or 3.) such conduct has the purpose or effect of unreasonably interfering with an individual's work performance or creating an intimidating, hostile, or offensive working environment.*[19]

Sexual harassment almost always involves elements of unequal power and coercion. Although most victims are women, sexual harassment can be directed at either males or females. Repeated incidents of sexual harassment generally result in a hostile, intimidating, or anxiety-producing work or educational environment.

Mooney, Knox, and Schacht indicate that sexual harassment can take two different forms;

(1) quid pro quo, in which an employer requires sexual favors in exchange for a promotion, salary increase, or any other employee benefit, and (2) the existence of a hostile environment that unreasonably interferes with job performance, as in the case of sexually explicit comments or insults being made to an employee. Common examples of sexual harassment include unwanted touching, the invasion of personal space, making sexual comments about a person's body or attire, and sexual joke telling.[20]

Sexual harassment can also occur over the Internet—by sending sexually explicit e-mails to co-workers or to other people, or by posting sexually explicit images of an individual on a website. The victim as well as the harasser may be a man or a woman, although adult women are usually the victims and adult men are usually the harassers.

Those found guilty of sexual harassment are subject to reprimand, dismissal, demotion, and other consequences at their place of employment. Unfortunately, even a successful protest sometimes further victimizes the victim. She must endure the unpleasantness of pursuing the complaint, and she may be viewed by some as having invited the advances. Some women who protest eventually are forced to seek a new job because of the discomfort they feel in the old workplace.

In recent years, corporate America has received several wake-up calls on sexual harassment. For example, in 1994 a San Francisco jury awarded a legal secretary $7.1 million in punitive damages after finding that her former employer failed to stop an attorney in the firm from harassing her.

In 1998 Astra AB in Boston agreed to pay nearly $10 million to more than 70 women to settle claims that its president and other executives replaced older female employees with beautiful, young single women who were then pressured into having sex. Also in 1998, Mitsubishi Motors agreed to pay a record $34 million to 350 women to settle allegations that women on the assembly line at its Illinois factory were groped and insulted and that managers did nothing to stop it.

In 2005 Boeing Co. agreed to pay 17,960 current and former female employees $72 million to dispose of their sex-discrimination class-action suit against the aerospace giant.

In June 1998, the U.S. Supreme Court ruled that an employer could be held liable when a supervisor sexually harasses a worker, even if the employee's job is not harmed. (However, if a company has a strong program in place to prevent and discipline harassment, that company has, according to the Supreme Court, some measure of protection from sexual harassment lawsuits.)

Critical Thinking Questions

Have you been a victim of sexual harassment? (Males, as well as females, can be victimized.) If so, did you effectively confront the harassment, or could you have done something different that would have more effectively confronted the harassment?

Traditional Sex-Role Expectations

Sex roles are learned patterns of behavior that are expected of the sexes in a given society. Sex-role expectations, which define how men and women are to behave and how they are to be treated by others, are based largely on stereotypes. *Stereotyping* involves attributing of fixed and usually inaccurate and unfavorable qualities to a category of people. Stereotyping makes it easier for discrimination (unequal treatment) to occur.

Critical Thinking Questions

Do you have traditional sex-role expectations? Could you improve your life by making changes in your sex-role expectations?

American women traditionally are expected to be affectionate, passive, conforming, sensitive, intuitive, and dependent—"sugar and spice and everything nice." They are supposed to be concerned primarily with domestic life, to be nurturing, to love to care for babies and young children, to fuss over their personal appearance, and to be self-sacrificing for their families. They should not appear ambitious, aggressive, competitive, or more intelligent than men. They should be ignorant about and uninterested in sports, economics, and politics. Also, they are not supposed to initiate relationships with men but are expected to be tender, feminine, emotional, and appreciative when in these relationships.

CASE EXHIBIT 13.4

Traditional Stereotypes of a Businessman and a Businesswoman

- He's aggressive; she's pushy.
- He's good at details; she's picky.
- He loses his temper because he's so involved in his job; she's bitchy.
- When he's depressed (or hung over), everyone tiptoes past his office; she's moody so it must be her "time of the month."
- He follows through; she doesn't know when to quit.
- He's confident; she's conceited.
- He stands firm; she's hard.
- He has judgment; she's prejudiced.

- He's a man of the world; she's "been around."
- He drinks because of excessive job pressure; she's a lush.
- He isn't afraid to say what he thinks; she's mouthy.
- He exercises authority diligently; she's power mad.
- He's close-mouthed; she's secretive.
- He's a stern taskmaster; she's hard to work for.
- He climbed the ladder to success; she slept her way to the top.

SOURCE: Author unknown.

There are also a number of traditional sex-role expectations for males in our society: A male is expected to be tough, fearless, logical, self-reliant, independent, and aggressive. He should have definite opinions on the major issues of the day and make authoritative decisions at work and at home. He is expected to be strong—a sturdy oak—and never to be depressed, vulnerable, or anxious. He is not supposed to be a "sissy"—to cry or openly display emotions that suggest vulnerability. He is expected to be the provider, the breadwinner. He should be competent in all situations, physically strong, athletic, confident, daring, brave, and forceful. He should be in a position to dominate any situation—to be a "Clint Eastwood."[21] He is supposed to initiate relationships with women and be dominant in these relationships. Men who are supported by their wives, or who earn less than their wives, are likely to experience feelings of shame and inadequacy.

Even very young boys are expected to be masculine. Parents and relatives are far more concerned when a boy is a "sissy" than when a girl is a "tomboy." A tomboy is expected to outgrow her "masculine" tendencies, but it is erroneously feared that a sissy will never fare well in our competitive society and may even become gay. (The right of a boy to wear his hair long had to be won in many court battles in this country, whereas hardly anyone is concerned when a girl wears her hair short.)

Is There a Biological Basis for Sexism?

Let's examine the sexist ideology that assumes the differences between men and women are the result

Peter Dazeley/Photographer's Choice RF/Getty Images

Are sex roles determined by biology? Or are human behavior patterns almost entirely learned and therefore flexible?

of biology—that anatomy equips men to play an active and dominant role in the world and women to play a passive and secondary role.

There are certain biological differences between men and women. Of course, there are the obvious anatomical, sexual, and reproductive differences. There are also hormonal differences. Each sex has

CASE EXHIBIT 13.5

Sex-Role Expectations Are Culturally Determined

In her classic study *Sex and Temperament in Three Primitive Societies*, Margaret Mead refuted the notion that sex-role expectations are biologically determined. The study was conducted among three tribes in New Guinea in the early 1930s. Mead demonstrated that many characteristics Americans classify as typically female or male are defined differently in these tribes.

Both sexes among the Arapesh would seem feminine to us. Both men and women are gentle, nurturant, and compliant. The personalities of males and females in this society are not sharply differentiated. Both girls and boys learn to be unaggressive, cooperative, and responsive to the needs and wants of others. Relations between husband and wife parallel the traditional mother–child relations in our society, with the Arapesh husband often seeing his role as providing training to his much younger wife.

In contrast, among the Mundugamor, both sexes would seem masculine to us. Both are headhunters and cannibals, are nonnurturant and aggressive, and actively initiate sexual involvement.

The most interesting society studied was the Tchambuli, which virtually reverses our traditional sex-role expectations and stereotypes. The men spend much more time than the women in grooming and decorating themselves and in painting, carving, and practicing dance steps. In contrast, the women are efficient, impersonal, unadorned, managerial, and brisk. They are the traders and have most of the economic power.

Mead concludes:

> We no longer have any basis for regarding such aspects of behavior as sex linked....Standardized personality differences between the sexes are...cultural creations to which each generation, male or female, is trained to conform.

SOURCE: Margaret Mead, *Sex and Temperament in Three Primitive Societies* (New York: Morrow, 1935).

both male and female hormones, but women have higher levels of female hormones and men have higher levels of male hormones. Research on some animal species (which may or may not be applicable to humans) has shown that if male hormones are injected into females, the females have a heightened sex drive and become more aggressive.[22] Scientists, however, see this hormonal difference as playing only a minor role in humans. This is because human behavior patterns are almost entirely learned, whereas behavior patterns in lower animals are more influenced by hormonal factors.[23]

Men, on the average, are taller and heavier than women and have greater physical strength. Women can tolerate pain better and have greater physical endurance (except in short-term feats of strength).[24] In most respects, women are physically healthier.[25] Females are less susceptible to most diseases and on the average live longer. Males have higher rates of fetal and infant mortality. Male fetuses can inherit a greater number of sex-linked weaknesses: More than 30 disorders have been found exclusively among males, including hemophilia, certain types of color blindness, and webbing of the toes.

Soon after birth, female babies tend be more content and less physically active.[26] As children develop, other differences appear, but it has not yet been determined whether the identified differences are due to inherited or learned factors. Girls learn to talk and read at an earlier age; they also become more docile and dependent and seem more intellectually mature (most remedial education classes have a large majority of boys). Boys are superior in elementary school on tasks requiring spatial, mechanical, and analytic ability, whereas girls are superior at tasks involving verbal capacities and numerical computation.[27] The basis for these differences is uncertain. Girls, for example, may be better at reading and language because they are encouraged to spend more time with adults and to read rather than to engage in competitive sports or similar activities.

There is considerable research supporting the position that sex-role differences are due primarily to socialization patterns.[28]

The fact that there are wide variations in sex-role expectations among cultures also suggests that sex roles are learned rather than biologically determined. (If all cultures defined sex-role expectations similarly, this would suggest a biological basis for sex-role distinctions.) Let's consider a few examples. Most cultures expect women to do most of the carrying of heavy objects, whereas in this country and in most European countries men are expected to do most of the lifting and carrying of heavy objects. In some societies, unlike ours, the men do most of the cooking. Not so long ago in Europe, it was the males who wore stockings, perfume, and silks. Men in Scotland still wear kilts (skirts). Among the

Maoris and the Trobrianders, it is the women who are expected to take the initiative in sexual activity.

Margaret Mead, in a classic study, examined sex-role expectations in three tribes in New Guinea. She found that one tribe required both males and females to behave in a way we would define as "masculine"; a second required both to behave in a "feminine" fashion; and the third had the females act "masculine" and the males act "feminine." Mead concluded that sex-role expectations are determined primarily by cultural learning experiences (see Case Exhibit 13.5).

Sex-Role Socialization

In the United States, sex-role socialization starts shortly after birth. Baby girls are dressed in pink, and baby boys are dressed in blue. Babies are given gender-related toys. Boys are bounced on the knee and handled roughly, whereas girls are cooed over. A child becomes aware that he is a "boy" or she is a "girl" long before noticing anatomical differences between the sexes.[28] Lawrence Kohlberg notes that children make basic decisions (based on what others tell them) that they are boys or girls and then select those activities that significant others (people they view as important to them) define as conforming to this self-concept.[29]

Many parents go to great lengths to socialize their young children according to sex-role expectations. Little boys are given toy trucks to play with, and girls are given dolls. Boys are encouraged to play ball; girls are urged to play house. Ruth Hartley notes:

> Girls gain approval ... by doing the rather undemanding things that are expected of them.... A girl need not be bright as long as she is docile and attractive.... This kind of treatment is likely to produce rather timid, unventuresome, unoriginal, conformist types.[30]

Young girls in many families are still raised by their parents to be mothers and homemakers and/or are encouraged to seek low-status, low-paid employment. The early socialization of boys, according to Hartley, is quite different:

> Almost from birth the boy has more problems to solve autonomously. In addition, he is required to limit his interest at a very early age to sex-appropriate objects and activities, while girls are permitted to amble their way to a similar status

at a more gradual and natural pace.... He is challenged to discover what he should do by being told what he should not do, as in the most frequently employed negative sanction, "Don't be a sissy!"... Interest in girlish things is generally forbidden and anxiety-provoking in American boyhood.... The boy is constantly open to a challenge to prove his masculinity. He must perform, adequately and publicly, a variety of physical feats that will have very little utility in most cases in adulthood. He is constantly under pressure to demonstrate mastery over the environment, and, concomitantly, to suppress expression of emotion.[31]

Boys are encouraged to play more competitive games than girls and to be outgoing and aggressive, whereas young girls are encouraged to be passive and reserved.[32] Young children are impressionable. Such sex-role stereotyping often becomes a self-fulfilling prophecy. According to Charles Cooley's "looking glass self-concept," people will come to view themselves as others relate to them.[33]

Research shows that some females are actually taught to fear success and achievement and to "play dumb" in order to "boost the male ego."[34] To be feminine, girls must display softness, helplessness, tenderness, understanding, and be generally nonassertive. Thus, adolescent and adult females are put in a double bind due to *femininity/achievement incompatibility*.[35] There is a traditional view in our society that a woman cannot be both feminine and achievement oriented. (Of course, this traditional view is an arbitrary one that has been a factor in leading women to play a submissive role; there is nothing intrinsically incompatible about femininity and achievement.)

A significant part of the socialization process occurs in school. Girls are often channeled into sewing, typing, and cooking classes, whereas boys are channeled into such classes as woodworking, printing, and mechanics. Most elementary and middle school teachers are female, whereas most principals are male.[36] Thus, children see men in superior decision-making positions and women in subordinate positions.

A review of more than 100 studies by the American Association of University Women found that:

- Although girls and boys start school with similar levels of skill and confidence, by the end of high school girls trail boys in science and math test scores.

- Teachers pay less attention to girls than to boys.
- Reports of sexual harassment of girls are increasing.
- Textbooks still ignore or stereotype women and girls and omit discussions of pressing problems such as sexual abuse.
- Some tests are biased against females and thereby limit their chances of obtaining scholarships.
- African American girls are particularly likely to be ignored or rebuffed in schools.[37]

Because boys are given more encouragement to be independent and assertive, they are more likely to act up and get into trouble.[38] Perhaps for this reason, studies of teacher–student interaction have found that boys get more attention from teachers than do girls.[39] Myra Sadker and associates put it this way, "Boys are the central figures . . . and girls are relegated to second-class participation."[40] Partly because of such socialization practices in school systems, males are much more apt when they enter college to major in fields such as science, mathematics, and engineering, which are most likely to lead directly to high-paying careers.

Textbooks in preschool, elementary, junior high, and high school portray female characters as more passive and dependent and less creative than males.[41]

Some guidance counselors advise students to pursue careers not just on the basis of their abilities, but also on the basis of traditional sex-role expectations. For example, a young girl who excels at math may be encouraged to be a teacher, whereas a young boy with equal skills may be urged to consider engineering. Janet Chafetz comments on such counseling practices:

> Counselors defend such practices on the basis of what youngsters may "realistically" expect to face in the future: marriage, child care, and a lack of opportunity in a number of career fields for females, and the need to support a family at the highest income and status levels possible for males. "Realism," however, has always been an excuse for maintaining the status quo, and it is no different in the case of sex role stereotypes. If, for instance, females do not prepare to enter previously masculine fields, such fields will remain male-dominated, allowing another generation of counselors to assure girls that females can't work in them. In addition, it is questionable whether counselors' notions of "reality" in fact keep pace with reality. There is undoubtedly a lag between

> expanding opportunities and changing sex role definitions on the one hand, and counselors' awareness of these phenomena on the other.[42]

Even contemporary theories in psychology describe women as more passive and emotional, lacking in abstract interests, and as having an instinctive tenderness for babies.[43] Although masculinity and femininity are largely learned roles, contemporary psychological theories subtly imply (erroneously) that sex-role differences are genetically determined. Sigmund Freud's theory of the development of the female personality is probably the most sexist and outrageous. According to Freud, young girls discover that their genitals differ from boys', which leads them to have "penis envy." Because of this difference, girls conclude that they are biologically inferior to males and then develop a passive, submissive personality as a way to adjust to interactions with males, whom they view as superior.[44]

There are many sexist implications built into the English language. The words we select greatly influence our interpretation of reality. The use of sexist language has been a significant factor in defining and maintaining the position of males as dominant in our society, with females assigned a supportive or submissive role. The following words and phrases portray males as dominant: *mankind, manned, manpower, chairman, congressman, businessman, mailman, salesman, foreman, policeman, the best man for the job,* and *man and wife.* There are other examples of how sexism has infiltrated the English language. Books in the past tended (there has been considerable improvement in recent years) to use the pronoun "he" to refer in a generic sense to a person when the gender is unspecified. On reaching adulthood, a man becomes "Mr." for the remainder of his life; this is a polite term that makes no reference to the status of a man's personal life. On the other hand, a woman starts as a "Miss" and then becomes a "Mrs." upon marriage, which clearly identifies her marital status. (The modern-day use of "Ms." is a desired nonsexist alternative term.) In addition, traditional customs assume a woman will, upon her marriage, use her husband's last name (instead of her family name).

The mass media, particularly in advertising, also play an important role in sex-role socialization. Women are frequently portrayed in commercials as being wives, mothers, or sex objects or as obsessed with getting a date. They used to be portrayed as invariably less intelligent and more dependent than men and were hardly ever shown in executive positions.

Some TV ads still depict women in traditional sex-role stereotypes, such as delighting in waxing their floors or in discovering a new detergent to get their families' white clothes whiter. Fortunately, some changes are occurring in the mass media's portrayal of women, reflecting changes in our society. Some commercials are now even reversing traditional roles. Because the mass media are important socialization vehicles, they can assist in changing attitudes about "proper" sex roles in the future.

Sadly, to this day, the media is still conveying that a woman who is valued in our society is one who is young, beautiful, and sensual. As a result, a woman's intelligence and accomplishments are largely devalued. Teenage women are socialized to believe they will be valued primarily because of their beauty and sensuality. Many young women resort to anorexia or bulimia to have a "thinner" appearance. TV, movies, and the Internet trivialize women and paint them in subtle and not-so-subtle ways as sex objects. Women are much more apt than men to seek to look younger through Botox and plastic surgery. Most women who are glamorized in movies, on TV, and in magazine ads are young and beautiful. The resulting message conveyed to girls and young women is that they can only become successful, self-assured, empowered, and civically engaged if they focus on developing a youthful look and becoming more physically attractive—rather than on further developing their intellectual capacities and on acquiring marketable skills and knowledge for a career. It is skills and knowledge that are necessary to excel in leadership positions in business and in the political arena. Is it any wonder there are so few women in leadership positions in business and in the political arena?

Critical Thinking Questions

What are your career aspirations? Are your aspirations partly influenced by traditional sex-role expectations?

Consequences of Sexism

Sexism is prejudice or discrimination against women. Although females represent a numerical majority in our society, they are considered a minority group because they are victims of discrimination on many fronts and have unequal access to valued resources.

Effects on Occupation and Income

Women tend to be concentrated in the lower-paying, lower-status positions: secretaries, child-care workers, receptionists, typists, nurses, hairdressers, bank tellers, cashiers, and file clerks. Men tend to be concentrated in higher-paying positions: lawyers, judges, engineers, airplane pilots, physicians, and dentists (see Table 13.1).

As noted earlier, full-time working women are paid about three-fourths of what full-time working men are paid.[45] Even though sex discrimination laws have been passed, job discrimination continues to be found in a number of studies.[46]

Women hold fewer than 20% of the nation's elective offices.[47] There has never been a woman president or vice president of the United States. The vast majority of senators and representatives in Congress are men. It is a rarity when a woman is elected governor in a state. Men still control the political processes to nominate candidates and to campaign for their election. The higher the status of an elective office, usually, the lower the percentage of women holding that position. The potential political clout of women, however, is immense because they constitute a majority of the nation's voters.

Women hold only 2% of the top management positions in American corporations and just 6% of the seats on corporate boards of directors.[48] Even successful female executives often complain about an invisible "glass ceiling" that seems to lock them out of the key positions of power. One study, based on interviews with 100 male and female executives from three major U.S. corporations, concluded that there was a clear double standard in promotions and that women had to perform significantly better than their male counterparts to get ahead.[49]

About two-thirds of the women who work outside the home in the United States are employed in the "low-paying" positions of housekeepers, secretaries, receptionists, telephone operators, clerks, and so on.[50] And overall, women earn less income than men in practically every job category.[51] It is true that differences in income between men and women by job category are due partly to seniority (men earn more because they've held their jobs longer), but studies taking seniority into account have found that women tend to receive less pay for doing the same job.[52]

There are probably many reasons for these occupational and income differences between men and

Table 13.1 Employment Positions Held by Women

POSITION	PERCENTAGE HELD BY WOMEN
Dental assistants	97.5
Secretaries	96.1
Dental hygienists	95.1
Child care workers	94.7
Teacher assistants	92.4
Hairdressers, cosmetologists	91.9
Registered nurses	91.1
Book keepers	90.9
Librarians	82.8
File clerks	82.0
Elementary and middle school teachers	81.8
Social workers	80.8
Cashiers	73.7
Waiters and waitresses	71.1
Psychologists	66.7
Authors	63.5
Pharmacists	53.0
Physicians	32.3
Lawyers	31.5
Chief executives	25.5
Dentists	25.5
Architects	24.4
Computer programmers	22.0
Clergy	17.5
Police officers	13.0
Civil engineers	9.7
Airplane pilots	5.2
Fire fighters	3.6
Carpenters	1.4
Electricians	1.5

SOURCE: U.S. Census Bureau, *Statistical Abstract of the United States: 2012* (Washington, DC, 2011).

women. Female children are socialized to seek lower-paying occupations and careers. For example, boys are encouraged to be lawyers and doctors, whereas girls are encouraged to be teachers and secretaries. Men and women are also "sex typed" for various jobs: Males seeking employment are encouraged by prospective employers to apply for higher-status positions, whereas women are encouraged to apply for lower-level positions.[53] Then there is the tendency for our society to assign lower pay to job categories in which women are concentrated: receptionists, secretaries, and typists. Nonetheless, lower pay for women holding the same jobs as men indicates that there are discriminatory practices occurring even after women are hired.

Horton, Leslie, and Larson provide additional reasons, stemming from sex-role socialization, for the job and income disparity between men and women:

> *Motivation for career advancement is difficult to measure, and rash generalization is dangerous. Yet there are good reasons to suspect that intense career ambitions have been less common among women than among men. Beginning in early socialization, most girls are trained to please and charm others; most boys are trained to impress and outdistance others. Boys are trained to dominate and lead; girls, to submit and follow. Boys are taught to make demands upon others; girls learn to serve others' needs. Boys are praised for their strength; girls, for their prettiness and graciousness. As adults, men in our society are evaluated primarily according to their career success ("Meet my son, the doctor"), while women have been evaluated primarily according to their skill in human relationships ("She has a handsome husband and three darling children"). Husbands who knowingly neglected their families to pursue career advancement (moonlighting, night school, weekends working at the office) were praised for their ambition, while wives who allowed their careers to interfere with family life were scolded and scorned. A woman's spectacular success might alienate men, and much has been written about the avoidance-of-success syndrome in women....This all has contributed to a lower level of career expectation among women than among men.[54]*

Effects on Human Interactions

The effects of sexism on human interactions are immense. Let's look at some examples.

Parents place more social restrictions on teenage daughters than on teenage sons. Daughters cannot stay out as late, their friends are more closely monitored, they are less likely to be given the family car for going out, and they are discouraged from participating in athletics.

Women are pressured to have the "Miss America" look—well-developed busts, shapely figures, and attractive features. Women who are judged less attractive, according to current American stereotypes, receive less attention from males, find it more difficult to get dates, and may even have less success at obtaining higher-status employment. The psychological costs are particularly severe when a woman reaches middle age. Socialized into believing her main function is child rearing and her main asset is her physical attractiveness, she often watches with despair as both her children and her youth leave her.

There are many double standards for male and female social interactions. If teenage boys are sexually active, they are viewed as "studs," whereas sexually active teenage girls may be called derogatory names. To a greater extent, males are allowed to be aggressive and to use vulgar language. There are social restrictions that discourage women from entering certain nightclubs and other places of entertainment. Married women who have an affair are usually subjected to more disapproval than are married men who do.

In male–female interactions, there is a tendency for the male to seek to be dominant and for the female either to seek an egalitarian relationship or to be manipulated into being submissive. For example, in dating, the male usually is expected to ask the female for a date and to choose what they will do on the date. Also, males often try to be "macho"; some females find that, to receive positive reinforcement and social acceptability, they must play along by being submissive, passive, or "feminine." When both husband and wife are working, the wife usually leaves her job and follows her husband to a new geographic area when he gets a job transfer.[55]

Often there are power struggles between males and females related to sex-role expectations. Marriage counselors are now seeing many couples in which the husband wants his wife to play a traditional role: stay at home, raise the children, and do the housework. If a wife does work, the husband often demands that the job not interfere with her doing the domestic tasks. He also perceives her job as a "second income" in contrast to a "career." Wives who want egalitarian relationships and who are becoming increasingly aware of the negative effects of sex-role stereotyping are likely to experience conflict with husbands who want them to fulfill the traditional wife role.

Women experience more depression and greater dissatisfaction in marriage than men.[56] Women are expected to make most of the adjustments necessary to keep the marriage intact. Middle-age women frequently suffer severe depression when many of their tasks as mothers and homemakers are phased out—especially if they do not have outside jobs.[57] Research demonstrates that employed wives are happier than full-time homemakers.[58] Women who are extensively battered by their husbands, yet continue to live in these circumstances for years, sadly document the extent to which some women feel trapped by social arrangements that perpetuate their dependency and submission.

Matina Horner found that many women are motivated to avoid success because they fear that the more ambitious and successful they are, the less feminine they will appear in their interactions with men.[59]

Sex-role stereotypes also contribute to women being treated as sex objects by some men and to women being sexually harassed at work, at school, and in other settings.

Of course, it is not just female stereotypes that cause difficulties in human interaction. Males also experience problems in living up to the "Clint Eastwood" image (described earlier). It is almost impossible for any male to meet such expectations. Yet there are considerable pressures on males to try—or suffer the consequences. Take the example of Senator Edmund Muskie in the Democratic presidential primary campaign in 1968. Senator Muskie was the leading candidate for the nomination. Then a newspaper in New England made some derogatory accusations about his wife and Muskie reacted by breaking down and crying in public. Very quickly the American public concluded that Muskie did not have the emotional stability to be president, and his popularity plummeted in the polls. Deborah David and Robert Brannon describe another example:

A friend explained to me that he broke down and cried in front of a colleague at the office after some personal tragedies and office frustrations. He explained, "The news of my crying was all over the office in an hour. At first, no one said anything. They just sort of looked. They couldn't handle the situation by talking about it. Before this, only girls had cried. One of the guys did joke, 'Hear you and Sally been crying lately, eh?' I guess that was a jibe at my masculinity, but the 'knowing silence' of the others indicated the same doubts. What really hurt was that two years later, when I was

CASE EXHIBIT 13.6

Consequences of Sexist Traditions: Rape and Murder of Wives in India

Fifteen-year-old Baskar was married in July 1997 to a stranger selected by her conservative Muslim family. As is traditional in India, Baskar's family sent a dowry (consisting of a refrigerator, furniture, and other household goods) to the family of the groom. However, the family could not afford one item that the groom had demanded—a motorcycle. On her wedding night, her drunken husband and three of his male friends took turns beating her and raping her, forcing her to crouch on all fours (simulating a motorcycle) as they victimized her.

A few years earlier, a young bride was burned to death because her in-laws were unhappy over her dowry. More than 5,000 women are killed every year in India because their in-laws consider the dowries they receive inadequate. Only a small percentage of the rapists and killers over dowry disputes

are ever punished, due to tradition. Reena Bannerjee, a women's rights activist who works with dowry disputes and rape victims, commented, "The position of women is so low that men consider them lower than the shoes they wear."

Bride burnings are fairly common in India. Often kerosene is poured on the bride, and then she is set on fire. In India brides generally move in with the husband's family after an arranged marriage. Burning the bride is common because in-laws can then claim it was a cooking accident.

SOURCES: Hema Shukla, "Women Seek Justice in a Land Where Their Voices Are Stifled," *Wisconsin State Journal*, Aug. 2, 1997, p. 10A. Celia W. Dugger, "Kerosene, Weapon of Choice for Attacks on Wives in India," *New York Times*, Dec. 26, 2000.

---

doing very well and being considered for a promotion, it was brought up again. My manager was looking over my evaluations, read a paragraph to himself, and said, 'What do you think about that crying incident?' You can bet that was the last time I let myself cry."[60]

Ruth Hartley notes that sex-role socialization of boys inevitably leads to personal conflicts in later years:

The boy is not adequately socialized for adulthood…. The boy is conditioned to live in an all-masculine society, defining his own self-image by rejecting whatever smacks of femininity. In adulthood, he will have to adjust to a heterosexual work world, perhaps even take orders from a female, a species he has been taught to despise as inferior. Finally, the emphasis on repression of the emotions, the high value of stoicism, leaves the boy wholly unprepared for the emotional closeness and intimate personal interaction now more and more expected of a lover and a spouse.[61]

Critical Thinking Questions

If you are a male, do you seek to be dominant in male–female interactions? If you are a female, have you ever decided to appear less successful at something in order to appear more feminine?

Men frequently feel they must put their careers first and thereby sharply limit the interactions and satisfactions received in being husbands and fathers. In contrast, women are traditionally expected to put their roles as wives and mothers first and thereby limit their growth, capacities, and satisfactions in other areas.

Men in this country are disadvantaged before the law in several areas. In some jurisdictions, husbands are legally required to provide financial support for their families, and failure to do so is grounds for divorce by the wife. If a marriage breaks up, courts usually grant custody of the children to the wife. In child custody battles, the father bears a heavier burden of proof that he is a fit parent than does the mother, and only in cases in which the mother is demonstrably negligent is the father's claim seriously considered. Alimony is much more frequently awarded to wives, even when both spouses can support themselves. Several men's groups have now formed in various regions of the country to advocate for equal treatment of men in these legal areas.

Sex-role stereotyping probably also plays a key role in the following statistics.[62] Men are more likely than women to commit suicide, are substantially more likely to be involved in violence, and commit far more crimes. Alcoholics and drug addicts are primarily men. Males also have higher rates of stress-related illnesses, such as heart disease, ulcers, and hypertension. The life expectancy for men in our society is several years less than for women. This shorter life expectancy stems partly from the pressures they face to succeed financially and from the fact that they are socialized not to vent their emotions. As a result, they experience more psychological stress, which leads to higher rates of stress-related illnesses and thus a shorter life span.

Because of male stereotypes, many men view themselves as failures when they cannot meet the financial needs of their families. Some men are badly beaten in fights because they felt they could not walk away and still be "real men." Many women find it frustrating to interact with men who are unable to be honest and open about their feelings. Not being able to live up to the "model man" image makes many men unhappy, depressed, and unfulfilled. Clearly, sex-role stereotyping has huge costs (financial, social, and personal) not only for women but also for men.

Maternal Wall

The term "maternal wall" refers to the problems women face in juggling their roles as employees with those of mothers and caregivers. Women tend to be the primary caretakers/caregivers of children and of relatives with health challenges. Working women who are caregivers experience considerable stress in trying to excel at both their jobs and in their caregiver roles. Some women with college degrees decide to leave fast-track professions/careers and take less demanding jobs—or take a few years off from working outside the home. Choosing that option adversely impacts their earning potentials in the future. Someone has to do the necessary work of raising children and caregiving. (It is sad that the reward for such vital work is often loss of career status, professional marginalization, and an increased risk of poverty.)

Recent Developments and a Look to the Future

A sex-role revolution is occurring in our society. Men as well as women are becoming aware of the negative effects of sex-role distinctions. Increasingly we see courses on this topic in high schools, vocational schools, and colleges. More and more women are entering the labor force.

Women are becoming more involved in athletics than they were in the past, and they are entering certain types of competition previously confined to males. Women are now playing basketball, football, baseball, and volleyball. There are increasing numbers of women in track and field events, swimming, boxing, wrestling, weight lifting, golf, tennis, and stock-car racing.

In 1983 Sandra Day O'Connor became the first woman justice on the U.S. Supreme Court. In 1984 Geraldine Ferraro was the first woman selected to be a vice presidential candidate for a major political party.

Women are also pursuing a number of professions and careers that previously were nearly all male: military officers, engineers, lawyers, judges, firefighters, physicians, dentists, accountants, administrators, police officers, managers. Entering these new professions often has presented obstacles.

Human interactions are also changing, with more women being assertive and seeking out egalitarian relationships with males. To some extent, men are also (more slowly) beginning to realize that sex-role stereotypes limit the opportunities open to them in terms of emotional expression, interpersonal relationships, occupations, and domestic activities.

Sexism and Social Work

EP 2.1.10a

Females have held, and currently do hold, a number of leadership positions in social work, serving as deans of graduate schools, chairs of undergraduate social work programs, directors of agencies, and presidents of national, state, and local social work organizations. There have also been a vast number of female authors of social work texts and professional journal articles. However, overall, males predominate in leadership positions in social work.

Because more than two-thirds of social workers are female, there is the perception that social work is a female-dominated profession.[63] Some different statistics suggest otherwise. Gibelman and Schervish analyzed the demographics of the membership of the National Association of Social Workers (NASW) and found that "male social workers disproportionately hold managerial positions, assume such positions earlier in their careers, and earn more money in these positions than do their female counterparts."[64] Female social workers earn about 80 cents for every dollar earned by male social workers.[65] O'Neill in 2001 reported the median income for female social workers is more than $10,000 less than for male social workers.[66]

Social Work's Response to Women's Issues

There is evidence that the profession is responding to women's issues. In 1973 the Delegate Assembly of NASW added sexism to poverty and racism as basic concerns and priorities for the profession. The Council on Social Work Education (CSWE) has required in accreditation standards for baccalaureate and master's programs that content on women's issues be included throughout the curriculum. CSWE also has an accreditation standard that prohibits gender discrimination in social work educational programs and mandates affirmative action programs for women administrators, faculty, students, and staff in social work educational programs.

The NASW Legal Defense Fund has provided financial support in sex discrimination cases. In addition, NASW supported the Equal Rights Amendment and is working on other issues related to sexism.

In practice there is some truth that social work has an emphasis on serving women because a majority of social work clients are women. About three-fourths of all people receiving public assistance and welfare payments are females.[67] Because women still primarily care for children, they are the main users of child welfare services. They are more likely to seek and receive counseling, and they are the major consumers of services for the aged. In addition, females are the primary consumers of family planning, pregnancy counseling, abortion services, rape crisis services, services from shelters for battered wives, and displaced homemaker services.

There are a number of reasons why more women than men are social work clients. For one thing, women outnumber men in the United States. Julia B. Rauch identifies another reason: "Most women in this country are socialized to accept weakness and dependence with more ease than men. The role of client is compatible with behaviors expected of women but is not congruent with men's expectations of themselves."[68] Women tend to need more services because poverty is a problem that disproportionately affects them; women who work full time are paid substantially less than men who work full time. Women also have higher rates of unemployment and are much more likely to be single heads of households.

Rauch summarizes a number of additional reasons why women are more likely to be social work clients:

> … teenage and unwanted pregnancies, postpartum depression, and sexual dysfunction; the need, resulting from the concentration of parenting functions in women's hands, for services for mothers who abuse or neglect their children and for the mothers of emotionally disturbed, learning disabled, mentally retarded, blind, or otherwise handicapped children; women's vulnerability to wife abuse and rape; the limitations of the wife-mother role and the "empty nest" syndrome; the practical and emotional stresses for women of separation or divorce and the difficulties of raising children alone; and the norm that women marry older men, which, in combination with women's longer life expectancy leads to widowhood and the stresses of bereavement, loss of the role of wife, and loneliness.[69]

It is important for social workers to understand that the traditional socialization process and the sex-role stereotypes in our society account for many of the problems that confront female, as well as male, clients. Workers should be skilled in helping clients to actualize themselves and to overcome rigid sex-role stereotypes. As noted earlier, many interaction problems between males and females in our society are consequences of sex-role stereotyping. One therapy approach that is widely used to help both men and women express themselves more effectively and gain skills in countering sex-role stereotypes is assertiveness training (described later in this chapter). Consciousness-raising groups, largely with women, are helping clients to become more aware of sex-role stereotypes, to establish a better self-concept, and to foster contact with others who are also working to end sexism.

The growing awareness of sexism and women's issues has led to the provision of improved services to groups that had been largely ignored: victims of rape, battered wives, women seeking abortions, husbands and wives with marital concerns, people with sexual dysfunctions, single-parent households headed by women, and displaced homemakers.[70]

A men's movement is slowly becoming more prominent in our society. Some men are concerned that women tend to see them as "success objects," as women are substantially more apt than men to believe that a well-paying job is an essential requirement for selecting a spouse.[71] Men are also concerned that when a divorce occurs, many courts routinely assume that the mother will make the better parent. As a result, the mother is usually given custody of the children, with the father having to pay to support them and often given only limited visitation rights in return. The men's movement also asserts that some feminists have a tendency toward "male bashing"; they claim such feminists perpetuate negative stereotypes of men and blame men for problems that are actually created by historical forces beyond the control of any person or group.

Sex-role stereotypes have been costly to society. They have prevented a number of people from assuming more productive roles and have resulted in the expenditure of substantial resources on emotional and physical problems generated by these stereotypes.

AP Photo/Peter Southwick

Women are advancing in areas in which their presence was all but unthinkable just a few years ago. Barbara Harris blesses her congregation after being ordained as the first female bishop in the history of the Episcopal Church.

Men also are taking on new roles and entering new careers. It is becoming increasingly common for men to accept equal responsibility for domestic tasks and for child rearing. In addition, we are now seeing more male nurses, secretaries, child-care workers, nursery school teachers, and flight attendants.[72]

In the past five decades, millions of Americans have begun to change their ideas about the "naturalness" of sex roles. Traditional discriminations are coming to be perceived as an irrational system that threatens women with lifelong inferiority and wasted potential and restricts men to the role of always being competitive, aggressive, and emotionally insensitive.

Our society is slowly moving toward gender equality, but as we have seen earlier in this chapter, substantial gender inequality continues to exist.

Some feminists and social scientists have urged that men and women be socialized to be flexible in their role playing and to express themselves as human beings rather than in traditional feminine or masculine ways.[73] This idea is called "androgyny," from *andro* (male) and *gyne* (female). The notion is to have people explore a broad range of role-playing possibilities and express emotions and behaviors without regard to sex-role stereotypes. People thus are encouraged to pursue tasks and careers at which they are most competent and with which they are most comfortable and to express the attitudes and emotions they really feel. If a male wants to be a cook or an elementary school teacher and a female wants to be a soldier or an athlete—and they're good at it—then it is functional for society if both develop their talents and are allowed to achieve everything they're capable of.

The Feminist Perspective on Therapy

Female social work authors have made substantial contributions to developing the feminist perspective on therapy. This perspective has been explored by a number of writers, including Nan Van Den Bergh and L. Cooper.[74]

Feminism is a social movement aimed at establishing, defining, and defending equal social, economic, and political rights for women. In addition, feminism seeks to establish equal opportunities for women in employment and education. A *feminist* is a person whose beliefs and behavior are based on feminism.

Barker defines "feminist social work" as "the integration of the *values*, skills, and knowledge of social work with a feminist orientation to help individuals and society overcome the emotional and social problems that result from *sex discrimination*."[75] Barker has also defined "feminist therapy":

A psychosocial treatment orientation in which the professional (usually a woman) helps the client (usually a woman) in individual or group settings to overcome the psychological and social problems largely encountered as a result of sex discrimination and sex role stereotyping. Feminist therapists help clients maximize potential, especially through consciousness-raising, eliminating sex stereotyping, and helping them become aware of the commonalities shared by all women.[76]

The following nine principles of feminist intervention have been identified.[77]

1. A client's problems should be viewed within a sociopolitical framework. Feminist intervention is concerned with the inequitable power relationships between women and men and is opposed to all "power-over" relationships, regardless of gender, race, class, age, and so on. Such relationships lead to oppression and domination. Feminism seeks to change all social, economic, and political structures based on relationships between "haves" and "have-nots." Another way of stating this principle is that "personal is political." Van Den Bergh comments:

This principle maintains that what a woman experiences in her personal life is directly related to societal dynamics that affect other women. In other words, an individual woman's experiences of pejorative comments based on sex and of blocked opportunities are directly related to societal sexism. For ethnic minority women, racism and classism also are factors that affect well-being.[78]

   A primary distinguishing characteristic of feminist treatment is helping the client to analyze how her problems are related to systematic difficulties experienced by women in a sexist, classist, and racist society.

2. Traditional sex roles are pathological, and clients need encouragement to free themselves from traditional gender-role bonds. Traditionally, women have been socialized to fill a "learned helplessness" role. Van Den Bergh describes the effects of such sex-role stereotyping:

Sex-role stereotypes suggest that women should be submissive, docile, receptive, and dependent. The message is one of helplessness; that women cannot take care of themselves and are dependent upon others for their well being. This sets up a dynamic in which a woman's locus of control is external to her self, preventing her from believing that she can acquire what she needs on her own in order to develop and self-actualize. In other words, oversubscription to sex-role stereotypes engenders a state of powerlessness in which a woman is likely to become involved in situations where she becomes victimized…. For example, because young girls are socialized to be helpless, when they become women they tend to have a limited repertoire of responses when under stress; e.g., they respond passively.[79]

In feminist treatment, clients are helped to see that, by internalizing traditional sex roles, they have set themselves up to play passive, submissive roles and to experience low self-esteem and self-hatred. The feminist approach encourages clients to make their own choices and to pursue the tasks and goals they desire rather than being constrained by traditional sex roles.

3. Intervention should focus on client empowerment. Van Den Bergh describes the empowerment process:

Helping women to acquire a sense of power, or the ability to affect outcomes in their lives, is a crucial component of feminist practice. Empowerment means acquiring knowledge, skills, and resources that enhance an individual's ability to control her own life and to influence others. Traditionally women have used indirect, covert techniques to get what they want, such as helplessness, dependency, coyness, and demureness.[80]

   Empowerment can be fostered in a variety of ways: (a) by helping the client to define her own needs and clarify her personal goals so that she can then derive a sense of purposefulness; (b) by providing the client with education and access to resources; (c) by helping the client to believe that the ability to change lies within herself—that alterations in her life will result only from her own undertakings; and (d) by focusing on the identification and enhancement of the client's strengths rather than pathologies. Empowered women are ones who have learned to control their environments in order to get what they need.

4. The self-esteem of clients should be enhanced. Self-esteem and self-confidence are essential for

empowerment. The worker should seek to be an encouraging person (as described in Chapter 4), helping clients to identify and recognize their unique qualities and strengths. Many clients with low self-esteem tend to blame themselves for everything that is wrong. For example, a battered woman typically blames herself for being battered. Such clients need to look more realistically at those areas for which they are blaming themselves and feeling guilt so they can distinguish where their responsibility for dysfunctional interactions ends and other individuals' begins.

5. Clients should be encouraged to develop their identity (sense of self) based on their own strengths, attributes, interests, and achievements. It is a serious mistake for women to define themselves in terms of their husbands or boyfriends, their children, their friends, or their relatives. Women need an independent identity that is not based on their relationships with others.

6. Clients need to value other women and to develop social support systems with them. In a society that devalues women, it is all too easy for some females to view other females as insignificant. With social support systems, women can vent their concerns and share their experiences and the solutions they've found to similar problems. They can serve as brokers in identifying resources, and they can provide emotional support and nurturance to one another.

7. Clients need to find an effective balance between work and personal relationships. Feminist intervention encourages both women and men to share in the nurturant aspects of their lives and in providing economic resources.

8. The nature of the relationship between practitioner and client should approach equality as much as possible. Feminist practitioners view themselves not as experts in resolving clients' problems but as catalysts in helping clients empower themselves. Feminist practitioners seek to eliminate dominant–submissive relationships. On this topic, Van Den Bergh notes:

Obviously, there is an innate power differential between practitioner and client because the former has expertise and training as an "authority." However, the feminist admonition is to avoid abusing that status; "abuse" in this sense might be, for example, taking all credit for client change, or using

terminology and nomenclature that are difficult for the client to understand.[81]

9. Clients should be helped to express themselves assertively. (The steps in assertiveness training are described in Case Exhibit 13.7.) As indicated earlier, many women are socialized to be passive and nonassertive. Through individual and group counseling, clients can become more assertive, which will increase their self-confidence and self-esteem. They will be better able to communicate their thoughts, feelings, and opinions. Also, learning to express oneself is an important component in empowerment.

Many women feel anger over being victimized by sex discrimination and gender stereotyping. Some of these women turn their angry feelings inward, which often results in depression. Assertiveness training can help such women recognize that they have a right to be angry; it can also help them identify and practice constructive ways of expressing their anger (that is, assertively rather than aggressively).

Future Directions of the Women's Movement

Coleman and Kerbo note that the women's movement has had considerable success in countering overt discrimination, but it now needs to focus on countering subtle forms of discrimination.

The modern feminist movement has scored some remarkable successes. Women's liberation and sexual equality are now widely discussed, and more and more women are entering occupations that were formerly closed to them. Through effective court and legislative action, feminists have successfully attacked employment and promotion practices that discriminate against women. Government-sponsored programs now encourage employers to hire and promote more women and members of minority groups, and the overall gap between men's and women's pay has declined. Feminists have even made some inroads into the sexual biases built into the English language. Women now often identify themselves as "Ms." rather than "Miss" or "Mrs.," and new sexually neutral words such as chairperson *and* humankind *are replacing the traditional masculine terms. As we have seen in this chapter, however, we are still a long way from full equality. The victories of the*

CASE EXHIBIT 13.7

Assertiveness Training

Do you handle put-downs well? Are you reluctant to express your feelings and opinions openly and honestly in a group? Are you frequently timid when interacting with people in positions of authority? Do you react constructively to criticism? Do you sometimes explode in anger when things go wrong, or are you able to remain calm? Do you find it difficult to maintain eye contact when talking? If you are uncomfortable with someone smoking near you, do you express your feelings? Are you timid in arranging a date or social event? For anyone who has trouble in any of these situations, there is, fortunately, a useful technique—assertiveness training—that enables people to become more effective in interpersonal interactions.

Assertiveness problems range from extreme shyness, introversion, and withdrawal to inappropriate rage that results in alienating others. A nonassertive person is often acquiescent, fearful, and afraid of expressing his or her real, spontaneous feelings in a variety of situations. Frequently, resentment and anxiety build up, resulting in general discomfort, feelings of low self-esteem, tension headaches, fatigue, and perhaps a destructive explosion of temper, anger, and aggression. Some people are overly shy and timid in nearly all interactions. Most of us, however, encounter occasional problems in isolated matters in which it would be to our benefit to be more assertive. For example, a bachelor may be quite effective and assertive in his job as a store manager but still be awkward and timid while attempting to arrange a date.

There are three basic styles of interacting with others: nonassertive, aggressive, and assertive. Characteristics of these styles have been summarized by Robert Alberti and Michael Emmons:

In the nonassertive style, you are likely to hesitate, speak softly, look away, avoid the issue, agree regardless of your own feelings, not express opinions, value yourself "below" others, and hurt yourself to avoid any chance of hurting others.

In the aggressive style, you typically answer before the other person is through talking, speak loudly and abusively, glare at the other person, speak "past" the issue (accusing, blaming, demeaning), vehemently expound your feelings and opinions, value yourself "above" others, and hurt others to avoid hurting yourself.

In the assertive style, you will answer spontaneously, speak with a conversational tone and volume, look at the other person, speak to the issue, openly express your personal feelings and opinions (anger, love, disagreement, sorrow), value yourself equal to others, and hurt neither yourself nor others.[a]

Examples of Behavior

You are driving with an acquaintance to another city to attend a conference. The acquaintance lights up a pipe, and you soon find the smoke irritating and the odor somewhat stifling. What are your choices?

1. Nonassertive response: You attempt to carry on a "cheery" conversation for the 3-hour trip without commenting about the smoke.
2. Aggressive response: You become increasingly irritated, finally exploding, "Either you put out that pipe, or I'll put it out for you—the odor is sickening."
3. Assertive response: You look directly at the acquaintance and in a firm, conversational tone state, "The smoke from your pipe is irritating me. I'd appreciate it if you put it away."

At a party with friends, during small-talk conversation, your husband gives you a subtle put-down by stating, "Wives always talk too much." What do you do?

1. Nonassertive response: You don't say anything but feel hurt and become quiet.
2. Aggressive response: You glare at him and angrily ask, "John, why are you always criticizing me?"
3. Assertive response: You carry on as usual, wait until the drive home, and then calmly look at him and say, "When we were at the party tonight, you said that wives always talk too much. I felt you were putting me down when you said that. What did you mean by that comment?"

Being Assertive

Simply stated, assertive behavior is expressing yourself without hurting or stepping on others. Assertiveness training is designed to help us realize, feel, and act on the assumption that we have the right to be ourselves and to express our feelings freely. Assertive responses generally are not aggressive responses. The distinction between these two types of interactions is important. If, for example, a wife has an overly critical mother-in-law, aggressive responses by the wife would include ridiculing the mother-in-law, intentionally doing things that she knows will upset the mother-in-law (not visiting, serving the type of food the mother-in-law dislikes, not cleaning the house), urging the husband to tell his mother to "shut up," and getting into loud verbal arguments with the mother-in-law. On the other hand, an effective assertive response would be to counter criticism by saying: "Jane, your criticism of me deeply hurts me. I know you're trying to help me when you give advice, but I feel when you do that you're criticizing me. I know you don't want me to make mistakes. But to grow, I need to make my own errors and learn from them. If you want to help me the most, let me do it myself and be responsible for the consequences. The type of relationship that I'd like to have with you is a close, adult relationship and not a mother–child relationship."

The steps for learning to become more assertive are as follows:[b]

1. Examine your interactions. Are there situations that you need to handle more assertively? Do you at times hold

(continued)

opinions and feelings within yourself for fear of what would happen if you expressed them? Do you occasionally lash out angrily at others? Studying your interactions is facilitated by keeping a diary for a week or longer. Record the situations in which you acted timidly, those in which you were aggressive, and those that you handled assertively.

2. Select those interactions in which it would be to your benefit to be more assertive. They may include situations in which you were overpolite or overly apologetic. Or perhaps you were timid and allowed others to take advantage of you, at the same time harboring feelings of resentment, anger, embarrassment, fear of others, or self-criticism for not having the courage to express yourself. Overly aggressive interactions in which you exploded in anger or walked over others also need to be dealt with. For *each* set of nonassertive or aggressive interactions, you can become more assertive, as shown in the next steps.

3. Concentrate on a specific incident in the past in which you were either nonassertive or aggressive. Close your eyes for a few minutes and vividly imagine the details, including what you and the other person said and how you felt at the time and afterward.

4. Write down and review your responses. Ask yourself the following questions to determine how you presented yourself:

   a. Eye contact: Did you look directly at the other person with a relaxed, steady gaze? Looking down or away suggests a lack of self-confidence. Glaring is an aggressive response.

   b. Gestures: Were your gestures appropriate, free flowing, and relaxed? Did they emphasize your messages effectively? Awkward stiffness suggests nervousness; other gestures (such as an angry fist) signal an aggressive reaction.

   c. Body posture: Did you show the importance of your message by directly facing the other person, by leaning toward that person, by holding your head erect, and by sitting or standing appropriately close?

   d. Facial expressions: Did your facial expressions show a stern, firm pose consistent with an assertive response?

   e. Voice tone and volume: Was your response stated in a firm, conversational tone? Shouting may suggest anger. Speaking softly suggests shyness, and a cracking voice suggests nervousness. By tape recording and listening to your voice, you can practice increasing or decreasing the volume.

   f. Speech fluency: Did your speech flow smoothly, clearly, and slowly? Rapid speech or hesitation in speaking suggests nervousness. Tape recording assertive responses that you want to try out for problem situations is a way to improve fluency.

   g. Timing: Were your verbal reactions to a problem situation stated at the most appropriate time for you and the other person to review the incident? Generally, spontaneous expressions are best, but certain situations should be handled at a later time (for example, challenging some of your boss's erroneous statements in private rather than in front of a group she or he is making a presentation to).

   h. Message content: For a problem situation, which of your responses were nonassertive or aggressive, and which were assertive? Study the content and consider why you responded in a nonassertive or aggressive style.

5. Observe one or more effective models. Watch the verbal and nonverbal approaches that are assertively used to handle the type of interactions with which you are having problems. Compare the consequences of their approach and yours. If possible, discuss their approach and their feelings about using it.

6. Make a list of various alternative approaches for being more assertive.

7. Close your eyes and visualize yourself using each of these alternative approaches. For each approach, think through what the full set of interactions would be, along with the consequences. Select an approach, or combination of approaches, that you believe will be most effective for you to use. Through imagery, practice this approach until you feel comfortable that it will work for you.

8. Role-play the approach with someone else, perhaps a friend or counselor. If certain segments of your approach appear clumsy, awkward, timid, or aggressive, practice modifications until you become comfortable with the approach. Obtain feedback from the other person about the strengths and shortcomings of your approach. Compare your interactions to the verbal/nonverbal guidelines for assertive behavior in Step 4. It may be useful for the other person to model through role playing one or more assertive strategies, which you would then, by reversing roles, practice using.

9. Repeat Steps 7 and 8 until you develop an assertive approach that you believe will work best for you and that you are comfortable with.

10. Use your approach in a real-life situation. The previous steps are designed to prepare you for the real event. Expect to be somewhat anxious when first trying to be assertive. If you are still too fearful of attempting to be assertive, repeat Steps 5 through 8. For those few individuals who fail to develop the needed confidence to try out being assertive, professional counseling is advised because expressing yourself effectively in interactions with others is essential for personal happiness.

11. Reflect on the effectiveness of your effort. Did you remain calm? Getting angry at times is a normal human emotion, and it needs to be expressed. However, the anger should be expressed in a constructive, assertive fashion. When expressed in a destructive, lashing-out fashion, it violates the rights of others. Considering the nonverbal/verbal guidelines for assertive behavior discussed in Step 4, what components of your responses were assertive,

(continued)

CASE EXHIBIT 13.7 *(continued)*

aggressive, and nonassertive? What were the consequences of your effort? How did you feel after trying out this new set of interactions? If possible, discuss how you did in regard to these questions with a friend who may have observed the interactions.

12. Expect some success but not complete personal satisfaction with your initial efforts. Experiencing personal growth and interacting more effectively with others will be a continual learning process. Quite appropriately, "pat yourself on the back" for the strengths of your approach—you earned it. But also note the areas in which you need to improve, and use the foregoing steps for improving your assertiveness efforts.

These steps systematically make sense but are not to be followed rigidly. Each person has to develop a process that works best for himself or herself.

The structure of this technique is relatively simple to understand. Considerable skill (common sense and ingenuity), however, is needed to determine what will be an effective assertive strategy when a real-life situation arises. The joy and pride derived from being able to express oneself assertively are truly life enriching.

SOURCE: From "How to Become More Assertive," in The Personal Problem Solver, Charles Zastrow and Dae Chang, eds. Copyright © 1977 by Prentice Hall. Reprinted by permission of Charles Zastrow.

aRobert E. Alberti and Michael L. Emmons, *Stand Up, Speak Out, Talk Back!* (New York: Pocket Books, 1975), p. 24.
bThese self-training steps are a modification of assertiveness training programs developed by Robert E. Alberti and Michael L. Emmons, *Your Perfect Right*, 9th ed. (San Luis Obispo, CA: Impact, 2008), and by Herbert Fensterheim and Jean Baer, *Don t Say Yes When You Want to Say No* (New York: Dell, 1975).

---

past have been won against the most obvious and direct forms of discrimination, and feminists must now face much more subtle forms of bias.[82]

The National Organization for Women (NOW) has been united in its determination to fight efforts to prohibit abortions. The women's movement views access to abortions as a basic right of women to decide what happens to their bodies and to their lives.

Women burdened by unwanted children often become dependent on their partners or on public assistance and find it very difficult to compete with men in the job market.

There is a debate in the women's movement about whether traditional roles held by women should be devalued. Advocates for modern roles emphasize equality and careers, yet some leaders of NOW assert that the role of homemaker should be given equal respect.

Critical Thinking Questions

Everyone is nonassertive in some situations in which it would be more effective to be more assertive. In what situations or interactions do you need to be more assertive? Read the guidelines for becoming more assertive in Case Exhibit 13.7. Are these guidelines potentially helpful to you?

One of the directions that the women's movement is taking is to seek help for single-parent families,

particularly low-income, female-headed families. There has been a feminization of poverty in this country, and an increasing proportion of poor people are women. It is almost impossible for single mothers to be "financially equal" to males in the job market when day care is highly expensive and when women who work full time are paid considerably less than men who work full time. The women's movement is certain to continue to advocate for increased financial support by the federal government for child care.

The women's movement has also been advocating for "comparable worth." Comparable worth involves the concept of "equal pay for comparable work" rather than "equal pay for equal work." Comparable worth asserts that the intrinsic value of different jobs, such as that of a secretary or plumber, can be measured. Those jobs that are evaluated to be of comparable value should receive comparable pay. If implemented, it is believed that the concept will reduce the disparities in pay between women and men who work full time. Jobs held mainly by women pay an average of 20% below equivalent jobs held mainly by men.[83] Some states (such as Wisconsin and Washington) have initiated efforts to develop comparable worth programs for state employees.

Another direction that the women's movement is taking is to encourage and support female candidates for public offices at federal, state, and local levels. The women's movement recognizes that achieving social equality depends partly on moving toward political equality.

Diane Kravetz (a prominent social work educator) urges the following:

> For the benefit of all women, social workers should actively work for changes in social policies, including: (1) passage of ... federal policies that will ensure equal opportunity and pay equity; (2) increasing the availability and affordability of child care, including employer-sponsored child care programs; (3) broadening employment options to include flextime, jobsharing, and parental leave to help families meet both family and work responsibilities; (4) enforcement of child support and alimony payments; and (5) improving women's health care, including working to maintain women's right to abortion, advocating for federal funding of family planning services and abortion, and preventing the further spread of AIDS to women and children.
>
> Most important, social workers need to eliminate sexism within the profession as it impacts on the lives of female clients and workers. Services and programs need to be evaluated to eliminate the presence of sexism as well as racism, class bias, and heterosexism.[84]

The women's movement has made important gains in improving the status of women in our society in the past five decades. It is clear that its general thrust toward equality will continue.

SUMMARY

The following summarizes this chapter's content as it relates to the chapter objectives presented at the beginning of the chapter. Objectives include the following:

A *Present a history of sex roles, sexism, and sexual harassment.*

In almost every known society, women have had lower status than men. Women have traditionally been assigned housework and child-rearing responsibilities and have been socialized to be passive, submissive, and feminine. The socialization process and sex-role stereotyping have led to a number of problems. There is sex discrimination in employment, with men who work full time being paid substantially more than women who work full time. There are double standards of conduct for males and females. There are power struggles between males and females because men are socialized to be dominant in interactions with women, whereas women often seek egalitarian relationships. Sex-role stereotyping and the traditional female role have led women to be unhappier in marriages and to be more depressed than men.

B *Describe traditional sex-role expectations.*

American women traditionally are expected to be affectionate, passive, conforming, sensitive, intuitive, and dependent—"sugar and spice and everything nice." They are supposed to be concerned primarily with domestic life, to be nurturing, to love to care for babies and young children, to fuss over their personal appearance, and to be self-sacrificing for their families. They should not appear ambitious, aggressive, competitive, or more intelligent than men. They should be ignorant about and uninterested in sports, economics, and politics. Also, they are not supposed to initiate relationships with men but are expected to be tender, feminine, emotional, and appreciative when in these relationships.

There are also a number of traditional sex-role expectations for males in our society: A male is expected to be tough, fearless, logical, self-reliant, independent, and aggressive. He should have definite opinions on the major issues of the day and make authoritative decisions at work and at home. He is expected to be strong—a sturdy oak—and never to be depressed, vulnerable, or anxious. He is not supposed to be a "sissy"—to cry or openly display emotions that suggest vulnerability. He is expected to be the provider, the breadwinner. He should be competent in all situations, physically strong, athletic, confident, daring, brave, and forceful. He should be in a position to dominate any situation.

He is supposed to initiate relationships with women and be dominant in these relationships.

C *Examine whether there is a biological basis for sexism.*

Sex-role expectations are determined primarily by cultural learning experiences.

D *Describe traditional sex-role socialization practices.*

Sex-role stereotyping is pervasive in our society, with aspects being found in child-rearing practices, the educational system, religion, contemporary psychological theories, our language, the mass media, the business world, marriage and family patterns, and our political system.

E *Examine the consequences of sexism for males and females.*

Women are victimized in a variety of areas: occupation and income, domestic responsibilities, human interactions, and maternal wall. Men are also victimized. For example, men frequently feel they must put their careers first and thereby sharply limit the interactions and satisfactions received in being husbands and fathers.

Men in this country are disadvantaged before the law in several areas. In some jurisdictions, husbands are legally required to provide financial support for their families, and failure to do so is grounds for divorce by the wife. If a marriage breaks up, courts usually grant custody of the children to the wife. In child custody battles, the father bears a heavier burden of proof that he is a fit parent than does the mother, and only in cases in which the mother is demonstrably negligent is the father's claim seriously considered. Alimony is much more frequently awarded to wives, even when both spouses can support themselves.

F *Describe the sex-role revolution in our society.*

The women's movement, which had a resurgence in the 1960s, is working to eliminate sex-role stereotypes and is revolutionizing the socialization process. A number of laws forbidding sex discrimination have been enacted. Women as well as men are now pursuing new careers and are taking on roles and tasks that run counter to traditional sex stereotypes. The androgyny notion is gaining strength. Androgynous people explore a broad range of role-playing possibilities and express emotions and behaviors without regard to sex-role stereotypes.

Interestingly, the women's movement also has had many payoffs for males. Men experience extreme difficulties and encounter many problems in trying to fulfill the stereotypes of the model-man role—to always be dominant and strong, to never be depressed or anxious, to hide emotions, to be the provider, to be self-reliant and aggressive, and to never cry. Men are gradually realizing that this stereotypical role limits their opportunities in terms of interpersonal relationships, occupations, emotional expression, and domestic activities. Sex-role stereotyping has huge costs for women, for men, and for society.

G *Present strategies for achieving sexual equality.*

True sexual equality means that people would be free to be themselves. To achieve sexual equality, actions must be taken in many areas. These strategies are summarized in this chapter.

H *Summarize social work's commitment to combating sexism.*

The social work profession has made commitments to eliminate sexism, both within its own ranks and in the broader society. Although over two-thirds of practicing social workers are female, more males are concentrated in administrative and other leadership positions in social work. Most social work clients are women. Social workers need to become skilled in helping clients to actualize themselves and to stop being negatively influenced by sex-role stereotypes.

Competency Notes

EP 2.1.3a Distinguish, appraise, and integrate multiple sources of knowledge, including research-based knowledge and practice wisdom.

EP 2.1.4a, b, c, d The competency "Engage diversity and difference in practice," and the four practice behaviors associated with this competency.

EP 2.1.5a, b, c The competency "Advance human rights and social and economic justice," and the three practice behaviors associated with this competency. (All of this chapter) This chapter presents a history of sex roles, sexism, and sexual harassment. It describes traditional sex-role expectations, and examines whether there is a biological basis for sexism. It describes traditional sex-role socialization practices, and examines the consequences of sexism on males and females. It describes the sex-role revolution in our society, and presents strategies for achieving sexual equality. It ends by summarizing social work's commitment to combating sexism.

EP 2.1.10a Substantively and affectively prepare for action with individuals, families, groups, organizations, and communities. (pp. 441-449) Introductory material is presented on social work practice to reduce sexism in our society. Material is presented on strategies for achieving sexual equality, feminist social work practice, and assertiveness training.

Media Resources

Additional resources for this chapter, including a chapter quiz, can be found on the Social Work Course Mate. Go to CengageBrain.com.

Notes

1. William Kornblum and Joseph Julian, *Social Problems*, 14th ed. (Boston: Pearson, 2012), p. 273.
2. Ibid., p. 259.
3. Ibid., p. 199.
4. Jean Stockard and Miriam M. Johnson, *Sex Roles* (Englewood Cliffs, NJ: Prentice Hall, 1980), pp. 19–42.
5. Kornblum and Julian, *Social Problems*, pp. 279–280.
6. Thomas Sullivan, Kenrick Thompson, Richard Wright, George Gross, and Dale Spady, *Social Problems: Divergent Perspectives* (New York: Wiley, 1980), p. 452.
7. Francine D. Blair, "Women in the Labor Force: An Overview," in *Women: A Feminist Perspective*, Jo Freeman, ed. (Palo Alto, CA: Mayfield, 1979), p. 272.
8. H. L. Rheingold and K. V. Cook, "The Contents of Boys' and Girls' Rooms as an Index of Parents' Behavior," *Child Development*, *46* (June 1975), p. 461.
9. Eleanor Maccoby and Carol Jacklin, *The Psychology of Sex Differences* (Stanford, CA: Stanford University Press, 1974).
10. Ibid.
11. Betty Friedan, *The Feminine Mystique* (New York: Dell, 1963).
12. Paul R. Horton, Gerald R. Leslie, and Richard F. Larson, *The Sociology of Social Problems*, 9th ed. (Englewood Cliffs, NJ: Prentice Hall, 1988), p. 252.
13. Sullivan et al., *Social Problems: Divergent Perspectives*, pp. 475–476.
14. Kornblum and Julian, *Social Problems*, pp. 280–281.
15. Linda A. Mooney, David Knox, and Caroline Schacht, *Understanding Social Problems*, 8th ed. (Belmont, CA: Wadsworth Cengage Learning, 2013), p. 338.
16. Equal Employment Opportunity Commission, *Sexual Harassment*, http://eeoc.gov/stats/harass.html.
17. Horton, Leslie, and Larson, *The Sociology of Social Problems*, p. 261.
18. Mooney, Knox, and Schacht, *Understanding Social Problems*, p. 338.
19. Amy Saltzman, "Hands Off at the Office," *U.S. News & World Report*, Aug. 1, 1988, pp. 56–58.
20. Mooney, Knox, and Schacht, *Understanding Social Problems*, p. 338.
21. Deborah S. David and Robert Brannon, eds., *The Forty-Nine Percent Majority: The Male Sex Role* (Reading, MA: Addison-Wesley, 1976).
22. Stockard and Johnson, *Sex Roles*, pp. 133–147.
23. Richard C. Friedman, Ralph M. Richart, and Raymond L. Vande Wiehe, eds., *Sex Differences in Behavior* (New York: Wiley, 1974).
24. See Shirly Weitz, *Sex Roles: Biological, Psychological, and Social Foundations* (New York: Oxford University Press, 1977); Betty Yorburg, *Sexual Identity: Sex Roles and Social Change* (New York: Wiley, 1974); Michael Teitelbaum, ed., *Sex Roles: Social and Biological Perspectives* (New York: Doubleday/Anchor, 1976).
25. Ibid.
26. Maccoby and Jacklin, *The Psychology of Sex Differences.*
27. Ibid.
28. Allan Katcher, "The Discrimination of Sex Differences by Young Children," *Journal of Genetic Psychology*, 87 (Sept. 1955), pp. 131–143.
29. Lawrence Kohlberg, "A Cognitive-Developmental Analysis of Children's Sex-Role Concepts and Attitudes," in *The Psychology of Sex Differences*, Maccoby and Jacklin, eds., pp. 82–173.
30. Ruth E. Hartley, "American Core Culture: Changes and Continuities," in *Sex Roles in Changing Society*, Georgene H. Seward and Robert C. Williamson, eds. (New York: Random House, 1970), pp. 140–141.
31. Ibid., p. 141.
32. Sullivan et al., *Social Problems*, pp. 460–465.
33. Charles H. Cooley, *Social Organization* (New York: Scribner's, 1909).
34. Matina Horner, "Fail: Bright Women," *Psychology Today*, Nov. 1969, pp. 36–38; Vivian Gornick, "Why Women Fear Success," *Ms.*, Spring 1972, pp. 50–53.
35. Janet S. Hyde, *Understanding Human Sexuality*, 5th ed. (New York: McGraw-Hill, 1994), pp. 385–394.
36. Kornblum and Julian, *Social Problems*, pp. 276–278.
37. American Association of University Women, *How Schools Shortchange Women: The A.A.U.W. Report* (Washington, DC: A.A.U.W. Educational Foundation, 1992).
38. James W. Coleman and Harold R. Kerbo, *Social Problems*, 10th ed. (Upper Saddle River, NJ: Vango, 2008), p. 250.
39. Ibid.

40. Myra Sadker, David Sadker, and Susan S. Klein, "Abolishing Misconceptions about Sex Equity in Education," *Theory into Practice*, 25 (Autumn 1986), p. 220.
41. Kornblum and Julian, *Social Problems*, pp. 276–278.
42. Janet S. Chafetz, *Masculine, Feminine or Human? An Overview of the Sociology of Sex Roles* (Itasca, IL: F. E. Peacock, 1974).
43. Kornblum and Julian, *Social Problems*, pp. 278–279.
44. Sigmund Freud, *A General Introduction to Psychoanalysis* (New York: Boni & Liveright, 1924).
45. Kornblum and Julian, *Social Problems*, pp. 270–272.
46. Ibid., pp. 270–272.
47. Mooney, Knox, and Schacht, *Understanding Social Problems*, p. 321.
48. James W. Coleman and Harold R. Kerbo, *Social Problems*, 10th ed. (Upper Saddle River, NJ: Vango, 2008), pp. 255–256.
49. Ann M. Morrison, "Up against a Glass Ceiling," *Los Angeles Times*, Aug. 23, 1987, sec. 1, p. 3.
50. Kornblum and Julian, *Social Problems*, pp. 271–273.
51. Ibid.
52. Ibid.
53. Ibid., pp. 271–273.
54. Horton, Leslie, and Larson, *The Sociology of Social Problems*, p. 258.
55. Ibid.
56. Kornblum and Julian, *Social Problems*, p. 278.
57. Ibid.
58. Ibid.
59. Matina S. Horner, "Femininity and Successful Achievement: A Basic Inconsistency," in *Feminine Personality and Conflict*, Judith M. Bardwich, ed. (Pacific Grove, CA: Brooks/Cole, 1970).
60. David and Brannon, *The Forty-Nine Percent Majority*, pp. 53–54.
61. Hartley, "American Core Culture," p. 142.
62. Kornblum and Julian, *Social Problems*.
63. John O'Neill, "Network Reports Membership Data," *NASW News*, Jan. 2001, pp. 1, 8.
64. M. Gibelman and P. H. Schervish, "The Glass Ceiling in Social Work: Is It Shatterproof?" *AFFILIA*, 8, no. 4 (1993), p. 443.

65. O'Neill, "Network Reports Membership Data," p. 8.
66. Ibid.
67. Diane Kravetz, "Social Work Practice with Women," in *Social Work: A Profession of Many Faces*, 9th ed., Armando Morales and Bradford W. Sheafor, eds. (Needham Heights, MA: Allyn & Bacon, 2001), pp. 241–265.
68. Julia B. Rauch, "Gender as a Factor in Practice," in *Social Work: A Profession of Many Faces*, 5th. ed., Armando Morales and Bradford W. Sheafor, eds. (Boston: Allyn & Bacon, 1989), p. 342.
69. Ibid., pp. 343–344.
70. Kravetz, "Social Work Practice with Women," pp. 241–265.
71. Mooney, Knox, and Schacht, *Understanding Social Problems*, pp. 335–338.
72. Ibid., pp. 335–338.
73. Ibid., pp. 335–338.
74. Nan Van Den Bergh and L. B. Cooper, "Feminist Social Work," in *The Encyclopedia of Social Work* (Washington, DC: NASW, 1987), pp. 610–618.
75. Robert L. Barker, *Social Work Dictionary*, 5th ed. (Washington, DC: NASW Press, 2003), p. 161.
76. Ibid.
77. Van Den Bergh and Cooper, "Feminist Social Work," pp. 610–618; Nan Van Den Bergh, "Feminist Treatment for People with Depression," in *Structuring Change*, K. Corcoran, ed. (Chicago: Lyceum, 1992), pp. 95–110; K. K. Kirst-Ashman and G. H. Hull, Jr., *Understanding Generalist Practice* (Chicago: Nelson-Hall, 1993), pp. 422–463.
78. Van Den Bergh, "Feminist Treatment for People with Depression," p. 103.
79. Ibid., p. 101.
80. Ibid., p. 104.
81. Ibid.
82. Coleman and Kerbo, *Social Problems*, p. 260.
83. Kornblum and Julian, *Social Problems*, p. 259.
84. Kravetz, "Social Work Practice with Women," p. 260.

CHAPTER **14**

Aging and Gerontological Services

453

The plight of older adults, so long overlooked, has now become recognized as a major social problem in the United States. Older adults face a number of social and personal problems: high rates of physical illness and emotional difficulties, poverty, malnutrition, lack of access to transportation, low status, lack of a meaningful role in our society, and inadequate housing. To a large extent, older adults are a "recently discovered" minority group. Like other minority groups, they are victims of job discrimination, are excluded from the mainstream of American life on the basis of supposed group characteristics, and are subjected to prejudice that is based on erroneous stereotypes. This chapter will:

Learning Objectives

EP 2.1.3a

A   Describe the specific problems faced by older adults.

B   Discuss current services to meet these problems. Also, note gaps in current services.

C   Describe the role of social work in providing services to older adults.

D   Discuss social and political changes needed to improve the status of older adults.

An Overview

Throughout time some tribal societies have abandoned their enfeebled old. The Crow, Creek, and Hopi Indians, for example, built special huts away from the tribe where the old were left to die. The Eskimo left their incapacitated elderly in snowbanks or forced them to paddle away in a kayak. The Siriono of the Bolivian forest simply left them behind when they moved on in search of food.[1] Even today the Ik of Uganda leave older people and disabled people to starve to death.[2] (Generally, the primary reason tribal societies have been forced to abandon older people is scarce resources.)

Although we might consider these customs shocking and barbaric, have we not also abandoned older adults? We encourage them to retire when many are still productive. All too often, when a person retires, his or her status, power, and self-esteem are lost. Also, in a physical sense, we seldom have a place for large numbers of older people. Community facilities—parks, subways, libraries—are oriented to serving children and young people. Most housing is designed and priced for the young couple with one or two children and an annual income in excess of $50,000. If older adults are not able to care for

themselves (and if their families are unable to care for them), we "store" them away from society in nursing homes. Moreover, we do little to relieve the financial problems of older adults; 1 out of 10 is poor.[3] About 1 out of 4 African Americans and 1 out of 5 Hispanic Americans aged 65 and over live below the poverty line.[4] (In a sense, our abandonment of older adults is more unethical than that of tribal societies who are motivated by survival pressures; we don't have such serious survival problems.)

A "Recently Discovered" Minority Group

Our society's treatment of older adults has only recently come to be viewed as a major social problem. In effect, older adults are a recently discovered minority group. Like other minority groups, they are subjected to job discrimination. The most striking example of age discrimination was the practice of mandatory retirement, whereby people were forced to leave their jobs once they reach a certain age.

The legal retirement age used to be 65. In 1978 Congress enacted legislation that raised the age to

CASE EXAMPLE 14.1

The Best Years of Your Life—Retirement

Tom Townsend had been with the ironworks plant for 42 years. Being promoted to supervisor 16 years ago had fulfilled his dreams, and there was nothing he wanted more than to be on the job and managing his crew. He has been married to Laura for the past 37 years. At first their marriage had some rough moments, but Laura and Tom grew accustomed to and comfortable with each other over the years. They have a traditional view of the role of women in society. Her main job has always been to maintain the home. They have two grown children who have moved away and now have homes of their own.

Life was at the factory for Tom. He didn't have time to develop other hobbies and interests, nor was he interested in picnics or socials. When he had time off from work, he used it to repair things around the house and to "tool up" for getting back to work. Television replaced talk in his home, and Tom usually spent weekends watching a variety of sports programs.

On May 18, Tom turned 70. The company marked the occasion with a retirement dinner that was well attended. Tom and Laura were there, along with their children and families, the members of Tom's crew and their wives, and the company managers and their wives. At first everyone was a little anxious because these people did not often get together with one another socially. The dinner, however, went fairly well. Tom was congratulated by everyone, received a gold watch, and made appropriate remarks about his years with the company. After a

few more cocktails, everyone went home. Tom was feeling sentimental, but also quite good about himself because everyone was acknowledging his contributions.

Tom awoke at 7 o'clock the next morning—the usual time for him to get ready for work. Then it hit him. He was retired, with nowhere to go and no reason to get up. His life at the plant was over. What should he do now? He didn't know.

He spent the next week following Laura around the house, getting on her nerves. At times he complained about feeling useless. Twice he commented that he wished he were dead. He went back to the plant to see his men, but they were too busy to talk. Besides, Bill, who had been promoted to supervisor, delighted in showing Tom how the department's productivity had increased and bored Tom with his plans for making changes to increase production further.

Long walks didn't help much, either. As he walked, he thought about his plight and became more depressed. What was he going to do? What could he find to occupy his time meaningfully? He looked into a mirror and saw his receding hairline and numerous wrinkles. More and more, he started to feel a variety of aches and pains. He thought to himself, "I guess I'm just a useless old man." He wondered what the future would hold. Would his company pension keep pace with increasing bills? Would he eventually be placed in a nursing home? What was he going to do with the remainder of his life? He just didn't know.

---

70 for most jobs. Then, in 1986, Congress (recognizing that mandatory retirement was overtly discriminatory against older adults) outlawed most mandatory retirement policies.

Older people are discriminated against in many ways. Older workers are erroneously believed to be less productive. Unemployed workers in their 50s and 60s have greater difficulty finding new jobs and remain unemployed much longer than younger unemployed workers. Older people are given no meaningful role in our society.

Ours is a youth-oriented society that devalues old people. We glorify the body beautiful and physical attractiveness and thereby shortchange older adults. Older persons are viewed as "out of touch with what's happening," and therefore their knowledge is seldom valued or sought. It is also erroneously believed that intellectual ability declines with age. Research shows, however, that intellectual capacity, barring organic problems, remains essentially unchanged until very late in life.[5]

Older adults are misperceived as senile, conservative, resistant to change, inflexible, incompetent, and burdensome to the young. Given opportunities, older adults usually prove such prejudicial concepts wrong.

Older adults generally react to prejudice against them in the same way as racial and ethnic minorities react—by displaying self-hatred and by being self-conscious, sensitive, and defensive about their social and cultural status.[6] (Cooley's concept of the looking-glass self suggests that if individuals frequently receive negative responses from others, they will eventually come to view themselves negatively.)

A New View of Aging

It is a mistake to view later adulthood as a time of inevitable physical and mental decline. Stereotyping later adulthood as an "awful" life stage is erroneous, and sadly is a factor in elders being treated as second-class citizens by some people who are younger.

On the whole, people today are living longer and faring better than at any time in history. In Japan, old age is a mark of status. For example, travelers to Japan are often asked their age when checking into hotels—to ensure that they receive proper deference if they are older adults.[7]

In the United States, older adults as a group are healthier, more numerous, and younger at heart than ever before. Many 70-year-olds think, act, and feel as 50-year-olds did two decades ago. On television older adults are less often portrayed as cranky and helpless, and now more often as respected and wise.

Definitions of Later Adulthood

Kornblum and Julian describe some of our myths and stereotypes about older adults:

> *Popular culture characterizes old people as senile, lacking in individuality, tranquil, unproductive, conservative, and resistant to change. These beliefs persist despite abundant evidence to the contrary.*[8]

On the other hand, the mass media portray some retired people as always traveling and playing golf, sunning themselves in warm climates in the winter, and being in good health and free of money worries. For the "young aging," particularly those in upper-income groups, there is some validity to this stereotype. But it is not the experience of most of the older adults in our society.

The social and physical needs of older adults have only recently been recognized. In earlier societies, few people survived to advanced ages. Life expectancy has increased dramatically in the United States since the turn of the 20th century—up from 49 years in 1900 to 78 years at present.[9] Also, in most other societies, in contrast to ours, older adults had some meaningful role to perform—as arbitrators and advisers, as landowners and leaders, as repositories of the wisdom of the tribe, as performers of tasks within their capabilities.

Chronological age is very important to us. Our passage through life is partially governed by our age. Chronological age dictates when we are deemed old enough to go to school, drive a car, marry, or vote. Our society has also generally selected 65 as the beginning of old age.

Members of nonliterate tribes often do not know how old they are. Old age is determined by physical and mental conditions, not by chronological age.

And their definitions of old age are more accurate than ours. Everyone is not in the same mental and physical condition at age 65. Aging is an individual process that occurs at different rates in different people, and social–psychological factors may retard or accelerate the physiological changes.

The process of aging is called *senescence*. Senescence affects different people at different rates. In addition, the rates of change in various body processes affected by aging vary among people. Visible signs of aging include the appearance of wrinkled skin, graying and thinning of hair, and stooped or shortened posture from compressed spinal disks.

As a person ages, blood vessels, tendons, the skin, and connective tissues lose their elasticity. Hardening of blood vessels and stiffening of joints occur. Bones become brittle and thin; hormonal activity and reflexes slow down. Many of the health problems faced by older adults result from a general decline of the circulatory system. Reduced blood supply impairs mental sharpness, interferes with balance, and reduces the effectiveness of the muscles and body organs. The probability of strokes and heart attacks also increases.

As a person ages, the muscles lose some of their strength, and coordination and endurance become more difficult. There is also a decline in the functioning of organs such as the lungs, the kidneys, and to a lesser extent, the brain. As senescence proceeds, hearing and vision capacities decline, food may not taste the same, the sense of touch may become less acute, and there may be a loss of memory of recent and past events. Fortunately, the degree to which one's body loses its vitality can be influenced by one's lifestyle. People who are mentally and physically active throughout their younger years remain more alert and vigorous in their later years.

A key fact to remember about senescence is that no dramatic decline need take place at one's 65th birthday—or at any other age. We are all slowly aging throughout our lives. The rate at which we age depends on many factors. Most older people are physically active and mentally alert. Unfortunately, in reading about the process of aging, you may get the impression that both the physical functioning and the mental functioning of the older person are reduced to a minimal level. This is seldom the case. Although functioning may slow somewhat, it remains at a high enough level to enable most older people to be physically active and mentally alert.

CASE EXHIBIT 14.1

Age Need Not Be a Barrier to Making Major Contributions

- At 77 Ronald Reagan was president of the United States.
- At 80 George Burns received his first Academy Award for his role in *The Sunshine Boys*.
- At 81 Benjamin Franklin mediated the compromise that led to the adoption of the U.S. Constitution.
- At 82 Winston Churchill finished his four-volume text *A History of the English-Speaking Peoples*.
- At 88 Konrad Adenauer was chancellor of Germany.
- At 88 Michelangelo designed the Church of Santa Maria degli Angeli.

- At 89 Arthur Rubinstein gave a critically acclaimed recital at Carnegie Hall in New York City.
- At 89 Albert Schweitzer was directing a hospital in Africa.
- At 90 Pablo Picasso was producing engravings and drawings.
- At 91 Eamon de Valera was president of Ireland.
- At 93 George Bernard Shaw wrote a play titled *Farfetched Fables*.
- At 100 Grandma Moses was still painting.

SOURCE: *U.S. News & World Report*, Sept. 1, 1980, pp. 52–53.

There is growing evidence that many of the effects of aging are neither irreversible nor inevitable. Rather, several of the supposed effects of aging are due largely to the inactivity that is often associated with aging. Learning to reduce stress, along with exercising and maintaining a healthful diet, can reverse, or at least hold in abeyance, many of the effects thought to be caused by aging. In one study, a group of 70-year-old inactive men participated in a daily exercise program, and at the end of a year, they had regained the physical fitness levels of 40-year-olds.[10]

In defining "old age," the federal government generally uses a chronological cutoff point—age 65—to separate older adults from others. There is nothing magical or particularly scientific about 65. In 1883 the Germans set age 65 as the criterion of aging for the world's first modern social security system for the elderly.[11] When the Social Security Act was passed in 1935, the United States also selected 65 as the eligibility age for retirement benefits based on the German model.

Older adults are an extremely diverse group, spanning a 35- to 40-year age range. This large range, by itself, leads to considerable diversity. Just as there are substantial differences between 20-year-olds and 50-year-olds, there are generally vast differences between those age 65 and those age 100.

An Increasing Older Adult Population

There are now more than 10 times as many people age 65 and older as there were at the turn of the 20th century (see Table 14.1). There are several reasons for the phenomenal growth of the older population. The improved care of expectant mothers and newborn infants has reduced the infant mortality rate, and vaccinations have prevented many life-threatening childhood illnesses, allowing an increased proportion of those born to live to adulthood. New drugs, better sanitation, and other medical advances have increased the life expectancy of Americans.

Another reason for the increasing proportion of older adults is that the birthrate is declining—fewer babies are being born, while more adults are reaching later adulthood. After World War II, a baby boom lasted from 1947 to 1960. Children born during these years flooded schools in the 1950s and 1960s. Then they moved into the labor market. After

Table 14.1 Number and Percentage of U.S. Population Age 65 and Older, 1900 to 2010 (projected)

	YEAR						
	1900	1950	1970	1980	1990	2000	2010
Number of older people (in millions)	3	12	20	25	31	35	39
Percentage of total population	4	8	9.5	11	12	13	14

SOURCE: **United States Bureau of the Census,** *Statistical Abstract of the United States, 2012* **(Washington, DC: U.S. Government Printing Office, 2011).**

1960, there was a baby bust, a sharp decline in birth-rates. The average number of children per woman went down from a high of 3.8 in 1957 to the current rate of about 2.0.[12]

The increased life expectancy along with the baby boom followed by the baby bust will significantly increase the median age of Americans in future years. The median age is increasing dramatically. The long-term implications are that the United States will undergo a number of cultural, social, and economic changes.

The "Old-Old"—The Fastest-Growing Age Group

As medical science makes strides in treating and preventing heart disease, cancer, strokes, and other killers, an increasing percentage of older adults are living into their 80s, 90s, and beyond. People age 85 and over constitute, proportionately, the fastest-growing age group in the United States.[13]

We are witnessing "the graying of America," also called "the aging of the aged." This population revolution is occurring rather quietly in our society. Older people are living longer due in part to better medical care, sanitation, and nutrition. People age 85 and older, who currently comprise 13% of the total older population, are the most rapidly growing segment of the U.S. population. Those over age 85 will increase by more than 500% by 2050, due largely to the aging of the 69 million baby boomers.[14] (From 1946 to 1964 there were an exceptionally large number of babies born in the United States.) Since 1965 the birth rates in the United States have declined substantially.

Many of the old-old suffer from a multiplicity of chronic illnesses. Common medical problems include arthritis, heart conditions, hypertension, osteoporosis (brittle bones), Alzheimer's disease, incontinence, hearing and vision problems, and depression.

The older an older adult becomes, the higher the probability that she or he will become a resident of a nursing home. Although only about 5% of older adults are currently in a nursing home, nearly one of five of those age 85 and over is living in a nursing home.[15] The cost to society for this care is high—more than $70,000 a year per person.[16]

Despite the widespread image of families dumping aged parents into nursing homes, most frail older people still live outside institutional walls with a spouse, a child, or a relative as the chief caregiver. Some middle-age people are now encountering simultaneous demands to put children through col-lege and to support an aging parent in a nursing home. (The term *sandwich generation* has recently been coined to refer to middle-age parents who are caught in the middle of trying to meet the needs of both their aging parents and their children.)

With people retiring at age 65 or 70 and then living to age 85 or 90, the number of years spent in retirement can be considerable. To maintain the same standard of living after retiring requires immense assets.

Rising health-care costs and super longevity have ignited controversy over whether to ration health care to the very old. For example, should people over age 75 be prohibited from receiving liver transplants or kidney dialysis? Discussion of euthanasia (the practice of killing individuals who are hopelessly sick or injured) has also been stirring increased debate. In 1984 Governor Richard Lamm of Colorado made the controversial statement that the terminally ill have a duty to die. Dr. Eisdor Fer stated:

> The problem is age-old and across cultures. Whenever society has had marginal economic resources, the oldest went first, and the old people bought that approach. The old Eskimo wasn't put on the ice floe; he just left of his own accord and never came back.[17]

Problems Faced by Older Adults

We have a personal stake in improving the status and life circumstances of older adults. They are what we are becoming. If we do not face and solve the problems of older adults *now*, we will be in dire straits in the future. Let's examine some of these problems.

Low Status

We have generally been unsuccessful in finding anything important or satisfying for older adults to do. In most nonliterate societies, older adults were respected and viewed as useful to their people to a much greater degree than is the case in our society. Industrialization and the growth of modern society have robbed the elderly of high status. Prior to industrialization, older people were the primary owners of property. Land was the most important source of power; therefore, older adults controlled much of the economic and political power. Now people earn their living primarily in the job market. The vast majority of older adults own little land and are viewed as providing no salable labor.

Later Adulthood Is the Age of Recompense

The following case example illustrates that how we live in our younger years largely determines how we will live in our later years.

Allen was a muscular, outgoing teenager. He was physically bigger than most of his classmates and starred in basketball, baseball, and football in high school. In football he was chosen all-state line-backer in his senior year. At age 16 he began drinking at least a six-pack of beer each day, and at 17 he began smoking. Because he was an athlete, he had to smoke and drink on the sly. But Allen was good at conning others, and he found it fairly easy to smoke, drink, party, and still play sports. That left little time for studying, but Allen was not interested in that anyway. He had other priori-ties. He received a football scholarship and went on to college. He did well in football and majored in partying. His grades suffered, and, when his college eligibility for football was used up, he dropped out. Shortly thereafter he married Rachel Rudow, a college sophomore. She soon became pregnant and dropped out of college.

Allen was devastated after leaving college. He had been a jock for ten years, the envy of his classmates. Now he couldn't find a job with status. After a variety of odd jobs, he signed on as a road construction worker. He liked working outdoors and also liked the macho-type guys he worked, smoked, drank, and partied with.

He had three children with Rachel, but he was not a good husband. He was seldom home, and, when he was, he was often drunk. After a stormy seven years of marriage (including numerous incidents of physical and verbal abuse), Rachel moved out and got a divorce. She and the children moved to Florida with her parents so that Allen could not continue to harass her and the children. Allen's drinking and smoking increased. He was smoking over two packs a day, and he sometimes drank a quart of whiskey also.

A few years later he fathered an out-of-wedlock child for whom he was required to pay child support. At age 39 he mar-ried Jane, who was only 20. They had two children together and stayed married for six years. Jane eventually left him, because she became fed up with being belted around when Allen was drunk. Allen now had a total of six children to help support, and he seldom saw any of them. He continued to drink and also ate to excess. His weight went up to 285 pounds, and by age 48 he was no longer able to keep up with the other road construction work-ers. He was discharged by the company.

The next several years saw Allen taking odd jobs as a carpen-ter. He didn't earn much, and he spent most of what he earned on alcohol. He was periodically embarrassed by being hauled into court for failure to pay child support. He also was dismayed be-cause he no longer had friends who wanted to get drunk with him. When he was 61, the doctor discovered that he had cirrhosis of the liver and informed Allen that he wouldn't live much longer if he continued to drink. Since Allen's whole life centered around drinking, he chose to continue. Allen also noticed that he had less energy and frequently had trouble breathing. The doctor indicated that he probably had damaged his lungs by smoking and now had a form of emphysema. The doctor lectured Allen on the need to stop smoking, but Allen didn't heed that advice either. His health continued to deteriorate, and he lost 57 pounds. At age 64, while drunk, he fell over backward and fractured his

skull. He was hospitalized for three and a half months. The injury permanently damaged his ability to walk and talk. He now is confined to a low-quality nursing home. He is no longer allowed to smoke or drink. He is frequently angry, impatient, and frustrated. He has no friends. The staff detests working with him; his grooming habits are atrocious, and he frequently yells obscen-ities. Allen frequently expresses a wish to die to escape his misery.

David, Allen's brother, has lived a vastly different life. David had a lean, almost puny muscular structure and did not excel at sports. Allen was his parents' favorite and had dazzled the young females in school and in the neighborhood. David had practically no dates in high school and was viewed as a prude. He did well in math and in the natural sciences. He spent much of his time studying and reading. He also liked taking radios and electrical appliances apart. At first he got into trouble because he was not skilled enough to put them back together. However, he soon be-came known in the neighborhood as someone who could fix ra-dios and electrical appliances.

David went on to college and studied electrical engineering. He had no social life but graduated with good grades in his ma-jor. He went to graduate school and earned a master's degree in electrical engineering. On graduation, he was hired as an engi-neer by Motorola in Chicago. He did well there and in four years was named manager of a unit. Three years later he was lured to RCA with an attractive salary offer. The group of engineers he worked with at RCA made some significant advances in televi-sion technology.

At RCA David began dating a secretary, Jenny McCann, and they were married when he was 36. Life became much smoother for David after that. He was paid well and enjoyed annual vacations with Jenny to such places as Hawaii, Paris, and the Bahamas. David and Jenny wanted to have children but could not. In David's early forties they adopted two children, both from Korea. They bought a house in the suburbs and also a sailboat. David and Jenny occasionally had some marital dis-agreements, but generally they got along well. In their middle adult years, one of their adopted sons, Kim, was tragically killed by a drunk driver. That death was a shock and very difficult for the whole family to come to terms with. But the intense grieving gradually lessened, and after a few years David and Jenny put their lives back together.

Now, at age 67, David is still working for RCA and loving it. In a few years he plans to retire and move to the Hawaiian is-land of Maui. David and Jenny have already purchased a condo-minium there. Their surviving son, Dae, has graduated from college and is working for a life insurance company. David is looking forward to retiring so he can move to Maui and get more involved in his hobbies of photography and model railroads. His health is good, and he has a positive outlook on life. He occasionally thinks about his brother and sends him a card at Christmas and on his birthday. But, since David never had much in common with Allen, he seldom visits him.

SOURCE: From Zastrow/Kirst-Ashman, Understanding Human Behavior and the Social Environment, 5E. © 2001 Cengage Learning.

In earlier societies, older adults were also valued because of the knowledge they possessed. Their experiences enabled them to supervise planting and harvesting and to pass on knowledge about hunting, housing, and craft making. They also played key roles in preserving and transmitting the culture. But the rapid advances of science and technology have tended to limit the value of older people's knowledge; books and other "memory-storing" devices have rendered older adults less valuable as storehouses of culture and records.

There are other reasons why the status of older adults has declined over time. Children no longer learn their future profession or trade from their parents; instead, these skills are acquired through institutions, such as the school system. In addition, the children of older adults are no longer dependent on their parents for their livelihood; they make their living through a trade or profession that is independent of their parents. Finally, older adults no longer perform tasks that are viewed as essential by society: Often the older workers' skills are viewed as outmoded even before these individuals retire.

Critical Thinking Question

Because older adults have had many more life experiences than young people, do you value the knowledge that older adults have?

The low status of older adults is closely associated with *ageism*, which refers to discrimination and prejudice against people simply because they are old. Today many people react negatively to older adults. Ageism is like sexism or racism because it involves intolerance and unfair treatment of all members of a particular social category.

Ageism is evident in our everyday language, by the use of terms that no racial or ethnic group would ever accept: *old buzzard, old biddy, old fart, old fogey.* From a rational view, ageism makes no sense; those who delight in discriminating against older adults will one day be old themselves. If you believe that "old age is ugly," you probably are guilty of ageism.

Critical Thinking Questions

Do you have negative stereotypes about being old? Do you dread being old? Are you guilty of ageism?

Early Retirement

Maintaining a high rate of employment is a major goal in our society. In many occupations, the supply of labor exceeds the demand. An often-used remedy for the oversupply of available employees is the encouragement of earlier retirement. Forced retirements often create financial and psychological burdens that retirees usually face without much assistance or preparation.

Our massive Social Security program supports early retirement, which can come as early as age 62. Pension plans of some companies and unions make it financially attractive to retire as early as age 55. Perhaps the extreme case is the armed forces, which permit retirement on full benefits after 20 years' service as early as age 38.

Many workers who retire early supplement their pension by taking another job, usually of lower status. About 86% of Americans 65 years of age and older are retired, even though many are intellectually and physically capable of working.[18]

Early retirement has some advantages to society, such as reducing the labor supply and allowing younger employees to advance faster. But there are also some serious disadvantages. For society the total bill for retirement pensions is already huge and still growing. For the retiree, it means facing a new life and status without much preparation or assistance. Although our society has developed formal institutions to prepare the young for the work world, it has not developed comparable avenues for preparing older adults for retirement. Being without a job in our work-oriented society is often a reality shock for older people.

In our society, we still view a person's worth partly by his or her work. People often develop their self-image (their sense of who they are) in terms of their occupation—"I am a teacher," "I am a barber," "I am a doctor." Because the later years generally provide no exciting new roles to replace the occupational roles lost on retirement, a retiree cannot proudly say, "I am a…" Instead, she or he must say, "I *was* a good …" The more a person's life revolves around work, the more difficult retirement is likely to be.

Retirement often removes people from the mainstream of life. It diminishes their social contacts and their status and places them in a *roleless role.* Individuals who were once valued as salespeople, plumbers, accountants, or secretaries are now considered non contributors in a roleless role on the fringe of society.

Several myths about the older worker have been widely accepted by both employers and the general public. Older workers are thought to be less healthy, clumsier, more prone to absenteeism, more accident prone, more forgetful, and slower in task performance.[19] Research has shown that these myths are erroneous. Older workers have lower turnover rates, produce at a steadier rate, make fewer mistakes, have lower absenteeism rates, have a more positive attitude toward their work, and have fewer on-the-job injuries than younger employees.[20] However, if the older worker does become ill, she or he usually takes somewhat longer to recover.[21]

Even though employers can no longer force a worker to retire, many exert subtle pressures on their older employees. Adjustment to retirement varies for different people. Retirees who are not worried about money and who are healthy are happier in retirement than those who miss their income and do not feel well enough to enjoy their leisure time. Many recent retirees relish the first long stretches of leisure time they have had since childhood. After a while, however, they may begin to feel restless, bored, and useless. Schick found that the most satisfied retirees tend to be physically fit people who are using their skills in part-time volunteer or paid work.[22]

Retirement appears to have little effect on physical health, but it sometimes affects mental health. Bossé, Aldwin, Levenson, and Ekerdt found that retirees are more likely than workers to report depression, obsessive–compulsive behavior, and physical symptoms that had no organic cause.[23] Workers who are pressured to retire before they want may feel anger and resentment and may feel out of step with younger workers. Also, workers who defer retirement for as long as possible because they enjoy their work may feel that no longer working is an immense loss after they have been pressured to retire.

On the other hand, some people's morale and life satisfaction remain stable through both working and retirement years. The effect of retirement on the lives of people has positive consequences for some and negative consequences for others.

The two most common problems associated with retirement are adjusting to a reduced income and missing one's former job. Those who have the most difficulty in adjusting tend to be rigid or overly identify with their work by viewing their job as their primary source of satisfaction and self-image. Those who are happiest are able to replace job prestige and financial status with values stressing self-development, personal relationships, and leisure activities.

The "golden age" of leisure following retirement appears to be largely a myth. Lawton found that life in retirement is likely to be sedentary, with TV viewing and sleep outranking such traditional leisure-time activities as gardening, sports, clubs, and other pastimes.[24] Many of older adults are poorly educated, which makes them less likely to enjoy reading or activities that focus on learning or self-improvement. A sharp reduction in income, fear of crime, lack of transportation, and reduced mobility also contribute to the sedentary lifestyle of older adults.

It would seem far better if workers who are still productive could stay on the job longer on a part or full-time basis rather than being pensioned off or forced to take another job of lower status. (This perspective will be expanded on later in this chapter.)

Societal Emphasis on Youth

Our society fears aging and old age more than most other societies do. Our emphasis on youth is indicated both by our dread of getting gray hair and wrinkles or becoming bald and by the pleasure we experience when someone guesses our age to be younger than it actually is. We place a high value on change and newness. European societies, on the other hand, place a higher value on preserving traditional customs and lifestyles. Our society also emphasizes mobility, action, and energy. We like to think we are doers.

But why this emphasis on youth in our society? The reasons are not fully clear. There appear to be several factors. Industrialization has resulted in a demand for laborers who are energetic and agile and have considerable strength. Rapid advances in technology and science have made past knowledge and certain specialized work skills (for example, that of a blacksmith) obsolete. Competition has always been a cornerstone of our society, reinforced by Darwin's notions on evolution and the survival of the fittest. The mass media portray youthfulness and a beautiful physique as highly valued in our society, and the advertising industry seeks to sell a variety of diet programs and products, numerous cosmetics, and a variety of exercise equipment and programs that claim to give the consumer a more youthful image.

Health Problems and Costs of Health Care

Old age is a social problem partly because of the high costs of health care. Most older adults have at least one chronic condition, and many have multiple conditions. The most frequent health problems are arthritis, hypertension, hearing and visual

CASE EXHIBIT 14.2

High Status for Older Adults in China, Japan, and Other Countries

An older Japanese American man celebrates his 102nd birthday with members of the Japanese American community. Traditionally, older adults in Japan are accorded great respect and status.

For many generations, older adults in Japan and China have experienced higher status than older adults in the United States. In both countries, older adults are integrated into their families much more than in this country. In Japan more than 75% of older adults live with their children, whereas in the United States most older adults live separately from their children.[a]

Older adults in Japan are accorded respect in a variety of ways. For example, the best seats in a home are apt to be reserved for older adults, cooking tends to cater to the tastes of older adults, and individuals bow to older adults.

However, Americans' images of older adults in Japan and China are somewhat idealized. Older adults, although more revered than in the United States, are not as revered and idealized as American stereotypes. Japan is now becoming more urbanized and Westernized. As a consequence, the proportion of older adults living with their children is decreasing, and older adults there are now often employed in lower-status jobs.

What factors are associated with whether older adults are accorded a position of high status in a culture? Five factors have been identified:

1. Older people are recognized as having valuable knowledge.
2. Older people control key family and community resources.
3. The culture is more collectivistic than individualistic.
4. The extended family is a common family arrangement in the culture, and older people are integrated into the extended family.
5. Older people are permitted and encouraged to engage in useful and valued functions as long as possible.

[a]John W. Santrock, *Life-Span Development*, 13th ed. (New York: McGraw-Hill, 2011).

impairments, heart disease, orthopedic impairments, sinusitis, cataracts, diabetes, and tinnitus (a sensation of hearing ringing or other noises).[25] Older people visit their doctors more frequently, spend a higher proportion of their income on prescribed drugs, and are hospitalized for longer periods than younger people. As might be expected, the health status of the old old (85 and over) is worse than that of the young old.

The medical expenses of an older person average more than four times those of a young adult.[26] This is partly because older adults suffer much more from long-term illnesses, such as cancer, heart problems, diabetes, and glaucoma.[27]

Of course, the physical process of aging (senescence) contributes to health problems. However, research in recent years has demonstrated that social and personal stresses also play a major role in causing diseases. Older adults face a wide range of stressful situations: loneliness, death of friends and family members, retirement, changes in living arrangements, loss of social status, reduced income, and a

decline in physical energy and physical capacities. Medical conditions may also result from substandard diets, inadequate exercise, cigarette smoking, and excessive alcohol intake. Flynn notes:

Critical Thinking Questions

Do you have older adults—friends relatives, neighbors—with whom you frequently communicate? If not, why not?

Studies of long-living peoples of the world show that neither heredity nor low prevalence of disease is a significant determinant of longevity. Four other factors are much more likely to predict long-term survival: (1) a clearly defined and valued role in society; (2) a positive self-perception; (3) sustained, moderate physical activity; and (4) abstinence from cigarette smoking. Studies in this country indicate that secure financial status,

Disengagement Theory: Response of Individuals and Society to Aging

In 1961 Elaine Cumming and William E. Henry coined the term *disengagement* to refer to a process whereby people respond to aging by gradually withdrawing from the various roles and social relationships they occupied in middle age.[a] Such disengagement is claimed to be functional for the individual because he or she is thought to gradually lose the energy and vitality to sustain all the roles and social relationships held in younger years.

The term *societal disengagement* has been coined to refer to the process whereby society withdraws from the aging person.[b] It is allegedly functional for our society—which values efficiency, competition, and individual achievement—to disengage from older adults, who have the least physical stamina and the highest death rate. Societal disengagement occurs in a variety of ways: Older people may not be sought out for leadership positions in organizations, their employers may try to force them to retire, their children may no longer want them involved in making family decisions, and the government may be more responsive to meeting the needs of people who are younger. (Actually, societal disengagement is often unintended and unrecognized by society.) Many older people do not handle forced role losses well. Some even try to escape with alcohol, drugs, or suicide.

With reference to the two terms just explained, *disengagement theory* hypothesizes a mutual disengagement or withdrawal between the individual and society. Disengagement theory has stimulated considerable interest and research. There is a good deal of controversy over whether disengagement is functional for older adults and for our society. Research has found that some people undeniably do voluntarily disengage

as they grow older. Yet disengagement is neither a universal nor an inevitable response to aging. Contrary to disengagement theory, most older people maintain extensive associations with friends. Most also maintain active involvements in organizations (such as church groups, fraternal organizations, and unions). Some older people, after retiring, develop new interests, expand their circle of friends, do volunteer work, and join clubs. Others *rebel* against society's stereotypes and refuse to be treated as if they had little to offer society. Many of these people are marshaling political resources to force society to adapt to their needs and skills.

A severe criticism of societal disengagement theory is that it can be used to justify both ageism and society's failure to help older adults maintain meaningful roles. Disengagement theory may, at best, be merely a description of the problems we must confront as we try to combat ageism.

In contrast to the disengagement theory of aging is the activity theory. It asserts that the more physically and mentally active older adults are, the more successfully they will age. There is considerable evidence that being physically and mentally active will help to maintain the physiological and psychological functions of older adults. Whereas disengagement theory expects older adults to slow down, activity theory urges them to remain physically and mentally active.

[a]Elaine Cumming and W. E. Henry, *Growing Old: The Process of Disengagement* (New York: Basic Books, 1961), p. 6.
[b]Robert C. Atchley, *Aging: Continuity and Change* (Belmont, CA: Wadsworth, 1983), p. 97.

social relationships, and high education are also important.[28]

(Health care for older adults is discussed further in Chapter 15.)

Financial Problems

Many older people live in poverty. A fair number lack adequate food, essential clothes and medicines, and perhaps even a telephone. One of every 10 older adults has an income below the poverty line.[29] Few have substantial savings or investments.

Poverty among older people varies dramatically by race, sex, marital status, ethnicity, and age. Women, the old-old, people of color, and those who are widowed or single are most likely to be poor.[30] Nine percent of older Whites are poor, compared to

23.7% of older African Americans and 19.5% of older Hispanics.[31]

Older women are more likely to be poor than older men. Nearly half of older Hispanic women, and 4 out of 10 older African American women are living in poverty.[32] (Women of color were more likely to have been working in low-paying jobs with no retirement plan.)

The financial problems of older people are compounded by additional factors. One factor is the high cost of health care, as previously discussed. A second factor is inflation. Inflation is especially devastating to those on fixed incomes. Most private pension benefits do not increase in size after a worker retires. For example, if living costs rise annually at 3.5%, after 20 years a person on a fixed pension would be able to buy one-half as many goods and services as he or she could at retirement.[33] Fortunately, in 1974, Congress enacted an automatic escalator clause in Social Security benefits, providing a 3% increase in payments when the consumer price index increased a like amount. However, Social Security benefits were never intended to make a person financially independent, and it is nearly impossible to live comfortably on monthly Social Security checks.

The most important source of income for the vast majority of older people is Social Security benefits, primarily the Old-Age Survivors, Disability, and Health Insurance (OASDHI) program. This program is described later in this chapter. The percent of older adults who receive Social Security is 95%; for 18% of them, Social Security is their only income.[34]

Fourteen percent of people age 65 and older are in the paid labor force in the United States, that is substantially lower than in 1950 but represents an increase since 1993.[35]

The Social Security system was never designed to be the main source of income for older adults. It was originally intended as a form of insurance that would *partially supplement* other assets when retirement, disability, or death of a wage-earning spouse occurred. Yet many older adults do not have investments, pensions, or savings to support them in retirement, and therefore, Social Security has become their major or sole source of income.

The U.S. Social Security system was developed in 1935. The system was fairly solvent until recently. During its first few decades, more money was paid into the system from Social Security taxes imposed on employers and employees than was paid out. This was due largely to the fact that life expectancy was only about 60 years of age. The life expectancy rate, however, has gradually increased to 78.[36] There is now a danger that the Social Security system will soon be paying out more than it takes in. Social Security taxes have increased sharply in recent years, but with the old old being the fastest-growing age group and with the proportion of older adults increasing in our society, the system may go bankrupt. Some projections have the fund being depleted around 2020.

Critical Thinking Question

What changes do you believe need to be made to keep the Social Security system solvent?

The *dependency ratio* is the number of societal members who are under 18 or are 65 and over compared with the number of people who are between 18 and 64. With the older adults proportion of the population increasing, nonworkers will represent a ballooning burden on workers. Authorities predict that by the year 2020 the dependency ratio will decline from the current level of about three workers for every nonworking person to a ratio of about 2 to 1.[37]

Clearly, serious problems exist with the system. First, as already noted, the benefits are too small to meet the financial needs of older adults. With payments from Social Security, an estimated 80% of retirees now live on less than half of their preretirement annual incomes. The monthly payments from Social Security are generally below the poverty line.[38] Second, it is unlikely that the monthly benefits will be raised much because the amount of Social Security taxes paid by employees is already quite high.

The nation faces some hard choices about how to keep the system solvent in future years. Benefits might be lowered, but this would even further impoverish recipients. Social Security taxes might be raised, but there is little public support for this because the maximum tax rate has already increased more than tenfold since 1970 (about $400 in 1970 to more than $5,000 currently per employee).[39]

One change that has been made in recent years in the Social Security system in an attempt to keep the system solvent is to gradually raise the age for full retirement benefits. For those born in 1937 or earlier, the age at which full retirement benefits will be received is 65. This age is gradually increased so that those born in 1960 or later have to be 67 years old to receive full retirement benefits.

A number of Republican members of Congress have proposed sharp cutbacks in Social Security, Medicaid, and Medicare benefits.

Loss of Family and Friends

Older people who are single are generally less well off than those who are married. The longer life span of women has left nearly 60% of women over age 65 without a spouse.[40] Gordon Moss and Walter Moss comment about the value of marriage for older persons:

They now have much more time for and are more dependent upon each other. Some marriages cannot handle this increased togetherness, but those that can become the major source of contentment

CASE EXHIBIT 14.4

Alzheimer's Disease

Tony Wilkins is 68 years old. Two years ago, his memory began to falter. As the months went by, he even forgot what his wedding day to Rose had been like. His grandchildren's visits slipped from his memory in 2 or 3 days.

The most familiar surroundings have become strange to him. Even his friends' homes seem like places he has never been before. When he walks down the streets in his neighborhood, he frequently becomes lost.

Tony is now quite confused. He has difficulty speaking and can no longer perform such elementary tasks as balancing his checkbook. At times Rose, who is taking care of him, is uncertain whether he knows who she is. All of this is very baffling for Tony. Until he retired 3 years ago, he had been an accountant and had excelled at remembering facts and details.

Tony has Alzheimer's disease. Although the disease sometimes strikes in middle age, most sufferers are over 65. About 5 million Americans have Alzheimer's disease, including 5% to 10% of all people over 65. Forty-seven percent of Americans over 85 years old have Alzheimer's disease.[a] The statistics indicate the disease affects the old-old to a greater extent than the younger-old.

Alzheimer's disease is named after Dr. Alois Alzheimer. In 1906, Dr. Alzheimer noticed changes in the brain tissue of a woman who had died having an unusual medical condition. Her symptoms included memory loss, unpredictable behavior, and language problems. After she died, he examined her brain and found many abnormal clumps (now called amyloid plaques) and tangled bundles of fibers (now called tangles). Plaques and tangles in the brain are two of the main features of this disease.

Alzheimer's disease is a degenerative brain disorder that causes gradual deterioration in intelligence, memory, awareness, and ability to control bodily functions. In its final stages, Alzheimer's leads to progressive paralysis and breathing difficulties. The breathing problems often result in pneumonia, the most frequent cause of death for Alzheimer's victims. Other symptoms include irritability, restlessness, agitation, and impairments of judgment.

Over a period lasting from as few as 5 years to as many as 20, the disease destroys brain cells. The changes in behavior displayed by those afflicted show some variation. Brownlee notes:

> One sufferer refuses to bathe or change clothes, another eats fried eggs without utensils, a third walks naked down the street, a fourth has the family's beloved cats put to sleep, while yet another mistakes paint for juice and drinks it. The outlandish acts committed by Alzheimer's patients take as many forms as there are people who suffer the disease. Yet, in every case, the bizarre behavior serves as a sign that the sufferer is regressing towards unawareness, a second childishness.[b]

The most prominent early symptom of Alzheimer's is memory loss, particularly for recent events. Other early symptoms (which are often overlooked) are a reduced ability to play a game of cards, reduced performance at sports, and sudden outbreaks of extravagance. More symptoms then develop—irritability, agitation, confusion, restlessness, and impairments of concentration, speech, and orientation. As the disease progresses, the symptoms become more disabling. Caregivers eventually have to provide 24-hour supervision, which is a tremendous burden. As the disease progresses in its final stages, nursing home placement is often necessary. Near the end, the patient usually cannot recognize family members, cannot understand or use language, and cannot eat without help.

Brownlee describes the mental and physical trauma that caregivers and family members of those afflicted experience:

> They live in a private hell, one that cannot be discussed with neighbors and friends in too much detail because the details are so devastating. They grieve even as their loved ones plunge them into a maelstrom of unreality, where mothers streak through the living room wearing nothing but a shower cap and garter belt and grandfathers try to punch their baby granddaughters.[c]

In addition, the patient's inability to reciprocate expressions of caring and affection robs relationships of intimacy.

Diagnosing the disease is difficult because the disorder has symptoms that are nearly identical to other forms of dementia. The only sure diagnosis at the present time is observation of tissue deep within the brain, which can be done only by autopsy after death. Doctors usually diagnose the disease in a living person by ruling out other conditions that could account for the symptoms.[d]

Researchers in recent years have made tremendous strides in identifying the causes of Alzheimer's disease. As of 1997, three different genes have been linked to causing the disease, and there may be additional genes associated with it. Yet having one or more of these genes does not always result in the development of this disorder. Therefore, researchers believe there must be some as yet unidentified "triggers" such as viral infections, biochemical deficiencies, high levels of stress, toxic poisons, exposure to radiation, and nutritional deficiencies. Scientists are now aware that genetic tendencies are a contributing factor because relatives of Alzheimer's patients have an increased risk of having the disease in the future.[e]

Scientists are also investigating other hypotheses as to what triggers Alzheimer's. One intriguing clue comes from the finding that victims of Down syndrome (a severe form of mental retardation due to a chromosome defect) who survive into their 30s frequently develop symptoms indistinguishable from those of Alzheimer's. Another recent clue is the discovery of fragments of amyloid in brains of persons who died from the disorder. Amyloid is a very tough protein that in normal amounts is necessary for cell growth throughout the body. Some researchers hypothesize that abnormal patches of this protein in the brain set up a chain reaction that progressively destroys brain cells. This amyloid protein is an abnormal

(continued)

product formed from a larger compound called amyloid precursor protein, or APP.

Researchers are now seeking to develop a test to detect Alzheimer's disease in its early stages. If they are successful, people will be better able to plan for their future care and make arrangements for their families while they still retain control of their mental faculties. Furthermore, if in fact Alzheimer's disease results from an accumulation of the amyloid protein and if the early accumulation of this protein can be detected, then it is likely that drugs can be developed to treat the disorder by blocking the formation of amyloid in the brain.[f]

Already, early diagnosis and treatment can slow the progress of the disease and improve the quality of life. Cholinesterase inhibitors, such as Aricept, can stabilize or slow symptoms for 6 months to a year in one-third to one-half of patients.[g] Behavioral therapies can improve communications, slow the deterioration in capabilities, and reduce disruptive behaviors. Certain drugs can lighten depression, relieve agitation, and assist patients in sleeping. Proper nourishment, appropriate exercise, physical therapy, and social interaction may slow the progression of the disease. Memory training and memory aids in the early stages may improve cognitive functioning. Also being tested for its effectiveness in protecting against Alzheimer's or slowing its progression are the herbal remedy ginko biloba, vitamins, anti-inflammatory drugs, and dietary intake of antioxidants (such as selenium). Especially helpful to patients and their families are emotional and social support provided by groups and professional counseling.

[a]Seth Borenstein, "Alzheimer's Struggle Is Gaining Ground," *Wisconsin State Journal*, Jul. 8, 2004, p 2A.
[b]S. Brownlee, "Alzheimer's: Is There Hope?" *U.S. News & World Report*, Aug. 12, 1991, pp. 40–49.
[c]Brownlee, "Alzheimer's: Is There Hope?" p. 48.
[d]L. L. Heston and J. A White, *Dementia* (New York: W. H. Freeman, 1983).
[e]Diane E. Papalia, Sally W. Olds, and Ruth D. Feldman, *Human Development*, 11th ed. (New York: McGraw-Hill, 2009), pp. 571–573.
[f]S.S. Sisodia, E. H. Kop, K. Beyreuthe, A. Unterbeck and D. L. Price, "Evidence That B-Amyloid Protein in Alzheimer's Disease Is Not Derived by Normal Processing," *Science*, 248 (Apr. 27, 1990), pp. 492–495.
[g]Papalia, Olds, and Feldman, *Human Development*, p. 652.

to both partners…. A good marriage, or a remarriage, provides the elderly person with companionship and emotional support, sex, the promise of care if he is sick, a focus for daily activities, and frequently greater financial independence. Sex roles often blur, and the husband actively helps in household chores.[41]

The older person's life becomes more isolated and lonely when close friends and relatives move away or die. Of course, later adulthood is a time when close friends are most likely to die.

The needs of aging parents can present some painful dilemmas for their children, especially if the parents are poor or in ill health. The children may have families of their own, with heavy demands on their time and finances. For people on tight budgets, deciding how to divide their resources among their parents, their own children, and themselves can be agonizing. Some face the difficult question of whether to maintain a parent within their home, to leave the parent living alone, to place the parent in a nursing home, or to place the parent in some other type of housing for older adults (such as a group home).

Substandard Housing

We hear so much about nursing homes that few people realize 95% of older adults do not live in nursing homes or in any other kind of institution.[42] About 80% of all older males are married and live with their wives.[43] Because females tend to outlive their spouses, about 40% of women over age 65 live alone.[44] Nearly 80% of older married couples maintain their own households—in apartments, mobile homes, condominiums, or their own houses.[45] When older adults do not maintain their own households, they most often live in the homes of relatives, primarily one of their children.

Older adults who live in rural areas generally have higher status than those in urban areas. People living on farms can retire gradually. Also, people whose income is in land, rather than in a job, can retain importance and esteem to an advanced age.

However, about three-quarters of our population reside in urban areas, where older people often live in poor-quality housing.[46] At least 30% of older adults live in substandard, deteriorating, or dilapidated housing.[47] Often urban older adults live in inner-city hotels or apartments with inadequate living conditions. Their neighborhoods may be decaying and crime-ridden, which makes them easy prey for thieves and muggers.

Fortunately, many mobile-home parks, retirement villages, assisted-living residences, and apartment complexes geared to the needs of older adults have been built throughout the country. Such housing communities provide a social center, security/protection, sometimes a daily hot meal, and perhaps a little help with maintenance.

Transportation

Only the more affluent and physically vigorous older adults can afford the luxury of owning and driving a car. The lack of convenient, inexpensive transportation is a problem faced by most older citizens.

Crime Victimization

Because of their reduced energy, strength, and agility, older adults are vulnerable to being victimized by crime, particularly robbery, aggravated assault, burglary, larceny, vandalism, and fraud. Many older people live in constant fear of being victimized, although reported victimization rates for older adults are actually lower than those for younger people. The true victimization rates for older adults may be considerably higher than official crime statistics indicate because many older individuals feel uneasy about becoming involved with the legal and criminal justice systems. Therefore, they may fail to report some of these crimes. Also, some older people are afraid of retaliation from the offenders if they report the crimes.

Sadly, some older adults are hesitant to leave their homes for fear that they will be mugged or that their homes will be burglarized while they are away.

Sexuality in Later Adulthood

There is a common misconception that older people lose their sexual drive. An older male who displays sexual interest is labeled a "dirty old man." When two older people exhibit normal heterosexual behavior, someone may comment, "Aren't they cute?" Yet many older people have a strong sexual interest and a satisfying sex life.[48] Sexual capacities, particularly in women, show little evidence of declining with age, and a large percentage of both older men and older women are capable of sexual relations.[49]

Noted sex researchers William Masters and Virginia Johnson see no reason why sexual activity cannot be enjoyed by older adults.[50] If sexual behavior does decline, it probably is due more to social reasons than to physical reasons. According to Masters and Johnson, the major deterrents to sexual activity when one is older are the lack of a partner, overindulgence in drinking or eating, boredom with one's partner, attitudes toward sex (such as the erroneous

©CLEO PHOTOGRAPHY/PhotoEdit

Residents of a private care facility share a kiss. Sexual capacities show little evidence of declining with age.

belief that sex is inappropriate for older adults), poor physical or mental health, attitudes toward menopause, and fear of poor performance.[51]

The attitudes of the younger generations frequently create problems for older adults. A widow or widower may face strong opposition to remarrying from other family members. Negative attitudes are often strongest when an older person becomes interested in someone younger who will become an heir if the older person dies. Older adults are sometimes informed that they should not be interested in members of the opposite sex and that they should not establish new sexual relationships when they have lost a mate.

Perhaps the best survey to date on the sexuality of older adults was commissioned by the American Association of Retired Persons.[52] It found that women over 60 are much less likely to have a sexual partner available; so they report lower frequencies of partnered activity. About 24% of the women and about 31% of the men ages 60 to 74 reported having intercourse at least weekly. For women 75 and over, 6.6% reported having intercourse at least weekly, compared to 19.1% for men 75 and over. It appears, then, that among older people who are healthy and who have regular opportunities for sexual expression, sexual activity may continue well past 75 years of age.

Papalia, Olds, and Feldman note:

The most important factor in maintaining sexual functioning is consistent sexual activity over the years. A healthy man who has been sexually active normally can continue some form of active sexual expression into his seventies or eighties. Women are physiologically able to be sexually active as long as they live; their main barrier to a fulfilling sexual life is likely to be lack of a partner.[53]

Fortunately, attitudes toward sexuality in later adulthood are changing. Merlin Taber notes:

With the changing attitudes of younger people to alternatives to the traditional family, some older people are finding informal arrangements for living together attractive. The couple who do not have a marriage ceremony can share all the companionship and sexual satisfactions without upsetting inheritance rights and retirement benefits. When they become aware of it, their children may accept such a pattern because they find it preferable to remarriage. We have no idea of the numbers that are involved, but the old as well as the young have new options as societal norms change. The popularity of living together without marriage will probably increase.[54]

Critical Thinking Question

If one of your grandparents were to die, would you want the surviving grandparent to become romantically involved with someone else?

Malnutrition

Older adults are the most uniformly undernourished segment of our population. There are a number of reasons for chronic malnutrition among older adults: transportation difficulties in getting to grocery stores; lack of knowledge about proper nutrition; lack of

money to purchase a well-balanced diet; poor teeth or lack of dentures, which can greatly limit one's diet; lack of incentive to prepare an appetizing meal when one is living alone; and inadequate cooking and storage facilities.

Depression and Other Emotional Problems

The older person is often a lonely person. Most people 70 years of age or older are widowed, divorced, or single. When someone has been married for many years and his or her spouse dies, a deep sense of loneliness usually occurs that seems unbearable. The years ahead often seem full of emptiness. It is not surprising, then, that depression is the most common emotional problem of older adults. Symptoms of depression include feelings of uselessness, of being a burden, of being unneeded, of loneliness, and of hopelessness. Somatic symptoms of depression include loss of weight and appetite, fatigue, insomnia, and constipation. It is often difficult to determine whether such somatic symptoms are due to depression or to an organic disorder.

Depression can alter the personality of an older person. Depressed people may become apathetic, withdrawn, and show a slowdown in behavioral actions. An older person's reluctance to respond to questions is apt to be due to depression rather than to the contrariness of old age.[55]

Those who have unresolved emotional problems in earlier life will generally continue to have them when older. Often these problems will be intensified by the added stresses of aging.

Two major barriers to good mental health in the later years are failure to bounce back from psychosocial losses (such as the death of a loved one) and failure to have meaningful life goals. Later adulthood is a time when there are drastic changes thrust on older adults that may create emotional problems: loss of a spouse, loss of friends and relatives through death or moving, poorer health, loss of accustomed income, and changing relationships with children and grandchildren.

Unfortunately, there is an erroneous assumption that *senility* and *mental illness* are inevitable and untreatable. On the contrary, older adults respond well to both individual and group counseling.[56] In addition, even many 90-year-olds show no sign of senility. Senility is by no means an inevitable part of growing old.

Older males have the highest suicide rate of any age group in the United States.[57]

CASE EXHIBIT 14.5

Triple Jeopardy: Being Female, African American, and Old

The poverty rate for older females is almost double that of older males.[a] Despite their positive status in the African American family and the African American culture, African American women over the age of 70 are one of the poorest population groups in the United States.[b] Three of five older African American women live alone, and most of them are widowed.[c] The poverty rate of this age group is related to ageism, sexism, and racism. In the past, these women tended to hold very low-paying jobs, some of which were not even covered by Social Security or, in the case of domestic service, were not apt to be reported by the employer even though the reporting is legally required.

Although many of these women are struggling (financially, socially, and physically), Edmonds notes they have shown remarkable adaptiveness, resilience, coping skills, and responsibility.[d] Extension of family networks helps them cope with the bare essentials of living and gives them a sense of being loved. African American churches have provided avenues for

meaningful social participation, social welfare services, feelings of power, and a sense of internal satisfaction. These women have also tended to live together in ethnic minority communities, giving them a sense of belonging. They have also tended to adhere to the American work ethic and have viewed their religion as a source of strength and support. Nonetheless, the income and health of older African American women (as well as that of other ethnic minority individuals) are important concerns in our aging society.

[a]William Kornblum and Joseph Julian, *Social Problems*, 12th ed. (Upper Saddle River, NJ: Pearson, 2007), pp. 310–312.
[b]Ibid.
[c]Ibid.
[d]M. Edmonds, "The Health of the Black Aged Female," in *Black Age*, Z. Harel, E. A. McKinney, and M. Williams, eds. (Newbury Park, CA: Sage Publications, 1990).

There are a variety of reasons why older adults have a high rate of suicide, including declining health, loss of status, reduced income, and lack of relationships with families and friends. The higher suicide rate for older males is thought to be due to the fact that males are more apt than females in our society to make work the central focus of their lives; once they retire, many no longer see a reason for living.

Death

Preoccupation with death—and particularly with the circumstances surrounding it—is an ongoing concern of older adults. They see their friends and relatives dying, and they dread the disability, pain, and long periods of suffering that may precede death. They generally hope for a death with dignity: in their own homes, with little suffering, with mental faculties intact, and with families and friends nearby. Older adults also worry about the costs of their final illness, the difficulties they may cause others by the manner of their death, and the financial resources to permit a dignified funeral.

In our society, we tend to wall off the dying with silence. (Perhaps we do so to avoid having to confront our own mortality.) In hospitals great efforts are made to separate the dying from the living. Often the medical staff attempts to shield the dying person from awareness of his or her impending death. Families, too, begin to treat the patient differently when

they know the end is near. (This different treatment often subtly informs the dying that death is imminent.)

Many authorities have urged our society to treat death more openly.[58] Such openness would enable dying persons to prepare for death better, perhaps by having additional time to reassess their lives. It would also give the dying person more time to become accepting of death and to make financial arrangements, such as drawing up a will. It would give family members time to make necessary arrangements (including financial ones), as well as time to redress old wrongs and heal misunderstandings. We all need to face, and come to terms with, our own eventual death. The popularity of courses in death and dying on college campuses shows that people feel a need to become more psychologically comfortable with facing death.

People in nonliterate societies were generally better prepared for death than we are. Margaret Mead notes:

In peasant communities where things didn't change and where people died in the beds they were born in, grandparents taught the young what the end of life was going to be. So you looked at your mother, if you were a girl, and you learned what it was like to be a bride, a young mother. Then you looked at your grandmother and knew what it was like to be old. Children learned what it was to age and die

CASE EXHIBIT 14.6

Ethical Issue: Should Assisted Suicide Be Legalized?

The technology of life-support equipment can keep people alive almost indefinitely. Respirators, artificial nutrition, intravenous hydration, and so-called miracle drugs not only sustain life but also trap many of the terminally ill in a degrading mental and physical condition. Such technology has raised a variety of ethical questions. Do people who are terminally ill and in severe pain have a right to die by refusing treatment? Increasingly, through "living wills," patients are able to express their wishes and refuse treatment. However, does someone in a long-term coma who has not signed a living will have a right to die? How should our society decide when to continue and when to stop life-support efforts? Courts and state legislatures are presently working through the legal complexities governing death and euthanasia.

Should assisted death, or assisted suicide, be legalized? As of 2003, only the Netherlands permitted physicians to give qualifying terminally ill patients a lethal dose of drugs. There is considerable controversy about assisted suicide in the United States. Hemlock Society founder Derek Humphry has written a do-it-yourself suicide manual that has become a best seller. (The Hemlock Society promotes active voluntary euthanasia.) Michigan doctor Jack Kevorkian has made national news by building a machine to help terminally ill people end their lives and by assisting a large number of them to do so.

On September 17, 1998, Dr. Kevorkian assisted Thomas Youk in dying by giving him a lethal injection. Mr. Youk was 52 years old and had an advanced case of Lou Gehrig's disease—a disease in which a patient eventually loses all muscle control. Kevorkian videotaped the death, and later showed it on CBS's "60 Minutes." Kevorkian was found guilty of second-degree murder and delivery of a controlled substance by a Michigan court. He was sentenced to 10 to 25 years. He served 8 years of this sentence. He was released in 2007, and died in 2011.

In the Netherlands, an informal, de facto arrangement made with prosecutors more than 25 years ago allows physicians there to help patients die, as long as certain safeguards are followed. The patient, for example, has to be terminally ill, in considerable pain, and mentally competent; she or he must also repeatedly express a wish to die.

Oregon's Death with Dignity Act was passed by voters in 1994. It allows doctors to prescribe lethal drugs at the request of terminally ill patients who have less than 6 months to live. Doctors may only prescribe a lethal dose, not administer it.

People in favor of assisted suicide argue that unnecessary long-term suffering is without merit and should not have to be endured. They argue that people have a right to a death with dignity, which means a death without excessive emotional and physical pain and without excessive mental, physical, and spiritual degradation. They see assisted suicide as affirming the principle of autonomy—upholding the individual's right to make decisions about his or her dying process. Allowing the

option of suicide for the terminally ill is perceived as the ultimate right of self-determination.

Opponents assert that suicide is unethical and is a mortal sin for which the deceased cannot receive forgiveness. They view assisted suicide as assisted murder. They maintain that modern health care can provide almost everyone a peaceful, pain-free, comfortable, and dignified end to life. Opponents believe that most terminally ill persons consider suicide not because they fear death but because they fear dying—pain, abandonment, and loss of control—all of which the hospice is designed to alleviate. Horror stories of intense suffering are most often the tragic results of medical mismanagement, they feel. Moreover, assisted-suicide legislation could easily result in the philosophy that the terminally ill have a *duty* to avoid being a financial and emotional burden to their families and to society. A health-care system intent on cutting costs could give subtle, even unintended, encouragement to a patient to die. Relatives of a terminally ill person receiving expensive medical care may put pressure on the person to choose physician-assisted suicide to avoid eroding the family's finances. There is concern that, if competent people are allowed to seek death, then pressure will grow to use the treatment-by-death option with adults in comas or with others who are mentally incompetent (such as the mentally ill and those who have a severe cognitive disability). Finally, many people worry that, if the "right to die" becomes recognized as a basic right in our society, then it can easily become a "duty to die" for the elderly, the sick, the poor, and others devalued by society.

Some authorities have sought to make a distinction between active euthanasia (assisting in suicide) and passive euthanasia (withholding or withdrawing treatment). In many states, it is legal for physicians and courts to honor a patient's wishes not to receive life-sustaining treatment.

A case of passive euthanasia involved Nancy Cruzan. On January 11, 1983, when this Missouri woman was 25, her car overturned. Her brain lost oxygen for 14 minutes following the accident, and for the next several years she was in a "persistent vegetative state," with no hope of recovery. A month after the accident, her parents, Joyce and Joe Cruzan, gave permission for a feeding tube to be inserted. In the months that followed, however, the parents gradually became convinced there was no point in keeping Nancy alive indefinitely in such a hopeless condition.

In 1986 they were shocked when a Missouri state judge informed them that they could be charged with murder for removing the feeding tube. The Cruzans appealed the decision all the way to the U.S. Supreme Court, requesting the Court to overturn a Missouri law that specifically prohibits withdrawal of food and water from hopelessly ill patients. In July 1990, the Supreme Court refused the Cruzans' request that their daughter's tube be removed but ruled that states could sanction the removal if there is "clear and convincing evidence" that the

(continued)

patient would have wished it. Cruzan's family subsequently found other witnesses to testify that Nancy would not have wanted to be kept alive in such a condition.

A Missouri judge decided that the testimony met the Supreme Court's test. The tube was disconnected in December 1990, and Nancy Cruzan died several days later, on December 26.

Currently, 10,000 Americans are in similar vegetative conditions, unable to communicate. Many of these individuals have virtually no chance to recover. Right-to-die questions will undoubtedly continue to be raised in many of these cases.

In June 1997, the U.S. Supreme Court ruled that terminally ill people do not have a constitutional right to doctor-assisted suicide. The Court upheld laws in New York and Washington state that make it a crime for doctors to give life-ending drugs to mentally competent but terminally ill patients who no

longer want to live. The judges in their ruling made it clear their decision does not permanently attempt to resolve the assisted-suicide issue, and they in fact urged debate on this issue to continue.

In 2001 then–Attorney General John Ashcroft issued a directive that Oregon's Death with Dignity Act violates the Federal Controlled Substances Act because the drugs used in physician-assisted suicide did not have a "legitimate medical purpose." The state of Oregon sued to prevent enforcement of the directive.

In January 2006, the U.S. Supreme Court ruled that the Bush administration's attempts to stop Oregon doctors from prescribing lethal doses were improper. The immediate legal impact of the court's ruling is clear: Oregon doctors may continue to prescribe lethal doses without fear of federal penalty.

while they were very small. They were prepared for the end of life at the beginning.[59]

(Unfortunately, in our society, many of us seek to deny our own deaths, even though we are all "terminal" from birth.)

In the modern United States, most people die in nursing homes or hospitals, surrounded by medical staff.[60] Such deaths often occur without dignity.

Critical Thinking Questions

Do you believe that the terminally ill have a right to die by refusing treatment? Do you believe that assisted suicide should be legalized? If you had a terminally ill close relative who was in intense pain and asked you to assist her or him in acquiring a lethal dose of drugs, how would you respond? Would you be willing to help? Or would you refuse?

Fortunately, the hospice movement allows the terminally ill to die with dignity—to live their final weeks in the way they want. Hospices originated in the Middle Ages among European religious groups who welcomed sick, tired, or hungry travelers.[61] Hospices today are located in a variety of settings—in a separate unit of a hospital, in a building independent of a hospital, or in the dying person's home. Medical services and social services are provided, and extensive efforts are made to allow the terminally ill to spend their remaining days as they choose. Hospices sometimes have educational and

entertainment programs, and visitors are common. Pain relievers are used extensively so that patients can live out their final days in relative comfort.

Hospices view the disease, not the patient, as terminal. The emphasis is on helping patients to use the time that is left rather than on trying to keep people alive as long as possible. Many hospice programs are set up to assist patients to live their remaining days in the home of their family. In addition to medical and visiting-nurse services, hospices have volunteers who help the patient and family members with services such as counseling, transportation, insurance forms and other paperwork, and respite care for family members. After patients die, many hospices offer bereavement services for the survivors.

Parent Abuse

Parent abuse refers to abuse of older parents by their children. It occurs most often when the parents live with the children or are dependent on them. This problem is described in more depth in Chapter 6.

Current Services

The problems of older adults are coming into the public spotlight. Many state governments now have an office on aging, and some municipalities and counties have established community councils on aging. Numerous universities have established centers for the study of gerontology, and nursing, medicine, sociology, social work, architecture, and other disciplines and professions have established fields of study on gerontology. (*Gerontology* is the scientific study of aging and the problems of older adults.) Government research grants encourage gerontological study by academicians. Publishers are now producing books and pamphlets to educate the public about older adults, and a few high schools are offering courses to help teenagers understand older adults and their circumstances.

Present services and programs for older adults are principally "maintenance" in nature; that is, they are primarily designed to meet basic physical needs. Nonetheless, there are a number of programs, often federally funded, that provide needed services to older adults. A few of these are briefly described in Case Exhibit 14.7.

Older Americans Act of 1965

The Older Americans Act of 1965 created an operating agency (Administration on Aging) within the Department of Health, Education and Welfare.* This law and its amendments are the bases for financial aid by the federal government to assist states and local communities in meeting the needs of older adults. The act was designed to secure the following for older adults:

1. An adequate income
2. Best possible physical and mental health
3. Suitable housing
4. Restorative services for those who require institutional care
5. Opportunity for employment
6. Retirement in health, honor, dignity
7. Pursuit of meaningful activity
8. Efficient community services
9. Immediate benefit from research knowledge to sustain and improve health and happiness
10. Freedom, independence, and the free exercise of individual initiative in planning and managing their own lives[62]

Although these objectives are commendable, the reality is that the goals have not been realized for many of our older adults.

Nursing Homes

Nursing homes were created as an alternative to expensive hospital care and are substantially supported by the federal government through Medicaid and Medicare. About 1.5 million older people now live in

extended-care facilities, making nursing homes a billion-dollar industry.[63] There are more patient beds in nursing homes than in hospitals.[64]

Nursing homes are classified according to the kind of care they provide. At one end of the scale are residential homes that offer primarily room and board, with some nonmedical care (such as help in dressing). At the other end of the scale are nursing-care centers that provide skilled nursing and medical attention 24 hours a day. The more skilled and extensive the medical care given, the more expensive the home. The costs per resident average more than $5,500 per month.[65] Although only a small percentage of older adults live permanently in nursing homes (about 5%), many more spend some time convalescing in them.

One scandal after another characterizes care in some nursing homes. Patients have been found lying in their own feces or urine. In some nursing homes, the food is so unappetizing that some residents refuse to eat it. Some homes have serious safety hazards. In some homes, boredom and apathy are common among staff as well as residents. A number of nursing homes fail to meet food sanitation standards and have problems administering drugs and providing personal hygiene for residents. A study in 2001 found that a third of the nursing homes in the United States were cited by state inspectors as being abusive to residents in 1999 and 2000.[66]

Donald Robinson conducted a nationwide investigation of nursing homes and concluded: "I learned that the majority of nursing homes are safe, well-run institutions that take good care of the sick people entrusted to them. Some are superb."[67] Robinson also noted a number of horrors and abuses in some of the homes. The abuses included giving new and unapproved drugs to patients without their consent, giving patients heavy doses of tranquilizers to keep them docile, stealing funds from patients, submitting phony cost reports to Medicare, and charging patients thousands of dollars to gain admission to a home. There were also instances of sexual abuse of patients by staff members.[68]

At present, people of all ages tend to be prejudiced against nursing homes, even those that are well run. Frank Moss describes the elderly person's view of nursing homes: "The average senior citizen looks at a nursing home as a human junkyard, as a prison—a kind of purgatory, halfway between society and the cemetery—or as the first step of an inevitable slide into oblivion."[69] To some degree there is reality to

---

*This department was renamed the Department of Health and Human Services in 1980.

Some Programs for Older Adults

- *Medicare:* Helps pay the medical and hospital expenses of older adults (described in Chapter 15).
- *Old Age, Survivors, Disability, and Health Insurance:* Provides monthly payments to eligible retired workers (described in Chapter 4).
- *Supplemental Security Income:* Provides a minimum income for indigent older adults (described in Chapter 4).
- *Medicaid:* Pays most medical expenses for low-income people (described in Chapter 15).
- *Food stamps:* Offset some of the food expenses for low-income people who qualify (described in Chapter 4).
- *Nursing Home Ombudsman Program:* Investigates and acts on concerns expressed by residents in nursing homes.
- *Meals on Wheels:* Provides hot and cold meals to housebound recipients who are incapable of obtaining or preparing their own meals but who can feed themselves.
- *Retired Senior Volunteer Program (RSVP):* Seeks to match work and service opportunities with older volunteers seeking them.
- *Foster Grandparent Program*: Pays older adults for part-time work in which they provide individual care and attention to ill and needy children and youths.
- *Service Corps of Retired Executives (SCORE):* Provides consulting services to small businesses. This program enables retired executives to retain meaningful functions in our society.
- *Senior citizens' centers, golden-age clubs, and similar groups:* Provide leisure-time and recreational activities for older adults.
- *Special bus rates:* Reduce bus transportation costs for older adults.
- *Congregate housing facilities:* Provide housing in private or government-subsidized rental apartment complexes, remodeled hotels to meet the needs of independent older adults, or mobile home parks designed for older adults. They provide meals, housekeeping, transportation, social and recreational activities, and sometimes health care.
- *Group homes:* Provide housing for some older residents. A group home is usually a house that is owned or rented by a social agency. Employees are hired to shop, cook, do heavy cleaning, drive, and give counseling. Residents take care of much of their own personal needs and take some responsibility for day-to-day tasks.
- *Assisted-living facilities:* Allow older adults to have semi-independent living. Older adults in such a facility live in their own rooms or apartments. Residents receive personal care (bathing, dressing, and grooming), meals, housekeeping, transportation, and social and recreational activities.
- *Foster care homes:* Are usually single-family residences where the owners of the home take in an unrelated older adult and are reimbursed for providing housing, meals, housekeeping, and personal care.
- *Continued-care retirement communities:* Are long-term housing facilities that are designed to provide a full range of accommodations and services for affluent older people as their needs change. A resident may start out living in an independent apartment; then move into a congregate housing unit with such services as cleaning, laundry, and meals; then move to an assisted living facility; and finally move into an adjoining nursing home.
- *Property tax relief:* Available to older adults in many states.
- *Special federal income-tax deduction:* For people over 65.
- *Housing projects for older adults:* Built by local sponsors with financial assistance provided by the Department of Housing and Urban Development.
- *Reduced rates at movie theaters and other places of entertainment:* Often offered voluntarily by individual owners.
- *Home health services:* Provide visiting-nurse services, physical therapy, drugs, laboratory services, and sickroom equipment.
- *Nutrition programs:* Provide meals for older adults at group "eating sites." (These meals are generally provided four or five times a week and usually are lunchtime meals. These programs improve the nutrition of older adults and offer opportunities for socialization.)
- *Homemaker services:* Provided in some communities to take care of household tasks that older adults are no longer able to do for themselves.
- *Day-care centers for older adults:* Provide activities that are determined by the needs of the group. (This service gives the family some relief from 24-hour care. Programs such as home health services, homemaker services, and daycare centers prevent or postpone institutionalization.)
- *Telephone reassurance:* Provided by volunteers, often older people, who telephone older people who live alone. (Such calls are a meaningful form of social contact for both parties and also ascertain whether any accidents or other serious problems have arisen that require emergency attention.)
- *Nursing homes:* Provide residential care and skilled nursing care for older adults who cannot take care of themselves or whose families can no longer take care of them.
- *Medicare Prescription Drug, Improvement and Modernization Act of 2003:* The program is designed to assist older adults (especially low-income older adults) in purchasing prescription drugs at lower costs. (Details of the plan are complex; information can be obtained from your local Social Security Administration office.)

The Villages, Florida: A Model Retirement Community

The Villages is a master-planned age-restricted retirement community that is located approximately 45 miles northwest of Orlando, Florida. Visitors will be astonished by the amenities that are offered. The Villages is the biggest and most popular retirement community in the world. About 90,000 people live there. It is one of the fastest-growing metropolitan areas in the United States. At least 80% of the homes must be occupied by at least one person who is 55 years of age or older. Persons under the age of 19 years are not permitted to reside within the Villages, but may visit for a maximum of 30 days per year—unless granted an exemption. The median age of the residents is approximately 66 years.

The Villages is a haven for those who seek an active retirement lifestyle. Perhaps the most popular activity is golf. There are 29 Executive Golf courses, and 10 Championship courses. Golf is free for the Villages, residents on all the Executive courses, but there is a small greens fee to play the Championship courses. All residents are automatically made members of each country club, allowing them to dine in the club restaurants and use the recreational facilities. Other popular activities include softball, bocce ball, tennis, basketball, pickle ball, and many others.

Although many residents have their own cars, one of the main sources of transportation is via a golf cart. Most residents have a golf cart, and many spend a few thousand dollars customizing the cart to suit their taste. The Villages is also famous for its recreational activities. There are literally thousands of clubs that residents can join. There are over 40 recreation centers, each with swimming pools, tennis courts, and assorted activities—including bocce ball, horseshoes, shuffleboard, card and board games, billiards, line dancing, and more. Arts and crafts provide major enjoyment for many of the residents. Art, music, pottery, dance, and woodworking are just a few examples of the many choices available.

Entertainment is widely available, with free nightly music on the two town squares. A third town square is currently being built. The town squares have numerous restaurants, and also a large range of shopping opportunities. Most large shopping chain facilities are available, such as Barnes and Noble, and Wal-Mart. Banks, service stations, and other service facilities are also available. The Villages is a medium-size city that is designed to meet the needs and dreams of retirees. Newcomers can buy their own homes, build their own homes, or rent for a while to test out the lifestyle.

The Villages began to be developed in the early 1960s by Harold Schwartz and H. Gray Morse. The Villages is a gated community that is known for its low crime rate. The majority of the numerous forms of recreation are paid for via a monthly amenities fee assessed to residents. The Villages operates three media properties, a TV station, a radio station, and a daily newspaper. The Villages will undoubtedly change—in a positive direction—the views of visitors as to the advantages of living in a retirement community!

---

the notion that nursing homes are places where the elderly wait to die.

The cost of care for impoverished nursing home residents is largely paid by the Medicaid program (described in Chapter 15). Because the federal government has set limits on what will be reimbursed under Medicaid, other problems may arise. There may be an effort to keep salary and wage levels as low as possible and the number of staff to a minimum. A nursing home may postpone repairs and improvements. Food is apt to be inexpensive dishes such as macaroni and cheese and may be high in fats and carbohydrates. Congress has mandated that every nursing home patient on Medicaid is entitled to a monthly personal spending allowance. The homes have control over these funds, and some homes keep this money.

A danger of nursing home care is the potential abuse of the residents by staff members. In a telephone survey of 577 nurses and nurses' aides, Pillemer and Moore heard many instances of abuse by staff.[70] More than one-third of the respondents stated they had seen other staff members physically abusing patients—pushing, shoving, pinching, hitting, or kicking them; throwing things at them; or restraining them more than necessary. Ten percent acknowledged committing one or more of these acts themselves. Psychological abuse was even more common, with 81% of the respondents indicating they had seen other staff members yelling at patients, insulting them, swearing at them, isolating them unnecessarily, threatening them, or refusing to give them food. Forty percent of the respondents acknowledged committing such abuse themselves!

Complaints about the physical facilities of nursing homes include not enough floor space or too many people in a room. The call light by the bed may be difficult to reach, or the toilets and showers may not be conveniently located. And the building may be in a state of decay.

Although the quality of nursing home care ranges from excellent to awful, nursing homes are needed, particularly for those requiring around-the-clock health care for an extended time. If nursing homes were abolished, other institutions such as hospitals would have to serve older adults. Life in nursing homes need not be bad. Where homes are properly administered, residents can expand their life experiences.

The ideal nursing home should be lively (with recreational, social, and educational programming), safe, hygienic, and attractive. It should offer stimulating activities and opportunities to socialize with people of both sexes and all ages. It should offer privacy so that (among other reasons) residents can be sexually active. It should offer a wide range of therapeutic, social, recreational, and rehabilitative services. The best-quality care tends to be provided by larger nonprofit facilities that have a high ratio of nurses to nurses' aides.[71]

In 2002 the Centers for Medicare and Medicaid Services created a website, www.medicare.gov, that posts unusually detailed information about the quality of care delivered by more than 17,000 nursing homes in all 50 states. The homes are rated on a number of "quality measures," including the percentage of patients with bed sores, weight loss, or pain; the percentage of patients who have registered complaints; and the percentage of patients who need extra help with daily activities. The percentages are adjusted so that a nursing home with many residents near death, for instance, won't be penalized for excessive weight loss. Families going through the draining chore of finding a good nursing home should find this information to be very useful.

At present only 5% of the elderly population reside in nursing homes. However, it is estimated that one of every five of us who live beyond age 65 will spend part of our life in a nursing home.[72]

Social Work and Older Adults

Social work education is taking a leading role in identifying the problems of older adults and is developing gerontological specializations within the curricula. Social workers are a significant part of the staff of most agencies serving older adults. Some states, for example, are now requiring that each nursing home employ a social worker.

Some of the services in which social workers have expertise in providing to older adults are the following:

- *Brokering services.* In any community, there is a wide range of services available, but few people are knowledgeable about the array of services or the eligibility requirements. Older adults are in special need of this "broker" service because some have difficulty with transportation and communication and others may be reluctant to request needed assistance to which they are entitled.

- *Case management or care management services.* Social workers are trained to assess the social service needs of a client and the client's family. When appropriate, the social worker case manages by arranging, coordinating, monitoring, evaluating, and advocating for a package of multiple services to meet the often complex needs of an elderly client. Common functions of most case management programs for older adults include case finding, prescreening, intake, assessment, goal setting, care planning, capacity building, care plan implementation, reassessment, and termination.

- *Advocacy.* Because of shortcomings in services to older adults in our society, social workers must at times advocate for needed services for older adults.

- *Individual and family counseling.* Counseling interventions focus on examination of the older client's needs and strengths, the family's needs and strengths, and the resources available to meet the identified needs.

- *Grief counseling.* Older adults are apt to need counseling for role loss (such as retirement or loss of self-sufficiency), loss of a significant other (such as a spouse, a child, or an adult sibling), and loss due to chronic health or mental health conditions.

- *Adult day-care services.* Social workers provide individual and family counseling, outreach and broker services, supportive services, group work services, and care planning services for older adults being served by adult day-care services.

- *Crisis intervention services.* Social workers providing crisis intervention seek to stabilize the crisis situation and connect the older person and the family to needed supportive services.

- *Adult foster care services.* Foster care and group homes are designed to help the older person remain in the community. Social workers providing foster care match foster families with an older person and monitor the quality of life for those living in foster care settings.

- *Adult protective services.* Social workers in adult protective services assess whether adults are at risk for personal harm or injury owing to the actions (or inactions) of others. At-risk circumstances include physical abuse, material (financial) abuse, psychological abuse, and neglect (in which caregivers withhold medications or nourishment or fail to provide basic care). If abuse or neglect is determined, then adult protective services workers develop, implement, and monitor a plan to stop the maltreatment.

- *Support and therapeutic groups.* In some settings, social workers facilitate the formation of support groups and therapeutic groups for older adults or for family members (some of whom may be caregivers). Support and therapeutic groups are useful for such issues as adjusting to retirement, coping with illnesses such as Alzheimer's disease, dealing with alcohol or other drug abuse, coping with a terminal illness, and coping with depression and other emotional difficulties.

- *Respite care.* Social workers are involved with the recruitment and training of respite care workers as well as identifying families in need of these services. When an older person requires 24-hour at-home care, respite services allow caregivers (such as the spouse or other family members) time away from caregiving responsibilities, which alleviates some of the stress involved in providing care around the clock.

- *Transportation and housing assistance.* Social workers operate as brokers for finding appropriate housing in the community and for arranging safe transportation services.

- *Social services in hospitals and nursing homes.* Social workers in these settings provide assessment of social needs; health education for the older person and the family; direct services (such as counseling) to the older person, the family, and significant others; advocacy; discharge planning; community liaison; participation in program planning; consultation on developing a therapeutic environment in the facility; and participation in developing care plans that maximize the older person's potential for independence.

The reader will note that there is some overlap in these descriptions of services provided by social workers to older adults. Because the older population is the most rapidly growing age group in our society, it is anticipated that services to older adults will significantly expand in the next few decades. This expansion will generate a number of new employment opportunities for social workers.

The Emergence of Older Adults as a Powerful Political Force

Despite all the maintenance programs that are now available, the key problems of older adults remain to be solved. A high proportion of older people do not have meaningful lives, respected status, adequate income, transportation, good living arrangements, a healthy diet, or adequate health care.

Our society has made gains in combating many kinds of prejudice, but ageism is still prevalent. Gordon and Walter Moss comment: "Just as we are learning that black can be beautiful, so we must learn that gray can be beautiful, too. In so learning, we may brighten the prospects of our own age."[73]

In the past, prejudice has been most effectively countered when those discriminated against joined together for political action. It therefore seems apparent that if major changes in the older adult's role in our society are to take place, similar action will be needed.

Older people are, in fact, becoming increasingly involved in political activism—and in some cases, even radical militancy. Two prominent organizations are the American Association of Retired Persons and its affiliated group, the National Retired Teachers Association. These groups, among others, are lobbying for the interests of older adults at local, state, and federal levels of government.

An action-oriented group that has caught the public's attention is the Gray Panthers. This organization argues that a fundamental flaw in our society is the emphasis on materialism and the consumption of goods and services rather than on improving the quality of life for all citizens (including older adults). The Gray Panthers are seeking to end ageism and to advance the goals of human freedom, human dignity, and self-development. This organization advocates social action techniques, including getting older adults to vote as a bloc for their concerns. The founder of the group, Maggie Kuhn (1905–1995), stated, "We are not mellow, sweet old people. We have got to effect change, and we have nothing to lose."[74]

There are clear indications that the politics of age have arrived. Older adults are one of the most politically organized and influential groups in the United States. The past 60 years have seen some significant steps toward securing a better life for older adults: increased Social Security payments, enactment of

Medicare and Medicaid programs, the emergence of hospices, and the expansion of a variety of other programs. With the clout of this powerful political bloc, additional changes to improve the status of older adults in our society can be expected.

In April 2005, the U.S. Supreme Court struck a major blow for age equality in the workplace when it ruled that a bulwark of civil rights laws against race and sex discrimination should also protect employees who bring suits in federal court under the Age Discrimination in Employment Act (ADEA). Plaintiffs can now bypass what is often the hardest-to-prove aspect of their cases—showing that their employer's discrimination was deliberate. The Supreme Court has now sent a message that age discrimination is a serious problem that must be attacked when it is unintentional as well as when it is intentional.[75]

Development of Social Roles for Older Adults

It is essential for our society to find a meaningful, productive role for older adults. At present, many companies' early retirement programs and society's stereotypic expectations of older adults often result in older citizens' being unproductive, inactive, dependent, and unfulfilled. There are several steps that can be taken to provide productive roles for older people.

Older adults who want to work and are still performing well should be encouraged to continue working well past age 65 or 70, even if only half time or part time. Two older people working half time could be allowed to fill a full-time position. New roles might also be created for older adults as consultants after they retire in the areas in which they possess special knowledge and expertise. For those who do retire, there should be educational and training programs to help them develop their interests and hobbies (such as photography) into new sources of income.

Working longer would have a number of payoffs for older adults and for society. Older people would continue to be productive, contributing citizens; they would have a meaningful role; they would continue to be physically and mentally active; they would have higher self-esteem; and they could break down the stereotypes of older adults being unproductive and a financial burden on society. And importantly, they would be paying into the Social Security system rather than drawing from it.

Objections to such a system may be raised by those who maintain that some older adults are no longer productive. This may be true, but some younger people are also unproductive. What is needed to make the proposed system work is realistic, objective, and behaviorally measurable levels of performance. Individuals at any age who do not meet those standards would be informed about the deficiencies and given training to improve. If the performance levels still were not met, discharge would be used as a last resort. (For example, if a tenured faculty member's performance is inadequate—as measured by students' course evaluations, peer faculty evaluations of teaching, record of public service, record of service to the department and to the campus, and record of publications—she or he would be informed of the deficiencies. Training and other resources to meet standards should be offered. If the performance then does not improve to acceptable levels, dismissal proceedings would be initiated. Some colleges and universities are now moving in this direction.)

Another objection that has been voiced about this new system is that older adults have worked most of their lives and therefore deserve to retire and live in leisure with a high standard of living. It would be nice if older adults really had this option. However, that is not realistic. Most older citizens do not have the financial resources after retiring to maintain a high standard of living. The only real options in our society are to work and thereby maintain a higher standard of living or to retire and have a lower standard of living.

Some progress is being made in keeping older adults in productive roles. Most members of the U.S. Supreme Court and many members of Congress are over age 70. In addition, numerous organizations have been formed to promote the productivity of older adults. Three examples are the Retired Senior Volunteer Program, the Service Corps of Retired Executives, and the Foster Grandparent Program.

The *Retired Senior Volunteer Program* (*RSVP*) offers people over age 60 the opportunity of doing volunteer service to meet community needs. RSVP agencies place volunteers in hospitals, schools, libraries, daycare centers, courts, nursing homes, and a variety of other organizations.

The *Service Corps of Retired Executives* (*SCORE*) offers retired businesspeople an opportunity to help owners of small businesses and managers of community organizations who are having management problems. Volunteers receive no pay but are reimbursed for out-of-pocket expenses.

The *Foster Grandparent Program* employs low-income older people to help provide personal, individual care to children who live in institutions. (Such children include those who have a severe cognitive disability, those who are emotionally disturbed, and those who have a developmental disability.) Foster grandparents are given special assignments in child care, speech therapy, physical therapy, or as teachers aides. This program has been shown to be of considerable benefit to both the children and the foster grandparents.[76] The children served become more outgoing and enjoy improved relationships with peers and staff. They have increased self-confidence, improved language skills, and decreased fear and insecurity. The foster grandparents have an additional (although small) source of income, increased feelings of vigor and youthfulness, an increased sense of personal worth, a feeling of being productive, and a renewed sense of personal growth and development. For society, foster grandparents provide a vast pool of relatively inexpensive labor that can be used to do needed work in the community.

The success of these programs illustrates that older adults can be productive in both paid and volunteer positions. In regard to using elderly volunteers in agencies, Robert Atchley makes the following recommendations to increase the opportunities for successful outcomes:

First, agencies must be flexible in matching the volunteer's background to assigned tasks. If the agency takes a broad perspective, useful work can be found for almost anyone. Second, volunteers must be trained. All too often agency personnel place unprepared volunteers in an unfamiliar setting. Then the volunteer's difficulty confirms the myth that you cannot expect good work from volunteers. Third, a variety of placement options should be offered to the volunteers. Some volunteers prefer to do familiar things; others want to do anything but familiar things. Fourth, training of volunteers should not make them feel that they are being tested. This point is particularly sensitive among working-class volunteers. Fifth, volunteers should get personal attention from the placement agency. There should be people (perhaps volunteers) who follow up on absences and who are willing to listen to the compliments, complaints, or experiences of the volunteers. Public recognition

from the community is an important reward for voluntary service. Finally, transportation to and from the placement should be provided.[77]

Surprisingly large numbers of recent retirees say they would like to be back at work.[78] Of recent retirees, half are satisfied, a quarter are unable to work because of their health or family situations, and a quarter (about 2 million people) say they would prefer working again over retirement.

Is there any evidence to support the hypothesis that productive activity, either paid or unpaid, is a key to aging well? Glass et al. compared nearly 1,200 men and women ages 70 to 79 who showed high physical and cognitive functioning ("successful agers") with 162 medium- and low-functioning adults in the same age group ("usual agers").[79] Nearly all successful agers and more than 9 out of 10 usual agers engaged in some form of productive activity. A key finding was that successful agers were far more productive than the usual agers. On average, the successful agers were more than three times as likely to engage in paid work, did almost four times as much volunteer work, did one-third more housework, and did twice as much yard work as the usual agers. The research supports the idea that engaging in productive activity is correlated with successful aging.

Many role models of productive older adults are now emerging. These role models are challenging the formerly pervasive picture of old age as a time of inevitable physical and mental decline. Many 70-year-olds are now acting, thinking, and feeling like 50-year-olds did a decade or two ago. One of these role models is John Glenn; see Case Exhibit 14.9.

Preparation for Later Adulthood

Growing old is a lifelong process. Turning 65 does not interrupt the continuities in what a person has been, presently is, and will be. Recognition of this fact should reduce the fear of growing old. For people of modest means who have prepared thoughtfully, later adulthood can be a period if not of luxury, then at least of reasonable comfort and pleasure.

Critical Thinking Question

Examine your current lifestyle. Are you living the kind of life that will lead to your later adulthood being a dream or a nightmare?

CASE EXHIBIT 14.9

John Glenn, One of the Many Productive Older Adults

John Glenn was born July 18, 1921, in Cambridge, Ohio. He entered the Naval Aviation Cadet Program in March 1942 and graduated from this program. He was commissioned in the Marine Corps in 1943. During his World War II service, he flew 59 combat missions. During the Korean War, he flew 63 missions. In the last 9 days of Fighting in Korea, Glenn downed three MIGs in combat. He was awarded the Distinguished Flying Cross on six occasions for his service during World War II and Korea.

In 1959 he was selected as a Project Mercury astronaut and became the first American to orbit the earth. He became a national hero. He retired from the Marine Corps on January 1, 1965, and became a business executive. In November 1974, he was elected to the U.S. Senate. He served there with distinction, retiring from the Senate in January 1999.

John Glenn was not yet done. He offered himself as a human guinea pig by volunteering to go on a 9-day mission on the space shuttle *Discovery* so that scientists could study the effects of space travel on an older adult. Candidates for space travel, of any age, have to pass stringent physical and mental tests. Glenn was in superb physical condition. He passed the examinations with flying colors and then spent nearly 500 hours in training.

Discovery blasted off from the Kennedy Space Center at Cape Canaveral, Florida, on October 29, 1998. John Glenn, at age 77, became a space pioneer (and national hero) for the second time. Nine days later, on November 7, *Discovery* returned to Earth. Glenn, though weak and wobbly, walked out of the shuttle on his own two feet. Within 4 days, he had fully recovered his balance and was completely back to normal. Among other accomplishments, this flight had an important side effect in that it challenged common negative stereotypes about aging.

Anthony Behar/BEHAR ANTHONY/SIPA/Newscom

John Glenn.

Our lives depend largely on our goals and our motivations to achieve those goals. How we live prior to retiring will determine whether later adulthood will be a nightmare or a dream. There are a number of areas we should attend to in our younger years:

- *Being physically and mentally active: Active Theory* asserts that the more physically and mentally active people are, the more successfully they will age. There is considerable evidence that being physically and mentally active helps to maintain the physiological, physiological, and intellectual functions of older people. Practically everyone needs to incorporate physical exercise into their daily lives.

  Just as physical exercise maintains the level of physiological functioning, mental exercise maintains cognitive functioning. There is considerable truth in the adage, "what you don't use, you lose."

- *Health:* A sound exercise plan and periodic health examinations are crucial to the prevention of chronic health problems. Also critically important in maintaining health is learning and using techniques to reduce psychological stress (see Chapter 15).
- *Finances:* Saving money for later years is important, as is learning to manage or budget money wisely.
- *Interests and hobbies:* Psychologically, people who are traumatized most by retirement are those whose self-image and life interests center around their work. Individuals who have meaningful hobbies and interests look forward to retirement so they can devote more of their time to these enjoyable activities.
- *Self-identity:* People who are comfortable and realistic about who they are and what they want out of life are better prepared, including in later years, to deal with stresses and crises that arise.

● *A view toward the future:* A person who dwells on the past or rests on past laurels is likely to find the later years depressing. On the other hand, a person who looks to the future is able to find new challenges and new satisfactions in later years. Looking toward the future involves planning for retirement, including deciding where you want to live and what you want to do with your free time.

● *Effective problem solving:* If a person learns to cope effectively with crises in younger years, these coping skills will remain when the person is older. Effective coping involves learning to approach problems realistically and constructively.

SUMMARY

The following summarizes this chapter's content as it relates to the chapter objectives presented at the beginning of the chapter. Objectives include the following:

A *Describe the specific problems faced by older adults.*

Aging is an individual process that occurs at different rates in different people. Chronological age is not an accurate measure of how physically fit or mentally alert an older person is.

People 65 and older now compose more than one-tenth of our population. The old-old are the fastest-growing age group in our society. Older adults encounter a number of problems in our society: low status, lack of a meaningful role, the social emphasis on youth, health problems, financial problems, loss of family and friends, inadequate housing, transportation problems, restrictive attitudes about expressing their sexuality, malnutrition, crime victimization, and emotional problems such as depression and concern with circumstances surrounding dying. Most older adults depend on Social Security as their major source of income. Yet monthly payments are inadequate, and the system is no longer financially sound.

B *Discuss current services to meet these problems. Also, note gaps in current services.*

A wide array of services is available, as summarized in the chapter. These services are primarily geared to maintaining older adults, often at or only slightly above a subsistence level of existence. Services provided in many of our nursing homes are inadequate,

and the level of care in some of these homes has been sharply criticized. Nursing homes have also been criticized as being "storage centers" for older adults so that members of our society can avoid coming face to face with their own mortality.

Although the level of care needs to be substantially improved, nursing homes are needed for older adults who cannot take care of themselves and/or for those whose families can no longer provide care. Most older persons, however, do not need nursing homes for permanent care or shelter. (It is not generally known that 95% of older adults live independently or with relatives, not in nursing homes.)

C *Describe the role of social work in providing services to older adults.*

In many ways, older adults are victims of ageism. Social workers play numerous roles in serving older adults, including that of an advocate to secure system changes that will better serve them. Increasingly, older adults are becoming politically active and are organizing to improve their status. In the future, there are likely to be a number of social, economic, and political changes that will improve the status of older adults.

D *Discuss social and political changes needed to improve the status of older adults.*

To provide older adults with a productive, meaningful role in our society, it is suggested that they be encouraged to work (either in paid jobs or as volunteers) as long as they are productive and have an interest in working to maintain their standard of living. Empowering older adults to be productive in their lives would have a number of personal payoffs for them and would also be highly beneficial to society.

Competency Notes

EP 2.1.3a Distinguish, appraise, and integrate multiple sources of knowledge, including research-based knowledge and practice wisdom. (All of this chapter) This chapter describes the problems faced by older adults, and discusses current services to meet these problems. Gaps in current services are noted. It describes the role of social work in providing services to older adults. It ends with a discussion of social and political changes needed to improve the status of older adults.

Media Resources

Additional resources for this chapter, including a chapter quiz, can be found on the Social Work CourseMate. Go to CengageBrain.com.

Notes

1. Gordon Moss and Walter Moss, *Growing Old* (New York: Pocket Books, 1975), p. 18.
2. Colin M. Turnbull, *The Mountain People* (New York: Simon & Schuster, 1972).
3. Linda A. Mooney, David Knox, and Caroline Schacht, *Understanding Social Problems*, 8th ed. (Belmont, CA: Wadsworth/Cengage Learning, 2013), p. 177.
4. William Kornblum and Joseph Julian, *Social Problems*, 14th ed. (Boston: Pearson, 2012), p. 309.
5. Diane E. Papalia, Sally W. Olds, and Ruth D. Feldman, *Human Development*, 11th ed. (New York: McGraw-Hill, 2009), pp. 589–591.
6. Milton L. Barron, "The Aged as a Quasi-Minority Group," in *The Other Minorities*, Edward Sagarin, ed. (Lexington, MA: Ginn, 1971), p. 149.
7. Papalia, Olds, and Feldman, *Human Development*, p. 550.
8. Kornblum and Julian, *Social Problems*, p. 305.
9. Papalia, Olds, and Feldman, *Human Development*, p. 553.
10. Joan Arehart-Triechel, "It's Never Too Late to Start Living Longer," *New Yorker*, Apr. 11, 1977, p. 38.
11. Thomas Sullivan, Kenrick Thompson, Richard Wright, George Gross, and Dale Spady, *Social Problems: Divergent Perspectives* (New York: Wiley, 1980), pp. 335–370.
12. U.S. Bureau of the Census, *Statistical Abstract of the United States, 2012* (Washington, DC: U.S. Government Printing Office, 2011).
13. Ibid.
14. Nancy Hooyman, *Selected Facts on Aging,* Gero-Ed Center (Washington, DC: National Center for Gerontological Social Work Education, 2007).
15. Papalia, Olds, and Feldman, *Human Development*.
16. Nursing Home Asset Protection, http://www.living-trusts.net/nursing-care.html.

17. Eisdor Fer, quoted in Alan S. Otten, "Ever More Americans Live into 80s and 90s, Causing Big Problems," *Wall Street Journal*, July 30, 1984, p. 10.
18. Papalia, Olds, and Feldman, *Human Development*, pp. 595–597.
19. Kornblum and Julian, *Social Problems*, pp. 305–306.
20. Ibid.
21. Ibid.
22. F. L. Schick, ed., *Statistical Handbook on Aging Americans* (Phoenix, AZ: Oryz, 1986).
23. R. Bossé, C. M. Aldwin, M. R. Levenson, and D. J. Ekerdt, "Mental Health Differences among Retirees and Workers: Findings from the Normative Aging Study," *Psychology and Aging*, 2 (1987), pp. 383–389.
24. M. P. Lawton, "Leisure Activities for the Aged," *Annals of the American Academy of Political and Social Science*, 438 (1978), pp. 71–79.
25. Papalia, Olds, and Feldman, *Human Development*, p. 566.
26. Ibid.
27. Ibid.
28. Marilyn L. Flynn, "Aging," in *Contemporary Social Work*, 2nd ed., Donald Brieland, Lela Costin, and Charles Atherton, eds. (New York: McGraw-Hill, 1980), p. 353.
29. Mooney, Knox, and Schacht, *Understanding Social Problems*, p. 177.
30. Ibid., pp. 384–386.
31. Ibid.
32. Ibid.
33. Ibid.
34. Hooyman, "Selected Facts on Aging."
35. Ibid.
36. Mooney, Knox, and Schacht, *Understanding Social Problems*, pp. 28–29.
37. Ibid.
38. Kornblum and Julian, *Social Problems*, p. 308.
39. Ibid.
40. Ibid., p. 310.
41. Moss and Moss, *Growing Old*, p. 47.
42. Kornblum and Julian, *Social Problems*, pp. 306–310.
43. Ibid.
44. Ibid.
45. Ibid.
46. Ibid.
47. Ibid.

48. Janet S. Hyde and John D. Delamater, *Understanding Human Sexuality*, 11th ed. (Boston: McGraw-Hill, 2011), pp. 256–261.

49. Ibid.

50. William H. Masters and Virginia E. Johnson, "The Human Sexual Response: The Aging Female and the Aging Male," in *Middle Age and Aging*, L. Neugarten, ed. (Chicago: University of Chicago Press, 1968).

51. Ibid., p. 269.

52. American Association of Retired Persons (AARP), *Modern Maturity Sexuality Study* (Washington, DC: Author, 1999).

53. Papalia, Olds, and Feldman, *Human Development* p. 565.

54. Merlin Taber, "The Aged," in *Contemporary Social Work*, Donald Brieland, Lela Costin, and Charles Atherton, eds. (New York: McGraw-Hill, 1975), p. 359.

55. Papalia, Olds, and Feldman, *Human Development*, p. 569.

56. B. M. Newman and P. R. Newman, *Development through Life: A Psychosocial Approach* (Pacific Grove, CA: Brooks/Cole, 1995).

57. Kornblum and Julian, *Social Problems*, pp. 302–303.

58. Papalia, Olds, and Feldman, *Human Development*, pp. 616–628.

59. Margaret Mead, "Dealing with the Aged: A New Style of Aging," *Current*, no. 136 (Jan. 1972), p. 44.

60. Papalia, Olds, and Feldman, *Human Development*.

61. Sullivan et al., *Social Problems*, p. 363.

62. *Older Americans Act of 1965, As Amended, Text and History* (Washington, DC: U.S. Department of Health, Education and Welfare, November 1970).

63. Papalia, Olds, and Feldman, *Human Development*, p. 601.

64. Ibid.

65. Nursing Home Asset Protection.

66. "Some Golden Years," *U.S. News & World Report*, Aug. 13, 2001, p. 8.

67. Donald Robinson, "The Crisis in Our Nursing Homes," *Parade*, Aug. 16, 1987, p. 13.

68. Ibid.

69. Frank Moss, "It's Hell to Be Old in the U.S.A.," *Parade*, July 17, 1977, p. 9.

70. K. Pillemer and D. W. Moore, "Abuse of Patients in Nursing Homes: Findings from a Survey of Staff," *Gerontologist*, 29 (1989), pp. 314–320.

71. Ibid.

72. Papalia, Olds, and Feldman, *Human Development*, p. 601.

73. Moss and Moss, *Growing Old*, p. 79.

74. Quoted in Robert N. Butler, *Why Survive? Being Old in America* (New York: Harper & Row, 1975), p. 341.

75. David Newman, "Breakthrough," *AARP Bulletin* (Washington, DC: AARP, May 2005), pp. 10–12.

76. Robert C. Atchley, *The Social Forces in Later Life: An Introduction to Social Gerontology*, 2nd ed. (Belmont, CA: Wadsworth, 1977), p. 267.

77. Ibid., p. 81.

78. Tamar Lewin, "Many Retirees Tire of Leisurely Lives, Seek New Jobs," *Wisconsin State Journal*, Apr. 22, 1990, p. 1A.

79. T. A. Glass, T. E. Seeman, A. R. Herzog, R. Kahn, and L. F. Berkman, "Change in Productive Activity in Late Adulthood: MacArthur Studies of Successful Aging," *Journal of Gerontology: Social Sciences*, 50B, pp. 65–66.

CHAPTER

Health Problems and Medical Social Services

CHAPTER OUTLINE

Health and happiness are what we want most in life. Wealthy people who develop a chronic illness often say they would, if given a choice, relinquish their riches for a return to health. Most Americans now consider proper medical care a basic human right for which society should pay if an individual cannot. The view that health care is a basic right rather than a privilege is of relatively recent origin. For example, in 1967 the president of the American Medical Association still asserted that health care should be available only to those who could afford it.[1] The view of health care as a right was expressed by former President Richard Nixon in his "Health Message of 1971":

> Just as our National Government has moved to provide equal opportunity in areas such as education, employment, and voting, so we must now work to expand the opportunity for all citizens to obtain a decent standard of medical care. We must do all we can to remove any racial, economic, social, or geographic barriers that now prevent any of our citizens from obtaining adequate health protection. For without good health, no man can fully utilize his other opportunities.[2]

Sadly, as we shall see, we still have primarily a two-tier health-care system in the United States: a quality one for those who can pay, and a less-than-adequate system for those who cannot pay. In 2010 Congress passed and President Obama signed the Health Care Reform Act. The provisions of the bill will be phased in over a period of several years. The Health Care Reform Act, known as Obamacare, moves the United States closer to universal health care. What will be the impact of Obamacare on health care in the United States? What will be the impact of Obamacare on our economy? This chapter will:

Learning Objectives

EP 2.1.3a

A   Briefly describe the health-care system in the United States.

B   Summarize problems in health care: profit orientation, limited attention to preventive medicine, unequal access to health services, health care for older adults, AIDS, use of life-sustaining equipment, and the high cost of medical care.

C   Describe Obamacare, which may (or may not) resolve many of the problems in our health-care system.

D   Describe medical social work.

Physical Illnesses and the Health-Care System

There are hundreds of thousands of different medical conditions ranging in severity from a minor scratch to a terminal illness. The causes are also nearly infinite: accidents, infections, birth defects, viruses, bacteria, the aging process, stress, poor nutrition, and so on.

Medical services in this country are organized into four basic components: physicians in private practice, group outpatient settings, hospital settings, and public health services.

Physicians in individual or solo practice are, proportionately, more often found in rural than in urban areas. Such a physician is usually a general practitioner who is trained to provide treatment for the more common medical ailments. Supervision of general practitioners is minimal or nil; they are primarily accountable only to patients. Except through referrals for consultation and occasional use of laboratories and hospitals, a physician in private practice works in relative isolation from colleagues.

Group outpatient settings can be organized in several ways. A group of general practitioners may share facilities, such as a waiting room, examining rooms, and a laboratory. Or each physician within a group may have a different specialty and complement the skills of the others. Because medical knowledge and treatment techniques have become so vast and diverse, it is now impossible for a physician to have in-depth knowledge of all areas. Another type of outpatient setting is one in which a third party (a university, union, business, or factory) employs a group of physicians to provide medical care for its constituency. In still another type, a group of doctors with the same specialty (for example, neurological surgery) provide services in the same facility.

A third subsystem of health care is the hospital setting, which has a wide range of laboratory facilities, specialized treatment equipment, inpatient care facilities, and highly skilled technicians. Hospitals employ diverse and numerous medical personnel. A hospital is generally the center of the medical care system in communities. Because of the spiraling costs of hospital care and the lack of sufficient beds, many communities have nursing homes and convalescent homes for people who require fairly extensive medical care but not inpatient hospital attention.

Public health services are organized on five levels: local (city or county), regional, state, national, and international. The majority of public health services in a community are provided through local health programs. The priorities in public health keep changing; as success is achieved in dealing with one problem, other problems emerge that demand attention. Public health services have virtually eliminated a number of communicable diseases in this country, such as tuberculosis, polio, and smallpox.

The focus of public health services is primarily preventive in nature. Services provided through local health departments include: (a) health counseling to families regarding family planning, prenatal and postpartum care, growth and development, nutrition, and medical care; (b) skilled nursing care and treatment for the acute and chronically ill; (c) physical rehabilitation to patients with strokes, arthritis, and similar medical conditions; (d) school health services to public and parochial institutions and liaison services among home, school, and community; (e) disease prevention and control; (f) immunization services; (g) referral of families and individuals to make maximum use of available community resources; (h) environmental sanitation, which involves developing and enforcing codes, rules, and regulations designed to maintain and/or improve conditions in the environment that affect health (this activity covers a broad area, including air and water pollution, food protection, waste material disposal, and sanitation of recreation facilities); (i) maintenance of an index of all area births, deaths, marriages, and current communicable diseases; and (j) health education and information services to stimulate the public to recognize existing health problems. In the United States, the vast majority of health-care services are private rather than public (that is, administered by the government).

Problems in Health Care

The health-care system in the United States faces a number of problems. These include a service orientation versus profit orientation, limited attention to preventive medicine, unequal access to health services, low-quality health care for older adults, AIDS, unnecessary or harmful care, use of life-sustaining equipment, and the high cost of medical care.

Service Orientation versus Profit Orientation

Most Americans believe that the only focus of health care is to keep people healthy by preventing diseases, illnesses, and impairments from occurring and by restoring to health as rapidly as possible those who do become ill. If this were the only objective, the health-care system would not receive very high grades. There are a number of countries that have a higher life expectancy than the United States.[3] Life expectancy is highly correlated with the quality of health care in a society. As a population's health improves because of better medical care and improved living conditions, the average age to which its members live rises. (On the other hand, the life expectancy in the United States is more than double that of some developing countries. For example, it is 78 in the United States, but 30 years in Swaziland,[4] and Japan has the highest life expectancy at 82 years.[5])

Another indicator of the quality of health care is the infant mortality rate. Thirty-four countries have a lower infant mortality rate than the United States.[6] The higher the rate at which newborns live in a country is directly correlated with the quality of health care provided to newborns and their mothers. (The infant mortality rate in the United States is, however, much lower than that in developing countries; in the United States, the infant mortality rate is about 6 per 1,000 live births, while in Sierra Leone it is about 180 per 1,000 live births.[7]) The infant mortality rate is determined by the number of deaths of children under 1 year of age per 1,000 live births in a calendar year.

The objectives of health-care providers in the United States are not only to restore and maintain health but also to make a profit. There are numerous statistics documenting that the system is prospering. Many of our more than 7,000 hospitals are among the most modern in the world. Physicians have the highest median income of any occupational group. They earn several times more than the average wage earner. The mean income of physicians is about $200,000 per year.[8] The average daily cost for a hospital bed has gone from $74 in 1970 to more than $900 currently.[9] One of the most profitable small businesses in this country is the private medical practice. Among the most profitable intermediate-size businesses are nursing homes. The pharmaceuticals industry, involving the manufacture and sale of drugs, has been one of the most profitable large industries in the country.

The United States spends more money on health care (in both absolute and proportionate terms) than any other country. Medical costs constitute 25% of our total production of goods and services.[10]

Consumers seeking immediate and inexpensive health care in our country are often frustrated and angered over high costs and delays. Access is particularly difficult in low-income neighborhoods in cities and smaller rural communities because health-care facilities tend to be located in affluent urban and suburban neighborhoods. The late Robert F. Kennedy described the health-care system in the United States as "a national failure" that is "providing poor quality care at high costs."[11]

Other industrialized nations regard medical care as a social service. This philosophy is based on the premise that the kind of care you receive depends on the kind of illness you have. In contrast, in the United States, the kind of medical care you receive depends not only on your illness but also on how much money you are able and willing to spend.

Emphasis on Treatment Rather Than on Prevention

Most of the major causes of death today in the United States are chronic diseases: heart disease, cancer, cerebrovascular disease (such as strokes), obstructive pulmonary disease, and the like (Table 15.1). Chronic diseases progress and persist over a long period of time. They may exist long before we are aware of them because often there are no symptoms in the early stages and because we tend to ignore early symptoms. Social, psychological, and environmental factors are important influences in the progression of these diseases. Heart disease, for example, is known to be associated with a diet high in saturated animal fats (beef, butter, and cheese), lack of consistent and vigorous exercise, heavy smoking, and stress.

A major problem is that modern medicine is oriented toward crisis medicine, which is geared to treating people *after they become ill*. The crisis approach is effective in coping with some types of medical conditions, such as acute problems (for example, injuries, influenza, or pneumonia). Unfortunately, with chronic diseases, once the symptoms manifest themselves, much of the damage has already been done, and it is often too late to affect a complete

Table 15.1 Ten Leading Causes of Death in the United States

RANK	PERCENTAGE OF TOTAL DEATHS
1. Heart disease	25.4
2. Cancer	23.2
3. Stroke (cerebrovascular diseases)	5.6
4. Chronic lower respiratory diseases	5.3
5. Accidents (unintentional injuries)	5.1
6. Alzheimer's disease	3.1
7. Diabetes	2.9
8. Influenza/Pneumonia	2.2
9. Kidney disease	1.9
10. Drug-induced deaths	1.6

SOURCE: U.S. Census Bureau, *Statistical Abstract of the United States: 2012* (Washington, DC, 2011).

CASE EXHIBIT 15.1

Health Practices and Longevity

The following 10 health practices have been found to be positively related to good health and longevity:

1. Eating breakfast
2. Eating regular meals and not snacking
3. Eating moderately to maintain normal weight
4. Exercising moderately
5. Not smoking
6. Drinking alcohol moderately or not at all
7. Sleeping regularly 7 to 8 hours a night
8. Avoiding the use of illegal drugs
9. Learning to cope with stress
10. Leading a healthy sexual life

SOURCE: Diane E. Papalia, Sally W. Olds, and Ruth D. Feldman, *Human Development*, 11th ed. (Boston: McGraw-Hill, 2009), pp. 567–569.

recovery. To curb the incapacitating effects of chronic diseases, the health-care delivery system needs to emphasize the prevention of illness before extensive damage occurs. To date, preventive medicine has had a lower priority than crisis-oriented medicine in terms of research funding, the allocation of healthcare personnel, and the construction of medical facilities. (There is more profit in treatment programs than in prevention programs.) This emphasis on treatment violates the commonsense notion that "an ounce of prevention is worth a pound of cure."

The kinds of health problems that we have in this country stem largely from our lifestyles. Millions of Americans smoke, drink, or eat to excess. Smoking is a serious health hazard. It has been linked to a long list of diseases, including heart disorders, ulcers, lung cancer, and emphysema. The life expectancy for heavy smokers (two or more packs a day) is several years less than that for nonsmokers.[12] Some authorities now believe that nicotine is more addictive than heroin or cocaine.[13] Secondhand smoke (breathing in the smoke from someone else who is smoking) is now recognized as a dangerous carcinogen.

The health hazards of alcohol abuse are described at length in Chapter 8. The life expectancy of alcoholics is 10 to 12 years lower than that of nonalcoholics.[14]

Our diet is another aspect of lifestyle that has a profound impact on health and life expectancy. We eat too many fatty foods (such as red meat) and not enough fruits, vegetables, and whole-grain products. Our sugar consumption should be reduced and the fiber in our diet increased.[15] In addition, we love high-calorie food and have a major tendency to overeat, both of which cause the serious problem of obesity. Research has found that obesity is associated with a variety of health problems, including high

blood pressure, high cholesterol levels, heart disease, and diabetes.[16] Two-thirds of all Americans are now estimated to be overweight.[17]

Medical research shows that regular exercise is essential to good health. Exercise reduces significantly the risk of heart disease, which is the leading cause of death in the United States.[18] Regular exercise is one of the best predictors of overall longevity; yet the majority of Americans do not exercise regularly.[19] An often quoted minimum guideline for exercise is 30 minutes a day at least three or four times per week.

Environmental factors also pose health risks. Our air and water are filled with thousands of toxic chemicals (caused by emissions from autos and factories) that create health hazards, such as cancer and emphysema. The fatality rate from automobile crashes is staggeringly high. Many such accidents are caused by driving while intoxicated.

Critical Thinking Question

Are you currently living a healthy lifestyle, or do you need to make some changes in order to be healthier?

Physicians often treat the symptoms of chronic illnesses rather than the underlying causes. Patients who are tense or anxious are prescribed tranquilizers rather than given therapy to reduce the psychological stress that is causing the tension. Patients who are depressed are prescribed antidepressant medication rather than being counseled to determine the underlying reasons for the depression. Patients with stress-related disorders (for example, ulcers, migraine headaches, insomnia, diarrhea, digestive problems, hypertension) are often prescribed medication rather than given therapy to change certain aspects of their lifestyles that would reduce the underlying psychological stress, which is a major factor in producing such problems.

In recent years, holistic programs, which are preventive in nature, have been established in industry, in hospitals, in school settings, in medical clinics, and elsewhere. Holistic medicine recognizes that our thinking processes function together with our bodies as an integrated unit, and it focuses on both our physical and psychological functions. The major determinants of most illnesses are our lifestyles (including exercise patterns, diet, sleep patterns, and, particularly, stress reaction patterns). Holistic medicine instructs people in proper exercises, proper diet, and techniques to reduce psychological stress in order to maintain health and curb the development of chronic disorders.

Thomas McKeown emphasized the responsibility that each person has (although it is often not recognized) in maintaining good health:

The role of individual medical care in preventing sickness and premature death is secondary to that of other influences, yet society's investment in health care is based on the premise that it is the major determinant. It is assumed that we are ill and are made well, but it is nearer the truth to say that we are well and are made ill. Few people think of themselves as having the major responsibility for their own health....

The public believes that health depends primarily on intervention by the doctor and that the essential requirement for health is the early discovery of disease. This concept should be replaced by recognition that disease often cannot be treated effectively, and that health is determined predominantly by the way of life individuals choose to follow. Among the important influences on health are the use of tobacco, the misuse of alcohol and drugs, excessive or unbalanced diets, and lack of exercise. With research, the list of significant behavioral influences will undoubtedly increase.[20]

Critical Thinking Questions

Some people know they have a medical condition that should be medically checked out, but (for a variety of reasons) they put off seeing a physician. Do you have a medical concern that you should have medically checked out? If so, why are you procrastinating in contacting a physician?

Unequal Access to Health Services

The use and availability of medical care are directly related to socioeconomic class and race. For example, the average life expectancy of White males is about 6 years longer than that for African American males, and the average life expectancy for White females is about 4 years longer than that for African American females.[21] In addition, the infant mortality rate for African Americans is more than twice that for Whites.[22] Non-Whites have higher rates of practically every illness than Whites;[23] a number of factors help explain this difference, as non-Whites have less access to health care, are exposed to discrimination in a variety of ways, and are apt to receive a lower quality of health care from the health-care delivery system.

Membership in a lower social class is also correlated with higher rates of illnesses. The poor are seriously ill more frequently and for longer periods of time. They have higher rates of untreated illnesses and higher mortality rates for almost all illnesses. Contrary to popular belief, the highest rates of heart disease occur among the lowest salaried, not among top-level executives and managers.[24] (Stress levels may in fact be higher among the poor, who continually face psychological stress from financial crises. Differences in diet, exercise, and lifestyle patterns may also be factors.)

Of course, these higher rates of illness among the poor are largely attributable to their inability to afford private, high-quality medical care. Because of the profit motive, health-care services are located primarily in affluent urban areas and in suburbs. The poor who live in rural areas or in urban, low-income regions therefore have much more difficulty in gaining access to medical care, especially if they have transportation barriers. In the United States, health-care services are provided on a *fee-for-service* basis. As a result, a two-tier system now exists; the upper tier serves the wealthy with high-quality care, and the lower tier serves the poor with inferior care.

When poor people do decide to seek treatment (often they wait until they are seriously ill), they tend to visit a clinic rather than a private or family physician. At the clinic, they may feel self-conscious about their appearance. Frequently they must wait for hours in crowded waiting rooms and generally receive impersonal care. A trusting relationship with a physician seldom develops. Doctors generally

CASE EXHIBIT 15.2

Understanding and Reducing Stress

Seaward documents that rational and positive thinking has a major impact in promoting healing and maintaining health and that irrational and negative thinking is a major determinant of stress-related illnesses. (Thinking is irrational if it does one or more of the following: is inconsistent with objective reality, hampers you in protecting your life, hampers you in achieving short and long-term goals, causes significant trouble with other people, and leads you to feel unwanted emotions.) Stress-related physiological and psychological disorders have now become our number-one health problem.[a]

A simplified description of the effect of our thinking processes in creating stress-related illnesses is outlined as follows:

Stressor {
Events or experiences
↓
Certain kinds of self-talk
(For example, "This is a very dangerous situation.")
↓

Stress {
Emotions
(Such as tenseness, anxiety, worry, alarm)
↓

Stress {
Physiological reactions
The alarm stage of the general stress reaction will occur. The physiological changes of this alarm stage include an accelerated heart and pulse rate, shallow respiration, perspiring hands, tenseness of the neck and upper back, a rise in red blood count for fighting infection, increased metabolism, and secretion of proinflammatory hormones.[b] The physiological reactions that most students experience prior to giving a speech before a group illustrate the components of this alarm stage.

↓

Stress-related disorders
(If the emotional and physiological reactions are intensive and long term, a stress-related disease is apt to develop—such as an ulcer, migraine headache, diarrhea, heart problems, digestive problems, cancer, hypertension, bronchial asthma, hay fever, arthritis, enuresis, certain skin problems, and/or constipation.)

According to the above formula, there are two components of a "stressor": (a) the event and (b) the self-talk that we give ourselves about that event. Stress is the emotional and physiological reaction to a stressor. Self-talk plays a key role in

producing stress. The self-talk approach enables us to understand how positive (as well as negative events) can lead to a stress reaction. For example:

Positive event
Receiving a promotion
↓

Self-talk
"I now will have additional responsibilities that I may or may not be able to handle."
"If I fail at these new responsibilities, I will be fired and will be a failure. My career plans will never be realized."
"This promotion will make others in the office jealous."
"I'm in big trouble."
↓

Emotion
Worry, tension, anxiety
↓

Physiological reaction
Alarm stage of the general stress reaction
↓

Stress-related disorder
After a prolonged period of self-talk worries, a stress-related illness (such as ulcers or high blood pressure) develops.

Stress can be reduced in three primary ways. One way is to identify irrational and negative self-talk and then give yourself rational self-challenges (see Chapter 5 for examples of this approach). A second way is to become involved in activities that you enjoy, which will lead you to stop your irrational thinking and instead focus on events you view more positively. For example, if you enjoy golf, playing golf will lead you to stop thinking about your day-to-day problems and instead lead you to think about the enjoyable experiences associated with golfing. Activities that are likely to stop your irrational thinking include hobbies, entertainment events, jogging and other exercise programs, biofeedback programs, muscle relaxation exercises, and meditation.[c] A third way to reduce stress is to change the event that is producing it (for example, taking a job that you view as having less pressure).

[a]Brian L. Seaward, *Managing Stress*, 4th ed. (Sudbury, MA: Jones and Bartlett Publishers, 2004).
[b]Hans Selye, *The Stress of Life* (New York: McGraw-Hill, 1965).
[c]These stress-reducing techniques are described in Seaward, *Managing Stress.*

come from the middle and upper classes and therefore may face barriers in establishing rapport with low-income and non-White patients. Seham notes:

In general, health professionals have little—if any— understanding of the lifestyle of the poor. For a doctor to advise a patient who is living in poverty to increase his intake of protein, without helping

him to work out how to do it, is useless. Similarly, to suggest to a working mother that she come to the clinic for weekly treatments, when the clinic hours coincide with her working hours, is tantamount to not providing treatment at all.[25]

Being poor promotes poor health. The poor cannot afford to eat properly, so inadequate diet makes

CASE EXHIBIT 15.3

Traumas and Stress Disorders

Physical trauma is an injury to the body caused by violence or accident, such as a fracture. Psychological trauma is an emotional wound or shock, often having long-lasting effects. Physical traumas often lead to psychological traumas.

Traumatic experiences often involve a threat to life or safety, but any situation that leaves one feeling overwhelmed and alone can be traumatic, even if it does not involve physical harm. It's not the objective facts that determine whether an event is traumatic, but one's subjective emotional experience of the event.

A stressful event is most likely to be traumatic if:

- It happened unexpectedly.
- One is unprepared for it.
- It happened repeatedly.
- One felt powerless to prevent it.
- Someone was intentionally cruel.

Traumas can come in a huge variety of ways. The following is a short list: serving in combat in the military, being physically or sexually abused as a child, a sexual assault, an auto accident, the breakup of a significant relationship, a humiliating or deeply disappointing experience, and the discovery of a life-threatening illness or disabling condition.

People are more likely to be traumatized by a stressful experience if they are already under a heavy stress load or have recently suffered a series of losses. Not all potentially traumatic events lead to lasting psychological and emotional damage. Some people rebound quickly from even the most shocking and tragic experiences, whereas others are devastated by experiences that appear on the surface to be "mildly upsetting."

Traumatic experiences in childhood can have a severe and long-lasting impact. Children who have been traumatized see the world as a dangerous and frightening place. When childhood trauma is unresolved, this sense of fear and helplessness carries over into adulthood, setting the stage for further trauma.

Emotional symptoms of trauma include:

- Denial, shock, or disbelief
- Anxiety and fear
- Withdrawing from others
- Feeling numb or disconnected
- Anger, irritability, and mood swings
- Confusion and difficulty concentrating
- Guilt, self-blame, and shame
- Feeling hopeless or sad

Physical symptoms of trauma include:

- Aches and pains
- Fatigue
- Muscle tension
- Being startled easily
- Racing heartbeat
- Agitation and edginess
- Difficulty concentrating

These emotional and physical symtoms gradually fade *if* the impacted person makes progress in coming to terms with the trauma. But even if the person is progressing in resolving the trauma, the person may be troubled from time to time by painful memories and emotions. Triggers for reliving the painful event include anniversaries of the event and sounds and images of the situation that remind the traumatized individual of the traumatic experience.

There are two stress disorders associated with severe traumas: acute stress disorder and posttraumatic stress disorder (PTSD). Acute stress disorder is an anxiety disorder in which fear and related symptoms are experienced soon after a traumatic event and last less than a month.

Posttraumatic stress disorder is an anxiety disorder in which fear and related symptoms continue to be experienced long after a traumatic event.

Primary symptoms of PTSD include flashbacks or intrusive memories, living in a constant state of "red alert," and avoid things that remind the impacted person of the traumatic event.

Working through trauma can be painful, scary, and potentially retraumatizing. The "healing" work is best done with a competent trauma expert. Trauma treatment involves:

- Processing the trauma memories and feelings
- Discharging the pent-up emotions/energy associated with the trauma
- Learning how to control strong emotions
- Rebuilding the capacity to trust other people

Treatment approaches for PTSD include the following:

- Cognitive-behavioral therapy, such as rational therapy (described in Chapter 5), in which the person learns to reframe the disturbing traumatic thoughts.
- Antianxiety drugs, which help control the anxieties and tensions associated with PTSD. Such medication provides some relief, but needs to be combined with a "talk" therapy approach.
- Eye movement desensitization and reprocessing (EMDR), which incorporates elements of cognitive-behavioral therapy, while the impacted persons move their eyes in a rhythmic manner from side to side while flooding their minds with images of the objects and situations they try to avoid. These back-and-forth eye movements are thought to work by "unfreezing" traumatic memories, which then can be processed and resolved.

CASE EXHIBIT 15.4

Our Thoughts Impact Our Physiological Functioning: Healing Thoughts versus Disease-Facilitating Thoughts

Diseases and medical conditions are caused by a variety of factors: what we eat; exposure to germs, viruses, and bacteria; genetics; too much or too little sun; lack of exercise; lack of sleep; and thoughts. The following are examples of how our thoughts impact our physiological functioning:

1. Under hypnosis, "I will feel no pain" → painless surgery without anesthesia.
2. Under hypnosis, "Something hot is burning my arm" → blister.
3. Deep breathing relaxation, "I am relaxing" → painless dental drilling without anesthesia.
4. "I no longer want to live" → death in a few years.
5. "I don't want to die yet" → ravaged by cancer, person continues to live.
6. When having a cold, "I must get all these things done" → cold lingers for weeks. When having a cold, "I will take time off to rest and relax" → cold ends after a few days.
7. Hangover, "This pain is killing me" → intense pain. Hangover, "I will relax and ignore the pain" → pain soon subsides (the same is true for most other headaches).
8. "I am worried about such and such," or "I have SO much to do tomorrow" → inability to fall asleep.
9. "I will have serious complications if I have this surgery" → greater likelihood of complications.
10. "This plane I'm going to fly on is going to crash" → anxiety, panic attacks. (Panic attacks, if frequent, will lead to a variety of illnesses, including hypertension and heart problems.)
11. A woman thinking she's pregnant, but she isn't → morning sickness and enlarged stomach.
12. Thinking relaxing thoughts → immune system functions well, fights off illnesses, and facilitates healing.

13. Thinking alarming thoughts (such as I miss___ SO much!) → high stress level → a variety of illnesses—such as heart problems, colitis, stomach problems, skin rashes, ulcers, aches and pains, headaches, cancer, colds, flus, and so forth. (Immune system is suppressed when a person is under high levels of stress.)
14. "I will do well today in this sport, by focusing on" → being good at tennis, golf, bowling, baseball, and so forth.
15. "I am too fat; by controlling my eating, I can control part of my life" → anorexia and a variety of health problems.
16. "By throwing up after eating I can maintain my weight and figure, and also enjoy the good taste of food" → bulimia and a variety of health problems.
17. "I need several drinks each day to get through the day and numb my pain" → alcoholism.
18. "I love food SO much, I don't care what happens to me" → compulsive overeating, obesity, diabetes, and a variety of other health problems.
19. "I need to get more work done, in a shorter time, for the next 10 years" → Type A personality, hypertension, heart problems, and strokes.
20. "I will never forgive___ for what s/he did," or "I'll get even with her/him if it's the last thing I do in life" → hostility, and heart problems and strokes.
21. "Sex is disgusting," or "My partner stinks," or "My partner is inept at lovemaking" → lack of sexual arousal, and other sexual dysfunctions.

NOTE: This exhibit suggests that positive and optimistic thoughts reduce stress, facilitate optimum functioning of our immune system, and have healing qualities. Negative thoughts increase stress levels, suppress the functioning of our immune system, and facilitate the chances of diseases developing.

them more susceptible to illnesses. They are more likely to live in the most polluted areas, so they are more susceptible to cancer, emphysema, and other respiratory diseases. They cannot afford proper housing, have less heat in the wintertime, and are more exposed to disease-carrying rodents and garbage. Their lives are more stress filled, particularly with respect to financial concerns. They are less likely to know about and use preventive health approaches. They are less likely to seek early treatment that would prevent a serious disorder from developing. Because they are sometimes treated with hostility and contempt by physicians and other

medical personnel, they are likely to avoid seeking medical help.

Low-Quality Health Care for Older Adults

As noted in Chapter 14, the proportion of older adults in our society is increasing dramatically, and the old-old (age 85 and over) are our fastest-growing age group. Today there is a crisis in health care for older adults for a variety of reasons.

Older adults are much more likely to have long-term illnesses. In the 1960s, the Medicare and Medicaid programs were created to pay for much of their medical expenses. However, in the 1980s, the Reagan and Bush administrations decided that the government could no longer pay the full costs of that care. As a result, cuts were made in eligibility for payments and limits were set for what the government will pay for a variety of medical procedures.[26]

Physicians are trained primarily in treating the young and are often less interested in serving older adults. Accordingly, when older adults become ill, they may not receive quality medical care.

Medical conditions of older adults are often misdiagnosed because doctors lack the specialized training to recognize the unique medical conditions of old people. Many older adults who are seriously ill do not get medical attention. One of the reasons physicians are less interested in treating older adults is that the Medicare program sets reimbursement limits on a variety of procedures. With younger patients, the fee-for-service system is much more profitable. There also are restrictions on hospital payments under Medicare.

Older adults who live in the community often have transportation difficulties in getting medical care. Those living in nursing homes sometimes receive inadequate care because health professionals are not interested in providing high-quality medical care for patients who no longer have much time to live. Medical care for our older adults is becoming a national embarrassment.

AIDS

Acquired immunodeficiency syndrome (AIDS) is a contagious, presently incurable disease that destroys the body's immune system. AIDS is caused by the human immunodeficiency virus (HIV), which is transmitted from one person to another primarily during sexual contact or through the sharing of intravenous drug needles and syringes.

A virus is a protein-coated package of genes that invades a healthy body cell and alters the normal genetic apparatus of the cell, causing it to reproduce the virus. In the process, the invaded cell is often killed. The HIV virus falls within a special category of viruses called *retroviruses*, so named because they reverse the usual order of reproduction within the cells they infect. HIV invades cells involved in the body's normal process of protecting itself from disease, and it causes these cells to produce more of the virus. Apparently HIV destroys normal white blood cells, which are supposed to fight off diseases invading the body. As a result, the body is left defenseless and can fall prey to other infections. The virus

devastates the body's immune or defense system so that other diseases occur and eventually cause death. Without a functioning immune system to combat germs, the affected person becomes vulnerable to bacteria, fungi, malignancies, and other viruses that may cause life-threatening illnesses, such as cancer, pneumonia, and meningitis.

In recent years, it has become clear that more than one virus is linked with the development of AIDS. The first virus to be identified, and the one that causes the largest number of AIDS cases, has been designated as human immunodeficiency virus type 1 (HIV-1). This virus appears to be the most virulent member of the growing family of AIDS and AIDS-related viruses. HIV is a formidable enemy in that it is constantly changing, or mutating, and is present in multiple strains. To simplify our discussion of AIDS in the following pages, we will refer to the infectious agent simply as HIV.

Most physicians today specialize in treating the young. The scarcity of doctors trained in geriatrics has compounded the crisis in health care for older adults.

HIV is a tiny delicate shred of genetic material. As far as scientists know, it can live only in a very limited environment. It prefers one type of cell—the T-helper cell in human blood. Outside of blood and other bodily fluids, the virus apparently dies.

Documented ways in which the AIDS virus can be transmitted are by having sexual intercourse with someone who has HIV, by using hypodermic needles that were also used by someone who has the virus, and by receiving contaminated blood transfusions or other products derived from contaminated blood. Babies can contract the AIDS virus before or at birth from their infected mothers and through breast milk.

HIV has been isolated in semen, blood, vaginal secretions, saliva, tears, breast milk, and urine. Only blood, semen, vaginal secretions, and to a much lesser extent, breast milk have been identified as capable of transmitting the AIDS virus. Many experts doubt whether there is enough of the virus present in tears and saliva for it to be transmitted in these fluids. Experts rule out casual kissing or swimming in pools as a means of contracting AIDS. Sneezing, coughing, crying, and shaking hands also have not proven to be dangerous. Only the exchange of body fluids (for example, through anal, oral, or genital intercourse) permits infection. The virus is very fragile and cannot survive long without a suitable environment, and it is not able to penetrate the skin. In sum, evidence has not shown that AIDS can be spread through any type of casual contact. You cannot get AIDS from doorknobs, toilets, or telephones. Also, it does not appear that HIV can be transmitted by blood-sucking insects such as mosquitos or ticks.

Few lesbians have contracted AIDS. Lesbians are at low risk unless they use intravenous drugs or have unsafe sexual contact with people in high-risk groups. Female-to-female transmission is possible, however, through vaginal secretions or blood.

Women who use sperm from an infected donor for artificial insemination are also at risk of infection. Donors should be screened by licensed sperm banks as a preventive measure.

After an individual is exposed to the virus, it usually becomes inactive. Once it is in the body, it apparently needs help to stay active. Such help might include the person's history of infections with certain other viruses, generally poor health, the abuse of certain recreational drugs (such as butyl nitrite), malnutrition, and genetic predisposition. For those

©Christian Martinez Kempin/Syldavia/iStockphoto.com

HIV may be transmitted by reusing contaminated needles and syringes.

who do develop AIDS, the mortality rate is very high.

In the early 1980s, the AIDS virus was transmitted in some cases through blood transfusions. Today the blood used in transfusions is tested for the presence of antibodies to the AIDS virus, making transmission in this way unlikely. Because antibodies do not form immediately after exposure to the virus, a newly infected person may unknowingly donate blood after becoming infected but before his or her antibody test becomes positive.

Most people infected by HIV will eventually develop AIDS. The length of time between initial infection of HIV and the appearance of AIDS symptoms is called the incubation period for the virus. The average incubation period (prior to the development of recent drugs) was estimated to be 7 to 11 years.[27] There is considerable variation, however, ranging from a few months (particularly for babies who are HIV positive) to 20 years or more.

The drug azidothymidine (AZT) has been found to delay the progress of the disease in some people. First synthesized in 1964 and initially developed as a cancer drug, AZT helps to extend life and provide hope. It does not cure AIDS, and there are some serious side effects with the drug. AZT or Retrovir (its brand name) must be taken every 4 hours both night and day. People often experience very uncomfortable side effects. These include nausea, headaches, anemia, lowered white blood cell counts, liver function changes, kidney effects, and bone marrow damage. The longer the drug is taken, the more likely the person is to experience side effects with increasing severity. Additionally, the drug is very difficult to manufacture, involving 17 chemical steps plus 6 more steps to make it marketable. The result is scarcity and high costs. Nonetheless, the existence of a drug that at least can delay the effects of such a devastating disease has provided hope and has fought the black curtain of pessimism that has shrouded AIDS.

Critical Thinking Question

Do you adhere to safe-sex practices, or are you putting yourself at risk for acquiring a sexually transmitted disease?

Other drugs to combat the AIDS virus are being developed. In 1991 the Food and Drug Administration approved didanosine (DDI) for treatment of adults and children with advanced AIDS who cannot tolerate or are not helped by AZT.[28] In 1995 and 1996, the Food and Drug Administration approved several drugs called protease inhibitors, which fight HIV by snipping an enzyme the virus needs before it can infect human blood cells. Combining AZT with some of these protease inhibitors is delaying substantially the progression of AIDS in people who are HIV infected.

In recent years another class of drugs called nonnucleoside reverse transcriptase inhibitors (NNRTIs) has been added to the arsenal of HIV drugs. Patients now mix and match these drugs in complicated, individually tailored combinations. These "cocktail" drugs are not cheap, costing $10,000 to $12,000 a year per patient.[29]

A major health problem involves people who are HIV positive but have no symptoms of AIDS. Most of these individuals have not been tested for the AIDS virus and therefore are unaware they have it. They may then infect others, although they experience no life-threatening symptoms themselves. The following is a summary of high-risk factors in contracting AIDS:

- Having multiple sex partners without using safe-sex practices (such as using condoms). The risk of infection increases according to the number of sexual partners, male or female. In considering the risks of acquiring AIDS, a person should heed the warning, "When you have sex with a new partner, you are going to bed not only with this person but also with all this person's previous sexual partners."
- Sharing intravenous needles. HIV may be transmitted by reusing contaminated needles and syringes.
- Having anal intercourse with an infected person.
- Having sex with prostitutes. Prostitutes are at high risk because they have multiple sex partners and often are intravenous drug users.

Sexually active heterosexual adolescents and young adults are increasingly becoming a high-risk group for contracting HIV. People in this age group tend to be sexually active with multiple sex partners. The risk of male-to-female transmission through sexual intercourse is higher than that of female-to-male. As noted, the risk of woman-to-woman transmission through sexual contact appears low. Although multiple exposures to HIV infection through sexual intercourse are not necessary for transmission, multiple sexual partners increase the likelihood that transmission will occur.

Lloyd describes the ways in which sexual transmission of HIV can be prevented or reduced:

Only two methods of completely preventing sexual transmission have been identified: (1) abstaining from sex or (2) having sexual relations only with a faithful and uninfected partner. The risk of infection through sexual intercourse can be reduced by practicing what has been called "safe sex," which is using a condom for all sexual penetration (vaginal, oral, and anal) whenever there is any doubt about a sexual partner's HIV status; engaging in nonpenetrative sexual activity; limiting the number of sexual partners; and avoiding sexual contact with people such as prostitutes who have had many partners.[30]

Some people believe that any contact with someone who is HIV positive will guarantee illness and death. Such fears are not justified. Body fluids

CASE EXHIBIT 15.5

Second Opinion Saved Her Life

Ruthann Robson was diagnosed with a rare (and usually fatal) cancer called abdominal liposarcoma. She was referred to a respected oncologist. The oncologist recommended two protocols of chemotherapy. Over the course of 4 months, the first chemotherapy treatment, and then the second, failed to shrink the malignant tumor on her side. The oncologist then became pessimistic about other forms of treatment, including those that Ms. Robson researched on the Internet. Ms. Robson, for example, suggested surgery, but her oncologist stated that the tumor was too large to be removed and that the cancer had metastasized to her liver. The oncologist's only suggestion, which she made repeatedly, was tranquilizers and a referral to a psychiatrist to help her deal with "it" (the oncologist's word for her upcoming death).

When Ms. Robson asked for a referral for a second opinion, the oncologist indicated that would be fruitless. "This is the most famous cancer center in the world," she was reminded.

In desperation, after many sleepless nights, Ms. Robson concluded her most rational alternative was to inform her oncologist she was leaving as a patient and request the name of another oncologist she could contact. With little objection, the first oncologist did provide the name of another oncologist at a different hospital.

The second oncologist and other medical personnel at that hospital saved her life. This oncologist concluded the tumor could be successfully removed by surgery. It was removed, and the cancer had not metastasized. Her liver was perfectly healthy. Since the surgery, Ruthann Robson has been cancer free. Ms. Robson believes she owes her life to questioning the "terminal diagnosis" of her first oncologist and getting a second opinion.

SOURCE: Ruthann Robson, "Leaving My Doctor Saved My Life," *Self*, May 2001, pp. 152–153.

(such as fresh blood, semen, urine, and vaginal secretions) infected with the virus must enter the bloodstream for the virus to be transmitted from one person to another. Gay men account for so many AIDS cases because they are likely to engage in anal intercourse. Anal intercourse often results in a tearing of the lining of the rectum, which allows infected semen to get into the bloodstream. Sharing a needle during mainlining a drug with someone who is carrying the virus is also dangerous because it involves transmission of blood. A small amount of the previous user's blood is often drawn into the needle and then injected directly into the bloodstream of the next user.

Currently, there is no evidence that the virus can be spread by "dry" mouth-to-mouth kissing. There is a theoretical risk of transmitting HIV through vigorous "wet" or deep tongue kissing, as infected blood may be transmitted from one person to the other.

Several tests have been developed to determine if a person has been exposed to the virus. These tests do not directly detect the virus—only the antibodies a person's immune system develops to fight the virus.

The origin of AIDS is unknown, although there have been a variety of speculations. (We probably never will be able to identify the origin, particularly now that AIDS has spread throughout the world.)

People with the AIDS virus are now classified as being either HIV asymptomatic (without symptoms of AIDS) or HIV symptomatic (with symptoms). HIV invades a group of white blood cells (lymphocytes) called T-helper cells or T-4 cells. These cells in turn produce other cells, which are critical to the body's immune response in fighting off infections. When HIV attacks T-4 helper cells, it stops them from producing immune cells that fight off disease. Instead, HIV converts T-4 cells so that they begin producing HIV. Eventually the infected person's number of healthy T-4 cells is so reduced that infections cannot be fought off.

Once a person is infected with HIV, several years usually go by before symptoms of AIDS appear. Initial symptoms include dry cough, abdominal discomfort, headaches, oral thrush, loss of appetite, fever, night sweats, weight loss, diarrhea, skin rashes, tiredness, swollen lymph nodes, and lack of resistance to infection. (Many other illnesses have similar symptoms, so it is irrational for people to conclude they are developing AIDS if they have some of these symptoms.) As AIDS progresses, the immune system is less and less capable of fighting off "opportunist" diseases, making the infected person vulnerable to a variety of cancers, nervous system degeneration, and infections caused by other viruses, bacteria, parasites, and fungi. Ordinarily, opportunistic infections are not life threatening to people with healthy immune systems, but they can be fatal to people with AIDS, whose immunological functioning has been severely compromised.

The serious diseases that afflict people with AIDS include Kaposi's sarcoma (an otherwise rare form of cancer that accounts for many AIDS deaths), pneumocystic carinii pneumonia (a lung disease that is also a major cause of AIDS deaths), and a variety of other generalized opportunistic infections, such as shingles (herpes zoster), encephalitis, severe fungal infections that cause a type of meningitis, yeast infections of the throat and esophagus, and infections of the lungs, intestines, and central nervous system. The incidence of tuberculosis, a disease once nearly eradicated in the United States, has escalated in recent years due largely to the epidemic of HIV infection and AIDS.

Initially, HIV infection was diagnosed as AIDS only when the immune system became so seriously impaired that the infected individual developed one or more severe, debilitating diseases, such as Kaposi's sarcoma or pneumocystic carinii pneumonia. However, on April 1, 1992, the Centers for Disease Control broadened its definition of AIDS; now anyone who is infected with HIV and has a helper T-cell count of 200 cells per cubic millimeter of blood or less is said to have AIDS, regardless of other symptoms that person may or may not have. (Normal helper T-cell counts in healthy people not infected with HIV range from 800 to 900 per cubic millimeter of blood.)

AIDS as a syndrome is not any one specific disease. It simply makes those infected by the virus increasingly more vulnerable to any disease that might come along. The process of AIDS involves a continuum whereby those affected become more and more vulnerable to devastating diseases.

In some patients, AIDS may attack the nervous system and cause damage to the brain. This deterioration, called AIDS-dementia complex, occurs gradually over a period of time (sometimes a few years). Several specific intellectual impairments may result from AIDS. These include inability to concentrate, forgetfulness, inability to think quickly and efficiently, visuospatial problems that make it difficult to get from place to place or to perform complex and simultaneous tasks, and slowed motor ability. It is interesting to note that while people with Alzheimer's disease experience deterioration in language capacity and the ability to learn, people with AIDS do not seem to be affected in these areas.

Contrary to popular belief, people who are HIV positive can live for an indeterminately long time. At this time there is no cure for AIDS. Currently, extensive research is being undertaken to better understand, prevent, and fight AIDS.

Prevention can be pursued in two major ways. First, people can abstain from activities and behaviors that put them at risk for contracting the disease. Second, scientists can work on developing a vaccine to prevent the disease, just as there are vaccines that prevent polio and measles. A vaccine might either block the virus from attacking a person's immune system or bolster the immune systems so that HIV is unable to invade it.

It is advisable to use a condom when having sexual intercourse with a new partner until you are certain the person is not HIV positive. You cannot acquire AIDS from someone who is not infected by HIV.

In June 1998, the U.S. Supreme Court ruled that people infected by HIV (including those having AIDS) are covered by the 1990 Americans with Disabilities Act, which protects those with a disability against discrimination in jobs, housing, and public accommodations.

AIDS is a global epidemic. AIDS is spreading at far different rates in different world regions. New HIV cases are slowly declining in North America. However, the infection is still at epidemic levels in Africa, and HIV incidence there is rising sharply.

HIV/AIDS has killed about 30 million people, and an estimated 40 million people worldwide are living with HIV infection.[31] About one-fourth of those living with HIV do not know they are infected.[32] HIV/AIDS is most prevalent in Africa, particularly sub-Saharan Africa. Africa is home to 60% of people infected with HIV.[33] About 1 in 12 African adults has HIV—most do not know they are infected.[34] It should be noted that millions of people are also infected with HIV in India, China, the Mediterranean region, Western Europe, Latin America, Russia, Eastern European countries, the Caribbean, and Central Asia. Mooney, Knox, and Schacht note:

The high rates of HIV in developing countries, particularly sub-Saharan Africa, are having alarming and devastating effects on societies. HIV/AIDS has reversed the gains in life expectancy made in sub-Saharan Africa, which peaked at 49 years in the late 1980s and fell to 46 years in 2005....

The HIV/AIDS epidemic creates an enormous burden for the limited health care resources of poor countries. Economic development is threatened by the HIV epidemic, which diverts national funds to health-related needs and reduces the size of a nation's workforce. AIDS deaths have left millions of orphans in the world....

Some scholars fear that AIDS-affected countries could become vulnerable to political instability as the growing number of orphans exacerbates poverty, and produces masses of poor young adults who are vulnerable to involvement in criminal activity and recruitment for insurgencies.[35]

The drugs used to treat an HIV infection are very expensive, which further complicates containing the HIV/AIDS epidemic in poor nations. Kornblum and Julian note:

Prospects for coping with the AIDS epidemic in poor nations are particularly gloomy because of the high cost of advanced treatments. In the United States the cost of the multidrug therapy that has proven effective in suppressing the deadly AIDS symptoms can average $750 a month. This is a fortune for people in poor nations like South Africa, where about 8 percent of the population is HIV positive and the annual per capita income is $6,000.[36]

Controversy over the Use of Life-Sustaining Equipment

Medical technology has made dramatic advances in this century. Today we can keep alive for months, and in many cases years, people who in the past would have died.

Even after a person's brain has stopped functioning, technology can keep the respiratory processes, the heart, the liver, and other vital organs functioning for months. The lives of those who are terminally ill can be prolonged for substantial periods of time, but they may experience considerable pain and will be in a deteriorated condition. Many controversial issues have arisen about the use of life-sustaining technology. How should death now be defined, as vital functions can be kept going even when the brain is dead? Some lawsuits have already been filed in organ donor cases in which organs allegedly were removed before the donor was deceased. Should the lives of the terminally ill be prolonged when there is practically no hope for recovery and the patients are in severe pain? Should society seek to keep alive people who have such a severe and profound cognitive disability that they cannot (and will never be able to) walk or sit up? Should abortion be mandatory if major genetic defects are detected in the fetus? When should life-prolonging efforts be used, and when should the patient be allowed to die? If terminally

ill people who are in severe pain want to end their life by suicide, should they be legally allowed to—and should others (such as physicians and close relatives) be legally allowed to assist in such suicides?

Because of the adverse consequences of being kept alive indefinitely when there is no hope of recovery, an increasing number of people are signing "living wills." In a living will, a person stipulates in writing that, if he or she becomes physically or mentally disabled from a life-threatening illness from which there is no reasonable expectation of recovery, she or he wants to be allowed to die and not be kept alive by artificial means. A living will is not binding, but it conveys a patient's wishes to those (such as relatives and attending physicians) who must make a decision about whether to use life-sustaining equipment. To complement living wills, a number of states have enacted legislation enabling adults to authorize (by filling out a Power of Attorney for Health Care form) other individuals (called health-care agents) to make health-care decisions on their behalf if they become incapacitated.

Critical Thinking Questions
Have you signed a living will? If not, why not?

The President's Commission for the Study of Ethical Problems in Medicine and Biomedical and Behavioral Research recommended in 1981 that all states define death as occurring when either of the following is judged to have taken place: (a) the irreversible cessation of circulatory and respiratory functions (this is essentially the definition used in the past) or (b) irreversible cessation of all functions of the entire brain, including the brainstem (this is a new definition). In adopting the "whole-brain concept," the commission rejected a more controversial argument that death should be deemed to occur when "higher-brain functions" (those controlling consciousness, thought, and emotions) are lost. Patients who have lost higher-brain functions but retain the brainstem functions can persist for years in a chronic vegetative state. Many states have now incorporated this definition of death into their statutes.

The High Cost of Medical Care

Health-care costs have risen dramatically in the past 40 years. Expenditures on health care as a percentage

CASE EXHIBIT 15.6

How Should Financial Resources Be Allocated?

Fiscal conservatives argue that our society cannot afford widespread use of medical technology to prolong the lives of people who will not be productive in the future. They point to cases such as that of Geri D., which they say is proof that too much money is already being spent in some health care situations.

At 5 months of age, Geri D. is in a residential facility for persons with a severe developmental disability. The annual cost there is more than $300,000. Geri was born prematurely with multiple medical problems, including cardiovascular dysfunc-

tions. Lifesaving technology kept her alive. She has a profound cognitive disability—she will never be able to sit up, a developmental milestone that children of average intelligence achieve at 6 months of age. Already, more than $250,000 has been spent on this child. By the time she becomes a young adult, more than $5 million will have been spent on keeping her alive.

With medical advances, our society will face increasingly difficult issues regarding how financial resources should be used.

of this country's total production of goods and services have increased from 9% in 1980 to 25% at the present time.[37] The United States spends more than $1 trillion a year on health care—an average of $6,947 per person each year for health care.[38] In comparison, Canada and Great Britain spend half as much.[39] The United States spends substantially more on health care per person than any other country. These high costs are now recognized as a matter of national concern. There are many reasons why health expenses are so high and continue to increase more rapidly than the rate of inflation.

First, as we've seen, one of the objectives of the health-care system is to make a profit. There are few controls designed to keep fees and prices down. Although the United States uses a marketplace approach to health care, ill consumers are not in a position to shop around for medical treatment. If they are suffering, their priority is to feel better, so they are willing to pay whatever a doctor chooses to charge. Most patients are not even informed before receiving treatment what the physician will charge. Fees for doctors' services are not advertised and therefore are not subjected to the competition that exists elsewhere in marketplace systems. Physicians have successfully established a public image in which they are so revered that most patients will sit for an hour in a waiting room without complaining and will be reluctant to ask questions about charges before receiving treatment. (The same individuals don't hesitate to voice their frustrations about having to stand in line for 5 minutes at a checkout counter in a store.)

Another factor in the high cost of health care is dramatic technological advances in lifesaving treatment interventions. New equipment, along with the

cost of highly skilled personnel to operate it, is expensive. Forty years ago, we did not have cobalt machines, heart pacemakers, magnetic resonance imaging (MRI) equipment, artificial heart valves, and microsurgical instruments that enable doctors to perform surgery under a microscope. Coleman and Kerbo note that there are huge profits in developing new medical procedures and new drugs, and as a result, attention has been diverted away from less expensive (and often more effective) techniques of preventive medicine.[40] Klein and Castleman assert, "The processes that drive medical research toward expensive treatments also turn it away from preventive measures that do not hold the promise of corporate profit."[41]

Yet another reason is the increased life span of Americans. Now a larger proportion of our population is old, and older adults require more health care than younger people. Many technically and professionally trained groups (such as nurses and physical therapists) are demanding salaries consistent with their training and responsibilities. These higher salaries are reflected, of course, in the overall costs of medical treatment.

Another contributor is the fact that third-party financing is increasingly paying medical bills. Historically, medical bills were primarily charged to and paid by consumers. Now most bills are charged to and paid by third parties, including private insurance companies and the public Medicare and Medicaid programs. Physicians are more likely to recommend expensive diagnostic and treatment procedures if they feel such procedures will not be a financial burden to the patient. Third-party payments also tempt some physicians to perform surgeries that may be unnecessary.

The increase in malpractice suits is also a contributing factor. Juries in many cases have awarded large settlements when malpractice is judged to have occurred. Physicians are required by law to carry malpractice insurance, with annual premiums ranging from $5,000 to more than $90,000, depending on a variety of factors—including geographic area and field of practice.[42] (Neurosurgeons and anesthesiologists are often charged the highest rates because their fields are considered "high risk.") These premium costs are, of course, passed on to consumers.

The tendency toward increased specialization by doctors is another factor. At present, about 92% of physicians have a specialty.[43] The growth of medical knowledge has encouraged specialization; it is impossible today for a physician to be an expert in all medical areas. However, specialists charge more than general practitioners to receive compensation for their additional training and expertise. Specialization also raises costs because patients often are required to consult with (and pay) two or more physicians for each illness that they have. (A serious additional problem caused by specialization is that medical care becomes impersonal, dehumanized, and fragmented because patients now rarely establish a trusting, long-term relationship with one physician.)

Hospital care is extremely expensive. Hospitals compete with one another to offer the most prestigious and expensive equipment, which often leads to a duplication of expensive and seldom-used technology. And hospitals, similar to physicians, are not subjected to fees set by consumers on a supply-and-demand basis. Patients generally are not able to shop around for the hospital they want to go to.

Hospitals, physicians, nursing home operators, and drug companies are politically powerful. Health-care providers are represented by such influential organizations as the American Medical Association, the Pharmaceutical Manufacturers Association, the American Hospital Association, and the American Association of Medical Schools. Health-care providers appear, at least at present, to have clout to prevent changes in health care that would sharply restrict their profits.

Financing Medical Care

Medical expenses are paid for by private insurance, through governmental programs, and by direct payments from the individual to the health-care provider. Most of the federal government health-care

bill is paid through Medicaid, SCHIP, and Medicare. (The government also participates in the health insurance of federal employees, provides medical programs for families of members of the armed forces, and supports Veterans Affairs hospitals.) The government is also beginning to participate in financing Obamacare.

Medicaid

This program was established in 1965 by an amendment (Title XIX) to the Social Security Act. Medicaid provides medical care primarily for recipients of public assistance. It enables states to make direct payments to hospitals, doctors, medical societies, and insurance agencies for services provided to those on public assistance. The federal government shares the expense with states on a 55% to 45% basis. Medical expenses that are covered include diagnosis and therapy performed by a surgeon, physician, and dentist; nursing services in the home or elsewhere; and medical supplies, drugs, and laboratory fees.

Under the Medicaid program, benefits vary from state to state. The original legislation encouraged states to include coverage of all self-supporting people whose marginal incomes made them unable to pay for medical care. However, this inclusion was not mandatory, and "medical indigence" has generally been defined by states to provide Medicaid coverage primarily to recipients of public assistance.

Although the stated purpose of Medicaid was to ensure adequate health care to the nation's poor and near poor, the program actually covers fewer than half of all poor families.[44] This is because the federal government has restricted eligibility in order to cut costs. In the past, hospitals supported the uninsured by charging paying patients more. But after years of soaring costs, government and private insurers have rebelled against "cost shifting" by setting limits on what they will pay for services provided in hospitals. Many hospitals, unable to support the cost of indigent care, are turning these patients away. *A two-tiered system of health care is emerging in this country based on the ability to pay.*[45]

State Children's Health Insurance Program (SCHIP)

SCHIP is a U.S. federal government program created in 1997 that gives funds to states in order to provide health insurance to families with children. The program is designed to cover uninsured children in families with incomes that are modest, but too high to qualify for Medicaid. Like Medicaid, SCHIP is a partnership between federal and state governments. The programs are run by the individual states according to requirements set by the federal Centers for Medicare and Medicaid Services.

Within broad federal guidelines, states are given flexibility in designing their SCHIP eligibility requirements and policies. Some states have received authority through waivers of statutory provisions to use SCHIP funds to cover the parents of children receiving benefits from both SCHIP and Medicaid, pregnant women, and other adults.

Medicare

Older adults are the age group most afflicted with illnesses. People over age 65 now make up 14% of the population, and the percentage is increasing each year.[46]

In 1965 Congress enacted Medicare (Title XVIII of the Social Security Act). Medicare helps older adults pay the high cost of health care. It has two parts: hospital insurance (Part A) and medical insurance (Part B). Everyone age 65 or older who is entitled to monthly benefits under the Old Age, Survivors, Disability, and Health Insurance program gets Part A automatically, without paying a monthly premium. Practically everyone in the United States age 65 or older is eligible for Part B. Part B is voluntary, and beneficiaries are charged a monthly premium. Disabled people under age 65 who have been getting Social Security benefits for 24 consecutive months or more are also eligible for both Part A and Part B, effective with the 25th month of disability.

Part A—hospital insurance—helps pay for time-limited care in a hospital, in a skilled nursing facility (home), and for home health visits (such as visiting nurses). Coverage is limited to 150 days in a hospital and to 100 days in a skilled nursing facility. If patients are able to be out of a hospital or nursing facility for 60 consecutive days following confinement, they are again eligible for coverage. Covered services in a hospital or skilled nursing facility include the cost of meals and a semiprivate room, regular nursing services, drugs, supplies, and appliances. Part A also covers home health care on a part-time or intermittent basis if beneficiaries meet the following conditions: They are homebound, in need of skilled nursing care or physical or speech therapy, and services are ordered and regularly reviewed by a physician. Finally, Part A covers up to 210 days of hospice care for a terminally ill Medicare beneficiary.

Part B—supplementary medical services—helps pay for physicians' services, outpatient hospital services in an emergency room, outpatient physical and speech therapy, and a number of other medical and health services prescribed by a doctor, such as diagnostic services, X-ray or other radiation treatments, and some ambulance services.

Each Medicare beneficiary can choose coverage from an "alphabet soup" of health plans. This variety includes preferred provider organizations, provider service organizations, point-of-service plans, private fee-for-service plans, and medical savings accounts. (It is beyond the scope of this text to give detailed descriptions of these plans.)

Private Insurance

All health-care costs are rapidly rising, including the costs of health insurance. People who are not covered through group plans at their place of employment are increasingly finding it difficult to purchase private health insurance. An estimated 46 million Americans do not have health insurance.[47]

The majority of the uninsured are full-time and part-time workers and their children. Older adults qualify for Medicare, and the very poor who are unemployed qualify for Medicaid.

Obamacare

Obamacare was passed in 2010. The passage was achieved after a year of highly contentious debate in Congress; Republican leaders were unanimous in their opposition to the bill. Until 2010, the United States was one of the few developed countries that did not have a public health insurance program that was available to most citizens. In the past five decades, some members of Congress and a number of organizations have pressed for passage of a national health insurance program in the United States.

Prior to Obamacare, many people in the United States subscribed to private insurance plans, which were available to employed people and their families. Those who were marginally employed or unemployed were often not covered by health insurance.

Hospitals cannot survive without assured income for services provided. Physicians, as well, need to be paid for their services. Alarmingly, more than 46 million Americans (in 2012) are without private or government-sponsored health insurance.[48]

Proponents of a national health insurance plan state the following reasons why a national health insurance plan is needed. The rapid rise in health and insurance costs makes it impossible for the poor, for those of marginal income, and even for middle-class families to pay for insurance or extensive medical bills. The poor who are not covered by Medicaid cannot pay for even moderate medical expenses; as a result, they often forgo early treatment and develop more serious medical conditions. Medicare covers short-term hospitalization expenses for older adults but not long-term expenses. Extensive medical treatment can wipe out substantial savings and force a family deeply into debt, thereby dramatically changing its standard of living and lifestyle.

Starting with Franklin Roosevelt, every president except Ronald Reagan, George Bush, and George W. Bush, has proposed a national health insurance program—finally in 2010 Obamacare was passed.

The main objection to national health insurance revolves around the cost to taxpayers and the effect such an expensive new program will have on the economy. There is concern that such a program will escalate the costs of health care in a manner similar to what has happened with Medicare and Medicaid.

We will now turn to the provisions of Obamacare. The bill that was passed is over 2,000 pages long; so it is complex and rather difficult to accurately and concisely summarize.

The provisions of the bill are "phased in" over a several-year time period—to allow time for insurance companies, hospitals, and other participants to prepare and adjust. (The "phase-in" also took account of the fact that Obamacare was passed during an era of a severe economic recession; it was projected that the economy would gradually improve and thereby be better able to adjust to the gradual increases in the costs of the program.)

In 2010, insurance companies were barred from denying coverage to adults and children with preexisting conditions. This ends the ability of health insurance providers to reject coverage for people with preexisting conditions (such as AIDs and asthma). In addition, children are now permitted to stay on their parents' health insurance plan up to age 26; this provision is an important change for families with college-age members. Annual premium limits are also barred, a provision that also protects the insured from having their insurance canceled when they are diagnosed with a catastrophic illness.

By 2014, the most significant measures of Obamacare will go into effect, as millions of citizens will be added to the rolls of those with medical insurance and medical benefits. Of the 46 million people in the United States without health insurance, it is estimated that 37 million will then be covered by health insurance.[49] Every citizen will be required by 2014 to have medical insurance. An IRS penalty of $750 per individual or 2% of income—whichever is greater—goes into effect for any citizen who is not covered by an employer or a public plan (such as Medicaid or Medicare), and who chooses not to purchase health insurance. The centerpiece of Obamacare is this individual mandate, a provision that makes it mandatory for every citizen to purchase health insurance. (Some conservatives argue that this individual mandate violates the U.S. Constitution, as it may exceed the constitutional boundaries of congressional power.)

In June 2012, the U.S. Supreme Court ruled that the individual insurance mandate is a "tax," and thereby upheld the legality of Obamacare. (Opponents had argued that the individual mandate was a "product" and thereby the government under Obamacare was illegally forcing Americans to buy a product against their will.)

Critical Thinking Question

Do you believe Obamacare will improve health care in the United States, and be cost-effective?

By 2018 all insurance plans must offer preventive care with no co-payments and no deductibles.

The act's provisions are intended to be funded by a variety of taxes and offsets. Major sources of revenue include a much-broadened Medicare tax on incomes over $200,000 for individuals, and over $250,000 for joint filers. There will be an annual fee on insurance providers, and a 40% tax on "Cadillac" insurance policies (such plans have an annual cost exceeding $10,200 for individuals or $27,500 for a family). There are also taxes on pharmaceuticals, and on high-cost diagnostic equipment. Offsets are from anticipated cost savings; for example, it is asserted that those currently without health insurance will now be more apt under Obamacare to receive diagnoses at earlier stages (such as for cancer), and thereby receive earlier treatment and less costly care.

Medical Social Work

Many public and private social welfare agencies (such as public welfare departments, adoption agencies, family service agencies, neighborhood centers, and probation and parole departments) are perceived as primary settings for social workers. They are *primary* because they are often managed by social workers and because social work is their primary service. Hospitals, medical clinics, and schools are, on the other hand, *secondary* settings because their primary service is not social work. But this secondary focus does not reduce their importance for social work because health care and education serve a vital function and expend a substantial proportion of our national resources. Because social workers are not administratively in charge of secondary settings, problems related to status and influence sometimes arise. In such settings, it is important for social workers to learn to work with those in control. American doctors are the highest-paid professional group in our society, and they tend to expect a status consis-

tent with their salary. Some allied health professionals who work with physicians state that many doctors expect "godlike" respect.

The main setting for medical social work is the hospital. Dr. Richard C. Cabot first introduced social services into the Massachusetts General Hospital in Boston in 1905. Now almost every hospital has a social services department. In fact, a social services department is required by the American Hospital Association as a condition for accreditation. Social workers provide not only direct casework with patients and their families but also group work with certain patients, consultation, and training of other professionals. They also are involved in planning and policy development within the hospital and with various health agencies. At times medical social workers teach medical school courses in which they convey their professional knowledge of the sociopsychological components of illnesses and of the treatment process.

It is becoming increasingly recognized that psychological processes are causative factors in nearly

Peggy Fox/Jupiterimages

Medical social workers provide direct casework with patients and their families as well as group work, consultation, and training of other professionals.

CASE EXAMPLE 15.1

An Illustration of Medical Social Work

Janet Ely was hospitalized to have a hysterectomy because she had a tumor in her uterus. She is an attractive, single, 22-year-old woman.

Before the surgery, the nursing staff noted that she was apprehensive, depressed, and anxious. Following the operation, Ms. Ely became even more agitated and withdrawn. Her physician, again, fully answered her questions related to her hysterectomy. However, Ms. Ely appeared very concerned and confused about her future, making statements such as, "No one will ever marry me now," "Life isn't worth living," "My family doesn't care about me—no one does," and "Oh, well, I'm going to die soon anyway." At this point, her doctor asked Ms. Ely if she would be willing to discuss her concerns with the social worker at the hospital, Vicki Vogel, and she indicated she would.

Ms. Vogel met with Ms. Ely on 5 of the remaining 7 days of her hospitalization. Ms. Ely had a number of problems, primarily involving plans for her future. She had alienated nearly all her relatives when, at age 17, she quit school in her senior year and began living with her 20-year-old boyfriend. A year and a half later, her boyfriend discovered that she was having an affair with another man and demanded that she leave. She went to live with the other man and became rather heavily involved in drinking and experimenting with drugs. A year ago, Ms. Ely left this man and moved to this area. She is now living with a divorced man.

Ms. Ely continued to have a number of questions related to her hysterectomy: Would her sex life be changed? Might the cancer recur? Would the hysterectomy affect her future as a woman? Can a person be orgasmic following a hysterectomy?

Ms. Vogel attempted to provide some answers and also arranged for Debra Nass (a 32-year-old woman who had a hysterectomy 3 1/2 years ago) to talk with Ms. Ely. Although some uncertainty remained (for example, the possible recurrence of a malignancy), Ms. Ely became more comfortable about having undergone the hysterectomy after talking to Ms. Nass.

However, Ms. Ely had a number of questions that she felt she needed to look at. She wondered why, when people were nice to her, she sometimes was "rotten" to them. For instance, she had lived with two different men, and each time she continued to have sexual relationships with other men. She also wondered what the future held for her. She was not skilled at a trade or a profession and did not know what kind of a career, if any, she desired. She was very confused about what she wanted out of life and also admitted that she had occasional blackouts from heavy drinking.

These problems were briefly discussed with Ms. Vogel. The focus of social services at this hospital, however, was limited to short-term crisis counseling. Because these complicated problems indicated that longer-term counseling was needed, Ms. Vogel suggested, and Ms. Ely agreed to, a referral to the mental health center in the area.

Several months later, Ms. Vogel heard from a friend of hers that Ms. Ely had gotten engaged, but "on the spur of the moment" moved with another man to live on the West Coast.

Thus, the immediate psychological crisis situation surrounding the hysterectomy appears to have been resolved. However, problems remain in Ms. Ely's relationships with others.

---

every illness—in stress-related illnesses, alcoholism, depression, drug addiction, heart conditions, hypertension, and susceptibility to viruses, bacteria, and other infections. The patient's emotions and motivation for recovery also substantially affect the treatment process. Sexually transmitted diseases (including AIDS) and cirrhosis of the liver, for instance, may evoke feelings of shame and guilt because of the stigma attached to these illnesses. People with heart conditions need to learn how to relax, avoid continued stressful conditions, and follow a prescribed diet. A miscarriage may result in a wide variety of emotional reactions that need to be dealt with. Adjusting to a chronic or permanent disability also evokes a variety of negative psychological reactions. Medical treatment teams depend on social workers to attend to social and psychological factors that are either contributing causes of medical ailments or side effects of a medical condition.

Physicians consider social work an allied medical discipline. Along with doctors, nurses, and other therapists, social workers take part in the study, diagnosis, and treatment-planning processes for patients. A medical social worker frequently obtains important information on the living conditions, environment, habits, personality, and income of patients. Because physicians are no longer as well acquainted with patients, such information is often vital in arriving at a diagnosis and a treatment plan. Through interviews with the patient and members of his or her family, the worker gains a perspective on the social and emotional components of the illness and how these components may affect treatment.

In medical social work (now often referred to as social work in the health field), widely varying problems and situations are encountered. Social workers engage in the following activities:

- Helping terminally ill patients and their families cope
- Counseling women who have had a mastectomy
- Helping a low-income wife from a distant area find lodging in the community while her husband undergoes heart surgery
- Counseling people who are so depressed they are contemplating suicide
- Helping a single woman who has just become a mother to plan for the future
- Providing genetic counseling for a young couple who gave birth to a child with a cognitive disability
- Helping an executive of a large company make plans for the future following a severe heart attack
- Counseling a woman about her emotional reactions following a miscarriage or a stillbirth
- Being a support person to a hospitalized person with AIDS and to his or her friends and relatives
- Finding living arrangements that will provide some medical attention for people who no longer need to be hospitalized
- Counseling alcoholics and drug addicts or making appropriate referrals to other agencies
- Counseling patients who are apprehensive about undergoing surgery
- Helping someone suddenly struck with a permanent disability to adjust and make plans for the future
- Meeting with relatives and friends of patients to help interpret the nature of the medical condition and perhaps to solicit their help in formulating a treatment plan to facilitate recovery
- Counseling someone with emphysema on how to stop smoking
- Counseling a rape victim concerning her psychological reactions
- Informing relatives about the medical condition of someone who has just had a severe automobile accident

While dealing with such problems and situations, the social worker is almost always a member of a medical team headed by a physician.

The job of a social worker in the health field is a dynamic one that requires continued study. With the dramatic expansion of new therapy approaches for medical conditions (for example, organ transplants, new prescription drugs, extensive new surgery techniques), it is essential that medical social workers keep informed about new technological approaches.

Social work in hospitals tends to be short term and crisis oriented because there is generally a fairly rapid turnover of patients. Social workers are often involved in discharge planning (for example, making arrangements for patients to return to their families or to a convalescent home). In recent years, there has been a trend throughout the country to reduce the length of hospital stays to cut the costs of hospitalization. This trend has increased the importance of discharge planning (and thus of the services of social workers) in hospitals.

At times hospital social workers must act as advocates to ensure that the rights of patients are secured and that their needs are best served. Although social workers in medical settings are involved primarily in direct services to patients and their families, there are occasions when they engage in activity planning, administration of programs (for example, directing a hospice program so that terminal patients can live their final months in dignity), research, and education of other professionals.

The development of specialized clinics and programs—for providing genetics counseling; abortion services; family planning; services to people with AIDS or to people who are HIV positive; services to rape victims; services to the terminally ill; and treatment for alcoholics, drug abusers, and people with eating disorders—has created new opportunities for social workers in the health field. Sometimes these programs are located in offices away from hospitals. Nursing homes also are increasingly employing social workers.

One of the emerging fields of practice for social workers is combating AIDS. Social workers are getting involved in advocating for programs that will assist in reducing discrimination against those who are HIV positive or who have AIDS. They are also involved in counseling those who test HIV positive and in providing services in hospitals, residential treatment centers, nursing homes, and hospices to those who have AIDS. Social workers have become case managers for many people with AIDS. The case manager works with the AIDS patient, her or his loved ones, providers of care, and payers of health-care expenses to make certain that pressing medical, financial, social, and other needs are met and to ensure that the most cost-effective care possible is provided. In serving people with AIDS, the trend is to have more and more of the medical care delivered outside the hospital or nursing home, often at home or in an outpatient clinic.

There is also a trend for group medical clinics, individual practitioners, family practice clinics, and prepaid health clinics to employ social workers as part of a team in diagnosing and treating patients. Increasingly, social workers in such settings are working with high-risk groups, playing a preventive as well as a therapeutic role. High-risk groups include teenage mothers, women requesting abortions, drug and alcohol abusers, people undergoing organ transplants, severely depressed or highly anxious people, people under stress, people attempting suicide, amputees, and individuals with an eating disorder.

Counseling the Terminally Ill

One of the most difficult tasks of doctors, nurses, social workers, and other allied professionals in the health field is to help a terminally ill patient deal with dying. Death is a frightening event, and the fear of death is felt universally in all cultures.

Most people in our society die in a hospital. This setting, in itself, is one of the primary reasons why dying is so hard. Health professionals are committed to recovery—to healing. When someone is found to have a terminal illness, medical personnel experience a sense of failure. In some cases, health professionals may feel guilty that they cannot do more or that they might have made a mistake that contributed to the terminal illness. Many health professionals are not comfortable in counseling the terminally ill. They feel insecure and do not know what to say or do. Often they have not come to terms with their own mortality; that is, they have not come to see death as an integral part of their lives. If a professional person views death as a frightening, horrible, taboo topic, she or he will never be able to face it calmly and helpfully with a patient.

Dr. Elisabeth Kübler-Ross (perhaps the foremost authority on death and dying in our era) has identified five stages that terminally ill patients may go through[50] (see Case Exhibit 15.7). These stages are not absolute; not everyone goes through every stage according to the sequence described. (Some patients never advance beyond the first or second stage, and some patients vacillate from stage to stage.)

Critical Thinking Question

Reflect on a serious loss that you experienced such as the death of a loved one or someone breaking up with you. Did you experience the emotional reactions identified by Elisabeth Kübler-Ross?

The one thing that usually persists through all five stages is hope—hope for a "miracle" cure. All terminally ill patients seem to have a little bit of hope and are supported and nourished by it, especially during their most difficult times. With respect to hope, the desired direction in counseling is to be honest with the patient about the probable outcome while allowing the person to hope for the million-to-one chance of recovery.

To work with the terminally ill requires maturity, which comes only from experience. The most important communication is the "door-opening interview," in which the counselor conveys verbally and nonverbally to the dying patient that she or he is ready and willing to share the dying person's concerns without fear and anxiety. A prerequisite is that the counselors have an attitude toward their own death with which they are comfortable.

Mwalimu Imara views dying as potentially the final stage of growth and gives a number of suggestions on how to come to terms with one's own dying.[51] Having a well-developed sense of identity (that is, a sense of who you are) is an important step. (Chapter 2 in this text discusses ways to develop a positive identity.) This requires arriving at realistic life goals that you will have pride in achieving. Without a blueprint of what will give meaning and direction to our lives, we will experience our lives as fragmented and aimless.

Imara indicates that a dying patient at the stage of acceptance corresponds to a person with a healthy identity. An individual who comes to accept a terminal illness has also arrived at a fairly well-thought-out sense of himself or herself. Death is the final stage of growth in that the patient finally develops a unified sense of self and accepts imminent death. (Ideally, people will develop a healthy identity long before the final crisis and thus be fairly prepared before that crisis arises.)

According to Imara, all of us experience separations and pains throughout life that lead to personal growth—for example, leaving family to attend kindergarten, leaving high school to seek work or attend college, leaving work and friends to seek a better position in a different geographical area, and experiencing romantic and perhaps marital separations. Imara indicates that "abandoning old ways and breaking old patterns is like dying, at least dying to old ways of life for an unknown new life of meaning and relationships. But living without change is not living at all, not growing at all."[52] Making changes in our lives also creates fears and anxieties in us. But if such changes lead to personal growth, we will be

CASE EXHIBIT 15.7

Five Stages of Dying in the Terminally Ill

The following stages identified by Dr. Elisabeth Kübler-Ross have been found to be a valuable paradigm in understanding a terminally ill person's behavior:

Stage 1: Denial. "It can't be." "No, not me." "There must be a mistake." This is generally the first reaction when a person learns she or he has a terminal illness. Dr. Kübler-Ross believes such a reaction is functional because it helps cushion the impact that death will soon be inevitable.

Stage 2: Rage and anger. "Why me!" "Look at the good things I've done and still need to do for the members of my family." "This just isn't fair!" Patients resent the fact that they will soon die while others remain healthy and alive. God is frequently a special target of the anger during this stage, as God is viewed as unfairly imposing a death sentence. Dr. Kübler-Ross believes that such anger is inevitable, and that the patient should be allowed to express such anger. And she adds, "God can take it."

During this stage, family and hospital staff frequently experience difficulty in coping with the anger, which is displaced in many directions. The patient may charge that the doctor is incompetent, that the hospital surroundings are inhumane, that the nurses are unconcerned about people, that there is too much noise, and so on. The underlying reasons generating the patient's anger need to be remembered during this stage. Reacting personally or angrily to the patient's anger will only feed into that hostile behavior. During this stage, conveying to the patient that she or he is an important person who is worthy of respect, time, and understanding will usually lead to a reduction of angry demands.

Stage 3: Bargaining. "I realize my death is inevitable, but if I could just live 6 months more I could ..." During this stage, patients come to accept their terminal illness but try to strike bargains (frequently with God) for more time. They promise to do something worthwhile or to be good in exchange for another month or year of life. Dr. Kübler-Ross indicates that even agnostics and atheists sometimes attempt to bargain with God during this stage.

Stage 4: Depression. "Yes, it will soon be over." "It's really sad, but true." The first phase of this stage is when the patient mourns things not done, past losses, and wrongs committed. This type of depression is frequently exacerbated by guilt or shame about acts of omission or commission. Counseling during this phase generally focuses on helping the patient to resolve feelings of guilt and shame. In some cases, this may involve helping family members to make realistic plans for

their future and to reassure the patient that vital unfinished situations are being taken care of.

The second phase of this stage is when the patient enters a state of "preparatory grief," in which she or he is getting ready for the inevitable by taking into account impending losses. During this stage, the patient should not be encouraged to be cheerful; this would interfere with the necessity for the patient to contemplate his or her impending death. During this phase, the patient generally becomes quiet and does not want to see visitors. The patient is in the process of losing everything and everybody she or he loves. If the patient is allowed to express this sorrow, final acceptance of death will be much easier. In addition, the patient will be grateful to those who are able to sit quietly nearby, without telling him or her not to be sad. According to Dr. Kübler-Ross, when a dying patient no longer continues to request to see someone to discuss his or her situation, it is a sign that unfinished business is completed and the patient has reached the final stage.

Stage 5: Acceptance. "I will soon pass on, and it's all right." Dr. Kübler-Ross describes this final stage as "not a happy stage, but neither is it unhappy. It's devoid of feelings but it's not resignation; it's really a victory." During this stage, visitors often are not desired because the patient no longer is in a talkative mood. Communications with a counselor may become more nonverbal than verbal. Patients may just want to hold the counselor's hand–to sit together in silence with someone who is comfortable in the presence of a dying person.

Dr. Kübler-Ross notes that some patients continue grieving about their terminal illness without ever reaching the final stage of acceptance. She also notes that not everyone will progress through these stages as presented here. There is often considerable movement back and forth among stages. For example, a patient may go from denial to depression, to rage and anger, back to denial, then to bargaining, then to depression, and so on.

Note: These emotional reactions are not limited to being informed that one has a terminal illness. The reactions are apt to occur in anyone who has experienced a serious loss. Have you gone through similar emotional reactions when you have had a loss—such as someone breaking up with you, not getting the grade you wanted, or getting a speeding ticket?

SOURCES: Elisabeth Kübler-Ross, *On Death and Dying* (New York: Macmillan, 1969); Elisabeth Kübler-Ross, ed., *Death: The Final Stage of Growth* (Englewood Cliffs, NJ: Prentice Hall, 1975).

better prepared to face new challenges and new changes. Through a willingness to risk the unknown, we undertake the search for ourselves. Overcoming fears and anxieties that arise from current challenges (and learning more about ourselves through these experiences) helps prepare us for the fears and anxieties that will arise when we learn that our death is near.

CASE EXHIBIT 15.8

How to Cope with Grief

Nearly all of us are currently grieving about a loss that we have had. It might be the end of a romantic relationship, moving away from friends and parents, the death of a pet, failing to get a grade we wanted, or someone's death. Many people who are grieving experience the same emotional reactions (described earlier in this chapter) that were identified by Elisabeth Kübler-Ross: denial, rage and anger, bargaining, depression, and acceptance.

If you are grieving, try whichever of the following suggestions you believe will be most useful.

- Crying is an acceptable and valuable expression of grief. Cry as you feel the need. Crying releases the tension that is part of grieving.
- Talking about your loss and your plans for the present and the future is very constructive. Sharing your grief with friends, family, the clergy, or a professional counselor is advisable. You may want to become involved with a support group of people who are having similar experiences. Talking about your grief eases loneliness, allows you to vent your feelings, and helps you to accept your loss and make constructive plans for the present and the future. Talking with close friends gives you a sense of security and brings you closer to others you love. Talking with others who have similar losses helps put your problems into perspective; you will see that you are not the only one with problems, and you will feel good about yourself when you assist others in handling their losses.
- Disabilities often cause us to examine and question our faith or philosophy of life. Do not become concerned if you begin questioning your beliefs. Talk about them. For many people, a religious faith provides help in accepting the loss.
- Writing out a rational self-analysis of your grief will help you to identify irrational thinking that is contributing to the grief. (Chapter 5 explains how to write a rational self-analysis.) Once your irrational thinking is identified, you can relieve much of your grief through rational challenges to your irrational thinking.
- Try not to dwell on how unhappy you feel. Become involved and active in life around you. Do not waste your time and energy on self-pity.
- If there are certain days of the year when you tend to grieve deeply (such as an anniversary of a disabling automobile accident), spend these days with family and friends who will give you support.

- You may feel that you have nothing to live for and may even think about suicide. Understand that many people who encounter severe losses feel this way. Seek to find assurance in the fact that a sense of purpose and meaning will return.
- Intense grief is very stressful, and stress can lead to a variety of illnesses, such as headaches, colitis, ulcers, colds, and flus. If you become ill, seek a physician's help and tell the doctor that your illness may be related to grief you are experiencing.
- Intense grief may also lead to sleeplessness, sexual difficulties, loss of appetite, or overeating. You may find you have little energy and cannot concentrate. All of these reactions are normal. Seek to focus on the fact that eventually a sense of purpose and meaning will return to your life. Such a return happens for practically everyone who suffers a serious loss.
- Seek during your grief to eat a balanced diet, to get ample rest, and to exercise moderately. Every person's grief is unique. If you are experiencing unusual physical reactions (such as nightmares), try not to become overly alarmed.
- Medication should be taken sparingly and only under the supervision of a physician. Avoid trying to relieve your grief with alcohol or other drugs. Many drugs are addictive and may stop or delay the necessary grieving process.
- Recognize that guilt, real or imagined, is a normal part of grief. Parents who have a child with a disability often feel guilty about things they have done or about things they think they should have done. If you are experiencing intense guilt, share it with friends or with a professional counselor. It might also be helpful to write a rational self-analysis on the guilt (see Chapter 5). Learn to forgive yourself. If you didn't make mistakes, you wouldn't be human.
- You may find that friends and relatives appear to be shunning you. If this is happening, they are probably uncomfortable around you because they do not know what to say or do. Take the initiative and talk with them about your loss. Tell them about ways in which you would like them to be supportive to you.
- If possible, put off making major decisions (changing jobs, moving away, and so on) until you become more emotionally relaxed. When you're highly emotional, you're likely to make unwise decisions.

SUMMARY

The following summarizes this chapter's content as it relates to the chapter objectives presented at the beginning of the chapter. Objectives include the following:

A *Briefly describe the health-care system in the United States.*

There are a number of problems with our health-care system. In contrast to other industrialized countries in which health care is viewed as having a service orientation, the health-care system in the United States has the dual (and sometimes conflicting) objectives of providing service and making a profit. The system is indeed prospering. The United States is now spending substantially more per capita on health care than are other industrialized nations. Yet a number of other countries have lower infant mortality rates and longer life expectancies than ours. Such statistics suggest that other countries are providing health care that is as good as (or better than) ours at a lower cost.

B *Summarize problems in health care: profit orientation, limited attention to preventive medicine, unequal access to health services, health care for older adults, AIDS, use of life-sustaining equipment, and the high cost of medical care.*

Our health-care system is focused on treating people *after* they become ill; little attention is given to preventing illnesses. It is increasingly being recognized that our lifestyles (including exercise, diet, sleep patterns, and stress reaction patterns) largely determine whether illness will occur and also influence the recovery process when an illness does occur. People need to realize that they, and not their physicians, have the major responsibility for their own health.

The poor and racial minorities have higher rates of illnesses and shorter life expectancies for a variety of reasons. Largely because of the profit motive, low-income areas in cities and rural areas are generally underserved by health-care services.

Health care for adults is becoming a national disgrace. Many older citizens lack access to quality care. Medical conditions of older adults are often misdiagnosed, and treatment is often inadequate.

AIDS has emerged as a major health problem. The two primary ways in which it is transmitted from one person to another are through sexual contact and through sharing of intravenous needles.

There are many misconceptions about AIDS that have led those who are HIV positive and those who have AIDS to be shunned and discriminated against.

The use of life-sustaining technology has raised a number of questions. Should such equipment be used to prolong the life of someone who is terminally ill and in considerable pain? How should death be defined? Should society seek to keep alive people who have such a profound cognitive disability that they will never be able to walk or even sit? Can society afford to continue to expand the use of such costly life-sustaining equipment? Should physician-assisted suicide for the terminally ill who want to die be legalized?

The high costs of medical care have become an issue of national concern. Illnesses now can threaten a family's financial stability. These high costs are also a threat to the economic stability of our country. There are a variety of reasons why medical expenses are so high, including the profit-making focus, high costs of technological advances, increased life expectancies of people, third-party financing, inadequate health-care planning, proliferation of malpractice suits, and increased specialization by doctors.

C *Describe Obamacare, which may (or may not) resolve many of the problems in our health-care system.*

Obamacare was passed in 2010. It is designed to provide health insurance to most of the 46 million people in the United States who do not currently have health insurance. The provisions of the program will gradually be phased in over a time period of several years. One of its emphases is on preventive health care.

D *Describe medical social work.*

Health care is a secondary setting for social work. In such a setting, social workers generally function as members of a team, and they need to learn to work with those in charge. Medical treatment teams are increasingly dependent on social workers to attend to sociopsychological factors that are either contributing causes of illnesses or side effects of a medical condition that must be dealt with to facilitate recovery. As a member of a medical team, social workers have an important role in diagnosing and treating medical conditions.

A social worker in the health field needs skills and knowledge about how to counsel people with a wide variety of medical conditions. Counseling the terminally ill requires a high level of emotional maturity, a well-thought-out identity, and a high level of competency in counseling.

Competency Notes

EP 2.1.3a Distinguish, appraise, and integrate multiple sources of knowledge, including research-based knowledge and practice wisdom. (All of this chapter) This chapter briefly describes the health-care system in the United States. It summarizes the following problems in health care: profit orientation, limited preventive medicine, unequal access to health services, health care for older adults, AIDS, use of life-sustaining equipment, and the high cost of medical care. It describes Obamacare, which may (or may not) resolve many of the problems in our health-care system. It ends with providing an introduction to medical social work.

Media Resources

Additional resources for this chapter, including a chapter quiz, can be found on the Social Work CourseMate. Go to CengageBrain.com.

Notes

1. Joseph Julian, *Social Problems*, 3rd ed. (Englewood Cliffs, NJ: Prentice Hall, 1980), p. 25.
2. Richard Nixon, "Special Message to Congress Proposing a National Health Strategy," Feb. 18, 1971, White House, p. 8.
3. Linda A. Mooney, David Knox, and Caroline Schacht, *Understanding Social Problems*, 8th ed. (Belmont, CA: Wadsworth/Cengage Learning, 2013), pp. 47–48.
4. Ibid.
5. Ibid.
6. Ibid.
7. Ibid.
8. *Occupational Outlook Handbook, 2010–11 Edition*, http://www.bls.gov/oco/ocos074.htm.
9. William Kornblum and Joseph Julian, *Social Problems*, 14th ed. (Boston: Pearson, 2012), pp. 36–37.
10. Ibid., p. 36.
11. Quoted in John A. Denton, *Medical Sociology* (Boston: Houghton Mifflin, 1978), p. 65.
12. J. John Palen, *Social Problems for the Twenty-First Century* (Boston: McGraw-Hill, 2001), p. 399.
13. James W. Coleman and Harold R. Kerbo, *Social Problems*, 10th ed. (Upper Saddle River, NJ: Vango Books, 2008), pp. 300–301.
14. Kornblum and Julian, *Social Problems*, p. 108.
15. Coleman and Kerbo, *Social Problems*, p. 135.
16. Ibid.
17. Ibid.
18. Ibid.
19. Ibid.
20. Thomas McKeown, "Determinants of Health," *Human Nature*, 1 (Apr. 1978), p. 66.
21. Kornblum and Julian, *Social Problems*, p. 33.
22. Ibid.
23. Ibid.
24. Ibid., p. 34.
25. Max Seham, *Blacks and American Medical Care* (Minneapolis, MN: University of Minnesota Press, 1973), pp. 22–23.
26. "Growing Old in America," ABC News Program Transcript (New York: Journal Graphics, Dec. 28, 1985).
27. G. A. Lloyd, "HIV/AIDS Overview," in *Encyclopedia of Social Work*, 19th ed. (Washington, DC: NASW, 1995).
28. C. Scanlan, "New AIDS Drug Wins OK by FDA," *Wisconsin State Journal*, Oct. 10, 1991, p. 3A.
29. Susan Brink, "Improved AIDS Treatments Bring Life and Hope—at a Cost," *U.S. News & World Report*, Jan. 29, 2001, pp. 44–45.
30. G. A. Lloyd, "AIDS and HIV: The Syndrome and the Virus," *Encyclopedia of Social Work: 1990 Supplement* (Silver Spring, MD: NASW, 1990), p. 25.
31. "Worldwide HIV & AIDS Statistics," http://www.avert.org/worldstats.htm.
32. Ibid.
33. Ibid.
34. Ibid.
35. Ibid.
36. Kornblum and Julian, *Social Problems*, p. 52.
37. Ibid., p. 36.
38. Ibid., p. 36.
39. Ibid., p. 36.
40. Coleman and Kerbo, *Social Problems*, pp. 152–153.
41. Jeffrey Klein and Michael Castleman, "The Profit Motive in Breast Cancer," *Los Angeles Times*, Apr. 4, 1994, p. B7.

42. Coleman and Kerbo, *Social Problems*, pp. 152–153.
43. Kornblum and Julian, *Social Problems*, p. 47.
44. Mooney, Knox, and Schacht, *Understanding Social Problems*, p. 45.
45. Ibid., pp. 44–46.
46. Kornblum and Julian, *Social Problems*, pp. 300–301.
47. Ibid., p. 60.
48. Ibid., p. 60.
49. Ibid., p. 60.
50. Elisabeth Kübler-Ross, *On Death and Dying* (New York: Macmillan, 1969).
51. Mwalimu Imara, "Dying as the Last Stage of Growth," in *Death: The Final Stage of Growth*, Elisabeth Kübler-Ross, ed. (Englewood Cliffs, NJ: Prentice Hall, 1975), pp. 147–163.
52. Ibid., p. 148.

CHAPTER

Physical and Mental Disabilities and Rehabilitation

CHAPTER OUTLINE

History of Rehabilitation Practices

Developmental Disabilities

Society's Reactions to Disabilities

Current Services

Roles of Social Workers

Empowering Consumers of Services

There are 50 million people with a disability in the United States—nearly one of five people.[1] People with a disability include those who:

Are temporarily injured (e.g., from severe burns, injuries to the back or spine, broken limbs).

Have a chronic physical disability (including people who use canes, crutches, walkers, braces, or wheelchairs; mobility-impaired older adults; and people with illnesses such as severe cardiovascular disorder, cerebral palsy, chronic arthritis, and AIDS).

Have a hearing disability.

Have a visual disability.

Have a mental disability (including an emotional disorder, a cognitive disability,* or a severe learning disability).[2]

This chapter will:

Learning Objectives

EP 2.1.3a

A   Provide a brief history of rehabilitation practices and of the ways different cultures have treated people with a disability.

B   Define and describe developmental disabilities.

C   Describe different levels of cognitive disability and summarize the causes.

D   Discuss our society's reactions to disabilities.

E   Identify current services for people with a disability.

F   Summarize the roles of social workers in working with clients who have a disability and their families.

History of Rehabilitation Practices

Society's willingness to help people with a disability has been determined largely by the perceived causes of the disability, existing medical knowledge, and general economic conditions. Ancient and modern religious faiths (including Christianity) have at times been an aid and at other times a detriment to viewing those with a disability as "people." Attitudes have ranged from perceiving people with a disability as possessed by demons to viewing them as saintlike, with the community having a responsibility to care for them.

The early Greeks promoted the philosophy of the unity of body and soul, with a blemish on one signifying a blemish on the other.[3] This philosophy led to a negative attitude toward those with a disability. The extreme implication of this doctrine was found in Sparta, where "the immature, the weak, and the damaged were eliminated purposefully."[4] Centuries later the Romans also put to death some people with a disability who were considered "unproductive."[5] In ancient history, there were almost no organized efforts to meet the needs of people with a cognitive disability. In early Greece and in the Roman Empire, mental illness was seen as stemming from demons entering the body, with exorcism being the primary treatment.[6]

During the Middle Ages, disabilities were seen either as the result of demonic possession or as God's punishment.[7] Modern Judeo-Christian values of

---

* Because the term *mental retardation* has negative connotations, the term *cognitive disability* will instead be used in this text. (Some organizations now prefer that *intellectual disability* be used instead of *cognitive disability*.)

charity and humanitarian treatment were generally absent during this period, partly as a result of poor economic conditions. About the only employment provided by feudal lords for people with a disability was that of court jester, a position considered suitable for those with a cognitive or physical disability.[8] The mentally ill continued to be viewed as possessed by demons, and cruelty was advocated and used to punish and drive out the demons.

The Elizabethan English Poor Laws of 1601 provided financial support for the involuntarily unemployed (including those with a disability). These Poor Laws were the first major secular-based relief effort for the poor and people with a disability.[9]

In early colonial America, conditions were not yet suitable for the development of rehabilitation programs. The colonists were barely able to earn a living from the soil; also, disability was viewed as the result of God's punishment.[10]

In the 19th century, gradual recognition was given to the needs of people with a disability in the United States. The first programs to help these people were developed around that time.

Thomas Gallaudet opened the first school for educating the deaf in this country in 1817 in Hartford, Connecticut.[11] Gallaudet demonstrated that the deaf could be taught to read and speak, which led to the opening of other schools for the deaf. The first school for the blind was opened in 1832 in Massachusetts.[12] The first sheltered-type work situation for the employment of the blind was established in 1850 in Massachusetts.[13]

Cognitive disability, before and during the early part of the 19th century, was thought to be inherited and therefore incurable.[14] In the first half of the 1800s, most people with a cognitive disability "were relegated to lunatic asylums, poorhouses, almshouses, or local jails."[15] Interest in providing services to those with a cognitive disability began in France, especially after the physician Jean Itard made considerable progress over a 5-year period in the early 1800s in educating a 12-year-old "wolf child" found in a forest. The boy was diagnosed as having a severe level of cognitive disability. When found, he was unsocialized and walked on all fours.[16] The philosophy of providing services to people with a cognitive disability gradually spread to this country. In 1848 the first residential school for people with a cognitive disability was established in Barge, Massachusetts.[17]

Unfortunately, the orientation toward people with a cognitive disability in the latter half of the 19th century switched from one of education and training to one of custodial care. A major reason for this change was the popularity of Social Darwinism, which asserted that it was far better for society to allow the poor and the weak to perish than to sustain their existence and encourage their proliferation through government-supported programs.[18] People with a cognitive disability were viewed as having defective genetic strains; as a result, sterilization was used extensively at the end of the 19th century.[19]

The first hospitals for the mentally ill were built in this country in the 1850s and 1860s.[20] Before this time, as Dorothea Dix had documented, the mentally ill were either kept "out of sight" in the homes of their families or confined in almshouses and local jails.[21] The living conditions of almshouses and mental hospitals were deplorable.

Until the latter half of the 19th century, people with a physical disability were either taken care of by their family or placed in almshouses. Toward the end of the 19th century, these people began to benefit from medical advances: antiseptic surgery, orthopedic surgery, heat and water therapy, braces, and exercise programs.[22] Around that same time, public funds began to be used for the education and training of children with a disability.[23]

The charity organization movement during the latter part of the 19th century created a structure not only for future social work practices but also for vocational rehabilitation casework.[24] These early organizations had a rehabilitation rather than a maintenance focus. The movement also advocated extensive investigation of each case and the use of individualized treatment determined by the needs of each client. Unfortunately, the volunteers who provided the services for charity organizations operated from the premise that the causes of poverty and of disabilities had moral roots; thus, the primary way to help was to urge those with a disability to become active members in a church (with the church then providing some social services).[25]

During the late 19th and early 20th centuries, few precautions were taken by industries to improve worker safety. As a result, a large number of people developed disabilities from poor working conditions and industrial accidents. To meet the tolls being taken by the Industrial Revolution, the first workers' compensation law was passed in 1910 in New York.[26]

In the early 20th century, large numbers of unskilled rural youths began flocking to cities seeking

Members of American Disabled for Attendant Programs Today (ADAPT) campaign for a change in funding practices. They believe public money should be transferred from payments for institutional care, particularly nursing home care, to community or home-based care.

employment. There were also increasing numbers of dislocated industrial workers who needed retraining. Therefore, the federal government passed the Smith-Hughes Act in 1917, which made federal monies available for vocational education programs and created the Federal Board of Vocational Education.[27] In 1918 the Soldier's Rehabilitation Act was passed, which was a program designed to rehabilitate veterans who had a disability.[28]

The federal Social Security Act of 1935 established the permanency of rehabilitation programs and instituted public assistance programs for the blind and for the disabled. The Barden-LaFollette Act of 1943 extended rehabilitation services to the mentally ill and to people with cognitive disabilities.[29]

During World War II, there was a severe labor shortage, which provided work opportunities to people with a disability. These people were able to demonstrate to thousands of employers that if placed in an appropriate job, they could perform well. This growing realization led in 1945 to the establishment of the President's Committee on Employment of the Handicapped.[30] After World War II, a number of other federal programs underscored society's growing belief that those with a disability could be productive workers and should be given the opportunities and training to demonstrate their work capacities.[31]

Spurred by the civil rights movement of the 1950s and 1960s, a new minority group began to be heard in the late 1960s and 1970s. People with a physical disability began speaking out, marching forth, and demanding equal rights. They have been seeking (including through legislation and lawsuits) an end to job discrimination, limited educational opportunities, architectural barriers, and societal discrimination. In 1973 Congress passed the Vocational Rehabilitation Act, one section of which prohibits discrimination against people with a disability by any program or organization receiving federal funds. Included in this legislation is an affirmative action policy (described in Chapter 12) in which employers who receive federal funds must demonstrate extensive efforts to hire those with a disability.

In 1990 Congress passed, and President Bush signed into law, the Americans with Disabilities Act. This act prohibits discrimination against those with a disability either in hiring or by limiting access to public accommodations (such as restaurants, stores, museums, and theaters). The law requires that new public buildings be accessible by those with a disability and that barriers in existing public buildings be removed if the changes can be accomplished without much difficulty or expense. Advocates of the law call it the most significant civil rights legislation since the 1964 act prohibiting discrimination based on race.[32]

The past 100 years has seen the development of numerous programs and technological advances to help people with a disability. Yet, as will be discussed, much remains to be done in changing society's attitudes toward people with a disability and in helping them to live satisfying and productive lives. Increasingly, people with a disability are receiving improved services that facilitate the development of their capacities.

Critical Thinking Questions

Do you have a disability, or does a member of your family have a disability? If so, have you or this person been a victim of discrimination because of the disability? How do you feel about such discrimination?

Developmental Disabilities

Developmental disability is a relatively recent term, and many people erroneously believe it to be synonymous with *cognitive disability*. However, it is a broader term that includes not only cognitive disabilities but also a variety of other conditions that occur before age 22 and hinder development. These conditions include infantile autism, cerebral palsy, and some cases of dyslexia (a learning disability).

The Rehabilitation, Comprehensive Services, and Developmental Disabilities Act (PL 95-602) of 1978 defines developmental disability as follows:

Developmental disability means a severe, chronic disability of a person which is attributable to a mental or physical impairment or combination of mental and physical impairment and

- *is manifest before twenty-two years of age*

- *is likely to continue indefinitely*
- *results in substantial functional limitations in three or more of the following areas of major life activity:*

  self-care
  receptive and expressive language
  learning
  mobility
  self-direction
  capacity for independent living
  economic self-sufficiency

- *and reflects the person's need for a combination and sequence of special, interdisciplinary, or generic care, treatment or other services which are of lifelong or extended duration and individually planned and coordinated.*[33]

Autism

Perhaps the most puzzling developmental disability is infantile autism. As yet, the causes of this disorder are unknown. David Rosenhan and Martin Seligman offer the following description:

*The essential feature of **autism** is that the child's ability to respond to others does not develop within the first thirty months of life. Even at that early age, gross impairment of communicative skills is already quite noticeable, as are the bizarre responses these children make to their environment. They lack interest in and responsiveness to people, and they fail to develop normal attachments. In infancy, these characteristics are manifested by their failure to cuddle, by lack of eye contact, or downright aversion to physical contact and affection. These children may fail entirely to develop language, and if language is acquired, often it will be characterized by **echolalia**—the tendency to repeat or echo immediately or after a brief period precisely what one has just heard—or **pronominal reversals**—the tendency to use "I" where "you" is meant, and vice-versa. Such children also react very poorly to change, either in their routines or in their environments.*[34]

Symptoms of autism appear early in life, before age 3. Autism affects about 1 in 150 children.[35] Approximately 80% of those affected are boys.[36] About 90% of individuals with autism have severe disabilities into adulthood and are unable to lead independent lives.[37]

There are several types of autism; The most common type is Asperger's disorder. Children with Asperger's disorder usually have normal or even high verbal intelligence, do good schoolwork, and are curious, but they have limited, fixed interests; repetitive speech and behavior; and difficulty understanding social and emotional cues.

The prevalence of autism has increased markedly since the mid-1970s. Why the dramatic increase? There is no agreed-upon explanation. Part of the increase may be due to increased awareness and more accurate diagnosis.

One of the approaches that is used with limited success in treating autism is behavioral therapy. Comer describes this approach:

Behavioral approaches have been used in cases of autism for more than 30 years to teach new, appropriate behaviors, including speech, social skills, classroom skills, and self-help skills, while reducing negative, dysfunctional ones. Most often, the therapists use modeling and operant conditioning. In modeling, they demonstrate a desired behavior and guide people with the disorder to imitate it. In operant conditioning, they reinforce such behaviors, first by shaping them—breaking them down so they can be learned step by step—and then rewarding each step clearly and consistently. . . . With careful planning and application these procedures often produce new, more functional behaviors.[38]

As noted, the causes of autism are still unknown. Autistic disorders run in families and seem to have a strong genetic basis.[39] However, environmental factors such as exposure to certain viruses or chemicals may trigger an inherited tendency toward autism.[40] The claim that autism is partially caused by the administration of the mumps-measles-rubella vaccine has not been substantiated.[41] Society needs to use a strengths approach with persons who are diagnosed as being autistic (see Case Exhibit 16.1).

Cognitive Disability

The largest subcategory of developmental disabilities is cognitive disability. It is a disorder that afflicts 3 of 100 children, two-thirds of whom are boys.[42] The disorder is somewhat difficult to define precisely or diagnose

---

CASE EXHIBIT 16.1

Temple Grandin, a Prominent PhD, Author, and Inventor Who Is Autistic

Temple Grandin was born August 29, 1947. She did not begin to speak until she was nearly 4 years old. Instead, she communicated her frustrations by screaming. At 3 years old she was labeled autistic, and doctors told her parents that she should be institutionalized.

Grandin's mother spoke to a doctor who suggested speech therapy. The mother hired a nanny who spent hours playing games with Grandin and her sister. At age 4, Grandin began talking, and making developmental progress. Grandin considers herself lucky to have had a supportive mother, and supportive mentors from primary school onwards. However, Grandin said that the middle and high school years were the worst years of her life. She was viewed as the "nerdy kid" whom everyone teased. At times, she was taunted by her peers calling her "tape recorder," as she would repeat things over and over again.

Temple Grandin graduated from Hampshire Country School, a boarding school in New Hampshire, in 1966. She earned her bachelor's degree in psychology from Franklin Pierce College in 1970; she received her master's degree in animal science from Arizona State University in 1975; and she received her doctoral degree in animal science in 1989 from the University of Illinois at Urbana–Champaign. She is a professor at Colorado State University.

She is a philosophical leader of both animal welfare and autism advocacy movements. Grandin advocates early interventions to address autism, and supportive teachers who can direct the fixations of autistic children in fruitful directions. She remains hypersensitive to noise and other sensory stimuli, she prefers "alone" time, and she has never married. She is a best-selling author on animal welfare and autism. She is an inventor of a number of livestock handling facilities that keep cattle calm and prevent them from getting hurt.

Temple Grandin's life story illustrates, that no one should be stereotyped as having "no hope for the future" because of receiving a physical/mental disability diagnosis, such as that of autism. She had supportive people in her early years (mother, teachers, mentors) that helped her focus on her strengths, rather than her limitations. She was listed in the 2010 *Time* magazine list of the 100 most influential people in the world in the category "Heroes."

Source: Temple Grandin, *The Way I See It*, 2nd ed. (Arlington, TX: Future Horizons, 2011).

accurately. The difficulty occurs because defining the concept of intelligence (which is at the core of cognitive disability) is problematic. The American Association on Mental Deficiency provides this definition:

> It is characterized by significantly subaverage intellectual functioning, existing concurrently with related limitations in two or more of the following applicable adaptive skill areas: communication, self-care, home living, social skills, community use, self-direction, health and safety, functional academics, leisure, and work. Mental retardation manifests before age eighteen.[43]

Levels of Cognitive Disability

The various levels of cognitive disability and the percentages of people affected at these levels are shown in Table 16.1. The IQ scores for this table are based on the Wechsler Intelligence Test. We'll now look at the functioning of people at these various levels.

Mild Cognitive Disability People at this level develop communication and social skills similar to other people's. Their cognitive disability is often not recognized until they are in the third or fourth grade, when they begin to have serious academic difficulties. With help they can acquire academic skills beyond the sixth-grade level. Other than intellectual functioning, their needs and abilities are indistinguishable from those of others. Special education programs in school often enable these children to acquire the vocational skills needed for performing unskilled and semiskilled jobs. As adults, many are employed and live somewhat independently.

Moderate Cognitive Disability Children at this level learn to talk and communicate during the preschool years. Unlike other children, however, they have difficulties learning social customs. They are unlikely to ever perform beyond second-grade level in academic subjects. Some have poor motor coordination. As adults they can learn to contribute to their own support by working at semiskilled or unskilled tasks in protected settings; many live in group homes.

Severe Cognitive Disability People at this level have major difficulties in communicative speech, and before the age of 5 they display considerable evidence of motor coordination problems. At special schools, they may learn to talk, and they can be trained in elementary hygiene. As adults they may be able to perform simple and unskilled job tasks under supervision in a protected setting. Most reside in group homes or in residential institutions.

Profound Cognitive Disability People at this level display severe disabilities in adaptive behavior. During the preschool years, they are able to master only the simplest motor tasks. Later some development of motor skills may occur, and they may learn some elementary self-care skills. This level of cognitive disability is often associated with severe physical deformities and central nervous system difficulties. Health and resistance to diseases are often poor. Life expectancy is substantially shortened. Children and adults at this level usually need custodial care.

Causes of Cognitive Disability

Hundreds of causes of cognitive disability have been identified, and we'll summarize some of the major ones. It should be noted that not everyone who is exposed to some of these factors will automatically experience a cognitive disability. For example, many children whose mothers drank heavily during gestation do not have a cognitive disability.

Cultural/Familial Cognitive Disability Accounting for about two-thirds of all cognitive disabilities,[44] this category stems from genetic and environmental influences. Most people in this category have a mild or moderate level of cognitive disability. Many of them have parents and siblings who also have a cognitive disability, suggesting that at least part of the disability is passed on through the genes.

The second major contributor to this type of cognitive disability is the restricted environment in which the individuals in this category live and develop. People who are raised in poverty have a much higher probability of experiencing this type of cognitive disability. Rosenhan and Seligman note:

Table 16.1 Levels of Cognitive Disability

LEVEL	PERCENTAGE OF PEOPLE WITH THIS LEVEL OF COGNITIVE DISABILITY	WECHSLER IQ SCORE
Mild	85	50–70
Moderate	10	35–49
Severe	4	20–34
Profound	1	Below 20

SOURCE: Ronald J. Comer, *Fundamentals of Abnormal Psychology*, 4th ed. (New York: Worth Publishers, 2005), pp. 440–441.

Lower-class mothers are more likely to give birth to premature infants with low birth weights, and low birth weight is a risk factor for retardation. Children from impoverished backgrounds also face a number of postnatal environmental challenges to intellectual growth. Some of these children ingest toxic levels of lead by eating fragments of lead-based paint that peel off the walls of the old buildings in which they live. In turn, exposure to lead is associated with retarded intellectual growth. In addition, children from lower-class families are more likely than upper-class children to be malnourished, to receive poor health care, and to suffer from a variety of illnesses across childhood. Such an environment inhibits the full development of the intellectual abilities a child does have.[45]

Environmental influences include poor prenatal care, frequent accidents, infections, poor health habits, malnutrition, and lack of stimulation. With cultural/familial cognitive disability, it is nearly impossible to determine for each affected person how much of the cognitive disability is due to genetic variables and how much is due to environmental variables.

Gestational Disorders Infants born prematurely (before 37 weeks of gestation) are at increased risk of having a cognitive disability. Many metropolitan centers have specialized clinics for pregnant women who are known to be at high risk of premature delivery, and most hospitals have neonatal intensive care units for infants who are born prematurely. These facilities reduce the risk of neurological damage as a result of gestational problems.

Toxemia Toxic (poisonous) substances in the blood during the gestation period pose a risk for both the pregnant woman and the fetus. Such substances include prescription drugs, cocaine and other illegal drugs, nicotine (from smoking), and alcohol.

A toxic disorder that has received considerable publicity is fetal alcohol syndrome (FAS). It is associated with heavy drinking (generally considered to be five or six drinks on occasion) during the gestation period. Pregnant women who occasionally have one or two drinks also place their fetus at some risk for FAS, which is characterized by facial and cranial abnormalities, possible heart defects, delayed physical and intellectual development, joint and limb

anomalies, decreased weight of the fetus, and increased risk of stillbirth.[46]

The risk of toxemia can be substantially reduced if pregnant women receive early, regular, and specialized care during pregnancy. Pregnant women should follow their physician's advice about which medications to take, and which to avoid, during pregnancy.

Infections during Gestation Certain infections that pregnant women contract may place the fetus at risk for having a cognitive disability. One of these infections, rubella (also called German measles), can result from the mother's exposure to the virus during the first trimester of pregnancy. The affected fetus is also at higher risk of being born with other congenital abnormalities, such as deafness, blindness, heart anomalies, and microcephalus. Mass immunization programs now provide childbearing women protection against rubella. Blood tests are also available to determine the level of protection a woman has against the virus; those who are unprotected can then become immunized before pregnancy.

Another infection of pregnant women that can prove devastating for the fetus is syphilis. Syphilis infection, like rubella, is passed on to the fetus through the placenta. The affected fetus is likely to be born with many physical anomalies in addition to a cognitive disability.

A virus that is affecting an increasing number of babies is the AIDS virus. Infants can be infected during gestation, at birth, or after birth from milk from an HIV-positive mother. AIDS infants tend to have a short life expectancy.

Postnatal Cerebral Infection A variety of viral and bacterial diseases, such as encephalitis and meningitis, can cause severe and irreversible brain damage, particularly if not treated in the early stages of infection. The AIDS virus may also lead to brain deterioration in older children and adults.

Chromosome Abnormalities The best-known and most common disorder in this category is Down syndrome. This condition arises because there are 47 chromosomes, rather than the usual 46, in the cells of those affected. The disorder does not appear to be inherited, although the reason for this chromosome abnormality is not known. The disorder occurs in children born to mothers of all ages but with higher frequency in children born to mothers over age 35. The risk of the disorder is about 1 in 1,500 for children born to mothers in their 20s; it increases to 1 in 40 when the mother is over 40 when the child is born.[47]

Down syndrome children and adults generally experience a moderate to severe level of cognitive disability. Their eyes are almond shaped and slanted, and they tend to have a round face. Many of those affected also have physical anomalies, which may include heart lesions and gastrointestinal difficulties.

There are a variety of other chromosomal abnormalities that may occur. In 1991 scientists discovered the gene that causes fragile X syndrome.[48] This gene was located on the X chromosome. Fragile X syndrome is the most common inherited form of cognitive disability. (Down syndrome is more common but does not run in families.) Symptoms of fragile X syndrome can range from mild learning disability to a severe level of cognitive disability, with serious behavioral problems. Some carriers are completely normal but can pass the gene that produces the syndrome to later generations. Fragile X syndrome is incurable. It occurs in 1 in 1,000 males and 1 in 600 females.[49]

Through a test called amniocentesis, prenatal detection of Down syndrome, other chromosome defects, and some metabolic disorders is possible. Although some small risk of miscarriage is involved, amniocentesis is a fairly simple procedure. A needle is inserted through the abdomen and into the uterus, and amniotic fluid is extracted for chromosome or chemical studies. The procedure should be performed in the first trimester of pregnancy if the mother is known to be at risk for having a child with a specific chromosome or metabolic condition. The test is recommended if the pregnant woman has a complicated medical or gestational history.

Another test, called chorionic villi sampling (CVS), has been developed to help identify certain fetal abnormalities. The test can be performed in a physician's office as early as the fifth week of gestation (which is several weeks earlier than amniocentesis can first be used). CVS is relatively simple to perform and under some conditions is a viable alternative to amniocentesis.

Metabolic Disorders   Phenylketonuria (PKU) is perhaps the best-known metabolic disease. The affected infant cannot metabolize phenylalanine, an essential building block of protein in food. As a result, phenylalanine and its derivative, phenyl pyruvic acid, build up in the body and rapidly poison the central nervous system, causing irreversible brain damage. About a third of such children cannot walk, about two-thirds never learn to talk, and more than half have a profound level of cognitive disability.[50] PKU results from the action of a recessive gene that is inherited from each parent. No test currently exists to identify the recessive gene in the parents. However, affected babies can be identified by a simple test of the urine about 3 weeks after birth. Once identified, the infants can be placed on a diet that controls the level of phenylalanine in their system until age 6, at which time the brain is nearly fully developed and their chances of surviving with normal intelligence and health are good.

Lipid storage disorders include Tay-Sachs disease, Hunter's disease, and Hurler's syndrome. These disorders involve a progressive degenerative process due to the accumulation of fatty substances in the cells that eventually leads to the death of the affected individuals. These conditions are inherited, and as yet effective treatment has not been developed. The incidence, however, has been greatly reduced through genetic counseling programs and prenatal diagnosis.

Disorders of Unknown Prenatal Influence   Of the numerous disorders in this category, two of the better known are hydrocephalus and microcephalus. Hydrocephalus involves a condition in which there is an increased amount of cerebrospinal fluid within the skull that will, unless treated, cause an enlargement of the skull. Neurosurgical techniques are now available that prevent brain damage by decreasing the pressure that causes it.

Microcephalus is a condition in which there is a reduced circumference of the head. In some cases, it may result from an inherited disorder; in other cases, it may result from fetal or neonatal brain damage.

Trauma to the Brain   Injury to the brain can occur at any time during prenatal, perinatal, or postnatal development. During the prenatal period, one source of injury is X-rays that the pregnant woman may have during gestation. If the fetus's brain is exposed to the X-rays, a severe level of cognitive disability may occur.

During the prenatal and perinatal periods, brain injury can result from deprivation of oxygen (anoxia) or from insufficient oxygen (hypoxia) to maintain functioning of the brain tissue. Such conditions destroy brain cells and may result in a cognitive disability. Shortage of oxygen may occur for a variety of reasons, including a knotted umbilical cord, premature separation of the placenta, or difficult birth as a result of a breech position.

Postnatal damage can result from an almost infinite number of causes. Brain injury can occur from a blow to the head while boxing or fighting, bicycle and automobile accidents, near drowning, football injuries, falls from a horse, battering by a parent, or any other damage to the head.

Critical Thinking Questions

Have you listened to, or told, jokes about people with a disability? Assume you have a disability; how would you feel if a cruel joke were told related to your disability?

These diverse causes of cognitive disability illustrate how fragile human life is. We are all one accident or one infection away from experiencing a severe cognitive disability. In reviewing the multitude of sources that may lead to having a child with a cognitive disability, it is important to have a positive attitude when one is about to become a mother or father.

The temptation is to think that with all the possibilities of having a child with a cognitive disability, it is impossible to believe that one could have a baby who is normal and healthy and stays that way through the entire developmental period. The risk of having a child with a cognitive disability is low, and every prospective parent should approach parenthood with optimism. Although precautions can be taken to decrease the chances of having a child with a cognitive disability, it can and does occur every day in families in which early and excellent prenatal care was sought, in which the mother stayed away from all agents known or suspected to be toxic, in which no illness occurred during the gestational period, and in which the birth was uncomplicated.

Society's Reactions to Disabilities

Our culture places a high value on having a beautiful body. We work out at health clubs, and we spend large proportions of our incomes on clothes, cosmetics, hairstylists, and special diets to look more attractive. Beauty is erroneously identified with goodness and ugliness with evil. Movies, television, and books portray heroes and heroines as physically attractive and villains as ugly. Snow White, for example, was lovely, whereas the evil witch was horrible looking. Children are erroneously taught that being physically attractive will lead to the good life, whereas having unattractive features is a sign of being inferior. Richardson found that young children rated people with a disability as "less desirable" than people without a disability.[51]

Unfortunately, this emphasis on the body beautiful has caused people with a disability to be the objects of cruel jokes and has occasionally led them to be either shunned or treated as inferior. According to C. H. Cooley, if people with a disability are related to as if they are inferior, second-class citizens, they are likely to come to view themselves as inferior and to have a negative self-concept.[52] Our society needs to reassess its values about the perfect physique. It would seem that other traits ought to be more important: honesty, integrity, a pleasant personality, responsibleness, kindness, and helpfulness.

Wright has noted that the emphasis on beautiful bodies has also led society to believe that people with a disability "ought" to feel inferior.[53] She has coined the term *the requirement of mourning* for this expectation of society. A person who spends a great deal of time, money, and effort to be physically attractive psychologically wants a person with a disability to mourn the disability because the "body beautiful" person needs feedback that it is worthwhile and important to strive to have an attractive physique.

Another consequence of this misplaced emphasis is that people with a disability are sometimes pitied as being less fortunate and given sympathy. Many people with a disability decry receiving pity and being patronized. They seek to be treated as equals.

Asch and Mudrick have noted that people with a disability are stigmatized and often treated as "not quite human" or "not normal."[54] The fear and aversion to disability that most people have often lead them to fear and reject people with a disability.[55] (Social workers have to recognize and challenge their own apprehensions of impairment in order to become effective change agents in combating prejudices against those with a disability.)

There is also a tendency in our society to conclude that a person with one kind of disability will have other kinds of disabilities. Nancy Weinberg has noted that people talk louder in the presence of someone who is blind, erroneously assuming that people who cannot see also have hearing problems.[56] Individuals with a physical disability are also erroneously assumed at times to have a cognitive disability. A 22-year-old college student in a wheelchair describes one example of this tendency:

> I'm in church with my father and my father is standing beside me and I'm in a wheelchair. I'm relatively intelligent, but I'm disabled. I'm sitting there like anyone else. And somebody comes up to my father and they're about as far away from me as from him and they say to my father, "How's he doing?" "Well he's looking pretty good." And I just want to kick him in the stomach.[57]

Receiving such responses from others may lead those with a physical disability to believe they are less intelligent and less effective in social interactions.

Studies have found that many people cut short their interactions with people who have a disability.[58] They are uncomfortable when a person with a disability is near because they are uncertain about what is appropriate and inappropriate to say and they fear offending the person. Usually they do not want to make any direct remarks about the disability. People show their discomfort in a variety of ways—through abrupt and superficial conversations, fixed stares away from the person with a disability, compulsive talking, or an artificial seriousness. Individuals with a disability are sensitive to such insincere interactions. Fred David describes a few encounters that produce interactional strains:

> I get suspicious when somebody says, "Let's go for a uh, ah [imitates confused and halting speech] push with me down the hall," or something like that. This to me is suspicious because it means that they're aware, really aware, that there's a wheelchair here, and that this is probably uppermost with them. . . . A lot of people in trying to show you that they don't care that you're in a chair will do crazy things. Oh, there's one person I know who constantly kicks my chair, as if to say "I don't care that you're in a wheelchair. I don't even know that it's there." But that is just an indication that he really knows it's there.[59]

People with a disability detest being treated as socially different simply because of their disability. It is important that all of us respect those who have a disability for a variety of reasons, one of which is that all of us have a vested interest in creating a society that respects those who have a disability. As we grow older, we almost certainly will eventually develop one or more disabilities, perhaps in hearing, in vision, in mobility, or in having a chronic illness. Right now, we are just an accident away from one.

These negative attitudes toward people who have a mental or physical disability have undoubtedly been a factor in preventing individuals with a disability from achieving their full potential. An empowerment approach emphasizes the importance of developing the potential capabilities of individuals with a disability. Case Exhibit 16.2 illustrates that having a mental or physical disability does not prevent people from excelling.

Critical Thinking Questions

Do you place a high value on having a beautiful body? If so, do you then devalue those who are less attractive or who have a disability?

Current Services

Numerous programs provide funds and services to people with a disability. Some of these are federally funded and administered at state or local levels.

Rehabilitation Centers

Rehabilitation centers serving those with a mental or physical disability provide a variety of services, generally including vocational evaluation, sheltered employment, work adjustment training, counseling services, and placement services. (This type of rehabilitation center used to be called a sheltered workshop.)

Vocational Evaluation

Clients are assessed on the basis of work behavior, physical capacities, social interaction, psychological functioning, and vocational goals and interests. Emphasis is on identifying the client's vocational assets and limitations. (In recent years, some rehabilitation centers have made a policy change. They now consider their "clients" to be "workers" or "employees." This shift has created a more efficient, work-oriented

---

CASE EXHIBIT 16.2

People with a Disability Who Have Become Famous

- Julius Caesar, Roman emperor, had epilepsy.
- George Patton, general, World War II hero, had dyslexia.
- George Washington, president, had a learning disability. He had immense difficulties in spelling.
- Goya, a Spanish painter (1746–1828) became deaf at age 46. He went on to create the most famous Spanish art of the 19th century.
- John Milton, English author/poet (1608–1674), became blind at age 43. He went on to create his most famous epic, *Paradise Lost*.
- Ludwig van Beethoven, famous musician and composer, had a serious hearing disorder.
- Helen Keller, who was blind, deaf, and mute, was an advocate for people with a disability and lived independently as an adult for more than three decades.
- Franklin D. Roosevelt had polio as a child, which resulted in a serious mobility disability. He went on to become governor of New York State and then was elected president of the United States for four terms.
- Winston Churchill, prime minister of Great Britain, had a learning disability.
- Thomas Edison, inventor, had a learning disability.

- Albert Einstein, mathematician/physicist, had a learning disability.
- Alexander Graham Bell, inventor, had a learning disability.
- Woodrow Wilson, president, was severely dyslexic.
- Ray Charles, singer and musician, was blind.
- Stevie Wonder, singer and musician, is blind.
- Cole Porter, composer, lost one of his legs in a horse-riding accident. He continued to compose a number of popular songs.
- Tony Melendez, Nicaraguan guitar player, singer, and songwriter, was born without arms.
- Stephen Hopkins was born with a mild case of cerebral palsy. He was one of the signers of the Declaration of Independence and then led militias in defense of the United States against the British.
- Chris Burke was born with Down syndrome. He became a TV star on the ABC hit sitcom *Life Goes On* (1989–1993).
- Jim Abbott, major league pitcher, was born without a right hand.
- Marlee Matlin, actress, is deaf.

These individuals illustrate that having a mental or physical disability does not stop people from making major contributions.

---

environment and helped the "employees" maximize their capacities for productive work.)

Sheltered Employment

These programs provide a work environment for individuals who are unable to secure or maintain jobs in the community. Clients are paid (often below the minimum-wage level) for work produced. Work tasks derive from various subcontract jobs from other industries in the community and allow for long-term vocational development and possible placement into competitive employment. There is periodic evaluation of clients' progress in meeting rehabilitation objectives to ensure maximum vocational and personal development.

Work Adjustment Training

Vocational training experiences are provided to clients who are not yet ready for competitive employment following their initial vocational evaluation. The program is conducted in a work setting, using various types of subcontract jobs secured from industries in the community. The employment is designed to train individuals in developing good work skills and appropriate behavior on the job. Counselors are

available to discuss problems, to assist learning new tasks, and to teach better work habits.

Counseling Services

Counseling services include individual, group, parent, and vocational guidance. Individual counseling stresses work and intervention goals applied to mutually determined problem areas. Group counseling focuses on peer interaction and development of social skills. Parent counseling acquaints parents with rehabilitation objectives, thus providing support in the home for the total rehabilitation program. Exposure to the work world, development of job-seeking skills, and identification of realistic goals are the major emphases of vocational counseling.

Placement Services

These programs assist clients in securing competitive employment. First, clients' work habits and skills are assessed. Then they receive training in searching for a job, applying for a job, and holding a job. Counselors then seek, together with clients, to place the clients with local employers. After placement, contact is maintained for a period of time to deal with any adjustment problems that may arise. At many work sites in the community, counselors serve as job coaches (often for a few weeks) to assist the clients in learning and performing the tasks of the positions for which they have been hired.

Respite Care

Respite care programs provide caregiving services to parents and other caregivers for people with a disability, giving primary caregivers a break from their responsibilities. Respite care can also provide support during crises such as a caregiver experiencing his or her own acute health problems.

Support Groups for Caregivers

Support groups allow caregivers to get together to share stories, concerns, and achievements with other caregivers who are experiencing similar challenges. Support groups can also assist in long-term planning for those who have a disability. A common concern of aging caregivers is what will happen to the person with a disability when the caregiver is no longer able to provide care.

Recreational Programs

Involvement in recreational activities is a factor in facilitating the emotional, physical, spiritual, and intellectual well-being of a person. The more active we are, mentally and physically, the better our quality of life. There are a variety of recreational programs for people with a disability: Special Olympics, summer camps, craft projects, and so-on. There are also a variety of programs that "mainstream" people with a disability, such as Boy Scouts, Girl Scouts, Boys and Girls Clubs, and 4-H clubs.

Educational Programs

Historically, many public schools either refused to serve children with a severe disability or segregated

Special Olympic events foster pride and self-worth for children and adults with developmental disabilities.

them in special programs. In 1975 Congress enacted the Education for All Handicapped Children Act (now known as Individuals with Disabilities Education Act.). This statute mandates that all local school districts provide full and appropriate educational opportunities to all children, including those with a disability. An individualized educational program designed to meet the unique needs of each child must be developed to provide instruction in the least restrictive environment that is feasible. The intent is to "mainstream" children with a disability so that they can participate as much as possible in regular educational programs. Most school districts now have "special educational programs" designed to meet the educational needs of children with a cognitive disability, emotionally disturbed children, children with learning disabilities, and children with a physical disability. Many states have schools for children with a hearing disability and for those with a visual disability. Often these specialized schools also provide statewide consultation for young children.

Residential Programs

Group Homes, Halfway Houses, and Nursing Homes

Many of these facilities provide living arrangements for children and adults with a disability who, for a variety of reasons, are unable to live with their families.

Residential Treatment Centers

Centers that provide residential care and treatment include mental hospitals, residential treatment centers for the emotionally disturbed, and centers for those with a developmental disability. The average length of stay varies among facilities and may range from several days to permanent care. Some of these residential facilities also serve clients on an outpatient basis, providing diagnostic, evaluative, and planning services.

Day-Care Centers

These centers provide day-care services to children with a cognitive disability, to the emotionally disturbed, and to children with a physical disability. The centers not only give the parents some relief time but also provide training in self-help, socialization, homemaking, communication, and leisure-time activities.

Hospital Services

Hospitals provide a variety of rehabilitation services for those with a disability, such as medical services, physical therapy, and speech therapy. For individuals who are severely injured or have a serious chronic illness, hospitals are often the entry point into the rehabilitation system.

Home Services

Meals on Wheels

This program provides hot and cold meals to housebound recipients who are incapable of obtaining or preparing their own meals but who can feed themselves.

Home Health Services

These programs provide visiting nurse services, drugs, physical therapy, laboratory services, and sickroom equipment.

Homemaker Services

In some communities, homemakers are available to do household tasks that people with a disability are unable to do for themselves.

Federal and State Assistance Programs

Vocational Rehabilitation Funding

Federal funding programs for rehabilitation have developed gradually in this country. Two of the key statutes were the Vocational Rehabilitation Act Amendments of 1973 and the Rehabilitation Act of 1975.[60] At present there are federal matching funds available to states for basic rehabilitation programs at the matching rate of 80% federal and 20% state. Individuals are eligible for vocational rehabilitation services if they have a mental or physical disability that substantially interferes with their capacity to obtain employment and if there is a reasonable expectation that services will enable them to obtain employment. Potential clients receive medical testing free of charge to assess the extent of their disability and to check their overall health. Rehabilitation counselors employed by the state review these results. Applicants found eligible may then receive, at state and federal expense, a variety of services:

- Special equipment, such as hearing aids, guide dogs, wheelchairs, canes, or prosthetics.
- Special training in such areas as sign language, vocational training, reading, or social adjustment.

This training may take place at a rehabilitation center, at a vocational school, at a public or private college, or on the job.
- Money for transportation and living expenses during the training period.
- Medical, surgical, and other services that will reduce the extent of the client's impairment.
- Individual counseling and guidance.
- Assistance in finding a suitable job or essential equipment, licenses, tools, or stock for a small business.
- Follow-up to smooth the client's entrance into employment.

Under this program, states are able to set priorities for categories of eligible clients who will be served when financial resources are limited. For example, states may assign a higher priority to clients who need medical restoration than to those who need psychological counseling. Each state also has the option of deciding whether an economic means test should be used to determine whether the applicant is entitled to certain services.

The amendments in 1992 to the Rehabilitation Act require that the services financed be aimed at individuals with the most severe disabilities. In addition to providing funds for the traditional rehabilitation areas of job counseling, retraining, and prosthetic and other assistive devices, the amendments authorize funding for "supported employment"—a service model in which a person with a severe disability works in a private-sector job with a "job coach" who eases the transition to independent employment.

Medicaid

This program (described in Chapter 15) covers medical expenses for low-income people.

Old Age, Survivors, Disability, and Health Insurance

This is a social insurance program (described in Chapter 4) for those who are no longer able to work following several years of covered employment.

Supplemental Security Income

This is a public assistance program (described in Chapter 4) for low-income people with a physical or mental disability.

Food Stamps

This program (described in Chapter 4) offsets some of the food expenses for low-income people who qualify.

Workers' Compensation Program

Workers injured or disabled on the job, and surviving dependents of workers who die as a result of such injury, are provided financial assistance to compensate for lost wages and to pay the cost of any required medical or rehabilitative care.

People with permanent disabilities arising from work injuries may receive a lump sum or a monthly payment in perpetuity from workers' compensation. Workers' compensation is not a federal program; laws in every state (except Texas) require employers to purchase workers' compensation insurance to cover the claims made by injured workers.

Roles of Social Workers

Social workers come in contact with people with a disability in two general ways.

First, they encounter them in settings in which the primary service focus is something other than rehabilitation. For example, workers at family counseling agencies usually see families with marital and interpersonal problems. One or more of these family members may have a disability. The disability may be unrelated to the family problems, or it may be an important contributing factor. In the latter case, the social worker's role is to help the family assess and understand the nature and impact of the disability and then develop effective strategies for handling the difficulties associated with the disability.

Second, social workers may be employed in settings that primarily serve people with a disability, such as rehabilitation centers, nursing homes, general hospitals, day-care centers for people with a disability, rehabilitation hospitals, and specialized schools (such as schools for people with a visual disability).

Rehabilitation for people with a physical or mental disability can be defined as restoration to the fullest physical, mental, social, vocational, and economic usefulness of which they are capable.[61] Programs focus on vocational training, vocational counseling, psychological adjustment, medical and physical restoration, and job placement. Clients, of course, differ in which of these services are needed. Some clients require help in all of these areas.

Many types of professionals provide rehabilitation services: physicians, nurses, clinical psychologists, physical therapists, psychiatrists, occupational therapists, recreational therapists, vocational counselors, speech therapists, hearing therapists, industrial arts teachers, social workers, special education teachers, and prosthetists. Most of these therapists focus on the physical functioning of the clients, whereas social workers focus primarily on their social functioning. In most rehabilitation settings, a team approach is used.

The major functions of social workers in rehabilitation settings are discussed in the following sections.

Counseling Clients

Counseling in this context involves helping clients adjust to their disability and to the rehabilitation programs at the agency. A wide range of problems may be covered: personal, interpersonal, family, financial, vocational adjustment, and educational adjustment.

Counseling Families

In some rehabilitation settings, the social worker is involved primarily in working with the family and not with the client, especially if the client is a young child. Counseling with the family involves helping them to understand the nature of the disability and the prognosis, to make the essential adjustments to help the client, and to deal with personal and interpersonal concerns associated with the disability. In such a role, a social worker provides information, comfort, understanding, counseling on specific concerns, and sometimes referral services.

Taking Social Histories

A social history contains information about the client's family background and present status. It includes information about what the client's family life was like before contact with the agency, what it is like now, and what it will probably be like in the future. A social history contains a history of the disability, positive and negative reactions of family members to the disability, significant family relationships, summary of strengths and weaknesses within the family for handling the disability, information on social skills of the client, a history of the client's functioning at school and at work, a history of services provided in the past, and a summary of the problems associated with the disability and concerns of family members (see Case Example 16.1). Information for the social history is gathered from the client, from family members, and from case records of other social and medical agencies that the client has had contact with.

CASE EXAMPLE 16.1

Social History of a Client at a Vocational Testing Division of a Rehabilitation Center

Hillside Vocational Training Center
Columbus, Ohio

Name: Jim Frey

Date of Birth: 6-30-93

Address: 550 S. Adams, Columbus

Telephone: 478-2346

Religion: Lutheran

Occupation: Unemployed

Race: Black

Marital Status: Single

Height: 5'10"

Weight: 180

Reason for Testing. On April 30, 2010, Jim Frey was involved in an automobile accident with his older brother, Bob. Bob was killed in the accident, and Jim's spine was severed. Jim was hospitalized for 3 months, spent 5 more months convalescing in a nursing home, and since that time has been living with his parents. Jim is paralyzed from the waist down. Following the accident, he was also severely depressed. He was referred to this agency by Lakeland Counseling Center, an agency from which Jim and his parents have been receiving counseling. Jim's depression has gradually decreased, and he is now seeking testing and vocational counseling to explore career opportunities.

Family Background and Early History. Jim's father, Donald Frey, has been an insurance salesman for the past 27 years. His mother, Joan Frey, has been a real estate broker for the past 14 years. Both Mr. and Mrs. Frey appear very concerned about their son's future, and both stated they are willing to do whatever they can to help. The Freys live in a middle-class neighborhood and have a home that is clean and well kept. The Freys appear to have considerable respect for each other and a good relationship.

The only children that the Freys had were Jim and Bob, with Bob being 2 years older. The Freys reported that both their children did well academically in school, and each had a number of friends. The boys were both active in intramural sports, with Bob being a second-string player on the basketball team in his junior and senior years. The most serious trouble that either of the boys had gotten into prior to the accident was Bob being arrested for setting off firecrackers around the 4th of July 5 years ago.

The automobile accident occurred late one evening after Jim and Bob had left a party in which alcoholic beverages were served. Their car hit a bridge abutment. Bob was killed instantly. The parents reported they were extremely distraught following this accident and felt their whole world had been shattered. They indicated they had few friends they socialized with, as they spent most of their time prior to the accident with their work and their children. They received counseling for grief and depression for 18 months from Lakeland Counseling Center. They indicated they discontinued counseling when the person they were seeing made a job transfer to the West Coast.

For nearly the past 2 years, Mr. and Mrs. Frey have been caring for Jim at home. Mrs. Frey indicated she has taken a leave of absence from her real estate position in order to care for her son. They acknowledged that caring for Jim has been "taxing," as he has been quite depressed and has required considerable physical attention. Only recently has he been able to get into and out of a wheelchair without assistance. The parents still mourn the loss of Bob but are increasingly becoming optimistic with the progress that Jim has been making, including a decrease in his depression, increased physical agility, and now a motivation to receive training for a career.

School Performance. Jim attended Franklin Elementary School, Stevens Junior High, and Randal High School. At the time of his accident, Jim was a senior. He was near graduation but as yet has not completed the coursework. School records show that Jim generally received *A*s and *B*s, with a few *C*s. Jim had an intelligence test in his sophomore year in which he achieved a score of 122. Before the accident, Jim was planning to attend college. He reportedly had a number of friends, and most continued to visit him for the first several months following the accident. But as time passed and as Jim's depression continued, his friends gradually stopped coming by to see him. At present he has no close friends.

General Health. Until the accident, his health was generally good. He had a hernia operation at age 10 and a broken collarbone at age 12. During the accident, Jim suffered a severed spine and is now partially paralyzed. He also had a variety of cuts from glass that required more than 80 stitches. Since the accident, he at times has experienced considerable pain connected with his injury and has been prone to catch flus and colds. Medical reports indicate Jim received intensive physical therapy while at the hospital and while convalescing in the nursing home. On returning to his home, Jim's parents were instructed on giving him a variety of exercises.

Dating History. Jim indicated he dated a number of young women before the accident. At the time of the accident, he was dating someone steadily (during his senior year). At first this person showed considerable interest in Jim and his circumstances. However, Jim stated that after a few months she started dating others, and her interest in continuing their relationship rapidly declined.

Employment History. Jim was a paperboy for a few years. Before the accident, he worked part time as a busboy at a restaurant. He has not worked since the accident.

Prior Contact with Social Agencies. Jim was hospitalized in 2010 for 3 months at St. Mary's Hospital. Records show he received extensive physical therapy and counseling for depression from the social work staff. Following this hospitalization, he was transferred to a group home, where he continued to receive physical therapy and counseling. Jim had fallen asleep on the fateful night when his brother was killed. For months after that, he was depressed and continued to feel guilty because

(continued)

he felt that, if he had stayed awake, he might have kept his brother awake. (The police concluded that the accident occurred after Bob had fallen asleep.) Jim also has been depressed over the breakup with his girlfriend, over the loss of other friends, and particularly over the shattered hopes and expectations for his future. After Jim returned home, his parents made arrangements with the referring agency (Lakeland Counseling Center) for Jim to receive counseling associated with his depression and also focused on his future. Reports received from Lakeland Counseling Center also indicated that his parents have expressed concerns in the past year that Jim may be drinking beer and other alcoholic beverages to excess.

General Impressions. Jim has made gradual progress in putting his life back together since his auto accident some 3 years ago. At times he is still somewhat depressed, but he now is making efforts to stop brooding about his past and is motivated to improve his situation. He is looking forward to the test results at the center, because he wants to receive training for a career. He is uncertain which career he desires to pursue and is uncertain which vocations or professions he is qualified to pursue. He is articulate and personable and appears to possess a high intellect. He has expressed a strong interest in graduating from high school and wonders whether he might have the capacities and financial resources to attend college. His parents appear supportive of his desires to seek a

higher education and stated they would be willing and able to provide some financial support.

Jim stated he is also interested in learning to drive and hopes to be able to secure a driver's license and an auto with assistive devices that would enable him to drive.

Jim's drinking was discussed with him. He stated that he may at times drink to excess, but he said this only happens when he is bored or depressed or has nothing to do. It would seem that Jim's drinking is a potential difficulty that should be monitored.

Jim has the support and encouragement of his parents. Jim's optimism about his future is indeed a positive sign. However, it is important for him to realize that testing is only the first step. Jim hopes to acquire the necessary training, employment, and financial resources to live independently of his parents. Although his parents are supportive, there are occasional conflicts between Jim and his parents, such as over his drinking. Jim may occasionally get discouraged when he encounters obstacles to arriving at the goals that he has set. It is at these times that he may need continued counseling to prevent the return of a long-term depression.

Respectfully submitted,

Frank Lia
Social Worker

Serving as Case Manager

As a case manager, a social worker coordinates needed services provided by a number of agencies, organizations, or facilities to clients. A person with a disability may require extensive services and resources, including those provided by systems of health care, mental health, rehabilitation, education, housing, employment, and other related systems. Because of the pervasive needs of clients with a disability, it is vital that one of the service providers, typically a social worker, be designated as case manager. Such an arrangement assigns responsibility for planning and orchestrating the delivery of services in a systematic and timely manner. As a case manager, the worker may provide services to a client in a variety of roles, including broker, advocate, counselor, teacher, community organizer, coordinator, and planner. Case managers assess the comprehensive needs of clients, connect them to appropriate services, and ensure that those services are provided effectively.

Serving as Liaison between the Family and the Agency

Keeping the lines of communication open is essential in any human service setting. In a rehabilitation setting, social workers generally have the responsibility to serve as liaison between the agency staff and the family. At times a worker arranges meetings between the staff and the family to discuss the client's disability, factors affecting rehabilitation, and future plans and services. In a hospital setting, it is the physician's responsibility to explain the particular medical condition to the client, but a social worker often discusses the implications of the medical condition with the client and the family. Implications covered include the likely effect the disability will have in the future on the capacity of the affected person to function at work, at school, in social situations, and within the family. To be an effective liaison, a social worker in a rehabilitative setting needs a basic knowledge of a variety of medical conditions and of medical terminology as well as an awareness of the implications of these medical conditions for emotional, physical, and social functioning.

Being a Broker

Often a social worker functions to link families with other community resources. To be an effective broker, a worker needs a knowledge of other community services, including the programs provided, eligibility requirements, and admission procedures. Clients may need a variety of services from other community agencies, such as financial assistance, wheelchairs, prosthetic services, day-care services, special job training, visiting nurse services, and transportation.

Doing Discharge Planning

In some rehabilitation settings, such as hospitals, social workers have major responsibility for discharge planning. If a client is unable to return home, arrangements must be made for placement in some other setting, such as a nursing home or a group home. Social workers often help clients and their families prepare for returning to the home or to some other facility. In this capacity, the social worker may arrange for financial aid and for such specialized care as home health care, day care, physical therapy, and job training.

(Empowering consumers of services is perhaps the most important role for social workers in their interactions with people with a disability. Because of its importance, it is described in the following separate section.)

Empowering Consumers of Services

People with physical or mental disabilities can live productive, fruitful, happy lives when they receive the support they need. In working with a person who has a disability, it is crucial to assess not only the severity and extent of the disability but also the strengths and special talents of that person.

Stevie Wonder has been among the most influential Black music artists over the past five decades.[62] He is a songwriter, producer, singer, and musician. He was inducted into the Rock and Roll Hall of Fame in 1989. He was born Steveland Judkins on May 13, 1950, in Saginaw Michigan. When born, he was suffering from retinopathy of prematurity, which eventually caused his retina to detach, resulting in his blindness. With the support and encouragement of his parents, he learned to play the piano at the age of 7. By the age of 9, he had also mastered playing drums and harmonica. After his family moved to Detroit in 1954, he joined a church choir and began to develop his singing potential. In 1961, at the age of 11, he was discovered by Ronnie White of the group The Miracles, who arranged an audition at Motown Records. Almost immediately he was signed by Berry Gordy to Motown Records, Clarence Paul came up with the "Wonder" surname, as Stevie at the time was being introduced as the "8th Wonder of the World." Clarence Paul also supervised his early recordings and helped him develop his singing talents and his talents as a multi-instrumentalist. Why did Stevie Wonder become one of our country's greatest entertainers? He certainly was born with immense musical potential. But he also had supportive parents and a number of mentors and advisers who helped him develop his potential.

Critical Thinking Question

Do you have an interest in a professional career in which you provide services to people with a disability?

This brief biography of Stevie Wonder demontrates that people with a disability also have strengths and special attributes. It obviously would be a serious mistake to conclude that every person with a disability has the potential to become a Stevie Wonder, but all of us have special talents and attributes that have the potential of being developed.

One of the most important challenges any social worker has in working with any population (including people on probation, school-age children, homeless people, and so on) is to focus on identifying and assisting in the development of the special talents and attributes of each person. The following are some principles that foster an empowerment approach.

View recipients of services as *consumers* rather than as clients. The term *consumer* implies greater power and choice than does the term *client*. As consumers, recipients of services should be able to choose their purchases or resource providers within a competitive market rather than having someone else make choices for them.

Normalization is the principle that every consumer, even those with the most severe disabilities should have a living and educational environment as close to "normal" as possible. Sadly, 60 (and more) years ago, people with developmental disabilities were often placed "out of sight and mind" in obscurely located institutions. In the 1970s and 1980s, communities started viewing people with mental and developmental disabilities as having the right to live as normally as possible. A parallel concept to normalization is *deinstitutionalization*, which is the process of moving people who are dependent for their physical and mental care from residential care facilities into the community. Community facilities that then provide care include group homes, family homes, and supported apartments. Normalization assumes that the more that people with developmental disabilities can be assimilated into the community and the more that they can be "mainstreamed," the better their quality of life will be.

A focus of empowering people with disabilities is to maximize self-determination and independence in the *least restrictive environment* that is feasible. The concept of least restrictive environment focuses on having consumers of services enjoy as much freedom as possible and on having consumers make as many decisions for themselves as they can. As much as possible, consumers are encouraged to make choices and decide what goals they wish to pursue and what supports and services they want. Consider Aaron, who is 19 years old and has muscular dystrophy. He wants to attend college and become a social worker. His vocational rehabilitation counselor and a social worker who is working with him and his family facilitate him in locating a campus with special services for students with disabilities and that also has an accredited social work program. He applies and is accepted. The campus's Center for Students with a Disability assists him in locating appropriate housing for his needs, having a personal attendant for 3 to 4 hours each day, and transportation with a van for him (with his wheelchair) to classes and other events.

Critical Thinking Question

We all know and interact with people with a disability. For the people you know who have a disability, what can you do that will assist in empowering them?

An empowerment approach also has a focus on *innovation*, which involves the identification, development, and application of new ideas. Innovative service provision involves creatively combining existing services depending on what an individual wishes to accomplish. It also involves creating new services for the special needs of consumers. For example, assistive computer technology systems have been developed for those who are dyslexic or visually impaired that can scan printed material into a computer, which then reads it aloud to the user. One such program is called Jaws and is a Windows-based program. Jaws makes it possible for a computer running Windows 95, 98, or NT to speak the information being displayed on the monitor.

Empowerment may involve *advocacy*. Hepworth, Rooney, Rooney, Storm–Gottfried, and Larsen have defined *advocacy* as:

> *the process of affecting or initiating change. This process involves working with or on the behalf of clients (1) to obtain services or resources that would not otherwise be provided; (2) to modify or influence policies, procedures, or practices that adversely affect groups or communities; and (3) to promote legislation or policies that will result in the provision of requisite resources or services.*[63]

When consumers are not getting their needs met, the social work practitioner has an obligation to advocate on their behalf. An illustration of successful advocacy was the efforts of Carlos Lopez, school social worker, to have his school district purchase Jaws software for middle school and high school students who are dyslexic or visually impaired. He advocated for this purchase with the directors of pupil services, principals in the district, district administrators, and eventually the district school board.

Facilitating and enhancing *family support* is another component of empowerment of people with a disability. The more family support that a person with a disability receives, the greater the chances that a person with a disability will actualize his or her capabilities and talents. Family members are often the primary caregivers for people with a disability. Social workers can assist caregivers in obtaining the services needed for the person with a disability and for the caregivers themselves. Such services include recreational programs, educational programs, respite care, conflict resolution resources, stress management programs, financial assistance programs, and quality health care.

SUMMARY

The following summarizes this chapter's content as it relates to the chapter objectives presented at the beginning of the chapter. Objectives include the following:

A *Provide a brief history of rehabilitation practices and of the ways different cultures have treated people with a disability.*

Throughout history the willingness of societies to care for the needs of those with a disability has always been largely determined by the perceived causes of the disability, the existing medical knowledge, and the general economic conditions. In the past, disability was often viewed as a result of demonic possession or as God's punishment.

People with a disability include those who are temporarily injured, those with a chronic physical disability, those with a hearing or visual disability, those who have an emotional disorder, those with a cognitive disability, those with a learning disability, and those with degenerative illnesses and chronic health disorders.

B *Define and describe developmental disabilities.*

Developmental disabilities are conditions that produce functional impairment as a result of disease, genetic disorder, or impaired growth pattern manifested before adulthood, are likely to continue indefinitely, and require specific and lifelong or extended care.

Developmental disabilities include cognitive disability, infantile autism, cerebral palsy, and a variety of other conditions that occur before adulthood.

C *Describe different levels of cognitive disability and summarize the causes.*

The levels of cognitive disability are mild, moderate, severe, and profound. Hundreds of causes of cognitive disability have been identified, and the chapter summarizes some of the major causes.

D *Discuss our society's reactions to disabilities.*

In the past 100 years, our society has made progress in better understanding the needs of people with a disability and in designing services to meet these needs. Yet there is still a general lack of acceptance of people with a disability; it is often related to our emphasis on the "body beautiful" in our society. People with a disability are still frequently pitied, shunned, or made the brunt of jokes. Our society has yet to learn that people with a disability want to be treated as peers. (All of us are only an accident away from having a disability.) Until people with a disability are given an opportunity, not only legally but also socially, to be treated as peers, social services will be only partially effective. Ideally, people with a disability should be limited only by the physical or mental restrictions of their disability. Sadly, the psychological and social obstacles faced by these people are often greater than their actual physical or mental limitations. Our society has yet to learn that a person with a disability is a person—a person who happens to have a disability.

E *Identify current services for people with a disability.*

Services include: rehabilitation centers, vocational evaluation, sheltered employment, work adjustment training, counseling services, placement services, respite care, support groups for caregivers, educational programs, group homes, halfway houses, nursing homes, residential treatment centers, day-care centers, hospital services, Meals on Wheels, home health services, homemaker services, and vocational rehabilitation.

F *Summarize the roles of social workers in working with clients who have a disability and their families.*

Social workers are only one of numerous groups of professionals who provide services to people with a disability. The roles of social workers in providing rehabilitative services include counseling people with a disability, counseling family members, gathering information through social histories, serving as case managers, serving as liaisons between the family and the agency, being brokers, and doing discharge planning. A final key role for social workers is empowering consumers of services. Components of empowering individuals with a disability include normalization, deinstitutionalization, least restrictive environment, innovation, advocacy, and family support.

Competency Notes

EP 2.1.3a Distinguish, appraise, and integrate multiple sources of knowledge, including research-based knowledge and practice wisdom. (All of this chapter) This chapter presents a history of rehabilitation practices and of the ways different cultures have treated people with a disability. It defines and describes developmental disabilities, and it describes different levels of cognitive disability and summarizes the causes. It discusses our society's reactions to disabilities, and identifies current services for people with a disability. It ends by summarizing the roles of social workers in providing services to clients who have a disability and their families.

Media Resources

Additional resources for this chapter, including a chapter quiz, can be found on the Social Work CourseMate. Go to CengageBrain.com.

Notes

1. William Kornblum and Joseph Julian, *Social Problems*, 14th ed. (Boston: Pearson, 2012), pp. 47–48.
2. Ibid.
3. G. L. Dickinson, *Greek View of Life* (New York: Collier Books, 1961), p. 95.
4. S. Nichtern, *Helping the Retarded Child* (New York: Grosset & Dunlap, 1974), p. 14.
5. J. F. Garrett, "Historical Background," in *Vocational Rehabilitation of the Disabled*, D. Malikin and H. Rusalem, eds. (New York: New York University Press, 1969), pp. 29–38.
6. J. C. Coleman, *Abnormal Psychology and Modern Life*, 3rd ed. (Glenview, IL: Scott, Foresman, 1964).
7. C. E. Obermann, *A History of Vocational Rehabilitation in America* (Minneapolis, MN: Dennison, 1964).
8. L. Kanner, *A History of the Care and Study of the Mentally Retarded* (Springfield, IL: Charles C. Thomas, 1964), p. 6.
9. M. Judge, "A Brief History of Social Services, Part I," *Social and Rehabilitation Record*, 3, no. 5 (Sept. 1976), pp. 2–8.
10. Stanford Rubin and Richard Roessler, *Foundations of the Vocational Rehabilitation Process* (Baltimore: University Park Press, 1978), p. 4.
11. A. F. Tyler, *Freedom s Ferment* (New York: Harper & Row, 1962), pp. 294–296.
12. J. Lenihan, "Disabled Americans: A History," *Performance* (a publication of The President's Committee on Employment of the Handicapped), 27 (1977), Bicentennial issue.
13. Obermann, *A History of Vocational Rehabilitation in America*, p. 333.
14. L. M. Dunn, "A Historical Review of the Retarded," in *Mental Retardation*, J. Rothstein,

15. Obermann, *A History of Vocational Rehabilitation in America*, p. 80.
16. Kanner, *A History of the Care and Study of the Mentally Retarded*, pp. 36–38.
17. Ibid., p. 39.
18. Rubin and Roessler, *Foundations of the Vocational Rehabilitation Process*, pp. 12–13.
19. Ibid., pp. 13–14.
20. Lenihan, "Disabled Americans: A History," pp. 28–37.
21. Tyler, *Freedom s Ferment*, p. 306.
22. Rubin and Roessler, *Foundations of the Vocational Rehabilitation Process*, pp. 8–9.
23. Ibid., pp. 10–11.
24. R. Lubove, *The Professional Altruist* (Cambridge, MA: Harvard University Press, 1965).
25. Ibid.
26. Obermann, *A History of Vocational Rehabilitation in America*, p. 121.
27. Rubin and Roessler, *Foundations of the Vocational Rehabilitation Process*, pp. 22–23.
28. Obermann, *A History of Vocational Rehabilitation in America*, pp. 155–157.
29. R. Thomas, "The Expanding Scope of Service," *Journal of Rehabilitation*, 36, no. 5 (1978), pp. 37–40.
30. Rubin and Roessler, *Foundations of the Vocational Rehabilitation Process*, pp. 30–32.
31. Ibid., pp. 32–45.
32. Gregory Spears, "Bush Inks Disabled Rights Bill," *Wisconsin State Journal*, July 27, 1990, p. 5A.
33. William E. Kiernan and Jack A. Stark, eds., *Pathways to Employment for Adults with Developmental Disabilities* (Baltimore: Brooks, 1986), pp. 12–15.
34. David L. Rosenhan and Martin E. P. Seligman, *Abnormal Psychology*, 3rd ed. (New York: Norton, 1995), p. 633.
35. Diane E. Papalia, Sally W. Olds, and Ruth D. Feldman, *Human Development*, 11th ed. (Boston: McGraw-Hill, 2009), pp. 122–123.
36. Ibid.
37. Ibid.
38. Ronald J. Comer, *Fundamentals of Abnormal Psychology*, 4th ed. (New York: Worth Publishers, 2005), p. 433.
39. Ibid.
40. Ibid.
41. Papalia, Olds, and Feldman, *Human Development*, pp.122–123.

42. Comer, *Fundamentals of Abnormal Psychology*, pp. 440–441.
43. Rosenhan and Seligman, *Abnormal Psychology*, p. 633.
44. Ibid., 630.
45. Ibid., pp. 630–631.
46. Papalia, Olds, and Feldman, p. 313.
47. Rosenhan and Seligman, *Abnormal Psychology*, p. 628.
48. Daniel Q. Haney, "Retardation Gene Discovered," *Wisconsin State Journal*, May 30, 1991, p. 1A.
49. Ibid.
50. Rosenhan and Seligman, *Abnormal Psychology*, p. 629.
51. S. Richardson et al., "Cultural Uniformity in Reaction to Physical Disabilities," *American Sociological Review*, 26 (Apr. 1961), pp. 241–247.
52. C. H. Cooley, *Human Nature and the Social Order* (New York: Scribner's, 1902).
53. Beatrice A. Wright, *Physical Disability: A Psychological Approach* (New York: Harper & Row, 1960), p. 259.
54. Adrienne Asch and Nancy R. Mudrick, "Disability," in *Encyclopedia of Social Work*, 19th ed. (Washington, DC: NASW, 1995), p. 753.
55. Ibid.
56. Nancy Weinberg, "Rehabilitation," in *Contemporary Social Work*, 2nd ed., Donald Brieland, Lela Costin, and Charles Atherton, eds. (New York: McGraw-Hill, 1980), p. 310.
57. Ibid.
58. R. Kleck, H. Ono, and A. H. Hastorf, "The Effects of Physical Deviance upon Face-to-Face Interaction," *Human Relations*, 19 (1966), pp. 425–436.
59. Fred David, "Deviance Disavowal: The Management of Strained Interaction by the Visibly Handicapped," in *The Other Side: Perspectives on Deviance*, Howard S. Becker, ed. (New York: Free Press, 1964), p. 123.
60. Rubin and Roessler, *Foundations of the Vocational Rehabilitation Process*, pp. 32–44.
61. Ibid.
62. "Stevie Wonder Page," available at http://www.soulwalking.co.uk/StevieWonder.html (accessed Jan. 10, 2009).
63. Dean H. Hepworth, Ronald H. Rooney, Glenda D. Rooney, Kimberly Storm-Gottfried, Jo Ann Larsen, *Direct Social Work Practice*, 7th ed. (Belmont, CA: Thomson, 2006), p. 428.

CHAPTER 17

Overpopulation, Misuse of the Environment, and Family Planning

Problems associated with overpopulation and despoiling of the environment threaten to reduce the quality of human life throughout the world. The seriousness of these problems is illustrated by the fact that some nations are contemplating the enactment of compulsory sterilization laws. This chapter will:

Learning Objectives

EP 2.1.3a

A   Describe the problems associated with rapid population growth throughout the world. Discuss pollution and misuse of the environment.

B   Summarize current efforts to curtail the growth of the world's population and to preserve the environment. Outline proposals that have been advanced for population control and for environmental protection in the future.

C   Provide suggestions for what each of us can do to save the earth.

D   Describe the role of social work in family planning.

The Population Crisis

There are now over 7 billion people living on earth[1] (see Case Exhibit 17.1). In 1930 there were 2 billion. The world's population is increasing at the rate of 1.2% per year, resulting in the addition of 80 million people per year[2] (see Table 17.1). The dangers of runaway population growth can be viewed in historical perspective by looking at the world's population in units of 1 billion people. It took all of human history until 1850 for the world's population to reach 1 billion, but the next unit of 1 billion was added in only 80 years (1850–1930). The unit after that was in 30 years (1930–1960), and the next occurred in only 15 years (1960–1975). Since 1975, 3 billion people have been added.[3]

Assuming a continued doubling rate of 65 years, by 2065 there will be 12 billion people. If this growth continued for 900 years, there would be 60 *million billion* people! This means that there would be about 100 people for each square yard of the earth's surface, including both land and water.[4]

Doubling Time and Population Growth

The rate at which the population doubles in a country, and in the world, has immense consequences. Doubling time is based on the extent to which the birthrate exceeds the death rate. Doubling times have a compound effect. Just as interest dollars earn interest, people added to the population produce more people. Table 17.2 shows the relationship

---

CASE EXHIBIT 17.1

Comprehending How Much I Billion Is

It is difficult to conceive how much 1 billion is. Many people cannot imagine the meaning of 1 billion, let alone 7 billion. The following may be useful:

• If you were to count to 1 billion, saying one number per second without stopping, it would take you 31.7 years.

• One billion minutes equals 1,901 years, so in a billion minutes from the year 2007, it will be the year 3908.

SOURCE: Linda A. Mooney, David Knox, and Caroline Schacht, *Understanding Social Problems* (Belmont, CA: Thomson Wadsworth, 2005), p. 394.

Table 17.1 Doubling Times of the World's Population

DATE	ESTIMATED WORLD POPULATION	TIME REQUIRED FOR POPULATION TO DOUBLE (IN YEARS)
8000 B.C.	5 million	
1650 A.D.	500 million	1,500
1850	1 billion	200
1930	2 billion	80
1975	4 billion	45
2000	6 billion	65
2011	7 billion	45

SOURCE: William Kornblum and Joseph Julian, *Social Problems*, 14th ed. (Boston: Pearson, 2012), pp. 414–417.

Table 17.2 Rate of Population Growth and Doubling Time

ANNUAL PERCENTAGE INCREASE	DOUBLING TIME (IN YEARS)
1.0	70
2.0	35
3.0	24
4.0	17

SOURCE: Paul Ehrlich, *The Population Bomb* (New York: Ballantine, 1971), p. 10.

between the annual population growth rate and the doubling time of the population. Thus, what seems a small population growth rate of 1.2% per year (the current rate in the world) leads to a dramatic doubling time of 65 years.[5] On a positive note, the doubling time has slowed from 45 years to 65 years in recent years.[6]

Doubling Time and Developing Countries

The countries experiencing the most severe doubling-time problems are the "developing countries" (also called Third World nations), which are just beginning to industrialize. Sadly, population growth is greatest in the countries that can least afford increases—that is, the countries that need to spend their resources on improving their economic conditions. Developing countries have more than two-thirds of the world's population and doubling times of about 20 to 35 years.[7] They tend to have primitive and inefficient agriculture, small gross national prod-

ucts, and high illiteracy rates. Their populations spend most of their time trying to meet basic subsistence needs, and many people are starving in these countries.

Developing countries are characterized by high birthrates and declining death rates. The trend in the past has been that when a country begins to industrialize, the death rate drops (people live longer) while the birthrate remains high for a substantial period of time. The result is rapid population growth. Unfortunately, developing countries, where people's living conditions most need improvement, are precisely the nations whose populations are increasing so rapidly that most people are scarcely better off than they were a generation ago. Nine of every 10 people added to the world's population are born in the poorer, developing countries.[8] Third World countries are much more likely than industrial countries to have a population explosion.

The population crisis in the world today is not due to families having more children than they did in the past; family size has not increased. However, more people are living to the age of fertility and beyond. In effect, more babies are growing to maturity to produce babies themselves. This change is due to several factors: advances in medicine, sanitation, and public health and the increased capacity to reduce the effects of famines, floods, droughts, and other natural disasters.

Lee Rainwater has noted that "the poor get children."[9] There is a vicious circle involving rapid population growth and poverty. Rapid population growth places an increasing strain on a nation's ability to feed and clothe its growing masses, which leads to poverty. Poverty, in turn, leads to a high birthrate, which leads to further population growth. Former World Bank President Robert S. McNamara warned: "Short of thermonuclear war itself, rampant population growth is the gravest issue the world faces over the decades ahead."[10]

Developed or industrialized countries have doubling times in the 50- to 200-year range.[11] In the United States in recent years, the birthrate has steadily decreased and is nearing a zero-population-growth rate (an average of two children per family). The basic reason for the longer doubling time in developed countries is that people decide to have fewer children (for financial and other reasons). The average cost of raising a child from birth to age 18 for a two-parent family is estimated to be $226,920 for food, shelter, and other necessities.[12]

Developed nations are characterized by both low birthrates and low death rates.

Critical Thinking Questions

Are you aware that if you decide to have two children, you and your spouse will spend more than $500,000 raising them? Are you aware, and appreciative, of your parents spending more than $200,000 to raise you?

The slower doubling times in industrialized countries in no way indicate that these nations are not part of the problem. If one looks at consumption rates of raw materials, they are the major culprit. People living in industrialized countries consume a majority of the raw materials on planet Earth.[13]

In many developing countries, families average seven or eight children.[14] As a result, these countries are increasingly populated by the young. Figure 17.1 indicates that one result of this younger population is that developing countries are much more likely than industrialized countries to have a population explosion.

An Optimal Population Size

A common question is, "What is the capacity of the world to support people?" To say that the population is too large or too small implies there is an optimal size, but no exact figure could accurately be considered the ideal population for the world.

Many variables and values would enter into specifying an optimal world population size, including preservation of a certain standard or quality of life, rate of consumption of nonrenewable raw materials, future technological breakthroughs in finding new energy and food sources, maintenance of "safe" levels of clean air and water, and public acceptance of the government's role (perhaps compulsory) in population control. The industrialized nations, with their high-consumption and high-waste economies, are using up more of the earth's raw materials and generating more pollution than are developing countries.

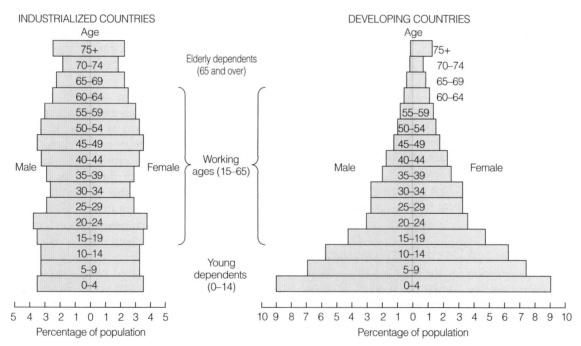

FIGURE 17.1 Age/Sex Population Pyramids: Industrialized and Developing Country Models

Because of consumption rates, adding 1 million people to industrialized countries is comparable to adding 30 million people to developing countries.[15]

With regard to the question of whether the earth is already overpopulated, Paul Ehrlich and Anne Ehrlich note:

> *The key to understanding overpopulation is not population density but the numbers of people in an area relative to its resources and the capacity of the environment to sustain human activities; that is, to the area's carrying capacity. When is an area overpopulated? When its population can't be maintained without rapidly depleting nonrenewable resources (or converting renewable resources into nonrenewable ones) and without degrading the capacity of the environment to support the population. In short, if the long-term carrying capacity of an area is clearly being degraded by its current human occupants, that area is overpopulated.*
>
> *By this standard, the entire planet and virtually every nation is already vastly overpopulated.*[16]

Problems of Overpopulation

A wide range of problems is associated with overpopulation. These include too little food, too little water, economic problems, international terrorism, crowding, immigration issues, too little energy, and shortages of other nonrenewable resources.

Too Little Food

An estimated three-quarters of a billion people today are undernourished—that is, slowly starving.[17] Malnourishment during childhood years can have devastating effects. It delays physical maturity, impairs brain development, reduces intelligence, and may produce dwarfism. An undernourished adult is listless, apathetic, and unable to work as vigorously as a well-fed adult. A number of diseases are caused directly by dietary deficiency, including beriberi, rickets, and marasmus. Malnutrition also lowers resistance to disease, so the malnourished are likely to have a number of other health problems. The danger of epidemics is always high in overpopulated areas where people are malnourished. In addition, the damage of malnutrition is passed from one generation to the next, as babies born to malnourished mothers are weaker and in poorer health than the babies of well-fed mothers.[18]

Even in the United States, many people are undernourished, with some dying of starvation.[19] In approximately the time it takes to read this sentence, four people will die (three of them children) from malnutrition.[20] The brain of an infant grows to 80% of its adult size within the first 3 years of life. If supplies of protein are inadequate during this period, the brain stops growing, and the damage is irreversible; such children suffer permanent cognitive disabilities.[21]

More than 200 years ago (in 1798), Thomas Malthus asserted that population growth, if left unchecked, would outstrip the food supply.[22] Malthus theorized that uncontrolled population growth increases in powers of 2: 1, 2, 4, 8, 16, 32, 64—that is, in a geometric ratio. In contrast, the food supply cannot possibly increase that fast. At best, the food supply increases in a steady additive fashion: 1, 2, 3, 4, 5, 6, 7—that is, in an arithmetic ratio. Inevitably, according to Malthus, population growth overtakes the growth in food supplies. Therefore, either population has to be controlled by society, or starvation, hunger, and poverty will be the unavoidable fate of most of the world's people. The fact that widespread starvation and poverty are indeed common in many countries today provides some evidence of the validity of Malthusian theory.

There has been an ongoing, heated controversy among scientists over whether technology will be able to substantially increase the world's food supply. Some scientists claim that we have already reached the limit, and technology is no longer able to increase the food supply to meet the needs of even a slowly growing world population. Others are predicting that future technology will provide food for a population 10 times as large as our current one.[23]

Which side is right? The verdict is not yet in. A few decades ago, a technological breakthrough led to a dramatic improvement in much more food produced per acre by new strains of wheat and rice. This "green revolution," however, requires increased use of fertilizers and water. Fertilizers are becoming scarce and more expensive, and many developing countries cannot afford costly irrigation systems. Lester Brown notes, "The old formula of combining more and more fertilizer with ever-higher yielding varieties that helped almost triple the world grain harvest from 1950 to 1990 is no longer working well and there is no new formula."[24]

Research on increasing the food supply is also taking other approaches. One effort is to investigate the feasibility of cultivating the tropical rain forests of Africa, South America, and Indonesia. These areas

CASE EXHIBIT 17.2

Compulsory Sterilization Laws

Overpopulation is now recognized as one of the severest problems affecting the preservation of the quality of human life. Some countries are now seriously considering enacting compulsory sterilization laws to control rapid population growth. One such country is India. In 1976 Maharashtra (a state in India) passed a compulsory sterilization law to limit family size. The law required all males under age 55 and all females under age 45 to be sterilized within 180 days of the birth of their third living child. Prison terms of up to 2 years could be assigned to those who failed to comply, although offenders were generally sterilized and then paroled. From April 1976 through December 1976, more than 7 million sterilizations reportedly were performed. This law was rescinded with the fall of Prime Minister Indira Gandhi's government in 1976. Nevertheless, it illustrates the desperation some countries feel to alleviate the pressures of unwanted population growth.

SOURCES: "Maharashtra Passes Family Size Limitation Measure," *Intercom*, 9 (Sept. 1976), p. 5; Lynn C. Landman, "Birth Control in India: The Carrot and the Rod?" *Family Planning Perspectives*, 9 (May–Jun. 1977), p. 102.

have large amounts of sunshine and water but poor soil (requiring large quantities of fertilizer) and severe insect infestations. Another effort is geared to finding new ways to harvest fish and plant life from the sea. The sea contains huge quantities of food, much of which is currently distasteful. Not only does more food need to be produced, but food distribution systems must be improved. In the United States, it is more than ironic that farmers are producing more food than Americans can consume, yet an estimated 45 million people in the country do not have enough to eat.[25]

Too Little Water

Somewhat surprisingly, fresh water is also in short supply in the world. Of the world's water, 97% is salt water; only 3% is fresh water.[26] Developed nations use substantially more water per person than developing nations. More than 1 billion people lack access to clean, fresh water.[27]

Economic Problems

In industrialized countries, rapid population growth reduces the standard of living and the quality of life by reducing the average per capita income.[28] Because birthrates are consistently higher among the lower-income groups, there are additional social and economic strains. Some authorities openly express alarm that high birthrates among poorer classes may lead to a reduction in average educational achievement and provide a threat to the values espoused by the middle and upper classes. Rapid population growth also leads to other problems: massive unemployment, air and water pollution, traffic jams, inadequate and insufficient housing, and so on.

Economic problems are even more serious in developing nations. Economic progress tends to be canceled out by the increased population. For poor countries to industrialize requires that the inhabitants invest (through either public or private funds) in capital items such as factories, tractors, and industrial equipment. Many developing nations do not even have the funds to provide adequate food for their people. Inability to invest in capital items practically guarantees that they will be unable to improve their people's standard of living.

Lack of funds also creates educational and political problems. Developing countries have a high proportion of school-age children but do not have the resources to provide enough schools. For example, Dr. Benson Morah describes the situation in Nigeria: "You have schools with 70 children in the classrooms, there are children sitting in the windows, children carrying their chairs to school."[29] As a result, in many countries a majority of children do not attend school. Illiteracy and lack of training further lock the inhabitants into poverty.

In addition, people who are poorly housed, hungry, and miserably clothed are likely to view the government as the protector of the rich and the oppressor of the poor. Such conditions often lead to political unrest, revolutions, and civil wars—as have been common in Africa, Asia, and South America.

The gap in living standards between industrialized and developing countries is wide and growing wider. In 2011, for example, the average per capita gross income was more than $40,000 in the United States; in some developing nations, it was less than $500.[30]

Ethiopian children are fed at a relief camp. Up to 20 million people, mostly children in developing countries, die of starvation each year.

International Terrorism

Rapid population growth is a factor that contributes to civil unrest, violence, and international strife. Overpopulation leads to higher unemployment, rapid urbanization, declining public health, environmental degradation, economic stagnation, and a large youthful population. Young people in Third World countries are in destitute poverty and have little hope for a better future; yet at the same time, they have a gnawing awareness that people in industrialized nations are much more affluent. Such conditions create an "Aspiration Bomb." Many young people see violence and terrorism as their only avenue for achieving a better life.

In a report on population, the U.S. National Security Council noted:

> *Recent experience, in Iran and other countries, shows that this younger age group, frequently unemployed and crowded into urban slums, is particularly susceptible to extremism, terrorism, and violence as outlets for frustration. On balance, these factors add up to a growing potential for social unrest, political instability, mass migrations, and possible conflicts over control of land and resources.*[31]

Werner Fornos makes the following comments about the perils of the "Aspiration Bomb":

> *Fully 60 percent of the Third World is under 20 years of age; half are 15 years or less. These population pressures create a volatile mixture of youthful aspirations that when coupled with economic and political frustrations help form a large pool of potential terrorists.*
>
> *The "Aspiration Bomb" may well present a greater threat to U.S. security than the atomic bomb. This is because while there is always the hope that mutual deterrence or common sense will preclude the use of nuclear weapons, there is no such countervailing influence against the violence and frustration embodied in the Aspiration Bomb.*[32]

Critical Thinking Questions

What strategies should the United States use to reduce global terrorism? Are you a supporter of the U.S. invasion of Iraq?

On September 11, 2001, terrorists hijacked four commercial planes. The terrorists flew two of the

Osama bin Laden and his Al Qaeda organization are thought to have committed numerous international acts of terrorism, including the destruction of the Twin Towers of the World Trade Center in New York City on September 11, 2001.

planes into the Twin Towers of the World Trade Center in New York City, completely destroying both 110-story towers. A third plane flew into the Pentagon in Washington, D.C., causing extensive damage; a fourth crashed in Pennsylvania. About 3,000 people were killed in these attacks. The United States and many other countries responded by declaring war on terrorism. Afghanistan was invaded by the United States and its allies, and the Taliban government, which supported terrorism, was removed from power. Several months later, the United States and its allies invaded Iraq and removed Saddam Hussein, who supported terrorism, from power; Osama bin Laden was killed on May 2, 2011, by U.S. Navy Seals and CIA operatives. The United States continues to fight terrorism (see Case Exhibit 17.3).

Crowding

Crowding has been described as a person's subjective judgment that he or she has insufficient space. Numerous studies have investigated the effects of crowding on animals. John Calhoun placed rats in laboratory pens and allowed them to breed until their number rose far beyond that found in their natural environment. Several behavioral changes took place. Many females became infertile, others began to abort, and some that bore offspring did not adequately care for their young.[33]

In other studies, overcrowding among animals has led them to become irritable, overly aggressive, nervous, inattentive to grooming, and messy, with some even resorting to cannibalism. In many cases, such negative behaviors continued when the animals were returned to a normal environment.[34]

Although animal research is suggestive, it is not necessarily applicable to humans. The effects of crowding on people have not been sufficiently researched. Some authorities believe it is a factor that leads to crime, emotional problems, incest, child abuse, suicide, violence, dirty streets, and polluted air. Other authorities assert that increases in these behaviors are due not to overcrowding but to poverty and to the breakdown in traditional values. Nonetheless, we should remember that *a delicate balance often exists between a population and an environment, and this balance can be drastically changed by a slight increase in population*. For example, adding one or two fish to a fully populated aquarium may result in a shortage of oxygen that kills most of the fish.[35]

Immigration Issues

Overpopulation also intensifies issues related to immigration. *Immigrate* means to enter a country of which one is not a native for permanent residence. Throughout the world, people living in poor nations dream of moving to the richer countries. Immigration to the United States has reached levels unmatched since early in the century. Other affluent countries have also experienced an influx of people from poorer nations.

It is often said that the United States is a nation of immigrants. Since the earliest days of European settlement, North America has attracted people from all over the world. Some, like the black slaves from Africa, were brought here against their will. Most other groups came in search of freedom from oppression and economic opportunities. In the past two centuries, millions of immigrants of different religions, races, cultures, and political views have come to the United States. This diversity is one of the attributes and strengths of American culture. The immense variety of dress, diet, and music in our society can be traced to the contributions of immigrants from many different cultures and nations.

CASE EXHIBIT 17.3

Social Work with Military Personnel, Veterans, and Their Families

A War Like None Other

On September 11, 2001, the United States and its citizens were forever changed. Men and women from around the country watched in horror as their country was under attack. The day began like any other; however, unbeknownst to many, four airplanes had been hijacked and were making their way to predetermined destinations in the largest terrorist attack to have ever taken place on U.S. soil. Shortly after 9:00 am (EST), the first hijacked airplane flew into the New York World Trade Center's North Tower. People watched in disbelief and confusion, only to see another plane deliberately crash into the South Tower a short time later. As the country was suspended in shock, a third hijacked plane intentionally crashed into the Pentagon. A fourth airplane had also been hijacked on that day. However, a courageous group of passengers had learned about the previous attacks and attempted to retake the plane from the hijackers, and selflessly crashed it in a vacant field in Pennsylvania, possibly saving numerous other lives. Nearly 3,000 people were killed on that September day, and many lives were forever changed.

Following the events of September 11, 2001, unlike at any other time in history, men and women felt the overwhelming need to serve and protect their country by joining the armed forces to defend their land and their people. Droves of patriotic citizens joined the U.S. Army, Marine Corps, Navy, and Air Force in an attempt to answer their call to duty and embark on what would become known as the Global War on Terror. Operation Enduring Freedom (OEF) began when the United States declared war on Afghanistan in October 2001. The United States later entered into a concurrent war in Iraq, in March 2003, which was named Operation Iraqi Freedom (OIF). In September 2010, OIF was renamed Operation New Dawn (OND) as the reigns of control changed and the Iraqi people took on more control in their country and the U.S. forces began to back out.

Social workers play a key role in working with service members and their families during the entire course of service: pre-deployment, deployment, and post-deployment. These times are often filled with anxiety, tension, anticipation, and a number of different stressors, not only for service members, but also for their families and communities. It is vital that as service providers, civilian social workers take the time to educate themselves about the military and the unique military culture that encompasses its members and their families.

Issues Facing Service Members, Veterans, and Their Families

Many current and returning service men and women are faced with psychosocial issues as a result of long and multiple deployments and exposure to combat, such as mental health issues, parenting and family conflict, domestic violence, homelessness, military sexual trauma, and substance abuse issues.[a]

Service members experience not only the visible physical injuries caused by combat, but also the invisible, often debilitating, psychological issues that war can leave behind. Some of the physical injuries incurred during war include amputated limbs, vision and hearing loss, brain and spinal cord damage, and traumatic brain injuries. Traumatic brain injuries have been termed the "signature injury" impacting soldiers due to the extensive amount of improvised explosive devices used during OEF and OIF.[b]

Traumatic brain injuries may not always be apparent to the individual who sustained the injury or the service provider working with the individual. However, Savitsky, Illingworth, and DuLaney state that these injuries can result in a number of different symptoms, such as "memory loss, short attention spans, muddled reasoning, headaches, confusion, anxiety, depression and irritability."[c] Individuals may also experience significant behavioral and personality changes as well.

Military men and women have an undying loyalty to their comrades, and when injured they are not only plagued by the physical injury, but also with the internal dilemma, and often guilt, of going home and leaving their unit behind in combat. Although service members are often injured during their tours of duty, 98% of the wounded soldiers fighting in the Iraq War survived, which is the highest survival rate of any war.[d] This survival rate contributes to a number of additional factors that may pose as stressors for the individual and family, which may include lengthy periods of rehabilitation, significant financial burdens related to medical care, and life-altering changes in the activities of daily living and relationships. All of these stressors impact a soldier's ability to heal and recuperate, but also may take a toll on mental health functioning.

Historically, military men and women have suffered from a number of different mental health disorders during and after tours of duty, and this is no different for military personnel who have served in OEF or OIF. Posttraumatic stress disorder (PTSD) is often associated with individuals who have been exposed to combat. Anxiety disorders may also be experienced by such individuals, resulting from the chronic threat of roadside bombs and improvised explosive devices used in OEF and OIF. Depression is also not uncommon for soldiers, as they experience long and extended tours of duty and time apart from their families. Although military personnel are a vulnerable population to the risks of mental health stressors, they may be more reluctant than other individuals to seek necessary treatment for problematic symptoms based on the fear of professional repercussions or social stigmas.

As rates of depression, anxiety, and other mental health disorders rise, so do the rates of attempted and completed suicides among service members and veterans. A recent study conducted by the Army Behavioral Health Integrated Data Environment reported a striking 80% increase in suicides among army personnel during the Iraq and Afghanistan wars. The study went on to state that service members who have been involved in prolonged combat operations, such as OEF and OIF, are more vulnerable to experience exaggerated levels of stress and stressful situations, which may contribute to an increase in mental health conditions and the risk of suicide.[e]

(continued)

Military service members may use and abuse alcohol and drugs, for similar reasons that civilian individuals do. Substances have historically been used for a number of reasons, including as a coping tool. Service members and veterans may also be likely to use substances as a means of coping with the stressors that they experience as a result of combat; however, the same stigma that negates service members from seeking treatment for mental health issues may also stop them from seeking substance abuse treatment.

OEF and OIF have also been unique in that more female service members than at any other time in history served in these wars. Female veterans are exposed to and experience similar stressors and conflicts as their male counterparts; however, women struggle with their role transition more than their male counterparts.[f] This can also be problematic and stressful because female service members are likely to have young children at home and to possibly be the primary caregivers for these children. The stress of this situation may take its toll on the female service member and her ability to perform while serving, and also have a significant impact on her family.

Unlike in any previous war, military families are facing multiple and extended deployments. This poses several concerns and creates stressors not only for the service member, but also for his or her family at home, including the children left behind. Van Pelt states that some of these stresses include, but are not limited to, the frequent absence of a parent, long-distance parenting, challenges that come up for the at-home parent, worrying about a deployed family member's safety, and continual changes in family roles.[g] Each of these stressors, often experienced in combination with one another, can create several problematic situations physically, emotionally, and mentally for affected individuals. DeAngelis notes that a family that is strongly connected prior to the time of military service will most likely fair far better than a family that is struggling with any of these stressors prior to service. The cohesiveness and strength of a family also contributes immensely to a soldier's ability to perform successfully while in battle.[h]

Children of military families often face very unique issues, such as frequent relocations, long periods of separation, and multiple times of single-parenting households.[i] Children may display problematic behaviors—physically, emotionally, mentally, behaviorally, or academically. Families and professionals should acknowledge the amount of stress that is experienced by these children and address these issues at home, in school, and in the community by offering extra support to children of military families.

Deployment of a family member is also a very stressful time for the parent or caregiver who remains at home and is left to take over the full parenting responsibilities. Savitsky et al. state that rates of "child maltreatment by Army wives during their husbands' deployment was more than three times the rate of child maltreatment by wives while their husbands were not deployed."[j] This statistic highlights the fact that the parent who remains at home may experience more stress while the other parent is deployed, and this could adversely impact the family unit.

Service men and women often struggle upon their return home in reuniting in their intimate relationships and family roles. Castro et al. define the "Battlemind as the soldier's inner strength to face fear and adversity in combat, with courage. The two components of Battlemind are self-confidence and mental toughness; strengths that all soldiers must have to successfully perform in combat."[k] The Battlemind is a critical aspect of survival in the combat zone; however, it can also be problematic upon post-deployment and result in displayed anger and family conflict when a service member returns home, posing challenges in intimate relationships. Many soldiers returning home have to relearn their role in the family and acknowledge that they have been gone for some time and have missed several events in their family's lives. The Battlemind may interfere negatively with this reintegration, as the stress of this transition affects a soldier and her or his family.

Military sexual trauma (MST) also impacts men and women who have served their country. MST is described as assault based on gender and could be displayed in repeated, threatening sexual harassment or intimidation. Twenty percent of female veterans report experiencing MST; however, when screening for MST with active-duty members, only 8% report incidents of MST.[l] This finding may support the idea that MST is occurring while members are actively serving, but they may not be reporting for a number of reasons, such as fear of possible repercussions.

Active-duty service members experience high workloads and often work around the clock. They have little downtime and much of their day is very structured. Service men and women are trained to be mission ready at all times, and little autonomy is found in their active-duty lifestyles. This constant sense of mission readiness may lead to a hypervigilent approach in daily activities, which may contribute to some anxiety and stress for soldiers while they are serving, but can also be problematic upon reintegration to civilian life. Service members may find this difficult when returning home to little structure and possible unemployment.

Providing Services to Service Members, Veterans, and Their Families

Service men and women are returning home from a war like none other. This has impacted not only the service members, but also their families as well as their communities. Social workers fulfill many roles in providing services to military personnel and to veterans.

As an *enabler*, a social worker assists military members and their families in identifying and clarifying their needs and problems, prior to, during, and after times of military service. The need for services can be identified during the assessment process, and screening for possible concerns and services of military men and women is very important at all stages of service. Upon return from a tour of duty, service members are often doing well—happy to be reunited with their families and thankful to be safely home. Oftentimes, these individuals display minimal issues or minimal services immediately after returning home. However, it may be several months or years

(continued)

later that issues arise, and services are needed for these individuals and their families at that time.[m]

When problematic issues are identified, social workers embrace the role of *empowerer*. Social workers empower those whom they serve by assisting them in developing the skills necessary to improve their quality of life. Clients may be empowered through counseling to develop anger management skills, establish skills to create environmental stability (such as parenting or vocational skills), and better cope with substance abuse challenges.

Military families, especially those in rural, isolated areas, may not be aware of services available to them. A social work *broker* will diligently work with a military family to make a linkage to services when needed. During the course of deployment, families often experience a number of stressors, and social work brokers can be the ones to link the family to resources, such as medical, financial, or other benefits or supports, which may be vital to the family's survival during the service member's absence.

As a primary goal of the social work field, workers continually *advocate* for the individuals whom they serve. Social workers take on the advocacy role by empowering military members and their families to be able to make their needs known and to get those needs met. Social workers could demonstrate this role in a number of ways. For example, a worker who is advocating for a military child at school may assist the school in understanding the child's needs and unique culture and address how to meet these needs adequately. Some service members may be reluctant to seek services or to allow their family members to do so, out of fear of professional repercussions and social stigma. It is important for social workers to advocate for clients and their families to overcome the long-standing stigma that prevents individuals from seeking needed services.

Activists are social workers who may focus their time at the local, state, and federal levels to bring attention to problematic issues in an attempt to secure changes in policies and procedures that will assist in meeting the needs of their clients. An example of activism would be a worker who assiduously works with policymakers and lawmakers to ensure that mental health or substance abuse services are available to service members who need them. Activism would also be displayed in a social worker bringing attention to the homeless veteran population and working to bring changes to this demographic.

As a *mediator*, a worker may provide services within a family, group, or community. If a family is experiencing interfamilial issues, such as at the time of reintegration, a worker may become involved to assist in addressing the conflict before these stressors escalate to domestic violence or issues related to child abuse and neglect.

A social worker could provide *negotiator* services to a family if issues (such as, housing, medical services, and other provided services) arise and the family is unable to manage these matters on its own. As a negotiator, social workers are aligned with the client and are working to meet the client's needs, often by negotiating with a third-party service provider.

As an *educator*, workers may be the ones to educate the family on the different issues that arise during the deployment cycle and how these could impact the family. A social worker may also provide education to schools and other service providers to enable them to provide more successful services to support children of military families. An educator may also work to educate a family on the signs and symptoms of problematic behaviors (such as mental health or substance abuse concerns) and to teach stress management techniques.

Military members and their families may find comfort and support within a group setting, and a social worker could take on the role of *group facilitator* to create this opportunity. Social workers could also facilitate a support network for parents who often spend long periods of time being single parents and may experience an increase in stress because of this. Isolation from a support network and services can significantly contribute to a family's inability to manage life during the already difficult time of deployment.

Social workers must also continue the vital role of *researcher* in the field of military social work and adapt their practices to the unique needs of the military culture and its members. Researchers will play an imperative part in identifying the long-term needs of these individuals, as well as the impact that combat and long and multiple deployments have on military members and their families. This important data will assist in determining the needed services and in developing the evidence-based practices needed to deliver them in the future.

SOURCE: This exhibit was written by Rachel Dunn, MSW, CAPSW, field coordinator for George Williams College of Aurora University.

[a]G. Gunter-Hunt, S. Daugherty-Dennis, K. Brunner, and J. Jaqua, *Bringing the War Home: The Impact of the War in Iraq and Afghanistan Military Service Members, Veterans and Families* (Madison, WI: National Association of Social Workers Wisconsin Chapter Home Study Program, 2012).

[b]L. Savitsky, M. Illingworth, and M. DulAney "Civilian Social Work: Serving the Military and Veterans Populations" *Social Work*, 54, no. 4, (2009), pp. 327–339.

[c] Ibid., p. 332.

[d]Ibid.

[e]C. Gann, "Suicides, Mental Health Woes Soar since Start of Iraq War." *ABC News*, http://news.yahoo.com (accessed March 7, 2012).

[f]Gunter-Hunt, Daugherty-Dennis, Brunner, and Jaqua, *Bringing the War Home*.

[g]J. Van Pelt, "Parental Deployment and Child Mental Health," *Social Work Today*, 11, no. 2, (2011), pp. 30–31.

[h]T. DeAngelis, "Social Workers Help Military Families," *National Association of Social Workers*, http://www.socialworkers.org/pressroom/events/peace/helpfamilies.asp.

[i]Savitzky, Illingworth, and DeLaney, "Civilian Social Work."

[j]Ibid., p. 330.

[k]C.A. Castro, C.W. Hoge, C.W. Milliken, D. McGurk, A. Adler, A. Cox, and P. Bliese, "Battlemind Training: Transitioning Home from Combat," presented at the Army Science Conference, Orlando, FL, November, 2006, http://www.dtic.mil/cgi-bin/GetTRDoc?AD=ADA481083, p. 1.

[l]Gunter-Hunt, Daugherty-Dennis, Brunner, and Jaqua, *Bringing the War Home*.

[m]Ibid.

Immigration has also contributed to some of the social problems that plague American society. Immigration has resulted in ethnic and racial conflict, exploitation of illegal aliens, competition among different ethnic groups for a "piece of the pie," and the stresses and costs associated with educating and caring for new arrivals.

The presence of illegal aliens (also called undocumented immigrants) is one of the most complex social issues in our country. The number of undocumented immigrants currently in the United States is unknown, as is the number of new arrivals each year. By far the largest percentage of undocumented immigrants are Mexicans and Central Americans.

The effects of illegal residents on the economy of the United States has been a topic of heated debate for decades. Some authorities argue that they take jobs away from native-born residents. Other authorities believe they are a boon to our economy as they perform distasteful work that U.S. citizens are reluctant to do—such as harvesting garden crops on their knees. They also maintain some industries by accepting lower wages and inferior working conditions. The survival of such industries stimulates growth in associated services, thereby creating more jobs. During economic recessions, undocumented immigrants are generally laid off or discharged more readily than citizens; they thereby help cushion the native-born population from economic uncertainty.

Undocumented immigrants are easily exploited by ruthless individuals who know that the immigrants cannot complain to authorities when they have been victimized. (If they went to the authorities, their illegal status might be discovered, which would subject them to deportation.) Although many undocumented immigrants are working in the United States, their employment is now illegal. In 1986 Congress passed the Immigration Reform and Control Act, under which employers are subject to civil penalties ranging from $250 to $10,000 for each illegal alien they hire.

The vast majority of the immigrants who arrive in the United States primarily settle in only a few cities and regions, such as the metropolitan areas of New York City, Los Angeles, Miami, and Chicago. The phenomenon of *chain migration* is the primary cause of this urban concentration. The term refers to the tendency of immigrants to migrate to areas where relatives and others from their home communities are already living. These relatives and acquaintances share the immigrants' culture and language (or dialect) and are available to help the immigrants adjust to the new surroundings. The clusters of immigrants in large cities greatly add to the costs of services in these areas, such as education, health care, job training, public housing, and adult English-language classes.

Now, as in the past, much of the opposition to immigration is based on racial and ethnic prejudice because most of the immigrants to the United States in recent decades have been people of color and non-Europeans. But there is a legitimate question as to whether immigrants raise the unemployment rate by adding to the competition for a limited number of jobs.

Sudden surges of political refugees or illegal immigrants may create special problems. For example, in 1980 Fidel Castro released a number of prisoners and residents of mental hospitals in Cuba; many of these individuals fled to southern Florida, particularly Miami. The influx taxed governmental services in southern Florida and also spurred several serious outbreaks of racial violence in the area during the 1980s.

An *immigrant* is a person who migrates to another country, usually for permanent residence. A *refugee* is a person who flees his or her country of origin or habitual residence because he or she has suffered persecution due to religion, race, political opinion, nationality, or because the person is a member of a persecuted social group.

In 1997 the respected National Academy of Sciences/National Research Council released a landmark report titled *The New Americans: Economic, Demographic, and Fiscal Effects of Immigration*. The report concluded immigration has a very small impact on the U.S. economy: "The costs to native-born workers are small, and so are the benefits."[36] The report found that immigrants have no negative effects on the wages of most Americans. There is one exception: the very low skilled. Workers with less than a high school degree (who represent about 15% of the workforce) earn wages that are somewhat lower (about 5%) than they would without competition from low-skilled immigrants. The study found that the other losers are taxpayers in California, Florida, Texas, and a few other states where most immigrants live. Taxpayers in these states end up paying more in taxes for the government services (primarily health care and public schools) used by the newcomers. The study also found that immigrants generate a growing share of taxes the longer they are here.[37]

In recent years several states, cities, and counties have passed a variety of laws and ordinances related to illegal immigration. (When the unemployment rate is high, as it has been in recent years, there often is an effort to deport undocumented immigrants, who some believe are taking jobs away from American citizens.) In 2006, Hazelton, Pennsylvania, passed a law to take business licenses away from employers who hire undocumented workers, and to fine any landlord $1,000 a day for renting to illegal immigrants. In 2010, Arizona passed an act (Support Our Law Enforcement and Safe Neighborhoods Act) that has the intent of enhancing the arrest and deportation of illegal immigrants. Federal law requires that legal immigrants carry registration papers with them at all times. Arizona's act makes failure to carry registration documents a state crime, and mandates police to verify the legal status of a person during arrests, detentions, and traffic stops if the police suspect the person is an illegal immigrant. Critics of the legislation say it encourages racial profiling, whereas supporters say the law prohibits the use of race as the sole basis for investigating immigration status. There have been protests in opposition to the law in nearly 100 U.S. cities—including boycotts and calls for boycotts of conferences and national events held in Arizona.

Passage of this Arizona act has prompted other states to consider adopting similar legislation. Surveys have found the act to have majority support in Arizona and nationwide.[38]

The Obama administration sued to block Arizona's law shortly after it passed in 2010, saying it interfered with federal authority over immigration. The law made it a state crime for illegal immigrants to seek work or fail to carry proper immigration papers. It also requires police officers to check immigration status and make warrantless arrests for immigration crimes in some cases. In June 2012, the U.S. Supreme Court upheld a key part of Arizona's law that allows police officers to ask about immigration status during stops. Other parts of the law, including a provision that made it a state crime for illegal immigrants to seek work, will remain blocked, as the justices affirmed the federal government's supremacy over immigration policy.

The Development, Relief and Education for Alien Minors Act (DREAM Act) was introduced in Congress in 2009. At the time of this revision, the act has not been passed. The DREAM Act allows some undocumented immigrants who were brought to the United States as children to apply for U.S. citizenship. If such children go to college or serve in the U.S. military when they are age-ready, they would (under DREAM) be allowed to apply for temporary legal status and eventually become eligible for U.S. citizenship. DREAM also would eliminate a federal provision that penalizes states that provide in-state tuition to undocumented immigrants.

Critical Thinking Questions

Do you support the DREAM Act? Do you support Arizona's Support Our Law Enforcement and Safe Neighborhoods Act?

Too Little Energy

Eight-tenths of all energy is provided by fossil fuel sources: oil, coal, and natural gas. Natural gas sources are rapidly being depleted. The domestic supply of oil in the United States is incapable of meeting our needs, and therefore, this country is heavily dependent on foreign sources. All the industrialized nations combined hold only 25% of the world's people but use an estimated 85% to 90% of the energy consumed each year.[39]

It has been estimated that the world's petroleum and natural gas reserves will be substantially depleted within a century.[40] In recent years there has been an increased recognition that the demand for oil worldwide was overtaking the barrels of oil that could be produced. As a result, there were dramatic increases worldwide in the price of gasoline. New sources of energy that work as well as fossil fuel sources will have to be found.

Shortages of Other Nonrenewable Resources

The world's mineral resources also contain elements that are essential for industrial production. These essential elements include copper, lead, zinc, tin, nickel, tungsten, mercury, chromium, manganese, cobalt, molybdenum, aluminum, platinum, iron, and helium. Consumption of these minerals is occurring so rapidly that reserve sources will eventually be depleted, expensive mining of low-quality ores will have to be undertaken, and substitutes will have to be found. As the developing countries continue to industrialize, the demand for these nonrenewable minerals will far exceed the supply.

The Theory of Demographic Transition

As noted, the rate of population growth is highest in developing countries. Researchers have observed that growth rates tend to decrease and then stabilize after a fairly high level of industrialization has been achieved. This observation is assumed to be true about population growth in general, and the assumption is called the *theory of demographic transition*. This transition is thought to take place in three stages:

1. *Preindustrial agricultural societies*. In this stage, there is a fairly stable population size. The societies have both high birth rates and high death rates.

2. *Developing societies that are beginning to industrialize*. In such societies, the birthrates remain high, but the death rates drop, leading to a rapid increase in the population. The death rates drop because these societies develop the medical capacities to keep people alive and increase the average life span.

3. *Developed industrial societies*. Such societies have both low birthrates and low death rates, resulting in a stable population once again. The low birthrates are thought to be due to people voluntarily limiting the number of children they have. Parents decide to have fewer children to maintain a higher standard of living for themselves and their children.

The theory of demographic transition gives hope that, as developing countries continue to industrialize, their high population growth rates will eventually decrease and then stabilize. However, the concept of demographic transition is merely a theoretical model. It is a summary statement of what happened in the United States and in many other industrialized nations. Because some past societies have had this demographic history does not necessarily mean that current developing nations will repeat the same patterns.

A variety of factors, including religious and cultural values, can affect the rate of population growth. In Japan, for example, certain values rapidly accelerated passage through the second stage in the demographic transition. At the end of World War II, Japan was a developing nation with a high birthrate. Two variables thrust Japan into the third stage of demographic transition. First, there was a general consensus that population control was needed. Second, abortion was not considered immoral (as it was in Western societies). As a result, from 1947 to 1957, the birthrate in Japan dropped from 34 children per 1,000 to 14 per 1,000, one of the sharpest declines on record. During this decade, half of all conceptions were terminated by abortion.[41] It is doubtful that such a rapid transition could be achieved in countries with cultural traditions that encourage large families.

With regard to stabilizing population growth, Ian Robertson notes:

The question is not whether population will stabilize—it will. If the global population exceeds the carrying capacity of the earth, death rates will rise and halt population growth. The issues are whether stability will result from a decrease in birth rates or an increase in death rates, how long it will take before stability occurs, and how many people will be here when this finally happens. The prospect of a demographic transition offers the hope that if certain preconditions are met, population growth rates in the developing world will be reduced by a decline in birth rates rather than the grim alternative.[42]

At present, tragically, most developing countries have become lodged in a "holding pattern" in the middle stage of demographic transition, with high birthrates and lowered death rates.[43] The longer these countries remain in this stage, the more the size of their populations will swell and the more difficult it will become for them to industrialize and complete the "demographic transition."

Problem Attitudes and Values

The Roman Catholic Church still objects to using any birth control approach except the rhythm method. In many countries, widely accepted values encourage parents to have large families. Abortions are still a controversial issue in our society. And many Americans believe that population growth is *not* a major issue requiring immediate attention.[44] With such attitudes and values, it is clear that overpopulation is not recognized as one of our most serious problems.

With regard to attitudes toward the use of birth control, Ehrlich and Ehrlich note:

We shouldn't delude ourselves: the population explosion will come to an end before very long. The only remaining question is whether it will be halted through the humane method of birth control, or by nature wiping out the surplus. We realize that religious and cultural opposition to birth control exists throughout the world; but we believe that people simply don't understand the choice that such opposition implies. Today, anyone opposing birth control is unknowingly voting to have the human population size controlled by a massive increase in early deaths.[45]

Critical Thinking Questions

Do you believe population growth is a major issue requiring immediate attention? If so, do you believe our government should promote the use of contraceptives to prevent unwanted pregnancies and to help slow the doubling-time rate of the world's population?

Two Countries with Severe Population Problems

India and China are two countries with immense overpopulation problems. If the population growth rate in the world is not curbed, most countries will face similar conditions in the future.

India

With an area about one-third the size of the United States, India has a population more than three times the size of ours; it has more than 1 billion people.[46] About 25 million babies are estimated to be born in India each year.[47]

India is also one of the world's poorest nations, with a per capita income of $1,527 per year.[48] Many of its citizens are malnourished and starving. The average Indian has a daily food intake of about 2,000 calories. (The minimum requirement for staying healthy is about 2,300 to 2,500 calories.) In some states in India, more than 100 of every 1,000 babies die because of inadequate prenatal care and delivery services, low levels of immunization among children, and a substantial proportion of high-risk births.[49]

In 1952 India became the first country in the world to adopt a public family planning program to reduce the birthrate. At first the program was poorly funded. In 1956, for example, total expenditures amounted to 1¢ per year for every 20 people. The principal contraceptive method that was promoted was the rhythm method, which is one of the least effective approaches. In the 1960s, vasectomies and the intrauterine device (IUD) were added to the techniques used. At the end of the 1960s, oral contraceptives were also added, although vasectomies and IUDs remain the preferred methods.

Although the birthrate has declined somewhat in India, birth control devices have not reduced the rate

Afternoon traffic jams the streets in Calcutta. India's population hit 1 billion in 1999.

Dibyangshu Sarkar/Afp/Getty Images

to the zero-growth level. A major reason is that most people using birth control techniques decide to do so only after they already have a large family.[50]

In 1976 the Indian government under Indira Gandhi decided to promote a more aggressive population control strategy. Public educational programs were developed to try to persuade Indians that their main problem was not too little food but too many people. The federal government threatened to dismiss civil service employees who had more than three children. Individual states were asked to pass bills requiring compulsory sterilization of parents after the birth of their third child. As we saw in Case Exhibit 17.2, one state, Maharashtra, passed such a law and began compulsory sterilization.

Critical Thinking Question

Do you believe some countries in the future will seek to reduce population growth rates by enacting compulsory sterilization laws?

In 1977, however, Mrs. Gandhi received a crushing electoral defeat, partly because of her government's record on civil liberties and partly because of the unpopularity of the population control programs. Following her defeat, the compulsory sterilization law in Maharashtra was rescinded.

India is projected to surpass China in population size by the year 2050, as India's growth rate is substantially higher than China's.[51] More than 80% of all Indians are Hindus. Hindu husbands frequently will not permit their wives to use contraceptives until they have produced at least two sons.[52] An additional 11% of the population are Muslims. Some Muslim religious leaders denounce birth control of any kind, but especially sterilization, because cutting the body is a violation of religious law.[53] The obsession for sons is so strong in India that, in order to prevent abortions of unwanted female fetuses, national law prohibits physicians from telling a pregnant woman the sex of the unborn child.[54]

Will India continue to race toward starvation and famine, or will it find politically acceptable approaches to controlling its population growth and begin to raise the standard of living for its citizens? Answers to such questions are of vital significance to all developing countries (and will also have substantial consequences for the rest of the world).

In recent years India has been experiencing one of the highest rates of economic growth in the world. The advent of the digital age and the large number of young and educated people fluent in English are gradually transforming India into an important "back office" destination for global outsourcing of customer services and financial services.

China

In terms of sheer size, China's population surpasses that of India. China already has more than 1.3 billion people—nearly one-fifth of the world's entire population.[55]

China's attitude about population growth has varied with time. For many years, the government considered its huge population an important military resource in any conflict with the former Soviet Union or the United States. Furthermore, it urged other developing nations to take the same view. As is common with many developing nations, China's standard of living is low, and much of the farming and factory work is done by hand.

Poor harvests and resulting food shortages (along with changes in the top leadership and a closer relationship with the United States) have convinced the Chinese government that population control is essential. The leaders are now promoting the view that limiting family size will improve the health and living conditions of all its citizens and will also liberate women from traditional restrictions. Propaganda posters advertise that an education and a good career are more easily attained with a small family.

Prior to the present policies on family size, Chinese women averaged three children each.[56] In 1980 China's government established a one-child-per-family policy. It raised the minimum legal age of marriage by 2 years, to 22 for men and 20 for women. In some higher-density areas, this minimum age is even older; in Beijing it is 28 for men and 25 for women.[57] (A higher minimum age for marriage is correlated with a smaller average family size.[58]) To have a large family is now regarded as disrespectful to the Communist party and to the country.

Women who become pregnant after the birth of their first child are sometimes pressured to have an abortion. China has also established a number of economic and social incentives for couples to have no more than one child, including income bonuses, priority consideration in urban housing assignments, subsidies in health care, promises of higher pensions, and private vegetable gardens for city residents. For couples who have more than two children, there are also disincentives, such as possible wage deduction to fund welfare programs.

China has greatly slowed its growth rate with these policies. China's current growth rate is down to about 1.1%—an extremely low rate for what is still a poor developing nation.[59] It is clear that China is now committed to an all-out effort to stabilize the size of its population, which is good news for the future of China (and for the rest of the world).

Yet new problems have emerged. Some fears have surfaced about the possibility of an emerging generation of spoiled and self-centered only children. Also, if the one-child policy were fully achieved, China would become a society without brothers, sisters, uncles, or aunts.[60] Chinese peasants have traditionally placed a high value on having sons, who live with the extended family throughout their lives. Daughters, on the other hand, are expected to move in with their husband's family and are therefore considered more of a burden than an asset. Having a son is also viewed as vitally important in continuing the family's name and heritage. As a result, the one-child policy has caused a startling increase in female infanticide because couples then are able, without government opposition, to attempt another pregnancy in the hope of having a male child. The pace of childbearing in China has decelerated faster than that in any other large developing country.[61]

Critical Thinking Question

Would you like to live in a society in which there were no brothers, sisters, uncles, or aunts?

Another problem related to female infanticide in China is that today there are nearly three men for every two women.[62] This statistic poses some obvious problems for unmarried Chinese men.

In recent years, China has opened its doors to the West, inviting tourists and Western technology and investments. Undoubtedly there will be unrest accompanied by political turmoil. (For example, in the 1970s, the Shah of Iran established governmental policies and programs to facilitate industrialization, using funds from the sale of its crude oil to foreign countries. These rapid changes led to political unrest, civil war, and the eventual ouster of the shah.) The future changes in China will have immense implications for the rest of the world.

Today, China is the fastest growing major economy in the world. China is also becoming one of the most visited countries in the world. It received increased attention worldwide when the summer Olympics were held in Beijing in 2008. China's economic success in recent years has been primarily due to manufacturing low-cost products. This is attributed to a combination of cheap labor, relatively high productivity, favorable economic policies of the government, good infrastructure, and a medium level of technology and skills of the populace.

Will coercive population control policies such as those in India and China eventually be needed in the United States? Ehrlich and Ehrlich note:

> We must hope that our government doesn't wait until it too decides that only coercive measures can solve America's population problem. One must always keep in mind that the price of personal freedom in making childbearing decisions may be the destruction of the world in which your children or grandchildren live. How many children a person has now has serious social consequences in all nations, and therefore is a legitimate concern of society as a whole.[63]

Environmental Problems

Higher concentrations of people in an area usually intensify environmental problems. In this section, we will examine the following issues: despoilment of the land, waste disposal (including radioactive and solid waste), air pollution, radioactive leaks from nuclear power plants, nuclear war, water pollution, acid rain, and general pollutants.

Despoilment of the Land

The scenic beauty of our land—as well as its long-term economic value—is being spoiled by a variety of short-term human efforts: strip mining of coal, oil drilling, clearing trees and forests, building highways, constructing oil pipelines, overgrazing by cattle and sheep, dumping garbage, littering, and erecting highway billboards. In nature there is often a delicate balance among the elements: Some fertile land needs trees and grass to retain moisture and fertility; grass-eating animals need grass to survive; carnivorous animals need the grass-eating animals; some birds need seed and insects; other birds feed on small animals or larger animals that have died; all are in need of water. Upsetting this balance often leads to destruction. Dinosaurs once ruled the earth, but all died from some as-yet-unknown environmental change. The Sahara Desert, fewer than 20,000 years ago, was a luxuriant forest. Overgrazing by domesticated sheep and goats and clearing of the forests were major factors in destroying the area.[64]

Deforestation is caused almost entirely by humans who log trees to get lumber and fuel and intentionally destroy the forests to make room for the farms and cities demanded by a growing population. Every year the world loses an area of tropical forest land that is comparable to the size of Wisconsin.[65] At this rate, virtually no tropical forests will be left in 30 or 40 years.[66] If the rain forests are destroyed, more than a million unique species of animals and plants will die with them.[67]

Paul and Anne Ehrlich describe what happens when forests are cleared:

Numerous animals that depend on the trees for food and shelter disappear. Many of the smaller forest plants depend on the trees for shade; they and the animals they support also disappear. With the removal of trees and plants, the soil is directly exposed to the elements, and it tends to erode faster. Loss of topsoil reduces the water-retaining capacity of an area, diminishes the supply of fresh water, causes silting of dams, and … flooding.… Deforestation … reduces the amount of water transferred from ground to air by the trees in the process known as "transpiration." This modifies the weather downwind of the area, usually making it more arid and subject to greater extremes of temperature.[68]

Some areas of the world are losing several inches of topsoil each year because of poor management that exposes the land to water and wind erosion. This is particularly alarming in light of the fact that it takes 300 to 1,000 years to produce 1 inch of topsoil under favorable conditions.[69] Each year 25 billion tons of topsoil are lost, primarily by erosion and by being washed into the sea.[70]

Forests, water, and soil are renewable resource systems that have "carrying capacities"—that is, levels at which they can provide maximum yields without injuring their capacity to repeat those yields. We can chop down only a certain number of trees in a forest each year without destroying the forest's capacity to replace those trees. Human populations in many parts of the world have grown so large that they are beginning to exceed the "carrying capacities" of their environments.[71]

Sometimes the environment is despoiled by human accidents. In April 2010, the *Deepwater Horizon* oil drilling rig (owned by Transocean and leased to BP) in the Gulf of Mexico exploded over the Macondo oil well. Eleven oil rig workers were killed, and 17 more were injured. The explosion opened a gusher of oil and methane gas into the Gulf. By the time the oil well was sealed months later, over 4 million barrels of oil had spilled into the Gulf, creating what probably was the worst environmental disaster in U.S. history. Dead birds, dolphins, whales, and fish were found covered in oil along the 650 miles of coastline that were impacted by the BP oil spill. In an attempt to lessen the impact of the oil slick, BP used nearly 2 million gallons of chemical dispersants (detergent-like compounds that break up spilled oil into tiny droplets that mix with water). Sadly, some of the 57 chemicals found in these dispersants can cause cancer, respiratory problems, and skin and eye irritation, and also are toxic to aquatic life. The fishing industry in the Gulf was devastated, coral formations were smothered, and the ecosystems in the Gulf were severely damaged.[72]

Sometimes the environment is intentionally despoiled by humans. Prior to being forced out of Kuwait in 1991 during the Gulf War, President Saddam Hussein of Iraq ordered his military forces to set 600 oil wells in Kuwait on fire. Billions of dollars of oil reserves were destroyed, skies were blackened for months, and the persistent smoke and fires had severe adverse effects on the quality of life for humans and animals in the region.

Waste Disposal

As of yet, our country does not have a safe way of disposing of radioactive waste material. Solid waste disposal also poses major problems.

Radioactive Wastes

The United States now has more than 100 nuclear power plants and plans to build more in the future.[73] A danger is that nuclear power plants generate radioactive nuclear wastes, and disposing of radioactive wastes is a complex problem. In large doses, radiation from these wastes can cause death; small doses may lead to cancer or birth deformities. These wastes are particularly hazardous because they remain radioactive for as long as 300,000 years. The Nuclear Regulatory Commission has considered various proposals for

A.J. SISCO/UPI/Newscom

Oil spills have the potential to kill numerous birds and marine species.

disposing of these wastes: firing them into space by rockets, burying them at sea, burying them in solid rock formations, and burying them in the deepest abandoned mines that can be found. An ultimate solution has not as yet been found. Such wastes are now generally put in concrete tanks and buried. A serious danger is that these tanks are built to last only for a couple of hundred years, not for the needed thousands.

Radioactive wastes remain boiling hot for years. Leakage from some of these waste tanks has already occurred. In 1974 one leaked for 51 days and raised the radiation count substantially above the minimum acceptable levels.[74] A crucial question is, with our current ways of disposing of nuclear wastes, are we creating a lethal problem for the future?

Solid Waste Disposal

So much public concern is focused on radioactive waste disposal that we sometimes overlook another serious disposal problem: good old-fashioned trash. Each year Americans junk billions of tons of wastes: food, glass, paper, plastics, cans, paints, dead animals, abandoned cars, old machinery, and a host of other things. We are often referred to as a "consumer society." More accurately, we are a throwaway society.

Solid wastes are ugly, unpleasant, and odorous. They pollute water that circulates through them and provide breeding grounds for rats and other noxious pests.

The two principal methods of solid waste disposal are landfills (that is, burying in the ground) and incineration. Many garbage-dumping areas, particularly in small towns, do not meet the sanitary standards set by the federal government.[75] In addition, improperly designed municipal incinerators are major contributors to urban air pollution.

Toxic Wastes

Toxic wastes, or residues, are a major problem. Toxic wastes result from the production of pesticides, plastics, paints, and other products. These wastes have typically been buried in pits or ditches. The famous case of Love Canal, near Niagara Falls (see Case Exhibit 17.4), arose when toxic residues that had been dumped into the unfinished canal seeped into the surrounding area and contaminated both the soil and the water.

CASE EXHIBIT 17.4

Tragedy at Love Canal

Love Canal was once a pleasant neighborhood of tree-lined streets in the city of Niagara Falls, New York. Up until the late 1970s, hardly anyone was concerned that the area had once been a chemical dumping ground. Over a 25-year period ending in 1953, Hooker Chemicals and Plastic Corporation had buried 20,000 tons of toxic substances in leaky drums. Among the chemicals dumped was highly lethal dioxin. In the late 1970s, it was noted that the residents of Love Canal had substantially higher rates of birth defects, cancer, miscarriages, chromosome damage, kidney failure, and death.

The neighborhood—homes, schools, and parks—had been built above the dump site. Families noted that bluish-black substances sometimes oozed through the ground. The substances were discovered to be toxic. Dumped pesticides and other poisons had polluted the groundwater, seeping up through the earth and into basements, creating hazardous vapors. Tests in certain basements found 80 different toxic chemicals to be present. It was also thought that contamination was occurring from eating home-grown garden vegetables.

In 1980 the Environmental Protection Agency conducted tests in the area and found it to have dangerously high levels of toxic substances. The residents of Love Canal were eventually evacuated. In 1985, after more than 6 years of litigation, 1,300 former residents were awarded payments totaling $20 million in compensation for health problems (including birth defects and cancers) suffered as a result of the contamination. In 1991, after extensive cleanup, some houses in the Love Canal area were declared habitable again. Most of the 900 families that originally lived in Love Canal have relocated.

Environmental experts acknowledge that the Love Canal disaster is not an isolated problem. Of the nearly 50,000 toxic-chemical dumps in the United States, more than 1,000 are considered potential health hazards.

SOURCES: "Living with Uncertainty: Saga of Love Canal Families," *U.S. News & World Report*, June 2, 1980, p. 32; William Kornblum and Joseph Julian, *Social Problems*, 14th ed. (Boston: Pearson, 2012), p. 467. http://www.epa.gov/history/topics/lovecanal/.

Global Warming

Global warming is the gradual increasing of average global air temperature. Average global surface temperatures have increased by about 0.74°C over the last century.[76] Although that increase may seem insignificant, it should be noted that average temperatures during the last Ice Age were only 5°C lower than they are today.[77]

The prevailing scientific view is that greenhouse gases—primarily carbon dioxide, nitrous oxide, and methane—accumulate in the atmosphere and act like glass in a greenhouse, thereby causing global warming. Global increases in carbon dioxide are due primarily to increases in the burning of gasoline, oil, and natural gas. As forests are cut down or burned, fewer trees are available to absorb the carbon dioxide (trees and other plant life use carbon dioxide and release oxygen into the air). Increases in methane and nitrous oxide are primarily due to agricultural practices.

The effects of global warming could be devastating. As ocean/sea levels rise, some island countries, as well as some barrier islands, will go under water and disappear. Low-lying coastal areas will become increasingly vulnerable to storm surges and flooding. Global warming is anticipated to affect regions in various ways. As average temperature rises, some areas will experience heavier rain, whereas other areas will become arid from receiving very little rain. Global warming will result in shifts of animal and plant habitats; some species may not survive.[78]

Air Pollution

Air pollution is most severe in large, densely populated industrial centers. Some cities (such as Los Angeles) occasionally have such dense smog that, even on clear days, there is a haze over the city. Moreover, not only city air but also the entire atmosphere of the earth is polluted to some degree.

Health Effects and Extent of Air Pollution

Not only does air pollution rot windshield wiper blades and nylon stockings, blacken skies and clothes, damage crops, and corrode paint and steel, it also kills people. Death rates are higher whenever and wherever smog occurs, especially for the very old, the very young, and those with respiratory ailments. Pollution contributes to a higher incidence of pneumonia, emphysema, lung cancer, and bronchitis. A 1952 London smog disaster was directly linked to some 4,000 deaths.[79] And such disasters are of substantially less significance than the far-reaching effects of day-to-day living in seriously polluted cities. Also, poor visibility caused by smog is recognized as a major factor in both airplane and automobile accidents.

Each year in the United States, we release into the air tons of pollutants, including carbon monoxide, hydrocarbons, oxides of nitrogen, oxides of sulfur, soot, and ashes. Cars emit many of these pollutants, industrial centers (particularly pulp and paper mills, petroleum refineries, chemical plants, and iron and steel mills) add a large share, and so do trash incineration and the burning of fuel for heating homes and offices.[80]

Air pollution is believed to contribute to the deaths of at least 50,000 Americans every year.[81] Valleys and closed air basins are more likely to have air pollution than plains and mountains. In the former areas, the air can become especially bad when a layer of warmer air moves over a layer of cooler air and seals in pollutants that would ordinarily rise into the upper atmosphere; this condition is known as *temperature inversion*.

Critical Thinking Questions

Are you living in a clean air environment? If not, what steps should you take to protect your health and improve your life expectancy?

Air Pollution and Environmental Changes

Air pollution may also be breaking down the earth's protective ozone layer. This layer surrounds the earth from an altitude of 8 to 30 miles above sea level and screens out many of the harmful rays from the sun. Some studies suggest that fluorocarbon gases (commonly used in refrigerating systems and aerosol spray cans) may be destroying the ozone layer.[82] If it is breaking down, there reportedly will be sharp increases in skin cancer and crop failure as well as changes in the world's climate. When these studies became public knowledge, the use of fluorocarbon spray cans by American consumers dropped sharply (demonstrating that individuals acting in concert can and do make a difference). Manufacturers responded to this drop in sales by developing spray cans without fluorocarbons. However, fluorocarbons are still used in coolants in refrigerators and air conditioners, for making plastic foams, and as cleaning solvents for microelectronic circuitry. Under certain conditions, these compounds escape into the atmosphere, rise high into the stratosphere, and set off chemical reactions that rapidly destroy ozone.

Radioactive Leaks from Nuclear Power Plants

We've already discussed one of the problems associated with nuclear energy: radioactive wastes. Another nuclear energy problem is the potential for radioactive leaks into the atmosphere. In the United States, there have been numerous malfunctions at nuclear power plants that have resulted in the release of minor amounts of radioactivity into the air.[83] In 1979 more than 200,000 residents had to be evacuated from the area surrounding the power plant at Three Mile Island, Pennsylvania. Radioactive leakage from a damaged reactor caused fear that an explosion might occur. In 1986 an explosion did occur at a nuclear power plant in Chernobyl, Ukraine. In 2011, an earthquake and subsequent tsunami in Japan caused a series of equipment failures and nuclear meltdowns at a nuclear power plant. (See Case Exhibit 17.5.)

Nuclear War

On the morning of August 6, 1945, adults in Hiroshima, Japan, were preparing to go to work. An American bomber was spotted overhead. Seconds later it dropped an atomic bomb, which exploded 2,000 feet above the center of the city. The destruction was devastating. The heat and force of the blast killed tens of thousands of people almost instantly. It also released radiation, which eventually killed more than 100,000 more people.[84] Numerous bombs have since been built that are 1,600 times more powerful than the one that destroyed Hiroshima.[85]

One of the greatest dangers to the survival of civilization is nuclear war. A nuclear war would have devastating effects on the environment and, according to many authorities, could end human civilization. Russia and the United States have the nuclear capacity to destroy each other several times over. Many other nations also possess nuclear bombs or are seeking to develop nuclear warheads or purchase them from other countries.[86]

If a nuclear war occurred, life forms located nearby would be killed instantly. Anyone or anything that initially survived would face death from a variety of sources. (Exposure to radiation may cause cancer and a variety of other fatal medical conditions.) Some scientists predict that survivors would face a "nuclear winter," in which a cloud of soot would block the sun over much of the earth, pushing temperatures far below freezing and preventing the

CASE EXHIBIT 17.5

Nuclear Power Plant Disasters in Chernobyl, Ukraine, and Japan

In spring 1986, there was an explosion and fire at a nuclear power plant in Chernobyl, Ukraine. The explosion blew off the top of the reactor and sent a radioactive plume across large parts of the former Soviet Union and much of Eastern and Western Europe. The 4,000°F fire burned in the reactor's graphite core for more than a week before it was extinguished. Within a few weeks after the disaster, more than 30 people had died from massive doses of radiation. Exposure to smaller amounts of radiation has resulted in early deaths for tens of thousands of other people from cancers of the bone marrow, breast, and thyroid.

The disaster occurred at a highly vulnerable place. Eighty miles from the site is the city of Kiev, which has a population of more than 2 million. Chernobyl is also near the breadbasket area of Russia; nearly half of that country's winter wheat is grown there. Much of the grass and animal feed in the area was contaminated with radioactive particles. Such accidents have alerted the public to the dangers of nuclear power plants and have slowed the growth of nuclear energy use. Whether to expand or curtail the development of nuclear plants is an international issue. It is an issue that illustrates the complexity of trying to choose between energy needs and physical safety, especially when experts are in sharp disagreement about the technological risks. Those exposed to radioactivity in Chernobyl would, if given a choice, undoubtedly opt for less energy over the current reality that they are now more likely to bear children with birth defects and more likely to die early from cancer.

On March 11, 2011, a 9.0-magnitude earthquake and resulting tsunami caused a series of equipment failures and nuclear meltdowns at the Fukushima Daiichi nuclear power plant in Japan. There was a major release of radioactive materials, causing widespread environmental and health damages. A mandatory evacuation was issued for people living within 12 miles of the plant. Those living outside this radius were advised to stay indoors, and close their doors and windows. They were also told to cover their mouths with masks, and avoid drinking tap water. A few weeks later, the evacuation zone was expanded to 18 miles or more, with about 20,000 being forced to leave their homes. High radioactive levels led the government to ban the sale of food grown in the area. More than 300 plant workers received significant radiation doses. A few workers died almost immediately. Future cancer deaths due to accumulated radiation exposures in the population living near Fukushima are anticipated. The Japanese government declared on December 16, 2011, that the plant was now stable, but that it would take decades to decontaminate the surrounding areas and to decommission (to remove from service) the plant. The amount of uranium released was equivalent to 20 Hiroshima bombs!

SOURCES: http://www.chernobyl-international.org; Linda A. Mooney, David Knox, and Caroline Schacht, *Understanding Social Problems*, 8th ed. (Belmont, CA: Wadsworth, 2013), pp. 412–413.

---

growth of most foods. Another worry is that the ozone layer would break down. Clearing of the cloud of soot would cause intense sun rays to penetrate humans and animals, resulting in skin cancer and other disorders. Another danger is that crops would be affected by radioactivity and would be potentially dangerous as food sources. Quite possibly, the initial survivors would face a slow, painful death. Their quality of life could slip to depths at which they would grub out a brute-like, barely human existence. The social infrastructure would unravel; that is, the industrial, educational, agricultural, transportation, health care, political, and communication systems would cease to function. Those who did survive would also face intense psychological stress from grief, despair, disorientation, hopelessness, and anger.[87]

How can a nuclear war be averted? This is perhaps one of the most important questions facing civilization. Fortunately, the chances of an all-out nuclear war appear to have lessened in recent years, primarily because of the improvement in relationships between the former Soviet Union and the

United States. Prior to the 1990s, these two superpowers were unable to agree on a nuclear disarmament plan. As a result, both countries built and stockpiled nuclear weapons that had the capacity to destroy each other several times over.

Only after Russia rejected communism and started to move toward a democratic form of government around 1990 were the two superpowers willing to trust each other sufficiently to make progress in reducing nuclear warheads. In 1993 Russia and the United States signed the Strategic Arms Reduction Treaty (START) agreement, which substantially reduced U.S. and Russian stockpiles of long-range nuclear missiles.[88] A major reason for this more cooperative relationship was the easing of mutually hostile ideologies. Once Russia moved toward democracy and away from a state-controlled economy, it became less ideologically opposed to the United States. At the same time, Russia's move toward democracy led the United States to give up its perception of Russia as "the evil empire." (This term was used by President Reagan in 1984 in referring to the former Soviet Union.)

Even though the threat of a nuclear holocaust resulting from the Cold War between the United States and the Soviet Union has greatly diminished, the possibility exists that nuclear bombs will be developed (and perhaps used) by nations in unstable areas of the world, such as in the Middle East. There is also the danger that radioactive materials will be stolen (or bought) by terrorist groups and converted into low-grade nuclear bombs. In 1994 German police arrested a Russian smuggler with more than 300 grams of plutonium in his baggage; it turned out to be a sample from 4 kilograms of plutonium that were being offered for sale for $250 million.[89] Such concerns suggest it is premature to celebrate the end of the threat of a nuclear holocaust. Certain countries have, or are believed to have, nuclear weapons: the United States, Russia, the United Kingdom, France, China, India, Pakistan, Israel, and North Korea. Iran is believed to be seeking to develop nuclear weapons.

Water Pollution

More than two-thirds of the earth's surface is covered by water. Water is continually cleansing itself by evaporating, forming clouds, and raining back to the earth. Unfortunately, people are contaminating the water supply faster than it can cleanse itself. As the population grows in a particular area, so does industry, which pours into the water a vast array of contaminants: detergents, sulfuric acid, lead, hydrofluoric acid, ammonia, and so on. Increased agricultural production also pollutes water with insecticides, herbicides, and nitrates (from fertilizers). The result is the spread of pollution in creeks, streams, and lakes; along coastlines; and—most seriously—in groundwater, where purification is almost impossible. Water pollution poses the threat of disease epidemics such as hepatitis and dysentery as well as poisoning by exotic chemicals. Some rivers and lakes are now so polluted that they cannot support fish and other organisms that require relatively clean, oxygen-rich water. These lakes and rivers are accurately described as "dead."

The United States has the dubious distinction of being the only country in the world with a river that has been called a fire hazard. So many industrial chemicals, oils, and other combustible pollutants have been dumped into the Cuyahoga River in Ohio that it has twice caught on fire.[90] Water quality in this river has improved in recent years.

Human waste is also a major contributor to water pollution. The sewage from New York City alone produces 5 million cubic yards of sludge a year, which is dumped into the ocean and now covers more than 15 square miles of ocean bottom.[91] An even bigger source of pollution is waste from oil refining, food processing, animal feedlots, textile and paper manufacturing, and other industries.

Acid Rain

There is a growing concern over acid rain. Formed from emissions from automobiles and industrial plants, acid rain has become a serious problem in eastern Canada, in the northeastern United States, and in many other countries.[92] It is created when sulfur and nitrogen oxides in emissions combine with moisture in the air to form sulfuric and nitric acids. Acid rain is killing fish in lakes and streams and is reducing the number of plant nutrients in the ground, thereby making soil less fertile. It has also damaged timber and may eventually start affecting synthetic structures, including classic architecture and sculptures. Scientists estimate that 50,000 lakes in the United States and Canada are now so polluted by acid rain that fish populations have been either destroyed or severely damaged.[93]

General Pollutants

Some substances—such as chlorinated hydrocarbons, lead, mercury, and fluorides—reach us in so many ways that they are considered *general pollutants*. Of the chlorinated hydrocarbons, DDT was used the longest but is now banned. DDT is a synthetic insecticide; chemically it breaks down slowly, and it will last for decades in soil. Unfortunately, the way DDT circulates in ecosystems leads to a concentration in carnivores (including humans); that is, it becomes increasingly concentrated as it is passed along a food chain. Following World War II, DDT was widely used as an insecticide until research with laboratory animals showed that it affects fertility, causes changes in brain functioning, and increases the incidence of cancer.[94]

The long-term effects of DDT (and of many other general pollutants) are still unknown. The substance is poisonous and may (or may not) lead to subtle physiological changes. An important question is: Among the thousands of chemicals currently being used, which ones will have unknown toxic side effects? In the United States, there are more than 62,000 chemical substances in commercial use, with 1,500 new chemicals being introduced each year. However, complete data on the health and environmental effects are known for only 7% of the chemicals produced in high volume.[95]

Radioactive wastes and certain poisons such as DDT also pose serious problems because of biological magnification. With this process (mentioned previously), the concentration of the substance increases as it ascends in the food chain. For example, Richard Curtis and Elizabeth Hogan found in a study of the Columbia River in the western United States that although the radioactivity of the water was at such low levels that it was nonhazardous, the radioactivity of river-related biological life forms was much higher and potentially hazardous:

> *...the radioactivity of the river plankton was 2,000 times greater; the radioactivity of the fish and ducks feeding on the plankton was 15,000 and 40,000 times greater, respectively; the radioactivity of young swallows fed on insects caught by their parents in the river was 500,000 times greater; the radioactivity of the egg yolks of water birds was more than a million times greater.*[96]

The radioactivity was thought to be due to isotopes released into the river from the nuclear power plant at Hanford, Washington.

DDT, many other pesticides, and radioactive material are cumulative poisons; that is, they are retained in the tissues of the organisms that consume them rather than excreted back into the environment. Thus, one never loses the poison of previous exposure, and future exposures compound the potential danger to the individual.

The use of pesticides by American farmers also has a number of adverse consequences. An article in *Newsweek* noted:

> *It's a bit of the devil's bargain. In exchange for using $3 billion worth of pesticides yearly, American farmers reap $12 billion worth of crops that might otherwise be lost to weeds and insects. Without the chemicals, millions of people might face food shortages. On the other hand, less than 1 percent of the poisons reach their target pests; the rest wind up as contaminants in water, residues on produce and poisonous fallout on farm workers. Worldwide, the compounds fatally poison an estimated 10,000 people a year and injure 400,000 more. Uncounted millions more may be at increased risk for cancer, reproductive problems and birth defects due to low-level, chronic exposure. We can't seem to do without pesticides; but can we live with their consequences?*[97]

Multiple chemical sensitivity (MCS) is also known as "environmental illness." It is a condition whereby some individuals experience adverse actions when exposed to low levels of chemicals found in commonly used substances (such as perfumes, housecleaning materials, fresh paint, vehicle exhaust, and numerous other petrochemical-based products). Symptoms include burning eyes, headaches, stomach distress, dizziness, loss of mental concentration, and breathing difficulties. Sufferers of MCS often avoid public places, or wear a protective breathing mask to avoid inhaling the chemical substances that they are sensitive to.

Chronic lead poisoning is also serious; it leads to loss of appetite, weakness, and apathy. It also causes lesions of the neuromuscular system, the circulatory system, the gastrointestinal tract, and the brain. Exposure to lead comes from a variety of sources: pesticides, lead pipes, and lead-contaminated food and water. Perhaps the most hazardous instance is when children eat paint containing lead. Most household paints today do not contain lead, but the danger still exists with older buildings and furniture that were painted with lead-based paint. Even when these buildings are painted over with lead-free paint, peeling may expose the original lead-based ones.

Exposure to high concentrations of mercury can cause blindness, deafness, loss of coordination, severe mental disorders, or even death. Mercury is added to the environment in many ways: It may leak into the water from industrial processes that produce chlorine; it is emitted by the pulp and paper industry; it is a primary ingredient of agricultural fungicides. Also, small amounts are released when fossil fuels are burned.

What Needs to Be Done

Up to now, we've merely been describing several national and international problems: overpopulation, food and water shortages, economic problems, international terrorism, crowding, energy shortages, shortages of nonrenewable resources, despoilment of the land, radioactive and solid waste disposal, toxic wastes, air pollution, radioactive leaks from nuclear power plants, nuclear war, water pollution, acid rain, and general pollutants. Now we'll look at a number of recommendations for confronting overpopulation and environmental problems.

Confronting Overpopulation

Limiting population growth will have a major positive effect on all of the problems discussed in this chapter. If the world's population growth is reversed to approach a zero-growth rate—or even a negative rate—it may give us the necessary time to find solutions to other problems. Limiting population growth is a key factor in maintaining our current quality of life.

How can the size of the population be limited? Dr. Paul Ehrlich suggests that, as the most affluent and influential superpower, the United States should become a model for population control by (a) setting a goal of a stable optimum population size for our country and displaying our determination to achieve this goal rapidly and (b) reversing our government's current "reward" system for having children. Specific measures include the following:

- No longer allowing income-tax deductions for children
- Placing a luxury tax on layettes, diapers, cribs, expensive toys, and diaper services
- Rewarding small families by such measures as giving "responsibility prizes" to each man who has a vasectomy after having two children
- Subsidizing adoptions and simplifying adoption procedures
- Guaranteeing the right of any woman to have an abortion
- Enacting a federal law to require sex education in schools, including material on the need for regulating the birthrate and on techniques of birth control
- Developing new contraceptives that are reliable and easy to use and do not have harmful side effects[98]

Bernard Berelson compiled a list of other proposals to control population:

- Adding temporary sterilants to water or food supplies, with doses of an antidote carefully rationed by the government to produce the desired population size (such sterilants are not yet in existence)
- Making sterilization of men with three or more living children compulsory
- Raising the minimum age for marriage
- Providing benefits (money, goods, or services) to couples who do not bear children for extended time periods
- Requiring that foreign countries establish effective population control programs before any foreign aid will be provided[99]

Some of these proposals appear too radical for most Americans to accept, and they conflict with the moral and ethical values of many citizens. But will we reach such an overpopulation crisis that they may be necessary in the future? Many developing nations are now instituting sex education and family planning programs, which (at least temporarily) are showing evidence of lowering birthrates. Ideally, the population control measures recommended by Berelson can be avoided.

In the United States, the vast majority of women who are sexually active and do not want to become pregnant use a modern contraceptive.[100]

A developing country that has had success in reducing the rate of population growth is Indonesia. It launched its national family planning program in the 1960s. Initially, Indonesia focused its efforts on informing its people (including the country's conservative religious leaders) of the problems associated with overpopulation and the advantages of a smaller family. The government's next effort shifted to making contraceptives available to everyone who wanted them. This effort was careful to respect the conservative sexual attitudes of most Indonesians. (For example, there was very little effort to promote the use of condoms because most Indonesians associate them with prostitution.) The government now offers incentives for the long-term use of contraceptives, including subsidies for government employees, valuable agricultural products, and even complimentary trips to Mecca (the holiest site of the Islamic religion). As a result of these efforts, Indonesia's birthrate has declined by about 45% in the past two decades.[101] Its current annual growth rate is about 1.3%, which is significantly lower than that of most other developing countries.[102]

The Abortion Controversy

If the world's population continues to grow at or near its present rate, the current debate over voluntary abortions may pale compared to controversies that will be generated if compulsory population control measures are needed.

The abortion controversy has been going on for five decades, but it was heightened in January 1973, when the U.S. Supreme Court, in a 7–2 decision, overruled state laws that prohibited or restricted a woman's right to obtain an abortion during the first 3 months of pregnancy. Suing under the assumed name of Jane Roe, a Texas resident argued that her state's law against abortion denied her a constitutional right. The Court agreed that the right of personal privacy includes the right to decide whether to have an abortion. However, the Court held that such

Pro-life or pro-choice? Abortion is one of the most divisive public issues today.

a right is not absolute and that states have the authority to impose restrictions after the third month. This decision, known as *Roe v. Wade*, also allowed states to prohibit abortions in the last 10 weeks of pregnancy (a time when there is a good chance that the fetus will live), except when the life or health of the mother is endangered.

In 1977 Congress passed, and President Carter signed into law, the so-called Hyde Amendment (named for its original sponsor, Representative Henry Hyde from Illinois). This amendment prohibits Medicaid spending for abortions except when a woman's life would be endangered by childbirth or in cases of promptly reported rape or incest. In June 1980, this amendment was upheld as constitutional in a 5–4 vote by the U.S. Supreme Court. The ruling means that the federal government and individual states do not have to pay for most abortions for women on welfare.

The Hyde Amendment is significant because more than one-third of the legal abortions performed in the United States between 1973 and 1977 were for women on welfare.[103] The passage of the amendment illustrates the strength of the anti-abortion forces in this country. Is it fair for middle- and upper-class women to have more access to abortions than lower-income women?

With the election of President Reagan in 1980, there was a move toward conservatism in our society. Certain groups, such as the Catholic Church and right-to-life groups, have been strongly urging that a constitutional amendment be passed to prohibit abortions, except in cases where the woman's life is endangered.

During the Reagan and George Bush administrations from 1980 to 1992, some liberal Supreme Court judges retired and were replaced by more conservative judges. As a result, the Supreme Court gradually assumed a more conservative (pro-life) position on the abortion issue. The waning of the Supreme Court majority recognizing a woman's right to an abortion

CASE EXHIBIT 17.6

Legal Abortion: Arguments Pro and Con

Against Legal Abortion

Human life begins at conception; therefore, abortion is murder. Even scientists have not reached a consensus on any other point in fetal development that can be considered the moment the fetus becomes a person. Life is a matter of fact, not religion or values.

We must pass a constitutional amendment to protect unborn babies from abortion. To say that the law will not be followed and therefore should not be made is like saying laws against murder should be repealed because people still get murdered.

Medicaid should not pay for abortion. It is wrong to try to eliminate poverty by killing the unborn children of the poor. Tax money should not be used for the controversial practice of aborting unwanted children. The decision not to have children should be made before one gets pregnant.

If you believe abortion is morally wrong, you are obligated to work for the passage of a "human life" amendment to the Constitution.

The right of the unborn to live supersedes any right of a woman to "control her own body."

The "abortion mentality" leads to infanticide, euthanasia, and the killing of individuals with a disability and older people.

Abortion causes psychological damage to women.

Women have abortions for their own convenience or "on a whim."

In a society in which contraceptives are so readily available, there should be no unwanted pregnancies and therefore no need for abortion.

In Favor of Legal Abortion

The belief in personhood at conception is a religious belief held by the Roman Catholic Church. Most Protestant and Jewish denominations regard the fetus as a potential human being, not a full-fledged person, and have made position statements in support of legal abortion. When the unborn becomes a person is a matter of religion and values, not absolute fact.

No law has ever stopped abortion, and no law ever will. The issue is not whether abortions will be done, but whether they will be done safely, by doctors, or dangerously, by back-alley butchers or by the women themselves. History has shown that anti-abortion laws are uniquely unenforceable and do not prevent abortions.

The original intent of Medicaid was to equalize medical services between the rich and the poor and to help the poor become independent and self-sufficient. To make them ineligible for abortion defies justice, common sense, and rational policy. Women burdened by unwanted children cannot get job training or go to work and are trapped in the poverty/welfare cycle. Neither abortion nor childbirth should be forced on poor women.

Many people who are personally opposed to abortion, including most Roman Catholics, believe it is wrong to impose their religious or moral beliefs on others.

For women to have equality with men, they must be autonomous and free to make an abortion decision. If women lose the right to have an abortion, their lives and lifestyles would substantially be determined by men and impregnation.

In countries where abortion has been legal for years, there is no evidence that respect for life has diminished or that legal abortion leads to the killing of any people. Infanticide, however, is prevalent in countries where the overburdened poor cannot control their childbearing and was also prevalent in Japan before abortion was legalized.

The Institute of Medicine of the National Academy of Sciences has concluded that abortion is not associated with a detectable increase in the incidence of mental illness. The depression and guilt feelings reported by some women are usually mild, temporary, and outweighed by feelings of relief. Such negative feelings would be substantially lessened if anti-abortion advocates were less vehement in expressing their beliefs. Women choosing abortion should be informed of the risks and benefits to the procedure and should decide for themselves what to do.

Right-to-life advocates dismiss unwanted pregnancy as a mere annoyance. The urgency of women's need to end unwanted pregnancy is measured by their willingness to risk death and mutilation, to spend huge sums of money, and to endure the indignities of illegal abortion. Women have abortions only when the alternative is unendurable. Women take both abortion and motherhood very seriously.

No birth control method is perfectly reliable, and for medical reasons many women cannot, or will not, use the most effective methods. Contraceptive information and services are not available to all women, particularly to teenagers, the poor, and rural women.

(continued)

CASE EXHIBIT 17.6 *(continued)*

Against Legal Abortion	In Favor of Legal Abortion
Abortion is not the safe and simple procedure we're told it is.	Before the 1973 Supreme Court rulings, in *Roe v. Wade*, illegal abortion was the leading cause of maternal death and mutilation. Having a legal abortion is medically less dangerous than giving birth.
Doctors make large profits from legal abortions.	Legal abortion is less costly and less profitable than illegal abortion was. Many legal abortions are done in nonprofit facilities. If it's not improper to "make money" on childbirth, it is not wrong to earn money by performing legal abortions.
Parents have the right and responsibility to guide their children to important decisions. A law requiring parental notification of a daughter's abortion would strengthen the family unit. (Many states have now passed parental consent laws that are consistent with this argument.)	Many teenagers voluntarily consult their parents, but some simply will not. Forcing the involvement of unsympathetic, authoritarian, or very moralistic parents in a teen's pregnancy (and sexuality) can damage the family unit beyond repair. Some family units are already under so much stress that knowledge of an unwed pregnancy could be disastrous.
Pro-abortionists are antifamily. Abortion destroys the American family.	The unwanted child of a teenage mother has little chance to grow up in a normal, happy American home. Instead, a new family is created: a child and her child, both destined for a life of poverty and hopelessness. Legal abortion helps women limit their families to the number of children they want and can afford, both emotionally and financially, and reduces the number of children born unwanted. Pro-choice is definitely profamily.

became clear in a 1989 decision, *Webster v. Reproductive Health Services.* The Supreme Court upheld a restrictive Missouri law that (a) prohibited state employees from assisting in abortions and prohibited abortions from being performed in state-owned hospitals and (b) banned abortions of *viable* fetuses. (The Missouri law viewed fetuses as viable if the woman was believed to be 20 or more weeks pregnant and a viability test showed the fetus could live.) The broader effect of the Court's decision was to throw the hot-potato issue of abortion back to state legislatures, many of which debated a variety of abortion bills.

In 1992 Bill Clinton was elected president. He had adhered to a pro-choice position on the abortion issue. President Clinton had the opportunity to appoint a few liberal judges to the Supreme Court.

President George W. Bush was elected in 2000. He supported a pro-life position. In 2008, Barack Obama was elected president; he supports a pro-choice position.

In 2007 the U.S. Supreme Court ruled that certain forms of late-term abortions could be declared illegal, regardless of the danger to the woman's health if the pregnancy were continued. This decision reversed years of precedent holding that a woman's risk of severe health consequences was more important than the life of the fetus.

By 2012, more than a dozen states had passed laws regulating or restricting abortions, which are designed to restrict access to abortion without directly challenging a woman's right to choose under the existing policy set forth in *Roe v. Wade.* For example, a recent Oklahoma law requires that a woman who wants an abortion must first view an ultrasound as a doctor or technician describes in detail the anatomical characteristics of the fetus.

More than 1 million women have an abortion each year in the United States.[104] About one in three women in the United States has had an abortion by age 45.[105]

The major objection to permitting abortions is based on perceptions of moral principles. The Catholic Church views abortion as one of the most important current moral issues. This church and various right-to-life groups condemn abortions as being synonymous with murder. They assert that life begins at conception—that there is no phase during pregnancy in which there is a distinct, qualitative difference in the development of the fetus. The Catholic Church views abortion as acceptable only when it is done to save the physical life of the mother. This type of abortion is justified on the principle of "double effect," which holds that a morally evil action (performing an abortion) is allowable when it is the side effect of a morally good action (saving the life of the mother). Case Exhibit 17.6 summarizes the arguments both for and against legal abortion.

If abortions were prohibited again, women would seek illegal abortions as they did in the past. Performed in a medical clinic or hospital, an abortion is a relatively safe operation, but performed under unsanitary conditions, perhaps by an inexperienced or unskilled abortionist, the operation is extremely dangerous and may even imperil the life of the woman. When abortions are illegal, some women attempt to self-abort. Self-induced abortions can be extremely dangerous. Women have tried such techniques as severe exercise, hot baths, and pelvic and intestinal irritants and have even attempted to lacerate the uterus with such sharp objects as hat pins, nail files, and knives.

Opponents of abortion argue that the "right to life" is basic and should in no way be infringed on. Proponents of abortion counter this view by arguing that there may be a more basic right than the right to life: the preservation of the quality of life. Given the overpopulation problem and the fact that abortion is an effective population control technique (in some countries, the number of abortions is approaching the number of live births), some authorities argue that abortion is a necessary measure (although less desirable than contraception) to preserve the quality of life. Unless life has quality, the right to life is meaningless.

Providing Family Planning Services

Family planning services are obviously essential programs for preventing unwanted pregnancies. Such services include birth control information and contraceptives, pregnancy testing, HIV testing and counseling, testing and counseling about other sexually transmitted diseases, sex education, abortion counseling and abortions, counseling on child spacing, sterilization information and operations, infertility counseling, and preparation for parenthood.

Governmental Programs

National family planning programs involve governmental efforts to lower birthrates by funding programs that provide birth control information and services. With family planning programs, families voluntarily decide whether to limit the number of children they have. Most countries, including both developing and developed nations, now have official family planning programs. This is a remarkable achievement because 70 years ago no developing country had such a program. (In fact, 70 years ago, several countries had programs with the opposite objective—to increase the birthrate and the rate of immigration.) Concern about world population growth clearly is a recent phenomenon.

Critical Thinking Question

The National Association of Social Workers has taken a policy position that it supports a woman's right to obtain a medically safe abortion under dignified circumstances. Do you support or oppose this policy position?

Despite these advances, only a few countries have established population control policies. (Population control is the deliberate regulation of the size of the population by society. Family planning, in contrast, is the regulation of births by individual families.) As we noted, India's population control program included a sterilization policy that was soon retracted after the ruling party failed to be reelected. Whether India will attempt to enact another population control policy is unclear; future population growth may be a decisive factor in determining whether such action is necessary.

Until President Lyndon Johnson's 1965 State of the Union Address, family planning was not considered a proper concern for our government. In that address, President Johnson stated that $5 spent on family planning was worth $100 invested in some other area of world economic development. In 1966 the federal government developed regulations that, for the first time, allowed federal funds to provide family planning services to welfare clients on a voluntary basis. The avowed purpose of this policy (which was widely criticized) was not phrased in terms of family planning goals. Rather, the stated objectives were to reduce the welfare burden by lowering the illegitimacy rate and to break the poverty cycle by decreasing the transmission of poverty from one generation to another.

The National Center for Family Planning Services was established by the passage of the Family Planning Services and Population Research Act of 1970. This act recognized that family planning was part of the delivery of comprehensive health services for all. In 1972 Congress mandated that family planning services be provided to all welfare recipients who

Table 17.3 Ranking of Effectiveness of Birth Control Methods in Preventing Pregnancies

METHOD	NUMBER OF PREGNANCIES PER 100 WOMEN DURING 1 YEAR OF USE
1. Abstinence	0
2. Norplant implant	Fewer than 1
3. Sterilization: Men, vasectomy	Fewer than 1
4. Depo-Provera (contraceptive injection)	Fewer than 1
5. Sterilization: Women, tubal ligation	Fewer than 1
6. IUD	2
7. Oral contraceptives (female)	5
8. Male condom	14
9. Withdrawal	19
10. Diaphragm	20
11. Cervical cap	20
12. Female condom	21
13. Natural family planning (rhythm)	25
14. Spermicide	26

NOTE: After the first seven listed methods, the risk of pregnancy for sexually active users sharply increases. (Sterilization for women, tubal ligation, is nearly 100% effective, although in very rare cases, the tubes may rejoin.)

SOURCE: "Comparing Effectiveness of Birth Control Methods," http://www.plannedparenthood.org.

desired them. At that time, contraceptive policy changes were also made, lifting restrictions on marital status and age for receiving birth control information and devices.

Private Agencies

In the United States, most family planning services in the past were provided by private agencies and organizations. The largest and best-known organization is Planned Parenthood. Founded by Margaret Sanger in 1916 with the opening of the first birth control clinic in Brooklyn, the organization now has clinics throughout the nation. Planned Parenthood offers the following: (a) medical services—physical examinations, Pap tests, urine and blood tests, screening for sexually transmitted diseases, all medically approved methods of contraception, and pregnancy testing; (b) counseling services—infertility, premarital, contraceptive, pregnancy, and sterilization for both males and females; and (c) educational services—sex education, contraceptive information (including effectiveness and side effects of the varied approaches), and breast self-examinations. (Table 17.3 shows a ranking of the effectiveness of various contraceptives in preventing pregnancies.)

Family planning services are now available in practically all areas in the United States from a variety of public and private organizations, including health departments, hospitals, physicians in private practice, Planned Parenthood affiliates, and other agencies such as community action groups and free clinics.

The Future

Violence against abortion clinics and family planning clinics has escalated in recent decades. Anti-abortion groups have picketed clinics, with the objective being to stop patients from using clinic services. Clinic physicians and other staff often receive threatening phone calls and have their own homes picketed. Abortion clinics, staff, and patients have been subjected to a number of incidents of violence involving bombings, arsons, vandalisms, burglaries, assaults, death threats, kidnappings, and stalkings. Violent tactics by anti-abortion supporters have even included incidents of shooting and killing staff at abortion clinics. It is ironic that some fringe elements of the right-to-life movement have resorted to murder to seek to force their views on others. Will such violence continue to escalate in the United States in the future?

CASE EXHIBIT 17.7

Medication Abortion

In September 2000, the U.S. Food and Drug Administration gave final approval to the use of RU-486. This pill, which induces abortion early in pregnancy, was developed and introduced in France. It is now widely used in France, Great Britain, Sweden, and China to induce abortions. RU-486 acts by impeding a hormone (progesterone) that is necessary for a fetus to stay implanted in the uterus. The pill works only until 7 weeks after conception. The drug has its limits; most notably, it takes longer to abort a pregnancy than a surgical abortion.

RU-486 has been named "mifepristone" in this country. When mifepristone is taken in conjunction with another drug, misoprostol, which causes uterine contractions that expel the embryo, the regimen is about 95% effective in terminating pregnancies when used within 7 weeks of conception. It generally takes three doctor's visits to complete a drug-induced abortion. During the initial visit a woman is examined; if everything is OK, she takes three mifepristone (brand name: Mifeprex) tablets. Two days later, she returns to the physician's office for a dose of misoprostol. Most women experience intense cramping and heavy bleeding soon after taking the second drug. Bleeding and spotting can last from 9 to 16 days and sometimes as long as a month. Nausea, headache, and diarrhea are also common side effects.

The embryo is usually expelled within 24 hours of taking the pills; a follow-up visit 2 weeks later confirms that the pregnancy has ended. In some cases, a surgical abortion is necessary because the abortion has not been completed or bleeding is too severe.

The right-to-life movement was successful in the late 1980s and early 1990s in keeping RU-486 from being legally distributed in the United States. The Food and Drug Administration banned the pill in 1989 after being pressured by anti-abortion groups.

In 1994 the U.S. government announced that an agreement had been reached with France's Roussel Uclaf, the company that originally patented the drug, permitting testing of the pill on 2,000 American women. The tests were successful.

Scientists who developed RU-486, as well as pro-choice groups, prefer not to call it an abortion method, but rather a method for the induction of menstruation or a contragestational drug. It cannot properly be called a contraceptive because it prevents gestation, not conception.

SOURCE: The Boston Women's Health Book Collective, *Our Bodies, Ourselves* (New York: A Touchstone Book, 2005), pp. 394–398.

The United States needs to resolve a number of family planning issues before it can have an effective national policy on family planning. Currently, there is considerable controversy about a number of issues associated with family planning: sex education in schools, provision of birth control information and devices for teenagers, approaches to prevent HIV and other sexually transmitted diseases, and abortions (including the issue of whether the federal government should pay for abortions for those who cannot afford them).

If problems associated with overpopulation continue to intensify, a national policy of population control may need to be developed. Several authorities are predicting dire consequences for the future of the world unless population control measures are implemented immediately. Other authorities discount overpopulation concerns and predict that technological advances will prevent cataclysmic effects from rapid population growth. If the latter authorities are mistaken, we may be forced in a few years to apply population control measures that now seem unethical and "inhumane."

Werner Fornos strongly urges the United States to fund international programs designed to slow population growth in developing countries:

If Americans now feel anguish over witnessing the recent human suffering and needless deaths in Ethiopia, just imagine a world in which virtually the entire Third World will be wracked by vast poverty and human misery....

And if Americans are now troubled by the specter of instability, revolution, and authoritarianism in the Third World, they have only to imagine the consequences of inaction, because the fragile seed of democracy cannot survive long in societies with escalating misery, crippled economies, and dying environments.

In shaping the federal budget, the U.S. Congress must ask not only how much it will cost to fund population programs, but also what will be the cost of not funding them.[106]

Confronting Environmental Problems

Although environmental problems are very serious, it would be a mistake to assume that the

CASE EXHIBIT 17.8

Morning-After Pills

What can a woman do when the following occurs?

- The condom breaks.
- She has sex and then realizes she forgot to take her pill.
- She is not taking the pill and then is raped.

Fortunately, a woman in such circumstances is no longer limited to waiting and worrying. There are now at least three safe and effective methods available to prevent a pregnancy, even after intercourse has taken place: combined birth control pills, progestin-only pills, and IUDs. All three of these methods can be used for emergency contraception (EC). The Boston Women's Health Book Collective notes:

> Anti-choice groups oppose EC and claim it is abortion which ends a pregnancy instead of contraception, which prevents one. However, EC works either by preventing ovulation or by preventing implantation of a fertilized egg in the uterus. The international medical community has said that pregnancy begins with implantation, so EC acts before pregnancy even occurs. (p. 374)

Combined Birth Control Pills. This approach uses estrogen and progestin in a higher dose than the "traditional" birth control pill. This method frequently causes nausea and discomfort, but users believe the possible protection is worth it. One brand name is called Preven.

Progestin-Only Pills. Progestin-only pills cause few, if any, side effects. One brand, Plan B, is available through health-care providers and also is available in some states without a prescription in pharmacies.

Both of these types of contraceptives prevent a pregnancy by changing a woman's hormone levels. The Boston Women's Health Book Collective describes these emergency contraceptive pills (ECPs):

> They give the body a short, high burst of synthetic hormones that disrupt hormone patterns needed for pregnancy. This prevents pregnancy by inhibiting ovulation or by disrupting egg and sperm transport, fertilization, or implantation. Most women can safely use emergency contraceptive pills even if we cannot use birth control pills as our regular method of birth control. ECPs can be used within five days of unprotected sexual intercourse. The sooner after unprotected intercourse they are taken, the more effective they are.

It is not advisable to use ECPs as your only protection against pregnancy if you are sexually active or planning to be, because they are not as effective as other contraceptive methods. Using ECPs frequently won't hurt you, but it will get expensive. (pp. 374–375)

IUDs. A copper IUD has proved very effective in preventing pregnancy if inserted within 7 days of unprotected intercourse. It appears to work by preventing the implantation of a fertilized egg. It reduces the risk of pregnancy by more than 99%. In addition, once inserted into the uterus, it can be left in place as the regular method of birth control for up to 10 years.

SOURCE: The Boston Women's Health Book Collective, *Our Bodies, Ourselves* (New York: A Touchstone Book, 2005), pp. 374–376.

---

environment is heading for catastrophe. In the late 1960s, the public began to wake up to the environmental problems we face. Dozens of organizations have since been formed (many of them with international memberships) that are working on everything from saving wild animals to recycling aluminum cans to developing new sources of energy.

Since the 1960s, there has been progress in a number of areas. Air quality has improved. Less sewage is being dumped into water. Most automobiles have emission control devices. Life expectancy in the United States has been rising, which is an indirect measure that environmental living conditions may be improving. Relationships between the United States and Russia have improved, which reduces the chances for a nuclear war. Obviously, however, much more needs to be done.

Energy development, preservation of the environment, and economic growth are interdependent

problems. Programs that advance one of these causes often aggravate the others. For example, the development of nuclear power plants led to the explosion in Chernobyl that may shorten the lives of tens of thousands of people who were exposed. Devices that clean exhaust from automobiles reduce air pollution but also decrease fuel economy and thereby more rapidly deplete oil reserves. Strip mining of coal increases available energy supplies but despoils the scenery. Effective environmental programs in the future will need to strike a balance among our competing objectives.

Environmentalists have been waging a political and educational campaign that has not only increased public awareness of environmental concerns but also prompted passage of significant legislation to protect the nation's air, land, and water. For example, the Clean Air Act of 1970 established the Environmental Protection Agency (EPA) and empowered

CASE EXHIBIT 17.9

Male Contraceptives

Why should females have the primary responsibility for using contraceptives? There may be a change in the future.

Because vasectomies are difficult to reverse, researchers have been seeking to develop male hormonal contraceptives (MHCs). Hormones, such as testosterone and progestins, are used in MHCs to turn off sperm production. MHCs could be

taken as a pill, as an injection, or as an implant. Researchers are currently testing MHCs to determine their effectiveness.

SOURCE: "Male Birth Control Pill Soon a Reality," http://www.msnbc .msn.com/id/3543478/ns/health-sexual_health.

---

it to set and enforce standards of environmental quality. However, since the 1980s, political opposition to environmental concerns has intensified. For example, some of the largest corporations in the world have sought to drill oil wells and dig mines in fragile wilderness areas or have sought to "get the government off their back" when they spewed pollutants into the air and water.[107] These businesses have spent millions of dollars to persuade the government to let them pursue such activities. Since the 1980s, environmentalists have struggled to preserve the gains made in the 1970s. Environmentalists, however, do not have the financial resources that large corporations do. Therefore, it is crucial for those concerned about preserving our environment to be aware of political issues in this area and to express their views to government leaders.

It is clear that in the future our environmental problems are not going to disappear on their own. In fact, left alone, existing problems are likely to increase, and new ones will arise. What can be done? Actions needed include changing values from consumption to conservation and developing new sources of energy.

Changing Values

We must realize that bigger is not necessarily better. We need to focus on preserving and conserving our resources rather than consuming them. George Ritzer notes:

We need a reorientation of American culture, a reorientation that may already be underway. Basically, we need to move away from a system that values things growing constantly bigger and better. We are no longer able to master and subdue all that surrounds us. Rather, we must learn to live more harmoniously with our environment. We need to learn to value and protect our environment

rather than seeing it as something to be exploited, raped and despoiled. Most importantly, we need to accept the idea that we are approaching the limits of what the environment can yield to us. At best, we can expect a steady state, at worst a marked decline in our style of life.... We need, in other words, to focus on, and invest in, resources that we can renew rather than the current propensity to exploit such nonrenewable resources as coal and oil.[108]

The move toward conserving resources can be put into action in a variety of ways. Garbage can be used as fuel for running mills to make recycled paper. Water in communities can be purified again and again so that it can continually be reused without being discharged into a river, lake, or ocean. Homes can be better insulated to conserve heat. Smaller cars can be driven at more energy-efficient speeds. People can ride trains and buses instead of cars. Newspapers, aluminum (especially cans), tin, cardboard, magazines, plastic, paper, and glass can be recycled to reduce the amount of solid-waste materials. Recycling a 4-foot stack of newspapers saves a 40-foot pine tree.[109] Aluminum recycling saves 95% of the energy needed to make new cans from raw materials.[110] Using recycled glass to make new glass reduces the amount of air and water pollution by 50% to 60% compared to producing glass from silica.[111] Our society needs to use the conservation measures that are already available. Each of us can make a difference in combating the environmental problems on this planet! (See Case Exhibit 17.10)

People in this country appear to be increasingly aware that all of us have a responsibility to preserve the environment. There is a continued interest in Earth Day, which was founded on April 22, 1970, and is recognized annually. The pesticide DDT has been banned.[112] Since 1970 the following progress

CASE EXHIBIT 17.10

What You Can Do to Help Save Planet Earth

You can make a difference! If everyone takes small steps, major improvements will occur. The following are simple things that you and your family members can do to help the earth:

- Use mugs instead of paper cups, washable cotton towels instead of paper towels, and cloth napkins rather than paper napkins.
- Use both sides of sheets of paper.
- To minimize solid waste, buy products in bulk or products that have the least amount of packaging. Packaging accounts for about 30% to 35% of our trash (U.S. output of garbage equals 400,000 tons every day).
- At the market, use paper bags (which you can recycle) instead of plastic bags. Plastics tend to be nonbiodegradable; they do not break down into innocuous materials.
- Buy products that are recyclable, reliable, repairable, refillable, and/or reusable. Avoid disposables. The new buzzword in waste management is "source reduction," which means buying wisely to minimize the consequences of consumption.
- Grow some of your own food, organically when possible. Plant deciduous shade trees (trees whose leaves fall off) that protect south- and west-facing windows from sun in summer but allow it in during winter. Plant and maintain trees, bushes, or shrubbery. Trees and shrubbery consume carbon dioxide and thereby reduce air pollution.
- Avoid use of Styrofoam cups, which tend to be nonbiodegradable.
- To save water, install sink faucet aerators and water-efficient showerheads. Such adjustments cut water use up to 80% without a noticeable decrease in performance. Repair leaky faucets.
- Take showers of fewer than 5 minutes instead of baths.
- Do not run water continuously when brushing your teeth or shaving.
- Consider ultra-low flush toilets, which use 60% to 90% less water than conventional models. Conserve water by placing a brick or a jug of water in the toilet's water tank.
- Where possible, use fluorescent bulbs rather than incandescent bulbs. Fluorescent bulbs use considerably less energy.
- Use cloth diapers for babies. Disposable diapers annually account for 18 billion tons of trash that, because of plastic content, will take 500 years to decompose. In addition, disposable diapers in landfills frequently contain fecal matter, which can harbor viruses (such as hepatitis) that may trickle into water supplies.
- Turn down the thermostat at night and when the house is empty. Close off and do not heat or cool unused rooms. Wear a sweater instead of turning up the heat. Keep windows (especially near thermostats) tightly shut.
- Turn the thermostat on the water heater down to 120°.
- When possible, use a clothesline instead of a dryer.
- Reduce the use of hazardous chemicals in your home. For example, instead of using ammonia-based cleaners, use a mixture of distilled vinegar, salt, and water for surface cleaning, and use baking soda and water for the bathroom.
- Don't buy motorized or electric tools or appliances when hand-powered ones are available.
- To conserve energy, wash clothes and other materials in warm water and rinse in cold water.
- Open blinds during the day for heat from the sun during cold weather, and close them at night to conserve heat. Close blinds during the day in hot weather to reduce air-conditioning costs.
- Bike, walk, carpool, or use public transit. If at all possible, try to live close to your work and shop close to home.
- Get a low-cost home energy audit from your utility company for suggestions for conserving energy.
- Check caulking around windows and doors, and add it where needed.
- Use latex paints (which are considerably less toxic to the environment) rather than oil-based paints.
- Buy and use cars that are fuel efficient. Keep your car well tuned so that it is fuel efficient. (Burning 1 gallon of gasoline produces nearly 20 pounds of carbon dioxide, which is a major source of the greenhouse effect that contributes to global warming.)
- Avoid use of aerosols and other products containing chlorofluorocarbons (CFCs). CFCs are depleting the protective ozone layer in the atmosphere. Such depletion has already led to sharp increases in rates of skin cancer caused by the sun's rays.
- Reduce food wastes, which are major contributors to garbage. Whenever possible, compost food wastes.
- Stop the delivery of junk mail. Your local post office will give you the address and instructions for writing to Direct Mail Marketing Association in New York City to request an end to junk mail delivery.
- Buy products that are made out of recycled paper. Buying recycled paper helps create a market for it.
- Do not litter.
- Cut the grass tall on your lawn. Short grass requires more water. Water lawns at night or early in the morning rather than during direct sunlight. (Watering in direct sunlight is wasteful because much of the water evaporates.)
- Recycle motor oil. Used oil is highly destructive to the environment when dumped and also is likely to contaminate nearby water supplies.
- Use soap detergents that are low in phosphates. Phosphates are toxic.
- Use dry cleaning sparingly because it is done with toxic chlorinated solvents.
- Be cautious in using chipboard, plywood, insulation, carpeting, and upholstery; they contain or can create toxic formaldehyde gas.
- Avoid purchasing products made from endangered species—for example, ivory, tortoise shells, and reptile skin.
- Buy eggs in paperboard cartons instead of plastic foam cartons (which tend to be nonbiodegradable).

(continued)

CASE EXHIBIT 17.10 *(continued)*

- Purchase meat, poultry, and other products that are wrapped in paper rather than plastic.
- Buy beverages in aluminum cans or glass bottles, and buy food in glass containers with metal lids instead of plastic. Return the bottles, cans, and glass for recycling.
- Do not put toxic waste products into garbage containers. If deposited into landfills, such products can trickle into nearby water reserves.

- Keep fireplace dampers closed (to reduce heat loss) unless there's a fire.

SOURCES: "A User's Guide to Saving the Planet," CBS television show, broadcast nationally on April 19, 1990; "What You Can Do to Help Earth," *Wisconsin State Journal*, Apr. 22, 1990, p. 1H; "Inspiring People to Take Responsibility for Earth," http://www.nwei.org.

---

has been made in the United States. Sulfur dioxide emissions have been cut substantially.[113] Auto emissions have been cleaned up dramatically, as catalytic converters have substantially cut the release into the air of hydrocarbons, carbon monoxide, and nitrogen oxides.[114] Lead has been removed from gasoline. Overall lead levels in the average American's blood have dropped by one-third since 1976.[115]

Critical Thinking Questions

How actively involved are you in helping to preserve the environment? Are you doing some of the things mentioned in Case Exhibit 17.10 to help save planet Earth?

Since the late 1980s, economic and political values have changed significantly in Eastern European countries. These changes have largely been based on former Soviet President Mikhail Gorbachev's concepts of *glasnost* and *perestroika*. Glasnost refers to greater openness and increased freedoms for people in the Eastern Bloc countries. Perestroika involves economic, social, and political reforms (restructuring) in these countries. Based on these principles, a number of these nations have rejected communism and are moving toward establishing democracies. Such restructuring is leading to improved relationships between Western and Eastern nations. There is now increased cooperation between Western and Eastern nations to overcome the problems that severely impact all inhabitants of this planet.

Finding New Sources of Energy

Reduction of pollution, population, and energy consumption will not alter the fact that much of our current energy comes from nonrenewable fuel sources. Sooner or later, we will have to find new sources of energy. In the meantime, it is crucial that all countries set a priority on conserving the earth's nonrenewable fuel sources.

Possible new sources of energy are nuclear energy, synthetic fuel, and solar energy.

Nuclear Energy   Nuclear energy is a potential solution to the energy shortage, but concerns over the safety of nuclear power plants have slowed construction of them. In March 1979, a near-disaster at the nuclear plant at Three Mile Island in Pennsylvania increased these concerns. Radioactive steam escaped, and there was a danger of a meltdown that probably would have killed many people in the area from lethal overdoses of radiation. The April 1986 explosion in Chernobyl was a much more serious accident; tens of thousands of inhabitants were exposed to radioactivity and face the threat of a shortened life span. In 2011, a massive earthquake and resulting tsunami caused a nuclear plant in Japan to have meltdowns.

Such accidents emphasize that safety in any nuclear power plant cannot be taken for granted. Nuclear energy out of control has the potential for large-scale disaster. A major question is whether future development of nuclear energy is worth the risks.

Synthetic Fuel   In 1980 the federal government passed legislation to create and finance a synthetic-fuel industry. The raw materials for synthetic fuel are in oil shale formations, coal deposits, and gooey-tar sands. The term *synthetic fuel* is actually a misnomer because its components have the same carbon base as crude oil. Coal, for example, will become gas if it is pulverized and then mixed with oxygen and steam under extreme heat. Shale is a dark-brown, fine-grained rock that contains carbon. Production problems are considerable; it is estimated that it takes 1.7 tons of shale to produce a barrel of oil and that it takes a ton of coal to produce two barrels of oil.[116] Whether synthetic fuel can be cost effective remains a major question. On a positive note, it is estimated that the United States has a 600-year supply of the raw materials for synthetic fuel.[117]

Solar Energy Solar energy is another potential solution to the world's energy crisis. Thousands of U.S. homes and offices are getting all or part of their heating and cooling from the sun.[118] Even the White House has a solar water-heating system on its roof. Another potential use of sunlight is direct conversion to electricity with photovoltaic cells, but at present this process is too expensive to be used widely. Solar energy is really an imitation of nature because all energy ultimately comes from the sun.

Wind Power Wind turbines, which turn wind energy into electricity, are increasingly being used in many countries. One disadvantage of wind turbines is that birds are killed when they fly into the blades. This bird mortality problem is being mitigated through the use of painted blades and slower rotational speeds.

Biofuel Biofuels are fuels derived from agricultural crops. For example, ethanol is an alcohol-based fuel that is produced by fermenting and distilling corn or sugar. It then can be added to gasoline, to reduce the amount of gasoline used while driving. One problem with ethanol fuel is that its production has led to an increased demand for corn. As a result, the price of corn has increased dramatically, resulting in higher food prices because many processed food items contain corn. Also, corn is in high demand as feed for animals.

Hybrid Cars and Hydrogen-Powered Vehicles It is clear that other fuel sources have to be found for automobiles because oil reserves are being depleted. Two options that the automobile industry is working on are hybrid cars and hydrogen-powered vehicles.

With the price of gasoline skyrocketing since 2005, hybrid cars are increasingly becoming popular. Japan is taking the lead in producing hybrids. Hybrids are a key cog in Toyota's strategy to become the world's biggest and most successful car maker.[119]

Hybrid vehicles combine electric motors and rechargeable batteries with a conventional gasoline engine to boost mileage by as much as 40%.[120] To save gasoline fuel, the gas engine shuts down when the car stops or coasts. It restarts immediately when the driver hits the accelerator. The electric motor drives the car at low speeds (at which gas engines are least efficient). The gas engine provides most of the energy at highway speeds.

A sealed battery pack powers the electric motor and recharges automatically. (The size of the sealed battery pack is one of the few disadvantages of a hybrid—it takes up about as much storage space as a spare tire.) Most battery packs are guaranteed to last at least 100,000 miles. In a hybrid, the heat energy generated by using the brakes is captured and used to recharge the battery pack. This "regenerative braking" helps make hybrids ideal for stop-and-go driving. Hybrids have other design features meant to reduce drag or weight, such as stiffer tires inflated to a higher pressure.

The race to develop hydrogen-powered vehicles has begun among the major automobile-producing companies. Hydrogen-powered vehicles require 90% fewer moving parts than hybrids.[121] With hydrogen-powered vehicles, fuel cells produce energy through a chemical reaction, like a battery, rather than combustion, so there's no need for camshafts, pistons, or dozens of other bits of machinery. Because the hydrogen fuel cell can be placed anywhere in the vehicle (not just under the hood), cars can be recast with better safety structures and more user-friendly interiors. Another advantage is that fuel cells emit no pollutants, only water vapor. Because hydrogen comes from other sources in addition to fossil fuels and can even be wrung out water, it could take the auto industry out of the competition for petroleum.

There are, however, several technological breakthroughs that are needed to mass-produce hydrogen-powered vehicles. One involves safety concerns. Hydrogen is highly volatile and flammable; it has been used to power rocket engines and make devastating bombs. A second concern is the high cost of manufacturing hydrogen fuel cells; currently, a host of expensive materials is required to manufacture the cells. A third concern is that currently hydrogen fuel cells weigh substantially more than an internal combustion engine. A fourth concern is the development of a fueling infrastructure; most commercial hydrogen currently is made as part of the processing of natural gas and is about 20% more expensive than a comparable amount of gasoline. In addition, the development of a national fueling infrastructure in the United States would require about 12,000 hydrogen fueling stations, at an estimated cost of $1 million a piece.[122]

Social Work and Family Planning

Social workers are concerned about overpopulation—about the problems it is creating now and the even greater problems it may create in the future. In almost every social service agency, social workers come in contact with clients who want and need family planning information. Social workers also must respond to controversial issues: providing abortion information and making referrals, responding to those who advocate involuntary sterilization of people who have a severe inherited disability, and setting up family planning clinics in high schools so that contraceptive information and devices are more readily accessible to teenagers.

Social workers are increasingly employed in settings in which the primary service is family planning. Many roles in family planning are well suited for social workers: premarital counseling; pregnancy counseling; provision of contraceptive information including effectiveness and side effects of the varied approaches; sex education services; counseling about sexually transmitted diseases; AIDS education and counseling; abortion counseling; infertility counseling; and community planning efforts to develop family planning services and create a community atmosphere that is accepting of family planning as a legitimate service.

There are several reasons for anticipating that family planning services will be expanded in future years, thereby creating new career opportunities for social workers. The general public is becoming increasingly aware of the dangers of overpopulation. There has been a growing acceptance in our society of contraceptives. The specter of AIDS has led to greater awareness that AIDS education and sex education are widely needed.

Social workers are being hired in specialized agencies that deal with family planning. These include Planned Parenthood, maternal and child health clinics, and agencies providing abortions and abortion counseling.

School social workers have become increasingly involved in family planning activities in connection with sex education for sexually active teenagers. Social workers in single-parent units of social services departments (also called human services departments) also provide family planning services. Other settings in which social workers counsel on family planning include pediatrics and gynecology departments in hospitals and clinics, child welfare agencies, and residential treatment facilities for teenagers.

Unfortunately, very few undergraduate and graduate social work programs have family planning courses. Some programs do provide family planning instructional units in other courses.

SUMMARY

The following summarizes this chapter's content as it relates to the chapter objectives presented at the beginning of the chapter. Objectives include the following.

A *Describe the problems associated with rapid population growth throughout the world. Discuss pollution and misuse of the environment.*

Problems associated with overpopulation and misuse of the environment are very serious and may have an adverse, dramatic effect on the quality of life in the future. The world's population has more than tripled in size since 1930. At current growth rates, the population will again double in the next 65 years. Already we are experiencing resource crises. Some of the problems associated with overpopulation and misuse of the environment are:

- Too little food. A large proportion of the people in the world are undernourished, and many are starving.
- Too little water. Fresh water is in short supply.
- Economic problems. Overpopulation lowers the average per capita income, reduces the standard of living, and often leads to political turmoil.
- International terrorism. Rapid population growth is a factor that contributes to civil unrest, violence, and international strife.
- Crowding. There is some evidence that the subjective feeling of insufficient space may be a factor in such problems as crime, emotional disturbances, suicide, violence, incest, and child abuse.
- Immigration issues. Immigration has resulted in ethnic and racial conflict, economic competition among different nationality groups, exploitation of undocumented immigrants, and the stresses and costs associated with education and caring for new arrivals.
- Too little energy. We currently have an energy crisis. Fossil fuel resources (oil, coal, and natural gas), which provide more than nine-tenths of the world's energy consumption, are rapidly being depleted.

- Depleted mineral resources. Essential elements such as copper, zinc, iron, and manganese are increasingly becoming short in supply.
- Despoiling of the land. Coal strip mining, oil drilling, deforestation, and overgrazing by cattle and sheep not only are unsightly but also cause devastating environmental damage when the delicate balance among nature's elements is interrupted.
- Radioactive wastes. As of yet, we have not found a safe way to dispose of nuclear wastes, which may create lethal problems in the future.
- Garbage. Increased consumption increases throwaways, the disposal of which often leads to air pollution, water pollution, and other undesirable environmental effects.
- Global warming. The earth's average global air temperature is rising. Such warming will melt glaciers, raise sea levels, adversely impact crop production, change climates, and cause flooding.
- Air pollution. In large industrial centers, air pollution is a health hazard. There are also growing concerns about the gradual depletion of the ozone layer, the greenhouse effect, and global warming.
- Water pollution. Water pollution is also a serious health hazard; some rivers and lakes are now so polluted that they cannot support fish and other organisms.
- Acid rain. Acid rain has damaged timber and is killing fish in lakes and streams.
- Radioactive leaks from nuclear power plants. Leaks and accidents at nuclear power plants in Japan, the Ukraine, and in the United States raise the question of whether nuclear energy is worth the risks.
- Nuclear war. The number of countries that have nuclear warheads is increasing, which makes nuclear war a threat to civilization.
- General pollutants. Increasingly, we are becoming aware of the harmful effects of such pollutants as lead, mercury, DDT, and other chlorinated hydrocarbons.

B *Summarize current efforts to curtail the growth of the world's population and to preserve the environment. Outline proposals that have been advanced for population control and for environmental protection in the future.*

Unless the size of the world's population is brought under control, the above problems will intensify. A number of proposals have been advanced to curtail the growth of the world's population, some of which, if implemented, would radically change current lifestyles. Proposals include subsidizing adoptions, expanding sex education in schools, developing safer contraceptives, enforcing compulsory sterilization of adults who have three or more children, raising the minimum age of marriage, no longer allowing tax deductions for children, making birth control information and devices more available, and making abortions more accessible. If nations are not successful in controlling the birthrate through voluntary family planning, pressure will mount for countries to adopt population control programs.

It is essential that we confront our environmental problems. Two primary actions that are needed are changing values toward conserving resources and developing new sources of energy, such as solar energy.

C *Provide suggestions for what each of us can do to save the earth.*

All of us can take steps to help save our earth. The chapter summarizes a number of these, such as buying products that are recyclable. Whatever happens to the earth will surely affect everyone. This chapter (and this text) ends with challenging you to work for the improvement of human living conditions.

D *Describe the role of social work in family planning.*

Family planning services are crucial to population control. Social workers are increasingly being employed in settings that offer family planning services. Family planning appears to be an emerging career field for social work, as many roles are well suited for social workers: premarital counseling, pregnancy counseling, provision of contraceptive information, sex education services, abortion counseling, counseling on sexually transmitted diseases, and community planning efforts to further develop family planning services.

Competency Notes

EP 2.1.3a Distinguish, appraise, and integrate multiple sources of knowledge, including research-based knowledge and practice wisdom. (All of this chapter) This chapter describes the problems associated with rapid population growth throughout the world. It discusses pollution and misuse of the environment. It summarizes current efforts to curtail the growth of the world's population and to preserve the environment. It outlines proposals that have been advanced for population control and for environmental protection in the future. It provides suggestions for what each of us can do to save the earth. It ends with describing the role of social work in family planning.

Media Resources

Additional resources for this chapter, including a chapter quiz, can be found on the Social Work CourseMate. Go to CengageBrain.com.

Notes

1. Linda A. Mooney, David Knox, and Caroline Schacht, *Understanding Social Problems*, 8th ed. (Belmont, CA: Wadsworth/Cengage Learning, 2013), p. 378.
2. William Kornblum and Joseph Julian, *Social Problems*, 14th ed. (Boston: Pearson, 2012), pp. 415–417.
3. Ibid., pp. 415–418.
4. Paul R. Ehrlich, *The Population Bomb* (New York: Ballantine, 1971), p. 4.
5. Mooney, Knox, and Schacht, *Understanding Social Problems*, pp. 378–380.
6. Ibid.
7. Werner Fornos, *Gaining People, Losing Ground* (Washington, DC: Population Institute, 1987), p. 57.
8. Mooney, Knox, and Schacht, *Understanding Social Problems*, pp. 378–380.
9. Lee Rainwater, *And the Poor Get Children* (Chicago: Quadrangle Books, 1960).
10. Quoted in Donald C. Bacon, "Poor vs. Rich: A Global Struggle," *U.S. News & World Report*, July 31, 1978, p. 57.
11. Fornos, *Gaining People, Losing Ground*, pp. 38–61.
12. "The Rising Cost of Raising a Child," http://money.cnn.com/2011/09/21/pf/cost_raising_child/index.htm.
13. Kornblum and Julian, *Social Problems*, pp. 459–470.
14. Ibid., pp. 415–417.
15. Paul Ehrlich and Anne Ehrlich, *The Population Explosion* (New York: Simon & Schuster, 1990).
16. Ibid., pp. 38–39.
17. Kornblum and Julian, *Social Problems*, p. 422.
18. Ibid.
19. Ibid.
20. Ehrlich and Ehrlich, *The Population Explosion*.
21. Ian Robertson, *Social Problems*, 2nd ed. (New York: Random House, 1980), p. 41.
22. Thomas R. Malthus, *On Population*, Gertrude Himmelfarb, ed. (New York: Modern Library, 1960), pp. 13–14. (Original edition published 1798.)
23. J. John Palen, *Social Problems for the Twenty-First Century* (Boston: McGraw-Hill, 2001), pp. 158–163.
24. Quoted in Paola Scommengna, "UN Food Summit Tries to Focus World Attention on Hunger," *Population Today*, November 1996, p. 2.
25. Kornblum and Julian, *Social Problems*, pp. 422–423.
26. Paul R. Ehrlich and Anne H. Ehrlich, *Population, Resources, Environment* (San Francisco: W. H. Freeman, 1970), p. 65.
27. Mooney, Knox, and Schacht, *Understanding Social Problems*, p. 418.
28. Fornos, *Gaining People, Losing Ground*, pp. 7–23.
29. Quoted in Fornos, *Gaining People, Losing Ground*, p. 10.
30. U.S. Bureau of the Census, *Statistical Abstract of the United States, 2012* (Washington, DC: U.S. Government Printing Office, 2011).
31. Quoted in Fornos, *Gaining People, Losing Ground*, pp. 20–21.
32. Fornos, *Gaining People, Losing Ground*, p. 21.
33. John B. Calhoun, "Population Density and Social Pathology," *Scientific American*, 206 (Feb. 1962), pp. 139–148.
34. Joseph Julian, *Social Problems*, 3rd ed. (Englewood Cliffs, NJ: Prentice Hall, 1980), p. 502.
35. Ibid.
36. Paul Glastris, "The Alien Payoff," *U.S. News & World Report*, May 26, 1997, p. 20.
37. Ibid., p. 21.
38. Mooney, Knox, and Schacht, *Understanding Social Problems*, pp. 277–278.
39. Ibid., p. 410.
40. Ibid.

41. Irene B. Taeuber, "Japan's Demographic Transition Reexamined," *Population Studies*, 14 (July 1960), p. 39.
42. Robertson, *Social Problems*, p. 43.
43. Fornos, *Gaining People, Losing Ground*, p. 5.
44. Kornblum and Julian, *Social Problems*, pp. 427–428.
45. Ehrlich and Ehrlich, *The Population Explosion*, p. 17.
46. http://www.indianchild.com/population_of_india.htm.
47. Ibid.
48. Ibid.
49. Ibid.
50. Ibid.
51. Ibid.
52. Ibid.
53. Ibid.
54. Ibid.
55. Kornblum and Julian, *Social Problems*, pp. 425–427.
56. Ibid.
57. Ibid.
58. Ibid.
59. Ibid.
60. Ibid.
61. Ibid.
62. Ibid.
63. Ehrlich and Ehrlich, *The Population Explosion*, p. 207.
64. Ibid.
65. James W. Coleman and Harold R. Kerbo, *Social Problems*, 10th ed. (Upper Saddle River, NJ: Vango Books, 2008), p. 404.
66. Ibid.
67. Ibid.
68. Ehrlich and Ehrlich, *The Population Explosion*, pp. 205–209.
69. Fornos, *Gaining People, Losing Ground*, pp. 45–46.
70. Ibid.
71. Ibid., p. 13.
72. Mooney, Knox, and Schacht, *Understanding Social Problems*, pp. 412–413.
73. Kornblum and Julian, *Social Problems*, pp. 467–468.
74. Robertson, *Social Problems*, p. 71.
75. Kornblum and Julian, *Social Problems*, p. 470.
76. Mooney, Knox and Schacht, *Understanding Social Problems*, pp. 414–416.
77. Ibid., p. 414.
78. Ibid., pp. 414–415.
79. Julian, *Social Problems*, p. 528.
80. Coleman and Kerbo, *Social Problems*, pp. 399–403.
81. Ibid.
82. Ibid.
83. Ibid., pp. 406–407.
84. Kornblum and Julian, *Social Problems*, pp. 490–491.
85. Ibid.
86. Ibid., pp. 523–526.
87. Orr Kelly, "Nuclear War's Horrors: Reality vs. Fiction," *U.S. News & World Report*, Nov. 28, 1983, pp. 85–86.
88. Barry Schwied, "U.S., Russia Seal Missile Deal," *Wisconsin State Journal*, Jan. 4, 1993, p. 1A.
89. Coleman and Kerbo, *Social Problems*, pp. 453–454.
90. Stacie Thomas, "The Cuyahoga Revisited" in *The Freeman: Ideas on Liberty*, May 2000.
91. Coleman and Kerbo, *Social Problems*, pp. 403–404.
92. Ehrlich and Ehrlich, *The Population Explosion*, pp. 123–124.
93. Ibid.
94. Ehrlich, *The Population Bomb*, pp. 31–35.
95. Mooney, Knox, and Schacht, *Understanding Social Problems*, pp. 418–419.
96. Richard Curtis and Elizabeth Hogan, *Perils of the Peaceful Atom* (New York: Ballantine, 1969), p. 194.
97. "Silent Spring Revisited," *Newsweek*, July 14, 1986, p. 72.
98. Ehrlich, *The Population Bomb*, pp. 127–145.
99. Bernard Berelson, "The Present State of Family Planning Programs," *Studies in Family Planning*, 57 (Sept. 1970), p. 2.
100. Kornblum and Julian, *Social Problems*, p. 424.
101. "Indonesia—Population," http://countrystudies.us/indonesia/32.htm.
102. Ibid.
103. "Abortion Foes Gain Victory," *Wisconsin State Journal*, July 1, 1980, sec. 1, p. 1.
104. Mooney, Knox, and Schacht, *Understanding Social Problems*, pp. 458–459.

105. The Boston Women's Health Book Collective, *Our Bodies, Ourselves* (New York: A Touchstone Book, 2005), p. 389.

106. Fornos, *Gaining People, Losing Ground*, p. 42.

107. Kornblum and Julian, *Social Problems*, pp. 470–471.

108. George Ritzer, *Social Problems*, 2nd ed. (New York: Random House, 1986), p. 556.

109. "Don't Throw a Good Thing Away," *Policyholder News*, 23, no. 1 (Spring 1990), p. 3.

110. Ibid.

111. Ibid.

112. Steven Thomma, "Some Problems Solved Since Earth Day in '70, But Now We Face New Troubles," *Wisconsin State Journal*, Apr. 22, 1994, p. 1D.

113. Kornblum and Julian, *Social Problems*, pp. 474–475.

114. Ibid.

115. Ibid.

116. "Fuels for America's Future," *U.S. News & World Report*, Aug. 13, 1979, p. 33.

117. Ibid.

118. Ibid.

119. Richard J. Newman, "Invasion of the Green Machines," *U.S. News & World Report*, May 9, 2005, pp. 49–54.

120. Mooney, Knox, and Schacht, *Understanding Social Problems*, p. 428

121. Ibid.

122. Ibid.

Your Future in Combating Human Problems

September 11, 2001, has changed lives in the United States, and throughout the world. On that day terrorists hijacked four commercial planes. They flew two of them into the Twin Towers of the World Trade Center in New York City, and flew another into the Pentagon. A fourth plane crashed in Pennsylvania. These events clearly indicate that we live in a global community—what happens in Afghanistan, Iraq, Saudi Arabia, and all other countries can significantly impact what happens in the United States. Since September 11, 2001, the United States, and many other countries, have declared war on terrorism.

All of us are alive on this planet for a relatively short time. However, during this time we have an opportunity to make a difference in improving the quality of life for others.

This text has described social work and social welfare. A major thrust has been to illustrate the social problems and the diverse fields of practice in which social workers and other human service professionals seek to combat human problems. Through case examples, I've tried to show some of the frustrations and gratifications encountered in social work practice. All of this information is designed to help you make a career decision about whether social work is a profession you want to pursue.

Test your interest by answering these questions:

1. Do you enjoy working closely and intensely with people?
2. Do you think you could cope with failure?
3. Do you think you would be willing to acquire the knowledge, skills, and values necessary to make life more meaningful to individuals, groups, families, organizations, and communities?
4. Do you think you would like a profession dedicated to social change and to combating social injustice?

If you honestly can answer yes to each of these questions, you may well have the potential to become an effective social worker.

Whether or not you decide to pursue a career in social work, the material in this text on social problems and social services will give you a framework for making responsible citizenship decisions. As a voter, you help decide which political officials will be elected to work for the expansion or the curtailment of social welfare services. You have the opportunity to be a volunteer for a human service agency, to serve on boards and committees of agencies, to participate in fund-raisers for human service programs, to become involved in legislative processes that address human issues, and to influence others in daily interactions about controversial social welfare issues. Changes in the structure and functioning of the social welfare system are inevitable. You can work for the improvement of human living conditions. As John F. Kennedy, in his 1961 Presidential Inaugural Address, so eloquently stated, "Ask not what your country can do for you. Ask what you can do for your country."*

---

*Quoted in James A. Henretta, W. Elliot Brownlee, David Brody, and Susan Ware, *America's History* (Chicago: Dorsey Press, 1987), p. 875.

What Do Social Workers Make?

Social work, as everyone knows, is not one of the highest-paying professions. What do social workers really make?

They make a teenager in a dysfunctional family find a focus in school and in his life. They locate two children to adopt for an infertile couple who yearn to be parents, and they rescue these two children from the alternative of being raised in a series of foster homes. They facilitate, through counseling, a marital couple problem-solving their marital issues, and thereby prevent a divorce.

They place a battered wife and her three children in a domestic violence shelter and then work with this family to find new directions in their lives. They empower a recently arrived Hmong refugee family living in poverty to learn English, to receive job training services, to be connected with necessary medical and dental care, and to find housing, and they place the parents in jobs that allow the family members to escape from poverty. They instruct and facilitate a young adult with anger management issues to learn to express her anger in an assertive manner and thereby empower her to get what she wants, rather than allowing her anger to get her involved in physical confrontations with others.

They empower a postpartum depressed mother with a young baby to challenge her negative and irrational thinking patterns and thereby alleviate the depression—and thereby also provide a better life for herself, her child, and her husband. They provide sexual assault services to a rape victim, and thereby help her put her life back together. They assist a suicidal gay teenager to become aware and accepting of his sexual orientation and to begin to develop a lifestyle that provides direction and meaning to his life.

They provide a diversion program for first-time offenders for shoplifting (and similar offenses) that provides restitution to the victims and also deters these offenders from committing future crimes. They help organizations to recognize institutional patterns of racism, and then make changes to reach out to better serve people of color.

They assist an older employee to make a solid financial plan for retiring and to also connect him with volunteer opportunities that will be gratifying for him and also benefit the community. They serve as a catalyst in a deteriorating community to form a grassroots organization to improve the neighborhood.

They provide family group conferencing to a family in which abuse is occurring, which empowers the family to end the abuse and keeps the family intact. They connect (broker) an alcoholic female in her 20s to join AA and start her one-day-at-a-time recovery. They empower a secretary to become assertive to confront her employer about the sexual innuendoes that he makes, which thereby ends the sexual harassment.

They provide hospice services to a terminally ill male cancer patient, thereby relieving the pain associated with the disease and helping him make the most of his remaining days; they also provide services to the family members to help them through this difficult time—and then provide bereavement services to the family members after the patient dies. They find a quality group home for an autistic young adult and also place him in a job at a fast-food restaurant and job-coach him until he learns how to do the tasks that are assigned. They inform a 16-year-old pregnant teenager of her options and help her make plans for the adoption option she selects.

What do social workers make? They get paid to help other people—that's something most people would be inclined to do anyway. They make more than most people will ever make. They make a difference.

Glossary

Absolute approach to poverty: An assumption that a certain amount of goods and services is essential to an individual's or family's welfare; those who do not have this minimum amount are viewed as poor

Absolute confidentiality: Confidentiality in which disclosures made to the professional are not shared with anyone else, except when authorized by the client in writing or required by law

Accountability: The process of evaluating the effectiveness of service programs

Acid rain: Created when sulfur and nitrogen oxides in emissions from automobiles and industrial plants combine with moisture in the air to form sulfuric and nitric acids

Activist: A worker who seeks institutional change; often the objective involves a shift in power and resources to a disadvantaged group

Ad hoc committee: A group, such as a task force, set up for one purpose and usually ceases functioning after completion of its task

Administration: Work that involves directing the overall program of a social service agency

Adoption and Safe Families Act (ASFA): A law passed in 1997 that reaffirmed the need to forge linkages between the child welfare system and other systems of support for families, and stresses that the child's health and safety shall be the paramount concern in determining what is reasonable and consistent with the plan for timely, permanent placement of a child

Advocate: A worker who seeks to empower a client or a citizens' group through securing a beneficial change in one or more institutional policies; in the school setting, a person who understands and is not intimated by large complicated systems and can help a family or child face the educational bureaucracy or deal with other social systems

Affirmative action programs: Programs that provide preferential hiring and admission requirements for minority applicants

Afrocentric perspective: Recognizes that African Americans have retained, to some degree, a number of elements of African life and values

Ageism: Discrimination and prejudice against people simply because they are old

AIDS (Acquired immunodeficiency syndrome): A contagious, presently incurable disease that destroys the body's immune system; caused by the human immunodeficiency virus (HIV)

AIDS-dementia complex: Deterioration of the brain caused by AIDS

Alienation: Worker alienation is the sense of meaninglessness and powerlessness that people experience when interacting with social institutions they consider oppressive and beyond their control

Alzheimer's disease: A degenerative brain disorder that causes gradual deterioration in intelligence, memory, awareness, and ability to control bodily functions

Americans with Disabilities Act: An act passed in 1990 that prohibited discrimination against people with a disability either in hiring or by limiting access to public accommodations

Amniocentesis: A genetic screening procedure in which a hollow needle is inserted through the abdominal wall and uterus of a pregnant female to obtain amniotic fluid for the determination of chromosomal abnormality. It is a test for prenatal detection of Down syndrome, other chromosome defects, and some metabolic disorders

Androgyny: A concept in which men and women can be flexible in their role playing and in expressing themselves as human beings rather than in traditional feminine or masculine ways

Anger rapist: A rapist who performs his act to discharge feelings of pent-up anger and rage; uses far more force than is necessary to gain sexual access to his victim because his aim is to hurt and debase his victim

Anglo-conformity: A perspective that assumes the desirability of maintaining modified English institutions, language, and culture as the dominant standard in American life

Anomie theory: A theory that views criminal behavior as resulting when an individual is prevented from achieving high-status goals in a society

Anorexia nervosa: A disorder characterized by the relentless pursuit of thinness through voluntary starvation

Anoxia: A condition that occurs when there is a deprivation of oxygen

Artificial insemination-donor (AID): The sperm donor is someone other than the husband

Artificial insemination-husband (AIH): The sperm donor is the woman's husband

Asperger's disorder: Children who usually have normal or even high verbal intelligence, do good schoolwork, and are curious, but have limited, fixed interests, repetitive speech and behavior, and difficulty understanding social and emotional cues

Aspiration bomb: When many young people in poverty in Third World countries are aware that people in industrialized nations are much more affluent and see violence and terrorism as their only avenue for achieving a better life

Assault: The unlawful application of physical force on another person

Assertiveness: Expressing yourself without hurting or stepping on others

Assisted-living facilities: Facilities that allow older adults to have semi-independent living with their own rooms or apartments and to receive personal care, meals, housekeeping, transportation, and social and recreational activities

Authoritarian: Inflexible, rigid, and a low tolerance for uncertainty; a great respect for authority figures and a quick submission to their will; place a high value on conventional behavior, and feel threatened by unconventional behavior in others

Autism: The child's ability to respond to others does not develop within the first 30 months of life

AZT (Azidothymidine): A drug that has been found to delay the progress of AIDS in some people but does not cure it

Barden-LaFollette Act: An act passed in 1943 that extended rehabilitation services to the mentally ill and to people with cognitive disabilities

Behavior specialist: A social worker who can systematically apply behavior modification principles

Biochemical genetics: The discipline that studies the mechanisms whereby genes control the development and maintenance of the organism

Biological magnification: The concentration of the substance increases as it ascends in the food chain

Bisexual: A person who is sexually attracted to members of either gender

Blended families: Two families joined by the marriage of one parent to another

Board of directors: An administrative group charged with responsibility for setting the policy that governs agency programs

Brady Bill: Passed in 1993, it requires that gun buyers wait 5 business days and undergo a background check by police

Broker: A social work role that links individuals and groups who need help with community services

Brown v. Board of Education: In 1954 the Supreme Court ruled in this case that racial segregation in public schools was unconstitutional

Bulimia nervosa: A disorder characterized by bingeing on large amounts of food and then purging (vomiting, the use of laxatives, or compulsive exercise)

Bullying: Being physically, emotionally, or verbally aggressive to another person

Case manager: A person designated to assume primary responsibility for assessing the needs of a client, arranging and coordinating the delivery of essential goods and services provided by other resources, and working directly with the client to ensure that the goods and services are provided in a timely manner; case managers must maintain close contact with clients (including sometimes acting to provide direct casework services) and with other service providers to ensure that plans for service delivery are in place and are subsequently delivered as planned

Chain migration: The tendency of immigrants to migrate to areas where relatives and others from their home communities are already living

Charity organization society (COS): An English innovation brought to Buffalo, New York, in 1877, when private agencies joined together to provide direct services to individuals and families, and to plan and coordinate the efforts of these agencies to combat the pressing social problems of cities

Charter schools: Publicly funded elementary or secondary schools in the United States that have been freed from the regulations, rules, and statutes that apply to other public schools in exchange for some type of accountability for producing certain results

Child Abuse Prevention and Treatment Act: Passed in January 1974 to provide direct assistance to states to help them develop child abuse and child neglect programs

Child molestation: The sexual abuse of a child by an adult; includes sexual intercourse, oral-genital contact, fondling, and behaviors such as exposing oneself to a child and photographing or viewing a child for the molester's erotic pleasure

Chorionic villi sampling (CVS): This test helps identify certain fetal abnormalities; it is a prenatal technique that involves taking a sample of cells from the chorionic villus and analyzing it for birth defects

Classical theory: A theory, based on hedonistic psychology, arguing that a person makes a decision about whether to engage in criminal activity based on the anticipated balance of pleasure and pain

Cloning: The process whereby a new organism is reproduced from the nucleus of a single cell

Cochran Gardens: A grassroots effort in St. Louis, Missouri, that turned a deteriorating housing project into a public housing project with flower-lined paths, and a clean neighborhood filled with trusting people who have a sense of pride in their community

Cognitive disability: A disability characterized by significantly subaverage intellectual functioning existing concurrently with related limitations in two or more of the following applicable adaptive skill areas: communication, self-care, home living, social skills, community use, self-direction, health and safety, functional academics, leisure, and work

Comarital sex: Mate swapping and other organized extramarital relations in which both spouses agree to participate

Coming out: Acknowledging to oneself, and then to others, that one is gay or lesbian

Commission on Global Social Work Education: A commission of the Council on Social Work Education that is composed of educators from around the country who are actively involved in teaching international content and initiating cross-national exchange programs

Committee: A group formed to deal with specific tasks or matters within an agency or organization

Community Mental Health Centers Act: An act, passed in 1963, that provided for transferring the care and treatment of the majority of mentally ill people from state hospitals to their home communities

Community organization: Work that is aimed at stimulating and assisting the local community to evaluate, plan, and coordinate efforts to provide for the community's health, welfare, and recreation needs

Community practice: The process of stimulating and assisting the local community to evaluate, plan, and coordinate its efforts to provide for the community's health, welfare, and recreation needs; various labels of practice include: social planning, community planning, locality development, community action, social action, macro practice, community organization, and community development

Comparable worth: A concept involving equal pay for comparable work instead of equal pay for equal work

Compulsive overeating: A disorder characterized by the irresistible urge to consume excessive amounts of food on a long-term basis

Computer crime: Crimes that involve the use of computers and the Internet to commit acts against people, public order, property, or morality

Computerized infant simulators: A teen pregnancy prevention program that involves realistic, life-sized computerized "dolls" that are programmed to cry at random intervals; the "baby" stops crying only when the caregiver "attends" to the doll by inserting a key into a slot in the simulator's back until it stops crying

Confidentiality: The implicit or explicit agreement between a professional and a client to maintain the privacy of information about the client

Conflict gangs: Gangs that are turf oriented; they engage in violent conflict with individuals of rival groups that invade their neighborhood or commit acts that they consider degrading or insulting

Conflict habituated relationship: A marriage in which the husband and wife frequently quarrel in private; they may also quarrel in public, or they may put up a façade of being compatible

Congregate housing facilities: An arrangement that provides housing in private or government-subsidized rental apartment complexes, remodeled hotels to meet the needs of independent older adults, or mobile home parks designed for older adults. They provide meals, housekeeping, transportation, social and recreational activities, and sometimes health care

Conservatives: People who tend to resist change, generally view individuals as autonomous, advocate a residual approach to social welfare programs, and revere the "traditional" nuclear family and try to devise policies to preserve it

Consultive management: Managers of this type consult with their employees and encourage them to think about job-related issues and contribute their own ideas before decisions are made

Continued-care retirement communities: Long-term housing facilities that are designed to provide a full range of accommodations and services for affluent older people as their needs change

Conversion therapy: The goal of this therapy is to convert gays' and lesbians' sexual orientation to heterosexuality

Coordinator: A worker who brings components together in some kind of organized manner

Corporate crime: A type of white-collar crime that includes illegal labor practices, insider trading, and environmental crimes

Council on Social Work Education: The national accrediting entity for baccalaureate and master's programs in social work—requires all undergraduate and graduate programs to train their students in generalist social work practice

Crime: An act committed or omitted in violation of a law

Criminal gangs: Gangs that have as a primary goal material gain through criminal activities, including theft of property from people or premises, extortion, fencing, and drug trafficking

Critical theory: Argues that the capitalist economic system is the root cause of our crime problem, but theory fails to explain why crime occurs in Communist societies

Cross-dresser: This term generally refers to men (in their private lives) who wear clothing and accessories designed for women. Cross-dressers are sometimes called "transvestites," but that term is considered pejorative

Cult-occult gangs: Gangs engaged in devil or evil worship

Cultural competence: Social workers need to become aware of culture and its pervasive influence, learn about their own cultures, recognize their own ethnocentricity, learn about other cultures, acquire cultural knowledge about their clients, and adapt social work skills and intervention approach accordingly

Cultural pluralism: A concept that implies a series of coexisting groups, each preserving its own tradition and culture but each loyal to an overarching American nation; it appears to be the form that race and ethnic relations are presently taking

Cumulative trauma disorders/repetitive motion disorders: Muscle, tendon, vascular, and nerve injuries that result from repeated or sustained actions or exertions of different body parts

Cyberbullying: Any bullying done through the use of technology

Day-care centers for older adults: Centers that provide activities determined by the needs of the group

DDT: A chlorinated hydrocarbon, synthetic insecticide (now banned) that chemically breaks down slowly and lasts in the soil for decades

De facto discrimination: Discrimination that actually exists, whether legal or not; this type of discrimination often results from powerful informal norms that are discriminatory

De' jure discrimination: Legal discrimination

Death with Dignity Act: An act passed by Oregon voters in 1994 that allows doctors to prescribe lethal drugs at the request of terminally ill patients who have less than 6 months to live—doctors may only prescribe a lethal dose, not administer it

Defense of Marriage Act: An act passed in 1996 that allows states to refuse to recognize gay marriages performed in other states and prevents one partner in a homosexual relationship from claiming benefits in the event of the other's death or disability; the act allows states to pass laws against same-sex marriages but does not oblige them to do so

Deinstitutionalization: A movement that resulted when mental health practitioners realized that mental hospitals, instead of "curing" the disturbed, were frequently perpetuating disturbed behavior via long-term hospitalization. It is the process of moving people who are dependent for their physical and mental care from residential care facilities into the community

Democratic management: Management of this type systematically allows employee groups to make a number of major decisions

Demonology: A theory that asserts that those who engage in deviant behavior are possessed by the devil

Dependency ratio: The number of societal members who are under 18 or are 65 and over, compared with the number of people who are between 18 and 64

Developmental disability: A broad term that includes cognitive disabilities and a variety of other conditions that occur before age 22 and hinder development (epilepsy, infantile autism, cerebral palsy, and some cases of dyslexia)

Developmental view: A process of planned social change designed to promote the well-being of the population as a whole in conjunction with a dynamic process of economic development

Deviant subcultures theory: Asserts that some groups develop their own attitudes, values, and perspectives that support criminal activity

Devitalized relationship: A marriage in which the husband and wife lack excitement or any real interest in each other or their marriage

Devolution revolution: Decisions about the provision of key social welfare programs are being transferred from the federal government to the state level

Didanosine (DDI): A treatment for adults and children with advanced AIDS who cannot tolerate or are not helped by AZT

Differential association theory: Criminal behavior is the result of a learning process that primarily occurs in small, intimate groups

Discharge planning: Social workers helping clients and their families prepare for returning to the home or to some other facility

Discrimination: Discrimination has two very different meanings; it may have the positive meaning of the power of making fine distinctions between two or more ideas, objects, situations or stimuli—however, in minority-group relations it is the unfair treatment of a person, racial group, or minority; it is an action based on prejudice

Disengagement: A process whereby people respond to aging by gradually withdrawing from the various roles and social relationships they occupied in middle age

Distal stimulation: A type of infant stimulation that involves looking and talking

Diversion programs: Programs developed to divert first-time or minor offenders from entering the criminal justice system; as an alternative, they receive services from community agencies

Double bind: A psychological dilemma in which the receiver of a message gets conflicting interpersonal communications from the sender or faces disparagement no matter what her or his response to a situation is

Doubling time: The rate at which the population doubles in the world; is based on the extent to which the birthrate exceeds the death rate

Down syndrome: Children and adults generally experience a moderate to severe level of cognitive disability, their eyes are almond shaped and slanted, and they tend to have a round face

Drag queen/king A drag queen is a mate who impersonates a female for entertainment purposes (typically singing and dancing to music). A drag king is a female who impersonates a male. Persons who "do drag" may or may not consider themselves transgender

Drift hypothesis: A theory that social class is not a cause but a consequence of mental disorder, and that mentally ill people who have a higher class level tend to drift downward to the lowest socioeconomic class because their illness results in a lowered social status and a decrease in earning power

Dual perspective: A concept in which all people are a part of two systems: (a) the dominant system, and (b) the nurturing system

Ecological approach: An approach to human behavior that integrates both treatment and reform by conceptualizing and emphasizing the dysfunctional transactions between people and their physical and social environments

Economic justice: An ideal condition in which all members of a society have the same opportunities to attain material goods, income, and wealth

Education for All Handicapped Children Act: Enacted in 1975, this mandates that all local school districts provide full and appropriate educational opportunities to all children, including those with a disability

Education groups: The focus of such groups is for members to acquire knowledge and learn more complex skills

Educational neglect: When a child is allowed to be excessively absent from school

Educator: A worker who gives information to clients and teaches them adaptive skills

Elder abuse: The physical or psychological mistreatment of older adults

Elizabethan Poor Law: Enacted in England in 1601; included three categories of relief recipients

(the able-bodied poor, the impotent poor, dependent children); these fundamental provisions were incorporated into the laws of the American colonies

Embezzlement: An offense in which an employee fraudulently converts some of the employer's funds to personal use through altering company records

Embryonic stem cells: Come from the inner cell mass of a blastocyst, the term for a fertilized egg 4 days after conception

Emergency contraception (EC): The three methods available (combined birth control pills, progestin-only pills, and IUDs) work either by preventing ovulation or by preventing implantation of a fertilized egg in the uterus

Emotional neglect: Failure to provide the child the emotional nurturing or emotional support necessary for the development of a sound personality

Employee assistance programs (EAPs): Most social services in the workplace are currently provided by EAPs, and include alcohol and drug abuse counseling, counseling for emotional difficulties, family counseling, career and education counseling, credit counseling, and retirement planning

Empowerer: A worker who helps individuals, families, groups, organizations, and communities increase their personal, interpersonal, socioeconomic, and political strength and influence through improving their circumstances

Empowerment: The process of helping individuals, families, groups, organizations, and communities to increase their interpersonal, personal, political, and socioeconomic strengths so that they can improve their circumstances

Empty-shell marriages: The spouses feel no strong attachments to each other, and outside pressures keep the marriage together rather than feelings of warmth and attraction between the partners

Enabler: A worker who helps individuals or groups to articulate their needs, clarify and identify their problems, explore resolution strategies, select and apply a strategy, and develop their capacities to deal with their own problems more effectively

Environmental neglect: A type of neglect in which the parents or guardians let a child live in filth, without proper clothing, unattended, unsupervised, or without proper nourishment

Environmental Protection Agency (EPA): Agency established in 1970 that was empowered to set and enforce standards of environmental quality; however, since the 1980s, political opposition to environmental concerns has intensified

Ethnic group: A group of people who share cultural characteristics, such as religion, language, dietary practices, national origin, and a common history, and who regard themselves as a distinct group

Ethnic-sensitive practice: Social work practice that seeks to incorporate understanding of diverse ethnic, cultural, and minority groups into the theories and principles that guide social work practice

Ethnocentrism: An orientation or set of beliefs that holds one's own culture, ethnic or racial group, or nation to be superior to others

Extended family: Consists of a number of relatives living together, such as parents, children, grandparents, great-grandparents, aunts, uncles, in-laws, and cousins

Facilitator: A role in which the worker may take on activities of a counselor, teacher, caregiver, and changer of specific behavior

Familism: The belief that the family takes precedence over the individual

Family: A kinship system of all relatives living together or recognized as a social unit

Family allowance program: A proposed welfare alternative program in which the government pays each family a set amount based on the number of children in the household

Family group conferencing: An approach to prevent child abuse or neglect that originated in New Zealand, and involves the parents' extended kinship network

Family Planning Services and Population Research Act: Passed in 1970, it recognized that family planning was part of the delivery of comprehensive health services for all; in 1972 contraceptive policy lifted restrictions on marital status and age for receiving birth control information and devices

Family preservation program: A model of intervention developed specifically for work with families

in which the placement of one or more of the children is imminent; services are provided in the client's home

Family sculpting: An assessment tool that involves a physical arrangement of the members of a family, with the placement of each person determined by an individual family member acting as director; the resulting tableau represents that person's symbolic view of family relationships

Family therapy: A type of group therapy aimed at helping families with interactional, behavioral, and emotional problems

Female genital mutilation (FGM): A practice, commonplace in more than half of the African countries and in parts of the Middle East, in which all or part of a girl's external genitalia is cut away to diminish sexual appetite in order to maintain a girl's virginity and marriageability

Feminine mystique: The negative self-concept, lack of direction, and low sense of self-worth among women

Feminist therapy: A psychosocial treatment orientation in which the professional helps the client in individual or group settings to overcome the psychological and social problems largely encountered as a result of sex discrimination and sex-role stereotyping

Financial abuse: The illegal or improper exploitation of the victim's assets or property

Fixated child molester: A type of child molester whose primary sexual object choice is children

Food stamps: A public assistance program designed to combat hunger and to improve the diets of low-income households by supplementing their food-purchasing ability. It offsets some of the food expenses for low-income people who qualify

Foster care: Type of service in which the goals are to protect the children, to rehabilitate the parents, and generally to return the children to their genetic parents as soon as it is feasible

Foster care homes: Usually single-family residences where the owners of the home take in an unrelated older adult and are reimbursed for providing housing, meals, housekeeping, and personal care

Foster Grandparent Program: Pays older adults for part-time work in which they provide individual care and attention to ill and needy children and youth

Frustration-aggression theory: Asserts that some frustrated people displace their anger and aggression onto a scapegoat; the scapegoat may not be limited to a particular person but may include a group of people, such as a minority group

Gay The term preferred by many people with a same-sex orientation, primarily males, in describing themselves and their sexual orientation; gay men prefer the term *gay* instead of *homosexual* because it does not have the negative connotations frequently associated with the word *homosexual*; the term *gay* is sometimes used to refer to both males and females who have a same-sex sexual orientation

Gay Liberation Movement: Composed of several groups and contends that homosexuality is not a perversion or sickness but is simply a different lifestyle

General Allotment Act: An act passed in 1887 that empowered Congress unilaterally to revise treaties made with Native Americans and opened the way for land-hungry Whites to take productive native land

General assistance: This public assistance program is supposed to serve those needing temporary, rather than long-term, financial support; the only public assistance program that receives no federal funds, as it is usually funded by property taxes

Generalist practice: Generalist practice is grounded in the liberal arts and the person-in-environment construct; to promote human and social well-being, generalist practitioners use a range of prevention and intervention methods in their practice with individuals, families, groups, organizations, and communities; the generalist practitioner identifies with the social work profession and applies ethical principles and critical thinking in practice; generalist practitioners incorporate diversity in their practice and advocate for human rights and social and economic justice; they recognize, support, and build on the strengths and resiliency of all human beings; they engage in research informed practice and are proactive in responding to the impact of context on professional practice

Gerontology: The scientific study of aging and the problems of older adults

GLBT: The term often used to refer collectively to gays, lesbians, bisexuals, and transgender individuals

Global warming: The increasing average global air temperature

Grassroots organizations: Community groups, composed of community residents who work together to improve their surroundings

Gray Panthers: An action-oriented group that argues that a fundamental flaw in our society is the emphasis on materialism and the consumption of goods and services rather than on improving the quality of life for all citizens; it is seeking to end ageism and to advance the goals of human freedom, human dignity, and self-development

Group facilitator: A worker who serves as a leader for group activity

Group home: Provides housing for some older residents, usually a house that is owned or rented by a social agency where residents take care of much of their own personal needs and take some responsibility for day-to-day tasks

Group therapy: Work that is aimed at facilitating the social, behavioral, and emotional adjustment of individuals through the group process

Group work: Social work that seeks to facilitate the intellectual, emotional, and social development of individuals through group activities

Hate crimes: Violent acts aimed at individuals or groups of a particular race, ethnicity, religion, sexual orientation, gender, identity, class, social status, age, political affiliation, nationality, or disability

Hawthorne effect: When subjects know they are participants in a study, this awareness may lead them to behave differently and thereby substantially influence the results of the study

Health Maintenance Organization (HMO): Managed care system that tends to have the two major functions of establishing policies and procedures that regulate benefits, payments, and providers, and employing gatekeepers to review and authorize services

Hemlock Society: An organization that promotes voluntary euthanasia and has a do-it-yourself suicide manual

Hermaphrodite: Person born with both male and female sexual characteristics but labeled either a male or a female at birth and then related to according to the gender on the birth certificate

Heterosexual: The sexual or erotic orientation of a person for members of the opposite sex

HIV (Human immunodeficiency virus): A virus transmitted from one person to another primarily during sexual contact or through the sharing of intravenous drug needles and syringes

HMOs: Prepaid health-care insurance plans that emphasize prevention—because the revenues are fixed, their incentives are to keep patients well because they benefit from patient wellness, not sickness

Holistic programs: Programs that recognize that our thinking processes function together with our bodies as an integrated unit

Home health services: Visiting-nurse services, physical therapy, drugs, laboratory services, and sickroom equipment are provided at home

Homemaker services: Provided in some communities to take care of household tasks that older adults are no longer able to do for themselves

Homicide: The unlawful killing of one person by another

Homophobia: The irrational fear or hatred of people oriented toward same-sex relationships

Homosexual: The sexual or erotic orientation of a person for members of the same sex; it should be noted that using the term *homosexual* to describe a gay or lesbian individual is offensive and is similar to using the "n-word" to describe African Americans

Hospice: A program that allows terminally ill people to die with dignity, to live their final weeks in the way they want

Housing assistance: Similar to food stamps and Medicaid, this public assistance program is an in-kind program rather than a cash program that provides public housing or helps with renting and even buying homes

Hull House: A settlement house established by Jane Addams in Chicago

Human rights: Human rights are commonly understood as inalienable fundamental rights to which a person is inherently entitled simply because he or she is a human being; human rights are universal (applicable everywhere) and egalitarian (the same for everyone); examples include: freedom of thought, freedom of religious choice, freedom of peaceful association, and liberty

Human services: A broader term than *social work* because it includes services such as library services, law enforcement, housing-code enforcement, consumer protection, and fire prevention and firefighting that are usually not considered social welfare services

Human trafficking: Internationally, this is the recruitment, transportation, or receipt of people for the purposes of slavery, forced labor, or servitude

Hyde Amendment: This amendment, passed in 1977 and upheld in 1980, prohibits Medicaid spending for abortions except when a woman's life would be endangered by childbirth or in cases of promptly reported rape or incest

Hydrocephalus: A condition in which there is an increased amount of cerebrospinal fluid within the skull that will, unless treated, cause an enlargement of the skull

Hypoxia: A condition that occurs when there is insufficient oxygen to the brain

Identity acceptance: A phase of sexual orientation identity development that occurs for lesbians or gays when they now conclude "I am gay or lesbian" and accept this identity

Identity comparison: A phase of sexual orientation identity development that occurs for lesbians or gays when they ponder whether "I *may* be gay or lesbian"

Identity confusion: A phase of sexual orientation identity development that occurs when a gay or lesbian person has had a history of assuming a heterosexual identity because heterosexuality is the expectation in our society

Identity formation: The process of determining who you are and what you want out of life

Identity pride: A phase of sexual orientation identity development that occurs when a gay or lesbian dichotomizes people into gays and lesbians (who are good and important people) and heterosexuals (who are apt to be intolerant and discriminating); a strong identification with the gay community

Identity synthesis: A phase of sexual orientation identity development for gays and lesbians when they no longer believe gays and lesbians are "us" and heterosexuals are "them" because they recognize that there are some good and supportive heterosexuals

Identity theft: The use of someone else's identification to obtain credit and purchase items; the average victim spends about 600 hours and $1,400 clearing her or his name and credit records after the crime has been committed

Identity tolerance: A sense of identity for a gay man or a lesbian in which the person comes to believe that "I probably am gay or lesbian in sexual orientation"

Ideology of individualism: The view that the rich are personally responsible for their success and that the poor are to blame for their failure

Illegal aliens: People who enter a country without documentation (also called undocumented immigrants)

I-messages: Nonblaming messages that communicate only how the sender believes the receiver is adversely affecting him or her

Immigrate: To enter a country of which one is not a native for permanent residence

Immigration Reform and Control Act: An act passed in 1986 that declared that employers are subject to civil penalties for each illegal alien they hire

Incest: Sexual relations between blood relatives

Income: The amount of money a person makes in a given year

Indian Child Welfare Act: Enacted in 1978, it seeks to protect Native American families and tribes by providing a legal mechanism for tribes to assume jurisdiction over Native American children who have been involuntarily removed by state and local authorities

Individual racism: The negative attitudes one person has about all members of a racial or ethnic group, often resulting in overt acts such as name-calling, social exclusion, or violence

Individualization: Viewing and treating each person as unique and worthwhile

Individualized education program (IEP) team: A school social worker might be involved in this type of group working on initial assessment of the child and the family, with the parents clinically, and in teacher observation, training, and support

Individuals with Disabilities Education Act (IDEA): Formerly known as the Education for All Handicapped Children Act, it was passed in 2004 and requires that public schools create an individualized education program (IEP) for each student who is found to be eligible for special education services; the cornerstone of a student's educational program

Infant mortality rate: Determined by the number of deaths of children under 1 year of age per 1,000 live births in a calendar year

Informed consent: Means a patient accepts treatment after receiving a full and understandable explanation of the treatment being offered and making a decision based on his or her own judgment of the risks and benefits of the treatment

Initiator: A worker who calls attention to a problem or to a potential problem

Insecurity and inferiority theory: Discrimination helps some insecure people feel better about themselves by putting down another group

Institutional discrimination: The unfair treatment of an individual that is due to the established operating procedures, policies, laws, or objectives of large organizations (such as governments, corporations, schools, police departments, and banks)

Institutional racism: Those policies, practices, or procedures embedded in bureaucratic structures that systematically lead to unequal outcomes for people of color

Institutional view: Asserts that social welfare programs are to be accepted as a proper, legitimate function of modern industrial society in helping individuals achieve self-fulfillment

Interactional model: An approach to emotional and behavioral problems that focuses on the processes of everyday social interaction and the effects of labeling on people

International Association of Schools of Social Work (IASSW): Promotes social work education and the development of high-quality educational programs around the world

International Federation of Social Workers (IFSW): Comprised of more than 50 professional membership associations

Intersex individuals Intersex persons are people who are born with atypical reproductive anatomies; they are sometimes called "hermaphrodites," but that term is considered pejorative

Jim Crow system: A rigid caste system in the southern United States that prescribed how African Americans were supposed to act in the presence of Whites, asserted White supremacy, embraced racial segregation, and denied political and legal rights to African Americans

Jones Act: In 1917 established the island of Puerto Rico as a commonwealth of the United States, with citizenship extended to Puerto Ricans living on the island

Kaposi's sarcoma: A rare form of cancer that accounts for many AIDS deaths

Labeling theory: Scheff's assertion that labeling is the most important determinant of people's displaying a chronic mental illness; asserts that criminals *learn* to break the law, and focuses on the process of branding people as criminals and on the effects of such labeling

Laissez-faire economic theory: Asserts that the economy and society in general would best prosper if businesses and industries were permitted to do whatever they desired to make a profit

Law: A formal social rule that is enforced by a political authority

Lesbian: A woman whose sexual or erotic orientation is for other women

Liberals: People who tend to believe that change is generally good, adhere to an institutional view of social welfare, and view the family as an evolving institution

Lipid storage disorders: Disorders involving a progressive degenerative process due to the accumulation of fatty substances in the cells; eventually leads to the death of affected individuals

Living will: A document in which a person stipulates in writing that if he or she becomes physically or mentally disabled from a life-threatening illness from which there is no reasonable expectation of recovery, she or he wants to be allowed to die and not be kept alive by artificial means

Lobotomies: Surgical slashing of the frontal section of the brain that was thought to "remove" mental illness

Locality development model: A model of community organization that asserts that community change can best be brought about through broad-based participation by a wide spectrum of people at the local community level (also called community development)

Lombrosian theory: Asserts that a criminal inherits certain physical abnormalities or stigmata, such as a scanty beard, low sensitivity to pain, distorted nose, large lips, or long arms, and that the more such stigmata a person has, the more he or she is predisposed to a criminal career; popular around the turn of the 20th century

Looking-glass self-concept: A concept developed by Cooley that means we develop our self-concept in terms of how other people react to us

Machismo: A strong sense of masculine pride

Macro practice: A type of social work that involves working with organizations and communities or seeking changes in statutes and social policies

Managed health care: A generic term used to describe a variety of methods of delivering and financing health-care services designed to contain the costs of service delivery while maintaining a defined level of quality of care

Marxist-Leninist theory: Assumes that all crime results from the exploitation of workers and from intense competition among people

Maternal wall: Refers to the problems women face in juggling their roles as employees with those of mothers and caregivers

Meals on Wheels: Provides hot and cold meals to housebound recipients who are incapable of obtaining or preparing their own meals but who can feed themselves

Means test: Assessment tool designed to ensure that individuals receiving assistance do not already have sufficient resources for a minimum level of subsistence

Mediator: A worker who provides intervention in disputes between parties to help them find compromises, reconcile differences, or reach mutually satisfactory agreements

Medicaid: A program established in 1965 by Title XIX amendment to the Social Security Act that provides medical care primarily for recipients of public assistance

Medical abortion: Mifepristone (formerly RU-486), when taken in conjunction with another drug, misoprostol, causes uterine contractions that expel the embryo

Medical model: An approach that views clients as patients—patients' problems are viewed as being inside the patient; views emotional and behavioral problems as mental illness, comparable to physical illness

Medical neglect: No effort is made to secure needed medical care for the child

Medical social work: The main setting is the hospital; workers here provide patients with direct casework, group work, planning and policy development, discharge planning, grief counseling, and many other services

Medicare: A program established in 1965 by Title XVIII of the Social Security Act; includes hospital insurance (Part A) and medical insurance (Part B)

Medicare Prescription Drug, Improvement and Modernization Act: The program was passed into law in 2003 and designed to assist older adults (especially low-income older adults) in purchasing prescription drugs at lower costs

Melting pot: A perspective that views the future American society not as a modified England but rather as a totally new blend, both culturally and biologically, of all the various groups that inhabit the United States

Mental deficiency theory: Asserts that criminal behavior results from "feeblemindedness," which was alleged to impair the capacity to acquire morality and self-control or to appreciate the meaning of laws; waned in popularity in the 1930s

Mesothelioma: A once rare form of cancer that has become relatively common among asbestos workers and is usually fatal

Mezzo practice: A type of social work that includes working with families and other small groups

Micro practice: A type of social work that involves working on a one-to-one basis with an individual

Microcephalus: A condition in which there is a reduced circumference of the head

Minority: A group, or a member of a group, of people of a distinct religious, ethnic, racial or other group that is smaller or less powerful than the society's controlling group

Model Cities Program: Part of the War on Poverty in the 1960s, tore down dilapidated housing and constructed comfortable living quarters, or renovated salvageable buildings; also had a variety of programs that provided job training and placement health-care services, social services, and education opportunities; the communities have again become slums, with living conditions as bleak or bleaker than at the start of the interventions

Monolithic code: Permits only one acceptable pattern of behavior

Morphological theory: Asserts that there is a fundamental relationship between psychological makeup and physical structure

Motivational interviewing: A counseling style for eliciting behavior change by helping clients explore and resolve ambivalence

Multiple chemical sensitivity (MCS): Also known as environmental illness; is a condition whereby individuals experience adverse reactions when exposed to low levels of chemicals found in everyday substances

National Association of Social Workers (NASW): An organization formed in 1955 that represents the social work profession in this country

National health insurance program: A plan in which public tax dollars are used to pay for medical care for all citizens; Great Britain, Canada, and many other countries have this type of plan

National Institute for Occupational Safety and Health (NIOSH): Created in the Department of Health and Human Services to research occupational hazards

Neglect: The deliberate failure or refusal to fulfill a caregiving obligation, such as denial of food or health care or abandoning the victim

Negotiator: A worker who brings together those who are in conflict over one or more issues and seeks to achieve bargaining and compromise to arrive at mutually acceptable agreements

Neoclassical theory: Accepted the basic notion of hedonistic calculations but urged that children and "lunatics" be exempt from punishment because of their inability to calculate pleasure and pain responsibly

New York Charity Organization Society: The first organization to offer training courses for social work

No Child Left Behind (NCLB): George W. Bush's education plan that was signed into law in 2002; has received mixed reviews

Nonintercourse Act: An 1870 act stating that any land transaction between Indians and others not approved by Congress is null and void

Non-nucleoside reverse transcriptase inhibitors (NNRTIs): A "cocktail" of drugs used for HIV

Normalization: The principle that every consumer, even those with the most severe disabilities, should have a living and educational environment as close to "normal" as possible

Nuclear family: A family that consists of a married couple and their children living together

Nursing Home Ombudsman Program: Investigates and acts on concerns expressed by residents in nursing homes

Nursing homes: Facilities that provide residential care and skilled nursing care for older adults who cannot take care of themselves or whose families can no longer take care of them

Obamacare: This Health Care Reform Act was passed in 2010; this complex act moves the United States closer to universal health care

Occupational Safety and Health Act: Established two new organizations to combat occupational hazards: the Occupational Safety and Health Administration (OSHA) and the National Institute for Occupational Safety and Health (NIOSH)

Occupational Safety and Health Administration (OSHA): Created in the Department of Labor to establish health standards for industry

Occupational social work: Social workers in the workplace; they are expected to be accountable by demonstrating that their services promote improved productivity, reduce tardiness and absenteeism, and make it easier to retain members of the company's workforce

Old Age, Survivors, Disability, and Health Insurance (OASDHI): A social insurance program created by the Social Security Act and usually referred to as Social Security by the public; designed to partially replace income that is lost when a worker retires or becomes disabled

Older American Act: Created in 1965, the Administration on Aging within the Department of Health, Education and Welfare (renamed the Department of Health and Human Services in 1980)

Open adoption: Adoption in which the genetic and adoptive parents become officially known to each other, and often remain in contact

Open marriage: The partners are free to have extramarital relationships or sex without betraying one another

Oppression: The unjust or cruel exercise of authority or power

Organization: A group of individuals gathered together to serve a particular purpose

Outsourcing: The practice of locating plants that produce products for U.S. markets in Third World nations where the corporation can take advantage of lower wage rates

Parens patriae: The state is ultimately a parent to all children

Parent abuse: Abuse of older parents by their children

Parents Anonymous (PA): A self-help, crisis intervention program for parents to meet, share their experiences and feelings, learn to control their emotions better, and have contact among members in crisis to prevent parents from abusing their children

Parents Without Partners (PWP): A self-help organization that serves divorced people, unwed mothers or fathers, and stepparents; partially a social group but also helps members with the adjustment problems of raising a family alone

Parole: The conditional release of a prisoner serving an indeterminate or unexpired sentence

Passive-congenial relationship: A marriage in which both partners are not happy but are content with their lives and generally feel adequate

Pedophilia: A sexual disorder characterized by recurrent sexual fantasies and urges or behaviors involving sexual activity with children

Personal Responsibility and Work Opportunity Reconciliation Act: Passed in 1996; ended the 60-year-old Aid to Families of Dependent Children (AFDC) and replaced it with Temporary Assistance to Needy Families (TANF)

Person-in-environment concept: An emphasis in the ecological model that stresses that people in our society continually interact with many systems

Phenylketonuria (PKU): An infant affected with this disorder cannot metabolize phenylalanine, an essential building block of protein in food

Phrenology: Belief that criminal behavior was related to the size and shape of the human skull; popular until the turn of the 20th century

PL 94-142: Formerly the Education for All Handicapped Children Act, this law mandated that all school districts identify students with these problems and then develop specialized programs to meet their needs

Planned Parenthood: The largest and best-known family planning organization, founded in 1916 by Margaret Sanger; had the first birth control clinic

Plea bargaining: For a plea of guilty, a suspect may receive a more lenient sentence, have certain charges dropped, or have the charge reduced to a less serious offense—more that 90% of convictions in the United States are obtained in this manner

Pneumocystic carinii: A lung disease that is also a major cause of AIDS deaths

Politics of creative disorder: A type of activism that operates on the edge of the dominant social system and includes school boycotts, rent strikes, job blockades, sit-ins, public marches, and product boycotts; based on nonviolent resistance

Politics of disorder: A type of activism that reflects alienation from the dominant culture and disillusionment with the political system, and includes mob uprising, riots, and other forms of violence

Politics of escape: A type of activism that is characterized by passionate rhetoric about how minorities are being victimized; the focus is not on arriving at solutions, and perhaps only provides an emotional release

Ponzi scheme: A fraudulent investment operation that involves paying abnormally high returns to investors out of the money paid in by subsequent investors, rather than from the profits from any real business

Posttraumatic stress disorder (PTSD): Caused by witnessing or experiencing a traumatic event; symptoms may include flashbacks, nightmares, feelings of detachment, irritability, trouble concentrating, and sleeplessness

Poverty line: The level of income that the federal government considers sufficient to meet basic requirements of food, shelter, and clothing

Power rapist: A rapist who is interested in possessing his victim sexually, not harming her; acts out of underlying feelings of inadequacy and is interested in controlling his victim; only uses the amount of force necessary to gain her compliance

Prejudice: A preconceived adverse opinion or judgment formed without just grounds or before sufficient knowledge

Prejudiced discriminator: A person who does not believe in the values of freedom and equality and consistently discriminates against other groups in both word and deed

Prejudiced nondiscriminator: A person who feels hostile to other groups but recognizes that law and social pressures are opposed to overt discrimination, so reluctantly does not translate prejudice into action

Presentence report: A document prepared by a probation and parole officer that is basically a social history of the offender that is prepared to help guide the judge in sentencing

Primary industry: Industry that involves the gathering or extracting of undeveloped natural resources

Probation: Suspending the sentence of a convicted offender and giving him or her freedom during good behavior under the supervision of a probation officer

Problem-solving and decision-making groups: Might be viewed as a subcategory of tasks groups; each participant often has some interest or stake in the process

Program research specialist: A social work role in which an important focus is on evidence-based practice; needs to look at the research and identify what programs actually produce what results

Projection: A psychological defense mechanism by which we attribute to others characteristics that we are unwilling to recognize in ourselves

Promise Neighborhoods: One of Barack Obama's proposals; to be modeled after the Harlem Children's Zone, which provides a network of services to an entire neighborhood from birth to college

Proposition 209: Voters in California, in 1996, passed this proposition that explicitly rejects the idea that women and other minority group members should receive special consideration when applying for jobs, government contracts, or university admission

Protective services: A specialized casework service to neglected, abused, exploited, or rejected children that is geared toward rehabilitation through identification and treatment of the motivating factors that underlie the problem

Protestant ethic: Emphasized the importance of hard work and asserted that it was morally wrong to engage in pleasurable activities of any kind

Protestant Reformation: Began in the 17th century; work became highly valued for the first time and since then work has continued to be viewed as honorable and having religious significance

Proximal stimulation: A type of infant stimulation that involves rocking and handling

Psychoanalytic theory: Not a single coherent theory but a variety of hypotheses postulating that delinquent behavior results when the restraining forces in the superego (one's conscience and self-ideal) and the ego (mediator among the superego, the id, and reality) are too weak to curb the instinctual, antisocial pressures from the id (source of psychic energy)

Psychodynamic problem-solving theory: Views deviant behavior as contrived by the personality as a way of dealing with some adjustment problem; situational factors are generally de-emphasized

Psychological abuse: The infliction of mental anguish by intimidating, humiliating, and threatening harm

Psychotropic drugs: Drugs including tranquilizers, antipsychotic drugs, and antidepressants used in reducing high levels of anxiety, depression, and tension

Public assistance programs: Benefits in these programs are paid from general government revenues and have a means test for applicants

Public health services: The majority of services to a community are provided through local health programs; the focus is primarily preventive in nature, and the priorities keep changing

Public-order crimes: These crimes constitute the largest category and include traffic violations, prostitution, vagrancy, pornography, gambling, drunkenness, curfew violations, loitering, use of illegal substances, and fornication

Quality circles: Work-improvement task forces in which managers and employees meet regularly to allow employees to air grievances, identify problems that hinder productivity, and offer suggestions for alleviating these concerns

Race: A group of people believed to have a common set of physical characteristics, but whose members may or may not share the sense of togetherness or identity that holds an ethnic group together

Racial discrimination: Racial discrimination involves denying to members of other racial groups equal access to opportunities, residential housing areas, membership in religious and social organizations, involvement in political activities, access to community services, and so on

Racism: The belief that race is the primary determinant of human capacities and traits and that racial differences produce an inherent superiority of a particular race; racism is frequently a basis of discrimination against members of other "racial" groups

Rape trauma syndrome: A series of emotional changes experienced by the victims of rape; the first phase (acute phase) begins immediately, followed by the long-term reorganization phase

Rational-emotive behavior therapy: Albert Ellis's therapy that includes the ABCs (A = Activating event → B = Your belief system → C = Your emotional consequence)

Rational self-analysis (RSA): An approach to changing unwanted emotions that is done by recording the event and self-talk on paper

Rational therapy: Potentially enables those who become skillful in rationally analyzing their self-talk to control or get rid of any undesirable emotion or any dysfunctional behavior

Recreation groups: Groups that provide activities for enjoyment and exercise

Recreation-skill group: Group whose objective is to improve a set of skills while at the same time providing enjoyment

Reform approach: Social work model in the 1960s that wanted to change systems to benefit clients

Regressed child molester: A person whose usual sexual interest is in adult partners, but when faced with massive stress, falls back emotionally and acts out sexually toward children to meet his needs; most incest perpetrators are of this type

Relative approach to poverty: An assumption that a person is poor when his or her income is substantially less than the average income of the population

Relative confidentiality: Confidentiality in which case records are often shared with other team professionals and supervisors; most social work practice follows this type of confidentiality

Religion: A term that refers to the formal institutional contexts of spiritual beliefs and practices

Requirement of mourning: A belief that people with disabilities "ought" to feel inferior

Researcher: A worker who studies the literature on topics of interest, evaluates the outcomes of one's practice, assesses the merits and shortcomings of programs, and studies community needs

Residual view: Asserts that social welfare services should be provided only when an individual's needs are not properly met through other societal institutions; has been characterized as "charity for unfortunates"

Respite care: Provides caregiving services to parents and other caregivers for people with a disability, giving primary caregivers a break from their responsibilities

Retired Senior Volunteer Program (RSVP): Seeks to match work and service opportunities with older volunteers seeking them

Retreatist gangs: Gangs whose focus is on getting "high" or "loaded" on alcohol, cocaine, marijuana, heroin, or other drugs; individuals tend to join this type of gang to secure continued access to drugs

Retroviruses: Reverse the usual order of reproduction within the cells they infect

Reverse discrimination: The possible result of affirmative action programs when qualified majority group members are sometimes arbitrarily excluded

Sadistic rapist: A rapist who eroticizes aggression; aggressive force creates sexual arousal; is enormously gratified by his victim's torment, pain, and suffering; his offenses often are ritualistic and involve bondage and torture, particularly to the sexual organs

Sandwich generation: Middle-aged parents who are caught in the middle of trying to meet the needs of both their aging parents and their children

School busing: A court-ordered proportion of non-Whites are bused to schools in White areas and a certain proportion of Whites are bused to schools in non-White areas with the objectives of providing equal educational opportunities and reducing racial prejudice through interaction

Secondary industry: Industry that involves turning raw materials into manufactured goods

Self-determination: Clients have the right to hold and express their own opinions and to act on them, as long as doing so does not infringe on the rights of others

Self-help groups: Voluntary, small-group structures for mutual aid and the accomplishment of a special purpose

Self-managing teams: Autonomous work groups that are given a high degree of decision-making authority and are expected to control their own behavior and work schedules; compensation usually based on the team's overall productivity

Self-neglect: Behaviors of a frail, depressed, or mentally incompetent older person that threaten her or his own safety or health

Self-talk theory: The reasons for any criminal act can be determined by examining what the offender was thinking prior to and during the time the crime was committed

Senescence: The process of aging

Sensitivity groups: Encounter groups, T (training)-groups, and sensitivity training (these terms are used somewhat synonymously) refer to group experiences in which people relate to one another in an intimate manner requiring self-disclosure

Serial marriages: A pattern of successive, temporary marriages

Service Corps of Retired Executives (SCORE): A program that provides consulting services to small businesses

Settlement houses: Workers lived in the impoverished neighborhoods and sought to improve conditions by using change techniques that are now referred to as social group work, social action, and community organization

Sex offenses: Include forcible rape, prostitution, soliciting, statutory rape, fornication, sodomy, homosexuality, adultery, and incest

Sex roles: Learned patterns of behavior that are expected of the sexes in a given society

Sex variances: Term used to refer to sexual expressions that are of concern to certain segments of our society

Sexism: Prejudice or discrimination against women

Sexual abuse: Nonconsensual sexual contact

Sexual harassment: Unwelcome sexual advances, requests for sexual favors, and other verbal and physical conduct of a sexual nature constitute sexual harassment when this conduct explicitly or implicitly affects an individual's employment, unreasonably interferes with an individual's employment, unreasonably interferes with an individual's work performance, or creates an intimidating, hostile, or offensive work environment

Sexual orientation: Sexual orientation is the direction of one's sexual interest toward members of the same, opposite, or both sexes; three aspects of sexual orientation are: attraction, behavior, and identity; sexual attraction may be to partners of the same or opposite sex or to both sexes; behavior refers to sexual activities with partners of the same or opposite sex, or with both sexes; identity refers to one's view of oneself as heterosexual, gay or lesbian, or bisexual

Sexual scripts: Behaviors that result from elaborate prior learning in which we acquire the etiquette of sexual behavior

Sheltered employment: Programs that provide a work environment for those who are unable to secure or maintain jobs in the community

Silent rape reaction: The trauma for nonreporters of rape is often intensified because they have no way of expressing or venting their feelings

Smith-Hughes Act: Passed in 1917, it made federal monies available for vocational education programs and created the Federal Board of Vocational Education

Social action model: A type of community organization that assumes that there is a disadvantaged (often oppressed) segment of the population that needs to be organized to pressure the power structure for increased resources or for social justice

Social casework: Social work aimed at helping individuals on a one-to-one basis to resolve personal and social problems

Social control theory: Assumes that all of us would "naturally" commit crimes and therefore must be constrained and controlled by society from breaking the law

Social conversation groups: Conversation in these groups is often loose and tends to drift aimlessly; there is no formal agenda; they are often used for testing purposes

Social Darwinism: The concept that it was far better for society to allow the poor and the weak to perish than to sustain their existence and encourage their proliferation through government-supported programs

Social disengagement: The process whereby society withdraws from the aging person

Social history: A document that contains information about the client's family background and present status

Social insurance programs: Programs financed by taxes on employees, employers, or both

Social justice: An ideal condition in which all members of a society have the same basic rights, protection, opportunities, obligations, and social benefits

Social planning model: A model of community organization that emphasizes the process of problem solving; assumes that community change is a complex industrial environment

Social stratification: The ranking of social classes, with the upper classes having by far the greatest access to the pleasures that money can buy

Social welfare institution: A nation's system of programs, benefits, and services that helps people meet those social, economic, educational, and health needs that are fundamental to the maintenance of society

Social work: The professional activity of helping individuals, groups, families, organizations, and communities to enhance or restore their capacity for social functioning and to create societal conditions favorable to their goals; requires knowledge of human development and behavior; of social, economic, and cultural institutions; and of the interaction of all these factors

Social worker: Graduates of schools of social work (with either bachelor's or master's degrees), who use their knowledge and skills to provide social services for clients, as defined by the National Association of Social Workers

Socialization groups: These groups generally seek to change members' attitudes and behaviors to a more socially acceptable direction

Society for the Prevention of Cruelty to Children: An organization formed in New York in the late 1800s to protect children from abuse and neglect

Society for the Prevention of Pauperism: An early social welfare organization, founded in 1820 by John Griscom, that was established to investigate the habits and circumstances of the poor, suggest plans by which the poor could help themselves, and encourage the poor to save and economize

Sociopath: A person who is thought to have no moral constraints against engaging in criminal activity, doing so whenever it is personally advantageous, even though others may be hurt

Soldier's Rehabilitation Act: Passed in 1918, it was designed to rehabilitate veterans who had a disability

Spirituality: The general human experience of developing a sense of meaning, purpose, and morality

State Children's Health Insurance Program (SCHIP): A U.S. federal government program, created in 1997, that gives funds to states in order to provide health insurance to families with children

Status offenses: Acts that are defined as illegal if committed by juveniles but not if committed by adults

Statutory rape: Sexual contact between a male who is of a legally responsible age and a female who is a willing participant but is below the legal age of consent

Stereotypes: Generalizations, or assumptions, that people make about the characteristics of all members of a group, based on an image (often wrong) about what people in that group are like

Stereotyping: Attributing fixed and usually inaccurate and unfavorable qualities to a category of people, which makes it easier for discrimination to occur

Stock trusts: Allow employees to buy or receive stock in the company, thereby becoming partial owners

Strategic Arms Reduction Treaty (START): An agreement signed by Russia and the United States in 1993 that substantially reduced the stockpiles of long-range nuclear missiles

Strengths perspective: Seeks to identify, use, build, and reinforce the abilities and strengths that people have, in contrast to the pathological perspective, which focuses on their deficiencies

Supplemental Security Income (SSI): In this public assistance program the federal government pays monthly checks to people in financial need who are 65 years of age and older or who are blind or disabled at any age

Surrogate motherhood: A surrogate gives birth to a baby conceived by artificial insemination; at birth the surrogate mother terminates her parental rights; and the child is then legally adopted by the sperm donor and his wife

Systems approach: A social work process that emphasizes looking beyond the client's presenting problems to assess the complexities and interrelationships of the client's life situation

Systems change specialist: A person in this role can help by linking people to systems and improving existing service and delivery mechanisms

Task force: A group established for a special purpose; usually disbanded after the task is completed

Task groups: Exist to achieve a specific set of tasks or objectives

Tea Party: The Tea Party is a political movement that is generally recognized as conservative and libertarian; the Tea Party endorses reduced government spending, opposition to many current taxation policies, and reduction of the federal budget deficit and of the national debt

Telephone reassurance: Volunteers telephone older people who live alone for social contact and also to ascertain whether any accidents or other serious problems have arisen that require emergency attention

Temperature inversion: Occurs when a layer of warmer air moves over a layer of cooler air and seals in pollutants that would ordinarily rise into the upper atmosphere

Temporary Assistance to Needy Families (TANF): This public assistance program replaced AFDC, with the assumption that in order to avoid a long-term welfare class, all jobless people should work

Ten Percent Society: A gay and lesbian organization that argues the incidence of homosexuality is 10%

Tertiary industry: Industry that involves service activities of one kind or another

Theft: Refers to illegally taking someone's property without the person's consent

T-helper/T-4 cells: HIV invades this group of white blood cells and converts more cells producing HIV

Theory of demographic transition: Asserts that growth rates tend to decrease and then stabilize after a fairly high level of industrialization has been achieved

Theory X managers: Managers who view employees as incapable of much growth

Theory Y managers: Managers who view employees as wanting to grow and develop by exerting physical and mental effort to accomplish work objectives to which they are committed

Therapy groups: Generally composed of members with rather severe emotional or personal problems

Toxemia: Toxic (poisonous) substances in the blood during the gestation period, including prescription drugs, cocaine and other illegal drugs, nicotine, and alcohol

Toxic Substances and Control Act: Enacted in 1976 and established systems and guidelines for screening and controlling dangerous substances

Toynbee Hall: The first settlement house in London, established in 1884

Transgender person: A person whose gender identity is the opposite of his or her biological gender

Transitional programs: Help inmates to maintain and develop strong ties to the noncriminal elements in their home communities

Transsexual individual A person who has a persistent desire to transition to living as, and being perceived as, the sex that is consistent with his or her gender identity; typically, this desire is driven by an extreme discomfort with his or her current sex; transsexuals transitioning from male to female are often referred to as "MTFs"; similarly female-to-female transsexuals are frequently referred to as "FTMs"

Truant officer: A social worker who often functions as an advocate for the child; there are times when acting as an agent of social control (the law, the system) need not be looked at negatively

Unemployment Insurance: A program of the Social Security Act, it provides benefits to workers who have been laid off or, in certain cases, fired; financed by a tax on employers

Unprejudiced discriminator: A person who is not personally prejudiced but may sometimes, reluctantly, discriminate against other groups because it seems socially or financially convenient to do so

Unprejudiced nondiscriminator: A person, in both belief and practice, who upholds American ideals of freedom and equality, is not prejudiced against other groups, and, on principle, will not discriminate against them

Values: Values are beliefs, preferences, or assumptions about what is desirable or good for people

Victorian morality: The moral values prominent in the later 19th and early 20th centuries in which sexuality was all but banished from discussion in respectable relationships, middle-and upper-class women were expected to be virgins before marriage, and it was thought that men were inherently more sexual than women

Vocational Rehabilitation Act: Passed in 1973, it prohibited discrimination against people with a disability by any program or organization receiving federal funds

Wealth: A person's total assets; real estate holdings, cash, stocks, bonds, and so forth

White-collar crime: Work-related offenses committed by people of high status

White flight: Whites leaving the inner cities and moving to suburbs

White supremacy: The belief, and promotion of the belief, that White people are superior to people of other racial backgrounds

Workers' Compensation Insurance: Provides both income and assistance in meeting medical expenses for injuries sustained on a job; by 1948 all states had adequate coverage

Worldview: One's perceptions of oneself in relation to other people, objects, institutions, and nature. It focuses on one's view of the world and one's role and place in it

Name Index

Subject Index